Lecture Notes in Artificial Intelligence 12842

Subseries of Lecture Notes in Computer Science

More information about this subseries at http://www.springer.com/series/1244

Anupam Das · Sara Negri (Eds.)

Automated Reasoning with Analytic Tableaux and Related Methods

30th International Conference, TABLEAUX 2021
Birmingham, UK, September 6–9, 2021
Proceedings

Springer

Editors
Anupam Das
University of Birmingham
Birmingham, UK

Sara Negri
University of Genoa
Genoa, Italy

ISSN 0302-9743 ISSN 1611-3349 (electronic)
Lecture Notes in Artificial Intelligence
ISBN 978-3-030-86058-5 ISBN 978-3-030-86059-2 (eBook)
https://doi.org/10.1007/978-3-030-86059-2

LNCS Sublibrary: SL7 – Artificial Intelligence

This Springer imprint is published by the registered company Springer Nature Switzerland AG
The registered company address is: Gewerbestrasse 11, 6330 Cham, Switzerland

Preface

TABLEAUX, the International Conference on Automated Reasoning with Analytic Tableaux and Related Methods, is a conference series that started in 1992 and has been held every year since then. The series brings together researchers interested in all aspects - theoretical foundations, implementation techniques, systems development, and applications - of the mechanization of reasoning with tableaux and related methods. Since 1995 proceedings of TABLEAUX have been published in Springer's LNCS/LNAI series.

TABLEAUX 2021 was the 30th edition of the conference series and was hosted by the University of Birmingham, UK, during September 6–9, 2021. It was co-located with the 13th International Symposium on Frontiers of Combining Systems (FroCoS 2021). Due to continued uncertainty caused by the COVID-19 pandemic, the conference was primarily held virtually, with facilities for hybrid participation available at the School of Computer Science, University of Birmingham.

The Program Committee received a total of 46 submissions, including 43 research papers and 3 system descriptions. Each submission received at least four peer reviews in a single-blind process and was evaluated during Program Committee discussions. Eventually 23 research papers and all 3 system descriptions were accepted for presentation at the conference.

This volume includes all the accepted research papers and system descriptions of TABLEAUX 2021. These include papers on proof theory, with deductive mechanisms ranging from tableaux, sequent calculi and variations thereof, and cyclic proofs. Their objects of inquiry are modal logics, including provability logic and tense logic, conditional logics, fuzzy logic, weak Kleene logic, and the study of properties such as cut elimination, termination of proof search, and the finite model property. Attention is paid to the development of proof systems from semantics, such as non-deterministic matrices and game-theoretic semantics. Several papers are concerned with tools for automated theorem proving for classical, intuitionistic, modal, and conditional logics, for the formalization of proofs and SAT solvers. This year's edition, particularly, saw an increase of research at the intersection of theorem proving and machine learning.

This volume also includes abstracts of invited talks presented at TABLEAUX 2021. The following five invited speakers were chosen by the Program Committee:

- Michael Benedikt (University of Oxford, UK). Joint with FroCoS 2021.
- Orna Kupferman (Hebrew University, Israel).
- Revantha Ramanayake (University of Gröningen, The Netherlands).
- Greg Restall (University of Melbourne, Australia, and University of St Andrews, UK).
- Renate Schmidt (University of Manchester, UK). Joint with FroCoS 2021.

Finally, the Program Committee selected winners of the following awards:

- **Best Paper.** Stepan Kuznetsov. *Complexity of a fragment of infinitary action logic with exponential via non-well-founded proofs.*
- **Best Paper by Junior Researcher(s).** Jan Rooduijn. *Cyclic hypersequent calculi for some modal logics with the master modality.*

The two awards were presented at the conference. Each award was generously financially supported by Springer.

We would like to thank all the people who contributed to making TABLEAUX 2021 a success. We thank the Program Committee and all additional reviewers for the time, professional effort, and expertise they invested to deliver the high scientific standards of the conference and these proceedings. We thank the invited speakers for their inspiring talks and the Steering Committee for their helpful advice. Finally, we thank all the authors for their excellent contributions.

We would like to thank Springer for sponsoring the conference and publishing these proceedings, UK Research and Innovation for absorbing additional organizational costs through funded projects[1], and the University of Birmingham for providing online and hybrid facilities. Thanks to them, registration to TABLEAUX 2021 was free of charge.

July 2021

Anupam Das
Sara Negri

[1] Structure vs. Invariants in Proofs, project reference MR/S035540/1.

Organization

Program Committee Chairs

Anupam Das	University of Birmingham, UK
Sara Negri	University of Genoa, Italy

Steering Committee

Agata Ciabattoni	Technical University Vienna, Austria
Cláudia Nalon	University of Brasília, Brazil
Hans de Nivelle	Nazarbayev University, Kazakhstan
Jens Otten	University of Oslo, Norway
Elaine Pimentel	Federal University of Rio Grande do Norte, Brazil
Andrei Popescu	University of Sheffield, UK
Anupam Das	University of Birmingham, UK
Dirk Pattinson	Australian National University, Australia

Program Committee

Bahareh Afshari	University of Amsterdam, The Netherlands, and University of Gothenburg, Sweden
Carlos Areces	Universidad Nacional de Córdoba, Argentina
Arnon Avron	Tel-Aviv University, Israel
Nick Bezhanishvili	University of Amsterdam, Netherlands
Patrick Blackburn	University of Roskilde, Denmark
Serenella Cerrito	Université d'Evry Val d'Essonne, France
Kaustuv Chaudhuri	Inria, France
Liron Cohen	Ben-Gurion University, Israel
Anupam Das	University of Birmingham, UK
Stéphane Demri	CNRS, France
Hans de Nivelle	Nazarbayev University, Kazakhstan
Valeria de Paiva	Topos Institute Berkeley, USA
Clare Dixon	University of Manchester, UK
Christian Fermüller	TU Wien, Austria
Didier Galmiche	Université de Lorraine, France
Silvio Ghilardi	Università degli Studi di Milano, Italy
Rajeev Goré	Australian National University, Australia
Andrzej Indrzejczak	University of Łódź, Poland
Hidenori Kurokawa	Kanazawa University, Japan
Stepan Kuznetsov	Russian Academy of Sciences, Russia
Björn Lellmann	SBA Research, Austria
Stéphane Graham-Lengrand	SRI International, USA

George Metcalfe	University of Bern, Switzerland
Neil Murray	University at Albany, USA
Cláudia Nalon	University of Brasília, Brazil
Sara Negri	University of Genoa, Italy
Nicola Olivetti	Aix-Marseille University, France
Eugenio Orlandelli	University of Bologna, Italy
Jens Otten	University of Oslo, Norway
Alessandra Palmigiano	Vrije Universiteit Amsterdam, The Netherlands
Dirk Pattinson	Australian National University, Australia
Frank Pfenning	Carnegie Mellon University, USA
Elaine Pimentel	Federal University of Rio Grande do Norte, Brazil
Andrei Popescu	University of Sheffield, UK
Gian Luca Pozzato	University of Turin, Italy
Giselle Reis	Carnegie Mellon University in Qatar, Qatar
Reuben Rowe	Royal Holloway, University of London, UK
José Espírito Santo	University of Minho, Portugal
Lutz Straßburger	Inria, France
Josef Urban	Czech Technical University in Prague, Czech Republic

Additional Reviewers

Matteo Acclavio
Patrick Baillot
Paolo Baldi
Valentin Cassano
Abhishek De
Tiziano Dalmonte
Jeremy Dawson
Santiago Escobar
Michael Färber
Raul Fervari
Robert Freiman
Sabine Frittella
Nathan Fulton
Francesco Genco
Guido Gherardi
Iris van der Giessen
Marianna Girlando
Giuseppe Greco
Edward Hermann Haeusler
Johannes Hafner
Natthapong Jungteerapanich
Martin Lange
Serafina Lapenta
Graham Leigh
Tim Lyon
Paolo Maffezioli
Joao Marcos
Johannes Marti
Andrea Mazzullo
Paulo Oliva
Francesco Paoli
Alexandra Pavlova
Edi Pavlovic
Adam Pease
Luís Pinto
Damien Pous
Michael Rawson
Giles Reger
Alexis Saurin
Igor Sedlar
Ian Shillito
Thomas Studer
Vasily Shangin
Apostolos Tzimoulis
Marco Volpe
Uwe Waldmann
Richard Zach
Anna Zamansky
Michał Zawidzki
Yoni Zohar

Abstracts of Invited Talks

The Strange Career of Interpolation and Definability

Michael Benedikt

University of Oxford, UK
michael.benedikt@gmail.com

Beth Definability, Craig Interpolation, and their variants have long been seen as an important topic in commmputational logic, telling us something about logical simplification. But the rationale for their significance has varied over time, and it is not even clear whether they should be best seen as a property of a logic or of a proof system. In this talk I will look back at the somewhat twisty evolution of the topic, highlighting some issues that have been underexplored. I'll also present some current work (joint with Pierre Pradic) aimed at filling some of the gaps. No background on interpolation or definability will be assumed in the talk.

Rational Synthesis

Orna Kupferman

Hebrew University, Israel
orna@cs.huji.ac.il

In the traditional approach to synthesis, the system has to satisfy its specification in all environments. Thus, the components that compose the environment can be seen as if their only objective is to conspire to fail the system. In real life, the components that compose the environment are often entities that have objectives of their own. The approach taken in the field of game theory is to assume that interacting agents are rational, and thus act to achieve their own objectives. Adding rationality to the synthesis setting softens the universal quantification on the environments, and motivates the study of rational synthesis. There, we seek a system that satisfies its specification in all rational environments. The above can be formalized in two different ways. The first is cooperative rational synthesis, where the desired output is a stable profile of strategies to all components in which the objective of the system is satisfied. The second is non-cooperative rational synthesis, where the desired output is a strategy for the system such that its objective is satisfied in every stable profile where she follows this strategy.

The talk introduces the two types of rational synthesis and surveys their game-theoretical aspects. In particular, we discuss quantitative rational synthesis and relate cooperative and non-cooperative rational synthesis with the two notions of equilibrium inefficiency in game theory, namely price of stability and price of anarchy.

The talk is based on joint work with Shaull Almagor, Dana Fisman, Yoad Lustig, Giuseppe Perelli, and Moshe Y. Vardi.

The Barter Trade in Structure and Cuts

Revantha Ramanayake

University of Gröningen, The Netherlands
d.r.s.ramanayake@rug.nl

Proof-based methods for reasoning about non-classical logics often rely on the subformula property and its consequent restriction on the space of proofs. Sequent calculi with the subformula property are a prominent success story, utilised for establishing consistency, decidability, complexity bounds, interpolation, automated reasoning and more. The bottleneck is the difficulty (or impossibility) finding such sequent calculi for the many non-classical logics of interest.

The response in the structural proof theory community since the 1960s was the formulation of an astonishing breadth of new and exotic proof formalisms: hypersequents, nested sequents, labelled sequents, display calculi are just a few examples. Each of these formalisms is obtained by extending the structural language of the sequent calculus in a way that enables the subformula property for more logics. This program has been very successful in terms of obtaining proof calculi with the subformula property for many logics but the yield has been modest in terms of new meta-logical results.

I will examine the trade that is the gain of cut-elimination (and consequent subformula property) at the cost of introducing new structure. Illustrating using hypersequent calculi, I will introduce a principled transformation that eliminates structure in favour of highly restricted cuts–parametrised by the end formula–in the sequent calculus and discuss what this means, for assessing the strength of the subformula property in an exotic formalism, and as a common framework for automated reasoning for non-classical logics. A concept of cut-restriction emerges that has cut-elimination as a special case.

Comparing Rules for Identity in Sequent Systems and Natural Deduction

Greg Restall

University of Melbourne, Australia, and University of St Andrews, UK
greg@consequently.org

It is straightforward to treat the identity predicate in models for first order predicate logic. Truth conditions for identity formulas are given by a natural clause: a formula $s = t$ is true (or satisfied by a variable assignment) in a model if and only if the denotations of the terms s and t (perhaps relative to the given variable assignment) are the same.

On the other hand, finding appropriate rules for identity in a sequent system or in a natural deduction proof setting leaves a number of questions open. Identity could be treated with introduction and elimination rules in natural deduction, or left and right rules, in a sequent calculus, as is standard for familiar logical concepts. On the other hand, since identity is a predicate and identity formulas are atomic, it is also very natural to treat identity by way of axiomatic sequents, rather than by inference rules. I will describe and discuss this phenomenon, and explore the relationships between different formulations of rules for the identity predicate, and attempt to account for some of the distinctive virtues of each different formulation.

Forgetting and Subontology Generation for the Medical Ontology SNOMED CT

Renate A. Schmidt

University of Manchester, UK
Renate.Schmidt@manchester.ac.uk

In this talk I discuss efforts in developing systems to provide automated support for content extraction for the medical ontology SNOMED CT. SNOMED CT is a large knowledge base of standardised, precise definitions of clinical terms and medical codes for use in electronic health records to allow consistent data capture at the point of care and meaningful processing of data across health care sectors. Since SNOMED CT is so large it has long been an aim to have the capability to compute smaller extracts of the ontology that are self-contained but restricted to a narrow focus, for example, kidney diseases, dentistry or vocabulary relevant for nursing. Such subontologies would make it easier to reuse and share content, to assist with new ontology creation, quality assurance, ontology update and debugging. In addition, reasoning tasks such as querying and classification take less time to execute over a smaller extract than over the original ontology.

The aim of our research is to compute extracts that are semantically complete in that they faithfully capture the knowledge in an ontology about a user-specified focus signature. This is a challenging problem, because the knowledge of an ontology is not only given by the explicitly stated axioms in the ontology but also all implicit knowledge that can be inferred from these axioms. Forgetting creates a compact representation of the implicit knowledge of an ontology over specified focus concepts and relations, by performing inferences on the non-focus (forgetting) signature. A number of PhD projects in our group have developed a series of forgetting tools and adaptations for use in applications such as logical difference computation and abduction in the context of description logic-based ontologies. These tools provided the basis for a series of industry projects in which we applied and further developed these for use cases of the medical ontology SNOMED CT. A workflow of different modularisation and forgetting methods was devised and thoroughly evaluated. With this workflow we managed to significantly improve the performance and success rates of our tools and provide a feasible way to compute faithful extracts of SNOMED CT.

Building on these experiences, in a current joint project with SNOMED Intl we have developed a new bespoke approach and prototype for computing subontologies of SNOMED CT. This approach is definition driven and returns concise encodings of descriptions of the specified focus concepts in a normal form according to modelling guidelines of SNOMED Intl. These can be efficiently computed and are significantly smaller than both forgetting solutions and subontologies computed by modularisation methods.

The talk will give an overview of this research spanning several years, focussing on key ideas, findings, experiences and practical challenges encountered.

Contents

Intuitionistic Modal Logics

Tableau Calculi

Tableaux and Restricted Quantification for Systems Related to Weak Kleene Logic

Thomas Macaulay Ferguson[1,2(✉)]

[1] ILLC, University of Amsterdam, Amsterdam, The Netherlands
[2] Arché Research Centre, University of St. Andrews, St. Andrews, Scotland
tferguson@gradcenter.cuny.edu

Abstract. Logic-driven applications like *knowledge representation* typically operate with the tools of classical, first-order logic. In these applications' standard, *extensional* domains—*e.g.*, knowledge bases representing product features—these deductive tools are suitable. However, there remain many domains for which these tools seem overly strong. If, *e.g.*, an artificial conversational agent maintains a knowledge base cataloging *e.g.* an interlocutor's *beliefs* or *goals*, it is unlikely that the model's contents are closed under Boolean logic. There exist propositional deductive systems whose notions of validity and equivalence more closely align with legitimate inferences over such *intentional* contexts. *E.g.*, philosophers like Kit Fine and Stephen Yablo have made compelling cases that Richard Angell's AC characterizes *synonymy*, under which such intentional contexts *should* be closed. In this paper, we adapt several of these systems by introducing sufficient quantification theory to support *e.g.* subsumption reasoning. Given the close relationship between these systems and *weak Kleene* logic, we initially define a novel theory of restricted quantifiers for weak Kleene logic and describe a sound and complete tableau proof theory. We extend the account of quantification and tableau calculi to two related systems: Angell's AC and Charles Daniel's $S^{\star}_{fde}$, providing new tools for modeling and reasoning about agents' mental states.

Keywords: Restricted quantifiers · Weak Kleene logic · Analytic containment

1 Introduction

Logic-oriented fields incorporating *semantics* and *reasoning* tend to rely on a fragment of the classical, first-order predicate calculus. *E.g.*, although description logics like $\mathcal{ALC}$ and $\mathcal{SROIQ}$ differ with respect to *expressivity*, they rest on the same Boolean semantic foundations. In most extensional contexts—*e.g.*, cases in which a knowledge base is interpreted as a collection of truths about a domain—inferences drawn on this foundation are appropriate. But knowledge

A. Das and S. Negri (Eds.): TABLEAUX 2021, LNAI 12842, pp. 3–19, 2021.
https://doi.org/10.1007/978-3-030-86059-2_1

bases representing *intentional* contexts may not be closed under classical validity; that φ is an agent's *belief* does not entail that every classical consequence of φ is counted as a belief as well.

Thus, semantic representations of such contexts would benefit from having access to weaker deductive bases that more closely align with the closure conditions for intentional contexts. One candidate is Richard Angell's logic of *analytic containment* AC of [1]. Philosophers like Fabrice Correia (in [5]), Kit Fine (in [9]), and Stephen Yablo (in [18]) have provided sustained arguments that AC characterizes a notion of fine-grained *synonymy*. A description logic based on AC would close an intentional context under synonymy, which is a plausible closure condition. Tools like description logics require at least enough quantification theory to describe class relations like *subsumption*, but convincing quantification theory has been lacking for these systems. It is our goal to open up new deductive bases for such applications by introducing sufficient quantification theory to support description logics, providing semantics and tableaux for several plausible deductive systems. The results of [7] show that AC and a closely related system of $\mathsf{S}^{\star}_{\mathtt{fde}}$ bear a very close relationship with weak Kleene logic wK. A theory of restricted quantification for wK could therefore be directly applied to provide these systems with the desired quantification; likewise, a tableau calculus for wK will form a foundation for tableau calculi for AC and $\mathsf{S}^{\star}_{\mathtt{fde}}$. (As we will describe, the matter of quantification in wK is itself a nontrivial problem, so such a theory is independently interesting.)

We will proceed by first examining wK, looking at some of the difficulties for quantification and providing semantics and tableaux for a reasonable theory of restricted quantification. We will conclude by showing how this work on wK can be leveraged to induce similar model theory and tableau calculi for AC and $\mathsf{S}^{\star}_{\mathtt{fde}}$.

2 Weak Kleene Logic

In [14], Kleene introduces three-valued matrices for connectives to account for cases in which a recursive procedure calculating truth values fails to converge:

> In this section, we shall introduce new senses of the propositional connectives, in which, *e.g.*, $Q(x) \vee R(x)$ will be defined in some cases when $Q(x)$ or $R(x)$ is undefined. It will be convenient to use truth tables, with three "truth values" $\mathfrak{t}$ ('true'), $\mathfrak{f}$ ('false') and $\mathfrak{e}$ ('undefined'), in describing the senses which the connectives shall now have [14, p. 332].

Kleene considers that for each predicate there is a "range of definition" over which it is then defined. For example, a predicate $Q(x)$ understood as a function with range $\{\mathfrak{t}, \mathfrak{f}\}$ may not converge for every argument. This is in line with the Halldén-Bochvar interpretation (in [11] or [2]), in which a predicate has a range of objects about which it may be meaningfully applied. A natural interpretation of these ranges is that $\varphi(c)$ evaluates to $\mathfrak{e}$ when an agent lacks *competence* with the concept $\varphi(x)$ and is unable to determine a truth value.

This interpretation accords with thinking about reasoning about beliefs; if an agent is not familiar with the use of a predicate—or does not have a clear grasp of how a predicate may apply to certain objects—an atomic formula may be viewed as not truth-evaluable.

2.1 The Propositional Case

We will first review the propositional basis of weak Kleene logic before embellishing with additional expressivity. For our propositional language, let **At** be a collection of propositional atomic formulas $\{p_0, ..., q_0, ...\}$ and let $\mathcal{L}$ be the language standardly defined by closing **At** under the unary $\sim$ and binary $\wedge$ and $\vee$.

To provide semantics, we first describe the weak Kleene truth tables over the set of truth values $\mathcal{V}_3 = \{\mathfrak{t}, \mathfrak{e}, \mathfrak{f}\}$:

Definition 1. *The* weak Kleene truth tables *are:*

$\sim$	
$\mathfrak{t}$	$\mathfrak{f}$
$\mathfrak{e}$	$\mathfrak{e}$
$\mathfrak{f}$	$\mathfrak{t}$

$\wedge$	$\mathfrak{t}$	$\mathfrak{e}$	$\mathfrak{f}$
$\mathfrak{t}$	$\mathfrak{t}$	$\mathfrak{e}$	$\mathfrak{f}$
$\mathfrak{e}$	$\mathfrak{e}$	$\mathfrak{e}$	$\mathfrak{e}$
$\mathfrak{f}$	$\mathfrak{f}$	$\mathfrak{e}$	$\mathfrak{f}$

$\vee$	$\mathfrak{t}$	$\mathfrak{e}$	$\mathfrak{f}$
$\mathfrak{t}$	$\mathfrak{t}$	$\mathfrak{e}$	$\mathfrak{t}$
$\mathfrak{e}$	$\mathfrak{e}$	$\mathfrak{e}$	$\mathfrak{e}$
$\mathfrak{f}$	$\mathfrak{t}$	$\mathfrak{e}$	$\mathfrak{f}$

The tables in Definition 1 induce the *weak Kleene truth functions.* For convenience, denote a connective's corresponding truth function by decorating it with a dot, *e.g.*, we write $\dot{\sim}\mathfrak{t}$ or $\mathcal{I}(\varphi) \mathbin{\dot{\wedge}} \mathcal{I}(\xi)$.

Definition 2. *A propositional weak Kleene interpretation $\mathcal{I}$ is a function $\mathcal{I} : \mathcal{L} \rightarrow \mathcal{V}_3$ respecting the conditions that:*

- $\mathcal{I}(\sim\varphi) = \dot{\sim}(\mathcal{I}(\varphi))$
- $\mathcal{I}(\varphi \wedge \psi) = \mathcal{I}(\varphi) \mathbin{\dot{\wedge}} \mathcal{I}(\psi)$
- $\mathcal{I}(\varphi \vee \psi) = \mathcal{I}(\varphi) \mathbin{\dot{\vee}} \mathcal{I}(\psi)$

Now, let us explore an account of restricted quantification.

2.2 Adding Restricted Quantifiers

Many applications for logical systems in semantics, artificial intelligence, or computer science presuppose some degree of quantification theory. For example, a description logic like $\mathcal{SROIQ}$ expresses the *subsumption* of one concept by another by making a universally quantified statement that every individual falling under once concept falls under the other. We thus have an interest in providing a quantification theory for the systems we are studying.

In practice, however, such applications are keenly concerned with *decidability* and *computational complexity*, meaning that the requirement is not for *full* first-order quantification, but rather the limited resources provided by *restricted quantifiers*. With an eye to allowing *e.g.* the representation of *concept subsumption* or *existential quantification of roles*, we then wish to consider a language of the form: Given a set $\mathbf{C}$ of individual constants and a set $\mathbf{R}$ of relation symbols, we define a language $\mathcal{L}'$ in the standard way, also introducing for any open formula $\varphi(x)$ and $\psi(x)$ the formulae $[\exists x\varphi(x)]\psi(x)$ ("some thing that is a φ is a ψ") and $[\forall x\varphi(x)]\psi(x)$ ("all φs are ψs") for restricted existential and universal quantification, respectively.

Intuitions concerning the *truth conditions* of these sentences are fairly clear. $[\exists x\varphi(x)]\psi(x)$ should be evaluated as $\mathfrak{t}$ if there is a $c \in \mathbf{C}$ such that $\varphi(c)$ and $\psi(c)$ are $\mathfrak{t}$; $[\forall x\varphi(x)]\psi(x)$ should be $\mathfrak{t}$ if there is a guarantee that any time $\varphi(c)$ is true, $\psi(c)$ will be true. If we follow typical interpretations of weak Kleene-like many-valued logics—*e.g.*, that of Halldén and Bochvar—we also allow for cases in which a quantified sentence receives the value $\mathfrak{e}$. The line we will take on this is that a sentence like $[\exists x\varphi(x)]\psi(x)$ is treated as not truth-evaluable precisely in case *there is no point of comparison between* $\varphi(x)$ and $\psi(x)$, that is, there is no individual for which both properties can be *meaningfully* considered. Absent such an individual, it is not clear how the necessary comparison could be carried out.

To formalize these desiderata about restricted quantification, let us consider a precise description of the expectations. Given the foregoing discussion, we would require of an interpretation $\mathcal{I}$ that it observes:

$$\mathcal{I}([\exists x\varphi(x)]\psi(x)) = \begin{cases} \mathfrak{t} & \text{if for some } c,\, \mathcal{I}(\varphi(c)) = \mathfrak{t} \;\&\; \mathcal{I}(\psi(c)) = \mathfrak{t} \\ \mathfrak{e} & \text{if for all } c,\, \text{either } \mathcal{I}(\varphi(c)) = \mathfrak{e} \text{ or } \mathcal{I}(\psi(c)) = \mathfrak{e} \\ \mathfrak{f} & \text{if } \begin{cases} \text{for all } c, \text{ if } \mathcal{I}(\varphi(c)) = \mathfrak{t} \text{ then } \mathcal{I}(\psi(c)) \neq \mathfrak{t} \text{ and} \\ \text{for some } c,\, \mathcal{I}(\varphi(c)) \neq \mathfrak{e} \;\&\; \mathcal{I}(\psi(c)) \neq \mathfrak{e} \end{cases} \end{cases}$$

$$\mathcal{I}([\forall x\varphi(x)]\psi(x)) = \begin{cases} \mathfrak{t} & \text{if } \begin{cases} \text{for all } c, \text{ if } \mathcal{I}(\varphi(c)) = \mathfrak{t} \text{ then } \mathcal{I}(\psi(c)) = \mathfrak{t} \text{ and} \\ \text{for some } c,\, \mathcal{I}(\varphi(c)) \neq \mathfrak{e} \;\&\; \mathcal{I}(\psi(c)) \neq \mathfrak{e} \end{cases} \\ \mathfrak{e} & \text{if for all } c,\, \text{either } \mathcal{I}(\varphi(c)) = \mathfrak{e} \text{ or } \mathcal{I}(\psi(c)) = \mathfrak{e} \\ \mathfrak{f} & \text{if } \begin{cases} \text{for some } c,\, \mathcal{I}(\varphi(c)) = \mathfrak{t} \;\&\; \mathcal{I}(\psi(c)) \neq \mathfrak{t} \text{ and} \\ \text{for some } c',\, \mathcal{I}(\varphi(c')) \neq \mathfrak{e} \;\&\; \mathcal{I}(\psi(c')) \neq \mathfrak{e} \end{cases} \end{cases}$$

To make definitions a bit more elegant, we generalize Carnielli's account of *distribution quantifiers* introduced in [4], where a quantifier is interpreted as a function mapping non-empty sets of truth values to truth values.

Au fond, evaluating restricted quantifiers involves considering for each c the truth values assigned to $\mathcal{I}(\varphi(c))$ and $\mathcal{I}(\psi(c))$; the distribution of these *pairs* of truth values, as it turns out, is sufficient to reproduce the above reasoning. This observation permits us to interpret a restricted quantifier as a function mapping sets of *pairs of truth values* to truth values.

Definition 3. *The* restricted Kleene quantifiers *are functions* $\dot{\exists}$ *and* $\dot{\forall}$ *mapping a nonempty sets* $X \subseteq \mathcal{V}_3^2$ *to truth values from* $\mathcal{V}_3$ *as follows:*

$$\dot{\exists}(X) = \begin{cases} \mathfrak{t} & \text{if } \langle \mathfrak{t}, \mathfrak{t} \rangle \in X \\ \mathfrak{e} & \text{if for all } \langle u, v \rangle \in X, \text{ either } u = \mathfrak{e} \text{ or } v = \mathfrak{e} \\ \mathfrak{f} & \text{if } \langle \mathfrak{t}, \mathfrak{t} \rangle \notin X \text{ \& for some } \langle u, v \rangle \in X, u \neq \mathfrak{e} \text{ and } v \neq \mathfrak{e} \end{cases}$$

$$\dot{\forall}(X) = \begin{cases} \mathfrak{t} & \text{if } \langle \mathfrak{t}, \mathfrak{f} \rangle, \langle \mathfrak{t}, \mathfrak{e} \rangle \notin X \text{ \& for some } \langle u, v \rangle \in X, u \neq \mathfrak{e} \text{ and } v \neq \mathfrak{e} \\ \mathfrak{e} & \text{if for all } \langle u, v \rangle \in X, \text{ either } u = \mathfrak{e} \text{ or } v = \mathfrak{e} \\ \mathfrak{f} & \text{if } \{\langle \mathfrak{t}, \mathfrak{f} \rangle, \langle \mathfrak{t}, \mathfrak{e} \rangle\} \cap X \neq \varnothing \text{ \& for some } \langle u, v \rangle \in X, u \neq \mathfrak{e} \text{ and } v \neq \mathfrak{e} \end{cases}$$

Definition 4. *A predicate weak Kleene interpretation* $\mathcal{I}$ *is a pair* $\langle \mathbf{C}^{\mathcal{I}}, \mathbf{R}^{\mathcal{I}} \rangle$ *where* $\mathbf{C}^{\mathcal{I}}$ *is a* domain *of individuals and* $\mathbf{R}^{\mathcal{I}}$ *is a collection of functions where* $\_^{\mathcal{I}}$ *assigns:*

- *every constant* c *an individual* $c^{\mathcal{I}} \in \mathbf{C}^{\mathcal{I}}$
- *every* n*-ary predicate* R *a function* $R^{\mathcal{I}} : (\mathbf{C}^{\mathcal{I}})^n \to \mathcal{V}_3$

In order to simplify matters, it is assumed that every element of $\mathbf{C}^{\mathcal{I}}$ *is* $c^{\mathcal{I}}$ *for some constant* c.

Definition 5. *A predicate weak Kleene interpretation induces a map from* $\mathcal{L}'$ *to* $\mathcal{V}_3$ *defined as in Definition 2 with the exception that for atomic formulae:*

- $\mathcal{I}(R(c_0, ..., c_{n-1})) = R^{\mathcal{I}}(c_0^{\mathcal{I}}, ..., c_{n-1}^{\mathcal{I}})$

and quantified formulae are evaluated as follows:

- $\mathcal{I}([\exists x \varphi(x)]\psi(x)) = \dot{\exists}(\{\langle \mathcal{I}(\varphi(c)), \mathcal{I}(\psi(c)) \rangle \mid c \in \mathbf{C}\})$
- $\mathcal{I}([\forall x \varphi(x)]\psi(x)) = \dot{\forall}(\{\langle \mathcal{I}(\varphi(c)), \mathcal{I}(\psi(c)) \rangle \mid c \in \mathbf{C}\})$

We note that although the above quantifiers align with reasonable intuitions about restricted quantifiers, DeMorgan's laws fail. Despite this, the quantifiers will satisfy DeMorgan's laws for $\mathsf{S}^{\star}_{\mathsf{fde}}$ and AC, as we will see in subsequent sections.

Validity is then described naturally as:

Definition 6. *Validity in* weak Kleene logic *is defined as truth preservation,* i.e.

$$\Gamma \vDash_{\mathsf{wK}} \varphi \text{ if for all } \mathsf{wK} \text{ interpretations such that } \mathcal{I}[\Gamma] = \{\mathfrak{t}\}, \mathcal{I}(\varphi) = \mathfrak{t}$$

where $\mathcal{I}[\Gamma] = \{\mathcal{I}(\varphi) \mid \varphi \in \Gamma\}$.

2.3 Brief Excursus on Quantification

We have mentioned that the emphasis on restricted quantifiers here is driven not only by the suitability to applications like description logics, but also by difficulties with the general theory of quantification in the weak Kleene setting. Given our concerns, the suitability of a quantification theory stands and falls with its treatment of sentences of the form $[\forall x\varphi(x)]\psi(x)$ and $[\exists x\varphi(x)]\psi(x)$, with standard (and intuitive) translations as $\forall x(\varphi(x) \supset \psi(x))$ (where $\supset$ is the defined material conditional) and $\exists x(\varphi(x) \wedge \psi(x))$, respectively. A special desideratum of full quantification theory on the weak Kleene basis, then, is the suitable interpretation of sentences of these forms.

We have several candidates from the three-valued Kleene family available to extend propositional weak Kleene logic. Most obvious are the strong Kleene and weak Kleene quantifiers, which are essentially infinitary conjunctions/disjunctions. To capture the semantic features, we will describe these as distribution quantifiers in the sense of [4], *i.e.*, functions from sets of truth values to truth values.

Definition 7. *The strong Kleene quantifiers are defined as:*

$$\exists(X) = \begin{cases} \mathfrak{t} & \textit{if } \mathfrak{t} \in X \\ \mathfrak{e} & \textit{if } \mathfrak{e} \in X \textit{ and } \mathfrak{t} \notin X \\ \mathfrak{f} & \textit{if } X = \{\mathfrak{f}\} \end{cases} \qquad \forall(X) = \begin{cases} \mathfrak{t} & \textit{if } X = \{\mathfrak{t}\} \\ \mathfrak{e} & \textit{if } \mathfrak{e} \in X \textit{ and } \mathfrak{f} \notin X \\ \mathfrak{f} & \textit{if } \mathfrak{f} \in X \end{cases}$$

Comparing Definition 7 to the strong Kleene tables of [14] makes clear that *e.g.*, strong Kleene existential quantification is essentially infinitary strong Kleene disjunction (and *mutatis mutandis* for universal quantification).

By applying this analogy to *weak* Kleene connectives, we can define *weak Kleene quantifiers* in a manner that carries over the hallmark features.[1] The weak quantifiers may be defined as follows.

Definition 8. *The weak Kleene quantifiers are defined as:*

$$\exists(X) = \begin{cases} \mathfrak{t} & \textit{if } \mathfrak{t} \in X \textit{ and } \mathfrak{e} \notin X \\ \mathfrak{e} & \textit{if } \mathfrak{e} \in X \\ \mathfrak{f} & \textit{if } X = \{\mathfrak{f}\} \end{cases} \qquad \forall(X) = \begin{cases} \mathfrak{t} & \textit{if } X = \{\mathfrak{t}\} \\ \mathfrak{e} & \textit{if } \mathfrak{e} \in X \\ \mathfrak{f} & \textit{if } \mathfrak{f} \in X \textit{ and } \mathfrak{e} \notin X \end{cases}$$

Upon examination, each set of quantifiers has properties that conflict with our intuitive understanding of the above first-order formulae, making neither account entirely suitable for our purposes.

If we look to universally quantified statements, the *strong* Kleene quantifiers seem to conflict with our intuitions. We might expect that $\forall x(\varphi(x) \supset \psi(x))$ should be considered *true* if it holds that whenever $\varphi(c)$ is evaluated as $\mathfrak{t}$, also $\psi(c)$ is evaluated as $\mathfrak{t}$. But this is contradicted in cases in which there exists *some* c' for which either $\varphi(c')$ or $\psi(c')$ is evaluated as $\mathfrak{e}$. In such a case, $\varphi(c') \supset \psi(c')$ will be evaluated as $\mathfrak{e}$, and $\forall x(\varphi(x) \supset \psi(x))$ will not be evaluated as $\mathfrak{t}$. As an example from the Halldén-Bochvar tradition, this is akin to saying that even though every thing that is a dog is a mammal, the fact that "the number two is a dog" is meaningless is sufficient to render "all dogs are mammals" meaningless.

[1] Although not frequently encountered in the literature, Malinowski describes them in [15].

In the existentially quantified case, the *weak* quantifiers diverge from expected behavior. According to the weak Kleene quantifiers, having a witness c for which $\varphi(c)$ and $\psi(c)$ are true is insufficient to establish the truth of the formula in case for some c', $\varphi(c')$ is evaluated as $\mathfrak{e}$. To provide a simple illustration, even if we know, *e.g.*, that both "Caesar is a skilled writer" and "Caesar is a general" are true, the fact that "the number two is a skilled writer" is meaningless propagates and renders "there exists a skilled writer who is a general" meaningless as well.

In short, both pairs of Kleene quantifiers conflict in some way with our intuitions.[2] There *are* potential alternatives to consider. In the context of strict-tolerant interpretations of weak Kleene, [8] considers Carnielli *et al.*'s quantifiers from [3], calling them "immune Kleene quantifiers" due to their being infinitary analogues of the immune connectives of [17]. The discussion in [8] suggests that it is plausible that the restricted quantifiers here respect the immune quantifiers. But this is left for another time.

2.4 Tableau Calculus for Weak Kleene Logic with Restricted Quantifiers

A tableau $\mathcal{T}$ is a tree with nodes that are decorated with a signed formula of the form $u : \varphi$. Although our truth values appear as signs, we also incorporate two additional signs to simplify the rules: $\mathfrak{m}$ and $\mathfrak{n}$. $\mathfrak{m}$—understood as "meaningful"—decorates a formula φ when both $\mathfrak{t} : \varphi$ and $\mathfrak{f} : \varphi$ are available for branching. Likewise, $\mathfrak{n}$—understood as "nontrue"—decorates a formula when both $\mathfrak{f} : \varphi$ and $\mathfrak{e} : \varphi$ are available.

Each node that is not a hypothesis is added to $\mathcal{T}$ by applying a rule to a *target* node. In describing the rules, we follow [4] in using $\circ$ to indicate that one or more items are to be added to the same branch and $+$ to indicate that new branches should be created for each formula in its scope.

Definition 9. *The tableau calculus* **wKrQ** *for weak Kleene with restricted quantifiers is captured by the following rules:*

$$\frac{v : \sim\varphi}{\dot{\sim} v : \varphi} \qquad \frac{\mathfrak{m} : \varphi}{\mathfrak{t} : \varphi + \mathfrak{f} : \varphi} \qquad \frac{\mathfrak{n} : \varphi}{\mathfrak{f} : \varphi + \mathfrak{e} : \varphi}$$

$$\frac{v : \varphi \wedge \psi}{+_{v_0 \dot{\wedge} v_1 = v}\{v_0 : \varphi \circ v_1 : \psi\}} \qquad \frac{v : \varphi \vee \psi}{+_{v_0 \dot{\vee} v_1 = v}\{v_0 : \varphi \circ v_1 : \psi\}}$$

$$\frac{\mathfrak{t} : [\exists\varphi(x)]\psi(x)}{\mathfrak{t} : \varphi(c) \circ \mathfrak{t} : \psi(c)} \quad \frac{\mathfrak{f} : [\exists\varphi(x)]\psi(x)}{\mathfrak{m} : \varphi(c) \circ \mathfrak{m} : \psi(c) \circ (\mathfrak{n} : \varphi(a) + \mathfrak{n} : \psi(a))} \quad \frac{\mathfrak{e} : [\exists\varphi(x)]\psi(x)}{\mathfrak{e} : \varphi(a) + \mathfrak{e} : \psi(a)}$$

$$\frac{\mathfrak{t} : [\forall\varphi(x)]\psi(x)}{\mathfrak{m} : \varphi(c) \circ \mathfrak{m} : \psi(c) \circ (\mathfrak{n} : \varphi(a) + \mathfrak{t} : \psi(a))} \quad \frac{\mathfrak{e} : [\forall\varphi(x)]\psi(x)}{\mathfrak{e} : \varphi(a) + \mathfrak{e} : \psi(a)}$$

[2] One qualification is in order, namely, that the critique emphasizes the *semantic interpretations*. Recent work by Andreas Fjellstad in [10] provides a very elegant *proof-theoretic* analysis but explicitly declines to "engage in the discussion" of interpretation.

$$\frac{\mathfrak{f} : [\forall \varphi(x)]\psi(x)}{\mathfrak{m} : \varphi(c) \circ \mathfrak{m} : \psi(c) \circ \mathfrak{t} : \varphi(c') \circ \mathfrak{n} : \psi(c')}$$

where v is any element of $\mathcal{V}_3$, c or c' are new to a branch, and a is arbitrary.

Definition 10. *A branch $\mathcal{B}$ of a tableau $\mathcal{T}$* closes *if there is a sentence φ and distinct $v, u \in \mathcal{V}_3$ such that both $v : \varphi$ and $u : \varphi$ appear on $\mathcal{B}$.*[3]

Definition 11. $\{\varphi_0, ..., \varphi_{n-1}\} \vdash_{\mathbf{wKrQ}} \varphi$ *when every branch of a tableau $\mathcal{T}$ with initial nodes $\{\mathfrak{t} : \varphi_0, ..., \mathfrak{t} : \varphi_{n-1}, \mathfrak{n} : \varphi\}$ closes.*

We now show soundness of **wKrQ**:

Theorem 1 (Soundness of wKrQ). *If $\Gamma \vdash_{\mathbf{wKrQ}} \varphi$ then $\Gamma \vDash_{\mathsf{wK}} \varphi$.*

Proof. Inspection confirms that each rule of **wKrQ** exhaustively characterizes the corresponding semantic conditions from Definitions 4 and 5. Thus, when every branch closes in a tableau proving $\Gamma \vdash \varphi$, this shows that no model $\mathcal{I}$ for which $\mathcal{I}[\Gamma] = \{\mathrm{t}\}$ and $\mathcal{I}(\varphi) \neq \mathrm{t}$ is possible, *i.e.*, $\Gamma \vDash_{\mathsf{wK}} \varphi$.

For completeness, we give several definitions and lemmas:

Definition 12. *Given a tableau with an open branch $\mathcal{B}$, we define the* branch interpretation $\mathcal{I}_{\mathcal{B}}$ *and domain $\mathbf{C}^{\mathcal{I}_{\mathcal{B}}}$ as follows:*

- *For all constants c appearing on the branch, $c^{\mathcal{I}_{\mathcal{B}}}$ is a unique element of $\mathbf{C}^{\mathcal{I}_{\mathcal{B}}}$*
- *For all relation symbols R and tuples $c_0, ..., c_{n-1}$ appearing on the branch,*
  $R^{\mathcal{I}_{\mathcal{B}}}(c_0^{\mathcal{I}_{\mathcal{B}}}, ..., c_{n-1}^{\mathcal{I}_{\mathcal{B}}}) = \begin{cases} v & \text{if } v : R(c_0, ..., c_{n-1}) \text{ is on } \mathcal{B} \\ \mathfrak{e} & \text{otherwise} \end{cases}$

Lemma 1. *For all sentences φ and $v \in \mathcal{V}_3$, if $v : \varphi$ is on $\mathcal{B}$, then $\mathcal{I}_{\mathcal{B}}(\varphi) = v$.*

Proof. As basis step, note that Definition 12 guarantees the property to hold of atomic sentences. As induction hypothesis, assume that the property holds for all subformulae of φ.

In case $\varphi = \sim\psi$, if $v : \sim\psi$ is on $\mathcal{B}$, then the appropriate rule from **wKrQ** must at some point be applied on the branch, whence $\dot{\sim} v : \psi$ is on the branch. By induction hypothesis, $\mathcal{I}_{\mathcal{B}}(\psi) = \dot{\sim} v$, whence $\mathcal{I}_{\mathcal{B}}(\sim\psi) = v$.

For binary connectives, we treat the case in which $v : \psi \wedge \xi$ is on $\mathcal{B}$. The rules then guarantee values v_0 and v_1 such that $v_0 : \psi$ and $v_1 : \xi$ are on $\mathcal{B}$. By the induction hypothesis, then, $\mathcal{I}_{\mathcal{B}}(\psi) = v_0$ and $\mathcal{I}_{\mathcal{B}}(\xi) = v_1$. But per Definition 9, v_0 and v_1 are selected just in case $v_0 \mathbin{\dot{\wedge}} v_1 = v$, whence $\mathcal{I}_{\mathcal{B}}(\psi \wedge \xi) = v$.

For the quantifiers, suppose that $v : [\exists x\psi(x)]\xi(x)$ is on $\mathcal{B}$. Then we consider a case for each possible choice of v:

[3] *N.b.* that the criterion for closure is that a formula appears signed with *distinct truth values* and not *distinct signs*. *E.g.*, $\mathfrak{m} : \varphi$ is merely a notational device for potential branching, so both $\mathfrak{m} : \varphi$ and $\mathfrak{t} : \varphi$ may harmoniously appear in an open branch.

- If $v = \mathfrak{t}$, then there is a constant c for which $\mathfrak{t} : \psi(c)$ and $\mathfrak{t} : \xi(c)$ are on $\mathcal{B}$. By induction hypothesis, also $\mathcal{I}_{\mathcal{B}}(\psi(c)) = \mathfrak{t}$ and $\mathcal{I}_{\mathcal{B}}(\xi(c)) = \mathfrak{t}$, whence $\mathcal{I}_{\mathcal{B}}([\exists x\psi(x)]\xi(x)) = \mathfrak{t}$.
- When $v = \mathfrak{e}$, for every constant c on $\mathcal{B}$, either $\mathfrak{e} : \psi(c)$ or $\mathfrak{e} : \xi(c)$ appears on $\mathcal{B}$. By choice of $\mathbf{C}^{\mathcal{I}_{\mathcal{B}}}$, for all c', either $\mathcal{I}_{\mathcal{B}}(\psi(c')) = \mathfrak{e}$ or $\mathcal{I}_{\mathcal{B}}(\xi(c')) = \mathfrak{e}$; that $\mathcal{I}_{\mathcal{B}}$ respects $\dot{\exists}$ thus guarantees that $\mathcal{I}_{\mathcal{B}}([\exists x\psi(x)]\xi(x)) = \mathfrak{e}$.
- That $v = \mathfrak{f}$ reveals two points about $\mathcal{B}$: One, there is a c for which both $\psi(c)$ and $\xi(c)$ appear on $\mathcal{B}$ signed by either $\mathfrak{t}$ or $\mathfrak{f}$. By induction hypothesis, this means that $\mathcal{I}_{\mathcal{B}}(\psi(c)) \neq \mathfrak{e}$ and $\mathcal{I}_{\mathcal{B}}(\xi(c)) \neq \mathfrak{e}$. Two, for no c' are both $\mathfrak{t} : \psi(c')$ and $\mathfrak{t} : \xi(c)'$ on $\mathcal{B}$; by the induction hypothesis, nor do both $\mathcal{I}_{\mathcal{B}}(\psi(c')) = \mathfrak{t}$ and $\mathcal{I}_{\mathcal{B}}(\xi(c')) = \mathfrak{t}$ hold for any c'. Between these two observations, the definition of $\dot{\exists}$, and induction hypothesis, $\mathcal{I}_{\mathcal{B}}([\exists\psi(x)]\xi(x)) = \mathfrak{f}$.

The cases of disjunction and the universal restricted quantifier follow from nearly identical reasoning.

Theorem 2 (Completeness of wKrQ). *If $\Gamma \vDash_{\mathsf{wK}} \varphi$ then $\Gamma \vdash_{\mathbf{wKrQ}} \varphi$.*

Proof. In line with the standard argument, we prove the contrapositive. Suppose that $\Gamma \nvdash_{\mathbf{wKrQ}} \varphi$. Then there is an open branch on a tableau including $\mathfrak{t} : \gamma_i$ for each $\gamma_i \in \Gamma$ but on which either $\mathfrak{f} : \varphi$ or $\mathfrak{e} : \varphi$ appears. By Lemma 1, $\mathcal{I}_{\mathcal{B}}(\gamma_i) = \mathfrak{t}$ for all $\gamma_i \in \Gamma$ but $\mathcal{I}_{\mathcal{B}}(\varphi) \neq \mathfrak{t}$. $\mathcal{I}_{\mathcal{B}}$ serves as a counterexample witnessing that $\Gamma \nvDash_{\mathsf{wK}} \varphi$.

3 Bilateral Logics Related to Weak Kleene Logic

Although we find the question of providing an intuitive quantification theory in the weak Kleene setting to be intriguing, weak Kleene logic seems to have little promise as a tool for *e.g.* semantic representation of intentional contexts. However, several logical frameworks that *are* obviously good candidates enjoy a close relationship to weak Kleene logic, allowing us to directly employ the results on wK.

We now examine two propositional logics related to wK: Charles Daniels' "first degree story logic" $\mathsf{S}^{\star}_{\mathtt{fde}}$ described in [6] and Richard Angell's logic of analytic containment AC described in [1]. Each is weaker than classical propositional logic and each has been offered as a notion of validity under which weak, non-veridical theories can be closed. [6] argues that *fictions* are closed under $\mathsf{S}^{\star}_{\mathtt{fde}}$; Correia in [5] and Fine in [9] have argued that AC preserves equivalence of facts, whence even classes of *e.g.* desires are closed under AC consequence. Both, therefore, are intriguing foundations for applications like description logics—*presuming the details of restricted quantification are worked out.*

As these two systems are less familiar than wK, it may help the reader to provide axiomatic presentations of propositional AC and $\mathsf{S}^{\star}_{\mathtt{fde}}$. As *consecution calculi*, the first-degree account of AC is determined by the following axioms:

AC1a $\varphi \vdash \sim\sim\varphi$
AC1b $\sim\sim\varphi \vdash \varphi$
AC2 $\varphi \vdash \varphi \wedge \varphi$
AC3 $\varphi \wedge \psi \vdash \varphi$
AC4 $\varphi \vee \psi \vdash \psi \vee \varphi$
AC5a $\varphi \vee (\psi \vee \xi) \vdash (\varphi \vee \psi) \vee \xi$
AC5b $(\varphi \vee \psi) \vee \xi \vdash \varphi \vee (\psi \vee \xi)$
AC6a $\varphi \vee (\psi \wedge \xi) \vdash (\varphi \vee \psi) \wedge (\varphi \vee \xi)$
AC6b $(\varphi \vee \psi) \wedge (\varphi \vee \xi) \vdash \varphi \vee (\psi \wedge \xi)$

and rules:
AC7 If $\varphi \vdash \psi$ and $\psi \vdash \varphi$ are derivable then $\sim\varphi \vdash \sim\psi$ is derivable
AC8 If $\varphi \vdash \psi$ is derivable then $\varphi \vee \xi \vdash \psi \vee \xi$ is derivable
AC9 If $\varphi \vdash \psi$ and $\psi \vdash \xi$ are derivable then $\varphi \vdash \xi$ is derivable

$\mathsf{S}^{\star}_{\mathtt{fde}}$ can be defined by adding the following:
S1 $\varphi \vdash \varphi \vee \sim\varphi$

For a multiple-premise formulation with finite premises Γ, provability of $\Gamma \vdash \varphi$ can be understood as derivability of $\bigwedge \Gamma \vdash \varphi$.

In [7], a tight connection between wK (on the one hand) and $\mathsf{S}^{\star}_{\mathtt{fde}}$ and AC (on the other) is described. This connection can be summarized as the idea that these two logics are essentially *bilateral*—tracking distinct values for both truth and falsity—with the calculation of truth values and falsity values being performed by parallel positive weak Kleene interpretations.

3.1 $\mathsf{S}^{\star}_{\mathtt{fde}}$ and AC

A semantic value for $\mathsf{S}^{\star}_{\mathtt{fde}}$ and AC is a pair $\langle u, v\rangle$ with $u, v \in \mathcal{V}_3$. We can read the first coordinate as an indicator of *corroborating* evidence for a formula and the second coordinate as representing whether there is *refuting* evidence. For example, that φ receives value $\langle \mathfrak{t}, \mathfrak{f}\rangle$ can be understood as "there exists evidence in favor of the truth of φ and no evidence refuting φ"; that it receives value $\langle \mathfrak{f}, \mathfrak{f}\rangle$ can be read as "there no evidence either supporting or refuting φ."

We define propositional interpretations for AC:

Definition 13. *A propositional* AC *interpretation $\mathcal{I}$ is a function $\mathcal{I} : \mathcal{L} \to \mathcal{V}_3 \times \mathcal{V}_3$. Let $\mathcal{I}_0$ and $\mathcal{I}_1$ denote functions mapping formulae φ to the first and second coordinates of $\mathcal{I}(\varphi)$.*

- $\mathcal{I}(\sim\varphi) = \langle \mathcal{I}_1(\varphi), \mathcal{I}_0(\varphi)\rangle$
- $\mathcal{I}(\varphi \wedge \psi) = \langle \mathcal{I}_0(\varphi) \dot{\wedge} \mathcal{I}_0(\psi), \mathcal{I}_1(\varphi) \dot{\vee} \mathcal{I}_1(\psi)\rangle$
- $\mathcal{I}(\varphi \vee \psi) = \langle \mathcal{I}_0(\varphi) \dot{\vee} \mathcal{I}_0(\psi), \mathcal{I}_1(\varphi) \dot{\wedge} \mathcal{I}_1(\psi)\rangle$

N.b. that negation is clearly a "toggle" negation in the sense of [13] as it simply exchanges the truth coordinate for the falsity coordinate. Moreover, the duality between *e.g.* conjunction and disjunction is respected by defining the falsity of a conjunction as the disjunction of the falsity values of the conjuncts.

Semantically, $\mathsf{S}^{\star}_{\mathtt{fde}}$ is yielded from AC by restricting the available values to $\hat{\mathcal{V}}^2_3 = \{\langle \mathfrak{t}, \mathfrak{t}\rangle, \langle \mathfrak{t}, \mathfrak{f}\rangle, \langle \mathfrak{f}, \mathfrak{t}\rangle, \langle \mathfrak{f}, \mathfrak{f}\rangle, \langle \mathfrak{e}, \mathfrak{e}\rangle\}$. From the Halldén-Bochvar perspective, this is equivalent to enforcing a condition that a formula is meaningless precisely when its negation is.

Definition 14. *A propositional* $\mathsf{S}^{\star}_{\mathtt{fde}}$ *interpretation* $\mathcal{I}$ *is an* AC *interpretation where atoms are mapped to the set* $\hat{\mathcal{V}}^2_3$.

We now enrich the propositional base with the needed expressivity.

3.2 Adding Restricted Quantifiers

The discussion of restricted quantification and the way that duals are reflected in the bilateral interpretation of truth values jointly lead to a natural interpretation of quantification in $\mathsf{S}^{\star}_{\mathtt{fde}}$ and AC.

Definition 15. *A predicate* AC *(respectively,* $\mathsf{S}^{\star}_{\mathtt{fde}}$*) interpretation is a function* $\mathcal{I}$ *from* $\mathcal{L}'$ *to* $\mathcal{V}^2_3$ *(respectively,* $\hat{\mathcal{V}}^2_3$*) evaluating connectives as in Definition 13 and respecting the following:*

$$\mathcal{I}([\exists x\varphi(x)]\psi(x)) = \langle \dot{\exists}(\{\langle \mathcal{I}_0(\varphi(c)), \mathcal{I}_0(\psi(c))\rangle \mid c \in \mathbf{C}\}), \dot{\forall}(\{\langle \mathcal{I}_0(\varphi(c)), \mathcal{I}_1(\psi(c))\rangle \mid c \in \mathbf{C}\})\rangle$$
$$\mathcal{I}([\forall x\varphi(x)]\psi(x)) = \langle \dot{\forall}(\{\langle \mathcal{I}_0(\varphi(c)), \mathcal{I}_0(\psi(c))\rangle \mid c \in \mathbf{C}\}), \dot{\exists}(\{\langle \mathcal{I}_0(\varphi(c)), \mathcal{I}_1(\psi(c))\rangle \mid c \in \mathbf{C}\})\rangle$$

The restricted quantifiers we have introduced are perfectly harmonious with the bilateral, weak Kleene-based interpretation from [7]. In the bilateral context, consider two notions—one weak, one strong—in which $[\exists x\varphi(x)]\psi(x)$ might be thought to be *false* in an interpretation. In a *weak* sense, the sentence might be considered *refuted* whenever searches for a c satisfying both $\varphi(x)$ and $\psi(x)$ have *failed*, *i.e.*, one has not successfully *verified* the sentence. In contrast, a *stronger* notion can be invoked, *i.e.*, that there is a *demonstration* that any c satisfying $\varphi(x)$ *must falsify* $\psi(x)$.

Such a distinction is reflected in the assignment of a bilateral truth value $\langle u, v\rangle \in \mathcal{V}^2_3$ to a quantified sentence $[\exists x\varphi(x)]\psi(x)$. As in the propositional case, the coordinates u and v represent the status of the *verification* and *falsification* of $[\exists x\varphi(x)]\psi(x)$, respectively. Thus, the *weak* notion of refutation described in the foregoing paragraph may be codified by the assignment of a value $\langle \mathfrak{f}, v\rangle$ to the sentence, *i.e.*, whenever it is *false* that the sentence has been *verified*. In contrast, the *strong* type of refutation of $[\exists x\varphi(x)]\psi(x)$ is reflected in its receipt of a value of the form $\langle v, \mathfrak{t}\rangle$, *i.e.*, there is *positive* information attesting to the *falsification* of the sentence.

The reader can confirm that the bilateral approach in fact improves on the presentation for wK inasmuch as DeMorgan's laws are reestablished; as $\mathsf{S}^{\star}_{\mathtt{fde}}$ and AC are our actual targets, this should relieve concerns about their failure in wK.

One further observation is required, establishing that $\hat{\mathcal{V}}^2_3$ is in fact closed under the bilateral interpretation of the restricted quantifiers.

Lemma 2. $\hat{\mathcal{V}}^2_3$*—the collection of* $\mathsf{S}^{\star}_{\mathtt{fde}}$ *truth values—is closed under the above interpretation of the restricted quantifiers.*

Proof. For a valuation $\mathcal{I}$ mapping all atomic formulae to one of the $\mathsf{S}^{\star}_{\mathtt{fde}}$ truth values, the atomic and literal cases form a basis step. Assume that for all subformulae ψ of φ, $\mathcal{I}_0(\psi) = \mathfrak{e}$ if and only if $\mathcal{I}_1(\psi) = \mathfrak{e}$. That the set is closed under negation and binary connectives is straightforward (see [7]), leaving only the quantifiers; we consider existential quantification, as universal quantification is analogous.

We show that the induction hypothesis entails that $\mathcal{I}_0([\exists x\varphi(x)]\psi(x)) = \mathfrak{e}$ occurs if and only if $\mathcal{I}_1([\exists x\varphi(x)]\psi(x)) = \mathfrak{e}$. Suppose that $\mathcal{I}_0([\exists x\varphi(x)]\psi(x)) = \mathfrak{e}$. By definition, this holds when for all $\langle u, v\rangle \in \{\langle \mathcal{I}_0(\varphi(c)), \mathcal{I}_0(\psi(c))\rangle \mid c \in \mathbf{C}\}$ either $u = \mathfrak{e}$ or $v = \mathfrak{e}$. By induction hypothesis, $\mathcal{I}_0(\psi(c)) = \mathfrak{e}$ precisely when $\mathcal{I}_1(\psi(c)) = \mathfrak{e}$. Thus, this holds if and only if the same can be said for each $\langle u, v\rangle \in \{\langle \mathcal{I}_0(\varphi(c)), \mathcal{I}_1(\psi(c))\rangle \mid c \in \mathbf{C}\}$. But this is just to say that $\mathcal{I}_1([\exists x\varphi(x)]\psi(x)) = \mathfrak{e}$.

We define validity in $\mathsf{S}^{\star}_{\mathtt{fde}}$ and AC jointly:

Definition 16. *Let* L *be either* $\mathsf{S}^{\star}_{\mathtt{fde}}$ *or* AC. *Then* L *validity is defined as truth preservation,*[4] i.e.

$$\Gamma \vDash_{\mathsf{L}} \varphi \textit{ if for all } \mathsf{L} \textit{ interpretations such that } \mathcal{I}_0[\Gamma] = \{\mathsf{t}\},\ \mathcal{I}_0(\varphi) = \mathsf{t}.$$

3.3 Tableau Calculi for $\mathsf{S}^{\star}_{\mathtt{fde}}$ and AC with Restricted Quantifiers

Rather than introduce signed tableau calculi with five or nine values for $\mathsf{S}^{\star}_{\mathtt{fde}}$ and AC, we leverage their close relationship with wK to supply tableaux.

A trick employed by Kamide in [12] for the study of the bilateral Nelson logic $\mathsf{N4}$ will play a role. Nelson's $\mathsf{N4}$ from [16] can be given a bilateral interpretation in which its measures of truth and falsity are being individually calculated by positive intuitionistic logic; Kamide shows that by introducing for each atomic parameter p a parameter $p^{\star}$ corresponding to p's *falsity value*, $\mathsf{N4}$ can be embedded into positive intuitionistic logic. As a similarly bilateral semantics, the trick can be employed in our case as well:

Definition 17. *For a language* $\mathcal{L}$, *let* $\mathcal{L}^{\star}$ *be the language that includes for every predicate* R *a predicate of the same arity* $R^{\star}$; *for a sentence* $\varphi \in \mathcal{L}$, *let* $\varphi^{\star} \in \mathcal{L}^{\star}$ *be:*

- $R(t_0, ..., t_{n-1})^{\star} = R(t_0, ..., t_{n-1})$ *and* $({\sim}R(t_0, ..., t_{n-1}))^{\star} = R^{\star}(t_0, ..., t_{n-1})$
- $({\sim}{\sim}\varphi)^{\star} = \varphi^{\star}$
- $(\varphi \wedge \psi)^{\star} = (\varphi)^{\star} \wedge (\psi)^{\star}$ *and* $(\varphi \vee \psi)^{\star} = (\varphi)^{\star} \vee (\psi)^{\star}$
- $[\forall x\varphi(x)]\psi(x))^{\star} = [\forall x(\varphi(x))^{\star}](\psi(x))^{\star}$
- $[\exists x\varphi(x)]\psi(x))^{\star} = [\exists x(\varphi(x))^{\star}](\psi(x))^{\star}$
- $({\sim}(\varphi \wedge \psi))^{\star} = ({\sim}\varphi)^{\star} \vee ({\sim}\psi)^{\star}$ *and* $({\sim}(\varphi \vee \psi))^{\star} = ({\sim}\varphi)^{\star} \wedge ({\sim}\psi)^{\star}$
- $({\sim}[\forall x\varphi(x)]\psi(x))^{\star} = [\exists x(\varphi(x))^{\star}]({\sim}\psi(x))^{\star}$
- $({\sim}[\exists x\varphi(x)]\psi(x))^{\star} = [\forall x(\varphi(x))^{\star}]({\sim}\psi(x))^{\star}$

[4] A reviewer has observed that alternative definitions could be considered, *e.g.*, requiring preservation of *non-refutability* in the second coordinate. Whether such alternatives determine distinct consequence relations is an interesting question.

For a set of sentences Γ, give $\Gamma^\star$ the natural definition as the translation of each element of Γ.

The techniques of [7] immediately adapt when restricted quantifiers are in play to yield the following lemmas:

Lemma 3. *For an* AC *interpretation $\mathcal{I}$, $\mathcal{I}(\varphi) = \mathcal{I}(\varphi^\star)$.*

Lemma 4. *$\Gamma \vDash_{\mathsf{AC}} \varphi$ iff $\Gamma^\star \vDash_{\mathsf{wK}} \varphi^\star$*

The tableau proof theory **ACrQ** is yielded by modifying Definition 9:

Definition 18. *Let* **wKrQ**$^+$ *be the result of dropping the $\sim$ rule from* **wKrQ**. *Then the tableau calculus* **ACrQ** *is defined by adding to* **wKrQ**$^+$*:*

$$\frac{v : {\sim}R(c_0, ..., c_{n-1})}{v : R^\star(c_0, ..., c_{n-1})} \qquad \frac{v : {\sim}R^\star(c_0, ..., c_{n-1})}{v : R(c_0, ..., c_{n-1})} \qquad \frac{v : {\sim}{\sim}\varphi}{v : \varphi}$$

$$\frac{v : {\sim}(\varphi \wedge \psi)}{v : ({\sim}\varphi \vee {\sim}\psi)} \qquad \frac{v : {\sim}(\varphi \vee \psi)}{v : ({\sim}\varphi \wedge {\sim}\psi)} \qquad \frac{v : {\sim}[\forall\varphi(x)]\psi(x)}{v : [\exists\varphi(x)]{\sim}\psi(x)} \qquad \frac{v : {\sim}[\exists\varphi(x)]\psi(x)}{v : [\forall\varphi(x)]{\sim}\psi(x)}$$

where v is any element of $\mathcal{V}_3$.

Lemma 5. *If $u : \varphi$ and $v : \psi$, for distinct u and v, are on a branch of an* **ACrQ** *tableau such that $\varphi^\star = \psi^\star$, then the branch will close.*

Proof. This clearly holds for atomic formulae, so take this as a basis step and assume that it holds for all subformulae of φ and ψ and their negations.

Now, if either φ and ψ are negated, applying negation elimination rules to the branch yields non-negated formulae, so assume them to not be negated. Importantly, that $\varphi^\star = \psi^\star$ ensures that φ and ψ will share a common primary logical operator.

For the case of a binary connective, suppose without loss of generality that $\varphi = \varphi_0 \wedge \varphi_1$ and $\psi = \psi_0 \wedge \psi_1$. Applying the conjunction rule to these nodes will yield a number of branches in which truth values are distributed to $u_0 : \varphi_0$, $u_1 : \varphi_1$, $v_0 : \psi_0$, and $v_1 : \psi_1$. But the *functionality* of $\dot{\wedge}$ ensures that in any such branch, either $u_0 \neq v_0$ or $u_1 \neq v_1$. Because $\varphi_i^\star = \psi_i^\star$ for each i, the induction hypothesis ensures that each branch will close.

Similar considerations apply to the case in which φ and ψ are quantified sentences; suppose them to be $[\exists x\varphi_0(x)]\varphi_1(x)$ and $[\exists x\psi_0(x)]\psi_1(x)$. No matter the values of u and v, applying the appropriate rules in the right order will result in assortment of branches in which $u_0 : \varphi_0(c)$, $u_1 : \varphi_1(c)$, $v_0 : \psi_0(c)$, and $v_1 : \psi_1(c)$ appear. But either $u_0 \neq v_0$ or $u_1 \neq v_1$ must hold in every such case and, by the induction hypothesis, any resulting branches will close.

Lemma 6. *$\Gamma \vdash_{\mathbf{ACrQ}} \varphi$ if and only if $\Gamma^\star \vdash_{\mathbf{ACrQ}} \varphi^\star$*

Proof. Take a tableau $\mathcal{T}$ and construct a new tableau $\mathcal{T}^{\circ}$ by replacing every node n with formula $u : \varphi$ by a node n° decorated with $u : \varphi^{\star}$. We first prove that the application of rules is preserved through the transformation. There are two cases to consider: those in which φ is negated and when it is not.

When φ is *not* negated then there must be one of the $\mathbf{wKrQ}^{+}$ rules that applies. In all such cases, φ and $\varphi^{\star}$ have the same primary logical operator, *e.g.*, when φ is a conjunction, $\varphi^{\star}$ is a conjunction. Thus, whenever a node n on $\mathcal{T}$ with a non-negated sentence $u : \varphi$ has children, the same rule will be applicable to n°. Moreover, the decomposition of complex sentences to subformulae induced by the rules are respected by the clauses defining $\_^{\star}$. In other words, if the application of a $\mathbf{wKrQ}^{+}$ rule to a node n decorated by $u : \varphi$ yields children $u_0 : \varphi_0, ..., u_{n-1} : \varphi_{n-1}$, the same rule, applied to n°, yields children $u_0 : \varphi_0^{\star}, ..., , u_{n-1} : \varphi_{n-1}^{\star}$.

When φ *is* negated, $\mathcal{T}$ must apply one of the proper **ACrQ** rules involving negation. In this case, both parent and child nodes in $\mathcal{T}^{\circ}$ will be decorated by the same signed formula. What was a negation rule in $\mathcal{T}$ will be a vacuous repetition in $\mathcal{T}^{\circ}$.

Importantly, whenever distinct $u : \varphi$ and $v : \varphi$ appear in a branch in $\mathcal{T}$, $u : \varphi^{\star}$ and $v : \varphi^{\star}$ will appear in that branch in $\mathcal{T}^{\circ}$, *i.e.*, a closed branch in $\mathcal{T}$ will remain closed in $\mathcal{T}^{\circ}$. This establishes the left-to-right direction of the lemma.

Because $\_^{\star}$ is not injective, $\mathcal{T}^{\circ}$ may identify many sentences that $\mathcal{T}$ sees as distinct. Thus, one may worry about cases in which $\mathcal{T}$ has an open branch that is closed in $\mathcal{T}^{\circ}$, precluding the right-to-left direction of the lemma. But Lemma 5 clears a path forward; if such a case occurs, $\mathcal{T}$ can be extended to a new tableau $\mathcal{T}'$ in which any such branches will ultimately be closed.

Given our results on wK, soundness of **ACrQ** is established:

Theorem 3 (Soundness of ACrQ). *If* $\Gamma \vdash_{\mathbf{ACrQ}} \varphi$ *then* $\Gamma \vDash_{\mathsf{AC}} \varphi$.

Proof. Suppose that $\mathcal{T}$ is a tableau demonstrating that $\Gamma \vdash_{\mathbf{ACrQ}} \varphi$. Then by Lemma 6, there is a closed **ACrQ** tableau showing that $\Gamma^{\star} \vdash_{\mathbf{ACrQ}} \varphi^{\star}$. But *this* proof involves no *properly* **ACrQ** rules—it is thus a $\mathbf{wKrQ}^{+}$ (and *a fortiori* a **wKrQ**) tableau. Thus, $\Gamma^{\star} \vdash_{\mathbf{wKrQ}} \varphi^{\star}$ and by Theorem 1, $\Gamma^{\star} \vDash_{\mathsf{wK}} \varphi^{\star}$. Finally, by Lemma 4, we conclude that $\Gamma \vDash_{\mathsf{AC}} \varphi$.

Completeness similarly follows from previous remarks:

Theorem 4 (Completeness of ACrQ). *If* $\Gamma \vDash_{\mathsf{AC}} \varphi$ *then* $\Gamma \vdash_{\mathbf{ACrQ}} \varphi$

Proof. We prove the contrapositive. Suppose that $\Gamma \nvdash_{\mathbf{ACrQ}} \varphi$. Then by Lemma 6, $\Gamma^{\star} \nvdash_{\mathbf{ACrQ}} \varphi^{\star}$. As negation is essentially eliminated, $\Gamma^{\star} \nvdash_{\mathbf{wKrQ}} \varphi^{\star}$, whence we infer the existence of a **wKrQ** tableau with an open branch $\mathcal{B}$. Definition 12 can then be applied to yield a weak Kleene branch model $\mathcal{I}_{\mathcal{B}}$ for which $\mathcal{I}_{\mathcal{B}}[\Gamma] = \{\mathsf{t}\}$ and $\mathcal{I}_{\mathcal{B}}(\varphi) \neq \mathsf{t}$.

$\mathcal{I}_{\mathcal{B}}$ induces an AC interpretation $\mathcal{I}_{\mathcal{B}}^{\bowtie}$ that preserves the interpretation of constants while bilaterally interpreting n-ary predicates so that $R^{\mathcal{I}_{\mathcal{B}}^{\bowtie}}(c_0^{\mathcal{I}_{\mathcal{B}}^{\bowtie}}, ..., c_{n-1}^{\mathcal{I}_{\mathcal{B}}^{\bowtie}}) = \langle R^{\mathcal{I}_{\mathcal{B}}}(c_0^{\mathcal{I}_{\mathcal{B}}}, ..., c_{n-1}^{\mathcal{I}_{\mathcal{B}}}), (R^{\star})^{\mathcal{I}_{\mathcal{B}}}(c_0^{\mathcal{I}_{\mathcal{B}}}, ..., c_{n-1}^{\mathcal{I}_{\mathcal{B}}})\rangle$. The semantic clauses ensure that $\mathcal{I}_{\mathcal{B}}^{\bowtie}$ verifies all of $\Gamma^{\star}$ while *failing* to verify $\varphi^{\star}$. By Lemma 3, this lifts to Γ and φ, whence we conclude that $\Gamma \nvDash_{\mathsf{AC}} \varphi$.

These results summarize the presentation of restricted quantification for AC. Now, we define an appropriate calculus for $\mathsf{S}^{\star}_{\mathtt{fde}}$:

Definition 19. *The tableau calculus* **SrQ** *for* $\mathsf{S}^{\star}_{\mathtt{fde}}$ *with restricted quantifiers is captured by adding the following rules to* **ACrQ** *where* $v \in \{\mathfrak{t}, \mathfrak{f}\}$*:*

$$\frac{\mathfrak{e} : R(c_0, ..., c_{n-1})}{\mathfrak{e} : R^{\star}(c_0, ..., c_{n-1})} \qquad \frac{\mathfrak{e} : R^{\star}(c_0, ..., c_{n-1})}{\mathfrak{e} : R(c_0, ..., c_{n-1})}$$

$$\frac{v : R(c_0, ..., c_{n-1})}{\mathfrak{m} : R^{\star}(c_0, ..., c_{n-1})} \qquad \frac{v : R^{\star}(c_0, ..., c_{n-1})}{\mathfrak{m} : R(c_0, ..., c_{n-1})}$$

with the proviso that an above rule may be applied to a formula $R(c_0, ..., c_{n-1})$ *or* $R^{\star}(c_0, ..., c_{n-1})$ at most once *on any branch.*

Thinking of the notation $\mathfrak{m}$ as indicating "*not* $\mathfrak{e}$" may aid in interpreting the above rules. That $R(c_0, ..., c_{n-1})$ is assigned *e.g.* $\mathfrak{t}$ establishes only that its mate $R^{\star}(c_0, ..., c_{n-1})$ is *not* $\mathfrak{e}$, entailing a branch on the two remaining values.

To show soundness and completeness, we first establish some results about a class of weak Kleene interpretations. Let $\mathfrak{S}$ denote the class of weak Kleene interpretations $\mathcal{I}$ over the broader language $\mathcal{L}^{\star}$ such that for all atomic sentences, $\mathcal{I}(R(c_0, ..., c_{n-1})) = \mathfrak{e}$ if and only if $\mathcal{I}(R^{\star}(c_0, ..., c_{n-1})) = \mathfrak{e}$. Furthermore, let $\vDash_{\mathfrak{S}}$ denote weak Kleene validity over the restricted class $\mathfrak{S}$.

Lemma 7. $\Gamma \vDash_{\mathsf{S}^{\star}_{\mathtt{fde}}} \varphi$ *iff* $\Gamma^{\star} \vDash_{\mathfrak{S}} \varphi^{\star}$

Proof. By definition, $\Gamma \vDash_{\mathsf{S}^{\star}_{\mathtt{fde}}} \varphi$ holds if and only if it holds in an AC interpretation over $\hat{\mathcal{V}}_3^2$, in which no formula will correspond to values $\langle \mathfrak{t}, \mathfrak{e} \rangle$, $\langle \mathfrak{f}, \mathfrak{e} \rangle$, $\langle \mathfrak{e}, \mathfrak{t} \rangle$, or $\langle \mathfrak{e}, \mathfrak{f} \rangle$. But the corresponding class of wK interpretations will be $\mathfrak{S}$. So the results of [7] that support Lemma 4 establish this lemma as well.

Lemma 8. *Let* $\mathcal{I}_{\mathcal{B}}$ *be a branch model defined on an open branch from an* **SrQ** *tableau. Then* $\mathcal{I}_{\mathcal{B}} \in \mathfrak{S}$*.*

Proof. Suppose that $\mathcal{I}_{\mathcal{B}}(R(c_0, ..., c_{n-1})) = \mathfrak{e}$. Then one of two cases must have occurred: First, suppose that for *no* $v \in \mathcal{V}_3$ does $v : R(c_0, ..., c_{n-1})$ appear on the branch. Then the rules of **SrQ** ensure that neither does a signed formula $u : R^{\star}(c_0, ..., c_{n-1})$ appear on $\mathcal{B}$. In the second case, $\mathfrak{e} : R(c_0, ..., c_{n-1})$ *does* appear on $\mathcal{B}$, in which case the **SrQ** rules guarantee that $\mathfrak{e} : R^{\star}(c_0, ..., c_{n-1})$ is on the branch. Either way, Definition 12 guarantees that $\mathcal{I}_{\mathcal{B}}(R^{\star}(c_0, ..., c_{n-1})) = \mathfrak{e}$.

Lemma 9. *Let* $\mathbf{wKrQ}^{\mathfrak{S}}$ *be the result of adding properly* **SrQ** *rules to* $\mathbf{wKrQ}^{+}$*. Then* $\mathbf{wKrQ}^{\mathfrak{S}}$ *is sound with respect to* $\mathfrak{S}$*.*

Proof. By Theorem 1, all rules of $\mathbf{wKrQ}^{+}$ respect the semantics. But the properly **SrQ** rules precisely correspond to the semantic conditions defining $\mathfrak{S}$.

Now we have the necessary lemmas to prove soundness and completeness:

Theorem 5 (Soundness of SrQ). *If* $\Gamma \vdash_{\mathbf{SrQ}} \varphi$ *then* $\Gamma \vDash_{\mathsf{S}^{\star}_{\mathtt{fde}}} \varphi$*.*

Proof. For any tableau demonstrating that $\Gamma \vdash_{\mathbf{SrQ}} \varphi$, Lemma 6 can be applied to generate a proof of $\Gamma^{\star} \vdash_{\mathbf{SrQ}} \varphi^{\star}$. This proof includes only properly **SrQ** rules, and is thus a $\mathbf{wKrQ}^{\mathfrak{S}}$ tableau. By Lemma 9, $\Gamma^{\star} \vDash_{\mathfrak{S}} \varphi^{\star}$. Finally, by Lemma 7, we conclude that $\Gamma \vDash_{\mathsf{S}^{\star}_{\mathtt{fde}}} \varphi$.

Theorem 6 (Completeness of SrQ). *If $\Gamma \vDash_{\mathsf{S}^{\star}_{\mathtt{fde}}} \varphi$ then $\Gamma \vdash_{\mathbf{SrQ}} \varphi$*

Proof. Suppose that $\Gamma \nvdash_{\mathbf{SrQ}} \varphi$. Just as in Theorem 4, we can extract a branch model $\mathcal{I}^{\bowtie}_{\mathcal{B}}$ from an **SrQ** tableau that does not close. By Lemma 8, $\mathcal{I}^{\bowtie}_{\mathcal{B}}$ is a member of $\mathfrak{S}$. By Lemma 7, $\Gamma \nvDash_{\mathsf{S}^{\star}_{\mathtt{fde}}} \varphi$.

4 Concluding Remarks

The deductive systems wK, $\mathsf{S}^{\star}_{\mathtt{fde}}$, and AC capture notions of validity and equivalence that are stricter than classical, Boolean logic. Given the interpretative and philosophical work on these systems, they are plausible candidates for modest closure conditions for intentional contexts, including collections of agents' *beliefs*, *knowledge*, or *goals*.

In this paper, we have introduced sufficient quantification theory for these systems to support applications like description logics. The end results envisioned are description logics that can felicitously and plausibly capture and reason about agents' intentional states. The present work has provided a formal foundation for these applications, but work remains to be done, *e.g.*, determining the complexity of deductions in the tableau calculi introduced in this paper and adapting them to calculi including the syntax of *e.g.* $\mathcal{ALC}$ or $\mathcal{SROIQ}$.

One concluding note on the matter of the complexity of determining validity: Definition 17 translates both systems into a positive logic and in the propositional case, this corresponds to classical validity in conjunction with a *variable-inclusion* property. Thus, validity in propositional $\mathsf{S}^{\star}_{\mathtt{fde}}$ or AC is polynomial-time reducible to classical validity. It is worth investigating whether a similar approach will work in the case of restricted quantification.

Acknowledgements. I appreciate the insights and thoughtful input of four reviewers, whose suggestions were very helpful in revising this paper.

References

1. Angell, R.B.: Three systems of first degree entailment. J. Symb. Log. **42**(1), 147–148 (1977)
2. Bochvar, D.A.: On a three-valued logical calculus and its application to the analysis of contradictions. Matematicheskii Sbornik **4**(2), 287–308 (1938)
3. Carnielli, W., Marcos, J., de Amo, S.: Formal inconsistency and evolutionary databases. Logic Log. Philos. **8**, 115–152 (2000)
4. Carnielli, W.A.: Systematization of finite many-valued logics through the method of tableaux. J. Symb. Log. **52**(2), 473–493 (1987)

5. Correia, F.: Grounding and truth functions. Logique et Anal. (N.S.) **53**(211), 251–279 (2010)
6. Daniels, C.: A note on negation. Erkenntnis **32**(3), 423–429 (1990)
7. Ferguson, T.M.: Faulty Belnap computers and subsystems of FDE. J. Logic Comput. **26**(5), 1617–1636 (2016)
8. Ferguson, T.M.: Secrecy, content, and quantification. Análisis Filosófico 1–14 (2021, to appear)
9. Fine, K.: Angellic content. J. Philos. Log. **45**(2), 199–226 (2016)
10. Fjellstad, A.: Structural proof theory for first-order weak Kleene logics. J. Appl. Non-Classical Logics **30**(3), 272–289 (2020)
11. Halldén, S.: The Logic of Nonsense. Lundequista Bokhandeln, Uppsala, Sweden (1949)
12. Kamide, N.: An embedding-based completeness proof for Nelson's paraconsistent logic. Bull. Section Logic **39**(3/4), 205–214 (2010)
13. Kapsner, A.: Logics and Falsifications. Springer, Cham (2014)
14. Kleene, S.C.: Introduction to Metamathematics. North-Holland Publishing Company, Amsterdam (1952)
15. Malinowski, G.: Many-valued logic. In: Jacquette, D. (ed.) A Companion to Philosophical Logic, pp. 545–561. Blackwell Publishing, Oxford (2002)
16. Nelson, D.: Negation and separation of concepts in constructive systems. In: Heyting, A. (ed.) Constructivity in Mathematics, pp. 208–225. North-Holland, Amsterdam (1959)
17. Szmuc, D., Da Re, B.: Immune logics. Australas. J. Log. **18**(1), 29–52 (2021)
18. Yablo, S.: Aboutness. Princeton University Press, Princeton (2014)

Constraint Tableaux for Two-Dimensional Fuzzy Logics

Marta Bílková[1], Sabine Frittella[2], and Daniil Kozhemiachenko[2](✉)

[1] The Czech Academy of Sciences, Institute of Computer Science, Prague, Czech Republic
bilkova@cs.cas.cz

[2] INSA Centre Val de Loire, Univ. Orléans, LIFO EA 4022, Bourges, France
{sabine.frittella,daniil.kozhemiachenko}@insa-cvl.fr

Abstract. We introduce two-dimensional logics based on Łukasiewicz and Gödel logics to formalize reasoning with graded, incomplete and inconsistent information. The logics are interpreted on matrices, where the common underlying structure is the bi-lattice (twisted) product of the $[0,1]$ interval. The first (resp. second) coordinate encodes the positive (resp. negative) information one has about a statement. We propose constraint tableaux that provide a modular framework to address their completeness and complexity.

Keywords: Constraint tableaux · Łukasiewicz logic · Gödel logic · Two-dimensional logics

1 Introduction

A two-dimensional treatment of uncertainty. Belnap-Dunn four-valued logic BD [5,11,27], also referred to as First Degree Entailment FDE, provides a logical framework to reason with both incomplete and inconsistent information. In BD, formulas are evaluated on the Belnap-Dunn square (Fig. 1, left) where the four values encode the information available about the formula: $\{t, f, b, n\}$ (true, false, both, neither). Hence, b and n correspond to inconsistent and incomplete information respectively. The shift in perspective lies in the values encoding the information available about the formula, and not the intrinsic truth or falsity of the formula which may not be accessible. This idea was generalized by introducing the algebraic notion of bilattices by Ginsberg [15] in the context of AI, and studied further in [21,29]. Bilattices contain two lattice orders simultaneously: a truth order, and an information order. Belnap-Dunn square, the smallest interlaced bilattice, can be seen as the product bilattice of the two-element lattice where the four values are seen as pairs of classical values which can be naturally interpreted as representing two independent dimensions of information –

The research of Marta Bílková was supported by RVO: 67985807. The research of Sabine Frittella and Daniil Kozhemiachenko was funded by the grant ANR JCJC 2019, project PRELAP (ANR-19-CE48-0006).

A. Das and S. Negri (Eds.): TABLEAUX 2021, LNAI 12842, pp. 20–37, 2021.
https://doi.org/10.1007/978-3-030-86059-2_2

the positive and the negative one. We can understand them as providing positive and negative support for statements independently.

Non-standard probabilities [12,22] extend the idea of independent positive and negative support of a statement in presence of uncertainty. They quantify evidence for and evidence against (the positive and negative probabilistic information about) a statement φ with a couple $p(\varphi) = (p^+(\varphi), p^-(\varphi)) \in [0,1] \times [0,1]$. The maps are such that $p^-(\varphi) = p^+(\neg\varphi)$, p^+ is a monotone map w.r.t. BD entailment relation, and satisfies the import-export axiom $p^+(\varphi \wedge \psi) + p^+(\varphi \vee \psi) = p^+(\varphi) + p^+(\psi)$. Since formulas are interpreted in BD, one cannot prove that $p(\neg\varphi) = 1 - p(\varphi)$, and $p(\varphi) = p(\neg\varphi) = 1$ can be the case when one has contradictory information about φ. The range of non-standard probabilities coincides with the carrier of the continuous extension of Belnap-Dunn square (Fig. 1, center), which we see as the product bilattice of the unit real interval $[0,1] \odot [0,1]$ in Subsect. 2.1.[1] We employ expansions of this algebra in Subsect. 2.2 to provide semantics to two-dimensional fuzzy logics.[2]

A Broader Motivation. This paper is a part of the project introduced in [6] aiming to develop a modular logical framework for reasoning based on uncertain, incomplete and inconsistent information. We model agents who build their epistemic attitudes (like beliefs) based on information aggregated from multiple sources. A convenient framework to formalize such reasoning is that of two-layer modal logics, first introduced in [13,20] and further developed in [4,7]. Roughly speaking, the lower layer of events or evidence encodes the information given by the sources, while the upper layer encodes reasoning with the agent's attitudes based on this information, and the modalities expressing the attitudes connect the two layers and are interpreted in terms of an uncertainty measure (like probability, belief function, etc.). In this article, we study two families of logics suitable for the upper layer.

The Logics. We aim at a two-dimensional formalism that separates the positive and negative dimensions of information or support not only on the level of evidence, but also on the level of reasoning with agent's epistemic attitudes. In [6], we have proposed examples of such two-layer modal logics of belief based on incomplete and inconsistent information. In the two-layer framework, the upper logic operates atomic propositions of the form $B\phi$ where ϕ is a formula of the lower layer (and the belief B modalities do not nest). Atomic propositions of the logics we propose here can therefore be given such an epistemic interpretation, depending on a choice of epistemic attitudes and the uncertainty measure used to quantify evidence for and evidence against a statement. The logics themselves then model graded reasoning with such epistemic attitudes.[3]

[1] In the context of Nelson's paraconsistent logics such product construction has been called twisted product of algebras [30], or twist structures [26, Chapter 8].

[2] We wish to stress we do not claim that non-standard probabilities are compositional or propose an algebraic interpretation of them.

[3] This is a natural point to enter the discussion whether reasoning about uncertainty can be adequately handled within truth-functional semantics (see e.g. [10]). Such discussion is however beyond the scope of the current paper.

In some scenarios, it is reasonable to represent agents attitudes as probabilities (e.g. a company reasoning with information based on statistical data). To model graded reasoning about such attitudes, we propose logics derived from Łukasiewicz logic [9, Chapter VI], mainly because its language allows to express the (non-standard) probability axioms which is crucial to obtain complete axiomatization of the resulting two-layer logics [6,20].

In other cases, the agent's aggregated attitude is not a probability. For instance, agents may be able to compare their belief on two different statements while not being necessarily able to say exactly to what extent they believe. Just as Łukasiewicz logic can be seen as a logic of measure or quantity, Gödel logic [9, Chapter VII] can be considered a logic of order. In this context it is therefore natural to consider Gödel logic as the starting point.

To comply with the two-dimensionality aim, we define the logics semantically, using expansions of the product bilattice $[0,1] \odot [0,1]$ with connectives derived from standard semantics of Łukasiewicz logic or Gödel logic. Two-dimensional treatment of implication is of a particular interest (as we explain more in detail in Remarks 1 and 3). We consider two possibilities: the first dualizes implication by co-implication, the second understands negative support of an implication as a conjunction of the positive support of the antecedent and the negative support of the consequent. The first option connects to one of Wansing's logic of [31], namely I_4C_4, and goes back to bi-intuitionistic logic [16,28], the second option connects to Nelson's logic $N4$ [25].

Depending on the choice of connectives, and the choice of the set of designated values on the resulting algebra, we encounter both logics which are paraconsistent and logics which are not. Before proceeding further, we need to clarify the notion of paraconsistency. Unless specified otherwise, we construe 'logic' as a set of valid formulas, not as sets of valid entailments. Hence, while not all logics considered in the paper lack explosion w.r.t. their entailment—$p, \neg p \models q$, in none of them $(p \wedge \neg p) \rightarrow q$ is valid. It is in this sense that we call the logics presented here 'paraconsistent'.

Proof Theory. Proof theory for many-valued logics is mostly presented in either of the following three forms. Hilbert style axiomatic calculi (cf., e.g. [20,23]); different versions of sequent and hypersequent calculi [18,23]; tableaux and decomposition calculi (cf., e.g. [19] for Łukasiewicz logic and [3] for Gödel logic).

Each of these proof formalisms has its own advantages: Hilbert calculi provide an explicit list of postulates which facilitates establishing the relations between different logics (e.g. whether one logic is an extension of another). The rules of (hyper)sequent calculi provide structural insights into the algebraic properties of the connectives of the given logic. On the other hand, tableaux and decomposition systems are easily automatisable and can be readily used to determine an upper bound on the complexity of the validity and satisfiability problems for the logic in question. Another advantage of the tableaux is that their semantical nature allows for a straightforward formalisation of different entailment relations defined on the same algebra. Since the logics we are going to introduce are hybrids between FDE and Łukasiewicz or Gödel logic, we opt for combining the constraint tableaux framework with the FDE-tableaux by D'Agostino [8].

Structure of the Paper. Section 2 presents preliminaries on bilattices and matrices and introduces the logics for a two dimensional treatment of uncertainty and their properties (proofs are in the Appendix). Section 3 presents the constraint tableaux for these logics and discusses their soundness and completeness, and the complexity of the proof search. Section 4 presents further lines of research.

2 The Logics for a Two-Dimensional Treatment of Uncertainty

2.1 Preliminaries

First, we describe the algebras we are going to use to interpret the logics. Their construction relays on the standard MV-algebra, and the standard Gödel algebra, which provide the standard semantics of Łukasiewicz and Gödel logic respectively (we refer the reader to [9, Chapters VI,VII] for a basic exposure to Gödel and Łukasiewicz logics and their standard semantics). In what follows, $[0,1]$ denotes the real unit interval with its natural order, and $[0,1]^{\mathsf{op}}$ denotes the interval with the reversed order.

The Standard MV-Algebra. $[0,1]_{\text{Ł}} = ([0,1], 0, \wedge, \vee, \&, \rightarrow_{\text{Ł}})$ is defined as follows: for all $a, b \in [0,1]$ the standard operations are given by

$$a \wedge b := \min(a,b) \qquad a\&b := \max(0, a+b-1)$$
$$a \vee b := \max(a,b) \qquad a \rightarrow_{\text{Ł}} b := \min(1, 1-a+b)$$

Moreover, we define the negation ${\sim_{\text{Ł}}} a := a \rightarrow_{\text{Ł}} 0$, the constant $1 :={\sim_{\text{Ł}}} 0$, the truncated sum $a \oplus b :={\sim_{\text{Ł}}} a \rightarrow_{\text{Ł}} b$, and the truncated subtraction $a \ominus b := a\&{\sim} b$.

The MV-algebra $[0,1]_{\text{Ł}}^{\mathsf{op}} = ([0,1]^{\mathsf{op}}, 1, \vee, \wedge, \oplus, \ominus)$ arises turning the standard MV-algebra upside down, and is isomorphic to it. Here, we have ${\sim_{\text{Ł}}} a := 1 \ominus a$.

The Standard Gödel Algebra. $[0,1]_{\mathsf{G}} = ([0,1], 0, \wedge, \vee, \rightarrow_{\mathsf{G}})$ is defined as follows: for all $a, b \in [0,1]$, the standard operations are given by $a \wedge b := \min(a,b)$, $a \vee b := \max(a,b)$, and the implication is defined as follows. We at the same time spell out a definition of a co-implication we shall need later on:

$$a \rightarrow_G b = \begin{cases} 1, & \text{if } a \leq b \\ b & \text{else} \end{cases} \qquad b \prec_G a = \begin{cases} 0, & \text{if } b \leq a \\ b & \text{else} \end{cases}$$

We define a negation ${\sim_{\mathsf{G}}} a := a \rightarrow_{\mathsf{G}} 0$, and $1 :={\sim_{\mathsf{G}}} 0$.

The algebra $[0,1]_{\mathsf{G}}^{\mathsf{op}} = ([0,1]^{\mathsf{op}}, 1, \vee, \wedge, \prec_{\mathsf{G}})$ arises by dualizing the standard Gödel algebra (in particular, similarly as $\rightarrow_G$ is the residuum of $\wedge$, $\prec_{\mathsf{G}}$ is the residuum of $\vee$). A negation can be defined on this algebra as $-_{\mathsf{G}} a := 1 \prec_{\mathsf{G}} a$.

Remark 1. Observe that $\ominus$ and $\prec_G$ are dual to $\to_{\text{Ł}}$ and $\to_G$ in the following sense.

$$a \leq b \oplus c \text{ iff } a \ominus b \leq c \qquad a\&b \leq c \text{ iff } a \leq b \to_{\text{Ł}} c$$
$$a \leq b \vee c \text{ iff } a \prec_G b \leq c \qquad a \wedge b \leq c \text{ iff } a \leq b \to_G c$$

As one can see, $\ominus$ and $\prec_G$ residuate disjunctions dually to how $\to_{\text{Ł}}$ and $\to_G$ residuate conjuctions. Taking these dualities into account, we will call $\ominus$ and $\prec_G$ *co-implications.*

Product Billatices. Given an arbitrary lattice $\mathbf{L} = (L, \wedge_L, \vee_L)$, we can construct the *product bilattice* $\mathbf{L} \odot \mathbf{L} = (L \times L, \wedge, \vee, \sqcap, \sqcup, \neg)$ [1,2]. In what follows, we essentially use the product bilattice $[0,1] \odot [0,1]$, constructed from the lattice $([0,1], \min, \max)$. We only consider the $\{\wedge, \vee, \neg\}$ reduct of this structure in this paper, and not to complicate notation denote it by $[0,1] \odot [0,1]$. It is defined as follows: for all $(a_1, a_2), (b_1, b_2) \in [0,1] \times [0,1]$,

$$\begin{aligned}
(a_1, a_2) \leq (b_1, b_2) &:= a_1 \leq b_1 \text{ and } b_2 \leq a_2 \\
\neg(a_1, a_2) &:= (a_2, a_1) \\
(a_1, a_2) \wedge (b_1, b_2) &:= (\min(a_1, b_1), \max(a_2, b_2)) \\
(a_1, a_2) \vee (b_1, b_2) &:= (\max(a_1, b_1), \min(a_2, b_2)).
\end{aligned}$$

We use expansions of $[0,1] \odot [0,1]$ by implication connectives derived from the Łukasiewicz or Gödel implication described above. Their positive support coincides with those of Ł and G implications. For the negative support, we consider two options. The first one dualizes the implication by the co-implication, the second results in negating implication by the conjunction of the positive part of the antecedent and the negative part of the consequent. For Łukasiewicz logics these result in:

$$(a_1, a_2) \to (b_1, b_2) := (a_1 \to_{\text{Ł}} b_1, b_2 \ominus a_2) \quad (a_1, a_2) \rightharpoonup (b_1, b_2) := (a_1 \to_{\text{Ł}} b_1, a_1 \& b_2)$$

For Gödel logics we obtain:

$$(a_1, a_2) \to (b_1, b_2) := (a_1 \to_{\mathsf{G}} b_1, b_2 \prec_{\mathsf{G}} a_2) \quad (a_1, a_2) \rightharpoonup (b_1, b_2) := (a_1 \to_{\mathsf{G}} b_1, a_1 \wedge b_2)$$

In the first option, the interpretation arises as the one on the product algebra $[0,1]_{\text{Ł}} \times [0,1]_{\text{Ł}}^{\mathsf{op}}$ or $[0,1]_{\mathsf{G}} \times [0,1]_{\mathsf{G}}^{\mathsf{op}}$. In the Gödel case, it relates to how the implication is interpreted in Wansing's logic I_4C_4 [31]. In the second option, $\rightharpoonup$ is not congruential, and a strong congruential implication can be defined as $(a \rightharpoonup b) \wedge (\neg b \rightharpoonup \neg a)$. The second option corresponds to how implication is interpreted in product residuated bilattices of [21]. In the Gödel case, it relates to how the implication is interpreted in Nelson's logic N4 [25].

- We denote by $[0,1]_{\text{Ł}} \odot [0,1]_{\text{Ł}}(\to)$ and $[0,1]_{\text{Ł}} \odot [0,1]_{\text{Ł}}(\rightharpoonup)$ the corresponding expansions of $[0,1] \odot [0,1]$ defined using the Łukasiewicz connectives.
- We denote by $[0,1]_{\mathsf{G}} \odot [0,1]_{\mathsf{G}}(\to)$ and $[0,1]_{\mathsf{G}} \odot [0,1]_{\mathsf{G}}(\rightharpoonup)$ the corresponding expansions of $[0,1] \odot [0,1]$ defined using the Gödel connectives.

2.2 The Logics

The logics considered in this paper are defined through matrix semantics [14]. We consider logical matrices of the form $(\mathbf{A}, D)$ where $\mathbf{A}$ is one of the four algebras described above, and $D \subseteq A$ is a set of designated values. As sets of designated values, we use various lattice filters of the form $(x, y)^{\uparrow} := \{(x', y') \mid x \leq x' \text{ and } y' \leq y\}$ (see Fig. 1, center). The motivation is the following: x represents the threshold of having enough evidence to say there is reasonable evidence supporting the truth of the formula, while y represents the threshold below which one considers not to have enough evidence to say that there is reasonable evidence supporting the falsity of the formula. Of particular interest are filters $(1, 0)^{\uparrow}$ (the evidence fully supports the formula and does not contradicts it) and $(1, 1)^{\uparrow}$ (there is some evidence that fully supports the formula).

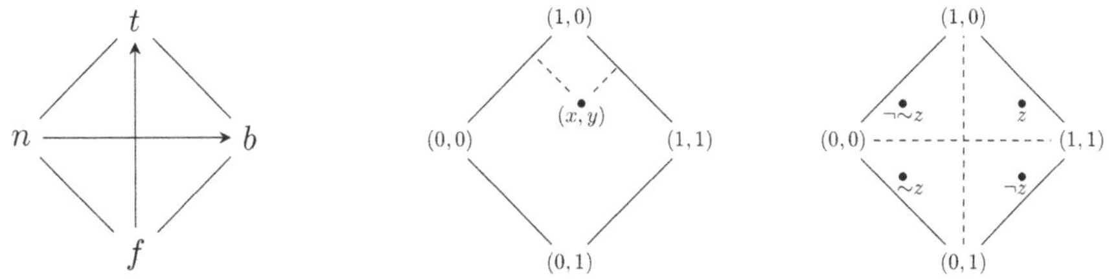

Fig. 1. Belnap-Dunn square **4** (left), its continuous probabilistic extension with the filter $(x, y)^{\uparrow}$ (center) and the geometric interpretation of $\neg$, $\sim$, and $\neg\!\sim$ for $Ł^2$ (right).

Each logical matrix determines the set of valid formulas in a given language (formulas, which are, for each valuation, designated), and a consequence relation (an entailment) between sets of formulas and formulas, defined as preservation of designated values. Regarding the two types of implication introduced in the previous subsection, the standard semantics of the logics is set as follows:

- Logics with the $\rightarrow$ implication in the language (i.e. the logics $Ł^2_{(x,y)}(\rightarrow)$ and $\mathsf{G}^2_{(x,y)}(\rightarrow)$ below) are given by the matrices $([0,1]_{Ł} \odot [0,1]_{Ł}(\rightarrow), (x, y)^{\uparrow})$ and $([0,1]_{\mathsf{G}} \odot [0,1]_{\mathsf{G}}(\rightarrow), (x, y)^{\uparrow})$ respectively.
- Logics with the $\multimap$ implication in the language (i.e. the logics $Ł^2_{(x,y)}(\multimap)$ and $\mathsf{G}^2_{(x,y)}(\multimap)$ below) are given by the matrices $([0,1]_{Ł} \odot [0,1]_{Ł}(\multimap), (x, y)^{\uparrow})$ and $([0,1]_{\mathsf{G}} \odot [0,1]_{\mathsf{G}}(\multimap), (x, y)^{\uparrow})$ respectively.

We however need to treat Łukasiewicz and Gödel logics separately. Therefore it is practical to define the language and semantics for them separately in a compact way as follows. We refer by $Ł^2$ to Łukasiewicz logics, and by G^2 to Gödel logics, specifying the filter in the subscript.

Definition 1 (Language and semantics of $Ł^2$). *We fix a countable set* Prop *of propositional letters and consider the following language:*

$$\phi := \mathbf{0} \mid p \mid \neg\phi \mid (\phi \wedge \phi) \mid (\phi \vee \phi) \mid (\phi \rightarrow \phi) \mid (\phi \multimap \phi)$$

where $p \in \mathsf{Prop}$. *We define* $\sim\phi := \phi \to \mathbf{0}$, $\sim_w\phi := \phi \rightarrowtriangle \mathbf{0}$, $\phi_1 \odot \phi_2 := \sim(\phi_1 \to \sim\phi_2)$, *and* $\phi_1 \leftrightarrow \phi_2 := (\phi_1 \to \phi_2) \odot (\phi_2 \to \phi_1)$.

Let $v : \mathsf{Prop} \to [0,1]\times[0,1]$, *and denote* v_1 *and* v_2 *its left and right coordinates, respectively. We extend* v *as follows.*

$$\begin{array}{rl} v(\mathbf{0}) = (0,1) & v(\phi_1 \wedge \phi_2) = (v_1(\phi_1) \wedge v_1(\phi_2), v_2(\phi_1) \vee v_2(\phi_2)) \\ v(\neg\phi) = (v_2(\phi), v_1(\phi)) & v(\phi_1 \vee \phi_2) = (v_1(\phi_1) \vee v_1(\phi_2), v_2(\phi_1) \wedge v_2(\phi_2)) \\ & v(\phi_1 \to \phi_2) = (v_1(\phi_1) \to_{\text{Ł}} v_1(\phi_2), v_2(\phi_2) \ominus v_2(\phi_1)) \\ & v(\phi_1 \rightarrowtriangle \phi_2) = (v_1(\phi_1) \to_{\text{Ł}} v_1(\phi_2), v_1(\phi_1) \mathbin{\&} v_2(\phi_2)) \end{array}$$

Notice that

$$\begin{aligned} v(\sim\phi) &= (1 - v_1(\phi), 1 - v_2(\phi)) \\ v(\phi_1 \odot \phi_2) &= (v_1(\phi_1) \mathbin{\&} v_1(\phi_2), v_2(\phi_1) \oplus v_2(\phi_2)) \\ v(\phi_1 \leftrightarrow \phi_2) &= (1 - |v_1(\phi_1) - v_1(\phi_2)|, |v_2(\phi_1) - v_2(\phi_2)|) \end{aligned}$$

Remark 2. In Sect. 2.3, we use the fact that $\neg$ corresponds to a symmetry w.r.t. the horizontal axis, $\sim$ to a symmetry w.r.t. the point $(0.5, 0.5)$, $\sim\neg$ and $\neg\sim$ are correspond to a symmetry w.r.t. the horizontal axis (see Fig. 1, right). From the meaning perspective, $\neg$ corresponds for swapping the positive and negative supports of the statement.

Definition 2 (Language and semantics of G^2). *We fix a countable set* Prop *of propositional letters and consider the following language:*

$$\phi := \mathbf{0} \mid \mathbf{1} \mid p \mid \neg\phi \mid (\phi \wedge \phi) \mid (\phi \vee \phi) \mid (\phi \to \phi) \mid (\phi \prec \phi) \mid (\phi \rightarrowtriangle \phi)$$

where $p \in \mathsf{Prop}$. *We define* $\sim\phi := \phi \to \mathbf{0}$, *and* $\sim_w\phi := \phi \rightarrowtriangle \mathbf{0}$.

Let $v : \mathsf{Prop} \to [0,1]\times[0,1]$, *and denote* v_1 *and* v_2 *its left and right coordinates, respectively. We extend* v *as follows.*

$$\begin{array}{rl} v(\mathbf{0}) = (0,1) & v(\phi_1 \wedge \phi_2) = (v_1(\phi_1) \wedge v_1(\phi_2), v_2(\phi_1) \vee v_2(\phi_2)) \\ v(\mathbf{1}) = (1,0) & v(\phi_1 \vee \phi_2) = (v_1(\phi_1) \vee v_1(\phi_2), v_2(\phi_1) \wedge v_2(\phi_2)) \\ v(\neg\phi) = (v_2(\phi), v_1(\phi)) & v(\phi_1 \to \phi_2) = (v_1(\phi_1) \to_{\mathsf{G}} v_1(\phi_2), v_2(\phi_2) \prec_{\mathsf{G}} v_2(\phi_1)) \\ & v(\phi_1 \rightarrowtriangle \phi_2) = (v_1(\phi_1) \to_{\mathsf{G}} v_1(\phi_2), v_1(\phi_1) \wedge v_2(\phi_2)) \end{array}$$

Remark 3 (Interpreting negations and (co-)implications). $\psi \to \psi'$ is positively supported in Ł^2 and G^2 is interpreted as 'positive evidence for ψ is not stronger than for ψ''. The negative support is obtained via co-implications. In the case Ł^2, $\ominus$ measures the difference between negative supports of ψ' and ψ. On the other hand, in G^2, the negative support of $\psi \to \psi'$ is non-zero (and in fact is equal to the negative support of ψ') when the negative support of ψ' is stronger than that of ψ.

On the other hand, $\rightarrowtriangle$ in both G^2 and Ł^2 could be considered as being closer to the more intuitive 'if . . . , then . . . ' in natural language. Thus, to obtain negative support of $\psi \rightarrowtriangle \psi'$, we use positive support of ψ and negative support of ψ'. Falsity of $\rightarrowtriangle$ is thus more related to the traditional understanding of implication being false when the antecedent is true and the consequent is false.

Definition 3 (Validity and consequence). *Let ϕ be a formula and Γ a set of formulas of* Ł^2 *(resp.* G^2*) and* $v[\Gamma] := \{v(\gamma) \mid \gamma \in \Gamma\}$*.*

- ϕ *is* $\text{Ł}^2_{(x,y)}$*-valid (resp.* $\mathsf{G}^2_{(x,y)}$*-valid) iff* $\forall v : v(\phi) \in (x,y)^{\uparrow}$*.*
- $\Gamma \vDash_{\text{Ł}^2_{(x,y)}} \phi$ *(resp.* $\Gamma \vDash_{\mathsf{G}^2_{(x,y)}} \phi$*) iff* $\forall v :$ *if* $v[\Gamma] \subseteq (x,y)^{\uparrow}$ *then* $v(\phi) \in (x,y)^{\uparrow}$*.*

Convention 1. *We introduce the following notation.*

- $\text{Ł}^2_{(x,y)}(\rightarrow)$ *stands for the* $\text{Ł}^2_{(x,y)}$ *logics over* $\{\mathbf{0}, \neg, \wedge, \vee, \rightarrow\}$*.*
- $\mathsf{G}^2_{(x,y)}(\rightarrow)$ *stands for the* $\mathsf{G}^2_{(x,y)}$ *logics over* $\{\mathbf{0}, \mathbf{1}, \neg, \wedge, \vee, \rightarrow, \prec\}$*.*
- $\text{Ł}^2_{(x,y)}(\multimap)$ *stands for the* $\text{Ł}^2_{(x,y)}$ *logics over* $\{\mathbf{0}, \neg, \wedge, \vee, \multimap\}$*.*
- $\mathsf{G}^2_{(x,y)}(\multimap)$ *stands for the* $\mathsf{G}^2_{(x,y)}$ *logics over* $\{\mathbf{0}, \mathbf{1}, \neg, \wedge, \vee, \multimap\}$*.*

We note that $\mathbf{0}$ *of* $\text{Ł}^2_{(x,y)}(\rightarrow)$ *can be defined as* $\neg(p \rightarrow p)$*. However, since there is no definition of* $\mathbf{0}$ *using* $\multimap$*, we leave it in both languages for the sake of preserving the same tableau rules for all logics. Likewise, although* $\mathbf{0}$ *and* $\mathbf{1}$ *are definable in* $\mathsf{G}^2_{(x,y)}(\rightarrow)$*, their presence in the language simplifies the proofs of their semantical properties (cf. Propositions 5 and 6).*

Remark 4. Let ϕ be a formula over $\{0, \wedge, \vee, \supset\}$ with $\supset$ being the Boolean implication. Denote $\phi^{\bullet}$ the formula obtained from it by substituting $\supset$ for $\rightarrow$, and ϕ° by substituting $\supset$ for $\multimap$. Since v_1's behave precisely like the valuations in Łukasiewicz (Gödel) logic, one can see that ϕ is Ł-valid (G-valid) iff $\phi^{\bullet}$ is $\text{Ł}^2_{(1,0)}(\rightarrow)$-valid ($\mathsf{G}^2_{(1,0)}(\rightarrow)$-valid). Furthermore, ϕ is Ł-valid (G-valid) iff ϕ° is $\text{Ł}^2_{(1,1)}(\multimap)$-valid ($\mathsf{G}^2_{(1,1)}(\multimap)$-valid). Thus, $\text{Ł}^2_{(1,0)}(\rightarrow)$ and $\text{Ł}^2_{(1,1)}(\multimap)$ are conservative extensions of Ł while $\mathsf{G}^2_{(1,0)}(\rightarrow)$ and $\mathsf{G}^2_{(1,1)}(\multimap)$ are conservative extensions of G.

Remark 5. Notice that if $v(p) = (1,1)$, then $v(p \multimap p) = (1,1)$ in $\mathsf{G}^2(\multimap)$ and $\text{Ł}^2(\multimap)$. Thus, if we refuse to consider $(1,1)$ as a designated value, the weak implication ceases to be reflexive. Therefore, $\text{Ł}^2_{(x,y)}(\multimap)$'s and $\mathsf{G}^2_{(x,y)}(\multimap)$'s with sets of designated values not containing $(1,1)$ do not extend Ł and G.

In order to work with extensions of Ł and G, we are going to consider only $\text{Ł}^2_{(x,y)}(\multimap)$'s and $\mathsf{G}^2_{(x,y)}(\multimap)$'s whose sets of designated values extend $(1,1)^{\uparrow}$, that is $\text{Ł}^2_{(x,1)}(\multimap)$ and $\mathsf{G}^2_{(x,1)}(\multimap)$. In the remainder of the article $\phi, \varphi, \chi, \psi$ denote formulas. Unless there is some ambiguity, we do not specify to which language they belong.

2.3 Semantical Properties of $\text{Ł}^2_{(x,y)}(\rightarrow)$

In this section, we are going to explore how the choice of $(x,y)^{\uparrow}$ affects the set of $\text{Ł}^2_{(x,y)}(\rightarrow)$-valid formulas. In particular, we are providing families of formulas differentiating different $\text{Ł}^2_{(x,y)}(\rightarrow)$-validities.

Definition 4 (Closure under conflation). *We say that a filter* D *of* $[0,1] \odot [0,1]$ *is* closed under conflation *if for any* $(x,y) \in D$*, we have* $(1-y, 1-x) \in D$*.*

In bilattices, the negation $\neg$ corresponds to a symmetry w.r.t. the horizontal axis and the conflation corresponds to a symmetry w.r.t. the vertical axis. Notice that a filter $(x, y)^{\uparrow}$ is closed under conflation iff $y = 1 - x$. In $\mathrm{Ł}^2_{(x,y)}(\rightarrow)$, conflation can be defined as $\neg\sim$ or equivalently $\sim\neg$ (cf. Fig. 1, right).

Proposition 1

- *Let* $y \geq 1 - x$. *Then* ϕ *is* $\mathrm{Ł}^2_{(x,y)}(\rightarrow)$*-valid iff* ϕ *is* $\mathrm{Ł}^2_{(x,1-x)}(\rightarrow)$*-valid.*
- *Let* $y < 1 - x$. *Then* ϕ *is* $\mathrm{Ł}^2_{(x,y)}(\rightarrow)$*-valid iff* ϕ *is* $\mathrm{Ł}^2_{(1-y,y)}(\rightarrow)$*-valid.*

The following statements show that by choosing different sets of designated values, we can alter the sets of tautologies.

Proposition 2. *Let* $m, n \in \{2, 3, \ldots\}$. *Then* $\mathrm{Ł}^2_{(\frac{m-1}{m},\frac{1}{m})} \subsetneq \mathrm{Ł}^2_{(\frac{n-1}{n},\frac{1}{n})}$ *iff* $m > n$.

Note, however, that while $\mathrm{Ł}_{(\frac{1}{2},\frac{1}{2})}$ validates $p \vee \sim p$, it does not collapse into classical logic as the following propositions show.

Proposition 3. *Let* $m, n \in \{3, 4, \ldots\}$. *Then* $\mathrm{Ł}^2_{(\frac{m-2}{2m},\frac{m+2}{2m})} \subsetneq \mathrm{Ł}^2_{(\frac{n-2}{2n},\frac{n+2}{2n})}$ *iff* $m > n$.

We end this subsection by noting that all $\mathrm{Ł}^2_{(x,y)}(\rightarrow)$'s where $(x, y)^{\uparrow}$ is prime are paraconsistent in the following sense: $p, \neg p \nvDash_{\mathrm{Ł}^2_{(x,y)}(\rightarrow)} q$. Furthermore, if $(\frac{1}{2}, \frac{1}{2}) \in (x, y)^{\uparrow}$, the logic is paraconsistent even w.r.t. $\sim$ since $p, \sim p \nvDash_{\mathrm{Ł}^2_{(x,y)}(\rightarrow)} q$. Last but not least, most $\mathrm{Ł}^2_{(x,y)}(\rightarrow)$'s are not closed under modus ponens.

Proposition 4. *Let* $\mathrm{Ł}^2_{(1,0)}(\rightarrow) \subsetneq \mathrm{Ł}^2_{(x,y)}(\rightarrow)$. *Then* $\mathrm{Ł}^2_{(x,y)}(\rightarrow)$ *is not closed under modus ponens.*

2.4 Semantical Properties of $\mathsf{G}^2(\rightarrow)$

In this section, we show that all $\mathsf{G}^2_{(x,y)}(\rightarrow)$ logics have the same set of valid formulas. This means that just as the original Gödel logic, $\mathsf{G}^2(\rightarrow)$ can be seen as the logic of comparative truth. Furthermore, the presence of the second dimension allows to interpret $\mathsf{G}^2(\rightarrow)$ as the logic of comparative truth and falsehood.

Proposition 5. *Let* ϕ *be a formula over* $\{\mathbf{0}, \mathbf{1}, \neg, \wedge, \vee, \rightarrow, \prec\}$. *For any* $v(p) = (x, y)$ *let* $v^*(p) = (1 - y, 1 - x)$. *Then* $v(\phi) = (x, y)$ *iff* $v^*(\phi) = (1 - y, 1 - x)$.

Proposition 6. *Let* ϕ *be a formula over* $\{\mathbf{0}, \mathbf{1}, \neg, \wedge, \vee, \rightarrow, \prec\}$ *such that* $v(\phi) \geq (x, y)$ *for any* v *and some fixed* $(x, y) \neq (0, 1)$. *Then* $v'(\phi) = (1, 0)$ *for any* v'.

The last three propositions show that in contrast to $\mathsf{L}^2(\rightarrow)$, the changing of the set of designated values does not change the set of valid formulas as long as the set remains a filter[4] on $[0, 1] \odot [0, 1]$ generated by a single point. However, while the sets of tautologies remain the same, the entailment relation can be made

[4] Notice that $p \vee \neg p$ would be valid for $D = [0, 1] \odot [0, 1] \setminus \{(0, 1)\}$. But D is not a filter.

paraconsistent. Indeed, it suffices to choose any prime $(x, y)^{\uparrow}$ and the entailment ceases to be explosive in the following sense: $p, \neg p \nvDash_{\mathsf{G}^2_{(x,y)}} q$.

Furthermore, the propositions have an important corollary which simplifies the construction of the tableaux proofs.

Corollary 1. *$v(\phi) = (1, 0)$ for any v iff $v'_1(\phi) = 1$ for any v'.*

3 Tableaux

First, we give a general definition of a constraint tableaux, then in Sects. 3.1 and 3.2, we introduce tableaux for $Ł^2$'s and G^2's.

Definition 5 (Constraint tableaux). *Let* Label *be a set of labels and* $\mathcal{L}$ *a set of formulas. A* constraint *is one of these three expressions:*

- Labelled formulas *of the form* $L : \phi$ *with* $L \in \mathsf{Label}$ *and* $\phi \in \mathcal{L}$,
- Numerical constraints *of the form* $c \leq d$ *or* $c < d$ *with* $c, d \in [0, 1]$,
- Formulaic constraints *of the form* $L : \phi \leqslant L' : \phi'$ *or* $L : \phi < L' : \phi'$ *with* $L, L' \in \mathsf{Label}$ *and* $\phi, \phi' \in \mathcal{L}$.

A constraint tableau *is a downward branching tree each branch of which is a non-empty set of constraints. Each branch* $\mathcal{B}$ *can be extended by applications of a given set of rules. If no rule application adds new entries to* $\mathcal{B}$*, it is called* complete.

As expected, in labelled formulas, L is some *set of values*. Thus, the intended interpretation of $L : \phi$ is 'ϕ has some value from L'. In formulaic constraints, L and L' are *components of ϕ's valuation*. Hence, the intended interpretation of $L : \phi \leqslant L' : \phi'$ is 'the component of ϕ's valuation denoted by L is less or equal to the component of ϕ''s valuation denoted by L''. The detailed interpretations of all types of entries for each tableau calculus are given in Definitions 6 and 8 as well as remarks 6 and 7.

Henceforth, we only state the rules and the closure conditions for branches. In what follows, we identify a branch with the set of entries that appear at some point on the branch.

Since our logics are hybrids between FDE and Ł (or G), we can combine the constraint tableaux framework with the FDE-tableaux by D'Agostino [8]. In particular, it means that we use two kinds of labelled formulas and formulaic constraints: those that concern the left coordinate (evidence for the statement) and those that concern the right coordinate (evidence against the statement).

3.1 Constraint Tableaux for $Ł^2$

Definition 6 (Constraint tableau for $Ł^2$—$\mathcal{T}\left(Ł^2_{(x,y)}\right)$). *Branches contain* labelled formulas *of the form* $\phi \leqslant_1 i$, $\phi \leqslant_2 i$, $\phi \geqslant_1 i$, *or* $\phi \geqslant_2 i$, *and* numerical constraints *of the form* $i \leq j$ *with* $i, j \in [0, 1]$. *We call* atomic labelled formulas *labelled formulas where* $\phi \in \mathsf{Prop}$.

$$\mathbf{0}\leqslant_1 \frac{\mathbf{0}\leqslant_1 i}{0\leq i} \qquad \mathbf{0}\leqslant_2 \frac{\mathbf{0}\leqslant_2 i}{1\leq i} \qquad \mathbf{0}\geqslant_1 \frac{\mathbf{0}\geqslant_1 i}{0\geq i} \qquad \mathbf{0}\geqslant_2 \frac{\mathbf{0}\geqslant_2 i}{1\geq i}$$

$$\neg\leqslant_1 \frac{\neg\phi\leqslant_1 i}{\phi\leqslant_2 i} \qquad \neg\leqslant_2 \frac{\neg\phi\leqslant_2 i}{\phi\leqslant_1 i} \qquad \neg\geqslant_1 \frac{\neg\phi\geqslant_1 i}{\phi\geqslant_2 i} \qquad \neg\geqslant_2 \frac{\neg\phi\geqslant_2 i}{\phi\geqslant_1 i}$$

$$\rightarrow\leqslant_1 \frac{\phi_1\rightarrow\phi_2\leqslant_1 i}{i\geq 1 \left| \begin{array}{c}\phi_1\geqslant_1 1-i+j\\ \phi_2\leqslant_1 j\\ j\leq i\end{array}\right.} \qquad \rightarrow\leqslant_2 \frac{\phi_1\rightarrow\phi_2\leqslant_2 i}{\begin{array}{c}\phi_1\geqslant_2 j\\ \phi_2\leqslant_2 i+j\end{array}}$$

$$\rightarrow\geqslant_1 \frac{\phi_1\rightarrow\phi_2\geqslant_1 i}{\begin{array}{c}\phi_1\leqslant_1 1-i+j\\ \phi_2\geqslant_1 j\end{array}} \qquad \rightarrow\geqslant_2 \frac{\phi_1\rightarrow\phi_2\geqslant_2 i}{i\leq 0 \left| \begin{array}{c}\phi_1\leqslant_2 j\\ \phi_2\geqslant_2 i+j\\ j\leq 1-i\end{array}\right.}$$

$$\rightarrowtriangle\leqslant_1 \frac{\phi_1\rightarrowtriangle\phi_2\leqslant_1 i}{i\geq 1 \left| \begin{array}{c}\phi_1\geqslant_1 1-i+j\\ \phi_2\leqslant_1 j\\ j\leq i\end{array}\right.} \qquad \rightarrowtriangle\leqslant_2 \frac{\phi_1\rightarrowtriangle\phi_2\leqslant_2 i}{\begin{array}{c}\phi_1\leqslant_2 i+j\\ \phi_2\leqslant_1 1-j\end{array}}$$

$$\rightarrowtriangle\geqslant_1 \frac{\phi_1\rightarrowtriangle\phi_2\geqslant_1 i}{\begin{array}{c}\phi_1\leqslant_1 1-i+j\\ \phi_2\geqslant_1 j\end{array}} \qquad \rightarrowtriangle\geqslant_2 \frac{\phi_1\rightarrowtriangle\phi_2\geqslant_2 i}{i\leq 0 \left| \begin{array}{c}\phi_1\geqslant_2 i+j\\ \phi_2\geqslant_1 1-j\\ j\leq 1-i\end{array}\right.}$$

$$\wedge\leqslant_1 \frac{\phi_1\wedge\phi_2\leqslant_1 i}{\phi_1\leqslant_1 i \mid \phi_2\leqslant_1 i} \qquad \wedge\leqslant_2 \frac{\phi_1\wedge\phi_2\leqslant_2 i}{\begin{array}{c}\phi_1\leqslant_2 i\\ \phi_2\leqslant_2 i\end{array}}$$

$$\wedge\geqslant_1 \frac{\phi_1\wedge\phi_2\geqslant_1 i}{\begin{array}{c}\phi_1\geqslant_1 i\\ \phi_2\geqslant_1 i\end{array}} \qquad \wedge\geqslant_2 \frac{\phi_1\wedge\phi_2\geqslant_2 i}{\phi_1\geqslant_2 i \mid \phi_2\geqslant_2 i}$$

$$\vee\leqslant_1 \frac{\phi_1\vee\phi_2\leqslant_1 i}{\begin{array}{c}\phi_1\leqslant_1 i\\ \phi_2\leqslant_1 i\end{array}} \qquad \vee\leqslant_2 \frac{\phi_1\vee\phi_2\leqslant_2 i}{\phi_1\leqslant_2 i \mid \phi_2\leqslant_2 i}$$

$$\vee\geqslant_1 \frac{\phi_1\vee\phi_2\geqslant_1 i}{\phi_1\geqslant_1 i \mid \phi_2\geqslant_1 i} \qquad \vee\geqslant_2 \frac{\phi_1\vee\phi_2\geqslant_2 i}{\begin{array}{c}\phi_1\geqslant_2 i\\ \phi_2\geqslant_2 i\end{array}}$$

Fig. 2. Rules of $\mathcal{T}\left(\text{Ł}^2_{(x,y)}\right)$. Vertical bars denote splitting of the branch.

Each branch can be extended by an application of one of the rules in Fig. 2 where $i, j \in [0,1]$. Let i's be in $[0,1]$ and x's be variables ranging over the real interval $[0,1]$. We define the translation τ from labelled formulas to linear inequalities as follows:

$$\tau(\phi \leqslant_1 i) = x^L_\phi \leq i;\ \tau(\phi \geqslant_1 i) = x^L_\phi \geq i;\ \tau(\phi \leqslant_2 i) = x^R_\phi \leq i;\ \tau(\phi \geqslant_2 i) = x^R_\phi \geq i$$

Let $\bullet \in \{\leqslant_1, \geqslant_1\}$ and $\circ \in \{\leqslant_2, \geqslant_2\}$. A tableau branch

$$\mathcal{B} = \{\phi_1 \circ i_1, \ldots, \phi_m \circ i_m, \phi'_1 \bullet j_1, \ldots, \phi'_n \bullet j_n, k_1 \leq l_1, \ldots, k_q \leq l_q\}$$

is closed *if the system of inequalities*

$$\tau(\phi_1 \circ i_1), \ldots, \tau(\phi_m \circ i_m), \tau(\phi'_1 \bullet j_1), \ldots, \tau(\phi'_n \bullet j_n), k_1 \leq l_1, \ldots, k_q \leq l_q$$

does not have solutions. Otherwise, $\mathcal{B}$ is open. *A tableau is* closed *if all its branches are closed.*

ϕ has a $\mathcal{T}\left(Ł^2_{(x,y)}\right)$ proof *if the tableaux beginning with $\{\phi \leqslant_1 c, c < x\}$ and $\{\phi \geqslant_2 d, d > y\}$ are both closed.*

Remark 6 (How to interpret the rules of $\mathcal{T}\left(Ł^2_{(x,y)}\right)$?). Consider for instance the rule $\to\leqslant_2$. It's meaning is: $v_2(\phi_1 \to \phi_2) \leq i$ iff there is $j \in [0,1]$ s.t. $v_2(\phi_1) \geq j$ and $v_2(\phi_2) \leq i + j$. While rule $\wedge\leqslant_1$ means $v_1(\phi_1 \wedge \phi_2) \leq i$ iff either $v_1(\phi_1) \leq i$ or $v_1(\phi_2) \leq i$.

To prove completeness and soundness, we need the following definitions.

Definition 7 (Satisfying valuation of a branch). *Let v be a valuation and $\mathrm{k} \in \{1,2\}$. v* satisfies *a labelled formula $\phi \leqslant_{\mathrm{k}} i$ (resp. $\phi \geqslant_{\mathrm{k}} i$) iff $v_{\mathrm{k}}(\phi) \leq i$ (resp. $v_{\mathrm{k}}(\phi) \geq i$). v* satisfies *a branch $\mathcal{B}$ iff v* satisfies *any labelled formula in $\mathcal{B}$. A branch $\mathcal{B}$ is* satisfiable *iff there is a valuation which satisfies it.*

Theorem 1 (Soundness and completeness). *ϕ is $Ł^2_{(x,y)}(\to)$-valid (resp. $Ł^2_{(x,y)}(\Rightarrow)$-valid) iff there is a $\mathcal{T}\left(Ł^2_{(x,y)}\right)$ proof for it.*

Proof. The soundness follows from the fact that no closed branch is realisable and that if a premise of the rule is realisable, then all labelled formulas are satisfied in at least one of the conclusions.

To show completeness, we proceed by contraposition. We need to show that complete open branches are satisfiable.

Assume that $\mathcal{B}$ is a complete open branch. We construct the satisfying valuation as follows. Let $* \in \{\leqslant_1, \geqslant_1, \leqslant_2, \geqslant_2\}$ and $p_1, \ldots, p_m$ be the propositional variables appearing in the atomic labelled formulas in $\mathcal{B}$. Let $\{p_1 * i_1, \ldots, p_m * i_n\}$ and $\{k_1 \leq l_1, \ldots, k_q \leq l_q\}$ be the sets of all atomic labelled formulas and all numerical constraints in $\mathcal{B}$. Notice that one variable might appear in many atomic labelled formulas, hence we might have $m \neq n$. Since $\mathcal{B}$ is complete and open, the following system of linear inequalities over the set of variables $\{x^L_{p_1}, x^R_{p_1}, \ldots, x^L_{p_m}, x^R_{p_m}\}$ must have at least one solution under the constrains listed:

$$\tau(p_1 * i_1), \ldots, \tau(p_m * i_n), k_1 \leq l_1, \ldots, k_q \leq l_q.$$

Let $c = (c_1^L, c_1^R, \ldots, c_m^L, c_m^R)$ be a solution to the above system of inequalities such that c_j^L (resp. c_j^R) is the value of $x_{p_j}^L$ (resp. $x_{p_j}^R$). Define the valuation v as follows: $v(p_j) = (c_j^L, c_j^R)$.

It remains to show by induction on ϕ that all formulas present at $\mathcal{B}$ are satisfied by v. The basis case of variables holds by construction of v. We consider only the most instructive case of $\phi_1 \to \phi_2 \geqslant_2 i$ as the other cases are straightforward.

Assume that $\phi_1 \to \phi_2 \geqslant_2 i \in \mathcal{B}$. Then, by completeness of $\mathcal{B}$, either $i \leq 0 \in \mathcal{B}$, in which case, $\phi_1 \to \phi_2 \geqslant_2 i$ is trivially satisfied, or $\phi_1 \leqslant_2 j, \phi_2 \geqslant_2 i + j \in \mathcal{B}$. Furthermore, by the induction hypothesis, v satisfies $\phi_1 \leqslant_2 j$ and $\phi_2 \geqslant_2 i + j$, and we also have that $j \leq 1 - i$. Now, to show that v satisfies $\phi_1 \to \phi_2 \geqslant_2 i$, recall from semantics that $v_2(\phi_1 \to \phi_2) = \max(0, v_2(\phi_2) - v_2(\phi_1))$.

Now, we have

$$\max(0, v_2(\phi_2) - v_2(\phi_1)) \geq \max(0, i + j - j) = \max(0, i) = i$$

as desired.

The cases of other connectives can be tackled in a similar fashion. □

3.2 Constraint Tableaux for $\mathbf{G}^2$

Definition 8 (Constraint tableaux for G^2—$\mathcal{T}(\mathsf{G}^2)$). *Let* $\lesssim\ \in \{<, \leqslant\}$ *and* $\gtrsim\ \in \{<, \leqslant\}$. *Branches contain:*

- formulaic constraints *of the form* $\mathbf{x} : \phi \lesssim \mathbf{x}' : \phi'$ *with* $\mathbf{x} \in \{1, 2\}$*;*
- numerical constraints *of the form* $c \lesssim c'$ *with* $c, c' \in \{1, 0\}$*;*
- labelled formulas *of the form* $\mathbf{x} : \phi * c$ *with* $* \in \{\lesssim, \gtrsim\}$.

We abbreviate all these types of entries with $\mathfrak{X} \lesssim \mathfrak{X}'$. *Each branch can be extended by an application of one of the rules in Fig. 3 where* $\mathbf{c} \neq \mathbf{c}'$, $c \neq c'$, $\mathbf{c}, \mathbf{c}' \in \{\mathbf{0}, \mathbf{1}\}$ *and* $c, c' \in \{0, 1\}$.

A tableau's branch $\mathcal{B}$ *is* closed *iff at least one of the following conditions applies:*

- *the transitive closure of* $\mathcal{B}$ *under* $\lesssim$ *contains* $\mathfrak{X} < \mathfrak{X}$,
- $0 \geqslant 1 \in \mathcal{B}$ *or* $\mathfrak{X} > 1 \in \mathcal{B}$ *or* $\mathfrak{X} < 0 \in \mathcal{B}$.

A tableau is closed *iff all its branches are closed. We say that there is a* tableau proof *of* ϕ *iff there is a closed tableau starting from* $1 : \phi < 1$.

Remark 7 (Interpretation of constraints). Formulaic constraint $\mathbf{x} : \phi \leqslant \mathbf{x}' : \phi'$ encodes the fact that $v_{\mathbf{x}}(\phi) \leq v_{\mathbf{x}'}(\phi')$, similarly labelled formula $\mathbf{x} : \phi \leqslant c$ encodes the fact that $v_{\mathbf{x}}(\phi) \leq c$.

Definition 9 (Satisfying valuation of a branch). *Let* $\mathbf{x}, \mathbf{x}' \in \{1, 2\}$. *Branch* $\mathcal{B}$ *is* satisfied *by a valuation* v *iff*

- $v_{\mathbf{x}}(\phi) \leq v_{\mathbf{x}'}(\phi')$ *for any* $\mathbf{x} : \phi \leqslant \mathbf{x}' : \phi' \in \mathcal{B}$ *and*
- $v_{\mathbf{x}}(\phi) \leq c$ *for any* $\mathbf{x} : \phi \leqslant c \in \mathcal{B}$ *s.t.* $c \in \{0, 1\}$.

$$\mathbf{c}_1\lesssim\frac{1:\mathbf{c}\lesssim\mathfrak{X}}{c\lesssim\mathfrak{X}}\qquad \mathbf{c}_2\lesssim\frac{2:\mathbf{c}\lesssim\mathfrak{X}}{c'\lesssim\mathfrak{X}}\qquad \mathbf{c}_1\gtrsim\frac{1:\mathbf{c}\gtrsim\mathfrak{X}}{c\gtrsim\mathfrak{X}}\qquad \mathbf{c}_2\gtrsim\frac{2:\mathbf{c}\gtrsim\mathfrak{X}}{c'\gtrsim\mathfrak{X}}$$

$$\neg_1\lesssim\frac{1:\neg\phi\lesssim\mathfrak{X}}{2:\phi\lesssim\mathfrak{X}}\qquad \neg_2\lesssim\frac{2:\neg\phi\lesssim\mathfrak{X}}{1:\phi\lesssim\mathfrak{X}}\qquad \neg_1\gtrsim\frac{1:\neg\phi\gtrsim\mathfrak{X}}{2:\phi\gtrsim\mathfrak{X}}\qquad \neg_2\gtrsim\frac{2:\neg\phi\gtrsim\mathfrak{X}}{1:\phi\gtrsim\mathfrak{X}}$$

$$\wedge_1\gtrsim\frac{1:\phi\wedge\phi'\gtrsim\mathfrak{X}}{\begin{array}{c}1:\phi\gtrsim\mathfrak{X}\\ 1:\phi'\gtrsim\mathfrak{X}\end{array}}\quad \wedge_2\lesssim\frac{2:\phi\wedge\phi'\lesssim\mathfrak{X}}{\begin{array}{c}2:\phi\lesssim\mathfrak{X}\\ 2:\phi'\lesssim\mathfrak{X}\end{array}}\quad \vee_1\lesssim\frac{1:\phi\vee\phi'\lesssim\mathfrak{X}}{\begin{array}{c}1:\phi\lesssim\mathfrak{X}\\ 1:\phi'\lesssim\mathfrak{X}\end{array}}\quad \vee_2\gtrsim\frac{2:\phi\vee\phi'\gtrsim\mathfrak{X}}{\begin{array}{c}2:\phi\gtrsim\mathfrak{X}\\ 2:\phi'\gtrsim\mathfrak{X}\end{array}}$$

$$\wedge_1\lesssim\frac{1:\phi\wedge\phi'\lesssim\mathfrak{X}}{1:\phi\lesssim\mathfrak{X}\mid 1:\phi'\lesssim\mathfrak{X}}\qquad \wedge_2\gtrsim\frac{2:\phi\wedge\phi'\gtrsim\mathfrak{X}}{2:\phi\gtrsim\mathfrak{X}\mid 2:\phi'\gtrsim\mathfrak{X}}$$

$$\vee_1\gtrsim\frac{1:\phi\vee\phi'\gtrsim\mathfrak{X}}{1:\phi\gtrsim\mathfrak{X}\mid 1:\phi'\gtrsim\mathfrak{X}}\qquad \vee_2\lesssim\frac{2:\phi\vee\phi'\lesssim\mathfrak{X}}{2:\phi\lesssim\mathfrak{X}\mid 2:\phi'\lesssim\mathfrak{X}}$$

$$\to_1\leqslant\frac{1:\phi\to\phi'\leqslant\mathfrak{X}}{\begin{array}{r|l} & \mathfrak{X}<1\\ \mathfrak{X}\geqslant 1 & 1:\phi'\leqslant\mathfrak{X}\\ & 1:\phi>1:\phi'\end{array}}\quad \to_1\gtrsim\frac{1:\phi\to\phi'\gtrsim\mathfrak{X}}{1:\phi\leqslant 1:\phi'\mid 1:\phi'\gtrsim\mathfrak{X}}\quad \to_1<\frac{1:\phi\to\phi'<\mathfrak{X}}{\begin{array}{c}1:\phi'<\mathfrak{X}\\ 1:\phi>1:\phi'\end{array}}$$

$$\to_2\lesssim\frac{2:\phi\to\phi'\lesssim\mathfrak{X}}{2:\phi'\leqslant 2:\phi\mid 2:\phi'\lesssim\mathfrak{X}}\quad \to_2\geqslant\frac{2:\phi\to\phi'\geqslant\mathfrak{X}}{\begin{array}{r|l} & \mathfrak{X}>0\\ \mathfrak{X}\leqslant 0 & 2:\phi'\geqslant\mathfrak{X}\\ & 2:\phi'>2:\phi\end{array}}\quad \to_2>\frac{2:\phi\to\phi'>\mathfrak{X}}{\begin{array}{c}2:\phi'>\mathfrak{X}\\ 2:\phi'>2:\phi\end{array}}$$

$$\prec_1\lesssim\frac{1:\phi\prec\phi'\lesssim\mathfrak{X}}{1:\phi\leqslant 1:\phi'\mid 1:\phi\lesssim\mathfrak{X}}\quad \prec_1>\frac{1:\phi\prec\phi'>\mathfrak{X}}{\begin{array}{c}1:\phi>\mathfrak{X}\\ 1:\phi>1:\phi'\end{array}}\quad \prec_1\geqslant\frac{1:\phi\prec\phi'\geqslant\mathfrak{X}}{\begin{array}{r|l} & \mathfrak{X}>0\\ \mathfrak{X}\leqslant 0 & 1:\phi\geqslant\mathfrak{X}\\ & 1:\phi>1:\phi'\end{array}}$$

$$\prec_2\gtrsim\frac{2:\phi\prec\phi'\gtrsim\mathfrak{X}}{2:\phi\gtrsim\mathfrak{X}\mid 2:\phi'\leqslant 2:\phi}\quad \prec_2\leqslant\frac{1:\phi\prec\phi'\leqslant\mathfrak{X}}{\begin{array}{r|l} & \mathfrak{X}<1\\ \mathfrak{X}\geqslant 1 & 2:\phi\leqslant\mathfrak{X}\\ & 2:\phi'>2:\phi\end{array}}\quad \prec_2<\frac{2:\phi\prec\phi'<\mathfrak{X}}{\begin{array}{c}2:\phi<\mathfrak{X}\\ 2:\phi<2:\phi'\end{array}}$$

$$\rightarrowtriangle_1\leqslant\frac{1:\phi\rightarrowtriangle\phi'\leqslant\mathfrak{X}}{\begin{array}{r|l} & \mathfrak{X}<1\\ \mathfrak{X}\geqslant 1 & 1:\phi'\leqslant\mathfrak{X}\\ & 1:\phi>1:\phi'\end{array}}\quad \rightarrowtriangle_1\gtrsim\frac{1:\phi\rightarrowtriangle\phi'\gtrsim\mathfrak{X}}{1:\phi\leqslant 1:\phi'\mid 1:\phi'\gtrsim\mathfrak{X}}\quad \rightarrowtriangle_1<\frac{1:\phi\rightarrowtriangle\phi'<\mathfrak{X}}{\begin{array}{c}1:\phi'<\mathfrak{X}\\ 1:\phi>1:\phi'\end{array}}$$

$$\rightarrowtriangle_2\lesssim\frac{2:\phi\rightarrowtriangle\phi'\lesssim\mathfrak{X}}{1:\phi\lesssim\mathfrak{X}\mid 2:\phi'\lesssim\mathfrak{X}}\qquad \rightarrowtriangle_2\gtrsim\frac{2:\phi\rightarrowtriangle\phi'\gtrsim\mathfrak{X}}{\begin{array}{c}1:\phi\gtrsim\mathfrak{X}\\ 2:\phi'\gtrsim\mathfrak{X}\end{array}}$$

Fig. 3. Rules of $\mathcal{T}\left(\mathsf{G}^2\right)$. Vertical bars denote branching; $\mathbf{c}\neq\mathbf{c}'$, $c\neq c'$, $\mathbf{c},\mathbf{c}'\in\{\mathbf{0},\mathbf{1}\}$, $c,c'\in\{0,1\}$.

Theorem 2 (Soundness and completeness). *ϕ is G^2-valid iff it has a $\mathcal{T}(\mathsf{G}^2)$ proof.*

Proof. For soundness, we check that if the premise of the rule is satisfied, then so is at least one of its conclusions.

For completeness, we show that every complete open branch $\mathcal{B}$ is satisfiable. We construct the satisfying valuation as follows. If $\mathbf{x} : p \geqslant 1 \in \mathcal{B}$, we set $v_1(p) = 1$. If $1 : p \leqslant 0 \in \mathcal{B}$, we set $v_1(p) = 0$. We do likewise for $2 : p \leqslant 0$ and $2 : p \geqslant 1$. To set the values of the remaining variables $q_1, \ldots, q_n$, we proceed as follows. Denote $\mathcal{B}^+$ the transitive closure of $\mathcal{B}$ under $\lesssim$ and let

$$[\mathbf{x} : q_i] = \left\{ \mathbf{x}' : q_j \;\middle|\; \begin{array}{c} (\mathbf{x} : q_i \leqslant \mathbf{x}' : q_j \in \mathcal{B}^+ \text{ or } \mathbf{x} : q_i \geqslant \mathbf{x}' : q_j \in \mathcal{B}^+) \\ \text{and} \\ \mathbf{x} : q_i < \mathbf{x}' : q_j \notin \mathcal{B}^+ \text{ and } \mathbf{x} : q_i > \mathbf{x}' : q_j \notin \mathcal{B}^+ \end{array} \right\}$$

It is clear that there are at most $2n$ $[\mathbf{x} : q_i]$'s since the only possible loop in $\mathcal{B}^+$ is $\mathbf{x} : r \leqslant \ldots \leqslant \mathbf{x} : r$, but in such a loop all elements belong to $[\mathbf{x} : r]$. We put $[\mathbf{x} : q_i] \preceq [\mathbf{x}' : q_j]$ iff there are $\mathbf{x} : r \in [\mathbf{x} : q_i]$ and $\mathbf{x}' : r' \in [\mathbf{x}' : q_j]$ s.t. $\mathbf{x} : r \leqslant \mathbf{x}' : r' \in \mathcal{B}^+$.

We now set the valuation of these variables as follows

$$v_{\mathbf{x}}(q_i) = \frac{|\{[\mathbf{x}' : q'] \mid [\mathbf{x}' : q'] \preceq [\mathbf{x} : q_i]\}|}{2n} \tag{$*$}$$

Thus, all constraints containing only variables are satisfied.

It remains to show that all other constraints are satisfied. For that, we prove that if at least one conclusion of the rule is satisfied, then so is the premise. We consider only the case of $\rightarrowtriangle_2\lesssim$. Let $1 : \phi_1 \lesssim \mathfrak{X}$ be satisfied. W.l.o.g., assume that $\mathfrak{X} = 2 : \psi$ and $\lesssim = <$. Thus, $v_1(\phi_1) < v_2(\psi)$. Recall that $v_2(\phi_1 \rightarrowtriangle \phi_2) = \min(v_1(\phi_1), v_2(\phi_2))$. Hence, $v_2(\phi_1 \rightarrowtriangle \phi_2) < v_2(\psi)$, and $2 : \phi_1 \rightarrowtriangle \phi_2 < 2 : \psi$ is satisfied as desired. By the same reasoning, we have that if $2 : \phi_2 \lesssim \mathfrak{X}$ is satisfied, then so is $2 : \phi_1 \rightarrowtriangle \phi_2 \lesssim \mathfrak{X}$.

The cases of other rules can be showed in the same fashion. □

3.3 Applications

Corollary 2. *Satisfiability for any $\mathrm{Ł}^2_{(x,y)}(\rightarrow)$ and $\mathrm{Ł}^2_{(x,1)}(\rightarrowtriangle)$ is $\mathcal{NP}$-complete while their validities are co$\mathcal{NP}$-complete.*

Proof. Let $|\phi|$ be the number of symbols in ϕ. Observe, from the proof of Theorem 1, that each tableau branch gives rise to two bounded mixed-integer programming problems (bMIP)—each of the length $O(\rho(|\phi|))$ for some polynomial ρ. Recall that bMIP is $\mathcal{NP}$-complete (cf. [17]). Thus we can non-deterministically guess an open branch and then solve its two bMIPs (one arising from inequalities with $\leqslant_1$, and the other from those with $\leqslant_2$). This yields the $\mathcal{NP}$- and co$\mathcal{NP}$-membership for satisfiability and validity, respectively.

To obtain the $\mathcal{NP}$-hardness, we use the same method as in [17,24]. For each classical formula ϕ one can construct a formula $\mathsf{two}(\phi)$ (cf. the detailed definition in [24, Lemmas 3.1–3.3]). Then by [24, Lemma 3.2], ϕ is classically valid iff $\phi^{\mathsf{C}} := \mathsf{two}(\phi) \supset \phi$ is Ł-valid. Furthermore, if ϕ^{C} is not valid, there is an Ł-valuation v such that $v(\phi^{\mathsf{C}}) = 0$. Recall that $\phi^{\bullet}$ (resp. ϕ°) denotes the formula obtained by substituting $\supset$ for $\to$ (resp. $\twoheadrightarrow$) in the formula ϕ (cf. Remark 4). Thus, ϕ is classically valid iff $(\phi^{\mathsf{C}})^{\bullet}$ is $\text{Ł}^2_{(1,0)}(\to)$-valid and $(\phi^{\mathsf{C}})^{\circ}$ is $\text{Ł}^2_{(1,1)}(\twoheadrightarrow)$-valid. Furthermore, if $(\phi^{\mathsf{C}})^{\bullet}$ is not valid, there is v' such that $v'((\phi^{\mathsf{C}})^{\bullet}) = (0,1)$, and $(\phi^{\mathsf{C}})^{\circ}$ is not valid, there is v' such that $v'((\phi^{\mathsf{C}})^{\bullet}) = (0,x)$ for some x. Since $(0,1)$ is not included in any non-trivial filter on $[0,1] \odot [0,1]$, and since no non-trivial filter can include $(1,1)$ and some $(0,x)$ simultaneously, we obtain

$$\vDash_{CPL} \phi \text{ iff } (\phi^{\mathsf{C}})^{\bullet} \text{ is } \text{Ł}^2_{(x,y)}(\to)\text{-valid iff } (\phi^{\mathsf{C}})^{\circ} \text{ is } \text{Ł}^2_{(x,y)}(\twoheadrightarrow)\text{-valid}$$

as desired. □

Remark 8 (Removing the branching). We have introduced branching rules in our tableaux in order to make them more intuitive. It is possible, however, to make all rules *linear* just as it was done originally in [17]. For example, the linear versions of $\to\leqslant_1$ and $\to\geqslant_2$ look as follows ($y \in \{0,1\}$):

$$\frac{\phi_1 \to \phi_2 \leqslant_1 i}{\begin{array}{ll}\phi_1 \geqslant_1 1-i+j-y & y \leqslant i\\ \phi_2 \leqslant_1 j+y & j \leqslant i\end{array}} \qquad \frac{\phi_1 \to \phi_2 \geqslant_2 i}{\begin{array}{ll}\phi_1 \leqslant_2 j+y & y \leqslant 1-i\\ \phi_2 \geqslant_2 i+j-y & j \leqslant 1-i\end{array}}$$

Other rules can be easily acquired since $\vee$ and $\wedge$ can be defined via $\to$ and $\mathbf{0}$ in the language of Ł^2. Rules without branching improve efficiency of the proof search by removing the need to guess the branch whose bMIP we should solve.

Corollary 3. *Satisfiability for* $\mathsf{G}^2(\to)$ *and* $\mathsf{G}^2(\twoheadrightarrow)$ *is* $\mathcal{NP}$*-complete.*

Proof. It follows from the Proof of Theorem 2 that the satisfiability of $\mathsf{G}^2(\to)$ and $\mathsf{G}^2(\twoheadrightarrow)$ is in $\mathcal{NP}$: we obtain the valuation from $(*)$, and it takes polynomial time to check that it indeed satisfies the formula.

The $\mathcal{NP}$-hardness follows since G^2's are conservative extensions of G whose satisfiability and validity are $\mathcal{NP}$- and *co*$\mathcal{NP}$-complete respectively. □

We can also use the tableaux to check whether a set Γ of assumptions entails a formula ϕ in the logics we consider. This yields the finite strong completeness for G^2's and Ł^2's by means of tableaux, and extends the complexity results to the finitary entailment.

Corollary 4. *Let* Γ *be a finite set of formulas. Then* $\Gamma \vDash_{\text{Ł}^2_{(x,y)}} \phi$ *iff the left tableau closes,* $\Gamma \vDash_{\mathsf{G}^2(\to)} \phi$ *iff the central tableau closes, and* $\Gamma \vDash_{\mathsf{G}^2(\twoheadrightarrow)} \phi$ *iff the left tableau closes.*

$$\bigcup_{\phi' \in \Delta} \{\phi' \geqslant_1 x, \phi' \leqslant_2 y\} \;\Big/\; \begin{array}{c|c}\phi \geqslant_1 c & \phi \geqslant_2 d\\ c < x & d > y\end{array}$$

$$\{1 : \phi' \geqslant 1, \phi' \leqslant 0 \mid \phi' \in \Gamma\} \;\Big/\; \begin{array}{c|c}1 : \phi < 1 & 2 : \phi > 0\end{array}$$

$$\{1 : \phi' \geqslant 1 \mid \phi' \in \Gamma\} \;\Big/\; 1 : \phi < 1$$

Thus, the finitary entailment for any of these logics is co$\mathcal{NP}$*-complete.*

4 Conclusions and Further Research

Using constraint tableaux, we have provided a modular treatment of the Łukasiewicz and Gödel based two-dimensional logics. Our next steps are: (1) to study the structural proof theory of these logics, and of the two layer logics introduced in [6]; (2) to study and compare the logics in terms of consequence relations, to provide a Hilbert style axiomatization (for those where modus ponens is sound), and to prove standard completeness—cases we understand so far are the following four: $Ł^2_{(1,1)}(\rightarrowtriangle)$, $Ł^2_{(1,0)}(\rightarrow)$ which is the logic $Ł_{(\neg)}$ of [6], $\mathsf{G}^2_{(1,0)}(\rightarrow)$ whose validities coincide with the axiomatic extension of Wansing's I_4C_4 [31] with the prelinearity axiom, and $\mathsf{G}^2_{(1,1)}(\rightarrowtriangle)$ whose consequence coincides with the axiomatic extension of Nelson's $N4^{\perp}$ [25,26] with the prelinearity axiom.

In a broader sense we naturally aim to provide a general treatment of two-dimensional graded logics. Indeed, within the research project introduced in [6], we want to develop a modular logical framework for reasoning based on heterogeneous information (such as crisp or fuzzy data, personal beliefs, etc.) that can be both incomplete and inconsistent. In addition, we do not wish to commit to a specific logic to model the reasoning of the agent(s), because different situations may call for different logics—modeling the reasoning of a group of experts is different from modeling the reasoning of the crowd. Doing so requires the ability to manipulate and combine logics for these different situations in a modular way.

References

1. Avron, A.: The structure of interlaced bilattices. Math. Struct. Comput. Sci. **6**(3), 287–299 (1996). https://doi.org/10.1017/S0960129500001018
2. Avron, A., Arieli, O.: Reasoning with logical bilattices. J. Logic Lang. Inform. **5**, 25–63 (1996)
3. Avron, A., Konikowska, B.: Decomposition proof systems for Gödel-Dummett logics. Stud. Logica. **69**(2), 197–219 (2001)
4. Baldi, P., Cintula, P., Noguera, C.: On two-layered modal logics for uncertainty (2020, manuscript)
5. Belnap, N.D.: How a computer should think. In: Omori, H., Wansing, H. (eds.) New Essays on Belnap-Dunn Logic. SL, vol. 418, pp. 35–53. Springer, Cham (2019). https://doi.org/10.1007/978-3-030-31136-0_4
6. Bílková, M., Frittella, S., Majer, O., Nazari, S.: Belief based on inconsistent information. In: Martins, M.A., Sedlár, I. (eds.) DaLi 2020. LNCS, vol. 12569, pp. 68–86. Springer, Cham (2020). https://doi.org/10.1007/978-3-030-65840-3_5
7. Cintula, P., Noguera, C.: Modal logics of uncertainty with two-layer syntax: a general completeness theorem. In: Proceedings of WoLLIC 2014, pp. 124–136 (2014)
8. D'Agostino, M.: Investigations into the Complexity of Some Propositional Calculi. Oxford University Computing Laboratory, Oxford (1990)
9. Di Nola, A., Leustean, I.: Łukasiewicz logic and MV-algebras. In: Cintula, P., Hajek, P., Noguera, C. (eds.) Handbook of Mathematical Fuzzy Logic, vol. 2. College Publications (2011)
10. Dubois, D.: On ignorance and contradiction considered as truth-values. Log. J. IGPL **16**(2), 195–216 (2008)

11. Dunn, J.M.: Intuitive semantics for first-degree entailments and 'coupled trees'. Philos. Stud. **29**(3), 149–168 (1976)
12. Dunn, J.M.: Contradictory information: too much of a good thing. J. Philos. Log. **39**, 425–452 (2010)
13. Fagin, R., Halpern, J.Y., Megiddo, N.: A logic for reasoning about probabilities. Inf. Comput. **87**, 78–128 (1990)
14. Font, J.: Abstract Algebraic Logic-An Introductory Textbook, Studies in Logic, vol. 60. College Publications, London (2016)
15. Ginsberg, M.: Multivalued logics: a uniform approach to reasoning in AI. Comput. Intell. **4**, 256–316 (1988)
16. Goré, R.: Dual intuitionistic logic revisited. In: Dyckhoff, R. (ed.) TABLEAUX 2000. LNCS (LNAI), vol. 1847, pp. 252–267. Springer, Heidelberg (2000). https://doi.org/10.1007/10722086_21
17. Hähnle, R.: Many-valued logic and mixed integer programming. Ann. Math. Artif. Intell. **12**(3–4), 231–263 (1994)
18. Hähnle, R.: Advanced many-valued logics. In: Gabbay, D., Guenthner, F. (eds.) Handbook of Philosophical Logic. HALO, vol. 2, pp. 297–395. Springer, Dordrecht (2001). https://doi.org/10.1007/978-94-017-0452-6_5
19. Hähnle, R.: Tableaux and related methods. In: Robinson, J.A., Voronkov, A. (eds.) Handbook of Automated Reasoning, vol. 2, pp. 100–178. Elsevier and MIT Press (2001). https://doi.org/10.1016/b978-044450813-3/50005-9
20. Hájek, P.: Metamathematics of Fuzzy Logic. Trends in Logic, vol. 4. Springer, Dordrecht (1998)
21. Jansana, R., Rivieccio, U.: Residuated bilattices. Soft. Comput. **16**(3), 493–504 (2012)
22. Klein, D., Majer, O., Rad, S.R.: Probabilities with gaps and gluts. J. Philos. Log. (2021). https://doi.org/10.1007/s10992-021-09592-x
23. Metcalfe, G., Olivetti, N., Gabbay, D.: Proof Theory for Fuzzy Logics. Applied Logic Series, vol. 36. Springer, Heidelberg (2008)
24. Mundici, D.: Satisfiability in many-valued sentential logic is NP-complete. Theor. Comput. Sci. **52**(1), 145–153 (1987). https://doi.org/10.1016/0304-3975(87)90083-1
25. Nelson, D.: Constructible falsity. J. Symb. Log. **14**(1), 16–26 (1949)
26. Odintsov, S.: Constructive Negations and Paraconsistency. Trends in Logic, vol. 26. Springer, Heidelbrg (2008)
27. Omori, H., Wansing, H.: 40 years of FDE: an introductory overview. Stud. Logica. **105**(6), 1021–1049 (2017). https://doi.org/10.1007/s11225-017-9748-6
28. Rauszer, C.: An algebraic and Kripke-style approach to a certain extension of intuitionistic logic. dissertation, Institute of Mathematics, Polish Academy of Sciences (1980)
29. Rivieccio, U.: An algebraic study of bilattice-based logics. Ph.D. thesis, University of Barcelona - University of Genoa (2010)
30. Vakarelov, D.: Notes on N-lattices and constructive logic with strong negation. Stud. Logica. **36**(1–2), 109–125 (1977)
31. Wansing, H.: Constructive negation, implication, and co-implication. J. Appl. Non-Classical Logics **18**(2–3), 341–364 (2008). https://doi.org/10.3166/jancl.18.341-364

Analytic Tableaux for Non-deterministic Semantics

Lukas Grätz[1,2(✉)]

[1] Technische Universität Darmstadt, Darmstadt, Germany
lukas.graetz@tu-darmstadt.de
[2] Universität Leipzig, Leipzig, Germany

Abstract. Analytic tableau systems for the family of non-deterministic semantics are introduced. These are based on tableaux for many-valued logics using sets-as-signs DNF representations. Karnaugh maps illustrate the construction of tableau rules. In contrast to classical many-valued tableaux, we add a rule called sign intersection. Soundness and completeness are shown. As an example demonstrates, some tableau systems would be incomplete without sign intersection. There is a correspondence to well-studied canonical calculi based on sequent systems: Tableau systems can be translated into canonical calculi, but not vice-versa (structural rules are missing on the tableau side).

Keywords: Tableaux · Non-deterministic semantics · Sets as signs · Signed logic · DNF representation

1 Introduction

As a generalization of many-valued logics, non-deterministic semantics has been successfully used to provide a semantics for a large variety of logics, including para-consistent logics [1], non-standard modal logics [12,22]. As shown there, some important logics do not have a deterministic finitely-valued semantics.

In this paper, a characterization of tableau systems for many-valued logics [16–18] is adapted to non-deterministic semantics. A previous approach is a special case within our framework [24].[1]

Tableaux are related to other Gentzen-style sequent systems, notably canonical calculi (Sect. 8).

Just a short warning, for those who may see this paper as a sheer exercise:

1. Admittedly, the tableau rule definition is a straightforward generalization.
2. An additional structural rule called *sign intersection* is added. Without sign intersection, some tableau systems would be incomplete (see Example 3). The rule itself had already been suggested to improve complexity of many-valued tableaux, see Note 4 below Definition 6.

[1] Also note that a tableau system for a particular non-deterministic semantics is already listed in [19, p. 211]. Unfortunately, we could not find out more about it; an approach to contact the author was unsuccessful.

A. Das and S. Negri (Eds.): TABLEAUX 2021, LNAI 12842, pp. 38–55, 2021.
https://doi.org/10.1007/978-3-030-86059-2_3

3. In this paper, soundness and completeness proofs are designed to be simple.
4. Generalized DNFs make use of (meta-level) modal operators.

Finally, it becomes an exercise to construct new tableau systems by using our framework for specific semantics in the literature.

The paper is organized as follows: After the preliminaries (Sect. 2), tableau rules are defined (Sect. 3), which are shown to be sound and complete (Sects. 5 and 6). The meta-logical representation of a tableau rule is a generalized DNF (Sect. 7). For finite valued semantics, tableau rules based on canonical DNF do always exist. More efficient rules with less branching can be constructed using generalized Karnaugh maps (Sect. 4).

2 Non-deterministic Semantics

This section provides self-contained notions, see [6] for in-depth descriptions.

A propositional language $\mathcal{L} = \langle P, C \rangle$ consists of a countable set of propositional variables $P = \{p_0, p_1, \dots\}$ and a set of logical connectives $\langle C, \alpha \rangle$ where α defines the arity $\alpha(\odot) \in \mathbb{N}$ of each connective $\odot \in C$. For a compact notation we write $\odot^{(a)}$ to indicate that $\odot \in C$ has arity a, e.g., $C = \{\neg^{(1)}, \rightarrow^{(2)}, \vee^{(2)}\}$.

The set of all formulas is denoted by For $\mathcal{L}$ and has the usual inductive definition: If $\odot^{(m)} \in C$ is a connective and $A_1, \dots, A_m \in$ For $\mathcal{L}$ are formulas, then $\odot(A_1, \dots, A_m) \in$ For $\mathcal{L}$ is also a formula.

Definition 1 (Nmatrix). *$\mathcal{M} = \langle \mathcal{V}, \mathcal{D}, \mathcal{O} \rangle$ is called* nmatrix, *where*

- *$\mathcal{V}$ is the set of* truth values,
- *$\mathcal{D} \subseteq \mathcal{V}$ is the subset of* designated values *(non-designated are $\mathcal{F} = \mathcal{V} \setminus \mathcal{D}$),*
- *$\mathcal{O}$ is the set of* non-deterministic truth functions.

The set $\mathcal{O}$ includes a non-deterministic truth function $\tilde{\odot}\colon \mathcal{V}^m \to (2^{\mathcal{V}} \setminus \emptyset)$ for each $\odot^{(m)} \in C$.

This generalizes the definition of a (many-valued) matrix, with a truth function $\tilde{\odot}\colon \mathcal{V}^m \to \mathcal{V}$ for each connective $\odot^{(m)} \in C$. Such a matrix is equivalent to a "deterministic" nmatrix, in which each truth function returns singletons only.

Note 1. Usually, see [29], the set of designated truth values $\mathcal{D}$ is required to be a non-empty proper subset of $\mathcal{V}$, since $\mathcal{D} = \emptyset$ or $\mathcal{D} = \mathcal{V}$ would make the semantics trivial. Nevertheless, we do not need this assumption in the following. Still, we will not introduce tableaux for "PNmatrices" [9] as we need $\tilde{\odot}(x_1, \dots, x_m) \neq \emptyset$ in Lemma 2.

Definition 2 (Valuation). *Let $\mathcal{M} = \langle \mathcal{V}, \mathcal{D}, \mathcal{O} \rangle$ be an nmatrix. A (dynamic)* valuation *in $\mathcal{M}$ is a function $v\colon$ For $\mathcal{L} \to \mathcal{V}$ such that for each $\odot^{(m)} \in C$ and $A_1, \dots, A_m \in$ For $\mathcal{L}$:*

$$v(\odot(A_1, \dots, A_m)) \in \tilde{\odot}(v(A_1), \dots, v(A_m))$$

Logical entailment is given by a Tarskian consequence relation:

Definition 3 ($\vDash_\mathcal{M}$). *The* semantic consequence relation

$$\varDelta \vDash_\mathcal{M} A$$

between $\varDelta \subseteq For\ \mathcal{L}$ *and* $A \in For\ \mathcal{L}$ *is defined as*

$$\forall v \in \mathsf{Val}^\mathcal{M}\colon\ (\forall B \in \varDelta\colon v(B) \in \mathcal{D}) \implies v(A) \in \mathcal{D}$$

where $\mathsf{Val}^\mathcal{M}$ *is the set of all valuations in* $\mathcal{M}$. *We say that a conclusion* A *follows from a set of premises* $\varDelta$ *in* $\mathcal{M}$.

3 Tableau System Definition

In this section and any following sections, let $\mathcal{M} = \langle \mathcal{V}, \mathcal{D}, \mathcal{O} \rangle$ be an nmatrix ($\mathcal{F} = \mathcal{V} \setminus \mathcal{D}$) and C be the set of connectives.

Definition 7 in this section generalizes tableau rules for many-valued semantics. The remaining definitions in this section are taken from the many-valued case, c.f. [18]; only the *sign intersection rule* is added here (again, see Note 4 for origins). The rest of the section is taken by Example 3, a tableau system for demonstration purposes.

Tableau systems are meant to formalize indirect proofs. Simple tableau systems (c.f. Definition 14 and Note 6) use signed formulas "x A" or "A takes the truth value x". Proving that a particular formula A is *valid* (i.e., $\vDash A$) would require separate tableaux with an assumption "x A" for each $x \in \mathcal{F}$. This formalizes separate indirect proofs for each $x \in \mathcal{F}$.

However, it is more natural to use only one indirect proof with the assumption that A takes any of the non-designated values. This assumption can be formalized using *sets as signs* [16–18] by the signed formula $\mathcal{F}\ A$. Although this paper covers sets as signs only, simple tableau systems can still be simulated using singleton sets as signs.

Definition 4 ($\mathbb{S}$, $\mathbb{S}^+$). *A* set of signs $\mathbb{S}$ for $\mathcal{M}$, *is a non-empty family of truth value sets* $\emptyset \neq \mathbb{S} \subseteq 2^\mathcal{V}$, *closed under intersection* $\{X \cap Y \mid X, Y \in \mathbb{S}\} = \mathbb{S}$. *Given* $\mathbb{S}$, *we call* $\mathbb{S}^+ = \mathbb{S} \setminus \{\emptyset\}$ *the* set of non-empty signs.

Note 2. In the following, we will define a particular set of signs either by $\mathbb{S}$ or by $\mathbb{S}^+$. Given $\mathbb{S}^+$, we usually get $\mathbb{S} = \mathbb{S}^+ \cup \{\emptyset\}$. Special cases with $\emptyset \notin \mathbb{S}$ are of little interest.

Example 1. The set of *simple signs* consists of all singletons $\mathbb{S}_1^+ = \{\{x\} \mid x \in \mathcal{V}\}$.

Example 2. The whole power set $\mathbb{S}_2 = 2^\mathcal{V}$ is also a candidate.

Definition 4 permits a finite set of signs even under an infinite number of truth values. In most of the proofs we require at least $\{\{x\} \mid x \in \mathcal{V}\} \subseteq \mathbb{S}$ or $\mathcal{D}, \mathcal{F} \in \mathbb{S}$. The following definition is taken from [7,14]:

Definition 5 (Signed formula). *Given* $X \in \mathbb{S}$ *and* $A \in For\ \mathcal{L}$, *the expression* $X\ A$ *is called a* signed formula *and has the following semantics:*

1. *We say a* signed formula $(X\ A)$ is true under a valuation v in $\mathcal{M}$ *if* $v(A) \in X$.
2. *Expressions over signed formulas and meta-connectives* ($\bigwedge\!\!\!\!\bigwedge$, $\bigvee\!\!\!\!\bigvee$, $\neg\!\!\!\neg$, $\Longleftrightarrow$, $\Longrightarrow$, $\Longleftarrow$) *have the semantics of classical propositional logic: For instance, if both* $(X\ A)$ *and* $(Y\ B)$ *are true under* v, *then* $(X\ A \bigwedge\!\!\!\!\bigwedge Y\ B)$ *is true under* v.

Note 3. Satisfiability and validity are adapted to signed formulas: A signed formula $(X\ A)$ is *satisfiable* or *consistent* iff there is a valuation v with $v(A) \in X$. A signed formula $(X\ A)$ is *valid* iff $v(A) \in X$ holds for all valuations v.

Definition 6 (Sign intersection). *The* sign intersection rule *can be applied to signed formulas* $(X\ A)$, $(Y\ A)$ *and returns* $(X \cap Y\ A)$.

$$\frac{\begin{array}{c} X\ A \\ Y\ A \end{array}}{X \cap Y\ A}$$

Note 4. Sign intersection was already known as "contraction rule" in [17]. The rule was renamed to prevent confusion with the well-known structural rule of the sequent calculus. Both rules follow the same idea to contract two instances with the same formula A into a single formula in their respective direction of proof. However, the direction is converse in analytic tableaux and (synthetic) sequent calculi. A structural rule with a similar effect to sign intersection is called *anti-contraction* by Ohnishi and Matsumoto [21], also known as "expansion" or "duplication", see [23, p. 61 ff].

Definition 7 (Tableau rule). *Given is a set of signs* $\mathbb{S}$ *for* $\mathcal{M}$. *Let* $Y \in \mathbb{S}^+$ *be a sign,* $\odot^{(m)} \in C$ *a connective,* $I_j \subseteq \{1, \ldots, m\}$ *index sets, and* $X_{j,i} \in \mathbb{S}^+$ *signs (for all* $j = 1, \ldots, k$ *and* $i \in I_j$*). Then*

$$\frac{Y\ \odot(A_1, \ldots, A_m)}{\{X_{1,i}\ A_i \mid i \in I_1\} \;\Big|\; \cdots \;\Big|\; \{X_{k,i}\ A_i \mid i \in I_k\}}$$

is a tableau rule for Y and $\tilde{\odot}$ *iff for all* $z_1, \ldots, z_m \in \mathcal{V}$:

$$Y \cap \tilde{\odot}(z_1, \ldots, z_m) \neq \emptyset \iff \bigvee_{j=1}^{k} \bigwedge_{i \in I_j} z_i \in X_{j,i} \tag{1}$$

As in [16], a tableau rule can also be written as function $\pi_{Y\odot}$.

Definition 8. *The* functional representation *of a tableau rule for* $Y\ \odot(A_1, \ldots, A_m)$ *(Definition 7) is given by a function* $\pi_{Y\odot}\colon (For\ \mathcal{L})^m \to \mathcal{P}(\mathcal{P}(\mathbb{S} \times For\ \mathcal{L}))$ *with:*

$$\pi_{Y\odot}(A_1, \ldots, A_m) = \Big\{ \{X_{j,i}\ A_i \mid i \in I_j\} \;\Big|\; j \in \{1 \ldots k\} \Big\}$$

Definition 9. *Each* $E \in \pi_{Y\odot}(A_1, \ldots, A_m)$ *is called an* extension *of the tableau rule* $\pi_{Y\odot}$ *(i.e., an extension* E *is a "column" in a tableau rule).*

Note 5. We distinguish between an extensionless rule $\pi_{Y\odot}(A_1, \ldots, A_m) = \emptyset$ and a rule with a single empty extension $\pi_{Y\odot}(A_1, \ldots, A_m) = \{\emptyset\}$ by using $\dfrac{Y\ \odot(A_1, \ldots, A_m)}{\times}$ for the former and $\dfrac{Y\ \odot(A_1, \ldots, A_m)}{}$ for the latter.

Definition 10 (Tableau system). *Let* $\mathcal{M} = \langle \mathcal{V}, \mathcal{D}, \mathcal{O} \rangle$ *be an nmatrix and* $\mathbb{S}(\subseteq 2^{\mathcal{V}})$ *be a set of signs. A* tableau system for $\mathcal{M}$ and $\mathbb{S}$ *consists of tableau rules for all* $X \in \mathbb{S}^+$ *and* $\odot \in C$ *and additionally, the sign intersection rule. We may define such a tableau system* $\Pi = \{\pi_{Y\odot} \mid X \in \mathbb{S}^+, \odot \in C\}$ *by its tableau rules.*

For the definition of a tableau proof tree, the reader is assumed to be familiar with basic notions of graph theory, namely *tree*, *node*, *root*, *leaf*, *child*, and *branch*. A branch is simply a path from the root to a leaf.

Definition 11. *Let* Θ *be a set of signed formulas. A* tableau proof tree for assumptions Θ in a tableau system Π *is a tree of signed formulas. Each node in the tableau tree is either an assumption or a result of a rule application from* Π*. Applying a tableau rule with* k *extensions on some signed formula in a branch results in* k *subbranches, containing all signed formulas of the respective extension. These subbranches are located below the previous leaf of the branch. The application of sign intersection on* $Y\ A$ *and* $X\ A$ *in a branch results in a new leaf* $(X \cap Y)\ A$*.*

Definition 12. *A branch of a tableau is* closed *iff either*

- *any empty-signed formula* $\emptyset\ A$ *occurs, or*
- *an extensionless rule* $\dfrac{Y\ \odot(A_1, \ldots, A_m)}{\times}$ *was applied, leaving no subbranches.*

A tableau is closed iff every branch is closed.

Definition 13. *A* proper leaf *in a tableau tree is a leaf that cannot be closed by applying an extensionless tableau rule.*

So to say, a proper leaf represents an end of a branch in the tree, while an improper leaf is just an inner node with zero children. Applying an extensionless tableau rule leads to the usual branching, just with zero continuing branches. A branch with $\emptyset\ A$ is closed since it is obviously unsatisfiable.

Definition 14 (Simple tableau system). *A* simple tableau system for $\mathcal{M}$ *corresponds to a tableau system for* $\mathcal{M}$ *and* $\mathbb{S}_1^+ = \{\{x\} \mid x \in \mathcal{V}\}$ *without sign intersection and with a modified closing condition: A branch is closed by either an extensionless rule, or two signed formulas* $\{x\}\ A$ *and* $\{y\}\ A$ *with* $x \neq y$*.*

Note 6. Instead of singleton signed formulas $\{x\}\ A$, formulas $x\ A$ with truth values $x \in \mathcal{V}$ as signs are used in the literature [11,14,18,24]. These are only a syntactical variant of simple tableau systems, as we observe. A collection of simple tableau systems for non-deterministic semantics is given in [24].

The following lemma shows that simple tableaux are equivalent to tableaux with singleton sets.

Lemma 1. *Let Π be a tableau system for $\mathcal{M}$ and $\mathbb{S}_1^+ = \{\{x\} \mid x \in \mathcal{V}\}$, and Π' be the corresponding simple tableau system for $\mathcal{M}$, then there is a tableau proof for a signed formula $\{x\}\ A$ in Π whenever there is a similar tableau proof for $\{x\}\ A$ in Π'.*

Proof. *Suppose that a tableau proof tree in Π has a sign intersection applied to $\{y\}\ B$ and $\{z\}\ B$ with $\{y\}, \{z\} \in \mathbb{S}_1$. Then either $y \neq z$ or $y = z$. In the former case, we get a closing condition with $\emptyset\ B$. In the letter case, sign intersection has no effect since $\{y\}\ B$ already occurs on the branch.*

Next, observe that closing conditions of Π and Π' can be mutually simulated: A closing in Π with $\emptyset\ B$ involves a previous sign intersection of $\{y\}\ B$ and $\{z\}\ B$—the simple tableau would already be closed without sign intersection. And a closing in Π' by $\{y\}\ B$ and $\{z\}\ B$ with $y \neq z$ can be simulated in Π by sign intersection and closing with $\emptyset\ B$. Of course, we do not have to simulate closing with an extensionless rule as this is part of both tableau variants.

Thus, we can translate tableau proofs in Π to proofs in Π' and vice versa.

For soundness see Sect. 5; for completeness see Sect. 6.

Example 3. Let $\mathcal{M}_3 = \langle\{0,1,2\}, \{1,2\}, \{\tilde{\sqsupset}, \tilde{\sim}\}\rangle$ be an nmatrix[2] with:

$\tilde{\sqsupset}$	0	1	2	$\tilde{\sim}$
0	2	2	2	2
1	0	0, 1	2	0, 2
2	0	0, 1	2	0

(2)

In this example, the signs are given by $\mathbb{S}_3^+ = \{\{0\}, \{0,1\}, \{1\}, \{1,2\}\}$ and the tableau calculus Π_3 consists of the following rules:

$$\frac{\{0\}\ A \sqsupset B}{\begin{array}{l}\{1,2\}\ A\\ \{0,1\}\ B\end{array}} \qquad \frac{\{0,1\}\ A \sqsupset B}{\begin{array}{l}\{1,2\}\ A\\ \{0,1\}\ B\end{array}} \qquad \frac{\{1\}\ A \sqsupset B}{\begin{array}{c}\{1,2\}\ A\\ \{1\}\ B\end{array}} \qquad \frac{\{1,2\}\ A \sqsupset B}{\{0\}\ A \mid \{1,2\}\ B}$$

$$\frac{\{0\} \sim A}{\{1,2\}\ A} \qquad \frac{\{0,1\} \sim A}{\{1,2\}\ A} \qquad \frac{\{1\} \sim A}{\times} \qquad \frac{\{1,2\} \sim A}{\{0,1\}\ A}$$

Observe that these rules satisfy (1) in Definition 7 (alternatively this can be checked visually using Karnaugh maps, see the next section).

To prove a certain formula, we have to assume that the formula is valuated to any non-designated value, and construct a closed tableau. For example, we prove $\models_{\mathcal{M}_3} {\sim}p \sqsupset {\sim}p$ by a tableau starting with assumption $\mathcal{F}\ {\sim}p \sqsupset {\sim}p$. This is shown in the left of Fig. 1.

[2] A usage of this nmatrix in a meaningful logic would be nice but is not intended.

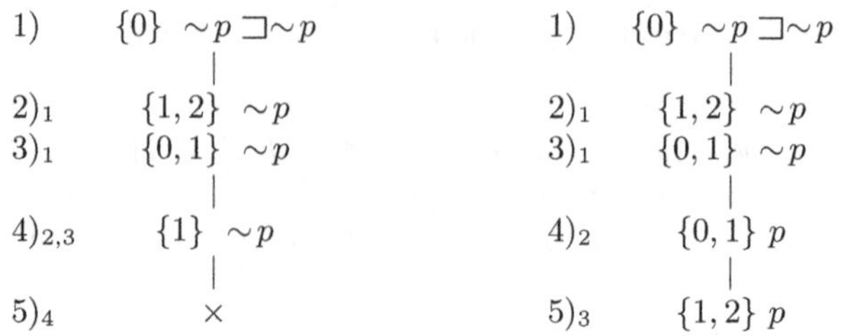

Fig. 1. Tableaux with assumption $\{0\}\ {\sim}p \sqsupset {\sim}p$ in tableau system Π_3 by Example 3 (the tree nodes are numbered, a subscript indicates that a node stems from a rule application on the nodes with given numbers). The closed tableau on the left uses sign intersection in node 4. The tableau on the right is open after *exhaustive* rule application without sign intersection. Thus, Π_3 without sign intersection is incomplete.

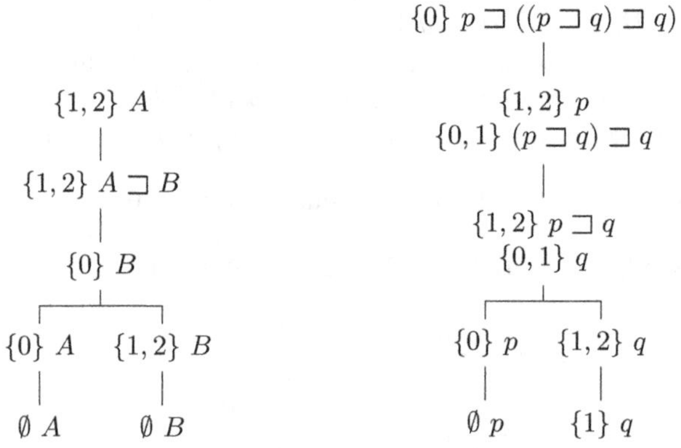

Fig. 2. Closed tableau in Π_3 (Example 3) for the consequence $A,\ A \sqsupset B \vDash B$ and open tableau in Π_3 with assumption $\{0\}\ p \sqsupset ((p \sqsupset q) \sqsupset q)$.

What happened if we would drop the sign intersection rule? On the right of Fig. 1, we *exhaustively* applied any tableau rule of Π_3 except sign intersection. By *exhaustive*, we mean that no further rule application adds a new signed formula on the proof tree. Thus, Π_3 would be incomplete without sign intersection!

We conclude that we need sign intersection for completeness of tableaux for non-deterministic semantics. In contrast, tableaux with sets as signs for many-valued semantics without sign intersection are sound and complete, c.f. [16].

A rule $B_1, \ldots, B_r \vDash_{\mathcal{M}} A$ can be proven by a tableau tree with assumptions $\mathcal{D}\ B_1$, …, $\mathcal{D}\ B_r$ and $\mathcal{F}\ A$. The proof tree for $A, A \sqsupset B \vDash_{\mathcal{M}_3} B$ (modus ponens) is given on the left of Fig. 2. On the other hand, $\vDash_{\mathcal{M}_3} p \sqsupset ((p \sqsupset q) \sqsupset q)$ does not hold. We can choose between $v(p) = 1$ or $v(p) = 2$ when constructing a valuation for the open branch in the open tableau on the right, e.g., $v(p) = 2$, $v(q) = 1$, $v(p \sqsupset q) = 1$, $v((p \sqsupset q) \sqsupset q) = 0$. Lemma 2 together with Lemma 3 give the general construction of valuations for countersatisfiability, see Sect. 6.

4 Rule Construction

As a consequence of (1) in Definition 7, the extensions of some signed formula $Y \odot (A_1, \ldots, A_m)$ have to cover those and only those cells whose return value sets that are not disjoint from Y. The construction could be done using a generalization of *Karnaugh maps* to many-valued logic [17], which corresponds to shading or colouring all matching cells in the nmatrix. Example 4 gives a demonstration.

Example 4. In this example, the construction of tableau rules for the nmatrix $\mathcal{M}_3$ is discussed ($\mathcal{M}_3$ was defined in Example 3).

A tableau rule for $\{0\} \sim A$ has to cover all cells of $\tilde{\sim}$, which contain the truth value 0. The tableau rule $\pi'_{\{0\}\sim}$ covers each cell with separate extensions. However, these extensions result in unnecessary branching in the tableau proof tree.

	$\tilde{\sim}$
0	2
1	0, 2
2	0

$$\frac{\{0\} \sim A}{\{1\}\ A \mid \{2\}\ A}\ \pi'_{\{0\}\sim}$$

	$\tilde{\sim}$
0	2
1	0, 2
2	0

$$\frac{\{0\} \sim A}{\{1,2\}\ A}\ \pi_{\{0\}\sim}$$

Using $\pi_{\{0\}\sim}$, the whole square is covered by a single extension.

The advantage of sets as signs becomes even more obvious when constructing a rule for $\{0\} \sqsupset$. This rule needs only one extension, whereas a version with simple signs would need four extensions.

When the set of signs includes a truth value set like $\{1, 2\}$, we have to construct tableau rules for these signs, too. A rule for $\{1, 2\}\ A \sqsupset B$ has to cover all cells of $\tilde{\sqsupset}$, which contain 1 or 2:

$\tilde{\sqsupset}$	0	1	2
0	2	2	2
1	0	0, 1	2
2	0	0, 1	2

$\tilde{\sqsupset}$	0	1	2
0	2	2	2
1	0	0, 1	2
2	0	0, 1	2

This is done by $\pi'_{\{1,2\}\sqsupset}$ or $\pi_{\{1,2\}\sqsupset}$:

$$\frac{\{1,2\}\ A \sqsupset B}{\begin{array}{l|l} \{0\}\ A & \{1,2\}\ B \\ \{0\}\ B & \end{array}}\ \pi'_{\{1,2\}\sqsupset}$$

$$\frac{\{1,2\}\ A \sqsupset B}{\{0\}\ A \mid \{1,2\}\ B}\ \pi_{\{1,2\}\sqsupset}$$

If $X \odot (A_1, \ldots, A_m)$ is valid, i.e., $X \supseteq \tilde{\odot}(z_1, \ldots, z_m)$ for all $z_1 \ldots z_m \in \mathcal{V}$, then the tableau rule has no condition on the subformulas. If $X \odot (A_1, \ldots, A_m)$ is unsatisfiable, i.e., $X \cap \tilde{\odot}(z_1, \ldots, z_m) = \emptyset$ for all $z_1 \ldots z_m \in \mathcal{V}$, then the current branch gets killed. To indicate the differences, we use blank space for the former and $\times$ for the latter. This is demonstrated by the following rules:

$$\frac{\{0,2\} \sim A}{}\ \pi_{\{0,2\}\sim} \qquad \frac{\{1\} \sim A}{\times}\ \pi_{\{1\}\sim}$$

Given any finitely-valued non-deterministic semantics, we can construct a tableau system with singleton or simple signs, see Corollary 4 in Sect. 7.

In some cases, it is possible to create tableau rules for infinitely many truth values. See [18] for tableaux based on infinitely many-valued (deterministic) semantics.

5 Soundness

Throughout this paper, we assume a tableau system Π for an nmatrix $\mathcal{M} = \langle \mathcal{V}, \mathcal{D}, \mathcal{O} \rangle$ and a set of signs $\mathbb{S}$ (Definition 10). We can construct such systems using the methods in Sect. 4. It is worth noting that soundness and completeness would be preserved if we added (redundant) tableau rules (still respecting Definition 7).

Theorem 1 (Strong soundness). *Assume $\mathcal{D}, \mathcal{F} \subseteq \mathbb{S}$. If there is a closed tableau for $\mathcal{D}\ B_1, \ldots, \mathcal{D}\ B_r, \mathcal{F}\ C_1$ then $B_1, \ldots, B_r \vDash_{\mathcal{M}} C_1$.*

Proof. Suppose by contraposition that $B_1, \ldots, B_r \nvDash_{\mathcal{M}} C_1$. Then there is a valuation v with $v(B_1), \ldots, v(B_r) \in \mathcal{D}$ and $v(C_1) \in \mathcal{F}$. Thus, the premises of the tableau for $\mathcal{D}\ B_1, \ldots, \mathcal{D}\ B_r, \mathcal{F}\ C_1$ are satisfiable.

Consider a branch where the first k signed formulas are satisfied by v, i.e., for $Y\ A$ we have $v(A) \in Y$. Whenever we apply a tableau rule for a signed formula $Y\ \odot(A_1, \ldots, A_m)$ on the branch that is satisfied by v, we have $v(\odot(A_1, \ldots, A_m)) \in Y$. Moreover, $v(\odot(A_1, \ldots, A_m)) \in \tilde{\odot}(v(A_1), \ldots, v(A_m))$ holds by the definition of a valuation and therefore

$$\exists j \in \{1, \ldots, k\} \colon \forall i \in I_j \colon v(A_i) \in X_{j,i}$$

by (1) in Definition 7. Hence there is a (sub) branch satisfied by v. Whenever we apply sign intersection on $X\ A$ and $Y\ A$, we have $v(A) \in X$ and $v(A) \in Y$, hence this branch also satisfies the signed formula $X \cap Y\ A$.

This shows that there is a branch which satisfies v (for any signed formula $X\ A$ on the branch, we have $v(A) \in X$). This branch must be open, since $\emptyset \neq \{v(A)\} \subseteq X$. Therefore, the tableau would not be closed.

Corollary 1. *By Theorem 1: If there is a closed tableau for $\mathcal{F}\ A$ then $\vDash_{\mathcal{M}} A$.*

6 Completeness

In [16], the completeness proof for many-valued sets as signs uses generalized Hintikka sets. In the following, Hintikka sets are generalized for non-deterministic semantics using a similar approach. The difference is that the additional sign intersection rule has to be met. We assume the same as in the previous section.

Definition 15. *A set of signed formulas $\Theta \subseteq (\mathbb{S} \cup \{\emptyset\}) \times For\ \mathcal{L}$ is called* satisfiable *iff there is a valuation v in $\mathcal{M}$ such that, for all $(X\ A) \in \Theta$, $v(A) \in X$.*

Definition 16. *A* Hintikka set *is any set $H \subseteq \mathbb{S} \times For\ \mathcal{L}$, which is closed under* sign intersection (3) *and* tableau rule application (4).

$$\forall (X\ A), (Y\ A) \in H\colon \quad (X \cap Y\ A) \in H \tag{3}$$
$$\forall (X\ \odot(A_1 \dots A_m)) \in H\colon \quad X \neq \emptyset \implies (\exists E \in \pi_{X\odot}(A_1 \dots A_m)\colon E \subseteq H) \tag{4}$$

Note that the following proofs would also hold if we added more (redundant) tableau rules $\pi'_{X\odot}$ to the tableau system but not to (4). This means, $\pi_{X\odot}$ would still be fixed in Definition 16.

Lemma 2 (Lindenbaum construction). *A Hintikka set H is satisfiable iff H does not include a formula with an empty sign $(\emptyset\ A) \notin H$.*

Proof. Assume $(\emptyset\ A) \in H$. Then H is unsatisfiable by definition.

Assume $(\emptyset\ A) \notin H$. We enumerate the set of formulas $\{B_1, B_2, \dots\} =$ For $\mathcal{L}$ such that for any $i \in \mathbb{N}$, all subformulas B_j of B_i have a lower index $j \leq i$. By choosing a value $v(B_i)$ where $v(B_1), \dots, v(B_{i-1})$ are already defined, we inductively construct a valuation v satisfying H:

For a propositional variable $B_i = p \in P$ choose any $v(p) \in X$ if there is a minimal X with $(X\ p) \in H$, otherwise choose any $v(p) \in \mathcal{V}$.

For a formula $B_i = \odot(A_1, \dots, A_m)$, choose any

$$v(\odot(A_1, \dots, A_m)) \in \tilde{\odot}(v(A_1), \dots, v(A_m)) \cap X$$

if there is a minimal X with $(X\ \odot(A_1, \dots, A_m)) \in H$, otherwise choose any

$$v(\odot(A_1, \dots, A_m)) \in \tilde{\odot}(v(A_1), \dots, v(A_m)).$$

For contradiction, assume two minimal signs $X \neq Y$ with $(X\ B_i), (Y B_i) \in H$ but then we would also have $(X \cap Y\ B_i) \in H$ by Definition 16.

It remains to show $\tilde{\odot}(v(A_1), \dots, v(A_m)) \cap X \neq \emptyset$ for any minimal X with $(X\ \odot(A_1, \dots, A_m)) \in H$. By (4) in Definition 16 we get $E \subseteq H$ with $E \in \pi_{X\odot}(A_1, \dots, A_m)$. Without loss of generality, let $E = \{X_i\ A_i \mid i \in I\}$ for a suitable index set $I \subseteq \{1, \dots, m\}$ and $X_i \in \mathbb{S}^+$ for all $i \in I$. By inductive construction of v, we already have $\bigwedge_{i \in I} v(A_i) \in X_i$, thus $\tilde{\odot}(v(A_1), \dots, v(A_m)) \cap X \neq \emptyset$ by (1) in Definition 7.

We can construct Hintikka sets for any tableau branch:

Lemma 3. *Let $\Theta \subseteq \mathbb{S} \times For\ \mathcal{L}$ be a finite set of signed formulas as assumptions. Then we can construct a finite tableau tree, such that the set of signed formulas Ω on every path from the root to a proper leaf is a Hintikka set with $\Omega \supseteq \Theta$.*

Proof. Starting from the root of an empty tableau proof tree, we create nodes for all assumptions $(X\ A) \in \Theta$. This guarantees $\Omega \supseteq \Theta$ for the set of signed formulas Ω on every path from root to leaf.

Suppose there is a leaf node with Ω not closed under tableau rule application, i.e., there is a formula $(X\ \odot(A_1, \dots, A_m)) \in \Omega$ such that (4) is violated. Now we apply tableau rule $\pi_{X\odot}$ on the former leaf to get finitely many child nodes. For Ω on each path of these child nodes we get $E \subseteq \Omega$ for some $E \in \pi_{X\odot}(A_1, \ldots, A_m)$. If there are no child nodes since $\pi_{X\odot}(A_1, \ldots, A_m) = \emptyset$, then the current node is not a *proper* leaf.

Suppose that there is a leaf node with Ω not closed under sign intersection, i.e., for two signed formulas $(X\ A), (Y\ A) \in \Omega$ we have $(X \cap Y\ A) \notin \Omega$. Then we apply sign intersection to get $(X \cap Y\ A)$ on the child node.

There are only finitely many combinations for sign intersection. Moreover, each rule application gives only finitely many subformulas. Therefore, the process terminates after finitely many rule applications. Thus, we have Hintikka sets on each proper leaf.

Note 7 (Construction of countersatisfiable valuations). We can always construct a tableau tree for $\mathcal{F}\ A$ with Hintikka sets by Lemma 3. By soundness, if $\not\models_{\mathcal{M}} A$ then this tableau tree has an open branch. Thus, we can construct a valuation v for that branch (with $v(A) \in \mathcal{F}$) by Lemma 2.

Theorem 2 (Strong completeness). *Let $\mathcal{D}, \mathcal{F} \in \mathbb{S}$ and $B_1, \ldots, B_r \models_{\mathcal{M}} C_1$. Then there is a finite, closed tableau for $\Theta = \{\mathcal{D}\ B_1, \ldots, \mathcal{D}\ B_r, \mathcal{F}\ C_1\}$.*

Proof. By Lemma 3 we can construct a tableau tree for Θ with Hintikka sets $H \supseteq \Theta$ on each path from root to a proper leaf. Assume that any of these sets is satisfiable by some v with $v(B_1), \ldots, v(B_r) \in \mathcal{D}$ and $v(C_1) \in \mathcal{F}$, then $B_1, \ldots, B_r \not\models_{\mathcal{M}} C_1$. This is a contradiction. Hence, by Lemma 2, we have $\emptyset\ A \in H$ for some formula A on every proper leaf. Thus, the tableau is closed.

Corollary 2. *If $\models_{\mathcal{M}} A$ then there is a closed tableau for $\mathcal{F}\ A$ by Theorem 2.*

7 DNF Representations

A DNF-like representation is already given in (1). Nevertheless, DNF representations for many-valued tableau rules are more compact and intuitive, using signed formulas $X_{k,i}\ A_i$ instead of set theory, see [18]. This requires a treatment of signed meta-logic [7,10,14,15], originally introduced as "partial normal forms" [25]. Incidentally, signed logic also facilitates to compare different calculi used for many-valued logic.

In the following, we will see how DNF (and CNF) representations can be adapted to non-deterministic semantics.

Depending on the $z_1, \ldots, z_m \in \mathcal{V}$, we can construct a valuation v such that $v(p_i) = z_i$ for $i \in \{1 \ldots m\}$. Hence (1) holds iff for all valuations v:

$$Y \cap \tilde{\odot}(v(p_1), \ldots, v(p_m)) \neq \emptyset \iff \bigvee_{j=1}^{k} \bigwedge_{i \in I_j} v(p_i) \in X_{j,i} \tag{5}$$

By Definition 2, we have $v(\odot(A_1, \ldots, A_m)) \in \tilde{\odot}(v(A_1), \ldots, v(A_m))$. Hence

$$v(\odot(p_1, \ldots, p_m)) \in Y \implies \bigvee_{j=1}^{k} \bigwedge_{i \in I_j} v(p_i) \in X_{j,i}$$

for all valuations v. By applying Definition 5 we get that

$$Y \odot (p_1, \ldots, p_m) \implies \bigvee\!\!\!\!\bigvee_{j=1}^{k} \bigwedge\!\!\!\!\bigwedge_{i \in I_j} X_{j,i}\, p_i \tag{6}$$

is true under all valuations v. This is one direction of the *DNF representation* for many-valued (deterministic) tableau rules, c.f. [18].

It is not hard to see that non-deterministic tableau rules do not respect the back direction $\Longleftarrow$ of (6). This can be demonstrated by the rule $\pi_{\{0\}\sim}$ as given in Example 4. For a valuation v with $v(p) = 1$, both $v(\sim p) = 0$ and $v(\sim p) = 2$ are possible.

In the non-deterministic case, we could loosely say that

$$Y \odot (p_1, \ldots, p_m) \text{ is possible } \Longleftrightarrow \bigvee\!\!\!\!\bigvee_{j=1}^{k} \bigwedge\!\!\!\!\bigwedge_{i \in I_j} X_{j,i}\, p_i,$$

since $v(\odot(A_1, \ldots, A_m)) \in Y$ is only a non-deterministic option (see also [14, Proposition 4.7]). Nevertheless, a DNF representation can be achieved by defining a meta-logical modality $\lozenge\!\!\!\lozenge$:

Definition 17. *For any signed formula X A, define the semantics of $\lozenge\!\!\!\lozenge(X\ A)$ and $\ (X\ A)$ by:*

$$\lozenge\!\!\!\lozenge(X\ p) \text{ is true under } v \Longleftrightarrow X \neq \emptyset$$
$$\lozenge\!\!\!\lozenge(X\ \odot(A_1, \ldots, A_m)) \text{ is true under } v \Longleftrightarrow X \cap \tilde{\odot}(v(A_1), \ldots, v(A_m)) \neq \emptyset$$
$$(X\ p) \text{ is true under } v \Longleftrightarrow X = \mathcal{V}$$
$$(X\ \odot(A_1, \ldots, A_m)) \text{ is true under } v \Longleftrightarrow X \supseteq \tilde{\odot}(v(A_1), \ldots, v(A_m))$$

for all valuations v in $\mathcal{M}$, $p \in P$, $(A_1, \ldots, A_m) \in$ For $\mathcal{L}^m$, and $\odot^{(m)} \in C$.

Note 8. Definition 17 gives the semantics for $\lozenge\!\!\!\lozenge\, \alpha$ and $\ \alpha$ only when α is a single signed formula. In contrast, classical meta-connectives $(\mathbb{A}, \mathbb{W}, \neg, \Longleftrightarrow, \Longrightarrow, \Longleftarrow)$ are inductively defined for any expression over signed formulas.

By applying Definition 5 and 17 on (5), we get that

$$\lozenge\!\!\!\lozenge(Y \odot (p_1, \ldots, p_m)) \Longleftrightarrow \bigvee\!\!\!\!\bigvee_{j=1}^{k} \bigwedge\!\!\!\!\bigwedge_{i \in I_j} X_{j,i}\, p_i \tag{7}$$

is true under all valuations v. This is the *DNF representation* we were after. Since X A implies $\lozenge\!\!\!\lozenge(X\ A)$, direction $\Longrightarrow$ in (6) is preserved.

In the following, we use $\overline{X} = \mathcal{V} \setminus X$ to denote the complement set of $X \subseteq \mathcal{V}$.

Corollary 3. $(X\ A) \iff \neg \Diamond(\overline{X}\ A)$ *for any signed formula* $X\ A$.

Dual tableaux (Sect. 8) and some other many-valued sequent systems have *CNF representations*. For an early use of such a representation, see [26, Lemma 1]. Using Corollary 3 and de Morgan's laws, a DNF representation for $Y\ A$ can be translated into a CNF representation for $\overline{Y}\ A$ (c.f. [7, p. 1371]):

$$(\overline{Y}\ \odot(p_1, \ldots, p_m)) \iff \bigwedge_{j=1}^{k} \bigvee_{i \in I_j} \overline{X_{j,i}}\ p_i \tag{8}$$

Note that the negation of a signed formula is a formula with a complement sign.

7.1 Canonical DNF

In Sect. 4 we left open how to construct tableau rules for any finitely-valued non-deterministic semantics. To show this, we are using *canonical DNF representations* as defined in the following. Canonical DNF representations are also known as *complete disjunctive truth conditions* [14, Definition 4.6].

Definition 18. *Let* $\mathcal{M} = \langle \mathcal{V}, \mathcal{D}, \mathcal{O} \rangle$ *be an nmatrix with a finite set of truth values* $|\mathcal{V}| < \infty$*. Then a* canonical DNF representation *for* $Y \subseteq \mathcal{V}$ *and* $\odot^{(m)} \in C$ *is defined as:*

$$\Diamond(Y\ \odot(p_1, \ldots, p_m)) \iff \bigvee_{\substack{(x_1,\ldots,x_m) \in \mathcal{V}^m \\ \tilde{\odot}(x_1,\ldots,x_m) \cap Y \neq \emptyset}} \bigwedge_{i=1}^{m} \{x_i\}\ p_i$$

Now it is easy to construct a tableau system based on canonical DNF representations for any finitely-many valued non-deterministic semantics. The following corollary is adapted from many valued logic, c.f. [26, Lemma 1] and [18, Theorem 20, Theorem 32].

Corollary 4. *Let* $\mathcal{M} = \langle \mathcal{V}, \mathcal{D}, \mathcal{O} \rangle$ *be an nmatrix with a finite set of truth values* $|\mathcal{V}| < \infty$ *and* $\mathbb{S}$ *be a set of signs with* $\{\{x\} \mid x \in \mathcal{V}\} \subseteq \mathbb{S}$*. Then we can construct a tableau system for* $\mathcal{M}$ *and* $\mathbb{S}$ *using canonical DNF representations.*

Note 9. A tableau rule of a canonical DNF representation has the form

$$\frac{Y\ \odot(A_1, \ldots, A_m)}{\begin{array}{c|c|c} \{x_{1,1}\}\ A_1 & & \{x_{k,1}\}\ A_1 \\ \vdots & \cdots & \vdots \\ \{x_{1,m}\}\ A_m & & \{x_{k,m}\}\ A_m \end{array}}$$

where $x_{1,1}, \ldots, x_{k,m} \in \mathcal{V}$ are the truth values satisfying $\odot(x_{j,1}, \ldots, x_{j,m}) \cap Y \neq \emptyset$ for $1 \leq j \leq k$.

These correspond to the tableau rules for non-deterministic semantics as defined in [24]. See there for further examples. Rules based on canonical DNF are far from being efficient as they involve extensions for every single cell in the Karnaugh map. In most cases, we could easily obtain much simpler rules.

8 Related Work

This section situates analytic tableau systems as defined in Sect. 3 in context with other tableau systems and *sequent systems*. A particular interest is in a class of sequent systems called *canonical calculi*. On the one hand, a canonical calculus is a source of a characteristic non-deterministic semantics, see [3–5,9]. On the other hand, tableau rules can be easily translated into a canonical calculus.

8.1 Analytic Tableaux for Many-Valued Logic

The tableaux described in the present paper generalize analytic tableaux for many-valued logic [18]. In particular: Tableaux with rules based on canonical DNF were defined in [28] (and in [24] for non-deterministic semantics). For tableaux with simple signs, see [11]. Tableaux with sets as signs were finally introduced in [16].

The following properties help to distinguish between analytic tableaux for many-valued logics and other tableaux, e.g., dual tableaux:

1. They are cut-free by construction.
2. They are conservative extensions of the signed tableaux for classical logic.
3. They are based on DNF representations.
4. For each pair of sign and connective, there is only one tableau rule.
5. They implement indirect proofs, i.e., closing conditions are primitive contradictions.

It is worth noting that all these properties are inherited to analytic tableaux for non-deterministic semantics, as defined in the previous sections.

8.2 Dual Tableaux

It is well known that classical two-valued tableaux were derived from cut-admissible Gentzen-style sequent systems; and it is easy to see the correspondence between both: A tableau is a sequent proof written upside down, where the sequents are given implicitly by the set of formulas between a node and the root of the tableau. For a signed tableau calculus see [27]. Formulas with sign **f** go to the right of a sequent, other formulas to the left side of a sequent.

For many-valued logics, the situation seems similar at first. Many-valued sequents were introduced in [26]. For m truth values, a sequent is divided into m parts, typically partitioned using the respective truth values as labels or signs. The corresponding *dual tableau* [8,18] (also known as *R-S system* [2,20]) inherits the signs from the sequent system. However, dual tableaux for two-valued sequent systems have signs **t** and **f** swapped in contrast to the classical signed tableau: The reason is that two-sided sequents are signed with **f** on the right and **t** on the left. Moreover, a dual tableau proof no longer represents an indirect proof: In particular, closing condition of dual tableaux are primitive *axioms* and not primitive *contradictions*.

Dual tableaux and analytic tableaux with simple signs are separate concepts. However, we can translate (propositional) dual tableaux with CNF representations into analytic tableaux with sets as signs. Recall Sect. 7: The negation of a DNF is a CNF with complement sets as signs.

8.3 Canonical Calculi

Canonical calculi (also known as *canonical labelled calculi* or *canonical signed calculi*) [2–5,9] are sequent systems whose introduction rules are *canonical* (not to be confused with canonical DNF). These are the "standard" introduction rules involving one connective and the respective signs for the formula and immediate subformulas. Further rules of a canonical calculus are the structural rules for cut and weakening, as well as primitive axioms. For the origins of definitions, rules and notations of canonical calculi we refer to [6].

An introduction rule is not required to have a CNF representation, i.e., it may violate $\Longrightarrow$ in (9). Nevertheless, introduction rules based on CNF representations are defined as follows (the syntax of canonical calculi is used here):

Definition 19. *Given CNF representation*

$$(S \ \odot (p_1, \ldots, p_m)) \iff \bigwedge_{j=1}^{k} \bigvee_{i \in I_j} Z_{j,i} \ p_i \tag{9}$$

the introduction rule based on the CNF representation is:

$$\frac{\Omega \cup \{Z_{1,i}{:}p_i \mid i \in I_1\} \qquad \cdots \qquad \Omega \cup \{Z_{k,i}{:}p_i \mid i \in I_k\}}{\Omega \cup \{S{:}\diamond(p_1, \ldots, p_m)\}}$$

Converting an analytic tableau system to a canonical calculus is straight forward. This is done by using the equivalent CNF representation (8) of a tableaux rule (with simple signs):

Theorem 3. *Given CNF representations for every connective $\odot^{(m)} \in C$ of an nmatrix $\mathcal{M}$ and singleton complement $\overline{\{x\}} \in \{\overline{\{x\}} \mid x \in V\}$, i.e.:*

$$(\overline{\{x\}} \ \odot (p_1, \ldots, p_m)) \iff \bigwedge_{j=1}^{k} \bigvee_{i \in I_j} Z_{j,i} \ p_i \tag{10}$$

Then the canonical calculus with introduction rules based on these CNF representations is sound and complete for $\mathcal{M}$.

Proof. The proof is omitted due to limited space.

Corollary 5. *Given a tableaux system with simple signs $\mathbb{S} = \{\{x\} \mid x \in V\}$, we can construct a sound and complete (Theorem 3) canonical calculus based on the equivalent CNF representations.*

Notably, the rule construction methods (Sect. 4) can be adapted to canonical calculi: We just have to translate DNF into CNF representations. See [2] for a different approach on rule construction, these rules do not necessarily have CNF representations.

In general, the other conversion direction (from canonical calculi to tableaux) does not work. This seems to be caused by missing structural rules in tableau systems with sets as signs (implicit for canonical calculi). Candidates are:

$$\frac{(X \cap Y)\ A}{\begin{array}{c} X\ A \\ Y\ A \end{array}}\ \textbf{sign split} \qquad\qquad \frac{}{X\ A \mid \overline{X}\ A}\ \textbf{PM}$$

8.4 Other Calculi

Rule **PM** is similar to the *principle of bivalence* used in the calculus **KE**, which corresponds to a cut [13]. A many-valued version is called *principle of multivalence* [17]. These calculi restrict branching to **PM** rule applications. This allows optimizing proof complexity. Also, there is *signed resolution* and *DPLL* [10].

8.5 Semantic Games

Although not directly providing efficient proof procedures, *semantic games* [14] have a close connection to tableaux and DNF/CNF representations.

9 Conclusion

Tableaux for non-deterministic semantics provide analytic methods for checking validity, satisfiability and related questions. There are two aspects, the construction of a tableau system and its rules and the tableau proofs itself. The framework is based on tableaux for many-valued semantics [18].

The difference lies in the formal condition on a tableau rule as discussed in Sect. 7. For a signed formula $\{y\} \odot(A_1, \ldots, A_m)$, i.e., $y = v(\odot(A_1, \ldots, A_m))$, the tableau rule needs to cover all cases of signed subformulas $\{x_1\}\ A_1, \ldots, \{x_m\}\ A_m$, in which we *possibly get* the signed formula. For classical many-valued logics, it is just *get*. Nevertheless, the process of rule construction is similar to many-valued logics, graphically by shading cells in the nmatrix (Sect. 4).

Corollary 4 shows that a tableau system for any finite-valued non-deterministic semantics can be given, generalizing a result from many-valued semantics. For infinite valued non-deterministic semantics, rule construction is a challenge.

Acknowledgements. I am indebted to Peter Steinacker for the supervision of my master's thesis and to Andreas Maletti, second reviewer, for spotting the mistake in my thesis which initiated the work on the present paper. I would like to thank Daniel Skurt, Hitoshi Omori, Reiner Hähnle, Richard Bubel, Elio La Rosa, Pawel Pawlowski for useful suggestions.

References

1. Avron, A., Arieli, O., Zamansky, A.: Theory of Effective Propositional Paraconsistent Logics. College Publications (2018)
2. Avron, A., Konikowska, B.: Multi-valued calculi for logics based on non-determinism. Log. J. IGPL **13**(4), 365–387 (2005). https://doi.org/10.1093/jigpal/jzi030
3. Avron, A., Lev, I.: Canonical propositional Gentzen-type systems. In: Goré, R., Leitsch, A., Nipkow, T. (eds.) IJCAR 2001. LNCS, vol. 2083, pp. 529–544. Springer, Heidelberg (2001). https://doi.org/10.1007/3-540-45744-5_45
4. Avron, A., Lev, I.: Non-deterministic multiple-valued structures. J. Log. Comput. **15**(3), 241–261 (2005). https://doi.org/10.1093/logcom/exi001
5. Avron, A., Zamansky, A.: Canonical signed calculi, non-deterministic matrices and cut-elimination. In: Artemov, S., Nerode, A. (eds.) LFCS 2009. LNCS, vol. 5407, pp. 31–45. Springer, Heidelberg (2008). https://doi.org/10.1007/978-3-540-92687-0_3
6. Avron, A., Zamansky, A.: Non-deterministic semantics for logical systems. In: Gabbay, D., Guenthner, F. (eds.) Handbook of Philosophical Logic, vol. 16, 2nd edn, pp. 227–304. Springer, Heidelberg (2011). https://doi.org/10.1007/978-94-007-0479-4_4
7. Baaz, M., Fermüller, C.G., Salzer, G.: Automated deduction for many-valued logics. In: Robinson, A., Voronkov, A. (eds.) Handbook of Automated Reasoning, vol. 2, chap. 19, pp. 1355–1402. Elsevier and MIT Press (2001)
8. Baaz, M., Fermüller, C.G., Zach, R.: Dual systems of sequents and tableaux for many-valued logics. Bull. EATCS **51**, 192–197 (1993)
9. Baaz, M., Lahav, O., Zamansky, A.: Finite-valued semantics for canonical labelled calculi. J. Autom. Reason. **51**(4), 401–430 (2013). https://doi.org/10.1007/s10817-013-9273-x
10. Beckert, B., Hähnle, R., Manyà, F.: The SAT problem of signed CNF formulas. In: Basin, D., D'Agostino, M., Gabbay, D.M., Matthews, S., Viganò, L. (eds.) Labelled Deduction. APLS, vol. 17, pp. 59–80. Springer, Dordrecht (2000). https://doi.org/10.1007/978-94-011-4040-9_3
11. Carnielli, W.A.: Systematization of finite many-valued logics through the method of tableaux. J. Symb. Log. **52**(2), 473–493 (1987). https://doi.org/10.2307/2274395
12. Coniglio, M.E., del Cerro, L.F., Newton, M.P.: Modal logic with non-deterministic semantics: part I–propositional case. Log. J. IGPL **28**(3), 281–315 (2020). https://doi.org/10.1093/jigpal/jzz027
13. D'Agostino, M., Mondadori, M.: The taming of the cut. Classical refutations with analytic cut. J. Log. Comput. **4**(3), 285–319 (1994). https://doi.org/10.1093/logcom/4.3.285
14. Fermüller, C.G.: On matrices, Nmatrices and games. J. Log. Comput. **26**(1), 189–211 (2016). https://doi.org/10.1093/logcom/ext024
15. Hähnle, R.: Advanced many-valued logics. In: Gabbay, D., Guenthner, F. (eds.) Handbook of Philosophical Logic, vol. 2, 2nd edn, pp. 297–395. Springer, Dordrecht (2001). https://doi.org/10.1007/978-94-017-0452-6_5
16. Hähnle, R.: Towards an efficient tableau proof procedure for multiple-valued logics. In: Börger, E., Kleine Büning, H., Richter, M.M., Schönfeld, W. (eds.) CSL 1990. LNCS, vol. 533, pp. 248–260. Springer, Heidelberg (1991). https://doi.org/10.1007/3-540-54487-9_62

17. Hähnle, R.: Automated Deduction in Multiple-valued Logics. Oxford University Press (1993)
18. Hähnle, R.: Tableaux for many-valued logics. In: D'Agostino, M., Gabbay, D.M., Hähnle, R., Posegga, J. (eds.) Handbook of Tableau Methods, pp. 529–580. Kluwer (1999)
19. Ivlev, J.V.: Modal'naja logika. Moskovskogo Univ, Izdat (1991). (in Russian)
20. Konikowska, B.: Two over three: a two-valued logic for software specification and validation over a three-valued predicate calculus. J. Appl. Non-Classical Log. **3**(1), 39–71 (1993). https://doi.org/10.1080/11663081.1993.10510795
21. Ohnishi, M., Matsumoto, K.: A system for strict implication. Ann. Jpn. Assoc. Philos. Sci. **2**(4), 183–188 (1964). https://doi.org/10.4288/jafpos1956.2.183
22. Omori, H., Skurt, D.: More modal semantics without possible worlds. IfCoLog J. Log. Appl. **3**(5), 815–846 (2016)
23. Paoli, F.: Substructural Logics: A Primer. Trends in Logic. Kluwer Academic Publishers (2002)
24. Pawlowski, P.: Tree-like proof systems for finitely-many valued non-deterministic consequence relations. Log. Univers. **14**(4), 407–420 (2020). https://doi.org/10.1007/s11787-020-00263-0
25. Rosser, J.B., Turquette, A.R.: Many-Valued Logics. North-Holland (1952)
26. Rouseau, G.: Sequents in many valued logic I. Fundam. Math. **60**(1), 23–33 (1967). https://doi.org/10.4064/fm-60-1-23-33
27. Smullyan, R.M.: First-Order Logic. Dover, 2 edn. (1995)
28. Surma, S.J.: An algorithm for axiomatizing every finite logic. In: Rine, D.C. (ed.) Computer Science and Multiple-Valued Logic, pp. 137–143. North-Holland Publishing Company (1977)
29. Zamansky, A., Avron, A.: Canonical signed calculi with multi-ary quantifiers. Ann. Pure Appl. Logic **163**(7), 951–960 (2012). https://doi.org/10.1016/j.apal.2011.09.006

Tableaux for Free Logics with Descriptions

Andrzej Indrzejczak[2] and Michał Zawidzki[1,2(✉)]

[1] Department of Computer Science, University of Oxford, Oxford, UK
[2] Department of Logic, University of Łódź, Łódź, Poland
andrzej.indrzejczak@filhist.uni.lodz.pl, michal.zawidzki@cs.ox.ac.uk

Abstract. The paper provides a tableau approach to definite descriptions. We focus on several formalizations of the so-called minimal free description theory (MFD) usually formulated axiomatically in the setting of free logic. We consider five analytic tableau systems corresponding to different kinds of free logic, including the logic of definedness applied in computer science and constructive mathematics for dealing with partial functions (here called *negative quasi-free logic*). The tableau systems formalise MFD based on PFL (positive free logic), NFL (negative free logic), PQFL and NQFL (the quasi-free counterparts of the former ones). Also the logic NQFL^- is taken into account, which is equivalent to NQFL, but whose language does not comprise the existence predicate. It is shown that all tableaux are sound and complete with respect to the semantics of these logics.

Keywords: Free logics · Definite descriptions · Analytic tableaux

1 Introduction

The topic of *definite descriptions* (DD) is of wide interest to philosophers, linguists, and logicians. On the other hand, in proof theory and automated deduction the number of formal systems and studies of their properties is relatively modest. In particular, there are several tableau calculi due to Bencivenga, Lambert and van Fraassen [3], Gumb [10], Bostock [5], Fitting and Mendelsohn [8], but all of them introduce DD by means of rather complex rules, and so, are not really in the spirit of tableau methodology. Quite a lot of natural deduction systems for DD have been provided, but only a few of them (namely Tennant's [29,30] and Kürbis' [19,20] works) deal with DD by means of rules which allow for finer proof analysis and provide normalization proofs. Cut-free sequent calculi for several theories of DD were provided by Indrzejczak [11–14] and recently also by Orlandelli [25].

Both authors are supported by the National Science Centre, Poland (grant number: DEC- 2017/25/B/HS1/01268). The second author is supported by the EPSRC projects OASIS (EP/S032347/1), AnaLOG (EP/P025943/1), and UK FIRES (EP/S019111/1), the SIRIUS Centre for Scalable Data Access, and Samsung Research UK.

A. Das and S. Negri (Eds.): TABLEAUX 2021, LNAI 12842, pp. 56–73, 2021.
https://doi.org/10.1007/978-3-030-86059-2_4

The number of theories of DD that have been proposed since Frege's and Russell's first accounts (see, e.g., a discussion in [27]) is enormous, however what we are concerned with in this paper is an adequate tableau characterization of DD, so due to space restrictions we omit a detailed presentation of different theories of DD and their philosophical or linguistic motivations. In particular, we confine ourselves to only one approach to DD, strongly connected with *free logic* and commonly called a *minimal free description theory* (MFD)[1]. It is based on the so-called Lambert's axiom (L):

$$\forall x(\imath x\varphi(x) = x \leftrightarrow \forall y(\varphi(y) \leftrightarrow y = x)). \qquad \text{(L)}$$

In fact, this axiom added to different kinds of free logics leads to significantly different theories of DD. We provide tableau calculi for four kinds of different free logics, called here PFL, NFL, PQFL, and NQFL (where N stands for *negative*, P for *positive*, Q for *quasi*). In negative free logics, in contrast to positive ones, atomic formulas with non-denoting terms are always evaluated as false or, equivalently, all predicates are strict, that is, defined only over denoting terms. Both PFL and NFL characterize absolutely free logics in the sense that variables may also fail to denote. On the other hand, NQFL and PQFL are systems for quasi-free logics in the sense that only descriptions can fail to denote; variables are always denoting.

Recently, cut-free sequent calculi for several free logics, yet without DD, have been presented by Pavlović and Gratzl [26] and by Indrzejczak [15]. In particular, in the latter work it has been shown that if we restrict instantiation in quantifier rules only to variables, we do not lose completeness, provided that some special rules are added. It makes it possible to characterize NQFL and PQFL by means of classical quantifier rules, which justifies our use of the term 'quasi free' (introduced therein). Yet even more importantly, such a restriction on quantifier rules allows us to extend this approach to MFD and preserve cut-freeness (see [14]). Since the above-referenced paper provides a purely proof-theoretic approach, completing the work with the semantic side and suitably defined adequate and analytic tableau systems seems to be a natural next research step. The aim of the present study is to make this step and fill the indicated gap.

We limit our considerations to the logics mentioned above as the most prominent representatives of the family of free logics. PFL is by all means the most popular version of free logic (see, e.g., [4,22], or [23]), applied mainly in philosophical studies and as the basis of formalization of modal first-order logics (see, e.g., Garson [9]). The original Lambert's version of MFD was proposed on the basis of PFL. The basic negative free logic NFL, known also as the *logic of existence* ([28]), was more popular in computer science and foundational studies [29,30].

Negative quasi-free logic NQFL is known as the *definedness logic* (or the *logic of partial terms*) by Beeson [2] and Feferman [7]. It has also been extensively studied and applied in computer science. Although it was originally developed in

[1] The reader may find a more fine-grained presentation of MFD and its extensions in Lambert's [21], Bencivenga's [4] or Lehmann's [23] works.

the context of constructive mathematics to deal with partial untyped combinatory and lambda calculi, Feferman rightly noticed that it works without changes in the classical setting (in fact, he was concerned only with classical semantics in [7]. PQFL is a positive variant of NQFL, that is, not requiring that all predicates are strict. It is interesting that its intuitionistic restricted version (no identity and DD) was studied proof-theoretically by Baaz and Iemhoff [1] and recently by Maffezioli and Orlandelli [24].

NQFL$^-$ is a variant of NQFL but formulated in the language without the existence predicate. Although the latter can be defined in all the considered logics, it is handy to keep it as primitive. However, in [15] it was shown that in quantifier rules for all free logics with identity, instantiation terms may be restricted to variables. That opens a possibility of discarding the existence predicate and simplifying the rules, at least for NQFL. Thus, this logic is presented here in two variants: as NQFL with the existence predicate (which allows to compare it with the remaining logics more easily), and then as NQFL$^-$ in an existence-free version with simpler rules. In fact NQFL$^-$ with the rules for descriptions on classical foundations appears to be equivalent also to the formalization of Russellian theory of descriptions provided by Kalish, Montague and Mar [18]; (see Indrzejczak [16] for a detailed explanation).

Lambert's axiom (L) was used as a basic way of formalizing DD in all the abovementioned logics, except for PQFL. However, on the ground of NFL, (and NQFL) it yields quite a strong theory of DD of essentially Russellian character. This follows from the fact that in NFL (NQFL) (L) is equivalent to the following formula:

$$\psi(\imath x\varphi(x)) \leftrightarrow \exists y(\forall x(\varphi(x) \leftrightarrow x = y) \wedge \psi(y)), \text{ where } \psi \text{ is atomic.} \quad \text{(R)}$$

(R) expresses the Russellian approach to characterizing DD and it was often attacked as being too strong. The left-to-right implication encodes that if we state something about a DD, it implies that this description denotes. According to Strawson's well-known criticism, if a DD is used as an argument of a predicate, its existence and uniqueness is presupposed rather than implied. Lambert's axiom is in general weaker than (R) and in PFL (PQFL) implies only the right-to-left implication of (R) which is commonly acceptable. The equivalence of (L) and (R) in NFL is a consequence of the fact that in NFL all predicates are strict, so the statement of an atomic formula implies that all terms occurring in it are denoting (see [14]).

Due to space limitations, we confine ourselves to logics which are founded on the classical core. Interestingly, cut-free sequent calculi in [14], after restricting sequents to at most one formula in the succedent and small refinements of some rules for DD, may also characterize their intuitionistic versions. In the case of tableaux adequate with respect to a given semantics, however, such small refinements do not suffice to obtain intuitionistic versions. Hence, we postpone completing this task, as well as the characterization of MFD on the basis of neutral free logics, to future work. In the latter case even the standard sequent calculus is not sufficient for a satisfactory proof-theoretic characterization.

In what follows, after a brief characterization of the syntax and semantics in Sect. 2, in Sect. 3 we provide five tableau calculi for the logics PFL, PQFL, NFL, NQFL, and NQFL$^-$. Adequacy of all systems is established in Sect. 4. In Sect. 5 we briefly compare our tableau calculi with alternative approaches, in particular with sequent calculi by Indrzejczak [14]. Finally we discuss some possible advantages of using DD instead of functional terms and present further lines of research.

2 Preliminaries

2.1 Syntax

For the logics PFL, NFL, PQFL, NQFL we consider sentences, that is, formulas with no free variables, built in the standard first-order language $\mathscr{L}$ with identity and the unary existence predicate E treated as logical constants and with no function symbols as primitives. The vocabulary of $\mathscr{L}$ consists of:

- a countably infinite set of bound individual variables $\mathsf{VAR} = \{x, y, z \ldots\}$,
- a countably infinite set of parametric (free) individual variables $\mathsf{PAR} = \{a, b, c, \ldots\}$,
- a countably infinite set of n-ary predicate symbols $\mathsf{PRED}^n = \{P^n, Q^n, R^n, \ldots\}$, for any non-negative integer n;
- a set of propositional connectives: $\neg$, $\wedge$,
- the universal quantifier $\forall$,
- the definite description operator $\imath$,
- the identity relation $=$,
- the existence predicate E,
- left and right parentheses: (,).

In the case of NQFL$^-$ we discard the existence predicate E from the language and refer to such a restricted language as $\mathscr{L}^-$.

A set of terms TERM and a set of formulas FOR (in the language of deduction) are defined simultaneously by the following context-free grammars:

$$\mathsf{TERM} \ni t \ ::= x \mid a \mid \imath x\varphi,$$
$$\mathsf{FOR} \ni \varphi \ ::= P(t_1, \ldots, t_n) \mid t_1 = t_2 \mid \mathtt{E}t \mid \neg\varphi \mid \varphi \wedge \varphi \mid \forall x\varphi,$$

where $x \in \mathsf{VAR}$, $a \in \mathsf{PAR}$, $P \in \mathsf{PRED}^n$, $t, t_1, \ldots, t_n \in \mathsf{TERM}$, and $\varphi \in \mathsf{FOR}$. The existential quantifier and other boolean connectives are introduced as standard abbreviations. Note that the absence of function symbols as primitives in $\mathscr{L}$ and $\mathscr{L}^-$ is due to the fact that they can be simulated by using the operator $\imath$ in the sense that every term of the form $f^n(t_1, \ldots, t_n)$ can be represented as $\imath x F^{n+1}(t_1, \ldots, t_n, x)$. On the other hand, not every (proper) description can be expressed using functional terms. For example, descriptions like 'the winner of the ultimate fight', 'the bear we have seen recently' can only be represented by constants.

2.2 Semantics

By a *model* we mean a structure $\mathcal{M} = \langle \mathcal{D}, \mathcal{D}_{\mathrm{E}}, \mathcal{I} \rangle$, where $\mathcal{D}_{\mathrm{E}}$ is a (possibly empty) subset of $\mathcal{D}$ and for each n-argument predicate P^n, $\mathcal{I}(P^n) \subseteq \mathcal{D}^n$. An *assignment* v is defined as $v : VAR \cup PAR \longrightarrow \mathcal{D}$ for PFL, NFL, and as $v : VAR \cup PAR \longrightarrow \mathcal{D}_{\mathrm{E}}$ for PQFL, NQFL, and NQFL$^-$. Thus, in proper free logics variables may fail to denote, which is not possible in quasi-free logics. An *x-variant* v' of v agrees with v on all arguments, save, possibly, x. We will write v^x_o to denote the x-variant of v with $v^x_o(x) = o$. The notion of *interpretation* $\mathcal{I}_v(t)$ of a term t under an assignment v is defined simultaneously with the notion of *satisfaction* of a formula φ under v, in symbols $\mathcal{M}, v \models \varphi$:

$$\begin{array}{rcl}
\mathcal{I}_v(x) = v(x), & & \\
\mathcal{I}_v(a) = v(a), & & \\
\mathcal{I}_v(\imath x\varphi) = o \in \mathcal{D}_{\mathrm{E}} & \text{iff} & \mathcal{M}, v^x_o \models \varphi, \text{ and for any } x\text{-variant } v' \text{ of } v, \\
 & & \text{if } \mathcal{M}, v' \models \varphi, \text{ then } v'(x) = o, \\
\mathcal{M}, v \models P^n(t_1, ..., t_n) & \text{iff} & \langle \mathcal{I}_v(t_1), \ldots, \mathcal{I}_v(t_n) \rangle \in \mathcal{I}(P^n) \\
 & & (\text{and } \mathcal{I}_v(t_i) \in \mathcal{D}_{\mathrm{E}}, i \leq n, \text{ for NFL, NQFL,} \\
 & & \text{and NQFL}^-), \\
\mathcal{M}, v \models t_1 = t_2 & \text{iff} & \mathcal{I}_v(t_1) = \mathcal{I}_v(t_2) \\
 & & (\text{and } \mathcal{I}_v(t_1), \mathcal{I}_v(t_2) \in \mathcal{D}_{\mathrm{E}}, \text{ for NFL, NQFL,} \\
 & & \text{and NQFL}^-), \\
\mathcal{M}, v \models \mathsf{E}t & \text{iff} & \mathcal{I}_v(t) \in \mathcal{D}_{\mathrm{E}}, \\
\mathcal{M}, v \models \neg\varphi & \text{iff} & \mathcal{M}, v \not\models \varphi, \\
\mathcal{M}, v \models \varphi \wedge \psi & \text{iff} & \mathcal{M}, v \models \varphi \text{ and } \mathcal{M}, v \models \psi, \\
\mathcal{M}, v \models \forall x\varphi & \text{iff} & \mathcal{M}, v^x_o \models \varphi, \text{ for all } o \in \mathcal{D}_{\mathrm{E}},
\end{array}$$

where $x \in$ VAR, $a \in$ PAR, $P^n \in$ PRED^n, and $t, t_1, \ldots, t_n \in$ TERM.

A formula φ is called *satisfiable* if there exist a model $\mathcal{M}$ and a valuation v such that $\mathcal{M}, v \models \varphi$. A formula is *valid* if, for all models $\mathcal{M}$ and valuations v, $\mathcal{M}, v \models \varphi$. In the remainder of the paper, instead of writing $\mathcal{M}, v \models \varphi_1, \ldots, \mathcal{M}, v \models \varphi_n$, we will write $\mathcal{M}, v \models \varphi_1, \ldots, \varphi_n$.

3 Tableau Calculi

In this section, we present tableau calculi for the considered logics for definite descriptions. For each logic L $\in$ {PFL, NFL, PQFL, NQFL, NQFL$^-$} we denote the tableau calculus for L by TC$_\mathsf{L}$.

A *tableau* $\mathcal{T}$ generated by a calculus TC$_\mathsf{L}$, for L $\in$ {PFL, NFL, PQFL, NQFL, NQFL$^-$}, is a *derivation tree* whose nodes are assigned formulas in a respective (deduction) language. A *branch of* $\mathcal{T}$ is a simple path from the root to a leaf of $\mathcal{T}$. For brevity, we identify each branch $\mathcal{B}$ with the set of formulas assigned to nodes constituting $\mathcal{B}$.

Our tableau calculi are composed of rules whose general form is as follows: $\frac{\Phi}{\Psi_1 | \ldots | \Psi_n}$, where Φ is the set of *premises* and each Ψ_i, for $i \in \{1, \ldots, n\}$, is a set of *conclusions*. If a rule has more than one set of conclusions, it is called a *branching* rule. Otherwise it is *non-branching*. Thus, if a rule $\frac{\Phi}{\Psi_1|\ldots|\Psi_n}$ is applied to Φ occurring on $\mathcal{B}$, $\mathcal{B}$ splits into n branches: $\mathcal{B} \cup \{\Psi_1\}, \ldots, \mathcal{B} \cup \{\Psi_n\}$. A rule (R) with Φ as the set of its premises is *applicable* to Φ occurring on a branch $\mathcal{B}$ if it has not yet been applied to Φ on $\mathcal{B}$. A set Φ is called (R)-*expanded* if (R) has already been applied to Φ. A term t is called *fresh* on a branch $\mathcal{B}$ if it has not yet occurred on $\mathcal{B}$. We call a branch $\mathcal{B}$ *closed* if the inconsistency symbol $\bot$ occurs on $\mathcal{B}$. If $\mathcal{B}$ is not closed, it is *open*. A branch is *fully expanded* if it is closed or no rules are applicable to (sets of) formulas occurring on $\mathcal{B}$. A tableau $\mathcal{T}$ is called closed if all of its branches are closed. Otherwise $\mathcal{T}$ is called open. Finally, $\mathcal{T}$ is fully expanded if all its branches are fully expanded. A *tableau proof* of a formula φ is a closed tableau with $\neg\varphi$ at its root. A formula φ is tableau-valid (with respect to the calculus $\mathsf{TC_L}$) if all fully expanded tableaux generated by $\mathsf{TC_L}$ with $\neg\varphi$ at the root are tableau proofs of φ. A tableau calculus $\mathsf{TC_L}$ is *sound* if, for each formula φ, whenever φ is tableau-valid wrt $\mathsf{TC_L}$, then it is valid. $\mathsf{TC_L}$ is *complete* if, for each formula φ, whenever φ is valid, then it is tableau-valid wrt $\mathsf{TC_L}$.

When presenting the rules, we adopt the following notational convention:

- metavariables φ, ψ stand for arbitrary formulas in $\mathscr{L}$ (or $\mathscr{L}^-$ if NQFL^- is considered),
- metavariables $t, t_1, \ldots, t_n$ represent arbitrary terms present on a branch,
- metavariables a, $a_1, \ldots, a_n$ denote fresh parameters,
- metavariables b, b_1, b_2 stand for an arbitrary parameters present on a branch,
- an expression $\varphi[x/t]$ represents the result of a correct substitution of all free occurrences of x within φ with a term t,
- $t_1 \neq t_2$ is an abbreviation for $\neg(t_1 = t_2)$,
- 'DD' is an abbreviation for 'definite description'.

The rules for tableau calculi $\mathsf{TC_{PFL}}$, $\mathsf{TC_{NFL}}$, $\mathsf{TC_{PQFL}}$, $\mathsf{TC_{NQFL}}$, and $\mathsf{TC_{NQFL}}^-$ are presented in Figs. 1 and 2. Intuitively, if a rule's name contains 'E' and the name of an operator, it is an elimination rule which removes the operator from the processed formula. On the other hand, if a rule's name contains 'I' and the name of an operator, it is an *introduction* rule which adds to the branch an expression featuring this operator. Moreover, we have three *closure* rules which close the branch as inconsistent, and two special *analytic cut* rules which make it possible to compare denotations of variables and definite descriptions.

A few words of comment on the rules displayed in Fig. 1 are in order. The propositional core of the calculi is known from tableaux for classical propositional logic. The rule $(\bot_1)$ closes a branch when a propositional inconsistency occurs thereon, whereas the remaining two closure rules, $(\bot_2)$ and $(\bot_3)$ rest on reflexivity of identity (possibly in a restricted form). The rules $(\forall E_1)$ and $(\neg\forall E_1)$ are standard rules for quantifier elimination in first-order logic. The remaining two rules for $\forall$, namely $(\forall E_2)$ and $(\neg\forall E_2)$, reflect the semantic condition saying that a term replacing a variable after quantifier elimination must denote an existing object. While in quasi-free logics it is ensured by the definition of

Rules

CPL

$$(\neg\neg E)\ \frac{\neg\neg\varphi}{\varphi} \qquad (\wedge E)\ \frac{\varphi\wedge\psi}{\varphi,\psi} \qquad (\neg\wedge E)\ \frac{\neg(\varphi\wedge\psi)}{\neg\varphi \mid \neg\psi}$$

$\bot$

$$(\bot_1)\ \frac{\varphi,\neg\varphi}{\bot} \qquad (\bot_2)\ \frac{t\neq t}{\bot} \qquad (\bot_3)\ \frac{b\neq b}{\bot}$$

$\forall$

$$(\forall E_1)\ \frac{\forall x\varphi}{\varphi[x/b]} \qquad (\neg\forall E_1)\ \frac{\neg\forall x\varphi}{\neg\varphi[x/a]} \qquad (\forall E_2)\ \frac{\forall x\varphi, \mathtt{E}b}{\varphi[x/b]} \qquad (\neg\forall E_2)\ \frac{\neg\forall x\varphi}{\mathtt{E}a, \neg\varphi[x/a]}$$

$=$

$$(=E)\ \frac{t_1\approx t_2, \varphi[x/t_1]}{\varphi[x/t_2]},\ t_1\approx t_2 \text{ stands for } t_1=t_2 \text{ or } t_2=t_1$$

$$(=I_1)\ \frac{P(t_1,\ldots,t_n)}{a_i=t_i},\ 1\leq i\leq n \text{ and } t_i \text{ is a DD} \qquad (=I_2)\ \frac{t_1=t_2}{a_i=t_i},\ 1\leq i\leq 2 \text{ and } t_i \text{ is a DD}$$

$$(cut_1)\ \frac{}{b=t \mid b\neq t},\ t \text{ is a DD} \qquad (cut_2)\ \frac{\mathtt{E}b}{b=t \mid b\neq t},\ t \text{ is a DD}$$

E

$$(\mathtt{E}E_1)\ \frac{\mathtt{E}t}{a=t},\ t \text{ is a DD} \qquad (\mathtt{E}E_2)\ \frac{\mathtt{E}t}{t=t}$$

$$(\mathtt{E}I_1)\ \frac{P(t_1,...,t_n)}{\mathtt{E}t_i},\ 1\leq i\leq n \text{ (and } t_i \text{ is a DD for NFL)}$$

$$(\mathtt{E}I_2)\ \frac{t_1=t_2}{\mathtt{E}t_i},\ 1\leq i\leq 2 \text{ (and } t_i \text{ is a DD for NFL)}$$

$$(\mathtt{E}I_3)\ \frac{}{\mathtt{E}b} \qquad (\mathtt{E}I_4)\ \frac{}{\mathtt{E}a},\ \text{if there are no parameters on the branch}$$

$\imath$

$$(\imath E_1)\ \frac{b_1=\imath x\varphi}{\varphi[x/b_1], \neg\varphi[x/b_2] \mid b_1=b_2, \varphi[x/b_1]} \qquad (\neg\imath E_1)\ \frac{b\neq\imath x\varphi}{\neg\varphi[x/b] \mid a\neq b, \varphi[x/a]}$$

$$(\imath E_2)\ \frac{b_1=\imath x\varphi, \mathtt{E}b_1, \mathtt{E}b_2}{\varphi[x/b_1], \neg\varphi[x/b_2] \mid b_1=b_2, \varphi[x/b_1]} \qquad (\neg\imath E_2)\ \frac{b\neq\imath x\varphi, \mathtt{E}b}{\neg\varphi[x/b] \mid a\neq b, \varphi[x/a], \mathtt{E}a}$$

Fig. 1. Tableau rules for $\mathsf{TC}_{\mathsf{PFL}}$, $\mathsf{TC}_{\mathsf{NFL}}$, $\mathsf{TC}_{\mathsf{PQFL}}$, $\mathsf{TC}_{\mathsf{NQFL}}$, and $\mathsf{TC}_{\mathsf{NQFL}^-}$

valuation, in the remaining (absolutely free) logics it needs to be secured by a separate existence formula. Note that all quantifier elimination rules admit only parameters as instances of bound variables. The $(=E)$-rule scheme ensures the substitutability of identical terms within arbitrary formulas, often called Leibniz' principle. One of its side effects is a guarantee that $=$ is symmetric in all calculi. $(=I_1)$ and $(=I_2)$, occurring only in $\mathsf{TC}_{\mathsf{NQFL}^-}$, which lacks the existence predicate E, make sure that each definite description occurring in a true atomic formula has a unique and existing denotation, by equating it with a fresh vari-

	PFL	PQFL	NFL	NQFL	NQFL$^-$
	$(\neg\neg E)$, $(\wedge E)$, $(\neg\wedge E)$, $(\bot_1)$, $(= E)$				
	$(\bot_2)$	$(\bot_2)$	$(\mathrm{E}E_2)$	$(\bot_3)$	$(\bot_3)$
	$(\forall E_2)$	$(\forall E_1)$	$(\forall E_2)$	$(\forall E_1)$	$(\forall E_1)$
	$(\neg\forall E_2)$	$(\neg\forall E_1)$	$(\neg\forall E_2)$	$(\neg\forall E_1)$	$(\neg\forall E_1)$
	(cut_2)	(cut_2)	(cut_2)	(cut_2)	(cut_1)
	$(\mathrm{E}E_1)$	$(\mathrm{E}E_1)$	$(\mathrm{E}E_1)$	$(\mathrm{E}E_1)$	
			$(\mathrm{E}I_1)$	$(\mathrm{E}I_1)$	$(= I_1)$
			$(\mathrm{E}I_2)$	$(\mathrm{E}I_2)$	$(= I_2)$
		$(\mathrm{E}I_3)$		$(\mathrm{E}I_3)$	
	$(\imath E_2)$	$(\imath E_1)$	$(\imath E_2)$	$(\imath E_1)$	$(\imath E_1)$
	$(\neg\imath E_2)$	$(\neg\imath E_1)$	$(\neg\imath E_2)$	$(\neg\imath E_1)$	$(\neg\imath E_1)$
non-empty domain assumption	$(\mathrm{E}I_4)$		$(\mathrm{E}I_4)$		

Fig. 2. Tableau calculi $\mathsf{TC}_{\mathsf{PFL}}$, $\mathsf{TC}_{\mathsf{NFL}}$, $\mathsf{TC}_{\mathsf{PQFL}}$, $\mathsf{TC}_{\mathsf{NQFL}}$, and $\mathsf{TC}_{\mathsf{NQFL}^-}$

able (which is always denoting in NQFL$^-$). (cut_1) and (cut_2) are a restricted form of analytic cut which, for each definite description and denoting variable checks whether their denotations are identical or distinct. $(\mathrm{E}E_1)$ works similarly to $(= I_1)$ and $(= I_2)$ with the caveat that it equates with a fresh variable a definite description that is known to be denoting. $(\mathrm{E}E_2)$, which is present only in $\mathsf{TC}_{\mathsf{NFL}}$, enforces reflexivity of identity among denoting terms. Intuitively, it allows us to prove that, for each non-denoting term t, a formula $t \neq t$ holds in NFL. The rules $(\mathrm{E}I_1)$ and $(\mathrm{E}I_2)$ reflect the semantic condition stating that each term which is an argument of a true atomic NQFL-formula, or each definite description occurring in such an NFL-formula, is denoting. $(\mathrm{E}I_3)$, on the other hand, refers to the definition of valuation in PQFL and NQFL, where variables are always mapped to existing objects. The rule $(\mathrm{E}I_4)$ introduces a fresh variable which is assumed to denote, provided that there are no parameters on the branch. Consequently, it guarantees that the non-empty domain assumption is satisfied, should we make it. The first pair of $\imath$-rules, $(\imath E_1)$ and $(\neg\imath E_1)$, eliminate an occurrence of a definite description provided that it appears as an argument of an identity. In $(\imath E_1)$ a formula defining the definite description must hold of b_1, hence this formula is present in both conclusions. A definite description is subsequently compared to each parameter b_2 occurring on a branch. If we assume that they are equal, it is also equal to b_1 (the right conclusion), otherwise φ does not hold of b_2, so we obtain its negation. In $(\neg\imath E_1)$ we assume that a denoting parameter b and a definite description have distinct denotations. It is either because the formula defining the definite description does not hold of b (the left conclusion) or because some other object satisfies this formula. To state the latter a fresh parameter a is introduced which satisfies φ, yet it is not equal to b. The second pair of $\imath$-rules, $(\imath E_2)$ and $(\neg\imath E_2)$, being a part of the calculi for proper free logics, work similarly, with the caveat that we need to additionally ensure, using the existence predicate E, that respective variables occurring in the premises of the rules are denoting. In PFL and NFL variables are not automatically guaranteed to denote, so such an additional condition is necessary for bringing the rules in line with the semantic condition for proper definite descriptions.

Since the rules in all calculi are closed under subformulas modulo substitution, adding single negations and adding equality to two terms already present on the branch one of which being a definite description and another one being a parameter, one can think of the calculi as *analytic* in an extended sense of the term.

4 Soundness and Completeness[2]

In order to prove soundness and completeness of the calculi $\mathsf{TC}_{\mathsf{PFL}}$, $\mathsf{TC}_{\mathsf{PQFL}}$, $\mathsf{TC}_{\mathsf{NFL}}$, $\mathsf{TC}_{\mathsf{NQFL}}$, and $\mathsf{TC}_{\mathsf{NQFL}^-}$ we need two well-known lemmas which we recall without proofs (see, e.g., [6, Sect. III.4 and III.8]).

Lemma 1 (Coincidence Lemma). *Let* $\varphi \in \mathsf{FOR}$, *let* $\mathscr{M} = \langle \mathscr{D}, \mathscr{D}_{\mathrm{E}}, \mathscr{I} \rangle$ *be a model, and let* v_1, v_2 *be assignments. If* $v_1(x) = v_2(x)$ *for each free variable* x *occurring in* φ, *then* $\mathscr{M}, v_1 \models \varphi$ *iff* $\mathscr{M}, v_2 \models \varphi$.

Lemma 2 (Substitution Lemma). *Let* $\varphi \in \mathsf{FOR}$, $t, t' \in \mathsf{TERM}$, *and let* $\mathscr{M} = \langle \mathscr{D}, \mathscr{D}_{\mathrm{E}}, \mathscr{I} \rangle$ *be a model. Then* $\mathscr{M}, v \models \varphi[x/t]$ *iff* $\mathscr{M}, v^x_{\mathscr{I}_v(t)} \models \varphi$.

4.1 Soundness

Let (R) $\frac{\Phi}{\Psi_1 | \ldots | \Psi_n}$ be a rule from a calculus TC_{L}. We say that (R) is *sound* if whenever Φ is L-satisfiable, then $\Phi \cup \Psi_i$ is L-satisfiable, for some $i \in \{1, \ldots, n\}$.

Lemma 3 *For each* $\mathsf{L} \in \{\mathsf{PFL}, \mathsf{PQFL}, \mathsf{NFL}, \mathsf{NQFL}, \mathsf{NQFL}^-\}$ *all rules of* TC_{L} *are sound.*

Proof. We confine ourselves to showing soundness of the rules for definite descriptions.

To prove soundness of $(\imath E_1)$ assume that $b_1 = \imath x\varphi$ is L-satisfiable, for $\mathsf{L} \in \{\mathsf{PQFL}, \mathsf{NQFL}, \mathsf{NQFL}^-\}$, that is, there exists a model $\mathscr{M} = \langle \mathscr{D}, \mathscr{D}_{\mathrm{E}}, \mathscr{I} \rangle$ and an assignment v such that $\mathscr{M}, v \models b_1 = \imath x\varphi$. Let $v(b_1) = o \in \mathscr{D}_{\mathrm{E}}$, then $\mathscr{I}_v(\imath x\varphi) = v(b_1) = o$ and by the satisfaction condition $\mathscr{M}, v^x_o \models \varphi$, and for any x-variant v' of v, if $\mathscr{M}, v' \models \varphi$, then $v'(x) = o$. The first conjunct guarantees,

[2] Full Versions of the Proofs of Lemmas 3 and 4 and Propositions 1 and 2 Can Be Found in [17].

by Substitution Lemma, that $\mathcal{M}, v \models \varphi[x/b_1]$, which holds for both conclusions. The second conjunct yields, for any $b_2 \in \mathcal{D}_{\mathsf{E}}$, that either $\mathcal{M}, v \not\models \varphi[x/b_2]$ or $\mathcal{M}, v \models b_1 = b_2$. The former case yields the left conclusion, whereas the latter case yields the right one. To show that $(\neg\imath E_1)$ is sound assume that $b \neq \imath x\varphi$ is L-satisfiable for $\mathsf{L} \in \{\mathsf{PQFL}, \mathsf{NQFL}, \mathsf{NQFL}^-\}$. Then, there exists a model $\mathcal{M} = \langle \mathcal{D}, \mathcal{D}_{\mathsf{E}}, \mathcal{I} \rangle$ and an assignment v such that $\mathcal{M}, v \models b \neq \imath x\varphi$. It means that $\mathcal{I}_v(\imath x\varphi) \neq v(b) = o \in \mathcal{D}_{\mathsf{E}}$. By the satisfaction condition $\mathcal{M}, v_o^x \not\models \varphi$, or for some x-variant v' of v, $\mathcal{M}, v' \models \varphi$ but $o' = v'(x) \neq v(x) = o$. In the first case, by Substitution Lemma, $\mathcal{M}, v \not\models \varphi[x/b]$, so the left conclusion is satisfied. If the second holds, then by Coincidence Lemma and Substitution Lemma we have that $\mathcal{M}, v \models \varphi[x/a]$ but $\mathcal{M}, v \models b \neq a$ for some fresh a.

Proofs for $(\imath E_2)$ and $(\neg\imath E_2)$, respectively, are conducted analogically with the following caveat. In PFL and NFL variables are not automatically guaranteed to denote, so the existence of a referrent object needs to be ensured externally. This is done by placing a variable in the scope of the existence predicate E. □

Now we are ready to prove the following theorem.

Theorem 1 (Soundness). *The tableau calculi $\mathsf{TC}_{\mathsf{PFL}}$, $\mathsf{TC}_{\mathsf{PQFL}}$, $\mathsf{TC}_{\mathsf{NFL}}$, $\mathsf{TC}_{\mathsf{NQFL}}$, and $\mathsf{TC}_{\mathsf{NQFL}^-}$ are sound.*

Proof. To show that for each L-formula φ, where $\mathsf{L} \in \{\mathsf{PFL}, \mathsf{PQFL}, \mathsf{NFL}, \mathsf{NQFL}, \mathsf{NQFL}^-\}$, if φ is tableau-valid, then it is valid. Let $\mathcal{T}$ be a proof of φ, that is, a closed tableau with $\neg\varphi$ at the root. Each branch of $\mathcal{T}$ has $\bot$ at the leaf, which is clearly L-unsatisfiable. By Lemma 3 we know that all the rules of TC_{L} are L-satisfiability preserving, and so, going from the bottom to the top of $\mathcal{T}$, at each node we have an L-unsatisfiable set of formulas. Thus, (a singleton set consisting of) $\neg\varphi$ is L-unsatisfiable. By the well known duality between satisfiability and validity we obtain that φ is L-valid. □

4.2 Completeness

In this section, we prove that, for each $\mathsf{L} \in \{\mathsf{PFL}, \mathsf{PQFL}, \mathsf{NFL}, \mathsf{NQFL}, \mathsf{NQFL}^-\}$, TC_{L} is complete. To that end we show that every open and fully expanded branch $\mathcal{B}$ of a TC_{L}-tableau $\mathcal{T}$ satisfies some syntactic conditions. Then we show how to construct an L-structure $\mathcal{M}_{\mathcal{B}}^{\mathsf{L}}$ and a function $v_{\mathcal{B}}^{\mathsf{L}}$ out of such an open and fully expanded branch, and show that $v_{\mathcal{B}}^{\mathsf{L}}$ is an L-valuation, and $\mathcal{M}_{\mathcal{B}}^{\mathsf{L}}$ is an L-model satisfying, for each L-formula φ occurring on $\mathcal{B}$, $\mathcal{M}_{\mathcal{B}}^{\mathsf{L}}, v_{\mathcal{B}}^{\mathsf{L}} \models \varphi$.

We assume that for each $\mathsf{L} \in \{\mathsf{PFL}, \mathsf{PQFL}, \mathsf{NFL}, \mathsf{NQFL}, \mathsf{NQFL}^-\}$, the calculus TC_{L} can be accompanied by a suitable *fair* procedure in the sense that whenever a rule can be applied, it will eventually be applied. For example, an algorithm from [8], with added steps for additional rules, can be applied to TC_{L}. Thus, a fully expanded, possibly infinite, branch $\mathcal{B}$ is *closed under rule application.*

Let $\mathcal{B}$ be an open and fully expanded branch of a TC_{L}-tableau $\mathcal{T}$, where $\mathsf{L} \in \{\mathsf{PFL}, \mathsf{PQFL}, \mathsf{NFL}, \mathsf{NQFL}, \mathsf{NQFL}^-\}$. Let $\mathsf{TERM}(\mathcal{B})$, $\mathsf{VAR}(\mathcal{B})$, and $\mathsf{PAR}(\mathcal{B})$ be the sets of, respectively, all terms occurring on $\mathcal{B}$ (that is, parameters and definite descriptions), all bound variables occurring on $\mathcal{B}$, and all parameters occurring on $\mathcal{B}$. We define a binary relation $\sim$ on $\mathsf{TERM}(\mathcal{B})$ in the following way:

$$\forall t_1, t_2 \in \mathsf{TERM}(\mathcal{B}) \quad \big[t_1 \sim t_2 \quad \text{iff} \quad (t_1 = t_2 \text{ occurs on } \mathcal{B} \;\text{ or }\; t_1 \text{ is } t_2)\big].$$

Proposition 1. *$\sim$ is an equivalence relation.*

Proposition 2. *For any $t_1, t_2 \in \mathsf{TERM}(\mathcal{B})$, if $t_1 \sim t_2$, then $\varphi[x/t_1] \in \mathcal{B}$ iff $\varphi[x/t_2] \in \mathcal{B}$, for all formulas φ.*

So equipped, we are ready to prove the cornerstone result of this section.

Lemma 4 (Satisfaction Lemma). *Let $\mathcal{T}$ be a TC_L-tableau, for $\mathsf{L} \in \{PFL, PQFL, NFL, NQFL, NQFL^-\}$, and let $\mathcal{B}$ be an open and fully expanded branch of $\mathcal{T}$. Then there exists a structure $\mathscr{M}^\mathsf{L}_\mathcal{B} = \langle \mathscr{D}^\mathsf{L}_\mathcal{B}, \mathscr{D}_\mathrm{E}{}^\mathsf{L}_\mathcal{B}, \mathscr{I}^\mathsf{L}_\mathcal{B}\rangle$ and a function $v^\mathsf{L}_\mathcal{B}$ such that:*

$$\textit{if} \qquad \psi \in \mathcal{B}, \qquad \textit{then} \qquad \mathscr{M}^\mathsf{L}_\mathcal{B}, v^\mathsf{L}_\mathcal{B} \models \psi. \qquad (\star)$$

Proof. We first show how to construct $\mathscr{M}^\mathsf{L}_\mathcal{B}$ and $v^\mathsf{L}_\mathcal{B}$. The latter object is assumed to serve as an assignment, which is normally defined for $\mathsf{VAR}(\mathcal{B}) \cup \mathsf{PAR}(\mathcal{B})$. The values of bound variables, however, are arbitrary, so for convenience we introduce an extra object $\boldsymbol{o} \notin \mathsf{TERM}(\mathcal{B})$ that will further play the role of their value. First we define $\mathscr{D}^\mathsf{L}_\mathcal{B}$ and $\mathscr{D}_\mathrm{E}{}^\mathsf{L}_\mathcal{B}$.

- $\mathscr{D}^\mathsf{L}_\mathcal{B} = \{[t]_\sim \mid t \in \mathsf{TERM}(\mathcal{B})\} \cup \{\boldsymbol{o}\}$.

For $\mathsf{L} \in \{\mathsf{PFL}, \mathsf{NFL}\}$:

- $\mathscr{D}_\mathrm{E}{}^\mathsf{L}_\mathcal{B} = \{[t]_\sim \in \mathscr{D}^\mathsf{L}_\mathcal{B} \mid \mathrm{E}t \in \mathcal{B}\}$ [hence $\boldsymbol{o} \in \mathscr{D}^\mathsf{L}_\mathcal{B} \setminus \mathscr{D}_\mathrm{E}{}^\mathsf{L}_\mathcal{B}$].

For $\mathsf{L} \in \{\mathsf{PQFL}, \mathsf{NQFL}\}$:

- $\mathscr{D}_\mathrm{E}{}^\mathsf{L}_\mathcal{B} = \{[t]_\sim \in \mathscr{D}^\mathsf{L}_\mathcal{B} \mid \mathrm{E}t \in \mathcal{B}\} \cup \{\boldsymbol{o}\}$.

For $\mathsf{L} \in \{\mathsf{NQFL}^-\}$:

- $\mathscr{D}_\mathrm{E}{}^\mathsf{L}_\mathcal{B} = \{[t]_\sim \in \mathscr{D}^\mathsf{L}_\mathcal{B} \mid t \in \mathsf{PAR}(\mathcal{B})\} \cup \{\boldsymbol{o}\}$.

Next, we define $v^\mathsf{L}_\mathcal{B}$ as a function mapping elements from $\mathsf{VAR}(\mathcal{B}) \cup \mathsf{PAR}(\mathcal{B})$ to $\mathscr{D}^\mathsf{L}_\mathcal{B}$ for PFL and NFL, and as a function from $\mathsf{VAR}(\mathcal{B}) \cup \mathsf{PAR}(\mathcal{B})$ to $\mathscr{D}_\mathrm{E}{}^\mathsf{L}_\mathcal{B}$ for PQFL, NQFL, and NQFL^-. We let

$$v^\mathsf{L}_\mathcal{B}(t) = \begin{cases} [t]_\sim, & \text{if } t \text{ is a parameter,} \\ \boldsymbol{o}, & \text{if } t \text{ is a bound variable.} \end{cases}$$

- $\mathscr{I}^\mathsf{L}_{\mathcal{B}_{v^\mathsf{L}_\mathcal{B}}}(t) = v^\mathsf{L}_\mathcal{B}(t)$, for each $t \in \mathsf{PAR}(\mathcal{B}) \cup \mathsf{VAR}(\mathcal{B})$;
- $\mathscr{I}^\mathsf{L}_{\mathcal{B}_{v^\mathsf{L}_\mathcal{B}}}(\imath x\varphi) = [t]_\sim$ iff $\varphi[x/t] \in \mathcal{B}$ and for any $b \in \mathsf{PAR}(\mathcal{B})$, if $\varphi[x/b] \in \mathcal{B}$, then $t = b \in \mathcal{B}$, for each $\imath x\varphi \in \mathsf{TERM}(\mathcal{B})$ and $t \in \mathsf{PAR}(\mathcal{B})$;
- $\mathscr{I}^\mathsf{L}_\mathcal{B}(P) = \{\langle \mathscr{I}^\mathsf{L}_{\mathcal{B}_{v^\mathsf{L}_\mathcal{B}}}(t_1), \ldots, \mathscr{I}^\mathsf{L}_{\mathcal{B}_{v^\mathsf{L}_\mathcal{B}}}(t_n)\rangle \mid P(t_1, \ldots, t_n) \in \mathcal{B}\}$.

We need to show that $v^{\mathsf{L}}_{\mathcal{B}}$ is a properly defined L-assignment.

Assignment $v^{\mathsf{L}}_{\mathcal{B}}$

First, we show that $v^{\mathsf{L}}_{\mathcal{B}}$ is a properly defined L-assignment, for L being any of the considered logics. First we prove that $v^{\mathsf{L}}_{\mathcal{B}}$ is a function on $\mathsf{VAR}(\mathcal{B})$. Totality of $v^{\mathsf{L}}_{\mathcal{B}}$ straightforwardly follows from its definition. Uniqueness of the value assigned by $v^{\mathsf{L}}_{\mathcal{B}}$ to each element of $\mathsf{VAR}(\mathcal{B}) \cup \mathsf{PAR}(\mathcal{B})$ is a consequence of two facts. First, $\sim$ is an equivalence relation, so equivalence classes of $\sim$ are pairwise disjoint. Secondly, $\mathscr{D}^{\mathsf{L}}_{\mathcal{B}}$ is non-empty. Indeed, without loss of generality we can assume that we check for validity of universally quantified formulas, that is, the input formula φ is of the form $\neg\forall x\psi$. By expandedness of $\mathcal{B}$ we get that the rules $(\neg\neg E)$, $(\wedge E)$, $(\neg \wedge E)$, $(\neg\forall_i)$, and $(\neg\forall_i)$, for $i \in \{1,2\}$, were applied on $\mathcal{B}$ to the point where an atomic formula or a negated atomic formula with a free term t, that is, a parameter or definite description, occurs on $\mathcal{B}$. Such a formula must finally occur on $\mathcal{B}$ as $\mathscr{L}$ does not contain the constants $\bot$ and $\top$ and an atomic formula of $\mathscr{L}$ is of one of the forms: $t_1 = t_2$, $P(t_1,\ldots,t_n)$, or $\mathtt{E}t$, where $t, t_1,\ldots,t_n$ are terms and P is an n-ary predicate symbol. Thus, an equivalence class of such a freely occurring term t is an element of $\mathscr{D}^{\mathsf{L}}_{\mathcal{B}}$.

For $\mathsf{L} \in \{\mathsf{PQFL}, \mathsf{NQFL}, \mathsf{NQFL}^-\}$ we additionally need to show that the image of $v^{\mathsf{L}}_{\mathcal{B}}$ is included in $\mathscr{D}\mathtt{E}^{\mathsf{L}}_{\mathcal{B}}$. But for the first two logics this is a straightforward consequence of presence of the rule $(\mathtt{E}I_3)$ in $\mathsf{TC}_{\mathsf{PQFL}}$ and $\mathsf{TC}_{\mathsf{NQFL}}$, which, for each parameter b on $\mathcal{B}$, introduces $\mathtt{E}b$ to $\mathcal{B}$, and the definition of $\mathscr{D}\mathtt{E}^{\mathsf{L}}_{\mathcal{B}}$ for both logics. In the last case the required inclusion rests solely on the definition of $\mathscr{D}\mathtt{E}^{\mathsf{NQFL}_-}_{\mathcal{B}}$.

Let us now show that $(\star)$ holds. The notion of satisfaction in $\mathscr{M}^{\mathsf{L}}_{\mathcal{B}}$ is defined as in Sect. 2.2. We proceed by induction on the complexity of ψ which is defined as the number of connectives and quantifiers occuring in ψ but not in the scope of the $\imath$-operator. We restrict attention to the cases where $\psi := t_1 = t_2$ and $\psi := t_1 \neq t_2$.

$\psi := t_1 = t_2$ Let $t_1, t_2 \in \mathsf{TERM}(\mathcal{B})$ and $t_1 = t_2 \in \mathcal{B}$. Let $\mathsf{L} \in \{\mathsf{PFL}, \mathsf{PQFL}\}$. By the definition of $\sim$, $[t_1]_\sim = [t_2]_\sim$, and so, by the definition of $\mathscr{I}^{\mathsf{L}}_{\mathcal{B}v^{\mathsf{L}}_{\mathcal{B}}}$, $\mathscr{I}^{\mathsf{L}}_{\mathcal{B}v^{\mathsf{L}}_{\mathcal{B}}}(t_1) = \mathscr{I}^{\mathsf{L}}_{\mathcal{B}v^{\mathsf{L}}_{\mathcal{B}}}(t_2)$. Thus, by the satisfaction condition for $=$-formulas in both logics, $\mathscr{M}^{\mathsf{L}}_{\mathcal{B}}, v^{\mathsf{L}}_{\mathcal{B}} \models t_1 = t_2$. Now let $\mathsf{L} \in \{\mathsf{NFL}, \mathsf{NQFL}\}$. By expandedness of $\mathcal{B}$ we know that the rule $(\mathtt{E}I_2)$ (NFL) or $(\mathtt{E}I_2)$ together with $(\mathtt{E}I_3)$ (NQFL) was applied to $t_1 = t_2$, thus yielding $\mathtt{E}t_1, \mathtt{E}t_2 \in \mathcal{B}$. By the proof of the case $\psi := \mathtt{E}t$ we know that $\mathscr{I}^{\mathsf{L}}_{\mathcal{B}v^{\mathsf{L}}_{\mathcal{B}}}(t_1) \in \mathscr{D}\mathtt{E}^{\mathsf{L}}_{\mathcal{B}}$ and $\mathscr{I}^{\mathsf{L}}_{\mathcal{B}v^{\mathsf{L}}_{\mathcal{B}}}(t_2) \in \mathscr{D}\mathtt{E}^{\mathsf{L}}_{\mathcal{B}}$. Moreover, by the definition of $\sim$ and $\mathscr{I}^{\mathsf{L}}_{\mathcal{B}v^{\mathsf{L}}_{\mathcal{B}}}$, $\mathscr{I}^{\mathsf{L}}_{\mathcal{B}v^{\mathsf{L}}_{\mathcal{B}}}(t_1) = \mathscr{I}^{\mathsf{L}}_{\mathcal{B}v^{\mathsf{L}}_{\mathcal{B}}}(t_2)$. Hence, by the satisfaction condition for $=$-formulas, $\mathscr{M}^{\mathsf{L}}_{\mathcal{B}}, v^{\mathsf{L}}_{\mathcal{B}} \models t_1 = t_2$. Finally, let $\mathsf{L} = \mathsf{NQFL}^-$. By expandedness of $\mathcal{B}$ the rule $(= I_2)$ was applied to $t_1 = t_2$, thus yielding $a_i = t_i$, for $1 \leq i \leq 2$ and t_i being a definite description. Without loss of generality assume that $t_1 \in \mathsf{PAR}(\mathcal{B})$ and t_2 is a definite description, so we have $t_1, a_2 \in \mathsf{PAR}(\mathcal{B})$ and $t_2 = a_2 \in \mathcal{B}$. By the definition of $\sim$ and $\mathscr{D}\mathtt{E}^{\mathsf{L}}_{\mathcal{B}}$ for $\mathsf{L} = \mathsf{NQFL}^-$ we get that $[t_1]_\sim \in \mathscr{D}\mathtt{E}^{\mathsf{L}}_{\mathcal{B}}$, $[t_2]_\sim = [a_2]_\sim \in \mathscr{D}\mathtt{E}^{\mathsf{L}}_{\mathcal{B}}$ and $[t_1]_\sim = [t_2]_\sim$. By the definition of $\mathscr{I}^{\mathsf{L}}_{\mathcal{B}v^{\mathsf{L}}_{\mathcal{B}}}$, $\mathscr{I}^{\mathsf{L}}_{\mathcal{B}v^{\mathsf{L}}_{\mathcal{B}}}(t_1), \mathscr{I}^{\mathsf{L}}_{\mathcal{B}v^{\mathsf{L}}_{\mathcal{B}}}(t_2) \in \mathscr{D}\mathtt{E}^{\mathsf{L}}_{\mathcal{B}}$ and $\mathscr{I}^{\mathsf{L}}_{\mathcal{B}v^{\mathsf{L}}_{\mathcal{B}}}(t_1) = \mathscr{I}^{\mathsf{L}}_{\mathcal{B}v^{\mathsf{L}}_{\mathcal{B}}}(t_2)$. Hence, by the satisfaction condition for $=$-formulas, $\mathscr{M}^{\mathsf{L}}_{\mathcal{B}}, v^{\mathsf{L}}_{\mathcal{B}} \models t_1 = t_2$.

$\psi := t_1 \neq t_2$ Let $t_1, t_2 \in \mathsf{TERM}(\mathcal{B})$ and $t_1 \neq t_2 \in \mathcal{B}$. Let $\mathsf{L} \in \{\mathsf{PFL}, \mathsf{PQFL}\}$. By openness of $\mathcal{B}$, t_1 and t_2 are distinct terms, for otherwise the rule $(\bot_2)$ would close $\mathcal{B}$. Again, by openness of $\mathcal{B}$, $t_1 = t_2 \notin \mathcal{B}$, so by the definition of $\sim$, $[t_1]_\sim \neq [t_2]_\sim$. Hence, by the definition of $\mathscr{I}^{\mathsf{L}}_{\mathcal{B}\,v^{\mathsf{L}}_{\mathcal{B}}}$, $\mathscr{I}^{\mathsf{L}}_{\mathcal{B}\,v^{\mathsf{L}}_{\mathcal{B}}}(t_1) \neq \mathscr{I}^{\mathsf{L}}_{\mathcal{B}\,v^{\mathsf{L}}_{\mathcal{B}}}(t_2)$. Thus, by the satisfaction condition for $=$-formulas in both logics, $\mathscr{M}^{\mathsf{L}}_{\mathcal{B}}, v^{\mathsf{L}}_{\mathcal{B}} \not\models t_1 = t_2$, and so, by the satisfaction condition for $\neg$-formulas, $\mathscr{M}^{\mathsf{L}}_{\mathcal{B}}, v^{\mathsf{L}}_{\mathcal{B}} \models t_1 \neq t_2$. Let $\mathsf{L} \in \{\mathsf{NFL}\}$. Clearly, either t_1 and t_2 are distinct, or identical. Assume, first, that t_1 and t_2 are distinct terms. Then we proceed with the proof similarly to the case for $\mathsf{L} \in \{\mathsf{PFL}, \mathsf{PQFL}\}$. Now, assume that $t_1 \neq t_2$ is of one of the forms $t \neq t$. We know that $\mathtt{E}t \notin \mathcal{B}$, for otherwise we could apply $(\mathtt{E}E_2)$ and close $\mathcal{B}$ with $(\bot_1)$. Then, by the definition of $\sim$ and $\mathscr{D}^{\mathsf{L}}_{\mathtt{E}\mathcal{B}}$, it follows that $[t]_\sim \notin \mathscr{D}^{\mathsf{L}}_{\mathtt{E}\mathcal{B}}$. By the definition of $\mathscr{I}^{\mathsf{L}}_{\mathcal{B}\,v^{\mathsf{L}}_{\mathcal{B}}}$ and the satisfaction condition for $=$-formulas, we get $\mathscr{M}^{\mathsf{L}}_{\mathcal{B}}, v^{\mathsf{L}}_{\mathcal{B}} \not\models t = t$. By the satisfaction condition for $\neg$-formulas we finally obtain $\mathscr{M}^{\mathsf{L}}_{\mathcal{B}}, v^{\mathsf{L}}_{\mathcal{B}} \models t \neq t$. Let $\mathsf{L} \in \{\mathsf{NQFL}, \mathsf{NQFL}^-\}$. Clearly, either t_1 and t_2 are distinct, or $t_1, t_2 \notin \mathsf{PAR}(\mathcal{B})$. Indeed, if $t_1 \neq t_2$ was of the form $b \neq b$ for $b \in \mathsf{PAR}(\mathcal{B})$, then $\mathcal{B}$ would be closed by an application of $(\bot_3)$. Assume, first, that t_1 and t_2 are distinct terms. Then we proceed with the proof similarly to the case for $\mathsf{L} \in \{\mathsf{PFL}, \mathsf{PQFL}\}$. Now, assume that $t_1 \neq t_2$ is of the form $\imath x\varphi \neq \imath x\varphi$. Let $\mathsf{L} = \mathsf{NQFL}$. Certainly, $\mathtt{E}\imath x\varphi \notin \mathcal{B}$, for otherwise $(\mathtt{E}E_1)$ would have been applied, yielding $a = \imath x\varphi$ and, through $(= E)$, $a \neq a$, thus closing $\mathcal{B}$. So, by the definition of $\sim$, $\mathscr{D}^{\mathsf{L}}_{\mathtt{E}\mathcal{B}}$, and $\mathscr{I}^{\mathsf{L}}_{\mathcal{B}\,v^{\mathsf{L}}_{\mathcal{B}}}$, we have $\mathscr{I}^{\mathsf{L}}_{\mathcal{B}\,v^{\mathsf{L}}_{\mathcal{B}}}(\imath x\varphi) \notin \mathscr{D}^{\mathsf{L}}_{\mathtt{E}\mathcal{B}}$. The rest of the proof is identical to the one for $\mathsf{L} = \mathsf{NFL}$. Let $\mathsf{L} = \mathsf{NQFL}^-$. For the same reasons as for NQFL, for each $b \in \mathsf{PAR}(\mathcal{B})$, $b = \imath x\varphi \notin \mathcal{B}$. Then, by the definition of $\sim$, $\mathscr{D}^{\mathsf{L}}_{\mathtt{E}\mathcal{B}}$, and $\mathscr{I}^{\mathsf{L}}_{\mathcal{B}\,v^{\mathsf{L}}_{\mathcal{B}}}$, $\mathscr{I}^{\mathsf{L}}_{\mathcal{B}\,v^{\mathsf{L}}_{\mathcal{B}}}(\imath x\varphi) \notin \mathscr{D}^{\mathsf{L}}_{\mathtt{E}\mathcal{B}}$. We conduct the rest of the proof similarly to the one for $\mathsf{L} \in \{\mathsf{NFL}, \mathsf{NQFL}\}$.

Interpretation $\mathscr{I}^{\mathsf{L}}_{\mathcal{B}\,v^{\mathsf{L}}_{\mathcal{B}}}(\imath x\varphi)$

The last thing we must show is that the condition for the interpretation of definite descriptions holds in $\mathscr{M}^{\mathsf{L}}_{\mathcal{B}}$. In terms of the induced model it amounts to the following condition:

$$\mathscr{I}^{\mathsf{L}}_{\mathcal{B}\,v^{\mathsf{L}}_{\mathcal{B}}}(\imath x\varphi) = [a]_\sim \in \mathscr{D}^{\mathsf{L}}_{\mathtt{E}\mathcal{B}} \quad \text{iff} \quad \mathscr{M}^{\mathsf{L}}_{\mathcal{B}}, v^{x\ \ \mathsf{L}}_{[a]_\sim\mathcal{B}} \models \varphi \text{ and for each } x\text{-variant } v'^{\mathsf{L}}_{\mathcal{B}} \text{ of } v^{\mathsf{L}}_{\mathcal{B}}, \text{ if } \mathscr{M}^{\mathsf{L}}_{\mathcal{B}}, v'^{\mathsf{L}}_{\mathcal{B}} \models \varphi, \text{ then } v'^{\mathsf{L}}_{\mathcal{B}}(x) = [a]_\sim. \quad (\dagger)$$

The right-hand side of (†), by Substitution Lemma, is equivalent to the condition that $\mathscr{M}^{\mathsf{L}}_{\mathcal{B}}, v^{\mathsf{L}}_{\mathcal{B}} \models \varphi[x/a]$ and for each b such that $[b]_\sim \in \mathscr{D}^{\mathsf{L}}_{\mathtt{E}\mathcal{B}}$, if $\mathscr{M}^{\mathsf{L}}_{\mathcal{B}}, v^{\mathsf{L}}_{\mathcal{B}} \models \varphi[x/b]$, then $[b]_\sim = [a]_\sim$, which will be applied in the proof. We show (†) for PQFL, NQFL, NQFL^-. For the remaining systems the proof is similar. First let us note the following:

Claim. Let $\mathcal{B}$ be a fully expanded branch of a TC_{L}-tableau $\mathcal{T}$, for $\mathsf{L} \in \{\mathsf{PFL}, \mathsf{PQFL}, \mathsf{NFL}, \mathsf{NQFL}, \mathsf{NQFL}^-\}$. Then the following holds:

$$\mathscr{I}^{\mathsf{L}}_{\mathcal{B}\,v^{\mathsf{L}}_{\mathcal{B}}}(\imath x\varphi) = [a]_\sim \text{ iff } \imath x\varphi = a \in \mathcal{B}.$$

Proof. $\Rightarrow$ By contraposition, assume that $\imath x\varphi = a \notin \mathcal{B}$. Then, by (cut_1), $\imath x\varphi \neq a \in \mathcal{B}$, which, by $(\star)$, yields that $\mathscr{M}^{\mathsf{L}}_{\mathcal{B}}, v^{\mathsf{L}}_{\mathcal{B}} \models \imath x\varphi \neq a$. Thus, $\mathscr{I}^{\mathsf{L}}_{\mathcal{B}v^{\mathsf{L}}_{\mathcal{B}}}(\imath x\varphi) \neq [a]_\sim$.

$\Leftarrow$ If we assume that $\imath x\varphi = a \in \mathcal{B}$, then, by $(\star)$, $\mathscr{M}^{\mathsf{L}}_{\mathcal{B}}, v^{\mathsf{L}}_{\mathcal{B}} \models \imath x\varphi = a$, and we are done.

Now let us prove $(\dagger)$:

$\Rightarrow$ Let $\mathscr{I}^{\mathsf{L}}_{\mathcal{B}v^{\mathsf{L}}_{\mathcal{B}}}(\imath x\varphi) = [a]_\sim \in \mathscr{D}^{\mathsf{L}}_{\mathrm{E}\mathcal{B}}$. Hence, by Claim, $\imath x\varphi = a \in \mathcal{B}$. By $(\imath E_1)$, either $\varphi[x/a] \in \mathcal{B}$ and $\neg\varphi[x/b] \in \mathcal{B}$, or $\varphi[x/a] \in \mathcal{B}$ and $a = b \in \mathcal{B}$, for every b. In both cases, by $(\star)$, $\mathscr{M}^{\mathsf{L}}_{\mathcal{B}}, v^{\mathsf{L}}_{\mathcal{B}} \models \varphi[x/a]$. Moreover, again by $(\star)$, either $\mathscr{M}^{\mathsf{L}}_{\mathcal{B}}, v^{\mathsf{L}}_{\mathcal{B}} \not\models \varphi[x/b]$ or $\mathscr{M}^{\mathsf{L}}_{\mathcal{B}}, v^{\mathsf{L}}_{\mathcal{B}} \models a = b$, for every b. Hence the second conjunct follows.

$\Leftarrow$ Assume that $\mathscr{M}^{\mathsf{L}}_{\mathcal{B}}, v^{\mathsf{L}}_{\mathcal{B}} \models \varphi[x/a]$ and for each $b \in \mathscr{D}^{\mathsf{L}}_{\mathrm{E}\mathcal{B}}$, if $\mathscr{M}^{\mathsf{L}}_{\mathcal{B}}, v^{\mathsf{L}}_{\mathcal{B}} \models \varphi[x/b]$, then $[b]_\sim = [a]_\sim$, but $\mathscr{I}^{\mathsf{L}}_{\mathcal{B}v^{\mathsf{L}}_{\mathcal{B}}}(\imath x\varphi) \neq [a]_\sim$. Hence, by Claim, $\imath x\varphi \neq a \in \mathcal{B}$. By $(\neg\imath E)$ we have either $\neg\varphi[x/a] \in \mathcal{B}$ or, for some b, $\varphi[x/b] \in \mathcal{B}$ and $a \neq b \in \mathcal{B}$. Both cases, by $(\star)$, lead to a contradiction. □

Theorem 2 (Completeness). *The tableau calculi* $\mathsf{TC}_{\mathsf{PFL}}$, $\mathsf{TC}_{\mathsf{PQFL}}$, $\mathsf{TC}_{\mathsf{NFL}}$, $\mathsf{TC}_{\mathsf{NQFL}}$, *and* $\mathsf{TC}_{\mathsf{NQFL}^-}$ *are complete.*

Proof. We prove the contrapositive of the usual completeness condition. Assume that a L-formula φ is not tableau-valid wrt TC_{L}. Then, there is a fully expanded TC_{L}-tableau which is not a tableau proof of φ. Thus, there exists an open branch $\mathcal{B}$ in $\mathcal{T}$ with $\neg\varphi$ at the root. By Satisfaction Lemma the structure $\mathscr{M}^{\mathsf{L}}_{\mathcal{B}} = \langle \mathscr{D}^{\mathsf{L}}_{\mathcal{B}}, \mathscr{D}^{\mathsf{L}}_{\mathrm{E}\mathcal{B}}, \mathscr{I}^{\mathsf{L}}_{\mathcal{B}} \rangle$ is an L-model and the function $v^{\mathsf{L}}_{\mathcal{B}} : \mathsf{VAR} \cup \mathsf{PAR}(\mathcal{B}) \longrightarrow \mathscr{D}^{\mathsf{L}}_{\mathcal{B}}$ is an Ł-assignment and since $\neg\varphi \in \mathcal{B}$, then $\mathscr{M}^{\mathsf{L}}_{\mathcal{B}}, v^{\mathsf{L}}_{\mathcal{B}} \models \neg\varphi$. By the usual duality between satisfiability and validity we obtain that φ is not valid, which yields the conclusion. □

5 Related Work

Alongside with the tableau systems mentioned in Sect. 1, which usually directly transform the conditions (L) or (R), two alternative approaches deserve a separate mention. One of them, although in the setting of labelled sequent calculus, has recently been presented by Orlandelli [25]. He provided an alternative formulation of modal theory of descriptions developed by Fitting and Mendelsohn in [8] in the form of a tableau system not enjoying the subformula property. Orlandelli's system, on the other hand, is cut-free and analytic. These properties are obtained at the cost of a significant enrichment of the technical machinery. In addition to ordinary strong labels (i.e., labels naming worlds and attached to formulas and relational atoms showing accessibility links between worlds), he is using special denotation atoms $D(t, x, w)$ to express that a term t in w denotes the same object as the one denoted by a variable x. This device is used to define rules for DD and for the λ-operator. Another cut-free formulation of the same theory of descriptions was developed by Indrzejczak [13] in the setting of hybrid modal language. The main difference is that instead of introducing external labelling apparatus, a richer language with nominal variables and sat-operators is used and descriptions are characterized by means of rules dealing with equalities, like in the present approach. MFD in all variants analyzed in the present paper is a much weaker theory of descriptions than the theory mentioned above, although the variants based on NQFL and NQFL$^-$ show some affinities with Fitting and Mendelsohn's theory. It would be an interesting task to embed MFD, as represented in positive free logic, in the modal setting using one of the two presented alternative approaches.

The tableau calculi devised in this paper, despite being based on the cut-free sequent calculi for the same logics, introduced in [14], go beyond straightforward transpositions of the rules presented therein. The main aim of [14] was to obtain sequent formalizations of free logics for which it is possible to prove the cut elimination theorem in a constructive way. Our main objective here is to construct calculi which are analytic and effective tools of proof search in respective logics. This basic difference has a significant impact on the way the sets of rules are built in both approaches, which we briefly summarize in what follows. First of all, in our tableau systems a restricted (to identities) form of analytic cut is present, whereas in the sequent calculus from [14] cut is in general constructively eliminable. However, cut-freeness of the latter systems leads to more complicated forms of some other rules. In particular:

1. The sequent counterpart of the tableau rule $(= E)$ is restricted to atomic formulas and has three premises instead of one.
2. Some sequent rules are replaced here by suitable closure rules.
3. All tableau rules for definite descriptions are different than the respective rules in sequent calculi.

What speaks in favour of tableaux presented in this paper is a decreased branching factor in comparison to the discussed sequent calculi. The price to be paid, however, is a restricted form of analytic cut which is necessary to ensure completeness of the calculi. Since eliminating the three-premise rule makes it necessary to add a restricted cut, we cannot be sure that it leads to simpler proof-trees in the general case, but, at least on the basis of several tested examples, it seems highly probable.

The presence of cut, even in a strictly limited form which does not destroy the subformula property, may be seen as a disadvantage. However, both cut rules could be dispensed with and replaced with two other rules expressing some form of Leibniz's law:

$$(RL_1)\ \frac{\neg\varphi[x/t]}{\neg\varphi[x/b] \mid b \neq t} \qquad (RL_2)\ \frac{\neg\varphi[x/t], \mathtt{E}b}{\neg\varphi[x/b] \mid b \neq t},$$

where t is a DD and φ is atomic (including $\mathtt{E}$ and $=$). On the other hand, in comparison to the above Leibniz's rules the proposed form of analytic cut seems to be a more direct solution without overhead costs. The cut-free and analytic characterization of Russellian theory of DD from [16] is essentially based on the introduction of a collection of special equality rules for every kind of involved terms. Only after we augment the calculus with this extra toolkit, it becomes possible to dispense with any form of cut. However, despite of some purely proof-theoretic advantages of this solution, it does not seem to bring any serious benefits in the tableau setting.

6 Conclusions

The role of definite descriptions in the field of proof theory and automated deduction has so far been underestimated. That is why it is important to stress advantages using them may bring. First of all, as we mentioned in Sect. 2, every complex term represented by means of functional terms can be equivalently expressed using a definite description. In the latter case we do not need extra bridge principles showing how the information encoded by functional terms is represented by predicates, whereas in the former case we do. For example such bridge principles are usually needed as enthymematic premises in an analysis of obviously valid arguments. Moreover, the presence of functions in formal languages often easily leads to generating infinite Herbrand models even when finite models are allowed. Let us illustrate this with a simple example. From $\forall x(a = f(x))$ we infer $a = f(a), a = f(f(a)), a = f(f(f(a))), \ldots$ On the other hand, from $\forall x(a = \imath y F(x, y))$ we obtain $a = \imath y F(a, y)$, and then $F(a, a), \neg F(a, a) \mid a = a, F(a, a)$, where the left branch gets closed, but the right one provides a finite, single-element model. Moreover, definite descriptions can be used to provide smooth definitions of new terms, and even new operators, in formal languages. For example, one may define the abstraction operator in set theory in an elegant way.

These virtues of definite descriptions have not hitherto been thoroughly examined mainly because of a lack of good formal systems expressing their theories. The presented tableau systems are a step towards filling this gap. They are analytic despite of the use of restricted cuts and, in effect, seem to provide handy proof-search tools. Further plans for research include:

1. designing and implementing a tool for automated proof-search and user-friendly proof-assistance;
2. investigating computational efficiency of such a tool; in particular, comparing it with well-known programs designed for standard languages with functional terms;
3. formalizing stronger theories of definite descriptions in standard language and in enriched languages (e.g., with modalities);
4. applying these systems to a formalization of elementary theories.

References

1. Baaz, M., Iemhoff, R.: Gentzen calculi for the existence predicate. Stud. Logica. **82**(1), 7–23 (2006). https://doi.org/10.1007/s11225-006-6603-6
2. Beeson, M.J.: Foundations of Constructive Mathematics. Metamathematical Studies, Springer, Heidelberg (1985)

3. Bencivenga, E., Lambert, K., van Fraasen, B.: Logic, Bivalence and Denotation. Ridgeview, Atascadero (1991)
4. Bencivenga, E.: Free logics. In: Gabbay, D.M., Guenthner, F. (eds.) Handbook of Philosophical Logic, pp. 147–196. Springer, Dordrecht (2002). https://doi.org/10.1007/978-94-017-0458-8_3
5. Bostock, D.: Intermediate Logic. Clarendon Press, Oxford (1997)
6. Ebbinghaus, H.D., Flum, J., Thomas, W.: Mathematical Logic. Undergraduate Texts in Mathematics, Springer, New York (1994). https://doi.org/10.1007/978-1-4757-2355-7
7. Feferman, S.: Definedness. Erkenntnis **43**, 295–320 (1995). https://doi.org/10.1007/BF01135376
8. Fitting, M., Mendelsohn, R.: First-Order Modal Logic. Kluwer, Dordrecht (1998). https://doi.org/10.1007/978-94-011-5292-1
9. Garson, J.W.: Modal Logic for Philosophers. Cambridge University Press, Cambridge (2006). https://doi.org/10.1017/CBO9780511617737
10. Gumb, R.: An extended joint consistency theorem for a nonconstructive logic of partial terms with definite descriptions. Stud. Logica. **69**(2), 279–292 (2001). https://doi.org/10.1023/A:1013822008159
11. Indrzejczak, A.: Cut-free modal theory of definite descriptions. In: Bezhanishvili, G., D'Agostino, G., Metcalfe, G., Studer, T. (eds.) Advances in Modal Logic 12, pp. 387–406. College Publications, London (2018)
12. Indrzejczak, A.: Fregean description theory in proof-theoretical setting. Log. Logical Philos. **28**(1), 137–155 (2019). https://doi.org/10.12775/LLP.2018.008
13. Indrzejczak, A.: Existence, definedness and definite descriptions in hybrid modal logic. In: Olivetti, N., Verbrugge, R., Negri, S., Sandu, G. (eds.) Advances in Modal Logic 13, pp. 349–368. College Publications, London (2020)
14. Indrzejczak, A.: Free definite description theory - sequent calculi and cut elimination. Log. Logical Philos. **29**(4), 505–539 (2020). https://doi.org/10.12775/LLP.2018.008
15. Indrzejczak, A.: Free logics are cut-free. Stud. Logica. **109**(4), 859–886 (2020). https://doi.org/10.1007/s11225-020-09929-8
16. Indrzejczak, A.: Russellian definite description theory - a proof theoretic approach. Rev. Symb. Logic 1–26 (2021). https://doi.org/10.1017/S1755020321000289
17. Indrzejczak, A., Zawidzki, M.: Tableaux for free logics with descriptions (2021). arXiv:2107.07228
18. Kalish, D., Montague, R., Mar, G.: Logic. Techniques of Formal Reasoning, 2nd edn. Oxford University Press, New York (1980)
19. Kürbis, N.: A binary quantifier for definite descriptions in intuitionist negative free logic: natural deduction and normalization. Bull. Section Log. **48**(2), 81–97 (2019). https://doi.org/10.18778/0138-0680.48.2.01
20. Kürbis, N.: Two treatments of definite descriptions in intuitionist negative free logic. Bull. Section Log. **48**(4), 299–317 (2019). https://doi.org/10.18778/0138-0680.48.4.04
21. Lambert, K.: A theory of definite descriptions. In: Lambert, K. (ed.) Philosophical Applications of Free Logic, pp. 17–27. Kluwer (1962)
22. Lambert, K.: Free logic and definite descriptions. In: Lambert, K. (ed.) New Essays in Free Logic, pp. 37–48. Springer, Dordrecht (2001). https://doi.org/10.1007/978-94-015-9761-6-2
23. Lehmann, S.: More free logic. In: Gabbay, D., Guenthner, F. (eds.) Handbook of Philosophical Logic, vol. 5, 2nd edn., pp. 197–259. Springer, Dordrecht (2002). https://doi.org/10.1007/978-94-017-0458-8-4

24. Maffezioli, P., Orlandelli, E.: Full cut elimination and interpolation for intuitionistic logic with existence predicate. Bull. Section Log. **48**(2), 137–158 (2019). https://doi.org/10.18778/0138-0680.48.2.04
25. Orlandelli, E.: Labelled calculi for quantified modal logics with definite descriptions. J. Logic Comput. (2021). https://doi.org/10.1093/logcom/exab018, exab018
26. Pavlović, E., Gratzl, N.: A more unified approach to free logics. J. Philos. Log. **50**(1), 117–148 (2020). https://doi.org/10.1007/s10992-020-09564-7
27. Pelletier, F.J., Linsky, B.: What is Frege's theory of descriptions? In: Linsky, B., Imaguire, G. (eds.) On Denoting: 1905–2005, pp. 195–250. Philosophia Verlag, Munich (2005)
28. Scott, D.: Identity and existence in intuitionistic logic. In: Fourman, M., Mulvey, C., Scott, D. (eds.) Applications of Sheaves, pp. 660–696. Springer, Heidelberg (1979). https://doi.org/10.1007/BFb0061839
29. Tennant, N.: Natural Logic. Edinburgh University Press, Edinburgh (1978)
30. Tennant, N.: A general theory of abstraction operators. Philos. Q. **54**(214), 105–133 (2004). https://doi.org/10.1111/j.0031-8094.2004.00344.x

CEGAR-Tableaux: Improved Modal Satisfiability via Modal Clause-Learning and SAT

Rajeev Goré[1](✉) and Cormac Kikkert[2]

[1] Vienna University of Technology, Vienna, Austria [2] Australian National University, Canberra, Australia
cormac.kikkert@anu.edu.au

Abstract. We present CEGAR-Tableaux, a tableaux-like method for propositional modal logics utilising SAT-solvers, modal clause-learning and multiple optimisations from modal and description logic tableaux calculi. We use the standard Counter-example Guided Abstract Refinement (CEGAR) strategy for SAT-solvers to mimic a tableau-like search strategy that explores a rooted tree-model with the classical propositional logic part of each Kripke world evaluated using a SAT-solver. Unlike modal SAT-solvers and modal resolution methods, we do not explicitly represent the accessibility relation but track it implicitly via recursion. By using "satisfiability under unit assumptions", we can iterate rather than "backtrack" over the satisfiable diamonds at the same modal level (context) of the tree model with one SAT-solver. By keeping modal contexts separate from one another, we add further refinements for reflexivity and transitivity which manipulate modal contexts once only. Our solver CEGARBox is, overall, the best for modal logics K, KT and S4 over the standard benchmarks, sometimes by orders of magnitude.

1 Introduction

The TABLEAUX and DL communities have strived for thirty years to provide practical theorem provers for non-classical logics while the SAT community has moved from efficiently solving SAT-problems with tens of propositional variables to solving problems with hundreds of variables. The "silver bullet" was conflict driven clause-learning [7,10]. Following Claessen and Rosén [1], Fiorentini et al. [3] and Goré et al. [5], we give a tableaux-like calculus containing "modal clause learning" to handle modal satisfiability, where a main procedure explores a rooted tree-model with worlds evaluated via an "oracle" SAT-solver. Our implementation, `CEGARBox`, uses multiple optimisations and, overall, is the best over the standard benchmarks, sometimes by orders of magnitude.

Consider monomodal logic with modal operators $\Box$ and $\Diamond$ with formulae defined from atoms $p \in Atm$ by the BNF grammar $\varphi ::= \bot \mid \top \mid p \mid \neg\varphi \mid \varphi \wedge \varphi \mid \varphi \vee \varphi \mid \Box\varphi \mid \Diamond\varphi$. Define $(\varphi_1 \rightarrow \varphi_2) := (\neg\varphi_1 \vee \varphi_2)$ and $\varphi_1 \leftrightarrow \varphi_2 := ((\varphi_1 \rightarrow$

R. Goré—Work supported by the FWF projects I 2982 and P 33548.

A. Das and S. Negri (Eds.): TABLEAUX 2021, LNAI 12842, pp. 74–91, 2021.
https://doi.org/10.1007/978-3-030-86059-2_5

$\varphi_2) \wedge (\varphi_2 \to \varphi_1))$. We assume familiarity with the Kripke semantics for modal logics in which the modal logic K, KT, K4 and S4 are respectively characterised by all; reflexive; transitive; and reflexive-transitive frames.

We thank Steve Blackburn, Ullrich Hustadt and Daniel Le Berre.

2 Modal Clausal Tableaux

Following Goré and Nguyen [4], we define modal clausal tableaux as follows.

A *literal* is an atom p or its negation $\neg p$: we use a to f and l for literals. We use A, B, C and D for a set of literals. We define $\bar{l} := \neg p$ if $l = p$ and $\bar{l} := p$ if $l = \neg p$ so that $\bar{\bar{l}} = l$. A formula is in negation normal form (NNF) if it is implication-free and negations appear only in front of atomic formulae. A formula φ can be converted into an at most polynomially longer formula $nnf(\varphi)$ in NNF so that φ is logically equivalent to $nnf(\varphi)$. Let $\overline{\varphi} := nnf(\neg\varphi)$.

A *cpl-clause* is a disjunction of literals. A formula $(\neg a \vee \Box b)$ is a box-clause and $(\neg c \vee \Diamond d)$ is a dia-clause. We usually write box-clauses as $a \to \Box b$ and dia-clauses as $c \to \Diamond d$ to convey that the literal b is "boxed" while the literal d is "diamonded" and that these implications "fire" from left to right if their antecedents are true. For any set w_0 of these three types of clauses, let $\mathcal{C}^{cpl}(w_0)$ and $\mathcal{C}^{\to\Box}(w_0)$ and $\mathcal{C}^{\to\Diamond}(w_0)$ be, respectively, the set of cpl-clauses, box-clauses and dia-clauses from w_0.

A modal context is a possibly empty sequence of box-like modalities: formally $\Box^0\varphi := \varphi$ and $\Box^{i+1} := \Box^i\Box\varphi$. Every cpl-clause, box-clause and dia-clause is a modal clause, and if φ is a modal clause then so is $\Box^i\varphi, i \geq 1$. Using ";" for set-union, a set w_0 of modal clauses can be partitioned into separate modal contexts via: $w_0 = \Box^0\mathcal{C}_0(w_0)\ ;\ \Box^1\mathcal{C}_1(w_0)\ ;\ \cdots\ ;\ \Box^n\mathcal{C}_n(w_0)$ where each set $\mathcal{C}_i$ contains only cpl-clauses, box-clauses and dia-clauses so $\mathcal{C}_0(w_0) = \mathcal{C}^{cpl}(w_0)\ ;\ \mathcal{C}^{\to\Box}(w_0)\ ;\ \mathcal{C}^{\to\Diamond}(w_0)$. Letting $\mathcal{MC} := \Box^0\mathcal{C}_1; \cdots ; \Box^{k-1}\mathcal{C}_k$, we gather the non-zero modal contexts via $w_0 = \mathcal{C}^{cpl}(w_0); \mathcal{C}^{\to\Box}(w_0); \mathcal{C}^{\to\Diamond}(w_0); \Box\mathcal{MC}(w_0)$.

A formula can be put into modal clausal form (or Mints [11] normal form) in linear time and space wrt length [4]. The resulting modal clauses are K-satisfiable iff the original formula is K-satisfiable [4].

We assume familiarity with the standard tableau calculi for modal logics K, KT, K4 and S4 using NNF. These calculi will also work for formulae in modal clausal form. In the modal rules, L is a finite set of literals, while X, Y, and Z are possibly empty sets of modal clauses:

$$(T)\ \frac{\Box\varphi; X}{\varphi; \Box\varphi; X} \qquad (K)\ \frac{\Diamond\varphi; \Box X; \Diamond Y; L}{\varphi; X} \qquad (K4)\ \frac{\Diamond\varphi; \Box X; \Diamond Y; L}{\varphi; X; \Box X}$$

Suppose we want to test the formula φ_0 for validity. We negate it and put the negation into nnf to obtain $\overline{\varphi_0} := nnf(\neg\varphi_0)$. We then put $\overline{\varphi_0}$ into modal clausal form to obtain w_0. Thus w_0 is the modal clausal form of $nnf(\neg\varphi_0)$. We then use the rules shown above to try to find a closed tableau, as usual. But there is an alternative which builds-in some aspects of modus ponens as explained next.

Given an example root node $w_0 := L \; ; \; \{c \to \Diamond d, c_1 \to \Diamond d_1\} \; ; \; \{a_1 \to \Box b_i, a_2 \to \Box b_2\} \; ; \; \Box\mathcal{MC}(w_0)$, where L is a set of literals and $\Box\mathcal{MC}(w_0)$ is arbitrary, consider the (transitional-but-modus-ponens-like) KE-rule [2] instance:

$$(jump) \; \frac{L \; ; \; c \to \Diamond d \; ; \; a_1 \to \Box b_1, a_2 \to \Box b_2 \; ; \; \Box\mathcal{MC}(w_0)}{d \; ; \; b_1 \; ; \; \mathcal{MC}(w_0)}$$

Proposition 1. *If* $(\{c, a_1, \overline{a_2}\} \subseteq L$, *then this (jump) rule instance is derivable.*

Instead of a derivation of (jump), we simply show how it mimics (K) viz:

L: the set of literals as in (K)
$\Diamond\varphi$: a principal diamond $(c \to \Diamond d) \in \mathcal{C}^{\to\Diamond}(w_0)$ which fires giving $\Diamond d$ if $c \in L$
$\Diamond Y$: non-principal dia-clauses $\{c_1 \to \Diamond d_1\} = \mathcal{C}^{\to\Diamond}(w_0) \setminus \{c \to \Diamond d\}$
$\Box X$: box-clauses $(a_1 \to \Box b_1) \subseteq \mathcal{C}^{\to\Box}(w_0)$ giving $\{\Box b_1\} \subseteq \Box X$ if $a_1 \subseteq L$
$\Box X$: the non-empty modal contexts $\Box\mathcal{MC}(w_0) \subseteq \Box X$ and
none: box-clauses $a_2 \to \Box b_2$ which are dormant if $\overline{a_2} \subseteq L$ and have no counterpart in the original (K) rule.

We will replace the tableaux rules for cpl with a SAT-solver (oracle) and replace (K) with a generalised variant of (jump) called (jump)/(restart) which uses modal clause-learning. We first explain SAT-solvers and the CEGAR procedure.

3 SAT-solvers and the CEGAR Procedure

A formula is in conjunctive normal form (CNF) if it is a conjunction of cpl-clauses. SAT-solvers are extremely efficient algorithms for determining the satisfiability of a set of formulae of classical propositional logic in CNF [16].

Incremental SAT-solvers are solvers which allow alternating between adding a clause to the SAT-solver and testing for satisfiability. Further, modern SAT-solvers, such as MiniSAT [14], allow testing for *Satisfiability Under Unit Assumptions*, with a set of literals $A = \{l_1, \cdots, l_n\}$ called unit assumptions. That is, if the SAT-solver is in some state σ after loading a set S of cpl-clauses into it, we can now query whether or not $S \cup A$ is classically satisfiable. Moreover, after computing the un/satisfiability of $S \cup A$, such a SAT-solver will "undo" its actions to return to its previous state σ. Using this feature, we can use one single SAT-solver in state σ to *iteratively* test the classical satisfiability of many different extensions $S \cup \{A_1\}, S \cup \{A_2\}, \cdots, S \cup \{A_m\}$ of a given S without their interfering with one another, as long as each A_i is a set of unit assumptions.

For example, if we are given the set $\Box B \; ; \; \Diamond d_1 \; ; \; \cdots \; ; \; \Diamond d_m \; ; \; \Box\mathcal{C}$ where each $B \cup \{d_i\}$ is a set of unit assumptions, and $\mathcal{C}$ is a set of arbitrary cpl-clauses, then we can initially load the SAT-solver with the cpl-clauses in $\mathcal{C}$ to put it in some state σ and then iteratively test the un/satisfiability of each set $B \; ; \; d_i \; ; \; \mathcal{C}$ for $i = 1, \cdots, m$ using just one SAT-solver which reuses the state σ, rather than using m separate SAT-solvers with states $B \; ; \; d_i \; ; \; \mathcal{C}$. We assume that the SAT-solver we use provides the following operations:

`addClause(s,C)`: adds the cpl-clause C as a constraint to the SAT-solver s.

`solve(s,A)`: accepts a set $A = \{l_1, \cdots, l_m\}$ of unit assumptions, and tries to find a classical valuation ϑ that satisfies the cpl-clauses added so far to s under the unit assumptions in A. The call returns one of two answers:
- (sat, ϑ): if it is possible to find such an assignment ϑ representing the literals that are true, and so we have that $A \subset \vartheta$
- (unsat, A'): if it is impossible to find such an assignment with $A' \subset A$ a, not necessarily unique, *unsatisfiable core* of A, which causes the classical unsatisfiability of $s \cup A$. Note that A' itself may be classically satisfiable. The smaller A' is the more efficient our algorithm becomes.

We also use the following operation as a shorthand to avoid complicating specifications with the intricacies of implementation:

$sat(\mathcal{C}, A)$: Creates a SAT-solver s, adds the set $\mathcal{C}$ of cpl-clauses to s, then returns `solve(s,A)` where A is a set of unit-assumptions (literals).

We use the SAT-solver MiniSat [14], in our implementation.

3.1 Counter-Example Guided Abstraction Refinement (CEGAR)

The standard way to use a SAT-solver, besides a direct translation, is called Counter-Example Guided Abstraction Refinement (CEGAR) which involves creating an under-abstraction ψ which is less constrained than the original formula φ. We use $\psi := \mathcal{C}^{cpl}(\varphi)$ as our under-abstraction. Using a SAT-solver, we check whether a classical valuation ϑ can be found for ψ. If not, then it is impossible to create a Kripke model for the more constrained φ, and we conclude that φ is modally unsatisfiable. Otherwise, we check whether the classical valuation ϑ can be extended into a Kripke model for φ. If so we conclude that φ is modally satisfiable. Else we refine the under-abstraction ψ to be closer to φ by learning new cpl-clauses from the classical unsatisfiable core, and repeat the whole procedure.

Some versions of CEGAR use an over-approximation or even both, but we elide details for brevity as the method of under-approximation is the one we use.

We now present two tableau-like rules and a rule-application search strategy to mimic modal clausal tableaux using a CEGAR approach.

4 CEGAR Tableaux: Modal Clause-Learning via SAT

We describe tableau-like rules which mimic CEGAR. Each rule has a single parent above the line and multiple children below the line with the traditional modal (rather than description logic) tableaux reading of "if the parent is modally satisfiable then so is at least one child". To handle "satisfiability under unit assumptions", let $\mathcal{A}(w_0) \subseteq w_0$ be a set of designated literals called **assumptions**.

local CPL satisfiability rule:

$$(\text{local})\ \frac{w_0 := \mathcal{A}(w_0)\ ;\ \mathcal{C}^{cpl}(w_0)\ ;\ \mathcal{C}^{\to\Box}(w_0)\ ;\ \mathcal{C}^{\to\Diamond}(w_0)\ ;\ \Box\mathcal{MC}(w_0)}{sat(\mathcal{C}^{cpl}(w_0), \mathcal{A}(w_0))}$$

where $sat(\mathcal{C}^{cpl}(w_0), \mathcal{A}(w_0))$ either returns "closed" because it finds an unsatisfiable core $\mathcal{A}'(w_0) \subseteq \mathcal{A}(w_0)$ of literals or returns "open" because it finds a classical valuation $\vartheta(w_0) \supseteq \mathcal{A}(w_0)$ such that $\vartheta(w_0) \models \mathcal{C}^{cpl}(w_0)$. We can implement $sat(\mathcal{C}^{cpl}(w_0), \mathcal{A}(w_0))$ with a SAT-solver via $\mathtt{sat}(\mathcal{C}^{cpl}(w_0),\ \mathcal{A}(w_0))$.

Proposition 2. *If the parent of the (local) rule is modally satisfiable at some world w via $\vartheta(w)$ then its subset, the child, is classically satisfiable under $\vartheta(w)$.*

modal (jump/restart) rule:

$$\frac{w_0 := \mathcal{A}(w_0)\ ;\ \mathcal{C}^{cpl}(w_0)\ ;\ \mathcal{C}^{\to\Box}(w_0)\ ;\ \mathcal{C}^{\to\Diamond}(w_0)\ ;\ \Box\mathcal{MC}(w_0)}{w_1 := d\ ;\ B\ ;\ \mathcal{MC}(w_0) \qquad w_0' := w_0\ ;\ \varphi(w_0)}\ \vartheta(w_0)$$

where $\vartheta(w_0) \supseteq \mathcal{A}(w_0)$ is a classical valuation such that $\vartheta(w_0) \models \mathcal{C}^{cpl}(w_0)$ and
(1) there is at least one "fired" diamond $(c \to \Diamond d) \in \mathcal{C}^{\to\Diamond}(w_0)$ & $\vartheta(w_0) \models c$
(jump): left child $w_1 := d; B; \mathcal{MC}(w_0)$ for the fired diamond $\Diamond d$ where the "fired" (un)boxes are
(2) $B := \{b \mid (a \to \Box b) \in \mathcal{C}^{\to\Box}(w_0) \text{ and } \vartheta(w_0) \models a\}$
(restart): right child $w_0' := w_0; \varphi(w_0)$ if the left child w_1 with $\mathcal{A}(w_1) = (d\ ;\ B)$ closes with an unsatisfiable core $\mathcal{A}'(w_1) \subseteq (d\ ;\ B)$ and

$$\begin{aligned} A_d(w_1)\ &:= \{d\} \cup \mathcal{A}'(w_1) \text{ is the unsatisfiable core of } w_1 \text{ extended with } d \\ CS(w_0) &:= \{e \mid \vartheta(w_0) \models e \ \&\ (e \to \Box f) \in \mathcal{C}^{\to\Box}(w_0) \ \&\ f \in A_d(w_1)\} \\ &\quad \cup \{e \mid \vartheta(w_0) \models e \ \&\ (e \to \Diamond f) \in \mathcal{C}^{\to\Diamond}(w_0) \ \&\ f \in A_d(w_1)\} \\ &= \{l_1, \ldots, l_n\} \supseteq \{c\} \text{ are the "culprits" from } w_0 \end{aligned}$$

and $\varphi(w_0) := (\neg l_1 \vee \ldots \vee \neg l_n)$ is the local learned cpl-clause $\varphi(w_0)$ with which we restart w_0 as w_0' to refine $\vartheta(w_0)$ since $\vartheta(w_0) \models c$ and the single diamond $\Diamond d$ that it fired leads to a counter example w_1 w.r.t. $\Box\mathcal{MC}(w_0)$.

The (local) and (jump)/(restart) rules are notionally applicable to any set w_0 of modal clauses except that the (jump/restart) rule is additionally parametrised by a classical valuation $\vartheta(w_0)$: that is, they form a "producer-consumer" pair. Thus the (local) rule searches for a classical valuation (using a SAT-solver that returns (sat, ϑ)), effectively finding an open branch of static rule applications. The (jump) rule then uses this valuation to mimic the (K) as follows.

Item (1) non-deterministically chooses a dia-clause $c \to \Diamond d$ from $\mathcal{C}^{\to\Diamond}(w_0)$ which "fires" because $\vartheta(w_0) \models c$ giving us the principal formula $\Diamond d$ of (K).

Item (2) collects each box-clause $a \to \Box b$ from $\mathcal{C}^{\to\Box}(w_0)$ which "fires" because $\vartheta(w_0) \models a$, and unboxes each $\Box b$ producing literals $B \subseteq X$ in the (K)-rule.

The left (jump) child $w_1 := d\ ;\ B\ ;\ \mathcal{MC}(w_0)$ mimics the conclusion of a (K)-rule instance with a premise $\Diamond d\ ;\ \Box B\ ;\ \Box\mathcal{MC}(w_0)$, so w_1 is the set of formulae which must be true at the R-successor of the premise w_0.

Applying these two rules **recursively** will either close w_1 or leave w_1 open. If w_1 stays open then w_1 is a putative R-successor in the underlying counter-model that we are exploring so we must choose some other dia-clause which is fired by $\vartheta(w_0)$: we must **iterate** over all such fired diamonds as we are looking for a closed tableau but if all choices stay open then we have a Kripke model.

Else, if w_1 closes then it will return an (there may be many) unsatisfiable core $\mathcal{A}'(w_1) \subseteq (d \ ; \ B)$, closing the tableau branch for $\Diamond d$ and pinpointing the unit assumptions from w_1 which cause branch closure, effectively building in a use-check as explained below.

In the "else" case, a traditional tableau would backtrack up to the next highest application of the ($\vee$)-rule. But we can be cleverer by learning a clause as follows. We extend the unsatisfiable core $\mathcal{A}(w_1)'$ to $A_d(w_1)$ to ensure that d is in $A_d(w_1)$ because $\Diamond d$ was the principal formula of the "jump" from w_0 to w_1. We now find the "culprits" $e \in \vartheta(w_0)$ by "unfiring" each $e \rightarrow \Box f$ and each $e \rightarrow \Diamond f$ that caused their f to be put into the extended unsatisfiable core $A_d(w_1)$ of the R-successor, thereby obtaining the conflict set $CS(w_0)$ (used in the proofs) of w_0. That is, we have moved from w_1 back to w_0.

We know there is at least one culprit in w_0, namely c, but in general $CS(w_0) = \{l_1, \cdots, l_n\} \supseteq \{c\}$. We therefore "switch off" at least one of these culprits by adding the disjunction of their negations $\varphi(w_0) := (\neg l_1 \vee \cdots \vee \neg l_n)$ as a new clause and restart w_0 as $w_0' := w_0 \ ; \ \varphi(w_0)$. Intuitively, rather than backtracking to the next highest disjunction, our traditional tableau procedure is effectively re-starting the Static rules on the new incarnation w_0' to find a "saturation" that is guaranteed to be different from $\vartheta(w_0)$. Traditional tableau would only be guaranteed to find a different "saturation" if they included use-check or cut.

Proposition 3. *If the parent w_0 of the (jump/restart) rule is K-satisfiable in a Kripke model with root valuation $\vartheta(w_0)$ then so is its left (jump) child w_1.*

Proposition 4. *If the (jump/restart) rule is applied with $\vartheta(w_0)$ and the right (restart) child w_0' is classically satisfied by $\vartheta(w_0')$ then $\vartheta(w_0')$ is a different classical valuation from $\vartheta(w_0)$, and all previous such restarts, as there is at least one literal l_i which is true in the previous valuation but false in the new one.*

Example 1. Consider the standard K axiom instance $\Box(p \rightarrow q) \rightarrow (\Box p \rightarrow \Box q)$. We negate it and obtain the negation normal form $\neg K$: $\Box(\neg p \vee q) \wedge \Box p \wedge \Diamond\neg q$. A legitimate clausal form of $\neg K$ for illustrative purposes is: $w_0 = \{a_1, a_1 \rightarrow \Box b_1, \Box(b_1 \rightarrow (\neg p \vee q)), a_2, a_2 \rightarrow \Box p, c_1, c_1 \rightarrow \Diamond\neg q\}$ with $\mathcal{A}(w_0) = \emptyset$ and $\mathcal{C}^{cpl}(w_0) = \{a_1, a_2, c_1\}$ and $\mathcal{C}^{\rightarrow\Box}(w_0) = \{a_1 \rightarrow \Box b_1, a_2 \rightarrow \Box p\}$ and $\mathcal{C}^{\rightarrow\Diamond}(w_0) = \{c_1 \rightarrow \Diamond\neg q\}$ and $\Box\mathcal{C}(w_0) = \{\Box(b_1 \rightarrow (\neg p \vee q))\}$. Our final optimised normal forming procedure produces something smaller. Figure 1 contains the search-space for the resulting closed tableau. If we try $\Box(p \rightarrow q) \rightarrow (\Box p \rightarrow \Box r)$ then $c_1 \rightarrow \Diamond\neg q$ above becomes $c_1 \rightarrow \Diamond\neg r$ and the tableau will remain open and will return a Kripke (counter-)model $w_0 R w_1$ with $\vartheta(w_0) = \{a_1, a_2, c_1\}$ and $\vartheta(w_1) = \{b_1, p, q, \neg r\}$ which falsifies $\Box(p \rightarrow q) \rightarrow (\Box p \rightarrow \Box r)$ at w_0.

4.1 Termination, Soundness and Completeness of the Strategy

We dub our search strategy as **CEGARTab** (in bold font).

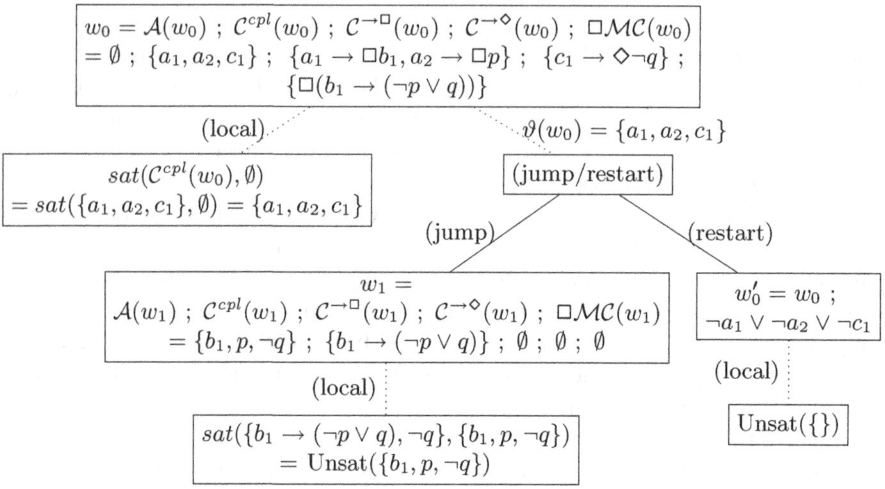

Fig. 1. The search-space for the negation ¬K of the K axiom $\Box(p \to q) \to (\Box p \to \Box q)$ where dotted lines indicate rule choices and solid lines indicate branching rules.

Each **iteration** in **CEGARTab** is finite because each node contains a finite number of dia-clauses. Thus the only way to not terminate is for **CEGARTab** to **recurse** for ever. But each **recursion** via the (jump) rule reduces the maximal modal degree of the formula set in the child node and each **recursion** via the (restart) rule enumerates a different classical valuation from the finite set of classical valuations for $\mathcal{C}^{cpl}(w_0)$. Thus **CEGARTab** must terminate.

Theorem 1. *For all sets of modal clauses $w_0 := nnf(\neg\varphi_0)$, **CEGARTab**$(w_0)$ returns closed iff w_0 is K-unsatisfiable (and hence φ_0 is K-valid).*

Proof. Both proofs proceed by a simple induction on the number of restarts.

Soundness: If the (local) rule returns closed then w_0 contains a classically unsatisfiable, and hence K-unsatisfiable, subset. Else there is a closed application of the (jump)/(restart) rule with learned clause $\varphi = (\neg l_1 \vee \cdots \vee \neg l_n)$. The induction hypothesis on the closed (jump) child implies that $w_0 \cup \neg\varphi$ is K-unsatisfiable. The induction hypothesis on the closed (restart) child implies that $w_0 \cup \varphi$ is K-unsatisfiable. Hence w_0 is K-unsatisfiable (and cut is admissible!).

Completeness: The open (local) rule returns $\vartheta(w_0)$. If the (jump)/(restart) rule is not applicable then there are no fired diamonds, and so the Kripke model is just a dead-end w_0 with $\vartheta(w_0)$. Else if the (jump) child is open then the induction hypothesis implies that we can extend $\vartheta(w_0)$ into Kripke sub-models for every diamond jump. Adding a new root with $\vartheta(w_0)$ that sees all these sub-models gives a Kripke model for w_0 itself. Else if the (jump) child is closed then the (restart) child with learned clause $\varphi = (\neg l_1 \vee \cdots \vee \neg l_n)$

is open. Then the induction hypothesis implies that $w_0; \varphi$ is K-satisfiable, which implies that w_0 is K-satisfiable. □

5   Implementation: Our Modal Satisfiability Tester CEGARBox

The only data-structures our base algorithm uses are a trie and lists. Memoisation, outlined in Sect. 7.2, was implemented using a binary tree.

5.1   Initialising a Trie During Normal Forming

Normal forming creates new atomic "names" p_ψ for certain subformulae ψ of the original formula: for example $\square\diamond(p_1 \wedge p_2)$ becomes a_1 ; $a_1 \rightarrow \square b_2$; $\square(b_2 \rightarrow \diamond d_3)$; $\square\square(d_3 \rightarrow p_1)$; $\square\square(d_3 \rightarrow p_2)$ [4] where a_1 names $\square\diamond(p_1 \wedge p_2)$ and d_3 names $(p_1 \wedge p_2)$. We make a linear recursive descent of the formula and store modal clauses in a trie where each trie-node represents a modal context. If we stored modal contexts, our normal form would be quadratic in size, and thus our algorithm would have a quadratic time and space complexity, as does the one from Goré and Nguyen [4]. Below is a trie that stores the above clauses:

$$\boxed{a_1 \ ; \ a_1 \rightarrow \square b_2} \xrightarrow{\square} \boxed{b_2 \rightarrow \diamond d_3} \xrightarrow{\square} \boxed{d_3 \rightarrow p_1 \ ; \ d_3 \rightarrow p_2}$$

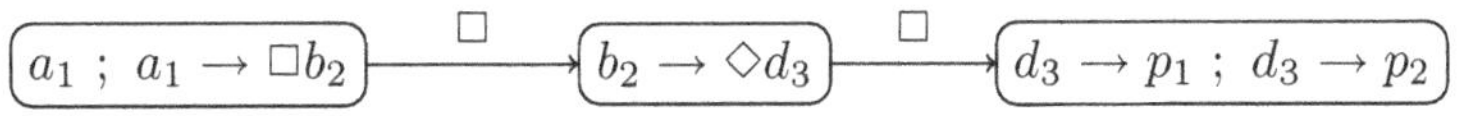

Each node of the trie at a given level (context) has the following components:

sat: A SAT-Solver initialised with the purely classical clauses $\mathcal{C}^{cpl}(.)$ in the node
BoxCl: the box clauses $\mathcal{C}^{\rightarrow\square}(.)$ of the form $a \rightarrow \square b$ in the node
DiaCl: the dia-clauses $\mathcal{C}^{\rightarrow\diamond}(.)$ of the form $c \rightarrow \diamond d$ in the node
Child(1): the node's (only) child node "containing" $\mathcal{MC}(.)$ as explained next.

Proposition 5. *If the input set of modal clauses is the set $w_0 := \mathcal{C}^{cpl}(w_0)$; $\mathcal{C}^{\rightarrow\square}(w_0)$; $\mathcal{C}^{\rightarrow\diamond}(w_0)$; $\square^1\mathcal{C}_1$; $\ldots$; $\square^k\mathcal{C}_k$ then the trie has depth equal to the maximal modal depth k of w_0 and $\forall i \geq 0$, `Trie.node` at depth i contains $\mathcal{C}_i := \mathcal{C}_i^{cpl}$; $\mathcal{C}_i^{\rightarrow\square}$; $\mathcal{C}_i^{\rightarrow\diamond}$ with `Trie.node.sat` $= \mathcal{C}_i^{cpl}$ and `Trie.node.BoxCl` $= \mathcal{C}_i^{\rightarrow\square}$ and `Trie.node.DiaCl` $= \mathcal{C}_i^{\rightarrow\diamond}$ and `Trie.node.Child(1)` $= \mathcal{C}_{i+1}$: as below.*

Logic	Trie Depth				Intuition where `TrieNode(i)` is i-th node of Trie
	0	1	$\cdots$	k	k is the maximum modal depth of the given w_0
K	$\mathcal{C}_0$	$\mathcal{C}_1$	$\cdots$	$\mathcal{C}_k$	finite chain with `TrieNode(k).child(1) = nil`

Algorithm 1 CEGARBox(A, TrieNode)

1: {Inputs: A is a set of unit assumptions and TrieNode is at level i in our trie}
2: Let $t_0 :=$ solve(TrieNode.sat, A) {*apply the (local) rule*}
3: **if** $t_0 =$ (unsat, A') **then**
4:    **return** Unsatisfiable(A')
5: **else if** $t_0 =$ (sat, ϑ) **then**
6:    {*Check box- and dia-clauses that fire under classical valuation* ϑ}
7:    **for** every $(c \to \Diamond d) \in$ TrieNode.DiaCl with $c \in \vartheta$ **do**
8:       Let $B = \{b \mid (a \to \Box b) \in$ TrieNode.BoxCl and $a \in \vartheta\}$
9:       {*apply the (jump) rule at next modal context*}
10:       **if** CEGARBox((d ; B), TrieNode.child(1)) = Unsatisfiable(X') **then**
11:          Let $C = \{c\} \cup \{a \mid (a \to \Box b) \in$ TrieNode.BoxCl and $a \in \vartheta$ and $b \in X'\}$
12:          { *Learn new clause* $\varphi := \neg C$}
13:          Let $\varphi := \bigvee_{l \in C} \neg l$
14:          addClause(TrieNode.sat, φ) {modify the i-th context globally}
15:          { *apply (restart)* }
16:          **return** CEGARBox(A, TrieNode)
17:       **end if**
18:    **end for**
19:    **return** Satisfiable {*because every fired diamond is fulfilled*}
20: **end if**

Fig. 2. The main algorithm of CEGARBox with A a set of unit assumptions

5.2 The Main Algorithm

Our algorithm follows Fiorentini et al.'s reworking [3] of intuit for propositional intuitionistic logic of Claessen and Rosén [1], which itself was "inspired" by bddtab of Goré et al. [5]. The pseudocode is in Fig. 2. Our implementation does **not** return an actual Kripke model, nor a closed tableau, as such, but it is trivial to extend it with the bookkeeping required to do so.

5.3 Inputs and Outputs

We write node.child(i) for the child labelled i of the trie rooted at node: as our logic is monomodal, $i = 1$. Similar to SAT-solvers we allow the use of a set of unit assumptions A. Our algorithm either returns Satisfiable, or Unsatisfiable(A'), where $A' \subset A$ is an unsatisfiable core of A.

We call CEGARBox(A, Trie) as the initial call with $A = \emptyset$.

Note that line 11 computes the correct conflict set as per the (jump)/(restart) rule because we ensure that no two box-clauses have the same RHS and no two dia-clauses have the same RHS, as explained later.

5.4 Use of Satisfiability Under Unit Assumptions

Note that in Line 10 of Fig. 2, we call the main algorithm recursively on Trie.child(1) with a set $X = (d\ ;\ B)$ of unit assumptions dependent

Logic	Trie Depth				Intuition where `TrieNode(i)` is i-th node of Trie
	0	1	$\cdots$	k	k is the maximum modal depth of the given w_0
K	$\mathcal{C}_0$	$\mathcal{C}_1$	$\cdots$	$\mathcal{C}_k$	finite chain with `TrieNode(k).child(1) = nil`
KT	$\mathcal{C}_0$	$\boldsymbol{\mathcal{C}}_1^k$	$\cdots$	$\boldsymbol{\mathcal{C}}_k^k$	descending chain with `TrieNode(k).child(1) = nil`
K4	$\mathcal{C}_0$	$\boldsymbol{\mathcal{C}}_1^1$	$\cdots$	$\boldsymbol{\mathcal{C}}_1^k$	ascending chain with `TrieNode(k).child(1) = TrieNode(k)`
S4	$\mathcal{C}_0; \boldsymbol{\mathcal{C}}_1^k$	$\boldsymbol{\mathcal{C}}_1^k$	$\cdots$	$\boldsymbol{\mathcal{C}}_1^k$	fixpoint at depth 1 with `TrieNode(1).child(1) = TrieNode(1)`

Fig. 3. The structure of the Trie for different logics with a modal context $\Box^0\mathcal{C}_0$; $\Box^1\mathcal{C}_1$; $\cdots$; $\Box^n\mathcal{C}_n$ and $\boldsymbol{\mathcal{C}}_i^n := \mathcal{C}_i$; $\cdots$; $\mathcal{C}_n$. For K, the modalised contexts form a descending chain $\boldsymbol{\mathcal{C}}_1^k \supseteq \boldsymbol{\mathcal{C}}_2^k \supseteq \cdots \supseteq \boldsymbol{\mathcal{C}}_k^k$ while for K4 (not implemented) they form an ascending chain $\boldsymbol{\mathcal{C}}_1^1 \subseteq \boldsymbol{\mathcal{C}}_1^2 \subseteq \cdots \subseteq \boldsymbol{\mathcal{C}}_1^k$. For S4, they are the constant $\boldsymbol{\mathcal{C}}_1^k$ after depth 1.

upon the fired dia-clause $c \to \Diamond d$. Moreover, this call is inside a for-loop which iterates over the fired diamonds. That is, if the set of fired diamonds is $\{c_1 \to \Diamond d_1, \cdots, c_n \to \Diamond d_n\}$, and the set of fired boxes gives $B = \{b \mid (a \to \Box b \in$ `Trie.BoxCl` and $a \in \vartheta\}$ then the putative n successor worlds must contain the unit assumption sets $X_1 = (d_1 \,;\, B)$ and $X_2 = (d_2 \,;\, B)$ up to $X_n = (d_n \,;\, B)$. We *iteratively* test the classical satisfiability of each set X_i ; `Trie.child(1)` by putting $X = (b_i \,;\, B)$ while keeping the parameter `Trie.child(1)` constant. This is sound because the sat-solver `Trie.child(1).sat` in `Trie.child(1)` undoes the assumptions it makes while computing the classical satisfiability of one set d_1 ; B ; `Trie.child(1)` (say) so that the same sat-solver `Trie.child(1).sat` can be reused for the next set d_2 ; B ; `Trie.child(1)` (say) without their interfering with each other. That is, this is only sound because our SAT-solver provides the ability to test for "satisfiability under unit assumptions".

5.5 Modal Clause Learning Modifies the Modal Context at Level i

Note that we learn a new cpl-clause in Line 14 via `addClause(Trie.sat,` φ`)`.

Consider a set of formulae and suppose that we saturate it using the traditional static tableau rules for cpl giving two OR-leaves, $\Diamond\varphi_1$; $\Box X_1$; $\Diamond Y_1$; L_1 and $\Diamond\varphi_2$; $\Box X_2$; $\Diamond Y_2$; L_2 where each L_i is a set of literals. Thus we can treat L_1/L_2 as a classical valuation ϑ_1/ϑ_2 which assigns all members of L_1/L_2 to true.

Suppose we try the successor φ_1 ; X_1 and find that it is modally unsatisfiable. Putting $\hat{X}_1$ for the conjunction of the members of X_1, we know that $\hat{X}_1 \to \neg\varphi_1$ is K-valid, independently of ϑ_1 itself. By necessition, we know that $\Box(\hat{X}_1 \to \neg\varphi_1)$ is K-valid. Goré et al. [5] tried to implement this insight into `bddtab` but it was refined nicely into the current form by Claessen and Rosén [1].

As explained previously, the i-th level of our `Trie` stores the cpl-clauses $\mathcal{C}_i^{cpl}$ from the i-th modal context $\Box^i\mathcal{C}_i$ inside the sat-solver `Trie.sat` at level i. Thus `addClause(Trie.sat,` φ`)` modifies the i-th modal context across level i.

We now describe extensions to handle the modal logics KT and S4.

6 Extensions to KT and S4

Three aspects of our framework handle modalities: the modal contexts $\Box\mathcal{MC} = \Box^1\mathcal{C}_1; \Box^2\mathcal{C}_2; \cdots ; \Box^k\mathcal{C}_k$ with $\mathcal{C}_i$ stored in the i-th level of the Trie; fired box-clauses $a \to \Box b$ when $\vartheta \models a$; and fired dia-clauses $c \to \Diamond d$ when $\vartheta \models c$.

Capturing Reflexivity. The characteristic axioms for reflexivity are $\Box\varphi \to \varphi$ and its dual $\varphi \to \Diamond\varphi$ so we make the following modification in these three aspects:

modal contexts: starting from level k, for all Trie nodes at levels $i \geq 1$, add `TrieNode.child(1)` to `TrieNode` so that the contexts in the `Trie` form a descending chain, building $\Box^i\mathcal{C}_i \to \mathcal{C}_i$ globally into the Trie, see Fig. 3

fired box-clauses: for every context $\mathcal{C}_i$ of modal clauses, if $(a \to \Box b) \in \mathcal{C}_i$, add the cpl-clause $(a \to b)$ to $\mathcal{C}_i$, building in the T-axiom $\Box b \to b$

fired dia-clauses: when calculating "fired" diamonds via "$(c \to \Diamond d) \in$ `Trie.DiaCl with` $c \in \vartheta$", add the extra condition "`and` $d \notin \vartheta$". Thus, $(c \to \Diamond d) \in \mathcal{C}^{cpl}(w_0)$ fires only if $\vartheta(w_0) \not\models d$ since w_0 is its own successor.

Termination is as before for K. Soundness is obvious. For completeness, take the reflexive closure of the tree-model created by our procedure. Why can the deepest world be made reflexive when `TrieNode(k)` is not its own child? It contains no box-clauses that fire so $\Box\varphi \to \varphi$ holds there vacuously.

Capturing Transitivity. Traditional proof-search in K4 can loop: e.g., the node $\{\Box\Diamond p, \Diamond p\}$ usually creates an infinite sequence of (K4)-successors each containing the set $\{p, \Box\Diamond p, \Diamond p\}$, leading to an infinite branch unless we check for ancestor loops. Thus the modal satisfiability of a given world depends not only on its assumptions but also on its ancestors because a world w might be modally satisfied only because some descendent v of w loops back to one of w's ancestors.

The characteristic axiom $\Box\varphi \to \Box\Box\varphi$ for transitivity implies that $\Box\varphi \to \Box^i\varphi$ for all $i \geq 1$. So the modal contexts form an ascending chain: see Fig. 3.

modal contexts: In the K4 `Trie`, the k-th level is its own child and level i contains $\mathcal{C}_1^n := \mathcal{C}_1 \ ; \ \cdots \ ; \ \mathcal{C}_n$ building in $\Box\varphi \to \Box\Box\varphi$;

fired box-clauses: In the i-th node of `Trie`, replace every box-clause $a \to \Box b$ with $a \to \Box P_b$, and add the modal clauses $P_b \to \Box P_b$ and $P_b \to b$ to every node of the Trie from $i+1$ to k where P_b is a new propositional variable for "persistent b", thereby encoding a finite state automaton that effectively turns $a \to \Box b$ into $a \to \Box^{j \geq i} b$, a technique from description logic tableaux;

ancestor loop-check: We add an additional input to `CEGARBox`, which is a list of the classical valuations found for the ancestors of the current world w_0. If w_0 requires us to fulfil $\Diamond d \ ; \ \Box B$, where $A = (d \ ; \ B)$ and some ancestor w_a, has $\vartheta(w_a) \models A$, then we can return satisfiable because we can just put $w_0 R w_a$.

Termination follows via ancestor loop-check. Soundness follows by noting that the above transformations are all sound. For completeness, we just take the transitive closure of our Kripke model.

Capturing Reflexivity and Transitivity Together. We add the changes for both KT and K4 as outlined above. The axiom $\Box\varphi \rightarrow \varphi$ made our Trie into a descending chain while the axiom $\Box\varphi \rightarrow \Box\Box\varphi$ made our Trie into an ascending chain, so adding both means that our Trie contains only two levels 0 and 1 with the second level being a fixed point. That is, level 1 is its own child with level 0 containing $\mathcal{C}_0$; $\mathcal{C}_1^n$ and level 1 containing $\mathcal{C}_1^n$: see Fig. 3.

Termination is by ancestor loop-check. Soundness follows by seeing that we are effectively encoding both of the (KT) and (K4) rules. For completeness, we just take the reflexive and transitive closure of our underlying Kripke model.

7 Optimisations Which Made `CEGARBox` faster

We utilise standard simplification techniques, truth propagation, formula sorting for the renaming process, and box lifting as described by Sebastiani and Vescovi [15]. We also used techniques from Nalon et al. [12] when normal forming to avoid new literals when old ones suffice. For modal logic K, this was implemented by keeping a map in every modal context that associates the literal l with the formula φ it names. Then when renaming any occurrence of φ, we check the map, and find l. For reflexivity, we can instead use a global map.

For brevity, we skip many small optimisations which allow us to avoid new literals, as each such literal potentially doubles the number of classical valuations the SAT-solvers need to search.

The running time of our algorithm depends on the number of box- and dia-clauses, so our final processing stage involves replacing these with cpl-clauses. Intuitively, the SAT-solver is better at handling cpl-clauses than `CEGARBox` is at handling modal clauses. We therefore do the following:

1. If two box-clauses $\{a_1 \rightarrow \Box b, a_2 \rightarrow \Box b\}$ or dia-clauses $\{a_1 \rightarrow \Diamond b, a_2 \rightarrow \Diamond b\}$, share a RHS b, create a new atomic formula p_a and replace them with $\{p_a \rightarrow \Box b / \Diamond b,\ a_1 \rightarrow p_a,\ a_2 \rightarrow p_a\}$ so that no two RHSs are the same.
2. If two box clauses $\{a \rightarrow \Box b, a \rightarrow \Box c\}$ share a LHS a, create a new literal p_a and replace these modal clauses with $a \rightarrow \Box p_a$, $\Box(p_a \rightarrow b)$, and $\Box(p_a \rightarrow c)$, thereby moving information from the box-clauses into the modal context;

We use negative polarity for all literals in MiniSAT so it sets unknown variables to false, thus decreasing the number of box- and dia-clauses that fire.

7.1 Reducing the Number of Dia-Clauses

We make minor changes to the algorithm of `CEGARBox` from Fig. 2. First, the previous optimisations mean that no two triggered dia-clauses have the same RHS, however, a triggered box $a \rightarrow \Box r$ and a triggered diamond clause $c \rightarrow \Diamond r$ may share the subformula r. Then, we can typically reduce the number of dia-clauses we have to consider. Let B and D be the set of RHSs of triggered box and dia-clauses, respectively. Instead of checking B ; d for every $d \in D$, we can skip those with $d \in B$, as any world created by another triggered diamond clause will contain d. For the case $D \setminus B = \emptyset$ with $D \neq \emptyset$, we just check one diamond clause, as this one world (if created) will contain D.

If a conflict set X' for some fired diamond contains literals only from box-clauses, we know the box-clauses have no consistent successor, so we can learn the appropriate clauses for all (fired and unfired) dia-clauses in one hit.

Finally, note that we can learn a new clause only when we find an unfulfillable dia-clause. We experimented with a heuristic to remember unfulfillable dia-clauses by tracking how many times a given dia-clause lead to Unsatisfiable, and sorted them highest to lowest. In general this lead to improvements, but for some benchmarks the overhead of sorting lead to a slower time. So we experimented with a quicker approximation which instead just moves a clause to the front of the list when it leads to Unsatisfiable, which also lead to performance improvements. However, placing the failed dia-clauses at the end also lead to performance improvements, and requires further investigation.

7.2 Memoisation of Satisfiable Assumptions

Memoisation of Satisfiable Assumptions in K. We can store which assumptions have lead to Satisfiable wrt each particular modal context. During proof search, if we find that the current unit assumptions have been found to be satisfiable in the given modal context, we can immediately return Satisfiable, saving time.

We call this exact-cache, as we only return Satisfiable if we find that the exact same assumptions have lead to Satisfiable before. Assumptions were stored in a Binary Tree based implementation of a set. We experimented with a "subset cache" approach which returns Satisfiable if the current assumptions is a subset of any cached assumptions. To get more matches, once we find that some unit assumptions leads to satisfiable we would store not the unit assumptions but rather the whole classical valuation instead. While this gave more matches, it was implemented with the slow process of checking each set in the cache individually, which made it slower than exact-cache. A faster way of implementing a subset check over a collection of sets may make "subset cache" more feasible.

Memoisation of Satisfiable Assumptions in KT. Descending chains mean that an assumptions set A that leads to Satisfiable in the modal context $\Box^i$ will also lead to Satisfiable in the modal context $\Box^{i+1}$. Thus we can use a global cache, instead of a cache for each modal context, and store the assumptions A as well as the smallest i for which it returns Satisfiable at modal context $\Box^i$. Then when searching the assumptions in the modal context $\Box^{j \geq i}$ we immediately return Satisfiable if the assumptions occurs in the cache.

Conversely, any clause learnt in the modal context $\Box^i$ applies to the modal context $\Box^{i-1}$ since context $\Box^i$ is a subset of context $\Box^{i-1}$: not implemented yet.

Loop-Check and Memoisation of Satisfiability in S4. Recall that traditional proof-search in S4 require a loop-check for termination.

Caching not just the assumptions of a world but also its ancestors would work, however it is unlikely matches would ever occur, leading to a limited speed up. Instead we take a different approach, that allows us to avoid storing any information related to ancestors in the cache. The idea is to store worlds only if every world reachable from it is modally satisfiable. That is, if a world w_1 has been deemed to be modally satisfiable, but uses a back edge to w_0, we will only add w_1 to the cache once w_0 has been shown to be modally satisfiable.

So we modify the proof search to look for maximally isolated subgraphs: that is, submodels with a world that reaches only its descendants. Formally, a world w such that there is no back edge connecting a descendent of w to an ancestor of w. When w becomes satisfiable, we add all its descendants to the cache.

7.3 Two Phase Caching

One problem with the previous approach is that in the worst case the highest world reachable by a world might be so high (e.g. the root), that the procedure never caches any worlds leading to no speed improvements.

Suppose world y is satisfiable if an ancestor world x is satisfiable. Previously, we only cache y if and when x becomes satisfiable but we can actually treat y as cached satisfiable for all descendants of x. Such two-phase caching means y is in a temporary cache until x becomes satisfiable, when it moves to a global cache.

Caution: we have to check for self contained models inside bigger ones.

8 Benchmarks and Issues with MOSAIC

We now outline various issues we found during our experiments. Our benchmarks are from Nalon et al. [12] and (corrected) Lagniez et al. [9]:

LWB: extended LWB benchmarks created by Nalon et al. [12] but which need to be generated *in situ* from their instructions as they can take up 14 GB;
3CNF: 1000 randomly generated $3CNF_K$ formulae over 3 to 10 propositional variables with modal depth 1 or 2 with 457 satisfiable and 464 unsatisfiable;
MQBF: the complete set of TANCS-2000 modalised random QBF formulae and the MQBF formulae provided by Kaminski and Tebbi.
KT and S4: the corrected extended benchmarks from MOSAIC.

The "new kid on the block" is MOSAIC, by Lagniez et al. [9]. But some of their extended LWB benchmark files were blank, unreadable, or lead to incorrect answers. We have confirmed these with Daniel Le Berre.

Daniel Le Berre sent us an executable binary for the latest version MOSAIC 2.4. Unfortunately, MOSAIC 2.4 returned wrong answers for many (corrected) benchmarks. Daniel Le Berre has retrospectively confirmed that MOSAIC 2.0 was also unsound. These issues undermine all of their experimental results [9].

We re-implemented the extended benchmark generator in python and confirmed that there were no differences with the original, smaller benchmarks.

9 Experimental Results

We used the following options: InKreSAT 1.0 - default; FaCT++ 1.6.3 - default; Spartacus 1.1.3 - default; BDDTab 1.0 - default; K_SP 0.1.3 - ordered; and Vampire 4.5.1 (OFT) (optimised functional translation) provided by Ullrich Hustadt. Our virtual machine had an Intel Xeon E5-2640@2.40 GHz CPU and 8GB of RAM. We also checked that all provers gave the same answers.

On the MQBF benchmarks, `ksp` is best, with `CEGARBox` second (Fig. 4). On the extended K-LWB benchmarks, `CEGARBox` is best (Fig. 4) with all 56 problems solved in the classes d4_n, d4_p, dum_n, dum_p, lin_n, path_n, path_p, poly_n, and poly_p within 15 s even though *"only the best current provers, if any at all, will be able to solve all the formulae within a time limit of 1000 CPU seconds"* [12]. No other prover managed to solve all 56 problems in any class. In 3CNF, `CEGARBox` triumphs after 1 s (Fig. 4). Over all K-benchmarks, `CEGARBox` at rougly 0.7 s beats every other prover at 15 s (Fig. 4). Indeed over all K-benchmarks, `CEGARBox` solves almost 2500 problems in just 15 s while Nalon et al. [13] report that no other prover solved more than about 2400 problems with 1000 s (16GB). For KT, `CEGARBox` dominates after 1 s (Fig. 5). For S4, `CEGARBox` is by far the best prover, beating every other prover within 0.25 s and solving over 600 problems in 15 s while the best other prover, `bddtab`, solves only 350 (Fig. 5).

10 Related Work

All SAT-based provers except `bddtab`, `intuit` and `CEGARBox` use explicit names for the reachability relation R: for example, a clause $r_{ij} \rightarrow \cdots$ encodes that "if world j is a successor of world i then ...". Instead, we put all formulae into their context while initialising the trie. Via the propositions about modal contexts, we can also move all formulae from modal contexts i to j directly. We believe that this is the reason for the massive improvement seen in our experiments.

As already stated, our approach is based on one from Claessen and Rosén [1], which itself was "inspired" by that of Goré et al. [5], so we articulate the differences. First, `intuit` handles propositional intuitionistic logic (Int), which is characterised by finite, rooted, reflexive and transitive Kripke models without any proper clusters, but as shown by Fiorentini et al. [3], `intuit` implements the loop-free sequent calculus g4ip so termination is not an issue. Second, the persistence property of Kripke models for Int allows them to propagate all formulae "along" the reachability relation using one incremental SAT-solver, while we must discard non-boxed formulae. Third, Claessen and Rosén outline "further work" for classical modal logics using only one SAT-solver, using a similar normal form, only one outermost $\Box$-context and a similar algorithm to ours, but we cannot find anything published about this work. They also do not mention reflexivity, transitivity, caching, loop-checking or optimisations. Thus our work is not "just an implementation of Claessen and Rosén".

InKreSAT [8] interleaves encoding phases with calls to an incremental SAT solver, but uses a labelled tableau calculus, and keeps an explicit encoding of R.

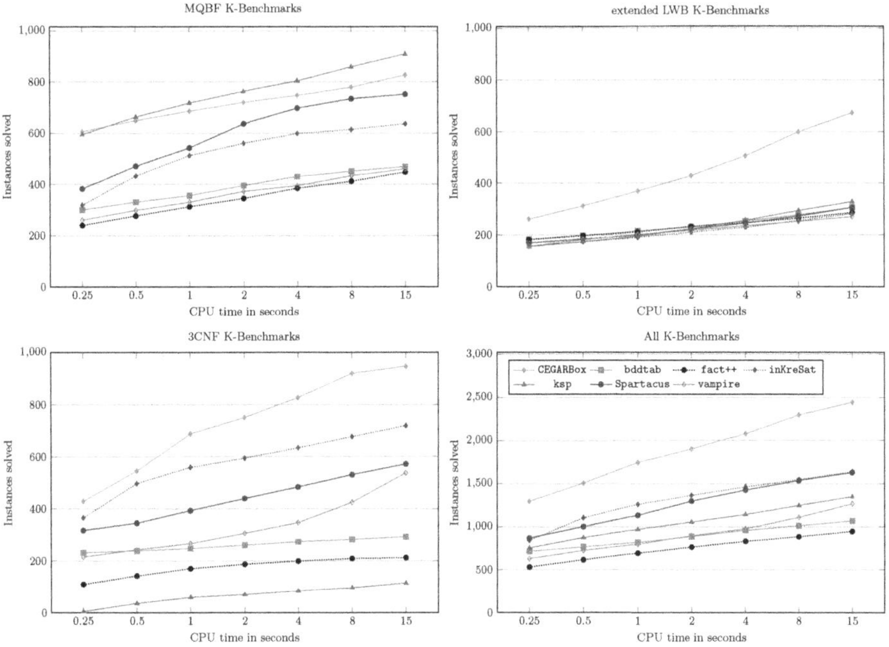

Fig. 4. Experimental results for the (extended) K benchmarks

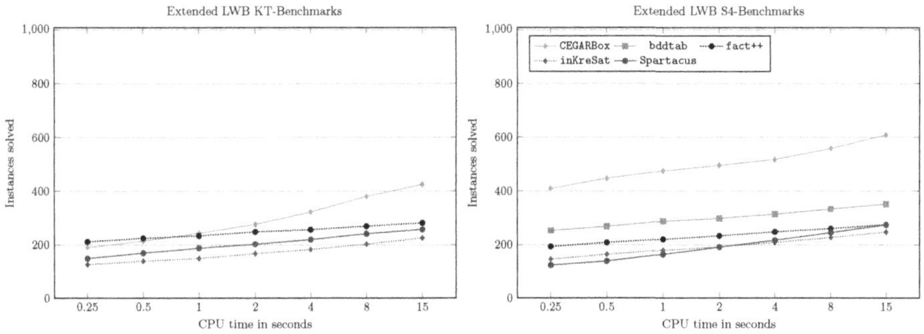

Fig. 5. Experimental results for the extended and corrected KT and S4 benchmarks

11 Further Work and Conclusions

Better heuristics for clause ordering will allow for both Sat and Unsat shortcuts. For example, we found it is possible to solve all instances of branch_p with one clause learnt per modal context but our final prover does not use this ordering.

Our K prover can be extended trivially to multi-modal logics, however for reflexive relations, the number of modal contexts a clause can belong to increases drastically, which most likely would slow down our prover as the number of different modalities increases. By ensuring that each subformula ψ is named uniquely with p_ψ, we can avoid keeping contexts and put $p_\psi \to \psi$ "globally". It is also easy to extend our prover to handle local and global assumptions. Symmetric relations require the notion of "too small" from Goré and Widmann [6].

Overall, `CEGARBox` is arguably the best prover for K, KT, and S4 on the standard benchmarks, sometimes by orders of magnitude.

Our repository is here: https://github.com/cormackikkert/CEGARBox.

Clearly, efficient SAT-based CEGAR-tableaux are possible for many different non-classical logics, including intuitionistic and modal (description) logics!

Finally, there is a very close connection between CEGAR-tableaux and the KE-tableaux of D'Agostino and Mondadori [2] which we are currently investigating. In particular, note that our proofs utilise a meta-level *semantic* cut-rule rather than a syntactic cut-rule: that is we have identified and absorbed all syntactic cuts required by KE-tableaux into the (jump)/(restart) rule!

Acknowledgment. Work supported by the FWF projects I 2982 and P 33548.

References

1. Claessen, K., Rosén, D.: SAT modulo intuitionistic implications. In: Davis, M., Fehnker, A., McIver, A., Voronkov, A. (eds.) LPAR 2015. LNCS, vol. 9450, pp. 622–637. Springer, Heidelberg (2015). https://doi.org/10.1007/978-3-662-48899-7_43
2. D'Agostino, M., Mondadori, M.: The taming of the cut. Classical refutations with analytic cut. J. Log. Comput. **4**(3), 285–319 (1994)
3. Fiorentini, C., Goré, R., Graham-Lengrand, S.: A proof-theoretic perspective on SMT-solving for intuitionistic propositional logic. In: Cerrito, S., Popescu, A. (eds.) TABLEAUX 2019. LNCS (LNAI), vol. 11714, pp. 111–129. Springer, Cham (2019). https://doi.org/10.1007/978-3-030-29026-9_7
4. Goré, R., Nguyen, L.A.: Clausal tableaux for multimodal logics of belief. Fundam. Informaticae **94**(1), 21–40 (2009)
5. Goré, R., Olesen, K., Thomson, J.: Implementing tableau calculi using BDDs: BDDTab system description. In: Demri, S., Kapur, D., Weidenbach, C. (eds.) IJCAR 2014. LNCS (LNAI), vol. 8562, pp. 337–343. Springer, Cham (2014). https://doi.org/10.1007/978-3-319-08587-6_25
6. Goré, R., Widmann, F.: Optimal and cut-free tableaux for propositional dynamic logic with converse. In: Giesl, J., Hähnle, R. (eds.) IJCAR 2010. LNCS (LNAI), vol. 6173, pp. 225–239. Springer, Heidelberg (2010). https://doi.org/10.1007/978-3-642-14203-1_20
7. Bayardo, Jr., R.J., Schrag, R.: Using CSP look-back techniques to solve real-world SAT instances. In: Kuipers, B., Webber, B.L. (eds.) Proceedings of the Fourteenth National Conference on Artificial Intelligence and Ninth Innovative Applications of Artificial Intelligence Conference, AAAI 97, IAAI 97, Providence, Rhode Island, USA, 27–31 July 1997, pp. 203–208. AAAI Press/The MIT Press (1997)
8. Kaminski, M., Tebbi, T.: InKreSAT: modal reasoning via incremental reduction to SAT. In: Bonacina, M.P. (ed.) CADE 2013. LNCS (LNAI), vol. 7898, pp. 436–442. Springer, Heidelberg (2013). https://doi.org/10.1007/978-3-642-38574-2_31

9. Lagniez, J.-M., Le Berre, D., de Lima, T., Montmirail, V.: A recursive shortcut for CEGAR: application to the modal logic K satisfiability problem. In: Sierra, C. (ed.) Proceedings of the Twenty-Sixth International Joint Conference on Artificial Intelligence, IJCAI 2017, Melbourne, Australia, 19–25 August 2017, pp. 674–680. ijcai.org (2017)
10. Marques-Silva, J.P., Sakallah, K.A.: GRASP - a new search algorithm for satisfiability. In: Rutenbar, R.A., Otten, R.H.J.M. (eds.) Proceedings of the 1996 IEEE/ACM International Conference on Computer-Aided Design, ICCAD 1996, San Jose, CA, USA, 10–14 November 1996, pp. 220–227. IEEE Computer Society/ACM (1996)
11. Mints, G.: Gentzen-type systems and resolution rules. In: Mints, G., Martin-Löf, P. (ed.) COLOG-88. LNCS, vol. 417, pp. 516–537. Springer (1988)
12. Nalon, C., Hustadt, U., Dixon, C.: KSP: a resolution-based prover for multimodal K, abridged report. In: Sierra, C. (ed.) Proceedings of the Twenty-Sixth International Joint Conference on Artificial Intelligence, IJCAI 2017, Melbourne, Australia, 19–25 August 2017, pp. 4919–4923. ijcai.org (2017)
13. Nalon, C., Hustadt, U., Dixon, C.: KSP: a resolution-based prover for multimodal K_n: architecture, refinements, strategies and experiments. J. Autom. Reason. **64**(3), 461–484 (2020)
14. Sörensson, N., Een, N.: http://minisat.se/Papers.html. Accessed 10 Feb 2020
15. Sebastiani, R., Tacchella, A.: SAT techniques for modal and description logics. In: Biere, A., Heule, M., van Maaren, H., Walsh, T. (eds.) Handbook of Satisfiability. Frontiers in Artificial Intelligence and Applications, vol. 185, pp. 781–824. IOS Press (2009)
16. Various. http://www.satcompetition.org/. Accessed 10 Feb 2020

Sequent Calculi

Proof-Theory and Semantics for a Theory of Definite Descriptions

Nils Kürbis[1,2(✉)]

[1] Department of Logic and Methodology of Science, University of Łódź, Łódź, Poland
nils.kurbis@filhist.uni.lodz.pl
[2] Department of Philosophie I, University of Bochum, Bochum, Germany
https://www.nilskurbis.weebly.com

Abstract. This paper presents a sequent calculus and a dual domain semantics for a theory of definite descriptions in which these expressions are formalised in the context of complete sentences by a binary quantifier I. I forms a formula from two formulas. $Ix[F, G]$ means 'The F is G'. This approach has the advantage of incorporating scope distinctions directly into the notation. Cut elimination is proved for a system of classical positive free logic with I and it is shown to be sound and complete for the semantics. The system has a number of novel features and is briefly compared to the usual approach of formalising 'the F' by a term forming operator. It does not coincide with Hintikka's and Lambert's preferred theories, but the divergence is well-motivated and attractive.

Keywords: Definite descriptions · Positive free logic · Proof theory · Sequent calculus · Cut elimination · Dual domain semantics

1 Introduction

A definite description is an expression of the form 'the F'. Accordingly, the most popular formalisations of the theory of definite descriptions treat them as term forming operators: the operator ι binds a variable and turns an open formula into a singular term ιxF. This treatment of definite descriptions goes back to Whitehead and Russell [34].[1] Whitehead and Russell, however, did not consider definite descriptions to be genuine singular terms: they only have meaning in the context of complete sentences in which they occur and disappear upon analysis: 'The F is G' is logically equivalent to 'There is one and only one F and it is

[1] Frege's treatment of the function that is a 'substitute for the definite article' is different. Frege's operator $\backslash$ applies to names of objects, not to (simple or complex) predicates or function symbols. Typically these names refer to the extensions of concepts, but this is not necessary. $\backslash\xi$ returns the unique object that falls under a concept, if ξ is a name of the extension of a concept under which a unique object falls, and its argument in all other cases. See [9, §11].

The research in this paper was funded by the Alexander von Humboldt Foundation.

A. Das and S. Negri (Eds.): TABLEAUX 2021, LNAI 12842, pp. 95–111, 2021.
https://doi.org/10.1007/978-3-030-86059-2_6

G'. Following the work of Hinitkka [12] and Lambert [25], many logicians prefer to formalise definite descriptions in a fashion where they are not straightforwardly eliminable. In such systems, ι is governed by what has come to be called *Lambert's Law*:

$$(LL) \quad \forall y(\iota xFx = y \leftrightarrow \forall x(Fx \leftrightarrow x = y))$$

The preferred logic of many free logicians is *positive free logic*, where formulas containing names that do not refer (to objects considered amongst those that exist) may be true. Then 'The F is G' is no longer equivalent to 'There is one and only one F and it is G'. In *negative free logic*, all atomic formulas containing non-denoting terms are false, and the Russellian analysis is again appropriate.

There is agreement amongst free logicians that (LL) formalises the minimal theory of definite descriptions. Lambert himself prefers a stronger theory [26] that in addition has the axiom:[2]

$$(FL) \quad t = \iota x(x = t)$$

There are a number of other axioms that have been considered, but these two will be the focus of the present investigation.[3] The proof theory of the theory of definite descriptions has received close study from the hands of Andrzej Indrzejczak.[4] In a series of papers, Indrzejczak has investigated various formalisations of theories of definite descriptions and provided cut free sequent calculi for them [14–17,19]. A cut free system of positive free logic of his will form the background to the present paper. It is presented in the next section.

Whitehead and Russell also note the need for marking scope distinctions to formalise the difference between 'The F is not G' and 'It is not the case that the F is G'. Free definite description theory in general ignores scope: the thought is that free logic says only very little about definite descriptions when they do not refer, and in case they do refer, scope distinctions no longer matter, as already pointed out by Whitehead and Russell.

Scope distinctions are, however, worth considering. The present paper proposes a proof-system and a semantics for a theory of definite descriptions in which scope distinctions are incorporated directly into the symbolism. 'The F is G' is formalised by a binary quantifier that takes two formulas and forms a formula $Ix[F, G]$ out of them. The notation is taken from Dummett [5, p.162]. It is also found in the work of Neale [31] and Bostock [2, Sec. 8.4]. The external negation 'It is not the case that the F is G' is formalised by $\neg Ix[F, G]$, the internal negation 'The F is not G' by $Ix[F, \neg G]$. Natural deduction proof-systems for this approach have been investigated by the present author in the context of intuitionist non-free as well as negative and positive free logic [20,21,23]. Rules suitable for a sequent calculus for classical positive free logic were formulated

[2] This axiom bears some resemblance to Frege's Basic Law VI, the sole axiom for his operator $\backslash$, which is $a = \backslash\acute{\varepsilon}(a = \varepsilon)$ [9, §18]. But see footnote 1.

[3] For a survey of various theories and their axioms, see [1,8,27,30].

[4] An earlier approach is by Czermak [4]. Gratzl provides a cut free proof system for Russell's theory of definite descriptions, including his method for marking scope [11].

in [22].[5] The latter system and its intuitionist counterpart were devised with the intention to stay close to the systems of Hintikka and Lambert. The results are rather complicated: I is governed by six rules, one right or introduction rule and five left or elimination rules. Despite their complexities, the systems remain proof-theoretically satisfactory as cut elimination and normalisation theorems hold for them. The present paper severs the ties to Hintikka and Lambert and considers alternative rules for I within classical positive free logic. The account proposed here is rather simpler than the previous ones: I is governed by one right rule, the same as before, but only two left rules. The result is a rather different formal theory from the perspective of the validities provable from the rules and compared to Hintikka's and Lambert's: the rules enforce the uniqueness of F, if $Ix[F,G]$ is true, but not its existence. The novelty of the present paper lies in the addition of these new rules for I to classical positive free logic,[6] the ensuing alternative theory of definite descriptions, and the provision of a sound and complete dual domain semantics for it.

The plan of this paper is as follows. The next section expounds Indrzejczak's sequent calculus formulation of classical positive free logic extended by rules governing the binary quantifier I. Section 3 discusses consequences of the theory and compares it to Hintikka's and Lambert's. Due to the absence of scope distinctions in axiomatisations of ι based on (LL), a direct comparison between the system proposed here and standard formalisations of definite descriptions is not very illuminating: $G(\iota xF)$ has no direct and natural correspondent, as $\neg G(\iota xF)$ corresponds to two formulas, the internal and the external negation of $Ix[F,G]$. Nonetheless, it is worth examining how the binary fares with respect to analogues of(LL) and (FL), when $\iota xA = y$ is rendered as a binary quantification $Ix[A, x = y]$. The latter formalises 'The A is identical to y', or 'The A is y' for short, which is exactly the reading one may give of $\iota xA = y$. To anticipate, while an analogue of (FL) is derivable in the system proposes here, only half of an analogue of (LL) is. Section 4 proves that cut is still eliminable from the extended system. Section 5 gives a formal semantics for classical positive free logic extended by I. Section 6 proves the soundness and completeness of the system. Some details of the completeness proof are relegated to the appendix for the online version of this paper [24]. Section 7 gives rules tableaux proof system.

2 A Deductive Calculus for Classical Positive Free Logic with a Binary Quantifier

Indrzejczak has provided a formalisation of classical positive free logic **CPF** in sequent calculus with desirable proof-theoretic properties: cut is eliminable from

[5] This paper also briefly considers rules for classical non-free and negative free logic.

[6] The rules are, in fact, those given for non-free classical logic at the end of [22]: it is a noteworthy result that, whereas in the context of this logic these rules are redundant and $Ix[F,G]$ definable in Russellian fashion as $\exists x(F \wedge \forall y(F^x_y \rightarrow x = y) \wedge G)$, added to classical positive free logic, the outcome is a theory of considerable logical and philosophical interest.

the system [18]. The definition of the language is standard. I will only consider $\to$, $\neg$, $\forall$ and a distinguished predicate symbol $\exists!$, the existence predicate, as primitives.[7] $\wedge$, $\vee$, $\exists$ are defined as usual. Free variables are distinguished from bound ones by the use of parameters $a, b, c \ldots$ for the former and $x, y, z \ldots$ for the latter. $t_1, t_2, t_3 \ldots$ range over the terms of the language, which are the parameters, constants, and complex terms formed from them and function symbols. For brevity I will write F or A instead of $F(x)$ or $A(x)$ etc., except in the case of the existence predicate, where I'll write $\exists!x$ etc. A^x_t is the result of substituting t for x in A, where it is assumed that no variable free in t becomes bound in A^x_t, i.e. that t is free for x in A. Γ, Δ denote finite multisets of formulas. The rules of **CPF** are as follows:

$$(\text{Ax}) \quad A \Rightarrow A \qquad\qquad \text{Cut}\ \frac{\Gamma \Rightarrow \Theta, A \qquad A, \Delta \Rightarrow \Lambda}{\Gamma, \Delta \Rightarrow \Theta, \Lambda}$$

$$(\text{LW})\ \frac{\Gamma \Rightarrow \Delta}{A, \Gamma \Rightarrow \Delta} \qquad\qquad (\text{RW})\ \frac{\Gamma \Rightarrow \Delta}{\Gamma \Rightarrow \Delta, A}$$

$$(\text{LC})\ \frac{A, A, \Gamma \Rightarrow \Delta}{A, \Gamma \Rightarrow \Delta} \qquad\qquad (\text{RC})\ \frac{\Gamma \Rightarrow \Delta, A, A}{\Gamma \Rightarrow \Delta, A}$$

$$(L\neg)\ \frac{\Gamma \Rightarrow \Delta, A}{\neg A, \Gamma \Rightarrow \Delta} \qquad\qquad (R\neg)\ \frac{A, \Gamma \Rightarrow \Delta}{\Gamma \Rightarrow \Delta, \neg A}$$

$$(L\to)\ \frac{\Gamma \Rightarrow \Delta, A \qquad B, \Gamma \Rightarrow \Delta}{A \to B, \Gamma \Rightarrow \Delta} \qquad (R\to)\ \frac{A, \Gamma \Rightarrow \Delta, B}{\Gamma \Rightarrow \Delta, A \to B}$$

$$(L\forall)\ \frac{A^x_t, \Gamma \Rightarrow \Delta}{\exists!t, \forall x A, \Gamma \Rightarrow \Delta} \qquad\qquad (R\forall)\ \frac{\exists!a, \Gamma \Rightarrow \Delta, A^x_a}{\Gamma \Rightarrow \Delta, \forall x A}$$

$$(=I)\ \frac{A^x_{t_2}, \Gamma \Rightarrow \Delta}{t_1 = t_2, A^x_{t_1}, \Gamma \Rightarrow \Delta} \qquad\qquad (=E)\ \frac{t = t, \Gamma \Rightarrow \Delta}{\Gamma \Rightarrow \Delta}$$

where in $(R\forall)$, a does not occur in the conclusion, and in $(L\forall)$, t is substitutable for x in A. In $(=I)$, A is atomic. The general case follows by induction.

To these we add rules for the binary quantifier I:

$$(RI)\ \frac{\Gamma \Rightarrow \Delta, A^x_t \qquad \Gamma \Rightarrow \Delta, B^x_t \qquad A^x_a, \Gamma \Rightarrow \Delta, a = t}{\Gamma \Rightarrow \Delta, Ix[A, B]}$$

[7] It would be possible to define $\exists!t$ as $\exists x\ x = t$, where $\exists$ may in turn be defined in terms of $\forall$ and $\neg$. However, treating it as primitive is formally and philosophically preferable: formally, it lends itself more easily to cut elimination, and philosophically, it permits to take existence as conceptually basic, with the quantifiers explained in terms of it: the attempted definition of $\exists!$ is arguably circular, as the rules of inference governing $\forall$, which explain its meaning, appeal to $\exists!$. The semantic clause for $\forall$, too, implicitly appeals to the concept of existence, as it ranges only over objects in the domain of the model which are considered to exist, that is, those of which $\exists!$ is true.

$$(LI^1)\quad \frac{A^x_a, B^x_a, \Gamma \Rightarrow \Delta}{Ix[A,B], \Gamma \Rightarrow \Delta}$$

$$(LI^2)\quad \frac{\Gamma \Rightarrow \Delta, A^x_{t_1} \qquad \Gamma \Rightarrow \Delta, A^x_{t_2} \qquad \Gamma \Rightarrow \Delta, C^x_{t_2}}{Ix[A,B], \Gamma \Rightarrow \Delta, C^x_{t_1}}$$

where in (RI) and (LI^1), a does not occur in the conclusion, and in (LI^2) C is an atomic formula. The general case follows by induction.

Vacuous quantification with I is allowed. If x is not free in A, then the truth of $Ix[A,B]$ requires or imposes a restriction on the domain: if there is only one object (existing or not), then, if A is true and B is true (of the object in the domain, if x is free in B), then $Ix[A,B]$ is true; and if $Ix[A,B]$ is true, then, if A is true, then there is only one object in the domain and B is true (of it, if x is free in B). If x is not free in B, then $Ix[A,B]$ is true if and only if a unique object (existing or not) is A and B is true.

Call the resulting system $\mathbf{CPF}^I$. Deductions are defined as usual, as certain trees with axioms at the top-nodes or leaves and the conclusion at the bottom-node or root. If a sequent $\Gamma \Rightarrow \Delta$ is deducible in $\mathbf{CPF}^I$, we write $\vdash \Gamma \Rightarrow \Delta$.

3 Consequences of the Formalisation

Call two formulas $\iota x A = y$ and $Ix[A, x = y]$ *analogues* of each other. They both formalise the same sentence 'The A is identical to y'. Similarly for $B(\iota x A)$ and $Ix[A,B]$, where we restrict B to atomic formulas to avoid complications regarding scope. Let $\mathbf{CPF}^\iota$ be $\mathbf{CPF}$ plus (LL) and (FL). Analogues provide a convenient means for comparisons between $\mathbf{CPF}^I$ and $\mathbf{CPF}^\iota$.

First we state the obvious. The Law of Identity $\Rightarrow t = t$ and Leibniz' Law $t_1 = t_2, A^x_{t_2} \Rightarrow A^x_{t_1}$ are derivable in $\mathbf{CPF}$:

$$\frac{t = t \Rightarrow t = t}{\Rightarrow t = t} \qquad \frac{\dfrac{\dfrac{A^x_{t_1} \Rightarrow A^x_{t_1}}{t_2 = t_1, A^x_{t_2} \Rightarrow A^x_{t_1}}}{t_1 = t_2, t_1 = t_1, A^x_{t_2} \Rightarrow A^x_{t_1}}}{t_1 = t_2, A^x_{t_2} \Rightarrow A^x_{t_1}}$$

$t_1 = t_2, A^x_{t_1} \Rightarrow A^x_{t_2}$ of course also holds, as established by step two of the left deduction through interchanging t_1 and t_2.

Leibniz' Law is no longer applicable to definite descriptions in the present framework, as definite descriptions are not analysed as singular terms but only in the context of complete sentences in which they occur. We can, however, mimic its use, as we can derive the sequents $Ix[A, x = t], B^x_t \Rightarrow Ix[A,B]$, $Ix[A, x = t], Ix[A,B], \Rightarrow B^x_t$ and $Ix[A, Iy[B, x = y]], Ix[A,C] \Rightarrow Ix[B,C]$. Using analogues, these correspond to instances of Leibniz' Law: $\iota x A = t, B^x_t \Rightarrow B(\iota x A)$, $\iota x A = t, B(\iota x A), \Rightarrow B^x_t$ and $\iota x A = \iota y B, C(\iota x A) \Rightarrow C(\iota y B)$. We'll prove the first for purposes of illustration. Double lines indicate applications of structural rules, in particular those needed to make the contexts of the rules identical by Thinning. Let Π be the following deduction in $\mathbf{CPF}^I$:

$$
\begin{array}{c}
A^x_b \Rightarrow A^x_b \qquad a = t, A^x_a \Rightarrow A^x_t \qquad \Rightarrow t = t \\
\hline\hline
Ix[A, x = t], A^x_b, a = t, A^x_a \Rightarrow b = t \\
\hline
Ix[A, x = t], Ix[A, x = t], A^x_b \Rightarrow b = t \\
\hline
Ix[A, x = t], A^x_b \Rightarrow b = t
\end{array}
$$

Then the following establishes the analogue of our instance of Leibniz' Law:

$$
\begin{array}{c}
a = t, A^x_a \Rightarrow A^x_t \qquad B^x_t \Rightarrow B^x_t \qquad \Pi \\
\hline\hline
a = t, A^x_a, B^x_t, Ix[A, x = t] \Rightarrow Ix[A, B] \\
\hline
Ix[A, x = t], B^x_t, Ix[A, x = t] \Rightarrow Ix[A, B] \\
\hline
Ix[A, x = t], B^x_t \Rightarrow Ix[A, B]
\end{array}
$$

To assess whether (LL) is provable, it is useful to have rules for the biconditional:

$$
(L\leftrightarrow) \quad \frac{\Gamma \Rightarrow \Delta, A, B \qquad A, B, \Gamma \Rightarrow \Delta}{A \leftrightarrow B, \Gamma \Rightarrow \Delta}
$$

$$
(R\leftrightarrow) \quad \frac{A, \Gamma \Rightarrow \Delta, B \qquad B, \Gamma \Rightarrow \Delta, A}{\Gamma \Rightarrow \Delta, A \leftrightarrow B}
$$

These are derivable from the rules for $\rightarrow$ given the usual definition of $\leftrightarrow$.

Next we derive one half of an analogue of (LL) in $\mathbf{CPF}^I$:

$$
\begin{array}{c}
\begin{array}{c}
A^x_a, a = b \Rightarrow A^x_b \qquad A^x_c \Rightarrow A^x_c \qquad \Rightarrow c = c \\
\hline\hline
Ix[A, x = b], A^x_a, a = b, A^x_c \Rightarrow c = b
\end{array}
\qquad A^x_a, a = b, c = b \Rightarrow A^x_c \\
\hline\hline
Ix[A, x = b], A^x_a, a = b \Rightarrow A^x_c \leftrightarrow c = b \\
\hline
\exists!c, Ix[A, x = b], A^x_a, a = b \Rightarrow A^x_c \leftrightarrow c = b \\
\hline
Ix[A, x = b], A^x_a, a = b \Rightarrow \forall x(A \leftrightarrow x = b) \\
\hline
Ix[A, x = b], Ix[A, x = b] \Rightarrow \forall x(A \leftrightarrow x = b) \\
\hline
Ix[A, x = b] \Rightarrow \forall x(A \leftrightarrow x = b) \\
\hline
\Rightarrow Ix[A, x = b] \rightarrow \forall x(A \leftrightarrow x = b) \\
\hline
\exists!b \Rightarrow Ix[A, x = b] \rightarrow \forall x(A \leftrightarrow x = b) \\
\hline
\Rightarrow \forall y(Ix[A, x = y] \rightarrow \forall x(A \leftrightarrow x = y))
\end{array}
$$

The left and rightmost leaves are derivable by Leibniz' Law.

The other half of (LL) is not derivable in $\mathbf{CPF}^I$. Intuitively, there being a unique *existing* A is not sufficient for $Ix[A, B]$, as there may also be *non-existing* As in addition. It is straightforward to give a countermodel with the semantics of Sect. 5.

$\Rightarrow Ix[x = t, x = t]$ follows by twice the Law of Identity and one application of (RI), where both A and B are $x = t$:

$$
\frac{\Rightarrow t = t \qquad \Rightarrow t = t \qquad a = t \Rightarrow a = t}{\Rightarrow Ix[x = t, x = t]}
$$

Thus the analogue of (FL) is derivable in $\mathbf{CPF}^I$. This is worth noting: Lambert calls (FL) 'an important theorem in traditional description theory' [26, p. 58], and, not being derivable in the minimal theory, is forced to add it as a further axiom.

The present theory of definite descriptions is thus not comparable to Hintikka's and Lambert's minimal theory: it contains only one half of the analogue (LL), but also the analogue of (FL). The first respect provides a sense in which the present theory is weaker than Lambert's preferred theory, the second one in which it is stronger, because the rules for I and $=$ yield the analogue of (FL) immediately, while in Lambert's theory, (FL) needs to be added as an extra axiom governing the definite description operator ι. The novelty of the present theory is shown by these features. In particular, the failure of the right to left half of (LL) is, arguably and *pace* Hintikka and Lambert, desirable, for the reason stated.

The theory does not allow the derivation of the analogue of $\iota xF = \iota xF$, $Ix[F, Iy[F, x = y]]$. This is a tolerable loss. As Russell is not identical to Whitehead, it is not difficult to accept that 'The author of *Principia Mathematica* = the author of *Principia Mathematica*' is not logically true. Reasons normally given for accepting $\iota xF = \iota xF$ is that it is an instance of the Law of Identity. These reasons, however, are not conclusive, as the example shows. $Ix[F, Iy[F, x = y]]$ is not an instance of the Law of Identity, and hence accepting that law does not force us to accept it. If more than two objects satisfy F, then it is false.

Its differences to Hintikka's and Lambert's theory of definite descriptions are advantages of the present proposal. It allows us to reject the claim that the author of *Principia Mathematica* is identical to the author of *Principia Mathematica* and to declare 'The author of *Principia Mathematica* smokes a pipe' to be false. If there is more than one A, existing or not, then $Ix[A, B]$ is false, whatever B may be: an identity, a predicate letter, a complex formula. The present theory provides principled reasons for declaring certain sentences containing definite descriptions to be false on which Hintikka and Lambert prefer to remain silent and for not having to accept some sentences they pronounce as logically true on grounds which one may well want to reject.

4 Cut Elimination for $\mathbf{CPF}^I$

We'll continue Indrzejczak's proof of cut elimination for **CPF** by adding the cases covering I. Let $d(A)$ be the degree of the formula A, that is the number of connectives occurring in it. $\exists!t$ is atomic, that is of degree 0. $d(\mathcal{D})$ is the degree of the highest degree of any cut formula in deduction $\mathcal{D}$. A^k denotes k occurrences of A, Γ^k k occurrences of the formulas in Γ. The height of a deduction is the largest number of rules applied above the conclusion, that is the number of nodes of a longest branch in the deduction. The proof appeals to the Substitution Lemma:

Lemma 1. *If* $\vdash_k \Gamma \Rightarrow \Delta$, *then* $\vdash_k \Gamma^a_t \Rightarrow \Delta^a_t$.

Its proof goes through as usual. Consequently, we can always rewrite deductions so that each application of $(R\forall)$, (RI) and (LI^1) has its own parameter that occurs nowhere else in the proof. In the following, it will be tacitly assumed that deductions have been treated accordingly.

Lemma 2 (Right Reduction). *If $\mathcal{D}_1 \vdash \Theta \Rightarrow \Lambda, A$, where A is principal, and $\mathcal{D}_2 \vdash A^k, \Gamma \Rightarrow \Delta$ have degrees $d(\mathcal{D}_1), d(\mathcal{D}_2) < d(A)$, then there is a proof $\mathcal{D} \vdash \Theta^k, \Gamma \Rightarrow \Lambda^k, \Delta$ with $d(\mathcal{D}) < d(A)$.*

Proof. By induction over the height of $\mathcal{D}_2$. The basis is trivial: if $d(\mathcal{D}_2) = 1$, then $A^k, \Gamma \Rightarrow \Delta$ is an axiom and hence $k = 1$, Γ is empty, and Δ consists of only one A; we need to show $\Theta \Rightarrow \Lambda, A$, but that is already proved by $\mathcal{D}_1$.

For the induction step, we consider the rules for I:

(I) The last step of $\mathcal{D}_2$ is by (RI). Then the occurrences A^k in the conclusion of $\mathcal{D}_2$ are parametric and occur in all three premises of (RI): apply the induction hypothesis to them and apply (RI) afterwards. The result is the desired proof $\mathcal{D}$.

(II) The last step of $\mathcal{D}_2$ is by (LI^1). There are two options:
(II.a) If the principal formula $Ix[F, G]$ of (LI^1) is not one of the A^k, then apply the induction hypothesis to the premises of (LI^1) and then apply (LI^1).
(II.b) If the principal formula $Ix[F, G]$ of (LI^1) is one of the A^k, then $\mathcal{D}_2$ ends with:

$$\frac{F^x_a, G^x_a, Ix[F, G]^{k-1}, \Gamma \Rightarrow \Delta}{Ix[F, G]^k, \Gamma \Rightarrow \Delta}$$

By induction hypothesis there is a deduction of $F^x_a, G^x_a, \Theta^{k-1}, \Gamma \Rightarrow \Lambda^{k-1}, \Delta$ with cut degree less than $d(A)$, and by the Substitution Lemma:

(1) $F^x_t, G^x_t, \Theta^{k-1}, \Gamma \Rightarrow \Lambda^{k-1}, \Delta$

A, i.e. $Ix[F, G]$, is principal in $\mathcal{D}_1$, so it ends with an application of (RI):

$$\frac{\Theta \Rightarrow \Lambda, F^x_t \qquad \Theta \Rightarrow \Lambda, G^x_t \qquad F^x_a, \Theta \Rightarrow \Lambda, a = t}{\Theta \Rightarrow \Lambda, Ix[F, G]}$$

Apply two cuts with (1) and the first and second premise, and conclude by contraction $\Theta^k, \Gamma \Rightarrow \Lambda^k, \Delta$.

(III) The last step of $\mathcal{D}_2$ is by (LI^2). In this case the succedent of the conclusion of $\mathcal{D}_2$ is Δ, C_{t_1}, where C_{t_1} is an atomic formula. There are two cases.
(III.a) The principal formula $Ix[F, G]$ of (LI^2) is not one of the A^k: apply the induction hypothesis to the premises of (LI^2) and then apply the rule.
(III.b) The principal formula $Ix[F, G]$ of (LI^2) is one of the A^k. Then $\mathcal{D}_2$ ends with:

$$\frac{Ix[F,G]^{k-1}, \Gamma \Rightarrow \Delta, F^x_{t_1} \qquad Ix[F,G]^{k-1}, \Gamma \Rightarrow \Delta, F^x_{t_2} \qquad Ix[F,G]^{k-1}, \Gamma \Rightarrow \Delta, C^x_{t_2}}{Ix[F,G]^k, \Gamma \Rightarrow \Delta, C_{t_1}}$$

By induction hypothesis, we have:

(1) $\Theta^{k-1}, \Gamma \Rightarrow \Lambda^{k-1}, \Delta, F^x_{t_1}$
(2) $\Theta^{k-1}, \Gamma \Rightarrow \Lambda^{k-1}, \Delta, F^x_{t_2}$
(3) $\Theta^{k-1}, \Gamma \Rightarrow \Lambda^{k-1}, \Delta, C^x_{t_2}$

A, i.e. $Ix[F,G]$, is principal in $\mathcal{D}_1$, so it ends with an application of (RI):

$$\frac{\Theta \Rightarrow \Lambda, F^x_t \qquad \Theta \Rightarrow \Lambda, G^x_t \qquad F^x_a, \Theta \Rightarrow \Lambda, a = t}{\Theta \Rightarrow \Lambda, Ix[F,G]}$$

The Substitution Lemma applied to the third premise gives

(5) $F^x_{t_1}, \Theta \Rightarrow \Lambda, t_1 = t$
(6) $F^x_{t_2}, \Theta \Rightarrow \Lambda, t_2 = t$

To show: $\vdash \Theta^k, \Gamma \Rightarrow \Lambda^k, \Delta, C_{t_1}$ with $d(\mathcal{D}) < d(Ix[F,G])$. Leibniz' Law gives

(7) $t_1 = t, t_2 = t \Rightarrow t_1 = t_2$
(8) $C_{t_2}, t_1 = t_2 \Rightarrow C_{t_1}$

Cuts with (1) and (5) and with (2) and (6) give $\Theta^k, \Gamma \Rightarrow \Lambda^k, \Delta, t_1 = t$ and $\Theta^k, \Gamma \Rightarrow \Lambda^k, \Delta, t_2 = t$, whence by Cut with (7) and contraction $\Theta^k, \Gamma \Rightarrow \Lambda^k, \Delta, t_1 = t_2$, and from the latter by Cuts with (3) and (8) and contraction $\Theta^k, \Gamma \Rightarrow \Lambda^k, \Delta, C_{t_1}$. As C_{t_2} in (LI^2) is restricted to atomic formulas, the degree of the ensuing deduction is less than $d(A)$, i.e. $d(Ix[F,G])$, which was to be proved.

This completes the proof of the Right Reduction Lemma.

Lemma 3 (Left Reduction). *If* $\mathcal{D}_1 \vdash \Gamma \Rightarrow \Delta, A^k$ *and* $\mathcal{D}_2 \vdash A, \Theta \Rightarrow \Lambda$ *have degrees* $d(\mathcal{D}_1), d(\mathcal{D}_2) < d(A)$, *then there is a proof* $\mathcal{D} \vdash \Gamma, \Theta^k \Rightarrow \Delta, \Lambda^k$ *with* $d(\mathcal{D}) < d(A)$.

Proof by induction over the height of $\mathcal{D}_1$. The basis is trivial, as then $\mathcal{D}_1$ is an axiom, and Γ consists of one occurrence of A and Δ is empty. What needs to be shown is that $A, \Theta \Rightarrow \Lambda$, which is already given by $\mathcal{D}_2$.

For the induction step, we distinguish two cases, and again we continue Indrzejczak's proof by adding the new cases arising through the addition of I.

(A) No A^k in the succedent of the conclusion of $\mathcal{D}_1$ is principal. Then we apply the induction hypothesis to the premises of the final rule applied in $\mathcal{D}_1$ and apply the final rule once more.

(B) Some A^k in the succedent of the conclusion of $\mathcal{D}_1$ is principal. Two options:

(I) The final rule applied in $\mathcal{D}_1$ is (RI):

$$\frac{\Gamma \Rightarrow \Delta, Ix[F,G]^{k-1}, F^x_t \qquad \Gamma \Rightarrow \Delta, Ix[F,G]^{k-1}, G^x_t \qquad F^x_a, \Gamma \Rightarrow \Delta, Ix[F,G]^{k-1}, a = t}{\Gamma \Rightarrow \Delta, Ix[F,G]^k}$$

By induction hypothesis, we have

(1) $\Gamma, \Theta^{k-1} \Rightarrow \Delta, \Lambda^{k-1}, F^x_t$
(2) $\Gamma, \Theta^{k-1} \Rightarrow \Delta, \Lambda^{k-1}, G^x_t$
(3) $F^x_a, \Gamma, \Theta^{k-1} \Rightarrow \Delta, \Lambda^{k-1}, a = t$

Apply (RI) with (1) to (3) as premises to conclude

(4) $\Gamma, \Theta^{k-1} \Rightarrow \Delta, \Lambda^{k-1}, Ix[F,G]$

Here $Ix[F,G]$ is principal, so apply the Right Reduction Lemma to the deduction concluding (4) and $\mathcal{D}_2$ (where $k = 1$) to conclude $\Gamma, \Theta^k \Rightarrow \Delta, \Lambda^k$.

(II) The final rule applied in $\mathcal{D}_1$ is (LI^2):

$$\frac{\Gamma \Rightarrow \Delta, {C_{t_1}}^{k-1}, F^x_{t_1} \qquad \Gamma \Rightarrow \Delta, {C_{t_1}}^{k-1}, F^x_{t_2} \qquad \Gamma \Rightarrow \Delta, {C_{t_1}}^{k-1}, C^x_{t_2}}{Ix[F,G], \Gamma \Rightarrow \Delta, {C_{t_1}}^k}$$

By induction hypothesis, we have

(1) $\Gamma, \Theta^{k-1} \Rightarrow \Delta, \Lambda^{k-1}, F^x_{t_1}$
(2) $\Gamma, \Theta^{k-1} \Rightarrow \Delta, \Lambda^{k-1}, F^x_{t_2}$
(3) $\Gamma, \Theta^{k-1} \Rightarrow \Delta, \Lambda^{k-1}, C^x_{t_2}$

Apply (LI^2) with (1) to (3) as premises to conclude:

(4) $Ix[F,G], \Gamma, \Theta^{k-1} \Rightarrow \Delta, \Lambda^{k-1}, C^x_{t_1}$

Here $C^x_{t_1}$ is principal, so apply the Right Reduction Lemma to the deduction concluding (4) and $\mathcal{D}_2$ (where $k = 1$) to conclude $Ix[F, G], \Gamma, \Theta^k \Rightarrow \Delta, \Lambda^k$.

This completes the proof of the Left Reduction Lemma.

Theorem 1 (Cut Elimination). *For every deduction in* $\mathbf{CPF}^I$, *there is a deduction that is free of cuts.*

Proof. The theorem follows from the Right and Left Reduction Lemmas by induction over the degree of the proof, with subsidiary inductions over the number of cut formulas of highest degree, as in Indrzejczak's paper.

5 Semantics for $\mathbf{CPF}^I$

For the purposes of providing a semantics for $\mathbf{CPF}^I$ it is convenient to modify the system slightly in the following way: free variables $x, y, z \ldots$ are allowed to occur in formulas, parameters are treated like constants, and constants may play the role of parameters if they occur parametrically in a deduction, that is, they fulfil the restrictions imposed in $(R\forall)$, (RI) and (LI^1). The restrictions for free variables in these rules are as for the parameters. Furthermore, for the purposes of this section, I take $\Rightarrow$ to have sets of sentences rather the multisets to its left and right. I'll write Γ, A to abbreviate $\Gamma \cup \{A\}$, $A, B, C \in \Delta$ for $\{A, B, C\} \subseteq \Delta$. The resulting modified system is evidently equivalent to the original formulation.

It is fairly obvious that the rules governing I enforce the uniqueness of A, if it is the case that $Ix[A, B]$, but not its existence. Arguing informally, it is immediate from (LI^2) that $Ix[A, B], A^x_a, A^x_b \Rightarrow a = b$, hence any As are identical; and if A^x_a is false, whatever a might be, then $A^x_a \Rightarrow \bot$, so by (LI^1), $Ix[A, B] \Rightarrow \bot$. But the rules do not permit us to determine whether the unique A exists or not. Conversely, to derive $Ix[A, B]$, we need a unique A that is B, but it is not required that it exists. Nonetheless, we will prove it rigorously by providing a sound and complete semantics for $\mathbf{CPF}^I$. I follow the popular proposal by [3, 28] and [29], where two domains are considered, an inner one and an outer one, the former the domain of existing objects, over which the universal quantifier ranges and of which $\exists!$ is true, and the latter the domain of 'non-existent' objects. I shall take the inner domain to be a subset of the outer domain.

The exposition of the formal semantics for $\mathbf{CPF}^I$ and the soundness and completeness proofs in the next section follow Enderton closely, with necessary adjustments to be suitable to free logic. Most of the following is well known and not new, but I'll be explicit about the details in order to demonstrate the semantics of I explicitly and precisely.

A *structure* $\mathfrak{A}$ is a function from the expressions of the language $\mathcal{L}$ of $\mathbf{CPF}^I$ to elements, a (possibly empty) subset, the sets of n-tuples of and operations on a non-empty set $|\mathfrak{A}|$, called the *domain of* $\mathfrak{A}$, such that:

1. $\mathfrak{A}$ assigns to the quantifier $\forall$ a (possibly empty) set $|\mathfrak{A}^{\forall}| \subseteq |\mathfrak{A}|$ called the *inner domain* or the *domain of quantification* of $\mathfrak{A}$.
2. $\mathfrak{A}$ assigns to the predicate $\exists!$ the set $|\mathfrak{A}^{\forall}|$.
3. $\mathfrak{A}$ assigns to each n-place predicate symbol P an n-ary relation $P^{\mathfrak{A}} \subseteq |\mathfrak{A}|^n$.
4. $\mathfrak{A}$ assigns to each constant symbol c an element $c^{\mathfrak{A}}$ of $|\mathfrak{A}|$.
5. $\mathfrak{A}$ assigns to each n-place function symbol f an n-ary operation $f^{\mathfrak{A}}$ on $|\mathfrak{A}|$, i.e. $f^{\mathfrak{A}} : |\mathfrak{A}|^n \to |\mathfrak{A}|$.

Next we define the notion of *satisfaction* of a formula B by a structure $\mathfrak{A}$. To handle free variables we employ a function $s : V \to |\mathfrak{A}|$ from the set of variables V of $\mathcal{L}$ to the domain of the structure. Suppose x occurs free in B. Informally, we say that $\mathfrak{A}$ satisfies B with s, if and only if the object of the domain of $\mathfrak{A}$ that s assigns to the variable x satisfies B, that is, if $s(x)$ is in the set $\mathfrak{A}$ assigns to B. We express this in symbols by $\vDash_{\mathfrak{A}} A\ [s]$. $\nvDash_{\mathfrak{A}} A\ [s]$ means that $\mathfrak{A}$ does not satisfy A with s. The formal definition of satisfaction is as follows.

First, s is extended by recursion it to a function $\overline{s}$ that assigns objects of $|\mathfrak{A}|$ to all terms of the language:

1. For each variable x, $\overline{s}(x) = s(x)$
2. For each constant symbol c, $\overline{s}(c) = c^{\mathfrak{A}}$.
3. For terms $t_1 \ldots t_n$, n-place function symbols f, $\overline{s}(ft_1 \ldots t_n) = f^{\mathfrak{A}}(\overline{s}(t_1) \ldots \overline{s}(t_n))$

Satisfaction is defined explicitly for the atomic formulas of $\mathcal{L}$:

1. $\vDash_{\mathfrak{A}} t_1 = t_2\ [s]$ iff $\overline{s}(t_1) = \overline{s}(t_2)$.
2. $\vDash_{\mathfrak{A}} \exists! t\ [s]$ iff $\overline{s}(t) \in |\mathfrak{A}^{\forall}|$.
3. For n-place predicate parameters P, $\vDash_{\mathfrak{A}} Pt_1 \ldots t_n\ [s]$ iff $\langle \overline{s}(t_1) \ldots \overline{s}(t_n) \rangle \in P^{\mathfrak{A}}$.

For the rest of the formulas, satisfaction is defined by recursion. Let $s(x|d)$ be like s, only that it assigns the element d of $|\mathfrak{A}|$ to the variable x:

1. For atomic formulas, as above.
2. $\vDash_{\mathfrak{A}} \neg A\ [s]$ iff $\nvDash_{\mathfrak{A}} A\ [s]$.
3. $\vDash_{\mathfrak{A}} A \to B\ [s]$ iff either $\nvDash_{\mathfrak{A}} A\ [s]$ or $\vDash_{\mathfrak{A}} B\ [s]$.
4. $\vDash_{\mathfrak{A}} \forall x A\ [s]$ iff for every $d \in |\mathfrak{A}^{\forall}|$, $\vDash_{\mathfrak{A}} A\ [s(x|d)]$.

This gives a semantics for **CPF**. For **CPF**^{I}, we add a clause for I:

5. $\vDash_{\mathfrak{A}} Ix[A, B]\ [s]$ iff there is $d \in |\mathfrak{A}|$ such that: $\vDash_{\mathfrak{A}} A\ [s(x|d)]$, there is no other $e \in |\mathfrak{A}|$ such that $\vDash_{\mathfrak{A}} A\ [s(x|e)]$, and $\vDash_{\mathfrak{A}} B\ [s(x|d)]$.

In other words, $\models_{\mathfrak{A}} Ix[F, G]\ [s]$ iff there is exactly one element in the domain of $\mathfrak{A}$ such that $\mathfrak{A}$ satisfies A with s modified to assign that element to x, and $\mathfrak{A}$ satisfies B with the same modified s.

We could define notions of validity, truth and falsity applicable to formulas, if we like, but won't need them in the following. A formula A is *valid* iff for every $\mathfrak{A}$ and every $s\colon V \to |\mathfrak{A}|$, $\models_{\mathfrak{A}} A\ [s]$. Call a formula with no free variables a sentence. A structure $\mathfrak{A}$ either satisfies a sentence σ with every function $s\colon V \to |\mathfrak{A}|$ or with none. If the former, σ is *true* in $\mathfrak{A}$, if the latter, σ is *false* in $\mathfrak{A}$. If the former, we may write $\models_{\mathfrak{A}} \sigma$ and say that $\mathfrak{A}$ is a model of σ.

More important are notions applicable to the sequents of the deductive system of $\mathbf{CPF}^I$. A sequent $\Gamma \Rightarrow \Delta$ is satisfied by a structure $\mathfrak{A}$ with a function $s\colon V \to |\mathfrak{A}|$ if and only if, if for all $A \in \Gamma$, $\models_{\mathfrak{A}} A\ [s]$, then for some $C \in \Delta$, $\models_{\mathfrak{A}} C\ [s]$. We symbolise this by $\models_{\mathfrak{A}} \Gamma \Rightarrow \Delta\ [s]$. A sequent $\Gamma \Rightarrow \Delta$ is *valid* iff it is satisfied by every structure with every function $s\colon V \to |\mathfrak{A}|$. In this case we write $\models \Gamma \Rightarrow \Delta$.

Sequents have finite sets to the left and right of $\Rightarrow$. We also need notions that apply to finite and infinite set.

A set of formulas Γ is *satisfiable* iff there is some structure $\mathfrak{A}$ and some function $s\colon V \to |\mathfrak{A}|$ such that $\mathfrak{A}$ satisfies every member of Γ with s.

A set of formulas Γ *deductively implies* a formula A, iff for some finite $\Gamma_0 \subseteq \Gamma$, $\vdash \Gamma \Rightarrow A$. If Γ deductively implies A, we record this fact by $\Gamma \vdash A$.

A set of formulas Γ *semantically implies* a formula A, iff for every structure $\mathfrak{A}$ and every function $s\colon V \to |\mathfrak{A}|$ such that $\mathfrak{A}$ satisfies every member of Γ with s, $\mathfrak{A}$ satisfies A with s. If Γ semantically implies A, we record this fact by $\Gamma \models A$.

6 Soundness and Completeness

I'll prove two pairs of soundness and completeness theorems: one pair shows that deducibility and validity of sequents coincide, and another that deductive and semantic implication coincide.

A formula A' is an *alphabetic variant* of a formula A if A and A' differ only in the choice of bound variables.

Lemma 4 (Existence of Alphabetic Variants). *For any formula A, term t and variable x, there is a formula A' such that $A \Rightarrow A'$ and $A' \Rightarrow A$ and t is substitutable for x in A'.*

Proof. Mutatis mutandis Enderton's proof goes through for $\mathbf{CPF}^I$, too [6, p. 126f].

Alphabetic variants are semantically equivalent: if A and A' are alphabetic variants, then $A \models A'$ and $A' \models A$.

Lemma 5 (The Substitution Lemma). $\models_{\mathfrak{A}} A^x_t\ [s]$ *iff* $\models_{\mathfrak{A}} A\ [s(x|\overline{s}(t))]$, *if t is free for x in A.*

Proof. See [6, p. 133f] and adjust.

Theorem 2 (Soundness for Sequents). *If* $\vdash \Gamma \Rightarrow \Delta$*, then* $\models \Gamma \Rightarrow \Delta$.

Proof. Standard, by induction over the complexity of deductions and observing that the axioms are valid and all rules preserve validity. In the appendix of [24], the soundness of the rules for the $\forall$ and I is proved.

Theorem 3 (Soundness for Sets). *If* $\Gamma \vdash A$*, then* $\Gamma \models A$.

Proof. If $\Gamma \vdash A$, then for some finite $\Gamma_0 \subseteq \Gamma$, $\vdash \Gamma_0 \Rightarrow A$. So by Theorem 2, $\models \Gamma_0 \Rightarrow A$. Suppose some structure $\mathfrak{A}$ satisfies all formulas of Γ with a function $s\colon V \rightarrow |\mathfrak{A}|$. Then $\mathfrak{A}$ satisfies Γ_o with s, hence, as $\models \Gamma_0 \Rightarrow A$, $\mathfrak{A}$ satisfies A with s, and so $\Gamma \models A$.

Some more definitions. Let $\bot$ represent an arbitrary contradiction. A set of formulas Γ is *inconsistent* iff $\Gamma \vdash \bot$. Γ is *consistent* iff it is not inconsistent. A set of formulas Γ is *maximal* iff for any formula A, either $A \in \Gamma$ or $\neg A \in \Gamma$. A set of formulas Γ is *deductively closed* iff, if $\Gamma \vdash A$, then $A \in \Gamma$.

Lemma 6. *Any maximally consistent set is deductively closed.*

Proof. Suppose Γ is maximal and $\Gamma \vdash A$ but $A \notin \Gamma$. Then for some finite $\Gamma_0 \subseteq \Gamma$, $\vdash \Gamma_0 \Rightarrow A$. By maximality of Γ, $\neg A \in \Gamma$, hence for some finite $\Gamma_1 \subseteq \Gamma$, $\vdash \Gamma_1 \Rightarrow \neg A$. Hence $\vdash \Gamma_0, \Gamma_1 \Rightarrow A \wedge \neg A$, and so $\Gamma \vdash \bot$. Contradiction.

Theorem 4. *Any consistent set of formulas* Δ *can be extended to a maximally consistent set* Δ^+ *such that:*
(a) for any formula A *and variable* x*, if* $\neg\forall x A \in \Delta^+$*, then for some constant* c*,* $\exists! c \in \Delta^+$ *and* $A^x_c \notin \Delta^+$*;*
(b) for any formulas A *and* B *and variable* x*, if* $Ix[A, B] \in \Delta^+$*, then for some constant* c*,* $A^x_c, B^x_c \in \Delta^+$ *and for all constants* d*, if* $A^x_d \in \Delta^+$*, then* $d = c \in \Delta^+$*.*
(c) for any formulas A *and* B *and variable* x*, if* $\neg Ix[A, B] \in \Delta^+$*, then for all constants* c*, either* $A^x_c \notin \Delta^+$*, or for some constant* d*,* $A^x_d \in \Delta^+$ *and* $d = c \notin \Delta^+$*, or* $B^x_c \notin \Delta^+$*.*

Proof is in the appendix of the online version [24].

Theorem 5. *If* Δ *is a consistent set of formulas, then* Δ *is satisfiable.*

Proof is in the appendix of the online version [24].

Theorem 6 (Completeness for Sequents). *If* $\models \Gamma \Rightarrow \Delta$*, then* $\vdash \Gamma \Rightarrow \Delta$.

Proof. Let $\neg\Delta$ be the negation of all formulas in Δ. If $\models \Gamma \Rightarrow \Delta$, then $\Gamma, \neg\Delta$ is not satisfiable. Hence by Theorem 5 it is inconsistent, and as they are both finite, $\vdash \Gamma, \neg\Delta \Rightarrow \bot$. Hence by the properties of negation $\vdash \Gamma \Rightarrow \Delta$.

Theorem 7 (Completeness for Sets). *If* $\Gamma \models A$*, then* $\Gamma \vdash A$.

Proof. Suppose $\Gamma \models A$. Then $\Gamma, \neg A$ is not satisfiable, hence by Theorem 5 it is inconsistent and $\Gamma, \neg A \vdash \bot$. So for some finite $\Sigma \subseteq \Gamma, \neg A$, $\Sigma \Rightarrow \bot$. If $\neg A \in \Sigma$, then by the deductive properties of negation, $\Sigma - \{\neg A\} \Rightarrow A$, and as $\Sigma - \{\neg A\}$ is certain to be a subset of Γ, $\Gamma \vdash A$. If $\neg A \notin \Sigma$, then $\Sigma \Rightarrow A$ by the properties of negation, and again $\Gamma \vdash A$.

7 Tableaux Rules

In this section, we'll extend Priest's tableaux system for classical positive free logic [32, Ch 13] by rules for I. His rules give a system equivalent to **CPF**:

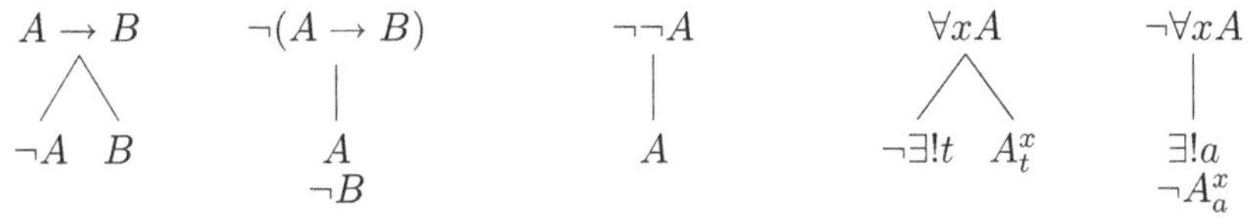

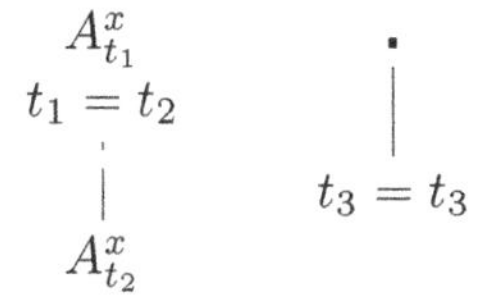

where t is any term on the branch (or a new one if there is none yet), a is new to the branch and t_3 is any term.

The binary quantifier I has the following rules:

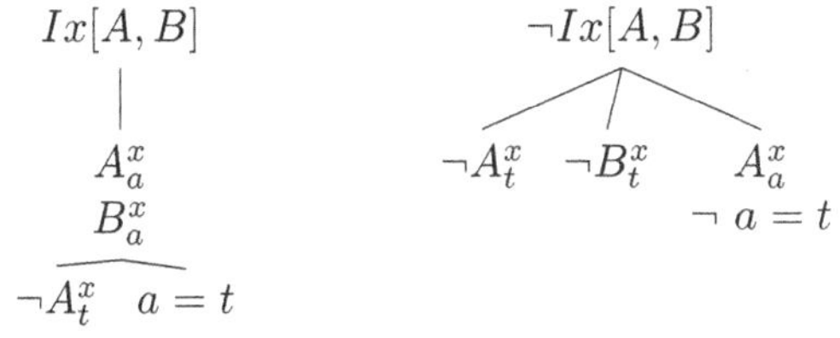

where a is new to the branch and t is any term on the branch (or a new one if there is none yet).

8 Conclusion

The theory of definite descriptions formulated here has some novel and attractive features. The proof-theory is simple and has desirable consequences. It differs from Hintikka's and Lambert's preferred theories in a well-motivated way. It lends itself to applications of formalisations in which scope distinctions are of importance. The distinction between internal and external negation has been mentioned in the introduction. Other, and particularly interesting, cases are found in modal discourse. There is a significant difference between 'It is possible the that present King of France is bald' and 'The present King of France is possibly bald'. In the present framework, the former is formalised by a formula such as $\Diamond Ix[Kx, Bx]$, the latter by $Ix[Kx, \Diamond Bx]$. The importance of scope distinctions in the context of modal logic was first pointed out by Smullyan [33]. His account was further developed by Hughes and Cresswell [13, p. 323ff]. Elaborate systems catering for definite descriptions in modal logic have been provided by

Fitting and Mendelsohn [7] and Garson [10]. In both of the latter systems, an operator for predicate abstraction is used to mark scope, but it serves no further purpose. Future research will investigate the addition of the binary quantifier I to quantified modal logic and compare the result to existing systems. In particular, as the present system incorporates scope distinctions directly into the formalism for representing definite descriptions, there is no need for additional means to mark scope. This promises economy and clarity in the formalism for representing definite descriptions where scope distinctions matter.

Acknowledgments. I would like to thank Andrzej Indrzejczak for comments on this paper and discussions of the proof-theory of definite descriptions in general. Some of this material was presented at Heinrich Wansing's and Hitoshi Omori's Work in Progress Seminar at the University of Bochum, to whom many thanks are due for support and insightful comments. Last but not least I must thank the referees for TABLEAUX 2021 for their thoughtful and considerate reports on this paper.

References

1. Bencivenga, E.: Free logics. In: Gabbay, D., Guenther, F. (eds.) Handbook of Philosophical Logic. Volume III: Alternatives to Classical Logic, pp. 373–426. Springer, Dortrecht (1986)
2. Bostock, D.: Intermediate Logic. Clarendon Press, Oxford (1997)
3. Cocchiarella, N.: A logic of actual and possible objects. J. Symb. Log. **31**(4), 668–689 (1966)
4. Czermak, J.: A logical calculus with definite descriptions. J. Philos. Log. **3**(3), 211–228 (1974)
5. Dummett, M.: Frege. Philosophy of Language, 2nd edn. Duckworth, London (1981)
6. Enderton, H.B.: A Mathematical Introduction to Logic, 2nd edn. Harcourt Academic Press, San Diego (2000)
7. Fitting, M., Mendelsohn, R.L.: First-Order Modal Logic. Kluwer, Dordrecht (1998)
8. van Fraassen, B.C.: On (the x) (x = lambert). In: Spohn, W., van Fraassen, B.C. (ed.) Existence and Explanation. Essays Presented in Honor of Karel Lambert. Kluwer, Dordrecht (1991)
9. Frege, G.: Grundgesetze der Arithmetik. Begriffsschriftlich abgeleited. I. Band. Jena: Hermann Pohle (1893)
10. Garson, J.W.: Modal Logic for Philosophers, 2nd edn. Cambridge University Press (2013)
11. Gratzl, N.: Incomplete symbols - definite descriptions revisited. J. Philos. Log. **44**(5), 489–506 (2015)
12. Hintikka, J.: Towards a theory of definite descriptions. Analysis **19**(4), 79–85 (1959)
13. Hughes, G., Cresswell, M.: A New Introduction to Modal Logic. Routledge (1996)
14. Indrzejczak, A.: Cut-free modal theory of definite descriptions. In: Bezhanishvili, G., D'Agostino, G.M., Studer, T. (eds.) Advances in Modal Logic, vol. 12, pp. 359–378. College Publications, London (2018)
15. Indrzejczak, A.: Fregean description theory in proof-theoretical setting. Logic Log. Philos. **28**(1), 137–155 (2018)
16. Indrzejczak, A.: Existence, definedness and definite descriptions in hybrid modal logic. In: Olivetti, N., Verbrugge, R., Negri, S., Sandu, G. (eds.) Advances in Modal Logic 13. College Publications, Rickmansworth (2020)

17. Indrzejczak, A.: Free definite description theory - sequent calculi and cut elimination. Log. Logical Philos. **29**(4), 505–539 (2020)
18. Indrzejczak, A.: Free logics are cut free. Stud. Logica. **109**(4), 859–886 (2020)
19. Indrzejczak, A.: Russellian definite description theory - a proof-theoretic approach. Forthcoming in the Review of Symbolic Logic (2021)
20. Kürbis, N.: A binary quantifier for definite descriptions in intuitionist negative free logic: Natural deduction and normalisation. Bull. Section Log. **48**(2), 81–97 (2019)
21. Kürbis, N.: Two treatments of definite descriptions in intuitionist negative free logic. Bull. Section Log. **48**(4), 299–318 (2019)
22. Kürbis, N.: A binary quantifier for definite descriptions for cut free free logics. Forthcoming in Studia Logica (2021)
23. Kürbis, N.: Definite descriptions in intuitionist positive free logic. Logic Log. Philos. **30**(2), 327–358 (2021)
24. Kürbis, N.: Proof-Theory and Semantics for a Theory of Definite Descriptions. Online version on arXiv arXiv:2108.03944 (2021)
25. Lambert, K.: Notes on "E!": II. Philos. Stud. **12**(1/2), 1–5 (1961)
26. Lambert, K.: Notes on "E!": III. Philos. Stud. **13**(4), 51–59 (1961)
27. Lambert, K.: Foundations of the hierarchy of positive free definite description theories. In: Free Logic. Selected Essays. Cambridge University Press (2004)
28. Leblanc, H., Thomason, R.: Completeness theorems for some presupposition-free logics. Fundam. Math. **62**, 125–164 (1968)
29. Meyer, R.K., Lambert, K.: Universally free logic and standard quantification theory. J. Symb. Log. **33**(1), 8–26 (1968)
30. Morscher, E., Simons, P.: Free logic: a fifty-year past and an open future. In: Morscher, E., Hieke, A. (eds.) New Essays in Free Logic in Honour of Karel Lambert. Kluwer, Dortrecht (2001)
31. Neale, S.: Descriptions. MIT Press, Cambridge (1990)
32. Priest, G.: An Introduction to Non-Classical Logic, 2nd edn. Cambridge University Press, Cambridge (2008)
33. Smullyan, A.: Modality and description. J. Symb. Log. **13**, 31–7 (1948)
34. Whitehead, A., Russell, B.: Principia Mathematica, vol. 1. Cambridge University Press, Cambridge (1910)

Basing Sequent Systems on Exclusive-Or

Arnon Avron(✉)

School of Computer Science, Tel Aviv University, 69978 Tel Aviv, Israel
aa@cs.tau.ac.il

Abstract. In the standard Gentzen-type systems for classical logic, the right hand side of a sequent is interpreted as the inclusive-or of its elements. In this paper we investigate what happens if the exclusive-or $\oplus$ is used instead. We provide corresponding analytic systems, and some of the decision procedures that are based on them. The latter are particularly efficient for the negation-equivalence fragment of classical logic.

Keywords: Analytic Gentzen-type proof systems · Cut-elimination · Translations · Hypersequents

1 Introduction

A Gentzen-type system G usually employs either single-conclusion sequents (like the system **LJ** for intuitionistic logic in [5]) or with multiple-conclusion ones (like the system **LK** for classical logic in [5]). The former has the form $\Gamma \Rightarrow \varphi$, where φ is a formula, Γ is a finite sequence (or sometimes a set or a multiset) of formulas, and $\Rightarrow$ is not a symbol of the language. The latter is of the form $\Gamma \Rightarrow \Delta$, where *both* Γ and Δ are finite sequences (sets, multisets) of formulas.

What is the meaning of a sequent? In the single-conclusion proof systems there is a straightforward interpretation: $\Gamma \Rightarrow \varphi$ usually expresses the fact that φ *follows* from Γ according to the corresponding logic **L**. This interpretation is independent of whether **L** is defined semantically (using the notion of a model) or proof-theoretically (e.g. using a Hilbert-type system). In contrast, a multiple-conclusion sequent does not have an obvious direct interpretation (especially when it is introduced by using some proof system). Therefore the meaning of a multiple-conclusion proof system G is usually given by some syntactic reduction of G to its single-conclusion fragment. This, in turn, is usually done by employing some *internal disjunction* [2], i.e. a binary connective $+$ for which it holds that $\vdash_G \Gamma \Rightarrow, \Delta_1, \varphi, \psi, \Delta_2$ iff $\vdash_G \Gamma \Rightarrow \Delta_1, \varphi + \psi, \Delta_2$. If such a connective $+$ is available, then the meaning of $\Gamma \Rightarrow \varphi_1, \ldots, \varphi_n$ in case $n > 0$ can be identified with the meaning of the single-conclusion sequent $\Gamma \Rightarrow \varphi_1 + \cdots + \varphi_n$. This leaves open, though, the interpretation of sequents of the form $\Gamma \Rightarrow$ (in which the r.h.s. is empty). This is usually solved by having an *internal negation* $\neg$ such that $\vdash_G \varphi, \Gamma \Rightarrow \Delta$ iff $\vdash_G \Gamma \Rightarrow \Delta, \neg\varphi$. In its presence one can internally interpret

This research was supported by The Israel Science Foundation (grant no. 550/19).

A. Das and S. Negri (Eds.): TABLEAUX 2021, LNAI 12842, pp. 112–128, 2021.
https://doi.org/10.1007/978-3-030-86059-2_7

every sequent $s = \varphi_1, \ldots, \varphi_n \Rightarrow \psi_1, \ldots, \psi_k$ such that $n + k > 0$ by the formula $\neg\varphi_1 + \cdots + \neg\varphi_n + \psi_1 + \cdots + \psi_k$.[1] (The empty sequent $\Rightarrow$ can be interpreted, e.g. as $\neg(\neg\varphi + \varphi)$, where φ is some formula.[2]).

As is well-known, for the standard Gentzen-type systems for classical logic the inclusive disjunction $\vee$ was chosen to serve as an internal disjunction, and the systems are designed accordingly, that is: by interpreting the r.h.s of a sequent as the inclusive-or of its elements. The goal of this paper is to investigate what kind of calculi are obtained if the exclusive-or $\oplus$ is chosen instead. We show that this interpretation too leads to corresponding analytic systems for classical logics, and to decision procedures that are based on them. The latter are very efficient, e.g., in the case of the negation-equivalence fragment of classical logic.

2 Preliminaries

In this section we review basic notions and facts about matrices (see e.g. [7,13]) and introduce the basic matrix which is relevant to the goals of this paper.

From now on we assume that all the propositional languages which we deal with have the same propositional variables, and that they are ordered in a sequence $P_1, P_2, \ldots$. We use p, q, r as meta-variables for propositional variables, and φ, ψ, τ as meta-variables for formulas.

Definition 1. A *matrix* for a language $\mathcal{L}$ is a triple $\langle \mathcal{V}, \mathcal{D}, \mathcal{O} \rangle$, where

- $\mathcal{V}$ is a non-empty set of truth values;
- $\mathcal{D}$ is a non-empty proper subset of $\mathcal{V}$ (whose elements are called the *designated* elements of $\mathcal{V}$);
- $\mathcal{O}$ is a function that associates an n-ary function $\widetilde{\diamond} : \mathcal{V}^n \to \mathcal{V}$ with every n-ary connective $\diamond$ of $\mathcal{L}$.

Definition 2. Let $\langle \mathcal{V}, \mathcal{D}, \mathcal{O} \rangle$ be a matrix for $\mathcal{L}$. A valuation in $\langle \mathcal{V}, \mathcal{D}, \mathcal{O} \rangle$ is a function v from the set of formulas of $\mathcal{L}$ to $\mathcal{V}$ such that the following condition is satisfied for every connective $\diamond$ of $\mathcal{L}$ and for every formulas $\psi_1, \ldots, \psi_n$ of $\mathcal{L}$ (where n is the arity of $\diamond$): $v(\diamond(\psi_1, \ldots, \psi_n)) = \widetilde{\diamond}(v(\psi_1), \ldots, v(\psi_n))$.

Definition 3. Let $\mathcal{M} = \langle \mathcal{V}, \mathcal{D}, \mathcal{O} \rangle$ be a matrix for $\mathcal{L}$.

- A valuation v in $\mathcal{M}$ is an $\mathcal{M}$-*model* of a formula φ ($v \models_{\mathcal{M}} \varphi$), if $v(\varphi) \in \mathcal{D}$.

[1] For being definite, we may assume here association to the right. In practice, this would not matter, since the interpretations of $+$ are almost always associative.

[2] In multiplicative linear logic and in many other logics, the empty sequent is interpreted by a special propositional constant $\bot$, such that $\Rightarrow$ and $\Rightarrow \bot$ are derivable from each other. In the logics we consider in this paper (as well as in plenty of others), the role of $\bot$ can be played by any formula of the form $\neg\tau$, where τ is a valid formula of the logic. In particular: we may take $\tau = \neg\varphi + \varphi$, since $\neg\varphi + \varphi$ is necessarily valid for every general consequence relation (in the sense of [2]) for which $+$ and $\neg$ are internal disjunction and negation, respectively.

- A valuation v in $\mathcal{M}$ is an $\mathcal{M}$*-model* of a theory (i.e. a set of sentences) $\mathcal{T}$ ($\nu \models _{\mathcal{M}}\mathcal{T}$) if it is an $\mathcal{M}$-model of every element of $\mathcal{T}$.
- A formula φ of $\mathcal{L}$ is *valid* in $\mathcal{M}$ if $v(\varphi) \in \mathcal{D}$ for every valuation v in $\mathcal{M}$.
- A formula φ of $\mathcal{L}$ *follows* in $\mathcal{M}$ from a theory $\mathcal{T}$ ($\mathcal{T} \vdash_{\mathcal{M}} \varphi$) if every $\mathcal{M}$-model of $\mathcal{T}$ is an $\mathcal{M}$-model of φ.

In this paper our main interest is in matrices for the following language:

Definition 4. $\mathcal{L}_{\oplus} = \{\oplus, \neg\}$

Definition 5. $\mathcal{M}_{\oplus}^{-}$ is the matrix $\langle \mathcal{V}, \mathcal{D}, \mathcal{O}\rangle$ for $\mathcal{L}_{\oplus}$ in which $\mathcal{V} = \{1, 0\}$, $\mathcal{D} = \{1\}$, $\tilde{\oplus} = \lambda a, b.(a+b)\ mod\ 2$ (i.e. $\tilde{\oplus}$ is the classical exclusive 'or'), $\tilde{\neg} = \lambda a.1 - a$ (i.e. $\tilde{\neg}$ is the classical negation).

The proof of the following lemma is straightforward.

Lemma 1. *$\tilde{\oplus}$ satisfies in $\mathcal{M}_{\oplus}^{-}$ the following identities:*

1. $a\tilde{\oplus}(b\tilde{\oplus}c) = (a\tilde{\oplus}b)\tilde{\oplus}c$ *(associativity);*
2. $a\tilde{\oplus}b = b\tilde{\oplus}a$ *(commutativity);*
3. $a\tilde{\oplus}0 = 0\tilde{\oplus}a = a$;
4. $a\tilde{\oplus}1 = 1\tilde{\oplus}a = 1 - a\ (= \tilde{\neg}a)$;
5. $a\tilde{\oplus}a = 0$.

Definition 6. Let $s = \varphi_1, \ldots, \varphi_n \Rightarrow \psi_1, \ldots, \psi_k$ be a sequent in a language $\mathcal{L}$ which extends $\mathcal{L}_{\oplus}$. Define:

$$\tau_s = \begin{cases} \neg\varphi_1 \oplus \cdots \oplus \neg\varphi_n \oplus \psi_1 \oplus \cdots \oplus \psi_k & n+k > 0 \\ \neg(\neg P_1 \oplus P_1) & n+k = 0 \end{cases}$$

Definition 7. Let v be a valuation in some matrix $\mathcal{M}$ for a language which includes $\mathcal{L}_{\oplus}$. v is extended to sequents by letting $v(s) = v(\tau_s)$. v is an $\mathcal{M}$*-model* of a sequent s ($v \models s$) if $v(s) \in \mathcal{D}$. v is an $\mathcal{M}$*-model* of a set S of sequents ($v \models S$) if $v \models s$ for every $s \in S$.

Lemma 2. *Let v be a valuation in $\mathcal{M}_{\oplus}^{-}$.*

1. $v \models \Gamma_1, \Gamma_2 \Rightarrow \Delta_1, \Delta_2$ *iff* $v(\Gamma_1 \Rightarrow \Delta_1) \neq v(\Gamma_2 \Rightarrow \Delta_2)$.
2. $v \models \Gamma \Rightarrow \Delta, \varphi$ *iff* $v(\Gamma \Rightarrow \Delta) \neq v(\varphi)$.
3. $v \models \varphi, \Gamma \Rightarrow \Delta$ *iff* $v(\Gamma \Rightarrow \Delta) = v(\varphi)$.
4. $v(\Rightarrow) = 0$.

Proof. Immediate from the definitions and Lemma 1. □

Note 1. Let $\varphi \leftrightarrow \psi = \neg(\varphi \oplus \psi)$. It is not difficult to see that $\leftrightarrow$ is interpreted in $\mathcal{M}_{\oplus}^{-}$ as the classical equivalence connective, that $\varphi \oplus \psi$ is equivalent there to $\neg(\varphi \leftrightarrow \psi)$, while $\varphi \leftrightarrow \psi$ is equivalent to $(\neg\varphi) \oplus \psi$ and to $\varphi \oplus (\neg\psi)$. Moreover: $\tau_{\varphi \Rightarrow \psi}$ (the internal interpretation of a sequent of the form $\varphi \Rightarrow \psi$) is $\varphi \leftrightarrow \psi$.

We now provide a useful criterion for being an $\mathcal{M}$-model of a sequent s:

Notation. We denote the set of natural numbers (including 0) by N, the set of even natural numbers by N_{even}, and the set of odd natural numbers by N_{odd}.

Definition 8. Let v be a valuation in $\mathcal{M}_{\oplus}^{-}$, and let $s = (\Gamma \Rightarrow \Delta)$. Define:

$$n_v(s) = \#(\{\varphi \in \Gamma \mid v(\varphi) = 0\}) + \#(\{\varphi \in \Delta \mid v(\varphi) = 1\})$$

(where $\#(X)$ denotes the cardinality of X).

Proposition 1. *Let v be a valuation in $\mathcal{M}_{\oplus}^{-}$. $v \models s$ iff $n_v(s) \in \mathsf{N}_{odd}$.*

Proof. An induction on n shows that Lemma 1 implies that the following holds for every $a_1, \ldots, a_n \in \{1, 0\}$:

$$a_1 \tilde{\oplus} \cdots \tilde{\oplus} a_n = \begin{cases} 0 & \#(\{i \mid a_i = 1\}) \in \mathsf{N}_{even} \\ 1 & \#(\{i \mid a_i = 1\}) \in \mathsf{N}_{odd} \end{cases}$$

Let v be a valuation v in $\mathcal{M}_{\oplus}^{-}$. Using an induction on $n_v(\Gamma \Rightarrow \Delta)$, it easily follows from this equation that if $n_v(\Gamma \Rightarrow \Delta)$ is in N_{odd} then $v \models \Gamma \Rightarrow \Delta$, while if it is in N_{even} then $v \not\models \Gamma \Rightarrow \Delta$. □

3 The Basic Systems

In this section we provide Gentzen-type sequential systems for $\vdash_{\mathcal{M}_{\oplus}^{-}}$, i.e. for the $\mathcal{L}_{\oplus}$-fragment of classical logic (where $\oplus$ denotes the exclusive-or). We start with the system $GCL_{\oplus}$ (Fig. 1), that differs from the standard Gentzen-type system for the $\{\neg, \vee\}$-fragment of classical logic only with respect to the form of the structural rules of weakening and contraction. In particular: the *logical* rules and the axioms of the two systems are identical.

Note 2. The presence of the two permutation rules ([P]) in $GCL_{\oplus}$ means that we are allowed to view the two sides of its sequents as if they are *multisets*. In what follows we indeed frequently (implicitly) treat them as such.

Note 3. Another possible description of $GCL_{\oplus}$ is that it is obtained from **MLL** (the multiplicative fragment of classical linear logic, where $\oplus$ denotes the multiplicative disjunction rather than the additive one) by the addition of the structural rules [2-D] and [2-W]. Nevertheless, the logic induced by $GCL_{\oplus}$ is not substructural in the strict sense, since [2-D] is not classically valid.

Note 4. The rule [2-D] is the *sole* rule of $GCL_{\oplus}$ which is not valid in the classical Gentzen-type system **LK**. This implies, of course, that it is not derivable from the other rules of $GCL_{\oplus}$. It should also be noted that while the rule [2-W] of $GCL_{\oplus}$ is obviously a weaker form of the weakening rule [W] of **LK**, [2-D] is completely different from the contraction rule of that system. Thus, although both rules eliminate some multiple occurrences of the same formula on one side

Axioms: $\varphi \Rightarrow \varphi$

Structural Rules:

$$[P] \quad \frac{\Gamma_1, \varphi, \psi, \Gamma_2 \Rightarrow \Delta}{\Gamma_1, \psi, \varphi, \Gamma_2 \Rightarrow \Delta} \quad \frac{\Gamma \Rightarrow \Delta_1, \varphi, \psi, \Delta_2}{\Gamma \Rightarrow \Delta_1, \psi, \varphi, \Delta_2}$$

$$[2\text{-W}] \quad \frac{\Gamma_1, \Gamma_2 \Rightarrow \Delta}{\Gamma_1, \psi, \psi, \Gamma_2 \Rightarrow \Delta} \quad \frac{\Gamma \Rightarrow \Delta_1, \Delta_2}{\Gamma \Rightarrow \Delta_1, \psi, \psi, \Delta_2}$$

$$[2\text{-D}] \quad \frac{\Gamma_1, \psi, \psi, \Gamma_2 \Rightarrow \Delta}{\Gamma_1, \Gamma_2 \Rightarrow \Delta} \quad \frac{\Gamma \Rightarrow \Delta_1, \psi, \psi, \Delta_2}{\Gamma \Rightarrow \Delta_1, \Delta_2}$$

$$[\text{Cut}] \quad \frac{\Gamma_1 \Rightarrow \Delta_1, \psi \qquad \Gamma_2, \psi \Rightarrow \Delta_2}{\Gamma_1, \Gamma_2 \Rightarrow \Delta_1, \Delta_2}$$

Logical Rules:

$$[\oplus\Rightarrow] \quad \frac{\varphi, \Gamma_1 \Rightarrow \Delta_1 \qquad \psi, \Gamma_2 \Rightarrow \Delta_2}{\varphi \oplus \psi, \Gamma_1, \Gamma_2 \Rightarrow \Delta_1, \Delta_2} \qquad [\Rightarrow\oplus] \quad \frac{\Gamma \Rightarrow \Delta, \varphi, \psi}{\Gamma \Rightarrow \Delta, \varphi \oplus \psi}$$

$$[\neg\Rightarrow] \quad \frac{\Gamma \Rightarrow \Delta, \varphi}{\Gamma, \neg\varphi \Rightarrow \Delta} \qquad [\Rightarrow\neg] \quad \frac{\Gamma, \varphi \Rightarrow \Delta}{\Gamma \Rightarrow \Delta, \neg\varphi}$$

Fig. 1. $GCL_{\oplus}$

of a sequent, none of them is derivable from the other. What is more: while the contraction rule is analytic[3], [2-D] in general is not. This means that $GCL_{\oplus}$ has *two* non-analytic rules: [Cut] and [2-D]. Hence an analogue of the classical cut-elimination theorem in the case of $GCL_{\oplus}$ should eliminate not only the former, but also the latter. In fact, eliminating [2-D] is more critical, since [Cut] is derivable using [2-D].[4] This is shown in the next proposition.

Proposition 2. [Cut] *is derivable from the other rules of* $GCL_{\oplus}$.

Proof. Here is a derivation of [Cut]:

$$\dfrac{\dfrac{\varphi \Rightarrow \varphi \qquad \dfrac{\varphi, \Gamma_2 \Rightarrow \Delta_2 \qquad \dfrac{\Gamma_1 \Rightarrow \Delta_1, \varphi}{\varphi, \varphi, \Gamma_1 \Rightarrow \Delta_1, \varphi}\,[2-W]}{\varphi, \varphi \oplus \varphi, \Gamma_1, \Gamma_2 \Rightarrow \Delta_1, \Delta_2, \varphi}\,[\oplus \Rightarrow]}{\varphi \oplus \varphi, \varphi \oplus \varphi, \Gamma_1, \Gamma_2 \Rightarrow \Delta_1, \Delta_2, \varphi, \varphi}\,[\oplus \Rightarrow]}{\Gamma_1, \Gamma_2 \Rightarrow \Delta_1, \Delta_2}\,[2-D]$$

Definition 9. Let G be a Gentzen-type system, and let $S \cup \{s\}$ be a set of sequents. We say that s is derivable from S in G ($S \vdash_G s$) if s is provable in

[3] Recall that a rule is analytic if every formula which occurs in one of its premises is a subformula of some formula in its conclusion.

[4] Nevertheless, for reasons that will become clear in Note 8, we prefer to leave it as one of the primitive rules of $GCL_{\oplus}$.

the system which is obtained from G by adding the sequents in S (but not their substitution instances) as new axioms.

Proposition 3 (Strong soundness of $GCL_{\oplus}$). *Let v be a valuation in $\mathcal{M}_{\oplus}^{-}$, and let $S \cup \{s\}$ be a set of sequents. If $S \vdash_{GCL_{\oplus}} s$ and $v \models S$ then $v \models s$.*

Proof. It suffices to show that the axioms of $GCL_{\oplus}$ are valid, and that if $v(s) = 1$ for every premise of some application of a rule of $GCL_{\oplus}$, then v assigns 1 also to the conclusion of that application. For most of the rules and axioms, this is immediate from the definitions and from Lemmas 1 and 2. Below is the proof in the less obvious case.

$[\oplus \Rightarrow]$ Suppose $v \models \varphi, \Gamma_1 \Rightarrow \Delta_1$ and $v \models \psi, \Gamma_2 \Rightarrow \Delta_2$. By Lemma 2, it follows that $v(\Gamma_1 \Rightarrow \Delta_1) = v(\varphi)$ and $v(\Gamma_2 \Rightarrow \Delta_2) = v(\psi)$. Hence $v(\Gamma_1, \Gamma_2 \Rightarrow \Delta_1, \Delta_2) = v(\Gamma_1 \Rightarrow \Delta_1) \tilde{\oplus} v(\Gamma_2 \Rightarrow \Delta_2) = v(\varphi) \tilde{\oplus} v(\psi)$, and so (again by Lemma 2) $v \models \varphi \oplus \psi, \Gamma_1, \Gamma_2 \Rightarrow \Delta_1, \Delta_2$. □

We shall show later that the converse of Proposition 3 holds only partially: $GCL_{\oplus}$ is complete for $\mathcal{M}_{\oplus}^{-}$, but not strongly so. Before that, we show another major drawback of $GCL_{\oplus}$.

Lemma 3. *$\vdash_{GCL_{\oplus}} \Gamma \Rightarrow \Gamma$ iff $\#(\Gamma)$ is odd.*

Proof. Suppose first that $\#(\Gamma)$ is odd. We prove that $\vdash_{GCL_{\oplus}} \Gamma \Rightarrow \Gamma$ by induction on $\#(\Gamma)$. This is obvious if $\#(\Gamma) = 1$. For the induction step, suppose $\vdash_{GCL_{\oplus}} \Gamma \Rightarrow \Gamma$. We derive $\Gamma, \varphi, \psi \Rightarrow \Gamma, \varphi, \psi$ as follows:

$$\dfrac{\dfrac{\Gamma \Rightarrow \Gamma}{\Gamma \Rightarrow \Gamma, \varphi, \varphi}\,[2-\mathrm{W}] \qquad \dfrac{\psi \Rightarrow \psi}{\varphi, \varphi, \psi \Rightarrow \psi}\,[2-\mathrm{W}]}{\Gamma, \varphi, \psi \Rightarrow \Gamma, \varphi, \psi}\,[\mathrm{Cut}]$$

Now suppose that $\#(\Gamma)$ is even. An easy induction on $\#(\Gamma)$ (using the fact that $v(\neg\varphi \oplus \varphi) = 1$ for every v and φ) shows that in this case $v(\Gamma \Rightarrow \Gamma) = 0$ for every v in $\mathcal{M}_{\oplus}^{-}$. Hence Proposition 3 imply that $\not\vdash_{GCL_{\oplus}} \Gamma \Rightarrow \Gamma$. □

Proposition 4. *Let $\Gamma \Rightarrow \Delta$ be a sequent with the following properties:*

- *Γ and Δ consist just of propositional variables.*
- *There are at least two distinct propositional variables that occur an odd number of times in both Γ and Δ.*

Then any proof in $GCL_{\oplus}$ of $\Gamma \Rightarrow \Delta$ contains either a cut, or some application of [2-D] in which the deleted formula is not a variable.

Proof. It is easy to see that the last inference of any proof of $\Gamma \Rightarrow \Delta$ is either some application of [2-D] in which the deleted formula is not a variable, or a cut, or it has a single premise which also has the above two properties of $\Gamma \Rightarrow \Delta$. Hence the proposition follows by an induction on the length of proofs. □

Corollary 1. *Let p_1 and p_2 be distinct propositional variables. The sequent $p_1, p_2, p_3 \Rightarrow p_1, p_2, p_3$ is provable in $GCL_\oplus$, but any proof of it contains a cut, or some application of* [2-D] *in which the deleted formula is not a variable.*

Proof. Immediate from Lemma 3 and Proposition 4. □

Corollary 1 shows that the non-analytic rules cannot be eliminated from all proofs in $GCL_\oplus$. Another drawback of $GCL_\oplus$ is that it has a rule ($[\oplus \Rightarrow]$) which is not invertible. (This would make it difficult for basing a useful tableaux system on it.) Therefore we provide in Fig. 2 an alternative system, $GCL^\star_\oplus$. Then we show that $GCL^\star_\oplus$ is equivalent to $GCL_\oplus$, but it does not share its drawbacks, and that the two systems are (weakly) complete for $\mathcal{M}^-_\oplus$.

Axioms: $\Gamma \Rightarrow \Gamma$ (provided that $\#(\Gamma)$ is odd.)

Structural Rules:

$$[P]\quad \frac{\Gamma_1, \varphi, \psi, \Gamma_2 \Rightarrow \Delta}{\Gamma_1, \psi, \varphi, \Gamma_2 \Rightarrow \Delta} \quad \frac{\Gamma \Rightarrow \Delta_1, \varphi, \psi, \Delta_2}{\Gamma \Rightarrow \Delta_1, \psi, \varphi, \Delta_2}$$

$$[2\text{-W}]\quad \frac{\Gamma_1, \Gamma_2 \Rightarrow \Delta}{\Gamma_1, \psi, \psi, \Gamma_2 \Rightarrow \Delta} \quad \frac{\Gamma \Rightarrow \Delta_1, \Delta_2}{\Gamma \Rightarrow \Delta_1, \psi, \psi, \Delta_2}$$

$$[2\text{-D}]\quad \frac{\Gamma_1, \psi, \psi, \Gamma_2 \Rightarrow \Delta}{\Gamma_1, \Gamma_2 \Rightarrow \Delta} \quad \frac{\Gamma \Rightarrow \Delta_1, \psi, \psi, \Delta_2}{\Gamma \Rightarrow \Delta_1, \Delta_2}$$

$$[Cut]\quad \frac{\Gamma_1 \Rightarrow \Delta_1, \psi \qquad \Gamma_2, \psi \Rightarrow \Delta_2}{\Gamma_1, \Gamma_2 \Rightarrow \Delta_1, \Delta_2}$$

Logical Rules:

$$[\oplus\Rightarrow]^\star\quad \frac{\varphi, \Gamma \Rightarrow \Delta, \psi}{\varphi \oplus \psi, \Gamma \Rightarrow \Delta} \qquad [\Rightarrow\oplus]\quad \frac{\Gamma \Rightarrow \Delta, \varphi, \psi}{\Gamma \Rightarrow \Delta, \varphi \oplus \psi}$$

$$[\neg\Rightarrow]\quad \frac{\Gamma \Rightarrow \Delta, \varphi}{\Gamma, \neg\varphi \Rightarrow \Delta} \qquad [\Rightarrow\neg]\quad \frac{\Gamma, \varphi \Rightarrow \Delta}{\Gamma \Rightarrow \Delta, \neg\varphi}$$

Fig. 2. $GCL^\star_\oplus$

Proposition 5. *$GCL^\star_\oplus$ and $GCL_\oplus$ are equivalent: $S \vdash_{GCL^\star_\oplus} s$ iff $S \vdash_{GCL_\oplus} s$.*

Proof. The following is a derivation in $GCL_\oplus$ of the rule $[\oplus\Rightarrow]^\star$ of $GCL^\star_\oplus$:

$$\cfrac{\cfrac{\varphi, \Gamma \Rightarrow \Delta, \psi \qquad \psi \Rightarrow \psi}{\varphi \oplus \psi, \Gamma \Rightarrow \Delta, \psi, \psi}\,[\oplus \Rightarrow]}{\varphi \oplus \psi, \Gamma \Rightarrow \Delta}\,[2-D]$$

That if $S \vdash_{GCL^\star_\oplus} s$ then $S \vdash_{GCL_\oplus} s$ follows from this and from Lemma 3.

To prove the converse, it suffices to show that the rule $[\oplus \Rightarrow]$ is derivable in $GCL^{\star}_{\oplus}$. Here is its derivation (where applications of [P] are omitted):

$$\dfrac{\dfrac{\dfrac{\varphi, \Gamma_1 \Rightarrow \Delta_1}{\varphi, \Gamma_1 \Rightarrow \Delta_1, \psi, \psi}\,[2-\mathrm{W}] \qquad \psi, \Gamma_2 \Rightarrow \Delta_2}{\varphi, \Gamma_1, \Gamma_2 \Rightarrow \Delta_1, \Delta_2, \psi}\,[\mathrm{Cut}]}{\varphi \oplus \psi, \Gamma_1, \Gamma_2 \Rightarrow \Delta_1, \Delta_2}\,[\oplus \Rightarrow]^{\star}$$

Corollary 2 (strong soundness of $GCL^{\star}_{\oplus}$). *Let v be a valuation in $\mathcal{M}^{-}_{\oplus}$. If $S \vdash_{GCL^{\star}_{\oplus}} s$ and $v \models S$ then $v \models s$.*

Proof. Immediate from Propositions 3 and 5. □

Proposition 6. *With the exception of* [Cut], *all the rules of $GCL^{\star}_{\oplus}$ which have a premise are invertible in it.*

Proof. The various cases are easy. As an example, here is a derivation of the premise of $[\oplus \Rightarrow]^{\star}$ from its conclusion. (Applications of [P] are not shown.)

$$\dfrac{\dfrac{\dfrac{\varphi \Rightarrow \varphi}{\varphi \Rightarrow \varphi, \psi, \psi}\,[2-\mathrm{W}]}{\varphi \Rightarrow \psi, \varphi \oplus \psi}\,[\Rightarrow \oplus] \qquad \varphi \oplus \psi, \Gamma \Rightarrow \Delta}{\varphi, \Gamma \Rightarrow \Delta, \psi}\,[\mathrm{Cut}]$$

Note 5. It is easy to see that all the results proved in this paper about $GCL^{\star}_{\oplus}$ would remain true had we taken $\leftrightarrow$ (Note 1) as primitive instead of $\oplus$, and replace the two rules for $\oplus$ in $GCL^{\star}_{\oplus}$ by the following two derived rules for $\leftrightarrow$:

$$[\leftrightarrow\Rightarrow]\ \dfrac{\Gamma \Rightarrow \Delta, \varphi, \psi}{\varphi \leftrightarrow \psi, \Gamma \Rightarrow \Delta} \qquad\qquad [\Rightarrow\leftrightarrow]\ \dfrac{\varphi, \Gamma \Rightarrow \Delta, \psi}{\Gamma \Rightarrow \Delta, \varphi \leftrightarrow \psi}$$

Note that these two rules for $\leftrightarrow$ are by far simpler than the rules for $\leftrightarrow$ in the usual Gentzen-type framework (based on inclusive-or):

$$\dfrac{\varphi, \psi, \Gamma_1 \Rightarrow \Delta_1 \quad \Gamma_2 \Rightarrow \Delta_2, \varphi, \psi}{\varphi \leftrightarrow \psi, \Gamma_1, \Gamma_2 \Rightarrow \Delta_1, \Delta_2} \qquad\qquad \dfrac{\varphi, \Gamma_1 \Rightarrow \Delta_1, \psi \quad \psi, \Gamma_2 \Rightarrow \Delta_2, \varphi}{\Gamma_1, \Gamma_2 \Rightarrow \Delta_1, \Delta_2, \varphi \leftrightarrow \psi}$$

Definition 10. A *clause* is a sequent which consists solely of propositional variables. A clause $\Gamma \Rightarrow \Delta$ is *reduced* if each propositional variable occurs at most once in Γ and at most once in Δ.

Lemma 4. *Any clause s is equivalent in $GCL_{\oplus}$ and $GCL^{\star}_{\oplus}$ to a unique (up to applications of* [P]*) reduced clause s' such that:*

- *s' is derivable from s using only applications of* [2-D].
- *s is derivable from s' using only applications of* [2-W].

Proof. Left to the reader. □

Proposition 7. *For every sequent $\Gamma \Rightarrow \Delta$ in $\mathcal{L}_\oplus$ we can effectively find a reduced clause which is equivalent to $\Gamma \Rightarrow \Delta$ in $GCL^\star_\oplus$, and from which $\Gamma \Rightarrow \Delta$ can be derived in $GCL^\star_\oplus$ without using either* [Cut] *or* [2-D].

Proof. This easily follows from Proposition 6 and Lemma 4. □

Note 6. The procedure implicit in the proof of Proposition 7 is particularly efficient, since all the rules of $GCL^\star_\oplus$ except [Cut] have a single premise. (Hence applying them backward amounts to producing a linear tableaux.)

Lemma 5. *A clause $\Gamma \Rightarrow \Delta$ is valid in $\mathcal{M}^-_\oplus$ iff it has the following properties:*

1. *Each propositional variable occurs in $\Gamma \Rightarrow \Delta$ an even number of times.*
2. $\#(\Gamma) \in \mathsf{N}_{odd}$.

Proof. It is easy to see that the reduced clause, to which $\Gamma \Rightarrow \Delta$ is equivalent according to Lemma 4, satisfies the above two conditions iff $\Gamma \Rightarrow \Delta$ does. Hence it suffices by Proposition 3 to prove the lemma under the assumption that $\Gamma \Rightarrow \Delta$ is reduced. In this case the satisfaction of the first condition by $\Gamma \Rightarrow \Delta$ means that $\Gamma = \Delta$. Therefore it immediately follows from Lemma 3 and Proposition 3 that if the two conditions are satisfied then $\Gamma \Rightarrow \Delta$ is valid in $\mathcal{M}^-_\oplus$.

For the converse, suppose that $\Gamma \Rightarrow \Delta$ does not satisfy the first condition. Assuming again that $\Gamma \Rightarrow \Delta$ is reduced, this means that there is a propositional variable p that occurs in $\Gamma \Rightarrow \Delta$ exactly once. Suppose without loss in generality that p occurs in Γ, but not in Δ. Let v be any valuation such that $v(p) \neq v(\Gamma - \{p\} \Rightarrow \Delta)$. (Such a valuation exists, since p does not occur in $\Gamma - \{p\} \Rightarrow \Delta$.) Then item 3 of Lemma 2 implies that $v \not\models \Gamma \Rightarrow \Delta$, and so $\Gamma \Rightarrow \Delta$ is not valid in $\mathcal{M}^-_\oplus$. It follows that if $\Gamma \Rightarrow \Delta$ is valid in $\mathcal{M}^-_\oplus$ then it satisfies the first condition. That it satisfies the second one too easily follows from that and from the fact that if $\#(\Gamma)$ is even then $v(\Gamma \Rightarrow \Gamma) = 0$ for every v in $\mathcal{M}^-_\oplus$. □

Note 7. Taking Note 6 into account, Proposition 7 and Lemma 5 provide us (with the help of Corollary 2) an efficient procedure for deciding whether a given sequent in $\mathcal{L}_\oplus$ is valid. By Note 5, this is true also for sequents in the negation-equivalence fragment of classical logic.[5]

Corollary 3. *A reduced clause $\Gamma \Rightarrow \Delta$ is valid in $\mathcal{M}^-_\oplus$ iff it can be derived from an axiom of $GCL^\star_\oplus$ using* [P].

Theorem 1. *A sequent $\Gamma \Rightarrow \Delta$ is valid in $\mathcal{M}^-_\oplus$ iff it has a proof in $GCL^\star_\oplus$ in which neither* [Cut] *nor* [2-D] *is used.*

[5] In particular: to use this procedure in order to check whether a formula ψ in the language of $\{\neg, \leftrightarrow\}$ is classically valid, we should first find a clause which is obtained from $\Rightarrow \psi$ by applying backward the logical rules of the system described in Note 5. Then we should check whether that clause satisfies the two conditions given in Lemma 5. It is not hard to see that this happens iff ψ satisfies the criterion of McKinsey and Mihailescu for validity of such formulas ([10], or [4], Corollary 1).

Proof. The 'if' part follows from Corollary 2. The converse follows from Proposition 7 and Corollary 3. □

Corollary 4. *A sequent is valid in* $\mathcal{M}_{\oplus}^{-}$ *iff it is provable in* $GCL_{\oplus}^{\star}$ *iff it is provable in* $GCL_{\oplus}$.

Corollary 5 (Cut-elimination and [2-D]-elimination). *If* $\vdash_{GCL_{\oplus}^{\star}} \Gamma \Rightarrow \Delta$, *then* $\Gamma \Rightarrow \Delta$ *has a proof in* $GCL_{\oplus}^{\star}$ *in which neither* [Cut] *nor* [2-D] *is used.*

Corollary 6. *Suppose that* $\vdash_{GCL_{\oplus}} s$. *Then* s *has a proof in* $GCL_{\oplus}$ *in which all applications of* [Cut] *and* [2-D] *are analytic.*

Proof. Use Proposition 3, Theorem 1, and the proof of Proposition 5. □

Note 8. Corollary 6 would have failed, had we not included [Cut] among the rules of $GCL_{\oplus}$ (despite Proposition 2).

Corollaries 5 and 6 can be strengthened as follows.

Theorem 2. *Let* $S \cup \{s\}$ *be a set of sequents, and assume that* $S \neq \{\Rightarrow\}$.

1. $S \vdash_{GCL_{\oplus}^{\star}} s$ *iff there is a proof in* $GCL_{\oplus}^{\star}$ *of* s *from* S *in which every application of* [Cut] *or* [2-D] *is on a formula in* $\Gamma \cup \Delta$ *for some* $\Gamma \Rightarrow \Delta \in S$.
2. *If* $S \vdash_{GCL_{\oplus}} s$ *then* s *has a proof from* S *in* $GCL_{\oplus}$ *in which all applications of* [Cut] *and* [2-D] *are analytic.*

Proof

1. Suppose that $s = \Gamma \Rightarrow \Delta$, and let $S' = \{\Gamma_1 \Rightarrow \Delta_1, \dots, \Gamma_n \Rightarrow \Delta_n\}$ be a finite subset of S such $S' \vdash_{GCL_{\oplus}^{\star}} s$. We prove the claim by induction on n. The case $n = 0$ is just Corollary 5. Suppose that the claim is true for n, we show it for $n+1$. So assume that $S' = \{\Gamma_1 \Rightarrow \Delta_1, \dots, \Gamma_n \Rightarrow \Delta_n, \Gamma_{n+1} \Rightarrow \Delta_{n+1}\}$, and $S' \vdash_{GCL_{\oplus}^{\star}} s$. There are three cases to consider.

   $\Gamma_{n+1} = \Delta_{n+1} = \emptyset$: Let τ be some formula in $\bigcup_{i=1}^{n}(\Gamma_i \cup \Delta_i)$. (Such a formula exists, since $S \neq \{\Rightarrow\}$). Take some proof-tree of s from S' in $GCL_{\oplus}^{\star}$, and transform it into another derivation in $GCL_{\oplus}^{\star}$ by replacing each premise of the form $\Rightarrow$ (i.e. $\Gamma_{n+1} \Rightarrow \Delta_{n+1}$) by the axiom $\tau \Rightarrow \tau$, and then apply in each node exactly the same rule with the same active formulas as in the original proof. Because of the context-independent ('pure' in the terminology of [2], 'multiplicative' in that of [6]) nature of the rules of $GCL_{\oplus}^{\star}$ (including [Cut]), we get by doing this a proof in $GCL_{\oplus}^{\star}$ from $\{\Gamma_1 \Rightarrow \Delta_1, \dots, \Gamma_n \Rightarrow \Delta_n\}$ of a sequent of the form $\Sigma, \Gamma \Rightarrow \Sigma, \Delta$, where $\Sigma = \tau, \dots, \tau$. Using [2-D], we get from this a proof in $GCL_{\oplus}^{\star}$ from $\{\Gamma_1 \Rightarrow \Delta_1, \dots, \Gamma_n \Rightarrow \Delta_n\}$ of either $\Gamma \Rightarrow \Delta$ or of $\tau, \Gamma \Rightarrow \tau, \Delta$. In the first case we directly apply the induction hypothesis to get a proof of $\Gamma \Rightarrow \Delta$ as required. In the second case we apply it to get such a proof for $\tau, \Gamma \Rightarrow \tau, \Delta$. By adding to that proof a Cut with $\Rightarrow \tau, \tau$ (which is derivable from the empty sequent $\Gamma_{n+1} \Rightarrow \Delta_{n+1}$ by [2-W]), followed by a permissible application of [2-D] on τ, we again get a proof of $\Gamma \Rightarrow \Delta$ as required.

$\Gamma_{n+1} \neq \emptyset$: Suppose, without loss in generality (due to the presence of [P]), that $\Gamma_{n+1} = \psi, \Gamma'_{n+1}$. Take some proof-tree of s from S' in $GCL^{\star}_{\oplus}$, and transform it into another derivation in $GCL^{\star}_{\oplus}$ like in the previous case, but this time replacing each premise of the form $\Gamma_{n+1} \Rightarrow \Delta_{n+1}$ by the valid sequent $\psi, \Gamma'_{n+1}, \Gamma'_{n+1} \Rightarrow \Delta_{n+1}, \Delta_{n+1}, \psi$, which is obtained (though not derived!) from $\Gamma_{n+1} \Rightarrow \Delta_{n+1}$ by adding Γ'_{n+1} to its l.h.s, and Δ_{n+1}, ψ to its r.h.s. As in the previous case, with the help of [2-D] we get by this transformation a proof in $GCL^{\star}_{\oplus}$ from $\{\Gamma_1 \Rightarrow \Delta_1, \ldots, \Gamma_n \Rightarrow \Delta_n\}$ of either $\Gamma \Rightarrow \Delta$ or of $\Gamma'_{n+1}, \Gamma \Rightarrow \Delta, \Delta_{n+1}, \psi$. By applying the induction hypothesis to this proof we get a proof from S as required of either $\Gamma \Rightarrow \Delta$ or of $\Gamma'_{n+1}, \Gamma \Rightarrow \Delta, \Delta_{n+1}, \psi$. In the first case we are done. In the second one we first add to this proof a permissible Cut on ψ of its end-sequent with $\Gamma_{n+1} \Rightarrow \Delta_{n+1}$, to get a proof as required of $\Gamma'_{n+1}, \Gamma'_{n+1}, \Gamma \Rightarrow \Delta, \Delta_{n+1}, \Delta_{n+1}$. Using permissible applications of [2-D], we finally get a proof as required of $\Gamma \Rightarrow \Delta$ in this case as well.

$\Delta_{n+1} \neq \emptyset$: We leave this case to the reader.

2. The proof is similar to that of the first part, using Corollary 6 instead of Corollary 5. □

Note 9. Theorem 2 is not true in case $S = \{\Rightarrow\}$. Thus $\{\Rightarrow\} \vdash_{GCL^{\star}_{\oplus}} P_1, P_2 \Rightarrow P_1, P_2$. (Apply [Cut] to $\Rightarrow P_2, P_2$ and $\Rightarrow P_2, P_2, P_1 \Rightarrow P_1$; The former is derivable from $\Rightarrow$ using [2-W], while the latter is derivable from the axiom $P_1 \Rightarrow P_1$ by [2-W].) Nevertheless, it is easy to see that it is impossible to derive it without using the [Cut] rule. However, by applying Theorem 2 to $\{\Rightarrow \varphi, \varphi\}$ (which is equivalent to $\{\Rightarrow\}$) we conclude that if $\{\Rightarrow\} \vdash_{GCL^{\star}_{\oplus}} s$ then there is a proof in $GCL^{\star}_{\oplus}$ of s from $\{\Rightarrow\}$ in which all applications of [Cut] and [2-D] are on φ, where the latter can arbitrarily be chosen.

4 Theorems on Strong Completeness

Corollary 4 is a weak completeness theorem for $GCL_{\oplus}$ ($GCL^{\star}_{\oplus}$). The next proposition implies that the corresponding strong completeness theorem fails.

Proposition 8. $\{\Rightarrow p, \Rightarrow \neg p\} \vdash_{\mathcal{M}^{-}_{\oplus}} \Rightarrow q$, *but* $\{\Rightarrow p, \Rightarrow \neg p\} \not\vdash_{GCL_{\oplus}} \Rightarrow q$.

Proof. The first part is obvious, since $\{\Rightarrow p, \Rightarrow \neg p\}$ has no model in $\mathcal{M}^{-}_{\oplus}$.

The second part is immediate from the following observation (that can be proved by an easy induction on length of proofs): if $S \vdash_{GCL_{\oplus}} s$, and the propositional variable q occurs an even number of times in every element of S, then it occurs an even number of times in s as well. □

The failure of $GCL_{\oplus}$ (or, equivalently, $GCL^{\star}_{\oplus}$) to be strongly complete for $\vdash_{\mathcal{M}^{-}_{\oplus}}$ raises two problems:

(A) To find semantics for which a strong soundness and completeness theorem for $GCL_{\oplus}$ ($GCL^{\star}_{\oplus}$) does obtain.

(B) To extend $GCL_{\oplus}$ or $GCL^{\star}_{\oplus}$ to a system which *is* strongly sound and complete with respect to $\mathcal{M}^{-}_{\oplus}$.

To solve problem **(A)**, we use the following matrix for $\mathcal{L}_{\oplus}$ from [4].

Definition 11. $\mathcal{M}^{id}_{\oplus}$ is the matrix $\langle \mathcal{V}, \mathcal{D}, \mathcal{O} \rangle$ for $\mathcal{L}_{\oplus}$ in which $\mathcal{V} = \{1, 0\}$, $\mathcal{D} = \{1\}$, $\tilde{\oplus}$ is the classical equivalence, and $\tilde{\neg}$ is the identity function.

Definition 12. Let v be a valuation in $\mathcal{M}^{id}_{\oplus}$, and let $s = (\Gamma \Rightarrow \Delta)$. Define:

$$n_v(s) = \#(\{\varphi \in \Gamma \mid v(\varphi) = 0\}) + \#(\{\varphi \in \Delta \mid v(\varphi) = 0\})$$

The proofs of the following lemmas and propositions about $\mathcal{M}^{id}_{\oplus}$ are similar to the proofs of their counterparts concerning $\mathcal{M}^{-}_{\oplus}$.

Lemma 6. *$\tilde{\oplus}$ satisfies in $\mathcal{M}^{id}_{\oplus}$ the following identities:*

1. $a\tilde{\oplus}(b\tilde{\oplus}c) = (a\tilde{\oplus}b)\tilde{\oplus}c$ *(associativity);*
2. $a\tilde{\oplus}b = b\tilde{\oplus}a$ *(commutativity);*
3. $a\tilde{\oplus}0 = 0\tilde{\oplus}a = 1 - a$*;*
4. $a\tilde{\oplus}1 = 1\tilde{\oplus}a = a$*;*
5. $a\tilde{\oplus}a = 1$.

Lemma 7. *Let v be a valuation in $\mathcal{M}^{id}_{\oplus}$.*

1. $v \models \Gamma_1, \Gamma_2 \Rightarrow \Delta_1, \Delta_2$ *iff* $v(\Gamma_1 \Rightarrow \Delta_1) = v(\Gamma_2 \Rightarrow \Delta_2)$.
2. $v \models \varphi, \Gamma \Rightarrow \Delta$ *iff* $v \models \Gamma \Rightarrow \Delta, \varphi$ *iff* $v(\Gamma \Rightarrow \Delta) = v(\varphi)$

Proposition 9. *Let v be a valuation in $\mathcal{M}^{id}_{\oplus}$. $v \models s$ iff $n_v(s) \in \mathsf{N}_{even}$.*

Proposition 10 (Strong soundness of $GCL_{\oplus}$). *Let v be a valuation in $\mathcal{M}^{id}_{\oplus}$, and let $S \cup \{s\}$ be a set of sequents. If $S \vdash_{GCL_{\oplus}} s$ and $v \models S$ then $v \models s$.*

Note 10. Since obviously $\{\Rightarrow p, \Rightarrow \neg p\} \not\vdash_{\mathcal{M}^{id}_{\oplus}} \Rightarrow q$, Proposition 10 provides another proof for the second part of Proposition 8.

In what follows we need the following:

Theorem 3 ([4]). *φ follows from $\mathcal{T}$ in both $\mathcal{M}^{-}_{\oplus}$ and $\mathcal{M}^{id}_{\oplus}$ ($\mathcal{T} \vdash_{\mathcal{M}^{-}_{\oplus}} \varphi$ and $\mathcal{T} \vdash_{\mathcal{M}^{id}_{\oplus}} \varphi$) iff there are $\psi_1, \ldots, \psi_n \in \mathcal{T}$ such that $\neg\psi_1 \oplus \cdots \oplus \neg\psi_n \oplus \varphi$ is valid in $\mathcal{M}^{-}_{\oplus}$, i.e. iff the sequent $\psi_1, \ldots, \psi_n \Rightarrow \varphi$ is valid in $\mathcal{M}^{-}_{\oplus}$.*

Corollary 7. *φ follows in $\mathcal{T}$ in both $\mathcal{M}^{-}_{\oplus}$ and $\mathcal{M}^{id}_{\oplus}$ iff there is a finite $\Gamma \subseteq \mathcal{T}$ such that $\vdash_{GCL_{\oplus}} \Gamma \Rightarrow \varphi$ ($\vdash_{GCL^{\star}_{\oplus}} \Gamma \Rightarrow \varphi$).*

Proof. Immediate from Theorem 3 and Corollary 4. □

Theorem 4. *Let $S \cup \{s\}$ be a set of sequents. $S \vdash_{GCL_{\oplus}} s$ ($S \vdash_{GCL^{\star}_{\oplus}} s$) iff both $S \vdash_{\mathcal{M}^{-}_{\oplus}} s$ and $S \vdash_{\mathcal{M}^{id}_{\oplus}} s$.*

Proof. The 'only if' part follows from Propositions 3 and 10.

For the converse, suppose that $S \vdash_{\mathcal{M}_{\oplus}^{-}} s$, and $S \vdash_{\mathcal{M}_{\oplus}^{id}} s$. This means that $\mathcal{T} \vdash_{\mathcal{M}_{\oplus}^{-}} \tau_{\Gamma\Rightarrow\Delta}$ and $\mathcal{T} \vdash_{\mathcal{M}_{\oplus}^{id}} \tau_{\Gamma\Rightarrow\Delta}$, where $s = \Gamma \Rightarrow \Delta$, and $\mathcal{T} = \{\tau_{s'} \mid s' \in S\}$. Hence Theorem 3 implies that there are $s_1, \ldots, s_n \in S$ such that the sequent $\tau_{s_1}, \ldots, \tau_{s_n} \Rightarrow \tau_{\Gamma\Rightarrow\Delta}$ is valid in $\mathcal{M}_{\oplus}^{-}$, and so also $\tau_{s_1}, \ldots, \tau_{s_n}, \Gamma \Rightarrow \Delta$ is valid in $\mathcal{M}_{\oplus}^{-}$. It follows by Corollary 4 that the latter sequent is provable in $GCL_{\oplus}$ ($GCL_{\oplus}^{\star}$). Now $\Rightarrow \tau_{s_i}$ is easily derivable in $GCL_{\oplus}$ ($GCL_{\oplus}^{\star}$) from s_i ($i = 1, \ldots, n$). By applying cuts to these n sequents and to $\tau_{s_1}, \ldots, \tau_{s_n}, \Gamma \Rightarrow \Delta$, we get a proof in $GCL_{\oplus}$ ($GCL_{\oplus}^{\star}$) of $\Gamma \Rightarrow \Delta$ from S. □

Next we turn to Problem **(B)**. The key for its solution is provided by the following proposition.

Proposition 11. *$\mathcal{T} \vdash_{\mathcal{M}_{\oplus}^{-}} \varphi$ iff there exists a finite $\Gamma \subseteq \mathcal{T}$ such that either $\vdash_{GCL_{\oplus}^{\star}} \Gamma \Rightarrow \varphi$ or $\vdash_{GCL_{\oplus}^{\star}} \Gamma \Rightarrow$.*

Proof. The if direction is obvious, since [Cut] is a sound rule, and $\Rightarrow$ has no models in $\mathcal{M}_{\oplus}^{-}$. For the converse, let $\mathcal{T} \vdash_{\mathcal{M}_{\oplus}^{-}} \varphi$. Then also $\mathcal{T}, \neg\varphi \vdash_{\mathcal{M}_{\oplus}^{-}} \varphi$. Since $\neg\varphi \vdash_{\mathcal{M}_{\oplus}^{id}} \varphi$, $\mathcal{T}, \neg\varphi \vdash_{\mathcal{M}_{\oplus}^{id}} \varphi$ as well. Hence Corollary 7 implies that there is $\Gamma \subseteq \mathcal{T} \cup \{\neg\varphi\}$ such that $\vdash_{GCL_{\oplus}^{\star}} \Gamma \Rightarrow \varphi$. If $\neg\varphi \notin \Gamma$ we are done. Otherwise $\Gamma = \Gamma' \cup \{\neg\varphi\}$, and $\vdash_{GCL_{\oplus}^{\star}} \Gamma', \neg\varphi \Rightarrow \varphi$. By applying [$\neg \Rightarrow$] followed by [D-2] on $\neg\varphi$, we get $\vdash_{GCL_{\oplus}^{\star}} \Gamma' \Rightarrow$. □

Theorem 5. *$S \vdash_{\mathcal{M}_{\oplus}^{-}} s$ iff either $S \vdash_{GCL_{\oplus}^{\star}} s$ or $S \vdash_{GCL_{\oplus}^{\star}} \Rightarrow$.*

Proof. The 'if' part follows from Corollary 2, and the fact that the empty sequent has no model in $\mathcal{M}_{\oplus}^{-}$. For the converse, let $S \vdash_{\mathcal{M}_{\oplus}^{-}} s$. Then by Proposition 11, there are $s_1, \ldots, s_n \in S$ such that either $\vdash_{GCL_{\oplus}^{\star}} \tau_{s_1}, \ldots, \tau_{s_n} \Rightarrow \tau_s$, or else $\vdash_{GCL_{\oplus}^{\star}} \tau_{s_1}, \ldots, \tau_{s_n} \Rightarrow$. Like in the proof of Theorem 4, in the first case we have that $S \vdash_{GCL_{\oplus}^{\star}} s$, while in the second case we get that $S \vdash_{GCL_{\oplus}^{\star}} \Rightarrow$. □

Definition 13. $GCL_{\oplus,\neg}$ ($GCL_{\oplus,\neg}^{\star}$) is the system which is obtained from $GCL_{\oplus}$ ($GCL_{\oplus}^{\star}$) by adding to it the following rule:

$$\frac{\Rightarrow}{\Gamma \Rightarrow \Delta}\,[\text{Triv}]$$

Corollary 8. *$GCL_{\oplus,\neg}$ ($GCL_{\oplus,\neg}^{\star}$) is strongly sound and complete for $\mathcal{M}_{\oplus}^{-}$.*

Note 11. From the proof of Theorem 5 it follows that if $S \vdash_{GCL_{\oplus,\neg}^{\star}} s$ then there is a proof in $GCL_{\oplus,\neg}^{\star}$ of s from S in which there is at most one application of [Triv], made (if at all) at the very end of the proof.

Note 12. It is straightforward to use Proposition 7, the first item of Theorem 2, and Note 2 in order to provide a resolution-based decision procedure for the question whether $S \vdash_{\mathcal{M}_{\oplus}^{-}} s$, where $S \cup \{s\}$ is a finite set of sequents. (This is particularly useful in the equivalence-negation context.)

5 Enhancing the Expressive Power of the System

In [8] it was proved that $\mathcal{L}_{\oplus}$ is not functionally complete for $\{1, 0\}$.[6] In particular: the classical (inclusive) disjunction is not available in it. In this section we describe how this problem can be overcome. We start with a method that allows us to enhance the expressive power of our systems without changing the underlying language: the use of hypersequents rather than simple sequents.[7]

Definition 14. A *hypersequent* is a finite multiset of ordinary sequents. The elements of this multiset are called its *components*. We denote by $s_1 \mid \cdots \mid s_n$ the hypersequent whose components are $s_1, \ldots, s_n$, and use H as a metavariable for (possibly empty) hypersequents.

Definition 15. Let $\mathcal{M}$ be a matrix for a language which includes $\mathcal{L}_{\oplus}$.

- A valuation v in $\mathcal{M}$ is an $\mathcal{M}$*-model* of a hypersequent H ($v \models H$) if v is an $\mathcal{M}$*-model* of some component of H.
- A hypersequent is $\mathcal{M}$*-valid* if every valuation v in $\mathcal{M}$ is an $\mathcal{M}$-model of it.
- A hypersequent H follows in $\mathcal{M}$ from a set $\mathcal{S}$ of hypersequents ($\mathcal{S} \vdash_{\mathcal{M}} H$) if every $\mathcal{M}$-model of $\mathcal{S}$ is also an $\mathcal{M}$-model of H.

Proposition 12. *Let $\mathcal{M}$ be a matrix for $\mathcal{L}$, $s_1, \ldots, s_n, s$ sequents of $\mathcal{L}$, and H a hypersequent of $\mathcal{L}$. If $s_1, \ldots, s_n \vdash_{\mathcal{M}} s$ then $\{H \mid s_1, \ldots, H \mid s_n\} \vdash_{\mathcal{M}} H \mid s$.*

In what follows, we identify a sequent s with the hypersequent $\{s\}$. The next theorem is then the key for developing a hypersequential system for $\mathcal{M}_{\oplus}^{-}$.

Theorem 6. *Let $H = \Gamma_1 \Rightarrow \Delta_1 \mid \cdots \mid \Gamma_n \Rightarrow \Delta_n$ ($n \geq 1$) be a hypersequent in $\mathcal{L}_{\oplus}$. $\vdash_{\mathcal{M}_{\oplus}^{-}} H$ iff there are $i_1, \ldots, i_k \in \{1, \ldots, n\}$ ($1 \leq k \leq n$) such that $\vdash_{GCL_{\oplus}^{\star}} \Gamma_{i_1}, \ldots, \Gamma_{i_k} \Rightarrow \Delta_{i_1}, \ldots, \Delta_{i_k}$.*

Proof. From the definitions it follows that $\Gamma_1 \Rightarrow \Delta_1 \mid \cdots \mid \Gamma_n \Rightarrow \Delta_n$ is valid iff

$$\{\neg\tau_{\Gamma_1 \Rightarrow \Delta_1}, \ldots, \neg\tau_{\Gamma_{n-1} \Rightarrow \Delta_{n-1}}\} \vdash_{\mathcal{M}_{\oplus}^{-}} \tau_{\Gamma_n \Rightarrow \Delta_n}$$

By Proposition 11, this is equivalent to the existence of $i_1, \ldots, i_l \in \{1, \ldots, n-1\}$ ($l \geq 0$) such that either $\vdash_{GCL_{\oplus}^{\star}} \neg\tau_{\Gamma_{i_1} \Rightarrow \Delta_{i_1}}, \ldots, \neg\tau_{\Gamma_{i_l} \Rightarrow \Delta_{i_l}} \Rightarrow \tau_{\Gamma_n \Rightarrow \Delta_n}$, or $\vdash_{GCL_{\oplus}^{\star}} \neg\tau_{\Gamma_{i_1} \Rightarrow \Delta_{i_1}}, \ldots, \neg\tau_{\Gamma_{i_l} \Rightarrow \Delta_{i_l}} \Rightarrow$. This, in turn, can be the case iff either $\vdash_{GCL_{\oplus}^{\star}} \Rightarrow \tau_{\Gamma_{i_1} \Rightarrow \Delta_{i_1}}, \ldots, \tau_{\Gamma_{i_l} \Rightarrow \Delta_{i_l}}, \tau_{\Gamma_n \Rightarrow \Delta_n}$, or $\vdash_{GCL_{\oplus}^{\star}} \Rightarrow \tau_{\Gamma_{i_1} \Rightarrow \Delta_{i_1}}, \ldots, \tau_{\Gamma_{i_l} \Rightarrow \Delta_{i_l}}$. By the invertibility of the logical rules of $GCL_{\oplus}^{\star}$, this happens iff either $\vdash_{GCL_{\oplus}^{\star}} \Gamma_{i_1}, \ldots, \Gamma_{i_l}, \Gamma_n \Rightarrow \Delta_{i_1}, \ldots, \Delta_{i_l}, \Delta_n$ or $\vdash_{GCL_{\oplus}^{\star}} \Gamma_{i_1}, \ldots, \Gamma_{i_l} \Rightarrow \Delta_{i_1}, \ldots, \Delta_{i_l}$. (So either $k = l + 1$ or $k = l$.) □

[6] An exact characterization of the expressive power of $\mathcal{L}_{\oplus}$ is given in [4].

[7] Hypersequents were independently introduced by Mints in [11], Pottinger in [12], and the author in [1] and [3]. Among other applications, they now provide the main framework for the proof theory of fuzzy logics ([9]).

Proposition 12 and Theorem 6 lead to the hypersequential extension $HGCL^{\star}_{\oplus}$ of $GCL^{\star}_{\oplus}$ which is presented in Fig. 3. It has the same axioms as $GCL^{\star}_{\oplus}$, as well as the hypersequential versions of all the rules of $GCL^{\star}_{\oplus}$. In addition, it has three new structural rules: the standard rules of external contraction ([EC]) and external weakening ([EW]), and the splitting rule [Sp]. (A hypersequential counterpart $HGCL_{\oplus}$ of $GCL_{\oplus}$ can be defined similarly, and again the two calculi can easily be shown to be equivalent using only analytic applications of rules.)

Axioms: $\Gamma \Rightarrow \Gamma$ (provided that $\#(\Gamma)$ is odd.)

Internal Structural Rules:

$$[\mathrm{P}]\quad \frac{H \mid \Gamma_1, \varphi, \psi, \Gamma_2 \Rightarrow \Delta}{H \mid \Gamma_1, \psi, \varphi, \Gamma_2 \Rightarrow \Delta} \qquad \frac{H \mid \Gamma \Rightarrow \Delta_1, \varphi, \psi, \Delta_2}{H \mid \Gamma \Rightarrow \Delta_1, \psi, \varphi, \Delta_2}$$

$$[\text{2-W}]\quad \frac{H \mid \Gamma_1, \Gamma_2 \Rightarrow \Delta}{H \mid \Gamma_1, \psi, \psi, \Gamma_2 \Rightarrow \Delta} \qquad \frac{H \mid \Gamma \Rightarrow \Delta_1, \Delta_2}{H \mid \Gamma \Rightarrow \Delta_1, \psi, \psi, \Delta_2}$$

$$[\text{2-D}]\quad \frac{H \mid \Gamma_1, \psi, \psi, \Gamma_2 \Rightarrow \Delta}{H \mid \Gamma_1, \Gamma_2 \Rightarrow \Delta} \qquad \frac{H \mid \Gamma \Rightarrow \Delta_1, \psi, \psi, \Delta_2}{H \mid \Gamma \Rightarrow \Delta_1, \Delta_2}$$

$$[\mathrm{Cut}]\quad \frac{H \mid \Gamma_1 \Rightarrow \Delta_1, \psi \qquad H \mid \Gamma_2, \psi \Rightarrow \Delta_2}{H \mid \Gamma_1, \Gamma_2 \Rightarrow \Delta_1, \Delta_2}$$

$$[\mathrm{Sp}]\quad \frac{H \mid \Gamma_1, \Gamma_2 \Rightarrow \Delta_1, \Delta_2}{H \mid \Gamma_1 \Rightarrow \Delta_1 \mid \Gamma_2 \Rightarrow \Delta_2}$$

External Structural Rules:

$$[\mathrm{EC}]\quad \frac{H \mid s \mid s}{H \mid s} \qquad [\mathrm{EW}]\quad \frac{H}{H \mid s}$$

Logical Rules:

$$[\oplus\Rightarrow]\quad \frac{H \mid \varphi, \Gamma \Rightarrow \Delta, \psi}{H \mid \varphi \oplus \psi, \Gamma \Rightarrow \Delta} \qquad [\Rightarrow\oplus]\quad \frac{H \mid \Gamma \Rightarrow \Delta, \varphi, \psi}{H \mid \Gamma \Rightarrow \Delta, \varphi \oplus \psi}$$

$$[\neg\Rightarrow]\quad \frac{H \mid \Gamma \Rightarrow \Delta, \varphi}{H \mid \Gamma, \neg\varphi \Rightarrow \Delta} \qquad [\Rightarrow\neg]\quad \frac{H \mid \Gamma, \varphi \Rightarrow \Delta}{H \mid \Gamma \Rightarrow \Delta, \neg\varphi}$$

Fig. 3. $HGCL^{\star}_{\oplus}$

Theorem 7. *A hypersequent H in $\mathcal{L}_{\oplus}$ is valid in $\mathcal{M}^{-}_{\oplus}$ iff it has a proof in $HGCL^{\star}_{\oplus}$ in which* [Cut], [2-D], *and* [EC] *are not used.*

Proof. This easily follows from Theorems 6 and 1. □

In order to generalize Theorem 7 to the consequence relation $\vdash_{\mathcal{M}^{-}_{\oplus}}$ between hypersequents, we add to $HGCL^{\star}_{\oplus}$ a counterpart of [Triv] (Definition 13).

Definition 16. The system $HGCL^{\star}_{\oplus,\neg}$ is obtained from $HGCL^{\star}_{\oplus}$ by the addition of the rule: from $H \mid\Rightarrow$ infer $H \mid \Gamma \Rightarrow \Delta$.

Theorem 8. *Let $\mathcal{S} \cup \{H\}$ be a set of hypersequents in $\mathcal{L}_{\oplus}$. $\mathcal{S} \vdash_{\mathcal{M}^{-}_{\oplus}} H$ iff there is a proof in $HGCL^{\star}_{\oplus,\neg}$ of H from $\mathcal{S}$ in which every application of* [Cut] *or* [2-D] *is on a formula in $\Gamma \cup \Delta$ for some component $\Gamma \Rightarrow \Delta$ of some element of $\mathcal{S}$.*

Proof (Outline). First, the proof of Theorem 6 can be extended without great difficulties to the following generalization: If $\mathcal{S}$ is a set of *sequents*, and $H = \Gamma_1 \Rightarrow \Delta_1 \mid \cdots \mid \Gamma_n \Rightarrow \Delta_n$ $(n \geq 1)$ is a hypersequent (all in $\mathcal{L}_{\oplus}$), then $\mathcal{S} \vdash_{\mathcal{M}^{-}_{\oplus}} H$ iff there is a proof from $\mathcal{S}$ in $GCL^{\star}_{\oplus}$ of either $\Rightarrow$, or of $\Gamma_{i_1}, \ldots, \Gamma_{i_k} \Rightarrow \Delta_{i_1}, \ldots, \Delta_{i_k}$ for some $i_1, \ldots, i_k \in \{1, \ldots, n\}$ $(1 \leq k \leq n)$. From Theorem 2 it follows that we may assume that this proof satisfies the condition given in the formulation of the theorem. The result for arbitrary set $\mathcal{S}$ of hypersequent follows now from the following easily established observations:

1. $\mathcal{S} \cup \{H_1 \mid H_2\} \vdash_{\mathcal{M}^{-}_{\oplus}} H$ iff $\mathcal{S} \cup \{H_1\} \vdash_{\mathcal{M}^{-}_{\oplus}} H$ and $\mathcal{S} \cup \{H_2\} \vdash_{\mathcal{M}^{-}_{\oplus}} H$.
2. Given proofs in $HGCL^{\star}_{\oplus,\neg}$ of H from $\mathcal{S} \cup \{H_1\}$ and from $\mathcal{S} \cup \{H_2\}$, we can combine them into a proof in $HGCL^{\star}_{\oplus,\neg}$ of H from $\mathcal{S} \cup \{H_1 \mid H_2\}$, which beside applications of [EC] uses exactly the same applications, with the same active formulas, of the axioms and rules used in the given proofs. □

We end this paper by explaining how the framework of hypersequents enables us to endow our system with the *full* power of propositional classical logic.

Definition 17. Let $\mathcal{L}_{Cl}$ be the language obtained by adding to $\mathcal{L}_{\oplus}$ the classical conjunction $\wedge$. $HGCL^{\star}_{\oplus,Cl}$ is the system in $\mathcal{L}_{Cl}$ which is obtained by adding to $HGCL^{\star}_{\oplus,\neg}$ the following two rules:

$$\frac{H \mid \Gamma \Rightarrow \Delta \mid \Gamma \Rightarrow \Delta, \varphi \quad H \mid \Gamma \Rightarrow \Delta \mid \Gamma \Rightarrow \Delta, \psi \quad H \mid \Gamma \Rightarrow \Delta, \varphi \mid \Gamma \Rightarrow \Delta, \psi}{H \mid \Gamma \Rightarrow \Delta, \varphi \wedge \psi}$$

$$\frac{H \mid \varphi, \Gamma \Rightarrow \Delta \mid \psi, \Gamma \Rightarrow \Delta, \psi \quad H \mid \varphi, \Gamma \Rightarrow \Delta, \varphi \mid \psi, \Gamma \Rightarrow \Delta \quad H \mid \varphi, \Gamma \Rightarrow \Delta \mid \psi, \Gamma \Rightarrow \Delta}{H \mid \varphi \wedge \psi, \Gamma \Rightarrow \Delta}$$

Theorem 9. *Let H be a hypersequent in $\mathcal{L}_{Cl}$. $\vdash_{\mathcal{M}^{-}_{\oplus}} H$ iff there is a proof in $HGCL^{\star}_{\oplus,Cl}$ of H in which there are no applications of* [Cut], [2-D], *or* [EC].

Proof. It is not difficult to check that like $HGCL^{\star}_{\oplus,\neg}$, all the logical rules of $HGCL^{\star}_{\oplus,Cl}$, *as well as all their inverses*, are strongly sound for the classical extension of $\mathcal{M}^{-}_{\oplus}$. (Note that each of the $\wedge$-rules has three inverses!) Hence for every hypersequent H one can construct a finite set S of clauses from which H can be derived using only logical rules, and H is valid iff all elements of S are valid. The theorem follows therefore from Theorem 7. □

Note 13. Unlike Theorem 7, Theorem 6 fails in the presence of $\wedge$. (A counterexample is given by $P_1 \Rightarrow P_1 \wedge P_2 \mid P_2 \Rightarrow P_1 \wedge P_2$.) In contrast, Theorem 8 *can* be generalized to $HGCL^{\star}_{\oplus,Cl}$. However, it is not really needed in order to use $HGCL^{\star}_{\oplus,Cl}$ for characterizing classical logic, since the following fact suffices: ψ classically follows from $\{\varphi_1, \ldots, \varphi_n\}$ iff $\vdash_{HGCL^{\star}_{\oplus,Cl}} \varphi_1 \Rightarrow\mid \cdots \mid \varphi_n \Rightarrow\mid\Rightarrow \psi$.

References

1. Avron, A.: A constructive analysis of RM. J. Symb. Log. **52**, 939–951 (1987)
2. Avron, A.: Simple consequence relations. Inf. Comput. **92**, 105–139 (1991)
3. Avron, A.: The method of hypersequents in proof theory of propositional non-classical logics. In: Hodges, W., Hyland, M., Steinhorn, C., Truss, J. (eds.) Logic: Foundations to Applications, pp. 1–32. Oxford Science Publications (1996)
4. Avron, A.: Implication, Equivalence, and Negation. Logical Investigations **27**, 31–45 (2021)
5. Gentzen, G.: Investigations into logical deduction, 1934. In: Szabo, M.E. (ed.) German. An English Translation Appears in 'The Collected Works of Gerhard Gentzen'. North-Holland (1969)
6. Girard, J.E.: Linear logic. Theor. Comput. Sci. **50**, 1–102 (1987)
7. Gottwald, S.: A Treatise on Many-Valued Logics, Studies in Logic and Computation, vol. 9. Research Studies Press, Baldock (2001)
8. Massey, G.J.: Negation, material equivalence, and conditioned nonconjunction: completeness and duality. Notre Dame J. Formal Log. **18**, 140–144 (1977)
9. Metcalfe, G., Olivetti, N., Gabbay, D.: Proof Theory for Fuzzy Logics. Springer, Heidelberg (2009)
10. Mihailescu, E.G.: Recherches sur la negation el l'équivalence dans le calcul des proposition. Annales scientiftques de l'Université de Jas **23**, 369–408 (1937)
11. Mints, G.E.: Some calculi of modal logic. Proc. Steklov Inst. Math. **98**, 97–122 (1968)
12. Pottinger, G.: Uniform, cut-free formulations of T, S4 and S5 (abstract). J. Symb. Log. **48**, 900 (1983)
13. Urquhart, A.: Many-valued logic. In: Gabbay, D., Guenthner, F. (eds.) Handbook of Philosophical Logic, vol. II, 2nd edn., pp. 249–295. Kluwer (2001)

Proof Search on Bilateralist Judgments over Non-deterministic Semantics

Vitor Greati[1(✉)], Sérgio Marcelino[2], and João Marcos[1]

[1] Universidade Federal do Rio Grande do Norte, Natal, Brazil
vitor.greati.017@ufrn.edu.br
[2] Instituto de Telecomunicações, Lisboa, Portugal

Abstract. The bilateralist approach to logical consequence maintains that judgments of different qualities should be taken into account in determining what-follows-from-what. We argue that such an approach may be actualized by a two-dimensional notion of entailment induced by semantic structures that also accommodate non-deterministic and partial interpretations, and propose a proof-theoretical apparatus to reason over bilateralist judgments using symmetrical two-dimensional analytical Hilbert-style calculi. We also provide a proof-search algorithm for finite analytic calculi that runs in at most exponential time, in general, and in polynomial time when only rules having at most one formula in the succedent are present in the concerned calculus.

Keywords: Bilateralism · Two-dimensional consequence · Proof search

1 Introduction

The conventional approach to bilateralism in logic treats denial as a primitive judgment, on a par with assertion. One way of allowing these two kinds of judgments to coexist without necessarily allowing them to interfere with one another is by considering a two-dimensional notion of consequence, in which the validity of logical statements obtains in terms of preservation of acceptance along one dimension and of rejection along the other. From a semantical standpoint, as we will show, this idea may be actualized by the canonical notion of entailment induced by a $\mathsf{B}^{\mathsf{PN}}_{\Sigma}$-matrix, a partial non-deterministic logical matrix in which the latter judgments, or cognitive attitudes, are represented by separate collections of truth-values. This will, in particular, allow for distinct Tarskian (one-dimensional, generalized) consequence relations to coinhabit the same logical structure while keeping their interactions disciplined.

A common practice for incorporating bilateralism into a proof formalism consists in attaching to the underlying formulas a force indicator or signal, say + for assertion and − for denial [15,22]. For example, the inference $-(A \to B) \vdash +A$ describes a rule in the bilateral axiomatization of classical logic given in [22], representing the impossibility of, at once, denying $A \to B$ while failing to assert A. In [9], a concurrent approach is offered that consists in working with

A. Das and S. Negri (Eds.): TABLEAUX 2021, LNAI 12842, pp. 129–146, 2021.
https://doi.org/10.1007/978-3-030-86059-2_8

a two-dimensional notion of consequence, allowing for the cognitive attitudes of acceptance and rejection to act over two separate logical dimensions and taking their interaction into consideration in determining the meaning of logical connectives and of the statements involving them. The aforementioned inference, for instance, would be expressed by the two-dimensional judgment $\frac{\varnothing}{\varnothing} \Big| \frac{A}{A \to B}$, which is intended to enforce that an agent is not expected to find reasons for rejecting $A \to B$ while failing to find reasons for accepting A. From a semantical standpoint, the latter notion of consequence may be induced by a two-dimensional logical matrix [7,9], whose associated two-dimensional canonical entailment relation very naturally embraces bilateralism and involves two possibly distinct collections of distinguished truth-values: the 'designated' values and the 'anti-designated' values, respectively equated with acceptance and rejection.

Non-deterministic logical matrices have been extensively investigated in recent years, and proved useful in the construction of effective semantics for many families of logics in a systematic and modular way [5,12,12,19]. As in [6], in the present paper the interpretations of the connectives in a matrix outputs (possibly empty) sets of values, instead of a single value. In our study, we explore an essential feature of (partial) non-deterministic semantics, namely *effectiveness*, to provide analytic axiomatizations for a very inclusive class of finite *monadic* two-dimensional matrices. The latter consist in matrices whose underlying linguistic resources are sufficiently expressive so as to uniquely characterize each of the underlying truth-values, in a similar vein as in [10,13]. In contrast to the multi-dimensional Gentzen-style calculi used in the literature to axiomatize many-valued logics in the context of bilateralism (and multilateralism) [16], we introduce much simpler two-dimensional symmetrical Hilbert-style calculi to the same effect and show how they give rise to derivations that do not conform to the received view that axiomatic proofs consist simply in 'sequences of formulas'. In our approach, indeed, extending to the bilateralist case the one-dimensional tree-derivation mechanism considered in [10,20,23], the inference rules, instead of manipulating metalinguistic objects, deal only with pairs of accepted/rejected formulas, and derivations are trees whose nodes come labelled with such pairs and result from expansions determined by the rules. As we will show, the *analyticity* of the axiomatizations that we extract from our two-dimensional (partial) non-deterministic matrices, using symmetrical rules that internalize 'case exhaustion', allows for bounded proof search, and the design of a simple recursive decision algorithm that runs in exponential time.

The paper is organized as follows: Sect. 2 introduces the basic concepts and terminology involved in two-dimensional notions of consequence and in symmetrical analytic Hilbert-style calculi. Section 3 presents the general axiomatization procedure for finite monadic matrices, illustrating it and highlighting its modularity via the correspondence between refining a matrix and adding rules to a sound symmetrical two-dimensional calculus. Then, Sect. 4 describes our proposed proof-search algorithm, proves its correctness and investigates its worst-case exponential asymptotic complexity. In the final remarks, we reflect upon the obtained results and indicate some directions for future developments. Detailed proofs of the main results may be found at https://tinyurl.com/21-GMM-Bilat.

2 Preliminaries

2.1 Languages

A *propositional signature* Σ is a family $\{\Sigma_k\}_{k\in\omega}$, where each Σ_k is a collection of k-*ary connectives*. Given a denumerable set $\mathcal{P} := \{p_i \mid i \in \omega\}$ of *propositional variables*, the *propositional language over* Σ *generated by* $\mathcal{P}$, $\mathbf{L}_\Sigma(\mathcal{P})$, is the absolutely free algebra over Σ freely generated by $\mathcal{P}$. The elements of $L_\Sigma(\mathcal{P})$, the carrier set of the latter algebra, are called *formulas* and will be indicated below by capital Roman letters. As usual, whenever there is no risk of confusion, we will omit braces and unions in collecting sets and formulas, and leave a blank space in place of $\varnothing$. For convenience, given $\Phi \subseteq L_\Sigma(\mathcal{P})$, the set of formulas not in Φ will be denoted by Φ^c. On any given language, we may define the functions subf and props, which output, respectively, the subformulas and the propositional variables occurring in a given formula, and define as well the function size, such that $\mathsf{size}(p) := 1$ for each $p \in \mathcal{P}$, and $\mathsf{size}(©(A_1,\ldots,A_k)) := 1 + \sum_{i=1}^{k} \mathsf{size}(A_i)$, for each $k \in \omega$ and $© \in \Sigma_k$. Moreover, as usual, endomorphisms on $\mathbf{L}_\Sigma(\mathcal{P})$ are called *substitutions*, and, given a formula $B \in L_\Sigma(\mathcal{P})$ with $\mathsf{props}(B) \subseteq \{p_{i_1},\ldots,p_{i_k}\}$, for some $k \in \omega$, we write $B(A_1,\ldots,A_k)$ for the image of B under a substitution σ where $\sigma(p_{i_j}) = A_j$, for all $1 \leq j \leq k$, and where $\sigma(p) = p$ otherwise; for a set Φ of one-variable formulas, we let $\Phi(A) := \{B(A) \mid B \in \Phi\}$.

2.2 Two-Dimensional Consequence Relations

Hereupon, we shall call B-*statement* any 2×2-place tuple $\left(\begin{array}{c:c}\Phi_{\text{И}} & \Phi_{\text{⅄}}\\ \hdashline \Phi_{\text{Y}} & \Phi_{\text{N}}\end{array}\right)$ of sets of formulas in a given language. By definition, a collection of B-statements will be said to constitute a B-*consequence relation* $\frac{\cdot}{\cdot}|\frac{\cdot}{\cdot}$ provided that any of the following conditions constitutes a sufficient guarantee for the *consequence judgment* $\frac{\Phi_{\text{И}}}{\Phi_{\text{Y}}}|\frac{\Phi_{\text{⅄}}}{\Phi_{\text{N}}}$ to be established:

(O) $\Phi_{\text{Y}} \cap \Phi_{\text{⅄}} \neq \varnothing$ or $\Phi_{\text{N}} \cap \Phi_{\text{И}} \neq \varnothing$

(D) $\frac{\Psi_{\text{И}}}{\Psi_{\text{Y}}}|\frac{\Psi_{\text{⅄}}}{\Psi_{\text{N}}}$ and $\Psi_\alpha \subseteq \Phi_\alpha$ for every $\alpha \in \{\text{Y}, \text{N}, \text{⅄}, \text{И}\}$

(C) $\frac{\Omega_{\text{Ƨ}}^c}{\Omega_{\text{S}}}|\frac{\Omega_{\text{S}}^c}{\Omega_{\text{Ƨ}}}$ for all $\Phi_{\text{Y}} \subseteq \Omega_{\text{S}} \subseteq \Phi_{\text{⅄}}^c$ and $\Phi_{\text{N}} \subseteq \Omega_{\text{Ƨ}} \subseteq \Phi_{\text{И}}^c$

(S) $\frac{\Psi_{\text{И}}}{\Psi_{\text{Y}}}|\frac{\Psi_{\text{⅄}}}{\Psi_{\text{N}}}$ and $\Phi_\alpha = \sigma(\Psi_\alpha)$ for every $\alpha \in \{\text{Y}, \text{N}, \text{⅄}, \text{И}\}$, for a substitution σ

In the above conditions, $\Phi_{\text{Y}}, \Phi_{\text{N}}, \Phi_{\text{⅄}}, \Phi_{\text{И}}$ denote arbitrary sets of formulas, that may intuitively be read as representing, respectively, collections of *accepted*, *rejected*, *non-accepted* and *non-rejected* formulas. It is not hard to check that such definition, employing the properties of (O)verlap, (D)ilution, (C)ut and (S)ubstitution-invariance, is equivalent to the one found in [9], and it generalizes the well-known abstract Tarskian one-dimensional account of logical consequence. In addition, a B-consequence relation will be called *finitary* when a consequence judgment $\frac{\Phi_{\text{И}}}{\Phi_{\text{Y}}}|\frac{\Phi_{\text{⅄}}}{\Phi_{\text{N}}}$ always implies that:

(F) $\frac{\Phi^{\mathsf{f}}_{\text{И}}}{\Phi^{\mathsf{f}}_{\mathsf{Y}}} \mid \frac{\Phi^{\mathsf{f}}_{\text{⅄}}}{\Phi^{\mathsf{f}}_{\mathsf{N}}}$, for some finite $\Phi^{\mathsf{f}}_{\alpha} \subseteq \Phi_{\alpha}$, for every $\alpha \in \{\mathsf{Y}, \mathsf{N}, \text{⅄}, \text{И}\}$

We will denote by $\frac{\cdot}{\cdot} \nmid \frac{\cdot}{\cdot}$ the complement of $\frac{\cdot}{\cdot} \mid \frac{\cdot}{\cdot}$, sometimes called the *compatibility relation* associated to $\frac{\cdot}{\cdot} \mid \frac{\cdot}{\cdot}$ (cf. [8]). Furthermore, we should note that later on we will sometimes write $\tilde{\mathsf{Y}}$ for ⅄, write $\tilde{\text{⅄}}$ for Y, write $\tilde{\mathsf{N}}$ for И, and write $\tilde{\text{И}}$ for N.

A B-consequence relation $\frac{\cdot}{\cdot} \mid \frac{\cdot}{\cdot}$ may be said to induce a 2-place relation $\cdot \rhd^{\mathsf{t}} \cdot$ over $\mathsf{Pow}(L_{\Sigma}(\mathcal{P}))$ by setting $\Phi_{\mathsf{Y}} \rhd^{\mathsf{t}} \Phi_{\text{⅄}}$ iff $\frac{\varnothing}{\Phi_{\mathsf{Y}}} \mid \frac{\Phi_{\text{⅄}}}{\varnothing}$. This is easily seen to constitute a generalized (one-dimensional) consequence relation. Another such relation is induced by setting $\Phi_{\mathsf{N}} \rhd^{\mathsf{f}} \Phi_{\text{И}}$ iff $\frac{\Phi_{\text{И}}}{\varnothing} \mid \frac{\varnothing}{\Phi_{\mathsf{N}}}$. Connected to that, we will say that $\cdot \rhd^{\mathsf{t}} \cdot$ *inhabits the* $\mathtt{t}$*-aspect of* $\frac{\cdot}{\cdot} \mid \frac{\cdot}{\cdot}$, and that $\cdot \rhd^{\mathsf{f}} \cdot$ *inhabits the* $\mathtt{f}$*-aspect of* $\frac{\cdot}{\cdot} \mid \frac{\cdot}{\cdot}$. These are but two of many possible aspects of interest of a given B-consequence relation; in principle, very different Tarskian —and also non-Tarskian!— logics may coinhabit the same given two-dimensional consequence relation (see [9]).

Finally, a B-consequence $\frac{\cdot}{\cdot} \mid \frac{\cdot}{\cdot}$ is said to be *decidable* when there is some *decision procedure* that takes a B-statement $\left(\frac{\Phi_{\text{И}}}{\Phi_{\mathsf{Y}}} \vdots \frac{\Phi_{\text{⅄}}}{\Phi_{\mathsf{N}}}\right)$ with finite component sets as input, outputs `true` when $\frac{\Phi_{\text{И}}}{\Phi_{\mathsf{Y}}} \mid \frac{\Phi_{\text{⅄}}}{\Phi_{\mathsf{N}}}$ is the case, and outputs `false` when $\frac{\Phi_{\text{И}}}{\Phi_{\mathsf{Y}}} \nmid \frac{\Phi_{\text{⅄}}}{\Phi_{\mathsf{N}}}$.

2.3 Two-Dimensional Non-deterministic Matrices

A *partial non-deterministic* B*–matrix* $\mathbb{M}$ *over a signature* Σ, or simply $\mathsf{B}^{\mathsf{PN}}_{\Sigma}$*-matrix*, is a structure $\langle \mathcal{V}^{\mathbb{M}}, \mathsf{Y}^{\mathbb{M}}, \mathsf{N}^{\mathbb{M}}, \cdot^{\mathbb{M}} \rangle$ where the set $\mathcal{V}^{\mathbb{M}}$ is said to contain *truth-values*, the sets $\mathsf{Y}^{\mathbb{M}}, \mathsf{N}^{\mathbb{M}} \subseteq \mathcal{V}^{\mathbb{M}}$ are said to contain, respectively, the *designated* and the *anti-designated* truth-values, and, for each $\mathrm{k} \in \omega$ and $\copyright \in \Sigma_{\mathrm{k}}$, the mapping $\copyright^{\mathbb{M}} : (\mathcal{V}^{\mathbb{M}})^{\mathrm{k}} \to \mathsf{Pow}(\mathcal{V}^{\mathbb{M}})$ is the *interpretation* of $\copyright$ in $\mathbb{M}$. For convenience, we define $\text{⅄}^{\mathbb{M}} := \mathcal{V}^{\mathbb{M}} \backslash \mathsf{Y}^{\mathbb{M}}$ and $\text{И}^{\mathbb{M}} := \mathcal{V}^{\mathbb{M}} \backslash \mathsf{N}^{\mathbb{M}}$. A $\mathsf{B}^{\mathsf{PN}}_{\Sigma}$-matrix is said to be *total* when $\varnothing$ is not in the range of the interpretation of any connective of Σ, *deterministic* when the range of any interpretation contains only singletons, also called *deterministic images*, and *fully indeterministic* if it allows for the maximum degree of non-determinism, that is, if $\copyright^{\mathbb{M}}(x_1, \ldots, x_{\mathrm{k}}) = \mathcal{V}^{\mathbb{M}}$ for each $\mathrm{k} \in \omega$ and $\copyright \in \Sigma_{\mathrm{k}}$, and all $x_1, \ldots, x_{\mathrm{k}} \in \mathcal{V}^{\mathbb{M}}$.

In the following definitions, $\mathbb{M}$ will represent an arbitrary $\mathsf{B}^{\mathsf{PN}}_{\Sigma}$*-matrix.*

Given a set of truth-values $\mathcal{X} \subseteq \mathcal{V}^{\mathbb{M}}$, the *sub–*$\mathsf{B}^{\mathsf{PN}}_{\Sigma}$*matrix* $\mathbb{M}_{\mathcal{X}}$ *induced by* $\mathcal{X}$ is the $\mathsf{B}^{\mathsf{PN}}_{\Sigma}$matrix $\langle \mathcal{X}, \mathsf{Y}^{\mathbb{M}} \cap \mathcal{X}, \mathsf{N}^{\mathbb{M}} \cap \mathcal{X}, \cdot^{\mathbb{M}_{\mathcal{X}}} \rangle$ such that $\copyright^{\mathbb{M}_{\mathcal{X}}}(x_1, \ldots, x_{\mathrm{k}}) := \copyright^{\mathbb{M}}(x_1, \ldots, x_{\mathrm{k}}) \cap \mathcal{X}$, for all $x_1, \ldots, x_{\mathrm{k}} \in \mathcal{X}$, $\mathrm{k} \in \omega$ and $\copyright \in \Sigma_{\mathrm{k}}$. The set of all subsets of the values of each non-empty total sub–$\mathsf{B}^{\mathsf{PN}}_{\Sigma}$matrix of $\mathbb{M}$ will be denoted by $\mathbb{T}_{\mathbb{M}}$, that is,

$$\mathbb{T}_{\mathbb{M}} := \bigcup_{\substack{\varnothing \neq \mathcal{X} \subseteq \mathcal{V}^{\mathbb{M}} \\ \mathbb{M}_{\mathcal{X}} \text{ total}}} \mathsf{Pow}(\mathcal{X}).$$

Check Example 3 for an illustration of the latter.

We shall call $\mathbb{M}$*-valuation* any mapping $v : L_{\Sigma}(\mathcal{P}) \to \mathcal{V}^{\mathbb{M}}$ such that $v(\copyright(A_1, \ldots, A_{\mathrm{k}})) \in \copyright^{\mathbb{M}}(v(A_1), \ldots, v(A_{\mathrm{k}}))$ for all $\mathrm{k} \in \omega$, $\copyright \in \Sigma_{\mathrm{k}}$ and

$A_1, \ldots, A_k \in L_\Sigma(\mathcal{P})$. As proved in [6], given a set $\Phi \subseteq L_\Sigma(\mathcal{P})$ closed under subformulas, any mapping $f : \Phi \to \mathcal{V}^{\mathbb{M}}$ extends to an $\mathbb{M}$-valuation provided that $f(©(A_1, \ldots, A_k)) \in ©^{\mathbb{M}}(f(A_1), \ldots, f(A_k))$, for every $©(A_1, \ldots, A_k) \in \Phi$, and $f(\Phi) \in \mathbb{T}_{\mathbb{M}}$. Notice that if we disregard the latter condition we obtain the property of *effectiveness* for total non-deterministic matrices ([2]); as this very condition holds for all such matrices, by making it explicit in the previous definition we obtain a generalization of effectiveness that also applies to partial non-deterministic matrices. Any formula $A \in L_\Sigma(\mathcal{P})$ with $\mathsf{props}(A) = \{p_{i_1}, \ldots, p_{i_k}\}$ may be interpreted on $\mathbb{M}$ as a k-ary mapping $A^{\mathbb{M}}$ such that $A^{\mathbb{M}}(x_1, \ldots, x_k) := \{v(A) \mid v \text{ is an } \mathbb{M}\text{-valuation and } v(p_{i_1}) = x_1, \ldots, v(p_{i_k}) = x_k\}$.

The B-*entailment relation induced by* $\mathbb{M}$ is a 2×2-place relation $\div|\div_{\mathbb{M}}$ over $L_\Sigma(\mathcal{P})$ such that:

(B-ent) $\dfrac{\Phi_{\text{И}}}{\Phi_{\mathsf{Y}}} \Big| \dfrac{\Phi_{\text{⅄}}}{\Phi_{\mathsf{N}}}\,\mathbb{M}$ iff there is no $\mathbb{M}$-valuation v such that $v(\Phi_\alpha) \subseteq \alpha^{\mathbb{M}}$ for every $\alpha \in \{\mathsf{Y}, \mathsf{N}, \text{⅄}, \text{И}\}$

for every $\Phi_{\mathsf{Y}}, \Phi_{\mathsf{N}}, \Phi_{\text{⅄}}, \Phi_{\text{И}} \subseteq L_\Sigma(\mathcal{P})$. Whenever $\frac{\Phi_{\text{И}}}{\Phi_{\mathsf{Y}}} | \frac{\Phi_{\text{⅄}}}{\Phi_{\mathsf{N}}}\,\mathbb{M}$, we say that the B-statement $\left(\frac{\Phi_{\text{И}}}{\Phi_{\mathsf{Y}}} \vdots \frac{\Phi_{\text{⅄}}}{\Phi_{\mathsf{N}}}\right)$ *holds* in $\mathbb{M}$. It is straightforward to check that (see [7]):

Proposition 1. *The* B-*entailment relation induced by a* $\mathsf{B}^{\mathsf{PN}}_{\Sigma}$-*matrix is a* B-*consequence relation.*

Example 1. Let $\mathcal{V}_4 := \{\mathbf{f}, \bot, \top, \mathbf{t}\}$, $\mathsf{Y}_4 := \{\top, \mathbf{t}\}$, $\mathsf{N}_4 := \{\top, \mathbf{f}\}$, and consider a signature Σ^{FDE} containing but two binary connectives, $\wedge$ and $\vee$, and one unary connective, $\neg$. Next, define the $\mathsf{B}^{\mathsf{PN}}_{\Sigma^{\text{FDE}}}$-matrix $\mathbb{I} := \langle \mathcal{V}_4, \mathsf{Y}_4, \mathsf{N}_4, \cdot^{\mathbb{I}} \rangle$ that interprets the latter connectives according to the following (non-deterministic) truth-tables (here and below, braces will be omitted from the images of the interpretations):

$\wedge^{\mathbb{I}}$	$\mathbf{f}$	$\bot$	$\top$	$\mathbf{t}$
$\mathbf{f}$	$\mathbf{f}$	$\mathbf{f}$	$\mathbf{f}$	$\mathbf{f}$
$\bot$	$\mathbf{f}$	$\mathbf{f}, \bot$	$\mathbf{f}$	$\mathbf{f}, \bot$
$\top$	$\mathbf{f}$	$\mathbf{f}$	$\top$	$\top$
$\mathbf{t}$	$\mathbf{f}$	$\mathbf{f}, \bot$	$\top$	$\mathbf{t}, \top$

$\vee^{\mathbb{I}}$	$\mathbf{f}$	$\bot$	$\top$	$\mathbf{t}$
$\mathbf{f}$	$\mathbf{f}, \top$	$\mathbf{t}, \bot$	$\top$	$\mathbf{t}$
$\bot$	$\mathbf{t}, \bot$	$\mathbf{t}, \bot$	$\mathbf{t}$	$\mathbf{t}$
$\top$	$\top$	$\mathbf{t}$	$\top$	$\mathbf{t}$
$\mathbf{t}$	$\mathbf{t}$	$\mathbf{t}$	$\mathbf{t}$	$\mathbf{t}$

	$\neg^{\mathbb{I}}$
$\mathbf{f}$	$\mathbf{t}$
$\bot$	$\bot$
$\top$	$\top$
$\mathbf{t}$	$\mathbf{f}$

The t-aspect of $\div|\div\,\mathbb{I}$ is inhabited by the logic introduced in [3], which incorporates some principles on how a processor would be expected to deal with information about an arbitrary set of formulas.

Given two $\mathsf{B}^{\mathsf{PN}}_{\Sigma}$-matrices $\mathbb{M}_1$ and $\mathbb{M}_2$, we say that $\mathbb{M}_2$ is a *refinement* of $\mathbb{M}_1$ when $\mathcal{V}^{\mathbb{M}_2} \subseteq \mathcal{V}^{\mathbb{M}_1}$ and $©^{\mathbb{M}_2}(x_1, \ldots, x_k) \subseteq ©^{\mathbb{M}_1}(x_1, \ldots, x_k)$ for each $k \in \omega$ and $© \in \Sigma_k$, and for every $x_1, \ldots, x_k \in \mathcal{V}^{\mathbb{M}_2}$. Also, we say that $\cdot^{\mathbb{M}_2}$ *agrees with* $\cdot^{\mathbb{M}_1}$ when both provide the same interpretations for the connectives of Σ. Evidently, every $\mathsf{B}^{\mathsf{PN}}_{\Sigma}$-matrix is a refinement of the corresponding fully indeterministic $\mathsf{B}^{\mathsf{PN}}_{\Sigma}$-matrix. In the examples that follow, we illustrate a couple of refinements of the

$\mathsf{B}^{\mathsf{PN}}_{\Sigma}$-matrix $\mathbb{I}$ presented in Example 1, giving rise to (two-dimensional versions of) other well-known logics.

Example 2. Let $\mathbb{E} := \langle \mathcal{V}_4, \mathsf{Y}_4, \mathsf{N}_4, \cdot^{\mathbb{E}} \rangle$ be the $\mathsf{B}^{\mathsf{PN}}_{\Sigma^{\mathrm{FDE}}}$-matrix consisting of a refinement of $\mathbb{I}$ with interpretations given by the following tables:

$\wedge^{\mathbb{E}}$	$\mathbf{f}$	$\bot$	$\top$	$\mathbf{t}$
$\mathbf{f}$	$\mathbf{f}$	$\mathbf{f}$	$\mathbf{f}$	$\mathbf{f}$
$\bot$	$\mathbf{f}$	$\bot$	$\mathbf{f}$	$\bot$
$\top$	$\mathbf{f}$	$\mathbf{f}$	$\top$	$\top$
$\mathbf{t}$	$\mathbf{f}$	$\bot$	$\top$	$\mathbf{t}$

$\vee^{\mathbb{E}}$	$\mathbf{f}$	$\bot$	$\top$	$\mathbf{t}$
$\mathbf{f}$	$\mathbf{f}$	$\bot$	$\top$	$\mathbf{t}$
$\bot$	$\bot$	$\bot$	$\mathbf{t}$	$\mathbf{t}$
$\top$	$\top$	$\mathbf{t}$	$\top$	$\mathbf{t}$
$\mathbf{t}$	$\mathbf{t}$	$\mathbf{t}$	$\mathbf{t}$	$\mathbf{t}$

	$\neg^{\mathbb{E}}$
$\mathbf{f}$	$\mathbf{t}$
$\bot$	$\bot$
$\top$	$\top$
$\mathbf{t}$	$\mathbf{f}$

One may readily see that these interpretations correspond to the ones of First Degree Entailment and that this $\mathsf{B}^{\mathsf{PN}}_{\Sigma^{\mathrm{FDE}}}$-matrix corresponds to the logic $\mathbf{E}^{\mathrm{B}}$ presented in [7].

Example 3. We may still refine $\mathbb{E}$ (and thus $\mathbb{I}$) a little more. Let $\mathbb{K} := \langle \mathcal{V}_4, \mathsf{Y}_4, \mathsf{N}_4, \cdot^{\mathbb{K}} \rangle$ be the $\mathsf{B}^{\mathsf{PN}}_{\Sigma^{\mathrm{FDE}}}$-matrix such that $\cdot^{\mathbb{K}}$ agrees with $\cdot^{\mathbb{E}}$ except that $\wedge^{\mathbb{K}}(\top,\bot) = \vee^{\mathbb{K}}(\top,\bot) = \wedge^{\mathbb{K}}(\bot,\top) = \vee^{\mathbb{K}}(\bot,\top) = \varnothing$. Note that $\mathbb{T}_{\mathbb{K}} = \{\mathcal{X} \subseteq \mathcal{V}_4 \mid \{\top,\bot\} \nsubseteq \mathcal{X}\}$. As shown in [10], Kleene's strong three-valued logic inhabits the t-aspect of $\div|\div\,\mathbb{K}$.

Example 4. Let $\mathcal{V}_5 := \{\mathrm{f}, \mathrm{F}, \mathrm{I}, \mathrm{T}, \mathrm{t}\}$, $\mathsf{Y}_5 := \{\mathrm{T}, \mathrm{I}, \mathrm{t}\}$, $\mathsf{N}_5 := \{\mathrm{T}, \mathrm{I}, \mathrm{f}\}$, and consider a signature Σ^{mCi} containing but three binary connectives, $\wedge$, $\vee$ and $\supset$, and two unary connectives, $\neg$ and $\circ$. Inspired by the 5-valued non-deterministic logical matrix presented in [1] for the logic of formal inconsistency called **mCi** [21], we define the $\mathsf{B}^{\mathsf{PN}}_{\Sigma^{\mathrm{mCi}}}$-matrix $\mathbb{P} := \langle \mathcal{V}_5, \mathsf{Y}_5, \mathsf{N}_5, \cdot^{\mathbb{P}} \rangle$ with the following interpretations:

$$\wedge^{\mathbb{P}}(x_1, x_2) := \begin{cases} \{\mathrm{f}\} & \text{if either } x_1 \notin \mathsf{Y}_5 \text{ or } x_2 \notin \mathsf{Y}_5 \\ \{\mathrm{t}, \mathrm{I}\} & \text{otherwise} \end{cases}$$

$$\vee^{\mathbb{P}}(x_1, x_2) := \begin{cases} \{\mathrm{t}, \mathrm{I}\} & \text{if either } x_1 \in \mathsf{Y}_5 \text{ or } x_2 \in \mathsf{Y}_5 \\ \{\mathrm{f}\} & \text{if } x_1, x_2 \notin \mathsf{Y}_5 \end{cases}$$

$$\supset^{\mathbb{P}}(x_1, x_2) := \begin{cases} \{\mathrm{t}, \mathrm{I}\} & \text{if either } x_1 \notin \mathsf{Y}_5 \text{ or } x_2 \in \mathsf{Y}_5 \\ \{\mathrm{f}\} & \text{if } x_1 \in \mathsf{Y}_5 \text{ and } x_2 \notin \mathsf{Y}_5 \end{cases}$$

	f	F	I	T	t
$\neg^{\mathbb{P}}$	t,I	T	t,I	F	f

	f	F	I	T	t
$\circ^{\mathbb{P}}$	T	T	F	T	T

We note that the logic **mCi** inhabits the t-aspect of $\div|\div\,\mathbb{P}$. It is worth pointing out that, up to now, no *finite* Hilbert-style calculus was known to axiomatize this logic; however, a finite two-dimensional symmetrical Hilbert-style calculus for **mCi** results smoothly from the procedure described in the next section.

Given $\mathcal{X}, \mathcal{Y} \subseteq \mathcal{V}^{\mathbb{M}}$ and $\alpha \in \{\mathsf{Y}, \mathsf{N}\}$, we say that $\mathcal{X}$ and $\mathcal{Y}$ are *α-separated*, denoted by $\mathcal{X} \#_{\alpha} \mathcal{Y}$, if $\mathcal{X} \subseteq \alpha^{\mathbb{M}}$ and $\mathcal{Y} \subseteq \mathcal{V}^{\mathbb{M}} \setminus \alpha^{\mathbb{M}}$, or vice-versa. Given two truth-values $x, y \in \mathcal{V}^{\mathbb{M}}$, a single-variable formula S is a *monadic separator for x and y* whenever $\mathrm{S}^{\mathbb{M}}(x) \#_{\alpha} \mathrm{S}^{\mathbb{M}}(y)$, for some $\alpha \in \{\mathsf{Y}, \mathsf{N}\}$. The $\mathsf{B}^{\mathsf{PN}}_{\Sigma}$-matrix $\mathbb{M}$ is said to be *monadic* when for each pair of distinct truth-values of $\mathbb{M}$ there is a monadic separator for these values.[1] We say that a set of single-variable formulas $\mathcal{D}^x$ *isolates x* whenever, for every $y \neq x$, there exists a monadic separator $\mathrm{S} \in \mathcal{D}^x$ for x and y. A *discriminator for* $\mathbb{M}$, then, is a family $\mathcal{D} := \{(\mathcal{D}^x_{\mathsf{Y}}, \mathcal{D}^x_{\text{⅄}}, \mathcal{D}^x_{\mathsf{N}}, \mathcal{D}^x_{\text{И}})\}_{x \in \mathcal{V}^{\mathbb{M}}}$ such that $\mathcal{D}^x := \bigcup_{\alpha} \mathcal{D}^x_{\alpha}$ isolates x and $\mathrm{S}^{\mathbb{M}}(x) \subseteq \alpha^{\mathbb{M}}$ whenever $\mathrm{S} \in \mathcal{D}^x_{\alpha}$. We denote the set $\bigcup_{x \in \mathcal{V}^{\mathbb{M}}} \mathcal{D}^x$ by $\mathcal{D}^{\bowtie}$ and say that $\mathcal{D}$ *is based on* $\mathcal{D}^{\bowtie}$.

Example 5. The tables below describe, respectively, a discriminator based on $\{\mathrm{p}\}$ for any $\mathsf{B}^{\mathsf{PN}}_{\Sigma}$-matrix of the form $\langle \mathcal{V}_4, \mathsf{Y}_4, \mathsf{N}_4, \cdot \rangle$ (see Examples 1, 2 and 3) and a discriminator for $\mathbb{P}$ based on $\{\mathrm{p}, \neg\mathrm{p}\}$ (of Example 4):

x	$\mathcal{D}^x_{\mathsf{Y}}$	$\mathcal{D}^x_{\text{⅄}}$	$\mathcal{D}^x_{\mathsf{N}}$	$\mathcal{D}^x_{\text{И}}$
f	∅	p	p	∅
⊥	∅	p	∅	p
⊤	p	∅	p	∅
t	p	∅	∅	p

x	$\mathcal{D}^x_{\mathsf{Y}}$	$\mathcal{D}^x_{\text{⅄}}$	$\mathcal{D}^x_{\mathsf{N}}$	$\mathcal{D}^x_{\text{И}}$
f	∅	p	p	∅
F	∅	p	∅	p
I	p, ¬p	∅	p	∅
T	p	¬p	p	∅
t	p	∅	∅	p

The following result —which will be instrumental, in particular, within the soundness proof of the axiomatizations that we will develop later on— shows that a discriminator is capable of uniquely characterizing each truth-value of the corresponding $\mathsf{B}^{\mathsf{PN}}_{\Sigma}$-matrix:

Lemma 1. *If* $\mathbb{M}$ *is a monadic* $\mathsf{B}^{\mathsf{PN}}_{\Sigma}$*-matrix and* $\mathcal{D}$ *is a discriminator for* $\mathbb{M}$*, then, for all* $\mathrm{A} \in \mathrm{L}_{\Sigma}(\mathcal{P})$, $x \in \mathcal{V}^{\mathbb{M}}$ *and* $\mathbb{M}$*-valuation* $\mathfrak{v}$,

$$\mathfrak{v}(\mathrm{A}) = x \quad \textit{iff} \quad \mathfrak{v}(\mathcal{D}^x_{\alpha}(\mathrm{A})) \subseteq \alpha^{\mathbb{M}} \textit{ and } \mathfrak{v}(\mathcal{D}^x_{\tilde{\alpha}}(\mathrm{A})) \subseteq \tilde{\alpha}^{\mathbb{M}} \textit{ for every } \alpha \in \{\mathsf{Y}, \mathsf{N}\}.$$

Proof. Analogous to the proof of Lemma 1 in [10].

2.4 Calculi for Two-Dimensional Statements

We may consider the B-statements themselves as the formal objects whose provability by a given (Hilbert-style) deductive proof system we will be interested upon. The B-statements with finite component sets will be hereupon called B-*sequents*. A *(Set^2–Set^2) rule schema* $\mathfrak{r} := \dfrac{\Phi_{\mathsf{Y}} \,;\, \Phi_{\mathsf{N}}}{\Phi_{\text{⅄}} \,;\, \Phi_{\text{И}}}$ is a B-statement $\left(\begin{smallmatrix} \Phi_{\text{И}} & \Phi_{\text{⅄}} \\ \Phi_{\mathsf{Y}} & \Phi_{\mathsf{N}} \end{smallmatrix}\right)$ that, when having its component sets subjected to a substitution σ, produce a *(rule) instance (with schema* $\mathfrak{r}$*)*, denoted simply by $\mathfrak{r}^{\sigma}$; for each rule

[1] Whether monadicity of a $\mathsf{B}^{\mathsf{PN}}_{\Sigma}$-matrix is decidable is still an open problem.

instance $\mathfrak{r}^{\sigma}$, the pair $(\sigma(\Phi_{\mathsf{Y}}), \sigma(\Phi_{\mathsf{N}}))$ is said to be the *antecedent* and the pair $(\sigma(\Phi_{\mathsf{⅄}}), \sigma(\Phi_{\mathsf{И}}))$ is said to be the *succedent* of $\mathfrak{r}^{\sigma}$. For later reference, we also set $\mathsf{branch}(\mathfrak{r}^{\sigma}) := |\sigma(\Phi_{\mathsf{⅄}}) \cup \sigma(\Phi_{\mathsf{И}})|$ and $\mathsf{size}(\mathfrak{r}^{\sigma}) := \sum_{\alpha} \mathsf{size}(\sigma(\Phi_{\alpha}))$, which extends to sets of rule instances in the natural way. Notice that our notation for rule schemas differs from that of B-statements with respect to the positioning of the sets of formulas. The purpose is to facilitate the development of proofs in tree form growing downwards from the premises to the conclusion as described in the sequel. B-statements, in turn, follow the notation for consequence judgements, which is motivated by the bilattice representation of the four logical values underlying a B-consequence relation [9], in addition to the desire of better expressing the possible interactions between the two dimensions.

A *(Set²–Set²) calculus* $\mathcal{C}$ is a collection of rule schemas. We shall sometimes refer to the set of all rule instances of a schema $\mathfrak{r}$ of $\mathcal{C}$ as an *inference rule (with schema* $\mathfrak{r}$*) of* $\mathcal{C}$. An inference rule with schema $\mathfrak{r} := \dfrac{\Phi_{\mathsf{Y}}\ ;\ \Phi_{\mathsf{N}}}{\Phi_{\mathsf{⅄}}\ ;\ \Phi_{\mathsf{И}}}$ is called *finitary* whenever Φ_{α} is finite for every $\alpha \in \{\mathsf{Y}, \mathsf{N}, \mathsf{⅄}, \mathsf{И}\}$. A calculus is finitary when each of its inference rules is finitary.

In order to explain what it means for a B-statement $\mathscr{s} := \begin{pmatrix}\Phi_{\mathsf{И}} & \Phi_{\mathsf{⅄}} \\ \Phi_{\mathsf{Y}} & \Phi_{\mathsf{N}}\end{pmatrix}$ to be provable—in other words, for its succedent $(\Phi_{\mathsf{⅄}}, \Phi_{\mathsf{И}})$ to follow from its antecedent $(\Phi_{\mathsf{Y}}, \Phi_{\mathsf{N}})$—using the inference rules of a calculus, we will first introduce the notion of a derivation structured in tree form. A *directed rooted tree* t is a poset $\langle \mathsf{nds}(t), \preceq^{t} \rangle$ such that, for every *node* $n \in \mathsf{nds}(t)$, the set $\mathsf{acts}^{t}(n) := \{n' \mid n' \prec^{t} n\}$ of the *ancestors* of n is well-ordered under $\prec^{t}$, and there is a single minimal element $\mathsf{rt}(t)$, called the *root* of t. We denote by $\mathsf{dcts}^{t}(n) := \{n' \mid n \prec^{t} n'\}$ the set of *descendants* of t, by $\mathsf{chn}^{t}(n)$ the minimal elements of $\mathsf{dcts}^{t}(n)$ (the *children* of n in t), and by $\mathsf{lvs}(t)$ the set of maximal elements of $\preceq^{t}$, the *leaves* of t. A rooted tree t is said to be *bounded* when every branch of t has a leaf. Moreover, we will call *labelled* a rooted tree t that comes equipped with a mapping ℓ^{t} : $\mathsf{nds}(t) \to \mathsf{Pow}(\mathrm{L}_{\Sigma}(\mathcal{P}))^{2} \cup \{\star\}$, each node n of t being *labelled with* $\ell^{t}(n)$. A node labelled with $\star$ is said to be *discontinued*. In what follows, labelled bounded rooted trees will be referred to simply as *trees*. A tree with a single node labelled with $\ell \in \mathsf{Pow}(\mathrm{L}_{\Sigma}(\mathcal{P}))^{2} \cup \{\star\}$ will be denoted by $\mathsf{sntree}(\ell)$.

Given a node n labelled with (Φ, Ψ) and given a formula A, we shall use $n_{\mathsf{S}}^{\mathrm{A}}$ to refer to a node labelled with $(\Phi \cup \{\mathrm{A}\}, \Psi)$ and use $n_{\mathsf{Ƨ}}^{\mathrm{A}}$ to refer to a node labelled with $(\Phi, \Psi \cup \{\mathrm{A}\})$. We say that a tree t is a $\mathcal{C}$-*derivation* provided that for each non-leaf node n of t labelled with $(\Psi_{\mathsf{Y}}, \Psi_{\mathsf{N}})$ there is an instance of an inference rule of $\mathcal{C}$, say $\mathfrak{r}^{\sigma} = \dfrac{\sigma(\Phi_{\mathsf{Y}})\ ;\ \sigma(\Phi_{\mathsf{N}})}{\sigma(\Phi_{\mathsf{⅄}})\ ;\ \sigma(\Phi_{\mathsf{И}})}$, that *expands* n or, equivalently, that is *applicable* to the label of n, meaning that $\sigma(\Phi_{\alpha}) \subseteq \Psi_{\alpha}$, for every $\alpha \in \{\mathsf{Y}, \mathsf{N}\}$, and

- if $\Phi_{\mathsf{⅄}} \cup \Phi_{\mathsf{И}} = \varnothing$, then $\mathsf{chn}^{t}(n) = \{n_{\star}\}$ and $\ell^{t}(n_{\star}) = \star$
- otherwise, $\mathsf{chn}^{t}(n) = \{n_{\mathsf{S}}^{\mathrm{A}} \mid \mathrm{A} \in \sigma(\Phi_{\mathsf{⅄}})\} \cup \{n_{\mathsf{Ƨ}}^{\mathrm{A}} \mid \mathrm{A} \in \sigma(\Phi_{\mathsf{И}})\}$

We should observe that, with our present notation, traditional Hilbert-style derivations (when only inference rules with a single formula in the succedent are applied) turn out to be linear trees; for all practical purposes, at any given node we may count with all the information from previous nodes in the branch, and, accordingly, a rule application with a single succedent just adds a new bit of information to that very branch.

Given a B-statement $\mathfrak{s} := \left(\begin{array}{c:c} \Phi_{\text{И}} & \Phi_{\text{⅄}} \\ \hdashline \Phi_{\mathsf{Y}} & \Phi_{\mathsf{N}} \end{array}\right)$ and a calculus $\mathcal{C}$, a $\mathcal{C}$-derivation t with $\ell^t(\mathsf{rt}(t)) = (\Psi_{\mathsf{Y}}, \Psi_{\mathsf{N}})$ is a $\mathcal{C}$-*proof* of $\mathfrak{s}$ provided that $\Psi_\alpha \subseteq \Phi_\alpha$ for every $\alpha \in \{\mathsf{Y}, \mathsf{N}\}$ and, for all $n \in \mathsf{lvs}(t)$ with $\ell^t(n) = (\Psi_{\text{⅄}}, \Psi_{\text{И}})$, we have $\Psi_\alpha \cap \Phi_\alpha \neq \varnothing$ for some $\alpha \in \{\text{⅄}, \text{И}\}$. We also say that a node is $(\Phi_{\text{⅄}}, \Phi_{\text{И}})$-*closed* when the latter condition holds for such node and we say that t is $(\Phi_{\text{⅄}}, \Phi_{\text{И}})$-*closed* when all of its leaf nodes are $(\Phi_{\text{⅄}}, \Phi_{\text{И}})$-closed. When a $\mathcal{C}$-proof exists for the B-statement $\mathfrak{s}$, we say that $\mathfrak{s}$ is $\mathcal{C}$-*provable*. The reader is referred to Example 10 in order to see some proofs of the form we have just described. A calculus $\mathcal{C}$ induces a $2{\times}2$-place relation $\frac{\cdot}{\cdot}|\frac{\cdot}{\cdot}\,\mathcal{C}$ over $\mathsf{Pow}(\mathrm{L}_\Sigma(\mathcal{P}))$ such that $\frac{\Phi_{\text{И}}}{\Phi_{\mathsf{Y}}}|\frac{\Phi_{\text{⅄}}}{\Phi_{\mathsf{N}}}\,\mathcal{C}$ whenever $\left(\begin{array}{c:c} \Phi_{\text{И}} & \Phi_{\text{⅄}} \\ \hdashline \Phi_{\mathsf{Y}} & \Phi_{\mathsf{N}} \end{array}\right)$ is $\mathcal{C}$-provable. As we point out in Proposition 2 below, this provides another realization (compare with Proposition 1) of a B-consequence relation.

Proposition 2. *Given a calculus $\mathcal{C}$, the $2{\times}2$-place relation $\frac{\cdot}{\cdot}|\frac{\cdot}{\cdot}\,\mathcal{C}$ is the smallest B-consequence containing the rules of $\mathcal{C}$.*

Given a collection R of rule instances, we say that a B-statement $\mathfrak{s}$ is R-provable whenever there is a proof of $\mathfrak{s}$ using only rule instances in R. We may define a $2{\times}2$-place relation $\frac{\cdot}{\cdot}|\frac{\cdot}{\cdot}\,\mathrm{R}$ by setting $\frac{\Phi_{\text{И}}}{\Phi_{\mathsf{Y}}}|\frac{\Phi_{\text{⅄}}}{\Phi_{\mathsf{N}}}\,\mathrm{R}$ to hold iff $\left(\begin{array}{c:c} \Phi_{\text{И}} & \Phi_{\text{⅄}} \\ \hdashline \Phi_{\mathsf{Y}} & \Phi_{\mathsf{N}} \end{array}\right)$ is R-provable. Although not necessarily substitution-invariant, one may readily check that this relation respects properties (O), (D) and (C).

Given a $\mathsf{B}^{\mathsf{PN}}_{\Sigma}$-matrix $\mathbb{M}$, we say that a calculus $\mathcal{C}$ is *sound* with respect to $\mathbb{M}$ whenever $\frac{\cdot}{\cdot}|\frac{\cdot}{\cdot}\,\mathcal{C} \subseteq \frac{\cdot}{\cdot}|\frac{\cdot}{\cdot}\,\mathbb{M}$ and say that it is *complete* with respect to $\mathbb{M}$ when the converse inclusion holds. Being sound and complete means that $\mathcal{C}$ *axiomatizes* $\mathbb{M}$.

Example 6. Any fully indeterministic $\mathsf{B}^{\mathsf{PN}}_{\Sigma}$-matrix is axiomatized by the empty set of rules.

Example 7. We present below a calculus that axiomatizes the $\mathsf{B}^{\mathsf{PN}}_{\Sigma}$-matrix $\mathbb{I}$ introduced in Example 1, resulting from the simplification of the calculus produced via the recipe described in Definition 1, given further ahead.

$$\frac{p\ ;\ }{p\vee q\ ;\ }\vee^4_1 \qquad \frac{q\ ;\ }{p\vee q\ ;\ }\vee^4_2 \qquad \frac{;\ p,q}{;\ p\vee q}\vee^4_3 \qquad \frac{;\ p\vee q}{;\ q}\vee^4_4 \qquad \frac{;\ p\vee q}{;\ p}\vee^4_5$$

$$\frac{p\wedge q\ ;\ }{p\ ;\ }\wedge^4_1 \qquad \frac{p\wedge q\ ;\ }{q\ ;\ }\wedge^4_2 \qquad \frac{p,q\ ;\ }{p\wedge q\ ;\ }\wedge^4_3 \qquad \frac{;\ q}{;\ p\wedge q}\wedge^4_4 \qquad \frac{;\ p}{;\ p\wedge q}\wedge^4_5$$

$$\frac{;\ \neg p}{p\ ;\ }\neg^4_1 \qquad \frac{;\ p}{\neg p\ ;\ }\neg^4_2 \qquad \frac{\neg p\ ;\ }{;\ p}\neg^4_3 \qquad \frac{p\ ;\ }{;\ \neg p}\neg^4_4$$

The next example illustrates how adding rules to an axiomatization of a $\mathsf{B}^{\mathsf{PN}}_{\Sigma}$-matrix $\mathbb{M}$ imposes refinements on $\mathbb{M}$ in order to guarantee soundness of these very rules. Such mechanism is essential to the axiomatization procedure presented in the next section.

Example 8. We obtain an axiomatization for $\mathbb{E}$ by adding rules $\frac{p \vee q\ ;}{p,q\ ;}\vee_6^4$ and $\frac{;\ p \wedge q}{;\ p,q}\wedge_6^4$ to the calculus of Example 7. If, in addition, we include the rule $\frac{q\ ;\ q}{p\ ;\ p}\mathrm{T}^4$ we axiomatize $\mathbb{K}$ (see Example 3).

Let us explain the intuition behind this mechanism considering the case of rule $\wedge_6^4$; the other rules will follow the same principle. What rule $\wedge_6^4$ enforces is that any refinement of $\mathbb{I}$ with respect to which this rule is sound must disallow valuations that assign values in $\{\bot, \mathbf{t}\}$ to formulas A and B while assigning a value in $\{\top, \mathbf{f}\}$ to $A \wedge B$, for otherwise such valuation would constitute a countermodel for that very rule. This is reflected in $\wedge^{\mathbb{E}}$ (Example 2) by the absence of the values from the set $\{\top, \mathbf{f}\}$ in the entries corresponding to the truth-value assignments in which both inputs belong to $\{\bot, \mathbf{t}\}$.

Example 9. By the same mechanism used in the previous example, in adding the rules $\frac{;}{p\ ;\ p}\bot\mathrm{E}$ and $\frac{p\ ;\ p}{;}\top\mathrm{E}$ to the axiomatization of $\mathbb{E}$, we force empty outputs on any truth-table entry whose input involves either $\bot$ or $\top$. It follows that Classical Logic inhabits the t-aspect of the resulting $\mathsf{B}_\Sigma^{\mathsf{PN}}$-matrix, hereby called $\mathbb{C}$.

Example 10. In Fig. 1, we offer proofs of $\left(\frac{\quad\ \vdots\ \neg p \vee \neg q}{\neg(p \wedge q)\ \vdots\quad}\right)$, $\left(\frac{s\ \vdots\ s}{r \wedge p\ \vdots\ p \vee q}\right)$ and $\left(\frac{\quad\ \vdots\quad}{p, \neg p\ \vdots\quad}\right)$, respectively, in the calculi for $\mathbb{E}$, $\mathbb{K}$ and $\mathbb{C}$ presented in the previous examples.

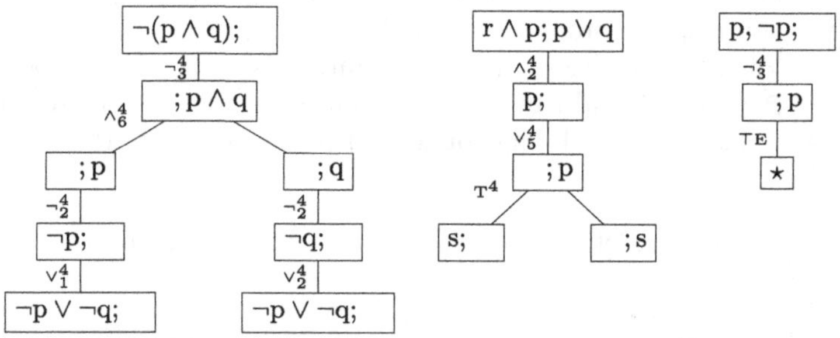

Fig. 1. Examples of derivations in tree form. For the sake of a cleaner presentation, we omit the formulas that are inherited when expanding a node.

We conclude this section by introducing the notion of (generalized) analyticity of a calculus, an important feature for proof-search procedures that is built in the axiomatizations delivered by the recipe of the next section. Given a B-statement $s := \left(\frac{\Phi_{\mathsf{И}}\ \vdots\ \Phi_{\mathsf{\lambda}}}{\Phi_{\mathsf{Y}}\ \vdots\ \Phi_{\mathsf{N}}}\right)$, let $\mathcal{S}(s) := \bigcup_{\alpha \in \{\mathsf{Y},\mathsf{N},\mathsf{\lambda},\mathsf{И}\}} \mathsf{subf}(\Phi_\alpha)$ be the collection of *subformulas of* s, and $\mathcal{S}^\Psi(s) := \mathcal{S}(s) \cup \{\sigma(A) \mid A \in \Psi, \sigma : \mathcal{P} \to \mathcal{S}(s)\}$ be the *generalized subformulas of* s *(with respect to* Ψ*)*. Define the $2{\times}2$-place relation $\div|\div\ {}^{\mathcal{S}^\Psi}_{\mathcal{C}}$ over $\mathsf{Pow}(L_\Sigma(\mathcal{P}))$ by setting $\frac{\Phi_{\mathsf{И}}}{\Phi_{\mathsf{Y}}}\Big|\frac{\Phi_{\mathsf{\lambda}}}{\Phi_{\mathsf{N}}}\ {}^{\mathcal{S}^\Psi}_{\mathcal{C}}$ iff there is a $\mathcal{C}$-proof t of $s := \left(\frac{\Phi_{\mathsf{И}}\ \vdots\ \Phi_{\mathsf{\lambda}}}{\Phi_{\mathsf{Y}}\ \vdots\ \Phi_{\mathsf{N}}}\right)$

such that $\ell^t(\mathsf{nds}(t)) \subseteq \mathsf{Pow}(\mathcal{S}^\Psi(\mathcal{s}))^2 \cup \{\star\}$. Such a proof is said to be Ψ-*analytic*. We say that $\mathcal{C}$ is Ψ-*analytic* in case $\frac{\Phi_{\text{И}}}{\Phi_{\mathsf{Y}}} | \frac{\Phi_{\text{⅄}}}{\Phi_{\mathsf{N}}} \, \mathcal{C}$ implies $\frac{\Phi_{\text{И}}}{\Phi_{\mathsf{Y}}} | \frac{\Phi_{\text{⅄}}}{\Phi_{\mathsf{N}}} \, {}^{\mathcal{S}^\Psi}_{\mathcal{C}}$. We will denote by $\mathcal{C}[\mathcal{s}]$ the set of all rule instances of $\mathcal{C}$ resulting from substitutions that only use formulas in $\mathcal{S}^\Psi(\mathcal{s})$.

3 Axiomatizing Monadic $\mathsf{B}^{\mathsf{PN}}_{\Sigma}$-matrices

We now describe four collections of rule schemas by which any sufficiently expressive $\mathsf{B}^{\mathsf{PN}}_{\Sigma}$-matrix $\mathbb{M}$ is constrained. Together, these schemas constitute a presentation of a calculus that will be denoted by $\mathcal{C}^{\mathcal{D}}$, where $\mathcal{D}$ is a discriminator for $\mathbb{M}$. The first collection, $\mathcal{C}^{\mathcal{D}}_{\exists}$, is intended to exclude all combinations of separators that do not correspond to truth-values. The second, $\mathcal{C}^{\mathcal{D}}_{\mathsf{D}}$, sets the combinations of separators that characterize acceptance apart from those that characterize non-acceptance, and sets the combinations of separators that characterize rejection apart from those that characterize non-rejection. The third one, $\mathcal{C}^{\mathcal{D}}_{\Sigma}$, fully describes, through appropriate refinements, the interpretation of the connectives of Σ in $\mathbb{M}$. At last, the rules in $\mathcal{C}^{\mathcal{D}}_{\mathbb{T}}$ guarantee that values belong to total sub-$\mathsf{B}^{\mathsf{PN}}_{\Sigma}$-matrices of $\mathbb{M}$.

In what follows, given $\mathcal{X} \subseteq \mathcal{V}^{\mathbb{M}}$, we shall use $\left(\dot{\mathcal{D}}^{\mathcal{X}}_{\mathsf{Y}}, \dot{\mathcal{D}}^{\mathcal{X}}_{\mathsf{N}}\right)$ to denote a pair of sets in which $\dot{\mathcal{D}}^{\mathcal{X}}_{\alpha}$, with $\alpha \in \{\mathsf{Y}, \mathsf{N}\}$, is obtained by choosing an element of $\mathcal{D}^{x}_{\alpha}$ for each $x \in \mathcal{X}$. Notice that, when $\mathcal{X} = \varnothing$, the only possibility is the pair $(\varnothing, \varnothing)$; moreover, when $\mathcal{D}^{x}_{\mathsf{Y}} \cup \mathcal{D}^{x}_{\mathsf{N}} = \varnothing$ for some $x \in \mathcal{X}$, no such pair exists. The pair $\left(\dot{\mathcal{D}}^{\mathcal{X}}_{\text{⅄}}, \dot{\mathcal{D}}^{\mathcal{X}}_{\text{И}}\right)$ shall be used analogously.

Definition 1. *Let* $\mathbb{M}$ *be a* $\mathsf{B}^{\mathsf{PN}}_{\Sigma}$-*matrix, and let* $\mathcal{D}$ *be a discriminator for* $\mathbb{M}$. *The calculus* $\mathcal{C}^{\mathcal{D}}$ *is presented by way of the following rule schemas:*

($\mathcal{C}^{\mathcal{D}}_{\exists}$) *for each* $\mathcal{X}_1 \subseteq \mathcal{V}^{\mathbb{M}}$ *and each possible choices of* $\left(\dot{\mathcal{D}}^{\mathcal{X}_0}_{\mathsf{Y}}, \dot{\mathcal{D}}^{\mathcal{X}_0}_{\mathsf{N}}\right)$ *and of* $\left(\dot{\mathcal{D}}^{\mathcal{X}_1}_{\text{⅄}}, \dot{\mathcal{D}}^{\mathcal{X}_1}_{\text{И}}\right)$, *with* $\mathcal{X}_0 := \mathcal{V}^{\mathbb{M}} \backslash \mathcal{X}_1$,

$$\frac{\dot{\mathcal{D}}^{\mathcal{X}_1}_{\text{⅄}} \; ; \; \dot{\mathcal{D}}^{\mathcal{X}_1}_{\text{И}}}{\dot{\mathcal{D}}^{\mathcal{X}_0}_{\mathsf{Y}} \; ; \; \dot{\mathcal{D}}^{\mathcal{X}_0}_{\mathsf{N}}}$$

($\mathcal{C}^{\mathcal{D}}_{\mathsf{D}}$) *for an arbitrary propositional variable* $\mathrm{p} \in \mathcal{P}$, *and for each* $x \in \mathcal{V}^{\mathbb{M}}$,

$$\frac{\mathcal{D}^{x}_{\mathsf{Y}}(\mathrm{p}), p_{\text{⅄}}(x) \; ; \; \mathcal{D}^{x}_{\mathsf{N}}(\mathrm{p})}{\mathcal{D}^{x}_{\text{⅄}}(\mathrm{p}), p_{\mathsf{Y}}(x) \; ; \; \mathcal{D}^{x}_{\text{И}}(\mathrm{p})} \qquad \frac{\mathcal{D}^{x}_{\mathsf{Y}}(\mathrm{p}) \; ; \; \mathcal{D}^{x}_{\mathsf{N}}(\mathrm{p}), p_{\text{И}}(x)}{\mathcal{D}^{x}_{\text{⅄}}(\mathrm{p}) \; ; \; \mathcal{D}^{x}_{\text{И}}(\mathrm{p}), p_{\mathsf{N}}(x)}$$

where, for $\alpha \in \{\mathsf{Y}, \mathsf{N}, \text{⅄}, \text{И}\}$, $p_\alpha : \mathcal{V}^{\mathbb{M}} \to \mathsf{Pow}(\{\mathrm{p}\})$ *is such that* $p_\alpha(x) = \{\mathrm{p}\}$ *iff* $x \in \alpha^{\mathbb{M}}$.

($\mathcal{C}^{\mathcal{D}}_{\Sigma}$) *for each* k*-ary connective* ©, *each sequence* $\mathrm{X} := (x_1, \ldots, x_k)$ *of truth-values of* $\mathbb{M}$, *each* $y \notin ©^{\mathbb{M}}\mathrm{X}$, *and for a sequence* $(p_1, \ldots, p_k)$ *of distinct propositional variables,*

$$\frac{\Theta^{©,\mathrm{X},y}_{\mathsf{Y}} \; ; \; \Theta^{©,\mathrm{X},y}_{\mathsf{N}}}{\Theta^{©,\mathrm{X},y}_{\text{⅄}} \; ; \; \Theta^{©,\mathrm{X},y}_{\text{И}}}$$

where each $\Theta^{©,\mathrm{X},y}_{\alpha} := \bigcup_{1 \le i \le k} \mathcal{D}^{x_i}_{\alpha}(p_i) \cup \mathcal{D}^{y}_{\alpha}(©(p_1, \ldots, p_k))$.

($\mathcal{C}^{\mathcal{D}}_{\mathbb{T}}$) *for each* $\mathcal{X} \notin \mathbb{T}_{\mathbb{M}}$ *and an arbitrary family* $\{p_x\}_{x \in \mathcal{X}}$ *of distinct propositional variables,*

$$\frac{\bigcup_{x \in \mathcal{X}} \mathcal{D}^{x}_{\mathsf{Y}}(p_x) \; ; \; \bigcup_{x \in \mathcal{X}} \mathcal{D}^{x}_{\mathsf{N}}(p_x)}{\bigcup_{x \in \mathcal{X}} \mathcal{D}^{x}_{\text{⅄}}(p_x) \; ; \; \bigcup_{x \in \mathcal{X}} \mathcal{D}^{x}_{\text{И}}(p_x)}.$$

Theorem 1. *If* $\mathcal{D}$ *is a discriminator for a* $\mathsf{B}^{\underline{PN}}_{\Sigma}$*-matrix* $\mathbb{M}$, *then the calculus* $\mathcal{C}^{\mathcal{D}}$ *is sound with respect to* $\mathbb{M}$.

Proof. We can show by contradiction that no $\mathbb{M}$-valuation can be a countermodel for the schemas in each of the groups of schemas of $\mathcal{C}^{\mathcal{D}}$. We detail the case of ($\mathcal{C}^{\mathcal{D}}_{\exists}$). Consider a schema $s := \dfrac{\dot{\mathcal{D}}^{\mathcal{X}_1}_{\text{⅄}} \; ; \; \dot{\mathcal{D}}^{\mathcal{X}_1}_{\text{И}}}{\dot{\mathcal{D}}^{\mathcal{X}_0}_{\mathsf{Y}} \; ; \; \dot{\mathcal{D}}^{\mathcal{X}_0}_{\mathsf{N}}}$, for some $\mathcal{X}_1 \subseteq \mathcal{V}^{\mathbb{M}}$ and some choice of $\left(\dot{\mathcal{D}}^{\mathcal{X}_0}_{\mathsf{Y}}, \dot{\mathcal{D}}^{\mathcal{X}_0}_{\mathsf{N}}\right)$ and $\left(\dot{\mathcal{D}}^{\mathcal{X}_1}_{\text{⅄}}, \dot{\mathcal{D}}^{\mathcal{X}_1}_{\text{И}}\right)$. Suppose that s does not hold in $\mathbb{M}$, with the valuation v witnessing this fact. We will prove that, given a propositional variable p, $v(p) \neq x$, for all $x \in \mathcal{V}^{\mathbb{M}}$, an absurd. For that purpose, let $x \in \mathcal{V}^{\mathbb{M}}$. In case $x \in \mathcal{X}_1$, there must be a separator S in $\mathcal{D}^{x}_{\tilde{\alpha}}$, for some $\alpha \in \{\mathsf{Y}, \mathsf{N}\}$, such that $v(S(p)) \in \alpha^{\mathbb{M}}$. By Lemma 1, this implies that $v(p) \neq x$. The reasoning is similar in case $x \in \mathcal{X}_0$.

In what follows, denote by $\mathcal{S}^{\mathcal{D}}$ the mapping $\mathcal{S}^{\mathcal{D}^{\bowtie}}$, which indicates what formulas may appear in a $\mathcal{D}^{\bowtie}$-analytic proof. In order to prove completeness and $\mathcal{D}^{\bowtie}$-analyticity of $\mathcal{C}^{\mathcal{D}}$ with respect to $\mathbb{M}$, we shall make use of Lemma 2 presented below, which contains four items, each one referring to a group of schemas of $\mathcal{C}^{\mathcal{D}}$. Intuitively, given a B-statement s and assuming that there is no $\mathcal{D}^{\bowtie}$-analytic proof of it in $\mathcal{C}^{\mathcal{D}}$, items 1 and 2 give us the resources to define a mapping $f : \mathsf{subf}(s) \to \mathcal{V}^{\mathbb{M}}$ that, by items 3 and 4, can be extended to a countermodel for s in $\mathbb{M}$.

Lemma 2. *For all* B*-statements* s *of the form* $\left(\begin{array}{c:c} \Omega^{c}_{\text{Ƨ}} & \Omega^{c}_{\mathsf{S}} \\ \hdashline \Omega_{\mathsf{S}} & \Omega_{\text{Ƨ}} \end{array}\right)$:

1. *if* $\frac{\Omega^{c}_{\text{Ƨ}}}{\Omega_{\mathsf{S}}} \ast \frac{\Omega^{c}_{\mathsf{S}}}{\Omega_{\text{Ƨ}}} {}^{\mathcal{S}^{\mathcal{D}}}_{\mathcal{C}^{\mathcal{D}}_{\exists}}$, *then for all* $A \in \mathsf{subf}(s)$ *there is an* $x \in \mathcal{V}^{\mathbb{M}}$ *such that* $\mathcal{D}^{x}_{\alpha}(A) \subseteq \Omega_{\beta}$ *and* $\mathcal{D}^{x}_{\tilde{\alpha}}(A) \subseteq \Omega^{c}_{\beta}$, *for* $(\alpha, \beta) \in \{(\mathsf{Y}, \mathsf{S}), (\mathsf{N}, \text{Ƨ})\}$;
2. *if* $\frac{\Omega^{c}_{\text{Ƨ}}}{\Omega_{\mathsf{S}}} \ast \frac{\Omega^{c}_{\mathsf{S}}}{\Omega_{\text{Ƨ}}} {}^{\mathcal{S}^{\mathcal{D}}}_{\mathcal{C}^{\mathcal{D}}_{\mathsf{D}}}$, *then for every* $A \in \mathsf{subf}(s)$ *and* $x \in \mathcal{V}^{\mathbb{M}}$ *such that* $\mathcal{D}^{x}_{\alpha}(A) \subseteq \Omega_{\beta}$ *and* $\mathcal{D}^{x}_{\tilde{\alpha}}(A) \subseteq \Omega^{c}_{\beta}$, *we have* $x \in \alpha^{\mathbb{M}}$ *iff* $A \in \Omega_{\beta}$, *for* $(\alpha, \beta) \in \{(\mathsf{Y}, \mathsf{S}), (\mathsf{N}, \text{Ƨ})\}$;

3. *if* $\frac{\Omega^{\mathsf{c}}_{\mathsf{Ɛ}}}{\Omega_{\mathsf{S}}} \ast \frac{\Omega^{\mathsf{c}}_{\mathsf{S}}}{\Omega_{\mathsf{Ɛ}}}\,{}^{\mathcal{S}^{\mathcal{D}}}_{\mathcal{C}^{\mathcal{D}}_{\Sigma}}$, *then for every* $© \in \Sigma_k$, $A := ©(A_1, \ldots, A_k) \in \mathsf{subf}(\mathfrak{s})$ *and* $x_1, \ldots, x_k \in \mathcal{V}^{\mathbb{M}}$ *with* $\mathcal{D}^{x_i}_{\alpha}(A_i) \subseteq \Omega_\beta$ *and* $\mathcal{D}^{x_i}_{\tilde{\alpha}}(A_i) \subseteq \Omega^{\mathsf{c}}_{\beta}$, *for each* $1 \leq i \leq k$ *and* $(\alpha, \beta) \in \{(\mathsf{Y}, \mathsf{S}), (\mathsf{N}, \mathsf{Ɛ})\}$, *we have that* $\mathcal{D}^{y}_{\alpha}(A) \subseteq \Omega_\beta$ *and* $\mathcal{D}^{y}_{\tilde{\alpha}}(A) \subseteq \Omega^{\mathsf{c}}_{\beta}$ *for each* $(\alpha, \beta) \in \{(\mathsf{Y}, \mathsf{S}), (\mathsf{N}, \mathsf{Ɛ})\}$ *implies* $y \in ©^{\mathbb{M}}(x_1, \ldots, x_k)$;
4. *if* $\frac{\Omega^{\mathsf{c}}_{\mathsf{Ɛ}}}{\Omega_{\mathsf{S}}} \ast \frac{\Omega^{\mathsf{c}}_{\mathsf{S}}}{\Omega_{\mathsf{Ɛ}}}\,{}^{\mathcal{S}^{\mathcal{D}}}_{\mathcal{C}^{\mathcal{D}}_{\mathbb{T}}}$, *then* $\{x \in \mathcal{V}^{\mathbb{M}} \mid \mathcal{D}^{x}_{\alpha}(A) \subseteq \Omega_\beta$ *and* $\mathcal{D}^{x}_{\tilde{\alpha}}(A) \subseteq \Omega^{\mathsf{c}}_{\beta}$, *for each* $(\alpha, \beta) \in \{(\mathsf{Y}, \mathsf{S}), (\mathsf{N}, \mathsf{Ɛ})\}$ *and* $A \in \mathsf{subf}(\mathfrak{s})\} \in \mathbb{T}_{\mathbb{M}}$.

Proof. The strategy to prove each item is the same: by contraposition, use the data from the assumptions to compose an instance of a rule schema of the corresponding group of rule schemas. We detail below the proof for the third item. Suppose that there is a connective $© \in \Sigma_k$, a formula $A := ©(A_1, \ldots, A_k) \in \mathsf{subf}(\mathfrak{s})$, a sequence $(x_1, \ldots, x_k)$ of truth-values with $\mathcal{D}^{x_i}_{\alpha}(A_i) \subseteq \Omega_\beta$ and $\mathcal{D}^{x_i}_{\tilde{\alpha}}(A_i) \subseteq \Omega^{\mathsf{c}}_{\beta}$ for each $1 \leq i \leq k$ and $(\alpha, \beta) \in \{(\mathsf{Y}, \mathsf{S}), (\mathsf{N}, \mathsf{Ɛ})\}$, and some $y \notin ©^{\mathbb{M}}(x_1, \ldots, x_k)$ such that $\mathcal{D}^{y}_{\alpha}(A) \subseteq \Omega_\beta$ and $\mathcal{D}^{y}_{\tilde{\alpha}}(A) \subseteq \Omega^{\mathsf{c}}_{\beta}$ for each $(\alpha, \beta) \in \{(\mathsf{Y}, \mathsf{S}), (\mathsf{N}, \mathsf{Ɛ})\}$. Then $\bigcup_{1 \leq i \leq k} \mathcal{D}^{x_i}_{\alpha}(A_i) \cup \mathcal{D}^{y}_{\alpha}(A) \subseteq \Omega_\beta \cap \mathcal{S}^{\mathcal{D}}(\mathfrak{s})$ and $\bigcup_{1 \leq i \leq k} \mathcal{D}^{x_i}_{\tilde{\alpha}}(A_i) \cup \mathcal{D}^{y}_{\tilde{\alpha}}(A) \subseteq \Omega^{\mathsf{c}}_{\beta} \cap \mathcal{S}^{\mathcal{D}}(\mathfrak{s})$ for each $(\alpha, \beta) \in \{(\mathsf{Y}, \mathsf{S}), (\mathsf{N}, \mathsf{Ɛ})\}$, and thus we have $\frac{\Omega^{\mathsf{c}}_{\mathsf{Ɛ}}}{\Omega_{\mathsf{S}}} \mid \frac{\Omega^{\mathsf{c}}_{\mathsf{S}}}{\Omega_{\mathsf{Ɛ}}}\,{}^{\mathcal{S}^{\mathcal{D}}}_{\mathcal{C}^{\mathcal{D}}_{\Sigma}}$.

Theorem 2. *If* $\mathcal{D}$ *is a discriminator for a* B^{PN}_{Σ}*-matrix* $\mathbb{M}$, *then the calculus* $\mathcal{C}^{\mathcal{D}}$ *is complete with respect to* $\mathbb{M}$. *Furthermore, this calculus is* $\mathcal{D}^{\bowtie}$*-analytic.*

Proof. Let $\mathfrak{s} := \left(\frac{\Phi_{\mathsf{И}} \,\vdots\, \Phi_{\mathsf{⅄}}}{\Phi_{\mathsf{Y}} \,\vdots\, \Phi_{\mathsf{N}}}\right)$ be a B-statement and suppose that (a) $\frac{\Phi_{\mathsf{И}}}{\Phi_{\mathsf{Y}}} \ast \frac{\Phi_{\mathsf{⅄}}}{\Phi_{\mathsf{N}}}\,{}^{\mathcal{S}^{\mathcal{D}}}_{\mathcal{C}^{\mathcal{D}}}$. Our goal is to build an $\mathbb{M}$-valuation witnessing $\frac{\Phi_{\mathsf{И}}}{\Phi_{\mathsf{Y}}} \ast \frac{\Phi_{\mathsf{⅄}}}{\Phi_{\mathsf{N}}}\,\mathbb{M}$. From (a), by (C), we have that (b) there are $\Phi_{\mathsf{Y}} \subseteq \Omega_{\mathsf{S}} \subseteq \Phi^{\mathsf{c}}_{\mathsf{⅄}}$ and $\Phi_{\mathsf{N}} \subseteq \Omega_{\mathsf{Ɛ}} \subseteq \Phi^{\mathsf{c}}_{\mathsf{И}}$ such that $\frac{\Omega^{\mathsf{c}}_{\mathsf{Ɛ}}}{\Omega_{\mathsf{S}}} \ast \frac{\Omega^{\mathsf{c}}_{\mathsf{S}}}{\Omega_{\mathsf{Ɛ}}}\,{}^{\mathcal{S}^{\mathcal{D}}}_{\mathcal{C}^{\mathcal{D}}}$. Consider then a mapping $f : \mathsf{subf}(\mathfrak{s}) \to \mathcal{V}^{\mathbb{M}}$ with (c) $f(A) \in \alpha^{\mathbb{M}}$ iff $A \in \Omega_\beta$, for $(\alpha, \beta) \in \{(\mathsf{Y}, \mathsf{S}), (\mathsf{N}, \mathsf{Ɛ})\}$, whose existence is guaranteed by items (1) and (2) of Lemma 2. Notice that items (3) and (4) of this same lemma imply, respectively, that $f(©(A_1, \ldots, A_k)) \in ©^{\mathbb{M}}(f(A_1), \ldots, f(A_k))$ for every $©(A_1, \ldots, A_k) \in \mathcal{S}^{\mathcal{D}}(\mathfrak{s})$, and $f(\mathsf{subf}(\mathfrak{s})) \in \mathbb{T}_{\mathbb{M}}$. Hence, f may be extended to an $\mathbb{M}$-valuation v and, from (b) and (c), we have $v(\Phi_\alpha) \subseteq \alpha^{\mathbb{M}}$ for each $\alpha \in \{\mathsf{Y}, \mathsf{N}, \mathsf{⅄}, \mathsf{И}\}$, so $\frac{\Phi_{\mathsf{И}}}{\Phi_{\mathsf{Y}}} \ast \frac{\Phi_{\mathsf{⅄}}}{\Phi_{\mathsf{N}}}\,\mathbb{M}$.

The calculi presented so far (Examples 7 and 8) were produced by means of the axiomatization procedure just described, followed by some simplifications consisting of removing instances of conditions (O) and (D), and using condition (C) on pairs of schemas having the forms $\frac{\Phi_{\mathsf{Y}}, A \;;\; \Phi_{\mathsf{N}}}{\Phi_{\mathsf{⅄}} \;;\; \Phi_{\mathsf{И}}}$ and $\frac{\Phi_{\mathsf{Y}} \;;\; \Phi_{\mathsf{N}}}{\Phi_{\mathsf{⅄}}, A \;;\; \Phi_{\mathsf{И}}}$, or the forms $\frac{\Phi_{\mathsf{Y}} \;;\; \Phi_{\mathsf{N}}}{\Phi_{\mathsf{⅄}} \;;\; \Phi_{\mathsf{И}}, A}$ and $\frac{\Phi_{\mathsf{Y}} \;;\; \Phi_{\mathsf{N}}, A}{\Phi_{\mathsf{⅄}} \;;\; \Phi_{\mathsf{И}}}$, yielding in either case the schema $\frac{\Phi_{\mathsf{Y}} \;;\; \Phi_{\mathsf{N}}}{\Phi_{\mathsf{⅄}} \;;\; \Phi_{\mathsf{И}}}$. By Theorem 2 and the fact that these simplifications preserve analyticity, it follows that such calculi are analytic. It is also worth mentioning that this same procedure may be applied to the matrix $\mathbb{P}$ in view of its monadicity (see a discriminator for it in Example 5), which means that we also obtain a *finite* Hilbert-style symmetrical axiomatization for **mCi**.

4 Proof Search in Two Dimensions

Throughout this section, let $\mathfrak{s} := \left(\frac{\Phi_{\text{И}} \,\vdots\, \Phi_{\text{⅄}}}{\Phi_{\mathsf{Y}} \,\vdots\, \Phi_{\mathsf{N}}}\right)$ be an arbitrary B-sequent, $\mathcal{C}$ be a finite and finitary calculus, and Ψ be a finite set of formulas. Notice that, whenever $\mathcal{C}$ is Ψ-analytic, it is enough to consider the rule instances in $\mathcal{C}[\mathfrak{s}]$ in order to provide a proof of $\mathfrak{s}$ in $\mathcal{C}$. Searching for such a proof is clearly a particular case of finding a proof of $\mathfrak{s}$ using only candidates in a finite set R of finitary rule instances. A proof-search algorithm for this more general setting is presented in Algorithm 1 by means of a function called Expand. The algorithm searches for a proof by expanding nodes that are not closed or discontinued using only instances in R that were not used yet in the branch of the node under expansion. As we shall see in the sequel, the order in which applicable instances are selected does not affect the result, although for sure smarter choice heuristics may well improve the performance of the algorithm in particular cases.

Algorithm 1: Proof search over a finite set of finitary rule instances

function Expand(F $:= (\Psi_{\mathsf{Y}}, \Psi_{\mathsf{N}})$, C $:= (\Phi_{\text{И}}, \Phi_{\text{⅄}})$, R):
  Input: antecedents in F, succedents in C and a finite set R of finitary rule instances
  $t \leftarrow \mathsf{sntree}(\mathrm{F})$
  if $\Psi_\alpha \cap \Phi_{\tilde{\alpha}} \neq \varnothing$ *for some* $\alpha \in \{\mathsf{Y}, \mathsf{N}\}$ **then return** t
  foreach *rule instance* $\mathsf{r}^\sigma := \dfrac{\Theta_{\mathsf{Y}} \,;\, \Theta_{\mathsf{N}}}{\Theta_{\text{⅄}} \,;\, \Theta_{\text{И}}} \in \mathrm{R}$ **do**
    if $\Theta_{\tilde{\alpha}} \cap \Psi_\alpha = \varnothing$ *and* $\Theta_\alpha \subseteq \Psi_\alpha$ *for each* $\alpha \in \{\mathsf{Y}, \mathsf{N}\}$ **then**
      if $\Theta_{\text{⅄}} \cup \Theta_{\text{И}} = \varnothing$ **then return** t *with a single child* $\mathsf{sntree}(\star)$
      foreach $\alpha \in \{\mathsf{Y}, \mathsf{N}\}$ *and* $\mathrm{A} \in \Theta_{\tilde{\alpha}}$ **do**
        $t' \leftarrow$ Expand($(\Psi_{\mathsf{Y}} \cup \mathrm{P}_{\mathsf{Y}}(\mathrm{A}), \Psi_{\mathsf{N}} \cup \mathrm{P}_{\mathsf{N}}(\mathrm{A}))$, C, $\mathrm{R} \setminus \{\mathsf{r}^\sigma\}$), where $\mathrm{P}_\alpha(\mathrm{A})$ is $\varnothing$ if $\mathrm{A} \notin \Theta_\alpha$ and $\{\mathrm{A}\}$ otherwise
        add $\mathsf{rt}(t')$ as a child of $\mathsf{rt}(t)$ in t
        if t' *is not* C*-closed* **then return** t
      if t *is* C*-closed* **then return** t
  return t

The following lemma (verifiable by induction on the size of R) proves the termination of Expand and its correctness. The subsequent result establishes the applicability of this algorithm for proof search over Ψ-analytic calculi.

Lemma 3. *Let* R *be a finite set of finitary rule instances. Then the procedure* Expand$((\Phi_{\mathsf{Y}}, \Phi_{\mathsf{N}}), (\Phi_{\text{⅄}}, \Phi_{\text{И}}), \mathrm{R})$ *always terminates, returning a tree that is* $(\Phi_{\text{⅄}}, \Phi_{\text{И}})$*-closed iff* $\frac{\Phi_{\text{И}}}{\Phi_{\mathsf{Y}}} \Big| \frac{\Phi_{\text{⅄}}}{\Phi_{\mathsf{N}}}\, \mathrm{R}$.

Lemma 4. *If $\mathcal{C}$ is Ψ-analytic, then* Expand *is a proof-search algorithm for $\mathcal{C}$ and a decision procedure for $\frac{\cdot}{\cdot}|\frac{\cdot}{\cdot}_{\mathcal{C}}$.*

Proof. We know that $\mathcal{C}[\mathfrak{s}]$ provides enough material for a derivation of $\mathfrak{s}$ to be produced, since $\mathcal{C}$ is Ψ-analytic. Clearly, such set is finite and contains only finitary rule instances, hence the present result is a direct consequence of Lemma 3.

The next results concern the complexity of Algorithm 1. In what follows, let R be a finite set of finitary rule instances, $\mathrm{b} := \max_{\mathfrak{r}^\sigma \in \mathrm{R}} \mathsf{branch}(\mathfrak{r}^\sigma)$, $\mathrm{s} := \mathsf{size}(\{\mathfrak{s}\} \cup \mathrm{R})$ and $\mathrm{n} := |\mathrm{R}|$. We shall use $\mathsf{p}(\mathrm{m})$ to refer to "a polynomial in m".

Lemma 5. *The worst-case running time of* $\textsc{Expand}((\Phi_{\mathsf{Y}}, \Phi_{\mathsf{N}}), (\Phi_{\text{⅄}}, \Phi_{\text{И}}), \mathrm{R})$ *is* $\mathrm{O}(\mathrm{b}^{\mathrm{n}} + \mathrm{n} \cdot \mathsf{p}(\mathrm{s}))$.

Proof. Let $\mathrm{T}(\mathrm{n}, \mathrm{s})$ be the worst-case running-time of Expand. Note that it occurs under three conditions: first, $\frac{\Phi_{\text{И}}}{\Phi_{\mathsf{Y}}}|\frac{\Phi_{\text{⅄}}}{\Phi_{\mathsf{N}}}\,\mathrm{R}$; second, the set R needs to be entirely inspected until an applicable rule instance is found; and third, such an instance does not have an empty set of succedents. Notice that $\mathrm{T}(0, \mathrm{s}) = \mathrm{c}_1 + \mathsf{p}(\mathrm{s})$ and, based on the assignments above and after some algebraic manipulations, we have, for $\mathrm{n} \geq 1$, $\mathrm{T}(\mathrm{n}, \mathrm{s}) \leq \mathrm{b} \cdot \mathrm{T}(\mathrm{n}-1, \mathrm{s} + \mathsf{p}(\mathrm{s})) + 2\mathrm{n} \cdot \mathsf{p}(\mathrm{s})$. It is then straightforward to check by induction on n that $\mathrm{T}(\mathrm{n}, \mathrm{s}) \in \mathrm{O}(\mathrm{b}^{\mathrm{n}} + \mathrm{n} \cdot \mathsf{p}(\mathrm{s}))$.

Theorem 3. *If $\mathcal{C}$ is Ψ-analytic,* Expand *is a proof-search algorithm for $\mathcal{C}$ that runs in exponential time in general, and in polynomial time if $\mathcal{C}$ contains only rules with at most one formula in the succedent.*

Proof. Clearly, the set of all instances of rules of $\mathcal{C}$ using only formulas in $\mathcal{S}^{\Psi}(\mathfrak{s})$ is finite and contains only finitary rule instances, and its size is polynomial in $\mathsf{size}(\mathfrak{s})$. The announced result then follows directly from Lemma 5.

The previous result makes the axiomatization procedure presented in Sect. 3 even more attractive, since it delivers a $\mathcal{D}^{\bowtie}$–analytic calculus for $\mathbb{M}$, where $\mathcal{D}^{\bowtie}$ is a finite set of formulas acting as separators. It follows then that Expand is a proof-search algorithm for such axiomatization running in at most exponential time. More than that, Expand outputs a tree with at least one open branch when the B-sequent $\mathfrak{s}$ of interest is not provable. From such branch, one may obtain a partition of $\mathcal{S}^{\mathcal{D}}(\mathfrak{s})$ and, by Proposition 2, define a mapping on $\mathsf{subf}(\mathfrak{s})$ that extends to an $\mathbb{M}$-valuation. It follows that the discussed algorithm may easily be adapted so as to deliver a countermodel when $\mathfrak{s}$ is unprovable. For experimenting with the axiomatization procedure and searching for proofs over the generated calculus, one can make use of the implementation that may be found at https://github.com/greati/logicantsy. We should also emphasize that, by Theorem 3 and the axiomatization procedure given in Sect. 3, we have:

Corollary 1. *Any finite monadic $\mathsf{B}^{\mathcal{PN}}_{\Sigma}$-matrix $\mathbb{M}$ whose induced axiomatization contains only rules with at most one succedent is decidable in polynomial time.*

By the above result, then, the B-entailment relation $\div|\div_{\mathbb{I}}$ (from Example 1) is decidable in polynomial time. Consequently, the same also holds for its t-aspect, which is inhabited by the 4-valued logic introduced in [3].

In addition, it is worth stressing that, although no better in the limiting cases, the axiomatization provided in Sect. 3 together with the algorithm presented in this section translate the problem of deciding a B-entailment relation into a purely symbolic procedure that may perform better than searching for $\mathbb{M}$-valuations in some cases.

We close with another complexity result concerning the decidability of $\div|\div_{\mathcal{C}}$, complementing the one given by the discussed algorithm; it follows by an argument similar to the one presented for the one-dimensional case in [18].

Theorem 4. *If $\mathcal{C}$ is Ψ-analytic, then the problem of deciding $\div|\div_{\mathcal{C}}$ is in* coNP.

5 Conclusion

In this paper, we approached bilateralism by exploring a two-dimensional notion of consequence, considering the cognitive attitudes of acceptance and rejection instead of the conventional speech acts of assertion and of denial. Our intervention has been two-fold: on the semantical front we have employed two-dimensional (partial) non-deterministic logical matrices, and on proof-theoretical grounds we have employed two-dimensional symmetrical proof formalisms which generalize traditional Hilbert-style calculi and their associated unilinear notion of derivation. As a result, and generalizing [10], we have provided an axiomatization procedure that delivers analytic calculi for a very expressive class of finite monadic matrices. On what concerns proof development, in spite of well-known evidence about the p-equivalence between Hilbert-style calculi and Gentzen-style calculi ([14]), die-hard popular belief concerning their 'deep inequivalence' seems hard to wash away. To counter that belief with facts, we developed for our calculi a general proof-search algorithm that was secured to run in exponential time.

We highlight that our two-dimensional proof-formalism differs in important respects from the many-placed sequent calculi used in [4] to axiomatize (one-dimensional total) non-deterministic matrices (requiring no sufficient expressiveness) and in [16] for approaching multilateralism. First, a many-placed sequent calculus is not Hilbert-style: rules manipulate complex objects whose structures involve contexts and considerably deviate from the shape of the consequence relation being captured; our calculi, on the other hand, are contained in their corresponding B-consequences. Second, when axiomatizing a matrix, the structure of many-placed sequents grows according to the number of values (n places for n truth-values); our rule schemas, in turn, remain with four places, and reflect the complexity of the underlying semantics in the complexity of the formulas being manipulated. Moreover, the study of many-placed sequents currently contemplates only one-dimensional consequence relations; extending them to the two-dimensional case is a line of research worth exploring.

As further future work, we envisage generalizing the two-dimensional notion of consequence relation by allowing logics over different languages ([17]) —for instance, conflating different logics or different fragments of some given logic of interest— to coinhabit the same logical structure, each one along its own dimension, while controlling their interaction at the object-language level, taking advantage of the framework and the results in [18]. This opens the doors for a line of investigation on whether or to what extent the individual characteristics of these ingredient logics, such as their decidability status, may be preserved. With respect to our proof search algorithm, an important research path to be explored would involve the design of heuristics for smarter choices of rule instances used to expand nodes during the search, as this may improve the performance of the algorithm on certain classes of logics. At last, we also expect to extend the present research so as to cover multidimensional notions of consequence, in order to provide increasingly general technical and philosophical grounds for the study of logical pluralism.

Acknowledgements. V. Greati and J. Marcos acknowledge support from CAPES (Brasil)—Finance Code 001 and CNPq (Brasil), respectively. S. Marcelino's research was done under the scope of Project UIDB/50008/2020 of Instituto de Telecomunicações (IT), financed by the applicable framework (FCT/MEC through national funds and cofunded by FEDER-PT2020).

References

1. Avron, A.: 5-valued non-deterministic semantics for the basic paraconsistent logic mCi. In: Studies in Logic, Grammar and Rhetoric, pp. 127–136 (2008)
2. Avron, A.: Multi-valued semantics: why and how. Stud. Logica. **92**(2), 163–182 (2009). https://doi.org/10.1007/s11225-009-9193-2
3. Avron, A., Ben-Naim, J., Konikowska, B.: Cut-free ordinary sequent calculi for logics having generalized finite-valued semantics. Log. Univers. **1**, 41–70 (2007). https://doi.org/10.1007/s11787-006-0003-6
4. Avron, A., Konikowska, B.: Multi-valued calculi for logics based on non-determinism. Logic J. IGPL **13**(4), 365–387 (2005). https://doi.org/10.1093/jigpal/jzi030
5. Avron, A., Zamansky, A.: Non-deterministic semantics for logical systems. In: Gabbay, D.M., Guenthner, F. (eds.) Handbook of Philosophical Logic, vol. 16, pp. 227–304. Springer, Dordrecht (2011). https://doi.org/10.1007/978-94-007-0479-4_4
6. Baaz, M., Lahav, O., Zamansky, A.: Finite-valued semantics for canonical labelled calculi. J. Autom. Reason. **51**(4), 401–430 (2013). https://doi.org/10.1007/s10817-013-9273-x
7. Blasio, C.: Revisitando a lógica de Dunn-Belnap. Manuscrito **40**, 99–126 (2017). https://doi.org/10.1590/0100-6045.2017.v40n2.cb
8. Blasio, C., Caleiro, C., Marcos, J.: What is a logical theory? On theories containing assertions and denials. Synthese (2019). https://doi.org/10.1007/s11229-019-02183-z
9. Blasio, C., Marcos, J., Wansing, H.: An inferentially many-valued two-dimensional notion of entailment. Bull. Sect. Logic **46**(9), 233–262 (2017). https://doi.org/10.18778/0138-0680.46.3.4.05
10. Caleiro, C., Marcelino, S.: Analytic calculi for monadic PNmatrices. In: Iemhoff, R., Moortgat, M., de Queiroz, R. (eds.) WoLLIC 2019. LNCS, vol. 11541, pp. 84–98. Springer, Heidelberg (2019). https://doi.org/10.1007/978-3-662-59533-6_6

11. Caleiro, C., Marcelino, S.: On Axioms and Rexpansions. In: Arieli, O., Zamansky, A. (eds.) Arnon Avron on Semantics and Proof Theory of Non-Classical Logics. OCL, vol. 21, pp. 39–69. Springer, Cham (2021). https://doi.org/10.1007/978-3-030-71258-7_3
12. Caleiro, C., Marcelino, S., Filipe, P.: Infectious semantics and analytic calculi for even more inclusion logics. In: IEEE International Symposium on Multiple-Valued Logic, pp. 224–229 (2020). https://doi.org/10.1109/ISMVL49045.2020.000-1
13. Caleiro, C., Marcos, J., Volpe, M.: Bivalent semantics, generalized compositionality and analytic classic-like tableaux for finite-valued logics. Theoret. Comput. Sci. **603**, 84–110 (2015). https://doi.org/10.1016/j.tcs.2015.07.016
14. Cook, S.A., Reckhow, R.A.: The relative efficiency of propositional proof systems. J. Symb. Log. **44**(1), 36–50 (1979). https://doi.org/10.2307/2273702
15. Drobyshevich, S.: Tarskian consequence relations bilaterally: some familiar notions. Synthese (2019). https://doi.org/10.1007/s11229-019-02267-w
16. Hjortland, O.T.: Speech acts, categoricity, and the meanings of logical connectives. Notre Dame J. Form. Logic **55**(4), 445–467 (2014). https://doi.org/10.1215/00294527-2798700
17. Humberstone, L.: Heterogeneous logic. Erkenntnis **29**(3), 395–435 (1988). https://doi.org/10.1007/BF00183072
18. Marcelino, S., Caleiro, C.: Decidability and complexity of fibred logics without shared connectives. Logic J. IGPL **24**(5), 673–707 (2016). https://doi.org/10.1093/jigpal/jzw033
19. Marcelino, S., Caleiro, C.: Disjoint fibring of non-deterministic matrices. In: Kennedy, J., de Queiroz, R.J.G.B. (eds.) WoLLIC 2017. LNCS, vol. 10388, pp. 242–255. Springer, Heidelberg (2017). https://doi.org/10.1007/978-3-662-55386-2_17
20. Marcelino, S., Caleiro, C.: Axiomatizing non-deterministic many-valued generalized consequence relations. Synthese (2019). https://doi.org/10.1007/s11229-019-02142-8
21. Marcos, J.: Possible-translations semantics for some weak classically-based paraconsistent logics. J. Appl. Non-Class. Logics **18**(1), 7–28 (2008). https://doi.org/10.3166/jancl.18.7-28
22. Rumfitt, I.: “Yes” and “No”. Mind **109**(436), 781–823 (2000). https://doi.org/10.1093/mind/109.436.781
23. Shoesmith, D.J., Smiley, T.J.: Multiple-Conclusion Logic. Cambridge University Press, Cambridge (1978). https://doi.org/10.1017/CBO9780511565687

From Input/Output Logics to Conditional Logics via Sequents – with Provers

Björn Lellmann(✉)

TU Wien, Vienna, Austria

Abstract. We consider cut-free sequent calculi for a number of deontic logics from the family of Input/Output logics. These sequent calculi provide a correspondence to the flat fragment of certain conditional logics. Two of the introduced calculi are non-standard in that they include non-derivability statements, and hence are interesting also from a purely technical perspective. We further modularise the calculi in an extended sequent framework. Proof search in the extended calculi is implemented in Prolog, providing seemingly the first automated reasoning systems for some of the considered logics.

Keywords: I/O logic · Conditional logic · Deontic logic · Sequent systems

1 Introduction

A formalism which has recently gained interest in the field of deontic logic is that of *Input/Output logics* [16,23]. Here, conditional obligations such as "If there is a dog, then there must be a fence" are treated as *Input-Output* pairs, intuitively converting their input (the conditions under which the conditional obligation holds, e.g., "there is a dog") into their output (what is obligatory under these conditions, e.g., "there is a fence"). In the Input/Output approach this conversion mechanism, called *detachment*, is taken as the core mechanism of deontic logics, and is used to analyse phenomena and problems of deontic logic including, e.g., Contrary-to-Duty reasoning (reasoning with and about violated norms) or deontic paradoxa and dilemmas. In this framework, an Input/Output logic is viewed as a "transformation engine", which converts an input, i.e., a state description, into an output, i.e., what should be the case, using a set of conditional obligations in the form of Input/Output pairs. As a main aspect of the Input/Output framework, the Input/Output pairs are given by a *meta-level* connective instead of an *object-level* connective as in, e.g., dyadic deontic logic or conditional logic. Different Input/Output logics are then obtained (on the syntactical side) by varying the mechanisms of obtaining new input-output pairs from a given set of these pairs.

This work has been supported by BRISE-Vienna (UIA04-081), a European Union Urban Innovative Actions project.

A. Das and S. Negri (Eds.): TABLEAUX 2021, LNAI 12842, pp. 147–164, 2021.
https://doi.org/10.1007/978-3-030-86059-2_9

While the more theoretical side of the basic Input/Output logics by now is rather well understood, their automated reasoning side has not yet been fully explored: The only more practical approaches in this direction so far seem to be the semantical embedding of some systems of Input/Output logic into Higher-Order logic enabling automation for these systems in [3] and a goal-directed method for deciding certain Input/Output logics introduced in [29]. However, the embedding into Higher-Order Logic makes use of an embedding of Input/Output logics into certain modal logics, and the goal-directed decision procedures are based heavily on the semantic characterisation of the logics.

Here we take a more proof-theoretic approach and exploit a strong similarity to the KLM framework for nonmonotonic reasoning [10]. Analogously to the notion of an Input/Output pair the KLM framework is based on a meta-level connective for *nonmonotonic inference*, written $\Gamma \mid\!\sim A$ and interpreted as "Γ nonmonotonically entails A". Different systems then are given by different rules for this connective. However, it has been observed already in *op. cit.*, that this meta-level connective corresponds to a dyadic object-level connective, specifically that of *conditional logics*, and that different systems in the KLM framework therefore correspond to the flat (i.e., unnested) fragment of various conditional logics. This of course opens up the possibility of transferring certain results from one framework to the other. In addition, the formulation in terms of an object-level connective facilitates the application of syntactic methods, in particular the construction and use of sequent systems.

In the present paper we will use the same idea to obtain axiomatisations for the logical connective corresponding to input/output pairs in certain Input/Output logics. With the aim of obtaining automated reasoning procedures we consider corresponding sequent systems for these logics. These correspondences are also interesting in their own right, because they yield a representation of certain Input/Output logics in conditional logics, resulting in an alternative semantics. Two of the sequent systems are in addition non-standard in that they mention underivability in the premisses, stemming from the fact that the corresponding Input/Output logics contain *consistency constraints* in the formulation of the rules. With respect to automated reasoning, we then consider a modification of the sequent systems which facilitates a prototype implementation.

Of course the idea of turning Input/Output pairs into logical connectives goes against the original idea of treating conditional obligations expressly at the meta-level [16]. While there are certainly good philosophical arguments to do so, here we do not take a stance on this matter and treat the connectives from a purely syntactical point of view.

2 Input/Output Logics and Their Sequent Calculi

We briefly recall the relevant Input/Output logics, henceforth also simply *I/O logics*, and then consider their sequent calculi. The reader is referred to [16,23] for more details on Input/Output logics including the semantics, motivation and philosophical discussion. We defer the technical results about the calculi to Sect. 3.

The set Prop of *propositional formulae* is given as usual by the grammar Prop ::= $\mathcal{V}$ | $\bot$ | $\top$ | $\neg$Prop | Prop $\wedge$ Prop | Prop $\vee$ Prop | Prop $\rightarrow$ Prop where $\mathcal{V}$ is a countable infinite set of *propositional variables*. We assume the usual conventions about binding strength of the operators, i.e., $\neg$ binds stronger than $\wedge$ binds stronger than $\vee$ binds stronger than $\rightarrow$.

Definition 1. *An* Input/Output pair, *short* I/O pair *is a tuple* (A, X), *where* $A, X \in$ Prop *are propositional formulae.*

In the following we only consider mainly *unconstrained* I/O logics (see, e.g., [23] for the details). From the purely syntactic point of view, these logics then are given by different rules for obtaining new I/O pairs from a given set of I/O pairs, captured in the form of different derivability relations. Here we consider the following I/O logics: *simple-minded output* deriv_1, *simple-minded throughput* deriv_1^+, *reusable output* deriv_3, and *reusable throughput* deriv_3^+ from [16], *simple-minded output without weakening* (or aggregative simple-minded output) $\mathsf{ag\_der}_1$ and *reusable output without weakening* (or aggregative reusable output) $\mathsf{ag\_der}_3$ from [26,30], and *simple minded output with consistency check* $\mathsf{c\_ag\_der}_1$ as well as *basic output with consistency check* $\mathsf{c\_ag\_der}_3$. from [24,25].

The rules are given in Fig. 1. Rule SI (*Strengthening of the Input*) corresponds to downwards monotonicity in the first argument of the pair operator, while WO (*Weakening of the Output*) corresponds to upwards monotonicity in the second argument. Rule OEQ (*Output Equivalence*) is the weaker version of the latter stating congruence in the second argument. Rules $\top$ (*Tautology*) and ID (*Identity*) are self-explanatory. Rule AND and its weaker version RAND (*Restricted AND*) state that conjunction distributes over the second argument, while the rules CT (*Cumulative Transitivity*), ACT (*Aggregative Cumulative Transitivity*) and RACT (*Restricted Aggregative Cumulative Transitivity*) state various weaker versions of transitivity. Note that since there is no nesting of the I/O pair operator, the entailment relation in the rules SI, OEQ and WO as well as the consistency requirement in the rules RAND and RACT range over classical propositional logic.

Definition 2. *Let* G *be a set of I/O pairs, and let* $\mathcal{L}$ *be one of* deriv_1, deriv_1^+, deriv_3, deriv_3^+, $\mathsf{ag\_der}_1$, $\mathsf{ag\_der}_3$. *An I/O pair* (A, X) *is* derivable from G in $\mathcal{L}$, *written* $G \vdash_{\mathcal{L}} (A, X)$, *iff there is a derivation in* $\mathcal{L}$ *with conclusion* (A, X) *whose leaves are I/O pairs from* G *or entailment or consistency statements true in classical propositional logic. Here as usual a* derivation in $\mathcal{L}$ *is a finite labelled directed tree, whose nodes are labelled with I/O pairs or statements about propositional logic such that the label of each node follows from the labels of its children using the rules of* $\mathcal{L}$ *as given in Fig. 2. For* $\mathcal{L}$ *one of* $\mathsf{c\_ag\_der}_1$ *or* $\mathsf{c\_ag\_der}_3$ *the definition is the same with the additional requirement that for all leaves* (B, Y) *of the derivation we have that* $B \wedge Y$ *is consistent.*

In order to formulate the sequent systems corresponding to such logics we internalise the I/O pairs using a corresponding logical connective $>$ as follows.

$$\frac{(A,X) \quad B \vdash A}{(B,X)}\ \mathsf{SI} \qquad \frac{(A,X) \quad X \vdash Y \quad Y \vdash X}{(A,Y)}\ \mathsf{OEQ} \qquad \frac{(A,X) \quad X \vdash Y}{(A,Y)}\ \mathsf{WO}$$

$$\frac{}{(\top,\top)}\ \mathsf{T} \qquad \frac{}{(A,A)}\ \mathsf{ID} \qquad \frac{(A,X) \quad (A \wedge X, Y)}{(A,Y)}\ \mathsf{CT}$$

$$\frac{(A,X) \quad (A,Y)}{(A, X \wedge Y)}\ \mathsf{AND} \qquad \frac{(A,X) \quad (A,Y) \quad A \wedge X \wedge Y \text{ consistent}}{(A, X \wedge Y)}\ \mathsf{RAND}$$

$$\frac{(A,X) \quad (A \wedge X, Y)}{(A, X \wedge Y)}\ \mathsf{ACT} \qquad \frac{(A,X) \quad (A \wedge X, Y) \quad A \wedge X \wedge Y \text{ consistent}}{(A, X \wedge Y)}\ \mathsf{RACT}$$

Fig. 1. I/O logic rules

Logic	SI	OEQ	WO	T	ID	RAND	AND	RACT	ACT	CT	Reference
deriv_1	✓	(✓)	✓	✓		(✓)	✓				[16]
deriv_1^+	✓	(✓)	✓	(✓)	✓	(✓)	✓				[16]
deriv_3	✓	(✓)	✓	✓		(✓)	✓	(✓)	(✓)	✓	[16]
deriv_3^+	✓	(✓)	✓	(✓)	✓	(✓)	✓	(✓)	(✓)	✓	[16]
$\mathsf{ag\_der}_1$	✓	✓				(✓)	✓				$\mathcal{D}_1$ in [26]
$\mathsf{ag\_der}_3$	✓	✓				(✓)	✓	(✓)	✓		$\mathcal{D}_3$ in [26]
$\mathsf{c\_ag\_der}_1$	✓	✓				✓					D_1 in [25]
$\mathsf{c\_ag\_der}_3$	✓	✓				(✓)		✓			D_3 in [25]

Fig. 2. The different I/O logics. Checkmarks in parentheses are implied.

Definition 3. *The set $\mathcal{F}$ of formulae in the* internalised I/O language *is given by $\mathcal{F} ::= \mathcal{V} \mid \bot \mid \top \mid \mathcal{F} \wedge \mathcal{F} \mid \mathcal{F} \vee \mathcal{F} \mid \mathcal{F} \to \mathcal{F} \mid \mathcal{F} > \mathcal{F}$. A* sequent *in the internalised I/O language is a tuple of multisets of formulae from $\mathcal{F}$, written $\Gamma \Rightarrow \Delta$.*

We assume that all propositional connectives bind stronger than $>$. The sequent systems considered below all contain the standard $\mathsf{G3p}$ rules for classical propositional logic given in Fig. 3 (see also [32]).

Converting the rules for the I/O pairs into sequent rules by simply moving the I/O pairs from the premisses to the antecedent of the conclusion yields the rules and axiomatic sequents in Fig. 4. Of course, replacing the sequent arrow in these with an implication yields Hilbert-style axiomatisations. Using the methods of [11,12,27] to absorb cuts between the conclusions of these rules into the rule set yields the rules in Fig. 5. To save space in the presentation of the rules we abuse notation and use set notation in the premisses. E.g., instead of writing

$$\frac{C \Rightarrow A_1 \quad C, B_1 \Rightarrow A_2 \quad C, B_1, B_2 \Rightarrow A_3 \quad B_1, B_2, B_3 \Rightarrow D}{(A_1 > B_1), (A_2 > B_2), (A_3 > B_3) \Rightarrow (C > D)}\ \mathsf{R}_3$$

$$\frac{}{\Gamma, \bot \Rightarrow \Delta}\ \bot_L \qquad \frac{}{\Gamma \Rightarrow \top, \Delta}\ \top_R \qquad \frac{}{\Gamma, p \Rightarrow p, \Delta}\ \mathsf{init} \qquad \frac{\Gamma \Rightarrow A, \Delta}{\Gamma, \neg A \Rightarrow \Delta}\ \neg_L \qquad \frac{\Gamma, A \Rightarrow \Delta}{\Gamma \Rightarrow \neg A, \Delta}\ \neg_R$$

$$\frac{\Gamma, B \Rightarrow \Delta \quad \Gamma \Rightarrow A, \Delta}{\Gamma, A \to B \Rightarrow \Delta}\ \to_L \qquad \frac{\Gamma, A \Rightarrow \Delta \quad \Gamma, B \Rightarrow \Delta}{\Gamma, A \vee B \Rightarrow \Delta}\ \vee_L \qquad \frac{\Gamma, A, B \Rightarrow \Delta}{\Gamma, A \wedge B \Rightarrow \Delta}\ \wedge_L$$

$$\frac{\Gamma, A \Rightarrow B, \Delta}{\Gamma \Rightarrow A \to B, \Delta}\ \to_R \qquad \frac{\Gamma \Rightarrow A, B, \Delta}{\Gamma \Rightarrow A \vee B, \Delta}\ \vee_R \qquad \frac{\Gamma \Rightarrow A, \Delta \quad \Gamma \Rightarrow B, \Delta}{\Gamma \Rightarrow A \wedge B, \Delta}\ \wedge_R$$

Fig. 3. The classical propositional sequent rules

$$\frac{B \Rightarrow A}{(A > X) \Rightarrow (B > X)}\ (\mathsf{SI}) \qquad \frac{X \Rightarrow Y \quad Y \Rightarrow X}{(A > X) \Rightarrow (A > Y)}\ (\mathsf{OEQ}) \qquad \frac{X \Rightarrow Y}{(A > X) \Rightarrow (A > Y)}\ (\mathsf{WO})$$

$$(\mathsf{T}) : \Rightarrow \top > \top \qquad (\mathsf{ID}) : \Rightarrow (A > A) \qquad (\mathsf{CT}) : (A > X) \wedge (A \wedge X > Y) \Rightarrow (A > Y)$$

$$(\mathsf{AND}) : (A > X) \wedge (A > Y) \Rightarrow (A > X \wedge Y)$$

$$(\mathsf{ACT}) : (A > X) \wedge (A \wedge X > Y) \Rightarrow (A > X \wedge Y)$$

$$\frac{A \wedge X \wedge Y \text{ consistent}}{(A > X) \wedge (A > Y) \Rightarrow (A > X \wedge Y)}\ (\mathsf{RAND})$$

$$\frac{A \wedge X \wedge Y \text{ consistent}}{(A > X) \wedge (A \wedge X > Y) \Rightarrow (A > X \wedge Y)}\ (\mathsf{RACT})$$

Fig. 4. Axioms and rules corresponding to the I/O rules

we write

$$\frac{\{C, B_1, \ldots, B_{i-1} \Rightarrow A_i : 1 \leq i \leq 3\} \quad B_1, B_2, B_3 \Rightarrow D}{(A_1 > B_1), (A_2 > B_2), (A_3 > B_3) \Rightarrow (C > D)}\ \mathsf{R}_3 \quad .$$

Note also that the systems include the special case of the rules for $n = 0$, i.e., the rules

$$\frac{\Rightarrow D}{\Gamma \Rightarrow (C > D), \Delta}\ \mathsf{CC}_0 \qquad \frac{C \Rightarrow D}{\Gamma \Rightarrow (C > D), \Delta}\ \mathsf{CCI}_0$$

which are the same as R_0 and RI_0, respectively. Most significantly, the rules $\mathsf{c\_ag\_CC}_n$ and $\mathsf{c\_ag\_R}_n$ include *underivability statements* of the form $\nvdash \Gamma \Rightarrow \Delta$ in the premisses. In order to capture this we use the following notion of derivability:

Definition 4. *A* proto-derivation for a sequent $\Gamma \Rightarrow \Delta$ in $\mathsf{G}_{\mathcal{L}}$ *is a finite directed labelled tree, where the root is labelled with* $\Gamma \Rightarrow \Delta$ *and:*

- *each internal node is labelled with a sequent, each leaf is labelled with a sequent or an* underivability statement *of the form* $\nvdash \Sigma \Rightarrow \Pi$

$$\frac{\{C \Rightarrow A_i : 1 \leq i \leq n\} \quad B_1, \ldots, B_n \Rightarrow D}{\Gamma, (A_1 > B_1), \ldots, (A_n > B_n) \Rightarrow (C > D), \Delta} \ \mathsf{CC}_n$$

$$\frac{\{C \Rightarrow A_i : 1 \leq i \leq n\} \quad B_1, \ldots, B_n, C \Rightarrow D}{\Gamma, (A_1 > B_1), \ldots, (A_n > B_n) \Rightarrow (C > D), \Delta} \ \mathsf{CCI}_n$$

$$\frac{\{C, B_1, \ldots, B_{i-1} \Rightarrow A_i : 1 \leq i \leq n\} \quad B_1, \ldots, B_n \Rightarrow D}{\Gamma, (A_1 > B_1), \ldots, (A_n > B_n) \Rightarrow (C > D), \Delta} \ \mathsf{R}_n$$

$$\frac{\{C, B_1, \ldots, B_{i-1} \Rightarrow A_i : 1 \leq i \leq n\} \quad B_1, \ldots, B_n, C \Rightarrow D}{\Gamma, (A_1 > B_1), \ldots, (A_n > B_n) \Rightarrow (C > D), \Delta} \ \mathsf{RI}_n$$

$$\frac{\{C \Rightarrow A_i : 1 \leq i \leq n\} \quad \{D \Rightarrow B_i : 1 \leq i \leq n\} \quad B_1, \ldots, B_n \Rightarrow D}{\Gamma, (A_1 > B_1), \ldots, (A_n > B_n) \Rightarrow (C > D), \Delta} \ \mathsf{ag\_CC}_n$$

$$\frac{\{C, B_1, \ldots, B_{i-1} \Rightarrow A_i : 1 \leq i \leq n\} \quad \{D \Rightarrow B_i : 1 \leq i \leq n\} \quad B_1, \ldots, B_n \Rightarrow D}{\Gamma, (A_1 > B_1), \ldots, (A_n > B_n) \Rightarrow (C > D), \Delta} \ \mathsf{ag\_R}_n$$

$$\frac{\{C \Rightarrow A_i : 1 \leq i \leq n\} \quad \{D \Rightarrow B_i : 1 \leq i \leq n\} \quad B_1, \ldots, B_n \Rightarrow D \quad \nvdash C, D \Rightarrow}{\Gamma, (A_1 > B_1), \ldots, (A_n > B_n) \Rightarrow (C > D), \Delta} \ \mathsf{c\_ag\_CC}_n$$

$$\frac{\{C, B_1, \ldots, B_{i-1} \Rightarrow A_i : 1 \leq i \leq n\} \quad \{D \Rightarrow B_i : 1 \leq i \leq n\} \quad B_1, \ldots, B_n \Rightarrow D \quad \nvdash C, D \Rightarrow}{\Gamma, (A_1 > B_1), \ldots, (A_n > B_n) \Rightarrow (C > D), \Delta} \ \mathsf{c\_ag\_R}_n$$

$\mathsf{G}_{\mathsf{deriv}_1}$	: $\{\mathsf{CC}_n : n \geq 0\}$	$\mathsf{G}_{\mathsf{deriv}_3}$	: $\{\mathsf{R}_n : n \geq 0\}$
$\mathsf{G}_{\mathsf{deriv}_1^+}$	: $\{\mathsf{CCI}_n : n \geq 0\}$	$\mathsf{G}_{\mathsf{deriv}_3^+}$	: $\{\mathsf{RI}_n : n \geq 0\}$
$\mathsf{G}_{\mathsf{ag\_der}_1}$	: $\{\mathsf{ag\_CC}_n : n \geq 1\}$	$\mathsf{G}_{\mathsf{ag\_der}_3}$	: $\{\mathsf{ag\_R}_n : n \geq 1\}$
$\mathsf{G}_{\mathsf{c\_ag\_der}_1}$	: $\{\mathsf{c\_ag\_CC}_n : n \geq 1\}$	$\mathsf{G}_{\mathsf{c\_ag\_der}_3}$	: $\{\mathsf{c\_ag\_R}_n : n \geq 1\}$

Fig. 5. Sequent rules for I/O logics

- *whenever a node has a standard sequent as its label, then that sequent follows from the labels of the node's children using the rules of* $\mathsf{G}_{\mathcal{L}}$

The depth *of a proto-derivation is the depth of the underlying tree. A proto-derivation in* $\mathsf{G}_{\mathcal{L}}$ *is* valid *if for every underivability statement* $\nvdash \Sigma \Rightarrow \Pi$ *there is no valid proto-derivation of* $\Sigma \Rightarrow \Pi$ *in* $\mathsf{G}_{\mathcal{L}}$. *A sequent is* derivable in $\mathsf{G}_{\mathcal{L}}$, *written* $\vdash_{\mathsf{G}_{\mathcal{L}}} \Gamma \Rightarrow \Delta$ *if there is a valid proto-derivation for it in* $\mathsf{G}_{\mathcal{L}}$.

Of course, since the definition of a valid proto-derivation makes use of the very same notion, we need to show that the concept is well defined.

Lemma 5. *Every proto-derivation in* $\mathsf{G}_{\mathcal{L}}$ *is valid or not valid, but not both.*

Proof. By induction on the *modal rank* of its conclusion $\Gamma \Rightarrow \Delta$, i.e., the maximal nesting depth of the modal operator $>$ in a formula in the sequent. All rules of $\mathsf{G}_{\mathcal{L}}$ have the *subformula property*, i.e., every formula occurring in its premisses is a subformula of a formula occurring in its conclusion. Hence, if the modal rank of the conclusion of a proto-derivation is 0, then only propositional rules occur in it, and hence no underivability statements. Thus it is automatically valid.

Suppose that the modal rank of the conclusion of a proto-derivation $\mathcal{D}$ is $n+1$. Then again by the subformula property and the fact that the underivability statements in the rules have strictly lower modal rank than their conclusions we obtain that all the underivability statements in $\mathcal{D}$ have modal rank at most n. By induction hypothesis every proto-derivation for the sequent in such an underivability statement is either valid or not valid, but not both. Thus for every sequent occurring in such an underivability statement either there is a valid proto-derivation or there is not, but not both. Hence the proto-derivation $\mathcal{D}$ is either valid or not, but not both. □

Since this definition of derivability is rather non-standard, some remarks are in order. First for the calculi without underivability statements the definition collapses to the standard notion of derivability in sequent systems. Hence the reader not interested in the calculi for $\mathsf{c\_ag\_der}_1$ and $\mathsf{c\_ag\_der}_3$ may mentally substitute the standard definition for the rest of the paper.

We could avoid underivability statements by considering an *antisequent calculus* for underivability along the lines of [4]. While for propositional rules this works well due to invertibility, for the modal rules we would need rules stating that for every modal rule which could have been used to derive a sequent at least one of its premisses is underivable. Since every ordered subset of modal formulae in a sequent corresponds to such a possible rule application, the number of premisses for the modal antisequent rules would become rather large. For the sake of a more compact presentation we therefore keep to the current formulation.

3 Technical Results and Correspondence

We now consider the properties of our calculi, starting with a number of standard results leading up to cut elimination and the correspondence to the I/O logics.

Lemma 6 (Generalised Initial Sequents). *Let $\mathcal{L}$ be one of the logics without consistency check. Then $\vdash_{\mathsf{G}_\mathcal{L}} \Gamma, A \Rightarrow A, \Delta$. If $\mathcal{L}$ is one of $\mathsf{c\_ag\_der}_1$ and $\mathsf{c\_ag\_der}_3$ then $\vdash_{\mathsf{G}_\mathcal{L}} \Gamma, A \Rightarrow A, \Delta$ for purely propositional A.*

Proof. By induction on the complexity of the formula A. In case A is of the form $C > D$ we use the modal rule with exactly one principal formula on the left hand side, e.g., in the calculus $\mathsf{G}_{\mathsf{deriv}_3^+}$ we have an application of the rule Rl_1 with conclusion $(C > D) \Rightarrow (C > D)$ and premisses $C \Rightarrow C$ and $D, C \Rightarrow D$. The premisses are derivable by induction hypothesis. □

Note that derivability of the generalised initial sequents does not hold unrestrictedly for the logics $\mathsf{c\_ag\_der}_1$ and $\mathsf{c\_ag\_der}_3$, because we cannot derive sequents $(A > B) \Rightarrow (A > B)$ where A and B are inconsistent. This includes examples such as $(\bot > \bot) \Rightarrow (\bot > \bot)$ or $(A > \neg A) \Rightarrow (A > \neg A)$. For the purpose of showing equivalence to I/O logics the form restricted to propositional formulae is enough, though, since I/O logics do not contain nested I/O pairs.

Lemma 7 (Invertibility of the propositional rules). *Let $\mathcal{L}$ be one of the logics considered. Then the propositional rules are* depth-preserving invertible, *i.e., whenever their conclusion is derivable with a proto-derivation of depth n, then so are their premisses.*

Proof. By induction on the depth of the proto-derivation, using the fact that the formulae with a propositional connective at the top level occur in the modal rules only as context formulae. □

Lemma 8 (Admissibility of the structural rules). *Let $\mathcal{L}$ be one of the logics considered. Then the structural rules of weakening, left contraction and right contraction below are* depth-preserving admissible, *i.e., whenever their premiss is derivable in depth n, then so is their conclusion.*

$$\frac{\Gamma \Rightarrow \Delta}{\Sigma, \Gamma \Rightarrow \Delta, \Pi}\ \mathsf{W} \qquad \frac{\Gamma, A, A \Rightarrow \Delta}{\Gamma, A \Rightarrow \Delta}\ \mathsf{ICL} \qquad \frac{\Gamma \Rightarrow A, A, \Delta}{\Gamma \Rightarrow A, \Delta}\ \mathsf{ICR}$$

Proof. By induction on the depth of the proto-derivation. In case the last applied rule is a propositional rule with the contracted formula principal, as usual we use depth-preserving invertibility of the propositional rules (Lemma 7). In case the last applied rule is a modal rule with both instances of the contracted formula principal, we apply contraction to the premisses followed by the version of the same modal rule with one principal formula less. Note that the modal rules only have one principal formula on the right hand side, hence we do not need to consider contractions between principal formulae on the right and avoid having to deal with contractions in the underivability statements. □

Theorem 9 (Cut Admissibility). *The cut rule is admissible in $\mathsf{G}_{\mathcal{L}}$, i.e.,*

$$\text{if } \vdash_{\mathsf{G}_{\mathcal{L}}} \Gamma \Rightarrow \Delta, A \text{ and } \vdash_{\mathsf{G}_{\mathcal{L}}} A, \Sigma \Rightarrow \Pi \text{ then } \vdash_{\mathsf{G}_{\mathcal{L}}} \Gamma, \Sigma \Rightarrow \Delta, \Pi\ .$$

Proof. As usual by double induction on the complexity of the cut formula A and the sum of the depths of the valid proto-derivations $\mathcal{D}_1$ of $\Gamma \Rightarrow \Delta, A$ and $\mathcal{D}_2$ of $A, \Sigma \Rightarrow \Pi$, see, e.g., [32]. The case where the complexity of A is 1, i.e., A is a propositional variable is standard, permuting the cut over the last applied rule in $\mathcal{D}_1$ using the induction hypothesis until that rule is init, then absorbing it into the last applied rule in $\mathcal{D}_2$. In case the complexity of A is $n + 1$ we distinguish cases according to the topmost connective of A. In the propositional case we follow the standard approach and use invertibility of the propositional rules (Lemma 7) to reduce the cut to cuts on formulae of smaller complexity, potentially followed by admissibility of Contraction (Lemma 8) to eliminate duplicate formulae.

The interesting case is where A is of the form $(C > D)$. Again we permute the cut over the last applied rule in $\mathcal{D}_1$ until the cut formula is principal there using the inner induction hypothesis, then do the same with $\mathcal{D}_2$. What is left to check is that cuts between the principal formulae of two modal rules can be reduced to cuts of smaller complexity. We only consider a complicated case here, the remaining cases are similar but simpler.

Suppose that $\mathcal{L}$ is $\mathsf{c\_ag\_der}_3$, and the last applied rules were $\mathsf{c\_ag\_R}_n$:

$$\frac{\{C, B_1, \ldots, B_{i-1} \Rightarrow A_i : i \leq n\} \quad \{D \Rightarrow B_i : i \leq n\} \quad B_1, \ldots, B_n \Rightarrow D \quad \nvdash C, D \Rightarrow}{(A_1 > B_1), \ldots, (A_n > B_n) \Rightarrow (C > D)}$$

and $\mathsf{c\_ag\_R}_m$:

$$\frac{\begin{array}{l} \{G, F_1, \ldots, F_{i-1} \Rightarrow E_i : i \leq k-1\} \\ \quad G, F_1, \ldots, F_{k-1} \Rightarrow C \\ \quad\quad \{G, F_1, \ldots, F_{k-1}, D, F_{k+1}, \ldots, F_{i-1} \Rightarrow E_i : k < i \leq m\} \\ \quad\quad\quad \{H \Rightarrow F_i : k \neq i \leq m\} \\ \quad\quad\quad\quad H \Rightarrow D \\ \quad\quad\quad\quad\quad F_1, \ldots, F_{k-1}, D, F_{k+1}, \ldots, F_m \Rightarrow H \\ \quad\quad\quad\quad\quad\quad \nvdash G, H \Rightarrow \end{array}}{(E_1 > F_1), \ldots, (E_{k-1} > F_{k-1}), (C > D), (E_{k+1} > F_{k+1}), \ldots, (E_m > F_m) \Rightarrow (G > H)}$$

Applying the induction hypothesis to cut on the formulae C and D we obtain:

$$\begin{array}{l} \{G, F_1, \ldots, F_{i-1} \Rightarrow E_i : i \leq k-1\} \\ \quad \{G, F_1, \ldots, F_{k-1}, B_1, \ldots, B_{i-1} \Rightarrow A_i : i \leq n\} \\ \quad\quad \{G, F_1, \ldots, F_{k-1}, B_1, \ldots, B_n, F_{k+1}, \ldots, F_{i-1} \Rightarrow E_i : k < i \leq m\} \\ \quad\quad\quad \{H \Rightarrow F_i : k \neq i \leq m\} \\ \quad\quad\quad\quad \{H \Rightarrow B_i : i \leq n\} \\ \quad\quad\quad\quad\quad F_1, \ldots, F_{k-1}, B_1, \ldots, B_n, F_{k+1}, \ldots, F_m \Rightarrow H \\ \quad\quad\quad\quad\quad\quad \nvdash G, H \Rightarrow \end{array}$$

and applying $\mathsf{c\_ag\_R}_{n+m-1}$ yields the desired $(E_1 > F_1), \ldots, (E_{k-1} > F_{k-1})$, $(A_1 > B_1), \ldots, (A_n > B_n), (E_{k+1} > F_{k+1}), \ldots (E_m > F_m) \Rightarrow (G > H)$. □

As usual, one of the main consequences of cut admissibilty is consistency:

Corollary 10 (Consistency). *The calculi are consistent, i.e.,* $\nvdash_{\mathsf{G}_{\mathcal{L}}} \Rightarrow \bot$.

Proof. All rules have the subformula property, and no rule introduces $\bot$. □

Lemma 11 (Derivability of the axioms). *Let $\mathcal{L}$ be one of the considered logics. Then the axioms and rules of Fig. 4 for the corresponding I/O rules are derivable in $\mathsf{G}_{\mathcal{L}}$, restricted to non-nested formulae for* $\mathsf{c\_ag\_der}_1$ *and* $\mathsf{c\_ag\_der}_3$.

Proof. The rules (SI) and (WO) are special cases of the rules CC_1, CCI_1, R_1 and RI_1 respectively. The rule (OEQ) is a special case of $\mathsf{ag\_CC}_1$ and $\mathsf{ag\_R}_1$. For (RACT) we have for purely propositional formulae A, B, C:

$$\dfrac{\dfrac{A \Rightarrow A \quad A, B \Rightarrow A \wedge B \quad B \wedge C \Rightarrow B \quad B \wedge C \Rightarrow C \quad B, C \Rightarrow B \wedge C \quad \nvdash A, B \wedge C \Rightarrow}{(A > B), (A \wedge B > C) \Rightarrow (A > B \wedge C)}\ \mathsf{c\_ag\_R}_2}{(A > B) \wedge (A \wedge B > C) \Rightarrow (A > B \wedge C)}\ \wedge_L$$

where the underivability premiss is the premiss of (RACT) and the other premisses are derivable using Lemma 6 since A, B, C are purely propositional. The case of (RAND) is similar, using $\mathsf{c\_ag\_CC}_1$. Deriving the axiomatic sequents is relatively straightforward using Lemma 6. □

Using cut admissibility we can finally show that the sequent systems indeed capture the corresponding I/O logics:

Theorem 12 (Equivalence). *Let $\mathcal{L}$ be one of the logics considered here. For every set $\{(A_1, X_1), \ldots, (A_n, X_n)\}$ of I/O pairs we have*

$$\{(A_1, X_1), \ldots, (A_n, X_n)\} \vdash_{\mathcal{L}} (A, X) \text{ iff } \vdash_{\mathsf{G}_{\mathcal{L}}} (A_1 > X_1), \ldots, (A_n > X_n) \Rightarrow (A > X) .$$

Proof. We use the fact that the construction of an I/O logic derivation corresponds to the construction of a sequent rules for $>$ using cuts.

The left to right direction is shown by induction on the depth of the I/O derivation, i.e., the maximal length of a branch in that derivation. We first consider an example of an I/O rule corresponding to an axiom from Fig. 4. Suppose that $\{(A_1, X_1), \ldots, (A_n, X_n)\} \vdash_{\mathcal{L}} (A, X)$ and that the last applied rule was CT. Then there are $\mathcal{P}_1, \mathcal{P}_2$ with $\mathcal{P}_1 \cup \mathcal{P}_2 = \{(A_1, X_1), \ldots, (A_n, X_n)\}$ and a formula Y such that $\mathcal{P}_1 \vdash_{\mathcal{L}} (A, Y)$ and $\mathcal{P}_2 \vdash_{\mathcal{L}} (A \wedge Y, X)$. Hence by induction hypothesis for the sets $\mathcal{P}_1^{>}$ and $\mathcal{P}_2^{>}$ of conditional formulae corresponding to the tuples in $\mathcal{P}_1$ and $\mathcal{P}_2$ respectively we have $\vdash_{\mathsf{G}_{\mathcal{L}}} \mathcal{P}_1^{>} \Rightarrow (A > Y)$ and $\vdash_{\mathsf{G}_{\mathcal{L}}} \mathcal{P}_2^{>} \Rightarrow (A \wedge Y > X)$. By Lemma 11 we have $\vdash_{\mathsf{G}_{\mathcal{L}}} (A > Y) \wedge (A \wedge Y > X) \Rightarrow (A > X)$, and hence by invertibility of the propositional rules also $\vdash_{\mathsf{G}_{\mathcal{L}}} (A > Y), (A \wedge Y > X) \Rightarrow (A > X)$. Applying cut admissibility (Theorem 9) twice we have $\vdash_{\mathsf{G}_{\mathcal{L}}} \mathcal{P}_1^{>}, \mathcal{P}_2^{>} \Rightarrow (A > X)$, and admissibility of contraction (Lemma 8) yields the result. The cases for the other I/O rules corresponding to axiomatic sequents are similar.

As an example of an I/O rule corresponding to a rule from Fig. 4, assume that the last applied I/O rule was WO. Thus there is an I/O pair (A, Y) with $\{(A_1, X_1), \ldots, (A_n, X_n)\} \vdash_{\mathcal{L}} (A, Y)$ and $Y \vdash X$. By induction hypothesis we have $\vdash_{\mathsf{G}_{\mathcal{L}}} (A_1 > X_1), \ldots, (A_n > X_n) \Rightarrow (A > Y)$. Since $Y \vdash X$ propositionally and the propositional rules of $\mathsf{G}_{\mathcal{L}}$ are complete for classical propositional logic we also have $\vdash_{\mathsf{G}_{\mathcal{L}}} Y \Rightarrow X$, and Lemma 11 yields $\vdash_{\mathsf{G}_{\mathcal{L}}} (A > Y) \Rightarrow (A > X)$. Now admissibility of the cut rule gives the result.

For the right to left direction we use an induction on n, i.e., the number of I/O formulae on the left hand side of the sequent. If $\vdash_{\mathsf{G}_{\mathcal{L}}} (A_1 > X_1), \ldots, (A_n > X_n) \Rightarrow (A > X)$, then the last applied rule must be a modal rule. Assume w.l.o.g. that all the $(A_i > X_i)$ are principal formulae (otherwise apply the induction hypothesis on the principal formulae). The base cases are those for $0 \leq n \leq 2$. In each case we distinguish subcases according to which rule was applied. We further use the fact that for propositional formulae we have $A \Rightarrow B$ iff $A \vdash B$.

Case $n = 0$: The last applied rule was one of $\mathsf{CC}_0, \mathsf{CCl}_0, \mathsf{R}_0, \mathsf{Rl}_0$. For an application of CC_0 or R_0 with premiss $\Rightarrow D$ and conclusion $\Rightarrow (C > D)$ we first obtain $(\top, \top)$ from $\top$, which together with $C \vdash \top$ yields $(C, \top)$ by SI. This together with $\top \vdash D$ yields (C, D) by WO. The case of CCl_0 or Rl_0 is even simpler, using ID and SI.

Case $n = 1$: The rules CC_1 and R_1 are straightforward using SI and WO. For the rule CCI_1 (and analogously for RI_1) we have:

$$\frac{C \Rightarrow A \quad B, C \Rightarrow D}{(A > B) \Rightarrow (C > D)} \,\mathsf{CCI}_1 \rightsquigarrow \frac{\dfrac{\dfrac{(A,B) \quad C \vdash A}{(C,B)}\,\mathsf{SI} \quad \dfrac{}{(C > C)}\,\mathsf{ID}}{(C, B \wedge C)}\,\mathsf{AND} \quad B \wedge C \vdash D}{(C,D)}\,\mathsf{WO}$$

For $\mathsf{ag\_CC}_1$ or $\mathsf{ag\_R}_1$ with premisses $C \Rightarrow A$ as well as $D \Rightarrow B$ and $B \Rightarrow D$ and conclusion $(A > B) \Rightarrow (C > D)$ we obtain (C, B) from (A, B) and $C \vdash A$ by SI. Together with $D \vdash B$ and $B \vdash D$ this yields (C, D) by OEQ. For $\mathsf{c\_ag\_CC}_1$ and $\mathsf{c\_ag\_R}_1$ we use the same derivation as for $\mathsf{ag\_CC}_1$. However, to ensure that we obtain a derivation valid in $\mathsf{c\_ag\_der}_1$ (resp. $\mathsf{c\_ag\_der}_3$) we need to check that none of the I/O pairs used as premisses is contradictory, i.e., specifically that $\nvdash A \wedge B \to \bot$. Assume that $\vdash A \wedge B \to \bot$. Then since $C \vdash A$ we also have $\vdash C \wedge B \to \bot$. Since moreover $D \vdash B$ and $B \vdash D$ we then obtain $\vdash C \wedge D \to \bot$, in contradiction to $\nvdash C, D \Rightarrow$. Thus $\nvdash A \wedge B \to \bot$.

Case $n = 2$: Rule CC_2 is straightforward using SI followed by AND and WO. For CCI_2 we also need to use ID and AND before WO. For R_2 we use SI followed by CT, AND and finally WO. For RI_2 we do the same but again insert ID and AND before the final application of WO. For $\mathsf{ag\_CC}_2$, suppose we have:

$$\frac{C \Rightarrow A_1 \quad C \Rightarrow A_2 \quad D \Rightarrow B_1 \quad D \Rightarrow B_2 \quad B_1, B_2 \Rightarrow D}{(A_1 > B_1), (A_2 > B_2) \Rightarrow (C > D)}\,\mathsf{ag\_CC}_2$$

Applying SI on (A_1, B_1) and $C \Rightarrow A_1$ yields (C, B_1) and similarly SI on (A_2, B_2) and $C \Rightarrow A_2$ yields (C, B_2). An application of AND then gives $(C, B_1 \wedge B_2)$, which together with $D \vdash B_1 \wedge B_2$ and $B_1 \wedge B_2 \vdash D$ by OEQ yields (C, D). The case of $\mathsf{ag\_R}_2$ is similar, using ACT instead of AND. For $\mathsf{c\_ag\_CC}_2$ we use the same derivation as for $\mathsf{ag\_CC}_2$. Additionally, we have to check that none of the I/O pairs occurring as assumptions of the derivation is inconsistent, i.e., that $\nvdash A_1 \wedge B_1 \to \bot$ and $\nvdash A_2 \wedge B_2 \to \bot$. From $\nvdash C, D \Rightarrow$ we obtain $\nvdash C \wedge D \to \bot$. Together with $\vdash C \leftrightarrow B_1 \wedge B_2$ this yields $\nvdash C \wedge B_1 \wedge B_2 \to \bot$. Since $C \vdash A_1$ and $C \vdash A_2$ this yields $\nvdash A_1 \wedge B_1 \wedge B_2 \to \bot$ and $\nvdash A_2 \wedge B_1 \wedge B_2 \to \bot$, and thus finally $\nvdash A_1 \wedge B_1 \to \bot$ and $\nvdash A_2 \wedge B_2 \to \bot$. The case of $\mathsf{c\_ag\_R}_2$ is analogous.

Case $n = m + 2$ *with* $m \geq 1$*:* We use essentially the method of proving soundness of "cuts between rules" from [11, Lem.2.4.5], using that the rules are constructed from smaller components via closure under cuts. I.e., for a rule with conclusion $(A_1 > B_1), \ldots, (A_{m+2} > B_{m+2}) \Rightarrow (C > D)$ we construct a formula $(E > F)$ such that both $(A_1 > B_1), \ldots, (A_m > B_m), (E > F) \Rightarrow (C > D)$ and $(A_{m+1} > B_{m+1}), (A_{m+2} > B_{m+2}) \Rightarrow (E > F)$ are derivable given the original premisses. Then by induction hypothesis we obtain $\{(A_1, B_1), \ldots, (A_m, B_m), (E, F)\} \vdash_{\mathcal{L}} (C, D)$ and $\{(A_{m+1}, B_{m+1}), (A_{m+2}, B_{m+2})\} \vdash_{\mathcal{L}} (E, F)$ Putting these together we then have $\{(A_1, B_1), \ldots, (A_{m+2}, B_{m+2})\} \vdash_{\mathcal{L}} (C, D)$. For space reasons we only give the formula (E, F), assuming the rules as in Fig. 5 with conclusion $(A_1 > B_1), \ldots, (A_{m+2} > B_{m+2}) \Rightarrow (C > D)$.

For CC_{m+2} we set $(E > F) = (C > B_{m+1} \wedge B_{m+2})$. For CCl_{m+2} we set $(E > F) = (C > C \wedge B_{m+1} \wedge B_{m+2})$. For R_{m+2} we use $(E > F) = (C \wedge \bigwedge_{i \leq m} B_i > B_{m+1} \wedge B_{m=2})$, and for Rl_{m+2} we set $(E > F) = (C \wedge \bigwedge_{i \leq m} B_i > C \wedge \bigwedge_{i \leq m+2} B_i)$. For $\mathsf{ag\_CC}_{m+2}$ and $\mathsf{c\_ag\_CC}_{m+2}$ we use $(E > F) = (C > (B_{m+1} \wedge B_{m+2}) \vee D)$. In the case of $\mathsf{c\_ag\_CC}_{m+2}$ we additionally need to show the underivability premisses, i.e., $\nvdash C, (B_{m+2} \wedge B_{m+2}) \vee D \Rightarrow$. This follows by invertibility of the propositional rules from $\nvdash C, D \Rightarrow$. Finally, for $\mathsf{ag\_R}_{m+2}$ and $\mathsf{c\_ag\_R}_{m+2}$ we set $(E > F) = (C \wedge \bigwedge_{i \leq m} B_i > (B_{m+1} \wedge B_{m+2}) \vee D)$. In the case of $\mathsf{c\_ag\_R}_{m+2}$ again we also need to show the underivability premiss, i.e., $\nvdash C \wedge \bigwedge_{i \leq m} B_i, (B_{m+1} \wedge B_{m+2}) \vee D \Rightarrow$. Assume otherwise. Then by invertibility of the propositional rules we also have $\vdash C, B_1, \ldots, B_{m+2} \Rightarrow$. Together with $\vdash D \Rightarrow B_i$ for $i \leq m+2$ and admissibility of cut and contraction this yields $\vdash C, D \Rightarrow$ in contradiction to the original premiss $\nvdash C, D \Rightarrow$. □

One benefit of the equivalence is that now we have a formal correspondence between certain I/O logics and the *conditional logics* or *dyadic deontic logics* obtained by adding (the Hilbert-style versions of) the axioms and rules of Fig. 4 to standard axioms for classical propositional logic:

Corollary 13. *For every finite set* $\{(A_i, X_i) : i \leq n\}$ *of I/O pairs we have* $\{(A_i, X_i) : i \leq n\} \vdash_{\mathcal{L}} (A, X)$ *iff* $\bigwedge_{i \leq n}(A_i > X_i) \to (A > X)$ *is a theorem of the conditional logic given by the corresponding axioms and rules of Fig. 4.*

Proof. The proof of Theorem 12 also shows that the sequent calculi are sound and complete for the logics given by the axioms and rules of Fig. 4 and the cut rule, and thus also the corresponding Hilbert-style systems. In particular, soundness is seen by converting the sequent rules into I/O derivations, then converting these into derivations using the axioms and rules of Fig. 4. □

This opens up new possibilities for comparing I/O logics to other conditional or dyadic deontic logics by investigating them in the same framework of Hilbert- or sequent systems, or by giving them semantics along the lines of [5]. As an example, Lewis' counterfactual logic $\mathbb{V}$ from [15] in the language with the dyadic *comparative plausibility* operator $\preccurlyeq$ has been equipped with a cut-free sequent system in [13]. The sequent rules for the operator $\preccurlyeq$ are given by the set $\{R_{n,m} : n \geq 1, m \geq 0\}$ for the rules

$$\frac{\{B_k \Rightarrow A_1, \ldots, A_n, D_1, \ldots, D_m : k \leq n\} \quad \{C_k \Rightarrow A_1, \ldots, A_n, D_1, \ldots, D_{k-1} : k \leq m\}}{\Gamma, (C_1 \preccurlyeq D_1), \ldots, (C_m \preccurlyeq D_m) \Rightarrow (A_1 \preccurlyeq B_1), \ldots, (A_n \preccurlyeq B_n), \Delta} R_{n,m}$$

Setting $n = 1$ we note that the structure of the premisses is the same as that of the rule Rl_m, only with flipped right and left hand sides. Thus we obtain:

Theorem 14. *We have* $\{(A_1, X_1), \ldots, (A_n, X_n)\} \vdash_{\mathsf{deriv}_3^+} (A, X)$ *if and only if* $\bigwedge_{i \leq n}(\neg A_i \preccurlyeq \neg X_i) \to (\neg A \preccurlyeq \neg X)$ *is a theorem of* $\mathbb{V}$.

Proof. Applications of the rule Rl_m are simulated in the system for $\mathbb{V}$ by negation rules followed by $R_{1,n}$. Vice versa, if $(\neg A_1 \preccurlyeq \neg X_1), \ldots, (\neg A_n \preccurlyeq X_n) \Rightarrow$

$(\neg A \preccurlyeq \neg X)$ is derivable in the system for $\mathbb{V}$, then w.l.o.g. it is the conclusion of an application of $\mathsf{R}_{1,n}$. Since the premisses are purely propositional, they are derivable in $\mathsf{G}_{\mathsf{deriv}_3^+}$. Using invertibility of the propositional rules we remove the negations, and then apply the rule RI_n. The full equivalence then follows from Theorem 12. □

Thus the I/O logic deriv_3^+ can be seen as the flat modal Horn fragment of conditional logic $\mathbb{V}$. This then yields an alternative semantics for deriv_3^+ in terms of the *sphere models* of [15] by simply spelling out the truth conditions for a formula $(\neg A \preccurlyeq \neg X)$.

4 Theorem Proving

One of the immediate benefits of the cut-free sequent calculi introduced above is that we immediately obtain an alternative decidability and complexity proof:

Theorem 15 (Decidability and Complexity). *Derivability in all the considered sequent systems is decidable in polynomial space.*

Proof. By a standard backwards proof search argument, e.g., the generic complexity result in [11, Thm. 2.7.8]. For the calculi with underivability statement we just need to flip the results for these statements. □

Since I/O pairs do not contain nested operators, the complexity for solving the entailment problem in I/O logics using our sequent calculi drops to the class Π_3^P of the polynomial hierarchy. However, since this is still above the optimal coNP-bounds following from [31] we do not consider this in detail here.

In terms of implementing our calculi, one suboptimal factor is that the number of principal formulae in the conclusion is unbounded, and that in contrast to, e.g., the rules for modal logic K the order of the principal formulae on the left hand side is crucial. We can obtain a more modular and arguably more elegant formulation by considering sequents with an additional *block*, in line with the idea of modularisation of sequent calculi in [14] and inspired by the blocks for nested sequent calculi in [1,8,19]. The main idea is to build up the sequent rules one formula at a time, starting with the principal formula on the right. The block is used to store the information during the building up of the rule.

Definition 16. *An* extended sequent *is a standard sequent possibly extended with a* block $[A > B : \Omega]$ *containing a formula* $A > B$ *and a multiset* Ω *of formulae. An extended sequent with a block is written* $\Gamma \Rightarrow \Delta, [A > B : \Omega]$.

The modal extended sequent rules then are given in Fig. 6, the modal part of the extended sequent calculi $\mathsf{EG}_{\mathcal{L}}$ is given in Fig. 7. In addition, all the calculi contain the standard propositional rules of Fig. 3. Note that this implies that the propositional rules can only be applied to standard sequents, i.e., sequents which do not contain a block. This is a design choice based purely on convenience, because it automatically separates the propositional and modal phases of a derivation, hence eliminating the need for a permutation-of-rules argument as in [14, Thm.4.3] when showing equivalence of the calculi. Note also the subtle difference between the rules jump and $\mathsf{jump}^{\mathsf{ag}}$: In the latter the left hand side of the premiss contains a formula B and hence cannot be empty. This ensures that the rule $\mathsf{jump}^{\mathsf{ag}}$ can not be applied immediately above the rule $>_R$, capturing the fact that aggregative logics do not satisfy the axiom $\top$ of Fig. 4 and hence their sequent rules from Fig. 5 have a non-empty left hand side in the conclusion. The same mechanism holds for the consistent version $\mathsf{jump}^{\mathsf{c\_ag}}$ of the rule.

$$\frac{\Gamma \Rightarrow \Delta, [C > D :]}{\Gamma \Rightarrow \Delta, C > D}\;>_R \qquad \frac{\Omega \Rightarrow D}{\Gamma \Rightarrow \Delta, [C > D : \Omega]}\;\mathsf{jump} \qquad \frac{\Omega, C \Rightarrow D}{\Gamma \Rightarrow \Delta, [C > D : \Omega]}\;\mathsf{jump}^+$$

$$\frac{C \Rightarrow A \quad \Gamma \Rightarrow \Delta, [C > D : \Omega, B]}{\Gamma, A > B \Rightarrow \Delta, [C > D : \Omega]}\;>_L \qquad \frac{C, \Omega \Rightarrow A \quad \Gamma \Rightarrow \Delta, [C > D : \Omega, B]}{\Gamma, A > B \Rightarrow \Delta, [C > D : \Omega]}\;>_L^3$$

$$\frac{C \Rightarrow A \quad D \Rightarrow B \quad \Gamma \Rightarrow \Delta, [C > D : \Omega, B]}{\Gamma, A > B \Rightarrow \Delta, [C > D : \Omega]}\;>_L^{\mathsf{ag}} \qquad \frac{\Omega, B \Rightarrow D}{\Gamma \Rightarrow \Delta, [C > D : \Omega, B]}\;\mathsf{jump}^{\mathsf{ag}}$$

$$\frac{C, \Omega \Rightarrow A \quad D \Rightarrow B \quad \Gamma \Rightarrow \Delta, [C > D : \Omega, B]}{\Gamma, A > B \Rightarrow \Delta, [C > D : \Omega]}\;>_L^{\mathsf{ag\_3}} \qquad \frac{\Omega, B \Rightarrow D \quad \not\vdash C, D \Rightarrow}{\Gamma \Rightarrow \Delta, [C > D : \Omega, B]}\;\mathsf{jump}^{\mathsf{c\_ag}}$$

Fig. 6. The extended sequent rules for internalised I/O logics

	$>_R$	$>_L$	$>_L^3$	$>_L^{\mathsf{ag}}$	$>_L^{\mathsf{ag\_3}}$	jump	jump^+	$\mathsf{jump}^{\mathsf{ag}}$	$\mathsf{jump}^{\mathsf{c\_ag}}$
$\mathsf{EG}_{\mathsf{deriv}_1}$	✓	✓				✓			
$\mathsf{EG}_{\mathsf{deriv}_1^+}$	✓	✓					✓		
$\mathsf{EG}_{\mathsf{deriv}_3}$	✓		✓			✓			
$\mathsf{EG}_{\mathsf{deriv}_3^+}$	✓		✓				✓		
$\mathsf{EG}_{\mathsf{ag\_der}_1}$	✓			✓				✓	
$\mathsf{EG}_{\mathsf{ag\_der}_3}$	✓				✓			✓	
$\mathsf{EG}_{\mathsf{c\_ag\_der}_1}$	✓			✓					✓
$\mathsf{EG}_{\mathsf{c\_ag\_der}_3}$	✓				✓				✓

Fig. 7. The exended sequent calculi

Proposition 17. *The standard sequent calculi and the extended sequent calculi are equivalent, i.e., a standard sequent is derivable in* $\mathsf{G}_{\mathcal{L}}$ *if and only if it is derivable in* $\mathsf{EG}_{\mathcal{L}}$.

Proof. To see that every sequent derivable in the standard sequent calculi is also derivable in the corresponding extended sequent calculi it is enough to show that the standard modal rules are derivable rules in the extended sequent calculi. We do this by first applying (bottom-up) the right rule for $>$, followed by a number of applications of the left rule for $>$ and finally an application of the corresponding jump rule. E.g., an application

$$\frac{\{C, B_1, \ldots, B_{i-1} \Rightarrow A_i : 1 \leq i \leq n\} \quad B_1, \ldots, B_n \Rightarrow D}{\Gamma, (A_1 > B_1), (A_2 > B_2), \ldots, (A_n > B_n) \Rightarrow (C > D), \Delta} \ \mathsf{R}_n$$

$$\frac{C, B_1, \ldots, B_{n-1} \Rightarrow A_n \quad \dfrac{B_1, \ldots, B_n \Rightarrow D}{\Gamma \Rightarrow \Delta, [C > D : B_1, \ldots, B_n]} \ \text{jump}}{\Gamma, (A_n > B_n) \Rightarrow \Delta, [(C > D) : B_1, \ldots, B_{n-1}]} \ >_L^3$$

$$\vdots$$

$$\frac{C \Rightarrow A_1 \quad \dfrac{C, B_1 \Rightarrow A_2 \quad \dfrac{\Gamma, (A_3 > B_3), \ldots, (A_n > B_n) \Rightarrow \Delta, [C > D : B_1, B_2]}{\Gamma, (A_2 > B_2), \ldots, (A_n > B_n) \Rightarrow \Delta, [(C > D) : B_1]} \ >_L^3}{\dfrac{\Gamma, (A_1 > B_1), (A_2 > B_2), \ldots, (A_n > B_n) \Rightarrow \Delta, [(C > D) :]}{\Gamma, (A_1 > B_1), (A_2 > B_2), \ldots, (A_n > B_n) \Rightarrow (C > D), \Delta}} \ >_L^3}{\quad} \ >_R$$

Fig. 8. The derivation of the sequent rule R_n

of the rule R_n is simulated by the derivation in Fig. 8. The other cases are similar. For the other direction, due to the fact that an extended sequent contains at most one block and the shape of the rules, the modal rules are applied only in blocks with an application of $>_R$ at the bottom, followed by a number of applications of the appropriate version of the $>_L$ rule and finally a single application of the appropriate version of the jump rule. Such blocks straightforwardly correspond to an application of the respective standard sequent rule, essentially reversing the simulation of that rule considered above.   □

A prototype implementation of proof search in the extended sequent calculi in SWI-Prolog[1] is available as IOCondProver both as a web interface[2] and as source code on GitHub[3]. The implementation uses the Lean methodology [2] to delegate proof search to Prolog's backtracking mechanism. In case proof search is successful it outputs a LaTeX file containing the derivation, which is automatically rendered to a PDF file in the web interface.

While decision procedures for some I/O logics have been given using a semantic embedding into Higher Order Logic [3], it seems like the only other approach to automated reasoning for the logics considered here is that of the I/O Logics Workbench [29], which in its current version captures the logics deriv_1, deriv_1^+, deriv_3 and deriv_3^+ but does not seem to capture the logics $\mathsf{ag\_der}_1$, $\mathsf{ag\_der}_3$,

---

[1] See https://www.swi-prolog.org.
[2] See http://subsell.logic.at/bprover/iocondprover/.
[3] See https://github.com/blellmann/iocondprover.

c_ag_der$_1$ or c_ag_der$_3$. In contrast to the proof theoretic approach underlying IOCondProver, the reasoning underlying the I/O Logics Workbench is based on the semantic characterisation of the I/O logics, using a module for the consequence relation of an underlying base logic. While this makes the I/O Logics Workbench easily adaptable to other base logics such as intuitionistic logic, it also makes it difficult to adapt to the full nested logics characterised by the sequent calculi considered here. The proof theoretic approach of IOCondProver has the additional advantage of certificates for derivable sequents in the form of a derivation. Since IOCondProver is merely a prototype implementation, the focus of this article is on the theoretical background, and in the absence of meaningful sets of benchmark formulae for I/O logics we do not consider a performance comparison with the I/O Logics Workbench here.

There are a number of calculi and theorem provers available both in the KLM-framework, see, e.g., [6,7,28] as well as in the framework of conditional logics, e.g., [9,18,20]. However, the vast majority of the available calculi and provers is based on KLM or conditional logics not corresponding to one of the I/O logics considered here. An exception is provided by the prover VINTE from [9], which implements proof search in an internal calculus for conditional logic $\mathbb{V}$. For the reasons given in the context of the I/O Logics Workbench we also do not consider performance comparisons with these provers here.

5 Conclusion

In this article we considered cut-free sequent calculi for a number of I/O logics including ones with consistency constraints. Two of the calculi are non-standard in that they contain underivability statements in the premisses. The calculi yield a correspondence of the original I/O logics to certain conditional logics and hence can form the basis of future comparisons between the two frameworks. We also considered modified versions of the calculi which are implemented in the prototype prover IOCondProver. For half of the considered logics this seems to be the first implementation available.

There are a number of possible directions for future research. The most obvious one is the extension to further I/O logics, in particular the logics deriv$_2$ and deriv$_4$, which result from deriv$_1$ and deriv$_3$ by adding essentially the axiom $(A > C) \wedge (B > C) \to (A \vee B > C)$. Since all the axioms for these logics have modal Horn form a cut-free sequent system immediately follows from the generic construction of [11, Sec. 4.1, Cor. 4.1.20]. The rules could even be made comprehensible by using the universal orders of derivation of [16, Sec. 8], since the order of applying I/O rules corresponds to an order in the construction of the sequent rules by cuts. Unfortunately Contraction might not be admissible in the resulting systems, and hence it is not clear that they can be used for automated reasoning. In contrast, it might be simpler to adapt the calculi considered here to the operators for *permissions* considered in [17,21]. Since the logics considered here are given by axioms in modal Horn form and do not involve disjunction it might also be straightforward to adapt them to intuitionistic instead of classical logic as the base logic in the spirit of [22]. Finally, it might be possible to exploit the sequent formulation in order to give a constructive proof of an analog of the Craig Interpolation Property for I/O logics, following the methods of [11,13].

Acknowledgements. This article would not have been possible without the many discussions on the topic with Leon van der Torre. I also thank the reviewers for their thorough reading and comments which helped to improve the article.

References

1. Alenda, R., Olivetti, N., Pozzato, G.L.: Nested sequent calculi for normal conditional logics. J. Log. Comput. **26**(1), 7–50 (2013). https://doi.org/10.1093/logcom/ext034
2. Becker, B., Posegga, J.: leanTAP: lean tableau-based deduction. J. Autom. Reason. **15**, 339–358 (1995). https://doi.org/10.1007/BF00881804
3. Benzmüller, C., Farjami, A., Meder, P., Parent, X.: I/O logics in HOL. J. Appl. Logics **6**(5), 715–754 (2019)
4. Bonatti, P.A., Olivetti, N.: Sequent calculi for propositional nonmonotonic logics. ACM Trans. Comput. Log. **3**, 226–278 (2002)
5. Chellas, B.F.: Modal Logic. Cambridge University Press, Cambridge (1980)
6. Giordano, L., Gliozzi, V., Olivetti, N., Pozzato, G.L.: Analytic tableaux calculi for KLM logics of nonmonotonic reasoning. ACM Trans. Comput. Log. **10**(3), 1–47 (2009)
7. Giordano, L., Gliozzi, V., Pozzato, G.L.: KLMLean 2.0: a theorem prover for KLM logics of nonmonotonic reasoning. In: Olivetti, N. (ed.) TABLEAUX 2007. LNCS (LNAI), vol. 4548, pp. 238–244. Springer, Heidelberg (2007). https://doi.org/10.1007/978-3-540-73099-6_19
8. Girlando, M., Lellmann, B., Olivetti, N., Pozzato, G.L.: Standard sequent calculi for Lewis' logics of counterfactuals. In: Michael, L., Kakas, A. (eds.) JELIA 2016. LNCS (LNAI), vol. 10021, pp. 272–287. Springer, Cham (2016). https://doi.org/10.1007/978-3-319-48758-8_18
9. Girlando, M., Lellmann, B., Olivetti, N., Pozzato, G.L., Vitalis, Q.: VINTE: an implementation of internal calculi for Lewis' logics of counterfactual reasoning. In: Schmidt, R.A., Nalon, C. (eds.) TABLEAUX 2017. LNCS (LNAI), vol. 10501, pp. 149–159. Springer, Cham (2017). https://doi.org/10.1007/978-3-319-66902-1_9
10. Kraus, S., Lehman, D., Magidor, M.: Nonmonotonic reasoning, preferential models and cumulative logics. Artif. Intell. **44**(1–2), 167–207 (1990)
11. Lellmann, B.: Sequent calculi with context restrictions and applications to conditional logic. Ph.D. thesis, Imperial College London (2013). http://hdl.handle.net/10044/1/18059
12. Lellmann, B., Pattinson, D.: Cut elimination for shallow modal logics. In: Brünnler, K., Metcalfe, G. (eds.) TABLEAUX 2011. LNCS (LNAI), vol. 6793, pp. 211–225. Springer, Heidelberg (2011). https://doi.org/10.1007/978-3-642-22119-4_17
13. Lellmann, B., Pattinson, D.: Sequent systems for Lewis' conditional logics. In: del Cerro, L.F., Herzig, A., Mengin, J. (eds.) JELIA 2012. LNCS (LNAI), vol. 7519, pp. 320–332. Springer, Heidelberg (2012). https://doi.org/10.1007/978-3-642-33353-8_25
14. Lellmann, B., Pimentel, E.: Modularisation of sequent calculi for normal and non-normal modalities. ACM Trans. Comput. Logic **20**(2), 7:1–7:46 (2019)

15. Lewis, D.: Counterfactuals. Blackwell (1973)
16. Makinson, D., van der Torre, L.: Input/Output logics. J. Philos. Log. **29**, 383–408 (2000). https://doi.org/10.1023/A:1004748624537
17. Makinson, D., van der Torre, L.: Permission from an input/output perspective. J. Philos. Log. **32**, 391–416 (2003). https://doi.org/10.1023/A:1024806529939
18. Olivetti, N., Pozzato, G.L.: CondLean 3.0: improving condlean for stronger conditional logics. In: Beckert, B. (ed.) TABLEAUX 2005. LNCS (LNAI), vol. 3702, pp. 328–332. Springer, Heidelberg (2005). https://doi.org/10.1007/11554554_27 http://www.springerlink.com/index/835jd3u9fx8klwy9.pdf
19. Olivetti, N., Pozzato, G.L.: A standard internal calculus for Lewis' counterfactual logics. In: De Nivelle, H. (ed.) TABLEAUX 2015. LNCS (LNAI), vol. 9323, pp. 270–286. Springer, Cham (2015). https://doi.org/10.1007/978-3-319-24312-2_19
20. Olivetti, N., Pozzato, G.L.: NESCOND: an implementation of nested sequent calculi for conditional logics. In: Demri, S., Kapur, D., Weidenbach, C. (eds.) IJCAR 2014. LNCS (LNAI), vol. 8562, pp. 511–518. Springer, Cham (2014). https://doi.org/10.1007/978-3-319-08587-6_39
21. Olszewski, M., Parent, X., van der Torre, L.: Input/Output logic with a consistency check - the case of permission. In: DEON 2020/2021. College Publications (2021)
22. Parent, X., Gabbay, D., Torre, L.: Intuitionistic basis for input/output logic. In: Hansson, S.O. (ed.) David Makinson on Classical Methods for Non-Classical Problems. OCL, vol. 3, pp. 263–286. Springer, Dordrecht (2014). https://doi.org/10.1007/978-94-007-7759-0_13
23. Parent, X., van der Torre, L.: Input/output logic. In: Gabbay, D., Horty, J., Parent, X., van der Meyden, R., van der Torre, L. (eds.) Handbook of Deontic Logic and Normative Systems, chap. 8, pp. 495–544. College Publications (2013)
24. Parent, X., van der Torre, L.: The pragmatic oddity in norm-based deontic logics. In: Governatori, G. (ed.) ICAIL 2017, pp. 169–178. Association for Computing Machinery (2017). https://doi.org/10.1145/3086512.3086529
25. Parent, X., van der Torre, L.: I/O logics with a consistency check. In: Broersen, J., Condoravdi, C., Nair, S., Pigozzi, G. (eds.) Deontic Logic and Normative Systems. DEON 2018, pp. 285–300. College Publications (2018)
26. Parent, X., van der Torre, L.: Input/Output logics without weakening. Filosofiska Notiser **6**(1), 189–208 (2019)
27. Pattinson, D., Schröder, L.: Generic modal cut elimination applied to conditional logics. Log. Methods Comput. Sci. **7**(1:4), 1–28 (2011)
28. Pozzato, G.L.: Conditional and Preferential Logics: Proof Methods and Theorem Proving. Frontiers in Artificial Intelligence and Applications, vol. 208. IOS Press, Amsterdam (2010)
29. Steen, A.: Goal-directed decision procedures for input/output logics. In: Liu, F., Marra, A., Portner, P., Putte, F.V.D. (eds.) DEON2020/2021. College Publications (2021, to appear)
30. Stolpe, A.: Normative consequence: the problem of keeping it whilst giving it up. In: van der Meyden, R., van der Torre, L. (eds.) DEON 2008. LNCS (LNAI), vol. 5076, pp. 174–188. Springer, Heidelberg (2008). https://doi.org/10.1007/978-3-540-70525-3_14
31. Sun, X., Robaldo, L.: On the complexity of input/output logic. J. Appl. Logic **25**, 69–88 (2017)
32. Troelstra, A.S., Schwichtenberg, H.: Basic Proof Theory. Cambridge Tracts in Theoretical Computer Science, vol. 43, 2nd edn. Cambridge University Press, Cambridge (2000)

Theorem Proving

Towards Finding Longer Proofs

Zsolt Zombori[1,2](✉), Adrián Csiszárik[1,2], Henryk Michalewski[3,4], Cezary Kaliszyk[3,5], and Josef Urban[6]

[1] Alfréd Rényi Institute of Mathematics, Budapest, Hungary
zombori@renyi.hu
[2] Eötvös Loránd University, Budapest, Hungary
[3] University of Warsaw, Warsaw, Poland
[4] Google Inc., Warsaw, Poland
[5] University of Innsbruck, Innsbruck, Austria
[6] Czech Technical University in Prague, Prague, Czech Republic

Abstract. We present a reinforcement learning (RL) based guidance system for automated theorem proving geared towards Finding Longer Proofs (FLoP). Unlike most learning based approaches, we focus on generalising from very little training data and achieving near complete confidence. We use several simple, structured datasets with very long proofs to show that FLoP can successfully generalise a single training proof to a large class of related problems. On these benchmarks, FLoP is competitive with strong theorem provers despite using very limited search, due to its ability to solve problems that are prohibitively long for other systems.

Keywords: Automated theorem proving · Machine learning · Reinforcement learning · Connection calculus

1 Introduction

Automated Theorem Proving (ATP) is the study of using machines for formal mathematical reasoning. It is related to general game playing, for example, the game of Go can be viewed as a simple formal system. Building on the recent success of machine learning, a growing trend in this field is to use learning methods to make theorem provers more powerful. Several research projects have shown that learning can be used to replace/surpass human-engineered heuristics. Despite huge improvements, interesting mathematical theorems remain elusive today. One crucial shortcoming of ATP systems is that they can typically find only relatively short proofs.

In this paper, we address this shortcoming and ask the question of how machine learning can be used to solve problems requiring very long inference chains. We argue that the fundamental reason why current ATP systems are limited to short proofs is that they focus on the search aspect of the task in the space of inference steps. It is very natural to see theorem proving as a search

A. Das and S. Negri (Eds.): TABLEAUX 2021, LNAI 12842, pp. 167–186, 2021.
https://doi.org/10.1007/978-3-030-86059-2_10

problem: each proof step involves a choice from a set of valid inferences, yielding a search space that grows exponentially with the length of the proof. Due to the exponential blowup, the search is bound to fail beyond a certain depth – except for special classes of problems where one of the smart human heuristics of the theorem prover allows for finding the solution without a search. As W. W. Bledsoe observed [7]: "Automated theorem proving ... is not the beautiful process we know as mathematics. This is 'cover your eyes with blinders and hunt through a cornfield for a diamond-shaped grain of corn'."

Approaches that try to avoid excessive search broadly fall into three categories: 1) Perform large steps, such as the invocation of tactics, decision procedures in SMT solvers [4], or other complex algorithms. This approach is widely used in interactive theorem provers, e.g. [5,13,30]. 2) Perform hierarchical reasoning by first creating a high-level proof plan and then gradually refine it to the calculus level, e.g. [10,29]. 3) Reason by analogy, e.g. [8,28].

Reasoning by analogy involves observing the proof of one problem, extracting the core idea, and successfully applying it to another. Note that using this formulation, success is barely dependent on proof length. On the other hand, establishing mappings between proofs is challenging and depends heavily on a proper data representation, which has been from the beginnings of ATP a major bottleneck for this approach. However, with the advent of machine learning methods capable of automatically discovering good data embeddings, the analogy approach seems worth revisiting.

In this work, we interpret analogical reasoning as building a model that internalises a proof and then successfully applies it to a class of related problems, without relying much on search. The trained model is supposed to know the proof of an unseen, yet familiar problem. This is a highly simplified approach which does not capture the full potential of analogy, but we argue that it is a meaningful start that will hopefully lead to more refined solutions. We select classes of problems where proofs are highly similar and trained humans can often generalize a single demonstration to the entire class, even if proof lengths greatly differ. We explore whether machine learning can yield similar generalization.

Many successful ATP systems, such as [11,17,19,31,36,52,56] implement the MaLARea [50,52] learning/reasoning loop (described later also as the DAgger [43] meta-algorithm). The MaLARea loop interleaves ATP runs based on the current models (*data collection phase*) with a *training phase*, in which these models are updated to fit the collected data.

An alternative family of reinforcement learning methods, including Temporal Difference (TD) learning [49], continuously update their models, allowing the system to bootstrap on itself. Such methods have so far been mostly ignored by the theorem proving community. In these methods, the search is usually replaced by rollouts. While MaLARea has been shown to yield good search heuristics, we argue that rollout based data collection is more suitable when the aim is to fully explore the space around a single problem without overfitting to it. Our work has the following contributions.

- We introduce a new theorem proving algorithm FLoP (Sect. 4) based on a TD algorithm[1] and the connection tableau calculus [6]. FLoP makes use of the curriculum learning algorithms presented by [40] and [44]. These techniques are well established in RL, however, they have never been applied to theorem proving before.
- We introduce a synthetic dataset of increasingly difficult arithmetic problems, as well as two datasets from the Logical Calculi domain of the TPTP [48] library, augmented with lemmata (Sect. 5).
- We show that when restricted to single shot evaluation – without search – FLoP performs very well, while another prover based on guided Monte Carlo Tree Search greatly degrades.
- We evaluate FLoP on our arithmetic benchmarks by training it on a single problem and show that it generalizes very well even when evaluated without search, allowing just a few proof attempts. This suggests that it has learned a simple form of reasoning by analogy.
- We use the arithmetic benchmarks to compare FLoP with state-of-the-art provers Vampire [25], E [46], leanCoP [32] guided by human-designed strategies, and with rlCoP [19] – an RL-based connection tableau prover. In the simple setup of unary encoding of numbers, FLoP is only outperformed by a portfolio (multi-strategy) mode of a single manually optimized rewriting-based system and only after trying several of its autoconfiguration heuristics. When using binary encoding, FLoP performs best, demonstrating its ability to generalize to long proofs.

Our datasets presented in Sect. 5 seem to be particularly suited for machine learning methods: some problems are algorithmically simple, with long solutions and strong shared structure (Robinson Arithmetic) while others are less similar, but hierarchically structured (Logical Calculi). Nevertheless, state-of-the-art systems struggle with solving some of the problems (see Sect. 6). Furthermore, our problems are much easier to analyze than typical heterogeneous proof corpora, hence promising better understanding of the current limits of theorem provers. The difficulty of our synthetic problems, as well as the proof lengths, are easily adjustable, yielding a scalable RL benchmark with interpretable failure modes.

Our code, datasets and all experiment configuration files are available at http://bit.ly/code_atpcurr[2]. Supplementary materials including screencasts with gameplays performed in our environments are available at the project webpage http://bit.ly/site_atpcurr.

2 Related Work

Theorem Proving by Analogy. Analogy has long been considered one of the most important heuristics in mathematical problem solving, e.g. [37,38]. It also gained

[1] In particular, we use Proximal Policy Optimization [45] (PPO), a variant of the policy gradient method, which uses Temporal Difference learning for optimization of the value function.

[2] This distribution does not include the fCoP theorem prover, which cannot yet be publicly released, however, a binary can be obtained upon request.

attention in automated theorem proving, e.g. [8,28], as an alternative of search-based methods. [8] defines analogical reasoning as "the proof of one theorem is used to guide the proof of a similar theorem by suggesting analogous steps". They rely on a user-provided matching between analogous concepts related to the two theorems and try to reuse the proof steps (adjusted modulo analogy) in the source proof during the construction of the target. [28] aim to achieve this on a higher level of abstraction by matching proof plans of a source and a target problem. As the proof plan is constructed, the plan of the source is searched for steps that can be transformed into a suitable step for the target. The set of allowable transformations are predefined and designed for a narrow domain. For example, the transformations given in [28] aim to carry a result, such as the Heine Borel theorem, stated in $\mathbb{R}^1$ over to $\mathbb{R}^2$. The characteristic feature of these systems is that search is performed on the meta level of plan mappings and proof step transformations. The search space is often defined ad hoc and is much smaller than that given by the inference rules of the calculus.

A machine learning system that is trained to guide a theorem prover is supposed to achieve a similar result, with two important improvements. First transformations are learned, without the need for manual engineering. Second, establishing mappings between proof steps (that can be transformed into each other) should result from learning of flexible and abstract features. The flexibility and abstraction allows for potentially reusing the same proof components several times, as well as using components from different proofs, which goes beyond earlier attempts that only establish direct matching between the two proofs.

Machine Learning Systems for Guiding Theorem Provers. A large body of research exists that aims to provide guidance for theorem provers via machine learning. FEMaLeCoP [18], rlCoP [19,31] plCoP [56] and lazyCoP [39] guide the leanCoP [32] compact connection tableau prover, which is also the system guided in our project. Learning based guidance is added to the saturation based E prover [46] in [11,15,16,26]. The HOList project [3,33] builds guidance on the tactic level[3] for the HOL Light [13] higher-order theorem prover. A distinctive feature of all these systems is that they rely heavily on an external search procedure, such as Monte Carlo Tree Search [24], or the search engine of the guided prover. Learning is aimed at making search more efficient and it is implemented in alternating iterations of proof search and model fitting, according to the DAgger [43] meta-algorithm, first used in MaLARea [52] for theorem proving. In contrast with the above, we use an algorithm which uses bootstrapping and learns from generated rollouts, aiming to learn to generate entire proof sequences in the leanCoP calculus. Such rollout based learning has so far been barely used in theorem proving, with the noteable exception of [12], developed in parallel with FLoP, which guides a saturation style prover using a simple policy gradient RL algorithm.

Concurrently with our work, [35,36,51] have used recurrent neural networks, attention and transformers to generate next proof steps. E.g., [36] report generalisation on problems with relatively short proofs. In line with emphasizing

[3] A tactic is a human-designed program which aggregates multiple proof steps.

analogy over search, their evaluation protocol only allows for limited search in a single proof attempt[4]. Our work employs much smaller neural models and focuses on generalizing to proofs with hundreds and thousands of steps (see Fig. 3).

Provers guiding the leanCoP Connection Tableau Calculus. As noted above, a series of learning systems guide the leanCoP connection calculus. Of these, we highlight three systems that use roughly the same learning setup: rlCoP [19], plCoP [56] and graphCoP [31]. In these systems, the value and policy functions of the guided MCTS algorithm are learned similarly to [1,47]. FLoP shares the same manually developed features [21] with rlCoP and plCoP, while graphCoP employs a graph neural network for feature extraction. We use these systems as an important baseline in Sect. 6. While the differences are important, they play little role in our current investigation and we refer to them jointly as *mcts-CoPs*.

By trying to match individual steps, these works all manipulate on the level of abstraction of a sequence of proof steps, instead of matching entire proof objects. This is a simplified approach that does not capture the full potential of analogy. Nevertheless, we argue that it is a meaningful start and we take the same approach in our work and interpret analogical reasoning as being able to produce a sequence of proof steps after having internalised a sequence of proof steps of an "analogous" problem. In our interpretation, we will put large emphasis proof construction without search: we ask what sort of machine learning scenarios allow for building a model that can internalize complex proof patterns and produce proofs for a class of problems (almost) without search.

A number of works have demonstrated how machine learning can enhance calculus level search of theorem provers. In this paper we intend to point out that machine learning is also well suited for analogical reasoning. We provide datasets and benchmarks which enforce very long proofs and in turn make the search very hard, emphasizing a need for reasoning via analogy.

3 The leanCoP Connection Tableau Calculus

FLoP provides guidance for of the very compact leanCoP [32] connection tableau calculus. The calculus was originally implemented in Prolog, but it also has an OCaml reimplementation fCoP [20] and FLoP can be used to guide both systems.

We briefly describe the connection tableau calculus, assuming basic first-order logic and theorem proving terminology [41]. The input is a (mathematical) problem consisting of *axioms* and *conjectures* formally stated in first-order logic (FOL). The calculus searches for *refutational proofs*, i.e. proofs showing that the axioms together with the negated conjectures are *unsatisfiable*. The FOL formulas are first translated to *clause normal form* (CNF), producing a set of first-order *clauses* consisting of *literals*, e.g. $\{\forall X, Y : (f(X)|r(X, Y|\neg f(Y)), f(a)\}$. Proof search starts with a *start clause* as a *goal* and proceeds by building a connection tableau by repeatedly applying *extension steps* and *reduction steps*.

The extension step connects (*unifies*) the *current goal* with a complementary literal of a new clause. This extends the *current branch*, possibly splitting

[4] A maximum of 4096 search nodes are allowed.

it into several branches if there are more literals in the new clause, and possibly *instantiating* some variables in the tableau. The reduction step connects the current goal to a complementary literal of the *active path*, thus *closing* the current branch. The proof is finished when all branches are closed. The extension and reduction steps are nondeterministic, requiring backtracking in the standard connection calculus. *Iterative deepening* is often used to ensure completeness. The project webpage shows an example *closed connection tableau*, i.e., a finished proof tree where every branch contains *complementary literals* (literals with opposite polarity). This shows that the set of clauses is unsatisfiable.

leanCoP represents theorem proving as a one-person game. The game ends with success if a proof is found. The prover has many choices to make along the way, in particular it can select from several valid extension and reduction steps. Whether a step is valid depends on the unification condition, i.e., if the current goal unifies with the negation of a literal in the corresponding clause. The full information about the game state consists of all previous proof steps, the partial proof tree (proof state) and the current goal.

The search space of the prover is exponentially large in the length of the proof. In leanCoP, the action space is roughly correlated with the size of the axiom set. While this can be large for large problems, typically only a few actions are available in any particular state.

4 FLoP – Main Algorithm

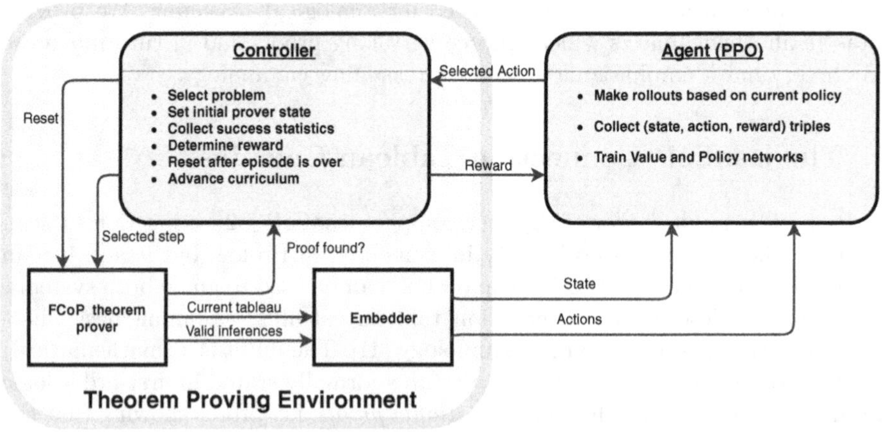

Fig. 1. Theorem proving as a reinforcement learning environment.

FLoP combines the connection tableau calculus with guidance based on Temporal Difference and curriculum learning. After each inference step, the prover engine returns its current state as well as the set of valid actions, i.e., valid inference steps that transform the current goal. The prover is encapsulated into a

Reinforcement Learning (RL) environment. In the following, we provide a brief summary of the relevant RL techniques.

4.1 Reinforcement Learning Fundamentals

Our RL summary is highly selective, aiming to describe Proximal Policy Optimization [45], the method used in FLoP. For further details, see [49].

Markov Decision Process. The mathematical foundation of the class of problems that Reinforcement Learning aims to solve is given by Markov Decision Processes (MDP). An MDP$(\mathcal{S}, \mathcal{A}, \mathcal{R}, \mathcal{P}, \gamma)$ describes a dynamic process and consists of the following components: $\mathcal{S}$ is the set of states, $\mathcal{A}$ is the set of actions, $\mathcal{R} : (\mathcal{S} \times \mathcal{A}) \rightarrow \mathbb{R}$ is a reward function, $\mathcal{P} : (\mathcal{S} \times \mathcal{A}) \rightarrow \mathcal{S}$ is the state transition function and γ is the discount factor. We assume that an agent interacts with this MDP, generating sequences of (s_t, a_t, r_t) state-action-reward tuples, called *trajectories*. The agent is equipped with a *policy* function $\pi : \mathcal{S} \rightarrow \mathcal{A}$ which determines which action it selects in a particular state. The aim of the agent is to maximize its total accumulated reward $\sum_{t \geq 0} \gamma^t r_t$. Several components of the model can be stochastic: the reward function, the transition function, as well as the policy. In such settings, the aim of the agent it to find the policy π^* that maximizes its cumulative expected reward, where future rewards are discounted with the γ discount factor:

$$\pi^* = \arg\max_{\pi} \mathbb{E}[\sum_{t \geq 0} \gamma^t r_t | \pi]$$

Policy Gradient. One successful family of methods solves this task by considering a parametric class of policy functions $\Pi = \{\pi_\Theta, \Theta \in \mathbb{R}^m\}$. We continuously sample trajectories from the current policy and optimize the parameters Θ via gradient descent based on the observed rewards. This is called *policy gradient*, and the RL literature contains numerous variants that differ in the details of optimization.

One well known difficulty of policy gradient is the large variance in the sampled trajectories, which makes convergence slow and requiring large number of training samples. A popular technique to reduce variance is to train a baseline model that estimates the expected reward from a given state and optimize the policy with respect to the excess reward on top of the baseline. This gives rise to the *actor-critic framework*. We train two models jointly: a *critic*: $V_\pi(s)$ that estimates the expected reward of trajectories starting from s given policy π and an *actor*, which is our policy π. Given some state s, we use the policy to sample an action a. We then sample further transitions to estimate the expected reward $Q_\pi(s, a)$ from state s after taking action a. We define *advantage* as the difference between these two expectations: $A_\pi(s, a) = Q_\pi(s, a) - V_\pi(s)$. Our optimization objective is then:

$$\min_{\Theta_V} \max_{\Theta_\pi} A_\pi(s, a)$$

where Θ_V and Θ_π are the parameters of the critic and the actor, respectively.

Proximal Policy Optimization. Policy gradient is an *on-policy* method, meaning that it optimizes the parameters of the policy based on trajectories sampled from the same policy. In contrast with *off-policy* methods, which extract samples through some other mechanism, policy gradient learning can be highly unstable. This is because the change in policy potentially invalidates the samples it was trained on. Proximal Policy Optimization [45] (PPO) addresses this problem by introducing a soft constraint on the magnitude of the policy updates.

We maintain two instances of the policy network: π_Θ which we aim to improve and $\pi_{\Theta_{old}}$ which we sample from. The ratio of the two policies gives us a measure of difference:

$$r_t(\Theta) = \frac{\pi_\Theta(a_t|s_t)}{\pi_{\Theta_{old}}(a_t|s_t)}$$

If this ratio lies outside of the range $[1-\epsilon, 1+\epsilon]$, then the advantage function is clipped:

$$r_t^*(\Theta) = \text{clip}(r_t(\Theta), 1-\epsilon, 1+\epsilon)$$
$$A_{\pi_\Theta}^*(s,a) = \min(r_t(\Theta)A_{\pi_{\Theta_{old}}}, r_t^*(\Theta)A_{\pi_{\Theta_{old}}})$$

The two networks are periodically synchronized to ensure that they are not too different. PPO has been shown to strike a good balance between simplicity and stability and is one of the most popular policy gradient methods.

4.2 Reinforcement Learning in FLoP

Theorem proving can be directly mapped into an MDP by treating prover states as states, inference steps as actions and proof attempts as trajectories. The only missing component is the reward function, which we set to be

$$\mathcal{R}(s,a) = \begin{cases} 1 \text{ if perfoming a in s finishes the proof} \\ 0 \text{ otherwise} \end{cases}$$

Other reward functions are also possible, though we argue that the selected one is most faithful to the task at hand: 1) we know very little about progress before we have found a proof, hence the zero reward for intermediary steps and 2) it is hard to tell if one proof is better than another, hence the binary nature of the rewards.

Reward maximization directly corresponds to finding a proof. Hence, we augment the core connection tableau calculus with a value (critic) and a policy (actor) model trained using PPO. Classical proof search is then replaced with generating proof attempts from the policy. Figure 1 shows the overall architecture of the system and Fig. 2 shows the policy and value network architectures. The state and the actions (formulae) are represented using previously developed features [21]. The features include (suitably hashed) triples, pairs, and singletons of adjacent nodes in the formula trees and the partial proof trees, as well as some global features: number of open goals, number of symbols in them, their maximum size and depth, length of the current path, and two most frequent symbols in open goals. This means that the proof states and the actions are presented as (sparse) fixed-length vectors.

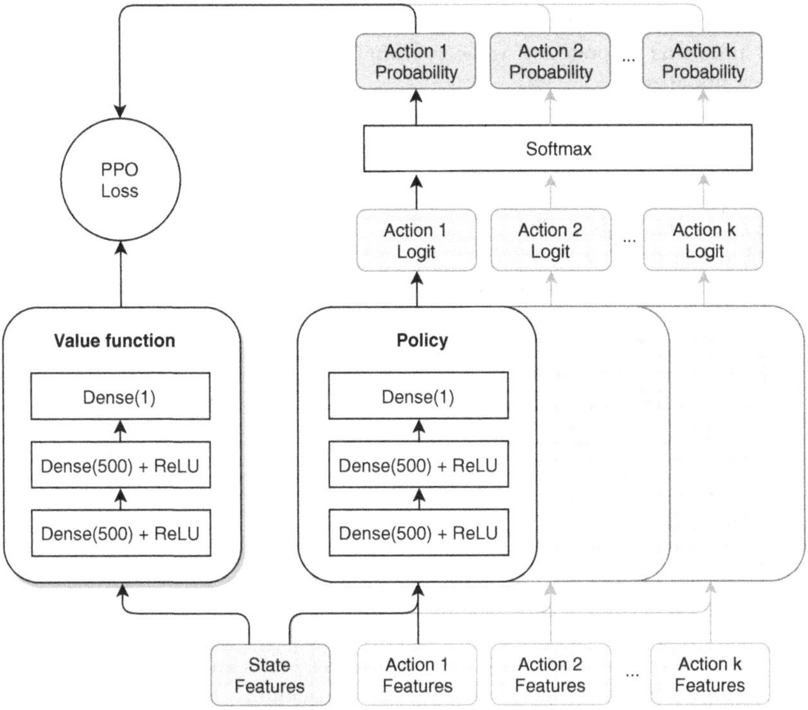

Fig. 2. Value and Policy network architectures in PPO. Their inputs are state and state-action pair features, respectively. The policy returns a score for each action, which are then normalized to a probability.

4.3 Curriculum Learning

A fundamental challenge for an RL system that learns to prove theorems from its own exploration is that rewards are sparse and binary. In case proofs are long, this makes learning nearly impossible. To tackle this, we use curriculum learning on the length of proofs in case a proof is available. Initially, we start exploration from near the end of the proof, making it easy to succeed and obtain positive reward. As the system gets more confident, we gradually move the starting state backwards along the given proof. This approach has already been successfully applied in many RL experiments. When there is no good alternative to the training proof, the system eventually learns those steps, while random exploration helps to identify alternatives and find novel proofs. Exploration also helps to learn steps that make the proof impossible to finish. We can start learning with or without training proofs. Each training problem can have its own curriculum schedule, which can be restarted when a new proof is found. Curriculum learning is an efficient tool for boosting rewards found during exploration.

Algorithm 1. FLoP: Main Learning Loop

Require: problems $\mathcal{P}$, policy π, value v, train steps $\in \mathbb{N}$, threshold $\in [0..1]$, episodes between updates: k $\in \mathbb{N}$

Ensure: trained policy π, trained value v, possibly proofs for some problems in $\mathcal{P}$

1: *curriculum* $\leftarrow$ dictionary such that for each $p \in P$ with proof Pr $curriculum[p] = \text{len}[Pr] - 1$
2: steps $\leftarrow 0$
3: **while** steps ¡ train steps **do**
4:    **for** j in 1..k **do**
5:       $p \leftarrow$ random problem from problem set $\mathcal{P}$ {An episode corresponds to a problem}
6:       initialize prover on problem p
7:       **if** p has stored proof **then**
8:          Take *curriculum*[p] proof steps according to stored proof
9:       **end if**
10:       **while** not episode over **do**
11:          $s', a'_1, a'_2 \dots a'_l \leftarrow$ Query prover for current state and valid actions
12:          $s, a_1, a_2 \dots a_l \leftarrow \text{feat}(s'), \text{feat}(a'_1), \text{feat}(a'_2) \dots \text{feat}(a'_l)$ {Extract features}
13:          Take action according to policy $\pi(a|s)$, observe reward r
14:          steps $\leftarrow$ steps + 1
15:       **end while**
16:       update success ratio for p
17:       **if** p is solved with proof Pr and no proof of p was known before **then**
18:          *curriculum*[p] $\leftarrow \text{len}(Pr) - 1$ {Start curriculum}
19:       **end if**
20:       **if** success rate for p ¿ threshold **then**
21:          *curriculum*[p] $\leftarrow$ *curriculum*[p] $- 1$ {Advance curriculum}
22:       **end if**
23:    **end for**
24:    Update policy π and value v
25: **end while**

4.4 Training Algorithm

Algorithm 1 gives an overview of the learning loop. First, in line 5 we sample a problem (in case there are multiple). In lines 6–9 we interact with the prover and ensure that its state corresponds to the one dictated by the current curriculum. In lines 10–15 we generate a proof attempt iterating 1) prover steps, 2) featurization, and 3) sampling a next action according to the policy. If a new problem is solved, we start the curriculum on it in lines 17–19. If performance on a given problem and curriculum reaches a threshold, we advance the curriculum in lines 20–22. In line 24 we update the policy and value models.

4.5 Implementation Details

Most of the FLoP system is implemented in the Python programming language, using the [14] RL framework. FLoP guides the fCoP [20] system, which is a reimplementation of leanCoP in the OCaml programming language. The communication between the guidance and prover components is provided via the C foreign language interface.

5 Datasets

To evaluate our system, we select simple classes of theorems with strong shared structure, giving a large room for learning-based improvement. Our five datasets are described in Table 1. The datasets are bundled into an OpenAI-gym [9] compliant environment and can be tested with modern RL algorithms.

Table 1. Three challenges defined in the theory of Robinson Arithmetic (RA) and two challenges from the Logical Calculi (LCL) domain of the TPTP library

Name	Theory	Size	Description
RA-1	RA	1800	Expressions of the form $N_1 + N_2 = N$, $N_1 \cdot N_2 = N$, where $0 \leq N_i < 30$. (Examples: $3+4=7$ or $5 \cdot 12=60$.)
RA-2	RA	1000	$T = N$, where $0 \leq N$, and T is a random expression with 3 operators and operands N_i such that $0 \leq N_i < 10$. (E.g.: $((3+4) \cdot 2)+6=20$.)
RA-3	RA	1000	$T_1 = T_2$, where T_1 and T_2 are random expressions with 3 operators and operands N_i such that $2 \leq N_i < 10$. E.g. $((3+4) \cdot 2)+6=((1+1) \cdot 5) \cdot 2$.)
LCL-Eq	LCL	890	TPTP domain: Logic Calculi (Equivalential) – extended with lemmata from E prover.
LCL-Imp	LCL	1204	TPTP domain: Logic Calculi (Implication/Falsehood 2 valued sentential) – extended with lemmata from E prover

Three datasets are built on the theory of Robinson Arithmetic [42], which defines addition and multiplication on the nonnegative integers. Despite its relative simplicity, this theory seems to be particularly suited for machine learning methods: solutions are long and repetitive, while also challenging for state-of-the-art systems (see Sect. 6). We examine both unary (24 actions) and binary (40 actions) encoding of numbers. The axioms of Robinson Arithmetic are given on the project webpage. Increasing the numbers in the conjecture greatly increases the length of the proof, making this dataset suitable for detecting the length boundary of various theorem provers.

Two datasets are extracted from the TPTP library, from the domain of Logical Calculi with condensed detachment (LCL). These theorems have been extensively studied from the early days of automated theorem proving, e.g. [22,27,34,55]. We run E prover with a large time limit on the problems and augment the dataset with lemmata extracted by E. As a result, many proofs of simpler problems can be directly used as parts of the proofs of harder problems. A direct analogy from one problem to the other is usually not possible, however, shallow search is often sufficient to connect the proofs of easier problems to the proof of harder ones.

The LCL domain in the TPTP [48] library consists of statements about various formal inference systems. LCL-Eq and LCL-Imp formalize properties of the Equivalential Calculus and the Implication and Falsum Calculus, respectively. Both are subsystems of the classical propositional calculus, restricting the set of allowed connectives to $\{\equiv\}$ and $\{\implies, \bot\}$. For both subsystems, the appropriate variant of the *condensed detachment* inference rule ($A, A \equiv B \vdash B$ and $A, A \implies B \vdash B$) constitutes a *strongly complete* inference system, i.e., whenever a formula semantically follows from a set of premises, it also follows from the set syntactically. A number of complete axiomatizations of both the Equivalential Calculus and the Implication and Falsum Calculus exist and the theorems in our datasets establish connections between them.

All arithmetic problems in our dataset are quite simple for humans, but in the case of logical calculi, some of the problems were posing a challenge for mathematicians (see [54]).

6 Experiments

Our experiments with Robinson arithmetic aim to demonstrate that in this highly structured dataset FLoP is capable of extracting a general proof pattern from one or two proofs and generalizing to related proofs of arbitrary length, using a restricted few-shot evaluation method (see below). Experiments 1, 2, and 3 compare FLoP with strong theorem provers using different fragments of the arithmetic dataset, varying the complexity of the axiomatization (unary vs. binary encoding of numbers) and the complexity of the target theorems (RA-1, RA-2, RA-3). FLoP is either the best or the second-best in each experiment. In each of these experiments, FLoP is allowed 100 proof attempts without backtracking: the first attempt is a deterministic run with a high time limit (1000 sec) that always selects the action maximizing the policy and the remaining 99 runs are stochastic samples from the policy with a time limit of 60 sec.

The LCL problems used in our experiments are less structured and success is dependent on search, even if the hierarchical composition of problems ensures that a relatively small search is sufficient to generalize from easier problems to harder ones. Consequently, we expect that search-based methods are better in this domain. However, when search is completely disallowed during evaluation, we show in Experiment 4 that FLoP performs much better than the mcts-CoPs. In Experiments 5 and 6 we demonstrate the benefit of using curriculum learning.

Our hyperparameters were selected using small grid searches. We checked standard RL parameters (e.g., the discount factor), parameters related to curriculum scheduling (e.g., local vs. global), neural network architectures (1–5 layers with 128–1024 neurons), feature sizes (64–1024) and training steps (10^5 – 10^8). Parameters used in the experiments are described in configuration files which are accessible along with the shared codebase.

Experiment 1: Comparison with Other Provers. We compare FLoP with a random model, two state-of-the-art saturation-style theorem provers (E 2.4, Vampire 4.3.0), a heuristic guided connection tableau prover (leanCoP 2.1), and rlCoP (one of the mcts-CoPs). Vampire, E, and leanCoP use human-designed strategies instead of learning. We use these provers in the configuration used for CASC, the yearly competition of fully automated theorem provers, employing a time limit of 60 sec. per problem. For E, we also report the results of the *auto-schedule* mode. For rlCoP we used the hyperparameters described in [19], only modifying the policy temperature from 2.5 to 1.5, as this works better with the Robinson datasets. The number of inferences in MCTS was limited to 200000. rlCoP was trained on the whole evaluation set, while FLoP was trained on a single problem: $1 \cdot 1 = 1$ and $1 \cdot 1 \cdot 1 = 1$ for RA-1 and RA-2, respectively.[5]

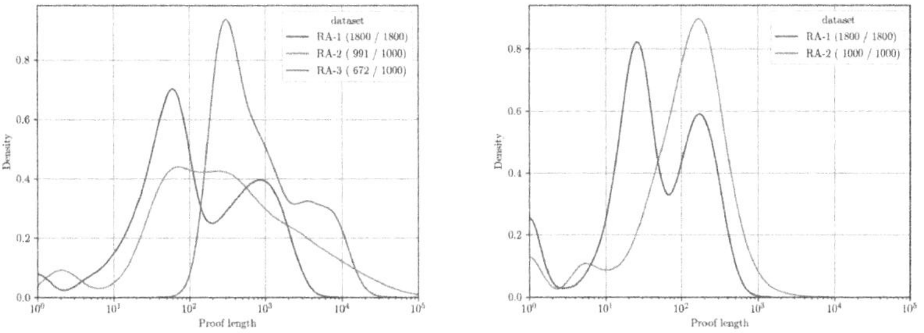

Fig. 3. Distributions of length of proofs found by FLoP. Note the logarithmic scale. **Left**: RA-1, RA-2 and RA-3 with average proof lengths 367, 2082, and 1864. **Right**: binary RA-1 and binary RA-2 with average proof lengths 85 and 179.

Success ratios are given in Table 2. FLoP is only outperformed by E's *auto-schedule*, which tries multiple strategies and finds one with the left-to-right ordering of all the addition and multiplication axioms. This solves all of our problems immediately without proof search by only rewriting to a normal form [2]. This demonstrates the power of equational theorem proving when a suitable term ordering exists and can be found by human-designed heuristics. This is, however, far from guaranteed in general even in such simple domains, as witnessed by Vampire's failure to find this ordering. To evaluate E without access to its built-in rewriting capability, we have renamed the equality to a new predicate 'eq' axiomatized exactly in the same way as in leanCoP. The auto-schedule mode then becomes somewhat weaker than the auto mode.

Table 2. Comparing a random model, Vampire, E, leanCoP, rlCoP and FLoP, with respect to success ratio for RA-1, RA-2 and RA-3 problems. Our method (FLoP) is marked in grey. E_1 – auto mode, E_2 – auto-schedule mode, E_3 – auto-schedule with renamed equality. The reason why FLoP did not reach 100% on RA-2 is that a few problems timeouted.

Dataset	Random	Vampire	E_1	E_2	E_3	leanCoP	rlCoP	FLoP
RA-1	0.04	0.60	0.60	**1.0**	0.54	0.22	0.86	**1.0**
RA-2	0.05	0.40	0.39	**1.0**	0.25	0.14	0.74	0.99
RA-3	0.00	0.34	0.28	**1.0**	0.22	0.01	0.41	0.67

[5] For a description of RA-3 training problems, see Experiment 2.

Experiment 2: Harder Arithmetic Expressions. RA-3 consists of arithmetic equalities with random expressions on both sides. This dataset is significantly more complex because there are many ways of proving the same problem. Proofs are longer, too. For FLoP, we examined various training sets and found that the system is very prone to overfitting. Most problems can be proven in many different ways, that vary greatly in terms of how well they foster generalization. It is true especially of easier problems that they can be proven with "shortcuts" that hinder generalization (see more on this on the project webpage). The harder the problems, the less likely they can be solved with such heuristic approaches, hence harder training problems promise better training signal. We demonstrate this by training FLoP on a few harder problems with proofs provided, making use of curriculum learning described in Sect. 4. A single longer training proof is sufficient to yield meaningful generalization. Adding one more training problem helps even more, as shows Table 3.

Figure 3 shows the distribution of the length of proofs found by FLoP. We can see that a large part of the problems requires thousands of steps to solve, highlighting the need to avoid search.

Table 3. Curriculum learning for RA-3 on two harder problems with proofs of 113 and 108 steps. We report success ratios and average proof lengths, based on 3 runs. Standard deviations are given in parenthesis.

Training problem	Succ	Len
$1 \cdot 2 + 1 + 1 = (1+1) \cdot 1 \cdot 2$	0.32(0.05)	566(14)
$1 \cdot 2 + 1 + 1 = (1+1) \cdot 1 \cdot 2$ $(1+1+1) \cdot 2 = 2 \cdot 1 + 2 + 2$	**0.67** (0.03)	1864(54)

For rlCoP, all RA-3 problems are too hard to solve without guidance within the inference limit, so we started with the version trained on the solutions of RA-2. Table 2 shows that FLoP is only outperformed by E's auto-schedule mode, which again finds the rewrite ordering that solves all problems without search.

Experiment 3: Binary Number Encoding. We experiment with Robinson Arithmetic using binary encoding of numbers. This makes the domain theory more complex: the total number of actions increases from 24 to 40.[6] On the other hand, proofs get shorter, as shows Fig. 3. Again, we train FLoP on a single proof: $3 \cdot 3 = 9$ and $(1 \cdot 2+1) \cdot 3 = 9$ for RA-1 and RA-2, respectively. Table 4 shows that provers get weaker, except for Vampire and FLoP. In particular, E is no longer capable of solving the problems with rewriting only. FLoP manages to generalize from a single proof to the whole dataset despite the increased action space and performs best in this experiment.

Table 4. Comparing Vampire, E (auto-schedule mode), leanCoP, rlCoP and FLoP, using binary encoding of numbers.

Dataset	Vampire	E	leanCoP	rlCoP	FLoP
RA-1	0.67	0.81	0.19	0.56	**1.0**
RA-2	0.62	0.62	0.13	0.12	**1.0**

Experiment 4: Search vs. Eager Evaluation. We compare FLoP with plCoP (one of the mcts-CoPs) using two different evaluation methods. After training both

[6] Note that only a subset of these is applicable in a given state.

Table 5. Comparing FLoP and plCoP using two different evaluation methods: 1) guided MCTS and 2) eager evaluation based on the policy model (Eager Policy). For plCoP we also evaluate based on the value model (Eager Value)

Prover	Eval	LCL-Eq	LCL-Imp	RA-1	RA-2
plCoP	MCTS	**47%**	**61%**	65%	48%
plCoP	Eager Policy	5%	5%	82%	49%
plCoP	Eager Value	1%	1%	3%	5%
FLoP	MCTS	19%	24%	61%	31%
FLoP	Eager Policy	19%	27%	**100%**	**99%**

systems on the whole dataset, we evaluate them using 1) MCTS and 2) eager evaluation, i.e. always select the action with the highest probability according to the policy model. Table 5 shows that plCoP performs better when search is allowed, especially for the more heterogeneous LCL problems. However, FLoP takes the upper hand in eager evaluation. For the LCL problems, plCoP collapses while FLoP is unaffected. This suggests that plCoP depends heavily on the search procedure it used for training. FLoP cannot make good use of MCTS, which is somewhat expected, since its policy and value networks were not trained for that purpose. For the arithmetic datasets, both systems benefit from not doing search because they reach proofs that are longer than what MCTS can reach. For FLoP, the removal of the depth limit reveals that it fully mastered the two problem classes, regardless of depth.

The performance of plCoP gets even worse if the eager evaluation is based on the value model, i.e., when we select the action whose successor state has the highest value score. We conjecture that this is because assigning a value to a never observed state is much harder than selecting from a smaller set of actions. These results are in line with our conjecture that the DAgger approach of plCoP is better for learning good search heuristics, while FLoP is better at internalizing a full proof pattern.

Experiment 5: Curriculum Learning vs only Exploration Based Learning. When training proofs are not available, the positive reward signal only occurs after the system solves a problem through exploration. Afterward, curriculum learning ensures that the system is continuously faced with a "reasonably" hard problem, alleviating the sparse reward challenge of theorem proving. We demonstrate this on the two LCL datasets. Here, before generating each rollout, we randomly select a problem from the entire dataset. We report the number of proofs found during training in Table 6. Curriculum

Table 6. Curriculum Learning compared with only exploration based learning, on the LCL-Eq and LCL-Imp datasets, using 10M and 30M inference limit, respectively. We report the ratio of proofs found during training. The results are averages of 2 runs.

Dataset	Curriculum	No curriculum
LCL-Eq	**0.24** (0)	0.23 (0.001)
LCL-Imp	**0.51** (0.002)	0.45 (0.003)

learning brings a small, but consistent improvement when compared with only exploration-based learning.

Experiment 6: Curriculum Learning vs. Supervised Learning. When training proofs are available, a natural baseline of curriculum learning is supervised learning on the proof steps. While such behavioral cloning sometimes leads to great performance, we show in Table 7 that it greatly depends on the quality of the given proof. We train RA-1 and RA-2 using the following training problems:

1. **RA-1** $1+1=2$, $1 \cdot 1 = 1$
2. **RA-2** $1+1=2$, $1 \cdot 1 = 1$, $1 \cdot 1 \cdot 1 = 1$

We take the "nice" proofs (5, 9 and 23 steps) of these problems and construct variants with 2-3 extra steps added. We observe that supervised learning degrades as superfluous steps are introduced, while FLoP's exploration allows the system to recover and find the original proofs.

Table 7. Curriculum Learning vs Supervised Learning trained on proofs with extra steps added for distraction.

Data	Proof Lengths	Supervised Succ.	Curriculum Succ.
RA-1	5, 9	0.98(0.04)	**1(0.01)**
	9, 11	0.52(0.08)	**0.98(0.01)**
RA-2	5, 9, 23	**0.85(0.04)**	0.76(0.02)
	9, 11, 25	0.59(0.08)	**0.76(0.01)**

7 Conclusion and Future Work

We have built FLoP, a proof guidance system based on a variant of temporal difference reinforcement learning, addressing the problem of finding long proofs in an exponential search space. Previous work [23,53] focused on finding long proofs with the help of human-designed heuristics. We showed that FLoP is capable of extracting proof patterns via learning and can generalise to much longer proofs, implementing a simple form of reasoning by analogy. We believe that mastering analogical reasoning is an important step in creating human-level automated mathematicians. We presented a set of theorem proving datasets that are suitably challenging for existing learning methods and are intended to become a general-purpose testing ground for reinforcement learning methods. We showed that FLoP can outperform strong theorem provers on some of these datasets. We find that curriculum learning is a useful component of the learning algorithm as it allows for amplifying training signal when proofs are long.

Acknowledgments. Adrián Csiszárik and Zsolt Zombori were supported by the European Union, co-financed by the European Social Fund (EFOP-3.6.3-VEKOP-16-2017-00002), the Hungarian National Excellence Grant 2018-1.2.1-NKP-00008 and by the Hungarian Ministry of Innovation and Technology NRDI Office within the framework of the Artificial Intelligence National Laboratory Program. Henryk Michalewski was supported by the Polish National Science Center grant UMO-2018/29/B/ST6/02959. Cezary Kaliszyk was supported by ERC grant no. 714034 *SMART*. Josef Urban was supported by the *AI4REASON* ERC Consolidator grant number 649043, and by the Czech project AI&Reasoning CZ.02.1.01/0.0/0.0/15_003/0000466 and the European Regional Development Fund.

This research was supported by the PL-Grid Infrastructure. In particular, quantitative results of FLoP reported in this paper were performed using the Prometheus supercomputer, located in the Academic Computer Center Cyfronet in the AGH University of Science and Technology in Kraków, Poland.

References

1. Anthony, T., Tian, Z., Barber, D.: Thinking fast and slow with deep learning and tree search. CoRR abs/1705.08439 (2017). http://arxiv.org/abs/1705.08439
2. Baader, F., Nipkow, T.: Term Rewriting and All That. Cambridge University Press, Cambridge (1998)
3. Bansal, K., Loos, S.M., Rabe, M.N., Szegedy, C., Wilcox, S.: HOList: an environment for machine learning of higher-order theorem proving (extended version). CoRR abs/1904.03241 (2019). http://arxiv.org/abs/1904.03241
4. Barrett, C., Tinelli, C.: Satisfiability modulo theories. In: Clarke, E., Henzinger, T., Veith, H., Bloem, R. (eds.) Handbook of Model Checking, pp. 305–343. Springer, Cham (2018). https://doi.org/10.1007/978-3-319-10575-8_11
5. Bertot, Y., Castran, P.: Interactive Theorem Proving and Program Development: Coq'Art The Calculus of Inductive Constructions, 1st edn. Springer, Heidelberg (2010). https://doi.org/10.1007/978-3-662-07964-5
6. Bibel, W., Eder, E., Fronhöfer, B.: Towards an advanced implementation of the connection method. In: Bundy, A. (ed.) Proceedings of the 8th International Joint Conference on Artificial Intelligence. Karlsruhe, FRG, August 1983, pp. 920–922. William Kaufmann (1983). http://ijcai.org/Proceedings/83-2/Papers/072.pdf
7. Bledsoe, W.W.: Some thoughts on proof discovery. In: Proceedings of the 1986 Symposium on Logic Programming, Salt Lake City, Utah, USA, 22–25 September 1986, pp. 2–10. IEEE-CS (1986)
8. Brock, B., Cooper, S., Pierce, W.: Analogical reasoning and proof discovery. In: Lusk, E., Overbeek, R. (eds.) CADE 1988. LNCS, vol. 310, pp. 454–468. Springer, Heidelberg (1988). https://doi.org/10.1007/BFb0012849
9. Brockman, G., et al.: OpenAI gym. CoRR abs/1606.01540 (2016). http://arxiv.org/abs/1606.01540
10. Bundy, A.: The use of explicit plans to guide inductive proofs. In: Lusk, E., Overbeek, R. (eds.) CADE 1988. LNCS, vol. 310, pp. 111–120. Springer, Heidelberg (1988). https://doi.org/10.1007/BFb0012826
11. Chvalovský, K., Jakubuv, J., Suda, M., Urban, J.: ENIGMA-NG: efficient neural and gradient-boosted inference guidance for E. CoRR abs/1903.03182 (2019). http://arxiv.org/abs/1903.03182
12. Crouse, M., et al.: A deep reinforcement learning approach to first-order logic theorem proving. Artificial Intelligence (2019)
13. Harrison, J.: HOL light: a tutorial introduction. In: Srivas, M., Camilleri, A. (eds.) FMCAD 1996. LNCS, vol. 1166, pp. 265–269. Springer, Heidelberg (1996). https://doi.org/10.1007/BFb0031814
14. Hill, A., et al.: Stable baselines (2018). https://github.com/hill-a/stable-baselines
15. Jakubův, J., Chvalovský, K., Olšák, M., Piotrowski, B., Suda, M., Urban, J.: ENIGMA anonymous: symbol-independent inference guiding machine (system description). In: Peltier, N., Sofronie-Stokkermans, V. (eds.) IJCAR 2020. LNCS (LNAI), vol. 12167, pp. 448–463. Springer, Cham (2020). https://doi.org/10.1007/978-3-030-51054-1_29

16. Jakubův, J., Urban, J.: ENIGMA: efficient learning-based inference guiding machine. In: Geuvers, H., England, M., Hasan, O., Rabe, F., Teschke, O. (eds.) CICM 2017. LNCS (LNAI), vol. 10383, pp. 292–302. Springer, Cham (2017). https://doi.org/10.1007/978-3-319-62075-6_20
17. Jakubuv, J., Urban, J.: Hammering mizar by learning clause guidance. In: Harrison, J., O'Leary, J., Tolmach, A. (eds.) 10th International Conference on Interactive Theorem Proving, ITP 2019, September 9–12, 2019, Portland, OR, USA. LIPIcs, vol. 141, pp. 34:1–34:8. Schloss Dagstuhl - Leibniz-Zentrum für Informatik (2019). https://doi.org/10.4230/LIPIcs.ITP.2019.34
18. Kaliszyk, C., Urban, J.: FEMaLeCoP: fairly efficient machine learning connection prover. In: Davis, M., Fehnker, A., McIver, A., Voronkov, A. (eds.) LPAR 2015. LNCS, vol. 9450, pp. 88–96. Springer, Heidelberg (2015). https://doi.org/10.1007/978-3-662-48899-7_7
19. Kaliszyk, C., Urban, J., Michalewski, H., Olsák, M.: Reinforcement learning of theorem proving. In: NeurIPS, pp. 8836–8847 (2018)
20. Kaliszyk, C., Urban, J., Vyskočil, J.: Certified connection tableaux proofs for HOL Light and TPTP. In: Proceedings of the 2015 Conference on Certified Programs and Proofs, CPP '15, pp. 59–66. ACM (2015). https://doi.org/10.1145/2676724.2693176. http://doi.acm.org/10.1145/2676724.2693176
21. Kaliszyk, C., Urban, J., Vyskočil, J.: Efficient semantic features for automated reasoning over large theories. In: Yang, Q., Wooldridge, M. (eds.) Proc. of the 24th International Joint Conference on Artificial Intelligence (IJCAI'15), pp. 3084–3090. AAAI Press (2015)
22. Kalman, J.A.: A shortest single axiom for the classical equivalential calculus. Notre Dame J. Form. Logic **19**(1), 141–144 (1978). https://doi.org/10.1305/ndjfl/1093888216
23. Kinyon, M., Veroff, R., Vojtěchovský, P.: Loops with abelian inner mapping groups: an application of automated deduction. In: Bonacina, M.P., Stickel, M.E. (eds.) Automated Reasoning and Mathematics. LNCS (LNAI), vol. 7788, pp. 151–164. Springer, Heidelberg (2013). https://doi.org/10.1007/978-3-642-36675-8_8
24. Kocsis, L., Szepesvári, C.: Bandit based Monte-Carlo planning. In: Fürnkranz, J., Scheffer, T., Spiliopoulou, M. (eds.) ECML 2006. LNCS (LNAI), vol. 4212, pp. 282–293. Springer, Heidelberg (2006). https://doi.org/10.1007/11871842_29
25. Kovács, L., Voronkov, A.: First-order theorem proving and Vampire. In: Sharygina, N., Veith, H. (eds.) CAV 2013. LNCS, vol. 8044, pp. 1–35. Springer, Heidelberg (2013). https://doi.org/10.1007/978-3-642-39799-8_1
26. Loos, S.M., Irving, G., Szegedy, C., Kaliszyk, C.: Deep network guided proof search. In: 21st International Conference on Logic for Programming, Artificial Intelligence, and Reasoning (LPAR) (2017)
27. McCune, W., Wos, L.: Experiments in automated deduction with condensed detachment. In: Kapur, D. (ed.) CADE 1992. LNCS, vol. 607, pp. 209–223. Springer, Heidelberg (1992). https://doi.org/10.1007/3-540-55602-8_167
28. Melis, E.: Theorem proving by analogy — A compelling example. In: Pinto-Ferreira, C., Mamede, N.J. (eds.) EPIA 1995. LNCS, vol. 990, pp. 261–272. Springer, Heidelberg (1995). https://doi.org/10.1007/3-540-60428-6_22
29. Melis, E., Siekmann, J.H.: Knowledge-based proof planning. Artif. Intell. **115**(1), 65–105 (1999). https://doi.org/10.1016/S0004-3702(99)00076-4
30. Nipkow, T., Wenzel, M., Paulson, L.C.: Isabelle/HOL: A Proof Assistant for Higher-Order Logic. Springer, Heidelberg (2002). https://doi.org/10.1007/3-540-45949-9

31. Olšák, M., Kaliszyk, C., Urban, J.: Property invariant embedding for automated reasoning. In: Giacomo, G.D., Catalá, A., Dilkina, B., Milano, M., Barro, S., Bugarín, A., Lang, J. (eds.) ECAI 2020–24th European Conference on Artificial Intelligence, 29 August-8 September 2020, Santiago de Compostela, Spain, August 29 - September 8, 2020 - Including 10th Conference on Prestigious Applications of Artificial Intelligence (PAIS 2020). Frontiers in Artificial Intelligence and Applications, vol. 325, pp. 1395–1402. IOS Press (2020). https://doi.org/10.3233/FAIA200244
32. Otten, J., Bibel, W.: leanCoP: lean connection-based theorem proving. J. Symb. Comput. **36**, 139–161 (2003)
33. Paliwal, A., Loos, S.M., Rabe, M.N., Bansal, K., Szegedy, C.: Graph representations for higher-order logic and theorem proving. CoRR abs/1905.10006 (2019). http://arxiv.org/abs/1905.10006
34. Peterson, J.G.: Shortest single axioms for the classical equivalential calculus. Notre Dame J. Formal Log. **17**(2), 267–271 (1976). https://doi.org/10.1305/ndjfl/1093887534
35. Piotrowski, B., Urban, J.: Guiding inferences in connection tableau by recurrent neural networks. In: Benzmüller, C., Miller, B. (eds.) CICM 2020. LNCS (LNAI), vol. 12236, pp. 309–314. Springer, Cham (2020). https://doi.org/10.1007/978-3-030-53518-6_23
36. Polu, S., Sutskever, I.: Generative language modeling for automated theorem proving. CoRR abs/2009.03393 (2020). https://arxiv.org/abs/2009.03393
37. Polya, G.: Mathematics and Plausible Reasoning. Introduction and Analogy in Mathematics, vol. 1. Princeton University Press, Princeton (1954)
38. Polya, G.: How to Solve It. Princeton University Press (1971). http://www.amazon.com/exec/obidos/redirect?tag=citeulike07-20&path=ASIN/0691023565
39. Rawson, M., Reger, G.: lazycop 0.1. EasyChair Preprint no. 3926 (2020, EasyChair)
40. Resnick, C., Raileanu, R., Kapoor, S., Peysakhovich, A., Cho, K., Bruna, J.: Backplay: "Man muss immer umkehren". CoRR abs/1807.06919 (2018). http://arxiv.org/abs/1807.06919
41. Robinson, A., Voronkov, A. (eds.): Handbook of Automated Reasoning. Elsevier Science Publishers B. V, Amsterdam (2001)
42. Robinson, R.M.: An essentially undecidable axiom system. In: Proceedings of the International Congress of Mathematics, pp. 729–730 (1950)
43. Ross, S., Gordon, G., Bagnell, D.: A reduction of imitation learning and structured prediction to no-regret online learning. In: Gordon, G., Dunson, D., Dudik, M. (eds.) Proceedings of the Fourteenth International Conference on Artificial Intelligence and Statistics. Proceedings of Machine Learning Research, vol. 15, pp. 627–635. PMLR, Fort Lauderdale (2011). http://proceedings.mlr.press/v15/ross11a.html
44. Salimans, T., Chen, R.: Learning Montezuma's Revenge from a single demonstration. CoRR abs/1812.03381 (2018). http://arxiv.org/abs/1812.03381
45. Schulman, J., Wolski, F., Dhariwal, P., Radford, A., Klimov, O.: Proximal policy optimization algorithms. CoRR abs/1707.06347 (2017)
46. Schulz, S.: System description: E 1.8. In: McMillan, K., Middeldorp, A., Voronkov, A. (eds.) LPAR 2013. LNCS, vol. 8312, pp. 735–743. Springer, Heidelberg (2013). https://doi.org/10.1007/978-3-642-45221-5_49
47. Silver, D., et al.: Mastering the game of go without human knowledge. Nature **550**, 354 (2017). https://doi.org/10.1038/nature24270
48. Sutcliffe, G.: The TPTP problem library and associated infrastructure. From CNF to TH0, TPTP v6.4.0. J. Autom. Reason. **59**(4), 483–502 (2017)

49. Sutton, R.S., Barto, A.G.: Reinforcement Learning: An Introduction, 2nd edn. The MIT Press (2018). http://incompleteideas.net/book/the-book-2nd.html
50. Urban, J.: MaLARea: a metasystem for automated reasoning in large theories. In: Sutcliffe, G., Urban, J., Schulz, S. (eds.) Proceedings of the CADE-21 Workshop on Empirically Successful Automated Reasoning in Large Theories, Bremen, Germany, 17th July 2007. CEUR Workshop Proceedings, vol. 257. CEUR-WS.org (2007). http://ceur-ws.org/Vol-257/05_Urban.pdf
51. Urban, J., Jakubův, J.: First neural conjecturing datasets and experiments. In: Benzmüller, C., Miller, B. (eds.) CICM 2020. LNCS (LNAI), vol. 12236, pp. 315–323. Springer, Cham (2020). https://doi.org/10.1007/978-3-030-53518-6_24
52. Urban, J., Sutcliffe, G., Pudlák, P., Vyskočil, J.: MaLARea SG1 - machine learner for automated reasoning with semantic guidance. In: Armando, A., Baumgartner, P., Dowek, G. (eds.) IJCAR 2008. LNCS (LNAI), vol. 5195, pp. 441–456. Springer, Heidelberg (2008). https://doi.org/10.1007/978-3-540-71070-7_37
53. Veroff, R.: Using hints to increase the effectiveness of an automated reasoning program: case studies. J. Autom. Reason. **16**(3), 223–239 (1996)
54. Wos, L., Winker, S., Smith, B., Veroff, R., Henschen, L.: A new use of an automated reasoning assistant: open questions in equivalential calculus and the study of infinite domains. Artifi. Intell. **22**(3), 303–356 (1984)
55. Wos, L.: Meeting the challenge of fifty years of logic. J. Autom. Reason. **6**(2), 213–232 (1990)
56. Zombori, Z., Urban, J., Brown, C.E.: Prolog technology reinforcement learning prover. In: Peltier, N., Sofronie-Stokkermans, V. (eds.) IJCAR 2020. LNCS (LNAI), vol. 12167, pp. 489–507. Springer, Cham (2020). https://doi.org/10.1007/978-3-030-51054-1_33

lazyCoP: Lazy Paramodulation Meets Neurally Guided Search

Michael Rawson(✉) and Giles Reger

The University of Manchester, Manchester, UK
michael@rawsons.uk

Abstract. State-of-the-art automated theorem provers explore large search spaces with carefully-engineered routines, but most do not learn from past experience as human mathematicians can. Unfortunately, machine-learned heuristics for theorem proving are typically either fast or accurate, not both. Therefore, systems must make a tradeoff between the quality of heuristic guidance and the reduction in inference rate required to use it. We present a system (lazyCoP) based on lazy paramodulation that is completely insulated from heuristic overhead, allowing the use of even deep neural networks with no measurable reduction in inference rate. Given 10 s to find proofs in a corpus of mathematics, the system improves from 64% to 70% when trained on its own proofs.

1 Introduction

The great majority of automatic theorem provers use some kind of heuristic search. This could be simple, such as the use of iterative deepening on a certain property to achieve completeness [25]; complex, as in hand-engineered schemes [8]; or even learned in some way [41]. Such heuristics are critical for system performance: an excellent heuristic could find a proof in linear time[1], while a poor heuristic increases search time drastically. Historically these routines have been engineered, rather than learned, resulting in fast yet disproportionately-effective heuristics like the age/weight schemes [35] used in systems like Vampire [15,29].

Learning a good heuristic from previous proof attempts has become more popular recently, and can achieve good results [4]. Techniques from machine learning can approximate complex functions that are difficult to discover or write down, but this comes at computational cost. This cost can result in an unfortunate outcome where a learned heuristic that appears promising during testing actually *degrades* performance when included in a concrete system, due to reduced inference throughput. Even assuming a heuristic is both fast and accurate, it is not always clear how to gainfully include predictions into existing target systems, particularly as a single wrong prediction can sometimes have disastrous results. Approaches are either ad-hoc or adapt existing techniques from other domains which are not necessarily well-suited to theorem proving.

[1] achieved by only making inferences used in the eventual proof.

A. Das and S. Negri (Eds.): TABLEAUX 2021, LNAI 12842, pp. 187–199, 2021.
https://doi.org/10.1007/978-3-030-86059-2_11

This paper presents a new system specifically designed to avoid these issues. lazyCoP (available online[2]) is an automatic theorem prover for first-order logic with equality in the connection tableaux family (Sect. 3). The system may use a policy learned end-to-end from previous proofs (Sect. 5) to bias a special-purpose backtracking search (Sect. 4.1) toward areas the policy considers promising. Performance penalties are eliminated by asynchronously evaluating the policy network on a coprocessor, such as commodity GPU hardware (Sect. 4.2).

The result is a system in which learned guidance has no measurable impact on inference rate (Sect. 6.1) and learns in a feedback loop from previous proofs on a set of training problems (Sect. 6.2). No manual features are used for learning, and the only manual heuristic used is "tableaux with fewer subgoals are more likely to lead to a proof". The system augmented with the final learned policy improves from 64% to 70% in real time under identical conditions.

2 Related Work

The rlCoP system introduced by Kaliszyk et al. [14] is the inspiration for this work and is most similar in spirit. In rlCoP, a connection tableaux system is guided by Monte-Carlo Tree Search (*MCTS* henceforth, as in work on two-player games [37]), learning both policy and value guidance with gradient-boosted trees from hand-engineered features. Learning from previous proofs or failures is a common approach for many different applications of machine learning to theorem proving, avoiding the need to generate data manually. For instance, all learned premise-selection systems we are aware of are trained using premises used by automated systems in existing proofs [12,42]. rlCoP sets up a feedback loop in which new information automatically found by the system is added to the training set in order to guide future iterations, as here.

Connection tableaux and classical first-order logic are popular settings for other internal guidance experiments—notably monteCoP [6], rlCoP, MaLeCoP [41], FEMaLeCoP [13], FLoP [43] and plCoP [44]—but internal guidance for other domains exist, including first-order saturation systems [4], SAT and QBF solvers [16,36], and systems for higher-order logics [1,5,7].

Performance is a recurring problem for systems with learned internal guidance. The authors of rlCoP exclude some kinds of learned models for performance reasons, and results are reported based on an inference, rather than time, limit. Loos et al. [19] report that the main bottleneck in the guided saturation-style system E [34] is the evaluation of inferences, and suggest a two-phase guided/unguided approach to theorem proving with learned guidance. Asynchronous evaluation was suggested in our earlier work on the same problem [28].

3 Unguided System

If an unguided system is completely hopeless, little progress can be made: very few positive training data can be generated from successful proofs, and the

[2] https://github.com/MichaelRawson/lazycop.

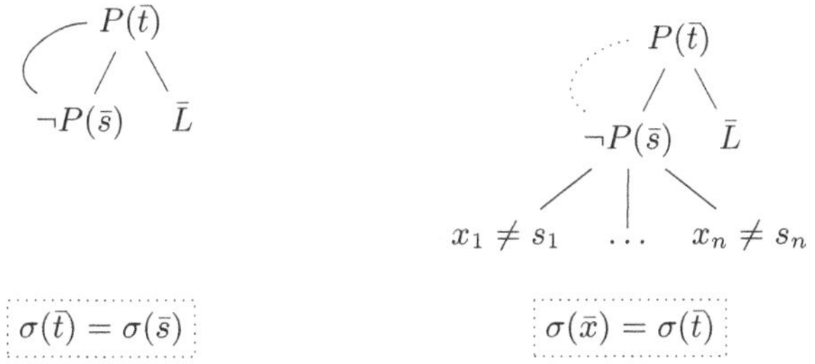

Fig. 1. Adding $\neg P(\bar{s}) \vee \bar{L}$ to a tableau where $P(\bar{t})$ is the current goal. The left tableau shows conventional "strict" extension, the right LPCT "lazy" extension.

learned guidance must be better still in order to achieve reasonable performance. However, it is not as simple as selecting a state-of-the-art theorem prover, as some are more amenable to guidance than others. Instead, there is a spectrum of different possible research directions, from attempting to guide weaker-yet-amenable systems up to meet stronger unguided systems, to integrating learning into already-strong systems which are not so easily improved by guidance.

The guidance scheme suggested here is designed for backtracking search, such as that found in systems based on connection calculi [18]. It is not clear how this could be adapted to a saturation theorem prover such as Vampire or E, which employ proof-confluent search with a time-sensitive choice point at the selection of a given clause. The basic system must therefore be as strong as possible while still allowing backtracking policy-guided search, and lazyCoP is purpose-built for this. A prototype version [31] entered the most recent CASC competition [39], and subsequent developments including a dedicated clausification routine have significantly improved performance.

3.1 Connection Tableaux

lazyCoP belongs to the connection-tableaux/model-elimination family [18] of theorem provers, which includes systems such as leanCoP [25] and SETHEO [2]. Such systems aim to *refute* a proposition by building a *closed tableau*: a tree of case-splits such that every path through the tree ends in a contradiction. *Connection* tableaux reduce the search space by constraining tableaux such that each addition to any given tableau must be *connected* in some way to the current leaf[3], as shown on the left-hand side of Fig. 1 where $P(\bar{t})$ connects to $\neg P(\bar{s})$. To *prove* a conjecture, it suffices to begin with the negated conjecture and build a closed tableau refuting it.

Since there is often more than one possible next step in building a tableau, not all of which lead to a proof, it is necessary to backtrack if a misstep is

[3] Usually this means that when adding a clause, there must be a literal with opposite sign that unifies with a leaf literal. Lazy paramodulation extends this notion to equality reasoning.

made. Typical connection systems often use some kind of iterative deepening to maintain completeness, but any fair scheme works: rlCoP uses MCTS for this purpose.

3.2 Lazy Paramodulation

Reasoning with equality has traditionally been a weak point of connection systems. The most widespread method for efficiently reasoning with equality, *paramodulation* [22], is incomplete in the obvious formulation for connection tableaux due to insufficient flexibility in the order of inferences. There have been various attempts to remedy this deficit, but as yet there is no conclusive solution.

lazyCoP uses the "lazy paramodulation" proof calculus LPCT [27], which relaxes some of the classical connection-tableaux rules in exchange for a paramodulation-like rule and some extra refinements. The basic idea is delaying unification to allow rewriting terms in the resulting disequations. For example, in the right-hand side of Fig. 1, it is not required that $P(\bar{t})$ unify with $P(\bar{s})$ immediately as in the classical calculus, instead deducing that at least one of the terms must not be equal. Terms may still be unified with a reflexivity rule dispatching goals of the form $t \neq s$.

This implementation detail of lazyCoP is not the main focus of this work: the vital feature of the proof calculus is backtracking proof search.

3.3 Calculus Refinements

To improve performance against the pure calculus, lazyCoP implements a number of well-known refinements of the classical predicate calculus (which are lifted to equalities where appropriate), including tautology deletion, various regularity conditions, and *folding up* [17], a way of re-using proofs of literals. Additionally, it is frequently the case that a unification is "lazy" when it could have been "strict"—such as in the case with no equality. lazyCoP therefore implements "lazy" and "strict" versions of every relevant inference rule, which shortens some proofs considerably. The resulting duplication is eliminated by not permitting "lazy" rules to simulate their "strict" counterparts.

It is not clear whether some refinements help or hinder the learned-guidance scenario. Some are definite improvements: folding up and strict rules decrease proof lengths and therefore increase the potential benefit of learned guidance. However, others, such as the regularity condition or the term ordering constraints in LPCT, are not as clear-cut. In some cases such refinements lengthen proofs significantly, outweighing the pruning effect, and previous work shows that guidance can partially replace these pruning mechanisms [9]. We leave all refinements switched on for this approach, but allowing the learned policy a greater amount of freedom is an interesting future direction.

Some techniques such as *restricted backtracking* [26] sacrifice completeness for performance. lazyCoP does not implement any approach known to be incomplete[4]: all problems attempted can be solved in principle.

4 Proof Search

Given a learned policy[5], we aim to use it to improve proof search outcomes. The *policy* $\pi(a \mid n)$ is a function from a tableau n and possible inferences a to a probability distribution. We work with an explicit search tree, each node of the tree representing an open tableau, although tableaux are not actually kept in memory for efficiency reasons. From each open tableau, there is a positive non-zero number of possible inferences (or *actions* in the reinforcement learning literature) which may be applied to generate a new child tableau. Nodes with zero possible inferences cannot be closed and are pruned from the tree. The root of the tree is an empty tableau, from which possible inferences are the *start clauses*, in this case clauses derived from the conjecture.

4.1 Policy-Guided Search

There are many possible tree search algorithms which can include some kind of learned heuristic. We experimented with the classical A^* informed-search procedure, although we found that it was difficult to learn a good heuristic function that was neither too conservative nor too aggressive. Other approaches might include the aforementioned MCTS, single-player adaptations of MCTS [33] single-agent approaches like that of LevinTS or LubyTS [24], or simply following a stochastic policy with restarts if no proof is found at some depth. While these approaches are no doubt interesting and provide theoretical guarantees, we did not find them to be necessary for our case.

Instead, we could simply employ best-first search, expanding the leaf node that the policy considers most likely first. If a leaf node n was obtained by taking actions a_i from ancestor nodes n_i, select

$$\operatorname*{argmax}_{n} \prod_{i} \pi(a_i \mid n_i)$$

Unfortunately, this simple scheme is not likely to recover if π makes a confident misprediction, and is even incomplete if any node has an infinite chain of single children beneath, where $\pi(a_j \mid n_j) = 1$ by definition. To correct this issue we take inspiration from rlCoP's initial value heuristic, where tableaux are exponentially

[4] It is not known whether lazyCoP's calculus with refinements is complete. For instance and to the best of our knowledge, Paskevich [27] leaves the compatibility of lazy paramodulation with the regularity condition an open question.

[5] no *value* function is employed: it is unclear how to adapt this to asynchronous evaluation, or how useful this would be in an asynchronous context.

less likely to be closed the more open branches they have. We model this idea as an exponential distribution

$$p(n) = \lambda e^{-\lambda g(n)}$$

where λ is a tunable parameter (set to 1 in our experiments here) and $g(n)$ is "number of open branches plus length of the path". Including "length of the path" in $g(n)$ makes little practical difference and makes the search procedure complete again. The two estimates are combined with a geometric mean so that nodes are selected by

$$\operatorname*{argmax}_{n} \sqrt{p(n) \prod_{i} \pi\left(a_i \mid n_i\right)}$$

In practice this expression is numerically difficult to evaluate, but in logarithmic space it is better-behaved, producing the final expansion criterion

$$\operatorname*{argmax}_{n} \left[\left(\sum_{i} \ln \pi\left(a_i \mid n_i\right)\right) - \lambda g(n)\right]$$

4.2 Asynchronous Policy Evaluation

The proof search routine above assumes that the policy is evaluated synchronously for each expanded node. As discussed in the introductory sections, this has a significant impact on performance, particularly so for computationally-expensive policies. Instead, evaluation is deferred and a separate CPU thread continuously arranges for nodes to be processed on a GPU, selecting the first non-evaluated node on the path to the current best leaf node. $\pi\left(a \mid n\right)$ is set to 1 for nodes not yet evaluated: applying a uniform distribution does not work well in practice.

It does not appear to be particularly important that all nodes are evaluated for a learned policy to improve search, perhaps because guidance at the top of the search tree has a disproportionate effect. Asynchronous policy evaluation allows use of policies that are orders of magnitude slower than expansion steps without reduction in inference rate.

5 Learned Policy

Section 4.1 describes biasing proof search with a learned policy, directing node expansions toward areas the policy considers useful. lazyCoP's policy is trained from its own proofs—at each non-trivial step[6] in a proof we record three things: (i) the tableau, (ii) available actions, and (iii) the action that lead to a proof. This procedure produces a training set of tableaux and actions which we use to train a neural-network based policy to predict the correct action. Learning from existing proofs in this way has advantages and disadvantages: each example's

[6] that is, states with more than one possible action.

label is guaranteed to lead to a proof, but it is not necessarily the shortest proof, nor can the training data express preference amongst other actions.

We train and evaluate using the same set of problems from the MPTP translation [40] of the Mizar Mathematical Library [10] into first-order logic with equality. There are 32,524 problems in total in the *M40k* set; we use the *M2k* subset of 2003 problems in order to iterate quickly. All problems have a labelled conjecture which lazyCoP is able to exploit so that search proceeds backward from the conjecture. Problems from the *M2k* set come from related articles in Mizar, suggesting a degree of similarity which may be exploited by learning.

5.1 Representing Tableaux with Actions

There are many possible ways to represent first-order logical data in neural networks. We use directed graphs paired with residual graph convolutions, as introduced for other similar tasks [30]. This approach has significant advantages for a first-order tableau system such as lazyCoP as it allows reconstructing an equivalent tableau (up to renaming) from a compact, pre-parsed representation invariant up to e.g. variable names.

Construction of directed graphs from tableaux is mostly typical for first-order representations [42], with a few problem-specific modifications. First, while occurrences of identical symbols and variables share nodes in the graph, identical compound terms do not: this is because they may be rewritten by equalities separately in LPCT. Additionally, variable binding is non-destructive in LPCT to implement a form of basic paramodulation. Bound variables therefore remain in place but have an outgoing edge attached to their binding.

Encoding actions is then straightforward. lazyCoP implements a small number of inference rules, such as reductions, extensions, reflexivity and so on. Each inference is attached to some terms or literals in the tableau to form a concrete action: rewriting $t = s$ in $L[p]$, for example, is represented as a node connected to the graph with an incoming edge from t and outgoing edge from p, uniquely identifying the inference.

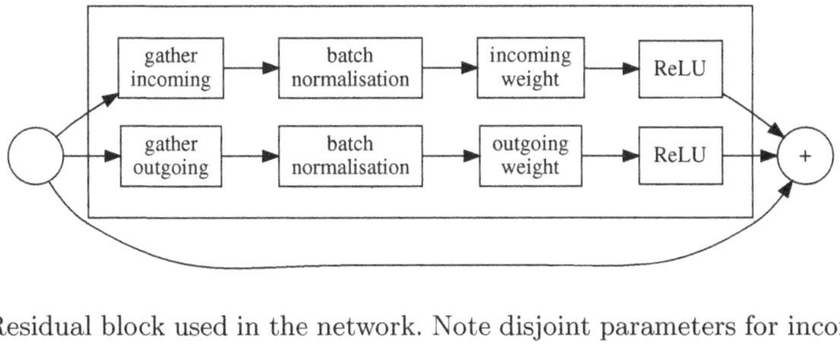

Fig. 2. Residual block used in the network. Note disjoint parameters for incoming and outgoing edges, both linear and normalisation layers.

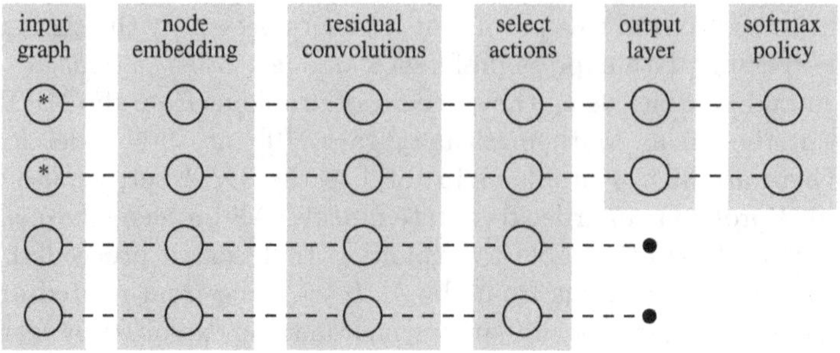

Fig. 3. Network diagram. As there is no pooling of any kind, data is processed at the node level until action nodes marked (*) are projected out.

5.2 Network Architecture

We use a residual version of the directed graph networks introduced in previous work [30] which allow the network to distinguish incoming and outgoing edges. The core of the network is the residual block shown in Fig. 2: this allows one round of message-passing from neighbouring nodes in the graph, treating incoming and outgoing edges separately before combining the results for the next layer. Batch normalisation [11] is inserted before the linear part of the convolution. The theoretical merits of this are unclear but it works well in practice. The complete network (Fig. 3) is, in order (Table 1):

Table 1. Network and training hyper-parameters.

Parameter	Value	Parameter	Value
Node dimension	64	Initial learning rate	0.01
Residual layers	24	Cycle batches	2000
		Batch size	64
		Momentum	0.9
		Weight decay	0.0001

Embedding. An embedding layer projects integer node labels into a real vector of the same size used in the convolutional layers.

Convolution layers. Several residual blocks combine and transform feature maps from neighbouring nodes, producing in particular a real vector for each action node.

Action projection. The vector for each action node is projected out, all other nodes are discarded at this point.

Output layer. Computes a single output value for each action.

Rectified linear units are used as non-linearities throughout.

5.3 Training

Training such a network on limited training examples from early iterations is challenging due to its tendency to memorise the training set if sufficient parameters are available and underfit drastically if they are not. This is perhaps a good argument for feature-based learning rather than the end-to-end approach we take here. However, the network can be made to train somewhat effectively by cosine annealing a high initial learning rate to 0 with "warm restarts" [20], repeating after a certain number of mini-batches. This has two benefits: the regularising effect of high learning rates somewhat reduces overfitting, and the network also trains faster.

5.4 Integration and Optimisation

After the network is trained, network weights are compiled into lazyCoP. The forward pass is re-implemented from scratch in CUDA [23], allowing a number of optimisations such as known array sizes, re-use of allocated buffers and the ability to profile for the specific workload. Additionally, batch normalisation layers' forward operation can be fused into the subsequent layer in this case, decreasing implementation complexity and increasing performance.

6 Experimental Results

We investigate two areas of practical interest: the effect of learned policy evaluations on inference rate, and whether this learning translates into improved performance on a training set of problems. Systems are only allowed 10 s of real time: this is relatively short, but a good approximation to real-world settings in which users of automatic "hammers" included in interactive theorem proving systems are unwilling to wait much longer than 30 s [3].

Table 2. Results from iterative training of lazyCoP's policy on *M2k*.

#	Proved	Cumulative	Steps
0	1,289	1,289	16,880
1	1,390	1,406	19,394
2	1,402	1,419	19,700
3	1,403	1,426	19,881

6.1 Inference Rates

There is no measurable decrease in inference rate when learned guidance is switched on. Occasionally the rate of inference even *improves*, perhaps due to guidance producing areas which are less productive or otherwise easier to explore. Running on `TOP001-1`, a non-theorem mid-sized topology problem from TPTP [38], unguided lazyCoP achieves around 62,000 expansions per second for 10 s at the time of writing on desktop hardware. Guided, the system evaluates around 200 policies per second and reaches inference speeds in excess of 70,000 expansions per second.

6.2 Effect of Guidance

We train lazyCoP iteratively on *M2k* as described in Sect. 5, training each iteration on the proofs produced by all previous iterations. Iteration 0 does not have access to a learned policy, iteration 1's policy is trained on iteration 0's proofs, iteration 2 on proofs from both iteration 0 and 1, etc. If there are two proofs for the same problem, the shorter proof is retained. The system is given 10 s of real time per problem, measured from program startup to the point of discovering a proof (but before output begins), and 16 GB memory on a desktop machine[7]. Table 2 shows the number of problems solved by that iteration, the number of problems proved by all previous iterations, and the total number of proof steps for training available after the iteration finishes.

7 Conclusion and Future Work

We have introduced a new system, lazyCoP which combines a lazy paramodulation-based connection tableau prover with *lazy* neural guidance. The neural guidance improves the underlying search from 64% to 70% without any measurable impact on inference rate. There are several future directions we will consider pursuing:

Scaling network and problem sets. It is very possible that a larger/deeper policy network would allow learning even better policies. This requires either more careful tuning or a larger set of problems such as *M40k* to avoid overfitting excessively.

Parallelism. Implementing both parallel search and parallel evaluation on today's multicore machines would have a beneficial impact on performance. Parallel search allows exploiting remaining cores to search faster and is a clear win, the explicit search tree of lazyCoP allowing for several easy schemes to inject parallelism. Parallel evaluation does not inherently improve performance, but does ensure that the coprocessor is always kept busy: at present there are short pauses while the evaluation thread propagates the previous evaluation and prepares another input. Using multiple host threads also allows hiding latency from e.g. coprocessor cache misses, increasing overall throughput at the expense of the speed of single evaluation.

[7] Intel® Core™ i7-6700 CPU @ 3.40 GHz, NVIDIA® GeForce® GT 730.

Incomplete modes. A system does not necessarily have to be complete to be useful [21]. leanCoP includes a powerful but incomplete restricted-backtracking mode, for example. As well as e.g. restricted backtracking, lazyCoP could implement a strategy in which parts of the search tree are progressively discarded as resource limits draw nearer, in a similar way to Vampire's *limited resource strategy* [32]. We expect this to help with finding extremely long proofs.

Generality. An anonymous reviewer suggested that with a little more effort this work could become a standalone tool for advising existing (backtracking) systems. We agree and thank the reviewer for the suggestion, although we also agree with the reviewer's assessment that existing systems would need to be modified somewhat.

References

1. Bansal, K., Loos, S., Rabe, M., Szegedy, C., Wilcox, S.: HOList: an environment for machine learning of higher order logic theorem proving. In: International Conference on Machine Learning, pp. 454–463 (2019)
2. Bayerl, S., Letz, R.: SETHEO: a sequential theorem prover for first-order logic. Esprit'87-Achievements and Impacts, part 1, pp. 721–735 (1987)
3. Böhme, S., Nipkow, T.: Sledgehammer: judgement day. In: Giesl, J., Hähnle, R. (eds.) IJCAR 2010. LNCS (LNAI), vol. 6173, pp. 107–121. Springer, Heidelberg (2010). https://doi.org/10.1007/978-3-642-14203-1_9
4. Chvalovský, K., Jakubův, J., Suda, M., Urban, J.: ENIGMA-NG: efficient neural and gradient-boosted inference guidance for E. In: Fontaine, P. (ed.) CADE 2019. LNCS (LNAI), vol. 11716, pp. 197–215. Springer, Cham (2019). https://doi.org/10.1007/978-3-030-29436-6_12
5. Färber, M., Brown, C.: Internal guidance for satallax. In: Olivetti, N., Tiwari, A. (eds.) IJCAR 2016. LNCS (LNAI), vol. 9706, pp. 349–361. Springer, Cham (2016). https://doi.org/10.1007/978-3-319-40229-1_24
6. Färber, M., Kaliszyk, C., Urban, J.: Monte-Carlo connection prover. In: Second Conference on Artificial Intelligence and Theorem Proving (2017)
7. Gauthier, T., Kaliszyk, C., Urban, J., Kumar, R., Norrish, M.: TacticToe: learning to prove with tactics. J. Autom. Reason. **65**(2), 257–286 (2021)
8. Gleiss, B., Suda, M.: Layered clause selection for theory reasoning. In: Peltier, N., Sofronie-Stokkermans, V. (eds.) IJCAR 2020. LNCS (LNAI), vol. 12166, pp. 402–409. Springer, Cham (2020). https://doi.org/10.1007/978-3-030-51074-9_23
9. Goertzel, Z.A.: Make E smart again (short paper). In: Peltier, N., Sofronie-Stokkermans, V. (eds.) IJCAR 2020. LNCS (LNAI), vol. 12167, pp. 408–415. Springer, Cham (2020). https://doi.org/10.1007/978-3-030-51054-1_26
10. Grabowski, A., Kornilowicz, A., Naumowicz, A.: Mizar in a nutshell. J. Formalized Reason. **3**(2), 153–245 (2010)
11. Ioffe, S., Szegedy, C.: Batch normalization: accelerating deep network training by reducing internal covariate shift. In: International Conference on Machine Learning, pp. 448–456 (2015)
12. Irving, G., Szegedy, C., Alemi, A.A., Eén, N., Chollet, F., Urban, J.: DeepMath – deep sequence models for premise selection. In: Advances in Neural Information Processing Systems, pp. 2235–2243 (2016)

13. Kaliszyk, C., Urban, J.: FEMaLeCoP: fairly efficient machine learning connection prover. In: Davis, M., Fehnker, A., McIver, A., Voronkov, A. (eds.) LPAR 2015. LNCS, vol. 9450, pp. 88–96. Springer, Heidelberg (2015). https://doi.org/10.1007/978-3-662-48899-7_7
14. Kaliszyk, C., Urban, J., Michalewski, H., Olšák, M.: Reinforcement learning of theorem proving. In: Advances in Neural Information Processing Systems, pp. 8822–8833 (2018)
15. Kovács, L., Voronkov, A.: First-order theorem proving and Vampire. In: Sharygina, N., Veith, H. (eds.) CAV 2013. LNCS, vol. 8044, pp. 1–35. Springer, Heidelberg (2013). https://doi.org/10.1007/978-3-642-39799-8_1
16. Lederman, G., Rabe, M., Seshia, S., Lee, E.A.: Learning heuristics for quantified boolean formulas through reinforcement learning. In: International Conference on Learning Representations (2020). https://openreview.net/forum?id=BJluxREKDB
17. Letz, R., Mayr, K., Goller, C.: Controlled integration of the cut rule into connection tableau calculi. J. Autom. Reason. **13**(3), 297–337 (1994)
18. Letz, R., Stenz, G.: Model elimination and connection tableau procedures. In: Handbook of Automated Reasoning, vol. 2. MIT Press (2001)
19. Loos, S., Irving, G., Szegedy, C., Kaliszyk, C.: Deep network guided proof search. In: LPAR-21. 21st International Conference on Logic for Programming, Artificial Intelligence and Reasoning, pp. 85–105 (2017)
20. Loshchilov, I., Hutter, F.: SGDR: stochastic gradient descent with warm restarts. In: 5th International Conference on Learning Representations (2017)
21. McCune, W., Wos, L.: Otter – the CADE-13 competition incarnations. J. Autom. Reason. **18**(2), 211–220 (1997)
22. Neuwenhuis, R., Rubio, A.: Paramodulation-based theorem proving. In: Handbook of Automated Reasoning, vol. 1. MIT Press (2001)
23. Nickolls, J., Buck, I., Garland, M., Skadron, K.: Scalable parallel programming with CUDA. ACM Queue **6**(2), 40–53 (2008)
24. Orseau, L., Lelis, L., Lattimore, T., Weber, T.: Single-agent policy tree search with guarantees. In: Advances in Neural Information Processing Systems, pp. 3201–3211 (2018)
25. Otten, J.: leanCoP 2.0 and ileanCoP 1.2: high performance lean theorem proving in classical and intuitionistic logic (system descriptions). In: Armando, A., Baumgartner, P., Dowek, G. (eds.) IJCAR 2008. LNCS (LNAI), vol. 5195, pp. 283–291. Springer, Heidelberg (2008). https://doi.org/10.1007/978-3-540-71070-7_23
26. Otten, J.: Restricting backtracking in connection calculi. AI Commun. **23**(2–3), 159–182 (2010)
27. Paskevich, A.: Connection tableaux with lazy paramodulation. J. Autom. Reason. **40**(2–3), 179–194 (2008)
28. Rawson, M., Reger, G.: A neurally-guided, parallel theorem prover. In: Herzig, A., Popescu, A. (eds.) FroCoS 2019. LNCS (LNAI), vol. 11715, pp. 40–56. Springer, Cham (2019). https://doi.org/10.1007/978-3-030-29007-8_3
29. Rawson, M., Reger, G.: Old or heavy? Decaying gracefully with age/weight shapes. In: Fontaine, P. (ed.) CADE 2019. LNCS (LNAI), vol. 11716, pp. 462–476. Springer, Cham (2019). https://doi.org/10.1007/978-3-030-29436-6_27
30. Rawson, M., Reger, G.: Directed graph networks for logical reasoning. In: Practical Aspects of Automated Reasoning (2020)
31. Rawson, M., Reger, G.: lazyCoP 0.1. EasyChair Preprint no. 3926 (EasyChair 2020) (2020)

32. Riazanov, A., Voronkov, A.: Limited resource strategy in resolution theorem proving. J. Symb. Comput. **36**(1–2), 101–115 (2003)
33. Schadd, M.P.D., Winands, M.H.M., van den Herik, H.J., Chaslot, G.M.J.-B., Uiterwijk, J.W.H.M.: Single-player Monte-Carlo tree search. In: van den Herik, H.J., Xu, X., Ma, Z., Winands, M.H.M. (eds.) CG 2008. LNCS, vol. 5131, pp. 1–12. Springer, Heidelberg (2008). https://doi.org/10.1007/978-3-540-87608-3_1
34. Schulz, S.: E - a brainiac theorem prover. AI Commun. **15**(2, 3), 111–126 (2002)
35. Schulz, S., Möhrmann, M.: Performance of clause selection heuristics for saturation-based theorem proving. In: Olivetti, N., Tiwari, A. (eds.) IJCAR 2016. LNCS (LNAI), vol. 9706, pp. 330–345. Springer, Cham (2016). https://doi.org/10.1007/978-3-319-40229-1_23
36. Selsam, D., Lamm, M., Bünz, B., Liang, P., de Moura, L., Dill, D.L.: Learning a SAT solver from single-bit supervision. arXiv preprint arXiv:1802.03685 (2018)
37. Silver, D., et al.: Mastering the game of Go with deep neural networks and tree search. Nature **529**(7587), 484–489 (2016)
38. Sutcliffe, G.: The TPTP problem library and associated infrastructure. J. Autom. Reason. **43**(4), 337 (2009). https://doi.org/10.1007/s10817-009-9143-8
39. Sutcliffe, G.: The CADE ATP system competition – CASC. AI Mag. **37**(2), 99–101 (2016)
40. Urban, J.: MPTP 0.2: design, implementation, and initial experiments. J. Autom. Reason. **37**(1–2), 21–43 (2006)
41. Urban, J., Vyskočil, J., Štěpánek, P.: MaLeCoP: machine learning connection prover. In: Brünnler, K., Metcalfe, G. (eds.) TABLEAUX 2011. LNCS (LNAI), vol. 6793, pp. 263–277. Springer, Heidelberg (2011). https://doi.org/10.1007/978-3-642-22119-4_21
42. Wang, M., Tang, Y., Wang, J., Deng, J.: Premise selection for theorem proving by deep graph embedding. In: Advances in Neural Information Processing Systems, pp. 2786–2796 (2017)
43. Zombori, Z., Csiszárik, A., Michalewski, H., Kaliszyk, C., Urban, J.: Towards finding longer proofs. arXiv preprint arXiv:1905.13100 (2019)
44. Zombori, Z., Urban, J., Brown, C.E.: Prolog technology reinforcement learning prover. In: Peltier, N., Sofronie-Stokkermans, V. (eds.) IJCAR 2020. LNCS (LNAI), vol. 12167, pp. 489–507. Springer, Cham (2020). https://doi.org/10.1007/978-3-030-51054-1_33

AC Simplifications and Closure Redundancies in the Superposition Calculus

André Duarte(✉) and Konstantin Korovin(✉)

The University of Manchester, Manchester, UK
{andre.duarte,konstantin.korovin}@manchester.ac.uk

Abstract. Reasoning in the presence of associativity and commutativity (AC) is well known to be challenging due to prolific nature of these axioms. Specialised treatment of AC axioms is mainly supported by provers for unit equality which are based on Knuth-Bendix completion. The main ingredient for dealing with AC in these provers are ground joinability criteria adapted for AC. In this paper we extend AC joinability from the context of unit equalities and Knuth-Bendix completion to the superposition calculus and full first-order logic. Our approach is based on an extension of the Bachmair-Ganzinger model construction and a new redundancy criterion which covers ground joinability. A by-product of our approach is a new criterion for applicability of demodulation which we call encompassment demodulation. This criterion is useful in any superposition theorem prover, independently of AC theories, and we demonstrate that it enables demodulation in many more cases, compared to the standard criterion.

Keywords: Superposition · Associativity-commutativity · Ground joinability · First-order theorem proving · Demodulation · iProver

1 Introduction

Associativity and commutativity (AC) axioms occur in many applications but efficient reasoning with them remain one of the major challenges in first-order theorem proving due to prolific nature of these axioms. Despite a number of theoretical advances specialised treatment of AC axioms is mainly supported by provers for unit equality such as Waldmeister [11], Twee [15] and MaedMax [19]. These provers are based on Knuth-Bendix completion, and the main ingredient for dealing with AC in these provers are ground joinability criteria adapted for AC [1,12]. Completeness proofs for ground joinability, known so far, are restricted to unit equalities, which limits applicability of these techniques. These proofs are based on proof transformations for unit rewriting which are not easily adaptable to the full first-order logic and also lack general redundancy criteria.

In this paper we extend ground AC joinability criteria from the context of Knuth-Bendix completion to the superposition calculus for full first-order logic.

A. Das and S. Negri (Eds.): TABLEAUX 2021, LNAI 12842, pp. 200–217, 2021.
https://doi.org/10.1007/978-3-030-86059-2_12

Our approach is based on an extension of the Bachmair-Ganzinger model construction [4] and a new redundancy criterion called closure redundancy. Closure redundancy allows for fine grained redundancy elimination which we show also covers ground AC joinability. We also introduced a new simplification called AC normalisation and showed that AC normalisation preserves completeness of the superposition calculus. Superposition calculus with the standard notion of redundancy can generate infinitely many non-redundant conclusions from AC axioms alone. Using our generalised notion of redundancy we can show that all of these inferences are redundant in the presence of a single extension axiom.

Using these results, superposition theorem provers for full first-order logic such as Vampire [10], E [14], SPASS [18], Zipperposition [17] and iProver [9] can incorporate AC simplifications without compromising completeness.

A by-product of our approach is a new criterion for applicability of demodulation which we call encompassment demodulation. Demodulation is one of the main simplification rules in the superposition-based reasoning and is a key ingredient in efficient first-order theorem provers. Our new demodulation criterion is useful independently of AC theories, and we demonstrate that it enables demodulation in many more cases, compared to the standard demodulation.

The main contributions of this paper include:

1. New redundancy criteria for the superposition calculus called closure redundancy.
2. Completeness proof of the superposition calculus with the closure redundancy.
3. Proof of admissibility of AC joinability and AC normalisation simplifications for the superposition calculus.
4. Encompassment demodulation and its admissibility for the superposition calculus.

In Sect. 2 we discuss preliminary notions, introduce closure orderings and prove properties of these orderings In Sect. 3 we introduce closure redundancy and prove the key theorem stating completeness of the superposition calculus with closure redundancy. In Sect. 4 we use closure redundancy to show that encompassment demodulation, AC joinability and AC normalisation are admissible simplifications. In Sect. 5 we show some experimental results and conclude in Sect. 6.

2 Preliminaries

We consider a signature consisting of a finite set of function symbols and the equality predicate as the only predicate symbol. We fix a countably infinite set of variables. First-order *terms* are defined in the usual manner. Terms without variables are called *ground terms*. A *literal* is an unordered pair of terms with either positive or negative polarity, written $s \approx t$ and $s \not\approx t$ respectively (we write $s \mathrel{\dot{\approx}} t$ to mean either of the former two). A *clause* is a multiset of literals. Collectively terms, literals, and clauses will be called *expressions*.

A *substitution* is a mapping from variables to terms which is the identity for all but a finitely many variables. If e is an expression, we denote application of a substitution σ by $e\sigma$, replacing all variables with their image in σ. Let $\mathrm{GSubs}(e) = \{\sigma \mid e\sigma \text{ is ground}\}$ be the set of *ground substitutions* for e. Overloading this notation for sets we write $\mathrm{GSubs}(E) = \{\sigma \mid \forall e \in E.\ e\sigma \text{ is ground}\}$. Finally, we write e.g. $\mathrm{GSubs}(e_1, e_2)$ instead of $\mathrm{GSubs}(\{e_1, e_2\})$.

An injective substitution θ with codomain being the set of variables is a *renaming*. Substitutions which are not renamings are called *proper*.

A substitution θ is *more general* than σ if $\theta\rho = \sigma$ for some proper substitution ρ. If s and t can be *unified*, that is, if there exists σ such that $s\sigma = t\sigma$, then there also exists the *most general unifier*, written $\mathrm{mgu}(s,t)$. A term s is said to be *more general* than t if there exists a substitution θ that makes $s\theta = t$ but there is no substitution σ such that $t\sigma = s$. We may also say that t is a *proper instance* of s. Two terms s and t are said to be *equal modulo renaming* if there exists a renaming θ such that $s\theta = t$. The relations "less general than", "equal modulo renaming", and their union are represented respectively by the symbols '$\sqsupset$', '$\equiv$', and '$\sqsupseteq$'.

A more refined notion of instance is that of *closure* [3]. Closures are pairs $t \cdot \sigma$ that are said to *represent* the term $t\sigma$ while retaining information about the original term and its instantiation. Closures where $t\sigma$ is ground are said to be *ground closures*. Let $\mathrm{GClos}(t) = \{t \cdot \sigma \mid t\sigma \text{ is ground}\}$ be the set of ground closures of t. Analogously to term closures, we define closures for other expressions such as literals and clauses, as a pair of an expression and a substitution. Overloading the notation for sets, if N is a set of clauses then $\mathrm{GClos}(N) = \bigcup_{C \in N} \mathrm{GClos}(C)$.

We write $s[t]$ if t is a *subterm* of s. If also $s \neq t$, then it is a *strict subterm*. We denote these relations by $s \trianglerighteq t$ and $s \triangleright t$ respectively. We write $s[t \mapsto t']_p$ to denote the term obtained from s by replacing t at the position p by t'. We omit the position when it clear from the context or irrelevant.

A relation '$\rightarrow$' over the set of terms is a *rewrite relation* if (i) $l \rightarrow r \Rightarrow l\sigma \rightarrow r\sigma$ and (ii) $l \rightarrow r \Rightarrow s[l] \rightarrow s[l \mapsto r]$. The members of a rewrite relation are called *rewrite rules*. The *reflexive-transitive closure* of a relation is the smallest reflexive-transitive relation which contains it. It is denoted by '$\xrightarrow{*}$'. Two terms are *joinable* ($s \downarrow t$)if $s \xrightarrow{*} u \xleftarrow{*} t$.

If a rewrite relation is also a strict ordering (transitive, irreflexive), then it is a *rewrite ordering*. A *reduction ordering* is a rewrite ordering which is well-founded. In this paper we consider reduction orderings which are total on ground terms, such orderings are also *simplification orderings* i.e., satisfy $s \triangleright t \Rightarrow s \succ t$.

For an ordering '$\succ$' over a set X, its *multiset extension* '$\succ\!\!\succ$' over multisets of X is given by: $A \succ\!\!\succ B$ iff $\forall x \in B.\ B(x) > A(x)\ \exists y \in A.\ y \succ x \wedge A(y) > B(y)$, where $A(x)$ is the number of occurrences of element x in multiset A. It is well known that the multiset extension of a well-founded (total) order is also a well-founded (respectively, total) order [6].

Orderings on Closures

In the following, let '$\succ_t$' be a reduction ordering which is total on ground terms. Examples of such orderings include KBO or LPO [2]. It is extended to an ordering on literals via $L \succ_l L'$ iff $M_l(L) \ggcurly_t M_l(L')$, where $M_l(s \approx t) = \{s, t\}$ and $M_l(s \not\approx t) = \{s, s, t, t\}$. It is further extended to an ordering on clauses via $C \succ_c D$ iff $C \ggcurly_l D$.

We extend this ordering to an ordering on ground closures. The idea is to "break ties", whenever two closures represent the same term, to make more general closures smaller in the ordering than more specific ones. The definitions follow.

$$s \cdot \sigma \succ_{tc} t \cdot \rho \quad \text{iff} \quad \begin{array}{l}\text{either } s\sigma \succ_t t\rho \\ \text{or else } s\sigma = t\rho \text{ and } s \sqsupset t.\end{array} \tag{1}$$

This is a well-founded ordering, since '$\succ_t$' and '$\sqsupset$' are also well-founded. However it is only a partial order even on ground closures (e.g., $f(x, b) \cdot (x \mapsto a) \bowtie f(a, y) \cdot (y \mapsto b)$), but it is well-known that any partial well-founded order can be extended to a total well-founded order (see e.g. [5]). Therefore we will assume that '$\succ_{tc}$' is extended to a total well-founded order on ground closures. Then let $M_{lc}((s \approx t) \cdot \theta) = \{s \cdot \theta, t \cdot \theta\}$ and $M_{lc}((s \not\approx t) \cdot \theta) = \{s \cdot \theta, s\theta \cdot id, t \cdot \theta, t\theta \cdot id\}$ in

$$L \cdot \sigma \succ_{lc} L' \cdot \rho \quad \text{iff} \quad M_{lc}(L \cdot \sigma) \ggcurly_{tc} M_{lc}(L' \cdot \rho), \tag{2}$$

and let $M_{cc}(C \cdot \sigma) = \{L \cdot \sigma\}$ if C is a unit clause $\{L\}$, and $M_{cc}(C \cdot \sigma) = \{L\sigma \cdot id \mid L \in C\}$ otherwise, in

$$C \cdot \sigma \succ_{cc} D \cdot \rho \quad \text{iff} \quad M_{cc}(C \cdot \sigma) \ggcurly_{lc} M_{cc}(D \cdot \rho). \tag{3}$$

Let us note that unit and non-unit clauses are treated differently in this ordering. Some properties that will be used throughout the paper follow.

Lemma 1. '$\succ_{tc}$', '$\succ_{lc}$', and '$\succ_{cc}$' are all well-founded and total on ground term closures, literal closures, and clause closures, respectively.

Proof. We have already established that $\succ_{tc}$ is well-founded by construction. '$\succ_{lc}$' and '$\succ_{cc}$' are derived from '$\succ_{tc}$' by multiset extension, so they are also well-founded. Similarly, '$\succ_{tc}$' is total on ground-terms on by construction, and '$\succ_{lc}$' and '$\succ_{cc}$' are derived from '$\succ_{tc}$' by multiset extension, so they are also total on ground literals/clauses. □

Lemma 2. Assume s, t are ground, then $s \cdot id \succ_{tc} t \cdot id \Leftrightarrow s \succ_t t$. Analogously for '$\succ_{lc}$' and '$\succ_{cc}$'.

Lemma 3. '$\succ_{tc}$' is an extension of '$\succ_t$', in that $s\sigma \succ_t t\rho \Rightarrow s \cdot \sigma \succ_{tc} t \cdot \rho$, however this is generally not the case for '$\succ_{lc}$' and '$\succ_{cc}$': $s\sigma \,\dot{\approx}\, t\sigma \succ_l u\rho \,\dot{\approx}\, v\rho \not\Rightarrow (s \,\dot{\approx}\, t) \cdot \sigma \succ_{lc} (u \,\dot{\approx}\, v) \cdot \rho$, and $C\sigma \succ_c D\rho \not\Rightarrow C \cdot \sigma \succ_{cc} D \cdot \rho$.

Proof. As an example, let $a \succ_t b$ and consider literal closures

$$(f(x) \approx a) \cdot x/a \qquad\qquad (f(a) \approx b) \cdot id \tag{4}$$

The literal represented by the one on the left is greater than the one represented by the one on the right, in '$\succ_l$'. However, the closure on the left is smaller than the one on the right, in '$\succ_{lc}$'. This is also an example for '$\succ_{cc}$' if these are two unit clauses. □

Lemma 4. $t\rho \cdot \sigma \succeq_{tc} t \cdot \rho\sigma$. *Analogously for '$\succ_{lc}$' and '$\succ_{cc}$'. In particular, $t\sigma \cdot id \succeq_{tc} t \cdot \sigma$ and analogously for '$\succ_{lc}$' and '$\succ_{cc}$'.*

Proof. From definition and the fact that $t\rho \sqsupseteq t$. □

Lemma 5. $t \cdot \sigma \succ_{tc} s \cdot id \Leftrightarrow t\sigma \succ_t s$.[1] *Analogously for '$\succ_{lc}$' and '$\succ_{cc}$'.*

Proof. For $t \cdot \sigma \succ_{tc} s \cdot id$ to hold, either $t\sigma \succ_t s$, or else $t\sigma = s$ but then $t \sqsupset s$ cannot hold. The $\Leftarrow$ direction follows from the definition. □

Lemma 6. *'$\succ_{tc}$' has the following property: $l \succ_t r \Rightarrow s[l] \cdot \theta \succ_{tc} s[l \mapsto r] \cdot \theta$. Analogously for '$\succ_{lc}$' and '$\succ_{cc}$'.*

Proof. For '$\succ_{tc}$': let $l \succ_t r$. By the fact that '$\succ_t$' is a rewrite relation, we have $l \succ_t r \Rightarrow s[l] \succ_t s[l \mapsto r] \Rightarrow s[l]\theta \succ_t s[l \mapsto r]\theta$. Then, by the definition of '$\succ_{tc}$', $s[l] \cdot \theta \succ_{tc} s[l \mapsto r] \cdot \theta$. For '$\succ_{lc}$' and '$\succ_{cc}$': by the above and by their definitions we have that the analogous properties also hold. □

Sometimes we will drop subscripts and use just '$\succ$' when it is obvious from the context: term, literals and clauses will be compared with '$\succ_t$', '$\succ_l$', '$\succ_c$' respectively, and corresponding closures with '$\succ_{tc}$', '$\succ_{lc}$', '$\succ_{cc}$'.

3 Model Construction

The superposition calculus comprises the following inference rules.

$$\text{Superposition} \qquad \frac{\underline{l \approx r} \vee C \quad \underline{s[u] \,\dot{\approx}\, t} \vee D}{(s[u \mapsto r] \,\dot{\approx}\, t \vee C \vee D)\theta}, \qquad \begin{array}{l}\text{where } \theta = \text{mgu}(l, u),\\ l\theta \not\preceq r\theta,\ s\theta \not\preceq t\theta,\\ \text{and } s \text{ not a variable,}\end{array} \tag{5}$$

$$\text{Eq. Resolution} \qquad \frac{\underline{s \not\approx t} \vee C}{C\theta}, \qquad \text{where } \theta = \text{mgu}(s, t), \tag{6}$$

$$\text{Eq. Factoring} \qquad \frac{\underline{s \approx t} \vee \underline{s' \approx t'} \vee C}{(s \approx t \vee t \not\approx t' \vee C)\theta}, \qquad \begin{array}{l}\text{where } \theta = \text{mgu}(s, s'),\\ s\theta \not\preceq t\theta \text{ and } t\theta \not\preceq t'\theta,\end{array} \tag{7}$$

and the selection function (underlined) selects at least one negative, or else all maximal (wrt. '$\succ_t$') literals in the clause.

The superposition calculus is refutationally complete wrt. the standard notion of redundancy [4, 13]. In the following, we refine the standard redundancy to closure redundancy and prove completeness in this case.

[1] But not, in general, $s \cdot id \succ_{tc} t \cdot \sigma \Leftrightarrow s \succ_t t\sigma$, e.g. $f(a) \cdot id \succ_{tc} f(x) \cdot (x \mapsto a)$.

Closure Redundancy. Let $\mathrm{GInsts}(C) = \{C\theta \mid C\theta \text{ is ground}\}$. In the standard definition of redundancy, a clause C is redundant in a set S if all $C\theta \in \mathrm{GInsts}(C)$ follow from smaller ground instances in $\mathrm{GInsts}(S)$. Unfortunately, this standard notion of redundancy does not cover many simplifications such as AC normalisation and a large class of demodulations (which we discuss in Sect. 4).

By modifying the notion of ordering between ground instances, using '$\succ_{cc}$' rather than '$\succ_c$', we adapt this redundancy notion to a closure-based one, which allows for such simplifications. We then show that superposition is still complete wrt. these redundancy criterion.

A clause C is *closure redundant* in a set S if all $C \cdot \theta \in \mathrm{GClos}(C)$ follow from smaller ground closures in $\mathrm{GClos}(S)$ (i.e., for all $C \cdot \theta \in \mathrm{GClos}(C)$ there exists a set $G \subseteq \mathrm{GClos}(S)$ such that $G \models C \cdot \theta$ and $\forall\, D \cdot \rho \in G.\, D \cdot \rho \prec_{cc} C \cdot \sigma$).

Although the definition of closure redundancy looks similar to the standard definition, consider the following example showing differences between them.

Example 1. Consider unit clauses $S = \{f(x) \approx g(x), g(b) \approx b\}$ where $f(x) \succ g(x) \succ b$. Then $f(b) \approx b$ is not redundant in S, in the standard sense, as it does not follow from any smaller (wrt. '$\succ_c$') ground instances of clauses in S, (it does follow from instances $f(b) \approx g(b)$, $g(b) \approx b$, but the former is bigger than $f(b) \approx b$). However, it is closure redundant in S, since its only ground instance $(f(b) \approx b) \cdot id$ follows from the smaller (wrt. '$\succ_{cc}$') closure instances: $(f(x) \approx g(x)) \cdot (x \mapsto b)$ and $(g(b) \approx b) \cdot id$. In other words, the new redundancy criterion allows demodulation even when the smaller side of the equation we demodulate with is greater than the smaller side of the target equation, provided that the matching substitution is proper. As we will see in Sect. 4 this considerably simplifies the applicability condition on demodulation and more crucially when dealing with theories such as AC it allows to use AC axioms to normalise clauses when standard demodulation is not be applicable.

Likewise, we extend the standard notion of redundant inference. An inference $C_1, \ldots, C_n \vdash D$ is *closure redundant* in a set S if, for all $\theta \in \mathrm{GSubs}(C_1, \ldots, C_n, D)$, the closure $D \cdot \theta$ follows from closures in $\mathrm{GClos}(S)$ which are smaller wrt. '$\succ_{cc}$' than the maximal element of $\{C_1 \cdot \theta, \ldots, C_n \cdot \theta\}$.

Let us establish the following connection between closure redundant inferences and closure redundant clauses. An inference $C_1, \ldots, C_n \vdash D$ is *reductive* if for all $\theta \in \mathrm{GSubs}(C_1, \ldots, C_n, D)$ we have $D \cdot \theta \prec_{cc} \max\{C_1 \cdot \theta, \ldots, C_n \cdot \theta\}$.

Lemma 7. If the conclusion of a reductive inference is in S or is closure redundant in S, then the inference is closure redundant in S. □

A set of clauses S is *saturated up to closure redundancy* if any inference $C_1, \ldots, C_n \vdash D$ with premises in S, which are all not redundant in S, is closure redundant in S. In the sequel, we refer to the new notion of closure redundancy as simply "redundancy", when it is clear form the context.

Theorem 1. The superposition inference system is refutationally complete wrt. closure redundancy, that is, if a set of clauses is saturated up to closure redundancy and does not contain the empty clause $\bot$, then it is satisfiable.

Proof. Let N be a set of clauses such that $\bot \notin N$, and $G = \text{GClos}(N)$. Let us assume N is saturated up to closure redundancy. We will build a model for G, and hence for N, as follows. A model is represented by a convergent term rewrite system (we will show convergence in Lemma 8), where a closure $C \cdot \theta$ is true in a given model R if at least one of its positive literals $(s \approx t) \cdot \theta$ has $s\theta \downarrow_R t\theta$, or if at least one of its negative literals $(s \not\approx t) \cdot \theta$ has $s\theta \not\downarrow_R t\theta$.

For each closure $C \cdot \theta \in G$, the partial model $R_{C\cdot\theta}$ is a rewrite system defined as $\bigcup_{D\cdot\sigma \prec_{cc} C\cdot\theta} \epsilon_{D\cdot\sigma}$. The total model R_∞ is thus $\bigcup_{D\cdot\sigma\in G} \epsilon_{D\cdot\sigma}$. For each $C \cdot \theta \in G$, the set $\epsilon_{C\cdot\theta}$ is defined recursively over $\prec_{cc}$ as follows. If:

$$
\begin{array}{l}
\text{a. } C \cdot \theta \text{ is false in } R_{C\cdot\theta}, \\
\text{b. } l\theta \approx r\theta \text{ strictly maximal in } C\theta, \\
\text{c. } l\theta \succ_t r\theta, \\
\text{d. } C \cdot \theta \setminus \{(l \approx r) \cdot \theta\} \text{ is false in } R_{C\cdot\theta} \cup \{l\theta \to r\theta\}, \\
\text{e. } l\theta \text{ is irreducible via } R_{C\cdot\theta},
\end{array}
\qquad (8)
$$

then $\epsilon_{C\cdot\theta} = \{l\theta \to r\theta\}$ and the closure is called *productive*, otherwise $\epsilon_{C\cdot\theta} = \emptyset$. Let also $R^{C\cdot\theta}$ be $R_{C\cdot\theta} \cup \epsilon_{C\cdot\theta}$.

Our goal is to show that R_∞ is a model for G. We will prove this by contradiction: if this is not the case, then there is a minimal (wrt. '$\succ_{cc}$') closure $C \cdot \theta$ such that $R_\infty \not\models C \cdot \theta$. We will show by case analysis how the existence of this closure leads to a contradiction, if the set is saturated up to redundancy. First, some lemmas.

Lemma 8. R_∞ and all $R_{C\cdot\theta}$ are convergent, i.e. terminating and confluent.

Proof. It is terminating since the rewrite relation is contained in $\succ_t$, which is well-founded. For confluence it is sufficient to show that left hand sides of rules in R_∞ are irreducible in R_∞. Assume that $l \to r$ and $l' \to r'$ are two rules produced by closures $C \cdot \theta$ and $D \cdot \sigma$ respectively. Assume l is reducible by $l' \to r'$. Then $l \trianglerighteq l'$, and since $\succ_t$ is a simplification order, then $l \succeq_t l'$. If $l \succ_t l'$ then by (8b) and (8c) we have $l \succ_t$ all terms in $D\sigma$, therefore all literal closures in $D\sigma \cdot id$ will be smaller than the literal closure in $C \cdot \theta$ which produced $l \to r$ (by Lemma 5), therefore $C \cdot \theta \succ_{cc} D\sigma \cdot id \succeq_{cc} D \cdot \sigma$ (see Lemma 4). But then $C \cdot \theta$ could not be productive due to (8e). If $l = l'$ then both rules can reduce each other, and again due to (8e) whichever closure is larger would not be productive. In either case we obtain a contradiction. □

Lemma 9. If $R^{C\cdot\theta} \models C \cdot \theta$, then $R_{D\cdot\sigma} \models C \cdot \theta$ for any $D \cdot \sigma \succ_{cc} C \cdot \theta$, and $R_\infty \models C \cdot \theta$.

Proof. If a positive literal $s \approx t$ of $C\theta$ is true in $R^{C\cdot\theta}$, then $s \downarrow_{R^{C\cdot\theta}} t$. Since no rules are ever removed during the model construction, then $s \downarrow_{R_{D\cdot\sigma}} t$ and $s \downarrow_{R_\infty} t$.

If a negative literal $(s \not\approx t) \cdot \theta$ of $C \cdot \theta$ is true in $R^{C\cdot\theta}$, then $s\theta \not\downarrow_{R^{C\cdot\theta}} t\theta$. Wlog. assume that $s\theta \succ_t t\theta$. Consider a productive closure $D \cdot \sigma \succ_{cc} C \cdot \theta$ that produced a rule $l\sigma \to r\sigma$. Let us show that $l\sigma \to r\sigma$ cannot reduce $s\theta \not\approx t\theta$. Assume otherwise. By (8b), $l\sigma \approx r\sigma$ is strictly maximal in $D\sigma$, so if $l\sigma \to r\sigma$ reduces either $t\theta$ or a strict subterm of $s\theta$, meaning $l\sigma \prec_t s\theta$, then clearly $s\theta \succ_t$ all terms in $D\sigma$, therefore $(s \not\approx t)\theta \cdot id \succeq_{lc} (s \not\approx t) \cdot \theta \succ_{lc}$ all literals in $D\sigma \cdot id \succeq_{lc}$ respective literals in $D \cdot \sigma$ (Lemmas 4 and 5), which contradicts $D \cdot \sigma \succ_{cc} C \cdot \theta$ regardless of whether any of them is unit. If $l\sigma = s\theta$, then $M_{lc}((s \not\approx t) \cdot \theta) = \{s \cdot \theta, t \cdot \theta, s\theta \cdot id, t\theta \cdot id\} \not\succ_{tc} \{l\sigma \cdot id, r\sigma \cdot id\} = M_{lc}((l \approx r)\sigma \cdot id)$, since $s\theta = l\sigma \succ_t t\sigma$ implies $s\theta \cdot id = l\sigma \cdot id$, and $s \cdot \theta \succ_{tc} r\sigma \cdot id$. Hence, by Lemma 4, $(s \not\approx t)\theta \cdot id \succeq_{lc} (s \not\approx t) \cdot \theta \succ_{lc} (l \approx r)\sigma \cdot id \succeq_{lc} (l \approx r) \cdot \sigma$, contradicting $D \cdot \sigma \succ_{cc} C \cdot \theta$ (again regardless of either of them being a unit). □

Lemma 10. *If $C \cdot \theta = (C' \vee l \approx r) \cdot \theta$ is productive, then $R_{D \cdot \sigma} \not\models C' \cdot \theta$ for any $D \cdot \sigma \succ_{cc} C \cdot \theta$, and $R_\infty \not\models C' \cdot \theta$.*

Proof. All literals in $C' \cdot \theta$ are false in $R^{C \cdot \theta}$ by (8d). For all negative literals $(s \not\approx t) \cdot \theta$ in $C' \cdot \theta$, if they are false then $s\theta \downarrow_{R^{C \cdot \theta}} t\theta$. Since no rules are ever removed during the model construction then $s\theta \downarrow_{R_{D \cdot \sigma}} t\theta$ and $s\theta \downarrow_{R_\infty} t\theta$.

For all positive literals $(s \approx t) \cdot \theta$ in $C' \cdot \theta$, if they are false in $R^{C \cdot \theta}$ then $s\theta \not\downarrow_{R^{C \cdot \theta}} t\theta$. Two cases arise. If $C \cdot \theta$ is unit, then $C' = \emptyset$, so $C' \cdot \theta$ is trivially false in any interpretation. If $C \cdot \theta$ is nonunit, then consider any productive closure $D \cdot \sigma \succ_{cc} C \cdot \theta$ that produces a rule $l'\sigma \to r'\sigma$, by definition $D \cdot \sigma \succ_{cc} C\theta \cdot id$ and by Lemma 5 $D\sigma \succ_c C\theta$. Since $l\theta \approx r\theta$ is strictly maximal in $C\theta$ then $l'\sigma \succ l\theta \succ$ any term in $C\theta$. Therefore $l'\sigma \to r'\sigma$ cannot reduce $s\theta$ or $t\theta$. □

We are now ready to prove the main proposition by induction on closures (see Lemma 1), namely that for all $C \cdot \theta \in G$ we have $R_\infty \models C \cdot \theta$. We will show a stronger result: that for all $C \cdot \theta \in G$ we have $R^{C \cdot \theta} \models C \cdot \theta$ (the former result follows from the latter by Lemma 9). If this is not the case, then there exists a minimal counterexample $C \cdot \theta \in G$ which is false in $R^{C \cdot \theta}$.

Notice that, since by induction hypothesis all closures $D \cdot \sigma \in G$ such that $D \cdot \sigma \prec_{cc} C \cdot \theta$ have $R^{D \cdot \sigma} \models D \cdot \sigma$, then by Lemma 9 we have $R_{C \cdot \theta} \models D \cdot \sigma$ (and $R^{C \cdot \theta} \models D \cdot \sigma$). Consider the following cases.

Case 1. *C is redundant.*

Proof. By definition, $C \cdot \theta$ follows from smaller closures in G. But if $C \cdot \theta$ is the minimal closure which is false in $R^{C \cdot \theta}$, then all smaller $D \cdot \sigma$ are true in $R^{D \cdot \sigma}$, which (as noted above) means that all smaller $D \cdot \sigma$ are true in $R_{C \cdot \theta}$, which means $C \cdot \theta$ is true in $R_{C \cdot \theta}$, which is a contradiction. □

Case 2. *C contains a variable x such that $x\theta$ is reducible.*

Proof. Then $R^{C \cdot \theta}$ contains a rule which reduces $x\theta$ to a term t. Let θ' be identical to θ except that it maps x to t. Then $C\theta' \prec C\theta$, so $C \cdot \theta' \prec C \cdot \theta$ (see Lemma 3), and therefore $C \cdot \theta'$ is true in $R_{C \cdot \theta}$. But $C \cdot \theta'$ is true in $R^{C \cdot \theta}$ iff $C \cdot \theta$ in $R^{C \cdot \theta}$, since $x\theta \downarrow_{R^{C \cdot \theta}} t$, therefore $C \cdot \theta$ is also true in $R^{C \cdot \theta}$, which is a contradiction. □

Case 3. *There is reductive inference $C, C_1, \ldots \vdash D$ which is redundant, such that $\{C, C_1, \ldots\} \subseteq N$, $C \cdot \theta$ is maximal in $\{C \cdot \theta\ , C_1 \cdot \theta\ , \ldots\}$, and $D \cdot \theta \models C \cdot \theta$.*

Proof. Then $D \cdot \theta$ is implied by closures in G smaller than $C \cdot \theta$. But since those closures are true in $R^{C \cdot \theta}$, then $D \cdot \theta$ is true, and since $D \cdot \theta$ implies $C \cdot \theta$, then $C \cdot \theta$ is true in $R^{C \cdot \theta}$, which is a contradiction. □

Case 4. Neither of the previous cases apply, and C contains a *negative* literal which is selected in the clause, i.e., $C \cdot \theta = (C' \vee s \not\approx t) \cdot \theta$ with $s \not\approx t$ selected in C.

Proof. Then either $s\theta \not\downarrow_{R_{C \cdot \theta}} t\theta$ and $C \cdot \theta$ is true and we are done, or else $s\theta \downarrow_{R_{C \cdot \theta}} t\theta$. Wlog., let us assume $s\theta \succeq t\theta$.

Subcase 4.1. $s\theta = t\theta$.

Proof. Then s and t are unifiable, meaning that there is an equality resolution inference

$$C' \vee s \not\approx t \vdash C'\sigma, \quad \text{with } \sigma = \text{mgu}(s, t), \tag{9}$$

with premise in N.

Take the instance $C'\sigma \cdot \rho$ of the conclusion such that $\sigma\rho = \theta$; it always exists since $\sigma = \text{mgu}(s, t)$. Also, since the mgu is idempotent [2] then $\sigma\theta = \sigma\sigma\rho = \sigma\rho$, so $C'\sigma \cdot \rho = C'\sigma \cdot \theta$. We show that $C \cdot \theta = (C' \vee s \not\approx t) \cdot \sigma\rho \succ C'\sigma \cdot \rho = C'\sigma \cdot \theta$. If C' is empty, then this is trivial. If C' has more than 1 element, then this is also trivial (see Lemma 2). If C' has exactly 1 element, then let $C' = \{s' \mathrel{\dot{\approx}} t'\}$. We have $(s' \mathrel{\dot{\approx}} t' \vee s \not\approx t) \cdot \sigma\rho \succ (s' \mathrel{\dot{\approx}} t')\sigma \cdot \rho$ if $(s' \mathrel{\dot{\approx}} t')\sigma\rho \cdot id \succeq (s' \mathrel{\dot{\approx}} t')\sigma \cdot \rho$, which is true by Lemma 4. Notice also that if $C'\sigma \cdot \rho$ is true then $(C' \vee \cdots) \cdot \sigma\rho$ must also be true.

Recall that Case 3 does not apply. But we have shown that this inference is reductive, with $C \in N$, $C \cdot \theta$ trivially maximal in $\{C \cdot \theta\}$, and that the instance $C'\sigma \cdot \theta$ of the conclusion implies $C \cdot \theta$. So for Case 3 not to apply the inference must be non-redundant. Also since Case 1 doesn't apply then the premise is not redundant. This means that the set is not saturated, which is a contradiction. □

Subcase 4.2. $s\theta \succ t\theta$.

Proof. Then (recall that $s\theta \downarrow_{R_{C \cdot \theta}} t\theta$) $s\theta$ must be reducible by some rule in $R^{C \cdot \theta}$. Since by (8b) the clause cannot be productive, it must be reducible by some rule in $R_{C \cdot \theta}$. Let us say that this rule is $l\theta \to r\theta$, produced by a closure $D \cdot \theta$ smaller than $C \cdot \theta$.[2] Therefore closure $D \cdot \theta$ must be of the form $(D' \vee l \approx r) \cdot \theta$, with $l\theta \approx r\theta$ maximal in $D\theta$, and $D' \cdot \theta$ false in $R_{D \cdot \theta}$. Also note that $D \cdot \theta$ cannot be redundant, or else it would follow from smaller closures, but those closures (which are smaller than $D \cdot \theta$ and therefore smaller than $C \cdot \theta$) would be true, so $D \cdot \theta$ would be also true in $R_{D \cdot \theta}$, so by (8a) it would not be productive.

Then $l\theta = u\theta$ for some subterm u of s, meaning l is unifiable with u, meaning there exists a superposition inference

$$D' \vee l \approx r\,,\, C' \vee s[u] \not\approx t \vdash (D' \vee C' \vee s[u \mapsto r] \not\approx t)\sigma, \quad \sigma = \text{mgu}(l, u), \tag{10}$$

[2] We can use the same substitution θ on both C and D by simply assuming wlog. that they have no variables in common.

Similar to what we did before, consider the instance $(D' \vee C' \vee s[u \mapsto r] \not\approx t)\sigma \cdot \rho$ with $\sigma\rho = \theta$.[3] We wish to show that this instance of the conclusion is smaller than $C \cdot \theta$ (an instance of the second premise), that is that

$$(C' \vee s \not\approx t) \cdot \sigma\rho \succ (D' \vee C' \vee s[u \mapsto r] \not\approx t)\sigma \cdot \rho. \quad (11)$$

Several cases arise:

- $C' \neq \emptyset$. Then both premise and conclusion are non-unit, so comparing them means comparing $C'\theta \vee s\theta \not\approx t\theta$ and $D'\theta \vee C'\theta \vee s\theta[u\theta \mapsto r\theta] \not\approx t\theta$ (Lemma 2), or after removing common elements, comparing $s\theta \not\approx t\theta$ and $D'\theta \vee s\theta[u\theta \mapsto r\theta] \not\approx t\theta$. This is true since (i) $l\theta \succ r\theta \Rightarrow s\theta[l\theta] \succ s\theta[l\theta \mapsto r\theta] \Rightarrow s\theta \not\approx t\theta \succ s\theta[l\theta \mapsto r\theta] \not\approx t\theta$, and (ii) $s\theta \succeq l\theta \succ r\theta$ and $l\theta \approx r\theta$ is greater than all literals in $D'\theta$, so $s\theta \not\approx t\theta$ is greater than all literals in $D'\theta$.
- $C' = \emptyset$ and $D' \neq \emptyset$. Then we need $(s \not\approx t) \cdot \sigma\rho \succ (D' \vee s[u \mapsto r] \not\approx t)\sigma\rho \cdot id$. By Lemma 5, this is true only if $s\theta \not\approx t\theta \succ D'\theta \vee s\theta[u\theta \mapsto r\theta] \not\approx t\theta$. To see that this is true we must also notice that, since $D \cdot \theta \prec C \cdot \theta$, then (again by Lemma 5) $D'\theta \vee l\theta \approx r\theta \prec s\theta \not\approx t\theta$ must also hold, so $\{s\theta \not\approx t\theta\} \succ D'\theta$. Then obviously $\{s\theta \not\approx t\theta\} \succ \{s\theta[u\theta \mapsto r\theta] \not\approx t\theta\}$.
- $C' = \emptyset$ and $D' = \emptyset$. Then simply $s\theta[u\theta] \succ s\theta[u\theta \mapsto r\theta]$ means $s[u] \cdot \sigma\rho \succ s[u \mapsto r]\sigma \cdot \rho$, which since $s\sigma\rho \succ t\sigma\rho$, means $(s[u] \not\approx t) \cdot \sigma\rho \succ (s[u \mapsto r] \not\approx t)\sigma \cdot \rho$.

In all these cases this instance of the conclusion is always smaller than the instance $C \cdot \theta$ of the second premise. Note also that $C \cdot \theta$ is maximal in $\{C \cdot \theta, D \cdot \theta\}$. Also, since $D' \cdot \theta$ is false in $R_{C \cdot \theta}$ (by Lemma 10) and $(s[u \mapsto r] \not\approx t) \cdot \theta$ is false in $R_{C \cdot \theta}$ (since $(s \not\approx t) \cdot \theta$ is in the false closure $C \cdot \theta$, $u\theta \downarrow_{R_{C \cdot \theta}} r\theta$, and the rewrite system is confluent), then in order for that instance of the conclusion to be true in $R_{C \cdot \theta}$ it must be the case that $C'\sigma \cdot \rho$ is true in $R_{C \cdot \theta}$. But if the latter is true then $C \cdot \theta = (C' \vee \cdots) \cdot \sigma\rho$ is true, in $R_{C \cdot \theta}$. In other words that instance of the conclusion implies $C \cdot \theta$. Therefore again, since Case 1 and Case 3 don't apply, we conclude that the inference is non-redundant with non-redundant premises, so the set is not saturated, which is a contradiction. □

This proves all subcases. □

Case 5. Neither of the previous cases apply, so all selected literals in C are positive, i.e., $C \cdot \theta = (C' \vee s \approx t) \cdot \theta$ with $s \approx t$ selected in C.

Proof. Then, since if the selection function doesn't select a negative literal then it must select all maximal ones, wlog. one of the selected literals $s \approx t$ must have $s\theta \approx t\theta$ is maximal in $C\theta$. Then if either $C' \cdot \theta$ is true in $R_{C \cdot \theta}$, or $\epsilon_{C \cdot \theta} = \{s\theta \to t\theta\}$, or $s\theta = t\theta$, then $C \cdot \theta$ is true in $R^{C \cdot \theta}$ and we are done. Otherwise, $\epsilon_{C \cdot \theta} = \emptyset$, $C' \cdot \theta$ is false in $R_{C \cdot \theta}$, and wlog. $s\theta \succ t\theta$. If $s \approx t$ is maximal in C then $s\theta \approx t\theta$ is maximal in $C\theta$.

---

[3] And again note that the mgu σ is idempotent so $(D' \vee C' \vee s[u \mapsto r] \not\approx t)\sigma \cdot \rho = (D' \vee C' \vee s[u \mapsto r] \not\approx t)\sigma \cdot \theta$.

Subcase 5.1. $s\theta \approx t\theta$ maximal but not strictly maximal in $C\theta$.

Proof. If this is the case, then there is at least one other maximal positive literal in the clause. Let $C \cdot \theta = (C'' \vee s \approx t \vee s' \approx t') \cdot \theta$, where $s\theta = s'\theta$ and $t\theta = t'\theta$. Therefore s and s' are unifiable and there is an equality factoring inference:

$$C'' \vee s \approx t \vee s' \approx t' \vdash (C'' \vee s \approx t \vee t \not\approx t')\sigma, \quad \text{with } \sigma = \text{mgu}(s, s'), \tag{12}$$

with $\sigma = \text{mgu}(s, s')$. Take the instance of the conclusion $(C'' \vee s \approx t \vee t \not\approx t')\sigma \cdot \rho$ with $\sigma\rho = \theta$. This is smaller than $C \cdot \theta$ (since $s'\theta \approx t'\theta \succ t\theta \not\approx t'\theta$, and Lemma 2 applies). Since $t\theta = t'\theta$ and $C''\sigma \cdot \rho$ is false in $R_{C\cdot\theta}$, this instance of the conclusion is true in $R_{C\cdot\theta}$ iff $(s\sigma \approx t\sigma) \cdot \rho$ is true in $R_{C\cdot\theta}$. But if the latter is true in $R_{C\cdot\theta}$ then $(s \approx t \vee \cdots) \cdot \sigma\rho$ also is. Therefore that instance of the conclusion implies $C \cdot \theta$. As such, and since again Cases 1 and 3 do not apply, we have a contradiction. □

Subcase 5.2. $s\theta \approx t\theta$ strictly maximal in $C\theta$, and $s\theta$ reducible (in $R_{C\cdot\theta}$).

Proof. This is similar to Subcase 4.2. If $s\theta$ is reducible, say by a rule $l\theta \rightarrow r\theta$, then (since $\epsilon_{C\cdot\theta} = \emptyset$) this is produced by some closure $D \cdot \theta$ smaller than $C \cdot \theta$, with $D \cdot \theta = (D' \vee l \approx r) \cdot \theta$, with the $l\theta \approx r\theta$ maximal in $D\theta$, and with $D' \cdot \theta$ false in $R_{D\cdot\theta}$.

Then there is a superposition inference

$$D' \vee l \approx r \,,\, C \vee s[u] \approx t \vdash (D' \vee C' \vee s[u \mapsto r] \approx t)\sigma, \quad \sigma = \text{mgu}(l, u), \tag{13}$$

Again taking the instance $(D' \vee C' \vee s[u \mapsto r] \approx t)\sigma \cdot \rho$ with $\sigma\rho = \theta$, we see that it is smaller than $C \cdot \theta$ (see discussion in Subcase 4.2). Furthermore since $D' \cdot \theta$ and $C' \cdot \theta$ are false in $R_{C\cdot\theta}$, then that instance of the conclusion is true in $R_{C\cdot\theta}$ iff $(s[u \mapsto r] \approx t)\sigma \cdot \rho$ is. But since also $u\theta \downarrow_{R_{C\cdot\theta}} r\theta$, then $(s[u \mapsto r] \approx t)\sigma \cdot \rho$ implies $(s[u] \approx t)\sigma \cdot \rho$. Therefore that instance of the conclusion implies $C \cdot \theta$. Again this means we have a contradiction. □

Subcase 5.3. $s\theta \approx t\theta$ strictly maximal in $C\theta$, and $s\theta$ irreducible (in $R_{C\cdot\theta}$).

Proof. Since $C \cdot \theta$ is not productive, and at the same time all criteria in (8) except (8d) are satisfied, it must be that (8d) is not, that is $C' \cdot \theta$ must be true in $R^{C\cdot\theta} = R_{C\cdot\theta} \cup \{s\theta \rightarrow t\theta\}$. Then this must mean we can write $C' \cdot \theta = (C'' \vee s' \approx t') \cdot \theta$, where the latter literal is the one that becomes true with the addition of $\{s\theta \rightarrow t\theta\}$, whereas without that rule it was false.

But this means that $s'\theta \downarrow_{R^{C\cdot\theta}} t'\theta$ such that any rewrite proof needs at least one step where $s\theta \rightarrow t\theta$ is used, since $s\theta$ is irreducible by $R_{C\cdot\theta}$. Wlog. say $s'\theta \succ t'\theta$. Since: (i) $s\theta \approx t\theta \succ s'\theta \approx t'\theta$, (ii) $s\theta \succ t\theta$, and (iii) $s'\theta \succ t'\theta$, then $s\theta \succeq s'\theta \succ t'\theta$, which implies $t'\theta \not\succeq s\theta$, which implies $s\theta \rightarrow t\theta$ can not be used to reduce $t'\theta$. Then the only way it can reduce $s'\theta$ or $t'\theta$ is if $s\theta = s'\theta$. This means there is an equality factoring inference:

$$C'' \vee s' \approx t' \vee s \approx t \vdash (C'' \vee s' \approx t' \vee t \not\approx t')\sigma, \quad \text{with } \sigma = \text{mgu}(s, s'). \tag{14}$$

Taking $\theta = \sigma\rho$, we see that the instance of the conclusion $(C'' \vee t \not\approx t' \vee s \approx t)$ $\sigma \cdot \rho$ is smaller than the instance of the $(C'' \vee s' \approx t' \vee s \approx t) \cdot \sigma\rho$.

But we have said that $s'\theta \downarrow_{R^{C \cdot \theta}} t'\theta$, where the first rewrite step had to take place by rewriting $s'\theta = s\theta \to t\theta$, and the rest of the rewrite proof then had to use only rules from $R_{C \cdot \theta}$. In other words, this means $t\theta \downarrow_{R_{C \cdot \theta}} t'\theta$. As such, the literal $(t \not\approx t') \cdot \theta$ is false in $R_{C \cdot \theta}$, and so the conclusion is true in $R_{C \cdot \theta}$ iff rest of the closure is true in $R_{C \cdot \theta}$. But if the rest of the closure $(C'' \vee s' \approx t')\sigma \cdot \rho$ then so is $C \cdot \theta$, so that instance of the conclusion implies $C \cdot \theta$. Once again, this leads to a contradiction since none Cases 1 and 3 apply and therefore the set must not be saturated. □

This proves all the subcases and the theorem. □

Remark: As part of this proof we have also shown that all inferences in the superposition system are reductive, so per Lemma 7 one way to make inferences redundant is simply to add the conclusion.

4 Redundancies

Now we will show three novel redundancy criteria whose proof is enabled by the framework we have just discussed. One is an extension of the demodulation rule, used in many different provers.

Demodulation

Recall the "standard" demodulation rule (a struck clause means that it can be removed from the set when the conclusion is added).

$$\text{Demodulation} \quad \frac{l \approx r \quad \cancel{C[l\theta]}}{C[l\theta \mapsto r\theta]}, \quad \begin{array}{l}\text{where } l\theta \succ r\theta \\ \text{and } \{l\theta \approx r\theta\} \prec C[l\theta].\end{array} \tag{15}$$

We show an extension which is also a redundancy in this framework.

$$\begin{array}{l}\text{Encompassment} \\ \text{Demodulation}\end{array} \quad \frac{l \approx r \quad \cancel{C[l\theta]}}{C[l\theta \mapsto r\theta]}, \quad \begin{array}{l}\text{where } l\theta \succ r\theta\text{, and} \\ \text{either } \{l\theta \approx r\theta\} \prec C[l\theta] \\ \text{or } l\theta \sqsupset l.\end{array} \tag{16}$$

Theorem 2. Encompassment demodulation is a sound and admissible simplification rule wrt. closure redundancy (a redundancy criterion is admissible if its struck premises are redundant wrt. the conclusion and the non-struck premises).

Proof. The proof can be found in the full version [8]. □

This theorem has many practical implications. Demodulation is widely used in superposition theorem provers, and improvement this criterion provides are two-fold.

First, it enables strictly more simplifying inferences to be performed where they previously could not. Let us re-consider Example 1 from Sect. 3. Standard demodulation is not applicable to $f(b)\approx b$ by clauses in $S = \{f(x)\approx g(x), g(b)\approx b\}$. However, we can simplify it to a tautology and remove it completely using encompassment demodulation. Our experimental results (Sect. 5) show that encompassment demodulation extends usual demodulation in many practical problems.

Second, it enables a faster way to check the applicability conditions. One of the considerable overheads in the standard demodulation is to check that the equation we are simplifying with is smaller than the clause we are simplifying. For this, right-hand side of the oriented equation needs to be compared in the ordering with all top terms in the clause. In the encompassment demodulation this expensive check is avoided in many cases. After obtaining the matching instantiation θ of the left side of the oriented equation, if it is not a renaming (a quick check) or the matching is strictly below the top position of the term, then we can immediately accept the inference and skip potentially expensive ordering checks.

Associative-Commutative Joinability

Let AC_f be

$$f(x, y) \approx f(y, x), \tag{17a}$$

$$f(x, f(y, z)) \approx f(f(x, y), z), \tag{17b}$$

$$f(x, f(y, z)) \approx f(y, f(x, z)). \tag{17c}$$

The first two axioms (17a) and (17b) define that f is an associative-commutative (AC) symbol. The third equation (17c) follows from those two and will be used to avoid any inferences between these axioms and more generally to justify AC joinability simplifications defined next.

We define the two following rules:

$$\text{AC joinability (pos)} \quad \frac{\cancel{s \approx t \vee C} \quad AC_f}{}, \quad \text{where } s \downarrow_{AC_f} t, \; s \approx t \vee C \text{ not in } AC_f, \tag{18a}$$

$$\text{AC joinability (neg)} \quad \frac{\cancel{s \not\approx t \vee C} \quad AC_f}{C}, \quad \text{where } s \downarrow_{AC_f} t, \tag{18b}$$

Theorem 3. AC joinability rules are sound and admissible simplification rules wrt. closure redundancy.

Proof. Let us prove rule (18a). We will show how, if $s \downarrow_{AC_f} t$, then all ground instances $(s \approx t) \cdot \theta$ are rewritable, via smaller instances of clauses in AC_f, to a smaller tautology or to a smaller instance of clauses in AC_f, meaning that $s \approx t$ is redundant wrt. closure redundancy. Using closure redundancy is essential, as instances of AC_f axioms used in the following rewriting process can be bigger than the clause we are simplifying in the usual term ordering, but as we will see they are smaller in the closure ordering.

For conciseness, let us denote $f(a, b)$ by ab in the sequel. We will assume that the term ordering has following properties: if $s \succ_t t$ then $st \succ_t ts$ and $s(tu) \succ_t t(su)$, and also that $(xy)z \succ_t x(yz)$. This conditions hold for most commonly used families of orderings, such as KBO or LPO [2].

First some definitions. Let subterms_f collect all "consecutive" f-subterms into a multiset, that is

$$\begin{aligned} &\text{if } u = f(s,t): && \text{subterms}_f(u) = \text{subterms}_f(s) \cup \text{subterms}_f(t), && \text{(19a)} \\ &\text{otherwise:} && \text{subterms}_f(u) = u. && \text{(19b)} \end{aligned}$$

so for example $\text{subterms}_f(a((bc)d)) = \{a, b, c, d\}$. Let us define sort_f as follows:

$$\text{sort}_f(u) = u''_1(\cdots u''_n), \quad \begin{array}{l} \text{where } \{u_1, \ldots, u_n\} = \text{subterms}_f(u) \\ \text{and } u'_i = \text{sort}_f(u_i) \\ \text{and } \{u''_1, \ldots\} = \{u'_1, \ldots\}, \\ \text{and } u''_1 \prec \cdots \prec u''_n. \end{array} \quad (20)$$

such that for example if $a \prec b \prec c$ then $\text{sort}_f(\,(ba)(g(cb))\,) = a(b(g(bc)))$. Note that we have $s \downarrow_{AC_f} t \Rightarrow \forall\theta \in \text{GSubs}(s,t).\ s\theta \downarrow_{AC_f} t\theta$, and $s \downarrow_{AC_f} t \Leftrightarrow \text{sort}_f(s) = \text{sort}_f(t)$. Therefore we will now show how, if $s \downarrow_{AC_f} t$, then for any ground instance $(s \approx t) \cdot \theta$, the closure $(s' \approx t') \cdot \theta$, with $s'\theta = \text{sort}_f(s\theta) = \text{sort}_f(t\theta) = t'\theta$, is either an instance of AC_f or a tautology, implied by smaller instances of clauses from AC_f.

For the cases where $|\text{subterms}_f(s)|$ is 1, 2, or 3, ad-hoc proofs are required. In the full version [8] we give such proofs for all cases with $\text{subterms}_f(s) = \{x\}$, $\{x, y\}$, and $\{x, y, z\}$. Then by Lemma 4 all cases with $|\text{subterms}(s)| \leq 3$ follow, since they will be an (equal or more specific) instance of some such case.

For the cases with $|\text{subterms}_f(s)| \geq 4$, consider any ground instance $(s \approx t) \cdot \theta$. First, exhaustively apply the rule $(xy)z \to x(yz)$ on all subterms of $s \approx t$. Since $(xy)z \succ x(yz)$, $s \succeq s'$ and $t \succeq t'$, then (Lemma 6) $(s \approx t) \cdot \theta \succeq (s' \approx t') \cdot \theta$. In order to show that $(s' \approx t') \cdot \theta$ and AC_f make $(s \approx t) \cdot \theta$ redundant, it remains to be shown that these rewrites were done by instances of (17b) which are also smaller than $(s \approx t) \cdot \theta$.

Since $|\text{subterms}_f(s)| \geq 4$, then any s or t where we can rewrite with $(xy)z \to x(yz)$ is in one of the following forms: (i) $(a_1a_2)(a_3a_4)$, in which case we can use an identical argument to encompassment demodulation since $(a_1a_2)(a_3a_4) \sqsupset (xy)z$, or (ii) a_1a_2 with the term being rewritten being a_2 or a subterm thereof, in which case the rewrite is also by a smaller instance.

After this, s' and t' are of the form $a_1(\cdots a_n)$. Now, since the closure is ground, for every adjacent pair of terms either $a_i\theta \prec a_{i+1}\theta$ or $a_i\theta \succ a_{i+1}\theta$ or $a_i\theta = a_{i+1}\theta$. This means we can always instantiate and apply one of (17a) or (17c) and "bubble sort" the AC terms until they become $a'_1(\cdots a'_n)$ with $a'_1\theta \prec \cdots \prec a'_n\theta$, where there is a bijection between $\{a_1, \ldots, a_n\}$ and $\{a'_1, \ldots, a'_n\}$, obtaining an $a'_1\theta(\cdots a'_n\theta) \preceq a_1\theta(\cdots a_n\theta)$.

Once again, these rewrites are done via smaller instances of AC_f, since we either rewrite with (17a) on a subterm, in the case of a_{n-1}/a_n, or with (17c) on a subterm, in the case of a_i/a_{i+1} with $2 \leq i \leq n-1$, or with (17c) on a less general term, in the case of a_1/a_2.

The process we have just described is done bottom-up on terms (meaning for instance $f(g(f(b,a)),c) \to f(g(f(a,b)),c) \to f(c,g(f(a,b))))$. Obviously, the rewrites on inner f-subterms are trivially done by smaller instances.

This concludes the process. Applying this on both sides yields the closure $(s' \approx t') \cdot \theta$ with $s'\theta = \mathrm{sort}_f(s\theta)$ and $t'\theta = \mathrm{sort}_f(t\theta)$, which we have shown is $\preceq (s \approx t) \cdot \theta$ and follows from it by smaller closures in $\mathrm{GClos}(AC_f)$. This can be done for all $\theta \in \mathrm{GSubs}(s,t)$. Thus $\mathrm{sort}_f(s,\theta) \approx \mathrm{sort}_f(t,\theta)$, a tautology, makes clause $s \approx t$ redundant, meaning any $s \approx t \vee C$ is redundant in AC_f. The same process proves rule (19a). □

AC Normalisation

We will now show some examples to motivate another simplification rule. Assume $a \prec b \prec c$. The demodulation rule already enables us to rewrite any occurrence of, for instance, $b(ca)$, or $(ac)b$ or any other such permutation, to $a(bc)$. However, take the term $b(xa)$. It cannot be simplified by demodulation. Yet it is easy to see that in any instance of a clause where it appears, it can be rewritten to a smaller $a(xb)$ via smaller instances of clauses in AC_f.

Such cases motivate the following simplification rule.[4]

$$\text{AC norm.} \quad \frac{\cancel{C[t_1(\cdots t_n)]} \quad AC_f}{C[t'_1(\cdots t'_n)]}, \quad \begin{array}{l}\text{where } t_1,\ldots,t_n \succ_{\mathrm{lex}} t'_1,\ldots,t'_n \\ \text{and } \{t_1,\ldots,t_n\} = \{t'_1,\ldots,t'_n\}\end{array} \tag{21}$$

Theorem 4. AC normalisation is a sound and admissible simplification rule wrt. closure redundancy.

Proof. The proof can be found in the full version [8]. □

In practice, this criterion can be implemented by applying the following function

$$\begin{aligned}\mathrm{norm}_f(s_1(\cdots s_n)) &= \begin{array}{l}\text{let } \mathrm{csort}_f(\mathrm{norm}_f(s_1),\ldots,\mathrm{norm}_f(s_n)) = (s'_1,\ldots,s'_n)\\ \text{in } s'_1(\cdots s'_n)\end{array}\\ \mathrm{norm}_f(g(t_1,\ldots,t_n)) &= g(\mathrm{norm}_f(t_1),\ldots,\mathrm{norm}_f(t_n)), \quad \text{if } g \neq f\end{aligned} \tag{22}$$

to all literals in the clause, where

$$\mathrm{csort}_f(s_1,\ldots,s_n) = \begin{cases} s_k +\!\!+ \, \mathrm{csort}^*_f(s_1,\ldots,s_n \setminus s_k) & \begin{array}{l}\text{if } \exists\, s_k \in \{s_1,\ldots,s_n\}.\ s_k \prec_t s_1\\ \text{and } s_k \text{ minimal in } \{s_1,\ldots,s_n\}\end{array}\\ s_1 +\!\!+ \, \mathrm{csort}_f(s_2,\ldots,s_n) & \text{otherwise}\end{cases} \tag{23}$$

and csort^*_f orders the list of terms using some total extension of the term ordering.

[4] Note we trivially assume all AC_f terms are right associative, since $(xy)z \to x(yz)$ is always oriented.

Some examples, assume $g(\ldots) \succ b \succ a$:

$$b(xa) \to a(xb) \tag{24a}$$
$$x(ba) \to x(ab) \tag{24b}$$
$$g(x)\,(ax) \to a(x\,g(x)) \tag{24c}$$
$$g(bx)\,g(ba) \to g(ab)\,g(bx) \tag{24d}$$

note the rhs may not be unique (e.g. in the first and third), since we are free to extend the term ordering in any (consistent) way.

The main advantages of applying this simplification rule are

- Strictly more redundant clauses found. For example, in the set $\{a(bx), a(xb), x(ab), b(xa), b(ax), x(ba)\}$, the latter three are redundant, instead of only the latter one.
- Faster implementation. Even for simplifications that were already allowed by demodulation, we avoid the work of searching in indices and instantiating the axioms to perform the rewrites. Also, we can avoid storing AC_f in the demodulation indices entirely. Since (17a) matches with all f-terms, and (17c) with all f-terms with 3 or more elements, this makes all queries on those indices faster.

5 Experimental Results

We implemented the simplifications developed in this paper – encompassment demodulation, AC joinability and AC normalisation – in a theorem prover for first-order logic, iProver [7,9].[5] iProver combines superposition with Inst-Gen and resolution calculi. For superposition iProver implements a range of simplifications including demodulation, light normalisation, subsumption and subsumption resolution. We run our experiments over FOF problems of the TPTP v7.4 library [16] (17 053 problems) on a cluster of Linux servers with 3 GHz 11 cores AMD CPUs, 128 GB memory, each problem was running on a single core with time limit 300 s.

In total iProver solved 10 358 problems. Encompassment demodulation (excluding cases when usual demodulation is applicable) was used in 7283 problems, ≥1000 times in 2343 problems, ≥10 000 in 1018 problems, and ≥100 000 in 272 problems. This is in addition to other places where usual demodulation is valid but an expensive ordering check is skipped.

There are 1366 problems containing 1 to 6 AC symbols, as detected by iProver. AC normalisation was applied in 1327 of these: ≥1000 times in 1047 problems, ≥10 000 times in 757 problems; and ≥100 000 times in 565 problems. AC joinability was applied in 1138 problems: ≥1000 times in 646, ≥10 000 times in 255 problems. We can conclude that new simplifications described in this paper were applicable in a large number of problems and were used many times.

[5] iProver is available at http://www.cs.man.ac.uk/~korovink/iprover.

6 Conclusion and Future Work

In this paper we extended the AC joinability criterion to the superposition calculus for full first-order logic. For this we introduced a new closure-based redundancy criterion and proved that it preserves completeness. Using this criterion we proved that AC joinability and AC normalisation simplifications preserve completeness of the superposition calculus. Using these results, superposition provers for full first-order logic can incorporate AC simplifications without compromising completeness. Moreover, we extended demodulation to encompassment demodulation, which enables simplification of more clauses (and faster), independent of AC theories.

We believe that the framework of closure redundancy can be used to prove many other interesting and useful redundancy criteria. For future work we are currently exploring other such applications, including more AC simplifications as well as general ground joinability criteria which can be incorporated in our framework.

References

1. Avenhaus, J., Hillenbrand, T., Löchner, B.: On using ground joinable equations in equational theorem proving. J. Symb. Comput. **36**(1,2), 217–233 (2003)
2. Baader, F., Nipkow, T.: Term Rewriting and All That. Cambridge University Press, Cambridge (1998)
3. Bachmair, L., Ganzinger, H., Lynch, C., Snyder, W.: Basic paramodulation. Inf. Comput. **121**(2), 172–192 (1995)
4. Bachmair, L., Ganzinger, H.: Rewrite-based equational theorem proving with selection and simplification. J. Log. Comput. **4**(3), 217–247 (1994)
5. Bonnet, R., Pouzet, M.: Linear extensions of ordered sets. In: Rival, I. (ed.) Ordered Sets. NATO Advanced Study Institutes Series (Series C – Mathematical and Physical Sciences), vol. 83, pp. 125–170. Springer, Dordrecht (1982). https://doi.org/10.1007/978-94-009-7798-3_4
6. Dershowitz, N., Manna, Z.: Proving termination with multiset orderings. Commun. ACM **22**(8), 465–476 (1979)
7. Duarte, A., Korovin, K.: Implementing superposition in iProver (system description). In: Peltier, N., Sofronie-Stokkermans, V. (eds.) IJCAR 2020. LNCS (LNAI), vol. 12167, pp. 388–397. Springer, Cham (2020). https://doi.org/10.1007/978-3-030-51054-1_24
8. Duarte, A., Korovin, K.: AC simplifications and closure redundancies in the superposition calculus. arXiv (2021). (full version)
9. Korovin, K.: iProver – an instantiation-based theorem prover for first-order logic (system description). In: Armando, A., Baumgartner, P., Dowek, G. (eds.) IJCAR 2008. LNCS (LNAI), vol. 5195, pp. 292–298. Springer, Heidelberg (2008). https://doi.org/10.1007/978-3-540-71070-7_24
10. Kovács, L., Voronkov, A.: First-order theorem proving and VAMPIRE. In: Sharygina, N., Veith, H. (eds.) CAV 2013. LNCS, vol. 8044, pp. 1–35. Springer, Heidelberg (2013). https://doi.org/10.1007/978-3-642-39799-8_1
11. Löchner, B., Hillenbrand, T.: A phytography of WALDMEISTER. AI Commun. **15**(2,3), 127–133 (2002)

12. Martin, U., Nipkow, T.: Ordered rewriting and confluence. In: Stickel, M.E. (ed.) CADE 1990. LNCS, vol. 449, pp. 366–380. Springer, Heidelberg (1990). https://doi.org/10.1007/3-540-52885-7_100
13. Nieuwenhuis, R., Rubio, A.: Paramodulation-based theorem proving. In: Robinson, J.A., Voronkov, A. (eds.) Handbook of Automated Reasoning, vol. 2, pp. 371–443. Elsevier and MIT Press (2001)
14. Schulz, S.: E–a brainiac theorem prover. AI Commun. **15**(23), 111–126 (2002)
15. Smallbone, N.: Twee: an equational theorem prover. In: Platzer, A., Sutcliffe, G. (eds.) CADE 2021. LNCS (LNAI), vol. 12699, pp. 602–613. Springer, Cham (2021). https://doi.org/10.1007/978-3-030-79876-5_35
16. Sutcliffe, G.: The TPTP problem library and associated infrastructure. From CNF to TH0, TPTP v6.4.0. J. Autom. Reason. **59**(4), 483–502 (2017)
17. Vukmirović, P., Bentkamp, A., Blanchette, J., Cruanes, S., Nummelin, V., Tourret, S.: Making higher-order superposition work. In: Platzer, A., Sutcliffe, G. (eds.) CADE 2021. LNCS (LNAI), vol. 12699, pp. 415–432. Springer, Cham (2021). https://doi.org/10.1007/978-3-030-79876-5_24
18. Weidenbach, C., Dimova, D., Fietzke, A., Kumar, R., Suda, M., Wischnewski, P.: SPASS version 3.5. In: Schmidt, R.A. (ed.) CADE 2009. LNCS (LNAI), vol. 5663, pp. 140–145. Springer, Heidelberg (2009). https://doi.org/10.1007/978-3-642-02959-2_10
19. Winkler, S., Moser, G.: MædMax: a maximal ordered completion tool. In: Galmiche, D., Schulz, S., Sebastiani, R. (eds.) IJCAR 2018. LNCS (LNAI), vol. 10900, pp. 472–480. Springer, Cham (2018). https://doi.org/10.1007/978-3-319-94205-6_31

The Role of Entropy in Guiding a Connection Prover

Zsolt Zombori[1,2](✉), Josef Urban[3], and Miroslav Olšák[4]

[1] Alfréd Rényi Institute of Mathematics, Budapest, Hungary
zombori@renyi.hu
[2] Eötvös Loránd University, Budapest, Hungary
[3] Czech Technical University in Prague, Prague, Czechia
[4] University of Innsbruck, Innsbruck, Austria

Abstract. In this work we study how to learn good algorithms for selecting reasoning steps in theorem proving. We explore this in the connection tableau calculus implemented by leanCoP where the partial tableau provides a clean and compact notion of a *state* to which a limited number of inferences can be applied. We start by incorporating a state-of-the-art learning algorithm — a graph neural network (GNN) – into the plCoP theorem prover. Then we use it to observe the system's behavior in a reinforcement learning setting, i.e., when learning inference guidance from successful Monte-Carlo tree searches on many problems. Despite its better pattern matching capability, the GNN initially performs worse than a simpler previously used learning algorithm. We observe that the simpler algorithm is less confident, i.e., its recommendations have higher entropy. This leads us to explore how the entropy of the inference selection implemented via the neural network influences the proof search. This is related to research in human decision-making under uncertainty, and in particular the *probability matching* theory. Our main result shows that a proper entropy regularization, i.e., training the GNN not to be overconfident, greatly improves plCoP's performance on a large mathematical corpus.

Keywords: Automated theorem proving · Machine learning · Reinforcement learning · Graph neural networks · Connection calculus · Entropy regularization

1 Introduction

Automated Theorem Proving (ATP) and Interactive Theorem Proving (ITP) are today increasingly benefiting from combinations with Machine Learning (ML) methods [44]. A number of learning-based inference guiding methods have been developed recently, starting with the leanCoP [33,34] style connection tableaux setting [12,23,25,32,35,46,51], later expanding into the E prover's [38,39] and Vampire's [28] superposition setting [9,18,19,29,42], and HOL's [15,16,41], Coq's [10] and Isabelle's [48] tactical settings [4,6,13,14,17,31,50].

A. Das and S. Negri (Eds.): TABLEAUX 2021, LNAI 12842, pp. 218–235, 2021.
https://doi.org/10.1007/978-3-030-86059-2_13

The connection tableau calculus as implemented by leanCoP is a very good framework for studying combinations of ML and ATP methods [5]. leanCoP has a compact Prolog implementation that is both easy to modify and surprisingly efficient. At the same time, unlike in the superposition and tactical setting, the partial tableau provides a clean and compact notion of a *state* to which a limited number of inferences (*actions*) can be applied. This has recently allowed the first experiments with AlphaZero [40] style Monte-Carlo tree search (MCTS) [12] and Reinforcement Learning (RL) [43] of theorem proving in the rlCoP [25], graphCoP [32] and plCoP [51] systems.

In this work, we start by extending plCoP with a state-of-the-art learning algorithm – a graph neural network (GNN) [32] – which was designed for processing logical formulae and exhibits several useful invariance properties, namely invariance under renaming of symbols, negation and reordering of clauses and literals. Despite its better pattern matching capability, the GNN initially performs worse than a simpler previously used learning algorithm based on gradient boosted trees (XGBoost [8]). We observe that the simpler algorithm is less confident about the inferences that should be applied to the proof states, i.e., its recommendations have higher entropy, leading to greater exploration of different inferences.

This leads us to analyze how the entropy of the inference selection implemented via the neural network influences the proof search. We try increasingly high penalties for overconfidence (low entropy) during the training of the GNN, using an approach called Maximum Entropy Reinforcement Learning [49]. For this, we need to be able to compare the entropy of proof states with different numbers of possible inferences (actions). We do that by introducing *normalized entropy*, which allows for comparing discrete distributions of different lengths. We make a rather surprising discovery that replacing the particular trained predictors by arbitrary (random) but entropy-normalized predictors that respect the inference ordering yields only slightly weaker ATP performance. This suggests that the correct ordering of possible inferences according to their utility in a given state plus the right amount of entropy capture most of the benefits of the learned guidance. In summary, our contributions are:

1. We integrate a fast logic-aware graph neural network into the plCoP system, allowing its use for guiding the choice of inferences (policy) and for estimating the provability of a partial connection tableau (value).
2. We adapt the graph construction algorithm to support the paramodulation inferences used in plCoP.
3. We analyze the entropy of the policy and its role in plCoP's performance.
4. We show that random policies with the right ordering and normalized entropy perform already quite well.
5. We do several smaller and larger evaluations over the standard corpus extracted from the Mizar Mathematical Library (MML) and show that the best entropy regularized GNN greatly improves over other learning-guided connection tableaux systems. In particular, we report 17.4% improvement on the Mizar40 evaluation set over rlCoP, the best previously published result.

The rest of the paper is structured as follows. Section 2 introduces in more detail the necessary background such as neural guidance of provers, the leanCoP setting, reinforcement learning and Monte-Carlo tree search, and Maximum Entropy learning. Section 3 discusses in more depth the use of Maximum Entropy learning in guiding MCTS-based theorem proving. Section 4 describes our new implementation and Sect. 5 experimentally evaluates the methods.

2 Background and Related Work

2.1 Neural Feature Extraction for Guiding Theorem Provers

Learning based ATP systems have for a long time explored suitable characterizations of mathematical objects, leading to solutions that process text directly (e.g. [2,4,29]) and solutions that rely on manually engineered features (e.g. [18,26]). Graph neural networks (GNN) [37] provide an alternative to both approaches: the graph representation allows for retaining the syntactic structure of mathematical objects, while also allowing for end-to-end (i.e., involving no manually designed features) training. However, improving over learning based on manual feature extraction has proven to be challenging with GNNs, especially in real time, as noted in several works (e.g. [9,11]). Usually it required high level of technical engineering. The GNN presented in [32] was designed to preserve many useful invariance properties of logical formulae and has demonstrated impressive improvement in guiding the leanCoP connection calculus compared with gradient boosted trees. We refer to this system as graphCoP.

2.2 Systems Guiding the leanCoP Theorem Prover

leanCoP [34] is a compact theorem prover for first-order logic, implementing connection tableau search. The proof search starts with a *start clause* as a *goal* and proceeds by building a connection tableau by applying *extension steps* and *reduction steps*. leanCoP uses iterative deepening to ensure completeness.

A series of learning systems guiding the leanCoP connection calculus have been developed recently. Of these, we highlight three that use roughly the same reinforcement learning setup: rlCoP [25], plCoP [51] and graphCoP [32]. These systems search for proofs using Monte Carlo Tree Search [7] and they train the *value* (the proof state quality) and the *policy* (the inference quality in a proof state) functions similarly to systems like AlphaZero [3,40]. rlCoP and plCoP use manually developed features [26] and gradient boosted trees (XGBoost [8]) for learning while graphCoP employs a GNN for end-to-end feature extraction and learning. This graph neural network was designed for processing mathematical formulae and has several useful invariance properties: the graph structure is invariant under renaming of symbols, negation and reordering of clauses and literals. In this paper, we incorporate the GNN of [32] into plCoP.

The plCoP system extends leanCoP with paramodulation steps that can handle equality predicates more efficiently. Let $t|_p$ denote the subterm of t at position

p and $t[u]_p$ denote the term obtained after replacing in t at position p by term u. Given a goal G and an input clause[1] $\{X \neq Y, B\}$, such that, for some position p there is a substitution σ such that $G|_p\sigma = X\sigma$, the paramodulation step changes G to $\{G[Y]_p\sigma, B\sigma\}$. Rewriting is allowed in both directions, i.e., the roles of X and Y can be switched.

2.3 Reinforcement Learning (RL)

Reinforcement learning (RL) [43] aims to find the optimal behaviour in an environment defined as a Markov Decision Process (MDP). An MDP$(\mathcal{S}, \mathcal{A}, \mathcal{R}, \mathcal{P}, \gamma)$ describes a dynamic process and consists of the following components: $\mathcal{S}$ is the set of possible states, $\mathcal{A}$ is the set of possible actions, $\mathcal{R} : (\mathcal{S} \times \mathcal{A}) \to \mathbb{R}$ is a reward function, $\mathcal{P} : (\mathcal{S} \times \mathcal{A}) \to \mathcal{S}$ is the state transition function and γ is the discount factor. We assume that an agent interacts with this MDP, generating sequences of (s_t, a_t, r_t) state-action-reward tuples, called *trajectories*. The agent is equipped with a *policy* function $\pi : \mathcal{S} \to \mathcal{A}$ which determines which action it selects in a particular state. The policy is often stochastic, i.e., it defines a probability distribution over inferences that are possible in a given state. The aim of the agent is to maximize its total accumulated reward $\sum_{t \geq 0} \gamma^t r_t$. Several components, such as the reward and transition functions, can be stochastic, in which case the aim of the agent it to find the policy π^* that maximizes its cumulative expected reward, where future rewards are discounted with the γ discount factor:

$$\pi^* = \arg\max_{\pi} \mathbb{E}\left[\sum_{t \geq 0} \gamma^t r_t | \pi\right]$$

2.4 Monte Carlo Tree Search (MCTS)

MCTS is a simple RL algorithm, which builds a search tree whose nodes are states and where edges represent actions. The aim of the search algorithm is to find trajectories (branches in the search tree) that yield high accumulated rewards. The search starts from a single root node, and new nodes are added iteratively. In each node i, we maintain the number of visits n_i, the total reward r_i, and the prior probability (estimated typically by a trained predictor) p_i of all its possible successors (in our case produced by the possible inferences). Each iteration, also called *playout*, involves the addition of a new leaf node.

The policy π used for selecting the actions of the playout is based on the standard UCT [27] (Upper Confidence Trees) formula (1): in each state we select the action with the maximal UCT value in the successor state. Once a new leaf state is created, we observe its reward and update its ancestors: visit counts are increased by 1 and rewards are increased by the reward of the leaf.

$$\text{UCT}(i) = \frac{r_i}{n_i} + cp \cdot p_i \cdot \sqrt{\frac{lnN}{n_i}} \tag{1}$$

[1] Assuming Disjunctive Normal Form.

In (1), N is the number of visits of the parent, and cp is a parameter that determines the balance between nodes with high reward (exploitation) and rarely visited nodes (exploration). In [3,40] MCTS is augmented with two learned functions. The *value* function estimates the accumulated reward obtainable from a state, and the leaf nodes are initialized with this value estimates. The second function predicts the prior probability of state-action pairs, which is usually referred to as the *policy*, with a slight abuse of terminology. When it can lead to confusion, we refer to this policy as π^M.

The plCoP, rlCoP and graphCoP systems use the MaLARea/DAgger [36,45] meta-learning algorithm to learn the policy and value functions. They interleave ATP runs based on the current policy and value (*data collection phase*) with a *training phase*, in which these functions are updated to fit the collected data. Such iterative interleaving of proving and learning has been used successfully in ATP systems such as MaLARea [45] and ENIGMA [20].

During the proof search we build a Monte Carlo tree for each training problem. Its nodes are the proof states (partial tableaux), and the edges represent inferences. Note that the Monte Carlo tree is thus different from the tableau trees. A branch of this Monte Carlo tree leading to a node with a closed tableau is a valid proof. Initially, the three leanCoP-based systems use somewhat different heuristic value and policy functions, later to be replaced with the learned guidance. To enforce deeper exploration, we perform a *bigstep* after a fixed number of playouts: the starting node of exploration is moved one level down towards the child with the highest value (called the *bigstep node*). Later MCTS steps thus only extend the subtree under the bigstep node. This in practice means no backtracking of the bigsteps, which in turn involves giving up completeness.

2.5 Maximum Entropy Reinforcement Learning

When training the policy, directly maximizing the expected utility on the action sequences observed by an RL agent (i.e., the training examples) can lead to instability. The policy can get stuck in local minima and become overconfident, preventing it from exploring the search space sufficiently when necessary to make good decisions. This has motivated using stochastic policies and several *regularization* (i.e., encouraging generality) techniques that ensure that all actions have a chance of being selected. Another motivation for properly regularized stochastic policy learning comes from experiments on humans and animals, suggesting that biological agents do not deterministically select the action with the greatest expected utility [47]: instead they randomly select actions with probability proportional to the expected utility, called *probability matching*. Consequently, action sequences that generate similar rewards tend to be similarly probable, i.e., we avoid making strong commitments whenever it is possible. Maximum Entropy Reinforcement Learning (MaxEnt RL), achieves probability matching by adding an entropy term to the loss function when the policy is trained:

$$\pi^* = \arg\max_{\pi} \mathbb{E}[\sum_{t\geq 0} \gamma^t r_t + \alpha H_\pi[a|s_t]|\pi]$$

where $H_\pi[a|s_t]$ is the Shannon entropy of the probability distribution over valid actions in state s_t:

$$H[p] = -\sum_{i=1}^{n} p_i \log(p_i)$$

and α is the entropy coefficient. This means that the training of the policy will be maximizing a weighted sum of the (discounted) rewards and of the entropy of the resulting distribution, thus discouraging overconfidence. The entropy term in the objective was first used in [49] and since then its benefit has been empirically demonstrated in several domains. It is particularly useful in dynamic environments, where some uncertainty remains, irrespective of the amount of exploration.

2.6 Kullback-Leibler Divergence

Shannon's entropy measures the uniformity of a single distribution. However, when contrasting different policies, we will need a measure to compare different distributions. For this, one of the most widely used options is the Kullback-Leibler (KL) divergence, also called *relative entropy*, which is a measure of how one probability distribution differs from a given reference distribution. For a discrete target distribution Q and a reference distribution P, the KL divergence is defined as:

$$KL(P\|Q) = \sum_{x} P(x) \log \frac{P(x)}{Q(x)}$$

This measure is zero exactly when P and Q are identical, otherwise it is positive. It can be infinite if there is some x such that $P(x) > 0$ and $Q(x) = 0$. A small $KL(P\|Q)$ means that the two distributions are similar on the domain where most of the probability mass of P lies. Note that $KL(P\|Q) \neq KL(Q\|P)$. For example, consider the following distributions:

$$P = [0.5, 0.47, 0.01, 0.01, 0.01]$$
$$Q = [0.96, 0.01, 0.01, 0.01, 0.01]$$

$KL(P\|Q) = 1.48$ and $KL(Q\|P) = 0.58$. When the summed terms are weighted according to P in $KL(P\|Q)$, the first two terms get large weight, while only the first term gets large weight in $KL(Q\|P)$. When both KL divergences are small, it is a good indicator of similarity of the two distributions.

3 Maximum Entropy for MCTS and Theorem Proving

In this section we discuss the entropy of the inference policy and its potential influence on the proof search. We also introduce a *normalized entropy* to correctly handle probability vectors of different lengths and argue that MaxEnt RL is more targeted and powerful than previously used temperature-based entropy control. Section 4 then describes our implementation.

3.1 Exploration and Entropy in MCTS

The MCTS implemented via the UCT formula has a built-in mechanism for balancing the *exploitation* of proof states that already have high rewards and the *exploration* of inferences whose effect is not yet known. This balancing serves to mitigate errors in the proof state value estimates. However, we need to do another balancing within exploration, between the different under-explored inference branches. This is estimated by the π^M policy predictor as the prior probabilities of the possible inferences. Hence, besides the ordering of the inferences that are possible from a given state, their exact prior probabilities are important as they determine how the exploration budget is split between them. This observation directs our attention to the entropy (uncertainty) of π^M and its relation to the theorem proving performance.

We argue that finding the right level of (un)certainty is particularly important for theorem proving. The goal of learning is to acquire inductive biases that allow the system to perform well on novel problems.[2] In many situations, however, it is not realistic to extract enough knowledge from the training data that justifies a high level of confidence. Sometimes, there is just not enough analogy between a new problem and the training problems, and we would like our guidance to be more conservative so that we can explore all directions equally. This makes a strong case for using MaxEnt RL, which gives tools for shaping the entropy (uncertainty) profile of our learned π^M policy predictor.

3.2 Normalized Entropy

In this work, we empirically demonstrate the importance of including the "right amount" of entropy when training the policy that guides the theorem prover. To the best of our knowledge, this is the first time that the effect of entropy regularization for MCTS in general and for theorem proving in particular is examined.

Using standard entropy for comparing probability vectors of different length would, however, be misleading. The same entropy value can mean very different uncertainty if the length of the vector changes. For example, consider the vectors

$$[0.34, 0.33, 0.33]$$
$$[0.73, 0.07, 0.05, 0.05, 0.05, 0.01, 0.01, 0.01, 0.01, 0.01]$$

Their entropy is roughly the same (1.1), despite the fact that the first is nearly uniform and the second centers around its first value. To make the uncertainty of these two vectors comparable, we introduce *normalized entropy*:

Definition 1. *Given a discrete probability vector* p *of length* n*, let* $H^*[p] = H[p]/\log(n)$ *denote the normalized entropy of* p*.*

[2] In this sense, theorem proving can be considered as a meta learning task.

Here, $\log(n)$ is the entropy of the uniform distribution when the length is n, hence it is the upper bound of $H[p]$. Consequently, $H^*[p] \in [0, 1]$. Furthermore, it is dimensionless, i.e., it does not depend on the base of the logarithm. The difference between the two distributions in the example above is better captured by their normalized entropy, which is 1 and 0.48.

3.3 Temperature-Based and Regularization-Based Entropy Control

An alternative mechanism for injecting entropy into the policy is through the softmax *temperature* parameter T. Our policy predictors (both XGBoost and GNN) output an unconstrained *logit* vector l, which is normalized to a probability vector p using the softmax function:

$$p_i = \frac{e^{\frac{l_i}{T}}}{\sum_{j=1}^{n} e^{\frac{l_j}{T}}}$$

Increasing the temperature flattens the probability curve, approaching the uniform distribution in the limit. On the other hand, if the temperature gets close to 0, then most of the probability mass concentrates on the most likely action.

While both higher temperature and entropy regularization increase the ultimate entropy of the policy, they work differently. The temperature acts globally and uniformly, flattening all inference probabilities estimated by the trained policy predictor. Entropy regularization, on the other hand, is part of the training process and it allows the neural network to learn distinguishing between situations with low and high uncertainty. In obvious situations, entropy regularization does not prevent the neural network from acquiring great certainty, while it will drive the network to more uniform predictions when there is no strong evidence against that in the training data. Hence, we expect entropy regularization to be more targeted and powerful than the temperature optimization. This is empirically demonstrated in Sect. 5.

4 Entropy Regularized Neural Guidance for plCoP

This section gives an overview of the training procedure, including how data is extracted from tableaux and Monte Carlo trees.

4.1 Neural Representation of the State and Inference Steps

The proof state in the leanCoP setting is roughly described by the partial tableau and by the set of input clauses corresponding to the initial axioms and conjecture. Each time we choose an extension step, we map the state into a hypergraph, as described in [32]. In more detail, we use the current goal (single literal), the active path leading to the current goal (set of literals), the set of all open goals (set of literals), and the input clauses in the hypergraph construction. The GNN processes the hypergraph and outputs a value prediction for the proof state in the range [0, 1]. It also outputs a probability distribution over all the literals of the axiom clauses that can be used for extension steps, i.e., that can be unified with the negation of the current goal literal.

The above method is used already in graphCoP, but the hypergraph construction algorithm used by graphCoP was designed to guide only the extension steps. Hence it expects the set of all clauses together with the information that identifies literals within the clauses that unify with the negation of the current goal. We adapt this to paramodulation by temporarily creating a clause for each valid paramodulation step that "simulates" the latter as an extension step. Suppose that the current goal is G and there is an input clause $\{X \neq Y, B\}$, such that, for some position p there is a substitution σ such that $G|_p\sigma = X\sigma$. There is a valid paramodulation step that replaces G with $\{G[Y]_p\sigma, B\sigma\}$. We simulate this step as an extension by adding clause $\{\neg G\sigma, G[Y]_p\sigma, B\sigma\}$ to the input clauses, when constructing the graph.

4.2 Training the Policy and Value Guidance for MCTS

As in plCoP, the value and policy estimates are stored in the MCTS nodes and are used for guiding proof search. The training data for learning policy (inference probabilities) and value (state quality) are also handled as in plCoP. They are extracted from the tableau states of the bigstep nodes. For each bigstep state, the value target is 1[3] if it leads to a proof and 0 otherwise. The policy targets at a particular proof state are the relative frequencies of the possible inferences, i.e., the children in the search tree.

For graphCoP, a single GNN was jointly trained to predict both the value and the policy [32]. However, we observed that training separate predictors yields a small improvement, hence we conduct our experiments in this setup. Consider a tableau state s for which we want to learn its target value v and target policy $p_1, \ldots, p_n$. Suppose that the partially trained value predictor outputs v' and the policy predictor outputs $p'_1, \ldots, p'_n$, then the objectives that we minimize are:

- **value objective**: $(v - v')^2$
- **policy objective**: $-\sum_{i=1}^{n} p_i \cdot \log(p'_i) - \alpha H[p']$

For more details of the graph construction and neural training we refer to [32]. In summary, we use the same setting as there, except for (i) extending guidance to paramodulation steps, (ii) training separate policy and value GNNs, (iii) increasing the number of neural layers in the GNN from 5 to 10,[4] and (iv) changing the policy training to encourage policies with higher entropy.

5 Experiments

We first introduce our datasets and other experimental settings (Sect. 5.1). Then we show the impact of entropy regularization (Sect. 5.2) and experimentally com-

[3] A discount factor of 0.99 is applied to positive rewards to favor shorter proofs.

[4] This is motivated by the experiments with the ENIGMA-GNN system [18], where 8–10 layers produce better results than 5 layers.

pare the entropies and other characteristics of the XGBoost and GNN predictors (Sect. 5.3). In Sect. 5.4, we show that random policies with the right ordering and normalized entropy perform already quite well. Section 5.5 then compares temperature-based entropy control with our approach. Finally, Sect. 5.6 evaluates the methods in a train/test scenario on the full Mizar40 dataset using several iterations of proving and learning.

5.1 Datasets and Common Settings

We evaluate our system[5] using the same datasets as those in [25]. The *Mizar40* dataset [22] consists of 32524 problems from the Mizar Mathematical Library that have been proven by several state-of-the-art ATPs used with many strategies and high time limits in the experiments described in [24]. Based on the proofs, the axioms were ATP-minimized, i.e., only those axioms were kept that were needed in any of the ATP proofs found. The smaller *M2k* dataset [21] consists of 2003 Mizar40 problems that come from related Mizar articles. Finally, we use the bushy (small) problems from the MPTP2078 benchmark [1], which contains just an article-based selection of Mizar problems, regardless of their solvability by a particular ATP system.

Unless otherwise specified, we use the same hyperparameters as described in [51], with the following important exceptions. To allow for faster experiments and put more emphasis on guidance instead of search, we reduce the per problem inference limit from 200000 to 20000 and the bigstep frequency from 2000 to 200. Hence the overall search budget is reduced by a factor of 10. We use a very large CPU time limit (300 s) intended to ensure that proof search terminates after exhausting the inference limit.

5.2 Experiment 1: Influence of Entropy Regularization

In this experiment, we examine the effect of regularizing the entropy of our policy predictor. We produce several variants of the GNN policy predictor which differ in the entropy coefficient α used in its training. Table 1 summarizes our results. We find that the entropy coefficient has a big impact on performance. By the 10th iteration, the best GNN predictor with $\alpha = 0.7$ is 17% better than the unregularized GNN and 5% better than XGBoost. Table 1 also shows the average entropy of the policies generated by the predictor during the proof search. Note that the average entropy of the best predictor in most iterations is reasonably close (often the closest) to the entropy of the XGBoost predictor. This suggests that one key strength of the XGBoost predictor is that it hits the "right" amount of entropy. Matching this entropy in the GNN with adequate regularization allows for matching and even surpassing XGBoost in performance.

---

[5] The new extensions described here and the experimental configuration files are publicly available at plCoP's repository: https://github.com/zsoltzombori/plcop.

Table 1. Number of problems solved (Succ) and average policy entropy (Ent) on the M2k dataset. α is the entropy loss term coefficient. Best models are marked with **boldface**, best GNN models are underlined.

Model	α	Iter 1		Iter 2		Iter 4		Iter 6		Iter 8		Iter 10	
		Ent	Succ	Ent	Succ	Ent	Succ	Ent	Succ	Ent	Succ	Ent	Succ
XGB		1.41	**790**	1.29	**956**	1.22	**1061**	1.19	1119	1.17	1147	1.14	1171
GNN	0	0.91	746	0.56	850	0.37	938	0.34	992	0.31	1021	0.32	1050
GNN	0.1	0.86	<u>787</u>	0.6	867	0.43	933	0.37	996	0.37	1031	0.38	1070
GNN	0.2	1.11	769	0.71	878	0.51	976	0.51	1045	0.49	1077	0.46	1114
GNN	0.3	1.05	736	0.8	868	0.7	991	0.73	1071	0.69	1109	0.78	1170
GNN	0.5	1.31	781	1.14	884	1.17	1015	1.13	1085	1.12	1144	1.06	1191
GNN	0.6	1.37	759	1.25	889	1.26	1040	1.21	1098	1.18	1150	1.19	1197
GNN	0.7	1.41	727	1.32	854	1.27	<u>1057</u>	1.22	<u>**1132**</u>	1.24	<u>**1184**</u>	1.2	<u>**1228**</u>
GNN	0.8	1.42	757	1.37	<u>912</u>	1.35	1029	1.32	1079	1.29	1111	1.3	1144
GNN	1.0	1.53	742	1.41	911	1.38	1032	1.35	1102	1.36	1144	1.35	1173
GNN	2.0	1.59	725	1.57	782	1.53	894	1.5	1007	1.5	1047	1.5	1086

5.3 Experiment 2: Relative Entropy on the Same Proof States

Table 1 reveals that there is a reasonable match in average entropy between XGBoost policies and our best GNN policies. Note, however, that this is in general measured on different proof states as the policies themselves determine what proof states the prover explores. To gain a deeper understanding, we create a separate dataset of proof states and compare the different GNNs from Experiment 1 with XGBoost on these proof states using the following four metrics: 1) fraction of proof states where the two predictors have the same most probable inference (Best), 2) fraction of proof states where the two predictors yield the same inference ordering (Order), and the average KL divergence (relative entropy) between the predictors in both directions: 3) $KL(X\|G)$ and 4) $KL(G\|X)$.[6] We contrast these metrics with the number of problems solved (Succ) by the corresponding entropy regularized GNN.

We perform this comparison using two datasets. These are the set of states visited by an unguided prover on the 1) M2k dataset and the 2) MPTP2078 bushy benchmark. The first set is part of the training corpus, while the second was never seen by the predictors before. The results can be seen in Table 2.

Changing the entropy coefficient mostly does not change the order of actions, as expected. For the two datasets, the GNN and the XGBoost predictors select the same best inference in around 80% and 58% of the states and yield exactly the same inference ordering in around 40% and 22% of the states. This reveals a significant diversity among the two predictor families, suggesting potential in combining them. We leave this direction for future work.

We find that the same level of entropy regularization ($\alpha = 0.7$) is the best when running both on the familiar (M2k) and the previously unseen

[6] X and G stand for the probability distributions predicted by XGBoost and GNN, respectively.

Table 2. Comparing the differently entropy-regularized GNN predictors (G) with XGBoost (X) on two fixed sets of proof states generated by running an unguided prover on the M2k and MPTP2078 benchmarks. All predictors were trained on M2k for 10 iterations. α is the entropy regularization coefficient. XGBoost solves 1171 (M2K) and 491 (MPTP2078) problems.

α	M2K					MPTP2078b				
	Succ	Best	Order	$KL(X\|G)$	$KL(G\|X)$	Succ	Best	Order	$KL(X\|G)$	$KL(G\|X)$
0	1050	0.81	0.43	0.52	2.9	230	0.56	0.22	0.97	4.5
0.1	1070	0.8	0.44	0.5	2.37	245	0.58	0.24	0.91	3.83
0.2	1114	0.81	0.42	0.47	1.66	256	0.56	0.24	0.88	2.82
0.3	1170	0.82	0.42	0.36	0.58	276	0.56	0.23	0.61	0.9
0.5	1191	0.82	0.42	0.24	0.28	335	0.59	0.23	0.41	0.43
0.6	1197	0.82	0.4	0.22	0.23	359	0.59	0.23	0.36	0.36
0.7	**1228**	0.82	0.4	0.22	0.21	**399**	0.58	0.22	0.34	0.32
0.8	1144	0.81	0.39	0.22	0.21	357	0.58	0.22	0.34	0.31
1.0	1173	0.82	0.4	0.24	0.21	363	0.58	0.22	0.33	0.29
2.0	1086	0.81	0.39	0.34	0.26	362	0.58	0.21	0.37	0.3

(MPTP2078) dataset. This is where the two directional KL divergences (relative entropies) roughly coincide and their sum is roughly minimal. These results make a stronger case for the hypothesis from Experiment 1, that the best GNN performance is obtained when the policy distributions are statistically close to those of the XGBoost predictor.

5.4 Experiment 3: Order and Entropy Are Largely Sufficient

Tables 1 and 2 demonstrate the importance of the entropy of the inference policy in ATP performance. To make this even more apparent, we design an experiment in which we remove a large part of the information contained in the inference policy, only preserving the inference ordering and the normalized entropy. The top two lines of Table 3 show the normalized entropy across iterations of the XGBoost and GNN predictors. Note that it is very stable. We select a target normalized entropy H^* and for each length l we generate a fixed random discrete probability p_l of length l whose normalized entropy is H^*. Finally, we run an MCTS evaluation in which each time our policy predictor emits a probability vector of length l, we replace it with p_l, permuted so that the ordering remains the same as in the original policy. Table 3 shows the ATP performance for the differently normalized entropy targets.

We find that the performance of this predictor is surprisingly good: its performance (1154) is only 1% worse than XGBoost (1171), 10% better than unregularized GNN (1050) and 6% worse than the best GNN (1228). This suggests that the right inference ordering plus the right amount of entropy capture most of the benefits of the learned inference guidance.

Table 3. Normalized entropy of the XGBoost and GNN predictors on M2k (top two rows) and number of problems solved by random policies constrained to have the same action ordering and fixed normalized entropy.

Iteration	0	1	2	3	4	5	6	7	8	9	10
XGBoost H^*	1	0.73	0.71	0.69	0.68	0.67	0.67	0.67	0.66	0.67	0.66
GNN ($\alpha = 0.7$) H^*	1	0.83	0.79	0.8	0.79	0.79	0.78	0.78	0.78	0.8	0.78
GNN $H^* = 0.6$	523	700	782	849	909	956	984	1019	1037	1059	**1083**
GNN $H^* = 0.7$	523	702	800	856	922	954	995	1040	1077	1110	**1129**
GNN $H^* = 0.8$	523	693	832	938	1023	1054	1086	1077	1115	1129	**1154**

5.5 Experiment 4: Temperature vs. Entropy Regularization

As noted in Sect. 3, tuning the softmax temperature is an alternative to entropy regularization. For XGBoost, the temperature was previously optimized to be $T = 2$ and all reported experiments use this number. For the GNN predictors, we used the default $T = 1$. In Table 4, we show how the ATP performance of the GNN changes after it has been trained for 10 iterations on the M2k dataset (without entropy regularization). Increasing the temperature brings some improvement, however, this is much smaller than the benefit of entropy regularization. This is true even if we take the best temperature ($T = 4$) and perform a full 10 iteration training with this temperature, as shown in Table 5. We obtain 3% improvement via the temperature optimization, compared with 17% improvement via the entropy regularization. We conclude that the effect of entropy regularization is much more refined and powerful than just flattening the probability curve.

Table 4. The effect of changing the temperature of an (unregularized) GNN predictor trained for 10 iterations on the M2k dataset on the number of problems solved.

Model	$T = 0.5$	$T = 1$	$T = 2$	$T = 3$	$T = 4$	$T = 5$
GNN	1036	1050	1057	1066	**1068**	1061

Table 5. Number of problems solved by the GNN trained for 10 iterations on the M2k dataset with different softmax temperatures.

Iteration	0	1	2	3	4	5	6	7	8	9	10
GNN $T = 1$	523	746	850	899	938	971	992	1012	1021	1023	**1050**
GNN $T = 4$	523	705	800	864	894	931	993	1017	1049	1065	**1079**

5.6 Experiment 5: Final Large Train/Test Evaluation on Mizar40

Finally, we perform a large evaluation of plCoP using XGBoost and GNN on the full Mizar40 dataset, and we compare its performance with rlCoP and graphCoP. This evaluation, including the training of the GNNs on the growing sets of proofs generated from the successive proving/learning iterations, takes over 10 days on a large multicore server, and the number of training policy/value examples extracted from the MCTS proof searches goes over 5M in the last iteration.

The 32524 problems are randomly split using a 9:1 ratio into 29272 training problems and 3252 evaluation problems. For consistency, we employ the same split that was used in [25]. Successive predictors are only trained on data extracted from the training problems, but we always evaluate the predictors on both the training and evaluation sets and report the number of proofs found for them. Our results can be found in Table 6, with plCoP/GNN solving in the last iteration 16906 training problems and 1767 evaluation problems. These are the highest numbers obtained so far with any learning-guided leanCoP-based system.

For training the GNN policy predictor, we use the entropy regularization coefficient ($\alpha = 0.7$) that worked best on M2k, without its further tuning on this larger dataset. Note that the resource limits are higher in Table 6 for rlCoP and also a bit different for graphCoP (which was run only for a few iterations), as we took their published results from [25,32] rather than rerunning the systems. Also, the evaluation of plCoP with GNN was stopped after iteration 8 due to our resource limits and the clear flattening of the performance on the evaluation set (1767 vs 1758 in the 8th vs 7th iteration).

Table 6. Comparing plCoP with XGBoost, plCoP with GNN, rlCoP and graphCoP on the Mizar40 training and evaluation set. rlCoP employs 200000 inference limit and 2000 bigstep frequency, plCoP uses 20000 inference limit and 200 bigstep frequency, graphCoP uses 200 depth limit and 200 bigstep frequency.

Iteration	0	1	2	3	4	5	6	7	8	9	10
Train set											
rlCoP	7348	12325	13749	14155	14363	14403	14431	14342	**14498**	14481	14487
graphCoP	4595	11978	**12648**	12642							
plCoP XGB	4904	8917	10600	11221	11536	11627	11938	11999	12085	12063	**12151**
plCoP GNN	4888	8704	12630	14566	15449	16002	16467	16745	**16906**		
Eval set											
rlCoP	804	1354	1519	1566	1595	**1624**	1586	1582	1591	1577	1621
graphCoP	510	1322	**1394**	1360							
plCoP XGB	554	947	1124	1158	1177	1204	1217	1210	1212	**1213**	1204
plCoP GNN	554	969	1375	1611	1650	1730	1742	1758	**1767**		

In particular, plCoP was given 20000 inferences per problem, i.e., one tenth of the inference limit used for rlCoP in [25]. For a fair comparison with rlCoP, we thus take the predictors (both XGBoost and GNN) used in the last plCoP iteration (iteration 10 for XGBoost and iteration 8 for GNN) and run plCoP with them on the evaluation set with 200000 inference limit and 2000 bigstep frequency, which corresponds to the limits used for rlCoP in [25]. To ensure that the system has enough time to exhaust its inference limit, we increase the timeout to 6000 s. plCoP with XGBoost then solves 1499 of the evaluation problems while plCoP with GNN solves **1907** (58.6%) of them. This is our final evaluation result, which is **17.4%** higher than the 1624 evaluation problems solved by rlCoP in the best previously published result so far [25].

6 Conclusion

We have extended the plCoP learning-based connection prover with a fast, logic-aware graph neural network (GNN) and explored how the GNN can learn good guidance for selecting inferences in this setting. We have identified the entropy of the inference selection predictor as a key driver of the ATP performance and shown that Maximum Entropy Reinforcement Learning largely improves the performance of the trained policy network, outperforming simpler temperature-based entropy increasing methods. To the best of our knowledge, this is the first time that the role of entropy in guiding a theorem prover has been analyzed.

We have discovered that replacing the particular trained predictors by arbitrary (random) but entropy-normalized predictors that respect the inference ordering yields only slightly weaker theorem proving performance than the best methods. This suggests that the right inference ordering plus the right amount of entropy capture most of the benefits of the learned inference guidance. In the large final train/test evaluation on the full Mizar40 benchmark our system improves by 17.4% over the best previously published result achieved by rlCoP.

Acknowledgments. ZZ was supported by the European Union, co-financed by the European Social Fund (EFOP-3.6.3-VEKOP-16-2017-00002), the Hungarian National Excellence Grant 2018-1.2.1-NKP-00008 and by the Hungarian Ministry of Innovation and Technology NRDI Office within the framework of the Artificial Intelligence National Laboratory Program. JU was funded by the *AI4REASON* ERC Consolidator grant nr. 649043 and the European Regional Development Fund under the Czech project AI&Reasoning CZ.02.1.01/0.0/0.0/15_003/0000466. MO was supported by the ERC starting grant no. 714034 SMART. We thank the TABLEAUX'21 reviewers for their thoughtful reviews and comments.

References

1. Alama, J., Heskes, T., Kühlwein, D., Tsivtsivadze, E., Urban, J.: Premise selection for mathematics by corpus analysis and kernel methods. J. Autom. Reason. **52**(2), 191–213 (2014)
2. Alemi, A.A., Chollet, F., Een, N., Irving, G., Szegedy, C., Urban, J.: DeepMath - deep sequence models for premise selection. In: Proceedings of the 30th International Conference on Neural Information Processing Systems, NIPS 2016, USA, pp. 2243–2251. Curran Associates Inc. (2016)

3. Anthony, T., Tian, Z., Barber, D.: Thinking fast and slow with deep learning and tree search. CoRR, abs/1705.08439 (2017)
4. Bansal, K., Loos, S.M., Rabe, M.N., Szegedy, C., Wilcox, S.: HOList: an environment for machine learning of higher order logic theorem proving. In: Chaudhuri, K., Salakhutdinov, R. (eds.) International Conference on Machine Learning, ICML 2019. Proceedings of Machine Learning Research, vol. 97, pp. 454–463. PMLR (2019)
5. Bibel, W.: A vision for automated deduction rooted in the connection method. In: Schmidt, R.A., Nalon, C. (eds.) TABLEAUX 2017. LNCS (LNAI), vol. 10501, pp. 3–21. Springer, Cham (2017). https://doi.org/10.1007/978-3-319-66902-1_1
6. Blaauwbroek, L., Urban, J., Geuvers, H.: Tactic learning and proving for the Coq proof assistant. In: Albert, E., Kovács, L. (eds.) LPAR 2020: 23rd International Conference on Logic for Programming, Artificial Intelligence and Reasoning. EPiC Series in Computing, vol. 73, pp. 138–150. EasyChair (2020)
7. Browne, C., et al.: A survey of Monte Carlo tree search methods. IEEE Trans. Comput. Intell. AI Games **4**, 1–43 (2012)
8. Chen, T., Guestrin, C.: XGBoost: a scalable tree boosting system. In: Proceedings of the 22Nd ACM SIGKDD International Conference on Knowledge Discovery and Data Mining, KDD 2016, New York, NY, USA, pp. 785–794. ACM (2016)
9. Chvalovský, K., Jakubův, J., Suda, M., Urban, J.: ENIGMA-NG: efficient neural and gradient-boosted inference guidance for E. In: Fontaine, P. (ed.) CADE 2019. LNCS (LNAI), vol. 11716, pp. 197–215. Springer, Cham (2019). https://doi.org/10.1007/978-3-030-29436-6_12
10. The Coq Proof Assistant. http://coq.inria.fr
11. Crouse, M., et al.: A deep reinforcement learning approach to first-order logic theorem proving. Artificial Intelligence (2019). arXiv
12. Färber, M., Kaliszyk, C., Urban, J.: Machine learning guidance for connection tableaux. J. Autom. Reason. **65**(2), 287–320 (2021)
13. Gauthier, T., Kaliszyk, C., Urban, J.: TacticToe: learning to reason with HOL4 tactics. In: Eiter, T., Sands, D. (eds.) LPAR-21. 21st International Conference on Logic for Programming, Artificial Intelligence and Reasoning. EPiC Series in Computing, vol. 46, pp. 125–143. EasyChair (2017)
14. Gauthier, T., Kaliszyk, C., Urban, J., Kumar, R., Norrish, M.: TacticToe: learning to prove with tactics. J. Autom. Reason. **65**(2), 257–286 (2021)
15. Gordon, M.J.C., Melham, T.F. (eds.): Introduction to HOL: A Theorem Proving Environment for Higher Order Logic. Cambridge University Press, Cambridge (1993)
16. Harrison, J.: HOL light: a tutorial introduction. In: Srivas, M., Camilleri, A. (eds.) FMCAD 1996. LNCS, vol. 1166, pp. 265–269. Springer, Heidelberg (1996). https://doi.org/10.1007/BFb0031814
17. Huang, D., Dhariwal, P., Song, D., Sutskever, I.: Gamepad: a learning environment for theorem proving. In: 7th International Conference on Learning Representations, ICLR 2019. OpenReview.net (2019)
18. Jakubův, J., Chvalovský, K., Olšák, M., Piotrowski, B., Suda, M., Urban, J.: ENIGMA anonymous: symbol-independent inference guiding machine (system description). In: Peltier, N., Sofronie-Stokkermans, V. (eds.) IJCAR 2020. LNCS (LNAI), vol. 12167, pp. 448–463. Springer, Cham (2020). https://doi.org/10.1007/978-3-030-51054-1_29

19. Jakubův, J., Urban, J.: ENIGMA: efficient learning-based inference guiding machine. In: Geuvers, H., England, M., Hasan, O., Rabe, F., Teschke, O. (eds.) CICM 2017. LNCS (LNAI), vol. 10383, pp. 292–302. Springer, Cham (2017). https://doi.org/10.1007/978-3-319-62075-6_20
20. Jakubuv, J., Urban, J.: Hammering Mizar by learning clause guidance. In: Harrison, J., O'Leary, J., Tolmach, A. (eds.) 10th International Conference on Interactive Theorem Proving, ITP 2019, Portland, OR, USA, 9–12 September 2019. LIPIcs, vol. 141, pp. 34:1–34:8. Schloss Dagstuhl - Leibniz-Zentrum für Informatik (2019)
21. Kaliszyk, C., Urban, J.: M2K dataset. https://github.com/JUrban/deepmath/blob/master/M2k_list
22. Kaliszyk, C., Urban, J.: Mizar40 dataset. https://github.com/JUrban/deepmath
23. Kaliszyk, C., Urban, J.: FEMaLeCoP: fairly efficient machine learning connection prover. In: Davis, M., Fehnker, A., McIver, A., Voronkov, A. (eds.) LPAR 2015. LNCS, vol. 9450, pp. 88–96. Springer, Heidelberg (2015). https://doi.org/10.1007/978-3-662-48899-7_7
24. Kaliszyk, C., Urban, J.: MizAR 40 for Mizar 40. J. Autom. Reason. **55**(3), 245–256 (2015). https://doi.org/10.1007/s10817-015-9330-8
25. Kaliszyk, C., Urban, J., Michalewski, H., Olšák, M.: Reinforcement learning of theorem proving. In: NeurIPS, pp. 8836–8847 (2018)
26. Kaliszyk, C., Urban, J., Vyskočil, J.: Efficient semantic features for automated reasoning over large theories. In: Yang, Q., Wooldridge, M. (eds.) IJCAI 2015, pp. 3084–3090. AAAI Press (2015)
27. Kocsis, L., Szepesvári, C.: Bandit based Monte-Carlo planning. In: Fürnkranz, J., Scheffer, T., Spiliopoulou, M. (eds.) ECML 2006. LNCS (LNAI), vol. 4212, pp. 282–293. Springer, Heidelberg (2006). https://doi.org/10.1007/11871842_29
28. Kovács, L., Voronkov, A.: First-order theorem proving and VAMPIRE. In: Sharygina, N., Veith, H. (eds.) CAV 2013. LNCS, vol. 8044, pp. 1–35. Springer, Heidelberg (2013). https://doi.org/10.1007/978-3-642-39799-8_1
29. Loos, S.M., Irving, G., Szegedy, C., Kaliszyk, C.: Deep network guided proof search. In: 21st International Conference on Logic for Programming, Artificial Intelligence, and Reasoning (LPAR) (2017)
30. Mohamed, O.A., Muñoz, C., Tahar, S. (eds.): TPHOLs 2008. LNCS, vol. 5170. Springer, Heidelberg (2008). https://doi.org/10.1007/978-3-540-71067-7
31. Nagashima, Y., He, Y.: PaMpeR: proof method recommendation system for Isabelle/HOL. In: Huchard, M., Kästner, C., Fraser, G. (eds.) Proceedings of the 33rd ACM/IEEE International Conference on Automated Software Engineering, ASE 2018, Montpellier, France, 3–7 September 2018, pp. 362–372. ACM (2018)
32. Olšák, M., Kaliszyk, C., Urban, J.: Property invariant embedding for automated reasoning. In: Giacomo, G.D., et al. (eds.) ECAI 2020–24th European Conference on Artificial Intelligence, Santiago de Compostela, Spain, 29 August-8 September 2020 - Including 10th Conference on Prestigious Applications of Artificial Intelligence (PAIS 2020). Frontiers in Artificial Intelligence and Applications, vol. 325, pp. 1395–1402. IOS Press (2020)
33. Otten, J.: leanCoP 2.0 and ileanCoP 1.2: high performance lean theorem proving in classical and intuitionistic logic (system descriptions). In: Armando, A., Baumgartner, P., Dowek, G. (eds.) IJCAR 2008. LNCS (LNAI), vol. 5195, pp. 283–291. Springer, Heidelberg (2008). https://doi.org/10.1007/978-3-540-71070-7_23
34. Otten, J., Bibel, W.: leanCoP: lean connection-based theorem proving. J. Symb. Comput. **36**, 139–161 (2003)
35. Rawson, M., Reger, G.: Automated theorem proving, fast and slow. EasyChair Preprint no. 4433. EasyChair (2020)

36. Ross, S., Gordon, G., Bagnell, D.: A reduction of imitation learning and structured prediction to no-regret online learning. In: Gordon, G., Dunson, D., Dudík, M. (eds.) Proceedings of the Fourteenth International Conference on Artificial Intelligence and Statistics. Proceedings of Machine Learning Research, Fort Lauderdale, FL, USA, 11–13 April 2011, vol. 15, pp. 627–635. PMLR (2011)
37. Scarselli, F., Gori, M., Tsoi, A.C., Hagenbuchner, M., Monfardini, G.: The graph neural network model. Trans. Neur. Netw. **20**(1), 61–80 (2009)
38. Schulz, S.: E - a Brainiac theorem prover. AI Commun. **15**(2–3), 111–126 (2002)
39. Schulz, S.: System description: E 1.8. In: McMillan, K., Middeldorp, A., Voronkov, A. (eds.) LPAR 2013. LNCS, vol. 8312, pp. 735–743. Springer, Heidelberg (2013). https://doi.org/10.1007/978-3-642-45221-5_49
40. Silver, D., et al.: Mastering the game of go without human knowledge. Nature **550**, 354 (2017)
41. Slind, K., Norrish, M.: A brief overview of HOL4. In: Mohamed et al. [30], pp. 28–32
42. Suda, M.: New techniques that improve Enigma-style clause selection guidance. In: International Conference on Automated Deduction, CADE 2021 (2021)
43. Sutton, R.S., Barto, A.G.: Reinforcement Learning: An Introduction, 2nd edn. The MIT Press, Cambridge (2018)
44. Urban, J.: ERC project AI4Reason final scientific report (2021). http://grid01.ciirc.cvut.cz/~mptp/ai4reason/PR_CORE_SCIENTIFIC_4.pdf
45. Urban, J., Sutcliffe, G., Pudlák, P., Vyskočil, J.: MaLARea SG1 - machine learner for automated reasoning with semantic guidance. In: IJCAR, pp. 441–456 (2008)
46. Urban, J., Vyskočil, J., Štěpánek, P.: MaLeCoP machine learning connection prover. In: Brünnler, K., Metcalfe, G. (eds.) TABLEAUX 2011. LNCS (LNAI), vol. 6793, pp. 263–277. Springer, Heidelberg (2011). https://doi.org/10.1007/978-3-642-22119-4_21
47. Vulkan, N.: An economist's perspective on probability matching. J. Econ. Surv. **14**(1), 101–118 (2000)
48. Wenzel, M., Paulson, L.C., Nipkow, T.: The Isabelle framework. In: Mohamed et al. [30], pp. 33–38
49. Williams, R.J., Peng, J.: Function optimization using connectionist reinforcement learning algorithms. Connect. Sci. **3**(3), 241–268 (1991)
50. Yang, K., Deng, J.: Learning to prove theorems via interacting with proof assistants. In: Chaudhuri, K., Salakhutdinov, R. (eds.) Proceedings of the 36th International Conference on Machine Learning, ICML 2019, Long Beach, California, USA, 9–15 June 2019. Proceedings of Machine Learning Research, vol. 97, pp. 6984–6994. PMLR (2019)
51. Zombori, Z., Urban, J., Brown, C.E.: Prolog technology reinforcement learning prover. In: Peltier, N., Sofronie-Stokkermans, V. (eds.) IJCAR 2020. LNCS (LNAI), vol. 12167, pp. 489–507. Springer, Cham (2020). https://doi.org/10.1007/978-3-030-51054-1_33

The nanoCoP 2.0 Connection Provers for Classical, Intuitionistic and Modal Logics

Jens Otten(✉)

Department of Informatics, University of Oslo, Oslo, Norway
jeotten@ifi.uio.no

Abstract. This paper introduces the *full* versions of the *non-clausal* connection provers nanoCoP for first-order classical logic, nanoCoP-i for first-order intuitionistic logic and nanoCoP-M for several first-order multimodal logics. The enhancements added to the core provers include several techniques to improve performance and usability, such as a strategy scheduling and the output of a detailed non-clausal connection proof for all covered logics. Experimental evaluations for all provers show the effectiveness of the integrated optimizations.

1 Introduction

The *non-clausal* connection calculus for classical logic [18] generalizes the *clausal* connection calculus [3,4,24] to arbitrary first-order formulae. By directly dealing with non-clausal formulae, a translation into a (disjunctive or conjunctive) clausal form can be avoided. Instead, the structure of the original input formula is preserved throughout the proof search. The non-clausal calculus combines the advantages of more natural (non-clausal) sequent and tableau calculi with the more systematic and goal-oriented proof search of connection calculi. Recently, the non-clausal connection calculus has been adapted and extended to first-order *intuitionistic* logic and several first-order *modal* logics [22]. This has been achieved by adding prefixes and a specialized prefix unification algorithm that captures the Kripke semantics of these non-classical logics.

Automated theorem provers that are based on these non-clausal calculi have been introduced as well: the nanoCoP (= *na*tural *no*n-clausal *Co*nnection *P*rover) series of provers for classical logic [20,21], first-order intuitionistic logic and several first-order modal logics [22]. While already the basic implementations of the non-clausal core calculi show a decent performance, these basic provers were missing important features in terms of performance and usability, e.g., output of readable connection proofs and further proof search optimizations, such as strategy scheduling, a technique that consecutively tries a set of different strategies when searching for a proof.

After a brief introduction of the non-clausal connection calculi (Sect. 2), the paper presents the most recent versions of the non-clausal connection provers nanoCoP, nanoCoP-i and nanoCoP-M together with the (minimalistic) source code of the Prolog core prover (Sect. 3). The main enhancements are the integration of several *lean* proof search optimizations, a strategy scheduling, the output

A. Das and S. Negri (Eds.): TABLEAUX 2021, LNAI 12842, pp. 236–249, 2021.
https://doi.org/10.1007/978-3-030-86059-2_14

of readable connection proofs, the extension of nanoCoP-M to multimodal logics, and a better support to run the provers on different Prolog platforms. The paper also presents a comprehensive practical evaluation of all provers on the standard problem libraries (Sect. 4).

2 Non-clausal Connection Calculi

A *(first-order) formula* (denoted by F, G, H) is built up from atomic formulae, the connectives $\neg$, $\wedge$, $\vee$, $\Rightarrow$, and the standard first-order quantifiers $\forall$ and $\exists$. A *(first-order) modal formula* might also include the modal operators $\Box$ and $\Diamond$. An *atomic formula* (denoted by A) is built up from predicate symbols (P, Q), function symbols (f, g) and term variables (x, y). A *literal* L has the form A or $\neg A$.

In the *clausal* connection calculus a matrix is a set of clauses, where a clause is a set of literals. The *non-clausal* connection calculus works on *non-clausal* matrices, in which a matrix M is a set of clauses and a clause C is a set of literals L and (sub)matrices. It can be seen as a representation of a formula in negation normal form.

For a formula F and polarity $pol \in \{0, 1\}$, the *classical non-clausal matrix* $M(F^{pol})$ of F^{pol} is defined inductively according to Table 1 ($: p$ and the last two lines are to be ignored). x^* is a new term variable, t^* is the Skolem term $f^*(x_1, \ldots, x_n)$ in which f^* is a new function symbol and $x_1, \ldots, x_n$ are all free variables in $(\forall x G)^0 : p$ or $(\exists x G)^1 : p$. The *(classical) non-clausal matrix* $M(F)$ of F is the classical non-clausal matrix $M(F^0)$.

In the *graphical representation* of a non-clausal matrix, its clauses are arranged horizontally, its literals and matrices are arranged vertically. A *connection* is a set $\{{A_1}^0, {A_2}^1\}$ of literals with the same predicate symbol but different polarities. A *term substitution* σ_T assigns terms to variables. A connection is σ_T*-complementary* iff $\sigma_T(A_1) = \sigma_T(A_2)$.

The axiom and the four rules of the *non-clausal connection calculus* are given in Fig. 1 (again, $: p_1$ and $: p_2$ are to be ignored). Compared to the formal *clausal* connection calculus [23], the extension rule is restricted to certain extension clauses and a *decomposition rule* is added that splits subgoal clauses; see [18,20] for details.

A clause C in a matrix M is an *extension clause (e-clause) of* M *with respect to* a set of literals *Path* iff either (a) C contains a literal of *path*, or (b) C is α-related to (i.e. occurs besides) all literals of *path* occurring in M, and if C has a parent clause, it contains a literal of *path*. In the clause β-$clause_{L_2}(C_2)$, the literal L_2 and all clauses that are α-related to (occur besides) L_2 are deleted from C_2, as these clauses do not need to be considered in the new subgoal clause in the premise of the extension rule. A *copy of the clause* C in the matrix M is made by renaming all *free variables* in C. $M[C_1 \backslash C_2]$ denotes the matrix M, in which the clause C_1 is replaced by the clause C_2.

Table 1. The definition of the (prefixed) non-clausal matrix for classical and modal logic

type	$F^{pol}:p$	$M(F^{pol}:p)$	type	$F^{pol}:p$	$M(F^{pol}:p)$
atomic	$A^0:p$	$\{\{A^0:p\}\}$	atomic	$A^1:p$	$\{\{A^1:p\}\}$
α	$(G\wedge H)^1:p$	$\{\{M(G^1:p)\}\},\{\{M(H^1:p)\}\}$	α	$(\neg G)^0:p$	$M(G^1:p)$
	$(G\vee H)^0:p$	$\{\{M(G^0:p)\}\},\{\{M(H^0:p)\}\}$		$(\neg G)^1:p$	$M(G^0:p)$
	$(G\Rightarrow H)^0{:}p$	$\{\{M(G^1:p)\}\},\{\{M(H^0:p)\}\}$	γ	$(\forall xG)^1:p$	$M(G[x\backslash x^*]^1:p)$
β	$(G\wedge H)^0:p$	$\{\{M(G^0:p),M(H^0:p)\}\}$		$(\exists xG)^0:p$	$M(G[x\backslash x^*]^0:p)$
	$(G\vee H)^1:p$	$\{\{M(G^1:p),M(H^1:p)\}\}$	δ	$(\forall xG)^0:p$	$M(G[x\backslash t^*]^0:p)$
	$(G\Rightarrow H)^1{:}p$	$\{\{M(G^0:p),M(H^1:p)\}\}$		$(\exists xG)^1:p$	$M(G[x\backslash t^*]^1:p)$
ν	$(\Box G)^1:p$	$M(G^1:pV^*)$	π	$(\Box G)^0:p$	$M(G^0:pa^*)$
	$(\Diamond G)^0:p$	$M(G^0:pV^*)$		$(\Diamond G)^1:p$	$M(G^1:pa^*)$

$$\textit{Axiom (A)}\quad \frac{}{\{\},M,\textit{Path}} \qquad \textit{Start (S)}\quad \frac{C_2,M,\{\}}{\varepsilon,M,\varepsilon}\ \text{ and } C_2 \text{ is copy of } C_1{\in}M$$

$$\textit{Reduction (R)}\quad \frac{C,M,\textit{Path}{\cup}\{L_2{:}\underline{p_2}\}}{C{\cup}\{L_1{:}\underline{p_1}\},M,\textit{Path}{\cup}\{L_2{:}\underline{p_2}\}}\ \text{ and } \{L_1{:}\underline{p_1},L_2{:}\underline{p_2}\} \text{ is } \sigma\text{-complementary}$$

$$\textit{Extension (E)}\quad \frac{C_3,M[C_1\backslash C_2],\textit{Path}{\cup}\{L_1{:}\underline{p_1}\}\qquad C,M,\textit{Path}}{C{\cup}\{L_1{:}\underline{p_1}\},M,\textit{Path}}$$

and $C_3{:=}\beta\text{-}clause_{L_2}(C_2)$, C_2 is copy of C_1, C_1 is e-clause of M wrt. $\textit{Path}{\cup}\{L_1{:}\underline{p_1}\}$, C_2 contains $L_2{:}\underline{p_2}$, $\{L_1{:}\underline{p_1},L_2{:}\underline{p_2}\}$ is σ-complementary

$$\textit{Decomposition (D)}\quad \frac{C{\cup}C_1,M,\textit{Path}}{C{\cup}\{M_1\},M,\textit{Path}}\ \text{ and } C_1{\in}M_1$$

Fig. 1. The non-clausal connection calculus for classical, intuitionistic and modal logic

The calculus works on tuples "$C, M, \textit{Path}$", where M is a non-clausal matrix, C is a (subgoal) clause or ε and (the active) *path* is a set of literals or ε. The *rigid* σ_T is calculated by using *term unification* whenever a connection is identified. A *non-clausal connection proof* of M is a proof of $\varepsilon, M, \varepsilon$ in the non-clausal connection calculus.

For *intuitionistic and modal logic*, the non-clausal matrix and the calculus are extended by prefixes, representing world paths in the Kripke semantics; see [22,30,31]. A *prefix* p is a string consisting of variables (V, W) and constants (a) and assigned to each literal. The *modal non-clausal matrix* $M(F^{pol}{:}p)$ *of a prefixed formula* $F^{pol}{:}p$ is defined according to Table 1. V^* is a new prefix variable, a^* is a prefix constant of the form $f^*(x_1,\ldots,x_n)$ in which f^* is a new function symbol and $x_1,\ldots,x_n$ are all free term and prefix variables in $(\Box G)^0:p$ or $(\Diamond G)^1:p$. The *modal non-clausal matrix* $M(F)$ of F is the modal non-clausal matrix $M(F^0:\varepsilon)$; see [22] for the *intuitionistic* case.

A *prefix substitution* σ_P assigns strings to prefix variables and is calculated by a *prefix unification* that depends on the specific non-classical logic. In intuitionistic and modal logic, a connection $\{L_1{:}p_1, L_2{:}p_2\}$ is σ-*complementary* iff both, its literals *and* prefixes can be unified under a combined substitution $\sigma = (\sigma_T, \sigma_P)$, i.e. additionally $\sigma_P(p_1) = \sigma_P(p_2)$ must hold. A *non-clausal connection proof* of M is a proof of $\varepsilon, M, \varepsilon$ in the calculus of Fig. 1 (with the underlined text included) with an *admissible* σ [22].

Example 1. The formula $P(a) \wedge (\forall y(P(y) \Rightarrow P(g(y))) \vee \neg(\Box Q \Rightarrow \Diamond Q)) \Rightarrow P(g(g(a)))$ has the following (modal) non-clausal matrix (empty prefix strings are not shown):

$$\{\{P(a)^1\}, \{\{\{P(y)^0, P(g(y))^1\}\}, \{\{Q^1 : V\}, \{Q^0 : W\}\}\}, \{P(g(g(a)))^0\}\}.$$

It has the following graphical representation and (graphical) connection proof with the substitutions $\sigma_T(y) = a$, $\sigma_T(y') = g(a)$ and $\sigma_P(V) = W$; literals of each connection are connected with a line. A *clausal* proof would need eleven instead of four connections.

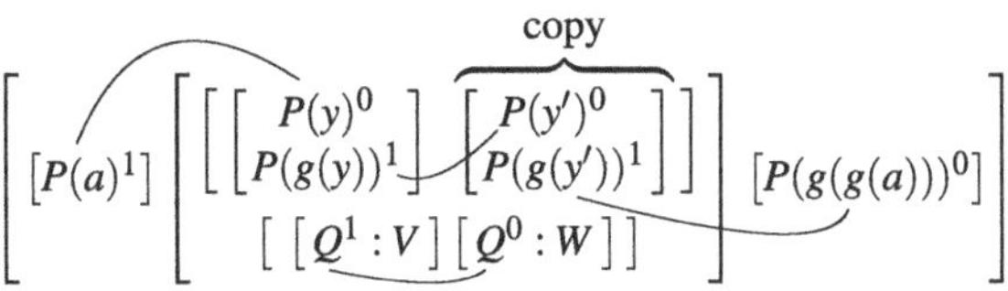

3 The Implementations

nanoCoP, nanoCoP-i and nanoCoP-M are theorem provers for first-order *classical* logic with equality, first-order *intuitionistic* logic with equality and several first-order *modal* logics, respectively.[1] They are very compact Prolog implementations of the basic non-clausal connection calculi extended by a few basic but effective optimizations.

3.1 Non-clausal Matrix

In the first step, the input formula F is translated into a non-clausal matrix M (see Table 1). Every (sub-)clause $(I, V, FV) : C$ and submatrix $J : M$ are marked with unique indices I and J, sets V of (free) term and prefix variables that are newly introduced in C and sets FV including pairs $x : pre(x)$ of free term variables and their prefixes, necessary to check if σ is admissible. In Prolog, literals with polarity 1 are marked with "-". In the second step, for every literal `Lit` in M the fact `lit(Lit,ClaB,ClaC,Grnd)` is asserted into Prolog's database where `ClaC` $\in M$ is the clause in which `Lit` occurs, `ClaB` is β-$clause_{Lit}$(`ClaC`), `Grnd` is `g` iff the smallest clause in which `Lit` occurs is ground.

Example 2. The (modal) formula from Example 1 is expressed in nanoCoP syntax as

```
( p(a) , ( all Y: (p(Y) => p(g(Y)) ) ; ~ (# q => * q) ) => p(g(g(a))) )
```

and is translated into the following (modal) non-clausal matrix

[1] Provers available under the GNU General Public License at http://leancop.de/nanocop/, http://leancop.de/nanocop-i/, and http://leancop.de/nanocop-m/.

```
(1)  prove(M,U,S,[(I^0)^V:X]) :-
(2)   ( m(scut,S) -> ( a([(I^0)^V^W:F|_],[!|_],M) ; m((I^0)^V^W:C,M),
(3)   posC(C,F) ) -> true ; ( a(Z,[!|_],M) -> m((I^0)^V^W:F,Z) ;
(4)   m((I^0)^V^W:C,M),posC(C,F) ) ), prove(F,M,[],[I^0],U,[],P,B,S,X),
(5)   a(B,W,D), domain_cond(D), prefix_unify(P).

(6)  prove(M,U,S,X) :- retract(p) -> ( m(comp(U),S) -> prove(M,1,[],X);
(7)   V is U+1, prove(M,V,S,X) ) ; m(comp(_),S) -> prove(M,1,[],X).

(8)  prove([],_,_,_,_,_,[],[],_,[]).

(9)  prove([J^K:M|C],H,P,T,U,Q,A,B,S,X) :- !, m(I^V^W:F,M),
(10)  prove(F,H,P,[I,J^K|T],U,Q,D,E,S,Y), prove(C,H,P,T,U,Q,N,O,S,Z),
(11)  a(N,D,A), a(W,E,R), a(O,R,B), X=[J^K:I^V:Y|Z].

(12) prove([L:J|C],H,P,T,U,Q,P1,V1,S,X) :-
(13)  X=[L:J,I^V:[N:O|Y]|Z], \+ (m(A,[L:J|C]),m(B,P),A==B), (-N=L;-L=N)
(14)  -> ( m(R,Q), L:J==R, D=[], Y=[], I=1, V=[], O=J, P4=[], V4=[] ;
(15)  m(R:O,P), R=N, D=[], Y=[], I=r, V=[], \+ \+ prefix_unify([J=O]),
(16)  P4=[J=O], V4=[] ; lit(N:O,E,F,G), ( G=g -> true ; length(P,K),K<U
(17)  -> true ; \+ p -> assert(p), fail ), \+ \+ prefix_unify([J=O]),
(18)  pe(E,F,H,T,I^V^W:D,M), prove(D,M,[L:J|P],[I|T],U,Q,P2,V2,S,Y),
(19)  P4=[J=O|P2], a(V2,W,V4) ), ( m(cut,S) -> ! ; true ),
(20)  prove(C,H,P,T,U,[L:J|Q],P3,V3,S,Z), a(P4,P3,P1), a(V3,V4,V1).

(21) pe((I^K)^V:E,N:C,H,T,D,M) :- a(A,[(I^L)^W:F|B],H), length(T,K),
(22)  ( E=[J^K:[G]|_], m(J^L,T), V=W, C=[_:[R|_]|_], a(U,[J^L:Y|X],F),
(23)  pe(G,R,Y,T,D,Z), a(U,[J^L:Z|X],S), a(A,[(I^L)^W:S|B],M) ;
(24)  (\+m(I^L,T);V\==W) -> D=(I^K)^V:E, a(A,[N:C|B],M) ).

(25) m(A,B) :- member(A,B). a(A,B,C) :- append(A,B,C).
```

Fig. 2. Source code of the nanoCoP, nanoCoP-i and nanoCoP-M core provers

```
[ (2^K)^[]^[]: [ -p(a): -[] ],
  (4^K)^[]^[]: [  5^K: [ (6^K)^[Y]^[Y:[]]: [ p(Y):[], -p(g(Y)): -[] ] ],
                 12^K: [ (13^K)^[V]^[]: [ -q: -[V] ], (16^K)^[W]^[]: [ q:[W] ] ] ],
 (18^K)^[]^[]: [ p(g(g(a))):[] ] ]
```

in which V and W are the prefix variables, the variable K is used to enumerate clauses.

3.2 nanoCoP for Classial Logic

The (minimalistic) source code of the nanoCoP core prover is shown in Fig. 2. The underlined code is necessary only for the non-classical provers and is to be ignored for the (classical) nanoCoP prover. The predicate prove(M,U,S,X) implements the start rule (lines 1–5). M is the matrix generated in the preprocessing step, U is the maximum size of the active path used for iterative deepening (lines 6–7), S specifies a strategy (see Sect. 3.5), and X contains the returned (compact) non-clausal connection proof.

The predicate `prove(Cla, Mat, Path, T, U, Q, S, X)` implements axiom (line 8), decomposition rule (lines 9–11), reduction rule (lines 12–15, 20), and extension rule (lines 12–13, 16–20) of the calculus in Fig. 1. It succeeds iff there is a proof for the tuple "`Cla, Mat, Path`" with |`Path`| < `U`. The predicate `pe` calculates an appropriate extension clause (lines 21–24). σ is stored implicitly by Prolog. Prolog's `member` and `append` predicates are abbreviated by `m` and `a`, respectively (line 25). The predicate `posC(C,F)` (invoked in line 3 and 4) calculates a *positive (start) clause* `F` of the clause `C`. It is implemented in seven lines of (non-minimalistic) code and is the only predicate of the core prover that is not included in the code in Fig. 2. The nanoCoP website includes a more readable version of the full source code.

3.3 nanoCoP-i for Intuitionistic Logic

For intuitionistic logic, prefixes are added to all literals in the non-clausal matrix (details in [22]) and to the non-clausal connection calculus. For nanoCoP-i, the underlined text in Fig. 2 is added to the classical nanoCoP prover; no other changes are done.

A list `P1` of prefix equations and a list `V1` of term variables (with their prefixes) are collected during the proof search and are added as arguments to the main predicate `prove(Cla, Mat, Path, T, U, Q, P1, V1, S, X)`. Two predicates need to be added to the code: `prefix_unify(P)` implements the prefix unification and `domain_cond(V)` checks whether σ is an admissible substitution.

3.4 nanoCoP-M for Multimodal Logics

For modal logic, prefixes are added to all literals in the non-clausal matrix (according to Table 1) and to the non-clausal connection calculus. The nanoCoP-M core prover shown in Fig. 2 has the same source code as the intuitionistic nanoCoP-i prover.

Again, `prefix_unify(P)` implements the prefix unification with respect to a specific modal logic and `domain_cond(V)` checks whether σ is an admissible substitution with respect to a specific domain condition. nanoCoP-M supports the modal logics D, T, S4, and S5 with varying, cumulative and constant domain condition; terms are considered rigid and local, the logical consequence relation is *local* [22,31].

For the modal logics D and T the *accessibility condition* $|\sigma_P(V)|{=}1$ and $|\sigma_P(V)|{\leq}1$, respectively, has to hold for all prefix variables V. There is no such restriction for the modal logic S4 and only the last prefix character is considered for the modal logic S5.

nanoCoP-M also supports heterogeneous multimodal logics. For *multimodal* logic, an index can be added to the modal operators $\Box$ and $\Diamond$, i.e. modal operators from the set $\{\Box_i, \Diamond_i \,|\, i \in I\!N\}$ are allowed. Modal operators with different indices can be assigned to different modal logics. See the nanoCoP-M website for more details.

3.5 Proof Search Optimizations

Following the *lean* methodology, a few basic but effective techniques are carefully selected and integrated into the nanoCoP, nanoCoP-i and nanoCoP-M provers.

Regularity and Lemmata. *Regularity* (line 13) and *lemmata* (line 14) are effective techniques for pruning the search space in *clausal* connection calculi [10] and were already included in the basic versions of the nanoCoP provers [20,22].

Restricted Backtracking. *Restricted backtracking* is an effective (but incomplete) technique to prune the search space in the (non-confluent) connection calculus [17]. Besides restricted backtracking for the extension and reduction rules ("`cut`") (line 19), restricted backtracking for the start rule ("`scut`") (lines 2–3) is now integrated as well, which cuts off backtracking over alternative start clauses in the connection calculus.

Conjecture Start Clauses. *Conjecture start clauses* ("`conj`") restricts the start rule for formulae of the form $(A_1 \wedge \ldots \wedge A_n) \Rightarrow C$ to clauses of the conjecture C (line 2 and 3), instead of the default positive clauses (line 3 and 4). This technique is in particular effective for formulae with many axioms A_i. This approach is incomplete for formulae with inconsistent/unsatisfiable axioms $A_1, \ldots, A_n$ and invalid conjecture C.

Reordering Clauses. *Reordering clauses* ("`reo(I)`") is a technique to modify (indirectly) the proof search order, which is in particular effective in combination with restricted backtracking. For non-clausal calculi it is important to produce diverse clause orders even for small sets of clauses, e.g., if a (sub)matrix contains only two or three clauses. It is done in a preprocessing step using a pseudo-randomized shuffle algorithm.

Strategy Scheduling. *Strategy scheduling* is a very effective technique that uses a sequence of different strategies to prove a formula. A strategy is specified in the argument `S` of the `prove` predicate. It is a list that contains a (possibly empty) subset of the options {`scut`,`cut`,`conj`, `reo`(I),`comp`(J)}, which effect the proof search as follows:

- `scut`: switches on restricted backtracking for start clauses,
- `cut`: switches on restricted backtracking for reduction/extension/lemma rule,
- `conj`: uses conjecture clauses as start clauses instead of positive clauses,
- `reo`(I) for $I \in \mathbb{N}$: reorders the clauses I times before the proof search starts,
- `comp`(J) for $J \in \mathbb{N}$: restarts the proof search using a complete search strategy, i.e. without `scut`, `cut`, and `conj`, if the path limit `U` exceeds J (lines 6–7).

A fixed strategy scheduling (sequence) is implemented using a shell script that invokes the Prolog prover. Comprehensive tests were performed in order to select a set of 20 strategies for nanoCoP and 12 strategies for nanoCoP-i and nanoCoP-M, respectively. The first three stategies used by nanoCoP, nanoCoP-i and nanoCoP-M are `[cut,comp(7)]`/`[reo(22),conj,cut]`/`[scut]`, `[cut,comp(6)]`/`[scut]`/`[scut,cut]`, and `[cut,comp(6)]`/`[cut]`/`[reo(20), conj,cut]`, respectively. The empty (and complete) strategy `[]` is the last one used by all three nanoCoP provers.

3.6 Proof Output

All three nanoCoP provers can output a detailed non-clausal connection proof. The nanoCoP core provers return a very compact (and hardly readable) non-clausal connection proof that has been further optimized in terms of size and included proof information. It is returned in the last argument `X` of the `prove` predicate in Fig. 2.

Example 3. For the (modal) formula from Example 1 and its non-clausal (modal) matrix given in Example 2, the nanoCoP-M core prover returns the following compact (modal) non-clausal connection proof

```
[ (18^0)^[]: [ p(g(g(a))):  [],
  (4^1)^[]: [ -p(g(g(a))): -[], 5^1: (6^1)^[g(a)]: [ p(g(a)):  [],
                                       (6^4)^[a]: [ -p(g(a)): -[], p(a):  [],
                                                    (2^5)^[]: [ -p(a): -[]] ] ],
              12^1: (13^1)^[[V]]: [ -q: -[[V]],
                      (16^4)^[V]: [ q:   [V] ] ] ] ] ]
```

in which the literals of the connections have been underlined. In the terms of the form `(I^K)^L:C`, `I` and `K` are the index and the instance (number) of the clause `C`, respectively, and `L` is a list that contains the substituted term and prefix variables.

Based on this returned compact proof, a detailed and more readable non-clausal connection proof is reconstructed in a separate module. As non-clausal connection proofs are closely related to proofs in Gentzen's LK/LJ sequent calculi [8] and Schütte's GS calculus [5], they can (rather) easily be translated into LK/LJ/GS proofs.

4 Experimental Evaluation

The optimizations described in Sect. 3 were integrated into the nanoCoP 2.0 provers and are evaluated on different benchmark libraries. All evaluations were conducted on a 2.3 GHz Xeon system with 32 GB of RAM running Linux 2.6.32. If not stated otherwise, ECLiPSe Prolog 5.10 was used for all provers implemented in Prolog.[2]

[2] ECLiPSe Prolog 5.x is available at https://eclipseclp.org/Distribution/Builds/. Newer versions of ECLiPSe Prolog are missing important features (e.g. the possibility to switch on a global occurs check) and have a significantly lower performance.

Table 2. Results on the first-order problems of the TPTP library

	leanTAP 2.3	leanCoP 2.2	E 2.4	nanoCoP 1.0	nanoCoP 2.0 SWI	nanoCoP 2.0	nanoCoP + leanCoP
Proved	555	2541	4377	2055	2132	**2500**	2709
0 to 1 s	520	1643	3152	1543	1325	**1573**	1590
1 to 10 s	20	369	780	277	317	**264**	294
10 to 100 s	15	529	445	235	490	**663**	825
Refuted	0	67	510	133	132	**133**	133
Total	555	2608	4887	2188	2264	**2633**	2842

nanoCoP. The classical nanoCoP prover was evaluated on all 8044 first-order (so-called FOF) problems in the TPTP library v6.4.0 [29]. Table 2 shows the results of the evaluation for a CPU time limit of 100 s. Besides nanoCoP 2.0, it includes the following provers: the lean tableau prover leanTAP 2.3 [1], the superposition prover E 2.4 [27] (using the options "`--proof-object -s --satauto`"), leanCoP 2.2 [17], and nanoCoP 1.0 [20]. It also includes the results of nanoCoP running on SWI Prolog 7.6.4 and the combined results of nanoCoP 2.0 and leanCoP 2.2.

nanoCoP 2.0 proves 22% more problems than nanoCoP 1.0 and 350% more problems than leanTAP, the other lean prover that is based on a non-clausal (tableau) calculus. E proves 75% more problems than nanoCoP 2.0. nanoCoP 2.0 performs significantly better on ECLiPSe Prolog than on SWI Prolog. The numbers in the last column indicate that nanoCoP 2.0 proves 168 problems that are not proven by leanCoP 2.2.

Optimizations. Table 3 shows the effectiveness of the different optimization techniques implemented in nanoCoP 2.0 on all 8044 FOF problems in the TPTP library v6.4.0 for a CPU time limit of 10 seconds. The following versions of nanoCoP are evaluated: a basic version without regularity and lemmata ("basic"), the standard version using regularity and lemmata (i.e. strategy `[]`), a version with conjecture start clauses (`[conj]`), two versions with restricted backtracking (`[scut]` and `[cut]`, respectively), nanoCoP 1.0 (which uses the single strategy `[cut,comp(6)]`), a "reo" version with reordering of clauses (using the strategy `[reo(22),conj,cut]`), and the full nanoCoP 2.0 prover using all of the described optimizations including strategy scheduling.

As different optimizations can be combined within the strategy scheduling, not only the total number of proved problems is given, but also the number of new problems proved compared to the "basic" or the standard nanoCoP version (using strategy `[]`).

Table 3. Evaluation of different optimization techniques

	"basic"	`[]`	`[conj]`	`[scut]`	`[cut]`	1.0	"reo"	2.0
Proved	1465	1516	1682	1598	1691	1820	1855	**2079**
New proved	–	64	253	248	421	409	260	**314**
Compared to	–	"basic"	`[]`	`[]`	`[]`	`[]`	1.0	1.0

Table 4. Results on the first-order problems of the ILTP library

	ileanTAP 1.17	ileanCoP 1.2	Slakje 2.14	nanoCoP-i 1.0	nanoCoP-i 2.0	nanoCoP-i + ileanCoP
Proved	314	782	1019	764	**839**	848
0 to 1 s	303	612	95	681	**676**	676
1 to 10 s	7	51	367	44	**47**	51
10 to 100 s	4	119	557	39	**116**	121
Refuted	4	78	363	89	89	91

nanoCoP-i. Table 4 shows the results of the evaluation on all 2550 first-order problems in the ILTP library v1.1.2 [26] for a CPU time limit of 100 s. Included are the provers ileanTAP 1.17, ileanCoP 1.2, Slakje 2.14, nanoCoP-i 1.0, nanoCoP-i 2.0 and the combined results of nanoCoP-i 2.0 and ileanCoP 1.2. ileanTAP [14] implements a prefixed free-variable tableau calculus and is written in Prolog; ileanCoP [15,16] is a compact Prolog prover that implements the prefixed *clausal* connection calculus; Slakje [6] uses a prover for classical logic to search for a classical proof and the GAPT system [7] to subsequently reconstruct an intuitionistic proof from the classical one. These are currently the fastest theorem provers for intuitionistic first-order logic (JProver, ft and ileanSeP prove significantly less problems than ileanCoP [16,22]).

nanoCoP-i 2.0 proves about 10% more problem than nanoCoP-i 1.0. It also proves more problem than ileanCoP, currently the fastest connection/tableau prover for first-order intuitionistic logic. Slakje proves the largest number of problems, but the proof reconstruction with GAPT shows a significant overhead. ileanCoP as well as nanoCoP-i prove significant more problems than Slakje within a time limit of 10 s.

nanoCoP-M. Table 5 shows the results of the evaluation on all 580 unimodal problems of the QMLTP library v1.1 [25]. Results are shown for the modal logics D, T, S4 and S5, and for the varying, cumulative, and constant domain variants. It includes the following provers: MleanTAP 1.3, MleanCoP 1.3, nanoCoP-M 1.0, and nanoCoP-M 2.0. MleanTAP [2] implements a prefixed tableau calculus; MleanCoP [19] implements a prefixed *clausal* connection calculus; both provers are written in Prolog. Up to the authors knowledge, these are currently the only provers for modal first-order logic (the sequent prover MleanSeP proves about the same number of problems as MleanTAP [19]).

nanoCoP-M 2.0 proves on average 16%, 4%, 11% and 6% more problems than nanoCoP-M 1.0 for the modal logics D, T, S4 and S5, respectively. It refutes about the same number of problems as nanoCoP-M 1.0. nanoCoP-M 2.0 also proves more problems than MleanCoP, which was so far the most successful prover on the QMLTP library [28]. The higher-order prover Leo-III [28] uses an embedding of modal logics into simple type theory in order to deal with a wide range of different (higher-order) modal logics. Leo-III does not support the QMLTP syntax, but previous evaluations show that it proves slightly fewer

Table 5. Results on the unimodal problems (varying/cumul./constant) of the QMLTP library

Logic	MleanTAP 1.3	—MleanCoP 1.3—		nanoCoP-M 1.0	—nanoCoP-M 2.0—	
	Proved	Proved	Refuted	Proved	Proved	Refuted
D	100/120/135	184/206/223	274/248/222	167/187/204	**193/213/230**	265/245/229
T	138/160/175	223/251/271	159/132/114	222/244/263	**231/253/273**	153/133/119
S4	169/205/220	286/349/363	127/96/83	271/321/336	**297/355/370**	124/98/85
S5	219/272/272	358/435/435	94/41/41	343/414/414	**365/440/440**	92/44/44

problems of the QMLTP library than MleanCoP [28]. nanoCoP 2.0 solves 17 of the 20 multimodal problems in the QMLTP library, all of them within one second.

5 Conclusion

In this paper the nanoCoP 2.0 provers for classical, intuitionistic and modal logics have been presented. They are very compact and modular Prolog implementations of the non-clausal connection calculi for classical and non-classical logics. The integration of a few effective optimization techniques improves performance significantly. Compared to the previous versions, the classical nanoCoP 2.0 system solves about 20% more problems from the TPTP library, the intuitionistic nanoCoP-i 2.0 and the modal nanoCoP-M 2.0 systems prove about 10% more problems from the ILTP and QMLTP libraries. Despite the overhead caused by the more complex non-clausal data structure, nanoCoP-i and nanoCoP-M prove more problems than the corresponding clausal provers ileanCoP and MleanCoP, and they are now among the fastest provers for these non-classical logics.

All nanoCoP 2.0 provers can provide detailed non-clausal connection proofs. Preliminary results show that on the non-clausal problems in the TPTP library, the non-clausal proofs of nanoCoP have on average only half the number of connections than the clausal proofs produced by leanCoP. The non-clausal proofs are also more "natural" as the structure of the original formula is preserved throughout the whole proof search. This makes them in particular interesting for applications where a human readable output or interaction is required. For example, the normative reasoner NAI uses MleanCoP at its backend in order to reason over legal texts formalized in a multimodal first-order logic [11,12]. nanoCoP-M 2.0, which now also supports heterogeneous multimodal logics, could be used in order to return a more natural human readable proof.

Future work includes the integration of better *refuting techniques* into the nanoCoP provers, which were so far not in the focus of the development. It also includes the extension to other modal logics, such as the *modal logic* K, for which a connection-based proof approach is more difficult as subformulae that are not involved in any connection might be relevant for a successful proof [31]. More straightforward is the development of connection calculi and provers for first-order *intuitionistic modal* logic. The presented calculi and provers are optimized for full *first-order* logic. Combining these with calculi for propositional logic might be promising as these calculi are entirely different from the first-order ones. Another future work is the integration of *learning techniques* into nanoCoP as already done in many (re-)implementations of leanCoP [9,13,32].

Acknowledgements. The author would like to thank Wolfgang Bibel for his helpful feedback.

References

1. Beckert, B., Posegga, J.: leanTAP: lean tableau-based deduction. J. Autom. Reason. **15**(3), 339–358 (1995)
2. Benzmüller, C., Otten, J., Raths, T.: Implementing and evaluating provers for first-order modal logics. In: De Raedt, L., et al. (eds.) 20th European Conference on Artificial Intelligence (ECAI 2012), pp. 163–168. IOS Press, Amsterdam (2012)
3. Bibel, W.: Matings in matrices. Commun. ACM **26**(11), 844–852 (1983)
4. Bibel, W.: Automated Theorem Proving. Artificial Intelligence, 2nd edn. F. Vieweg und Sohn, Wiesbaden (1987)
5. Bibel, W., Otten, J.: From Schütte's formal systems to modern automated deduction. In: Kahle, R., Rathjen, M. (eds.) The Legacy of Kurt Schütte, pp. 217–251. Springer, Cham (2020). https://doi.org/10.1007/978-3-030-49424-7_13
6. Ebner, G.: Herbrand constructivization for automated intuitionistic theorem proving. In: Cerrito, S., Popescu, A. (eds.) TABLEAUX 2019. LNCS (LNAI), vol. 11714, pp. 355–373. Springer, Cham (2019). https://doi.org/10.1007/978-3-030-29026-9_20
7. Ebner, G., Hetzl, S., Reis, G., Riener, M., Wolfsteiner, S., Zivota, S.: System description: GAPT 2.0. In: Olivetti, N., Tiwari, A. (eds.) IJCAR 2016. LNCS (LNAI), vol. 9706, pp. 293–301. Springer, Cham (2016). https://doi.org/10.1007/978-3-319-40229-1_20
8. Gentzen, G.: Untersuchungen über das Logische Schließen. Math. Z. **39**(176–210), 405–431 (1935)
9. Kaliszyk, C., Urban, J.: FEMaLeCoP: fairly efficient machine learning connection prover. In: Davis, M., Fehnker, A., McIver, A., Voronkov, A. (eds.) LPAR 2015. LNCS, vol. 9450, pp. 88–96. Springer, Heidelberg (2015). https://doi.org/10.1007/978-3-662-48899-7_7
10. Letz, R., Stenz, G.: Model elimination and connection tableau procedures. In: Robinson, A., Voronkov, A. (eds.) Handbook of Automated Reasoning, pp. 2015–2112. Elsevier Science, Amsterdam (2001)
11. Libal, T., Pascucci, M.: Automated reasoning in normative detachment structures with ideal conditions. In: Seventeenth International Conference on Artificial Intelligence and Law, ICAIL 2019, pp. 63–72. Association for Computing Machinery, New York (2019)
12. Libal, T., Steen, A.: The NAI suite - drafting and reasoning over legal texts. In: Araszkiewicz, M., Rodríguez-Doncel, V. (eds.) 32nd International Conference on Legal Knowledge and Information Systems (JURIX 2019). Frontiers in Artificial Intelligence and Applications, vol. 322, pp. 243–246. IOS Press, Amsterdam (2019)
13. Olšák, M., Kaliszyk, C., Urban, J.: Property invariant embedding for automated reasoning. In: Giacomo, G.D., et al. (eds.) ECAI 2020. Frontiers in Artificial Intelligence and Applications, vol. 325, pp. 1395–1402. IOS Press, Amsterdam (2020)

14. Otten, J.: ileanTAP: an intuitionistic theorem prover. In: Galmiche, D. (ed.) TABLEAUX 1997. LNCS, vol. 1227, pp. 307–312. Springer, Heidelberg (1997). https://doi.org/10.1007/BFb0027422
15. Otten, J.: Clausal connection-based theorem proving in intuitionistic first-order logic. In: Beckert, B. (ed.) TABLEAUX 2005. LNCS (LNAI), vol. 3702, pp. 245–261. Springer, Heidelberg (2005). https://doi.org/10.1007/11554554_19
16. Otten, J.: leanCoP 2.0 and ileanCoP 1.2: high performance lean theorem proving in classical and intuitionistic logic (system descriptions). In: Armando, A., Baumgartner, P., Dowek, G. (eds.) IJCAR 2008. LNCS (LNAI), vol. 5195, pp. 283–291. Springer, Heidelberg (2008). https://doi.org/10.1007/978-3-540-71070-7_23
17. Otten, J.: Restricting backtracking in connection calculi. AI Commun. **23**(2–3), 159–182 (2010)
18. Otten, J.: A non-clausal connection calculus. In: Brünnler, K., Metcalfe, G. (eds.) TABLEAUX 2011. LNCS (LNAI), vol. 6793, pp. 226–241. Springer, Heidelberg (2011). https://doi.org/10.1007/978-3-642-22119-4_18
19. Otten, J.: MleanCoP: a connection prover for first-order modal logic. In: Demri, S., Kapur, D., Weidenbach, C. (eds.) IJCAR 2014. LNCS (LNAI), vol. 8562, pp. 269–276. Springer, Cham (2014). https://doi.org/10.1007/978-3-319-08587-6_20
20. Otten, J.: nanoCoP: a non-clausal connection prover. In: Olivetti, N., Tiwari, A. (eds.) IJCAR 2016. LNCS (LNAI), vol. 9706, pp. 302–312. Springer, Cham (2016). https://doi.org/10.1007/978-3-319-40229-1_21
21. Otten, J.: nanoCoP: natural non-clausal theorem proving. In: Sierra, C. (ed.) Proceedings of the Twenty-Sixth International Joint Conference on Artificial Intelligence, IJCAI-17, Sister Conference Best Paper Track. pp. 4924–4928. IJCAI (2017)
22. Otten, J.: Non-clausal connection calculi for non-classical logics. In: Schmidt, R.A., Nalon, C. (eds.) TABLEAUX 2017. LNCS (LNAI), vol. 10501, pp. 209–227. Springer, Cham (2017). https://doi.org/10.1007/978-3-319-66902-1_13
23. Otten, J., Bibel, W.: leanCoP: lean connection-based theorem proving. J. Symb. Comput. **36**(1–2), 139–161 (2003)
24. Otten, J., Bibel, W.: Advances in connection-based automated theorem proving. In: Hinchey, M.G., Bowen, J.P., Olderog, E.-R. (eds.) Provably Correct Systems. NMSSE, pp. 211–241. Springer, Cham (2017). https://doi.org/10.1007/978-3-319-48628-4_9
25. Raths, T., Otten, J.: The QMLTP problem library for first-order modal logics. In: Gramlich, B., Miller, D., Sattler, U. (eds.) IJCAR 2012. LNCS (LNAI), vol. 7364, pp. 454–461. Springer, Heidelberg (2012). https://doi.org/10.1007/978-3-642-31365-3_35
26. Raths, T., Otten, J., Kreitz, C.: The ILTP problem library for intuitionistic logic. J. Autom. Reason. **38**, 261–271 (2007)
27. Schulz, S., Cruanes, S., Vukmirović, P.: Faster, higher, stronger: E 2.3. In: Fontaine, P. (ed.) CADE 2019. LNCS (LNAI), vol. 11716, pp. 495–507. Springer, Cham (2019). https://doi.org/10.1007/978-3-030-29436-6_29
28. Steen, A., Benzmüller, C.: The higher-order prover Leo-III. In: Galmiche, D., Schulz, S., Sebastiani, R. (eds.) IJCAR 2018. LNCS (LNAI), vol. 10900, pp. 108–116. Springer, Cham (2018). https://doi.org/10.1007/978-3-319-94205-6_8
29. Sutcliffe, G.: The TPTP problem library and associated infrastructure. J. Autom. Reason. **59**(4), 483–502 (2017)
30. Waaler, A.: Connections in nonclassical logics. In: Robinson, A., Voronkov, A. (eds.) Handbook of Automated Reasoning, pp. 1487–1578. Elsevier Science, Amsterdam (2001)

31. Wallen, L.A.: Automated Deduction in Nonclassical Logics. MIT Press, Cambridge (1990)
32. Zombori, Z., Urban, J., Brown, C.E.: Prolog technology reinforcement learning prover. In: Peltier, N., Sofronie-Stokkermans, V. (eds.) IJCAR 2020. LNCS (LNAI), vol. 12167, pp. 489–507. Springer, Cham (2020). https://doi.org/10.1007/978-3-030-51054-1_33

Eliminating Models During Model Elimination

Michael Rawson(✉) and Giles Reger

University of Manchester, Manchester, UK
michael@rawsons.uk, giles.reger@manchester.ac.uk

Abstract. We investigate the integration of SAT technology into clausal connection-tableau systems for classical first-order logic. Clauses present in tableaux during backtracking search are heuristically grounded and added to an incremental SAT solver. If the solver reports an unsatisfiable set of ground clauses at any point, search may be halted and a proof reported. This technique alone is surprisingly effective, but also supports further refinements "for free". In particular we further investigate depth control of randomised search based on grounded clauses, and a kind of ground lemmata rule derived from the partial SAT model.

Keywords: Connection tableaux · Boolean satisfiability · Instantiation

1 Introduction

The style of heuristic search in backtracking/iterative-deepening theorem provers for first-order logic, often used in conjunction with connection tableaux, is very different from the search found in saturation-style systems, often used with superposition calculi. Both approaches have their strengths and weaknesses, and typically perform well on different kinds of domains and problems.

One possible weakness of backtracking systems is that very little search effort expended in failing to find a proof can be reused, and in fact many popular backtracking systems "learn" almost nothing as search progresses. Contrast this with saturation systems, where deduced formulae are typically retained indefinitely, and even formulae not used in the final proof can aid proof search via mechanisms such as subsumption. Fixing this defect in backtracking systems generally and efficiently is not easy, and if taken to extremes results in a saturation system.

However, *ground* reasoning is typically more efficient than full first-order reasoning. This suggests something of a compromise: first-order search remains backtracking in nature, but a ground approximation to first-order information is retained and used to aid future first-order search. More concretely, we heuristically ground the clauses that make up tableaux constructed during backtracking search, then insert these grounded clauses into an incremental SAT solver, where they stay for the entire duration of proof search.

A. Das and S. Negri (Eds.): TABLEAUX 2021, LNAI 12842, pp. 250–265, 2021.
https://doi.org/10.1007/978-3-030-86059-2_15

This extra effort is compensated by the ability to report proofs found at the ground level (Sect. 4); a good heuristic for controlling a combination of restricted backtracking, randomisation and iterative deepening (Sect. 5); and a partial assignment of literals that can be skipped, focussing proof search (Sect. 6). We build a testbed system (Sect. 3) and experimentally evaluate our approach against a baseline and other systems (Sect. 8), showing that the overhead of grounding clauses pays off handsomely in practice.

2 Preliminaries

The following relates to fully-automatic theorem provers for classical first-order logic (with equality) with the usual syntax and semantics [46]. We focus particularly on systems implementing connection tableaux calculi and systems that use ground reasoning tools such as SAT or SMT solvers to accelerate or improve first-order search.

2.1 Connection Tableau Systems

The connection tableau[1] calculus [27] is chiefly a restriction on clausal free-variable tableaux requiring all additions to tableaux be *connected* to leaf literals: that is, extension clauses must contain a unifiable literal of opposite sign. This is an extremely strong restriction on general clause tableaux, which remains complete but loses proof confluence, necessitating backtracking search to build closed connection tableaux. Backtracking may be reduced in exchange for a loss of completeness with *restricted backtracking* schemes [32]. Figure 1 shows the basic rules of the calculus: tableaux begin with a *start* clause; a leaf may be closed by *reduction* if there is a unifiable literal of opposite sign in the current branch; and *extension* clauses may be added to the tableau if they are connected to the current leaf literal.

Competitive connection systems such as the SEquential THEOrem prover SETHEO [5] and, later, leanCoP [31] typically employ a number of optimising preprocessing steps, calculus refinements, search heuristics and efficient implementation techniques to improve performance on problems of interest. We note here a whole area of research designed to re-use work performed in other areas of backtracking search, such as failure caching [27], to which our work has similar aims but a different method.

As well as good performance in exchange for little complexity, such systems have a number of advantages: they are simple to implement (particularly in Prolog), often leading to a relatively small "trusted computing base" which can be easily certified [23,51]; they cope well with a large number of axioms due to a goal-directed search style; and their memory use remains low, or even constant. They can often be adapted for other domains and research areas, such as intuitionistic logic [31], modal logic [33], non-clausal reasoning [34], machine learning for theorem proving [17,22], and low-resource computing [35].

[1] also known as, or closely related to, the *connection method* [6], *model elimination* [28], and/or the method of *matings* [2].

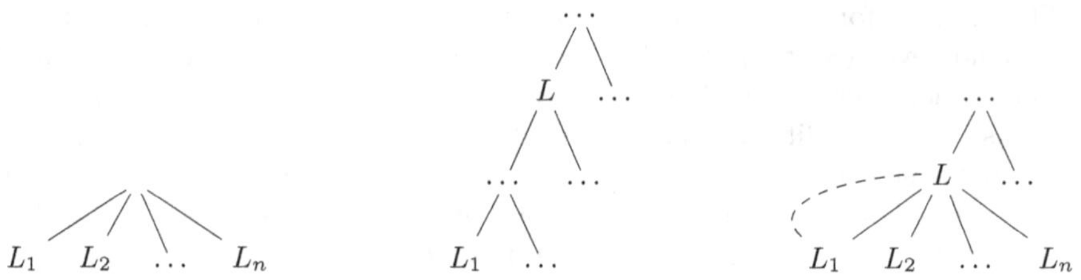

Fig. 1. The three inference rules of the clausal connection tableau calculus: *start*, *reduction*, and *extension*. In the *start* and *extension* rules, $C = L_1 \vee L_2 \vee \cdots \vee L_n$ is a fresh copy of a clause. In the *reduction* and *extension* rules, the global unifier is refined such that $\sigma(\neg L) = \sigma(L_1)$. i.e. L and L_1 are *connected* (illustrated by dashed lines).

2.2 Boolean Satisfiability

Boolean satisfiability (SAT) is a well-known NP-complete problem [10]. We will concisely phrase the problem as "given a set of propositional clauses, find an assignment of propositional variables such that each clause is satisfied, or report their unsatisfiability". Despite the computational difficulty, SAT solvers have improved rapidly [9] and can now quickly solve SAT instances previously considered impractically large or hard [3]. Arguably the major driving force behind this improvement is the realisation that most useful problems are not merely random, but contain structure that can be exploited by carefully-designed heuristics.

One such heuristic, *conflict-driven clause learning* (CDCL), in which new clauses are "learned" from a certain conflicting section of search space, is particularly effective [29]. It also allows for SAT solvers to become *incremental*, so that recomputing satisfiability as new clauses are added to the set is a cheaper operation. SAT is also often used as an "assembly language" for richer or harder problems. We discuss SAT for aiding first-order reasoning below, but Satisfiability Modulo Theories (SMT) [14] and bounded model checking [8] are two well-known applications from other domains.

2.3 Ground Support for First-Order Reasoning

The use of SAT solvers to provide ground support within first-order reasoning has been previously explored in various ways. In some approaches the main reasoning method is by reduction to SAT. For example, finite model finding methods [12,40] iteratively ground a first-order problem with a growing set of domain constants in order to find a finite model. Or the Instance Generation calculus [24,25], which approximates the unsatisfiability problem for sets of first-order clauses by a sequence of propositional problems: a propositional abstraction is iteratively refined by the addition of new instances. More naïvely, there are also cases where near-propositional problems can be decided directly via grounding [43]. Going beyond first-order reasoning, Satallax [11] is a higher-order prover that reasons via reduction to a series of SAT problems.

The previous approaches use SAT solvers as black boxes, as opposed to the more fine-grained approach taken by the Model Evolution Calculus [4] which interleaves instance generation with DPLL-style reasoning. In an unusual twist, the CHEWTPTP system uses a clever incremental ground encoding [15] of connection tableaux *search* such that at some point the ground solver may return propositional assignments representing closed connection tableaux.

Other first-order reasoning methods utilise SAT solvers to aid a separate proof search method, as in this paper. The AVATAR [37,49] framework implemented within Vampire [26,38] uses a SAT or SMT solver to organise the process of clause splitting within saturation-based search. The global subsumption simplification technique [24,39] uses a SAT solver to replace a clause by a subclause if the subclause holds globally, which can be under-approximated by propositional reasoning.

Finally, the saturation-based E theorem prover [45] has been extended with a lightweight technique that periodically grounds the search space and checks for propositional unsatisfiability [44]. This work is closest to what we propose in this work but in the context of saturation-based methods.

2.4 First-Order Benchmarks

We use several first-order benchmark problem sets to evaluate work experimentally. By "TPTP", we mean the provable FOF fragment (7,609 problems) of the Thousands of Problems for Theorem Provers set [47] 7.3.0. The MPTP2078 challenge [1] provides 2078 problems translated from the Mizar Mathematical Library [18] by the MPTP system [48], in two forms: "bushy", where problems are typically smaller and contain only relevant premises; and "chainy" where problems contain all preceding results. *M2k* is a slightly-easier set of 2003 related problems used for development [22], also originating from Mizar and MPTP.

3 Research Vehicle: SATCoP

We require a testbed for our experiments with the techniques outlined. In principle we could have modified e.g. leanCoP to take advantage of the "lean Prolog technology" approach (and we hope to explore this direction in future), but for these first experiments we found it easier to use an imperative language and our own system. We refer to the basic system described below as SATCoP_0, and to the system improved with additional SAT-based techniques as SATCoP.

SATCoP_0 implements the clausal connection tableau calculus. A simple clause normal form translation without definitions [32] translates general first-order formulae into clauses, and equality (if present) is then axiomatised in the usual way. No other preprocessing, such as reordering of clauses, takes place. Search starts with clauses derived from the conjecture[2], and proceeds by iterative deepening

[2] Unless there are no such clauses or *all* clauses stem from the conjecture, in which case positive clauses are used instead.

Algorithm 1: sketch of the basic $\mathsf{SATCoP_0}$ search routine

```
σ_U = ∅; // global tableaux-level unifier, modified by unify()
limit = 0; // depth limit for iterative deepening

function start() : bool is
    loop
        foreach C ∈ start clauses do
            if prove-all(ϵ, C) then return true ;
            σ_U = ∅; // reset σ_U to try again
        limit = limit + 1;

function prove-all(path, clause) : bool is
    foreach literal ∈ clause do
        if ¬prove(path, literal) then return false ;
    return true

function prove(path, goal) is
    // apply the reduction rule (restricted backtracking)
    foreach L ∈ path do
        if sign(goal) ≠ sign(L) and unify(goal, ¬L) then return true ;
    // limit search depth
    if |path| ≥ limit then return false ;
    // apply the extension rule (restricted backtracking)
    σ'_U = σ_U;
    foreach fresh copy C of a problem clause do
        foreach L ∈ C do
            if sign(goal) ≠ sign(L) and unify(goal, ¬L) then
                if prove-all(append(path, goal), C \ {L}) then return true ;
                σ_U = σ'_U; // reset σ_U to try again
                continue
```

on the length of the path. When trying to close a branch, reduction steps are tried before extension steps, and backtracking is restricted [32] in the style that Färber calls REI in his description of backtracking schemes [16]. The regularity condition [27] is enforced and some clause-level tautologies are eliminated. No intra-tableau mechanisms for re-use of intermediate results (such as *lemmata* or *folding up*) are implemented as this would overlap somewhat with Sect. 6, but in principle nothing prevents implementing this for further performance. For readers not familiar with connection systems and restricted backtracking, Algorithm 1 provides a sketch of the search routine.

The concrete system owes many implementation techniques to the Bare Metal Tableaux Prover [21]. In any case, the precise details of the basic system are not critically important here: we present the effect of each different techniques and final performance by experimental evaluation in Sect. 8. We expect these methods to be generally applicable to similar connection systems, at least for classical first-order logic, given a careful implementation.

4 Grounding Clausal Tableaux

A clausal tableaux (not necessarily closed) is built from instances of clauses derived from the negated input problem. In the first-order case, tableau variables represent a concrete ground term that is yet to be fully determined. As a result, any given tableaux represents a multiset of partially-instantiated clauses. Tableaux operations have pleasant interpretations in this setting: clauses added to tableaux are added to the set, and unifications within the tableau monotonically refine the instantiation of clauses in the set.

Backtracking search for closed clausal tableaux can therefore be seen as producing a *stream* of clauses with various instantiations: each inference rule produces a tableau built from a certain multiset of clauses, each of which can be fed into the stream. It is a sound deduction to apply any grounding substitution scheme to each clause, mapping remaining variables to ground terms.

To see this, consider a clause C in the input problem containing variables $\bar{x}$. During backtracking search, C is added to the tableau by applying a renaming substitution σ_R, mapping $\bar{x}$ to variables fresh for the tableau. Then, a number of unification steps results in a tableau-level unifier σ_U from tableau variables to arbitrary terms constructed over the signature and tableau variables. Finally, a grounding substitution σ_G maps tableau variables to arbitrary members of the Herbrand universe. Trivially, the composite substitution $\sigma = \sigma_G \circ \sigma_U \circ \sigma_R$ is a grounding substitution and

$$(\forall \bar{x}.C) \Rightarrow C\sigma$$

is a tautology, so $C\sigma$ is both a ground clause and a valid deduction from $\forall \bar{x}.C$.

Ground atoms can be bijectively mapped to propositional variables, obtaining a propositional approximation to the partially-instantiated clause present in the tableau. In this way, backtracking tableaux search over premises produces a stream of ground clauses such that if the ground approximation is unsatisfiable, so are the premises.

4.1 Reporting Unsatisfiability

This stream of ground clauses does not seem immediately useful. However, by inserting this stream of grounded clauses into a SAT solver, it can report when the clauses seen so far are unsatisfiable, witnessing a proof. Often this state occurs significantly before finding a closed connection tableau, which makes the technique potentially useful. We modify the basic system to perform an iterative deepening step, generating a large number of clauses from backtracking, and inserting clauses continuously. Before increasing the depth limit, we first query the SAT solver to check the current status. This appears to be a good tradeoff between reporting unsatisfiability early, and wastefully querying the solver.

4.2 Grounding Schemes

There are a large number of possible choices for the grounding scheme σ_G, and in fact using a whole family of grounding schemes to ground each clause multiply is sound, if potentially wasteful. The simplest scheme is to map every variable to a fresh constant, and in fact this works quite well immediately. Schulz [44] suggests choosing the most frequent constant from the conjecture, and we use this suggestion here, achieving a slight increase in performance over the simple scheme. If there is no constant in the conjecture, we fall back to the fresh constant.

4.3 SAT Solving

SAT *solving*, rather than the grounding procedure or backtracking search, is by far the biggest bottleneck in the resulting system. Additionally, the SAT instances generated by our approach are quite unusual: there are a large number of propositional variables, but conflicts are relatively rare until the clause set becomes unsatisfiable. Further, when new clauses are added, the existing model can often be extended to satisfy the new clauses without backtracking. When the clauses do become unsatisfiable, the unsatisfiable core is typically fairly small compared to the clause space.

After some initial experimentation with an off-the-shelf solver, PicoSAT [7], we found that *in this specific case* we can improve performance by implementing a custom SAT routine. We stress that we do not claim to improve on e.g. PicoSAT's general SAT performance or any similar claim. The custom routine is a more-or-less standard CDCL solver, with the following tweaks:

- The only possible mode is incremental.
- The next decision variable is always chosen as the unassigned variable first produced from proof search. This is both cheap to implement and difficult to beat with more sophisticated heuristics such as VSIDS, we hypothesise because variables introduced sooner are "closer to the conjecture".
- Conflict analysis backtracks through (and possibly resolves with) the entire trail, effectively restarting after every conflict. Since conflicts happen rarely, but it is critical that forced variables are assigned as soon as possible to avoid more conflicts later, this seems to be a good tradeoff in practice.
- The solver does not automatically restart on receiving new clauses. First, it tries to satisfy the new clauses by extending the current assignment, and only if a conflict is reached does it restart.
- Since conflicts are rare and the clause space is already huge, no effort is made to delete the relatively-small number of learned clauses.

4.4 A Note on Proofs

Connection tableau systems have access to an obvious and explicit proof object, the closed tableau. Typically this is also the smallest such with respect to the iterative deepening condition. Unfortunately, this is not the case here: to write a proof we must first obtain an unsatisfiable core (not necessarily minimal, but the smaller the better) from the SAT solver. By storing both the first-order atom that corresponds to a propositional variable, and the first-order premise that was instantiated to a propositional clause, an unsatisfiable set of ground instantiations of first-order clauses can be reported in exchange for a small amount of memory. These can be transformed into a proof by a ground reasoning system.

5 Randomisation and Depth Control

Randomisation of the search order is known to markedly increase performance of connection systems in the presence of restricted backtracking, exploited to great effect in the randoCoP system [36]. The idea here is roughly that if restricted backtracking renders a connection system unable to close a tableau, changing the order of clauses or the order of literals within those clauses may help as a different part of search space is explored. We found a modification of this idea particularly helpful for SATCoP and further allows a powerful depth-control heuristic.

randoCoP randomises both the order of premises and the order of literals within clauses, then runs the leanCoP-based core uninterrupted on the resulting problem, restarting from scratch frequently. Restarting from scratch is not so helpful in our case as we lose the propositional information we have worked so hard to achieve. It can also be wasteful with very large axiom sets as the entire set must be shuffled repeatedly, even though most will not be touched.

Instead, we take an ad-hoc randomisation approach: when there is a list of literals or clauses to be tried, we shuffle them[3]. We shuffle the order of literals in *start* or *extension* clauses, and also the order in which extensions are tried. The order in which the path is traversed looking for reductions is another possible shuffling area, but this does not seem to make much difference in practice.

Randomising search means that it is very likely that after an iterative deepening step generates some propositional clauses, running another iterative deepening step *at the same level* will still yield more propositional clauses from a different part of the search space found by randomisation. This feature of search suggests an optimisation: remain at the same iterative deepening level until no more new propositional clauses are found. As the next iterative deepening level has potentially exponentially many more states to explore, only increasing the search depth when absolutely necessary can be helpful.

6 Model-Based Lemmata

Our final technique is perhaps the most interesting, but easiest to explain. In order to reach an unsatisfiable set of ground clauses, the SAT solver's model must be forced to change until no more models are available. With this in mind, if we have a goal literal G at the leaf of a connection tableau, and its corresponding propositional literal is assigned false in the current model, refuting it will not change the model and is wasted effort from this perspective. To avoid this, we consider ground literals that are assigned false at the SAT level to be solved and skip them, in a similar way to the *lemmata* refinement for connection tableaux.

[3] pseudo-random shuffle such that results are reproducible.

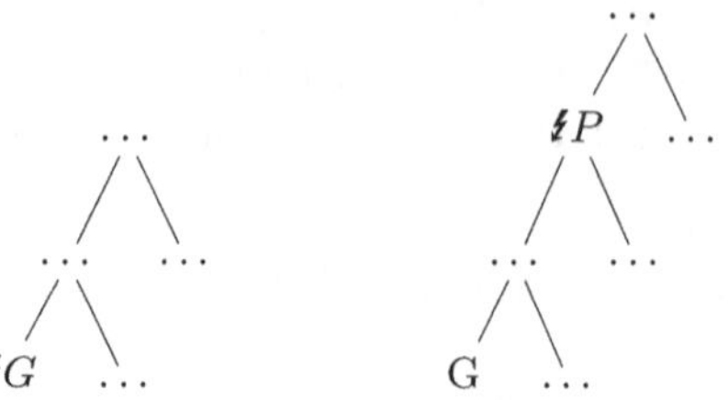

Fig. 2. If the abstraction of a ground goal G is assigned false in the current SAT model, refuting it can be skipped, as this will not force a change in the model. Generalising, if any ground path literal P is assigned false, the whole sub-tableau can be skipped.

We call this technique "model-based lemmata" due to this similarity, but the effect on proof search is not as clear. Literals may change assignment several times during proof search, although if refuted by a sub-tableau the literal will be *forced* false. Further, it is no longer sound to consider closed tableaux as a proof, as they may contain ground literals that have been skipped and therefore we can rely only on the SAT solver reporting unsatisfiability. An interesting side-effect is that iterative deepening steps do not take as long due to skipped literals: this may well have a positive effect on proof search by itself.

There is also a natural generalisation of this idea which we implement: if there are path literals $P_1, P_2, \ldots P_n$ available and the goal literal is G, we essentially try to refute the conjunction $P_1 \wedge P_2 \wedge \ldots \wedge P_n \wedge G$, or to show $P_1 \wedge P_2 \wedge \ldots \wedge P_n \Rightarrow \neg G$ if you prefer. If *any* of the path literals P_i become ground and assigned false through unification, these can also be skipped, closing an entire sub-tableau. The general idea is illustrated in Fig. 2.

7 First Impressions

Algorithm 2 extends that given in Algorithm 1 with the additions discussed in Sects. 4–6. New lines are marked with a $\rightarrow$. The resulting system is implemented in Rust and is available online[4].

Initial impressions of the resulting system are positive. Compared to the baseline system the most obvious change is an increase in memory use (SAT data and mapping information has to be kept somewhere), but this is not typically excessive, and is comparable to saturation systems. The majority of problems that the baseline system solved can now be solved in fewer steps, which typically also results in a shorter time-to-proof.

Practical performance on other problems also appears improved, particularly in cases where the SAT approach is very helpful. `PUZ010-1`, "who owns the zebra?" from the TPTP library contains a large number of nearly-ground axioms and a completely ground conjecture formed from a large disjunction of literals.

[4] https://github.com/MichaelRawson/satcop commit `65122a99e08648f5b2e331280d0a0011e73a0836` is discussed here.

Algorithm 2: sketch of the exended SATCoP search routine

```
  σ_U = ∅; // global tableaux-level unifier, modified by unify()
  limit = 0; // depth limit for iterative deepening
→ ground = ∅; // set of propositional clauses produced so far
→ new = ∅; // new propositional clauses produced this iteration
→ model = ∅; // partial propositional model of ground
  function start() : bool is
      // add start clauses to the grounding
→     foreach clause ∈ start clauses do
→         ground = ground ∪ {(clause)σ_G};
      loop
          foreach C ∈ start clauses do
→             shuffle C;
→             prove-all(ϵ, C);
              σ_U = ∅; // reset σ_U
→         if (new \ ground) ≠ ∅ then
→             ground = ground ∪ new;
→             new = ∅
          else
              limit = limit + 1; // only increase limit if no new clauses
→         if there is a model satisfying ground then
→             set model
          else
              // unsat propositional clauses: found a proof!
→             return true
  function prove-all(path, clause) : bool is
      foreach literal ∈ clause do
          if ¬prove(path, literal) then return false ;
      return true
  function prove(path, goal) is
      // model-based lemmata
→     foreach L ∈ path ∪ {goal} do
→         if (L)σ_U is ground and assigned false in model then return true;
      foreach L ∈ path do
          if sign(goal) ≠ sign(L) and unify(goal, ¬L) then
→             ground all clauses in the tableau and add them to new;
              return true
      // limit search depth
      if |path| ≥ limit then return false ;
      σ'_U = σ_U;
→     foreach fresh copy C of a problem clause in random order do
→         shuffle C;
          foreach L ∈ C do
              if sign(goal) ≠ sign(L) and unify(goal, ¬L) then
→                 ground all clauses in the tableau and add them to new;
                  if prove-all(append(path, goal), C \ {L}) then return true ;
                  σ_U = σ'_U; // reset σ_U to try again
                  continue
```

The unaided system cannot solve this problem in reasonable time[5], but the SAT-assisted system solves it near-instantaneously, producing a proof consisting of 322 grounded clauses.

It is not only problems tailor-made for SAT, either. GRP001-2 is a unit equality version of a problem from group theory, "if the square of every element is identity, the system is commutative". This problem is much easier for rewriting systems that specially handle equality: VAMPIRE solves this immediately, but the baseline system cannot solve it at all. However, with the enhancements described, SATCoP solves this in 4 s with no specialised equality handling.

8 Experimental Evaluation

We run two experiments to determine the practical effect of the preceding work. The first runs various configurations of SATCoP to evaluate different techniques from Sects. 4–6 against each other. The second compares SATCoP against other systems. All experiments are run on a desktop machine clocked at 3.4 GHz.

8.1 System Configurations

We run the state-of-the-art saturation system VAMPIRE [26] 4.5.1, and the strong connection system leanCoP [31] 2.1[6] to provide a comparison. Both of these systems expose options which can drastically alter proof search, and further both provide *portfolio modes* in which a number of different option combinations are tried in sequence. Inventing and evaluating good portfolios is a hard problem in itself, which we avoid here by running all systems with a fixed set of options: we stress that the results presented here do not necessarily reflect the "competition strength" of a system. VAMPIRE runs in its default mode, which entails a limited resource strategy [41], AVATAR [49], and a number of other search parameters. leanCoP was configured with `[cut,conj]`—that is, a restricted backtracking strategy, starting from clauses relating to conjectures—which more closely reflects SATCoP_0's strategy, but may not be the strongest available.

In the presence of large axiom sets containing extraneous axioms, saturation systems can sometimes choke. SInE [19] heuristically selects some subset of axioms that may be relevant for proving a conjecture, which can significantly accelerate proof search, provided that no necessary axiom is removed. VAMPIRE (SInE) runs SInE-style axiom selection with an additional flag.

8.2 Results and Discussion

We use 1-second runs on the *M2k* set of 2003 problems throughout development to quickly gauge practical effectiveness. Table 1 shows the effect produced by

[5] It is interesting to note that the saturation-based VAMPIRE theorem prover also fails to solve this problem in reasonable time without support from a SAT solver.

[6] run with SWI Prolog 7.6.4 [50].

Table 1. Problems from the *M2k* set solved in 1 s by all possible combinations of techniques. "grounding" is the method described in Sect. 4, "shuffle" the ad-hoc randomisation described in Sect. 5, "depth control" the modification of iterative deepening presented in the same section, and "model lemmata" the topic of Sect. 6.

Grounding	Shuffle	Depth control	Model lemmata	Solved
				886
✓				998
	✓			957
✓	✓			1135
✓	✓	✓		1173
✓			✓	1061
✓	✓		✓	1189
✓	✓	✓	✓	1252

Table 2. Problems solved in 10 s by existing systems and SATCoP on a variety of first-order benchmark sets. SATCoP_0 is SATCoP without any of the techniques described—i.e. a more standard connection system—for direct comparison.

	TPTP solved	Unique solved	Bushy solved	Unique	Chainy solved	Unique
Vampire	3650	388	1162	132	402	6
Vampire (SInE)	3013	258	781	34	550	109
leanCoP	1946	22	648	18	272	7
SATCoP_0	1837	8	564	0	221	0
SATCoP	3049	282	953	52	505	101
Benchmark size	7609		2078		2078	

different combinations of the techniques discussed here. Note that some combinations are omitted as nonsensical: for example, it is not possible to control iterative deepening as in Sect. 5 without grounding clauses, and without randomisation it is possible but provides no benefit.

We are pleased that the union of all techniques described performs the best, and that all produce some amount of benefit. It is interesting to note that some *combinations* are disproportionately effective, suggesting a synergising effect. Grounding clauses and randomisation gain 112 and 71 problems respectively over SATCoP_0, but combined gain 249. One might conjecture about *why* this happens—perhaps randomisation produces a larger number of ground clauses and thereby increases the likelihood of unsatisfiability—but in any event the outcome is encouraging.

We now compare our final system SATCoP against SATCoP_0 and other representative systems. We allow a 10-second time limit and evaluate the TPTP, "bushy" and "chainy" problem sets discussed in Sect. 2.4. Table 2 shows these data: the "solved" column is the number of problems solved for a given solver/set combination, while "unique" is the number of problems in a set *only that system and no other* solved.

9 Conclusions and Future Directions

We are pleasantly surprised at the improvement in performance achieved by very simple application of ground reasoning techniques to a connection tableau system. Further performance improvements can be obtained for relatively little effort using the existing ground information, which we demonstrate through final evaluation on a number of benchmark problem sets.

While the resulting system is not quite as concise as some of the beautiful systems achieved in Prolog, it is certainly effective and remains compact compared to state-of-the-art saturation systems. It is also possible that future investigations could make use of the "lean Prolog technology" approach, combined either with a Prolog implementation of CDCL [42], Prolog bindings to an existing SAT solver [13], or even (with some modification) constraint logic programming [20].

The SAT world also merits further investigation: SAT instances generated by our system are relatively unusual, and are mostly easily-satisfiable, until very suddenly they are not. A WalkSAT-like solver with some amount of clause learning [30] may improve SAT-level performance. SMT is another interesting direction, particularly for the theory of equality and uninterpreted functions. Application to other logics is a related topic we would like to investigate further: some seem quite achievable, such as some kind of support for arithmetic theories, but we acknowledge that intuitionistic logic may present a challenge.

9.1 A Note from the Future

Since submission, we have been busy preparing SATCoP for competition at CASC-28. Some ideas were found to further improve performance from that reported here. We report these modifications here both for interest and to document them in context for the competition.

- Our custom SAT routine is fast on the type of incremental SAT problems generated by SATCoP, but is not a good general SAT routine. We implement a new routine which first tries a few rounds of stochastic local search, then falls back to PicoSAT if we fail to find a satisfying assignment. This makes the common case very fast, allows solving the harder SAT problems quickly, and is much simpler than the approach described above.
- This improved routine allows us to continuously solve the SAT problem as clauses are added, rather than at each iterative deepening step.
- We restrict application of "model-based lemmata" to ground literals above. We can relax this restriction, allowing a sort of "literal selection" technique in which the first goal literal assigned true from a clause is attempted.
- Multiple CPU cores can be usefully occupied by launching multiple proof search attempts with different pseudo-random seeds.

References

1. Alama, J., Heskes, T., Kühlwein, D., Tsivtsivadze, E., Urban, J.: Premise selection for mathematics by corpus analysis and kernel methods. J. Autom. Reason. **52**(2), 191–213 (2014). https://doi.org/10.1007/s10817-013-9286-5
2. Andrews, P.B.: Theorem proving via general matings. J. ACM (JACM) **28**(2), 193–214 (1981)
3. Balyo, T., Froleyks, N., Heule, M.J., Iser, M., Järvisalo, M., Suda, M.: Proceedings of SAT Competition 2020: solver and benchmark descriptions (2020)
4. Baumgartner, P., Tinelli, C.: The model evolution calculus. In: Baader, F. (ed.) CADE 2003. LNCS (LNAI), vol. 2741, pp. 350–364. Springer, Heidelberg (2003). https://doi.org/10.1007/978-3-540-45085-6_32
5. Bayerl, S., Letz, R.: SETHEO: a sequential theorem prover for first-order logic. In: Esprit'87-Achievements and Impacts, part 1, pp. 721–735 (1987)
6. Bibel, W.: Automated Theorem Proving. Springer, Heidelberg (2013)
7. Biere, A.: PicoSAT essentials. J. Satisf. Boolean Model. Comput. **4**(2–4), 75–97 (2008)
8. Biere, A., Cimatti, A., Clarke, E.M., Strichman, O., Zhu, Y.: Bounded model checking (2003)
9. Biere, A., Ganesh, V., Grohe, M., Nordström, J., Williams, R.: Theory and practice of SAT solving (Dagstuhl Seminar 15171). In: Dagstuhl Reports. Schloss Dagstuhl-Leibniz-Zentrum fuer Informatik (2015)
10. Biere, A., Heule, M., van Maaren, H.: Handbook of satisfiability, vol. 185, IOS press (2009)
11. Brown, C.E.: Reducing higher-order theorem proving to a sequence of SAT problems. J. Autom. Reason. **51**(1), 57–77 (2013). https://doi.org/10.1007/s10817-013-9283-8
12. Claessen, K., Sorensson, N.: New techniques that improve MACE-style model finding. In: Model Computation (2003)
13. Codish, M., Lagoon, V., Stuckey, P.J.: Logic programming with satisfiability. Theory Pract. Logic Program. **8**(1), 121 (2008)
14. De Moura, L., Bjørner, N.: Satisfiability modulo theories: introduction and applications. Commun. ACM **54**(9), 69–77 (2011)
15. Deshane, T., Hu, W., Jablonski, P., Lin, H., Lynch, C., McGregor, R.E.: Encoding first order proofs in SAT. In: Pfenning, F. (ed.) CADE 2007. LNCS (LNAI), vol. 4603, pp. 476–491. Springer, Heidelberg (2007). https://doi.org/10.1007/978-3-540-73595-3_35
16. Färber, M.: A curiously effective backtracking strategy for connection tableaux. CoRR abs/2106.13722 (2021). https://arxiv.org/abs/2106.13722
17. Färber, M., Kaliszyk, C., Urban, J.: Machine learning guidance for connection tableaux. J. Autom. Reason. **65**(2), 287–320 (2021). https://doi.org/10.1007/s10817-020-09576-7
18. Grabowski, A., Korniłowicz, A., Naumowicz, A.: Four decades of Mizar. J. Autom. Reason. **55**(3), 191–198 (2015). https://doi.org/10.1007/s10817-015-9345-1
19. Hoder, K., Voronkov, A.: Sine qua non for large theory reasoning. In: Bjørner, N., Sofronie-Stokkermans, V. (eds.) CADE 2011. LNCS (LNAI), vol. 6803, pp. 299–314. Springer, Heidelberg (2011). https://doi.org/10.1007/978-3-642-22438-6_23
20. Jaffar, J., Lassez, J.L.: Constraint logic programming. In: Proceedings of the 14th ACM SIGACT-SIGPLAN symposium on Principles of programming languages, pp. 111–119 (1987)

21. Kaliszyk, C.: Efficient low-level connection tableaux. In: De Nivelle, H. (ed.) TABLEAUX 2015. LNCS (LNAI), vol. 9323, pp. 102–111. Springer, Cham (2015). https://doi.org/10.1007/978-3-319-24312-2_8
22. Kaliszyk, C., Urban, J., Michalewski, H., Olšák, M.: Reinforcement learning of theorem proving. In: Proceedings of the 32nd International Conference on Neural Information Processing Systems, pp. 8836–8847 (2018)
23. Kaliszyk, C., Urban, J., Vyskočil, J.: Certified connection tableaux proofs for HOL Light and TPTP. In: Proceedings of the 2015 Conference on Certified Programs and Proofs, pp. 59–66 (2015)
24. Korovin, K.: Instantiation-based automated reasoning: from theory to practice. In: Schmidt, R.A. (ed.) CADE 2009. LNCS (LNAI), vol. 5663, pp. 163–166. Springer, Heidelberg (2009). https://doi.org/10.1007/978-3-642-02959-2_14
25. Korovin, K.: Inst-Gen – a modular approach to instantiation-based automated reasoning. In: Voronkov, A., Weidenbach, C. (eds.) Programming Logics. LNCS, vol. 7797, pp. 239–270. Springer, Heidelberg (2013). https://doi.org/10.1007/978-3-642-37651-1_10
26. Kovács, L., Voronkov, A.: First-order theorem proving and Vampire. In: Sharygina, N., Veith, H. (eds.) CAV 2013. LNCS, vol. 8044, pp. 1–35. Springer, Heidelberg (2013). https://doi.org/10.1007/978-3-642-39799-8_1
27. Letz, R., Stenz, G.: Model elimination and connection tableau procedures. In: Handbook of Automated Reasoning, pp. 2015–2114. Elsevier (2001)
28. Loveland, D.W.: Mechanical theorem-proving by model elimination. In: Siekmann, J.H., Wrightson, G. (eds.) Automation of Reasoning, pp. 117–134. Springer, Heidelberg (1968). https://doi.org/10.1007/978-3-642-81955-1_8
29. Marques-Silva, J.P., Sakallah, K.A.: GRASP: a search algorithm for propositional satisfiability. IEEE Trans. Comput. **48**(5), 506–521 (1999)
30. McDonald, A., et al.: Parallel WalkSAT with clause learning. Data analysis project papers (2009)
31. Otten, J.: leanCoP 2.0 and ileanCoP 1.2: high performance lean theorem proving in classical and intuitionistic logic (system descriptions). In: Armando, A., Baumgartner, P., Dowek, G. (eds.) IJCAR 2008. LNCS (LNAI), vol. 5195, pp. 283–291. Springer, Heidelberg (2008). https://doi.org/10.1007/978-3-540-71070-7_23
32. Otten, J.: Restricting backtracking in connection calculi. AI Commun. **23**(2–3), 159–182 (2010)
33. Otten, J.: MleanCoP: a connection prover for first-order modal logic. In: Demri, S., Kapur, D., Weidenbach, C. (eds.) IJCAR 2014. LNCS (LNAI), vol. 8562, pp. 269–276. Springer, Cham (2014). https://doi.org/10.1007/978-3-319-08587-6_20
34. Otten, J.: nanoCoP: a non-clausal connection prover. In: Olivetti, N., Tiwari, A. (eds.) IJCAR 2016. LNCS (LNAI), vol. 9706, pp. 302–312. Springer, Cham (2016). https://doi.org/10.1007/978-3-319-40229-1_21
35. Otten, J.: The pocket reasoner – automatic reasoning on small devices. In: Norwegian Informatics Conference, NIK (2018)
36. Raths, T., Otten, J.: randoCoP: randomizing the proof search order in the connection calculus. In: First International Workshop on Practical Aspects of Automated Reasoning, pp. 94–103 (2008). http://ceur-ws.org/Vol-373/
37. Reger, G., Bjorner, N., Suda, M., Voronkov, A.: AVATAR modulo theories. In: Benzmüller, C., Sutcliffe, G., Rojas, R. (eds.) GCAI 2016. 2nd Global Conference on Artificial Intelligence. EPiC Series in Computing, vol. 41, pp. 39–52. EasyChair (2016). https://doi.org/10.29007/k6tp. https://easychair.org/publications/paper/7

38. Reger, G., Suda, M.: The uses of SAT solvers in Vampire. In: Kovács, L., Voronkov, A. (eds.) Proceedings of the 1st and 2nd Vampire Workshops, Vampire@VSL 2014, Vienna, Austria, July 23, 2014 / Vampire@CADE 2015, Berlin, Germany, 2 August 2015. EPiC Series in Computing, vol. 38, pp. 63–69. EasyChair (2015). https://easychair.org/publications/paper/ZG9
39. Reger, G., Suda, M.: Global subsumption revisited (briefly). In: Kovacs, L., Voronkov, A. (eds.) Vampire 2016. Proceedings of the 3rd Vampire Workshop. EPiC Series in Computing, vol. 44, pp. 61–73. EasyChair (2017). https://doi.org/10.29007/qcd7. https://easychair.org/publications/paper/QDj
40. Reger, G., Suda, M., Voronkov, A.: Finding finite models in multi-sorted first-order logic. In: Creignou, N., Le Berre, D. (eds.) SAT 2016. LNCS, vol. 9710, pp. 323–341. Springer, Cham (2016). https://doi.org/10.1007/978-3-319-40970-2_20
41. Riazanov, A., Voronkov, A.: Limited resource strategy in resolution theorem proving. J. Symb. Comput. **36**(1–2), 101–115 (2003)
42. Robbins, E., King, A., Howe, J.M.: Backjumping is exception handling. Theory Pract. Logic Program. **21**, 1–20 (2020)
43. Schulz, S.: A comparison of different techniques for grounding near-propositional CNF formulae. In: FLAIRS Conference, pp. 72–76 (2002)
44. Schulz, S.: Light-weight integration of SAT solving into first-order reasoners – first experiments. Vampire, pp. 9–19 (2017)
45. Schulz, S., Cruanes, S., Vukmirović, P.: Faster, higher, stronger: E 2.3. In: Fontaine, P. (ed.) CADE 2019. LNCS (LNAI), vol. 11716, pp. 495–507. Springer, Cham (2019). https://doi.org/10.1007/978-3-030-29436-6_29
46. Smullyan, R.M.: First-order logic. Courier Corporation (1995)
47. Sutcliffe, G.: The TPTP problem library and associated infrastructure. J. Autom. Reason. **43**(4), 337 (2009). https://doi.org/10.1007/s10817-017-9407-7
48. Urban, J.: MPTP 0.2: design, implementation, and initial experiments. J. Autom. Reason. **37**(1–2), 21–43 (2006). https://doi.org/10.1007/s10817-006-9032-3
49. Voronkov, A.: AVATAR: the architecture for first-order theorem provers. In: Biere, A., Bloem, R. (eds.) CAV 2014. LNCS, vol. 8559, pp. 696–710. Springer, Cham (2014). https://doi.org/10.1007/978-3-319-08867-9_46
50. Wielemaker, J.: SWI-Prolog version 7 extensions. In: Workshop on Implementation of Constraint and Logic Programming Systems and Logic-based Methods in Programming Environments, vol. 109. Citeseer (2014)
51. Zombori, Z., Urban, J., Brown, C.E.: Prolog technology reinforcement learning prover. In: Peltier, N., Sofronie-Stokkermans, V. (eds.) IJCAR 2020. LNCS (LNAI), vol. 12167, pp. 489–507. Springer, Cham (2020). https://doi.org/10.1007/978-3-030-51054-1_33

Learning Theorem Proving Components

Karel Chvalovský[1], Jan Jakubův[1,2(✉)], Miroslav Olšák[2], and Josef Urban[1]

[1] Czech Technical University in Prague, Prague, Czechia
karel@chvalovsky.cz
[2] University of Innsbruck, Innsbruck, Austria
mirek@olsak.net

Abstract. Saturation-style automated theorem provers (ATPs) based on the given clause procedure are today the strongest general reasoners for classical first-order logic. The clause selection heuristics in such systems are, however, often evaluating clauses in isolation, ignoring other clauses. This has changed recently by equipping the E/ENIGMA system with a graph neural network (GNN) that chooses the next given clause based on its evaluation in the context of previously selected clauses. In this work, we describe several algorithms and experiments with ENIGMA, advancing the idea of contextual evaluation based on learning important components of the graph of clauses.

Keywords: Automated theorem proving · Machine learning · Neural networks · Decision trees · Saturation-style proving

1 Introduction: Clause Selection and Context

Clause selection is a crucial part of saturation-style [29] automated theorem provers (ATPs) such as E [32], Vampire [20], and Prover9 [22]. These systems, implementing the given-clause [21] algorithm, provide the strongest methods for proving lemmas in large interactive theorem prover (ITP) libraries [4], and occasionally prove open conjectures in specialized parts of mathematics [19].

Clause selection heuristics have a long history of research, going back to a number of experiments done with the Otter system [24]. Systems such as Prover9 and E have eventually developed extensive domain-specific languages for clause selection heuristics, allowing application of sophisticated algorithms based on a number of different ideas [13,23,27,31,35] and their automated improvement [15,30,34]. These algorithms are, however, often evaluating clauses in isolation, ignoring other clauses selected in the proof search, and thus largely neglecting the notion of a *(proof) state* and its obvious importance for choosing the next *action* (clause).

This has changed recently with equipping the E/ENIGMA [6,14] system with a logic-aware graph neural network (GNN) [25], where the next given clause is

A. Das and S. Negri (Eds.): TABLEAUX 2021, LNAI 12842, pp. 266–278, 2021.
https://doi.org/10.1007/978-3-030-86059-2_16

chosen based on its evaluation in the context of previously selected clauses [12]. In more details, in GNN-ENIGMA, the generated clauses are not ranked immediately and independently on other clauses. Instead, they are judged by the GNN in larger batches and with respect to a large number of already selected clauses (*context*). The GNN estimates collectively the most useful subset of the context and new clauses by several rounds of message passing. The message-passing algorithm takes into account the connections between symbols, terms, subterms, atoms, literals, and clauses. It is trained on many previous proof searches, and it estimates which clauses will collectively benefit the proof search in the best way.

In the rest of the paper, we describe several algorithms and experiments with ENIGMA and GNN-based algorithms, advancing the idea of contextual evaluation. In Sect. 2, we give an overview of the learning-based ENIGMA clause selection in E, focusing on the recently added context-based evaluation by GNNs. Section 3 introduces the first variant of our context-based algorithms called *leapfrogging*. These algorithms interleave saturation-style ATP runs with external context-based evaluations and clause filtering. Section 4 introduces the second variant of our context-based algorithms, based on learning from past interactions between clauses and splitting the proof search into separate components. Section 5 discusses technical details, and Sect. 6 evaluates the methods.

2 ENIGMA and Learning Context-Based Guidance

This section summarizes our previous Graph Neural Network (GNN) ENIGMA *anonymization* architecture [12], which was previously successfully used for a given clause guidance within E Prover [16]. In this context, anonymization means guidance independent on specific symbol names.

Saturation-based ATPs, such as E, employ a *given-clause loop*. The input first-order logic problem is translated into a refutationally-equivalent set of clauses, and a search for a contradiction is initiated. Starting with the initial set of clauses, one clause is selected (*given*) for processing, and all possible inferences with all previously processed clauses are derived. This extends the set of clauses available for processing, and the loop repeats until (1) the contradiction (empty clause) is derived, or (2) there are no clauses left for processing (that is, the input problem is not provable), or (3) resources (time, memory, or user patience) are exhausted. As the selection of the right clauses for processing is essential for a success, our approach is to guide the clause selection within an ATP by sophisticated machine learning methods.

For the clause selection with ENIGMA Anonymous, we train a GNN classifier for symbol-independent clause embeddings from a large number of previous successful E proof searches. From every successful proof search, we extract the set of all processed clauses, and we label the clauses that appear in the final proof as *positive* while the remaining (unnecessarily processed) clauses as *negative*. These training data are turned into a tensor representation (one- and two-dimensional variable-length vectors), which encapsulate clause syntax trees by abstracting from specific symbol names while preserving information about symbol relations. Each tensor represents a set of clauses as a graph with three types of nodes (for terms/subterms, clauses, and symbols), and passes initial embeddings through a fixed number of message-passing (graph convolution) layers. Additionally, the conjecture clauses of the problem to be proved are incorporated into the graph to allow for conjecture-dependent clause classification.

Once a GNN classifier is trained from a large number of proof searches, it is utilized in a new proof search to evaluate the clauses to be processed and to select the best given clause as follows. Instead of evaluating the clauses one by one, as is the case in the alternative ENIGMA Anonymous decision tree classifiers, we postpone clause evaluation until a specific number of clauses to be evaluated is collected. These clauses form the *query* part and the size of the query is passed to the prover as a parameter. The query clauses are extended with clauses forming a *context*, that is, a specific number of clauses already processed during the current proof search. In particular, we use the first n clauses processed during the proof search as the context. The context size n is another parameter passed to the prover. After adding the conjecture and context clauses to the query, their tensor representation is computed and sent to the GNN for evaluation. The GNN applies several graph convolution (message passing) layers getting an embedding of every clause. Each clause is combined through a single fully connected layer with an embedding of the conjecture, and finally transformed into a single score (*logit*), which is sent back to the prover. The prover then processes the clauses with better (higher) scores in advance. For details, see [12,25].

3 Leapfrogging

The first class of algorithms is based on the idea that the graph-based evaluation of a particular clause may significantly change as new clauses are produced and the context changes. It corresponds to the human-based mathematical exploration, in which initial actions can be done with relatively low confidence and following only uncertain hunches. After some amount of initial exploration is done, clearer patterns often appear, allowing re-evaluation of the approach, focusing on the most promising directions, and discarding of less useful ideas.

In tableau-based provers such as leanCoP [26] with a compact notion of state, such methods can be approximated in a reinforcement learning setting by the notion of *big steps* [18] in the Monte-Carlo tree search (MCTS), implementing the standard *explore/exploit* paradigm [10]. In the saturation setting, our proposed algorithm uses short standard saturation runs at the exploration phase, after which the set of processed (selected) clauses is reevaluated and a decision on its most useful subset is made by the GNN. These two phases are iterated in a procedure that we call *leapfrogging*.

In more detail, leapfrogging is implemented as follows (see also Algorithm 1). Given a clausal problem consisting of a set of initial clauses $S = S_0$, an initial saturation-style search (in our case E/ENIGMA) is run on S with an abstract time limit. We may use a fixed limit (e.g., 1000 nontrivial processed clauses)

Algorithm 1: The Leapfrogging algorithm with a fixed saturation limit

Input: $AxiomClauses$, $NegConjectureClauses$, $SaturationLimit$, $IterationLimit$, $PremiseSelector$;

$S_0 = AxiomClauses \cup NegConjectureClauses$;
for $i = 0$ **to** $IterationLimit$ **do**
  $(L_{i+1}, Result) = Saturate(S_i, SaturationLimit)$;
  if $Result = Unsatisfiable$ **then return** $Unsatisfiable$;
  else if $Result = Satisfiable$ **then**
    if $i{=}0$ **then return** Satisfiable;
    else return $Unknown$;
  else // $Result = Unknown$
    $S_{i+1} = PremiseSelector(L_{i+1}, NegConjectureClauses)$;
    $S_{i+1} = S_{i+1} \cup NegConjectureClauses$;
return $Unknown$;

for all runs, or change (e.g. increase) the limits gradually. If the initial run results in a proof or saturation within the limit, the algorithm is finished. If not, we inspect the set of clauses created in the run. We can inspect the set of all generated clauses, or a smaller set, such as the set of all processed clauses. So far, we used the latter because it is typically much smaller and better suits our training methods. This (*large*) set is denoted as L_0. Then we apply a trained graph-based predictor to L_0, which selects a smaller *most promising* subset of L_0, denoted as S_1. We may or may not automatically include also the initial negated conjecture clauses or the whole initial set S_0 in S_1. S_1 is then used as an input to the next limited saturation run of E/ENIGMA. This process is iterated, producing gradually sets S_i and L_i.

A particularly simple version of leapfrogging uses GNN-guided ENIGMA for the saturation "jumps", and omits the external selection, thus setting $S_{i+1} := L_i$. This may seem meaningless with deterministic clause selection heuristics that do not use context: the next saturation run may be selecting the same clauses and ending up with $S_{i+1} = S_i$. Already in the standard ATP setting this is, however, easy to make less deterministic, as done, for example, in the randoCoP system [28]. The GNN-guided ENIGMA will typically also make different choices with the new input set L_0 than with the input set S_0.

A more involved version of leapfrogging, however, makes use of a nontrivial trained graph-based predictor that will reduce L_i to S_{i+1} such that $S_{i+1} \subsetneq L_i$. For this, we use an external evaluation run of a GNN, which has been trained in the same way as the GNN used inside ENIGMA: on sets of *positive* and *negative* processed clauses extracted from many successful proof runs. Here, the positive clauses are those that end up being part of the proof, and the negative ones are the remaining processed clauses. This is also very similar to an external *premise selection* [2] done with the GNNs [25], with the difference that the inputs are now clauses instead of formulas.

4 Learning Reasoning Components

The second class of algorithms is based on learning important components in the graph of clauses. This is again motivated by an analogy with solving mathematical problems, which often have well-separated reasoning and computational components. Examples include numerical calculations, computing derivatives and integrals, performing Boolean algebra in various settings, sequences of standard rewriting and normalization operations in various algebraic theories, etc. Such components of the larger problem can be often solved mostly in isolation from the other components, and only their results are then used together to connect them and solve the larger problem.

Human-designed problem solving architectures addressing such decomposition include, e.g., SMT systems, systems such as MetiTarski [1], and a tactic-based learning-guided proof search in systems such as TacticToe [9]. In all these systems, the component procedures or tactics are, however, *human-designed* and (often painstakingly) human-implemented, with a lot of care both for the components and for the algorithms that merge their results. This approach seems hard to scale to the large number of combinations of complex algorithms, decision procedures and reasoning heuristics used in research-level mathematics, and other complex reasoning domains.

Our new approach is to instead start to *learn* such *targeted components*, expressed as sets of clauses that perform targeted reasoning and computation within the saturation framework. We also want to learn the merging of the results of the components automatically. This is quite ambitious, but there seems to be growing evidence that such targeted components are being learned in many iterations of GNN-guided proving followed by retraining of the GNNs in our recent large iterative evaluation over Mizar.[1] In these experiments, we have significantly extended our previously published results [12],[2] eventually automatically proving 73.5% (more than 40k) of the Mizar theorems. In particular, there are many examples shown on the project Github page demonstrating that the GNN is learning to solve more and more involved computations in problems involving differentiation, integration, boolean algebra, algebraic rewriting, etc. Our initial approach is therefore to (i) use the GNN to learn to identify interacting reasoning components, (ii) use graph-based and clustering-based algorithms to split the set of clauses into components based on the GNN predictions, (iii) run saturation on the components independently, (iv) possibly merge the most important parts of the components, and (v) iterate. See the Split and Merge Algorithm 2.

5 Clustering Methods

Here we propose two modifications of our previous GNN architecture, described in Sect. 2, for the identification of interacting reasoning components, and we

[1] https://github.com/ai4reason/ATP_Proofs.
[2] The publication of this large evaluation is in preparation.

Algorithm 2: The Split and Merge algorithm

Input: $AxiomClauses$, $NegConjectureClauses$, $SaturationLimit$,
$\quad\quad IterationLimit$, $PremiseSelector$, $ClusteringAlgo$;

1 $S_0 = AxiomClauses \cup NegConjectureClauses$;

2 **for** $i = 0$ **to** $IterationLimit$ **do**

3 $\quad$ $(L_i, Result) = Saturate(S_i, SaturationLimit)$;

4 $\quad$ **if** $Result = Unsatisfiable$ **then return** $Unsatisfiable$;

5 $\quad$ **else if** $Result = Satisfiable$ **then**

6 $\quad\quad$ **if** $i=0$ **then return** Satisfiable;

7 $\quad\quad$ **else return** $Unknown$;

8 $\quad$ **else** // $Result = Unknown$

9 $\quad\quad$ $(C_i^1, ..., C_i^K) = ClusteringAlgo(L_i)$;   // Split to components

10 $\quad\quad$ **for** $j = 1$ **to** K **do**

11 $\quad\quad\quad$ $(L_i^j, Result^j) = Saturate(C_i^j, SaturationLimit)$;   // Run each

12 $\quad\quad\quad$ **if** $Result^j = Unsatisfiable$ **then return** $Unsatisfiable$;

13 $\quad\quad$ $S_{i+1} = PremiseSelector(\bigcup\limits_{j=1}^{K} L_i^j, NegConjectureClauses)$;   // Merge

14 $\quad\quad$ $S_{i+1} = S_{i+1} \cup NegConjectureClauses$;

15 **return** $Unknown$;

describe their intended use. The overall methodology to detect and utilize reasoning components is as follows. To produce the training data, we run E with a fixed limit of N given clause loops. For each solved problem, we output not only the proof, but the full derivation tree of all clauses *generated* during the proof search. These will provide training data to train a GNN classifier. For unproved problems, we output the N given clauses *processed* during the search. These data from unsuccessful proof searches are then used for the prediction of interacting components. This is the start of the Split and Merge Algorithm 2.

The training data are extracted from successful proof searches as follows. From each derivation tree, we extract all clause pairs C_i and C_j which interacted during the proof search, that is, the pairs which were used to infer another clause. All pairs (C_i, C_j) which were used to infer a proof clause are marked as *positive* while the remaining clause pairs as *negative*. Such clauses with the information about their positive/negative pairing are used to train a GNN predictor.

The trained GNN predictor will guide the construction of clusters, where clauses resembling positively linked clauses should end up within the same cluster. We obtain the data for predictions from the above unsuccessful proof searches (with the fixed limit of N processed clauses), and they contain N processed clauses for every problem. We want to assign each pair of clauses (C_i, C_j) a score $l_{i,j}$ which describes the likelihood of inferring a useful clause from C_i and C_j. These scores are the basis for the clustering algorithms.

We experiment with two slightly different GNN architectures for the identification of reasoning components. Let d be the dimension of the final clause embedding, and let c_i, c_j be the embeddings of clauses C_i, C_j respectively. Then the two architectures—differently computing the score $l_{i,j}$—are as follows:

1. We pass both c_i, c_j through a linear layer (with biases, without an activation function) with the output dimension n, resulting in d_i, d_j. Then we calculate $l_{i,j} = d_i \cdot d_j/\sqrt{n}$.
2. We pass both c_i, c_j through a linear layer with the output dimension $2n$, resulting in d'_i, d'_j. Then we calculate $l_{i,j} = d_i \cdot \text{rev}(d_j)/\sqrt{n}$ where rev represents reversing the vector.

Mathematically, this corresponds to $l_{i,j} = c_i^T A c_j + v^T(c_i + c_j) + b$ where v^T are n-dimensional vectors for clause evaluation, b is a scalar bias, and A is an $n \times n$ matrix which is symmetric and positive definite in architecture 1, and just symmetric in architecture 2. For training, we pass the value $l_{i,j}$ through sigmoid and binary cross entropy loss.

5.1 Clustering

To split the clauses into separate components, we use standard clustering algorithms. However, in our case, it is likely that some clauses should be shared among various components, and hence we are also interested in methods capable of such overlapping assignments.

Of course, the crucial precondition for splitting clauses into components is defining the similarity between clauses, or even better, a distance between them. We have at least two straightforward options here—to define the distance between two clauses as the distance between their embeddings (vectors) or use the matrix $L = (l_{ij})$ as a similarity measure, which approximates the likelihood that clauses i and j interact in the proof. A simple way to produce distances from L is to treat each row of L as a vector and define the distance between two clauses as the (Euclidean) distance between the corresponding rows of L.

Another approach is to use directly the intended meaning of matrix L, the likelihood that two given clauses appear in a proof, and to produce a weighted graph from L, where vertices are clauses and edges are assigned weights according to L. Moreover, we can remove edges that have weights below some threshold, expressing that such clauses do not interact. In this way, we obtain a weighted graph that can be clustered into components. The following paragraphs briefly describe the clustering algorithms used in the experiments.

k-Means. A widely used clustering method is k-means. The goal is to separate vectors into k clusters in such a way that their within-cluster variance is minimal. Although k-means is a popular clustering method, it suffers from numerous well-known problems. For example, it assumes that we know the correct number of clusters in advance, the clusters are of similar sizes, and they are nonoverlapping. Although these assumptions are not satisfied in our case, we used k-means from SciPY [36] as a well-known baseline.

Table 1. Four leapfrogging runs with different GNN-ENIGMAs

GNN-strategy	Original-60s-run	Leapfrogging (300-500-60s)	Union	Added-by-lfrg
G_1	2711	2218	3370	659
G_2	2516	2426	3393	877
G_3	2655	2463	3512	857
G_4	2477	2268	3276	799

Soft k-Means. It is possible to modify k-means in such a way that overlapping clusters (also called soft clusters) are allowed.[3] An example is the Fuzzy C-Means (FCM) algorithm [3] that generalizes k-means by adding the membership function for each point. This function scores how much each point belongs to a cluster, and it is possible to adjust the degree of overlap between the clusters. We used the `fuzzy-c-means` package [7] for our experiments.

Graph Clustering. We have experimented with the cluster application from the popular Graphviz visualisation software [8], which can split a graph into clusters using the methods described in [5]. The graphs are clustered based on the *modularity* measure which considers the density of links inside a cluster compared to links between clusters. It is possible to either directly specify the intended number of clusters (soft constraint), or base the number of clusters on their modularity. We also experimented with clustering using the *modularity quality*.[4] Moreover, by removing some highly connected vertices (clauses) before clustering and adding them into all clusters, we can produce overlapping clusters.

6 Evaluation

6.1 Leapfrogging

The first leapfrogging experiment is done as follows:

1. We stop GNN-ENIGMA after 300 processed clauses and print them.
2. We restart with the 300 clauses used as input, stop at 500 clauses and print the 500 clauses.
3. We restart with the 500 clauses, and do a final run for 60 s.

This is done on a set of 28k *hard* Mizar problems that we have been trying to prove with many different methods in a large ongoing evaluation over the full Mizar corpus.[5] We try with four differently trained and parameterized GNNs, denoted as $G_1, \ldots, G_4$. The summary of the runs is given in Table 1.

[3] Another popular way how to generalize k-means (and assign a point to more than one cluster) is to use Gaussian mixture models.

[4] https://gitlab.com/graphviz/graphviz/-/blob/main/lib/sparse/mq.h.

[5] Details are at https://github.com/ai4reason/ATP_Proofs.

Table 2. Clustering 3000 problems for evaluation

Method	#clusters	Newly solved problems
k-means	2	67
k-means	3	78
Soft k-means	2	63
Soft k-means	3	93
Graphviz	≤ 4	111

We see that the methods indeed achieve high complementarity to the original GNN strategies. This is most likely thanks to the different context in which the GNN sees the initial clauses in the subsequent runs.

6.2 Splitting and Merging

The initial experimental evaluation[6] is done on a large benchmark of 57880 Mizar40 [17] problems[7] exported to first-order logic by MPTP [33]. We use a subset of 52k Mizar40 [17] problems for training. To produce the training data, we run E with a well-performing GNN guidance, and with the limit of 1000 given clause loops. Within this limit, around 20k of the training problems are solved. For the 32k unproved training problems, we output the 1000 given clauses *processed* during the search. As described in Sect. 5, we train a

Fig. 1. Differentiation – T16_FDIFF_5

[6] On a server with 36 hyperthreading Intel(R) Xeon(R) Gold 6140 CPU @ 2.30 GHz cores, 755 GB of memory, and 4 NVIDIA GeForce GTX 1080 Ti GPUs.

[7] http://grid01.ciirc.cvut.cz/~mptp/1147/MPTP2/problems_small_consist.tar.gz.

Fig. 2. Associativity of gcd by many rewrites – T48_NEWTON

GNN predictor on the 20k successful runs, and use it to predict the interactions between the processed clauses of the unsuccessful runs. Since the evaluation on the full set of the 32k unsolved problems would be too resource-intensive, we limit this to its randomly chosen 3000-big subset. Table 2 shows the performance of the clustering methods in solving the problems in the first Split phase. The strongest method is the Graphviz-based graph clustering. In more detail, the `cluster` tool gives us on the GNN graph predictions up to four graph components. We run again with a 1000-given clause limit on them newly solving altogether 111 problems inside the components of the 3000. Then we choose this clustering for an experiment with the Merge phase. We merge the components of the remaining unsolved 2889 problems and use our GNN for a premise-selection-style final choice of the jointly best subset of the clauses produced by all the components (line 13 of Algorithm 2). We use four thresholds for the premise selection, and run again with a 1000-given clause limit on each of such premise selections (line 3 of Algorithm 2). This run on the merged components yields another 66 new proofs. Many of the newly found proofs indeed show frequent computational patterns. Examples include the proofs of Mizar problems `T16_FDIFF_5` (Fig. 1),[8] `T48_NEWTON` (Fig. 2),[9] `T10_MATRIX_4`,[10] `T11_VECTSP_2`,[11] `T125_RVSUM_1`,[12] `T13_BCIALG_3`,[13] and `T14_FUZZY_2`.[14]

[8] http://grid01.ciirc.cvut.cz/~mptp/7.13.01_4.181.1147/html/fdiff_5.html#T16.
[9] http://grid01.ciirc.cvut.cz/~mptp/7.13.01_4.181.1147/html/newton.html#T48.
[10] http://grid01.ciirc.cvut.cz/~mptp/7.13.01_4.181.1147/html/matrix_4.html#T10.
[11] http://grid01.ciirc.cvut.cz/~mptp/7.13.01_4.181.1147/html/vectsp_2.html#T11.
[12] http://grid01.ciirc.cvut.cz/~mptp/7.13.01_4.181.1147/html/rvsum_1.html#T125.
[13] http://grid01.ciirc.cvut.cz/~mptp/7.13.01_4.181.1147/html/bcialg_3.html#T13.
[14] http://grid01.ciirc.cvut.cz/~mptp/7.13.01_4.181.1147/html/fuzzy_2.html#T14.

7 Conclusion

We have described several algorithms advancing the idea of contextual evaluation based on learning important components of the graph of clauses. The first leapfrogging experiments already show very encouraging results on the Mizar dataset, providing many complementary solutions. The component-based algorithm also produces new solutions and there are clearly many further methods and experiments that can be tried in this setting. We believe that this approach may eventually lead to using large mathematical libraries for automated learning of nontrivial components, algorithms, and decision procedures involved in mathematical reasoning.

Acknowledgments. Supported by the ERC Consolidator grant *AI4REASON* no. 649043 (JJ, JU), by the Czech project AI & Reasoning CZ.02.1.01/0.0/0.0/15_003/0000466 and the European Regional Development Fund (KC, JU), by the ERC Starting grant *SMART* no. 714034 (JJ, MO), and by the Czech MEYS under the ERC CZ project *POSTMAN* no. LL1902 (JJ).

References

1. Akbarpour, B., Paulson, L.C.: MetiTarski: an automatic theorem prover for real-valued special functions. J. Autom. Reasoning **44**(3), 175–205 (2010)
2. Alama, J., Heskes, T., Kühlwein, D., Tsivtsivadze, E., Urban, J.: Premise selection for mathematics by corpus analysis and kernel methods. J. Autom. Reason. **52**(2), 191–213 (2013). https://doi.org/10.1007/s10817-013-9286-5
3. Bezdek, J.C., Ehrlich, R., Full, W.: FCM: the fuzzy c-means clustering algorithm. Comput. Geosci. **10**(2), 191–203 (1984). https://doi.org/10.1016/0098-3004(84)90020-7. https://www.sciencedirect.com/science/article/pii/0098300484900207
4. Blanchette, J.C., Kaliszyk, C., Paulson, L.C., Urban, J.: Hammering towards QED. J. Formalized Reason. **9**(1), 101–148 (2016). https://doi.org/10.6092/issn.1972-5787/4593. http://dx.doi.org/10.6092/issn.1972-5787/4593
5. Blondel, V.D., Guillaume, J.L., Lambiotte, R., Lefebvre, E.: Fast unfolding of communities in large networks. J. Stat. Mech: Theory Exp. **2008**(10), P10008 (2008)
6. Chvalovský, K., Jakubův, J., Suda, M., Urban, J.: ENIGMA-NG: efficient neural and gradient-boosted inference guidance for E. In: Fontaine, P. (ed.) CADE 2019. LNCS (LNAI), vol. 11716, pp. 197–215. Springer, Cham (2019). https://doi.org/10.1007/978-3-030-29436-6_12
7. Dias, M.L.D.: fuzzy-c-means: an implementation of fuzzy *c*-means clustering algorithm. (2019). https://doi.org/10.5281/zenodo.3066222. https://git.io/fuzzy-c-means
8. Ellson, J., Gansner, E.R., Koutsofios, E., North, S.C., Woodhull, G.: Graphviz and dynagraph - static and dynamic graph drawing tools. In: Jünger, M., Mutzel, P. (eds.) Graph Drawing Software, pp. 127–148. Springer, Heidelberg (2004). https://doi.org/10.1007/978-3-642-18638-7_6

9. Gauthier, T., Kaliszyk, C., Urban, J.: TacticToe: learning to reason with HOL4 tactics. In: Eiter, T., Sands, D. (eds.) LPAR-21, 21st International Conference on Logic for Programming, Artificial Intelligence and Reasoning, Maun, Botswana, 7–12 May 2017. EPiC Series in Computing, vol. 46, pp. 125–143. EasyChair (2017). http://www.easychair.org/publications/paper/340355
10. Gittins, J.C.: Bandit processes and dynamic allocation indices. J. Roy. Stat. Soc. Ser. B (Methodol.) 148–177 (1979)
11. Gottlob, G., Sutcliffe, G., Voronkov, A. (eds.): Global Conference on Artificial Intelligence, GCAI 2015, Tbilisi, Georgia, 16–19 October 2015. EPiC Series in Computing, vol. 36. EasyChair (2015). http://www.easychair.org/publications/volume/GCAI_2015
12. Jakubův, J., Chvalovský, K., Olšák, M., Piotrowski, B., Suda, M., Urban, J.: ENIGMA anonymous: symbol-independent inference guiding machine (system description). In: Peltier, N., Sofronie-Stokkermans, V. (eds.) IJCAR 2020. LNCS (LNAI), vol. 12167, pp. 448–463. Springer, Cham (2020). https://doi.org/10.1007/978-3-030-51054-1_29
13. Jakubův, J., Urban, J.: Extending E prover with similarity based clause selection strategies. In: Kohlhase, M., Johansson, M., Miller, B., de de Moura, L., Tompa, F. (eds.) CICM 2016. LNCS (LNAI), vol. 9791, pp. 151–156. Springer, Cham (2016). https://doi.org/10.1007/978-3-319-42547-4_11
14. Jakubův, J., Urban, J.: ENIGMA: efficient learning-based inference guiding machine. In: Geuvers, H., England, M., Hasan, O., Rabe, F., Teschke, O. (eds.) CICM 2017. LNCS (LNAI), vol. 10383, pp. 292–302. Springer, Cham (2017). https://doi.org/10.1007/978-3-319-62075-6_20
15. Jakubův, J., Urban, J.: Hierarchical invention of theorem proving strategies. AI Commun. **31**(3), 237–250 (2018). https://doi.org/10.3233/AIC-180761
16. Jakubův, J., Urban, J.: Hammering Mizar by learning clause guidance. In: Harrison, J., O'Leary, J., Tolmach, A. (eds.) 10th International Conference on Interactive Theorem Proving, ITP 2019, 9–12 September 2019, Portland, OR, USA. LIPIcs, vol. 141, pp. 34:1–34:8. Schloss Dagstuhl - Leibniz-Zentrum für Informatik (2019). https://doi.org/10.4230/LIPIcs.ITP.2019.34
17. Kaliszyk, C., Urban, J.: MizAR 40 for Mizar 40. J. Autom. Reason. **55**(3), 245–256 (2015). https://doi.org/10.1007/s10817-015-9330-8
18. Kaliszyk, C., Urban, J., Michalewski, H., sák, M.O.: Reinforcement learning of theorem proving. In: Advances in Neural Information Processing Systems 31: Annual Conference on Neural Information Processing Systems 2018, NeurIPS 2018, 3–8 December 2018, Montréal, Canada, pp. 8836–8847 (2018). http://papers.nips.cc/paper/8098-reinforcement-learning-of-theorem-proving
19. Kinyon, M., Veroff, R., Vojtěchovský, P.: Loops with abelian inner mapping groups: an application of automated deduction. In: Bonacina, M.P., Stickel, M.E. (eds.) Automated Reasoning and Mathematics. LNCS (LNAI), vol. 7788, pp. 151–164. Springer, Heidelberg (2013). https://doi.org/10.1007/978-3-642-36675-8_8
20. Kovács, L., Voronkov, A.: First-order theorem proving and VAMPIRE. In: Sharygina, N., Veith, H. (eds.) CAV 2013. LNCS, vol. 8044, pp. 1–35. Springer, Heidelberg (2013). https://doi.org/10.1007/978-3-642-39799-8_1
21. McCune, W.: Otter 2.0. In: Stickel, M.E. (ed.) CADE 1990. LNCS, vol. 449, pp. 663–664. Springer, Heidelberg (1990). https://doi.org/10.1007/3-540-52885-7_131
22. McCune, W.: Prover9 and Mace4 (2005–2010). http://www.cs.unm.edu/~mccune/prover9/

23. McCune, W.: Semantic guidance for saturation provers. In: Calmet, J., Ida, T., Wang, D. (eds.) AISC 2006. LNCS (LNAI), vol. 4120, pp. 18–24. Springer, Heidelberg (2006). https://doi.org/10.1007/11856290_4
24. McCune, W.: Otter 3.3 reference manual. Technical report ANL/MSC-TM-263, Argonne National Laboratory, Argonne, USA (2003)
25. Olšák, M., Kaliszyk, C., Urban, J.: Property invariant embedding for automated reasoning. In: Giacomo, G.D., et al. (eds.) ECAI 2020–24th European Conference on Artificial Intelligence, 29 August–8 September 2020, Santiago de Compostela, Spain, 29 August–8 September 2020 - Including 10th Conference on Prestigious Applications of Artificial Intelligence (PAIS 2020). Frontiers in Artificial Intelligence and Applications, vol. 325, pp. 1395–1402. IOS Press (2020). https://doi.org/10.3233/FAIA200244
26. Otten, J., Bibel, W.: leanCoP: lean connection-based theorem proving. J. Symb. Comput. **36**(1–2), 139–161 (2003)
27. Quaife, A.: Automated Development of Fundamental Mathematical Theories. Kluwer Academic Publishers (1992)
28. Raths, T., Otten, J.: randocop: randomizing the proof search order in the connection calculus. In: Konev, B., Schmidt, R.A., Schulz, S. (eds.) Proceedings of the First International Workshop on Practical Aspects of Automated Reasoning, Sydney, Australia, 10–11 August 2008. CEUR Workshop Proceedings, vol. 373. CEUR-WS.org (2008). http://ceur-ws.org/Vol-373/paper-08.pdf
29. Robinson, J.A., Voronkov, A. (eds.): Handbook of Automated Reasoning (in 2 volumes). Elsevier and MIT Press (2001)
30. Schäfer, S., Schulz, S.: Breeding theorem proving heuristics with genetic algorithms. In: Gottlob et al. [11], pp. 263–274. http://www.easychair.org/publications/paper/Breeding_Theorem_Proving_Heuristics_with_Genetic_Algorithms
31. Schulz, S.: E - a brainiac theorem prover. AI Commun. **15**(2–3), 111–126 (2002)
32. Schulz, S.: System description: E 1.8. In: McMillan, K., Middeldorp, A., Voronkov, A. (eds.) LPAR 2013. LNCS, vol. 8312, pp. 735–743. Springer, Heidelberg (2013). https://doi.org/10.1007/978-3-642-45221-5_49
33. Urban, J.: MPTP 0.2: design, implementation, and initial experiments. J. Autom. Reasoning **37**(1–2), 21–43 (2006)
34. Urban, J.: BliStr: the blind strategymaker. In: Gottlob et al. [11], pp. 312–319. http://www.easychair.org/publications/paper/BliStr_The_Blind_Strategymaker
35. Veroff, R.: Using hints to increase the effectiveness of an automated reasoning program: case studies. J. Autom. Reason. **16**(3), 223–239 (1996)
36. Virtanen, P., et al.: SciPy 1.0 contributors: SciPy 1.0: fundamental algorithms for scientific computing in python. Nat. Methods **17**, 261–272 (2020). https://doi.org/10.1038/s41592-019-0686-2

Formalized Proofs

A Formally Verified Cut-Elimination Procedure for Linear Nested Sequents for Tense Logic

Caitlin D'Abrera[1], Jeremy Dawson[1(✉)], and Rajeev Goré[2]

[1] School of Computing, The Australian National University, Canberra, Australia
{caitlin.dabrera,Jeremy.Dawson}@anu.edu.au
[2] Vienna University of Technology, Vienna, Austria

Abstract. We port Dawson and Goré's general framework of deep embeddings of derivability from Isabelle to Coq. By using lists instead of multisets to encode sequents, we enable the encoding of genuinely substructural logics in which some combination of exchange, weakening and contraction are not admissible. We then show how to extend the framework to encode the linear nested sequent calculus $\mathsf{LNS}_{\mathsf{Kt}}$ of Goré and Lellmann for the tense logic Kt and prove cut-elimination and all required proof-theoretic theorems in Coq, based on their pen-and-paper proofs. Finally, we extract the proof of the cut-elimination theorem to obtain a formally verified Haskell program that produces cut-free derivations from those with cut. We believe it is the first published formally verified computer program for eliminating cuts in any proof calculus.

Keywords: Formalised proof theory · Cut-elimination · Linear nested sequent calculus · Tense logic · Coq · Extraction · Program synthesis

1 Introduction

Traditional styles of proof calculi for capturing the notion of logical derivations include Hilbert calculi, natural deduction [19], sequent calculi [19] and tableau calculi [7]. More recent and elaborate styles include display calculi [1,3], labelled sequents [14] and nested sequent calculi [10]. Each style has strengths and weaknesses: expressivity, complexity, ease of use, and philosophical motivations.

Consider the interesting case of systems for tense logics. After previously published failed attempts at providing sequent calculi that satisfy cut-elimination, more complex systems were produced in the forms of display calculi, nested sequents and labelled sequents. Goré and Lellmann [8] provide a simpler calculus, $\mathsf{LNS}_{\mathsf{Kt}}$, using linear nested sequents (LNS) for the minimal tense logic Kt that

C. D'Abrera—Supported by an Australian Government Research Training Program Scholarship.
R. Goré—Work supported by the FWF projects I 2982 and P 33548.

A. Das and S. Negri (Eds.): TABLEAUX 2021, LNAI 12842, pp. 281–298, 2021.
https://doi.org/10.1007/978-3-030-86059-2_17

does not require the heavy machinery found in the other more complex systems. Their LNS calculus is a cut-free system and they proved cut-admissibility.

But, as is well-known, proofs of cut-admissibility are notoriously "case heavy" with many similar cases which are often "left to the reader". The cut-admissibility proof of Goré and Lellmann [8] is no exception and involves a complicated simultaneous induction over four sub-cases. One way of verifying its correctness is to formalise it in a modern interactive proof assistant, as explained next.

Dawson and Goré [6] gave an elegant embedding of a general framework for derivability in Isabelle/HOL, applicable to many styles of proof calculi, including many extensions of the sequent calculus [4]. But they used Isabelle/HOL 2007 and it would require a complete rewrite of that material to use it in modern Isabelle, which may indeed not be possible. So we ported this work to Coq and adapted it to allow the handling of genuinely substructural notions such as exchange, which the aforementioned Isabelle/HOL formalisation lacked. We extended this Coq framework to encode linear nested sequents and $\mathsf{LNS}_{\mathsf{Kt}}$, and proved in Coq the standard structural proof-theoretic theorems up to and including cut-admissibility, based on the original pen-and-paper proofs [8].

Constructively proving cut-elimination in Coq permits us to extract the procedure into a Haskell program that computes cut-free derivations from those with cut. The full proof of cut-elimination in a pen-and-paper setting is already large because it involves so many cases, and adding the extra cases that emerge as part of the task of formalising has made this theorem a good candidate for verification, particularly as multiple mistakes were found. As far as we know, ours is the first published extracted program for performing cut-elimination.

Our Coq code was developed with Coq 8.8.2 (October 2018) and tested with Coq 8.10.2 (Nov 2019): https://github.com/caitlindabrera/LNS-for-Kt.

2 Preliminaries

Formulae of normal modal tense logics are built from a given set *Atm* of atomic formulae via the following BNF grammar where $p \in Atm$: $A := p \mid \bot \mid A \to A \mid \Box A \mid \blacksquare A$. We assume that the reader is familiar with their associated Kripke semantics or their standard Hilbert calculus [8].

We define linear nested sequents as in [8] before giving the full calculus.

2.1 A Linear Nested Sequent Calculus for Kt

Definition 1. *A* sequent *is an expression* $\Gamma \Rightarrow \Delta$ *where the* antecedent Γ *and the* succedent Δ *are finite, possibly empty, multisets of formulae. We write* ϵ *to stand for an empty antecedent or succedent to avoid confusion. A* linear nested sequent *is a sequence of sequents where each adjacent pair is connected by* $\nearrow$ *or* $\swarrow$*. The sequents that occur within such a linear nested sequent are* components.

$$\frac{\mathcal{G} \updownarrow \Gamma \Rightarrow \Delta, A \swarrow \Sigma \Rightarrow \Pi, \Box A \quad \mathcal{G} \updownarrow \Gamma \Rightarrow \Delta \swarrow \Sigma \Rightarrow \Pi, \Box A \nearrow \epsilon \Rightarrow A}{\mathcal{G} \updownarrow \Gamma \Rightarrow \Delta \swarrow \Sigma \Rightarrow \Pi, \Box A}\ \Box^1_R$$

$$\frac{\mathcal{G} \updownarrow \Gamma \Rightarrow \Delta, A \nearrow \Sigma \Rightarrow \Pi, \blacksquare A \quad \mathcal{G} \updownarrow \Gamma \Rightarrow \Delta \nearrow \Sigma \Rightarrow \Pi, \blacksquare A \swarrow \epsilon \Rightarrow A}{\mathcal{G} \updownarrow \Gamma \Rightarrow \Delta \nearrow \Sigma \Rightarrow \Pi, \blacksquare A}\ \blacksquare^1_R$$

$$\frac{\mathcal{G} \nearrow \Gamma \Rightarrow \Delta, \Box A \nearrow \epsilon \Rightarrow A}{\mathcal{G} \nearrow \Gamma \Rightarrow \Delta, \Box A}\ \Box^2_R \qquad \frac{\mathcal{G} \swarrow \Gamma \Rightarrow \Delta, \blacksquare A \swarrow \epsilon \Rightarrow A}{\mathcal{G} \swarrow \Gamma \Rightarrow \Delta, \blacksquare A}\ \blacksquare^2_R$$

$$\frac{\mathcal{G} \updownarrow \Gamma, \Box A \Rightarrow \Delta \nearrow \Sigma, A \Rightarrow \Pi}{\mathcal{G} \updownarrow \Gamma, \Box A \Rightarrow \Delta \nearrow \Sigma \Rightarrow \Pi}\ \Box^1_L \qquad \frac{\mathcal{G} \updownarrow \Gamma, \blacksquare A \Rightarrow \Delta \swarrow \Sigma, A \Rightarrow \Pi}{\mathcal{G} \updownarrow \Gamma, \blacksquare A \Rightarrow \Delta \swarrow \Sigma \Rightarrow \Pi}\ \blacksquare^1_L$$

$$\frac{\mathcal{G} \updownarrow \Gamma, A \Rightarrow \Delta}{\mathcal{G} \updownarrow \Gamma \Rightarrow \Delta \swarrow \Sigma, \Box A \Rightarrow \Pi}\ \Box^2_L \qquad \frac{\mathcal{G} \updownarrow \Gamma, A \Rightarrow \Delta}{\mathcal{G} \updownarrow \Gamma \Rightarrow \Delta \nearrow \Sigma, \blacksquare A \Rightarrow \Pi}\ \blacksquare^2_L$$

$$\frac{}{\mathcal{G} \updownarrow \Gamma, p \Rightarrow p, \Delta}\ (id) \qquad \frac{}{\mathcal{G} \updownarrow \Gamma, \bot \Rightarrow \Delta}\ \bot_L \qquad \frac{\mathcal{G}}{\mathcal{G} \updownarrow \Gamma \Rightarrow \Delta}\ \mathsf{EW}$$

$$\frac{\mathcal{G} \updownarrow \Gamma, A \Rightarrow \Delta, A \to B, B}{\mathcal{G} \updownarrow \Gamma \Rightarrow \Delta, A \to B}\ \to_R \qquad \frac{\mathcal{G} \updownarrow \Gamma, A \to B, B \Rightarrow \Delta \quad \mathcal{G} \updownarrow \Gamma, A \to B \Rightarrow \Delta, A}{\mathcal{G} \updownarrow \Gamma, A \to B \Rightarrow \Delta}\ \to_L$$

Fig. 1. The system LNS$_{\mathsf{Kt}}$ where $\updownarrow$ stands for either $\nearrow$ or $\swarrow$

We use lower case letters (p, q, r) for atomic formulae, upper case letters (A, B, C) for formulae, capital Greek letters $(\Gamma, \Delta, \Sigma, \Pi)$ for finite multisets of formulae and calligraphic capital letters $(\mathcal{G}, \mathcal{H})$ for LNSs, unless otherwise stated. We often write $\mathcal{G}$ for a possibly empty *context*: e.g., $\mathcal{G} \nearrow \Gamma \Rightarrow \Delta$ stands for $\Gamma \Rightarrow \Delta$ if $\mathcal{G}$ is empty, and for $\Sigma \Rightarrow \Pi \swarrow \Omega \Rightarrow \Theta \nearrow \Gamma \Rightarrow \Delta$ if $\mathcal{G}$ is the LNS $\Sigma \Rightarrow \Pi \swarrow \Omega \Rightarrow \Theta$.

The rules of LNS$_{\mathsf{Kt}}$ [8] are in Fig. 1. Each rule has a number of *premisses* above the line and a single *conclusion* below it. The single formula in the conclusion is the *principal* formula and the formulae in the premisses are the *side-formulae.*

Intuitively, each component of a linear nested sequent corresponds to a world of a Kripke model, and the structural connectives $\nearrow$ and $\swarrow$ between components corresponds to the relations R and R^{-1} that connect these worlds. We can then think of a Kripke model forcing a LNS $\mathcal{G}$ if for every connected sequence of worlds corresponding to the structure of $\mathcal{G}$, one of those worlds forces its corresponding sequent component. See [8] for the formal detail.

Every instance of the (id) and $\bot_L$ rules is a *derivation* of depth 1. If (ρ) is an n-ary rule and there are n premiss derivations $\mathcal{D}_1, \cdots, \mathcal{D}_n$, each of depth $d_1, \cdots, d_n$, with respective conclusions $c_1, \cdots, c_n$, and $c_1, \cdots, c_n / c_0$ is an instance of (ρ) then $\mathcal{D}_1, \cdots, \mathcal{D}_n / c_0$ is a derivation of depth $1 + max\{d_1, \cdots, d_n\}$. We use $\mathsf{dp}(\mathcal{D})$ for the depth of derivation $\mathcal{D}$.

We generalise "derivations" to allow for "unfinished leaves", by which we simply mean leaf sequents from a given set that are considered separate to any zero-premiss rules in the system. We write $\mathcal{D} \vdash^{\mathsf{prems}}_{\mathsf{rls}} \mathcal{G}$ to mean that $\mathcal{D}$ is a derivation of the LNS $\mathcal{G}$ in the calculus with rule set rls, allowing for unfinished leaves prems. We further write $\mathcal{D} \vdash_{\mathsf{rls}} \mathcal{G}$ when prems is empty and thus $\mathcal{D}$ must be a finished proof with no unfinished leaves. In both cases, we may omit the

$\mathcal{D}$ to mean that there exists a derivation $\mathcal{D}$ such that $\mathcal{D} \vdash^{\mathsf{prems}}_{\mathsf{rls}} \mathcal{G}$ or $\mathcal{D} \vdash_{\mathsf{rls}} \mathcal{G}$, respectively. We simply write $\mathcal{D} \vdash \mathcal{G}$ if $\mathcal{D}$ is a derivation in $\mathsf{LNS_{Kt}}$ of the linear nested sequent $\mathcal{G}$, and $\vdash \mathcal{G}$ if there is a derivation $\mathcal{D}$ with $\mathcal{D} \vdash \mathcal{G}$.

Example 1. Consider the LNS $\epsilon \Rightarrow r \to \blacksquare\neg\Box\neg r$ where $r \to \blacksquare\neg\Box\neg r$ is the formula $r \to \blacksquare\Diamond r$ with the definition of $\Diamond$ expanded. The following is a non-trivial derivation that demonstrates the use of some of the box rules to move formulae between different components. Note that it uses the provably admissible rules $\neg_L$, $\neg_R$ and weakening.

$$\dfrac{\dfrac{\dfrac{\dfrac{\dfrac{\dfrac{\dfrac{}{r, \neg r \Rightarrow r, \blacksquare\neg\Box\neg r}\,(\mathrm{id})}{r, \neg r \Rightarrow \blacksquare\neg\Box\neg r}\,\neg_L}{r \Rightarrow \blacksquare\neg\Box\neg r \swarrow \Box\neg r \Rightarrow \neg\Box\neg r}\,\Box^2_L}{r \Rightarrow \blacksquare\neg\Box\neg r \swarrow \epsilon \Rightarrow \neg\Box\neg r}\,\neg_R}{r \Rightarrow \blacksquare\neg\Box\neg r}\,\blacksquare^2_R}{r \Rightarrow r \to \blacksquare\neg\Box\neg r, \blacksquare\neg\Box\neg r}\,\mathrm{weak}}{\epsilon \Rightarrow r \to \blacksquare\neg\Box\neg r}\,\to_R$$

3 Encoding Formulae, Sequents and LNSs

Having seen the pen-and-paper definition of the calculus, we turn to our Coq formalisation. We start with a set of proposition variables, `V : Set`, which corresponds to *Atm*, over which we build our formulae, `PropF V`:

```
Inductive PropF (V : Set) : Type :=
  | Bot   : PropF V
  | Var   : V -> PropF V
  | WBox  : PropF V -> PropF V
  | BBox  : PropF V -> PropF V
  | Imp   : PropF V -> PropF V -> PropF V.
```

Here we are creating a new type called `PropF`, and so we would encode, for example, the infix formula $\Box(p \to q) \to (\Box p \to \Box q)$ using prefix notation by the term `Imp (WBox (Imp (Var p) (Var q))) (Imp (WBox (Var p)) (WBox (Var q)))`.

Recall our sequents consist of multisets. To model this we chose lists and later proved exchange lemmas that enable us to move formulae around in any order without compromising derivability. See Sect. 6 for further details. Thus the multiset Γ of formulae is encoded as a term with type `list (PropF V)` and sequents, which have the form $\Gamma \Rightarrow \Delta$, have type `seq`:

```
Definition rel (W : Type) : Type := W * W. (* ie, prod W W *)
Definition seq {V : Set} := rel (list (PropF V)).
```

Here, `prod W W`, also written `W * W`, is the Cartesian product $W \times W$, and so an `s` of type `seq` is a pair of lists of formulae such as `pair` Γ Δ, also written (Γ, Δ).

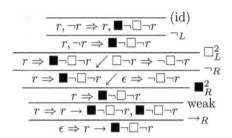

In Coq, `list` comes pre-defined as expected, where `a :: b :: c :: nil` encodes the list $[a, b, c]$. We can append list `l1` to list `l2` by the `++` operator. For a function `f : A -> B`, and a list `l : list A`, the result of `map f l` is got by applying `f` to each member of `l`. We use these extensively throughout our formalisation, as can be seen in the definitions for `nslclext` and `nslclrule` in Sect. 4.

Coq allows "implicit arguments" where certain arguments for some functions can usually be inferred and are not given. Typical examples are the first arguments of the list operators `++` and `::`, which state the type of the list members. The symbol `@` preceding a function name, as in `@seq V`, indicates that all arguments are given explicitly. In the code above, braces as in `{V : Set}`, as opposed to parentheses as in `(W : Type)`, indicates `V` is to be an implicit argument.

We defined the type `LNS` to encode LNSs as lists of pairs of sequents and directions, where the latter is defined to have two inhabitants corresponding to the $\nearrow$ and $\swarrow$ arrows:

```
Inductive dir : Type :=   | fwd : dir  | bac : dir.
Definition LNS {V : Set} := list ((@seq V) * dir).
```

There is an extra direction in the type for LNS: for n components there should only be $n-1$ directions. We ignore the first direction: so $\Gamma \Rightarrow \Delta \nearrow \Sigma \Rightarrow \Pi$ is encoded by $[(\Gamma,\ \Delta,$ `fwd`$),\ (\Sigma,\ \Pi,$ `fwd`$)]$ and $[(\Gamma,\ \Delta,$ `bac`$),\ (\Sigma,\ \Pi,$ `fwd`$)]$.

4 Encoding the $\mathsf{LNS_{Kt}}$ Calculus

A rule instance couples a list `ps` of premises with a conclusion `c`. We define a type `rlsT W := list W -> W -> Type` so that `rlsT ps c` is the type of all rule instances with list of premises `ps` and conclusion `c`. Our aim then is to encode a collection of permissible rule schemas – in our case the rules of $\mathsf{LNS_{Kt}}$ – by defining the type `LNSKt_rules` which has type `rlsT (@LNS V)`.

To do so, we encoded sub-collections of rules called `b2rrules`, `b1rrules`, `b2lrules`, `b1lrules`, `EW_rule` and `rs_prop` which correspond to the boxed rules, external weakening and the remaining propositional rules, respectively.

Consider `b2lrules` with `WBox2Ls` corresponding to $\Box^2_L$ and `BBox2Ls` to $\blacksquare^2_L$:

```
Inductive b2lrules (V : Set) : rlsT (@LNS V) :=
| WBox2Ls : forall A d Γ1 Γ2 Σ1 Σ2 Δ Π, b2lrules
  [ [((Γ1 ++ A :: Γ2), Δ, d)] ]
  [((Γ1 ++ Γ2), Δ, d) ; ((Σ1 ++ WBox A :: Σ2), Π, bac)]
| BBox2Ls : forall A d Γ1 Γ2 Σ1 Σ2 Δ Π, b2lrules
  [[((Γ1 ++ A :: Γ2), Δ, d) ]]
  [((Γ1 ++ Γ2), K1, d) ; ((Σ1 ++ BBox A :: Σ2), Π, fwd)].
```

The first `WBox2Ls` says that any rule instance that has one premise (encoded as a singleton list of LNSs) of the form $\Gamma_1, A, \Gamma_2 \Rightarrow \Delta$ and conclusion of the form $\Gamma_1, \Gamma_2 \Rightarrow \Delta \swarrow \Sigma_1, \Box A, \Sigma_2 \Rightarrow \Pi$ is permitted. Thus although the official rule has an antecedent multiset Γ, A, we present it as the list Γ_1, A, Γ_2 instead to align the pen-and-paper presentation and Coq presentation.

Note that we encode only those components containing principal or side formulae i.e. the last two components of the conclusion. So `WBox2Ls` encodes the rule instance below left. Ultimately we want the full context version below right.

$$\frac{\Gamma_1, A, \Gamma_2 \Rightarrow \Delta}{\Gamma_1, \Gamma_2 \Rightarrow \Delta \swarrow \Sigma_1, \Box A, \Sigma_2 \Rightarrow \Pi} \qquad \frac{\mathcal{G} \updownarrow \Gamma_1, A, \Gamma_2 \Rightarrow \Delta}{\mathcal{G} \updownarrow \Gamma_1, \Gamma_2 \Rightarrow \Delta \swarrow \Sigma_1, \Box A, \Sigma_2 \Rightarrow \Pi}\ \Box^2_L$$

To obtain the right one from the left, we define `nslcext` and `nclcrule`, where `nslcext` extends an LNS `ls` with a given context `G` to the left. We use `nclcrule` to extend the collection of rule instances defined by `b2lrules` to allow for the uniform adding of contexts with `nslcext` into premises and conclusions.

```
Definition nslclext W (G ls : list W) := G ++ ls.

Inductive nslclrule W (sr : rlsT (list W)) : rlsT (list W) :=
| NSlclctxt : forall ps c G, sr ps c ->
  nslclrule sr (map (nslclext G) ps) (nslclext G c).
```

If `r` is of type `nslclrule W sr` then it must be obtained by adding a (possibly empty) context to all the premises and conclusion of a rule instance of `sr`.

So `nslclrule (@b2lrules V) ps c` captures that the premise list `ps` and conclusion `c` form an instance of an extended version of a rule from `b2lrules` via uniform context addition, giving the full version of $\Box_L^2$ on the right above.

We can then define the full $\mathsf{LNS_{Kt}}$ rule set with `b2rrules` and the other corresponding subcollections by the following `LNSKt_rules` definition:

```
Inductive LNSKt_rules {V : Set} : rlsT (@LNS V) :=
| b2r  : forall ps c, nslclrule (@b2rrules V) ps c ->
  LNSKt_rules ps c
| b1r  : forall ps c, nslclrule (@b1rrules V) ps c ->
  LNSKt_rules ps c
| b2l  : forall ps c, nslclrule (@b2lrules V) ps c ->
  LNSKt_rules ps c
| b1l  : forall ps c, nslclrule (@b1lrules V) ps c ->
  LNSKt_rules ps c
| nEW  : forall ps c, nslclrule (@EW_rule V) ps c ->
  LNSKt_rules ps c
| prop : forall ps c, nslcrule (seqrule (@rs_prop V)) ps c ->
  LNSKt_rules ps c.
```

The `b2l` case reads: if the premise list `ps` and conclusion `c` form an extended instance of `b2lrules`, then `ps/c` is also a rule instance of `LNSKt_rules`. The other rules work in much the same way. The exceptions are the `prop` rules as `rs_prop` captures an even more refined rule skeleton for $\rightarrow_L$, $\rightarrow_R$, $\bot_L$ and (id) and requires the addition of a sequent level context (Γs and Δs) via `seqrule` [6]. We leave it to the reader to see the original code for details of the remaining rules.

5 Encoding Derivability

Our notion of derivability follows Dawson and Goré's formalisation in Isabelle [6]:

```
Inductive derrec X (rules : list X -> X -> Type) (prems : X -> Type) :
X -> Type :=
| dpI  : forall concl, prems concl -> derrec rules prems concl
| derI : forall ps concl, rules ps concl ->
         dersrec rules prems ps -> derrec rules prems concl
with dersrec X (rules : list X -> X -> Type) (prems : X -> Type) :
list X -> Type :=
| dlNil  : dersrec rules prems []
| dlCons : forall seq seqs, derrec rules prems seq ->
           dersrec rules prems seqs ->
           dersrec rules prems (seq :: seqs).
```

The X is the type of objects about which we are reasoning: formulae in natural deduction calculi, sequents in sequent calculi, etc. In our case, we will instantiate X with the type LNS of LNSs. Then `D : derrec X rules prems concl` encodes $\mathtt{D} \vdash_{\mathtt{rules}}^{\mathtt{prems}} \mathtt{concl}$. But, by a complication of Coq, X is an "implicit argument" and must be omitted in the line above. Think of `prems` as a characteristic function for set membership. Likewise `rules`, where the set is a set of pairs (each pair being a list of premises and a conclusion).

A conclusion `concl` is derivable from a set `prems` of premises if

`dpI`: `concl` is a member of the set `prems`, or
`derI`: there is a rule inferring `concl` from a list `ps`, and each `p` in `ps` is derivable

The notion `derrec` is defined mutually with `dersrec` which asserts that a list of conclusions is derivable instead of just one as in `derrec`. Thus `dersrec X rules prems concls`, using constructors `dlNil` and `dlCons`, holds if all members of `concls` are derivable via `derrec`.

In contrast to encodings that define both derivability and calculus rules in the one definition (for example [2,21]), `derrec` gives a modular framework where X, `rules` and `prems` can be arbitrary. Thus `derrec` can be used for a variety of calculi where we can prove lemmas which are generic to multiple calculi satisfing certain conditions, rather than having to prove the same lemmas over and over for different calculi.

Interlude: Doing this in Coq Versus Isabelle/HOL. We can contrast how this works out in Coq compared with our previous work in Isabelle/HOL. In Coq, as `derrec ... concl` is a `Type`, it represents the derivation tree showing that `concl` is derivable. This means we can define the height or size of a derivation tree, as needed to do proofs by induction on height or size of a derivation. (We note that doing this specifically requires using `Type`, not `Prop`, for `derrec`, `dersrec`, etc.)

By contrast, in Isabelle we had to define a separate data structure to describe a derivation tree (essentially a rose tree of sequents), specify the condition of its validity (that each node is a rule of the system), and prove that such a tree exists iff the endsequent `concl` satisfies `derrec ... concl`.

However the derivation tree that Coq gives us for free has problems not shared by the Isabelle/HOL derivation tree: namely, the derivation trees next up from the endsequent (ie the trees deriving the premises of the bottom rule of the tree) do not form a list, because they are not of the same type, as their conclusions are all different. Navigating around such difficulties was not easy.

In our cut-elimination context we were mostly working with Coq proofs that required all leaves to be obtained via the (*id*) or $\bot_L$ rules, and so we regularly instantiated `prems : X -> Type` with the empty characteristic function `(fun _ => False)`. The "wrappers" `pf` (proof) and `pfs` (proofs) encode such derivations:

```
Definition pf {X : Type} rules concl :=
  @derrec X rules (fun _ => False) concl.

Definition pfs {X : Type} rules concls :=
  @dersrec X rules (fun _ => False) concls.
```

Then, pf_LNSKt and pfs_LNSKt are the "proofs" with rules being LNSKt_rules:

```
Definition pf_LNSKt {V : Set} ns :=
  derrec (@LNSKt_rules V) (fun _ => False) ns.

Definition pfs_LNSKt {V : Set} lns :=
  dersrec (@LNSKt_rules V) (fun _ => False) lns.
```

6 Proof Theoretic Properties of LNSKt

We proved LNSKt_exchL and LNSKt_exchR as the admissibility of left and right internal exchange of formulae but show only left exchange for brevity:

Lemma 1 (Left internal exchange of $\mathsf{LNS_{Kt}}$). *If* $\vdash \mathcal{G} \updownarrow_1 \Gamma_1, \Gamma_2, \Gamma_3, \Gamma_4 \Rightarrow \Delta \updownarrow_2 \mathcal{K}$ *then* $\vdash \mathcal{G} \updownarrow_1 \Gamma_1, \Gamma_3, \Gamma_2, \Gamma_4 \Rightarrow \Delta \updownarrow_2 \mathcal{K}$.

```
Definition can_gen_swapL {V : Set} (rules : rlsT (@LNS V)) ns :=
  forall G K s d Γ1 Γ2 Γ3 Γ4 Δ,
  ns = G ++ (s, d) :: K ->
  s = pair (Γ1 ++ Γ2 ++ Γ3 ++ Γ4) Δ ->
  pf rules (G ++ (pair (Γ1 ++ Γ3 ++ Γ2 ++ Γ4) Δ, d) :: K).

Lemma LNSKt_exchL: forall (V : Set) ns (D : @pf_LNSKt V ns),
  can_gen_swapL (@LNSKt_rules V) ns.
```

Thus if LNS ns is derivable, then so is any LNS which permutes two adjacent sublists $\Gamma 2$ and $\Gamma 3$ on the left – all within $\mathsf{LNS_{Kt}}$ with no unfinished leaves.

On paper, Lemma 1 is immediate as the Γs and Δs are multisets so that Γ_2, Γ_3 is identical to Γ_3, Γ_2. In our Coq formalisation however, we chose to encode the Γs and Δs instead by lists and prove left and right internal exchange so LNSKt_exchL was not immediate.

Our proof is a standard induction on the structure of D using the inductive hypothesis automatically generated by Coq that the required result holds for the premises of the final (bottom) rule application. This is a weaker principle than induction on the depth of D with an inductive hypothesis that the required result holds for the conclusions of any derivation of lesser depth.

The remaining proof theoretic properties, internal weakening and contraction, are stated in the original paper as Lemma 13. As with left-exchange, we used a "can_gen" conclusion and a standard induction. See the code for details.

We are now ready to tackle cut-elimination.

7 Cut-Elimination via Cut-Admissibility

Goré and Lellmann [8] proved cut-admissibility in their cut-free calculus and we follow suit. Using cut-admissibility, we additionally prove cut-elimination. To state cut-admissibility for LNSs, we must merge two LNSs in the following way:

Definition 2. *The* merge *of two linear nested sequents is defined via the following, where we assume $\mathcal{G}$ and $\mathcal{H}$ to be non-empty:*

$$\begin{aligned}(\Gamma \Rightarrow \Delta) \oplus (\Sigma \Rightarrow \Pi) &:= \Gamma, \Sigma \Rightarrow \Delta, \Pi \\ (\Gamma \Rightarrow \Delta) \oplus (\Sigma \Rightarrow \Pi \updownarrow \mathcal{H}) &:= \Gamma, \Sigma \Rightarrow \Delta, \Pi \updownarrow \mathcal{H} \\ (\Gamma \Rightarrow \Delta \updownarrow \mathcal{H}) \oplus (\Sigma \Rightarrow \Pi) &:= \Gamma, \Sigma \Rightarrow \Delta, \Pi \updownarrow \mathcal{H} \\ (\Gamma \Rightarrow \Delta \nearrow \mathcal{G}) \oplus (\Sigma \Rightarrow \Pi \nearrow \mathcal{H}) &:= \Gamma, \Sigma \Rightarrow \Delta, \Pi \nearrow (\mathcal{G} \oplus \mathcal{H}) \\ (\Gamma \Rightarrow \Delta \swarrow \mathcal{G}) \oplus (\Sigma \Rightarrow \Pi \swarrow \mathcal{H}) &:= \Gamma, \Sigma \Rightarrow \Delta, \Pi \swarrow (\mathcal{G} \oplus \mathcal{H}) .\end{aligned}$$

Our Coq encoding of merge is as follows:

```
Inductive merge {V : Set} :
(@LNS V) -> (@LNS V) -> (@LNS V) -> Type :=
| merge_nilL ns1 ns2 ns3 : ns1 = [] -> ns3 = ns2 -> merge ns1 ns2 ns3
| merge_nilR ns1 ns2 ns3 : ns2 = [] -> ns3 = ns1 -> merge ns1 ns2 ns3
| merge_step Γ Δ Σ Π d ns1 ns2 ns3 ns4 ns5 ns6 s1 s2 s3 :
  s1 = (Γ,Δ,d) -> s2 = (Σ,Π,d) -> s3 = (Γ ++ Σ, Δ ++ Π,d) ->
  merge ns1 ns2 ns3 -> ns4 = s1 :: ns1 ->
  ns5 = s2 :: ns2 -> ns6 = s3 :: ns3 ->
  merge ns4 ns5 ns6.
```

Thus `merge ns1 ns2 ns3` encodes that `ns3` is the merge of `ns1` and `ns2`. Our Coq definition allows either the left or right LNS to be empty.

Note also that both pen-and-paper and Coq definitions are only well-defined for LNSs that are in some sense *structurally equivalent*, where the arrows of the two LNSs correspond. The original paper allowed LNSs of possibly differing lengths to be structurally equivalent. We instead used a strong version for only equal length LNSs as this was all that was needed. Doing so simplified some of the proofs. Alternatively we could define `merge` to hold only for structurally equivalent sequents. But where convenient, we conform to the original paper.

Definition 3. *Two LNSs $S_1 \updownarrow_1^S \dots \updownarrow_{n-1}^S S_n$ and $T_1 \updownarrow_1^T \dots \updownarrow_{n-1}^T T_n$ are* structurally equivalent *if we have $\updownarrow_i^S = \updownarrow_i^T$ for every i.*

```
Inductive struct_equiv_str {V : Set} : (@LNS V) -> (@LNS V) -> Type :=
| se_nil2 : struct_equiv_str [] []
| se_step2 Γ1 Δ1 d Γ2 Δ2 ns1 ns2 ns3 ns4 :
ns3 = ((Γ1, Δ1, d) :: ns1) -> ns4 = ((Γ2, Δ2, d) :: ns2) ->
struct_equiv_str ns1 ns2 -> struct_equiv_str ns3 ns4.
```

Our cut-admissibility theorem is called cut-elimination in the original paper.

7.1 Cut-Admissibility

The cut rule, where the premiss and conclusion LNSs are structurally equivalent:

$$\frac{\mathcal{G} \updownarrow \Gamma \Rightarrow \Delta, A \qquad \mathcal{H} \updownarrow A, \Sigma \Rightarrow \Pi}{\mathcal{G} \oplus \mathcal{H} \updownarrow \Gamma, \Sigma \Rightarrow \Delta, \Pi}\ \mathsf{Cut}$$

Theorem 1 (Cut-admissibility). *For structurally equivalent LNSs $\mathcal{G}$ and $\mathcal{H}$, if $\vdash \mathcal{G} \updownarrow \Gamma \Rightarrow \Delta, A$ and $\vdash \mathcal{H} \updownarrow A, \Sigma \Rightarrow \Pi$, then also $\vdash \mathcal{G} \oplus \mathcal{H} \updownarrow \Gamma, \Sigma \Rightarrow \Delta, \Pi$.*

```
Definition can_gen_cut {V : Set} (rules : rlsT (@LNS V)) ns1 ns2 :=
  forall G1 G2 G3 s1 s2 d Γ Δ1 Δ2 Σ1 Σ2 Π A,
  ns1 = G1 ++ [(s1, d)] -> s1 = pair Γ (Δ1++[A]++Δ2) ->
  ns2 = G2 ++ [(s2, d)] -> s2 = pair (Σ1++[A]++Σ2) Π ->
  merge G1 G2 G3 -> struct_equiv_str G1 G2 ->
  pf rules (G3 ++ [(Γ++Σ1++Σ2, Δ1++Δ2++Π, d)]).

Theorem LNSKt_cut_admissibility : forall (V : Set) ns1 ns2
  (D1 : pf_LNSKt ns1) (D2 : pf_LNSKt ns2),
  can_gen_cut (@LNSKt_rules V) ns1 ns2.
```

So `LNSKt_cut_admissibility` states that if two structurally-equivalent LNSs are (cut-free) derivable from `LNSKt_rules` then so is the structurally-equivalent LNS obtained by applying the cut rule to their conclusions (i.e. no cut in the rules).

Our Coq code follows the original paper where cut-admissibility is a corollary of the huge `Lemma_Sixteen`, thus transfering all heavy lifting to this mega lemma.

7.2 The Main Lemma: "Lemma Sixteen"

The so-called Lemma Sixteen is defined as follows.

Lemma 2. *The following statements hold for every n, m where we always assume that $\mathcal{G}$ and $\mathcal{H}$ are structurally equivalent:*

($\mathsf{SR}_\Box(n,m)$) *Suppose that all of the following hold:*
- $\mathcal{D}_1 \vdash \mathcal{G} \updownarrow_1 \Gamma \Rightarrow \Delta, \Box A$ *with* $\Box A$ *principal in the last rule in* $\mathcal{D}_1$
- $\mathcal{D}_2 \vdash \mathcal{H} \updownarrow_1 \Box A, \Sigma \Rightarrow \Pi \updownarrow_2 \mathcal{I}$
- *there is a derivation of* $\mathcal{G} \oplus \mathcal{H} \updownarrow_1 \Gamma, \Sigma \Rightarrow \Delta, \Pi \nearrow \epsilon \Rightarrow A$
- $\mathsf{dp}(\mathcal{D}_1) + \mathsf{dp}(\mathcal{D}_2) \leq m$
- $|\Box A| \leq n$.

Then there is a derivation of $\mathcal{G} \oplus \mathcal{H} \updownarrow_1 \Gamma, \Sigma \Rightarrow \Delta, \Pi \updownarrow_2 \mathcal{I}$.

($\mathsf{SR}_\blacksquare(n,m)$) *Suppose that all of the following hold:*
- $\mathcal{D}_1 \vdash \mathcal{G} \updownarrow_1 \Gamma \Rightarrow \Delta, \blacksquare A$ *with* $\blacksquare A$ *principal in the last rule in* $\mathcal{D}_1$
- $\mathcal{D}_2 \vdash \mathcal{H} \updownarrow_1 \blacksquare A, \Sigma \Rightarrow \Pi \updownarrow_2 \mathcal{I}$
- $\mathsf{dp}(\mathcal{D}_1) + \mathsf{dp}(\mathcal{D}_2) \leq m$
- *there is a derivation of* $\mathcal{G} \oplus \mathcal{H} \updownarrow_1 \Gamma, \Sigma \Rightarrow \Delta, \Pi \swarrow \epsilon \Rightarrow A$
- $|\blacksquare A| \leq n$.

Then there is a derivation of $\mathcal{G} \oplus \mathcal{H} \updownarrow_1 \Gamma, \Sigma \Rightarrow \Delta, \Pi \updownarrow_2 \mathcal{I}$.

($\mathsf{SR}_p(n,m)$) *Suppose that all of the following hold:*
- $\mathcal{D}_1 \vdash \mathcal{G} \updownarrow_1 \Gamma \Rightarrow \Delta, A$ *with* A *principal in the last applied rule in* $\mathcal{D}_1$
- $\mathcal{D}_2 \vdash \mathcal{H} \updownarrow_1 A, \Sigma \Rightarrow \Pi \updownarrow_2 \mathcal{I}$
- $\mathsf{dp}(\mathcal{D}_1) + \mathsf{dp}(\mathcal{D}_2) \leq m$
- $|A| \leq n$
- *A not of the form* $\Box B$ *or* $\blacksquare B$.

Then there is a derivation of $\mathcal{G} \oplus \mathcal{H} \updownarrow_1 \Gamma, \Sigma \Rightarrow \Delta, \Pi \updownarrow_2 \mathcal{I}$.

($\mathsf{SL}(n,m)$) *Suppose that all of the following hold:*
- $\mathcal{D}_1 \vdash \mathcal{G} \updownarrow_1 \Gamma \Rightarrow \Delta, A \updownarrow_2 \mathcal{I}$
- $\mathcal{D}_2 \vdash \mathcal{H} \updownarrow_1 A, \Sigma \Rightarrow \Pi$

– $\mathsf{dp}(\mathcal{D}_1) + \mathsf{dp}(\mathcal{D}_2) \leq m$
– $|A| \leq n$.

Then there is a derivation of $\mathcal{G} \oplus \mathcal{H} \updownarrow_1 \Gamma, \Sigma \Rightarrow \Delta, \Pi \updownarrow_2 \mathcal{I}$.

We show only the encoding corresponding to one of the parts, $\mathsf{SR}_\Box(n, m)$.

```
Definition SR_wb_pre (n m : nat) := forall {V : Set}
  G Γ Δ1 Δ2 H Σ1 Σ2 Π I GH (A : PropF V) d
  (D1 : pf_LNSKt (G ++ [(Γ, Δ1 ++ [WBox A] ++ Δ2,d)]))
  (D2 : pf_LNSKt (H ++ [(Σ1 ++ [WBox A] ++ Σ2, Π, d)] ++ I))
  (D3 : pf_LNSKt
        (GH ++ [(Γ ++ Σ1 ++ Σ2, Δ1 ++ Δ2 ++ Π, d)] ++
           [([],[A],fwd)])),
  principal_WBR D1 (WBox A) Γ Δ1 Δ2 ->
  ((dp D1) + (dp D2))%nat <= m ->
  struct_equiv_str G H ->
  merge G H GH ->
  fsize (WBox A) <= n ->
  pf_LNSKt (GH ++ [(Γ ++ Σ1 ++ Σ2, Δ1 ++ Δ2 ++ Π, d)] ++ I).

Definition SR_wb (nm : nat * nat) :=
  let (n,m) := nm in SR_wb_pre n m.

Lemma Lemma_Sixteen : forall (nm : nat * nat),
  SR_wb nm * SR_bb nm * SR_p nm * SL nm.
```

We had to state that $\Box A$ is principal in the last rule in $\mathcal{D}_1$. That is, although there may be other occurrences of $\Box A$ in $\mathcal{G} \updownarrow_1 \Gamma \Rightarrow \Delta, \Box A$, it is that particular displayed occurrence that is principal. To capture this, we defined `principal_WBR` which is specifically designed for white box formulae that occur on the right side of the sequent in the last component (hence `WBR` standing for White Box Right). Moreover, the statement `principal_WBR D1 (WBox A)` $\Gamma\, \Delta1\, \Delta2$ carries all required information of where the principal `WBox A` sits, in particular that it sits between $\Delta1$ and $\Delta2$. This is a requirement specific to our implementation based on lists. We have analogous definitions for the other cases: `principal_BBR` and `principal_not_box_R`. The full code contains these definitions and others we have omitted here, including depth of derivation `dp` and formula size `fsize`.

The Coq `Lemma_Sixteen` uses `*` as a `Type`-level conjunction as in the earlier example to enable extraction. All four parts of Lemma Sixteen are proved simultaneously by induction on the pair (n, m) in the lexicographic ordering, as in the original proof. Please refer to the code for our definitions of this lexicographic ordering `lt_lex_nat` and our induction principle `wf_lt_lex_nat_induction`.

The need to prove all four components of Lemma Sixteen simultaneously is of course because the different parts depend on induction hypotheses of the other components. The proof works through a lot of different cases, often multiple layers of cases going at once. Given that there are already four sublemmas to prove as well as the copious number of cases, the pen-and-paper proof is large and the Coq proof is, understandably, even larger.

Coq is useful to check the subtle details for each case, and it is unsurprising that our work highlighted multiple mistakes in the original proof. These ranged from incorrect arrow directions, incorrect rule applications, to omissions of conditions such as structural equivalence and same length of LNSs. Fortunately all were easily resolved. We have confirmed these with the original authors.

For example, in $\mathsf{SR}_{\Box}(n,m)$ ($\mathsf{SR}_{\blacksquare}(n,m)$), where we have $\updownarrow_1$ the original paper had $\nearrow$ ($\swarrow$), but there were indeed cases which require our more general version.

Cut-admissibility follows from ($\mathsf{SL}(n,m)$), and leads easily to cut-elimination.

7.3 Cut-Elimination

We encoded the cut rule in Coq as follows where we don't encode the skeleton of cut and then fill in contexts using **nslclrule** because the premises do not share linear nested sequent level contexts *i.e.* $\mathcal{G}$ and $\mathcal{H}$ may differ:

```
Inductive Cut_rule {V : Set} : rlsT (@LNS V) :=
| Cut : forall G H GH s1 s2 s3 ns1 ns2 ns3 d Γ Δ1 Δ2 Σ1 Σ2 Π A,
  ns1 =  G ++ [(s1, d)] -> s1 = (Γ, (Δ1++[A]++Δ2)) ->
  ns2 =  H ++ [(s2, d)] -> s2 = ((Σ1++[A]++Σ2), Π) ->
  ns3 = GH ++ [(s3, d)] -> s3 = ((Γ++Σ1++Σ2), (Δ1++Δ2++Π)) ->
  merge G H GH -> struct_equiv_str G H ->
  Cut_rule [ns1 ; ns2] ns3.
```

We then defined the calculus $\mathsf{LNS}_{\mathsf{Kt+Cut}}$ as $\mathsf{LNS}_{\mathsf{Kt}}$ plus Cut in Coq:

```
Inductive LNSKt_cut_rules {V : Set} : rlsT (@LNS V) :=
| LNSKt_rules_woc :
  forall ps c, LNSKt_rules ps c    -> LNSKt_cut_rules ps c
| LNSKt_rules_wc   :
  forall ps c, (@Cut_rule V) ps c -> LNSKt_cut_rules ps c.
```

The first constructor (`_woc` for "without cut") includes all **LNSKt_rules** and the second constructor (`_wc` for "with cut") adds the cut rule. We then specialised **LNSKt_cut_rules** to have no unfinished leaves as for **LNSKt_rules**:

```
Definition pf_LNSKt_cut {V : Set} ns :=
  derrec (@LNSKt_cut_rules V) (fun _ => False) ns.
```

The cut-elimination theorem allows us to eliminate Cut applications:

Theorem 2. *For every LNS* $\mathcal{G}$*, if* $\vdash_{\mathsf{LNS}_{\mathsf{Kt+Cut}}} \mathcal{G}$ *then* $\vdash_{\mathsf{LNS}_{\mathsf{Kt}}} \mathcal{G}$.

```
Theorem LNSKt_cut_elimination :
  forall {V:Set} (ns:@LNS V), pf_LNSKt_cut ns -> pf_LNSKt ns.
```

The original paper stopped at cut-admissibility (though they called it cut-elimination), so we produced our own proof in the standard way by induction on the depth of the derivation with cut. As usual, we start with a derivation with cuts, eliminate the cut application with smallest depth using cut-admissibility, and repeat the procedure in the resulting (transformed) derivation!

8 Extraction

The form of the cut-elimination theorem in Coq enables us to utilise Coq's extraction facility to synthesise a Haskell program that computes cut-free derivations from those with cut. Specifically, we can use Coq to distill the algorithmic content of our cut-elimination theorem in order to automatically produce a Haskell function that computes cut-free derivation from those without cut.

The file cut_elimination_theorem.v imports the necessary libraries and sets the language to Haskell, after which we extract into separate Haskell modules:

```
Require Import cut.
Require Import Extraction.
Extraction Language Haskell.

Separate Extraction LNSKt_cut_elimination.
```

This process automatically produces 47 Haskell modules, with the final cut-elimination function, `coq_LNSKt_cut_elimination`, specified in the Cut.hs module.

To use `coq_LNSKt_cut_elimination`, we have to specify how the required objects should be printed, and so we hand-coded a simple printing module that can be easily checked, called Main_thm.hs, which imports Cut.hs. Once Main_thm.hs is loaded, one can then use the cut-elimination function by calling `coq_LNSKt_cut_elimination` with the appropriate input.

Given that `coq_LNSKt_cut_elimination` requires inputs that are fairly large and can be difficult to write, our preferred method is to encode the desired examples in Coq before extraction, and then use extraction on both the cut-elimination theorem as well as that example derivation. That way, we benefit from Coq's type checker on the example derivation as well as the cut-elimination function. Let us illustrate with an example.

Consider the following derivation that uses the cut rule:

$$\dfrac{\dfrac{\dfrac{}{\Box p \Rightarrow \epsilon \nearrow p \Rightarrow p}\ \text{(id)}}{\Box p \Rightarrow \epsilon \nearrow \epsilon \Rightarrow p}\ \Box^1_L \qquad \dfrac{\dfrac{}{\epsilon \Rightarrow \epsilon \nearrow p, q \Rightarrow p, q \to p}\ \text{(id)}}{\epsilon \Rightarrow \epsilon \nearrow p \Rightarrow q \to p}\ \to_R}{\Box p \Rightarrow \epsilon \nearrow \epsilon \Rightarrow q \to p}\ \text{Cut}$$

In file cut_extraction_example_pre.v, we hand-coded this derivation in about 100 lines. Each rule instance requires an easy Coq proof to identify the rule, its principal and side-formulae and their locations in the premises and conclusion. For example, lemma `pf3_000` tells us *how* `concl3_000` follows from no premisses, where `concl3_000` corresponds to the conclusion of the left (id) instance above:

```
Definition concl3_000 :=
[ ([WBox (Var 0)], [], fwd) ; ([Var 0], [Var 0], fwd) ].

Lemma pf3_000 : LNSKt_cut_rules [] concl3_000.
```

This proof term is required by the cut-elimination function because it makes decisions depending on the form of `pf3_000`: thus we cannot elide it during extraction. The need for the user to specify these proof terms while specifying the full derivation is why we prefer to encode them on the Coq side. So Coq checks their type and the extraction mechanism converts everything to Haskell code.

Then we build up the final derivation, `example3`, by putting together these proof terms, premisses and conclusions. See the full code for details of how this is done. We then define `cut_example3` to perform cut-elimination on `example3`:

```
Definition cut_example3 := LNSKt_cut_elimination example3.
```

Extracting using cut_elimination_theorem.v extracts the cut-elimination function only. Instead, we ask users to compile cut_elimination_example.v, thereby extracting both the cut-elimination function and the example derivation `example3`:

```
Separate Extraction cut_example3.
```

This produces a Haskell module containing the example derivation code: extracting `example3` will not produce Haskell code for the cut-elimination procedure.

Beside the Main_thm.hs printing file, we have written Main_example.hs which is identical except for an import statement that gives access to the example derivation. Once this is loaded, we can call `cut_example3` (or the longer version `coq_LNSKt_cut_elimination example3`) which outputs the cut-free derivation:

```
derI
  (derI
    (derI (dlNil)
         ([(([[.] p 0], []), fwd) ::
           (([p 0 :: p 1], [p 1 --> p 0 :: p 0]), fwd)])
         (Id))
    ([(([[.] p 0], []), fwd) :: (([p 0], [p 1 --> p 0]), fwd)])
    (ImpR))
  ([(([[.] p 0], []), fwd) :: (([], [p 1 --> p 0]), fwd)])
  (WBox1Ls)
```

Adding line breaks and indentation, the code above is the cut-free derivation:

$$\cfrac{\cfrac{\cfrac{}{\Box p \Rightarrow \epsilon \nearrow p, q \Rightarrow q \to p, p}\,(\text{id})}{\Box p \Rightarrow \epsilon \nearrow p \Rightarrow q \to p}\,\to_R}{\Box p \Rightarrow \epsilon \nearrow \epsilon \Rightarrow q \to p}\,\Box_L^1$$

Each `derI` in the above code is a rule application that takes in three arguments: the subderivation of the premise, the conclusion and the name of the rule.

Clearly, the linear representation is not easy to read and a tree style representation would be better. See Sect. 10 for more discussion on this. Note that our printing instructions for the output derivation in the Main files exclude the printing of the proof terms like `pf3_000`. We did this because 1) logicians read this information off naturally from concrete derivations without it being explicitly stated; and 2) it gives a cleaner, easier to read derivation.

By consulting README.txt, readers can input their own derivations, extract, and behold the verified cut-free output derivations from `coq_LNSKt_cut_elimination`.

9 Related Work

Chaudhuri et al. [2] cover the related work well, so we concentrate only on work which formalises meta-theory, as opposed to formalised proof-search.

The work of Pfenning [16], Graham-Lengrand [9], Simmons [17] and Urban [20] all represent sequents as formulae of the meta-logic where, for example, a sequent $A, B \Rightarrow \varphi$ becomes the meta-logical formula `hyp A -> hyp A -> conc phi` [16]. Since the meta-logic is intuitionistic, the sequent calculi inherit exchange, weakening and contraction.

Arbitrary contexts follow by encoding rule skeletons using `->` to encode the horizontal line separating premises and conclusions. These methods cannot handle calculi that lack some combination of weakening, contraction and exchange, nor do they include extraction.

At the next level are encodings which build sequents out of multisets. Dawson and Goré [6] prove mix-elimination for the provability logic GL using Isabelle/HOL. Xavier et al. [21] prove cut-elimination and other meta-theoretic properties of (commutative) linear logic in Coq by extending the standard library for multisets with additional theorems and tactics. Multisets preclude non-commutativity. There is no extraction in either.

At the next level is work where sequents are built from lists, but with extra machinery added to regain commutativity. Tews [18] uses setoids, while Chaudhuri et al. [2] and Larchey-Wendling [11,12] build-in "permutability" explicitly. All these could be extended to handle non-commutative logics, but none do. Only Larchey-Wendling [11] allows extraction, though this has not been published.

Miller and Pimentel [13] explored embedding various object logics into linear logic, and gave "cut-coherence" conditions for the cut-admissibility of linear logic to carry over to an object logic. Olarte et al. [15] extended this work to allow object logics with modalities using a LNS presentation of SLL (a linear logic with subexponentials). A Coq encoding of this work would require us to first encode the syntax of (subexponential) linear logic, and then encode our object logic (sequents) as formulae of linear logic. Encoding into linear logic cannot handle non-commutative substructural logics but does allow us to omit weakening and contraction, which can then be regained via (sub)exponentials.

Our work has numerous advantages: (1) our notion of derivability is parametric on a set of objects `X` which could be formulae, sequents, or other structures; (2) using lists allows us to handle genuinely substructural logics in which some combination of weakening, contraction and exchange (commutativity) are missing, with Dawson and Goré's previous work [5] allowing us to even capture non-associativity if required; and (3) our use of `Type`, rather than `Prop`, in Coq allows us to extract a formally verified computer program to perform cut-elimination.

10 Conclusion and Future Work

We have transported and extended from Isabelle to Coq Dawson and Goré's [6] encodings of general notion of derivability which is usable for many different kinds of proof systems. We applied this to the linear nested sequent calculus $\mathsf{LNS_{Kt}}$ that was given by Goré and Lellmann [8] for tense logic and formalised the calculus along with all structural proof theoretic properties up to and including their proof of cut-admissibility (called cut-elimination in the original paper).

We uncovered multiple small mistakes but none were major and all were easily amended. The original authors accepted the corrections.

We proved cut-elimination from cut-admissibility and extracted a formally verified Haskell program that computes cut-free derivations from those with cut. We hand-coded Haskell Main files to provide requisite printing instructions in order to display the outputs.

Our Coq encodings are modular and allow us to prove meta-theoretic lemmas for arbitrary `rules` that satisfy certain conditions, which can then be applied to specific calculi. For example, in the proof of left internal exchange, the case where the last rule applied was a rule in `rs_prop` was proved not restricted to just `LNSKt_rules` but more generally for any `rules` provided that the last rule skeleton applied satisfied the `rules_L_oeT` condition, those for which every conclusion has at most one formula on the left. Thus our work has the potential to lead to a Coq library for proof theory that is applicable to a broad range of logics and calculi with results proved in the aforementioned generic way. Most formalisations that we have encountered do not enjoy such modularity (e.g. [2,21]).

This modularity of our encodings is in part due to our capturing not just derivability but derivations as first class citizens with corresponding proof terms. The deep embedding of derivations also enables extraction of the cut-elimination procedure into Haskell, and as such an alternative approach using a shallow embedding (e.g. [16]) would not suffice.

Recall that we encoded multisets in our context with lists and then proved exchange. First, our framework can then handle noncommutative logics and, secondly, gives us access to the libraries of basic reasoning about lists where other multiset libraries seemed to be lacking. The trade-off of this general framework is that in our specific $\mathsf{LNS}_{\mathsf{Kt}}$ context where exchange is admitted we faced needless difficulties relating to where a particular formula is located in a sequent. It is worth exploring a formalisation where `list` is replaced in `Definition seq := rel (list (PropF V))` to an encoding of multisets (e.g. [21]), or which utilises the Permutation library (e.g. [12]). In that case, we would expect to see simpler proofs and less complex and more efficient tactics. This may also translate to a more efficient extracted cut-elimination function which would not need to perform rearrangements on lists of formulae.

Related, we haven't yet performed any tests on efficiency of the extracted function nor attempted to make significant improvements in this area. While we consider this interesting, it is also part of a bigger picture of comparing efficiencies of verified and unverified implementations, which contributes to answering how realistic it is to prefer the former kind over the latter. We are still in early stages of program synthesis of formalised proof-theory and consider this an avenue worthy of further investigation.

Another aspect in this bigger picture of usability is the readability of the extracted function. The printing instructions in the Haskell Main files employ a linear representation to type-check and display the output, which is difficult to read. Alternatively, we could write tree-style printing instructions, import pre-existing Haskell libraries, use a format such as the LaTeX package bussproofs, or even develop a nice graphical user interface. The further down the spectrum of readability you move, the more you compromise on trustworthiness. In its current form, our work adopts a conservative approach on the trustworthy end of the spectrum but we do acknowledge there is scope here to improve usability.

We believe that our work has the potential to lead to a Coq library for deeply embedded and extractable proof theory for the huge number of truly substructural logics in the literature where some combination of weakening, contraction and exchange are not admissible.

References

1. Belnap, N.: Display logic. J. Philos. Log. **11**, 375–417 (1982)
2. Chaudhuri, K., Lima, L., Reis, G.: Formalized meta-theory of sequent calculi for linear logics. TCS **781**, 24–38 (2019)
3. Dawson, J.E., Brotherston, J., Goré, R.: Machine-checked interpolation theorems for substructural logics using display calculi. In: Olivetti, N., Tiwari, A. (eds.) IJCAR 2016. LNCS (LNAI), vol. 9706, pp. 452–468. Springer, Cham (2016). https://doi.org/10.1007/978-3-319-40229-1_31
4. Dawson, J.E., Clouston, R., Goré, R., Tiu, A.: From display calculi to deep nested sequent calculi: formalised for full intuitionistic linear logic. In: Diaz, J., Lanese, I., Sangiorgi, D. (eds.) TCS 2014. LNCS, vol. 8705, pp. 250–264. Springer, Heidelberg (2014). https://doi.org/10.1007/978-3-662-44602-7_20
5. Dawson, J.E., Goré, R.: Formalised cut admissibility for display logic. In: Carreño, V.A., Muñoz, C.A., Tahar, S. (eds.) TPHOLs 2002. LNCS, vol. 2410, pp. 131–147. Springer, Heidelberg (2002). https://doi.org/10.1007/3-540-45685-6_10
6. Dawson, J.E., Goré, R.: Generic methods for formalising sequent calculi applied to provability logic. In: Fermüller, C.G., Voronkov, A. (eds.) LPAR 2010. LNCS, vol. 6397, pp. 263–277. Springer, Heidelberg (2010). https://doi.org/10.1007/978-3-642-16242-8_19
7. Goré, R.: Tableau methods for modal and temporal logics. In: D'Agostino, M., Gabbay, D., Haehnle, R., Posegga, J. (eds.) Handbook of Tableau Methods, Kluwer, pp. 297–396 (1999)
8. Goré, R., Lellmann, B.: Syntactic cut-elimination and backward proof-search for tense logic via linear nested sequents. In: Cerrito, S., Popescu, A. (eds.) TABLEAUX 2019. LNCS (LNAI), vol. 11714, pp. 185–202. Springer, Cham (2019). https://doi.org/10.1007/978-3-030-29026-9_11
9. Graham-Lengrand, S.: Polarities & focussing: a journey from realisability to automated reasoning, Habilitation Thesis, Université Paris-Sud (2014)
10. Kashima, R.: Cut-free sequent calculi for some tense logics. Stud. Log. **53**(1), 119–136 (1994)
11. Larchey-Wendling, D.: Semantic cut elimination. https://github.com/. DmxLarchey/Coq-Phase-Semantics/blob/master/coq.type/cut_elim.v
12. Larchey-Wendling, D.: Constructive decision via redundancy-free proof-search. J. Autom. Reason. **64**(7), 1197–1219 (2020)
13. Miller, D., Pimentel, E.: A formal framework for specifying sequent calculus proof systems. Theor. Comput. Sci. **474**, 98–116 (2013)
14. Negri, S.: Proof analysis in modal logic. J. Philos. Logic **34**(5–6), 507–544 (2005)
15. Olarte, C., Pimentel, E., Xavier, B.: A fresh view of linear logic as a logical framework. In: LSFA 2020. ENTCS, vol. 351, pp. 143–165. Elsevier (2020)
16. Pfenning, F.: Structural cut elimination. In: LICS 1995, pp. 156–166. IEEE Computer Society (1995)
17. Simmons, R.J.: Structural focalization. ACM Trans. Comput. Log. **15**(3), 21:1–21:33 (2014)
18. Tews, H.: Formalizing cut elimination of coalgebraic logics in Coq. In: Galmiche, D., Larchey-Wendling, D. (eds.) TABLEAUX 2013. LNCS (LNAI), vol. 8123, pp. 257–272. Springer, Heidelberg (2013). https://doi.org/10.1007/978-3-642-40537-2_22
19. Troelstra, A., Schwichtenberg, H.: Basic Proof Theory. Number 43 in Cambridge Tracts in Theoretical Computer Science. Cambridge University Press (1996)

20. Urban, C., Zhu, B.: Revisiting cut-elimination: one difficult proof is really a proof. In: Voronkov, A. (ed.) RTA 2008. LNCS, vol. 5117, pp. 409–424. Springer, Heidelberg (2008). https://doi.org/10.1007/978-3-540-70590-1_28
21. Xavier, B., Olarte, C., Reis, G., Nigam, V.: Mechanizing focused linear logic in Coq. In: LSFA 2017. ENTCS, vol. 338, pp. 219–236. Elsevier (2017)

Cut-Elimination for Provability Logic by Terminating Proof-Search: Formalised and Deconstructed Using Coq

Rajeev Goré[3], Revantha Ramanayake[2], and Ian Shillito[1](✉)

[1] Australian National University, Canberra, ACT, Australia
ian.shillito@anu.edu.au
[2] University of Groningen, Groningen, The Netherlands
d.r.s.ramanayake@rug.nl
[3] Technische Universität Wien, Vienna, Austria

Abstract. Recently, Brighton gave another cut-admissibility proof for the standard set-based sequent calculus GLS for modal provability logic GL. One of the two induction measures that Brighton uses is novel: the maximum height of regress trees in an auxiliary calculus called RGL. Tautology elimination is established rather than direct cut-admissibility, and at some points the input derivation appears to be ignored in favour of a derivation obtained by backward proof-search. By formalising the GLS calculus and the proofs in Coq, we show that: (1) the use of the novel measure is problematic under the usual interpretation of the Gentzen comma as set union, and a multiset-based sequent calculus provides a more natural formulation; (2) the detour through tautology elimination is unnecessary; and (3) we can use the same induction argument without regress trees to obtain a direct proof of cut-admissibility that is faithful to the input derivation.

Keywords: Provability logic · Cut admissibility · Interactive theorem proving · Proof theory

1 Introduction

Propositional modal provability logics extend the basic normal modal logic K with axioms which interpret the $\Box$ connective as the mathematical notion of being "provable" in Peano Arithmetic [1,16]. There are several variants with characteristic axioms named after Gödel, Löb and Grzegorczyk:

Name	Characteristic Axiom
GL	$\Box(\Box p \to p) \to \Box p$
Go	$\Box(\Box(p \to \Box p) \to p) \to \Box p$
Grz	$\Box(\Box(p \to \Box p) \to p) \to p$

While the "provability" interpretation is now well-understood, the proof-theory of these logics is intricate and somewhat controversial as we explain next.

A. Das and S. Negri (Eds.): TABLEAUX 2021, LNAI 12842, pp. 299–313, 2021.
https://doi.org/10.1007/978-3-030-86059-2_18

Following Gentzen [5,6], the literature abounds with proofs of cut-admissibility for various sequent calculi based on the size of the cut-formula and the height of the premise derivations. But these measures looked, at first sight, inadequate for proving cut-elimination for the standard set-based sequent calculus GLS for provability logic GL so Valentini introduced a third novel measure called width, and showed that cut-elimination for GLS could be obtained via a triple induction over size, height and width [17].

Controversy arose when it was (erroneously) claimed that Valentini's proofs contained a gap and various authors provided alternative proofs of cut-elimination in response [2,10–12,14]. The question was resolved in Valentini's favour [7], with all proofs later verified using an interactive theorem prover Isabelle/HOL [4].

The cut-elimination proof for the logic Go (due to Goré and Ramanayake [8] via a deeper analysis of the structure of derivations, and subsequently by Savateev and Shamkanov [15] via non-well founded-proofs) is even more intricate. The proof-theory of provability logics can therefore be described as complex.

Recently, Brighton [3] provided yet another proof of cut-admissibility for GLS which is significantly simpler than any of the existing proofs of cut-admissibility in the literature. It uses a double induction with the traditional size of the cut-formula as primary measure. The secondary measure is called the "maximum height of regress trees" and it is a novel measure defined using a backward proof-search procedure for GLS called RGL, based on regress trees/regressants.

Backward proof-search can often be employed to obtain cut-free completeness with respect to the Kripke semantics of a logic. However, cut-elimination is *not* a result directly obtained by the use of backward proof-search. For this reason Brighton's method is intriguing from a structural proof theoretic perspective. Even more so because, from a tableaux perspective, the RGL calculus is nothing but the backward proof-search decision procedure for GL that is well-known to be cut-free complete with respect to the Kripke semantics of GL. Unfortunately, Brighton's arguments is clouded by various issues that become apparent when studying them in detail.

We first explain why Brighton's use of a set-based sequent calculus leads to confusion, and explain how this can be clarified using multisets. We then show that the special calculus RGL on regress trees can be replaced by a standard proof-search procedure PSGLS on GLS itself. Putting this all together, we replace Brighton's detour through tautology elimination [9] with a direct proof of cut-admissibility for GL making use of the maximum height of a derivation (the existence of the latter follows from the termination of backward proof-search). Noting that Brighton's proof seems to ignore the structure of the given cut-free derivations of the premises, and since such a shortcoming undermines cut-elimination as a procedure that manipulates the given derivations to produce a cut-free derivation, we take particular care to highlight the local nature of our transformations. All of our claims have been formally verified in the interactive theorem prover Coq (https://github.com/ianshil/CE_GLS.git).

2 Various Issues with the Method Used by Brighton

Although Brighton's work is extremely appealing, we have already mentioned that the argument and the proof technique supporting it require further clarifications. Let us exhibit the two main elements that appeared through the formalisation process to be responsible for this unclarity.

First, as the sequents that are used are based on sets, the rule for implication on the right, presented below on the left, is just a notation for the rule on the right where the comma is interpreted as set union.

$$\frac{A, X \Rightarrow Y, B}{X \Rightarrow Y, A \to B} \qquad \frac{\{A\} \cup X \Rightarrow Y \cup \{B\}}{X \Rightarrow Y \cup \{A \to B\}}\ (\to\text{R})$$

However, it is well-known that $(\to\text{R})$ contains an implicit contraction [7]. As a consequence, $(\to\text{R})$ could be reapplied as many times as one wants above $\Rightarrow p \to q$ on the formula $p \to q$. That implies the existence of derivations of all heights for this sequent, as shown below.

$$\dfrac{\dfrac{\{p\} \cup \emptyset \Rightarrow \emptyset \cup \{q\} \cup \{p \to q\}}{\{p\} \cup \emptyset \Rightarrow \emptyset \cup \{q\} \cup \{p \to q\}}\ (\to\text{R})}{\emptyset \Rightarrow \emptyset \cup \{p \to q\}}\ (\to\text{R})$$

Brighton's argument requires (and proves) that all sequents have a derivation of maximum height - this would contradict our observation above. For his argument to hold, it must therefore be the case that Brighton is not using the usual interpretation for the rules $(\to\text{R})$ and $(\to\text{L})$.

The only reasonable option seems to be that Brighton intends for the comma to be interpreted as *disjoint union*. This amounts to the following rule.

$$\frac{\{A\} \cup X \Rightarrow (Y \setminus \{A \to B\}) \cup \{B\}}{X \Rightarrow Y \cup \{A \to B\}}\ (\to\text{R}_{\text{Dis}})$$

If that was the case, a proof that the calculus is complete for GL under this interpretation is required. Moreover, further issues arise with this interpretation.

For example, it is not true in general that the premise of the sequent $\Gamma \Rightarrow \Delta, B \to C$ via the rule $(\to\text{R}_{\text{Dis}})$ is $B, \Gamma \Rightarrow \Delta, C$ (Case 2 of Theorem 1 of Brighton's article). Indeed, if $B \to C \in \Delta$ then $B, \Gamma \Rightarrow \Delta, C$ and $B, \Gamma \Rightarrow (\Delta \setminus \{B \to C\}), C$ would be different. This issue seems repairable. However the situation is undesirable given the sensitivity of structural proof theory to small syntactic details, and especially given the history of cut-elimination for GL.

Second, Brighton provides an unusual argument for the admissibility of cut. In order to obtain a proof of the latter, Brighton proves a result equivalent to it in the case of classical calculi: tautology elimination. More precisely, this lemma has the following shape: if $A \to A, X \Rightarrow Y$ is provable then so is $X \Rightarrow Y$. On inspection, it is clear that a procedure for tautology elimination can easily be turned into a procedure for cut-elimination, and *vice versa*. Given the proximity between these results, arguing for the admissibility of cut by proving tautology elimination seems to be an unnecessary detour.

3 Preliminaries

Let $\mathbb{V} = \{p, q, r \dots\}$ be an infinite set of propositional variables. Modal formulae are defined by the following grammar.

$$A ::= p \in \mathbb{V} \mid \bot \mid A \to A \mid \Box A$$

We use a minimal set of connectives since it is well-known that the other connectives can be defined from these.

We define the *size* of a formula by the number of symbols it contains. We say that a formula A is a *boxed formula* if it has $\Box$ as its main connective. A boxed multiset contains only boxed formulae. For a set $X = \{A_1, \dots, A_n\}$, define $\boxtimes X = \{A_1, \Box A_1, \dots, A_n, \Box A_n\}$. We denote the set of subformulae of a formula A by $\mathrm{Sub}(A)$. We abuse the notation to designate the set of subformulae of all formulae in the set X by $\mathrm{Sub}(X)$. In what follows we use the letters $A, B, C, \dots$ for formulae and $X, Y, Z, \dots$ for multisets of formulae.

The Hilbert calculus for the basic normal modal logic K extends a Hilbert-calculus for classical propositional logic with the axiom $\Box(p \to q) \to (\Box p \to \Box q)$ and the inference rule of necessitation: from A infer $\Box A$. Gödel-Löb logic GL is obtained by the addition of the axiom $\Box(\Box p \to p) \to \Box p$ to K.

A *sequent* is a pair of multisets of formulae, denoted $X \Rightarrow Y$. For multisets X and Y, the multiset sum $X \uplus Y$ is the multiset whose multiplicity (at each formula) is a sum of the multiplicities of X and Y. We write X, Y to mean $X \uplus Y$. For a formula A, we write A, X and X, A to mean $\{A\} \uplus X$.

A *sequent calculus* consists of a finite set of *sequent rule schemas*. Each rule schema consists of a conclusion sequent and some number of premise sequents. If a rule schema has no premise sequents, then it is called an initial sequent. The conclusion and premises are built in the usual way from propositional-variables, formula-variables and multiset-variables. A *rule instance* is obtained by uniformly instantiating every variable in the rule schema with a concrete object of that type. This is the standard definition from structural proof theory.

Definition 1 (Derivation/Proof). *A* derivation *of a sequent s in the sequent calculus C is a finite tree of sequents such that (i) the root node is s; and (ii) each interior node and its direct children are the conclusion and premise(s) of a rule instance in C.*

A proof *is a derivation where every leaf is an instance of an initial sequent.*

In what follows, it should be clear from context whether the word "proof" refers to the object defined in Definition 1, or to the meta-level notion. We say that a sequent is *provable* in C if it has a proof in C.

Definition 2 (Height). *The* height *of a derivation δ, noted $h(\delta)$, is the maximum number of nodes on a path from root to leaf.*

The sequent calculus GLS is given in Fig. 1.

$$\frac{}{p, X \Rightarrow Y, p}\ (\text{IdP}) \qquad \frac{}{\bot, X \Rightarrow Y}\ (\bot\text{L})$$

$$\frac{X \Rightarrow Y, A \qquad B, X \Rightarrow Y}{A \to B, X \Rightarrow Y}\ (\to\text{L}) \qquad \frac{A, X \Rightarrow Y, B}{X \Rightarrow Y, A \to B}\ (\to\text{R})$$

$$\frac{\boxtimes X, \Box B \Rightarrow B}{W, \Box X \Rightarrow \Box B, \Box Y, Z}\ (\text{GLR})$$

Fig. 1. The sequent calculus GLS. Here, W and Z do not contain any boxed formulae.

In a rule instance of (→L) or (→R), the formula instantiating the featured $A \to B$ is the *principal formula* of that instance. In (IdP), a propositional variable instantiating either featured occurrence of p is principal. In a rule instance of (GLR), the formula $\Box B$ is called the *diagonal formula* [13].

Example 1. The following are examples of derivations in GLS. Note that while the first and second examples are derivations, the third is a proof.

$$p \Rightarrow q \to r \qquad \frac{p, q \Rightarrow r}{p \Rightarrow q \to r}\ (\to\text{R}) \qquad \frac{\dfrac{}{\Box p, p, \Box p \Rightarrow p}\ (\text{IdP})}{\Box p \Rightarrow \Box p}\ (\text{GLR})$$

Example 2. A special example of derivation in GLS is the following:

$$\frac{\dfrac{\Box A \to A, \Box(\Box A \to A), A, A, \Box A, \Box A, \Box A \Rightarrow A}{\Box(\Box A \to A), A, \Box A, \Box A \Rightarrow A, \Box A}\ (\text{GLR}) \qquad \Box(\Box A \to A), A, A, \Box A, \Box A \Rightarrow A}{\Box A \to A, \Box(\Box A \to A), A, \Box A, \Box A \Rightarrow A}\ (\to\text{L})$$

By noticing the identity modulo formula multiplicities between the topmost and the lowest sequents, it appears that the sequence of application of rules in the above could be iterated indefinitely on the topmost sequent.

Finally, we consider the additive cut rule.

$$\frac{X \Rightarrow Y, A \qquad A, X \Rightarrow Y}{X \Rightarrow Y}\ (\text{cut})$$

In the above, we call A the *cut-formula*. It easily follows that GLS + (cut) is a sequent calculus for GL [13].

Theorem 1. *For all A we have: $A \in$ GL iff $\Rightarrow A$ is provable in* GLS + *(cut).*

4 Properties Of GLS

We need some lemmas that are commonly used in proof theory. Straightforward inductions on the structure of formulae or derivations are used to prove them.

Lemma 1. *For all X, Y and A, the sequent $A, X \Rightarrow Y, A$ has a proof.*

Lemma 2 (Height-preserving admissibility of weakening). *For all X, Y, A and B:*

(i) If $X \Rightarrow Y$ has a proof π in GLS*, then $X \Rightarrow Y, A$ has a proof π_0 in* GLS *such that $h(\pi_0) \leq h(\pi)$.*
(ii) If $X \Rightarrow Y$ has a proof π in GLS*, then $A, X \Rightarrow Y$ has a proof π_0 in* GLS *such that $h(\pi_0) \leq h(\pi)$.*

Lemma 3 (Height-preserving invertibility of the implication rules). *For all X, Y, A and B:*

(i) If $A \to B, X \Rightarrow Y$ has a proof π in GLS*, then $X \Rightarrow Y, A$ and $B, X \Rightarrow Y$ have proofs π_0 and π_1 in* GLS *such that $h(\pi_0) \leq h(\pi)$ and $h(\pi_1) \leq h(\pi)$.*
(ii) If $X \Rightarrow Y, A \to B$ has a proof π in GLS*, then $A, X \Rightarrow Y, B$ has a proof π_0 in* GLS *such that $h(\pi_0) \leq h(\pi)$.*

Lemma 4 (Height-preserving admissibility of contraction). *For all X, Y, A and B:*

(i) If $X \Rightarrow Y, A, A$ has a proof π in GLS*, then $X \Rightarrow Y, A$ has a proof π_0 in* GLS *such that $h(\pi_0) \leq h(\pi)$.*
(ii) If $A, A, X \Rightarrow Y$ has a proof π in GLS *of height n, then $A, X \Rightarrow Y$ has a proof π_0 in* GLS *such that $h(\pi_0) \leq h(\pi)$.*

In the following section we will introduce a proof-search procedure for GLS which terminates. This will allow us to define the maximum height of a derivation of a sequent with respect to this procedure. Later on this will constitute the secondary induction measure in the proof of admissibility of cut.

5 PSGLS: A Terminating Proof-Search

Given a sequent calculus C, one can define a proof-search procedure on C by imposing further constraints on the applicability of the rules of C. This procedure captures a subset of the set of all derivations of C, i.e. those which are built using the restricted version of the rules of C. Consequently, a proof-search procedure can be identified with the calculus PSC consisting of these restricted rules of C, under the condition that PSC allows to decide the provability of sequents in C.

The sequent calculus PSGLS restricts the rules of GLS in the following way.

1. An additional identity rule (IdB), derivable in GLS as shown in Lemma 1, is introduced.

$$\frac{}{\Box A, X \Rightarrow Y, \Box A}\ (\text{IdB})$$

2. The conclusion of the rule (GLR) is not permitted to be an instance of either (IdP) or ($\bot$L) or (IdB). This restriction ensures that repetitions (even in the weak sense of Example 2) of a sequent along a branch are forbidden.

By inspection, a sequent is provable in PSGLS if and only if it is provable in GLS. The remainder of this section is devoted to showing that each sequent has a derivation of maximum height in PSGLS (something that does not hold of GLS). This crucial result is not thoroughly proved in Brighton's work.

It is easy to prove that if there is a measure that decreases, given a well-founded order, upwards through the rules of PSGLS, then each sequent has a derivation of maximum height in PSGLS. We need the following definition.

Definition 3. *For a sequent $X \Rightarrow Y$:*

1. *Let $\iota(X \Rightarrow Y)$ be the* number of occurrences of "$\rightarrow$" *in $X \Rightarrow Y$.*
2. *Let $\beta(X \Rightarrow Y)$ be the* usable boxes *of $X \Rightarrow Y$ where:*

$$\beta(X \Rightarrow Y) := \{\Box A \mid \Box A \in Sub(X \cup Y)\} \setminus \{\Box A \mid \Box A \in X\}$$

3. *The tuple $(Card(\beta(X \Rightarrow Y)), \iota(X \Rightarrow Y))$, where $Card(U)$ is the cardinality of the set U, is denoted $\Theta(X \Rightarrow Y)$.*

The notion of usable boxes of a sequent $X \Rightarrow Y$ is the set of boxed formulae of $X \Rightarrow Y$ minus the boxed formulae in X. Intuitively, this notion captures the set of boxed formulae of a sequent s which might be the diagonal formula of an instance of (GLR) in a derivation of s in PSGLS.

We proceed to prove that the measure Θ decreases on the usual component-wise ordering on n-tuples, which is well-known to be well-founded, upwards through the rules of PSGLS.

Lemma 5. *Let s_0 and $s_1, ..., s_n$ be sequents. If there is an instance of a rule r of* PSGLS *of the following form, then $\Theta(s_i) < \Theta(s_0)$ for $1 \leq i \leq n$.*

$$\frac{s_1 \quad \dots \quad s_n}{s_0}\, r$$

Proof. We reason by case analysis on r:

1. If r is (IdP) or (IdB) or ($\bot$L), then we are done as there is no premise.
2. If r is ($\rightarrow$R), then it must have the following form.

$$\frac{X, A \Rightarrow Y, B}{X \Rightarrow Y, A \rightarrow B}\,(\rightarrow\text{R})$$

   Then we distinguish two cases. If A is boxed, then $\{\Box B \mid \Box B \in X\} \subseteq \{\Box B \mid \Box B \in X \cup \{A\}\}$. As a consequence, we have that $\beta(X, A \Rightarrow Y, B) \subseteq \beta(X \Rightarrow Y, A \rightarrow B)$ hence Card$(\beta(X, A \Rightarrow Y, B)) \leq$ Card$(\beta(X \Rightarrow Y, A \rightarrow B))$. If Card$(\beta(X, A \Rightarrow Y, B)) <$ Card$(\beta(X \Rightarrow Y, A \rightarrow B))$ then we are done. If Card$(\beta(X, A \Rightarrow Y, B)) =$ Card$(\beta(X \Rightarrow Y, A \rightarrow B))$, then we can see that $\iota(X, A \Rightarrow Y, B) = \iota(X \Rightarrow Y, A \rightarrow B) - 1$ hence $\Theta(X, A \Rightarrow Y, B) < \Theta(X \Rightarrow Y, A \rightarrow B)$. If A is not boxed, then obviously we get that Card$(\beta(X, A \Rightarrow Y, B)) =$ Card$(\beta(X \Rightarrow Y, A \rightarrow B))$ but also $\iota(X, A \Rightarrow Y, B) = \iota(X \Rightarrow Y, A \rightarrow B) - 1$ hence $\Theta(X, A \Rightarrow Y, B) < \Theta(X \Rightarrow Y, A \rightarrow B)$.

3. If r is $(\rightarrow \mathrm{L})$, then it must have the following form.

$$\frac{X \Rightarrow Y, A \qquad B, X \Rightarrow Y}{A \rightarrow B, X \Rightarrow Y} (\rightarrow \mathrm{L})$$

   We can easily establish that $\Theta(X \Rightarrow Y, A) < \Theta(A \rightarrow B, X \Rightarrow Y)$ as one implication symbol is deleted while the cardinality of usable boxes stays the same. To prove that $\Theta(B, X \Rightarrow Y) < \Theta(A \rightarrow B, X \Rightarrow Y)$ we reason as in (2).
4. If r is (GLR) then it must have the following form.

$$\frac{\boxtimes X, \Box B \Rightarrow B}{W, \Box X \Rightarrow \Box B, \Box Y, Z} (\mathrm{GLR})$$

   Clearly, we have that $\{\Box A \mid \Box A \in \mathrm{Sub}(\boxtimes X \cup \{\Box B\} \cup \{B\})\} \subseteq \{\Box A \mid \Box A \in \mathrm{Sub}(W \cup \Box X \cup \{\Box B\} \cup \Box Y \cup Z)\}$. Also, given that we consider a derivation in PSGLS, we can note that (IdB) is not applicable on $W, \Box X \Rightarrow \Box B, \Box Y, Z$ by assumption, hence $\Box B \notin \Box X$. Consequently, we get $\{\Box A \mid \Box A \in W \cup \Box X\} \subset \{\Box A \mid \Box A \in \boxtimes X \cup \{\Box B\}\}$. An easy set-theoretic argument leads to $\beta(\boxtimes X, \Box B \Rightarrow B) \subset \beta(W, \Box X \Rightarrow \Box B, \Box Y, Z)$. As a consequence we obtain $\mathrm{Card}(\beta(\boxtimes X, \Box B \Rightarrow B)) < \mathrm{Card}(\beta(W, \Box X \Rightarrow \Box B, \Box Y, Z))$, hence $\Theta(\boxtimes X, \Box B \Rightarrow B) < \Theta(W, \Box X \Rightarrow \Box B, \Box Y, Z)$.

Q.E.D.

The previous lemma implies the existence of a derivation in PSGLS of maximum height for all sequent. We present the formalisation of that theorem, called `PSGLS_termin` in Coq:

```
Theorem PSGLS_termin :
 forall (s : rel (list (MPropF V))),
 existsT2 (DMax: derrec PSGLS_rules (fun _ => True) s),
 (is_mhd DMax).
```

We first universally quantify (`forall`) over the sequent `s`: a *pair* (`rel`) of *lists* (`list`) of *formulae* (`MPropF V`) obtained from the set $\mathbb{V}$ (`V`). Note that while our pen-and-paper proof defines sequents using multisets, our formalisation defines them using lists. The equivalence of these approaches is witnessed by our proof of the derivability of exchange given in our formalisation. Second, we specify that there exists (`existsT2`) an inhabitant `DMax` of the type `derrec PSGLS_rules ( fun _ => True) s`. This is the type of all derivations of s in PSGLS. The ternary function `derrec` outputs a type of finite trees, i.e. derivations in our case, taking as input a set of rules (`PSGLS_rules`), a function describing the set of allowed leaves (`(fun _ => True)`), and the sequent at the root `s`. Third, we state that `DMax` satisfies the property `is_mhd`: it is a derivation of maximum height for the sequent `s`. This formalisation thus corresponds to the following:

Theorem 2. *Every sequent s has a derivation in* PSGLS *of maximum height.*

Proof. We reason by strong induction on the ordered pair $\Theta(s)$. As the applicability of the rules of PSGLS is decidable, we distinguish two cases:

(I) No PSGLS rule is applicable to s. Then the derivation of maximum height sought after is simply the derivation constituted of s solely, which is the only derivation for s.
(II) Some PSGLS rule is applicable to s. Either only initial rules are applicable, in which case the derivation of maximum height sought after is simply the derivation of height 1 constituted of the application of the applicable initial rule to s. Or, some other rules than the initial rules are applicable. Then consider the finite list $Prems(s)$ of all sequents s_0 such that there is an application of a PSGLS rule r with s as conclusion of r and s_0 as premise of r. By Lemma 5 we know that every element s_0 in the list $Prem(s)$ is such that $\Theta(s_0) < \Theta(s)$. Consequently, the induction hypothesis allows us to consider the derivation of maximum height of all the sequents in $Prem(s)$. As $Prem(s)$ is finite, there must be an element s_{max} of $Prem(s)$ such that its derivation of maximum height is higher or of same height than the derivation of maximum height of all sequents in $Prem(s)$. It thus suffices to pick that s_{max}, use its derivation of maximum height, and apply the appropriate rule to obtain s as a conclusion: this is by choice the derivation of maximum height of s.

Q.E.D.

As the previous lemma implies the existence of a derivation δ of maximum height in PSGLS for any sequent s, we are entitled to let $\text{mhd}(s)$ denote the height of δ. Similarly to Brighton, we later use $\text{mhd}(s)$ as the secondary induction measure used in the proof of admissibility of cut.

Before proving the only property we need from $\text{mhd}(s)$, let us interpret the previous lemma from the point of view of the proof-search procedure underlying PSGLS. The existence of a derivation of maximum height for each sequent in PSGLS shows that in the backward application of rules of PSGLS on a sequent, i.e. the carrying of the proof-search procedure, a halting point has to be encountered. As a consequence, the proof-search procedure is *terminating.*

While this is the essence of the content of the previous lemma, we effectively only use the fact that $\text{mhd}(s)$ decreases upwards in the rules of PSGLS.

Lemma 6. *If r is a rule instance from* PSGLS *with conclusion s_0 and s_1 as one of the premises, then $mhd(s_1) < mhd(s_0)$.*

Proof. Suppose that $\text{mhd}(s_1) \geq \text{mhd}(s_0)$. Let δ_0 and δ_1 be the derivations of, respectively, s_0 and s_1 witnessing Theorem 2. Then the following δ_2 is derivation of s_0 of height $\text{mhd}(s_1) + 1$.

$$\dfrac{\begin{array}{c}\vdots d \\ s_1\end{array} \qquad \dots}{s_0}\ r$$

Because of the maximality of δ_0, we get that the height of δ_0 is greater than the height of δ_2, i.e. $\text{mhd}(s_1) + 1 \leq \text{mhd}(s_0)$. As our initial assumption implies that $\text{mhd}(s_1) + 1 > \text{mhd}(s_0)$, we reached a contradiction. Q.E.D.

Coq is constructive, so how does it allow a proof by contradiction? It can do a proof by contradiction (without having to introduce classical axioms) when dealing with an expression of the decidable fragment. Here, $\mathrm{mhd}(s_1) < \mathrm{mhd}(s_0)$ can be decided because mhd is computable.

6 Cut-Elimination for GLS

We are ready to state and prove our main theorem. It is formalised in Coq in the following way:

```
Theorem GLS_cut_adm : forall A X0 X1 Y0 Y1,
 (derrec GLS_rules (fun _ =>False) (X0++X1,Y0++A::Y1))->
 (derrec GLS_rules (fun _ =>False) (X0++A::X1,Y0++Y1))->
 (derrec GLS_rules (fun _ =>False) (X0++X1,Y0++Y1)).
```

The usual operations on lists "append" and "cons" are respectively represented by `++` and `::`. Sequents are *pairs of lists*, so e.g. `(X0++X1,Y0++Y1)` corresponds to $X_0, X_1 \Rightarrow Y_0, Y_1$. This time `derrec` takes the set of rules `GLS_rules` and the characteristic function `(fun _ => False)` as arguments. So, each line states the existence of a *proof* in GLS. The additive cut rule is formalised in Coq as follows.

$$\frac{(\mathtt{X_0{+}{+}X_1,Y_0{+}{+}A{:}{:}Y_1}) \qquad (\mathtt{X_0{+}{+}A{:}{:}X_1,Y_0{+}{+}Y_1})}{(\mathtt{X_0{+}{+}X_1,Y_0{+}{+}Y_1})}$$

It is now clear that this statement formalises the following theorem:

Theorem 3. *The additive cut rule is admissible in* GLS.

Proof. Let d_1 (with last rule r_1) and d_2 (with last rule r_2) be proofs in GLS of $X \Rightarrow Y, A$ and $A, X \Rightarrow Y$ respectively, as shown below.

$$\frac{d_1}{X \Rightarrow Y, A}\, r_1 \qquad \frac{d_2}{A, X \Rightarrow Y}\, r_2$$

It suffices to show that there is a proof in GLS of $X \Rightarrow Y$. We reason by strong primary induction (PI) on the size of the cut-formula A, giving the primary inductive hypothesis (PIH), and strong secondary induction (SI) on $\mathrm{mhd}(s)$ of the conclusion of a cut, giving the secondary inductive hypothesis (SIH).

There are five cases to consider for r_1: one for each rule in GLS. We separate them by using Roman numerals. The SIH is invoked in all of the following cases: (III-a), (III-b-1), (III-b-2), (IV) and (V-a-2).

(I) $\mathbf{r_1}$ =(IdP): If A is not principal in r_1, then the latter must have the following form.

$$\frac{}{X_0, p \Rightarrow Y_0, p, A}\,(\mathrm{IdP})$$

where $X_0, p = X$ and $Y_0, p = Y$. Thus, we have that the sequent $X \Rightarrow Y$ is of the form $X_0, p \Rightarrow Y_0, p$, and is an instance of an initial sequent. So we are done.

If A principal in r_1, i.e. $A = p$, then $X \Rightarrow Y$ is of the form $X_0, p \Rightarrow Y$. Thus, the conclusion of r_2 is of the form $X_0, p, p \Rightarrow Y$. We can consequently apply Lemma 4 (ii) to obtain a proof of $X_0, p \Rightarrow Y$.

(II) $\mathbf{r_1}$ =($\bot$L): Then r_1 must have the following form.

$$\frac{}{X_0, \bot \Rightarrow Y, A}\ (\bot\text{L})$$

where $X_0, \bot = X$. Thus, we have that the sequent $X \Rightarrow Y$ is of the form $X_0, \bot \Rightarrow Y$, and is an instance of an initial sequent. So we are done.

(III) $\mathbf{r_1}$ =($\rightarrow$ R): We distinguish two cases.

(III-a) If A is not principal in r_1, then the latter must have the following form.

$$\frac{X, B \Rightarrow Y_0, C, A}{X \Rightarrow Y_0, B \rightarrow C, A}\ (\rightarrow\text{R})$$

where $Y_0, B \rightarrow C = Y$. Thus, we have that the sequent $X \Rightarrow Y$ and $A, X \Rightarrow Y$ are respectively of the form $X \Rightarrow Y_0, B \rightarrow C$ and $A, X \Rightarrow Y_0, B \rightarrow C$. We can apply Lemma 3 (ii) on the proof of the latter to get a proof of $A, X, B \Rightarrow Y_0, C$. Thus proceed as follows.

$$\dfrac{\dfrac{X, B \Rightarrow Y_0, C, A \qquad A, X, B \Rightarrow Y_0, C}{X, B \Rightarrow Y_0, C}\ \text{SIH}}{X \Rightarrow Y_0, B \rightarrow C}\ (\rightarrow\text{R})$$

Note that the use of SIH is justified here since the last rule in this proof is an instance of ($\rightarrow$R) in PSGLS and hence $\text{mhd}(X, B \Rightarrow Y_0, C) < \text{mhd}(X \Rightarrow Y_0, B \rightarrow C)$ by Lemma 6.

(III-b) If A principal in r_1, i.e. $A = B \rightarrow C$, then r_1 must have the following form.

$$\frac{B, X \Rightarrow Y, C}{X \Rightarrow Y, B \rightarrow C}\ (\rightarrow\text{R})$$

The conclusion of r_2 must be of the form $B \rightarrow C, X \Rightarrow Y$. In that case, we distinguish two further cases. In the first case, $B \rightarrow C$ is principal in r_2. Consequently the latter must have the following form.

$$\frac{X \Rightarrow Y, B \qquad C, X \Rightarrow Y}{B \rightarrow C, X \Rightarrow Y}\ (\rightarrow\text{L})$$

Proceed as follows.

$$\dfrac{X \Rightarrow Y, B \qquad \dfrac{B, X \Rightarrow Y, C \qquad \dfrac{C, X \Rightarrow Y}{C, B, X \Rightarrow Y}\ \text{Lem.2 (ii)}}{B, X \Rightarrow Y}\ \text{PIH}}{X \Rightarrow Y}\ \text{PIH}$$

In the second case, $B \to C$ is not principal in r_2. In the cases where r_2 is one of (IdP) and ($\bot$L) proceed respectively as in **(I)** and **(II)** when the cut-formula is not principal in the rule considered. We are left with the cases where r_2 is one of ($\to$R), ($\to$L) and (GLR).

(III-b-1) If r_2 is ($\to$R) then it must have the following form.

$$\frac{B \to C, D, X \Rightarrow Y_0, E}{B \to C, X \Rightarrow Y_0, D \to E}\ (\to\text{R})$$

where $Y_0, D \to E = Y$. In that case, note that the provable sequent $X \Rightarrow Y, B \to C$ is of the form $X \Rightarrow Y_0, D \to E, B \to C$. We can use Lemma 3 (ii) on the proof of the latter to get a proof of $D, X \Rightarrow Y_0, E, B \to C$. Proceed as follows.

$$\frac{\dfrac{D, X \Rightarrow Y_0, E, B \to C \qquad B \to C, D, X \Rightarrow Y_0, E}{D, X \Rightarrow Y_0, E}\ \text{SIH}}{X \Rightarrow Y_0, D \to E}\ (\to\text{R})$$

Note that the use of SIH is justified here as the last rule in this proof is effectively an instance of ($\to$R) in PSGLS, hence $\text{mhd}(X, D \Rightarrow Y_0, E) < \text{mhd}(X \Rightarrow Y_0, D \to E)$ by Lemma 6.

(III-b-2) If r_2 is ($\to$L) then it must have the following form.

$$\frac{B \to C, X_0 \Rightarrow Y, D \qquad B \to C, E, X_0 \Rightarrow Y}{B \to C, D \to E, X_0 \Rightarrow Y}\ (\to\text{L})$$

where $X_0, D \to E = X$. In that case, note that the provable sequent $X \Rightarrow Y, B \to C$ is of the form $X_0, D \to E \Rightarrow Y, B \to C$. We can use Lemma 3 (i) on the proof of the latter to get proofs of both $X_0 \Rightarrow Y, D, B \to C$ and $X_0, E \Rightarrow Y, B \to C$. Thus proceed as follows.

$$\frac{\dfrac{X_0 \Rightarrow Y, D, B \to C \qquad B \to C, X_0 \Rightarrow Y, D}{X_0 \Rightarrow Y, D}\ \text{SIH} \qquad \dfrac{X_0, E \Rightarrow Y, B \to C \qquad B \to C, E, X_0 \Rightarrow Y}{X_0, E \Rightarrow Y}\ \text{SIH}}{X_0, D \to E \Rightarrow Y}\ (\to\text{L})$$

Note that both uses of SIH are justified here as the last rule in this proof is effectively an instance of ($\to$L) in PSGLS, hence $\text{mhd}(X_0 \Rightarrow Y, D) < \text{mhd}(X_0, D \to E \Rightarrow Y)$ and $\text{mhd}(X_0, E \Rightarrow Y) < \text{mhd}(X_0, D \to E \Rightarrow Y)$ by Lemma 6.

(III-b-3) If r_2 is (GLR) then it must have the following form.

$$\frac{\boxtimes X_0, \Box D \Rightarrow D}{W, B \to C, \Box X_0 \Rightarrow \Box D, \Box Y_0, Z}\ (\text{GLR})$$

where $W, \Box X_0 = X$ and $\Box D, \Box Y_0, Z = Y$. In that case, note that the sequent $X \Rightarrow Y$ is of the form $W, \Box X_0 \Rightarrow \Box D, \Box Y_0, Z$. To obtain a proof of the latter, we apply the rule (GLR) on the premise of r_2 without weakening $B \to C$:

$$\frac{\boxtimes X_0, \Box D \Rightarrow D}{W, \Box X_0 \Rightarrow \Box D, \Box Y_0, Z}\ (\text{GLR})$$

(IV) $\mathbf{r_1} = (\to \mathbf{L})$: Then r_1 must have the following form.

$$\dfrac{X_0 \Rightarrow Y, B, A \qquad C, X_0 \Rightarrow Y, A}{B \to C, X_0 \Rightarrow Y, A}\ (\to\text{L})$$

where $B \to C, X_0 = X$. Thus, we have that the sequents $X \Rightarrow Y$ and $A, X \Rightarrow Y$ are respectively of the form $B \to C, X_0 \Rightarrow Y$ and $A, B \to C, X_0 \Rightarrow Y$. It thus suffices to apply Lemma 3 (i) on the proof of the latter to obtain proofs of both $A, X_0 \Rightarrow Y, B$ and $A, C, X_0 \Rightarrow Y$, and then proceed as follows.

$$\dfrac{\dfrac{X_0 \Rightarrow Y, B, A \qquad A, X_0 \Rightarrow Y, B}{X_0 \Rightarrow Y, B}\ \text{SIH} \qquad \dfrac{C, X_0 \Rightarrow Y, A \qquad A, C, X_0 \Rightarrow Y}{C, X_0 \Rightarrow Y}\ \text{SIH}}{B \to C, X_0 \Rightarrow Y}\ (\to\text{L})$$

Note that both uses of SIH are justified here as the last rule in this proof is effectively an instance of ($\to$L) in PSGLS, hence $\text{mhd}(X_0 \Rightarrow Y, B) < \text{mhd}(B \to C, X_0 \Rightarrow Y)$ and $\text{mhd}(C, X_0 \Rightarrow Y) < \text{mhd}(B \to C, X_0 \Rightarrow Y)$ by Lemma 6.

(V) $\mathbf{r_1}$ =(GLR): Then we distinguish two cases.

(V-a) A is the diagonal formula in r_1:

$$\dfrac{\boxtimes X_0, \Box B \Rightarrow B}{W, \Box X_0 \Rightarrow \Box B, \Box Y_0, Z}\ (\text{GLR})$$

where $A = \Box B$ and $W, \Box X_0 = X$ and $\Box Y_0, Z = Y$. Thus, we have that the sequents $X \Rightarrow Y$ and $A, X \Rightarrow Y$ are respectively of the form $W, \Box X_0 \Rightarrow \Box Y_0, Z$ and $\Box B, W, \Box X_0 \Rightarrow \Box Y_0, Z$. We now consider r_2. If r_2 is one of (IdP), ($\bot$L), ($\to$R) and ($\to$L) then respectively proceed as in (I), (II), (III) and (IV) when the cut-formula is not principal in the rules considered by using SIH. We are consequently left to consider the case when r_2 is (GLR). Then r_2 is of the following form:

$$\dfrac{B, \Box B, \boxtimes X_0, \Box C \Rightarrow C}{W, \Box B, \Box X_0 \Rightarrow \Box C, \Box Y_1, Z}\ (\text{GLR})$$

where $\Box C, \Box Y_1 = \Box Y_0$. In this situation, we distinguish two sub-cases.

(V-a-1) One of the rules (IdP), ($\bot$L) or (IdB) is applicable to $W, \Box X_0 \Rightarrow \Box C, \Box Y_1, Z$, then we are done for the two first cases as it suffices to apply the corresponding rules to obtain a proof of the conclusion of the cut-rule. For the case of (IdB) it suffices to apply Lemma 1.

(V-a-2) None of these rules is applicable to $W, \Box X_0 \Rightarrow \Box C, \Box Y_1, Z$ (NoInit). Then, proceed as follows.

$$\dfrac{\dfrac{\dfrac{\dfrac{\boxtimes X_0, \Box B \Rightarrow B}{\Box X_0 \Rightarrow \Box B}\ (\text{GLR})}{\boxtimes X_0, \Box C \Rightarrow C, \Box B}\ \text{Lem.2} \qquad \dfrac{\dfrac{\dfrac{\boxtimes X_0, \Box B \Rightarrow B}{\boxtimes X_0, \Box B, \Box C \Rightarrow C, B}\ \text{Lem.2} \qquad B, \Box B, \boxtimes X_0, \Box C \Rightarrow C}{\boxtimes X_0, \Box B, \Box C \Rightarrow C}\ \text{PIH}}{}}{\boxtimes X_0, \Box C \Rightarrow C}\ \text{SIH}}{W, \Box X_0 \Rightarrow \Box C, \Box Y_1, Z}\ (\text{GLR})$$

Note that the use of SIH is justified here as the assumption NoInit ensures that the last rule in this proof is effectively an instance of (GLR) in PSGLS, hence $\text{mhd}(\boxtimes X_0, \Box C \Rightarrow C) < \text{mhd}(W, \Box X_0 \Rightarrow \Box C, \Box Y_1, Z)$ by Lemma 6.

(V-b) A is not the diagonal formula in r_1:

$$\frac{\boxtimes X_0, \Box C \Rightarrow C}{W, \Box X_0 \Rightarrow \Box C, A, \Box Y_0, Z} \text{ (GLR)}$$

where $W, \Box X_0 = X$ and $\Box C, \Box Y_0, Z = Y$. In that case, note that the sequent $X \Rightarrow Y$ is of the form $W, \Box X_0 \Rightarrow \Box C, \Box Y_0, Z$. To obtain a proof of the latter, we apply the rule (GLR) on the premise of r_1 without weakening $\Box B$:

$$\frac{\boxtimes X_0, \Box C \Rightarrow C}{W, \Box X_0 \Rightarrow \Box C, \Box Y_0, Z} \text{ (GLR)}$$

Q.E.D.

The proof of cut-admissibility given here establishes that any topmost cut in a proof in GLS + (cut) is eliminable. By iterating this argument we obtain also cut-elimination for GLS + (cut).

7 Conclusion

We have seen how the termination of backward proof-search can be exploited to obtain cut-elimination. The proof technique used in this paper was first described by Brighton. It is particularly interesting because the termination of backward proof-search is close to a semantic proof of completeness, and the latter is typically much simpler to achieve than a proof of cut-elimination. This makes it particularly interesting to investigate the applicability of this technique to other logics such as Go or intuitionistic GL (using the Dyckhoff calculus for intuitionistic logic since it has terminating backward proof-search).

Our work may appear to beg the following question: if we first need to show semantic cut-free completeness to use this technique, then we already know that every instance of cut is admissible, so, what is the point? Note that this misses the mark. We chose to introduce PSGLS in order to clarify the role of terminating proof-search in the argument, and to demonstrate that the additional notion of regress tree was not essential. In particular, we did not have to show that PSGLS was complete for our purposes.

However, note that it is possible to establish cut-elimination directly without relying on an auxiliary proof calculus such as PSGLS. By isolating the subset of GLS derivations that are also PSGLS derivations, one can use the maximum height on that subset to define the induction measure, and adapt the proofs accordingly.

Acknowledgements. Work supported by the FWF project P33548, CogniGron research center, and the Ubbo Emmius Funds (University of Groningen). Work supported by the FWF projects I 2982 and P 33548.

References

1. Boolos, G.: The Unprovability of Consistency: An Essay in Modal Logic. Cambridge University Press, Cambridge (1979)
2. Borga, M.: On some proof theoretical properties of the modal logic GL. Stud. Logica. **42**(4), 453–459 (1983)
3. Brighton, J.: Cut elimination for GLS using the terminability of its regress process. J. Philos. Log. **45**(2), 147–153 (2016)
4. Dawson, J.E., Goré, R.: Generic methods for formalising sequent calculi applied to provability logic. In: Fermüller, C.G., Voronkov, A. (eds.) LPAR 2010. LNCS, vol. 6397, pp. 263–277. Springer, Heidelberg (2010). https://doi.org/10.1007/978-3-642-16242-8_19
5. Gentzen, G.: Untersuchungen über das logische schließen. II. Math. Zeitschrift **39**, 176–210, 405–431 (1935)
6. Gentzen, G.: Investigations into logical deduction. In: Szabo, M.E. (ed.) The Collected Papers of Gerhard Gentzen, volume 55 of Studies in Logic and the Foundations of Mathematics, pp. 68–131. Elsevier (1969)
7. Goré, R., Ramanayake, R.: Valentini's cut-elimination for provability logic resolved. Rev. Symb. Log. **5**(2), 212–238 (2012)
8. Goré, R., Ramanayake, R.: Cut-elimination for weak Grzegorczyk logic Go. Stud. Log. **102**(1), 1–27 (2014)
9. Indrzejczak, A.: Tautology elimination, cut elimination, and S5. Logic Log. Philos. **26**(4), 461–471 (2017)
10. Mints, G.: Cut elimination for provability logic. In: Collegium Logicum 2005: Cut-Elimination (2005)
11. Negri, S.: Proof analysis in modal logic. J. Philos. Log. **34**(5–6), 507–544 (2005)
12. Negri, S.: Proofs and countermodels in non-classical logics. Log. Univers. **8**(1), 25–60 (2014)
13. Sambin, G., Valentini, S.: The modal logic of provability: the sequential approach. J. Philos. Log. **11**, 311–342 (1982)
14. Sasaki, K.: Löb's axiom and cut-elimination theorem. Acad. Math. Sci. Inf. Eng. Nanzan Univ. **1**, 91–98 (2001)
15. Savateev, Y., Shamkanov, D.: Cut elimination for the weak modal Grzegorczyk logic via non-well-founded proofs. In: Iemhoff, R., Moortgat, M., de Queiroz, R. (eds.) WoLLIC 2019. LNCS, vol. 11541, pp. 569–583. Springer, Heidelberg (2019). https://doi.org/10.1007/978-3-662-59533-6_34
16. Solovay, R.: Provability interpretations of modal logic. Israel J. Math. **25**, 287–304 (1976)
17. Valentini, S.: The modal logic of provability: cut-elimination. J. Philos. Log. **12**, 471–476 (1983)

References

Non-Wellfounded Proofs

Complexity of a Fragment of Infinitary Action Logic with Exponential via Non-well-founded Proofs

Stepan L. Kuznetsov(✉)

Steklov Mathematical Institute of RAS, Moscow, Russia
sk@mi-ras.ru

Abstract. Infinitary action logic ($\mathbf{ACT}_\omega$) can be viewed as an extension of the multiplicative-additive Lambek calculus (**MALC**) with iteration (Kleene star) governed by an omega-rule (Buszkowski, Palka 2007). An alternative formulation utilizes non-well-founded proofs instead of the omega-rule (Das, Pous 2017). Another unary operation commonly added to **MALC** is the exponential. We consider a system which has both Kleene star and the exponential. In general, this system is of a very high complexity level: it is Π_1^1-complete (Kuznetsov, Speranski 2020), while $\mathbf{ACT}_\omega$ itself is Π_1^0-complete. As a reasonable intermediate logic, we consider the fragment where Kleene star is not allowed to appear in the scope of the exponential. For this fragment we manage to construct a formulation based on non-well-founded proofs, with an easily checkable correctness criterion. Using this formulation, we prove that this fragment indeed has strictly intermediate complexity, namely, we prove a Π_2^0 lower bound and a Δ_1^1 upper bound. We also prove a negative result that this fragment does not enjoy Palka's *-elimination property, which would have given a Π_2^0 upper bound as well.

Keywords: Infinitary action logic · Exponential modality · Non-well-founded proofs

1 Introduction

The concept of *action lattice,* which combines the lattice structure, the structure of a residuated monoid, and iteration operation (Kleene star), goes back to Pratt [19] and Kozen [11]. Infinitary action logic [4], denoted by $\mathbf{ACT}_\omega$, axiomatizes the atomic (equational) theory of a specific class of action lattices, namely the *-continuous ones. In a *-continuous action lattice, iteration is defined as a limit: $a^* = \sup\{a^n \mid n \geq 0\}$, rather than a fixpoint.

On the logical side, *-continuity is reflected by infinitary proof mechansims in calculi for $\mathbf{ACT}_\omega$. Thus, the original calculus by Buszkowski and Palka [4]

The work was supported by the Russian Science Foundation, in cooperation with the Austrian Science Fund, under grant RSF–FWF 20-41-05002.

A. Das and S. Negri (Eds.): TABLEAUX 2021, LNAI 12842, pp. 317–334, 2021.
https://doi.org/10.1007/978-3-030-86059-2_19

uses an ω-rule, and a more recent system by Das and Pous [5] is a calculus with non-well-founded derivations (that is, proofs may have infinitely long branches, obeying certain correctness conditions). The usage of such infinitary mechansims is inevitable, since the set of theorems of $\mathbf{ACT}_\omega$ is not recursively enumerable. Namely, it is Π_1^0-hard [3].

Calculi for $\mathbf{ACT}_\omega$ are based on the sequential axiomatization of the inequational theory of residuated lattices without iteration. This calculus is a well-known substructural logic, namely, the multiplicative-additive ("full") Lambek calculus, **MALC** [6]. In its turn, **MALC** can be viewed as a non-commutative intuitionistic variant of the multiplicative-additive fragment of Girard's [7] linear logic. Following the ideas of linear logic, **MALC** can be extended with the exponential modality. In this paper, we continue the line of research of [15] and consider a system with *both* Kleene star and exponential, that is, the extension of $\mathbf{ACT}_\omega$ with the exponential modality. This system will be denoted by $\mathbf{!ACT}_\omega$.

As a matter of notation, Kleene star is written in the postfix form, A^*, while exponential is prefix, $!A$.

The full $\mathbf{!ACT}_\omega$ system, combining two powerful modalities, has a very high complexity level. Namely, it is Π_1^1-complete [15]. The interesting lower bound, Π_1^1-hardness, is proved by encoding the Horn theory of *-continuous Kleene algebras, Π_1^1-completeness of which was proved by Kozen [12]. (The upper bound is established by a general argument valid for a wide class of systems.)

On the other hand, fragments of $\mathbf{!ACT}_\omega$ including only one modality, being undecidable, have quite modest complexity. Namely, $\mathbf{ACT}_\omega$ (includes *, but not !) is Π_1^0-complete [3,18] and **!MALC**, the extension of **MALC** with !, being a variant of linear logic, is Σ_1^0-complete [16]. The Π_1^0 upper bound also extends to a system which includes !, but allows its application only to very simple formulae [14].

This huge complexity gap between the bimodal $\mathbf{!ACT}_\omega$ and its unimodal subsystems, $\mathbf{ACT}_\omega$ and **!MALC**, motivates searching for reasonable fragments of $\mathbf{!ACT}_\omega$ which make use of both * and ! and enjoy an intermediate complexity level, *i.e.*, strictly between Δ_2^0 (which is above both Π_1^0 and Σ_1^0) and Π_1^1.

In this paper we study such a fragment of $\mathbf{!ACT}_\omega$, which is delimited by the following restriction:

no subformula of the form B^* appears inside a subformula of the form $!A$.

(For cut-free derivations, it does not matter whether we impose this restriction only on the goal sequent or on all sequents in its derivation.)

In what follows, we call this restriction the *independence constraint*, meaning "independence" of * from the structural rules offered by ! (most importantly, the contraction rule). The corresponding fragment of $\mathbf{!ACT}_\omega$ will be denoted by $\mathbf{!ACT}_\omega^-$.

For $\mathbf{!ACT}_\omega^-$, we develop a calculus with non-well-founded proofs, extending the system introduced by Das and Pous [5] for $\mathbf{ACT}_\omega$. Using this system, we establish a Σ_1^1 upper bound for $\mathbf{!ACT}_\omega^-$. Being a conservative fragment of $\mathbf{!ACT}_\omega$, however, this system is also Π_1^1-bounded. Thus, it belongs to Δ_1^1, which is strictly below Π_1^1. On the other hand, we prove a Π_2^0-hardness result, and Π_2^0 is strictly above Δ_2^0. Thus, $\mathbf{!ACT}_\omega^-$ is indeed the desired example of an intermediate system. Its exact complexity, however, is still an open question, and we show how some natural approaches to solving this question fail.

2 Formulation of $\mathbf{!ACT}_\omega$

Let us start with a traditional formulation of $\mathbf{!ACT}_\omega$ as a calculus with an ω-rule [15].

Formulae of $\mathbf{!ACT}_\omega$ are built from a countable set of variables $p_1, p_2, p_3, \ldots$ (we also use letters p, q, r, s, t for variables) and constants $\mathbf{1}$ and $\mathbf{0}$ using the following connectives: $\cdot$, $\backslash$, $/$, $\vee$, $\wedge$ (binary connectives), and * and $!$ (unary connectives, also called modalities). As a matter of notation, * is written in the postfix form: A^*, while $!$ is written in the prefix one: $!A$. Sequents are expressions of the form $\Pi \vdash B$, where B is a formula and Π is a finite (possibly empty) sequence of formulae. (Due to the non-commutative nature of our calculi, the ordering in Π matters.) In what follows, capital Latin letters denote formulae and capital Greek letters stand for sequences of formulae.

The core subsystem of $\mathbf{!ACT}_\omega$ is **MALC**, a finitary calculus with the following axioms and rules of inference:

$$\frac{}{A \vdash A}\ \mathrm{Id} \qquad \frac{}{\Gamma, \mathbf{0}, \Delta \vdash B}\ \mathbf{0}_\mathrm{L} \qquad \frac{\Gamma, \Delta \vdash B}{\Gamma, \mathbf{1}, \Delta \vdash B}\ \mathbf{1}_\mathrm{L} \qquad \frac{}{\vdash \mathbf{1}}\ \mathbf{1}_\mathrm{R}$$

$$\frac{\Pi \vdash A \quad \Gamma, B, \Delta \vdash C}{\Gamma, \Pi, A \backslash B, \Delta \vdash C}\ \backslash_\mathrm{L} \qquad \frac{A, \Pi \vdash B}{\Pi \vdash A \backslash B}\ \backslash_\mathrm{R} \qquad \frac{\Gamma, A, B, \Delta \vdash C}{\Gamma, A \cdot B, \Delta \vdash C}\ \cdot_\mathrm{L}$$

$$\frac{\Pi \vdash A \quad \Gamma, B, \Delta \vdash C}{\Gamma, B / A, \Pi, \Delta \vdash C}\ /_\mathrm{L} \qquad \frac{\Pi, A \vdash B}{\Pi \vdash B / A}\ /_\mathrm{R} \qquad \frac{\Pi \vdash A \quad \Delta \vdash B}{\Pi, \Delta \vdash A \cdot B}\ \cdot_\mathrm{R}$$

$$\frac{\Gamma, A, \Delta \vdash C}{\Gamma, A \wedge B, \Delta \vdash C}\ \wedge_{\mathrm{L}1} \qquad \frac{\Gamma, B, \Delta \vdash C}{\Gamma, A \wedge B, \Delta \vdash C}\ \wedge_{\mathrm{L}2} \qquad \frac{\Pi \vdash A \quad \Pi \vdash B}{\Pi \vdash A \wedge B}\ \wedge_\mathrm{R}$$

$$\frac{\Gamma, A, \Delta \vdash C \quad \Gamma, B, \Delta \vdash C}{\Gamma, A \vee B, \Delta \vdash C}\ \vee_\mathrm{L} \qquad \frac{\Pi \vdash A}{\Pi \vdash A \vee B}\ \vee_{\mathrm{R}1} \qquad \frac{\Pi \vdash B}{\Pi \vdash A \vee B}\ \vee_{\mathrm{R}2}$$

$$\frac{\Pi \vdash A \quad \Gamma, A, \Delta \vdash C}{\Gamma, \Pi, \Delta \vdash C}\ \mathrm{Cut}$$

Kleene star is axiomatized by the following rules, which yield $\mathbf{ACT}_\omega$. Here and further $A^n = \underbrace{A, \ldots, A}_{n \text{ times}}$; A^0 is the empty sequence.

$$\frac{\left(\Gamma, A^n, \Delta \vdash C\right)_{n=0}^{\infty}}{\Gamma, A^*, \Delta \vdash C}\ {*}_{\mathrm{L}\omega} \qquad \frac{\Pi_1 \vdash A \quad \ldots \quad \Pi_n \vdash A}{\Pi_1, \ldots, \Pi_n \vdash A^*}\ {*}_{\mathrm{R}n}$$

Here ${*}_{\mathrm{L}\omega}$ is a ω-rule, it has countably many premises; ${*}_{\mathrm{R}n}$ is an infinite series of finitary rules, one for each $n \geq 0$. In particular, ${*}_{\mathrm{R}0}$ is the axiom $\vdash A^*$.

Finally, the following logical and structural rules control the exponential:

$$\frac{\Gamma, A, \Delta \vdash C}{\Gamma, !A, \Delta \vdash C}\ !_{\mathrm{L}} \qquad \frac{!A_1, \ldots, !A_n \vdash B}{!A_1, \ldots, !A_n \vdash !B}\ !_{\mathrm{R}} \qquad \frac{\Gamma, \Delta \vdash C}{\Gamma, !A, \Delta \vdash C}\ !_{\mathrm{W}}$$

$$\frac{\Gamma, B, !A, \Delta \vdash C}{\Gamma, !A, B, \Delta \vdash C}\ !_{\mathrm{P}1} \qquad \frac{\Gamma, !A, B, \Delta \vdash C}{\Gamma, B, !A, \Delta \vdash C}\ !_{\mathrm{P}2} \qquad \frac{\Gamma, !A, !A, \Delta \vdash C}{\Gamma, !A, \Delta \vdash C}\ !_{\mathrm{C}}$$

The cut rule is eliminable by a standard technique combining Gentzen's mix rule and transfinite induction; see [15] for details. Cut elimination yields the subformula property: any formula used in a cut-free derivation is a subformula of the goal sequent.

Remark 1. As in [15], the choice of rules for the exponential follows Girard's linear logic [7], adapted to the non-commutative setting. Since we heavily use results from [15] (cut elimination, complexity bounds), it is important to keep the rules the same. For infinitary action logic extended by other variants of exponential modalities, complexity and structural proof theory questions are left open for future research. A particularly interesting variant is the system with multiplexing instead of contraction [10], that is, $!A$ gets decomposed into several copies of A rather than split into two copies of $!A$.

As for permutation rules ($!_{\mathrm{P}1}$ and $!_{\mathrm{P}2}$), it is crucial that only !-formulae are allowed to commute. This keeps the system non-commutative and allows encoding of Kleene algebras and thus yields the lower complexity bounds. For fully commutative systems, with $A \cdot B \vdash B \cdot A$ for any A and B, the corresponding complexity questions are open.

Remark 2. While the present paper is purely syntactical, let us make a short remark on semantics for the given systems. Infinitary action logic without the exponential, $\mathbf{ACT}_\omega$, enjoys a natural algebraic interpretation on *-continuous residuated Kleene lattices [4]. Standard examples of such lattices include algebras of formal languages (language models) and the ones of binary relations (relational models). These natural examples do not yield complete semantics even for **MALC**, because the distributivity law for $\vee$ and $\wedge$ is not derivable in such substructural systems (see [17]). There exists, however, a generalization of language models based on so-called syntactic concept lattices [21]. These models give completeness for **MALC**, and it is probably easily extendable to $\mathbf{ACT}_\omega$.

For the exponential modality, possible kinds of semantics are more involved. For **!MALC**, let us notice phase semantics [8] and quantale semantics [20]; the latter needs the distributivity law for $\vee$ and $\wedge$. Extending these (or other) kinds of semantics to $\mathbf{!ACT}_\omega$ is an open issue; that is why in this paper we use only syntactic arguments, even where semantic ones could seem more appropriate.

3 Non-well-founded Proofs

Now let us follow Das and Pous [5] and define a system which uses non-well-founded proofs instead of the ω-rule. Let us denote this formulation by $\mathbf{!ACT}_\infty^\sim$. The tilde in the notation reflects the fact that in the full language this system is **not** sound w.r.t. $\mathbf{!ACT}_\omega$, see Example 1 below. This is due to the fact that the correctness condition used in $\mathbf{!ACT}_\infty^\sim$ is too weak. However, for sequents obeying the independence constraint we shall prove equivalence (Theorem 1 below); the corresponding fragment will be denoted by $\mathbf{!ACT}_\infty^-$.

In whole, the relations between systems which appear in this paper can be depicted by the following diagram:

$$\begin{array}{ccccccc} & \nearrow & \mathbf{ACT}_\omega & \searrow & & & \\ \mathbf{MALC} & & & & \mathbf{!ACT}_\omega^- = \mathbf{!ACT}_\infty^- & \longrightarrow \mathbf{!ACT}_\omega & \dashrightarrow \mathbf{!ACT}_\infty^\sim \\ & \searrow & \mathbf{!MALC} & \nearrow & & & \end{array}$$

Here solid arrows mean *conservative* extensions: that is, the smaller system is obtained from the bigger one by a proper restriction of the formula language. In contrast, the dashed arrow is non-conservative: both $\mathbf{!ACT}_\omega$ and $\mathbf{!ACT}_\infty^\sim$ operate in the same language, but $\mathbf{!ACT}_\infty^\sim$ has strictly more derivable sequents.

In order to define $\mathbf{!ACT}_\infty^\sim$, we replace (in the ruleset of $\mathbf{!ACT}_\omega$) $*_{\mathrm{L}\omega}$ and $*_{\mathrm{R}n}$ with the following three finitary rules:

$$\frac{\Gamma, \Delta \vdash C \quad \Gamma, A, A^*, \Delta \vdash C}{\Gamma, A^*, \Delta \vdash C}\ *_{\mathrm{L}} \qquad \frac{}{\vdash A^*}\ *_{\mathrm{R}0} \qquad \frac{\Pi \vdash A \quad \Delta \vdash A^*}{\Pi, \Delta \vdash A^*}\ *_{\mathrm{R}}$$

In $*_{\mathrm{R}}$, one can always suppose that Π is non-empty: otherwise the conclusion coincides with the right premise, and the rule is meaningless. We also remove the cut rule; our system is cut-free by construction.

As a tradeoff for having only finitary rules, infinite *derivation branches* are now allowed, which makes proofs possibly non-well-founded. Thus, the proof tree is now "high" rather than "wide."

Remark 3. Let us emphasize that we do not restrict ourselves to cyclic (regular) non-well-founded proofs, and our derivations are *really infinite*. This is inevitable due to complexity considerations: even $\mathbf{ACT}_\omega$ is outside Σ_1^0, so finite (in particular, circular) proofs are insufficient. Thus, the fragment allowing only cyclic proofs is a proper one, and, complexitywise, it is Σ_1^0-complete, since it includes Pratt's inductive action logic, which is already Σ_1^0-hard [13].

Not all possible non-well-founded proof trees are correct, but only those which satisfy the following correctness condition which is called **-fairness.* A non-well-founded proof is *-fair, if every infinite path includes an infinite number of $*_{\mathrm{L}}$ applications on which the path turns to the right premise. A finite proof is always considered *-fair.

Notice that in our setting, unlike the one of [5], *-fairness is indeed essential. Without !, in the absence of cut, the only possible source of a non-*-fair proof is the usage of $*_{\mathrm{R}}$ with an empty Π. As noticed above, however, such applications can be just globally disallowed. In contrast, structural rules for !, namely, $!_{\mathrm{P1}}$, $!_{\mathrm{P2}}$, and $!_{\mathrm{C}}$ allow developing infinite proof branches which do not use $*_{\mathrm{L}}$. The usage of $!_{\mathrm{P1}}$ and $!_{\mathrm{P2}}$ could be somehow normalized, in order to prevent such effects, but for $!_{\mathrm{C}}$ it is unavoidable.

A sequent is provable in $\mathbf{!ACT}^{\sim}_{\infty}$ if and only if it has a *-fair proof.

The system defined above operates in the full language without any restrictions. However, as we have already mentioned, the equivalence between $\mathbf{!ACT}^{\sim}_{\infty}$ and $\mathbf{!ACT}_{\omega}$ is going to be valid only for sequents which obey the independence constraint. The corresponding fragment of $\mathbf{!ACT}^{\sim}_{\infty}$ will be naturally denoted as $\mathbf{!ACT}^{-}_{\infty}$.

Theorem 1. *A sequent obeying the independence constraint is provable (has a *-fair proof) in* $\mathbf{!ACT}^{\sim}_{\infty}$ *if and only if it is provable in* $\mathbf{!ACT}_{\omega}$.

Before proving this theorem, let us show that the independence constraint is essential for the "only if" direction (the "if" one, from $\mathbf{!ACT}_{\omega}$ to $\mathbf{!ACT}^{\sim}_{\infty}$, holds for arbitrary sequents).

Example 1. The sequent $s, !(s \setminus (p^* \cdot ((p^+ \setminus \mathbf{1}) \wedge q) \cdot s)) \vdash q \cdot s$, where $p^+ = p \cdot p^*$, has a *-fair proof in $\mathbf{!ACT}^{\sim}_{\infty}$, but it is not derivable in $\mathbf{!ACT}_{\omega}$. Here is the *-fair non-well-founded proof, in which A stands for $s \setminus (p^* \cdot ((p^+ \setminus \mathbf{1}) \wedge q) \cdot s)$:

$$
\dfrac{\dfrac{s \vdash s \qquad \dfrac{\dfrac{\dfrac{q \vdash q \quad s \vdash s}{q, s \vdash q \cdot s}\,{\cdot_{\mathrm{R}}}}{(p^+ \setminus \mathbf{1}) \wedge q, s, !A \vdash q \cdot s}\,{!_{\mathrm{W}}, \wedge_{\mathrm{L2}}} \qquad \dfrac{\dfrac{\dfrac{p \vdash p \quad p^* \vdash p^*}{p, p^* \vdash p^+}\,{\cdot_{\mathrm{R}}} \qquad \dfrac{\dfrac{\vdots}{s, !A \vdash q \cdot s}}{\mathbf{1}, s, !A \vdash q \cdot s}\,{\mathbf{1}_{\mathrm{L}}}}{p, p^*, p^+ \setminus \mathbf{1}, s, !A \vdash q \cdot s}\,{\setminus_{\mathrm{L}}}}{p, p^*, (p^+ \setminus \mathbf{1}) \wedge q, s, !A \vdash q \cdot s}\,{\wedge_{\mathrm{L1}}}}{p^*, (p^+ \setminus \mathbf{1}) \wedge q, s, !A \vdash q \cdot s}\,{*_{\mathrm{L}}}}{s, s \setminus (p^* \cdot ((p^+ \setminus \mathbf{1}) \wedge q) \cdot s), !A \vdash q \cdot s}\,{\cdot_{\mathrm{L}}, \setminus_{\mathrm{L}}}}{s, !A \vdash q \cdot s}\,{!_{\mathrm{L}}, !_{\mathrm{C}}}
$$

In order to prove that this sequent is not derivable in $\mathbf{!ACT}_{\omega}$, let us first take $p \vdash p^*$ (which is easily derivable) and obtain $!(s \setminus (p \cdot ((p^+ \setminus \mathbf{1}) \wedge q) \cdot s)) \vdash !A$ by monotonicity of the corresponding operations. Next, if $s, !A \vdash q \cdot s$ were derivable, we could have derived $s, !(s \setminus (p \cdot ((p^+ \setminus \mathbf{1}) \wedge q) \cdot s)) \vdash q \cdot s$ using cut. The latter sequent does not include negative occurrences of * (that is, those which could be introduced by $*_{\mathrm{L}\omega}$, not $*_{\mathrm{R}n}$). Thus, after cut elimination we get a finite derivation.

Now let us notice that the "branching" rules $\vee_L$ and $\wedge_R$ cannot be applied due to the (polarized) subformula property: there are no occurrences of $\vee$, and the only one of $\wedge$ is introduced by $\wedge_L$. Therefore, the occurrence of q in the right-hand side gets uniquely propagated upwards, and there is a unique axiom $q \vdash q$ in the derivation. Hence, while there could be several copies of $(p^+ \setminus \mathbf{1}) \wedge q$ (due to $!_C$), exactly one such copy gets decomposed using $\wedge_{L2}$ yielding q. Let us call the corresponding copy of the formula $A' = s \setminus (p \cdot ((p^+ \setminus \mathbf{1}) \wedge q) \cdot s)$ the *principal* one.

Moreover, the $q \vdash q$ axiom leaf is the end of the "rightmost path," that is, the path which always goes to the right premise of $\setminus_L$. Now let us take a look at the leftmost occurrence of p from the principal copy of A'. We claim that this occurrence also follows the "rightmost path," that is, always goes to the right premise of $\setminus_L$.

Indeed, this p could go to the left premise only in the case when a copy of $!A'$ penetrates between p and q and gets decomposed there. But in this case we get a left premise of the form $\Gamma, p \vdash s$, which could not be derivable, since Γ does not contain / which could take p apart from s.

This argument yields contradiction: the occurrence of p in question traces upwards along the "rightmost path" until its end, but in the end there is no p, just $q \vdash q$. □

Remark 4. The reason why $\mathbf{!ACT}_\infty^\sim$ is not sound (that is, equivalent to $\mathbf{!ACT}_\omega$) without the independence constraint is the fact that *-fairness, in general, is too weak a correctness condition for non-well-founded proofs. Das and Pous [5] present another correctness condition: for each infinite path, there should be a trace of *the same* formula of the form A^*, which undergoes $*_L$ infinitely many times. We leave it as an open question whether imposing this stronger correctness condition on $\mathbf{!ACT}_\infty^\sim$ yields a system equivalent to $\mathbf{!ACT}_\omega$. For our purposes, however, this is not needed: we already know that the full $\mathbf{!ACT}_\infty^\sim$ is Π_1^1-complete, so there is no hope to obtain better complexity upper bounds using non-well-founded proofs. (In particular, checking existence of valid traces requires quantification over infinite paths, which is already at least Π_1^1.) In contrast, the easily checkable *-fairness condition will allow us to obtain such upper bounds for $\mathbf{!ACT}_\omega^-$, which we are going to do in the next section.

Our proof of Theorem 1 basically reuses the ideas of Das and Pous [5]. However, in the presence of the exponential with its $!_C$ rule, we have to use different induction parameters. Namely, now one cannot just say that for each rule, except $*_L$, the premises are structurally simpler than the conclusion.

In what follows, we essentially use the fact that there is no cut rule in $\mathbf{!ACT}_\infty^\sim$. This is by design. Cut elimination issues (that is, whether one can add cut without altering theoremhood) for non-well-founded proofs are quite subtle and therefore left beyond the scope of this paper.

In order to prove Theorem 1, let us introduce several useful notions.

Let π be a proof in $\mathbf{!ACT}_\infty^\sim$. Cutting off its branches immediately below the lowermost applications of $*_L$ yields its *0-fragment,* denoted by π_0. Notice that if

π is *-fair, then π_0 is a finite tree: otherwise π includes an infinite path without applications of $*_{\mathrm{L}}$. The height of π_0 will be denoted by h_0.

Next, let us define the **-rank* for formulae and sequents. A *-rank will be a sequence of natural numbers $(r_0, r_1, r_2, \ldots)$, which is infinite, but only a finite number of r_i's are non-zero. On such sequences, we define two operations, sum and lifting, and constants:

$$(r_0, r_1, \ldots) \oplus (s_0, s_1, \ldots) = (r_0 + s_0, r_1 + s_1, \ldots) \qquad o = (0, 0, 0, 0, \ldots)$$
$$(r_0, r_1, r_2, \ldots)\!\uparrow = (0, r_0, r_1, r_2, \ldots) \qquad \iota = (1, 0, 0, 0, \ldots)$$

For a formula A or a sequent $\Pi \vdash B$, its *-rank, denoted by $\sigma(A)$ or $\sigma(\Pi \vdash B)$ respectively, is defined recursively:

$$\sigma(p_i) = \sigma(\mathbf{0}) = \sigma(\mathbf{1}) = o$$
$$\sigma(A \setminus B) = \sigma(B \,/\, A) = \sigma(A \cdot B) = \sigma(A \wedge B) = \sigma(A \vee B) = \sigma(A) \oplus \sigma(B)$$
$$\sigma(!A) = \sigma(A)$$
$$\sigma(A^*) = \sigma(A)\!\uparrow \oplus\, \iota$$
$$\sigma(A_1, \ldots, A_n \vdash B) = \sigma(A_1) \oplus \ldots \oplus \sigma(A_n) \oplus \sigma(B)$$

Notice that if we are under the independence constraint, then $\sigma(!A) = o$.

Finally, we define the strict anti-lexicographical (that is, lexicographical 'from right to left') order on ranks: $(r_0, r_1, r_2, \ldots) \prec (s_0, s_1, s_2, \ldots)$, if there exists such an i that $r_i < s_i$ and $r_j = s_j$ for all $j > i$. It is easy to see that this order is linear. Moreover, on *-ranks (but not on arbitrary infinite sequences) it is also well-founded. Thus, transfinite induction on *-ranks is legal.

We start proving Theorem 1 by establishing invertibility of the ω-rule, $*_{\mathrm{L}\omega}$, in the system with non-well-founded proofs.

Lemma 1. *If $\Gamma, A^*, \Delta \vdash C$ is derivable in $\mathbf{!ACT}^{\sim}_{\infty}$ (that is, it has a *-fair proof), then so are sequents $\Gamma, A^n, \Delta \vdash C$ for all $n \geq 0$.*

Proof. Recall that our derivation is an infinite *tree*, not a graph with cycles. We proceed by induction on n. For $n = 0$, we trace the "active" occurrence of A^* upwards along the proof tree and remove it, until we reach applications of $*_{\mathrm{L}}$ which introduce it. At such application, we just take the left premise (which, after removing A^*, coincides with the conclusion) and cut off the whole subtree which derives the right premise. The resulting tree is still *-fair, since its infinite branches do not contain the "active" A^*.

For the induction step, again, we replace "active" occurrences of A^* with A^{n+1}, up to applications of $*_{\mathrm{L}}$ which introduce the "active" A^*:

$$\frac{\Phi, \Theta \vdash B \quad \Phi, A, A^*, \Theta \vdash B}{\Phi, A^*, \Theta \vdash B}\ *_{\mathrm{L}}$$

Now we cut off the left subtree and apply the induction hypothesis to the right one. This yields derivability of $\Phi, A, A^n, \Theta \vdash B$, which is exactly $\Phi, A^{n+1}, \Theta \vdash$

B. The *-fairness condition is again preserved: infinite paths either end up in subtrees deriving formulae of the form $\Phi, A, A^n, \Theta \vdash B$, which are *-fair by induction hypothesis, or do not include the "active" A^*. □

Now we are ready to prove Theorem 1.

Proof (of Theorem 1). The interesting direction is the "only if" one, from $\mathbf{!ACT}_\infty^-$ to $\mathbf{!ACT}_\omega^-$. Let $\Psi \vdash C$ be a sequent derivable in $\mathbf{!ACT}_\infty^\sim$ and obeying the independence constraint. We proceed by nested induction. The outer induction parameter is $\sigma(\Psi \vdash C)$, the *-rank of the sequent in question. The inner one is h_0, the height of the 0-fragment of its proof in $\mathbf{!ACT}_\infty^\sim$.

Consider two cases.

Case 1. $\Psi \vdash C$ is of the form $\Gamma, A^*, \Delta \vdash C$. Lemma 1 yields derivability of $\Gamma, A^n, \Delta \vdash C$ for any $n \geq 0$. Notice that the latter sequents have a smaller *-rank. Indeed, A^n contributes $\sigma(A) \oplus \ldots \oplus \sigma(A)$ to the *-rank of the sequent, and this is always strictly less than $\sigma(A^*)$. (If $\sigma(A) \neq o$, then the last non-zero element of $\sigma(A)\uparrow$ has a bigger index than that of $\sigma(A)$. For $\sigma(A) = o$, the "$\oplus \iota$" in the definition of $\sigma(A^*)$ helps.) Thus, by induction hypothesis sequents $\Gamma, A^n, \Delta \vdash C$ are derivable in $\mathbf{!ACT}_\omega$, and by $*_{\mathrm{L}\omega}$ we derive $\Gamma, A^*, \Delta \vdash C$.

Case 2. $\Psi \vdash C$ is not of the form $\Gamma, A^*, \Delta \vdash C$. If it is an axiom, then it is also an axiom of $\mathbf{!ACT}_\omega$, and we finish the proof. Otherwise, the lowermost rule applied in the proof of $\Psi \vdash C$ is not $*_{\mathrm{L}}$, and its premises have proofs with a smaller h_0. We also notice that the premises could not have bigger *-ranks. Here the independence constraint is crucial: $\sigma(!A) = o$, so $!_{\mathrm{C}}$ could not increase the *-rank. Other rules just use subformulae of $\Psi \vdash C$. By induction hypothesis, the premises of the lowermost rule are derivable in $\mathbf{!ACT}_\omega$. If the lowermost rule is not $*_{\mathrm{R}}$, then it is also valid in $\mathbf{!ACT}_\omega$, and we finish the proof by applying it. The $*_{\mathrm{R}}$ rule is simulated using cut (where $\Psi = \Pi, \Delta$ and $C = A^*$):

$$\dfrac{\dfrac{\Pi \vdash A \quad \Delta \vdash A^*}{\Pi, \Delta \vdash A \cdot A^*}\,{\cdot_{\mathrm{R}}} \qquad \dfrac{\dfrac{\left(A^{n+1} \vdash A^*\right)_{n=0}^{\infty}}{A, A^* \vdash A^*}\,{*_{\mathrm{L}\omega}}}{A \cdot A^* \vdash A^*}\,{\cdot_{\mathrm{L}}}}{\Pi, \Delta \vdash A^*}\,\mathrm{Cut}$$

(Here each $A^{n+1} \vdash A^*$ is derived using the appropriate $*_{\mathrm{R}(n+1)}$.) Cut can be then eliminated using the cut-elimination theorem for $\mathbf{!ACT}_\omega$ [15].

The "if" direction, from $\mathbf{!ACT}_\omega$ to $\mathbf{!ACT}_\infty^\sim$, is easier. The $*_{\mathrm{R}n}$ rule is simulated by a finite series of $*_{\mathrm{R}}$, followed by $*_{\mathrm{R}0}$. The $*_{\mathrm{L}\omega}$ rule gets replaced by an infinite path of $*_{\mathrm{L}}$ applications (which yields *-fairness). Other rules and axioms of $\mathbf{!ACT}_\omega$ are valid in $\mathbf{!ACT}_\infty^\sim$ as well. □

4 Complexity

Being an easily checkable correctness condition, *-fairness allows us to obtain a non-trivial complexity upper bound on $\mathbf{!ACT}_\infty^-$, and thus on $\mathbf{!ACT}_\omega^-$.

Theorem 2. *The derivability problem for* $!\mathbf{ACT}_\omega^-$ *(that is, derivability in* $!\mathbf{ACT}_\omega$ *for sequents which obey the independence constraint) belongs to the* Σ_1^1 *complexity class.*

Proof. Recall that Σ_1^1 allows one second-order existential quantifier. We shall quantify over functions which map natural numbers to finite derivation trees (fragments of a proof). Such functions can be encoded as sets of natural numbers in a standard way.

Let us call a finite derivation tree π_n a subproof of level n, if it is constructed according to the rules of $!\mathbf{ACT}_\infty^\sim$, and each path from the root either reaches an axiom, or undergoes $*_\mathrm{L}$, turning to the right premise, at least n times. In the second case, the leaf node at which the path terminates may contain an arbitrary sequent. Let $\mathscr{S}_n$ denote the set of all subproofs of level n.

We claim that a sequent $\Psi \vdash C$ is provable in $!\mathbf{ACT}_\infty^\sim$ if and only if there exists a function $F\colon \mathbb{N} \to \bigcup_{n \in \mathbb{N}} \mathscr{S}_n$, $F\colon n \mapsto \pi_n$, such that:

1. each $\pi_n = F(n)$ is a subproof of level n;
2. each π_{n+1} is an extension of π_n (that is, π_n is a subtree in π_{n+1}).

Indeed, for the "only if" part one just takes the *-fair non-well-founded proof of $\Psi \vdash C$, denoted by π, and lets $F(n) = \pi_n$ be its n-fragment. The n-fragment is defined similarly to the 0-fragment: each infinite path gets cut off immediately below the $(n+1)$-st of the applications of $*_\mathrm{L}$ where the path turns right. Since π is *-fair, each π_n is finite, and indeed $\pi_0, \pi_1, \pi_2, \ldots$ is a growing chain of subproofs of corresponding levels.

For the "if" part, let π be the union of π_n's. This is of course a possibly non-well-founded tree which is constructed according to inference rules of $!\mathbf{ACT}_\infty^\sim$. Each leaf holds an axiom: otherwise the finite path to this leaf includes, for some k, at most k applications of $*_\mathrm{L}$, and this path could not belong to π_{k+1}. Finally, each infinite path should traverse all π_n's (since each of them is finite). Therefore, for any n it includes a least n applications of $*_\mathrm{L}$ on which the path turns right. This gives *-fairness.

Conditions 1–2 on the function F (that is, on the sequence $\pi_0, \pi_1, \pi_2, \ldots$) are arithmetical.

If the sequent $\Psi \vdash C$ obeys the independence constraint, then its derivability in $!\mathbf{ACT}_\infty^\sim$ is equivalent to derivability in $!\mathbf{ACT}_\omega$ (Theorem 1). Thus, we get the desired complexity upper bound for the fragment $!\mathbf{ACT}_\omega^-$. □

Corollary 1. *The derivability problem for* $!\mathbf{ACT}_\omega^-$ *belongs to the* Δ_1^1 *complexity class. Thus, this fragment is hyperarithmetical, unlike the complete system* $!\mathbf{ACT}_\omega$.

Proof. $\Delta_1^1 = \Sigma_1^1 \cap \Pi_1^1$. The Σ_1^1 upper bound has just been proved. On the other hand, $!\mathbf{ACT}_\omega^-$ is a conservative fragment of $!\mathbf{ACT}_\omega$, and therefore inherits its Π_1^1 complexity upper bound [15]. □

Thus, $!\mathbf{ACT}_\omega^-$ is a fragment whose complexity is strictly less than that of the full system $!\mathbf{ACT}_\omega$. Now let us prove a lower bound which shows that $!\mathbf{ACT}_\omega^-$

is strictly harder than $\mathbf{ACT}_\omega$, the system without !, and **!MALC**, the system without *.

Theorem 3. *The derivability problem for* $\mathbf{!ACT}_\omega^-$ *is* Π_2^0*-hard.*

The proof of Theorem 3 is based on the idea that the exponential modality, !, allows internalizing derivability from a finite number of hypotheses ("extra axioms") in the style of deduction theorem. (For **MALC** itself, the deduction theorem does not hold due to the lack of structural rules, which are restored under !.) Thus, encoding the Lambek calculus with extra axioms [2] allows proving Σ_1^0-completeness of the Lambek calculus with exponential [16]. For $\mathbf{ACT}_\omega$, derivation from hypotheses is Π_1^1-hard, so we get the same lower bound for the "pure" derivation problem for $\mathbf{!ACT}_\omega$ [15].

In $\mathbf{!ACT}_\omega^-$, however, the usage of ! is restricted to formulae without Kleene star. Thus, we could only encode derivations from hypotheses which do not include Kleene star (are *-free). Kozen [12] proves exactly the result we need, for *-continuous Kleene algebras. The language of Kleene algebras includes only the following connectives[1]: $\cdot$, $\vee$, *, and constants $\mathbf{0}$ and $\mathbf{1}$. Let $A_1, B_1, \ldots, A_n, B_n, C, D$ be formulae in the language of Kleene algebras, and let $A_1, B_1, \ldots, A_n, B_n$ be *-free. Under these assumptions, deciding whether a Horn clause of the form $(A_1 = B_1 \mathbin{\&} \ldots \mathbin{\&} A_n = B_n) \Rightarrow C = D$ is generally true in all *-continuous Kleene algebras is a Π_2^0-complete problem.

We can consider inequations instead of equations, that is, clauses of the form $(A_1 \preceq B_1 \mathbin{\&} \ldots \mathbin{\&} A_n \preceq B_n) \Rightarrow C \preceq D$, where $\preceq$ will be reflected by the sequential arrow $\vdash$. For such clauses, the problem is also Π_2^0-complete, which can be shown by an inspection of Kozen's proof [12]. Namely, Kozen's construction uses such formulae that $C = D$ is equivalent (if the Horn premises hold) to $C \preceq D$. The premises, $(A_1 = B_1 \mathbin{\&} \ldots \mathbin{\&} A_n = B_n)$, can be equivalently replaced by $(A_1 \preceq B_1 \mathbin{\&} B_1 \preceq A_1 \mathbin{\&} \ldots \mathbin{\&} A_n \preceq B_n \mathbin{\&} B_n \preceq A_n)$.

Kozen's result, however, is formulated semantically. Thus, in order to transfer it to our syntactical formulations, we shall need a soundness-and-completeness result. Moreover, the language in Kozen's setting is smaller, so we have to care for conservativity. Below we explain the proof accurately. We follow the line of the Π_1^1-hardness proof from [15], imposing *-freeness of the premises $(A_i \preceq B_i)$.

Let $\mathbf{KA}_\omega$ denote a calculus defined by the following axioms and rules, taken from $\mathbf{ACT}_\omega$: Id, $\vee_L$, $\vee_{R1}$, $\vee_{R2}$, $\cdot_L$, $\cdot_R$, $^*_{L\omega}$, $^*_{Rn}$, $\mathbf{1}_L$, $\mathbf{1}_R$, $\mathbf{0}_L$, and Cut. Sequents of $\mathbf{KA}_\omega$ are naturally interpreted on partially ordered algebraic structures in the language $\cdot$, $\vee$, *, $\mathbf{0}$, $\mathbf{1}$. Indeed, connectives are interpreted as corresponding operations, and $\vdash$ corresponds to the partial order, $\preceq$. By definition, a **-continuous Kleene algebra* is such an algebraic structure, in which all theorems of $\mathbf{KA}_\omega$ are generally true.

Let $\mathcal{E} = \{A_1 \vdash B_1, \ldots, A_n \vdash B_n\}$, where A_i and B_i are *-free formulae in the language of Kleene algebras, and let C and D be arbitrary formulae in this language.

[1] Kozen uses a different notation.

Lemma 2. *The following are equivalent.*

1. *The sequent $C \vdash D$ is true under any interpretation in a *-continuous Kleene algebra, under which all sequents from $\mathcal{E}$ are true. In other words, the Horn clause $(A_1 \preceq B_1 \,\&\, \ldots \,\&\, A_n \preceq B_n) \Rightarrow C \preceq D$ is generally true in all *-continuous Kleene algebras.*
2. *$C \vdash D$ is derivable in $\mathbf{KA}_\omega$ from the set of hypotheses $\mathcal{E}$.*
3. *The sequent $!(A_1 \setminus B_1), \ldots, !(A_n \setminus B_n), C \vdash D$ is derivable in $\mathbf{!ACT}_\omega$.*

This lemma immediately yields Theorem 3: checking statement 1 is a Π_2^0-hard problem due to Kozen [12], and statement 3 is actually a statement of derivability in $\mathbf{!ACT}_\omega^-$, since A_i and B_i are *-free.

Proof (of Lemma 2). $\boxed{1 \Rightarrow 2}$ Suppose that $C \vdash D$ is not derivable in $\mathbf{KA}_\omega$ from $\mathcal{E}$. Construct the Lindenbaum–Tarski algebra $LT_\mathcal{E}$ in the following way. For formulae F and G let $F \approx_\mathcal{E} G$, if $F \vdash G$ and $G \vdash F$ are both derivable in $\mathbf{KA}_\omega$ from $\mathcal{E}$. This is indeed an equivalence relation. The elements of $LT_\mathcal{E}$ are equivalence classes of the form $[F]_{\approx_\mathcal{E}}$. Operations are defined in a natural way: $[F]_{\approx_\mathcal{E}} \cdot [G]_{\approx_\mathcal{E}} = [F \cdot G]_{\approx_\mathcal{E}}$ and similarly for others. Finally, $[F]_{\approx_\mathcal{E}} \preceq [G]_{\approx_\mathcal{E}}$ if $F \vdash G$ is derivable in $\mathbf{KA}_\omega$ from $\mathcal{E}$. Correctness of these definitions is checked in a routine way. (Notice that the cut rule in $\mathbf{KA}_\omega$ is crucial here. In the presence of hypotheses, namely $\mathcal{E}$, the cut rule is in general not eliminable.)

Now, $LT_\mathcal{E}$ is a *-continuous Kleene algebra. Let us interpret each formula F as $[F]_{\approx\mathcal{E}}$. Correctness, again, is checked routinely. Under this interpretation, all sequents from $\mathcal{E}$ are true, while $C \vdash D$ is not. Contradiction.

$\boxed{2 \Rightarrow 3}$ Let us take the proof of $C \vdash D$ from $\mathcal{E}$ in $\mathbf{KA}_\omega$ and add the prefix $!(A_1 \setminus B_1), \ldots, !(A_n \setminus B_n)$ to each sequent. The rule applications remain valid, provided we add $!_{\mathrm{P}1}$ and $!_\mathrm{C}$ applications to rules with several premises. Sequents from $\mathcal{E}$ now become derivable: for $!(A_1 \setminus B_1), \ldots, !(A_n \setminus B_n), A_i \vdash B_i$, one just weakens all $!(A_j \setminus B_j)$ for $j \neq i$, moves $!(A_i \setminus B_i)$ to the right of A_i and removes the !. This yields a derivable sequent $A_i, A_i \setminus B_i \vdash B_i$.

$\boxed{3 \Rightarrow 1}$ Given a proof of $!(A_1 \setminus B_1), \ldots, !(A_n \setminus B_n), C \vdash D$ in $\mathbf{!ACT}_\omega$, let us eliminate cuts. In the cut-free proof, we erase all formulae including $\setminus$. In the resulting tree, all formulae are in the language of Kleene algebras. All rules operating ! have trivialized, and applications of $\setminus_\mathrm{L}$ turn into:

$$\frac{\Pi \vdash A_i \quad \Gamma, B_i, \Delta \vdash F}{\Gamma, \Pi, \Delta \vdash F}$$

($A_i \setminus B_i$ was erased). This is simulated in $\mathbf{KA}_\omega$ using cuts and formulae from $\mathcal{E}$:

$$\frac{\Pi \vdash A_i \qquad \dfrac{A_i \vdash B_i \quad \Gamma, B_i, \Delta \vdash F}{\Gamma, A_i, \Delta \vdash F}\,\mathrm{Cut}}{\Gamma, \Pi, \Delta \vdash F}\,\mathrm{Cut}$$

Thus, $C \vdash D$ is derivable in $\mathbf{KA}_\omega$ from $\mathcal{E}$. □

5 Issues with *-Elimination

In this section we discuss why attempts to prove better upper bounds for $\mathbf{!ACT}_\omega^-$ (namely, Π_2^0), based on extending proofs for the Π_1^0 upper bound for $\mathbf{ACT}_\omega$, fail.

Das and Pous [5] prove the Π_1^0 upper bound for $\mathbf{ACT}_\omega$ using the following argument: a sequent is derivable if and only if for any n there exists a partial derivation tree of height n. This argument is valid for the system without !, since it can be formulated as a non-well-founded system without *any* correctness conditions. For $\mathbf{!ACT}_\infty^-$, however, *-fairness is crucial, since otherwise we could get infinite paths built using $!_{\mathrm{C}}$ instead of $*_{\mathrm{L}}$.

Thus, analysis of subproofs yields only a Σ_1^1 upper bound, as explained in the previous section. Notice that in the proof of Theorem 2 it is crucial to require that each next π_{n+1} is an extension of π_n. One could try to relax this condition and require just the existence, for any n, of a valid subproof π_n of level n. This condition is a Π_2^0 one. However, construction of the infinite proof π from these subproofs will not work. Indeed, for each subproof of level n there are infinitely many "successor" subproofs of level $n+1$ (due to $!_{\mathrm{C}}$). Thus, Kőnig's lemma is not applicable here. In fact, the sequent in Example 2 below has subproofs of all levels, but is not derivable.

Palka's [18] proof of the upper Π_1^0 complexity bound on $\mathbf{ACT}_\omega$ is based on the following **-elimination* technique. Let $A^{\bullet m} = \underbrace{A \cdot \ldots \cdot A}_{m \text{ times}}$ and $A^{\bullet 0} = \mathbf{1}$.[2]
For each sequent, we define its *n-th approximation* by replacing each negative occurrence of A^* with a finite disjunction $\mathbf{1} \vee A \vee A^{\bullet 2} \vee \ldots \vee A^{\bullet n}$. Formally, this is done by the following recursive definition:

$$
\begin{array}{ll}
N_n(p_i) = p_i & P_n(p_i) = p_i \\
N_n(\mathbf{0}) = \mathbf{0} & P_n(\mathbf{0}) = \mathbf{0} \\
N_n(\mathbf{1}) = \mathbf{1} & P_n(\mathbf{1}) = \mathbf{1} \\
N_n(A \setminus B) = P_n(A) \setminus N_n(B) & P_n(A \setminus B) = N_n(A) \setminus P_n(B) \\
N_n(B \,/\, A) = N_n(B) \,/\, P_n(A) & P_n(B \,/\, A) = P_n(B) \,/\, N_n(A) \\
N_n(A \cdot B) = N_n(A) \cdot N_n(B) & P_n(A \cdot B) = P_n(A) \cdot P_n(B) \\
N_n(A \wedge B) = N_n(A) \wedge N_n(B) & P_n(A \wedge B) = P_n(A) \wedge P_n(B) \\
N_n(A \vee B) = N_n(A) \vee N_n(B) & P_n(A \vee B) = P_n(A) \vee P_n(B) \\
\multicolumn{2}{l}{N_n(A^*) = \mathbf{1} \vee N_n(A) \vee (N_n(A))^{\bullet 2} \vee \ldots \vee (N_n(A))^{\bullet n}} \\
 & P_n(A^*) = (P_n(A))^*
\end{array}
$$

The n-th approximation of $A_1, \ldots, A_k \vdash B$ is $N_n(A_1), \ldots, N_n(A_k) \vdash P_n(B)$.

Palka has proved the *-elimination theorem: a sequent is derivable in $\mathbf{ACT}_\omega$ if and only if so are all its approximations. The non-trivial direction here is the "if" one. This yields the desired Π_1^0 upper bound, since derivations of n-th approximations never include the ω-rule, and the derivability problem for such sequents is algorithmically decidable.

---

[2] For accuracy, we distinguish A^m as a sequence from $A^{\bullet m}$ as one formula. In fact, they are of course equivalent.

One could try to extend the notion of n-th approximation to $\mathbf{!ACT}_\omega$:

$$N_n(!A) = !N_n(A) \qquad P_n(!A) = !P_n(A).$$

Now the derivability problem for sequents of the form $N_n(A_1), \ldots, N_n(A_k) \vdash P_n(B)$ becomes undecidable (since it includes $\mathbf{!MALC}$), but it is still in Σ_1^0 (recursively enumerable). Thus if the *-elimination lemma could have been extended to $\mathbf{!ACT}_\omega$, we would enjoy a Π_2^0 upper bound, which coincides with the lower one (Theorem 3).

However, the following example shows that it is not the case.

Example 2. The sequent

$$s, !(s \setminus ((\mathbf{1} \wedge q) \cdot s)), s \setminus t, t \setminus (q \setminus \mathbf{1})^* \vdash \mathbf{1}$$

is not derivable in $\mathbf{!ACT}_\omega$, but all its approximations are.

The idea behind this example is as follows: the "key and lock" variables s and t enforce decomposing of $(q \setminus \mathbf{1})^*$ (using $*_{\mathrm{L}\omega}$) *after* performing contractions and decomposing all copies of $!(s \setminus ((\mathbf{1} \wedge q) \cdot s))$. Since ! is roughly $\exists$ and * is roughly $\forall$, this yields the order of quantifiers $\exists\forall$, which is Σ_2^0, not Π_2^0.

The "key and lock" technique goes back to Lincoln et al. [16].

The n-th approximation of the sequent in question is as follows:

$$s, !(s \setminus ((\mathbf{1} \wedge q) \cdot s)), s \setminus t, t \setminus (\mathbf{1} \vee (q \setminus \mathbf{1}) \vee (q \setminus \mathbf{1})^2 \vee \ldots \vee (q \setminus \mathbf{1})^n) \vdash \mathbf{1}$$

Its proof is routine. We start as follows:

$$\dfrac{s \vdash s \quad \dfrac{t \vdash t \quad (\mathbf{1} \wedge q)^n, \mathbf{1} \vee (q \setminus \mathbf{1}) \vee \ldots \vee (q \setminus \mathbf{1})^n \vdash \mathbf{1}}{(\mathbf{1} \wedge q)^n, t, t \setminus (\mathbf{1} \vee (q \setminus \mathbf{1}) \vee \ldots \vee (q \setminus \mathbf{1})^n) \vdash \mathbf{1}} \setminus L}{(\mathbf{1} \wedge q)^n, s, s \setminus t, t \setminus (\mathbf{1} \vee (q \setminus \mathbf{1}) \vee \ldots \vee (q \setminus \mathbf{1})^n) \vdash \mathbf{1}} \setminus L$$

$$\vdots$$

$$\dfrac{\dfrac{\dfrac{s \vdash s \quad \dfrac{\mathbf{1} \wedge q, s, (s \setminus ((\mathbf{1} \wedge q) \cdot s))^{n-1}, s \setminus t, t \setminus \ldots \vdash \mathbf{1}}{(\mathbf{1} \wedge q) \cdot s, (s \setminus ((\mathbf{1} \wedge q) \cdot s))^{n-1}, s \setminus t, t \setminus \ldots \vdash \mathbf{1}} \cdot L}{s, (s \setminus ((\mathbf{1} \wedge q) \cdot s))^n, s \setminus t, t \setminus (\mathbf{1} \vee (q \setminus \mathbf{1}) \vee (q \setminus \mathbf{1})^2 \vee \ldots \vee (q \setminus \mathbf{1})^n) \vdash \mathbf{1}} \setminus L}{s, (!(s \setminus ((\mathbf{1} \wedge q) \cdot s)))^n, s \setminus t, t \setminus (\mathbf{1} \vee (q \setminus \mathbf{1}) \vee (q \setminus \mathbf{1})^2 \vee \ldots \vee (q \setminus \mathbf{1})^n) \vdash \mathbf{1}} \,!L\ n \text{ times}}{s, !(s \setminus ((\mathbf{1} \wedge q) \cdot s)), s \setminus t, t \setminus (\mathbf{1} \vee (q \setminus \mathbf{1}) \vee (q \setminus \mathbf{1})^2 \vee \ldots \vee (q \setminus \mathbf{1})^n) \vdash \mathbf{1}} \,!C\ n-1 \text{ times}$$

Now, after decomposing the $\vee$'s in the topmost sequent, we need to derive all sequents of the form

$$(\mathbf{1} \wedge q)^n, (q \setminus \mathbf{1})^k \vdash \mathbf{1},$$

where $k = 0, \ldots, n$. We decompose the $\wedge$'s, taking k times q and $(n-k)$ times $\mathbf{1}$. The resulting sequent,

$$\mathbf{1}^{n-k}, q^k, (q \setminus \mathbf{1})^k \vdash \mathbf{1},$$

is easily derivable using $\setminus_{\mathrm{L}}$ and $\mathbf{1}_{\mathrm{L}}$.

In order to prove non-derivability of the original sequent,

$$s, !(s \setminus ((\mathbf{1} \wedge q) \cdot s)), s \setminus t, t \setminus (q \setminus \mathbf{1})^* \vdash \mathbf{1},$$

let us trace occurrences of the main $\setminus$ connective in $t \setminus (q \setminus \mathbf{1})^*$ up to its decomposition (using $\setminus_{\mathrm{L}}$). Below this decomposition, the only rules which could be applied are $\setminus_{\mathrm{L}}$, $\wedge_{\mathrm{L}}$, and rules for !. Thus, the trace does not branch.

Also notice that at each application of $\setminus_{\mathrm{L}}$ the formula $t \setminus (q \setminus \mathbf{1})^*$ should go to the right premise. (Notice that these applications of $\setminus_{\mathrm{L}}$ decompose other formulae, not $t \setminus (q \setminus \mathbf{1})^*$, since we are still below the decomposition of this formula.) This follows from the fact that in any sequent in our derivation the numbers of s and t occurrences should both be even. Indeed, such pairs of occurrences originate in axioms, and since in $s \setminus ((\mathbf{1} \wedge q) \cdot s)$ there are no t's and two s's, applying $!_{\mathrm{W}}$ and $!_{\mathrm{C}}$ does not alter this parity invariant. Now, if $t \setminus (q \setminus \mathbf{1})^*$ goes to the left premise of $\setminus_{\mathrm{L}}$, then this left premise either includes only one t, or an odd number of s's, contradiction.

Thus, the application of $\setminus_{\mathrm{L}}$ which decomposes $t \setminus (q \setminus \mathbf{1})^*$ looks as follows:

$$\frac{\Pi \vdash t \quad \Gamma, (q \setminus \mathbf{1})^*, \Delta \vdash \mathbf{1}}{\Gamma, \Pi, t \setminus (q \setminus \mathbf{1})^*, \Delta \vdash \mathbf{1}} \setminus_{\mathrm{L}}$$

Here formulae in Γ, Π, and Δ can be of the following forms: s, $!(s \setminus ((\mathbf{1} \wedge q) \cdot s))$, $s \setminus ((\mathbf{1} \wedge q) \cdot s)$, $(\mathbf{1} \wedge q) \cdot s$, $\mathbf{1} \wedge q$, $\mathbf{1}$, q, $s \setminus t$ and t. Moreover, there could be only one $s \setminus t$ or t (since it cannot be replicated by $!_{\mathrm{C}}$), and we could remove occurrences of $\mathbf{1}$, since $\mathbf{1}_{\mathrm{L}}$ is invertible (by cut with $\vdash \mathbf{1}$). Next, we also could immediately decompose $(\mathbf{1} \wedge q) \cdot s$, by invertibility of $\cdot_{\mathrm{L}}$ (again, using cut).

More interestingly, the occurrence of s (as a separate formula) also has to be unique. The reasoning for this is as follows. In order to get a new s, we have had to decompose $s \setminus ((\mathbf{1} \wedge q) \cdot s)$ by $\setminus_{\mathrm{L}}$. Let us introduce a counter for s which takes care of polarity: in $s \setminus A$, s is counted as -1, in other cases as $+1$. Such a counter for s should always be zero. Thus, when one decomposes $s \setminus ((\mathbf{1} \wedge q) \cdot s)$, the previous lonely s should go to the left premise, and in the right premise we again have only one $(\mathbf{1} \wedge q) \cdot s$, and, immediately applying $\cdot_{\mathrm{L}}$, get a unique lonely s.

Consider two cases.

Case 1. There is an occurrence of $s \setminus t$. (And, see above, it is unique.) Since the number of t's should be even, this occurrence goes to left premise, $\Pi \vdash t$. Since the number of s's should be even, the unique occurrence of s also goes to $\Pi \vdash t$. Thus, Γ and Δ could include only copies of $!(s \setminus ((\mathbf{1} \wedge q) \cdot s))$, $s \setminus ((\mathbf{1} \wedge q) \cdot s)$, $\mathbf{1} \wedge q$, and q. Due to the parity condition on s, we could not now decompose $s \setminus ((\mathbf{1} \wedge q) \cdot s)$. Therefore, there are actually no formulae of this form in Γ, Δ, and all formulae of the form $!(s \setminus ((\mathbf{1} \wedge q) \cdot s))$ should be eventually weakened. Thus, Γ and Δ include only copies of $\mathbf{1} \wedge q$ and q.

However, the $*_{\mathrm{L}\omega}$ rule is invertible (cut with $A^n \vdash A^*$), therefore, *all* sequents of the form $\Gamma, (q \setminus \mathbf{1})^m, \Delta \vdash \mathbf{1}$ should be derivable. Now let Γ and Δ include k formulae, each of the form $\mathbf{1} \wedge q$ or q. Taking $m > k$ yields a non-derivable sequent.

Case 2. There is a (unique) occurrence of t. In this case, there is no $s \setminus t$, and, by the parity condition for s, no lonely s. Thus, Γ and Δ could again include only copies of $!(s \setminus ((\mathbf{1} \wedge q) \cdot s))$, $s \setminus ((\mathbf{1} \wedge q) \cdot s)$, $\mathbf{1} \wedge q$, and q. Now we proceed exactly as in Case 1. □

In general, the "key and lock" technique allows imposing arbitrary priority on decomposition of ! and *. Since these connectives are in effect $\exists$ and $\forall$ quantifiers, this leads to a conjecture that our Π_2^0-hardness result can be strengthened to a higher, arithmetical lower bound. The important consideration here is that the independence constraint does not prevent us from simulating quantifier alternation. For example, $\exists\forall\exists$ could be simulated as to $s, !(s \setminus (A \cdot s)), s \setminus t, (t \setminus (B \cdot t))^*, t \setminus q, !(q \setminus (C \cdot q)), q \setminus \mathbf{1} \vdash D$, which roughly corresponds to $\exists n \, \forall m \, \exists k \, (A^n, B^m, C^k \vdash D)$.

6 Concluding Remarks

In this paper, we have considered infinitary action logic extended with exponential, that is, a bimodal extension of the multiplicative-additive Lambek calculus with both Kleene star with an ω-rule and the exponential modality from linear logic. The full system is Π_1^1-complete, while its unimodal fragments are below Δ_2^0: Π_1^0-complete and Σ_1^0-complete. This complexity gap motivates us to find a natural intermediate system, whose complexity is strictly in between. Such system, denoted by $\mathbf{!ACT}_\omega^-$, is naturally achieved by imposing the so-called *independence constraint:* the Kleene star is not allowed to appear in the scope of the exponential modality.

The independence constraint allows us to construct a well-behaved non-well-founded proof system, extending the one by Das and Pous [5]. This non-well-founded proof system has a very simple correctness condition, *-fairness, which gives a Σ_1^1 complexity upper bound. Together with the Π_1^1 upper bound for the full system, we get Δ_1^1.

For a lower bound, we get Π_2^0-hardness, by encoding the Horn theory for *-continuous Kleene algebra with *-free premises [12]. An attempt to apply Palka's [18] approach to prove a Π_2^0 upper bound, however, fails.

We conclude with several directions of further research.

1. The actual complexity of $\mathbf{!ACT}_\omega^-$ remains open, and we suppose that tighter lower bounds could be achieved. Namely, we conjecture an arithmetical lower bound, but still have no idea whether the system is in fact arithmetical or hyperarithmetical.
2. The non-well-founded proof system described in this paper is sound for $\mathbf{!ACT}_\omega^-$, but not for the full $\mathbf{!ACT}_\omega$. The question of developing a good non-well-founded proof system which is equivalent to the full $\mathbf{!ACT}_\omega$ and studying its proof-theoretic properties (mainly cut elimination), though not needed for complexity purposes, is interesting on its own right.
3. It should be not hard to extend our results to systems with several subexponential modalities instead of one exponential, see [9].

4. Finally, transferring the results of the present paper to the commutative case is also an open issue. Being interesting on its own, it is also motivated by related work. Namely, the μ**MALL** system [1] allows encoding of both Kleene star and exponential, but in a commutative setting. Thus, porting our results to the commutative setting would also say something about infinitary extensions of μ**MALL**.

Acknowledgments. The author is grateful to Anupam Das and Stanislav Speranski for fruitful discussions. The author also thanks the reviewers for thorough consideration of the paper and many valuable suggestions.

References

1. Baelde, D.: Least and greatest fixed points in linear logic. ACM Trans. Comput. Log. **13**(1), 2:1–2:44 (2012)
2. Buszkowski, W.: Lambek calculus with nonlogical axioms. In: Casadio, C., et al. (eds.) Language and Grammar, Studies in Mathematical Linguistics and Natural Language, pp. 77–93. CSLI Publications (2002)
3. Buszkowski, W.: On action logic: equational theories of action algebras. J. Log. Comput. **17**(1), 199–217 (2007)
4. Buszkowski, W., Palka, E.: Infinitary action logic: complexity, models and grammars. Stud. Logica **89**(1), 1–18 (2008)
5. Das, A., Pous, D.: Non-well-founded proof theory for (Kleene+action) (algebras+lattices). In: 27th EACSL Annual Conference on Computer Science Logic (CSL 2018). Leibniz International Proceedings in Informatics (LIPIcs), vol. 119, pp. 19:1–19:18. Schloss Dagstuhl-Leibniz-Zentrum für Informatik, Dagstuhl, Germany (2018). https://doi.org/10.4230/LIPIcs.CSL.2018.19
6. Galatos, N., Jipsen, P., Kowalski, T., Ono, H.: Residuated Lattices: An Algebraic Glimpse at Substructural Logics. Studies in Logic and the Foundations of Mathematics, vol. 151. Elsevier (2007)
7. Girard, J.Y.: Linear logic. Theoret. Comput. Sci. **50**(1), 1–102 (1987)
8. de Groote, P.: On the expressive power of the Lambek calculus extended with a structural modality. In: Casadio, C., et al. (eds.) Language and Grammar. Studies in Mathematical Linguistics and Natural Language, CSLI Lecture Notes, vol. 168, pp. 95–111 (2005)
9. Kanovich, M., Kuznetsov, S., Nigam, V., Scedrov, A.: Subexponentials in non-commutative linear logic. Math. Struct. Comput. Sci. **29**(8), 1217–1249 (2019)
10. Kanovich, M., Kuznetsov, S., Nigam, V., Scedrov, A.: Soft subexponentials and multiplexing. In: Peltier, N., Sofronie-Stokkermans, V. (eds.) IJCAR 2020. LNCS (LNAI), vol. 12166, pp. 500–517. Springer, Cham (2020). https://doi.org/10.1007/978-3-030-51074-9_29
11. Kozen, D.: On action algebras. In: van Eijck, J., Visser, A. (eds.) Logic and Information Flow, pp. 78–88. MIT Press (1994)
12. Kozen, D.: On the complexity of reasoning in Kleene algebra. Inf. Comput. **179**, 152–162 (2002)
13. Kuznetsov, S.: Action logic is undecidable. ACM Trans. Comput. Log. **22**(2), 10:1–10:26 (2021)

14. Kuznetsov, S.L.: A Π_1^0-bounded fragment of infinitary action logic with exponential. In: Nigam, V., et al. (eds.) Logic, Language, and Security. LNCS, vol. 12300, pp. 3–16. Springer, Cham (2020). https://doi.org/10.1007/978-3-030-62077-6_1
15. Kuznetsov, S.L., Speranski, S.O.: Infinitary action logic with exponentiation. arXiv preprint arXiv:2001.06863 (2020, submitted)
16. Lincoln, P., Mitchell, J., Scedrov, A., Shankar, N.: Decision problems for propositional linear logic. Ann. Pure Appl. Logic **56**(1–3), 239–311 (1992)
17. Ono, H., Komori, Y.: Logics without contraction rule. J. Symb. Log. **50**(1), 169–201 (1985)
18. Palka, E.: An infinitary sequent system for the equational theory of *-continuous action lattices. Fund. Inform. **78**(2), 295–309 (2007)
19. Pratt, V.: Action logic and pure induction. In: van Eijck, J. (ed.) JELIA 1990. LNCS, vol. 478, pp. 97–120. Springer, Heidelberg (1991). https://doi.org/10.1007/BFb0018436
20. Rogozin, D.: Quantale semantics of Lambek calculus with subexponential modalities. arXiv preprint arXiv:1908.01055 (2019)
21. Wurm, C.: Language-theoretic and finite relation models for the (full) Lambek calculus. J. Logic Lang. Inform. **26**(2), 179–214 (2017)

Uniform Interpolation from Cyclic Proofs: The Case of Modal Mu-Calculus

Bahareh Afshari[1,2(✉)], Graham E. Leigh[2], and Guillermo Menéndez Turata[1]

[1] Institute for Logic, Language and Computation, University of Amsterdam, Amsterdam, The Netherlands
{b.afshari,g.m.t.menendezturata}@uva.nl

[2] Department of Philosophy, Linguistics and Theory of Science, University of Gothenburg, Gothenburg, Sweden
graham.leigh@gu.se

Abstract. We show how to construct uniform interpolants in the context of the modal mu-calculus. D'Agostino and Hollenberg (2000) were the first to prove that this logic has the uniform interpolation property, employing a combination of semantic and syntactic methods. This article outlines a purely proof-theoretic approach to the problem based on insights from the cyclic proof theory of mu-calculus. We argue the approach has the potential to lend itself to other temporal and fixed point logics.

Keywords: Modal mu-calculus · Sequent calculus · Uniform interpolation · Cyclic proofs

1 Introduction

Uniform interpolation is frequently listed among the most desirable properties a logic may have. Let $\mathsf{Voc}(\varphi)$ denote the non-logical vocabulary of a formula φ.[1] A logic has the uniform interpolation property if given any formula φ and vocabulary $V \subseteq \mathsf{Voc}(\varphi)$, there exists a formula I with $\mathsf{Voc}(I) \subseteq V$, the *uniform interpolant*, such that for every ψ with $\mathsf{Voc}(\psi) \cap \mathsf{Voc}(\varphi) \subseteq V$ we have

$$\varphi \to \psi \text{ is valid iff } I \to \psi \text{ is valid.}$$

Upon inspection one sees that uniform interpolation is tightly knitted to deeper semantic considerations. Uniform interpolants simulate quantification. For example, in the case of propositional logic, if $\mathsf{Voc}(\varphi) \setminus V$ is a set of propositional constants $\{p_1, \ldots, p_k\}$ then the formula I above expresses $\exists p_1 \cdots \exists p_k \varphi$. This also

[1] This definition depends on the choice of underlying logic. For example, in the case of polymodal logic, $\mathsf{Voc}(\varphi)$ is the set of propositional constants and modal actions occurring in φ.

Supported by the Knut and Alice Wallenberg Foundation [2015.0179] and the Swedish Research Council [2016-03502 & 2017-05111]. The authors would like to thank the anonymous referees for their valuable comments.

A. Das and S. Negri (Eds.): TABLEAUX 2021, LNAI 12842, pp. 335–353, 2021.
https://doi.org/10.1007/978-3-030-86059-2_20

somewhat goes to explain why it is a challenging question: it does not reside entirely in the realm of syntax or semantics, thereby limiting the techniques available to tackle the problem.

A considerable body of research has been devoted to studying interpolation properties of logics, and the landscape is moderately clear [13,24]. Nevertheless, though perhaps not so surprising, proofs of uniform interpolation differ wildly from one system to another, leaving the question yet open for a number of interesting logical systems. There have been efforts to find general frameworks to attack the problem. Iemhoff [25,26] identifies sufficient (but not necessary) conditions on the form of proof systems that entail uniform interpolation. In modal logics, uniform interpolation is intimately connected to the definability of bisimulation quantifiers [16,43].

From a proof-theoretic perspective, the idea that uniform interpolation is tied to provability is a natural one. Thinking about Craig interpolation for the moment, if a 'nice' proof of a valid implication $\varphi \to \psi$ is available, one may succeed in defining an interpolant by induction on the proof-tree, starting from leaves and proceeding to the implication at the root. This method has recently been applied even to fixed point logics admitting cyclic proofs [2,38]. In contrast, for uniform interpolation, there is no single proof to work from but a collection of proofs to accommodate: a witness to each valid implication $\varphi \to \psi$ where the vocabulary of ψ is constrained. Working over a set of prospective proofs and relying on the structural properties of sequent calculus is the essence of Pitts' seminal result on uniform interpolation for intuitionistic logic [35].

In this article, we adapt Pitts' technique to the modal μ-calculus, a fixed point modal logic with an elegant mathematical theory that holds a prominent place among temporal logics. Uniform interpolation for the modal μ-calculus was established by D'Agostino and Hollenberg [14]. Their proof utilises modal automata [27] to show definability of bisimulation quantifiers in modal μ-calculus [35,43] (see also [15,16]). With this form of second-order quantification, uniform interpolants can be readily defined.

One may wonder why Pitts' method has not been exploited for the modal μ-calculus. A notable appeal of such a syntactic method is the direct construction of interpolants, without recourse to intermediate structures such as automata. One possible answer is that the method applies only in a setting where one can argue inductively over the cut-free derivations of a *finitary* system. In other words, the approach is helpless in the context of non-analytic or infinitary proofs.

While it is feasible to design analytic (complete) tableaux systems for many fixed point logics, they are often infinitary, i.e., the proof-tree can have infinite branches. The first deductive system for the μ-calculus for which completeness was established is indeed a system of ill-founded (cut-free) derivations, due to Niwiński and Walukiewicz [34]. With the advance of cyclic proof theory in recent years, it has been possible to obtain finite proof graphs that can witness validity. For modal μ-calculus specifically, an annotated goal-oriented system was given by Jungteerapanich [28] and Stirling [41] and it is a reformulation of that system which is utilised in the present work. A different cyclic proof system based on the

Jungteerapanich–Stirling system was exploited to establish Lyndon interpolation for the modal μ-calculus [2], a strengthening of Craig interpolation not implied by uniform interpolation. It is unclear whether the argument in [2] can be applied to uniform interpolation as the proof system employed lacks the requisite uniformity for a Pitts-style treatment.

The main ideas and concepts we present are not specific to modal μ-calculus but do rely on two of its essential features: the existence of (cyclic) analytic tableaux and expression of fixed points. As such we anticipate that the main argument is applicable to other logics admitting regular proof trees. That project, however, is reserved for future investigation.

Outline. In the next section we give a brief account of the syntax of μ-calculus and its equivalent formulation in terms of systems of equations which greatly facilitate defining interpolants. Section 3 presents our version of the Jungteerapanich–Stirling calculus and related concepts including that of a proof invariant and proofs in normal form. In Sect. 4 we describe the overall idea of the method and a key ingredient of our approach: construction of an interpolation 'template' for a formula encoding information about prospective proofs involving this formula. Section 5 is dedicated to the definition of the uniform interpolant and the verification of the main theorem is carried out in the subsequent section. In the conclusion we expand on some points already touched on in the introduction and further research questions of interest.

2 The Modal μ-calculus

Fix a countably infinite set Var of *variables* $X, Y, \dots$ and a set Act of *modal actions* $a, b, \dots$. The *formulas of the modal μ-calculus* are given by the following grammar:

$$\varphi := \top \mid \bot \mid X \mid \varphi \wedge \varphi \mid \varphi \vee \varphi \mid [a]\varphi \mid \langle a\rangle\varphi \mid \mu X\varphi \mid \nu X\varphi,$$

where X ranges over Var and a over Act. The language does not contain propositional constant symbols as these may be encoded by additional modal actions.

Formulas are denoted by lower-case Greek letters $\varphi, \psi, \chi, \dots$, and finite sets of formulas by upper-case Greek letters $\Gamma, \Delta, \Sigma, \dots$. An *atom* is either $\top$ or $\bot$. A *quantifier-free* formula is one built from atoms and variables via modal operators $[a]$, $\langle a\rangle$ and connectives $\wedge$ and $\vee$. A $[a]$*-formula* is one of the form $[a]\varphi$. A $[\cdot]$*-formula* is a $[a]$-formula for any $a \in \mathsf{Act}$. $\langle a\rangle$- and $\langle\cdot\rangle$-formulas are defined analogously. A *modal* formula is either a $[\cdot]$- or a $\langle\cdot\rangle$-formula. Define $[a]\Gamma = \{[a]\gamma \mid \gamma \in \Gamma\}$ and $\langle a\rangle\Gamma$ similarly.

An occurrence of a variable X in a formula φ is *bound* if it is within the scope of a quantifier σX for some $\sigma \in \{\mu, \nu\}$, and it is *free* otherwise. A formula is *closed* if no variable occurs free in it. A set of formulas is *closed* if every element is closed. We say that φ is *well-named* if no variable in φ occurs both free and bound and no variable is bound more than once. Each bound variable X of a well-named formula φ uniquely identifies a subformula $\sigma_X X\varphi_X$ of φ. When no ambiguity arises we express this association as $X =_{\sigma_X} \varphi_X$. A formula

φ is *guarded* if, for any subformula $\sigma X\psi$ of φ, every occurrence of X in ψ is within a modal subformula of ψ. It is well known that every formula of the modal μ-calculus is equivalent to a guarded one. A finite set of formulas Γ is *closed/guarded/well-named* if and only if the conjunction of elements $\bigwedge_{\gamma\in\Gamma}\gamma$ is.

It will be convenient to utilise a more succinct notation for μ-calculus formulas. Modal/hierarchical equational systems provide an expressively equivalent formalism meeting our needs. For the purpose of this article, a *modal equational system* is a pair $(\varphi, \mathcal{E})$ where φ is a quantifier-free formula over a set of variables $V_\mathcal{E}$ and $\mathcal{E}$ is a set of equations $\{X =_{p_X} \varphi_X \mid X \in V_\mathcal{E}\}$ where φ_X is a quantifier-free formula over $V_\mathcal{E}$ and $p_X \in \mathbb{N}$ for each $X \in V_\mathcal{E}$. The system $(\varphi, \mathcal{E})$ uniquely determines a μ-calculus formula $\varphi_\mathcal{E}$ given as follows. Let $V_\mathcal{E} = \{X_0, \dots, X_n\}$ where $p_{X_i} \leq p_{X_j}$ for each $i < j \leq n$. The formula $\varphi_\mathcal{E}$ is specified by recursively substituting $\sigma_i X_i \varphi_{X_i}$ for X_i in all equations starting from $i = n$ where $\sigma_i = \mu$ iff p_{X_i} is odd. In other words, the equations $X_i =_{p_{X_i}} \varphi_{X_i}$ of $(\varphi, \mathcal{E})$ correspond to associations $X_i =_{\sigma_i} \hat{\varphi}_{X_i}$ in $\varphi_\mathcal{E}$ where $\hat{\varphi}_{X_i}$ is a substitution instance of φ_{X_i}, and the ordering of the priorities corresponds to the subsumption order of $\varphi_\mathcal{E}$. We refer the reader to [21, §8.3.4] for details. In the following, whenever a system $(\varphi, \mathcal{E})$ is referred to as a formula we mean the formula $\varphi_\mathcal{E}$ described above.

We assume the reader is familiar with denotational semantics for formulas of μ-calculus over, for example, labelled transition systems (see, e.g. [21, §8.1.2]). A formula whose denotation over every labelled transition system is the set of states of the system is called *valid*.

3 The JS proof system

Based on tableaux for satisfiability by Jungteerapanich [28], Stirling [41] introduces a sound and complete tableau-style proof system for the modal μ-calculus in which formulas are enriched with annotations that keep track of fixed point unfoldings. In this section we present a Gentzen-style, two-sided version of the Jungteerapanich–Stirling system.

A *(plain) sequent* is a pair (Γ, Δ), henceforth written $\Gamma \Rightarrow \Delta$, where Γ and Δ are finite sets of formulas. A sequent $\Gamma \Rightarrow \Delta$ is *closed/guarded/well-named* iff $\Gamma \cup \Delta$ is closed/guarded/well-named. A closed sequent $\Gamma \Rightarrow \Delta$ is *valid* if the induced formula $\bigwedge_{\gamma\in\Gamma}\gamma \rightarrow \bigvee_{\delta\in\Delta}\delta$ is valid, where the connective $\rightarrow$ is defined in terms of disjunction and negation (the latter expressed via de Morgan duality). When working with sequents we shall frequently abbreviate $\Gamma \cup \Delta$ to Γ, Δ and $\Gamma, \{\varphi\}$ to Γ, φ.

For every $X \in \mathsf{Var}$ let a countably infinite set $\mathsf{N}_X = \{x_0, x_1, \dots\}$ of *names* for X be fixed such that $\mathsf{N}_X \cap \mathsf{N}_Y = \varnothing$ if $X \neq Y$. We denote names for variables $X, Y, Z, \dots$ by $x, y, z, \dots$ respectively (possibly with indices) and let $\mathsf{N} = \bigcup_{X\in\mathsf{Var}} \mathsf{N}_X$. An *annotation* is a finite sequence of pairwise distinct names in N. Given an annotation u we denote by $|u|$ the length of u. An *annotated* formula is a pair (u, φ), henceforth written φ^u, where φ is a formula and u is an annotation for variables occurring in φ. A name x occurs in Γ if x occurs in the annotation of some formula in Γ. An *(annotated) sequent* is a triple (Θ, Γ, Δ), henceforth written $\Theta : \Gamma \Rightarrow \Delta$, where Θ is an annotation in names for variables in $\Gamma \cup \Delta$, and Γ and Δ are finite sets of annotated formulae such that every name in Θ occurs in $\Gamma \cup \Delta$. The annotation Θ is called the *control* of $\Theta : \Gamma \Rightarrow \Delta$. We identify annotated sequents whose control is empty with plain sequents.

Let φ be closed and well-named. Fix an arbitrary linear ordering of the variables in φ, say $X_1 \lhd X_2 \lhd \cdots \lhd X_n$, compatible with the subsumption ordering on φ, i.e., such that $i < j$ implies φ_{X_i} is not a subformula of φ_{X_j}. If φ is given as an equational system, $\lhd$ can be chosen as any linear order such that $p_X < p_Y$ implies $X \lhd Y$. Given an annotation u for variables in φ, we denote by $u{\restriction}X_i$ the result of removing from u all names for $X_{i+1},\ldots,X_n$.

We now define the JS sequent calculus. The system operates on annotated sequents, i.e., expressions $\Theta : \Gamma \Rightarrow \Delta$ defined above. The axioms and rules of JS are given in Fig. 1. Applications of the rules are subject to three restrictions:

- Θ' is the subsequence of Θ given by removing any name which does not occur in the sequent whose control is Θ'. This applies to the rules LW, RW, Lμ, Rμ, Lν, Rν, LMod, RMod, LReset and RReset.
- In Lμ and Rν x is a name for the variable X not occurring in Θ, and $\Theta' x$ is the concatenation of Θ' and the annotation consisting of the single name x.
- In LReset$_z$ and RReset$_z$ the names z, z_1, ..., z_k all name the same variable; the other annotations (u, u_1, ..., u_k) are arbitrary.
- In LReset$_z$ the name z may not occur in Γ and in RReset$_z$ the name z may not occur in Δ.

By Mod (Reset) we denote either LMod or RMod (resp., LReset or RReset).

Definition 1. *A derivation of a closed and well-named sequent $\Gamma \Rightarrow \Delta$ is a finite tree P of annotated sequents in accordance with the rules of* JS *(subject to the restrictions above) with root $\Gamma \Rightarrow \Delta$, together with a map $l \mapsto c_l$ which assigns to every non-axiomatic leaf $l \in P$ a vertex $c_l <_P l$, where $<_P$ denotes the ancestor relation of P, such that the sequents at l and c_l are identical. We refer to c_l as the* companion *of l and to l as a* repeat.

A proof in the JS calculus is a derivation for which all repeat leaves fulfil a correctness condition that we now define.

Definition 2 (Invariant; Successful repeat). *Let P be a* JS *derivation and l a repeat leaf of P with companion c_l. Let Θ be the longest common prefix of all controls on the path $[c_l, l]_P$ from c_l to l. The* invariant *of l, in symbols* $\mathsf{inv}_P(l)$, *is the shortest prefix of Θ of the form ux where* Reset$_x$ *occurs on the path $[c_l, l]$. If no such prefix exists, define* $\mathsf{inv}_P(l) = \Theta$. *The repeat leaf l is* successful *iff* $\mathsf{inv}_P(l)$ *is of the first form above.*

The notion of an invariant for a repeat leaf does not feature in the presentations of the calculus in [28,41]. However, it is an easy exercise to show that a repeat is successful in the sense above if and only if it is successful in the sense of [41].

Definition 3 (JS **proof).** *A proof is a* JS *derivation P such that every non-axiomatic leaf is a successful repeat.*

$$\mathsf{Ax}_\bot\ \frac{}{\Theta : \Gamma, \bot^u \Rightarrow \Delta} \qquad \mathsf{Ax}_\top\ \frac{}{\Theta : \Gamma \Rightarrow \top^u, \Delta}$$

$$\mathsf{LW}\ \frac{\Theta' : \Gamma \Rightarrow \Delta}{\Theta : \Gamma, \Pi \Rightarrow \Delta} \qquad \mathsf{RW}\ \frac{\Theta' : \Gamma \Rightarrow \Delta}{\Theta : \Gamma \Rightarrow \Sigma, \Delta}$$

$$\mathsf{L}\wedge\ \frac{\Theta : \Gamma, \varphi^u, \psi^u \Rightarrow \Delta}{\Theta : \Gamma, \varphi \wedge \psi^u \Rightarrow \Delta} \qquad \mathsf{R}\vee\ \frac{\Theta : \Gamma \Rightarrow \varphi^u, \psi^u, \Delta}{\Theta : \Gamma \Rightarrow \varphi \vee \psi^u, \Delta}$$

$$\mathsf{L}\vee\ \frac{\Theta : \Gamma, \varphi^u \Rightarrow \Delta \qquad \Theta : \Gamma, \psi^u \Rightarrow \Delta}{\Theta : \Gamma, \varphi \vee \psi^u \Rightarrow \Delta} \qquad \mathsf{R}\wedge\ \frac{\Theta : \Gamma \Rightarrow \varphi^u, \Delta \qquad \Theta : \Gamma \Rightarrow \psi^u, \Delta}{\Theta : \Gamma \Rightarrow \varphi \wedge \psi^u, \Delta}$$

$$\mathsf{L}\mu\ \frac{\Theta' x : \Gamma, \varphi^{(u\restriction X)x} \Rightarrow \Delta}{\Theta : \Gamma, X^u \Rightarrow \Delta}\ X =_\mu \varphi \qquad \mathsf{R}\mu\ \frac{\Theta' : \Gamma \Rightarrow \varphi^{u\restriction X}, \Delta}{\Theta : \Gamma \Rightarrow X^u, \Delta}\ X =_\mu \varphi$$

$$\mathsf{L}\nu\ \frac{\Theta' : \Gamma, \varphi^{u\restriction X} \Rightarrow \Delta}{\Theta : \Gamma, X^u \Rightarrow \Delta}\ X =_\nu \varphi \qquad \mathsf{R}\nu\ \frac{\Theta' x : \Gamma \Rightarrow \varphi^{(u\restriction X)x}, \Delta}{\Theta : \Gamma \Rightarrow X^u, \Delta}\ X =_\nu \varphi$$

$$\mathsf{LMod}\ \frac{\Theta' : \Gamma, \varphi^u \Rightarrow \Delta}{\Theta : [a]\Gamma, \Pi, \langle a \rangle \varphi^u \Rightarrow \langle a \rangle \Delta, \Sigma} \qquad \mathsf{RMod}\ \frac{\Theta' : \Gamma \Rightarrow \varphi^u, \Delta}{\Theta : [a]\Gamma, \Pi \Rightarrow [a]\varphi^u, \langle a \rangle \Delta, \Sigma}$$

$$\mathsf{LReset}_z\ \frac{\Theta' : \Gamma, \varphi_1^{uz}, \ldots, \varphi_k^{uz} \Rightarrow \Delta}{\Theta : \Gamma, \varphi_1^{uzz_1u_1}, \ldots, \varphi_k^{uzz_ku_k} \Rightarrow \Delta} \qquad \mathsf{RReset}_z\ \frac{\Theta' : \Gamma \Rightarrow \varphi_1^{uz}, \ldots, \varphi_k^{uz}, \Delta}{\Theta : \Gamma \Rightarrow \varphi_1^{uzz_1u_1}, \ldots, \varphi_k^{uzz_ku_k}, \Delta}$$

Fig. 1. Rules of the JS system.

The role of the annotations is to keep track of unfoldings of fixpoint variables. Figure 2 shows a proof of the valid formula $\nu Z \mu X([a]Z \vee \langle a \rangle X)$ with corresponding modal equational system $(Z, \{Z =_0 X,\ X =_1 [a]Z \vee \langle a \rangle X\})$. The name z is preserved and reset in between the companion node and the repeat, so the repeat is successful.

We write $P \vdash \Gamma \Rightarrow \Delta$ to express that P is a proof of the (closed, well-named) sequent $\Gamma \Rightarrow \Delta$, and $\mathsf{JS} \vdash \Gamma \Rightarrow \Delta$ if and only if there exists a proof of $\Gamma \Rightarrow \Delta$. The following can be proved by reduction of the two-sided calculus JS to its one-sided fragment and appealing to the main result of [41].

Theorem 1. JS *is sound and complete with respect to validity for closed, well-named and guarded sequents.*

Before turning to the statement and proof of uniform interpolation, we present some important restrictions on applications of the rules of JS which does not affect the completeness theorem above. Following these observations, we establish a property of JS proofs which plays a crucial role in our proof of the uniform interpolation property. The property in question is that a finite unfolding of a JS proof – given by identifying repeat leaves with their companions – is a JS proof, and an invariant for a leaf in the unfolding is the invariant of some leaf in the original proof.

$$
\begin{array}{ll}
 & z : \varnothing \Rightarrow X^{z} \\
\hline
\mathsf{RReset}_z & zz' : \varnothing \Rightarrow X^{zz'} \\
\hline
\mathsf{RW} & zz' : \varnothing \Rightarrow X^{zz'}, X^{z} \\
\hline
\mathsf{R}\nu & z : \varnothing \Rightarrow Z^{z}, X^{z} \\
\hline
\mathsf{RMod} & z : \varnothing \Rightarrow [a]Z^{z}, \langle a \rangle X^{z} \\
\hline
\mathsf{R}\vee & z : \varnothing \Rightarrow ([a]Z \vee \langle a \rangle X)^{z} \\
\hline
\mathsf{R}\mu & z : \varnothing \Rightarrow X^{z} \\
\hline
\mathsf{R}\nu & : \varnothing \Rightarrow Z
\end{array}
$$

Fig. 2. A JS proof of $\nu Z \mu X([a]Z \vee \langle a \rangle X)$.

The structural rules of weakening are also implicit in our formulation of the modal rules LMod and RMod. Any JS proof can be converted into a proof without LW or RW. Although the argument is straightforward, some care is required as altering sequents in a JS proof can result in leaves and companions no longer being identical sequents. Weakening, however, serves a special purpose in the Jungteerapanich–Stirling calculus as a rule for maintaining a bound on the size of sequents in proof-search. To show completeness for JS a proof is constructed in which the left and right weakening rules are utilised in a specific form for eliminating (reading the rule from conclusion to premise) an occurrence of a formula if it occurs with two (distinct) annotations:

$$
\mathsf{LThin}\ \frac{\Theta' : \Gamma, \varphi^{u} \Rightarrow \Delta}{\Theta : \Gamma, \varphi^{u}, \varphi^{v} \Rightarrow \Delta}\ u \sqsubset_{\Theta} v \qquad \mathsf{RThin}\ \frac{\Theta' : \Gamma \Rightarrow \varphi^{u}, \Delta}{\Theta : \Gamma \Rightarrow \varphi^{u}, \varphi^{v}, \Delta}\ u \sqsubset_{\Theta} v
$$

LThin and RThin are referred to as *thinning rules.* As before, in both inferences Θ' denotes the result of removing from Θ any name which does not occur in $\Gamma \cup \Delta \cup \{\varphi^{u}\}$. The relation $\sqsubset_{\Theta}$ is a total ordering on subsequences of Θ defined as follows. If Θ is an annotation and u, v are subsequences of Θ, set $u <_{\Theta} v$ iff u precedes v in the lexicographic ordering induced by Θ. Then define $u \sqsubset_{\Theta} v$ as either $u <_{\Theta} v$ or there is some variable X such that $v{\restriction}X$ is a proper prefix of $u{\restriction}X$. We refer the reader to [29, §4.3] for the proof that $\sqsubset_{\Theta}$ is a total order on subsequences of Θ.

In the presence of the thinning rules, Stirling's completeness proof for the one-sided system shows it is possible to dispense entirely with weakening, both in the explicit form of LW and RW and implicitly in the modal inferences. Moreover, provided sequents are guarded it suffices that the conclusion to the modal rules LMod and RMod is a sequent of modal formulas and atoms only.

Further restrictions can be imposed on proofs in JS. These are outlined by the next definition. The first three restrictions mirror standard conditions that can be imposed on analytic sequent calculi for basic modal logic. Conditions 4 and 5 enforce uniformity on the rules manipulating annotations. The final condition places a similar condition on the logical inferences, with the effect that two incomparable vertices of a normal proof which are labelled by the same annotated sequent have identical sub-proof up to repeat leafs. The requirement is trivial for proofs of quantifier-free formulas; for quantified formulas it is a corollary of the fact that JS proofs are closed under unravelling repeat leaves.

Definition 4 (Normal proof). *A* JS *proof P is normal if the following conditions hold of P.*

1. *The only applications of weakening are the thinning rules.*
2. LMod *or* RMod *is permitted only in cases where (referring to the form of the rule in Fig. 1) Π consists of only $\top$, $\langle\cdot\rangle$-formulas and $[c]$-formulas for $c \neq a$, and Σ of only $\bot$, $[\cdot]$-formulas, and $\langle c\rangle$-formulas for $c \neq a$.*
3. *Any sequent which is an instance of an axiom is a leaf.*
4. *In instances of $\mathsf{L}\mu$ and $\mathsf{R}\nu$, x is the first name in N_X not occurring in Θ.*
5. *If a sequent $\Theta : \Gamma \Rightarrow \Delta$ in P can be realised as the conclusion of an instance of* LThin, RThin, LReset *or* RReset *then the sequent is the conclusion of this rule in P, with the thinning rules having precedence over reset rules.*
6. *Any two non-repeat vertices of P labelled by the same sequent are instances of the same rule instantiation.*

The following is a direct consequence of the completeness theorem for the one-sided fragment of JS by Stirling [41].

Theorem 2. *A closed, well-named and guarded sequent $\Gamma \Rightarrow \Delta$ is valid iff there exists a normal* JS *proof of $\Gamma \Rightarrow \Delta$.*

We conclude this section with two results concerning the definition of invariant of a repeat leaf.

Fix a JS derivation P and let Rep_P be the set of repeat leaves of P. We define two relations on elements of Rep_P. The first is a reflexive and transitive relation $\preceq$ given by setting $l \preceq l'$ if $\mathsf{inv}_P(l)$ is a prefix of $\mathsf{inv}_P(l')$. The second relation $\rightsquigarrow$ is defined as reachability between repeat vertices: $l \rightsquigarrow l'$ iff $c_l <_P l'$, i.e., there is a (simple) path in P from the companion of l to l'. Note that $\rightsquigarrow$ need not be symmetric or transitive.

The following two observations link invariants to the 'unfolding' of JS proofs. Both results are immediate consequences of our notion of invariant.

Proposition 1. *For every infinite $\rightsquigarrow$-chain $l_0 \rightsquigarrow l_1 \rightsquigarrow \cdots$ there exists $k \geq 0$ such that $l_k \preceq l_j$ for all $j \geq k$.*

Proposition 2. *Let P be a proof and $l \in \mathrm{Rep}_P$. The result of inserting a copy of the sub-derivation of P with root c_l at the leaf l is a* JS *proof. Any invariant of a repeat in the resulting proof is an invariant of a repeat in P.*

4 Uniform Interpolation

With the proof system now fixed, we present the statement of uniform interpolation that will be proved. The *vocabulary* of a formula φ, in symbols $\mathsf{Voc}(\varphi)$, is the set of modal actions occurring in φ. The vocabulary of a set of formulas Φ is $\mathsf{Voc}(\Phi) = \bigcup_{\varphi\in\Phi} \mathsf{Voc}(\varphi)$. In the following $\vdash \Gamma \Rightarrow \Delta$ expresses $\mathsf{JS} \vdash \Gamma \Rightarrow \Delta$.

Theorem 3. *Let Γ be a finite well-named set of modal μ-calculus formulas and $V \subseteq \mathsf{Voc}(\Gamma)$. There exists a formula I such that: (i) $\mathsf{Voc}(I) \subseteq V$, (ii) $\vdash \Gamma \Rightarrow I$, and (iii) for every Δ such that $\Gamma \Rightarrow \Delta$ is a well-named sequent and $\mathsf{Voc}(\Delta) \cap \mathsf{Voc}(\Gamma) \subseteq V$, if $\vdash \Gamma \Rightarrow \Delta$, then $\vdash I \Rightarrow \Delta$.*

We call the formula I of Theorem 3 the *(uniform) interpolant of Γ relative to V*. Mention of the fixed vocabulary V will be suppressed when it can be inferred from context. Note that the statement of uniform interpolation in Theorem 3 is equivalent to the version on page 1.

The Craig interpolation property is a special case of uniform interpolation.

Corollary 1. *If $\vdash \Gamma \Rightarrow \Delta$ and $\Gamma \Rightarrow \Delta$ is well-named then there exists a formula I such that $\mathsf{Voc}(I) \subseteq \mathsf{Voc}(\Gamma) \cap \mathsf{Voc}(\Delta)$, $\vdash \Gamma \Rightarrow I$ and $\vdash I \Rightarrow \Delta$.*

Proof. Let $\Gamma \Rightarrow \Delta$ be given and set $V = \mathsf{Voc}(\Gamma) \cap \mathsf{Voc}(\Delta)$. The uniform interpolant I for this choice of Γ and V satisfies the desired properties.

The remainder of this article is concerned with the proof of Theorem 3. Section 5 covers the construction of the interpolant in detail; the verification is the focus of Sect. 6. In the present section we overview the basic strategy in the simple case Γ is quantifier-free. In what immediately follows, sequents are expressions $\Theta : \Pi \Rightarrow \Delta$ where Π is a finite set of unannotated formulas and Θ only names variables in Δ. In particular, Θ is empty if Δ is empty, in which case the control will not be mentioned.

Let $V \subseteq \mathsf{Voc}(\Gamma)$ be fixed. The uniform interpolant I_Γ for Γ and V is constructed by recursion on the syntactic complexity of Γ. Preempting the incorporation of fixed points into Γ, we take a slightly less direct approach to the definition of I_Γ than necessary. Indeed, for quantifier-free sequents the construction of interpolants is among the simplest examples of obtaining uniform interpolants from a terminating proof system, as presented in [26].

We consider a derivation tree for the sequent $\Gamma \Rightarrow \varnothing$ according to the rules $\mathsf{Ax}_\bot$, $\mathsf{L}\wedge$, $\mathsf{L}\vee$ and a modification of the modal inferences which we detail shortly. A derivation tree with root $\Gamma \Rightarrow \varnothing$ that is maximal in the sense that every leaf is an instance of $\mathsf{Ax}_\bot$ or a sequent $\varnothing \Rightarrow \varnothing$ is called an *interpolation template for Γ*. The modal inference we utilise is an amalgamation of the left and right modal inferences, named the *global modal rule*, GMod:

$$\mathsf{GMod}\ \frac{\{\Gamma_i, \pi \Rightarrow \varnothing \mid i \leq n \wedge \pi \in \Pi_i\} \quad \{\Gamma_i \Rightarrow \varnothing \mid i \leq n \wedge a_i \in V\} \quad \varnothing \Rightarrow \varnothing}{[a_0]\Gamma_0, \langle a_0\rangle \Pi_0, \ldots, [a_n]\Gamma_n, \langle a_n\rangle \Pi_n, \Sigma \Rightarrow \varnothing}$$

Applications of the rule are subject to the restriction that $a_0, \ldots, a_n$ are distinct actions and $\Sigma \subseteq \{\top\}$. The sets Γ_i and Π_i are permitted to be empty.

Unlike LMod and RMod, the GMod rule is branching and involves three forms of premise: sequents $\Gamma_i, \pi \Rightarrow \varnothing$ for $i \leq n$ and $\pi \in \Pi_i$, called *active premises*; sequents $\Gamma_i \Rightarrow \varnothing$ for $i \leq n$ and $a_i \in V$, called *passive premises*; and the *trivial premise* $\varnothing \Rightarrow \varnothing$. The active and passive premises encode maximal instances of LMod and RMod respectively assuming an appropriate (but unspecified) instantiation of the consequent in both premise and conclusion. The trivial premise corresponds to an instance of RMod for an action label in $\mathsf{Act} \setminus V$, as any such application of RMod yields a premise with empty antecedent. In practice, the trivial premise may be safely ignored because it takes no part in the construction of the uniform interpolant; its presence is merely a technical convenience for tracing paths in a proof of $\Gamma \Rightarrow \Delta$ onto the interpolation template.

The desired connection between the three modality rules is formally expressed by the next lemma, the proof of which is straightforward. Restricting to the case $\Delta = \varnothing$, the lemma shows that a proof of a sequent $\Gamma \Rightarrow \varnothing$ (if one exists) is encoded within an interpolation template for Γ.

Lemma 1. *Let Γ be quantifier-free and $V \subseteq \mathsf{Voc}(\Gamma)$. There exists an interpolation template T for Γ such that for every Δ, if $\Gamma \Rightarrow \Delta$ is valid and $\mathsf{Voc}(\Delta) \cap \mathsf{Voc}(\Gamma) \subseteq V$, then there exists a normal proof $P \vdash \Gamma \Rightarrow \Delta$ satisfying the following condition. For every path $(\Gamma_i \Rightarrow \Delta_i)_{i<N}$ through P there exists a path $(\Gamma_{k_i} \Rightarrow \varnothing)_{i<N'}$ through T where $(k_i)_{i<N'}$ is strictly increasing and $\Gamma_{k_i+j} = \Gamma_{k_i}$ for all $j < k_{i+1} - k_i$.*

From an interpolation template T_Γ satisfying the above lemma it is possible to read off a uniform interpolant for Γ and V. We show that each vertex of $u \in T_\Gamma$ can be associated a formula I_u fulfilling the three conditions of Theorem 3 relative to the sequent at u. The construction of I_u begins at the leaves of T_Γ. In the following, u is assumed to be labelled by the sequent $\Pi \Rightarrow \varnothing$.

If u is a leaf, then either $\bot \in \Pi$ or $\Pi = \varnothing$. In the former case set $I_u = \bot$, in the latter $I_u = \top$. Either way, $\Pi \Rightarrow I_u$ is an axiom of JS. Now suppose u is a non-leaf vertex of T_Γ. Thus $\Pi \Rightarrow \varnothing$ together with the labels of immediate successors to u corresponds to an instance of either L$\wedge$, L$\vee$ or GMod. We consider each case in turn. The simpler of the three inferences is L$\wedge$. In this case u has a unique successor, v say, in T_Γ which we may assume is a sequent $\Pi', \varphi, \psi \Rightarrow \varnothing$ where $\Pi = \Pi' \cup \{\varphi \wedge \psi\}$. Define $I_u = I_v$. That $\vdash \Pi \Rightarrow I_u$ follows immediately from the induction hypothesis. A more informative case is L$\vee$. Here u has two immediate successors in T_Γ, u_0 and u_1 say, labelled by $\Pi', \varphi \Rightarrow \varnothing$ and $\Pi', \psi \Rightarrow \varnothing$ respectively where $\Pi = \Pi' \cup \{\varphi \vee \psi\}$. Choose $I_u = I_{u_0} \vee I_{u_1}$. From $\vdash \Pi', \varphi \Rightarrow I_{u_0}$ and $\vdash \Pi', \psi \Rightarrow I_{u_1}$ we deduce $\vdash \Pi \Rightarrow I_u$ by applications of RW, L$\vee$ and R$\vee$.

The final case in the construction is an instance of GMod which we may assume has the form on the previous page, i.e., Π is

$$\Pi = [a_0]\Gamma_0, \langle a_0 \rangle \Pi_0, \ldots, [a_n]\Gamma_n, \langle a_n \rangle \Pi_n, \Sigma \tag{1}$$

where $a_0, \ldots, a_n$ are distinct modal actions and $\Sigma \subseteq \{\top\}$. Let the actions be ordered such that $V = \{a_0, \ldots, a_k\}$ for some $k \leq n$. For each $i \leq n$ and $\pi \in \Pi_i$ let u_i^π be the immediate successor of u for the active premise $\Gamma_i, \pi \Rightarrow \varnothing$ and u_i the immediate successor for the passive premise $\Gamma_i \Rightarrow \varnothing$. We may ignore the trivial premise. A natural candidate for I_u is the formula

$$I_u^* = \bigwedge_{i \leq k} ([a_i] I_{u_i} \wedge \bigwedge_{\pi \in \Pi_i} \langle a_i \rangle I_{u_i^\pi}) \tag{2}$$

Restricting the conjunction to $i \leq k$ ensures $\mathsf{Voc}(I_u^*) \subseteq V$. Given $\vdash \Gamma_i, \pi \Rightarrow I_{u_i^\pi}$ for each $i \leq n$ and $\pi \in \Pi_i$, an application of LMod yields $\vdash \Pi \Rightarrow \langle a_i \rangle I_{u_i^\pi}$. Likewise, $\Pi \Rightarrow [a_i] I_{u_i}$ can be deduced from $\Gamma_i \Rightarrow I_{u_i}$ by RMod. So $\vdash \Pi \Rightarrow I_u^*$.

It is not difficult to show however that requirement (iii) of Theorem 3 can fail for this choice of interpolant, for example if $\Pi = \langle b \rangle \varphi$ where $b \notin V$ and φ is unsatisfiable. The conjunction in (2) would be empty and $I_u^* = \top$. So $\vdash \Pi \Rightarrow \bot$ but not $\vdash I_u^* \Rightarrow \bot$. The failure of I^* to be a uniform interpolant of Π stems from the possibility of modal actions outside V being relevant in a proof of $\Pi \Rightarrow \Delta$. If Γ_i, π is unsatisfiable for some $\pi \in \Pi_i$, then $\bot$ suffices as the choice of I_u but I_u^* may not. With this consideration in mind, define $I_u = \bot$ if $\vdash \Gamma_i, \pi \Rightarrow \varnothing$ for some $k \leq i \leq n$ and some $\pi \in \Pi_i$. Otherwise, set $I_u = I_u^*$.[2]

Let us conclude by establishing condition (iii) of the theorem. Let Δ be any set of guarded formulas such that $\mathsf{Voc}(\Delta) \cap \mathsf{Voc}(\Gamma) \subseteq V$ and suppose $\vdash \Gamma \Rightarrow \Delta$. Lemma 1 provides a normal proof $P \vdash \Gamma \Rightarrow \Delta$ and an assignment $f \colon P \to T_\Gamma$ of vertices in the interpolation template to vertices in P such that $u \in P$ and $f(u) \in T_\Gamma$ have the same antecedent. Moreover, paths through P correspond to paths through T_Γ (the latter expanded with repetitions). If $\Theta_u : \Gamma_u \Rightarrow \Delta_u$ denotes the label of $u \in P$, we claim $\vdash \Theta_u : I_{f(u)} \Rightarrow \Delta_u$.

Suppose $u \in P$ is a leaf. Then $\Theta_u : \Gamma_u \Rightarrow \Delta_u$ is either an instance of an axiom or is a repeat leaf of P. In the case of an axiom $\vdash \Theta_u : I_{f(u)} \Rightarrow \Delta_u$ holds because $I_{f(u)} = \bot$ if $\bot \in \Gamma_u$. If u is a repeat we observe that since Δ is guarded and Γ is quantifier-free, $\Gamma_u = \varnothing$. But then $I_{f(u)} = \bot$ and $\vdash \Theta_u : I_{f(u)} \Rightarrow \Delta_u$.

The only non-leaf case which is not straightforward is the modal rules, LMod or RMod. By the normality of P, the sets Γ_u and Δ_u are modal. Suppose

$$\Gamma_u = [a_0]\Gamma_0, \langle a_0 \rangle \Pi_0, \ldots, [a_n]\Gamma_n, \langle a_n \rangle \Pi_n, \Sigma$$
$$\Delta_u = [b_0]\Lambda_0, \langle b_0 \rangle \Delta_0, \ldots, [a_m]\Lambda_m, \langle b_m \rangle \Delta_m, \Sigma'$$

where we assume $k \leq \min\{m, n\}$ is such that $a_i = b_i$ for each $i \leq k$ and $\{a_{k+1}, \ldots, a_n\} \cap \{b_{k+1}, \ldots, b_n\} = \varnothing$. The premise to this inference can take one of four forms, depending on which formula of $\Gamma_u \Rightarrow \Delta_u$ is principal and which modal action the rule effected:

1. $\vdash \Gamma_i, \pi \Rightarrow \Delta_i$ for some $i \leq k$ and $\pi \in \Pi_i$.
2. $\vdash \Gamma_i \Rightarrow \lambda, \Delta_i$ for some $i \leq k$ and $\lambda \in \Lambda_i$.
3. $\vdash \Gamma_i, \pi \Rightarrow \varnothing$ for some $k < i \leq n$ and $\pi \in \Pi_i$.
4. $\vdash \varnothing \Rightarrow \lambda, \Delta_i$ for some $k < i \leq m$ and $\lambda \in \Lambda_i$.

If $I_{f(u)} = \bot$ then $\Theta_u : I_{f(u)} \Rightarrow \Delta_u$ is an axiom. Otherwise, $I_{f(u)} = I_{f(u)}^*$ (where vertices u_i^π and u_i in (2) refer to the active and passive premises of $f(u)$ in T_Γ) and the third scenario does not apply. In the first two cases $\Theta_u : I_{f(u)} \Rightarrow \Delta_u$ is a consequence of the induction hypothesis; in case 4, by RMod and LW.

Thus, we have shown that the formula I_r where r is the root of the interpolation template T_Γ is a uniform interpolant for Γ and V, if Γ is quantifier-free.

[2] The case distinction based on the provability of $\Gamma_i, \pi \Rightarrow \varnothing$ brings into question the computational cost of constructing uniform interpolants. Lemmas 1 and 3, however, provide that provability of sequents with empty consequent is implicit in the interpolation template.

5 Constructing the Interpolant

We are, of course, interested in obtaining interpolants for formulas containing quantifiers. The basic idea behind the interpolation template remains the same and can be generalised to incorporate the fixed point inferences $\mathsf{L}\mu$ and $\mathsf{L}\nu$, and the annotation management rules LThin and LReset. The construction, and subsequent verification, of interpolants from these templates is more subtle however. In order to ensure interpolation templates remain finite trees – so that interpolants can be defined recursively from leaf to root – it is necessary to treat them as we do cyclic proofs by permitting leaves with non-trivial sequent, i.e., sequents that are neither empty nor instances of $\mathsf{Ax}_\bot$. These leaves will be subject to path-based repeat condition in the style of JS proofs. Even with a suitable repeat condition, there remains the question of how to present an interpolant to a repeat leaf prior to knowing the intended interpolant for the companion vertex. We return to this question after clarifying the interpolation templates.

Fix a finite well-named set of guarded formulas Γ and vocabulary $V \subseteq \mathsf{Voc}(\Gamma)$. An *interpolation template for* Γ is a tree of *annotated* sequents of the form $\Theta : \Pi \Rightarrow \varnothing$ with root $\Gamma \Rightarrow \varnothing$ subject to the rules $\mathsf{L}\vee$, $\mathsf{L}\wedge$, $\mathsf{L}\mu$, $\mathsf{L}\nu$, LThin, LReset and GMod. The final rule is adapted to annotated sequents in the natural way in analogy with the rules LMod and RMod. We require interpolation templates to be a normal derivation.[3] As mentioned, three kinds of leaf are permitted in T_Γ: instances of $\mathsf{Ax}_\bot$, empty sequents $\varnothing \Rightarrow \varnothing$, and 'repeat' sequents. The requirements of a repeat is as follows: A leaf $u \in T_\Gamma$ is a repeat if and only if there exists a vertex $c_u <_{T_\Gamma} u$ (called the companion of u) labelled by the same (annotated) sequent. Every repeat leaf can be assigned an invariant according to Definition 2 which is called *successful* if the invariant ends in a name that is reset on the path between companion and leaf.

The restriction to normal proofs has the effect that interpolation templates can be assumed to be finite. The conditions, in especial conditions 4 and 5 concerning annotations, ensure that a maximal path through an interpolation template reaches either an axiom, empty sequent or a sequent which is repeated on the path. Such a repeat can be treated as a repeat leaf. The argument is identical to the proof of termination of proof search in [28,41].

Lemma 2. *Every guarded and well-named sequent $\Gamma \Rightarrow \varnothing$ admits a finite interpolation template.*

Henceforth we assume a fixed interpolation template T_Γ for a set Γ and vocabulary V. The path property of Lemma 1 also generalises to the quantified case. The result is analogous although now a path through a (normal) proof of $\Gamma \Rightarrow \Delta$ will in general trace out a path through the *unravelling* of T_Γ.

Lemma 3. *If $\Gamma \Rightarrow \Delta$ is a valid well-named and guarded sequent and $\mathsf{Voc}(\Gamma) \cap \mathsf{Voc}(\Delta) \subseteq V$, then there exists a normal proof $P \vdash \Gamma \Rightarrow \Delta$ such that for every*

[3] We assume Definition 4 is generalised to derivations with GMod. No additional restrictions are necessary to accommodate this rule

path $(\Theta_i : \Gamma_i \Rightarrow \Delta_i)_{i \leq N}$ *through* P *there is a sequence of vertices* $(u_i)_{i \leq N'}$ *from* T_Γ *with labels* $(\Theta'_{k_i} : \Gamma_{k_i} \Rightarrow \varnothing)_{i \leq N'}$ *where for every* $i < N'$:

1. u_{i+1} *is an immediate successor of* u_i *or* u_i *is a repeat and* u_{i+1} *is an immediate successor of the companion of* u_i.
2. $k_i < k_{i+1}$, *and for each* $j < k_{i+1} - k_i$ *we have* $\Gamma_{k_i+j} = \Gamma_{k_i}$ *and* Θ'_{k_i} *is the restriction of* Θ_{k_i+j} *to names for variables in* Γ_{k_i}.

Given an interpolation template T_Γ, we now assign an interpolant to each vertex of T_Γ. The definition proceeds in two stages. First, we assign to each $u \in T_\Gamma$ a formula I_u called the *pre-interpolant for* u. This is defined by recursion through T_Γ following essentially the same construction as before. Second, by considering the collection of all pre-interpolants it is possible to isolate a uniform interpolant for Γ.

Once we have decided on pre-interpolants for the repeat leaves of T_Γ, the construction of I_u can proceed by the same process as in the quantifier-free case. However, it is convenient to deal with trivial interpolants for instances of GMod as a special case before the more general recursive construction. Recall that if u is the conclusion of GMod we set $I_u = \bot$ if at least one active premise to this rule is valid (as a plain sequent). Lemma 3 confirms that as in the quantifier-free case, this question can be answered by inspection of the interpolation template directly (we omit the details here). With trivial instances of GMod pre-interpolated, we proceed with the recursive construction. Suppose $u \in T_\Gamma$ has not yet been assigned a pre-interpolant. If u sits above an application of GMod which has already been assigned (trivial) interpolant, $I_u = \bot$. In the case u is a repeat I_u is chosen to be a fresh variable symbol X_u uniquely associated to the leaf u. In all other cases, define I_u follows the same construction as before. The 'extra' derivation rules not covered before (Lμ, Lν, LThin and LReset) are all unary and we define $I_u = I_{u_0}$ where u_0 is the immediate successor to u.

Thus we have an interpolation template T_Γ and a pre-interpolant I_u for each $u \in T_\Gamma$, both relative to a choice of vocabulary $V \subseteq \mathsf{Voc}(\Gamma)$. The pre-interpolant I_u is a quantifier-free formula in variables $X_{u_1}, \ldots, X_{u_k}$ where $u_1, \ldots, u_k$ lists the repeat leaves above u. Let Rep_Γ be the set of repeat leaves of T_Γ and set r to be the root of T_Γ. The uniform interpolant for Γ is defined as the formula represented by the modal equational system

$$I_\Gamma = (I_r, \mathcal{E}_\Gamma) \text{ where } \mathcal{E}_\Gamma = \{X_u =_{p_u} I_{c_u} \mid u \in \mathrm{Rep}_\Gamma\}.$$

It remains to define the priority function $u \mapsto p_u$ on repeats. For this fix an enumeration $\{u_1, \ldots, u_n\}$ of Rep_Γ consistent with the relation $\preceq$ introduced in Sect. 3 and such that if $\mathsf{inv}(u_i) = \mathsf{inv}(u_j)$ for $i < j$ then either u_i is successful or u_j is unsuccessful. Define $p_{u_i} = 2i - 1$ if u_i is successful and $p_{u_j} = 2i$ otherwise.

6 Verifying the Interpolant

In this section we present the argument that I_Γ fulfils the requirements of Theorem 3. Inspection of the definition confirms that the interpolant is in the appropriate language: $\mathsf{Voc}(I_\Gamma) \subseteq V$. We address (ii) and (iii) of the theorem in turn beginning with the former. Due to constraints of space, we omit the technical details. Let T_Γ be a finite interpolation template satisfying Lemma 3.

Proposition 3. $\mathsf{JS} \vdash \Gamma \Rightarrow I_\Gamma$.

Proof. We begin by removing from T_Γ all vertices above the instances of GMod which were assigned trivial pre-interpolant by the construction. Let T^* be this tree. We assume the label of $u \in T^*$ is $\Theta_u : \Pi_u \Rightarrow \varnothing$. The strategy is to show $\vdash \Theta_u : \Pi_u \Rightarrow I_u$ for every $u \in T^*$ where I_u identifies the formula expressed by the equational system $(I_u, \mathcal{E}_\Gamma)$. For vertices of T^* lacking a repeat leaf as a successor, the claim follows the argument given in Sect. 4. Repeats in T^* will be accounted for via the equations $X_l = I_{c_l}$ and the creation of proof cycles.

The claimed JS proof $P \vdash \Gamma \Rightarrow I_\Gamma$ is defined as follows. Begin by identifying the repeat leaves of T^* with their companions to form a graph which we unravel to an infinite tree T^ω. At each sequent in T^ω instantiate the consequent by the assigned pre-interpolant and insert rules from JS between vertices to obtain an infinite JS derivation. Vertices arising from leaves of T^* will have the form $\Theta_l : \Pi_l \Rightarrow X_l$, whereby inserting (unannotated) instances of $\mathsf{R}\mu$ or $\mathsf{R}\nu$ allows them to be connected with their 'companion' sequent $\Theta_l : \Pi_l \Rightarrow I_{c_l}$. Applications of $\mathsf{R}\nu$ inserted in this way are annotated according to the normality condition 4 of Definition 4 and the names propagate through the derivation according to the JS rules (with applications of RReset inserted whenever possible). P is formed by pruning this tree on each path at the first repeated annotated sequent where a variable X_l of the pre-interpolant is principal provided that $l \preceq l'$ for every subsequent variable $X_{l'}$ active on the path.

That the process results in a finite JS derivation is straightforward to verify. To see that P is a proof, consider an arbitrary repeat leaf $l \in P$ and its companion $c_l \in P$. The path $[c_l, l]_P$, when projected to a sequence of vertices of T_Γ, identifies a $\rightsquigarrow$-chain $l_0 \rightsquigarrow l_1 \rightsquigarrow \cdots \rightsquigarrow l_n$ of repeat leaves of T_Γ. Given that repeats in T_Γ are associated unique variables, l and c_l must correspond to the same vertex of T_Γ, meaning $l_n \rightsquigarrow l_0$. Proposition 1 allows us to assume, without loss of generality, that $l_0 \preceq l_i$ for every $i \leq n$ and $p_{l_0} = \min\{p_{l_i} \mid i \leq n\}$. If p_{l_0} is even, meaning l_0 is unsuccessful in T_Γ, then X_{l_0} is of type ν and thus its unfoldings in P introduce names for X_{l_0}. Since $p_{l_0} \leq p_{l_i}$ for all $i \leq n$, the unfoldings of $X_{l_1}, \ldots, X_{l_n}$ preserve the names for X_{l_0} and each unfolding of X_{l_0} removes the names for the other variables, whence we can find a name for X_{l_0} preserved and reset in $[c_l, l]_P$. And if p_{l_0} is odd, then l_0 is successful in T_Γ, so, since $l_0 \preceq l_i$ for every $i \leq n$, the name on the antecedent witnessing the success of l_0 in T_Γ is preserved and reset in $[c_l, l]_P$.

The third clause of Theorem 3 is proved by a similar argument. We transform, using Lemma 3, a given proof $P \vdash \Gamma \Rightarrow \Delta$ into a derivation $P_I \vdash I_\Gamma \Rightarrow \Delta$ by replacing the antecedent of each sequent with the chosen pre-interpolant and observe that any repeat leaf of P_I whose success in P is on account of the variables from Γ is successful by virtue of a variable in I_Γ.

Proposition 4. *Suppose $\Gamma \Rightarrow \Delta$ is a well-named and guarded sequent such that* $\mathsf{Voc}(\Gamma) \cap \mathsf{Voc}(\Delta) \subseteq V$. *Then $\vdash \Gamma \Rightarrow \Delta$ implies $\vdash I_\Gamma \Rightarrow \Delta$*

Proof. Fix Δ satisfying the requirements and a normal JS proof $P \vdash \Gamma \Rightarrow \Delta$ given by Lemma 3. A derivation $P_I \vdash I_\Gamma \Rightarrow \Delta$ is obtained in two steps. First, P is converted into an ill-founded 'derivation' P_I^ω with the desired root sequent by unravelling P, replacing every antecedent by the corresponding pre-interpolant formula given by Lemma 3, correcting the 'left'-rules between vertices and adjusting the control of each vertex accordingly. Observe that the control of a vertex $u \in P_I^\omega$ and the control of the sequent corresponding to u in P are identical when restricted to variables from the consequent, i.e., variables in Δ. They differ, however, in that names of variables from Γ are no longer present in P_I^ω and that names for variables of the pre-interpolant have been inserted. Following the annotation strategy for normal proofs, it follows that every infinite path in P_I^ω contains a repeated annotated sequent which can be marked as a repeat leaf, thus obtaining a finite JS derivation P_I.

It remains to show that P_I is a proof. Let $l \in P_I$ be a repeat leaf with companion $c_l \in P_I$. As in the previous argument, tracing $[c_l, l]_{P_I}$ onto T_Γ yields a $\rightsquigarrow$-cycle $l_0 \rightsquigarrow l_1 \rightsquigarrow \cdots \rightsquigarrow l_n \rightsquigarrow l_0$ of repeat leaves of T_Γ and by Proposition 1 we may assume that $l_0 \preceq l_i$ for every $i \leq n$ and $p_{l_0} = \min\{p_{l_i} \mid i \leq n\}$. If p_{l_0} is odd, then l is a successful repeat because the unfoldings of X_{l_0} remove the names for any other variable X_{l_i} and introduce a new name for X_{l_0}, whence a name for X_{l_0} is preserved and reset in $[c_l, l]_{P_I}$. Therefore, suppose p_{l_0} is even, meaning that l_0 is not a successful leaf of T_Γ. But given that P is a proof, it follows that l is successful due to a name for a variable in Δ being preserved and reset on the path $[c_l, l]_{P_I}$.

7 Conclusion

We introduced the notion of an *interpolation template* for formulas of the modal μ-calculus and showed that these describe uniform interpolants. Interpolation templates are finite (cyclic) derivation trees in a sequent calculus based on the Jungteerapanich–Stirling annotated proof system of [28,41]. Uniform interpolants arise from encoding the structure of interpolation templates as formulas of the μ-calculus.

Interpolation templates can be given for a wide range of modal and temporal logics simply by embedding them into the modal μ-calculus. This holds even for logics that lack the uniform interpolation property, such as propositional dynamic logic PDL and the alternation-free fragment of the μ-calculus. Although uniform interpolants can still be constructed by the method given, these will be formulas of the μ-calculus that can not be expressed within the syntax of the logic in question. Nevertheless, it would be informative to investigate the interpolants that arise from templates for these logics as a way of shedding light on the complexity and expressivity of fragments of the μ-calculus. A natural question is whether uniform interpolants generated from, say, alternation-free formulas are of bounded complexity or exhaust the quantifier hierarchy of the modal μ-calculus.

We also expect our approach can be directly applied to logics without a detour via modal μ-calculus. A key requirement is the existence of a sound and complete cyclic sequent calculus from which one can define interpolation templates. While there are many examples of cyclic sequent calculi[4] not all are directly amenable to our methods. Our notion of interpolation templates presupposes an analytic calculus satisfying an appropriate sub-formula property. On the other hand, constructing interpolants from templates assumes a highly expressive logic, namely the definability of fixed points for the formulas arising from interpolation templates. From these perspectives, two logics in particular stand out as interesting candidates for investigation: Gödel–Löb provability logic GL and bisimulation quantifier logic BQL. The former logic admits an analytic cyclic sequent calculus which has been utilised to prove Craig interpolation for GL [38]. Bisimulation quantifier logic is the extension of propositional dynamic logic PDL with bisimulation quantifiers [15]. Although BQL is expressively equivalent to μ-calculus [14], the reduction is highly complex and a direct treatment of BQL will be an interesting contribution of cyclic proof theory to modal logic.

Uniform interpolation is intimately connected with quantification [14,35,43]. For modal logics the appropriate notion of quantification is (propositional) bisimulation quantifiers. In the present framework where propositional constants are replaced by modal actions, it is natural to consider quantifiers ranging over modal actions. Thus the formula $\exists a\varphi$ expresses that $\varphi[b/a]$, the result of substituting the modal action b for a in φ, holds for some $b \in \mathsf{Act}$, and similarly for the universal quantifier $\forall a\varphi$. To basic modal logic we may add the logical axiom $\vdash \varphi[b/a] \rightarrow \exists a\varphi$ and the rule 'from $\vdash \varphi \rightarrow \psi$ infer $\vdash \exists a\varphi \rightarrow \psi$,' where ψ is any formula in which a does not occur free (using the usual definition of free occurrences of variables). The universal quantifier is treated symmetrically. Having access to action quantifiers, the formula $\exists a\varphi$ is nothing more than a uniform interpolant for φ with respect to the vocabulary $\mathsf{Voc}(\varphi) \setminus \{a\}$. As such, our construction of uniform interpolants provides a new proof of the definability of bisimulation quantifiers in the modal μ-calculus, a result first established in [14] via automata theoretic methods.

Another direction of research arises in the area of description logics and knowledge representation, where uniform interpolation plays an important tool in reducing the search space for querying ontologies [6,12,33]. In the case of acyclic TBoxes uniform interpolants often exist but there seems to be no uniform approach for dealing with cyclic constraints [5]. We have left aside complexity considerations in the present study but it is an important factor for the methodology to have practical applications for tableaux-based algorithms. At this stage, our expectation is that the complexity may well not be favourable for modal μ-calculus. Nevertheless we hope the approach can contribute to database-related reasoning problems in the context of less expressive logics.

---

[4] A non-exhaustive list of cyclic proofs systems include: *first-order logic with inductive definitions* [8,9,11], *arithmetic* [7,17,39], *linear logic* [3,4,20], *modal and dynamic logics* [1,22,23,28,30,38,40,41,44], *program semantics* [37], *automated theorem proving* [10,36,42], *higher-order logic* [31] and *algebras and lattices* [18,19,32].

References

1. Afshari, B., Leigh, G.E.: Cut-free completeness for modal mu-calculus. In: 32nd Annual ACM/IEEE Symposium on Logic in Computer Science, LICS 2017, Reykjavik, Iceland, 20–23 June 2017, pp. 1–12. IEEE Computer Society (2017)
2. Afshari, B., Leigh, G.E.: Lyndon interpolation for modal mu-calculus. In: Post-Proceedings of TbiLLC 2019. (to appear)
3. Baelde, D., Doumane, A., Kuperberg, D., Saurin, A.: Bouncing threads for infinitary and circular proofs (2020). https://arxiv.org/abs/2005.08257
4. Baelde, D., Doumane, A., Saurin, A.: Infinitary proof theory: the multiplicative additive case. In: Talbot, J., Regnier, L. (eds.) 25th EACSL Annual Conference on Computer Science Logic, CSL 2016, August 29–September 1 2016, Marseille, France. LIPIcs, vol. 62, pp. 42:1–42:17. Schloss Dagstuhl - Leibniz-Zentrum für Informatik (2016)
5. Benedikt, M.: How can reasoners simplify database querying (and why haven't they done it yet)? In: den Bussche, J.V., Arenas, M. (eds.) Proceedings of the 37th ACM SIGMOD-SIGACT-SIGAI Symposium on Principles of Database Systems, Houston, TX, USA, 10–15 June 2018, pp. 1–15. ACM (2018)
6. Benedikt, M., ten Cate, B., Vanden Boom, M.: Interpolation with decidable fixpoint logics. In: 30th Annual ACM/IEEE Symposium on Logic in Computer Science, LICS 2015, Kyoto, Japan, 6–10 July 2015, pp. 378–389. IEEE Computer Society (2015)
7. Berardi, S., Tatsuta, M.: Equivalence of inductive definitions and cyclic proofs under arithmetic. In: 32nd Annual ACM/IEEE Symposium on Logic in Computer Science, LICS 2017, Reykjavik, Iceland, 20–23 June 2017, pp. 1–12. IEEE Computer Society (2017)
8. Berardi, S., Tatsuta, M.: Classical system of Martin-Löf's inductive definitions is not equivalent to cyclic proofs. Log. Methods Comput. Sci. **15**(3), 1:1–1:39 (2019)
9. Brotherston, J.: Cyclic proofs for first-order logic with inductive definitions. In: Beckert, B. (ed.) TABLEAUX 2005. LNCS (LNAI), vol. 3702, pp. 78–92. Springer, Heidelberg (2005). https://doi.org/10.1007/11554554_8
10. Brotherston, J., Gorogiannis, N., Petersen, R.L.: A generic cyclic theorem prover. In: Jhala, R., Igarashi, A. (eds.) APLAS 2012. LNCS, vol. 7705, pp. 350–367. Springer, Heidelberg (2012). https://doi.org/10.1007/978-3-642-35182-2_25
11. Brotherston, J., Simpson, A.: Sequent calculi for induction and infinite descent. J. Log. Comput. **21**(6), 1177–1216 (2011)
12. ten Cate, B., Franconi, E., Seylan, I.: Beth definability in expressive description logics. J. Artif. Intell. Res. **48**, 347–414 (2013)
13. D'Agostino, G.: Interpolation in non-classical logics. Synthese **164**(3), 421–435 (2008)
14. D'Agostino, G., Hollenberg, M.: Logical questions concerning the μ-calculus. J. Symb. Log. **65**(1), 310–332 (2000)
15. D'Agostino, G., Lenzi, G.: An axiomatization of bisimulation quantifiers via the mu-calculus. Theor. Comput. Sci. **338**(1–3), 64–95 (2005)
16. D'Agostino, G., Lenzi, G.: Bisimulation quantifiers and uniform interpolation for guarded first order logic. Theor. Comput. Sci. **563**, 75–85 (2015)
17. Das, A.: On the logical complexity of cyclic arithmetic. Log. Methods Comput. Sci. **16**(1), 10:1–10:25 (2020)
18. Das, A., Pous, D.: A cut-free cyclic proof system for Kleene algebra. In: Schmidt, R.A., Nalon, C. (eds.) TABLEAUX 2017. LNCS (LNAI), vol. 10501, pp. 261–277. Springer, Cham (2017). https://doi.org/10.1007/978-3-319-66902-1_16

19. Das, A., Pous, D.: Non-wellfounded proof theory for (kleene+action)(algebras+lattices). In: Ghica, D.R., Jung, A. (eds.) 27th EACSL Annual Conference on Computer Science Logic, CSL 2018, 4–7 September 2018, Birmingham, UK. LIPIcs, vol. 119, pp. 19:1–19:18. Schloss Dagstuhl - Leibniz-Zentrum für Informatik (2018)
20. De, A., Saurin, A.: Infinets: the parallel syntax for non-wellfounded proof-theory. In: Cerrito, S., Popescu, A. (eds.) TABLEAUX 2019. LNCS (LNAI), vol. 11714, pp. 297–316. Springer, Cham (2019). https://doi.org/10.1007/978-3-030-29026-9_17
21. Demri, S., Goranko, V., Lange, M.: Temporal Logics in Computer Science: Finite-State Systems, vol. 58. Cambridge University Press, Cambridge (2016)
22. Docherty, S., Rowe, R.N.S.: A non-wellfounded, labelled proof system for propositional dynamic logic. In: Cerrito, S., Popescu, A. (eds.) TABLEAUX 2019. LNCS (LNAI), vol. 11714, pp. 335–352. Springer, Cham (2019). https://doi.org/10.1007/978-3-030-29026-9_19
23. Enqvist, S., Hansen, H.H., Kupke, C., Marti, J., Venema, Y.: Completeness for game logic. In: 34th Annual ACM/IEEE Symposium on Logic in Computer Science, LICS 2019, Vancouver, BC, Canada, 24–27 June 2019, pp. 1–13. IEEE (2019)
24. Gabbay, D.M., Maksimova, L.: Interpolation and Definability. Modal and Intuitionistic Logic. Oxford University Press, Oxford (2005) Logic. Oxford University Press, Oxford (2005)
25. Iemhoff, R.: Uniform interpolation and sequent calculi in modal logic. Arch. Math. Log. **58**(1–2), 155–181 (2019)
26. Iemhoff, R.: Uniform interpolation and the existence of sequent calculi. Ann. Pure Appl. Log. **170**(11), 102711 (2019)
27. Janin, D., Walukiewicz, I.: Automata for the modal μ-calculus and related results. In: Wiedermann, J., Hájek, P. (eds.) MFCS 1995. LNCS, vol. 969, pp. 552–562. Springer, Heidelberg (1995). https://doi.org/10.1007/3-540-60246-1_160
28. Jungteerapanich, N.: A tableau system for the modal μ-calculus. In: Giese, M., Waaler, A. (eds.) TABLEAUX 2009. LNCS (LNAI), vol. 5607, pp. 220–234. Springer, Heidelberg (2009). https://doi.org/10.1007/978-3-642-02716-1_17
29. Jungteerapanich, N.: Tableau systems for the modal μ-calculus. Ph.D. thesis, University of Edinburgh (2010)
30. Kokkinis, I., Studer, T.: Cyclic proofs for linear temporal logic. In: Probst, D., Schuster, P. (eds.) Concepts of Proof in Mathematics, Philosophy, and Computer Science, Ontos Mathematical Logic, vol. 6, pp. 171–192. De Gruyter (2016)
31. Kori, M., Tsukada, T., Kobayashi, N.: A cyclic proof system for HFL_N. In: Baier, C., Goubault-Larrecq, J. (eds.) 29th EACSL Annual Conference on Computer Science Logic, CSL 2021, 25–28 January 2021, Ljubljana, Slovenia (Virtual Conference). LIPIcs, vol. 183, pp. 29:1–29:22. Schloss Dagstuhl - Leibniz-Zentrum für Informatik (2021)
32. Kuznetsov, S.: Half a way towards circular proofs for Kleene lattices (2019). circularity in Syntax and Semantics
33. Lutz, C., Wolter, F.: Foundations for uniform interpolation and forgetting in expressive description logics. In: Walsh, T. (ed.) IJCAI 2011, Proceedings of the 22nd International Joint Conference on Artificial Intelligence, Barcelona, Catalonia, Spain, 16–22 July 2011, pp. 989–995. IJCAI/AAAI (2011)
34. Niwinski, D., Walukiewicz, I.: Games for the mu-calculus. Theor. Comput. Sci. **163**(1 & 2), 99–116 (1996)
35. Pitts, A.M.: On an interpretation of second order quantification in first order intuitionistic propositional logic. J. Symb. Log. **57**(1), 33–52 (1992)

36. Rowe, R.N.S., Brotherston, J.: Realizability in cyclic proof: extracting ordering information for infinite descent. In: Schmidt, R.A., Nalon, C. (eds.) TABLEAUX 2017. LNCS (LNAI), vol. 10501, pp. 295–310. Springer, Cham (2017). https://doi.org/10.1007/978-3-319-66902-1_18
37. Santocanale, L.: A calculus of circular proofs and its categorical semantics. In: Nielsen, M., Engberg, U. (eds.) FoSSaCS 2002. LNCS, vol. 2303, pp. 357–371. Springer, Heidelberg (2002). https://doi.org/10.1007/3-540-45931-6_25
38. Shamkanov, D.: Circular proofs for the Gödel-Löb provability logic. Math. Notes **96**, 575–585 (2014)
39. Simpson, A.: Cyclic arithmetic is equivalent to Peano Arithmetic. In: Esparza, J., Murawski, A.S. (eds.) FoSSaCS 2017. LNCS, vol. 10203, pp. 283–300. Springer, Heidelberg (2017). https://doi.org/10.1007/978-3-662-54458-7_17
40. Sprenger, C., Dam, M.: On the structure of inductive reasoning: circular and tree-shaped proofs in the μ-calculus. In: Gordon, A.D. (ed.) FoSSaCS 2003. LNCS, vol. 2620, pp. 425–440. Springer, Heidelberg (2003). https://doi.org/10.1007/3-540-36576-1_27
41. Stirling, C.: A tableau proof system with names for modal mu-calculus. In: Voronkov, A., Korovina, M.V. (eds.) HOWARD-60: A Festschrift on the Occasion of Howard Barringer's 60th Birthday, EPiC Series in Computing, vol. 42, pp. 306–318. EasyChair (2014)
42. Tellez, G., Brotherston, J.: Automatically verifying temporal properties of pointer programs with cyclic proof. J. Autom. Reason. **64**(3), 555–578 (2020)
43. Visser, A.: Bisimulations, model descriptions and propositional quantifiers. Logic Group Preprint Series no. 161, Utrecht (1996)
44. Visser, A.: Cyclic Henkin logic (2021). https://arxiv.org/abs/2101.11462v1

Cyclic Hypersequent Calculi for Some Modal Logics with the Master Modality

Jan Rooduijn(✉)

University of Amsterdam, Amsterdam, Netherlands
j.m.w.rooduijn@uva.nl
https://staff.fnwi.uva.nl/j.m.w.rooduijn/

Abstract. At LICS 2013, O. Lahav introduced a technique to uniformly construct cut-free hypersequent calculi for basic modal logics characterised by frames satisfying so-called 'simple' first-order conditions. We investigate the generalisation of this technique to modal logics with the master modality (a.k.a. reflexive-transitive closure modality). The (co)inductive nature of this modality is accounted for through the use of non-well-founded proofs, which are made cyclic using focus-style annotations. We show that the peculiarities of hypersequents hinder the usual method of completeness via infinitary proof-search. Instead, we construct countermodels from maximally unprovable hypersequents. We show that this yields completeness for a small (yet infinite) subset of simple frame conditions.

Keywords: Hypersequent calculi · Modal logic · Master modality · Non-well-founded proofs · Cyclic proofs

1 Introduction

Cyclic and *non-well-founded* proofs have turned out to be highly effective in the proof theory of modal fixpoint logics. They have been applied to obtain proof-theoretic proofs of known results, such as the completeness of Kozen's axiomatisation of the modal μ-calculus [1], and Lyndon interpolation for Gödel-Löb logic [12]. Moreover, cyclic proof systems have been constructed for logics for which until then no proof system was known, *e.g.* Game Logic [7] and the hybrid μ-calculus [6]. The key advantage of cyclic proof systems over systems with explicit (co)induction rules, is that they enjoy a variant of the subformula property. Among other benefits, this makes them more suitable for proof search. Although cyclic proof systems have by now been devised for many modal fixpoint logics, little work has been done on constructing such systems in a uniform way. In particular, there is no general method to obtain cyclic proof systems for modal fixpoint logics characterised by various classes of frames. This paper attempts to take a first step in that direction.

This research has been made possible by a grant from the Dutch Research Council NWO, project nr. 617.001.857.

A. Das and S. Negri (Eds.): TABLEAUX 2021, LNAI 12842, pp. 354–370, 2021.
https://doi.org/10.1007/978-3-030-86059-2_21

Already without fixpoints, many modal logics call for a deviation from the standard sequent calculus. A typical example is the modal logic $\mathsf{S5}$ (characterised by frames whose accessibility relation is an equivalence relation), for which obtaining a cut-free calculus in the standard sequent system is notoriously difficult. Several alternatives have been proposed, most of which equip ordinary sequents with extra structure, often echoing the Kripke semantics (for an overview we refer the reader to Chap. 4 of [8]). The alternative that arguably stays closest to Gentzen's original approach is that of *hypersequents*, which are nothing but finite disjunctions of sequents. Already with this minor modification, many more modal logics, including $\mathsf{S5}$, can be given a sound and complete proof system. In [10], Ori Lahav presents a systematic method for constructing hypersequent calculi for any extension of one of the modal logics K, $\mathsf{K4}$ or KB, characterised by frames satisfying any finite number of so-called *simple* frame conditions.

In this paper we adapt Lahav's method to uniformly obtain cyclic proof systems for a comparatively simple modal fixpoint logic: *unimodal logic with the master modality.* This language, denoted ML^*, augments the basic modal language with a modality $\boxtimes$, which is to be thought of as the reflexive-transitive closure of the basic modality $\Box$. For each finite set $\mathcal{C}$ of simple frame conditions we uniformly construct both an infinitary and a cyclic hypersequent calculus for ML^* interpreted on the class of $\mathcal{C}$-frames. In the cyclic systems, sequents are annotated using a focus mechanism originally due to Lange and Stirling (see *e.g.* [11]). All systems are proven to be sound, but completeness is only proven for a subset of the simple frame conditions which we shall call *equable.* While many simple frame conditions are not equable, there are infinitely many equable frame conditions, including: seriality, reflexivity, directedness and universality. As a corollary, we obtain decidability for each of these logics.

As for related work, a finitary analytic proof system for ML^* interpreted on the class of all frames is given in [5]. In [3], a cyclic proof system is presented for LTL and CTL, two modal fixpoint logics that are interpreted on restricted frames classes. In [9], a general method is given for constructing sound and complete Hilbert systems for ML^* interpreted on various frame classes, but this concerns non-analytic systems having both a cut-rule and an explicit induction rule. Another notable example of related work is [4], where, like here, cyclic proofs are combined with some calculus that extends the ordinary sequent calculus. However, they use labelled sequents rather than hypersequents and do not consider multiple logics at once.

In Sect. 2 we introduce the syntax and semantics of ML^* and define simple and equable frame conditions. In Sect. 3 we introduce our hypersequent calculi. Section 4 proves soundness for all calculi. Finally, in Sect. 5 completeness is proven for those calculi that contain only rules for equable frame classes.

2 Preliminaries

For the rest of this article, we fix a countable set of P of *propositional variables.*

Definition 1. *The syntax* ML^* *of* modal $*$-formulas *over* P *is generated by:*

$$\varphi ::= p \mid \bot \mid \varphi \to \varphi \mid \Box\varphi \mid \boxast\varphi$$

where $p \in \mathsf{P}$.

As usual, formulas will be interpreted in Kripke models. We will refer to modal $*$-formulas as just *formulas.*

Definition 2. *A* Kripke frame *is a pair* (S, R) *consisting of a set* S *of* states *together with an* accessibility relation $R \subseteq S \times S$*. A* Kripke model *is a triple* (S, R, V)*, where* (S, R) *is a* Kripke frame *and* $V : \mathsf{P} \to \mathcal{P}(S)$ *a valuation function.*

Formulas are interpreted in Kripke models in the usual way, with the following additional clause for $\boxast$:

$$\mathbb{S}, s \Vdash \boxast\psi \;:\Leftrightarrow\; \text{for all } t \in S \text{ such that } sR^*t\text{: } \mathbb{S}, t \Vdash \psi$$

where R^* is the reflexive-transitive closure of R. Whenever the intended the model $\mathbb{S}$ is clear from the context, we will simply write $s \Vdash \varphi$ instead of $\mathbb{S}, s \Vdash \varphi$.

Let L_1 be the first-order language with equality and a single relation symbol R. In contrast to ML^*, we let L_1 include the propositional connectives $\wedge$, $\vee$ and $\neg$. A *frame condition* then is nothing but an L_1-sentence. For Θ a set of frame conditions, a Kripke frame (S, R) is said to be a *Θ-frame* whenever, when regarded an L_1-structure, the frame (S, R) satisfies each sentence φ in Θ. A Kripke model will be called a *Θ-model* whenever its underlying frame is a Θ-frame.

The following definitions and proposition are taken from [10].

Definition 3. *A frame condition is called n-*simple *whenever it is of the form* $\forall s_1 \cdots s_n \exists u \varphi$*, where* φ *is built up using the connectives* $\vee$ *and* $\wedge$ *from atomic formulas of the form* $s_i R u$ *and* $s_i = u$ *with* $1 \leq i \leq n$.

Definition 4. *Given* $n \in \omega$*, an* abstract n-simple frame condition *is a finite non-empty set* C *consisting of pairs* $(C_R, C_=)$ *of subsets* $C_R, C_= \subseteq \{1, \ldots, n\}$ *such that at least one of* C_R *and* $C_=$ *is non-empty.*

Definition 5. *The* interpretation *of some abstract n-simple frame condition C is the following first-order formula:*

$$\forall s_1 \cdots s_n \exists u \bigvee_{(C_R, C_=) \in C} \Big(\bigwedge_{i \in C_R} s_i R u \wedge \bigwedge_{j \in C_=} s_j = u \Big).$$

Using disjunctive normal forms, the following proposition is immediate.

Proposition 1. *Any n-simple frame condition is equivalent to the interpretation of some abstract n-simple frame condition.*

In the following, we use the general term *(abstract) simple frame condition* to encapsulate every (abstract) frame condition that is n-simple for some $n \in \omega$. For the sake simplicity we will sometimes blur the distinction between an abstract frame condition C and its interpretation. In particular, for $\mathcal{C}$ a finite set of abstract simple frame conditions and Θ the set of their interpretations, we often use the terms $\mathcal{C}$-model and $\mathcal{C}$-frame where we mean Θ-model and Θ-frame.

We close this section by defining the subclasses of the class of simple frame conditions, to which we will restrict most of our attention for the rest of this paper.

Definition 6. *An abstract n-simple frame condition C is called:*

- equality-free *if $C_= = \emptyset$ for all $(C_R, C_=) \in C$;*
- disjunction-free *if C is a singleton;*
- equable *if for some $U \subseteq \{1, \ldots, n\}$, we have $U = C_=$ for all $(C_R, C_=) \in C$.*

Clearly if C is equality-free or disjunction-free, then it is equable. It turns out that the converse is also true (up to logical equivalence). The verification of this fact is left to the reader. Some examples of equable frame conditions are *reflexivity*, given by $C = \{\langle\{1\}, \{1\}\rangle\}$, and *k-bounded top width*, which is given by $C = \{\langle\{i, j\}, \emptyset\rangle : 1 \leq i < j \leq k\}$ for any $k \geq 2$. An example of a simple frame condition which is *not* equable is $C = \{\langle\{1\}, \{2\}\rangle, \langle\{2\}, \{1\}\rangle\}$, which in [10] is called *linearity*. For more examples of simple frame conditions, we refer the reader to the aforementioned article.

3 Infinitary and Cyclic Hypersequent Calculi

In this section we introduce families of infinitary and cyclic hypersequent calculi for ML^* interpreted on classes of Θ-models, where Θ is an arbitrary set of simple frame conditions.

3.1 Hypersequents and Pre-proofs

Definition 7. *A* sequent *is an ordered pair (Γ, Δ) of finite sets of formulas, usually written $\Gamma \Rightarrow \Delta$. A* hypersequent *is a finite set $\{\sigma_0, \ldots, \sigma_n\}$ of sequents, usually written $\sigma_0 \mid \cdots \mid \sigma_n$.*

We adopt the convention of using shorthand notation for singleton formulas and sequents. For instance, we write $\Gamma, \varphi \Rightarrow \psi, \Delta$ where we mean $\{\varphi\} \cup \Gamma \Rightarrow \{\psi\} \cup \Delta$, and the hypersequent $H \cup \{\sigma\}$ may be written as $H \mid \sigma$.

(Hyper)sequents are interpreted in Kripke models as follows.

Definition 8. *Let $\mathbb{S}$ be a Kripke model. Then:*

- *A sequent $\Gamma \Rightarrow \Delta$ is said to be* satisfied *at a state s of $\mathbb{S}$ whenever:*
  If $s \Vdash \varphi$ for all $\varphi \in \Gamma$, then $s \Vdash \psi$ for some $\psi \in \Delta$.
- *A sequent is* valid *in $\mathbb{S}$ if it is satisfied at every state of $\mathbb{S}$.*
- *A hypersequent H is* valid *in $\mathbb{S}$ if there is a $\sigma \in H$ which is valid in $\mathbb{S}$.*

A hypersequent valid in all $\mathcal{C}$-models will be called *$\mathcal{C}$-valid*.

The following hypersequent calculus is an expansion by two additional fixpoint rules of the system HK given in [10] for basic modal logic.

Definition 9. *The hypersequent calculus* HK^* *has the following axioms and rules.*

$$\mathsf{id}\ \frac{}{\varphi \Rightarrow \varphi} \qquad\qquad \bot\ \frac{}{\bot \Rightarrow}$$

$$\mathsf{iw}_L\ \frac{H \mid \Gamma \Rightarrow \Delta}{H \mid \Gamma, \varphi \Rightarrow \Delta} \qquad \mathsf{iw}_R\ \frac{H \mid \Gamma \Rightarrow \Delta}{H \mid \Gamma \Rightarrow \varphi, \Delta} \qquad \mathsf{ew}\ \frac{H}{H \mid \Gamma \Rightarrow \Delta}$$

$$\to_L\ \frac{H \mid \Gamma, \psi \Rightarrow \Delta \qquad H \mid \Gamma \Rightarrow \varphi, \Delta}{H \mid \Gamma, \varphi \to \psi \Rightarrow \Delta} \qquad \to_R\ \frac{H \mid \Gamma, \varphi \Rightarrow \psi, \Delta}{H \mid \Gamma \Rightarrow \varphi \to \psi, \Delta}$$

$$\Box\ \frac{H \mid \Gamma \Rightarrow \varphi}{H \mid \Box\Gamma \Rightarrow \Box\varphi} \qquad \mathsf{cut}\ \frac{H \mid \Gamma_1, \varphi \Rightarrow \Delta_1 \qquad H \mid \Gamma_2 \Rightarrow \varphi, \Delta_2}{H \mid \Gamma_1, \Gamma_2 \Rightarrow \Delta_1, \Delta_2}$$

$$\boxast_L\ \frac{H \mid \Gamma, \varphi, \Box\boxast\varphi \Rightarrow \Delta}{H \mid \Gamma, \boxast\varphi \Rightarrow \Delta} \qquad \boxast_R\ \frac{H \mid \Gamma \Rightarrow \varphi, \Delta \qquad H \mid \Gamma \Rightarrow \Box\boxast\varphi, \Delta}{H \mid \Gamma \Rightarrow \boxast\varphi, \Delta}$$

Following [10], we augment HK^* with rules corresponding to certain simple frame conditions.

Definition 10. *Let C be an abstract n-simple frame condition. The rule* $\mathsf{r}_C^{\mathsf{HK}^*}$ induced *by C is defined as follows:*

$$\mathsf{r}_C^{\mathsf{HK}^*}\ \frac{\{H \mid \bigcup_{i \in C_R} \Gamma_i', \bigcup_{j \in C_=} \Gamma_j \Rightarrow \bigcup_{j \in C_=} \Delta_j : (C_R, C_=) \in C\}}{H \mid \Box\Gamma_1', \Gamma_1 \Rightarrow \Delta_1 \mid \cdots \mid \Box\Gamma_n', \Gamma_n \Rightarrow \Delta_n}$$

Given a finite set $\mathcal{C}$ of abstract simple frame conditions, we let $\mathsf{HK}^* + \mathsf{R}_{\mathcal{C}}$ be the system HK^* augmented with the rules $\mathsf{r}_C^{\mathsf{HK}^*}$ for each $C \in \mathcal{C}$.

In any application of some rule of $\mathsf{HK}^* + \mathsf{R}_{\mathcal{C}}$, the sequents outside of the context H are called *active*. Furthermore, the *active* formulas of an active sequent are those that occur outside of Γ and Δ. All other formulas and sequents are called *inactive*. Note that due to the fact the (hyper)sequents are sets, the contexts H might also contain active sequents (and likewise Γ and Δ might contain active formulas). In the case of $\mathsf{r}_C^{\mathsf{HK}^*}$, the i-th active sequent in the conclusion is said to have *index* i and the premiss corresponding to $(C_R, C_=) \in C$ is said to have *index* $(C_R, C_=)$. Here the fact that hypersequents are sets means that one sequent might have multiple indices.

For the rest of this paper we assume that $\mathcal{C}$ is an arbitrary finite set of simple frame conditions, unless specified otherwise.

Definition 11. *An* $\mathsf{HK}^* + \mathsf{R}_{\mathcal{C}}$-pre-proof *is a (possibly infinite) derivation in* $\mathsf{HK}^* + \mathsf{R}_{\mathcal{C}}$.

For any $\mathsf{HK}^* + \mathsf{R}_{\mathcal{C}}$-pre-proof π with root H, we say that π is a $\mathsf{HK}^* + \mathsf{R}_{\mathcal{C}}$-pre-proof *of* H.

This derivation system has a property akin to the subformula property.

Definition 12. *The* closure *of a set Φ of formulas is the least $\Psi \supseteq \Phi$ such that:*

(i) If $\varphi \to \psi \in \Psi$, then $\varphi, \psi \in \Psi$;
(ii) If $\Box\varphi \in \Psi$, then $\varphi \in \Psi$;
(iii) If $\boxast\varphi \in \Psi$, then $\varphi, \Box\boxast\varphi \in \Psi$.

We write $Cl(\Phi)$ for the closure of Φ. It is easy to see that Cl is a closure operator and that the closure of any finite set of formulas is finite. The following lemma can be verified by direct inspection of the rules.

Lemma 1. *Let π be a cut-free $\mathsf{HK}^* + \mathsf{R}_{\mathcal{C}}$-pre-proof of H. Any formula occurring in π belongs to the closure of the set of formulas occurring in H.*

3.2 Infinitary Proofs with Trace Condition

It is not hard to show that the system $\mathsf{HK}^* + \mathsf{R}_{\mathcal{C}}$ need not be sound with respect to all Kripke models based on a $\mathcal{C}$-frame. In fact, already when $\mathcal{C}$ is empty there are infinite pre-proofs of invalid hypersequents. We therefore need a way to recognize valid infinite proofs. The technical treatment in this section takes inspiration from [4], which in turn follows [2].

We use $\Box^n\varphi$ as a shorthand for the formula φ preceded by n instances of $\Box$.

Definition 13. *A formula φ is said to be a* trace formula *if it is of the form $\Box^i\boxast\psi$ for $i \in \{0, 1\}$. If $i = 1$, we say that φ is* unfolded.

Definition 14. *A* trace value *is either the* empty trace value *ϵ, or a pair (φ, σ), where σ is a sequent and φ a trace formula in the right-hand side of σ.*

If τ is the empty trace value or $\tau = (\varphi, \sigma)$ such that the sequent σ belongs to some hypersequent H, then τ is said to be a trace value *for* H.

Definition 15. *Let (H, H') be a pair consisting of the conclusion and a premiss, respectively, of an application of a some rule r of $\mathsf{HK}^* + \mathsf{R}_{\mathcal{C}}$ and let τ and τ' be trace values for H and H'. The pair (τ, τ') is called a* trace pair *for (H, H') if one of τ and τ' is the empty trace value, or one of the following conditions holds for $\tau = (\varphi, \sigma)$ and $\tau = (\varphi', \sigma')$:*

1. *σ' is an inactive sequent equal to σ and $\varphi = \varphi'$.*
2. *σ and σ' are active sequents and one of the following holds:*
   - *(a) r is among $\mathsf{iw}_L, \mathsf{iw}_R, \mathsf{cut}, \to_L, \to_R, \boxast_L, \boxast_R$ and $\varphi' = \varphi$.*
   - *(b) $\mathsf{r} \in \{\mathsf{r}_C^{\mathsf{HK}^*} \mid C \in \mathcal{C}\}$, the index of σ is in $C_=$, where $(C_R, C_=)$ is the index of H', and $\varphi = \varphi'$.*
   - *(c) r is $\Box$ and $\Box\varphi' = \varphi$.*
   - *(d) r is $\boxast_R$, φ is active, H' is the right-hand premiss, and $\varphi' = \Box\varphi$.*

When (τ, τ') is a trace pair by virtue of item 2(d), it will be called an unfolding.

Remark 1. There are several subtleties involved with Definition 15:

- Consider the following inference, where every trace value is marked.

$$\boxtimes_R \frac{p \Rightarrow \overbrace{\Box\boxtimes p}^{\tau_3} \mid p \Rightarrow \overbrace{\boxtimes p}^{\tau_4} \mid p \Rightarrow p \qquad p \Rightarrow \overbrace{\boxtimes p}^{\tau_5} \mid p \Rightarrow \overbrace{\Box\boxtimes p}^{\tau_6}}{p \Rightarrow \underbrace{\Box\boxtimes p}_{\tau_1} \mid p \Rightarrow \underbrace{\boxtimes p}_{\tau_2}}$$

  The trace value τ_1 does *not* form a trace pair with τ_6, because the sequent belonging to τ_6 is active, whereas the one belonging to τ_1 is not. In contrast, since the sequent of τ_5 is inactive, the pair (τ_2, τ_5) is a trace value, even though τ_2 is active. The other trace pairs are (τ_1, τ_3), (τ_2, τ_4) and (τ_2, τ_6) is a trace pair, with the latter being an unfolding.
- In case (2)(c), the shape of the rule $\Box$ forces σ' to be of the form $\Gamma \Rightarrow \varphi'$, where σ is of the form $\Box\Gamma \Rightarrow \Box\varphi'$.

Definition 16. *A* trace *is a sequence of trace pairs. A trace is called* good *if it contains finitely many empty trace values and infinitely many unfoldings.*

Definition 17. *A path $(H_i)_{i\in I}$ in some proof is said to be* covered *by a trace $(\tau_i)_{i\in I}$ if (τ_i, τ_{i+1}) is a trace pair for (H_i, H_{i+1}) for each $i \in I$ such that $i+1 \in I$.*

Definition 18. *An* $\mathsf{HK}^*_{\mathsf{inf}} + \mathsf{R}_C$-proof *is an $\mathsf{HK}^* + \mathsf{R}_C$-pre-proof of which every infinite branch is covered by a good trace.*

A hypersequent H will be called $\mathsf{HK}^*_{\mathsf{inf}} + \mathsf{R}_C$-provable if there is an $\mathsf{HK}^*_{\mathsf{inf}} + \mathsf{R}_C$-proof whose root is labelled by H.

3.3 Cyclic Proofs

In this section we assume that C is a finite set of equable frame conditions.

Definition 19. *An* annotated hypersequent *is a hypersequent H together with a trace value τ for H. We call τ an* annotation, *say that H is* annotated *by τ and write $\tau \vdash H$.*

In proof trees, we often simplify notation by, instead of writing $\tau \vdash$, putting the formula designated by τ between square brackets. This formula is then said to be *in focus*. When τ is empty, we signify this by putting no formula between brackets.

Definition 20. *The derivation system $\mathsf{HK}^*_{\mathsf{circ}} + \mathsf{R}_C$ is obtained from $\mathsf{HK}^* + \mathsf{R}_C$ by making the following adaptations:*

1. *The basic judgments are annotated hypersequents.*
2. *If H is derivable from $H_1, \ldots, H_n$ by some rule r of $\mathsf{HK}^* + \mathsf{R}_C$, then $\tau \vdash H$ is derivable from $\tau_1 \vdash H_1, \ldots, \tau_n \vdash H_n$ by r in $\mathsf{HK}^*_{\mathsf{circ}} + \mathsf{R}_C$ if and only if the pair (τ, τ_i) is a trace pair for (H, H_i).*

3. The following structural rule, called focus change, *is added:*

$$\mathsf{fc}\,\frac{\tau \vdash H}{\tau' \vdash H}$$

Here τ and τ' may be any two trace values for H.

Although the rules of the derivation system $\mathsf{HK}^*_{\mathsf{circ}} + \mathsf{R}_{\mathcal{C}}$ are given in an indirect fashion, it is clearly decidable whether some given inference is a valid rule application.

Whenever some leaf l of some derivation in $\mathsf{HK}^*_{\mathsf{circ}} + \mathsf{R}_{\mathcal{C}}$ is the conclusion of an application of id or $\bot$, we say that l is an *axiomatic* leaf.

Definition 21. *An* $\mathsf{HK}^*_{\mathsf{circ}} + \mathsf{R}_{\mathcal{C}}$-proof *is a finite derivation π in $\mathsf{HK}^*_{\mathsf{circ}} + \mathsf{R}_{\mathcal{C}}$ together with a back edge map f assigning to each non-axiomatic leaf l of π a node $f(l)$ such that:*

- *$f(l)$ is a proper ancestor of l, labelled by the same annotated hypersequent.*
- *For each step $\langle \tau \vdash H, \tau' \vdash H' \rangle$ on the path between $f(l)$ and l, it holds that τ' is not empty and the surrounding rule application is not* fc.
- *For some step $\langle \tau \vdash H, \tau' \vdash H' \rangle$ on the path between $f(l)$ and l it holds that (τ, τ') is an unfolding.*

An (unannotated) hypersequent H will be called $\mathsf{HK}^*_{\mathsf{circ}} + \mathsf{R}_{\mathcal{C}}$*-provable* if there is an $\mathsf{HK}^*_{\mathsf{circ}} + \mathsf{R}_{\mathcal{C}}$-proof with root $\tau \vdash H$, where τ may be any annotation. Note that, by the availability of fc, this is equivalent to there being an $\mathsf{HK}^*_{\mathsf{circ}} + \mathsf{R}_{\mathcal{C}}$-proof whose root is annotated by the empty trace value.

Definition 22. *Let (T, f) be a finite tree with back edges. The* one-step dependency order *$\preceq_1$ on $\mathsf{ran}(f)$ is given by:*

$$u \preceq_1 v :\Leftrightarrow u \text{ lies on the path between } v \text{ and } v' \text{ for some } v' \in f^{-1}(v).$$

The dependency order *$\preceq$ on $\mathsf{ran}(f)$ is defined as the transitive closure of $\preceq_1$.*

For α a sequence, we let $\mathrm{Inf}(\alpha)$ denote the set of elements occurring infinitely often in α. The proof of the following lemma is omitted to conserve space.

Lemma 2. *For any infinite path α through some finite tree with back edges (T, f), the set $\mathrm{Inf}(\alpha) \cap \mathsf{ran}(f)$ has a $\preceq$-greatest element.*

Proposition 2. *If H is $\mathsf{HK}^*_{\mathsf{circ}} + \mathsf{R}_{\mathcal{C}}$-provable, then H is $\mathsf{HK}^*_{\mathsf{inf}} + \mathsf{R}_{\mathcal{C}}$-provable.*

Proof. Let (π, f) be an $\mathsf{HK}^*_{\mathsf{circ}} + \mathsf{R}_{\mathcal{C}}$-proof with root $\tau \vdash H$. We let π_0 be the $\mathsf{HK}^*_{\mathsf{inf}} + \mathsf{R}_{\mathcal{C}}$-proof obtained by unravelling (π, f) and removing all annotations and applications of fc. It suffices to show that every infinite branch γ of π_0 is covered by a good trace. To that end, note that any such γ corresponds to an infinite path ρ through (π, f). Let $\preceq$ be the dependency order on $\mathsf{ran}(f)$ given in Definition 22. For any two $u, v \in \mathsf{ran}(f)$ such that $u \preceq v$, it holds that the focus rule is not applied on the path from v to u, because this path is an initial segment of the path from v to a leaf l with $f(l) = v$. By Lemma 2, the set

$\mathsf{Inf}(\rho) \cap \mathsf{ran}(f)$ must contain a $\preceq$-greatest element u_0. It follows that from some point in ρ every node has a formula in focus and the focus rule is not applied. Since, moreover, the node u_0 is visited infinitely often, an unfolding happens infinitely often on the trace corresponding to the formulas in focus on this tail of ρ. Therefore, the infinite branch γ is covered by a good trace, as required. □

4 Soundness

This section is devoted to proving the following soundness theorem. Again, our treatment is based on [4].

Theorem 1. *Let $\mathcal{C}$ be a finite set of abstract simple frame conditions. If a hypersequent is $\mathsf{HK}^*_{\mathsf{inf}} + \mathsf{R}_{\mathcal{C}}$-provable, then it is valid in every $\mathcal{C}$-model.*

Definition 23. *Let H be a hypersequent and $\mathbb{S}$ a Kripke model. A* countermodel state assignment (cmsa) *of H in $\mathbb{S}$ is a function $\alpha : H \to S$ assigning to each sequent σ of H a state $\alpha(\sigma)$ of $\mathbb{S}$ in which σ is not satisfied.*

Clearly for every model $\mathbb{S}$ in which H is invalid, there is a cmsa of H in $\mathbb{S}$.

Definition 24. *Let α be a cmsa of H in $\mathbb{S}$ and let $\tau := (\Box^i \boxast \psi, \sigma)$ be a non-empty trace value in H. The* weight *of τ with respect to α is given by*

$$\mu_\alpha(\tau) := \min\{n \in \omega : \mathbb{S}, \alpha(\sigma) \not\Vdash \Box^i \Box^n \psi\}.$$

Note that the minimum taken in the above definition always exists by the fact that α is assumed to be a cmsa.

Lemma 3. *Let H be the conclusion of an application of some rule r of $\mathsf{HK}^* + \mathsf{R}_{\mathcal{C}}$ with premisses $H_1, \ldots, H_n$ and let $\mathbb{S}$ be a $\mathcal{C}$-model. For every cmsa α of H in $\mathbb{S}$, there is a premiss H_k and a cmsa α_k of H_k in $\mathbb{S}$ such that for every trace pair (τ, τ_k) for (H, H_k) consisting of non-empty trace values, it holds that*

$$\mu_{\alpha_k}(\tau_k) \leq \mu_\alpha(\tau),$$

and if (τ, τ_k) is an unfolding, then this inequality is strict.

Proof. For the choice of H_k and α_k we make a case distinction on the rule r of $\mathsf{HK}^* + \mathsf{R}_{\mathcal{C}}$ that is applied. We first define α_k only on the active sequent of H_k (if it exists). Because of space issues, we only treat three cases, leaving the others to the reader.

- $\mathsf{r} = \Box$. There is a single premiss H_1 and there are two active sequents $\sigma \in H$ and $\sigma_1 \in H_1$. Moreover, the sequent σ is of the form $\Box\Gamma \Rightarrow \Box\varphi$. Since α is a cmsa, there must be some state s_1 for which it holds that $\alpha(\sigma) R s_1$ and $s_1 \not\Vdash \varphi$. If φ is not of the form $\boxast\psi$, we pick any such s_1 and put $\alpha_1(\sigma_1) := s_1$. If, on the other hand, the formula φ is of the form $\boxast\psi$, then we need to take a bit more care in picking the successor s_1 of $\alpha(\sigma)$. By definition, it holds that $\alpha(\sigma) \not\Vdash \Box\Box^{\mu_\alpha(\sigma, \Box\varphi)}\psi$. Thus it has a successor s_1 such that $s_1 \not\Vdash \Box^{\mu_\alpha(\sigma, \Box\varphi)}\psi$. We set $\alpha_1(\sigma_1) := s_1$.

- $\mathsf{r} = \mathsf{r}_C^{\mathsf{HK}^*}$ for some n-simple $C \in \mathcal{C}$. Let $\sigma_1, \ldots, \sigma_n$ be the active sequents in H. By the fact that $\mathbb{S}$ is a $\mathcal{C}$-model, there must be some state s of $\mathbb{S}$ and pair $(C_R, C_=) \in C$ such that for all $i \in C_R$ it holds that $\alpha(\sigma_i) R s$ and for all $j \in C_=$ that $\alpha(\sigma_j) = s$. As premiss we pick the H_k corresponding to this $(C_R, C_=) \in C$ and we set: $\alpha_k(\bigcup_{i \in C_R} \Gamma_i', \bigcup_{j \in C_=} \Gamma_j \Rightarrow \bigcup_{j \in C_=} \Delta_j) := s$.
- $\mathsf{r} = \boxplus_R$. Then H has an active sequent σ of the form $\Gamma \Rightarrow \boxplus\varphi, \Delta$, and there are two premisses H_1 and H_2, with as active sequent respectively $\sigma_1 = \Gamma \Rightarrow \varphi, \Delta$ and $\sigma_2 = \Gamma \Rightarrow \Box\boxplus\varphi, \Delta$. If $\alpha(\sigma) \not\Vdash \varphi$, we pick H_1 and set $\alpha_1(\sigma_1) := \alpha(\sigma)$. If, on the other hand, we have $\alpha(\sigma) \not\Vdash \Box\boxplus\varphi$, then we pick H_2 and set $\alpha_2(\sigma_2) := \alpha(\sigma)$.

To complete the definition of α_k, for each inactive sequent $\sigma_k \in H_k$, we put $\alpha_k(\sigma_k) := \alpha(\sigma_k)$. We leave it to the reader to verify that in each case α_k is a cmsa of H_k in $\mathbb{S}$.

It remains to verify the condition on trace pairs (τ, τ_k) for (H, H_k). First note that if τ_k is inactive, then τ and τ_k must have the same underlying sequent. By definition, it follows that $\mu_{\alpha_k}(\tau_k) = \mu_\alpha(\tau)$.

For trace pairs between active sequents, we only cover the case $\mathsf{r} = \boxplus_R$, leaving the other cases to the reader. Suppose that $\langle(\varphi, \sigma), (\varphi_k, \sigma_k)\rangle$ is a trace pair for (H, H_k) such that both σ and σ_k are active sequents in an application of $\boxplus_R$. By the definition of α_k given above, it holds that $\alpha(\sigma) = \alpha_k(\sigma_k)$. If $\varphi_k = \varphi$, then clearly $\mu_\alpha(\varphi, \sigma) = \mu_{\alpha_k}(\varphi_k, \sigma_k)$. If, on the other hand, the trace pair is an unfolding, then φ is active and H_k is the right-hand premiss. It follows there is some ψ such that $\varphi = \boxplus\psi$ and $\varphi_k = \Box\boxplus\psi$. Therefore we have that $\mu_{\alpha_k}(\varphi_k, \sigma_k) = \mu_\alpha(\varphi, \sigma) - 1 < \mu_\alpha(\varphi, \sigma)$, as required. □

Proof of Theorem 1. Suppose, towards a contradiction, that some $\mathsf{HK}^*_{\mathsf{inf}} + \mathsf{R}_\mathcal{C}$-provable hypersequent H is $\mathcal{C}$-invalid. Then there is a cmsa α of H in some model $\mathbb{S}$. Repeatedly applying Lemma 3, we obtain a branch $H = H_0, H_1, H_2 \ldots$ in the proof of H, with for each H_i a cmsa α_i of H_i in $\mathbb{S}$. Note that this branch must be infinite, for otherwise the final H_i is an axiom, contradicting the fact that it has a cmsa. Moreover, by the condition of infinite branches it contains a good trace $\overline{\tau}$ which from some point, say, from the hypersequent H_k, contains no empty trace values. By construction, we have $\mu_{\alpha_k}(\tau_0) \leq \mu_{\alpha_{k+1}}(\tau_1) \leq \mu_{\alpha_{k+2}}(\tau_2) \leq \ldots$ and, since infinitely many unfoldings occur on $\overline{\tau}$, this inequality is strict infinitely often. Clearly we have reached the desired contradiction.

Question 1. Suppose we weaken Condition 2 of Definition 15 to allow σ to be inactive, provided that it is equal to σ'. The pair (τ_1, τ_6) of Remark 1 then becomes a trace pair. Is the system $\mathsf{HK}^*_{\mathsf{inf}} + \mathsf{R}_\mathcal{C}$ still sound for any finite $\mathcal{C}$?

5 Completeness

In this section we prove cut-free completeness for $\mathsf{HK}^*_{\mathsf{circ}} + \mathsf{R}_\mathcal{C}$, where $\mathcal{C}$ is any finite set of equable frame conditions. Our method is an adaptation of the one in [10]. We close the section with a brief explanation for why the more common method of completeness via infinitary proof search is hard to apply to our hypersequent calculi.

5.1 Completeness of $\mathsf{HK}^*_{\mathsf{circ}} + \mathsf{R}_C$ for Equable C

This subsection will be devoted to proving the following theorem, which is the main theorem of this paper.

Theorem 2. *Let C be a finite set of equable frame conditions. If a hypersequent is valid in every C-model, then it has a cut-free $\mathsf{HK}^*_{\mathsf{circ}} + \mathsf{R}_C$-proof.*

We will prove this theorem by constructing a countermodel for each unprovable hypersequent. For Γ a set of formulas, we define $\Box^{-1}\Gamma := \{\varphi \mid \Box\varphi \in \Gamma\}$.

Definition 25. *Let H be a hypersequent. The* canonical model $\mathbb{S}^H$ *for H is the model (S, R, V) given by:*

- $S := H$.
- $\Gamma_1 \Rightarrow \Delta_1 R \Gamma_2 \Rightarrow \Delta_2 :\Leftrightarrow \Box^{-1}\Gamma_1 \subseteq \Gamma_2$.
- $V(p) := \{\Gamma \Rightarrow \Delta \mid p \in \Gamma\}$.

The key property of canonical models is that, for certain unprovable hypersequents H, they satisfy a *Truth Lemma*, with the consequence that H is invalid in the canonical model $\mathbb{S}^H$ of H. The bulk of this subsection concerns constructing such unprovable hypersequents and establishing the Truth Lemma.

Definition 26. *Let Σ be a finite closed set of formulas. An (annotated) (hyper)sequent is said to be a* Σ-(annotated) (hyper)sequent *if it contains only formulas from Σ.*

For the rest of this section we assume an arbitrary finite closed set of formulas Σ. First, we want our unprovable hypersequent to satisfy the following saturation properties.

Definition 27. *A sequent $\Gamma \Rightarrow \Delta$ is said to be* propositionally saturated *if the following closure conditions hold:*

(i) $\bot \notin \Gamma$.
(ii) $\Gamma \cap \Delta = \emptyset$.
(iii) *If $\varphi_1 \to \varphi_2 \in \Gamma$, then $\varphi_2 \in \Gamma$ or $\varphi_1 \in \Delta$.*
(iv) *If $\varphi_1 \to \varphi_2 \in \Delta$, then $\varphi_1 \in \Gamma$ and $\varphi_2 \in \Delta$.*
(v) *If $\boxplus\varphi \in \Gamma$, then $\varphi \in \Gamma$ and $\Box\boxplus\varphi \in \Gamma$.*
(vi) *If $\boxplus\varphi \in \Delta$, then $\varphi \in \Delta$ or $\Box\boxplus\varphi \in \Delta$.*

A hypersequent is propositionally saturated *whenever each of its sequents is.*

Definition 28. *Let C be a finite set of abstract simple frame conditions. A hypersequent H is said to be* C-presaturated *if $\mathbb{S}^H$ is a C-model. If, moreover, the hypersequent H is propositionally saturated, it is be said to be* C-saturated.

An annotated hypersequent will be called *C-(pre)saturated* whenever the underlying hypersequent is.

Definition 29. *Let $\Gamma_1 \Rightarrow \Delta_1$ and $\Gamma_2 \Rightarrow \Delta_2$ be sequents and let H_1, H_2 be hypersequents. We define:*

- $\Gamma_1 \Rightarrow \Delta_1 \sqsubseteq \Gamma_2 \Rightarrow \Delta_2$ *if* $\Gamma_1 \subseteq \Gamma_2$ *and* $\Delta_1 \subseteq \Delta_2$.
- $H_1 \sqsubseteq H_2$ *if for all* $\sigma_1 \in H_1$, *there is some* $\sigma_2 \in H_2$ *such that* $\sigma_1 \sqsubseteq \sigma_2$.

If two (hyper)sequents are related by $\sqsubseteq$, *we say that the former is* encompassed *by the latter.*

The following definition and lemmas are based on the notion of a *propositional retract* in [5].

Definition 30. *Let $\mathcal{C}$ be a finite set of simple frame conditions. A* retract *of an annotated Σ-hypersequent $(\varphi, \sigma) \vdash H \mid \sigma$ is a finite set $\mathcal{H}$ consisting of annotated Σ-hypersequents of the form $(\varphi, \sigma') \vdash H \mid \sigma'$ with $\sigma \sqsubseteq \sigma'$, such that $(\varphi, \sigma) \vdash H \mid \sigma$ is derivable from $\mathcal{H}$ in $\mathsf{HK}^*_{\mathsf{circ}} + \mathsf{R}_\mathcal{C}$ without using the rules $\Box$, fc, and cut. Moreover, the retract $\mathcal{H}$ is said to be* $\mathcal{C}$-saturated *if for every $(\varphi, \sigma') \vdash H' \in \mathcal{H}$ such that $\sigma' \sqsubseteq H$ it holds that H' is $\mathcal{C}$-saturated.*

The following crucial lemma is the only part of the completeness proof where we rely on the restriction to equable frame conditions.

Lemma 4. *Let $\mathcal{C}$ be a finite set of equable frame conditions and H a $\mathcal{C}$-saturated hypersequent. Then any annotated Σ-hypersequent $(\varphi, \sigma) \vdash H \mid \sigma$ has a $\mathcal{C}$-saturated retract.*

Proof. We say that a retract $\mathcal{H}$ is *$\mathcal{C}$-presaturated (propositionally saturated)* if for every $(\varphi, \sigma') \vdash H' \in \mathcal{H}$ such that $\sigma' \sqsubseteq H$ it holds that H' is $\mathcal{C}$-presaturated (propositionally saturated). The proof rests on the following two claims.

1. Any annotated Σ-hypersequent has a propositionally saturated retract.
2. For $\mathcal{C}$ a finite set of equable frame conditions, and H a $\mathcal{C}$-presaturated hypersequent, any annotated Σ-hypersequent $(\varphi, \sigma) \vdash H \mid \sigma$ has a $\mathcal{C}$-presaturated retract.

The proof of Claim 1 is analogous to the proof of Lemma 6.1 in [5]. For Claim 2, we argue by induction on the number of Σ-formulas not occurring in the sequent σ. If $\sigma \not\sqsubseteq H$ or if $H \mid \sigma$ is already $\mathcal{C}$-presaturated, then we simply set $\mathcal{H} := \{H \mid \sigma\}$.

Now suppose, towards a contradiction, that $\sigma \sqsubseteq H$ and $H \mid \sigma$ is not $\mathcal{C}$-presaturated, that is:

> There is an n-simple $C \in \mathcal{C}$ and a list $(\Gamma_k \Rightarrow \Delta_k)_{1 \le k \le n}$ of sequents in $H \cup \{\sigma\}$ such that for every $\Gamma \Rightarrow \Delta \in H \cup \{\sigma\}$ and $(C_R, C_=) \in C$ there is an $i \in C_R$ s.t. $\Box^{-1}\Gamma_i \not\subseteq \Gamma$ or a $j \in C_=$ s.t. $\Gamma_j \Rightarrow \Delta_j \neq \Gamma \Rightarrow \Delta$. (1)

For the rest of this proof we fix a condition $C \in \mathcal{C}$ and a list $(\Gamma_k \Rightarrow \Delta_k)_{1 \le k \le n}$ that witness (1).

Since $\sigma \sqsubseteq H$, there is a sequent $\overline{\sigma} \in H$ such that $\sigma \sqsubseteq \overline{\sigma}$. Let $(\overline{\Gamma_k} \Rightarrow \overline{\Delta_k})_{1 \le k \le n}$ be the list obtained by replacing in $(\Gamma_k \Rightarrow \Delta_k)_{1 \le k \le n}$ each occurrence of σ by $\overline{\sigma}$.

By the $\mathcal{C}$-presaturation of H, there must be some $(C_R, C_=) \in C$ and $\overline{\Gamma} \Rightarrow \overline{\Delta} \in H$ such that it holds for each $i \in C_R$ that $\Box^{-1}\overline{\Gamma_i} \subseteq \overline{\Gamma}$ and for each $j \in C_=$ that $\overline{\Gamma_j} \Rightarrow \overline{\Delta_j} = \overline{\Gamma} \Rightarrow \overline{\Delta}$.

It follows for every $i \in C_R$ that $\Box^{-1}\Gamma_i \subseteq \Box^{-1}\overline{\Gamma_i} \subseteq \overline{\Gamma}$. Thus, by the fact that $H \mid \sigma$ is not $\mathcal{C}$-presaturated, there must be some $k \in C_=$ such that $\Gamma_k \Rightarrow \Delta_k \neq \overline{\Gamma_k} \Rightarrow \overline{\Delta_k}$. By construction this can only be the case if $\Gamma_k \Rightarrow \Delta_k = \sigma$.

Now consider the following inference.

$$\mathsf{r}_C^{\mathsf{HK}^*}\ \frac{\{H \mid \bigcup_{i\in C_R} \Box^{-1}\Gamma_i, \bigcup_{j\in C_=} \Gamma_j \Rightarrow [\varphi], \bigcup_{j\in C_=} \Delta_j : (C_R, C_=) \in C\}}{H \mid \Gamma_k \Rightarrow [\varphi], \Delta_k}$$

Observe that the right-hand side of each premiss contains φ. The reason is that φ belongs to the right-hand side of $\sigma = \Gamma_k \Rightarrow \Delta_k$ and, by equability, $k \in C_=$ for every $(C_R, C_=) \in C$. We claim that for any $(C_R, C_=) \in C$, the Σ-sequent

$$\sigma_R := \bigcup_{i\in C_R} \Box^{-1}\Gamma_i \cup \bigcup_{j\in C_=} \Gamma_j \Rightarrow \bigcup_{j\in C_=} \Delta_j$$

is such that $\sigma \sqsubset \sigma_R$, whence contains strictly less Σ-formulas than σ. Note that no information is lost by indexing σ_R solely by R, since, by equability, for each $(C_R^1, C_=^1), (C_R^2, C_=^2) \in C$ it holds that $C_=^1 = C_=^2$. Since $k \in C_=$, we already have $\sigma \sqsubseteq \sigma_R$. Now suppose, towards a contradiction, that $\sigma = \sigma_R$. Then by (1), there must be some $j \in C_=$ such that $\Gamma_j \Rightarrow \Delta_j \neq \sigma$. It follows that

$$\begin{aligned} \Gamma_j \Rightarrow \Delta_j &= \overline{\Gamma_j} \Rightarrow \overline{\Delta_j} && \text{(because } \Gamma_j \Rightarrow \Delta_j \neq \sigma) \\ &= \overline{\Gamma_k} \Rightarrow \overline{\Gamma_k} && \text{(because } j, k \in C_=) \\ &= \overline{\sigma}. \end{aligned}$$

But then $\overline{\sigma} \sqsubseteq \sigma$, so $\sigma = \overline{\sigma}$ and $H \mid \sigma = H$, contradicting the assumption that $H \mid \sigma$ is not $\mathcal{C}$-presaturated.

Finally, the induction hypothesis gives, for each $(C_R, C_=) \in C$, a suitable retract $\mathcal{H}_R$ of $(\varphi, \sigma_R) \vdash H \mid \sigma_R$. We put:

$$\mathcal{H} := \bigcup_{(C_R, C_=)\in C} \mathcal{H}_R,$$

which finishes the proof of Claim 2.

The main statement of the lemma can now be proven from claims 1 and 2 by a straightforward induction. □

Definition 31. *Let $\mathcal{C}$ be some finite set of abstract simple frame conditions. A Σ-hypersequent H is called $\mathcal{C}$-*maximal *if the following hold:*

(i) There is no cut-free $\mathsf{HK}^*_{\mathsf{circ}} + \mathsf{R}_{\mathcal{C}}$-proof of H.
(ii) H is $\mathcal{C}$-saturated.
(iii) H is $\subseteq$-maximal as a Σ-hypersequent satisfying both (i) and (ii).
(iv) For every Σ-sequent σ:

Either $\sigma \sqsubseteq H$ or there is a cut-free $\mathsf{HK}^*_{\mathsf{circ}} + \mathsf{R}_{\mathcal{C}}$-proof of $H \mid \sigma$.

Because of space limitations the proof of the following lemma is only sketched.

Lemma 5. *Let $\mathcal{C}$ be some finite set of abstract simple frame conditions. Then any hypersequent H which has no cut-free $\mathsf{HK}^*_{\mathsf{circ}} + \mathsf{R}_{\mathcal{C}}$-proof, can be $\sqsubseteq$-extended to be $\mathcal{C}$-maximal.*

Proof (sketch). In the same way as one can prove Lemma 2 of [10], it can be shown that there is a Σ-hypersequent H_0 such that $H \sqsubseteq H_0$ and H_0 satisfies conditions (i) and (iv) of $\mathcal{C}$-maximality. Using similar arguments as in the proof of Theorem 3 of [10], it can then be shown that H_0 also satisfies condition (ii). Finally, taking a $\subseteq$-maximal extension of H_0 with respect to conditions (i) and (ii) breaks neither condition (iv) nor the encompassing of H. □

We will prove our Truth Lemma for the canonical models of $\mathcal{C}$-maximal hypersequents. We first prove the following existence lemma.

Lemma 6. *For $\mathcal{C}$ a finite set of equable simple frame conditions, let H be a $\mathcal{C}$-maximal Σ-hypersequent, and let $\mathbb{S}$ be its canonical model. Then for every sequent $\sigma := \Gamma \Rightarrow \Delta \in H$ the following hold:*

(i) For all $\Box\psi \in \Sigma$:
If $\Box\psi \in \Delta$, then there is $\sigma' := \Gamma' \Rightarrow \Delta' \in H$ such that $\sigma R \sigma'$ and $\psi \in \Delta'$.
(ii) For all $\boxast\psi \in \Sigma$:
If $\boxast\psi \in \Delta$, then there is $\sigma' := \Gamma' \Rightarrow \Delta' \in H$ such that $\sigma R^* \sigma'$ and $\psi \in \Delta'$.

Proof. We leave the proof of item (i) to the reader. For item (ii), define

$$\mathcal{S} := \{\Gamma' \Rightarrow \Delta' \in H : \sigma R^* \Gamma' \Rightarrow \Delta' \text{ and, } \psi \in \Delta' \text{ or } \Box\boxast\psi \in \Delta'\}.$$

We must show that $\mathcal{S}$ contains a sequent $\Gamma' \Rightarrow \Delta'$ with $\psi \in \Delta'$. Assume that this is not the case. We will reach a contradiction by constructing a cut-free $\mathsf{HK}^*_{\mathsf{circ}} + \mathsf{R}_{\mathcal{C}}$-proof (π, f) of H.

Since $\sigma \in \mathcal{S}$, we have $\Box\boxast\psi \in \Delta$ by our assumption. We begin the construction of (π, f) as follows:

$$\cfrac{\cfrac{\vdots}{\cfrac{\cfrac{\cfrac{\vdots}{\cfrac{\cfrac{\cfrac{\overset{(\pi_1, f_1)}{H \mid \Box^{-1}\Gamma \Rightarrow \psi} \qquad \overset{\pi_2}{H \mid \Box^{-1}\Gamma \Rightarrow [\Box\boxast\psi]}}{H \mid \Box^{-1}\Gamma \Rightarrow [\boxast\psi]}\,\boxast_R}{H \mid \Box\Box^{-1}\Gamma \Rightarrow [\Box\boxast\psi]}\,\Box}{}\,\mathsf{iw}_L}}{H \mid \Gamma \Rightarrow [\Box\boxast\psi]}\,\mathsf{iw}_L}{}\,\mathsf{iw}_R}}{H \mid \Gamma \Rightarrow \Delta, [\Box\boxast\psi]}\,\mathsf{iw}_R$$

The cut-free $\mathsf{HK}^* + \mathsf{R}_{\mathcal{C}}$ proof (π_1, f_1) is obtained by the $\mathcal{C}$-maximality of H and the fact that $\Box^{-1}\Gamma \Rightarrow \psi \not\sqsubseteq H$. The latter must be the case, for otherwise there would be a $\Gamma_1 \Rightarrow \Delta_1 \in H$ such that $\Box^{-1}\Gamma \Rightarrow \psi \sqsubseteq \Gamma_1 \Rightarrow \Delta_1$. But that would mean that $\Gamma_1 \Rightarrow \Delta_1 \in \mathcal{S}$ with $\psi \in \Delta_1$, which we assumed not to be the case.

We invoke Lemma 4 to obtain a retract $\mathcal{H}$ of $H \mid \Box^{-1}\Gamma \Rightarrow \Box\circledast\psi$ and let π_2 be the derivation of this hypersequent from $\mathcal{H}$. By construction, every annotated hypersequent in $\mathcal{H}$ is of the form $(\Box\circledast\psi, \sigma') \vdash H \mid \sigma'$ where $\sigma' \sqsupseteq \Box^{-1}\Gamma \Rightarrow \Box\circledast\psi$. Furthermore, the sequent σ' is such that $\sigma' \not\sqsubseteq H$ or $H \mid \sigma'$ is $\mathcal{C}$-saturated. By the $\mathcal{C}$-maximality of H this means that either $H \mid \sigma'$ has a cut-free $\mathsf{HK}^*_{\mathsf{circ}} + \mathsf{R}_{\mathcal{C}}$-proof, or $\sigma' \in H$.

To every leaf of π_2 that has a cut-free $\mathsf{HK}^*_{\mathsf{circ}} + \mathsf{R}_{\mathcal{C}}$-proof, we append that proof. Observe that any other leaf is of the form $(\Box\circledast\psi, \sigma') \vdash H \mid \sigma'$ for some $\sigma' \in \mathcal{S}$. To each such leaf we recursively apply the above procedure. By the finiteness of $\mathcal{S}$, every branch created in this way must at some point encounter the same annotated hypersequent $(\Box\circledast\psi, \sigma') \vdash H \mid \sigma'$ twice, for some in $\sigma' \in \mathcal{S}$. Whenever that happens, we add a back edge from the second encounter to the first and terminate the procedure for this branch. Notice that between target of the newly added back edge and its source the focus rule is not applied, there is always a formula in focus, and at least one unfolding happens on the induced trace.

After finitely many steps this procedure terminates for every branch and we obtain a cut-free $\mathsf{HK}^*_{\mathsf{circ}} + \mathsf{R}_{\mathcal{C}}$-proof of H, giving the desired contradiction. □

The following Truth Lemma is now proven using a straightforward induction, which we leave to the reader.

Lemma 7. *Let $\mathbb{S}^H$ be the canonical model for some $\mathcal{C}$-maximal Σ-hypersequent H. Then for all $\sigma := \Gamma \Rightarrow \Delta \in S^H$ and $\varphi \in \Sigma$ the following hold:*

(a) If $\varphi \in \Gamma$, then $\mathbb{S}^H, s \Vdash \varphi$.
(b) If $\varphi \in \Delta$, then $\mathbb{S}^H, s \nVdash \varphi$.

Proof of Theorem 2. We argue by contraposition. Suppose H has no cut-free $\mathsf{HK}^*_{\mathsf{circ}} + \mathsf{R}_{\mathcal{C}}$-proof. Let Σ be a finite closed set such that H is a Σ-sequent. By Lemma 5, there is a $\mathcal{C}$-maximal Σ-hypersequent H_0 encompassing H.

We claim that the canonical model $\mathbb{S}^{H_0}$ for H_0 is a countermodel to H. Indeed, let $\sigma \in H$, then there is $\sigma_0 := \Gamma_0 \Rightarrow \Delta_0 \in H_0$ such that $\sigma \sqsubseteq \sigma_0$. By Lemma 7, we have for each $\varphi \in \Gamma_0$ that $\mathbb{S}^{H_0}, s_0 \Vdash \varphi$ and for each $\psi \in \Delta_0$ that $\mathbb{S}^{H_0}, s_0 \nVdash \psi$. Thus σ_0 is not valid in $\mathbb{S}^{H_0}$, and the same holds for σ. Since σ was taken arbitrarily, the hypersequent H is not valid in $\mathbb{S}^{H_0}$.

Finally, the result follows that fact that, by $\mathcal{C}$-saturation, the model $\mathbb{S}^{H_0}$ is a $\mathcal{C}$-model. □

Question 2. For which other finite sets $\mathcal{C}$ of simple (not necessarily equable) frame conditions is $\mathsf{HK}^*_{\mathsf{circ}} + \mathsf{R}_{\mathcal{C}}$ cut-free complete?

Corollary 1. *For $\mathcal{C}$ a finite set of equable frame conditions, the logic obtained by interpreting* ML^* *on the class of $\mathcal{C}$-frames is decidable.*

Proof. Let H be an arbitrary hypersequent. Then H is a Σ-hypersequent for some finite closed set Σ. If H is invalid in some $\mathcal{C}$-model, then, by Theorem 1, it follows that H cannot have a cut-free $\mathsf{HK}^*_{\mathsf{circ}} + \mathsf{R}_{\mathcal{C}}$-proof. By the same reasoning as in the proof of Theorem 2 we obtain a model $\mathbb{S}^{H_0}$ in which H is not valid. Since the size of this model is by construction bounded by the size of Σ, we can decide the $\mathcal{C}$-validity of H by checking its validity in finitely many models.

Question 3. Is the size of the smallest cut-free $\mathsf{HK}^*_{\mathsf{circ}} + \mathsf{R}_{\mathcal{C}}$-proof of some $\mathcal{C}$-valid Σ-hypersequent also bounded by the size of Σ? We conjecture that this question can be answered positively by showing that for every cut-free $\mathsf{HK}^*_{\mathsf{circ}} + \mathsf{R}_{\mathcal{C}}$-proof, there is a cut-free $\mathsf{HK}^*_{\mathsf{circ}} + \mathsf{R}_{\mathcal{C}}$-proof of the same hypersequent, with the property that every branch contains at most one annotated hypersequent twice (in which case these two occurrences are connected by a back edge) and no annotated hypersequent more than twice.

5.2 Completeness via (Infinitary) Proof Search

A standard method for proving completeness of non-well-founded proof systems is via infinitary proof search. Roughly, the idea is to find some proof-search strategy such that a countermodel can be extracted from a failed attempt, *i.e.* an attempt that does not yield a proof. Then, since soundness entails that the proof-search must fail for any invalid hypersequent, completeness follows. This is also the method used to prove completeness in [4].

In this subsection we briefly sketch a complication that arises when one tries to apply this method to our hypersequent calculi. Because this already occurs in the case of $\mathsf{HK}^*_{\mathsf{inf}}$ (without additional rules for frame conditions), we restrict our attention to this system.

Suppose we obtain a pre-proof π from the failure of an application of some proof-search strategy for $\mathsf{HK}^*_{\mathsf{inf}}$ to the hypersequent H. The problem arises in the case that π is infinite. In this case we wish to use the fact that π has a branch β which is *not* covered by a good trace, in order to extract a countermodel. One might for example try to take the canonical model $\mathbb{S}^H$ of some hypersequent H that occurs infinitely often on β. To prove an analogue of part (ii) of Lemma 6 for $\mathbb{S}^H$, we would have to show that any $\boxast\psi \in \Delta$ for some $\Gamma \Rightarrow \Delta$ in H is not unfolded infinitely often on β. The proof-search strategy would then ensure that at some point in the branch β the rule $\boxast_R$ is applied to $\boxast\psi$ in $\Gamma \Rightarrow \Delta$ and the branch β continues through the premiss on the left-hand side. This would give us a state $\Gamma' \Rightarrow \Delta'$ in $\mathbb{S}^H$ such that $\Gamma \Rightarrow \Delta R^* \Gamma' \Rightarrow \Delta'$ and $\psi \in \Delta'$. The problem is that we cannot guarantee that $\boxast\psi$ is not unfolded infinitely often, because we might repeatedly lose its trace due to that trace being overtaken by some other active sequent (cf. Remark 1 and Question 1).

6 Conclusion

In this paper we have constructed sound and complete infinitary and cyclic proof systems for ML^* interpreted on any frame class characterised by a finite number of equable frame conditions.

In future work we wish to extend this to non-equable frame conditions. We conjecture that there are cases in which the single focus-style annotations are not sufficient, and one must turn a more complex annotating mechanism.

We would also like to extend this work to more expressive fragments of the modal μ-calculus, such as polymodal logic with the master modality, PDL, the alternation-free modal μ-calculus, or even the modal μ-calculus itself.

Another avenue for further research is to see whether our hypersequent calculi can be used to establish Craig interpolation for their respective logics.

Finally, we wish to combine non-well-founded proof theory with other enrichments of ordinary Gentzen sequents, such as nested sequents. It would be interesting to better understand which of such systems combine well with non-well-founded proof theory and why.

References

1. Afshari, B., Leigh, G.E.: Cut-free completeness for modal mu-calculus. In: Proceedings of the 32nd Annual ACM/IEEE Symposium on Logic in Computer Science. LICS 2017 (2017)
2. Brotherston, J., Simpson, A.: Sequent calculi for induction and infinite descent. J. Log. Comput. **21**(6), 1177–1216 (2011)
3. Brünnler, K., Lange, M.: Cut-free sequent systems for temporal logic. J. Log. Algebr. Program. **76**(2), 216–225 (2008)
4. Docherty, S., Rowe, R.N.S.: A non-wellfounded, labelled proof system for propositional dynamic logic. In: Cerrito, S., Popescu, A. (eds.) TABLEAUX 2019. LNCS (LNAI), vol. 11714, pp. 335–352. Springer, Cham (2019). https://doi.org/10.1007/978-3-030-29026-9_19
5. Doczkal, C., Smolka, G.: Constructive completeness for modal logic with transitive closure. In: Hawblitzel, C., Miller, D. (eds.) CPP 2012. LNCS, vol. 7679, pp. 224–239. Springer, Heidelberg (2012). https://doi.org/10.1007/978-3-642-35308-6_18
6. Enqvist, S.: A circular proof system for the hybrid mu-calculus. arXiv preprint arXiv:2001.04971 (2020)
7. Enqvist, S., Hansen, H.H., Kupke, C., Marti, J., Venema, Y.: Completeness for game logic. In: 2019 34th Annual ACM/IEEE Symposium on Logic in computer Science (LICS), pp. 1–13. IEEE (2019)
8. Indrzejczak, A.: Sequents and Trees: An Introduction to the Theory and Applications of Propositional Sequent Calculi. Springer Nature, Basingstoke (2020)
9. Kikot, S., Shapirovsky, I., Zolin, E.: Completeness of logics with the transitive closure modality and related logics. arXiv preprint arXiv:2011.02205 (2020)
10. Lahav, O.: From frame properties to hypersequent rules in modal logics. In: 2013 28th Annual ACM/IEEE Symposium on Logic in Computer Science, pp. 408–417. IEEE (2013)
11. Lange, M., Stirling, C.: Focus games for satisfiability and completeness of temporal logic. In: Proceedings 16th Annual IEEE Symposium on Logic in Computer Science, pp. 357–365. IEEE (2001)
12. Shamkanov, D.S.: Circular proofs for the Gödel-Löb provability logic. Math. Notes **96**(3), 575–585 (2014)

A Focus System for the Alternation-Free μ-Calculus

Johannes Marti and Yde Venema(✉)

ILLC, University of Amsterdam,
P.O. Box 94242, 1090 GE Amsterdam, The Netherlands
y.venema@uva.nl

Abstract. We introduce a cut-free sequent calculus for the alternation-free fragment of the modal μ-calculus. This system allows both for infinite and for finite, circular proofs and uses a simple focus mechanism to control the unravelling of fixpoints along infinite branches. We show that the proof system is sound and complete for the set of guarded valid formulas of the alternation-free μ-calculus.

Keywords: Alternation-free mu-calculus · Infinitary proof system · Circular proof system · Soundness · Completeness

The modal μ-calculus $\mathcal{L}_\mu$, introduced in its present form by Kozen [16], is an extension of basic modal logic with least and greatest fixpoint operators. In the theory of formal program verification the formalism serves as a general specification language for describing properties of reactive systems, embedding many well-known logics such as LTL, CTL, CTL* and PDL. In fact, restricted to bisimulation-invariant properties, $\mathcal{L}_\mu$ has the same expressive power as monadic second-order logic [13], while it still has very reasonable computational properties, such as an EXPTIME-complete satisfiability problem [9]. Furthermore, the modal μ-calculus has many attractive logical properties, and interesting connections with for instance the theory of automata and infinite games. In particular, $\mathcal{L}_\mu$-formulas can be effectively represented as alternating tree automata, and vice versa [12,26]. We refer to [4,5,10] for some surveys.

In this paper we contribute to the study of the modal μ-calculus by investigating one of its fragments. The theory of the full language is riddled with combinatorial intricacies involving the interaction between least- and greatest fixpoint operators. This interaction also lies at the root of the main drawback of the formalism, viz., that its formulas are not always easy to decipher. The *alternation-free μ-calculus* is the fragment $\mathcal{L}_\mu^{af}$ of $\mathcal{L}_\mu$ in which there is no real interaction between least and greatest fixpoint operators. This restriction comes with a decrease in expressive power, but many interesting logics, including LTL,

The authors want to thank the anonymous reviewers for many helpful comments.
J. Marti—The research of this author has been made possible by a grant from the Dutch Research Council NWO, project nr. 617.001.857.

A. Das and S. Negri (Eds.): TABLEAUX 2021, LNAI 12842, pp. 371–388, 2021.
https://doi.org/10.1007/978-3-030-86059-2_22

CTL and PDL still embed into $\mathcal{L}_{\mu}^{af}$. Moreover, the expressive power of the full μ-calculus collapses to that $\mathcal{L}_{\mu}^{af}$ on some interesting classes of structures, such as transitive ones [2] or the ones with restricted connectivity [11]. The latter case generalises the particularly interesting example of the *linear time* μ-calculus [15]. Other reasons to study the alternation-free μ-calculus are that it corresponds in expressive power to a natural class of parity automata, viz., the ones with a so-called *weak* acceptance condition [19], and to the bisimulation-invariant fragment of the so-called *noetherian* variation of monadic second-order logic [6].

The problem that we address here is that of obtaining good proof systems for the alternation-free μ-calculus. Finding derivation systems for the full μ-calculus and proving their soundness and completeness is a notoriously difficult task, and successful applications of proof-theoretic techniques were few and far between for a long time. Kozen [16] introduced a natural axiomatisation for the full μ-calculus, and this system was proved to be complete by Walukiewicz [25]; Kozen's system, however, is a Hilbert-style axiomatisation. Niwiński & Walukiewicz [21] introduced some interesting tableau games, but these have a rather infinitary character. The same applies to the proof systems investigated by Dax et alii [7] and by Studer [24]. Fairly recently, however, Afshari & Leigh [1] obtained completeness of Kozen's axiomatisation using a series of cut-free *circular* derivation systems. A crucial ingredient for their results is an earlier proof system, developed by Jungteerapanich and Stirling [14,23]. This system uses an intricate mechanism for annotating formulas to detect after finitely many steps when a branch of a proof may develop into a successful infinite branch in the sense of Niwínski & Walukiewicz' tableaux, thus obtaining a finite but circular proof.

In this paper we show that the approach of [14,23] can be significantly simplified in the setting of the alternation-free μ-calculus. In our proof system it suffices to annotate formulas with just one bit of information, indicating whether a formula is *in focus* or not. This terminology is taken from the focus games for logics such as LTL and CTL by Lange & Stirling [17]. These are tableau-based games where every sequent of the tableau contains exactly one formula in focus; we generalise this so that a proof node may feature a *set* of formulas in focus. This focus mechanism is used to detect successful trails of fixpoint formulas in infinite branches of the proof (and seems to be unrelated to the literature on focused proof systems starting with [3]).

The bookkeeping of annotations in our system is very simple: as we follow the trail of a formula when moving up from the root in a Focus proof, we basically keep the annotation unchanged, with two exceptions. First, when we unfold a *least* fixpoint formula, we always drop the focus from its residual unfolding—whereas unfolding a *greatest* fixpoint formula has no influence on the annotations. And second, there are *focus change rules*, which put previously unfocused formulas into focus, or vice versa; their use however, is very restricted.

In this paper we introduce Focus_{∞} and Focus as, respectively, an infinite and a finite but circular version of our focus proof system. We first show the equivalence of these two systems. Our main result concerns the soundness and completeness of Focus_{∞}; as an intermediate step in the proof we use a version of Niwiński & Walukiewicz' tableau games. Below we summarise the main line of argumentation in the paper (the number refers to the Theorem)

$$\vdash_{\mathsf{Focus}} \Phi \overset{1}{\Longleftrightarrow} \vdash_{\mathsf{Focus}_\infty} \Phi \overset{5,6}{\Longleftrightarrow} \Phi \in Win_{Prover}(\mathcal{G}(\mathbb{T})) \overset{4}{\Longleftrightarrow} \Phi \text{ is valid.}$$

Here Φ denotes an arbitrary sequent of guarded alternation-free formulas.

Finally, although it may not be visible at the surface, our approach is heavily influenced by ideas from automata theory. Here we follow Jungteerapanich [14], whose annotations can be seen to encode a deterministic ω-automaton that recognises successful branches of infinite proofs. Where such an encoding in the setting of the full μ-calculus involves some version of the *Safra construction* [22], in the case of alternation-free formulas a much simpler mechanism suffices. Basically, our one-bit focus mechanism encodes the determisation procedure for weak ω-automata, as described in e.g. [8, Theorem 15.2.1].

Related versions More background and proof details can be found in our technical report [18].

1 Preliminaries

The modal μ-calculus. The *formulas* of the language $\mathcal{L}_\mu$ of the modal μ-calculus are generated by the grammar

$$\varphi ::= p \mid \overline{p} \mid \bot \mid \top \mid (\varphi \vee \varphi) \mid (\varphi \wedge \varphi) \mid \Diamond\varphi \mid \Box\varphi \mid \mu x\, \varphi \mid \nu x\, \varphi,$$

where p and x are taken from a fixed set Prop of propositional variables and in formulas of the form $\mu x.\varphi$ and $\nu x.\varphi$ there are no occurrences of $\overline{x}$ in φ. It is well known that one can define a negation $\overline{\varphi} \in \mathcal{L}_\mu$ of any formula $\varphi \in \mathcal{L}_\mu$.

Formulas of the form $\mu x.\varphi$ ($\nu x.\varphi$) are called *μ-formulas* (*ν-formulas*, respectively); formulas of either kind are called *fixpoint formulas*. The operators μ and ν are called *fixpoint operators*. We use $\eta \in \{\mu, \nu\}$ to denote an arbitrary fixpoint operator and write $\overline{\eta} := \nu$ if $\eta = \mu$ and $\overline{\eta} = \mu$ if $\eta = \nu$. Formulas that are of the form $\Box\varphi$ or $\Diamond\varphi$ are called *modal*. Formulas of the form $\varphi \wedge \psi$ or $\varphi \vee \psi$ are called *boolean*. Formulas of the form p or $\overline{p}$ for some $p \in \mathsf{Prop}$ are called *literals* and the set of all literals is denoted by Lit; a formula is *atomic* if it is either a literal or an atomic constant, that is, $\top$ or $\bot$. We use standard notation and terminology for the binding of variables by the fixpoint operators and for substitutions. Given a fixpoint formula $\xi = \eta x.\chi$ we define its *unfolding* as the formula $\chi[\xi/x]$.

For every formula $\varphi \in \mathcal{L}_\mu$ we define the set $\mathsf{Clos}_0(\varphi)$ as follows

$$\begin{array}{llll}
\mathsf{Clos}_0(p) & := \varnothing & \mathsf{Clos}_0(\overline{p}) & := \varnothing \\
\mathsf{Clos}_0(\psi_0 \wedge \psi_1) & := \{\psi_0, \psi_1\} & \mathsf{Clos}_0(\psi_0 \vee \psi_1) & := \{\psi_0, \psi_1\} \\
\mathsf{Clos}_0(\Box\psi) & := \{\psi\} & \mathsf{Clos}_0(\Diamond\psi) & := \{\psi\} \\
\mathsf{Clos}_0(\mu x.\psi) & := \{\psi[\mu x.\psi/x]\} & \mathsf{Clos}_0(\nu x.\psi) & := \{\psi[\nu x.\psi/x]\}
\end{array}$$

If $\psi \in \mathsf{Clos}_0(\varphi)$ we call ψ a *residual* of φ and sometimes write $\varphi \to_C \psi$. We define the *closure* $\mathsf{Clos}(\varphi) \subseteq \mathcal{L}_\mu$ of φ as the least set Σ containing φ that is closed in the sense that $\mathsf{Clos}_0(\psi) \subseteq \Sigma$ for all $\psi \in \Sigma$. We define $\mathsf{Clos}(\Phi) = \bigcup_{\varphi \in \Phi} \mathsf{Clos}(\varphi)$ for any $\Phi \subseteq \mathcal{L}_\mu$. It is well known that $\mathsf{Clos}(\Phi)$ is finite iff Φ is finite. A *trace* is a sequence $(\varphi_n)_{n<\kappa}$, with $\kappa \leq \omega$, of formulas such that $\varphi_n \to_C \varphi_{n+1}$, for all n such that $n+1 < \kappa$. If $\tau = (\varphi_n)_{n<\kappa}$ is an infinite trace, then there is a unique formula φ_τ that occurs infinitely often on τ and is a subformula of φ_n for cofinitely many n. This formula is always a fixpoint formula, and where it is of the form $\varphi_\tau = \eta x.\psi$ we call τ an *η-trace.*

A formula $\varphi \in \mathcal{L}_\mu$ is *guarded* if in every subformula $\eta x.\psi$ of φ all free occurrences of x in ψ are in the scope of a modality. It is well known that every formula can be transformed into an equivalent guarded formula, and one may verify that all formulas in the closure of a guarded formula are also guarded.

The semantics of the modal μ-calculus is given in terms of *(Kripke) models* $\mathbb{S} = (S, R, V)$, where S is a set whose elements are called *worlds* or *states*, $R \subseteq S \times S$ is a binary relation on S and $V : \mathsf{Prop} \to \mathcal{P}S$ is a function called the *valuation function.* The *meaning* $[\![\varphi]\!]^{\mathbb{S}} \subseteq S$ of a formula $\varphi \in \mathcal{L}_\mu$ relative to a model $\mathbb{S}$ is defined by induction on the complexity of φ:

$$
\begin{array}{llll}
[\![p]\!]^{\mathbb{S}} & := V(p) & [\![\overline{p}]\!]^{\mathbb{S}} & := S \setminus V(p) \\
[\![\bot]\!]^{\mathbb{S}} & := \varnothing & [\![\top]\!]^{\mathbb{S}} & := S \\
[\![\varphi \vee \psi]\!]^{\mathbb{S}} & := [\![\varphi]\!]^{\mathbb{S}} \cup [\![\psi]\!]^{\mathbb{S}} & [\![\varphi \wedge \psi]\!]^{\mathbb{S}} & := [\![\varphi]\!]^{\mathbb{S}} \cap [\![\psi]\!]^{\mathbb{S}} \\
[\![\Diamond\varphi]\!]^{\mathbb{S}} & := \{s \in S \mid R[s] \cap [\![\varphi]\!]^{\mathbb{S}} \neq \varnothing\} & [\![\Box\varphi]\!]^{\mathbb{S}} & := \{s \in S \mid R[s] \subseteq [\![\varphi]\!]^{\mathbb{S}}\} \\
[\![\mu x.\varphi]\!]^{\mathbb{S}} & := \bigcap\{U \subseteq S \mid [\![\varphi]\!]^{\mathbb{S}[x \mapsto U]} \subseteq U\} & [\![\nu x.\varphi]\!]^{\mathbb{S}} & := \bigcup\{U \subseteq S \mid [\![\varphi]\!]^{\mathbb{S}[x \mapsto U]} \supseteq U\}.
\end{array}
$$

Here, $\mathbb{S}[x \mapsto U]$ for some $U \subseteq S$ denotes the model (S, R, V'), where $V'(x) = U$ and $V'(p) = V(p)$ for all $p \in \mathsf{Prop}$ with $p \neq x$. We say that φ *is true* at s if $s \in [\![\varphi]\!]^{\mathbb{S}}$. A formula $\varphi \in \mathcal{L}_\mu$ is valid if $[\![\varphi]\!]^{\mathbb{S}} = S$ holds in all models $\mathbb{S}$ and two formulas $\varphi, \psi \in \mathcal{L}_\mu$ are *equivalent* if $[\![\varphi]\!]^{\mathbb{S}} = [\![\psi]\!]^{\mathbb{S}}$ for all models $\mathbb{S}$.

The Alternation-Free Fragment. Following the approach by Niwiński [20], we call a formula ξ alternation free if it satisfies the following: if ξ has a subformula $\eta x.\varphi$ then no free occurrence of x in φ can be in the scope of an $\overline{\eta}$-operator in φ. We let $\mathcal{L}_\mu^{af}$ denote the set of all alternation-free formulas. For an inductive definition of this set we refer to [18].

Example 1. For some examples of alternation-free formulas, observe that $\mathcal{L}_\mu^{af}$ contains all basic modal (i.e., fixpoint-free) formulas, as well as all $\mathcal{L}_\mu$-formulas that use μ-operators or ν-operators, but not both, and all modal and boolean combinations of such formulas. For a slightly more sophisticated example, consider the formula $\xi = \mu x.(\nu y.p \wedge \Box y) \wedge \Diamond x$. This formula does feature an alternating chain of fixpoint operators, in the sense that the ν-formula $\varphi = \nu y.p \wedge \Box y$ is a subformula of the μ-formula ξ. However, since the variable x does not occur in φ, this formula does belong to $\mathcal{L}_\mu^{af}$.

The language $\mathcal{L}_\mu^{af}$ is closed under taking respectively negations, unfoldings, subformulas and guarded equivalents of formulas. It follows from this that the closure operation restricts to alternation-free formulas. The next observation formulates an essential simplification of traces in the case of $\mathcal{L}_{\mu}^{af}$-formulas.

Proposition 1. *For any infinite trace* $\tau = (\varphi_n)_{n<\omega}$ *of* $\mathcal{L}_{\mu}^{af}$*-formulas the following are equivalent: (1)* τ *is an* η*-trace; (2)* φ_n *is an* η*-formula, for infinitely many* n*; (3)* φ_n *is an* $\overline{\eta}$*-formula, for at most finitely many* n*.*

2 The Focus System

In this section we introduce our annotated proof system for the alternation-free μ-calculus. We consider two versions of the system, which we call Focus and Focus_∞, respectively. Focus_∞ is a proof system that allows proofs to be based on infinite, but finitely branching trees. The focus mechanism that is implemented by the annotations of formulas helps ensuring that all the infinite branches in a Focus_∞ proof are of the right shape. The proof system Focus can be seen as a finite variant of Focus_∞. The proof trees in this system are finite, but the system is circular in that it contains a discharge rule that allows to discharge a leaf of the tree if the same sequent is reached again closer to the root of the tree. As we will see, the two systems are equivalent in the sense that we may transform proofs in either variant into proofs of the other kind. We generally take a root-first perspective in proof search.

2.1 The Proof Systems Focus and Focus_∞

A *sequent* $(\Phi, \Psi, \ldots)$ is a finite set of guarded formulas, intuitively to be read *disjunctively*. We use standard notational conventions for sequents, e.g., we usually write $\varphi_1, \ldots, \varphi_i$ for the sequent $\{\varphi_1, \ldots, \varphi_i\}$, and $\varphi_1, \ldots, \varphi_i, \Phi$ for $\{\varphi_1, \ldots, \varphi_i\} \cup \Phi$. Given a sequent Φ we write $\Diamond\Phi$ for the sequent $\Diamond\Phi := \{\Diamond\varphi \mid \varphi \in \Phi\}$.

An *annotated formula* is a pair $(\varphi, a) \in \mathcal{L}_{\mu}^{af} \times \{f, u\}$; we usually write φ^a instead of (φ, a) and call a the *annotation* of φ. Given $a \in \{f, u\}$ we let $\overline{a}$ be its alternative, i.e., we define $\overline{u} := f$ and $\overline{f} := u$. Formulas annotated with f/u are said to be *in focus/out of focus*, respectively. A finite set of annotated formulas is called an *annotated sequent* $(\Sigma, \Gamma, \Delta, \ldots)$. In practice we will often be sloppy and refer to annotated sequents as sequents. Given a sequent Φ, we define $\Phi^a := \{\varphi^a \mid \varphi \in \Phi\}$. Conversely, we set $\widetilde{\Sigma} := \{\varphi \mid \varphi^a \in \Sigma, \text{ for some } a\}$. We abbreviate $\Sigma^f := \widetilde{\Sigma}^f$.

The proof rules of our focus proof systems Focus and Focus_∞ are given in Fig. 1. We use standard terminology when talking about proof rules. Every (application of a) rule has one *conclusion* and a finite (possibly zero) number of *premises*. *Axioms* are rules without premises. The *principal* formula of a rule application is the formula in the conclusion to which the rule is applied. As non-obvious cases we have that all formulas are principal in the conclusion of the rule $\mathsf{R}_\Box$ and that the rule $\mathsf{D}^\times$ has no principal formula. In all cases other than

$$\frac{}{p^a, \overline{p}^b}\,\mathsf{Ax1} \qquad \frac{}{\top^a}\,\mathsf{Ax2} \qquad \frac{\varphi^a, \psi^a, \Sigma}{(\varphi \vee \psi)^a, \Sigma}\,\mathsf{R}_\vee \qquad \frac{\varphi^a, \Sigma \quad \psi^a, \Sigma}{(\varphi \wedge \psi)^a, \Sigma}\,\mathsf{R}_\wedge \qquad \frac{\varphi^a, \Sigma}{\Box\varphi^a, \Diamond\Sigma}\,\mathsf{R}_\Box$$

$$\frac{\varphi[\mu x.\varphi/x]^u, \Sigma}{\mu x.\varphi^a, \Sigma}\,\mathsf{R}_\mu \qquad \frac{\varphi[\nu x.\varphi/x]^a, \Sigma}{\nu x.\varphi^a, \Sigma}\,\mathsf{R}_\nu \qquad \frac{\Sigma}{\varphi^a, \Sigma}\,\mathsf{W} \qquad \frac{\varphi^f, \Sigma}{\varphi^u, \Sigma}\,\mathsf{F} \qquad \frac{\varphi^u, \Sigma}{\varphi^f, \Sigma}\,\mathsf{U}$$

$$\begin{array}{c} [\Sigma]^{\mathsf{x}} \\ \vdots \\ \dfrac{\Sigma}{\Sigma}\,\mathsf{D}^{\mathsf{x}} \end{array}$$

Fig. 1. Proof rules of the focus system

the rule W the principal formula develops into one or more *residual* formulas in each of the premises. Principal and residual formulas are also called *active*.

Here are some more specific comments about the individual proof rules. The boolean rules ($\mathsf{R}_\wedge$ and $\mathsf{R}_\vee$) are fairly standard; observe that the annotation of the active formula is simply inherited by its subformulas. The fixpoint rules (R_μ and R_ν) simply unfold the fixpoint formulas; note, however, the difference between R_μ and R_ν when it comes to the annotations: in R_ν the annotation of the active ν-formula remains the same under unfolding, while in R_μ, the active μ-formula *loses focus* when it gets unfolded. The box rule $\mathsf{R}_\Box$ is the standard modal rule in one-sided sequent systems; the annotation of any formula in the consequent and its residual in the antecedent are the same.

The rule W is a standard *weakening rule*. Next to R_μ, the *focus rules* F and U are the only rules that change the annotations of formulas.[1] Finally, the *discharge rule* D is a special proof rule that allows us to discharge an assumption if it is repeating a sequent that occurs further down in the proof. Every application D^{x} of this rule is marked by a so-called *discharge token* x that is taken from some fixed infinite set $\mathcal{D} = \{\mathsf{x}, \mathsf{y}, \mathsf{z}, \dots\}$. In Fig. 1 this is suggested by the notation $[\Sigma]^{\mathsf{x}}$. The precise conditions under which D^{x} can be employed are explained in Definition 1 below.

Definition 1. *A* pre-proof $\Pi = (T, P, \Sigma, \mathsf{R})$ *is a quadruple such that* (T, P) *is a, possibly infinite, tree with nodes* T *and parent relation* P *(with* Puv *meaning that* u *is the parent of* v*).* Σ *is a function that maps every node* $u \in T$ *to a non-empty annotated sequent* Σ_u*; and*

$$\mathsf{R} : T \to \{\mathsf{Ax1}, \mathsf{Ax2}, \mathsf{R}_\vee, \mathsf{R}_\wedge, \mathsf{R}_\Box, \mathsf{R}_\mu, \mathsf{R}_\nu, \mathsf{W}, \mathsf{F}, \mathsf{U}\} \cup \{\mathsf{D}^{\mathsf{x}} \mid \mathsf{x} \in \mathcal{D}\} \cup \mathcal{D} \cup \{\star\},$$

is a map that assigns to every node u *of* T *its* label $\mathsf{R}(u)$*, which is either (i) the name of a proof rule, (ii) a discharge token or (iii) the symbol* $\star$*.*

To qualify as a pre-proof, Π *is required to satisfy the following conditions:*

[1] The rule U is not really needed—in fact we prove completeness without it. We include U because of its convenience for constructing proofs.

1. *If a node is labelled with the name of a proof rule then it has as many children as the proof rule has premises, and the annotated sequents at the node and its children match the specification of the proof rules in Fig. 1.*
2. *If a node is labelled with a discharge token or with* $\star$ *then it is a leaf. We call such nodes* non-axiomatic leaves *as opposed to the* axiomatic leaves *that are labelled with one of the axioms,* $\mathsf{Ax1}$ *or* $\mathsf{Ax2}$.
3. *For every leaf* l *that is labelled with a discharge token* $\mathsf{x} \in \mathcal{D}$ *there is exactly one node* u *in* Π *that is labelled with* D^{x}. *This node* u, *as well as its (unique) child, is a proper ancestor of* l *and satisfies* $\Sigma_u = \Sigma_l$. *In this situation we call* l *a* discharged leaf, *and* u *its* companion; *we write* c *for the function that maps a discharged leaf* l *to its companion* $c(l)$.
4. *If* l *is a discharged leaf with companion* $c(l)$ *then the path from* $c(l)$ *to* l *contains (4a) no application of the focus rules and (4b) at least one application of* $\mathsf{R}_\Box$, *while (4c) every node on this path features a formula in focus.*

Non-axiomatic leaves that are labelled with $\star$ *(and thus not discharged), are called* open, *as are the associated sequents. We call a pre-proof a* proof in Focus *if it is finite and does not have any open assumptions.*

A infinite branch $\beta = (v_n)_{n\in\omega}$ *is* successful *if there are infinitely many applications of* $\mathsf{R}_\Box$ *on* β *and there is some* i *such that for all* $j \geq i$ *the annotated sequent at* v_j *contains at least one formula that is in focus and none of the focus rules* F *and* U *is applied at* v_j. *A pre-proof is a* Focus_∞-proof *if it does not have any non-axiomatic leaves and all its infinite branches are successful.*

A plain sequent Φ *is* derivable *in* Focus, *notation:* $\vdash_{\mathsf{Focus}} \Phi$, *if there is a* Focus *proof for* Φ^f; *and similarly for* Focus_∞.

The idea behind the success condition on infinite branches (and the corresponding *path condition* 4 on finite Focus-proofs) is to force any infinite branch in a Focus_∞-proof (respectively, in the unravelling of a Focus-proof) to contain an infinite trace of formulas in focus. Since μ-formulas lose their focus when unfolded, such a trace then must be a ν-trace; and because of Proposition 1, every ν-trace will be of this form.

As an example of a Focus-proof consider the proof of the formula $\varphi \vee \psi$ in Fig. 2, where $\varphi = \nu x.\Diamond(p \wedge x) \vee \Box(q \wedge x)$ and $\psi = \mu y.\Diamond((\overline{p} \wedge \overline{q}) \vee y)$. This example illustrates a crucial difference between our system and the ones from [17]. Whereas the sequents of [17] have exactly one formula in focus, it is crucial for us to allow for multiple formulas to be in focus at one single sequent. In the proof from Fig. 2 both $\Diamond(p \wedge \varphi)$ and $\Box(q \wedge \varphi)$ need to be in focus at the sequent where $\mathsf{R}_\Box$ is applied. It is only above the application of $\mathsf{R}_\Box$, when the conjunction $\overline{p} \wedge \overline{q}$ is decomposed, that we know which of $p \wedge \varphi$ and $q \wedge \varphi$ needs to be in focus.

We close this section with a first observation about (pre-)proofs in this system. The (completely routine) proof is omitted.

Proposition 2. *Let* $\Pi = (T, P, \Sigma, \mathsf{R})$ *be some pre-proof with root* r. *Then all formulas occurring in* Π *belong to* $\mathsf{Clos}(\widetilde{\Sigma}_r)$.

$$
\dfrac{
\dfrac{
\dfrac{
\dfrac{\overline{\phantom{p^f,\overline{p}^u}}}{p^f,\overline{p}^u}\;\mathsf{Ax1}
}{p^f,\overline{p}^u,\psi^u}\;\mathsf{W}
\qquad
\dfrac{[\varphi^f,\psi^u]^\times}{\varphi^f,\overline{p}^u,\psi^u}\;\mathsf{W}
}{p\wedge\varphi^f,\overline{p}^u,\psi^u}\;\mathsf{R_\wedge}
}{p\wedge\varphi^f,q\wedge\varphi^f,\overline{p}^u,\psi^u}\;\mathsf{W}
\qquad\qquad
\dfrac{
\dfrac{
\dfrac{
\dfrac{\overline{\phantom{q^f,\overline{q}^u}}}{q^f,\overline{q}^u}\;\mathsf{Ax1}
}{q^f,\overline{q}^u,\psi^u}\;\mathsf{W}
\qquad
\dfrac{[\varphi^f,\psi^u]^\times}{\varphi^f,\overline{q}^u,\psi^u}\;\mathsf{W}
}{q\wedge\varphi^f,\overline{q}^u,\psi^u}\;\mathsf{R_\wedge}
}{p\wedge\varphi^f,q\wedge\varphi^f,\overline{q}^u,\psi^u}\;\mathsf{W}
}{
\dfrac{
\dfrac{
\dfrac{
\dfrac{
\dfrac{
\dfrac{p\wedge\varphi^f,q\wedge\varphi^f,\overline{p}\wedge\overline{q}^u,\psi^u}{p\wedge\varphi^f,q\wedge\varphi^f,(\overline{p}\wedge\overline{q})\vee\psi^u}\;\mathsf{R_\vee}
}{\Diamond(p\wedge\varphi)^f,\Box(q\wedge\varphi)^f,\Diamond((\overline{p}\wedge\overline{q})\vee\psi)^u}\;\mathsf{R_\Box}
}{\Diamond(p\wedge\varphi)^f,\Box(q\wedge\varphi)^f,\psi^u}\;\mathsf{R_\mu}
}{\Diamond(p\wedge\varphi)\vee\Box(q\wedge\varphi)^f,\psi^u}\;\mathsf{R_\vee}
}{\varphi^f,\psi^u}\;\mathsf{R_\nu}
}{
\dfrac{
\dfrac{\varphi^f,\psi^u}{\varphi^f,\psi^f}\;\mathsf{U}
}{\varphi\vee\psi^f}\;\mathsf{R_\vee}
}\;\mathsf{D^\times}
}\;\mathsf{R_\wedge}
$$

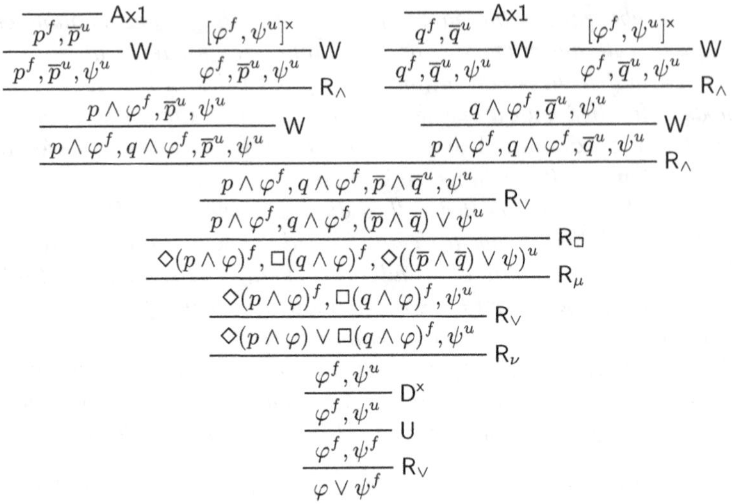

Fig. 2. A Focus-proof

2.2   Circular and Infinite Proofs

We first show that Focus_∞ and Focus are the infinitary and circular version of the same proof system, and derive the same annotated sequents.

Theorem 1. *Let Γ be an annotated sequent. Then Γ is provable in Focus iff it is provable in Focus_∞.*

Proof. (Sketch) The proof of the implication from left to right is based on a straightforward construction that (iteratively) *unravels* a given Focus-proof around its discharged leaves, creating a Focus_∞-proof in the limit.

For the opposite direction, fix a Focus_∞ pre-proof $\Pi = (T, P, \Sigma, \mathsf{R})$. If Π is finite we are done, so assume otherwise. A node u in Π is called a *successful repeat* if it has a proper ancestor t such that $\Sigma_t = \Sigma_u$, $\mathsf{R}(t) \neq \mathsf{D}$, and the path $[t, u]$ in Π satisfies condition 1 of Definition 1. It is then obvious by the definitions and Proposition 2 that every branch $\beta \in B^\infty$ contains a successful repeat. Define, for any $\tau \in B^\infty$, the number $\mathsf{l}(\tau) \in \omega$ as the least number $n \in \omega$ such that $\tau(n)$ is a successful repeat. This means that $\tau(\mathsf{l}(\tau))$ is the first successful repeat on τ. It is then possible to show, using König's Lemma, that the set

$$\widehat{Y} := \{\tau(\mathsf{l}(\tau)) \mid \tau \in B^\infty\}$$

is finite. Every element $l \in \widehat{Y}$ is a successful repeat; we may thus define a companion map $c : \widehat{Y} \to T$ by setting $c(l)$ to be the *first* ancestor t of l witnessing that l is a successful repeat. The map c takes care of the circular part of the finite tree (T', P') that will support the Focus-proof Π' of Γ. For a full and precise definition of Π' we have to add all ancestors of nodes in $\widehat{Y}$, and add a finite well-founded part, but this is not difficult. $\qquad\square$

2.3 Thin and Progressive Proofs

When we prove the soundness of our proof system it will be convenient to work with (infinite) proofs that are in a certain normal form.

Definition 2. *An annotated sequent Σ is* thin *if there is no formula $\varphi \in \mathcal{L}_{\mu}^{af}$ such that $\varphi^f \in \Sigma$ and $\varphi^u \in \Sigma$. Given an annotated sequent Σ, we define its* thinning

$$\Sigma^- := \{\varphi^f \mid \varphi^f \in \Sigma\} \cup \{\varphi^u \mid \varphi^u \in \Sigma, \varphi^f \notin \Sigma\}.$$

A pre-proof $\Pi = (T, P, \Sigma, \mathsf{R})$ is thin *if for all $v \in T$ with $\varphi^f, \varphi^u \in \Sigma_v$ we have that $\mathsf{R}_v = \mathsf{W}$ and $\varphi^u \notin \Sigma_u$ for the unique u with Pvu.*

Note that one may obtain the thinning Σ^- from an annotated sequent Σ by removing the *unfocused* versions of the formulas with a double occurrence in Σ. Since $\Sigma^- \subseteq \Sigma$, one may derive Σ from Σ^- through a series of weakenings.

Definition 3. *An application of a boolean or fixpoint rule at a node u in a pre-proof $\Pi = (T, P, \Sigma, \mathsf{R})$ is* progressive *if for the principal formula $\varphi^a \in \Sigma_u$ it holds that $\varphi^a \notin \Sigma_v$ for all v with Puv.*[2] *Π itself is* progressive *if all applications of the boolean rules and the fixpoint rules in Π are progressive.*

Our main result here is the following.

Theorem 2. *Let Φ be some sequent. If Φ is derivable in* Focus *or* Focus_∞ *then it has a thin and progressive proof, both in* Focus *and in* Focus_∞.

3 Tableaux and Tableau Games

To prove soundness and completeness, as an intermediate step we use a (fairly straightforward) adaptation of Niwiński & Walukiewicz' tableau games [21].

Tableaux. We first introduce tableaux, which are the graphs over which the tableau game is played. The nodes of a tableau for some sequent Φ are labelled with sequents consisting of formulas taken from the closure of Φ. Our system is based on the rules in Fig. 3, where the tableau rules Ax1, Ax2, $\mathsf{R}_\vee$, $\mathsf{R}_\wedge$, R_μ and R_ν are direct counterparts of the focus proof rules with the same name.

The *modal rule* M can be seen as a game-theoretic version of the box rule $\mathsf{R}_\Box$ from the focus system, differing from it in two ways. First of all, the number of premises of M is not fixed, but depends on the number of box formulas in the conclusion; as a special case, if the conclusion contains no box formula at all, then the rule has an empty set of premises, similar to an axiom. Second, the rule M does allow side formulas in the consequent that are not modal; note however, that M has as its *side condition* (†) that this set Ψ contains atomic formulas only, and that it is *locally falsifiable*, i.e., Ψ does not contain $\top$ and there is no proposition letter p such that both p and $\overline{p}$ belong to Ψ. This side condition guarantees that M is only applicable if no other tableau rule is.

[2] Note that since we assume guardedness, the principal formula is different from its residuals.

$$\frac{}{p, \overline{p}, \Phi}\,\mathsf{Ax1} \qquad \frac{}{\top, \Phi}\,\mathsf{Ax2} \qquad \frac{\varphi, \psi, \Phi}{\varphi \vee \psi, \Phi}\,\mathsf{R}_\vee \qquad \frac{\varphi, \Phi \qquad \psi, \Phi}{\varphi \wedge \psi, \Phi}\,\mathsf{R}_\wedge$$

$$(\dagger)\,\frac{\varphi_1, \Phi \qquad \dots \qquad \varphi_n, \Phi}{\Psi, \Box\varphi_1, \dots, \Box\varphi_n, \Diamond\Phi}\,\mathsf{M} \qquad \frac{\varphi[\mu x.\varphi/x], \Phi}{\mu x.\varphi, \Phi}\,\mathsf{R}_\mu \qquad \frac{\varphi[\nu x.\varphi/x], \Phi}{\nu x.\varphi, \Phi}\,\mathsf{R}_\nu$$

Fig. 3. Rules of the tableau system

Definition 4. *A* tableau *is a quintuple* $\mathbb{T} = (V, E, \Phi, \mathsf{Q}, v_I)$, *where* (V, E) *is a directed graph,* $v_I \in V$ *is the* root *of the tableau,* Φ *maps every node* v *to a non-empty sequent* Φ_v, *and* $\mathsf{Q} : V \to \{\mathsf{Ax1}, \mathsf{Ax2}, \mathsf{R}_\vee, \mathsf{R}_\wedge, \mathsf{M}, \mathsf{R}_\mu, \mathsf{R}_\nu\}$ *associates a proof rule* Q_v *with each node* v *in* V. *Tableaux must satisfy the following:*

1. *If* $\mathsf{Q}(u) = \mathsf{R}$ *then the sequents at the node* u *and its successors match the specification of* R *as in Fig. 3.*
2. *If* $\mathsf{Q}(u) = \mathsf{M}$ *then the side condition* $(\dagger)$ *of* M *is met.*
3. *In any application of the rules* $\mathsf{R}_\vee, \mathsf{R}_\wedge, \mathsf{R}_\mu$ *and* R_ν, *the principal formula is not an element of the context* Φ.

A tableau $\mathbb{T}$ *is a* tableau for a sequent Φ *if* Φ *is the sequent of the root of* $\mathbb{T}$.

The following can easily be proved.

Proposition 3. *There is a tree-based tableau for every sequent* Φ.

Crucially, one needs to keep track of the development of individual formulas along infinite paths in a tableau. Fix a tableau $\mathbb{T} = (V, E, \Phi, \mathsf{Q}, v_I)$.

Definition 5. *For all nodes* $u, v \in V$ *such that* Euv *we define the* active trail relation $\mathsf{A}_{u,v} \subseteq \Phi_u \times \Phi_v$ *and the* passive trail relation $\mathsf{P}_{u,v} \subseteq \Phi_u \times \Phi_v$, *via the following case distinction:*

Case $\mathsf{Q}_u = \mathsf{R}_\vee$: *With* $\Phi_u = \{\varphi \vee \psi\} \uplus \Psi$ *and* $\Phi_v = \{\varphi, \psi\} \cup \Psi$, *we define* $\mathsf{A}_{u,v} = \{(\varphi \vee \psi, \varphi), (\varphi \vee \psi, \psi)\}$ *and* $\mathsf{P}_{u,v} = \Delta_\Psi$, *where* $\Delta_\Psi = \{(\varphi, \varphi) \mid \varphi \in \Psi\}$.
Case $\mathsf{Q}_u = \mathsf{R}_\wedge$: *With* $\Phi_u = \{\varphi_0 \wedge \varphi_1\} \uplus \Psi$ *and* v *corresponding to the conjunct* φ_i, *we set* $\mathsf{A}_{u,v} = \{(\varphi_0 \wedge \varphi_1, \varphi_i)\}$ *and* $\mathsf{P}_{u,v} = \Delta_\Psi$.
Case $\mathsf{Q}_u = \mathsf{R}_\eta$: *With* $\Phi_u = \{\eta x.\varphi\} \uplus \Psi$ *and* $\Phi_v = \{\varphi[\eta x.\varphi/x]\} \cup \Psi$, *we define* $\mathsf{A}_{u,v} = \{(\eta x.\varphi, \varphi[\eta x.\varphi/x])\}$ *and* $\mathsf{P}_{u,v} = \Delta_\Psi$.
Case $\mathsf{Q}_u = \mathsf{M}$: *With* $\Phi_u = \Psi \cup \{\Box\varphi_1, \dots, \Box\varphi_n\} \cup \Diamond\Phi$ *and* $\Phi_v = \{\varphi_v\} \cup \Phi$, *we define* $\mathsf{A}_{u,v} = \{(\Box\varphi_v, \varphi_v)\} \cup \{(\Diamond\varphi, \varphi) \mid \varphi \in \Phi\}$ *and* $\mathsf{P}_{u,v} = \varnothing$.

Finally, we define the general trail relation *as* $\mathsf{T}_{u,v} := \mathsf{A}_{u,v} \cup \mathsf{P}_{u,v}$.

Definition 6. *A* path *in* $\mathbb{T}$ *is simply a path in the underlying graph* (V, E) *of* $\mathbb{T}$. *A* trail *on such a path* $\pi = (v_n)_{n<\kappa}$ *is a sequence* $\tau = (\varphi_n)_{n<\kappa}$ *of formulas such that* $(\varphi_i, \varphi_{i+1}) \in \mathsf{T}_{v_i, v_{i+1}}$, *whenever* $i + 1 < \kappa$. *The* tightening $\widehat{\tau}$ *is obtained from* τ *by removing all* φ_{i+1} *from* τ *for which* $(\varphi_i, \varphi_{i+1})$ *belongs to the passive trail relation* $\mathsf{P}_{v_i, v_{i+1}}$.

Because of guardedness, any infinite path π in $\mathbb{T}$ witnesses infinitely many applications of the rule M; and for any trail $(\varphi_n)_{n<\omega}$ on π there are infinitely many i such that $(\varphi_i, \varphi_{i+1}) \in \mathsf{A}_{v_i, v_{i+1}}$. Furthermore, for any two nodes u, v with Euv and $(\varphi, \psi) \in \mathsf{T}_{u,v}$, we have either $(\varphi, \psi) \in \mathsf{A}_{u,v}$ and $\psi \in \mathsf{Clos}_0(\varphi)$, or $(\varphi, \psi) \in \mathsf{P}_{u,v}$ and $\varphi = \psi$. It is then not difficult to see that tightened trails are *traces*, and that the tightening of an infinite trail is infinite.

Definition 7. *Let $\tau = (\varphi_n)_{n<\omega}$ be an infinite trail on the path $\pi = (v_n)_{n<\omega}$ in some tableau $\mathbb{T}$. Then we call τ an η-*trail *if its tightening $\widehat{\tau}$ is an η-trace.*

Tableau Games. With each tableau $\mathbb{T}$ we associate a *tableau game* $\mathcal{G}(\mathbb{T})$, with two players, *Prover* (female) and *Refuter* (male).

Definition 8. *Given a tableau $\mathbb{T} = (V, E, \Phi, \mathsf{Q}, v_I)$, the* tableau game *$\mathcal{G}(\mathbb{T})$ is the (initialised) board game $\mathcal{G}(\mathbb{T}) = (V, E, O, \mathcal{M}_\nu, v_I)$ defined as follows. O is a partial map that assigns an* owner *$O(v)$ to some positions $v \in V$. Refuter owns all positions that are labelled with one of the axioms,* Ax1 *or* Ax2*, or with the rule $\mathsf{R}_\wedge$; Prover owns all position labelled with* M*; O is undefined on all other positions. In this context v_I will be called the* initial *position of the game.*

The set $\mathcal{M}_\nu$ is the winning condition *of the game (for Prover); it is defined as the set of infinite paths through the graph that carry a ν-trail.*

A *match* of the game consists of the two players moving a token from one position to another, starting at the initial position, and following the edge relation E. The owner of a position is responsible for moving the token from that position to an adjacent one (that is, an E-successor); in case this is impossible because the node has no E-successors, the player *gets stuck* and immediately loses the match. For instance, Refuter loses as soon as the token reaches an axiomatic leaf labelled Ax1 or Ax2; similarly, Prover loses at any modal node without successors. If the token reaches a position that is not owned by a player, that is, a node of $\mathbb{T}$ that is labelled with the proof rule $\mathsf{R}_\vee$, R_μ or R_ν, the token automatically moves to the unique successor of the position. If neither player gets stuck, the resulting match is infinite; we declare Prover to be its winner if the match, as an E-path, belongs to the set $\mathcal{M}_\nu$, that is, if it carries a ν-trail.

Finally, a *winning* strategy for a player P in $\mathcal{G}(\mathbb{T})$ is a way of playing that guarantees that P wins the resulting match, no matter how P's opponent plays.

Remark 1. If $\mathbb{T}$ is *tree-based* we may identify strategies for either player with *subtrees* S of $\mathbb{T}$ that contain the root of $\mathbb{T}$ and, for any node s in S, (1) contain exactly one successor of s in case the player owns the position s, and (2) contain all successors of s in case the player's opponent owns the position s.

The observations below are essentially due to Niwiński & Walukiewicz [21].

Theorem 3 (Determinacy). *Let $\mathbb{T}$ be a some tableau. Then precisely one of the players has a winning strategy in $\mathcal{G}(\mathbb{T})$.*

Theorem 4 (Adequacy). *Let $\mathbb{T}$ be a tableau for a sequent Φ. Then Refuter (Prover, respectively) has a winning strategy in $\mathcal{G}(\mathbb{T})$ iff the formula $\bigvee \Phi$ is refutable (valid, respectively).*

Corollary 1. *Let $\mathbb{T}$ and $\mathbb{T}'$ be two tableaux for the same sequent. Then Prover has a winning strategy in $\mathcal{G}(\mathbb{T})$ iff she has a winning strategy in $\mathcal{G}(\mathbb{T}')$.*

4 Soundness

In this section we establish the soundness of our system. Because of Theorem 4 and Theorem 1 it suffices to prove the following.

Theorem 5. *Let Φ be some sequent. If Φ is provable in Focus_∞ then there is some tableau $\mathbb{T}$ for Φ such that Prover has a winning strategy in $\mathcal{G}(\mathbb{T})$.*

We will prove the soundness theorem by transforming a thin and progressive Focus_∞-proof of Φ into a winning strategy for Prover in the tableau game associated with some tableau for Φ. We first adapt the notion of trail from tableaux to the setting of Focus_∞-proofs.

Definition 9. *Let $\Pi = (T, P, \Sigma, \mathsf{R})$ be a thin and progressive proof in Focus_∞. For all nodes $u, v \in V$ such that Puv we define the* active trail relation $\mathsf{A}_{u,v} \subseteq \Sigma_u \times \Sigma_v$ *and the* passive trail relation $\mathsf{P}_{u,v} \subseteq \Sigma_u \times \Sigma_v$, *via the following case distinction:*

Case $\mathsf{R}(u) = \mathsf{R}_\vee$: With $\Sigma_u = \{(\varphi \vee \psi)^a\} \uplus \Gamma$ and $\Sigma_v = \{\varphi^a, \psi^a\} \cup \Gamma$, we define $\mathsf{A}_{u,v} := \{((\varphi \vee \psi)^a, \varphi^a), ((\varphi \vee \psi)^a, \psi^a)\}$ and $\mathsf{P}_{u,v} := \Delta_\Gamma$.

In the cases where $\mathsf{R}(u) \in \{\mathsf{R}_\wedge, \mathsf{R}_\mu, \mathsf{R}_\nu, \mathsf{R}_\Box\}$ we proceed analogously.

Case $\mathsf{R}(u) = \mathsf{W}$: With $\Sigma_u = \Sigma_v \uplus \{\varphi^a\}$, we set $\mathsf{A}_{u,v} := \varnothing$ and $\mathsf{P}_{u,v} := \Delta_{\Sigma_v}$.

Case $\mathsf{R}(u) \in \{\mathsf{F}, \mathsf{U}\}$: With $\Sigma_u = \{\varphi^a\} \cup \Gamma$ and $\Sigma_v = \{\varphi^{\overline{a}}\} \cup \Gamma$, we define $\mathsf{A}_{u,v} = \varnothing$ and $\mathsf{P}_{u,v} = \{(\varphi^a, \varphi^{\overline{a}})\} \cup \Delta_\Gamma$.

We also define the general trail relation $\mathsf{T}_{u,v} := \mathsf{A}_{u,v} \cup \mathsf{P}_{u,v}$.

We inductively extend the trail relation $\mathsf{T}_{u,v}$ to any two nodes such that P^*uv by putting $\mathsf{T}_{u,u} := \Delta_{\Sigma_u}$, and if Puw and P^*wv then $\mathsf{T}_{u,v} := \mathsf{T}_{u,w} \,;\, \mathsf{T}_{w,v}$, where ; denotes relational composition.

As in the case of tableaux, we will be specifically interested in infinite trails and their tighentings. These are defined in exactly the same way as for tableaux.

The following observation concerns a central feature of our focus mechanism.

Proposition 4. *Every infinite branch in a thin and progressive Focus_∞-proof carries a ν-trail.*

Proof. Consider an infinite branch $\alpha = (v_n)_{n \in \omega}$ in some thin and progressive Focus_∞-proof $\Pi = (T, P, \Sigma, \mathsf{R})$. Then α is successful by assumption, so that we may fix a k such that for every $j \geq k$, the sequent Σ_{v_j} contains a formula in focus, and $\mathsf{R}(v_j)$ is not a focus rule. We claim that

$$\text{for every } j \geq k \text{ and } \psi^f \in \Sigma_{v_{j+1}} \text{ there is a } \chi^f \in \Sigma_{v_j} \text{ with } (\chi^f, \psi^f) \in \mathsf{T}_{v_j, v_{j+1}}. \tag{1}$$

To see this, let $j \geq k$ and $\psi^f \in \Sigma_{v_{j+1}}$. It is obvious that there is some annotated formula $\chi^a \in \Sigma_{v_j}$ with $(\chi^a, \psi^f) \in \mathsf{T}_{v_j,v_{j+1}}$. The key observation is now that in fact $a = f$, and this holds because the only way that we could have $(\chi^u, \psi^f) \in \mathsf{T}_{v_j,v_{j+1}}$ is if we applied the focus rule at v_j, which would contradict our assumption on the nodes v_j for $j \geq k$.

Now consider the graph (V, E) where

$$V := \{(j, \varphi) \mid k \leq j < \omega \text{ and } \varphi^f \in \Sigma_{v_j}\},$$
$$E := \big\{((j, \varphi), (j+1, \psi)) \mid (\varphi^f, \psi^f) \in \mathsf{T}_{v_j,v_{j+1}}\big\}$$

This graph is directed, acyclic, infinite and finitely branching. Furthermore, it follows by (1) that every node (j, φ) is reachable in (V, E) from some node (k, ψ). Then by a (variation of) König's Lemma there is an infinite path $(n, \varphi^f_n)_{n \in \omega}$ in this graph. The induced sequence $\tau := (\varphi^f_n)_{n \in \omega}$ is a trail on α by definition of E. By the fact that α features infinitely many applications of $\mathsf{R}_\Box$, the tightening $\widehat{\tau}$ of τ must be infinite, and so τ is either a μ-trail or a ν-trail. But τ cannot feature infinitely many μ-formulas, simply because the rule R_μ attaches the label u to the unfolding of a μ-formula. This means that τ cannot be a μ-trail, and hence it must be a ν-trail. □

Proof of Theorem 5. Let $\Pi = (T, P, \Sigma, \mathsf{R})$ be a Focus_∞-proof for Φ^f. By Theorem 2 we may assume without loss of generality that Π is thin and progressive. We will construct a tableau $\mathbb{T} = (V, E, \Phi, \mathsf{Q}, v_I)$ and a winning strategy for Prover in $\mathcal{G}(\mathbb{T})$. Our construction will be such that (V, E) is a (generally infinite) tree, of which the winning strategy $S \subseteq V$ for Prover is a subtree, as in Remark 1.

In addition to the tableau $\mathbb{T}$ we define a function $g : S \to T$ satisfying the following three conditions, which will allow us to lift the ν-trails from Π to S:

1. If Euv then $P^* g(u) g(v)$.
2. The sequent $\Sigma_{g(u)}$ is thin, and $\widetilde{\Sigma}_{g(u)} \subseteq \Phi_u$.
3. If Euv and $(\psi^b, \varphi^a) \in \mathsf{T}^{\Pi}_{g(u),g(v)}$ then $(\psi, \varphi) \in \mathsf{T}^{\mathbb{T}}_{u,v}$.

The construction of $\mathbb{T}$, S and g is guided by the structure of Π and proceeds via an induction that starts from the root and in every step adds children to one of the nodes in the subtree S that is not yet an axiom. Nodes of $\mathbb{T}$ that are not in S are always immediately completely extended using Proposition 3, and thus need not be taken along in the inductive construction.

At step $n \in \omega$ of the construction, we are dealing with finite approximating objects $\mathbb{T}_n$, S_n and $g_n : S_n \to T$, and in the limit these will yield $\mathbb{T}$, S and g. Each $\mathbb{T}_n$ will be a *pre-tableau*, that is, an object as defined in Definition 4, except that we do not require the rule labelling to be defined for every leaf of the tree. The basic idea underlying the construction is that step n will take care of one such undetermined leaf of $\mathbb{T}_n$, say, l; the precise details of the construction (which are spelled out in [18]) depend on the nature of the proof rule applied in Π at the node $g_n(l)$.

It remains to be seen that S is a winning strategy for Prover in $\mathcal{G}(\mathbb{T})$. It is clear that she wins all finite matches that are played according to S because by construction all leaves in S are axioms. To show that she wins all infinite matches too, consider an infinite path $\beta = (v_n)_{n\in\omega}$ in S. We need to show that β contains a ν-trail. Using condition 1 it follows that there is an infinite path $\alpha = (t_n)_{n\in\omega}$ in Π such that for every $i \in \omega$ we have that $g(v_i) = t_{k_i}$ for some $k_i \in \omega$, and, moreover, $k_i \leq k_j$ if $i \leq j$. By Proposition 4 the infinite path α contains a ν-trail $\tau = \varphi_0^{a_0}\varphi_1^{a_1}\cdots$. With condition 3 it follows that $\tau' := \varphi_{k_0}\varphi_{k_1}\varphi_{k_2}\cdots$ is a trail on β. By Proposition 1, τ contains only finitely many μ-formulas; from this it is immediate that τ' also features at most finitely many μ-formulas. Thus, using Proposition 1 a second time, we find that τ' is a ν-trail, as required. □

5 Completeness

In this section we show that the focus systems are complete. Because of Theorem 4 and Theorem 1 it suffices to prove the following.

Theorem 6. *If Prover has a winning strategy in some tableau game for a sequent Φ then Φ is provable in* Focus_∞.

Proof. Let $\mathbb{T} = (V, E, \Phi, \mathsf{Q}, v_I)$ be a tableau for Φ and let S be a winning strategy for Prover in $\mathcal{G}(\mathbb{T})$. Because of Proposition 3, Corollary 1 and Remark 1, we may assume that $\mathbb{T}$ is tree based, with root v_I, and that $S \subseteq V$ is a subtree of $\mathbb{T}$. We will construct a Focus_∞-proof $\Pi = (T, P, \Sigma, \mathsf{R})$ for Φ^f.

Applications of the focus rules in Π will be very restricted. To start with, the unfocus rule U will not be used at all, and the focus rule F will only occur in the form of the following *total* focus rule F^t which is easily seen to be derivable as a series of successive applications of F:

$$\frac{\Phi^f}{\Phi^u}\ \mathsf{F}^t$$

We construct the pre-proof Π of Φ^f together with a function $g : S \to T$ in such a way that the following conditions are satisfied:

1. If Evu then $P^+g(v)g(u)$.
2. For every $v \in S$ and every infinite branch $\beta = (v_n)_{n\in\omega}$ in Π with $v_0 = g(v)$ there is some $i \in \omega$ and some $u \in S$ such that Evu and $g(u) = v_i$.
3. For every $\varphi \in \Phi_v$ there is a unique $a_\varphi \in \{f, u\}$ such that $\varphi^{a_\varphi} \in \Sigma_{g(v)}$. In particular, $\Sigma_{g(v)}$ is thin.
4. If Evu and $(\varphi, \psi) \in \mathsf{T}_{v,u}$ then $(\varphi^{a_\varphi}, \psi^{a_\psi}) \in \mathsf{T}_{g(v),g(u)}$.
5. If Evu, and s and t are nodes on the path from $g(v)$ to $g(u)$ such that P^+st, $(\chi^a, \varphi^f) \in \mathsf{T}_{g(v),s}$ for some $a \in \{f, u\}$ and $(\varphi^f, \psi^u) \in \mathsf{T}_{s,t}$, then $\chi = \varphi$ and χ is a μ-formula.
6. If α is an infinite branch of Π and F^t is applicable at some node on α, then F^t is applied at some later node on α.

We construct Π and g as the limit of finite stages, where at stage i we have constructed a finite pre-proof Π_i and a partial function $g_i : S \to \Pi_i$. At every stage we make sure that g_i and Π_i satisfy the following conditions:

7. All open leaves of Π_i are in the range of g_i.
8. All nodes $v \in S$ for which $g_i(v)$ is defined satisfy $\Phi_v = \widetilde{\Sigma}_{g_i(v)}$.

In the base case we define Π_0 to consist of just one node r that is labelled with the sequent Φ^f. The partial function g_0 maps r to v_I. Clearly, this satisfies the conditions 7 and 8.

In the inductive step we consider any open leaf m of Π_i, which has a minimal distance from the root of Π_i. This ensures that in the limit every open leaf is eventually treated, so that Π will not have any open leaves. By condition 7 there is a $u \in S$ such that $g(u) = m$. Our plan is to extend the proof Π_i at the open leaf m to mirror the rule that is applied at u in $\mathbb{T}$. In general this is possible because by condition 8 the formulas in the annotated sequent at $m = g_i(u)$ are the same as the formulas at u. All children of u that are in S should then be mapped by g_{i+1} to new open leaves in Π_{i+1}. Two technical issues feature in all the cases.

First, to ensure that condition 6 is satisfied by our construction we will apply F^t at m, whenever it is applicable. Thus, we need to check whether all formulas in the sequent of m are annotated with u. If this is the case then we apply the total focus rule and proceed with its premise n; otherwise we just proceed with $n = m$. Note that in either case the sequent at n contains the same formulas as the sequent at m and if $n \neq m$ then the trace relation relates the formulas at n in an obvious way to those at m. The second technical issue is that to ensure condition 3 we may need to apply W to the new leaves of Π_{i+1}. For the details of the construction, which are based on a straightforward case distinction depending on the rule $\mathsf{Q}(u)$, we refer to the technical report [18].

We define $\Pi = (T, P, \Sigma, \mathsf{R})$ and the function $g : S \to T$ as the limit of the structures Π_i and the maps g_i, respectively. The proof that g and Π satisfy the conditions 1–6, is fairly routine; details can be found in [18].

It is more interesting to see why Π is a correct Focus_∞-proof. Leaving the routine argument as to why Π is a pre-proof to the reader, we concentrate on the proof that every infinite branch of Π is successful. Let $\beta = (v_n)_{n\in\omega}$ be such a branch. Based on our construction it will not be hard to see that β witnesses infinitely many application of the box rule $\mathsf{R}_\Box$. Our key claim is that

$$\text{from some moment on, every sequent on } \beta \text{ contains a formula in focus.} \quad (2)$$

By condition 2 we can link β to a branch $\alpha = (t_n)_{n\in\omega}$ in S such that there are $0 = k_0 < k_1 < k_2 < \cdots$ with $g(t_i) = v_{k_i}$ for all $i < \omega$. Because α, as a match of the tableau game, is won by Prover, it contains a ν-trail $(\varphi_n)_{n\in\omega}$, so by condition 4 we obtain an annotated trail $\tau = (\psi_n^{a_n})_{n\in\omega}$ on β such that $\varphi_i = \psi_{k_i}$ for all i. Then by Proposition 1 τ is a ν-trail as well; in particular, it contains *no* μ-formulas after a certain moment k.

Now distinguish cases. If β has no application of F^t after k, then by condition 6 this rule is not applicable any more, so that by its definition β must witness a formula in focus at every node v_n with $n \geq k$ indeed. On the other hand, if $\mathsf{R}(v_n) = \mathsf{F}^t$ for $n \geq k$, then at stage $n+1$ every formula is in focus . In particular, we find $a_{n+1} = f$, and since no μ-formula is unfolded on τ after this, we may show that τ keeps passing through formulas in focus from this moment on.

This proves (2), and, again by condition 6, we may conclude that β features only finitely many applications of F^t. Since all applications of F in Π are part of F^t, and the unfocus rule U is not used anywhere in Π, β is successful indeed. □

6 Conclusion and Questions

In this paper we saw that the idea of placing formulas in *focus* can be extended from the setting of logics like LTL and CTL [17] to that of the alternation-free modal μ-calculus: we designed a very simple and natural, cut-free sequent system which is sound and complete for all validities in the language consisting of all (guarded) formulas in the alternation-free fragment $\mathcal{L}_\mu^{af}$ of the modal μ-calculus.

In a follow-up paper we use the Focus system to show that the alternation-free fragment enjoys the Craig Interpolation Theorem. Clearly, these results support the claim that $\mathcal{L}_\mu^{af}$ is an interesting logic with good meta-logical properties.

Below we list questions for future research. To start with, we based our soundness and completeness proofs on Niwiński & Walukiewicz' tableau games [21]. A reviewer suggested that our proofs might be simplified by connecting to the non-wellfounded proof system of Studer [24]. We leave this for future work.

Probably the most obvious question is whether the restriction to guarded formulas can be lifted. Note that guardedness is related to the condition that successful branches in a Focus_∞-proof feature infinitely many applications of the rule $\mathsf{R}_\Box$, which plays a crucial role in the soundness proof (cf. Proposition 4). Without guardedness, this condition would be too strong since it would disqualify any proof for a valid formula like $\nu x.x$.

Note that our proof systems are cut free, and that it follows from our soundness and completeness results that the cut rule is admissible. It would be of interest to see whether this can also be proved constructively, corresponding to a cut elimination procedure for the version of the system with the cut rule.

Another question is whether we may tidy up the focus proof system, in the same way that Afshari & Leigh did with the Jungteerapanich-Stirling system [1, 14,23]. As a corollary of this it should be possible to obtain an annotation-free sequent system for the alternation-free fragment of the μ-calculus, and to prove completeness of Kozen's axiomatisation for $\mathcal{L}_\mu^{af}$.

It is straightforward to generalise our result to the alternation-free fragment of variants of the modal μ-calculus, such as the polymodal or the monotone μ-calculus. Of particular interest is the *linear time μ-calculus* (i.e., where both $\Diamond$ and $\Box$ are the next time operator), since in this setting the alternation-free μ-calculus is known to have the same expressive power as the full language. It would be interesting to prove a general result for *coalgebraic modal μ-calculi*.

Moving in a somewhat different direction, we are interested to see to which degree the focus system can serve as a basis for sound and complete derivation systems for the alternation-free validities in classes of frames satisfying various kinds of frame conditions.

References

1. Afshari, B., Leigh, G.: Cut-free completeness for modal mu-calculus. In: Proceedings of the 32nd Annual ACM/IEEE Symposium on Logic In Computer Science (LICS 2017), pp. 1–12. IEEE Computer Society (2017)
2. Alberucci, L., Facchini, A.: The modal μ-calculus over restricted classes of transition systems. J. Symb. Log. **74**(4), 1367–1400 (2009)
3. Andreoli, J.: Logic programming with focusing proofs in linear logic. J. Log. Comput. **2**, 297–347 (1992)
4. Arnold, A., Niwiński, D.: Rudiments of μ-calculus. Studies in Logic and the Foundations of Mathematics, vol. 146. North-Holland Publishing Co., Amsterdam (2001)
5. Bradfield, J., Stirling, C.: Modal μ-calculi. In: van Benthem, J., Blackburn, P., Wolter, F. (eds.) Handbook of Modal Logic, pp. 721–756. Elsevier (2006)
6. Carreiro, F., Facchini, A., Venema, Y., Zanasi, F.: The power of the weak. ACM Trans. Comput. Log. **21**(2):15:1–15:47 (2020)
7. Dax, C., Hofmann, M., Lange, M.: A proof system for the linear time μ-calculus. In: Arun-Kumar, S., Garg, N. (eds.) International Conference on Foundations of Software Technology and Theoretical Computer Science, Lecture Notes in Computer Science, pp. 273–284 (2006)
8. Demri, S., Goranko, V., Lange, M.: Temporal Logics in Computer Science: Finite-State Systems. Cambridge Tracts in Theoretical Computer Science. Cambridge University Press, Cambridge (2016)
9. Emerson, E.A., Jutla, C.S.: The complexity of tree automata and logics of programs. SIAM J. Comput. **29**(1), 132–158 (1999)
10. Grädel, E., Thomas, W., Wilke, T. (eds.): Automata, Logic, and Infinite Games, volume 2500 of LNCS. Springer, Heidelberg (2002)
11. Gutierrez, J., Klaedtke, F., Lange, M.: The *mu*-calculus alternation hierarchy collapses over structures with restricted connectivity. Theor. Comput. Sci. **560**, 292–306 (2014)
12. Janin, D., Walukiewicz, I.: Automata for the modal μ-calculus and related results. In: Wiedermann J., Hájek P. (eds.) Mathematical Foundations of Computer Science 1995. MFCS 1995. LNCS, vol. 969, pp. 552–562. Springer, Berlin, Heidelberg (1995). https://doi.org/10.1007/3-540-60246-1_160
13. Janin D., Walukiewicz I.: On the expressive completeness of the propositional mu-calculus with respect to monadic second order logic. In: Montanari, U., Sassone, V. (eds.) CONCUR 1996: Concurrency Theory. CONCUR 1996. Lecture Notes in Computer Science, vol. 1119, pp. 263–277 (1996). Springer, Berlin, Heidelberg. https://doi.org/10.1007/3-540-61604-7_60
14. Jungteerapanich, N.: Tableau systems for the modal μ-calculus. PhD thesis, School of Informatics; The University of Edinburgh (2010)
15. Kaivola, R.: Axiomatising linear time mu-calculus. In: Lee, I., Smolka, S.A. (eds.) CONCUR 1995. LNCS, vol. 962, pp. 423–437. Springer, Heidelberg (1995). https://doi.org/10.1007/3-540-60218-6_32
16. Kozen, D.: Results on the propositional μ-calculus. Theor. Comput. Sci. **27**, 333–354 (1983)

17. Lange, M., Stirling, C.: Focus games for satisfiability and completeness of temporal logic. In: Proceedings of the 16th International Conference on Logic in Computer Science (LICS 2001), pp. 357–365. IEEE Computer Society (2001)
18. Marti, J., Venema, Y.: Focus-style proof systems and interpolation for the alternation-free μ-calculus. CoRR, abs/2103.01671 (2021)
19. Muller, D.E., Saoudi, A., Schupp, P.E.: Alternating automata, the weak monadic theory of trees and its complexity. Theor. Comput. Sci. **97**(2), 233–234 (1992)
20. Niwiński, D.: On fixed-point clones. In: Kott, L. (ed.) ICALP 1986. LNCS, vol. 226, pp. 464–473. Springer, Heidelberg (1986). https://doi.org/10.1007/3-540-16761-7_96
21. Niwínski, D., Walukiewicz, I.: Games for the μ-calculus. Theor. Comput. Sci. **163**, 99–116 (1996)
22. Safra, S.: On the complexity of ω-automata. In: Proceedings of the 29th Symposium on the Foundations of Computer Science, pp. 319–327. IEEE Computer Society Press (1988)
23. Stirling, C.: A tableau proof system with names for modal mu-calculus. In: Voronkov, A., Korovina, M.V. (eds.) HOWARD-60: A Festschrift on the Occasion of Howard Barringer's 60th Birthday, vol. 42, pp. 306–318 (2014)
24. Studer, T.: On the proof theory of the modal mu-calculus. Stud. Logica **89**(3), 343–363 (2008)
25. Walukiewicz, I.: On completeness of the mu-calculus. In: Proceedings of the Eighth Annual Symposium on Logic in Computer Science (LICS 1993), pp. 136–146. IEEE Computer Society (1993)
26. Wilke, T.: Alternating tree automata, parity games, and modal μ-calculus. Bull. Belgian Math. Soc. **8**, 359–391 (2001)

Intuitionistic Modal Logics

Terminating Calculi and Countermodels for Constructive Modal Logics

Tiziano Dalmonte[1(✉)], Charles Grellois[2], and Nicola Olivetti[2]

[1] Technische Universität Wien, Vienna, Austria
tiziano@logic.at
[2] Aix-Marseille University, Université de Toulon, CNRS, LIS, Marseille, France
{charles.grellois,nicola.olivetti}@lis-lab.fr

Abstract. We investigate terminating sequent calculi for constructive modal logics CK and CCDL in the style of Dyckhoff's calculi for intuitionistic logic. We first present strictly terminating calculi for these logics. Our calculi provide immediately a decision procedure for the respective logics and have good proof-theoretical properties, namely they allow for a syntactic proof of cut admissibility. We then present refutation calculi for non-provability in both logics. Their main feature is that they support direct countermodel extraction: each refutation directly defines a finite countermodel of the refuted formula in a natural neighbourhood semantics for these logics.

Keywords: Modal logic · Intuitionistic logic · Constructive modal logics · Sequent calculus · Refutation · Countermodels

1 Introduction

Intuitionistic modal logic has a long history going back to the pioneering work by Fitch [8] in the late 40's and then by Prawitz [20] in the 60's. It is not possible to retrace here the whole history. It is now clear that there are two traditions leading to two distinct families of systems. The first one, called Intuitionistic modal logics have been introduced by Fischer Servi [7] and Plotkin and Stirling [19] and then systematised by Simpson [21] whose main goal is to define an analogous of classical modalities justified from an intuitionistic meta-theory. Simpson's basic systems is modal logic IK, intended to be the intuitionistic counterpart of minimal normal modal logic K. The second one, called Constructive modal logics, are mainly motivated by their applications to computer science, such as the type-theoretic interpretations (Curry-Howard correspondence, typed lambda

We thank the reviewers for very accurate comments and corrections that helped us to improve the first version of this paper. This work has been partially supported by the ANR-FWF project TICAMORE ANR-16-CE91-0002-01; FWF I 2982. Dalmonte is supported by a Ernst Mach worldwide grant implemented by the OeAD, Austria Agency for Education and Internationalisation, and financed by BMBWF.

A. Das and S. Negri (Eds.): TABLEAUX 2021, LNAI 12842, pp. 391–408, 2021.
https://doi.org/10.1007/978-3-030-86059-2_23

calculi), verification and knowledge representation, together with their mathematical semantics. This second tradition has been developed independently, first by Wijesekera [23] who proposed the system CCDL (Constructive Concurrent Dynamic logic), and then by Bellin, De Paiva, and Ritter [2], among the others who proposed the logic CK (Constructive K) as the basic system for a constructive account of modality (see also the survey [22] and the references therein). Wijesekera's propositional CCDL was originally motivated as a logic of partial observations of concurrent actions, whereas CK can be also interpreted as a logic of contextual reasoning [16]. From an axiomatic point of view all systems (including Simpson's IK) share the same $\Box$-fragment, but they differ on the interpretation of diamond and interaction between the two modalities, in particular CCDL rejects diamond distribution over disjunction:

$$\Diamond(A \vee B) \rightarrow \Diamond A \vee \Diamond B$$

which is an axiom of IK, in addition CK further rejects its nullary version:

$$\neg\Diamond\bot$$

which is valid in CCDL.

The system CK has been extensively investigated from a proof-theoretical point of view: in addition to its Gentzen sequent calculus, a natural deduction system for it has been proposed [2], which leads to a type-theoretical interpretation of CK within an extended Lambda-calculus. Further proof systems for CK exist in the form of nested sequent calculus [1] and focused 2-sequent calculus [17], whereas a tableaux calculus for full CCDL is presented in [24].

From a semantical point of view, both CCDL and CK enjoy a Kripke semantics in terms of bi-relational Kripke models [16,23], although in order to accommodate the failure of $\neg\Diamond\bot$ Kripke models for CK must be equipped with "inconsistent" worlds which force $\bot$. The failure of distribution of $\Diamond$ over disjunction makes $\Diamond$ a non-normal modality, so that it does not come as a surprise that the semantic tools for non-normal modal logics can be employed for analysing these logics. For CCDL Kojima [15] has proposed a semantics in terms of intuitionistic neighbourhood models (see also [11] for neighbourhood models of intuitionistic logics with only $\Box$). More recently an alternative semantics in terms of neighbourhood models has been provided in [3], in that semantics models are equipped with two neighbourhood functions for interpreting the two modalities, this semantics accounts uniformly both CCDL and CK without the need of "inconsistent" worlds. Moreover in both cases finite neighbourhood models can be transformed into relational models of the corresponding logics (but the obtained model may be much larger). This is the intended semantics for both CCDL and CK we consider in this work.

Despite the amount of research on proof systems, decision procedures based on proof systems have not been studied,[1] and there is no work on countermodel

[1] Decidability for these logics follows from the finite model property established in Mendler and de Paiva [16] and Dalmonte et al. [3].

generation from failed derivations in sequent calculi neither for CK, nor for CCDL, which is the aim of this work. We are interested here in developing terminating proof systems that can be used also to extract countermodels from failed proof search. Our starting point is the calculus G4ip′ proposed by Dyckhoff [4]: his calculus has the form of a multiple-succedent sequent calculus comprising special decomposition rules; its main feature is that it is terminating in itself, without any control on proof-search. This calculus has been extended by Iemhoff [13] to intuitionistic/constructive modal logic, but only for the □-fragment (on which all systems, namely Simpson's IK, CCDL and CK coincide). Extending Iemhoff's work, our first contribution is the proposition of terminating calculi for both CK and CCDL in their full language with both modalities. The two calculi provide then immediately a decision procedure for the respective logics. Moreover the calculi have good proof theoretical properties, first of all they allow a syntactic proof of cut-elimination.

Next we define a refutation calculus which allows for countermodel extraction. Our starting point is the refutation calculus CRIP for intuitionistic logic proposed by Pinto and Dyckhoff [18]: in this calculus a derivation, or better a refutation, directly provides a countermodel of the root-formula. In Pinto and Dyckhoff's view: Kripke countermodels are witnesses of refutations, as much as lambda terms are witnesses of proofs. We propose terminating refutation calculi for both CK and CCDL. From one refutation in these calculi it can be defined *directly* a countermodel of the checked formula/sequent, namely a countermodel in the neighbourhood semantics mentioned above. In contrast we are not aware of any calculus for any of these two logics which allows for countermodel extraction within the original relational semantics.

The fact that a refutation corresponds directly to a neighbourhood countermodel confirms the significance of the neighbourhood semantics for these logics, thereby extending Pinto and Dyckhoff's views: neighbourhood countermodels are *the* natural witnesses of refutations for constructive modal logics.

2 Constructive Modal Logics and Their Semantics

In this section we present the constructive modal logics CK and CCDL in the form of axiomatic systems as well as their neighbourhood semantics. CK and CCDL are defined in a propositional modal language $\mathcal{L}$ based on a set $Atm = \{p_1, p_2, p_3, ...\}$ of countably many propositional variables; the *well-formed formulas* of $\mathcal{L}$ are generated by the following grammar, where p_i is any element of Atm:

$$A ::= p_i \mid \bot \mid A \wedge A \mid A \vee A \mid A \supset A \mid \Box A \mid \Diamond A.$$

In the following, we call 'atomic formulas' the propositional variables and $\bot$, we call 'atomic implication' every implication whose antecedent is an atomic formula, finally we call '□-formula', resp. '◇-formula', every formula whose outermost connective is □, resp. ◇. As usual we define $\neg A$ as $A \supset \bot$.

Definition 1. *The logic* CK *is defined by extending (any axiomatisation of) intuitionistic propositional logic, formulated in the modal language $\mathcal{L}$, with the following modal axioms and rules:*

$$Nec\,\frac{A}{\Box A} \qquad K_\Box\ \Box(A \supset B) \supset (\Box A \supset \Box B) \qquad K_\Diamond\ \Box(A \supset B) \supset (\Diamond A \supset \Diamond B).$$

The logic CCDL *is defined by extending* CK *with the additional axiom*

$$N_\Diamond\ \neg\Diamond\bot.$$

In the following we denote by C* any of the two logics. CK and CCDL have both relational [16,23] and neighbourhood semantics [3,15]. Independently from its interest in itself, one of the advantages of the neighbourhood semantics is that, as we shall see, our refutation calculi directly build a neighbourhood countermodel of every refuted formula, whether the same does not seem to be the case with relational models. Here we consider a minor variation of the neighbourhood semantics of [3] (as explained below) which allows for a more immediate extraction of countermodels from the calculi.

Definition 2. *A* neighbourhood model *for* CK *is a tuple $\mathcal{M} = \langle \mathcal{W}, \preceq, \mathcal{N}_\Box, \mathcal{N}_\Diamond, \mathcal{V}\rangle$ where: $\mathcal{W}$ is a non-empty set; $\preceq$ is a preorder over $\mathcal{W}$; $\mathcal{V}$ is a valuation function $Atm \to \mathcal{P}(\mathcal{W})$ satisfying the hereditary condition:*

$$\text{if } w \in \mathcal{V}(p) \text{ and } w \preceq v, \text{ then } v \in \mathcal{V}(p);$$

and $\mathcal{N}_\Box$ and $\mathcal{N}_\Diamond$ are two neighbourhood functions $\mathcal{W} \longrightarrow \mathcal{P}(\mathcal{P}(\mathcal{W}))$ satisfying the following conditions:

if $w \preceq v$, then $\mathcal{N}_\Box(w) \subseteq \mathcal{N}_\Box(v)$ and $\mathcal{N}_\Diamond(w) \subseteq \mathcal{N}_\Diamond(v)$	*($\Box$- and $\Diamond$-monotonicity)*
if $\alpha \in \mathcal{N}_\Box(w)$ and $\alpha \subseteq \beta$, then $\beta \in \mathcal{N}_\Box(w)$	*($\Box$-supplementation)*
if $\alpha \in \mathcal{N}_\Diamond(w)$ and $\alpha \subseteq \beta$, then $\beta \in \mathcal{N}_\Diamond(w)$	*($\Diamond$-supplementation)*
$\mathcal{W} \in \mathcal{N}_\Box(w)$	*($\Box$-containing the unit)*
if $\alpha, \beta \in \mathcal{N}_\Box(w)$, then $\alpha \cap \beta \in \mathcal{N}_\Box(w)$	*($\Box$-intersection closure)*
if $\alpha \in \mathcal{N}_\Box(w)$ and $\beta \in \mathcal{N}_\Diamond(w)$, then $\alpha \cap \beta \in \mathcal{N}_\Diamond(w)$	*($\Box\Diamond$-intersection closure)*

A neighbourhood model for CCDL *is any neighbourhood model for* CK *where $\mathcal{N}_\Diamond$ satisfies the following additional condition:*

$$\emptyset \notin \mathcal{N}_\Diamond(w) \quad (\Diamond\text{-consistency}).$$

The forcing relation $\mathcal{M}, w \Vdash A$ is defined as follows, where $[\![B]\!]$ denotes the set $\{v \in \mathcal{W} \mid \mathcal{M}, v \Vdash B\}$ of the worlds forcing B in $\mathcal{M}$:

$\mathcal{M}, w \Vdash p$	*iff*	$w \in \mathcal{V}(p)$;
$\mathcal{M}, w \nVdash \bot$;		
$\mathcal{M}, w \Vdash B \wedge C$	*iff*	$\mathcal{M}, w \Vdash A$ *and* $\mathcal{M}, w \Vdash B$;
$\mathcal{M}, w \Vdash B \vee C$	*iff*	$\mathcal{M}, w \Vdash A$ *or* $\mathcal{M}, w \Vdash B$;
$\mathcal{M}, w \Vdash B \supset C$	*iff*	*for every* $v \succeq w$, $\mathcal{M}, v \Vdash B$ *implies* $\mathcal{M}, v \Vdash C$;
$\mathcal{M}, w \Vdash \Box B$	*iff*	$[\![B]\!] \in \mathcal{N}_\Box(w)$;
$\mathcal{M}, w \Vdash \Diamond B$	*iff*	$[\![B]\!] \in \mathcal{N}_\Diamond(w)$.

$$\mathsf{init}\ \frac{}{\Gamma, p \Rightarrow p, \Delta} \qquad \mathsf{L}\bot\ \frac{}{\Gamma, \bot \Rightarrow \Delta} \qquad \mathsf{R}\wedge\ \frac{\Gamma \Rightarrow A, \Delta \quad \Gamma \Rightarrow B, \Delta}{\Gamma \Rightarrow A \wedge B, \Delta}$$

$$\mathsf{L}\wedge\ \frac{\Gamma, A, B \Rightarrow \Delta}{\Gamma, A \wedge B \Rightarrow \Delta} \qquad \mathsf{R}\vee\ \frac{\Gamma \Rightarrow A, B, \Delta}{\Gamma \Rightarrow A \vee B, \Delta} \qquad \mathsf{L}\vee\ \frac{\Gamma, A \Rightarrow \Delta \quad \Gamma, B \Rightarrow \Delta}{\Gamma, A \vee B \Rightarrow \Delta}$$

$$\mathsf{R}\supset\ \frac{\Gamma, A \Rightarrow B}{\Gamma \Rightarrow A \supset B, \Delta} \qquad \mathsf{L0}\supset\ \frac{\Gamma, p, B \Rightarrow \Delta}{\Gamma, p, p \supset B \Rightarrow \Delta} \qquad \mathsf{L}\wedge\supset\ \frac{\Gamma, C \supset (D \supset B) \Rightarrow \Delta}{\Gamma, (C \wedge D) \supset B \Rightarrow \Delta}$$

$$\mathsf{L}\vee\supset\ \frac{\Gamma, C \supset B, D \supset B \Rightarrow \Delta}{\Gamma, (C \vee D) \supset B \Rightarrow \Delta} \qquad \mathsf{L}\supset\supset\ \frac{\Gamma, C, D \supset B \Rightarrow D \quad \Gamma, B \Rightarrow \Delta}{\Gamma, (C \supset D) \supset B \Rightarrow \Delta}$$

Fig. 1. Rules of G4ip′ [4,5].

In the following we simply write $w \Vdash A$ when $\mathcal{M}$ is clear from the context. It is easy to prove that neighbourhood models for CK and CCDL satisfy the *hereditary property* (cf. [3]):

$$\text{for all } A \in \mathcal{L}, \text{ if } w \Vdash A \text{ and } w \preceq v, \text{ then } v \Vdash A.$$

Moreover, the equivalence of this semantics with the one of [3] can be easily shown with model transformations. Given a model $\mathcal{M} = \langle \mathcal{W}, \preceq, \mathcal{N}_\Box, \mathcal{N}_\Diamond, \mathcal{V} \rangle$ either as in Definition 2 or of the kind of [3], an equivalent model of the other kind can be obtained by taking the same $\mathcal{W}$, $\preceq$, $\mathcal{N}_\Box$ and $\mathcal{V}$, and defining $\mathcal{N}'_\Diamond(w) = \{\alpha \subseteq \mathcal{W} \mid \mathcal{W} \setminus \alpha \notin \mathcal{N}_\Diamond(w)\}$ for every $w \in \mathcal{W}$. By relying on the completeness result of [3] we then have:

Theorem 1. *The logics* CK *and* CCDL *are sound and complete with respect to the corresponding neighbourhood models.*

3 Sequent Calculi

In this section we present G4-style sequent calculi for the logics CK and CCDL. The calculi have the property that for every rule the complexity of the premiss(es) is strictly lower than the complexity of the conclusion (with respect to a suitable notion of complexity). From this it follows that bottom-up proof search always terminates. We show that the structural rules of weakening, contraction, and cut are admissible, and obtain thereby a proof of completeness of the calculi with respect to the axiomatic systems. As a consequence, bottom-up proof search in the calculi provides a decision procedure for the logics.

In the following, we denote by capital Greek letters $\Gamma, \Delta, \Sigma, \Pi$ possibly empty *multisets* of formulas of $\mathcal{L}$. If Γ is the multiset $A_1, ..., A_n$, we respectively denote by $\Box\Gamma$ and $\Diamond\Gamma$ the multisets $\Box A_1, ..., \Box A_n$ and $\Diamond A_1, ..., \Diamond A_n$ (whence $\Box\Gamma$ and $\Diamond\Gamma$ only contain $\Box$-, resp. $\Diamond$-, formulas). We call *sequent* any pair $\Gamma \Rightarrow \Delta$ of multisets of formulas. As usual, sequents are interpreted in the language $\mathcal{L}$ as

$$\mathsf{K}_\Box\ \frac{\Sigma \Rightarrow B}{\Gamma, \Box\Sigma \Rightarrow \Box B, \Delta} \qquad \mathsf{K}_\Diamond\ \frac{\Sigma, B \Rightarrow C}{\Gamma, \Box\Sigma, \Diamond B \Rightarrow \Diamond C, \Delta} \qquad \mathsf{N}_\Diamond\ \frac{\Sigma, B \Rightarrow}{\Gamma, \Box\Sigma, \Diamond B \Rightarrow \Delta}$$

$$\mathsf{L\Box\supset}\ \frac{\Sigma \Rightarrow C \qquad \Gamma, \Box\Sigma, B \Rightarrow \Delta}{\Gamma, \Box\Sigma, \Box C \supset B \Rightarrow \Delta} \qquad \mathsf{L\Diamond\supset}\ \frac{\Sigma, D \Rightarrow C \qquad \Gamma, \Box\Sigma, \Diamond D, B \Rightarrow \Delta}{\Gamma, \Box\Sigma, \Diamond D, \Diamond C \supset B \Rightarrow \Delta}$$

Fig. 2. Modal rules of G4.CK and G4.CCDL.

$$\dfrac{\dfrac{\dfrac{\dfrac{\dfrac{}{q, p \Rightarrow q}\,\mathsf{init}}{p \supset q, p \Rightarrow q}\,\mathsf{L0\supset}}{\Box(p \supset q), \Box p \Rightarrow \Box q}\,\mathsf{K}_\Box}{\Box(p \supset q) \Rightarrow \Box p \supset \Box q}\,\mathsf{R\supset}}{\Rightarrow \Box(p \supset q) \supset (\Box p \supset \Box q)}\,\mathsf{R\supset} \qquad \dfrac{\dfrac{\dfrac{\dfrac{\dfrac{}{q, p \Rightarrow q}\,\mathsf{init}}{p \supset q, p \Rightarrow q}\,\mathsf{L0\supset}}{\Box(p \supset q), \Diamond p \Rightarrow \Diamond q}\,\mathsf{K}_\Diamond}{\Box(p \supset q) \Rightarrow \Diamond p \supset \Diamond q}\,\mathsf{R\supset}}{\Rightarrow \Box(p \supset q) \supset (\Diamond p \supset \Diamond q)}\,\mathsf{R\supset} \qquad \dfrac{\dfrac{\dfrac{}{\bot \Rightarrow}\,\mathsf{L\bot}}{\Diamond\bot \Rightarrow \bot}\,\mathsf{N}_\Diamond}{\Rightarrow \Diamond\bot \supset \bot}\,\mathsf{R\supset}$$

Fig. 3. Derivations of $K_\Box$ and $K_\Diamond$ in G4.C* and of $N_\Diamond$ in G4.CK.

$\bigwedge \Gamma \supset \bigvee \Delta$ if Γ is non-empty, and are interpreted as $\bigvee \Delta$ if Γ is empty, where $\bigvee \emptyset$ is interpreted as $\bot$. We consider the following notions of weight of formulas and multiset ordering of sequents.

Definition 3 (Weight of formulas and multiset ordering of sequents). *For every formula A of $\mathcal{L}$, its weight $wg(A)$ is defined as follows: $wg(\bot) = 0$; $wg(p_i) = 1$ for every $p_i \in Atm$; $wg(A \supset B) = wg(A) + wg(B) + 1$; $wg(A \wedge B) = wg(A) + wg(B) + 2$; $wg(A \vee B) = wg(A) + wg(B) + 3$; and $wg(\Box A) = wg(\Diamond A) = wg(A) + 1$. Then we define $\Gamma \ll \Sigma$ iff Γ is the result of replacing one or more formulas in Σ by zero or more formulas of lower weight; and $\Gamma \Rightarrow \Delta \ll \Sigma \Rightarrow \Pi$ iff $\Gamma, \Delta \ll \Sigma, \Pi$.*

In Fig. 1 it is displayed Dyckhoff's multi-succedent sequent calculus G4ip′ for intuitionistic logic [4], with the rule L⊃⊃ formulated as in [5]. The main peculiarity of Dyckhoff's calculus is that it terminates without need of loop-checking. This is obtained by considering four left implication rules rather than a single one, namely one rule for every possible outermost connective in the antecedent of the principal implication. As a consequence, the resulting calculus has the property that the premisses of every rule have a smaller complexity than the conclusion with respect to the multiset ordering of Definition 3.

By extending Dyckhoff's calculus with suitable rules for the modalities we now define the calculi G4.CK and G4.CCDL for constructive modal logics.

Definition 4. *The calculi* G4.CK *and* G4.CCDL *are defined by extending the calculus* G4ip′ *in Fig. 1 with the following sets of rules from Fig. 2:*

$$\mathsf{G4.CK} := \mathsf{G4ip'} \cup \{\mathsf{K}_\Box, \mathsf{K}_\Diamond, \mathsf{L\Box\supset}, \mathsf{L\Diamond\supset}\}.$$
$$\mathsf{G4.CCDL} := \mathsf{G4.CK} \cup \{\mathsf{N}_\Diamond\}.$$

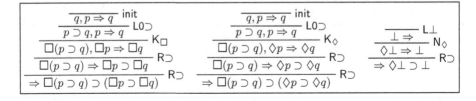

The rules $K_\Box$, $K_\Diamond$, and $N_\Diamond$ are the multi-conclusion formulation of the standard modal rules of sequent calculi for CK and CCDL (see e.g. [23]). In the spirit of G4ip′, the calculi G4.CK and G4.CCDL also contain two additional left implication rules, namely $L\Box\supset$ and $L\Diamond\supset$, which take care of the $\Box$- or $\Diamond$-formulas occurring in the antecedent of an implication. The rule $L\Box\supset$ comes from [13] where a G4-stlyle calculus for the intuitionistic monomodal $\Box$-version of logic K is presented. Since this logic coincides with the $\Diamond$-free fragment of CK and CCDL the same rule is also adequate for our calculi. Moreover, the rule $L\Diamond\supset$ reflects the different behaviour of the modality $\Diamond$, which is captured in the calculus by the rule $K_\Diamond$, and requires the presence of a $\Diamond$-formula in addition to the principal implication. We point out that multi-succedent sequents are not necessary in order to define sequent calculi for CK, nor for CCDL: indeed analogous calculi could be formulated extending Dyckhoff's single-succedent calculus G4ip [4]. The reason for considering the multi-succedent version of the calculus is that it allows for a more immediate transformation into a refutation calculus, as we will see in the next section.

Some examples of derivation in the calculi G4.C* are displayed in Fig. 3. It is easy to see that for every rule of G4.C*, the premisses have a smaller complexity than the conclusion with respect to the multiset ordering of Definition 3 (in particular the premisses of the modal rules only contain subformulas of formulas in the conclusion). Therefore it holds:

Theorem 2. *Backward proof search in* G4.C* *always terminates after a finite number of steps.*

We now prove that the calculi G4.C* are equivalent to the corresponding axiomatic systems. On the one hand, it is possible to show that all the rules of G4.C* are derivable in C*. As an example, the derivation of the rule $L\Diamond\supset$ in C* is as follows:

1.	$\bigwedge\Sigma\wedge D\supset C$	(assumption)
2.	$\bigwedge\Sigma\supset(D\supset C)$	(1, IPL)
3.	$\Box\bigwedge\Sigma\supset\Box(D\supset C)$	(2, $Nec+K_\Box$)
4.	$\bigwedge\Box\Sigma\supset\Box(D\supset C)$	(3, $Nec+K_\Box$)
5.	$\bigwedge\Box\Sigma\supset(\Diamond D\supset\Diamond C)$	(4, $K_\Diamond$)
6.	$\bigwedge\Box\Sigma\wedge\Diamond D\supset\Diamond C$	(5, IPL)
7.	$\bigwedge\Gamma\wedge\bigwedge\Box\Sigma\wedge\Diamond D\wedge(\Diamond C\supset B)\supset$ $\bigwedge\Gamma\wedge\bigwedge\Box\Sigma\wedge\Diamond D\wedge(\bigwedge\Box\Sigma\wedge\Diamond D\supset\Diamond C)\wedge(\Diamond C\supset B)$	(6, IPL)
8.	$\bigwedge\Gamma\wedge\bigwedge\Box\Sigma\wedge\Diamond D\wedge(\bigwedge\Box\Sigma\wedge\Diamond D\supset\Diamond C)\wedge(\Diamond C\supset B)\supset$ $\bigwedge\Gamma\wedge\bigwedge\Box\Sigma\wedge\Diamond D\wedge B$	(IPL)
9.	$\bigwedge\Gamma\wedge\bigwedge\Box\Sigma\wedge\Diamond D\wedge B\supset\bigvee\Delta$	(assumption)
10.	$\bigwedge\Gamma\wedge\bigwedge\Box\Sigma\wedge\Diamond D\wedge(\Diamond C\supset B)\supset\bigvee\Delta$	(7,8,9, IPL)

We now prove that G4.C* is complete with respect to C*. We remark that Dyckhoff's original completeness proof of G4ip′ [4], as well as Iemhoff's completeness proof of intuitionistic monomodal calculi [13], are indirect as they rely on the completeness of G3-style calculi. An alternative proof of the completeness of G4ip′ with no reference to other kinds of calculi is provided in [5] by showing that the calculus in itself is syntactically complete with respect to the axiomatization: as usual the argument relies on a direct of proof of cut-admissibility within the calculus G4ip′. We follow here this latter approach as it can be modularly extended to our calculi.

As usual, we say that a rule is *admissible* in G4.C* if whenever the premisses are derivable, the conclusion is also derivable, and that a single-premiss rule is *height-preserving admissible* (hp-admissible for short) if whenever the premiss is derivable, then the conclusion is derivable with a derivation of at most the same height. Moreover, we say that a rule $\dfrac{S_1 \quad \ldots \quad S_n}{S'}$ is *height-preserving invertible* (hp-invertible) *with respect to the premiss* S_i if the rule $\dfrac{S'}{S_i}$ is hp-admissible, and that it is *height-preserving invertible* (tout court) if it is hp-invertible with respect to all its premisses. One can easily prove the following:

Lemma 1. *The rules* L∧, R∧, L∨, R∨, L0⊃, L∧⊃, L∨⊃ *are height-preserving invertible. The rules* L⊃⊃, L□⊃, *and* L◇⊃ *are height-preserving invertible with respect to the right premiss.*

We now prove admissibility of the structural rules in G4.C*.

Proposition 1. *The following weakening rules are height-preserving admissible in* G4.C*, *moreover, the following contraction rules are admissible in* G4.C*:

$$\mathsf{Lwk}\,\frac{\Gamma \Rightarrow \Delta}{\Gamma, A \Rightarrow \Delta} \qquad \mathsf{Rwk}\,\frac{\Gamma \Rightarrow \Delta}{\Gamma \Rightarrow A, \Delta} \qquad \mathsf{Lctr}\,\frac{\Gamma, A, A \Rightarrow \Delta}{\Gamma, A \Rightarrow \Delta} \qquad \mathsf{Rctr}\,\frac{\Gamma \Rightarrow A, A, \Delta}{\Gamma \Rightarrow A, \Delta}$$

Proof. Hp-admissibility of weakening is straightforward. For contraction the proof extends the one of [5] for G4ip′ and proceeds by induction on the height of the derivation of the premiss of contraction and case analysis. The proof is standard if the contracted formula is not principal in the last rule application in the derivation of the premiss of contraction. The cases where the contracted formula is principal and the last rule applied is a rule of G4ip′ are covered in [5], in particular it is easy to see that the rule in Lemma 7.5 [5] is still admissible in G4.C*. Finally, for the modal rules we consider as an example the following application of contraction to the formula $\Diamond C \supset B$ which is obtained by L◇⊃ (on the left). The derivation is converted as follows (on the right) with an application of the hp-invertibilty of L◇⊃ with respect to the right premiss:

$$\dfrac{\dfrac{\Sigma, D \Rightarrow C \qquad \Gamma, \Box\Sigma, \Diamond D, B, \Diamond C \supset B \Rightarrow \Delta}{\Gamma, \Box\Sigma, \Diamond D, \Diamond C \supset B, \Diamond C \supset B \Rightarrow \Delta}\,\mathsf{L\Diamond\supset}}{\Gamma, \Box\Sigma, \Diamond D, \Diamond C \supset B \Rightarrow \Delta}\,\mathsf{Lctr} \quad \rightsquigarrow \quad \dfrac{\Sigma, D \Rightarrow C \qquad \dfrac{\dfrac{\Gamma, \Box\Sigma, \Diamond D, B, \Diamond C \supset B \Rightarrow \Delta}{\Gamma, \Box\Sigma, \Diamond D, B, B \Rightarrow \Delta}\,\mathsf{L\Diamond\supset^{i}}}{\Gamma, \Box\Sigma, \Diamond D, B \Rightarrow \Delta}\,\mathsf{Lctr}}{\Gamma, \Box\Sigma, \Diamond D, \Diamond C \supset B \Rightarrow \Delta}\,\mathsf{L\Diamond\supset}$$

□

Theorem 3 (Cut elimination). *The following cut rule is admissible in* G4.C*:

$$\mathsf{cut}\,\frac{\Gamma \Rightarrow A, \Delta \qquad \Gamma', A \Rightarrow \Delta'}{\Gamma, \Gamma' \Rightarrow \Delta, \Delta'}$$

Proof. As usual we proceed by induction on the lexicographically ordered pairs (c, h), where c is the weight of the cut formulas (cf. Definition 3), and $h = h_1 + h_2$, called cut height, is the sum of the heights h_1 and h_2 of the derivations of the premisses of cut. As before, the proof extends the one in [5] for G4ip′, and distinguishes some cases according to whether the cut formula is or not principal in the last rules applied in the derivation of the premisses of cut. We only show a few most relevant cases. (i) The cut formula is not principal in the last rule applied in the derivation of one premiss. As an example we consider:

$$\dfrac{\Gamma \Rightarrow A, \Delta \qquad \dfrac{\Sigma, B \Rightarrow C \qquad \Gamma', A, \Box\Sigma, \Diamond B, D \Rightarrow \Delta'}{\Gamma', A, \Box\Sigma, \Diamond B, \Diamond C \supset D \Rightarrow \Delta'}\,\mathsf{L\Diamond\supset}}{\Gamma, \Gamma', \Box\Sigma, \Diamond B, \Diamond C \supset D \Rightarrow \Delta, \Delta'}\,\mathsf{cut}$$

$$\rightsquigarrow$$

$$\dfrac{\Sigma, B \Rightarrow C \qquad \dfrac{\Gamma \Rightarrow A, \Delta \qquad \Gamma', A, \Box\Sigma, \Diamond B, D \Rightarrow \Delta'}{\Gamma, \Gamma', \Box\Sigma, \Diamond B, D \Rightarrow \Delta, \Delta'}\,\mathsf{cut}}{\Gamma, \Gamma', \Box\Sigma, \Diamond B, \Diamond C \supset D \Rightarrow \Delta, \Delta'}\,\mathsf{L\Diamond\supset}$$

(ii) The cut formula is principal in the last rule applied in the derivation of both premisses. We consider the following two cases, where R^* denotes multiple applications of the rule R. The other cases are similar and left to the reader.

(R⊃; L◇⊃)

$$\dfrac{\dfrac{\Gamma, \Diamond A \Rightarrow B}{\Gamma \Rightarrow \Diamond A \supset B, \Delta}\,\mathsf{R\supset} \qquad \dfrac{\Sigma, C \Rightarrow A \qquad \Gamma', \Box\Sigma, \Diamond C, B \Rightarrow \Delta'}{\Gamma', \Box\Sigma, \Diamond C, \Diamond A \supset B \Rightarrow \Delta'}\,\mathsf{L\Diamond\supset}}{\Gamma, \Gamma', \Box\Sigma, \Diamond C \Rightarrow \Delta, \Delta'}\,\mathsf{cut}$$

$$\rightsquigarrow$$

$$\dfrac{\dfrac{\dfrac{\dfrac{\Sigma, C \Rightarrow A}{\Box\Sigma, \Diamond C \Rightarrow \Diamond A}\,\mathsf{K_\Diamond} \qquad \Gamma, \Diamond A \Rightarrow B}{\Gamma, \Box\Sigma, \Diamond C \Rightarrow B}\,\mathsf{cut} \qquad \Gamma', \Box\Sigma, \Diamond C, B \Rightarrow \Delta'}{\Gamma, \Gamma', \Box\Sigma, \Box\Sigma, \Diamond C, \Diamond C \Rightarrow \Delta'}\,\mathsf{cut}}{\Gamma, \Gamma', \Box\Sigma, \Diamond C \Rightarrow \Delta, \Delta'}\,\mathsf{Lctr}^* + \mathsf{Rwk}^*$$

(K◇; L◇⊃)

$$\dfrac{\dfrac{\Sigma, A \Rightarrow B}{\Gamma, \Box\Sigma, \Diamond A \Rightarrow \Diamond B, \Delta}\,\mathsf{K_\Diamond} \qquad \dfrac{\Pi, B \Rightarrow C \qquad \Gamma', \Box\Pi, \Diamond B, D \Rightarrow \Delta'}{\Gamma', \Box\Pi, \Diamond B, \Diamond C \supset D \Rightarrow \Delta'}\,\mathsf{L\Diamond\supset}}{\Gamma, \Gamma', \Box\Sigma, \Box\Pi, \Diamond A, \Diamond C \supset D \Rightarrow \Delta, \Delta'}\,\mathsf{cut}$$

$$\rightsquigarrow$$

$$\dfrac{\dfrac{\Sigma, A \Rightarrow B \qquad \Pi, B \Rightarrow C}{\Sigma, \Pi, A \Rightarrow C}\,\mathsf{cut} \qquad \dfrac{\Gamma, \Box\Sigma, \Diamond A \Rightarrow \Diamond B, \Delta \qquad \Gamma', \Box\Pi, \Diamond B, D \Rightarrow \Delta'}{\Gamma, \Gamma', \Box\Sigma, \Box\Pi, \Diamond A, D \Rightarrow \Delta, \Delta'}\,\mathsf{cut}}{\Gamma, \Gamma', \Box\Sigma, \Box\Pi, \Diamond A, \Diamond C \supset D \Rightarrow \Delta, \Delta'}\,\mathsf{L\Diamond\supset}$$

□

Given the admissibility of cut and the derivability in G4.C* of the axioms and the modal rule of C* we obtain the following result:

Theorem 4 (Soundness and completeness). *$\Gamma \Rightarrow \Delta$ is derivable in* G4.C* *if and only if $\bigwedge \Gamma \supset \bigvee \Delta$ is derivable in* C*.

Proof. From right to left: For the intuitionistic axioms we refer to [5]. The derivations of specific instances of the modal axioms are displayed in Fig. 3. Since initial sequents can be generalised to arbitrary formulas, the same derivations can be applied to derive any instances of $K_\Box$ and $K_\Diamond$. Finally, the derivability of the rule *Nec* follows immediately from the rule $\mathsf{K}_\Box$, whereas modus ponens is simulated by cut in the usual way. For the opposite direction: We have shown above the derivation of the rule $\mathsf{L}\Diamond\supset$ in C^*. The derivation of $\mathsf{L}\Box\supset$ is similar, whereas the derivations of $\mathsf{K}_\Box$, $\mathsf{K}_\Diamond$, and $\mathsf{N}_\Diamond$ are standard and can be found in [23]. □

4 Refutation Calculi and Countermodel Construction

We shall now present refutation calculi for constructive modal logics CK and CCDL. These calculi can be seen as dual of the sequent calculi G4.CK and G4.CCDL of the previous section: instead of deriving all valid formulas, the refutation calculi allow one to *refute* all formulas which are *non-theorems* of the logics. We will further show that every refutation in these calculi explicitly constructs a neighbourhood countermodel of the refuted formula.

Refutation calculi handle so-called *anti-sequents*, which are pairs $\Gamma \not\Rightarrow \Delta$ of multiset of formulas of $\mathcal{L}$. Intuitively, the anti-sequent $\Gamma \not\Rightarrow \Delta$ expresses that $\bigvee \Delta$ does not follow from $\bigwedge \Gamma$, or equivalently that $\bigwedge \Gamma \supset \bigvee \Delta$ is not valid. The refutation calculi Ref.CK and Ref.CCDL of constructive modal logics extend the refutation calculus for intuitionistic logic by Pinto and Dyckhoff [18] in the following way.

Definition 5. *The refutation calculi* Ref.CK *and* Ref.CCDL *are defined by the following sets of rules from Fig. 4:*

$$\begin{aligned}\mathsf{Ref.CK} &:= \{\mathsf{init}, \mathsf{init}_{\mathsf{CK}}, \mathsf{L}\wedge, \mathsf{R}\wedge_1, \mathsf{R}\wedge_2, \mathsf{L}\vee_1, \mathsf{L}\vee_2, \mathsf{R}\vee, \mathsf{L0}\supset, \mathsf{L}\wedge\supset, \mathsf{L}\vee\supset,\\ &\quad\ \mathsf{L}\supset\supset, \mathsf{L}\Box\supset, \mathsf{L}\Diamond\supset, \mathsf{nip}\}.\\ \mathsf{Ref.CCDL} &:= \{\mathsf{init}, \mathsf{L}\wedge, \mathsf{R}\wedge_1, \mathsf{R}\wedge_2, \mathsf{L}\vee_1, \mathsf{L}\vee_2, \mathsf{R}\vee, \mathsf{L0}\supset, \mathsf{L}\wedge\supset, \mathsf{L}\vee\supset, \mathsf{L}\supset\supset,\\ &\quad\ \mathsf{L}\Box\supset, \mathsf{L}\Diamond\supset, \mathsf{nip}, \mathsf{nip}_{\mathsf{CCDL}}\}.\end{aligned}$$

Similarly to the refutation calculus in [18], the initial anti-sequents (or axioms) of Ref.C^* are all the pairs $\Gamma \not\Rightarrow \Delta$ such that the corresponding sequent $\Gamma \Rightarrow \Delta$ is neither an axiom of G4.C^*, nor the conclusion of any rule of G4.C^*. Concerning the other rules, every rule different from nip and $\mathsf{nip}_{\mathsf{CCDL}}$ corresponds to an invertible premiss of some rule of G4.C^* (more precisely, to a rule (more precisely, to a rule $\frac{S'}{S_i}$ such that the G4.C^* rule (more precisely, to a rule $\frac{S_1 \quad \dots \quad S_n}{S'}$ is invertible with respect to S_i), whereas nip and $\mathsf{nip}_{\mathsf{CCDL}}$ deal at the same time with all the non-invertible premisses of the rules of G4.C^*. Given their application conditions, the rules nip and $\mathsf{nip}_{\mathsf{CCDL}}$ are (bottom-up) applicable only when no invertible rule of G4.C^* is applicable. Observe that the rules nip and $\mathsf{nip}_{\mathsf{CCDL}}$ only differ with respect to the premisses where only $\Diamond$-formulas are principal. In particular, $\mathsf{nip}_{\mathsf{CCDL}}$ allows one to reduce the anti-sequents where no $\Diamond$-formula occurs in the consequent, which is allowed by the logic CCDL but is not allowed by CK. The idea is that in Ref.CCDL the rule nip is applied when Δ contains $\Diamond$-formulas, whereas $\mathsf{nip}_{\mathsf{CCDL}}$ is applied when Δ does not contain $\Diamond$-formulas. Two examples of refutations in Ref.C^* of formulas which are valid in

$$\mathsf{init}\ \frac{}{\Gamma, \Box\Gamma' \not\Rightarrow \Diamond\Delta, \Delta'} \qquad \mathsf{init}_{\mathsf{CK}}\ \frac{}{\Gamma, \Box\Gamma', \Diamond\Gamma'' \not\Rightarrow \Delta}$$

$$\mathsf{L}\wedge\ \frac{\Gamma, A, B \not\Rightarrow \Delta}{\Gamma, A \wedge B \not\Rightarrow \Delta} \qquad \mathsf{R}\wedge_1\ \frac{\Gamma \not\Rightarrow A, \Delta}{\Gamma \not\Rightarrow A \wedge B, \Delta} \qquad \mathsf{R}\wedge_2\ \frac{\Gamma \not\Rightarrow B, \Delta}{\Gamma \not\Rightarrow A \wedge B, \Delta}$$

$$\mathsf{L}\vee_1\ \frac{\Gamma, A \not\Rightarrow \Delta}{\Gamma, A \vee B \not\Rightarrow \Delta} \qquad \mathsf{L}\vee_2\ \frac{\Gamma, B \not\Rightarrow \Delta}{\Gamma, A \vee B \not\Rightarrow \Delta} \qquad \mathsf{R}\vee\ \frac{\Gamma \not\Rightarrow A, B, \Delta}{\Gamma \not\Rightarrow A \vee B, \Delta}$$

$$\mathsf{L0}\supset\ \frac{\Gamma, p, B \not\Rightarrow \Delta}{\Gamma, p, p \supset B \not\Rightarrow \Delta} \qquad \mathsf{L}\wedge\supset\ \frac{\Gamma, C \supset (D \supset B) \not\Rightarrow \Delta}{\Gamma, (C \wedge D) \supset B \not\Rightarrow \Delta} \qquad \mathsf{L}\vee\supset\ \frac{\Gamma, C \supset B, D \supset B \not\Rightarrow \Delta}{\Gamma, (C \vee D) \supset B \not\Rightarrow \Delta}$$

$$\mathsf{L}\supset\supset\ \frac{\Gamma, B \not\Rightarrow \Delta}{\Gamma, (C \supset D) \supset B \not\Rightarrow \Delta} \qquad \mathsf{L}\Box\supset\ \frac{\Gamma, B \not\Rightarrow \Delta}{\Gamma, \Box C \supset B \not\Rightarrow \Delta} \qquad \mathsf{L}\Diamond\supset\ \frac{\Gamma, \Diamond D, B \not\Rightarrow \Delta}{\Gamma, \Diamond D, \Diamond C \supset B \not\Rightarrow \Delta}$$

$$\mathsf{nip}\ \frac{\begin{array}{ll} \{\Gamma^{\Box} \not\Rightarrow A \mid \Box A \supset B \in \Gamma\} & \{\Gamma^{\Box} \not\Rightarrow A \mid \Box A \in \Delta\} \\ \{\Gamma^{\Box}, C \not\Rightarrow A \mid \Diamond A \supset B, \Diamond C \in \Gamma\} & \{\Gamma^{\Box}, A \not\Rightarrow B \mid \Diamond A \in \Gamma, \Diamond B \in \Delta\} \\ \{\Gamma', D \supset B, C \not\Rightarrow D \mid (C \supset D) \supset B \in \Gamma\} & \{\Gamma, A \not\Rightarrow B \mid A \supset B \in \Delta\} \end{array}}{\Gamma \not\Rightarrow \Delta}$$

$$\mathsf{nip}_{\mathsf{CCDL}}\ \frac{\begin{array}{ll} \{\Gamma^{\Box} \not\Rightarrow A \mid \Box A \supset B \in \Gamma\} & \{\Gamma^{\Box} \not\Rightarrow A \mid \Box A \in \Delta\} \\ \{\Gamma^{\Box}, C \not\Rightarrow A \mid \Diamond A \supset B, \Diamond C \in \Gamma\} & \{\Gamma^{\Box}, A \not\Rightarrow \ \mid \Diamond A \in \Gamma\} \\ \{\Gamma', D \supset B, C \not\Rightarrow D \mid (C \supset D) \supset B \in \Gamma\} & \{\Gamma, A \not\Rightarrow B \mid A \supset B \in \Delta\} \end{array}}{\Gamma \not\Rightarrow \Delta}$$

where • $\Gamma' = \Gamma \setminus \{(C \supset D) \supset B\}$, and
• if $\Box A_1, ..., \Box A_n$ are *all* the $\Box$-formulas of Γ, then $\Gamma^{\Box} = A_1, ..., A_n$.

Application conditions:

• init and $\mathsf{init}_{\mathsf{CK}}$: (i) Γ contains only propositional variables, atomic implications, and implications of the form $\Diamond A \supset B$; (ii) Δ contains only atomic formulas; (iii) if $p \supset A \in \Gamma$, then $p \notin \Gamma$; (iv) if Γ contains an implication $\Diamond A \supset B$, then $\Diamond\Gamma'' = \emptyset$; (v) $\Gamma \cap \Delta = \emptyset$.

• nip: (i) Γ does not contain $\bot$, conjunctions, disjunctions, and implications of the form $(C \wedge D) \supset B$ or $(C \vee D) \supset B$; (ii) Δ does not contain conjunctions and disjunctions; (iii) if $p \supset A \in \Gamma$, then $p \notin \Gamma$; (iv) if $p \in \Gamma$, then $p \notin \Delta$.

• $\mathsf{nip}_{\mathsf{CCDL}}$: conditions of nip, plus (v) Δ does not contain $\Diamond$-formulas.

• nip and $\mathsf{nip}_{\mathsf{CCDL}}$ must have at least one premiss.

Fig. 4. Rules of Ref.CK and Ref.CCDL.

$$\dfrac{\dfrac{\dfrac{\dfrac{}{p \not\Rightarrow q}\,\mathsf{init}}{\not\Rightarrow p \supset q}\,\mathsf{nip}}{\Diamond p \supset \Box q \not\Rightarrow \Box(p \supset q)}\,\mathsf{nip}}{\not\Rightarrow (\Diamond p \supset \Box q) \supset \Box(p \supset q)}\,\mathsf{nip} \qquad \dfrac{\dfrac{\dfrac{\mathsf{L}\vee\,\dfrac{\mathsf{init}\,\dfrac{}{q \not\Rightarrow p}}{p \vee q \not\Rightarrow p} \qquad \dfrac{\dfrac{}{p \not\Rightarrow q}\,\mathsf{init}}{p \vee q \not\Rightarrow q}\,\mathsf{L}\vee}{\Diamond(p \vee q) \not\Rightarrow \Diamond p, \Diamond q}\,\mathsf{nip}}{\Diamond(p \vee q) \not\Rightarrow \Diamond p \vee \Diamond q}\,\mathsf{R}\vee}{\not\Rightarrow \Diamond(p \vee q) \supset \Diamond p \vee \Diamond q}\,\mathsf{nip}$$

Fig. 5. Examples of refutations in Ref.C*.

intuitionistic modal logics but are not valid in constructive ones are displayed in Fig. 5.

Note that similarly to G4.C*, for every rule of Ref.C* the premisses have a smaller complexity than the conclusion with respect to the multiset ordering of Definition 3. Therefore we have:

Theorem 5. *Backward proof search in* Ref.C* *is terminating.*

We can prove that the refutation calculi Ref.CK and Ref.CCDL are the dual of the sequent calculi G4.CK and G4.CCDL, in the sense that an anti-sequent $\Gamma \not\Rightarrow \Delta$ is derivable in a refutation calculus if and only if the sequent $\Gamma \Rightarrow \Delta$ is not derivable in the corresponding sequent calculus. It follows that the refutation calculi are complete with respect to the sets of non-valid formulas in the neighbourhood semantics for CK and CCDL.

Theorem 6. $\Gamma \not\Rightarrow \Delta$ *is derivable in* Ref.C* *if and only if* $\Gamma \Rightarrow \Delta$ *is not derivable in* G4.C*.

We now show that every refutation of $\Gamma \not\Rightarrow \Delta$ provides a neighbourhood countermodel of $\Gamma \Rightarrow \Delta$. We thereby obtain a constructive proof of the completeness of the refutation calculi Ref.C* (and indirectly also of the calculi G4.C*) with respect to the neighbourhood semantics of C*. In order to define the countermodel construction, we enrich the anti-sequents occurring in a refutation with annotations that represent the worlds of a model in the following manner.

Definition 6. *An* annotation *is a finite sequence of natural numbers* $n_1.n_2. \dots .n_k$. *An* annotated anti-sequent *is an expression* $\Gamma \not\Rightarrow^\sigma \Delta$, *where* $\Gamma \not\Rightarrow \Delta$ *is an anti-sequent and* σ *is an annotation. An* annotated refutation *is a refutation where all sequents are annotated according to the following prescriptions:*

- *The root anti-sequent* $\Gamma \not\Rightarrow \Delta$ *is annotated with the initial annotation* 1.
- *If the conclusion of any rule different from* nip *or* $\mathsf{nip}_{\mathsf{CCDL}}$ *is annotated with* σ, *then its premiss has the same annotation* σ.
- *If the conclusion of* nip *or* $\mathsf{nip}_{\mathsf{CCDL}}$ *is annotated with* σ, *then its premisses are annotated as follows:*
  - *The premisses obtained from formulas* $(C \supset D) \supset B$ *on the left of the conclusion, or formulas* $A \supset B$ *on the right, are annotated each with a different annotation* $\sigma.n$ *not already occurring in the refutation.*
  - *The premisses obtained from any other formulas are annotated each with a different annotation* k *not already occurring in the refutation.*

As an example, the annotated versions of the refutations in Fig. 5 are displayed in Fig. 6. Note that every refutation in Ref.C* can be easily annotated according to Definition 6.

For any annotated refutation $\mathscr{R}$ of $\Gamma \not\Rightarrow^1 \Delta$ in Ref.C*, we denote[2]

$$\Gamma^\sigma = \bigcup\{\Gamma \mid \Gamma \not\Rightarrow^\sigma \Delta \in \mathscr{R}\} \text{and } \Delta^\sigma = \bigcup\{\Delta \mid \Gamma \not\Rightarrow^\sigma \Delta \in \mathscr{R}\}.$$

We now show how to extract a countermodel from an annotated refutation of $\Gamma \not\Rightarrow^1 \Delta$. Intuitively, every annotation corresponds to a world of the model. The rules in which the premiss and conclusion have the same annotation (i.e., all the rules but nip and $\mathsf{nip}_{\mathsf{CCDL}}$) are "local" as they deal with a single world. By contrast, bottom-up applications of nip and $\mathsf{nip}_{\mathsf{CCDL}}$ create new worlds: the premisses annotated with $\sigma.n$ (i.e., those generated by non-modal $\supset$-formulas occurring in the conclusion) represent worlds related through $\preceq$ to the world σ at the conclusion, whereas the other premisses represent worlds belonging to some neighbourhood of σ. The formal definition is as follows.

Definition 7 (Countermodel extraction). *Let $\mathscr{R}$ be an annotated refutation of $\Gamma \not\Rightarrow^1 \Delta$. The* countermodel *determined by $\mathscr{R}$ is defined as follows.*

- *$\mathcal{W}$ = the set of annotations occurring in $\mathscr{R}$.*
- *$\sigma \preceq \rho$ iff $\rho = \sigma.\pi$ for some possibly empty annotation π.*
- *$\mathcal{V}(p) = \{\sigma \in \mathcal{W} \mid p \in \Gamma^\sigma\}$.*
- *For every $\Box A, \Diamond A$ occurring in $\mathscr{R}$, $A^+ = \{\sigma \in \mathcal{W} \mid A \in \Gamma^\sigma\}$.*
- *For every $\sigma \in \mathcal{W}$, $\mathcal{N}_\Box(\sigma)$ and $\mathcal{N}_\Diamond(\sigma)$ are defined as follows:*
  - *If there are no $\Box$-formulas in Γ^σ, then:*
    - * $\mathcal{N}_\Box(\sigma) = \{\mathcal{W}\}$.
    - * $\mathcal{N}_\Diamond(\sigma) = \{\alpha \subseteq \mathcal{W} \mid$ there is $\Diamond B \in \Gamma^\sigma$ s.t. $B^+ \subseteq \alpha\}$.
  - *Otherwise, if $\Box A_1, ..., \Box A_n$ are* all *the $\Box$-formulas in Γ^σ, then:*
    - * $\mathcal{N}_\Box(\sigma) = \{\alpha \subseteq \mathcal{W} \mid A_1^+ \cap ... \cap A_n^+ \subseteq \alpha\}$.
    - * $\mathcal{N}_\Diamond(\sigma) = \{\alpha \subseteq \mathcal{W} \mid$ there is $\Diamond B \in \Gamma^\sigma$ s.t. $A_1^+ \cap ... \cap A_n^+ \cap B^+ \subseteq \alpha\}$.

Observe that $\mathcal{N}_\Diamond(\sigma) = \emptyset$ if there are no $\Diamond$-formulas in Γ^σ.

Theorem 7. *If $\mathscr{R}$ is an annotated refutation of $\Gamma \not\Rightarrow^1 \Delta$ in* Ref.C*, *and $\mathcal{M}$ is the model extracted from $\mathscr{R}$ according to Definition 7, then $\mathcal{M}$ is a neighbourhood model for* C* *and it is a countermodel of $\Gamma \Rightarrow \Delta$.*

Proof. We first prove that $\mathcal{M}$ is a neighbourhood model for C*. From the definition of $\mathcal{M}$ it immediately follows that $\mathcal{N}_\Box$ and $\mathcal{N}_\Diamond$ are supplemented, and $\mathcal{N}_\Box$ is closed under intersection and contains the unit. For Ref.CCDL we also have $\emptyset \notin \mathcal{N}_\Diamond(\sigma)$, since if $\Diamond B \in \Gamma^\sigma$, then by $\mathsf{nip}_{\mathsf{CCDL}}$ and the annotation procedure there is $n \in \mathcal{W}$ such that $n \in \bigcap\{A^+ \mid \Box A \in \Gamma^\sigma\} \cap B^+$, thus for every $\alpha \in \mathcal{N}_\Diamond(\sigma)$, $\alpha \neq \emptyset$. Moreover, if $\alpha \in \mathcal{N}_\Box(\sigma)$ and $\beta \in \mathcal{N}_\Diamond(\sigma)$, then if Γ^σ contains $\Box$-formulas we have $\bigcap\{A^+ \mid \Box A \in \Gamma^\sigma\} \subseteq \alpha$ and $\bigcap\{A^+ \mid \Box A \in \Gamma^\sigma\} \cap B^+ \subseteq \beta$ for some $\Diamond B \in \Gamma^\sigma$. Then $\bigcap\{A^+ \mid \Box A \in \Gamma^\sigma\} \cap B^+ \subseteq \alpha \cap \beta$, thus $\alpha \cap \beta \in \mathcal{N}_\Diamond(\sigma)$. Moreover, $\mathcal{N}_\Box$ and $\mathcal{N}_\Diamond$ are monotonic with respect to $\preceq$. For instance, if $\alpha \in \mathcal{N}_\Box(\sigma)$ and $\sigma.\pi \in \mathcal{W}$,

[2] To be precise, the sets Γ^σ and Δ^σ depend on the refutation $\mathscr{R}$. In order not to burden the notation we avoid explicit reference to $\mathscr{R}$ as it is clear from the context.

then $\alpha = \mathcal{W}$ or $A_1^+ \cap ... \cap A_n^+ \subseteq \alpha$, where $\Box A_1, ..., \Box A_n$ are all the $\Box$-formulas in Γ^σ. In the first case, $\mathcal{W} \in \mathcal{N}_\Box(\sigma.\pi)$. In the second case, by nip and $\mathsf{nip_{CCDL}}$ $\Box A_1, ..., \Box A_n \in \Gamma^{\sigma.\pi}$. Then $\bigcap\{B^+ \mid \Box B \in \Gamma^{\sigma.\pi}\} \subseteq \bigcap\{A^+ \mid \Box A \in \Gamma^\sigma\} \subseteq \alpha$, thus $\alpha \in \mathcal{N}_\Box(\sigma.\pi)$. Finally $\mathcal{V}$ satisfies the hereditary condition: if $\sigma \Vdash p$, then $p \in \Gamma^\sigma$. By the rules and the annotation procedure it follows that $p \in \Gamma^{\sigma.\pi}$ for every $\sigma.\pi \in \mathcal{W}$, thus $\sigma.\pi \Vdash p$. Observe that since $\mathcal{M}$ is a neighbourhood model for C^* it satisfies the ereditary property for every $A \in \mathcal{L}$.

Now we prove that for every formula A and every annotation σ occurring in $\mathcal{R}$, if $A \in \Gamma^\sigma$, then $\sigma \Vdash A$, and if $A \in \Delta^\sigma$, then $\sigma \nVdash A$. In order to carry on the proof we need the notion of "height of a label": we consider the forest of labels $F_\mathcal{R}$ generated by the labels σ in $\mathcal{R}$ with their immediate successors $\sigma.1, ..., \sigma.n$ (the root of each tree is a unitary label); we then define the height of a label σ as its height in $F_\mathcal{R}$. The two claims are proven simultaneously by induction on the pairs (c, h), where c is the weight of A (Definition 3), and h is the height of σ.

The basic case ($A \equiv p, \bot$) is trivial. If Γ or Δ contains a conjuction or a disjunction, or Γ contains an implication of the form $(C \wedge D) \supset B$ or $(C \vee D) \supset B$, then the claim easily follows from the i.h. and the structure of refutations. For instance, if $(C \wedge D) \supset B \in \Gamma^\sigma$, then $C \supset (D \supset B) \in \Gamma^\sigma$, and by i.h., $\sigma \Vdash C \supset (D \supset B)$, thus $\sigma \Vdash (C \wedge D) \supset B$.

If $B \supset C \in \Delta^\sigma$, then by the rule nip or $\mathsf{nip_{CCDL}}$ and the annotation procedure there is $\sigma.n \in \mathcal{W}$ such that $B \in \Gamma^{\sigma.n}$ and $C \in \Delta^{\sigma.n}$, thus by i.h. $\sigma.n \Vdash B$ and $\sigma.n \nVdash C$, then since $\sigma \preceq \sigma.n$ it follows that $\sigma \nVdash B \supset C$.

If $p \supset B \in \Gamma^\sigma$, then for every chain of worlds starting from σ either there is no world τ in the chain such that $p \in \Gamma^\tau$, or there is a $\preceq$-minimal world π with $\sigma \preceq \pi$ such that $p \in \Gamma^\pi$. In the first case, by definition p is false in every world of the chain. In the second case, $\rho \nVdash p$ for every $\rho \neq \pi$ such that $\sigma \preceq \rho \preceq \pi$, moreover there is $\Gamma \not\Rightarrow^\pi \Delta$ in $\mathcal{R}$ such that $p \in \Gamma$. Furthermore, by nip or $\mathsf{nip_{CCDL}}$ $p \supset B \in \Gamma$, then by $\mathsf{L0}\supset$ and the application conditions there is $\Gamma' \not\Rightarrow^\pi \Delta'$ such that $B \in \Gamma'$, thus $B \in \Gamma^\pi$. By i.h. it follows $\pi \Vdash B$, and by the ereditary property we have $\omega \Vdash B$ for every ω such that $\pi \preceq \omega$. Therefore for every τ such that $\sigma \preceq \tau$, $\tau \nVdash p$ or $\tau \Vdash B$, thus $\sigma \Vdash p \supset B$.

If $(C \supset D) \supset B \in \Gamma^\sigma$, then if $B \in \Gamma^\sigma$, then by i.h. $\sigma \Vdash B$, and by the hereditary property $\rho \Vdash B$ for every ρ such that $\rho \preceq \sigma$. If instead $B \notin \Gamma^\sigma$, then by nip or $\mathsf{nip_{CCDL}}$ there is $\sigma.k \in \mathcal{W}$ such that $D \supset B, C \in \Gamma^{\sigma.k}$ and $D \in \Gamma^{\sigma.k}$, moreover for every other immediate successor $\sigma.m$ of σ, $(C \supset D) \supset B \in \Gamma^{\sigma.m}$. By i.h. $\sigma.m \Vdash (C \supset D) \supset B$, that is, for every π such that $\sigma.m \preceq \pi$, $\pi \Vdash C \supset D$ implies $\pi \Vdash B$. Moreover, by i.h. $\sigma.n \Vdash D \supset B$, $\sigma.n \Vdash C$, and $\sigma.n \nVdash D$. Thus $\sigma \nVdash C \supset B$, and by the hereditary property, for every successor τ of $\sigma.n$, $\tau \Vdash C \wedge (D \supset B)$. Then if $\tau \Vdash C \supset D$ we have $\tau \Vdash D$, thus $\tau \Vdash B$. Therefore for every ρ such that $\sigma \preceq \rho$, $\rho \Vdash C \supset D$ implies $\rho \Vdash B$. Then $\sigma \Vdash (C \supset D) \supset B$.

If $\Box C \supset B \in \Gamma^\sigma$, then if $B \in \Gamma^\sigma$, then by i.h. $\sigma \Vdash B$, and by the hereditary property $\rho \Vdash B$ for every ρ such that $\rho \preceq \sigma$. If instead $B \notin \Gamma^\sigma$, then by nip or $\mathsf{nip_{CCDL}}$ for every immediate successor $\sigma.k$ of σ, $\Box C \supset B \in \Gamma^{\sigma.k}$, then by i.h. $\sigma.k \Vdash \Box C \supset B$, moreover there is $n \in \mathcal{W}$ such that $C \in \Delta^n$ and for every

1. Annotated refutation and countermodel for $(\Diamond p \supset \Box q) \supset \Box(p \supset q)$:

$$\dfrac{\dfrac{\dfrac{\dfrac{}{p \not\Rightarrow^{2.1} q}\,\textsf{init}}{\not\Rightarrow^{2} p \supset q}\,\textsf{nip}}{\Diamond p \supset \Box q \not\Rightarrow^{1.1} \Box(p \supset q)}\,\textsf{nip}}{\not\Rightarrow^{1} (\Diamond p \supset \Box q) \supset \Box(p \supset q)}\,\textsf{nip}$$

$\mathcal{W} = \{1, 1.1, 2, 2.1\}$. $1 \preceq 1.1$. $2 \preceq 2.1$.
$\mathcal{V}(p) = \{2.1\}$. $\mathcal{V}(q) = \emptyset$.
$\mathcal{N}_\Box(w) = \{\mathcal{W}\}$ for every $w \in \mathcal{W}$.
$\mathcal{N}_\Diamond(w) = \emptyset$ for every $w \in \mathcal{W}$.

2. Annotated refutation and countermodel for $\Diamond(p \vee q) \supset \Diamond p \vee \Diamond q$:

$$\dfrac{\dfrac{\dfrac{\dfrac{\dfrac{}{q \not\Rightarrow^{2} p}\,\textsf{init}}{p \vee q \not\Rightarrow^{2} p}\,\textsf{L}\vee \quad \dfrac{\dfrac{}{p \not\Rightarrow^{3} q}\,\textsf{init}}{p \vee q \not\Rightarrow^{3} q}\,\textsf{L}\vee}{\Diamond(p \vee q) \not\Rightarrow^{1.1} \Diamond p, \Diamond q}\,\textsf{nip}}{\Diamond(p \vee q) \not\Rightarrow^{1.1} \Diamond p \vee \Diamond q}\,\textsf{R}\vee}{\not\Rightarrow^{1} \Diamond(p \vee q) \supset \Diamond p \vee \Diamond q}\,\textsf{nip}$$

$\mathcal{W} = \{1, 1.1, 2, 3\}$. $1 \preceq 1.1$.
$\mathcal{V}(p) = \{3\}$. $\mathcal{V}(q) = \{2\}$.
$\mathcal{N}_\Box(w) = \{\mathcal{W}\}$ for every $w \in \mathcal{W}$.
$\mathcal{N}_\Diamond(w) = \emptyset$ for every $w \in \mathcal{W}$, $w \neq 1.1$.
$\mathcal{N}_\Diamond(1.1) = \{\alpha \mid (p \vee q)^+ \subseteq \alpha\} =$
$\{\{2, 3\}, \{2, 3, 1\}, \{2, 3, 1.1\}, \{2, 3, 1, 1.1\}\}$.

3. Annotated refutation and countermodel for $\Diamond\bot \supset \bot$ in Ref.CK:

$$\dfrac{\dfrac{}{\Diamond\bot \not\Rightarrow^{1.1} \bot}\,\textsf{init}_{\textsf{CK}}}{\not\Rightarrow^{1} \Diamond\bot \supset \bot}\,\textsf{nip}$$

$\mathcal{W} = \{1, 1.1\}$. $1 \preceq 1.1$.
$\mathcal{N}_\Box(1) = \{\mathcal{W}\}$. $\mathcal{N}_\Box(1.1) = \{\mathcal{W}\}$.
$\mathcal{N}_\Diamond(1) = \emptyset$. $\mathcal{N}_\Diamond(1.1) = \mathcal{P}(\mathcal{W})$.

Fig. 6. Annotated refutations and countermodels.

$\Box D \in \Gamma^\sigma$, $D \in \Gamma^n$. Then by i.h. $\bigcap\{D^+ \mid \Box D \in \Gamma^\sigma\} \not\subseteq [\![C]\!]$, thus $[\![C]\!] \notin \mathcal{N}_\Box(\sigma)$, therefore $\sigma \not\Vdash \Box C$. Then for every ρ such that $\sigma \preceq \rho$, $\rho \not\Vdash \Box C$ or $\rho \Vdash B$, therefore $\sigma \Vdash \Box C \supset B$.

If $\Diamond C \supset B \in \Gamma^\sigma$, then if $B \in \Gamma^\sigma$, then by i.h. $\sigma \Vdash B$, and by the hereditary property $\rho \Vdash B$ for every ρ such that $\rho \preceq \sigma$. If instead $B \notin \Gamma^\sigma$, then by nip or nip$_{\textsf{CCDL}}$ for every immediate successor $\sigma.k$ of σ, $\Box D \supset B \in \Gamma^{\sigma.k}$, then by i.h. $\sigma.k \Vdash \Box D \supset B$. Moreover, if there is no $\Diamond$-formula in Γ^σ, then $\mathcal{N}_\Diamond(\sigma) = \emptyset$, whence $\sigma \not\Vdash \Diamond C$. Otherwise for every $\Diamond D \in \Gamma^\sigma$, by nip or nip$_{\textsf{CCDL}}$ there is $n \in \mathcal{W}$ such that $D \in \Gamma^n$, $C \in \Delta^n$, and $E \in \Gamma^n$ for every $\Box E \in \Gamma^\sigma$. Then by i.h. $\bigcap\{E^+ \mid \Box E \in \Gamma^\sigma\} \cap D^+ \not\subseteq [\![C]\!]$, thus $[\![C]\!] \notin \mathcal{N}_\Diamond(\sigma)$, therefore $\sigma \not\Vdash \Diamond C$. Then for every ρ such that $\sigma \preceq \rho$, $\rho \not\Vdash \Diamond C$ or $\rho \Vdash B$, therefore $\sigma \Vdash \Diamond C \supset B$.

If $\Box B \in \Gamma^\sigma$ (resp. $\Diamond B \in \Gamma^\sigma$), then by i.h. $B^+ \subseteq [\![B]\!]$, and by definition $[\![B]\!] \in \mathcal{N}_\Box(\sigma)$ (resp. $\mathcal{N}_\Diamond(\sigma)$), so $\sigma \Vdash \Box B$ (resp. $\sigma \Vdash \Diamond B$).

If $\Box B \in \Delta^\sigma$, then by the rule nip or nip$_{\textsf{CCDL}}$ there is $n \in \mathcal{W}$ such that $B \in \Delta^n$ and for every $\Box C \in \Gamma^\sigma$, $C \in \Gamma^n$. Then by i.h. $\bigcap\{C^+ \mid \Box C \in \Gamma^\sigma\} \not\subseteq [\![B]\!]$, thus $[\![B]\!] \notin \mathcal{N}_\Box(\sigma)$, therefore $\sigma \not\Vdash \Box B$.

If $\Diamond B \in \Delta^\sigma$, then if there is no $\Diamond C \in \Gamma^\sigma$, then $\mathcal{N}_\Diamond(\sigma) = \emptyset$, thus $\sigma \not\Vdash \Diamond B$. If instead there is $\Diamond C \in \Gamma^\sigma$, then by the rule nip, for every $\Diamond C \in \Gamma^\sigma$ there is $n \in \mathcal{W}$ such that $B \in \Delta^n$, $C \in \Gamma^n$, and $D \in \Gamma^n$ for every $\Box D \in \Gamma^\sigma$. Then by i.h. $\bigcap\{D^+ \mid \Box C \in \Gamma^\sigma\} \cap C^+ \not\subseteq [\![B]\!]$, thus $[\![B]\!] \notin \mathcal{N}_\Diamond(\sigma)$, therefore $\sigma \not\Vdash \Diamond B$. $\square$

Some relevant examples of refutations of non-valid formulas and corresponding countermodels are displayed in Fig. 6.

As shown in [3], every neighbourhood model for CK or CCDL can be transformed into an equivalent relational model.[3] For instance, by applying the transformation to the last model in Fig. 6 we obtain a relational model $\langle \mathcal{W}', \preceq', \mathcal{R}, \mathcal{V}' \rangle$ for CK, where $\mathcal{W}' = \{(1, \{1, 1.1\}), (1.1, \{1, 1.1, f\}), (f, \{f\})\}$; $(1, \{1, 1.1\}) \preceq' (1.1, \{1, 1.1, f\})$; $(1.1, \{1, 1.1, f\})\mathcal{R}(f, \{f\})$; and $(f, \{f\}) \Vdash \bot$. Moreover, a simplified transformation is possible for the models where $\mathcal{N}_\Diamond$ is empty, whence in particular for neighbourhood models for the $\Box$-fragment of the logics. The simplified transformation generates relational models of the same size as the original neighbourhood ones. By contrast, the general transformation can produce relational models that are exponentially larger than the original neighbourhood ones. It follows that the 1-1 correspondence between the premisses of the non-invertible rules in a refutation and the worlds of the extracted countermodel is not preserved in the relational semantics. For this reason, while it is possible to directly extract relational models from refutations for the $\Box$-fragment of the two logics,[4] the same does not seem possible for CK and CCDL with both $\Box$ and $\Diamond$. In this sense neighbourhood models are the natural semantics of our refutation calculi.

5 Conclusion and Future Work

In this paper we have proposed terminating sequent calculi for constructive modal logics CK and CCDL. First we have presented the calculi G4.CK and G4.CCDL which extend both Dyckhoff's calculus for intuitionistic logic and Iemhoff's one for the $\Box$-fragment of IK. Our calculi provide a decision procedure for the respective logics. They have also good proof-theoretical properties, as they allow for a syntactic proof of cut admissibility. Then we have proposed dual refutation calculi for non-provability. The dual calculi are likewise terminating. Their main interest is that they support direct countermodel extraction: each refutation uniquely determines a finite neighbourhood countermodel of the refuted formula in the semantics defined in [3].

There are a number of issues that we intend to explore in future work. We have already mentioned the issue of transforming a neighbourhood countermodel into a "small" relational countermodel. There are also some computational issues: although the exact complexity of CK and CCDL has not been explicitly stated, we strongly conjecture that both are in PSPACE, in this hypothesis, the calculi G4.CK and G4.CCDL would not be optimal, since a derivation may have an exponential size, the same happens within Dyckhoff's G4ip′; this naturally leads to the issue of studying refinements of our calculi, following the line of [6] which would match (and establish) the PSPACE upper bound. Moreover, we believe that our terminating calculi are very suitable for implementation: a theorem prover based on them would expand the realm of intuitionistic modal

[3] The transformation in [3] must be slightly modified given the alternative formulation of the neighbourhood semantics.

[4] As an example, an extraction of relational countermodels from failed proofs in a G4-calculus for Intuitionistic Strong Löb Logic with only $\Box$ is presented in [9].

theorem proving, in addition to the recent prover presented in [10]. Following Iemhoff [14] we also intend to use our terminating calculi to prove constructively the uniform interpolation property for both CK and CCDL.

Finally, we plan to extend our calculi to other (non-normal) intuitionistic modal logics in two directions: on the one hand to subsystems of CK and CCDL defined in [3], and on the other hand their extensions with axioms of the standard modal cube. To this regard, nested sequents for the standard cube extensions of CK have been proposed in [1], but terminating calculi of the kind considered here have not been investigated yet for them. A further direction could be to study a constructive version of Bi-Intuitionistic Logic with tense modalities [12]. The investigation of refutation calculi for these logics, along the lines of this work, would of course presuppose the extension of the neighbourhood semantics itself to these logics, a non-trivial task which may have an independent interest.

References

1. Arisaka, R., Das, A., Straßburger, L.: On nested sequents for constructive modal logics. Log. Methods Comput. Sci. **11**(3), 1–33 (2015)
2. Bellin, G., De Paiva, V., Ritter, E.: Extended Curry-Howard correspondence for a basic constructive modal logic. In: Proceedings of Methods for Modalities, vol. 2 (2001)
3. Dalmonte, T., Grellois, C., Olivetti, N.: Intuitionistic non-normal modal logics: a general framework. J. Philos. Log. **49**(5), 833–882 (2020)
4. Dyckhoff, R.: Contraction-free sequent calculi for intuitionistic logic. J. Symb. Log. **57**(3), 795–807 (1992)
5. Dyckhoff, R., Negri, S.: Admissibility of structural rules for contraction-free systems of intuitionistic logic. J. Symb. Log. **65**(4), 1499–1518 (2000)
6. Ferrari, M., Fiorentini, C., Fiorino, G.: Contraction-free linear depth sequent calculi for intuitionistic propositional logic with the subformula property and minimal depth counter-models. J. Autom. Reason. **51**(2), 129–149 (2013)
7. Fischer Servi, G.: Semantics for a class of intuitionistic modal calculi. In: Dalla Chiara, M.L. (ed.) Italian Studies in the Philosophy of Science. BSPS, vol. 47, pp. 59–72. Springer, Dordrecht (1980). https://doi.org/10.1007/978-94-009-8937-5_5
8. Fitch, F.B.: Intuitionistic modal logic with quantifiers. J. Symb. Log. **14**(4), 113–118 (1950)
9. van der Giessen, I., Iemhoff, R.: Proof theory for intuitionistic strong Löb logic. arXiv preprint arXiv:2011.10383 (2020)
10. Girlando, M., Straßburger, L.: MOIN: a nested sequent theorem prover for intuitionistic modal logics (system description). In: Peltier, N., Sofronie-Stokkermans, V. (eds.) IJCAR 2020. LNCS (LNAI), vol. 12167, pp. 398–407. Springer, Cham (2020). https://doi.org/10.1007/978-3-030-51054-1_25
11. Goldblatt, R.I.: Grothendieck topology as geometric modality. Math. Log. Q. **27**(31–35), 495–529 (1981)
12. Goré, R., Postniece, L., Tiu, A.: Cut-elimination and proof search for biintuitionistic tense logic. In: Shehtman, V., Beklemishev, L., Goranko, V. (eds.) Advances in Modal Logic 8, pp. 156–177. College Publications (2010)
13. Iemhoff, R.: Terminating sequent calculi for two intuitionistic modal logics. J. Log. Comput. **28**(7), 1701–1712 (2018)

14. Iemhoff, R.: Uniform interpolation and the existence of sequent calculi. Ann. Pure Appl. Log. **170**(11), 102711 (2019)
15. Kojima, K.: Relational and neighborhood semantics for intuitionistic modal logic. Rep. Math. Log. **47**, 87–113 (2012)
16. Mendler, M., De Paiva, V.: Constructive CK for contexts. Context Representation and Reasoning (CRR-2005) 13 (2005)
17. Mendler, M., Scheele, S.: Cut-free Gentzen calculus for multimodal CK. Inf. Comput. **209**(12), 1465–1490 (2011)
18. Pinto, L., Dyckhoff, R.: Loop-free construction of counter-models for intuitionistic propositional logic. In: Symposia Gaussiana, Conference A, pp. 225–232 (1995)
19. Plotkin, G., Stirling, C.: A framework for intuitionistic modal logics. In: Proceedings of the 1st Conference on Theoretical Aspects of Reasoning about Knowledge (TARK), pp. 399–406 (1986)
20. Prawitz, D.: Natural Deduction: A Proof-Theoretical Study. Almqvist & Wiksell (1965)
21. Simpson, A.K.: The Proof Theory and Semantics of Intuitionistic Modal Logic. PhD thesis, School of Informatics, University of Edinburgh (1994)
22. Stewart, C., de Paiva, V., Alechina, N.: Intuitionistic modal logic: a 15-year retrospective. J. Log. Comput. **28**(5), 873–882 (2018)
23. Wijesekera, D.: Constructive modal logics I. Ann. Pure Appl. Log. **50**(3), 271–301 (1990)
24. Wijesekera, D., Nerode, A.: Tableaux for constructive concurrent dynamic logic. Ann. Pure Appl. Log. **135**(1–3), 1–72 (2005)

Nested Sequents for Intuitionistic Modal Logics via Structural Refinement

Tim S. Lyon(✉)

Computational Logic Group, Institute of Artificial Intelligence, Technische Universität Dresden, Dresden, Germany
timothy_stephen.lyon@tu-dresden.de

Abstract. We employ a recently developed methodology—called *structural refinement*—to extract nested sequent systems for a sizable class of intuitionistic modal logics from their respective labelled sequent systems. This method can be seen as a means by which labelled sequent systems can be transformed into nested sequent systems through the introduction of propagation rules and the elimination of structural rules, followed by a notational translation. The nested systems we obtain incorporate propagation rules that are parameterized with formal grammars, and which encode certain frame conditions expressible as first-order Horn formulae that correspond to a subclass of the Scott-Lemmon axioms. We show that our nested systems are sound, cut-free complete, and admit hp-admissibility of typical structural rules.

Keywords: Bi-relational model · Intuitionistic modal logic · Labelled sequent · Nested sequent · Proof theory · Propagation rule · Refinement

1 Introduction

Intuitionistic modal logics enable intuitionistic reasoning with the intensional operators $\Diamond$ and $\Box$. While a variety of different intuitionistic modal logics have been proposed [1,9,28,30,31], we focus on those defined in [28], which extend the intuitionistic modal logic IK with Scott-Lemmon axioms [20]. These logics were placed on a firm philosophical footing in [31] due to their satisfaction of certain requirements that one might reasonably impose upon an intuitionistic version of modal logic. Although such logics are interesting in their own right, intuitionistic modal logics have proven useful in practical applications: having been applied in the verification of computer hardware [8], to facilitate reasoning about functional programs [27], and in defining programming languages [7].

The development of intuitionistic modal logics naturally gave rise to an accompanying proof theory. Labelled natural deduction and sequent systems

Work supported by the European Research Council (ERC) Consolidator Grant 771779 (DeciGUT).

A. Das and S. Negri (Eds.): TABLEAUX 2021, LNAI 12842, pp. 409–427, 2021.
https://doi.org/10.1007/978-3-030-86059-2_24

were provided for IK extended with geometric axioms in [31]. In [13] and [14], label-free natural deduction systems and tree-sequent calculi were respectively provided for extensions of IK with combinations of the reflexivity axiom (T), symmetry axiom (B), transitivity axiom (4), and Euclidean axiom (5). In [32], nested sequent systems were proposed for all logics within the intuitionistic modal cube (i.e. logics axiomatized by extending IK with a subset of the axioms T, B, 4, 5, and the seriality axiom D). Such systems provide a suitable basis for developing automated reasoning and proof-search methods, having been used—in particular—to establish the decidability of logics within the intuitionistic modal cube [14,31].

With the exception of the systems introduced in [31], the drawback of the aforementioned proof systems is that they are rather limited, only being defined for a handful of logics. Indeed, in a recent paper on nested systems for intuitionistic modal logics [25], the authors leave open the problem of defining rules within the nested sequent formalism that allow for the capture of logics *outside* the intuitionistic modal cube. Accomplishing such a task would prove beneficial, since systems built within the nested formalism tend to be more economical (viz. they utilize simpler data structures) than those built within the labelled formalism, and have proven well-suited for the construction of analytic calculi [2,3,19], for writing decision algorithms [14,33], and for verifying interpolation [12,24].

In this paper, we answer the open problem of [25] to a large extent, and provide cut-free nested sequent systems for extensions of IK with what we call *Horn-Scott-Lemmon axioms (HSLs)*, namely, axioms of the form $(\Diamond^n \Box A \supset \Box^k A) \land (\Diamond^k A \supset \Box^n \Diamond A)$. We obtain such systems through the recently developed *structural refinement* methodology [21], which consists of transforming a labelled sequent system into a nested system through the introduction of *propagation rules* (cf. [4,10]) and the elimination of structural rules, followed by a notational translation. The propagation rules operate by viewing labelled sequents (which encode binary labelled graphs) as automata, allowing for formulae to be propagated along a path in the underlying graph of a labelled sequent, so long as the path is encoded by a string derivable in a certain formal grammar. The refinement methodology grew out of works relating labelled systems to 'more refined' or nested systems [5,18,23,26]. Also, the propagation rules we use are largely based upon the work of [17,33], where such rules were used in the setting of display and nested calculi. These rules were then transported to the labelled setting to prove the decidability of agency logics [23], to establish translations between calculi within various proof-theoretic formalisms [6], and to provide a basis for the structural refinement methodology [21].

This paper accomplishes the following: First, we show that structural refinement can be used to extract nested sequent systems from Simpson's labelled sequent systems [31] with proofs in the latter formalism algorithmically translatable into proofs of the nested formalism. Second, we provide sound and cut-free complete nested sequent systems for a considerable class of intuitionistic modal logics, and show that such systems admit the height-preserving admissibility (which we refer to as *hp-admissibility*) of certain structural rules (e.g. forms of weakening and contraction). Third, we provide an answer to the open problem of [25] to a large degree, giving a straightforward procedure for transforming axioms (viz. HSLs) into propagation/logical rules.

We have organized this paper accordingly: In Sect. 2, we define the intuitionistic modal logics considered, along with their axiomatizations and semantics. In Sect. 3, we introduce fundamental concepts in grammar theory that are needed for the definition of our propagation rules. We then introduce Simpson's labelled sequent calculi for intuitionistic modal logics in Sect. 4, and show how to structurally refine them in Sect. 5. Last, in Sect. 6, we translate the refined labelled systems of the previous section into sound and cut-free complete nested sequent systems admitting the hp-admissibility of certain structural rules.

2 Logical Preliminaries

In this section, we introduce the language, semantics, and axiomatization for the intuitionistic modal logic IK [28].[1] Moreover, we also introduce extensions of IK (referred to as *intuitionistic modal logics* more generally) with the seriality axiom D and axioms that we refer to as *Horn-Scott-Lemmon Axioms (HSLs)*.

We define our intuitionistic modal language $\mathcal{L}$ to be the set of formulae generated via the following BNF grammar:

$$A ::= p \mid \bot \mid A \vee A \mid A \wedge A \mid A \supset A \mid \Diamond A \mid \Box A$$

where p ranges over the set of propositional atoms $\Phi := \{p, q, r, \dots\}$. We use A, B, C, ... (occasionally annotated) to range over formulae in $\mathcal{L}$, and define ${\sim}A := A \supset \bot$ and $A \equiv B := (A \supset B) \wedge (B \supset A)$. For $n \in \mathbb{N}$, we use $\Diamond^n A$ and $\Box^n A$ to represent the formula A prefixed with a sequence of n diamonds or boxes, respectively. We interpret such formulae on *bi-relational models* [28,31]:

Definition 1 (Bi-relational Model [28]**).** *We define a* bi-relational model *to be a tuple* $M := (W, \leq, R, V)$ *such that:*

- W *is a non-empty set of* worlds $w, u, v, \dots$ *(potentially annotated);*
- *The* intuitionistic relation $\leq \subseteq W \times W$ *is reflexive and transitive;*
- *The* accessibility relation $R \subseteq W \times W$ *satisfies:*
  - *(F1) For all* $w, v, v' \in W$, *if* wRv *and* $v \leq v'$, *then there exists a* $w' \in W$ *such that* $w \leq w'$ *and* $w'Rv'$*;*
  - *(F2) For all* $w, w', v \in W$, *if* $w \leq w'$ *and* wRv, *then there exists a* $v' \in W$ *such that* $w'Rv'$ *and* $v \leq v'$*;*
- $V : W \to 2^{\Phi}$ *is a* valuation function *satisfying the* monotonicity condition*: For each* $w, u \in W$, *if* $w \leq u$, *then* $V(w) \subseteq V(u)$.

Formulae from $\mathcal{L}$ may then be interpreted over bi-relational models as specified by the semantic clauses below.

[1] See Simpson's 1994 PhD Thesis [31] for a detailed introduction and discussion of IK.

Definition 2 (Semantic Clauses [28]). *Let M be a bi-relational model with $w \in W$ of M. The* satisfaction relation $M, w \Vdash A$ *is defined recursively:*

- $M, w \Vdash p$ *iff* $p \in V(w)$, *for* $p \in \Phi$;
- $M, w \not\Vdash \bot$;
- $M, w \Vdash A \vee B$ *iff* $M, w \Vdash A$ *or* $M, w \Vdash B$;
- $M, w \Vdash A \wedge B$ *iff* $M, w \Vdash A$ *and* $M, w \Vdash B$;
- $M, w \Vdash A \supset B$ *iff for all* $w' \in W$, *if* $w \leq w'$ *and* $M, w' \Vdash A$, *then* $M, w' \Vdash B$;
- $M, w \Vdash \Diamond A$ *iff there exists a* $v \in W$ *such that* wRv *and* $M, v \Vdash A$;
- $M, w \Vdash \Box A$ *iff for all* $w', v' \in W$, *if* $w \leq w'$ *and* $w'Rv'$, *then* $M, v' \Vdash A$.

We say that a formula A is globally true on M, *written* $M \Vdash A$, *iff* $M, u \Vdash A$ *for all worlds* $u \in W$ *of* M, *and we say that a formula A is* valid, *written* $\Vdash A$, *iff A is globally true on all bi-relational models.*

As shown by Plotkin and Stirling in [28], the validities of IK are axiomatizable:

Definition 3 (Axiomatization [28]). *We define the axiomatization* HIK *as:*

A0 *All theorems of propositional intuitionistic logic*

A1 $\Box(A \supset B) \supset (\Box A \supset \Box B)$

A2 $\Box(A \supset B) \supset (\Diamond A \supset \Diamond B)$

A3 $\sim\Diamond\bot$

A4 $\Diamond(A \vee B) \supset (\Diamond A \vee \Diamond B)$

A5 $(\Diamond A \supset \Box B) \supset \Box(A \supset B)$

R0 $\dfrac{A \qquad A \supset B}{B}$ *(mp)*

R1 $\dfrac{A}{\Box A}$ *(nec)*

We define IK *to be the smallest set of formulae closed under substitutions of the above axioms and applications of the inference rules, and define A to be a* theorem *of* IK *iff* $A \in$ IK.

We also consider extensions of HIK with sets $\mathcal{A}$ of the following axioms:

$$\mathrm{D} : \Box A \supset \Diamond A \quad \mathrm{HSL} : (\Diamond^n \Box A \supset \Box^k A) \wedge (\Diamond^k A \supset \Box^n \Diamond A)$$

The above left axiom is referred to as the *seriality axiom* D and axioms of the form above right are referred to as *Horn-Scott-Lemmon axioms (*HSLs*)*, which we use $\phi(n, k)$ to denote.[2] For the remainder of the paper, we use $\mathcal{A}$ to denote an arbitrary set of the above axioms, that is:

$$\mathcal{A} \subseteq \{\mathrm{D}\} \cup \{(\Diamond^n \Box A \supset \Box^k A) \wedge (\Diamond^k A \supset \Box^n \Diamond A) \mid n, k \in \mathbb{N}\}$$

The set of HSLs includes well-known axioms such as:

$$\mathrm{T} : (A \supset \Diamond A) \wedge (\Box A \supset A) \quad 4 : (\Diamond\Diamond A \supset \Diamond A) \wedge (\Box A \supset \Box\Box A)$$

$$\mathrm{B} : (\Diamond\Box A \supset A) \wedge (A \supset \Box\Diamond A) \quad 5 : (\Diamond\Box A \supset \Box A) \wedge (\Diamond A \supset \Box\Diamond A)$$

[2] We note that the term *Horn-Scott-Lemmon axiom* arises from the fact that such axioms form a proper subclass of the well-known *Scott-Lemmon Axioms* [20] and are associated with frame conditions that are expressible as Horn formulae [31, Sect. 7.2].

Axiom	Frame Condition
$\Box A \supset \Diamond A$	$\forall w \exists u(wRu)$
$(\Diamond^n \Box A \supset \Box^k A) \land (\Diamond^k A \supset \Box^n \Diamond A)$	$\forall w, u, v(wR^n u \land wR^k v \supset uRv)$

Fig. 1. Axioms and their related frame conditions. We note that when $n = 0$, the related frame condition is $\forall w, v(wR^k v \supset wRv)$, when $k = 0$, the related frame condition is $\forall w, u(wR^n u \supset uRw)$, and when $n = k = 0$, the related frame condition is $\forall w(wRw)$.

The work of Simpson [31] establishes that any extension of HIK with a set $\mathcal{A}$ of axioms is sound and complete relative to a subclass of the bi-relational models. In particular, the extension of HIK with a set $\mathcal{A}$ of axioms is sound and complete relative to the set of bi-relational models satisfying the frame conditions related to the axioms of $\mathcal{A}$, as specified in Fig. 1.[3] We define axiomatic extensions of HIK along with their corresponding models below:

Definition 4 (Extensions, Bi-relational $\mathcal{A}$-model, $\mathcal{A}$-valid). *The axiomatization* $\mathsf{HIK}(\mathcal{A})$ *is defined to be* HIK *extended with the axioms from $\mathcal{A}$, and we define the* logic $\mathsf{IK}(\mathcal{A})$ *to be the smallest set of formulae closed under substitutions of the axioms of* $\mathsf{HIK}(\mathcal{A})$ *and applications of the inference rules. Also, a* theorem *of* $\mathsf{IK}(\mathcal{A})$ *is a formula A such that $A \in \mathsf{IK}(\mathcal{A})$. Moreover, we define a* bi-relational $\mathcal{A}$-model *to be a bi-relational model satisfying each frame condition related to an axiom $A \in \mathcal{A}$ (as specified in Fig. 1). Last, a formula A is* $\mathcal{A}$-valid *iff it is globally true on all $\mathcal{A}$-models.*

Remark 1. We note that $\mathsf{HIK} = \mathsf{HIK}(\emptyset)$ and that a bi-relational $\emptyset$-model is a bi-relational model.

Theorem 1 (Soundness and Completeness [31]). *A formula is a theorem of* $\mathsf{HIK}(\mathcal{A})$ *iff it is valid in all $\mathcal{A}$-frames.*

Proof. Follows from Theorem 6.2.1 and Theorem 8.1.4 of [31]. □

3 Grammar Theoretic Preliminaries

As will be seen later on (viz. in Sect. 5 and 6), a central component to our refinement methodology—i.e. the extraction of nested calculi from labelled—is the use of inference rules whose applicability is determined on the basis of strings generated by a formal grammar. We therefore introduce grammar-theoretic notions that are essential to the functionality of such rules.

We let Σ be our *alphabet* consisting of the *characters* $\Diamond$ and $\blacklozenge$, that is, $\Sigma := \{\Diamond, \blacklozenge\}$. The symbols $\Diamond$ and $\blacklozenge$ will be used to encode information about

[3] We note that the axioms we consider do not *characterize* the set of frames satisfying the frame properties related to the axioms as they do in the classical setting. For more details concerning this point, see [31, p. 56], and for details concerning the proper characterization results of the above axioms, see [28].

the accessibility relation R of a bi-relational model in certain inference rules of our calculi. In particular, $\Diamond$ will be used to encode information about what is happening in the *future* of the accessibility relation, and $\blacklozenge$ will be used to encode information about what is happening in the *past* of the accessibility relation. We note that such symbols have been chosen due to their analogous meaning in the context of tense logics [17,19]. Also, following [17], we let $\langle ? \rangle \in \Sigma$ and $\langle ? \rangle^{-1} \in \Sigma \setminus \{\langle ? \rangle\}$, i.e. $\Diamond^{-1} := \blacklozenge$ and $\blacklozenge^{-1} := \Diamond$; we refer to $\Diamond$ and $\blacklozenge$ as *converses* of one another. We may define *strings* over our alphabet Σ accordingly:

Definition 5 (Σ^*). *We let $\cdot$ be the* concatenation operation *with ε the* empty string. *We define the set Σ^* of* strings over Σ *to be the smallest set such that:*

- $\Sigma \cup \{\varepsilon\} \subseteq \Sigma^*$
- *If $s \in \Sigma^*$ and $\langle ? \rangle \in \Sigma$, then $s \cdot \langle ? \rangle \in \Sigma^*$*

For a set Σ^* of strings, we use $s, t, r, \ldots$. (potentially annotated) to represent strings in Σ^*. Also, the empty string ε is taken to be the identity element for the concatenation operation, i.e. $s \cdot \varepsilon = \varepsilon \cdot s = s$ for $s \in \Sigma^*$. Furthermore, we will not explicitly mention the concatenation operation in practice and let $st := s \cdot t$, that is, we denote concatenation by simply gluing two strings together. Beyond concatenation, another useful operation to define on strings is the *converse operation*, adapted from [33].

Definition 6 (String Converse). *We extend the converse operation to strings as follows:*

- $\varepsilon^{-1} := \varepsilon$;
- *If $s = \langle ? \rangle_1 \cdots \langle ? \rangle_n$, then $s^{-1} := \langle ? \rangle_n^{-1} \cdots \langle ? \rangle_1^{-1}$.*

We let $\langle ? \rangle^n$ denote a string consisting of n copies of $\langle ? \rangle$, which is ε when $n = 0$. Making use of such notation, we can compactly define the notion of an $\mathcal{A}$*-grammar*, which encodes information contained in a set $\mathcal{A}$ of axioms, and which will be employed in the definition of certain inference rules (see Sect. 5).

Definition 7 ($\mathcal{A}$-grammar). *We define an $\mathcal{A}$-*grammar *to be a set $g(\mathcal{A})$ such that:*

$$(\Diamond \longrightarrow \blacklozenge^n \Diamond^k), (\blacklozenge \longrightarrow \blacklozenge^k \Diamond^n) \in g(\mathcal{A}) \text{ iff } (\Diamond^n \Box A \supset \Box^k A) \land (\Diamond^k A \supset \Box^n \Diamond A) \in \mathcal{A}.$$

We call rules of the form $\langle ? \rangle \longrightarrow s$ production rules, *where $\langle ? \rangle \in \Sigma$ and $s \in \Sigma^*$.*

An $\mathcal{A}$-grammar $g(\mathcal{A})$ is a type of *Semi-Thue system* (cf. [29]), i.e. it is a string re-writing system. For example, assuming that $\langle ? \rangle \longrightarrow s \in g(\mathcal{A})$, we may derive the string tsr from $t\langle ? \rangle r$ in one-step by applying the mentioned production rule. As usual, through successive applications of production rules to a string $s \in \Sigma^*$, one obtains derivations of new strings, the collection of which, determines a language. We make such notions precise by means of the following definition:

Definition 8 (Derivation, Language). *Let $g(\mathcal{A})$ be an $\mathcal{A}$-grammar. The* one-step derivation relation $\longrightarrow_{g(\mathcal{A})}$ *holds between two strings s and t in Σ^*, written $s \longrightarrow_{g(\mathcal{A})} t$, iff there exist $s', t' \in \Sigma^*$ and $\langle ? \rangle \longrightarrow r \in S$ such that $s = s'\langle ? \rangle t'$ and $t = s'rt'$. The* derivation relation $\longrightarrow^*_{g(\mathcal{A})}$ *is defined to be the reflexive and transitive closure of $\longrightarrow_{g(\mathcal{A})}$. For two strings $s, t \in \Sigma^*$, we refer to $s \longrightarrow^*_{g(\mathcal{A})} t$ as a* derivation of t from s, *and define its* length *to be equal to the minimal number of one-step derivations needed to derive t from s in $g(\mathcal{A})$. Last, for a string $s \in \Sigma^*$, the* language of s relative to $g(\mathcal{A})$ *is defined to be the set $L_{g(\mathcal{A})}(s) := \{t \mid s \longrightarrow^*_{g(\mathcal{A})} t\}$.*

4 Labelled Sequent Systems

We introduce equivalent variants of Simpson's labelled sequent systems for intuitionistic modal logics [31], which are uniformly presented in Fig. 2. We use the name $\mathbf{L}_{\Box\Diamond}(\mathcal{A})$ to denote a labelled system as opposed to Simpson's name $\mathbf{L}_{\Box\Diamond}(\mathcal{T})$ since we define each system relative to a set $\mathcal{A}$ of axioms (cf. [31]). The sole difference between Simpson's original systems and the systems presented here is that we copy principal formulae into the premises of some rules. This minor change will facilitate our work in the subsequent section.

Simpson's systems make use of a denumerable set $Lab := \{w, u, v, \ldots\}$ of *labels* (which we sometimes annotate), as well as two distinct types of formulae: *labelled formulae*, which are of the form $w : A$ with $w \in Lab$ and $A \in \mathcal{L}$, and *relational atoms*, which are of the form wRu for $w, u \in Lab$. We define a *labelled sequent* to be a formula of the form $\mathcal{R}, \Gamma \vdash w : A$, where $\mathcal{R}$ is a (potentially empty) multiset of relational atoms, and Γ is a (potentially empty) multiset of labelled formulae. Also, we define a sequence of relational atoms $wR^n u := wRw_1, w_1Rw_2, \ldots, w_{n-1}Ru$, for $n \in \mathbb{N}$, and note that $wR^0u := (w = u)$.

We refer to the (id) and $(\bot_l)$ rules as *initial rules*, to the (d) and $(S_{n,k})$ rules as *structural rules*, and to the remaining rules in Fig. 2 as *logical rules*. Our use of the term *structural rules* in reference to (d) and $(S_{n,k})$ is consistent with the use of the term in the literature on proof systems for modal and related logics [2, 6, 16, 17] and is based on the fact that such rules manipulate the underlying data structure of sequents as opposed to introducing more complex logical formulae. Also, we point out that the $(S_{n,k})$ rules form a proper subclass of Simpson's (S_χ) *geometric structural rules* (see [31, p. 126]) used to generate labelled sequent systems for IK extended with any number of *geometric axioms*. When $n = 0$ or $k = 0$ in an HSL, i.e. when $\phi(0, k) \in \mathcal{A}$, $\phi(n, 0) \in \mathcal{A}$, or $\phi(0, 0) \in \mathcal{A}$, the structural rules $(S_{0,k})$, $(S_{n,0})$, and $(S_{0,0})$ are defined accordingly:

$$\frac{\mathcal{R}, wR^k v, wRv, \Gamma \vdash z : A}{\mathcal{R}, wR^k v, \Gamma \vdash z : A}\ (S_{0,k}) \qquad \frac{\mathcal{R}, wR^n u, uRw, \Gamma \vdash z : A}{\mathcal{R}, wR^n u, \Gamma \vdash z : A}\ (S_{n,0})$$

$$\frac{\mathcal{R}, wRw, \Gamma \vdash z : A}{\mathcal{R}, \Gamma \vdash z : A}\ (S_{0,0})$$

Let us now define the semantics for our labelled sequents, and then we state the soundness and completeness theorem for $\mathbf{L}_{\Box\Diamond}(\mathcal{A})$.

$$\frac{}{\mathcal{R}, w : p, \Gamma \vdash w : p}\ (id) \qquad \frac{}{\mathcal{R}, w : \bot, \Gamma \vdash u : A}\ (\bot_l)$$

$$\frac{\mathcal{R}, \Gamma, w : A \vdash u : C \qquad \mathcal{R}, \Gamma, w : B \vdash u : C}{\mathcal{R}, \Gamma, w : A \vee B \vdash u : C}\ (\vee_l) \qquad \frac{\mathcal{R}, \Gamma \vdash w : A_i}{\mathcal{R}, \Gamma \vdash w : A_1 \vee A_2}\ (\vee_r)\ i \in \{1, 2\}$$

$$\frac{\mathcal{R}, \Gamma, w : A, w : B \vdash u : C}{\mathcal{R}\Gamma, w : A \wedge B \vdash u : C}\ (\wedge_l) \qquad \frac{\mathcal{R}, \Gamma \vdash w : A \qquad \mathcal{R}, \Gamma \vdash w : B}{\mathcal{R}, \Gamma \vdash w : A \wedge B}\ (\wedge_r)$$

$$\frac{\mathcal{R}, \Gamma, w : A \supset B \vdash w : A \qquad \mathcal{R}, \Gamma, w : B \vdash u : C}{\mathcal{R}, \Gamma, w : A \supset B \vdash u : C}\ (\supset_l) \qquad \frac{\mathcal{R}, \Gamma, w : A \vdash w : B}{\mathcal{R}, \Gamma \vdash w : A \supset B}\ (\supset_r)$$

$$\frac{\mathcal{R}, wRu, \Gamma, u : A \vdash v : B}{\mathcal{R}, \Gamma, w : \Diamond A \vdash v : B}\ (\Diamond_l)^{\dagger} \qquad \frac{\mathcal{R}, wRu, \Gamma \vdash u : A}{\mathcal{R}, wRu, \Gamma \vdash w : \Diamond A}\ (\Diamond_r)$$

$$\frac{\mathcal{R}, wRu, \Gamma \vdash u : A}{\mathcal{R}, \Gamma \vdash w : \Box A}\ (\Box_r)^{\dagger} \qquad \frac{\mathcal{R}, wRu, \Gamma, w : \Box A, u : A \vdash v : C}{\mathcal{R}, wRu, \Gamma, w : \Box A \vdash v : C}\ (\Box_l)$$

$$\frac{\mathcal{R}, wRu, \Gamma \vdash v : A}{\mathcal{R}, \Gamma \vdash v : A}\ (d)^{\dagger} \qquad \frac{\mathcal{R}, wR^n u, wR^k v, uRv, \Gamma \vdash z : A}{\mathcal{R}, wR^n u, wR^k v, \Gamma \vdash z : A}\ (S_{n,k})$$

Fig. 2. The labelled calculi $\mathbf{L}_{\Box\Diamond}(\mathcal{A})$. We have (d) as a rule in the calculus, if $\mathrm{D} \in \mathcal{A}$, and $(S_{n,k})$ as a rule in the calculus, for each $\phi(n,k) \in \mathcal{A}$. The side condition † states that u must be an *eigenvariable*, i.e. u may not occur in the conclusion.

Definition 9 (Labelled Sequent Semantics). *Let* $M := (W, \leq, R, V)$ *be a bi-relational* $\mathcal{A}$*-model with* $I : Lab \mapsto W$ *an* interpretation function *mapping labels to worlds. We define the* satisfaction *of relational atoms and labelled formulae:*

- $M, I \models wRu$ *iff* $I(w)RI(u)$;
- $M, I \models w : A$ *iff* $M, I(w) \Vdash A$.

A labelled sequent $\Lambda := \mathcal{R}, \Gamma \vdash v : B$ *is* satisfied *in* M *with* I*, written* $M, I \models \Lambda$*, iff if* $M, I \models wRu$ *for all* $wRu \in \mathcal{R}$ *and* $M, I \models w : A$ *for all* $w : A \in \Gamma$*, then* $M, I \models v : B$*. A labelled sequent* Λ *is* falsified *in* M *with* I *iff* $M, I \not\models \Lambda$*, that is,* Λ *is not satisfied by* M *with* I*.*

Last, a labelled sequent Λ *is* $\mathcal{A}$-valid*, written* $\models_{\mathcal{A}} \Lambda$*, iff it is satisfiable in every bi-relational* $\mathcal{A}$*-model* M *with every interpretation function* I*. We say that a labelled sequent* Λ *is* $\mathcal{A}$-invalid *iff* $\not\models_{\mathcal{A}} \Lambda$*, i.e.* Λ *is not* $\mathcal{A}$*-valid.*

Theorem 2 ($\mathbf{L}_{\Box\Diamond}(\mathcal{A})$ Soundness and Completeness). $\mathcal{R}, \Gamma \vdash w : A$ *is derivable in* $\mathbf{L}_{\Box\Diamond}(\mathcal{A})$ *iff* $\mathcal{R}, \Gamma \vdash w : A$ *is* $\mathcal{A}$*-valid.*

Proof. Follows from Theorem 7.2.1 and Theorem 8.1.4 of [31]. □

5 Structural Refinement

We show how to *structurally refine* the labelled systems introduced in the previous section, that is, we implement a methodology introduced and applied in [6,21–23] (referred to as *structural refinement*, or *refinement* more simply) for simplifying labelled systems and/or permitting the extraction of nested systems. The methodology consists of eliminating structural rules (viz. the $(S_{n,k})$ rules in our setting) through the addition of *propagation rules* (cf. [4,10,31]) to the labelled calculi, begetting systems that are translatable into nested systems.

The propagation rules we introduce are based on those of [6,17,22,23,33], and operate by viewing a labelled sequent as an automaton, allowing for the propagation of a formula (when applied bottom-up) from a label w to a label u given that a certain path of relational atoms exists between w and u (corresponding to a string generated by an $\mathcal{A}$-grammar). We note that Simpson likewise introduced a variation of these rules, named $(\Diamond R)_{\mathcal{T}_H}$ and $(\Box L)_{\mathcal{T}_H}$ (see [31, p. 126]), by closing the relational atoms of a sequent under the frame conditions related to each HSL $\phi(n,k) \in \mathcal{A}$. We opt to use propagation rules based on formal grammars however because such rules permit the formulation of nested systems outside the class of HSL extensions of IK, thus setting the stage for the construction of nested systems for even broader classes of logics in future work.[4]

The definition of our propagation rules is built atop the notions introduced in the following two definitions:

Definition 10 (Propagation Graph). *The* propagation graph $PG(\mathcal{R})$ *of a multiset of relational atoms* $\mathcal{R}$ *is defined recursively on the structure of* $\mathcal{R}$*:*

- $PG(\emptyset) := (\emptyset, \emptyset)$;
- $PG(wRu) := (\{w, u\}, \{(w, \Diamond, u), (u, \blacklozenge, w)\})$;
- $PG(\mathcal{R}_1, \mathcal{R}_2) := (V_1 \cup V_2, E_1 \cup E_2)$ *where* $PG_x(\mathcal{R}_i) = (V_i, E_i)$.

We will often write $w \in PG(\mathcal{R})$ *to mean* $w \in V$*, and* $(w, \langle ? \rangle, u) \in PG(\mathcal{R})$ *to mean* $(w, \langle ? \rangle, u) \in E$.

Definition 11 (Propagation Path). *We define a* propagation path from w_1 to w_n in $PG(\mathcal{R}) := (V, E)$ *to be a sequence of the following form:*

$$\pi(w_1, w_n) := w_1, \langle ? \rangle_1, w_2, \langle ? \rangle_2, \dots, \langle ? \rangle_{n-1}, w_n$$

such that $(w_1, \langle ? \rangle_1, w_2), (w_2, \langle ? \rangle_2, w_3), \dots, (w_{n-1}, \langle ? \rangle_{n-1}, w_n) \in E$. *Given a propagation path of the above form, we define its* converse *as shown below top and its* string *as shown below bottom:*

$$\pi^{-1}(w_n, w_1) := w_n, \langle ? \rangle_{n-1}^{-1}, w_{n-1}, \langle ? \rangle_{n-2}^{-1}, \dots, \langle ? \rangle_1^{-1}, w_1$$

$$s_\pi(w_1, w_n) := \langle ? \rangle_1 \langle ? \rangle_2 \cdots \langle ? \rangle_{n-1}$$

Last, we let $\lambda(w, w) := w$ *represent an* empty path *with the string of the empty path defined as* $s_\lambda(w, w) := \varepsilon$.

[4] For instance, we could define our propagation rules relative to the formal grammar $\{\Diamond \longrightarrow \Diamond\blacklozenge\}$, which would give a calculus for a logic outside the class of HSL extensions of IK.

$$\frac{\mathcal{R}, \Gamma \vdash u : A}{\mathcal{R}, \Gamma \vdash w : \Diamond A} \ (p_{\Diamond}) \quad \textit{only if } \exists \pi(w,u) \in PG(\mathcal{R})(s_{\pi}(w,u) \in L_{g(\mathcal{A})}(\Diamond))$$

$$\frac{\mathcal{R}, \Gamma, w : \Box A, u : A \vdash v : B}{\mathcal{R}, \Gamma, w : \Box A \vdash v : B} \ (p_{\Box}) \quad \textit{only if } \exists \pi(w,u) \in PG(\mathcal{R})(s_{\pi}(w,u) \in L_{g(\mathcal{A})}(\Diamond))$$

Fig. 3. Propagation rules.

We are now in a position to define the operation of our propagation rules $(p_{\Diamond})$ and $(p_{\Box})$, which are displayed in Fig. 3. Each propagation rule $(p_{\Diamond})$ and $(p_{\Box})$ is applicable only if *there exists a propagation path* $\pi(w,u)$ *from* w *to* u *in the propagation graph* $PG(\mathcal{R})$ *such that the string* $s_{\pi}(w,u)$ *is in the language* $L_{g(\mathcal{A})}(\Diamond)$. We express this statement compactly by making use of its equivalent first-order representation:

$$\exists \pi(w,u) \in PG(\mathcal{R})(s_{\pi}(w,u) \in L_{g(\mathcal{A})}(\Diamond))$$

We provide further intuition regarding such rules by means of an example:

Example 1. Let $\mathcal{R} := vRu, uRw$. We give a graphical depiction of $PG(\mathcal{R})$:

$\Lambda := vRu, uRw, w : \Box p, u : p \vdash v : p \supset q$

Let $\mathcal{A} := \{(\Diamond^2 \Box A \supset \Box^1 A) \wedge (\Diamond^1 A \supset \Box^2 \Diamond A)\}$, so that the corresponding $\mathcal{A}$-grammar is $g(\mathcal{A}) = \{\Diamond \longrightarrow \blacklozenge\blacklozenge\Diamond, \blacklozenge \longrightarrow \blacklozenge\Diamond\Diamond\}$. Then, the path $\pi(w,u) := w, \blacklozenge, u, \blacklozenge, v, \Diamond, u$ exists between w and u. The first production rule of $g(\mathcal{A})$ implies that $s_{\pi}(w,u) = \blacklozenge\blacklozenge\Diamond \in L_{g(\mathcal{A})}(\Diamond)$. Therefore, we are permitted to (top-down) apply the propagation rule $(p_{\Box})$ to Λ to delete the labelled formula $u : p$, letting us derive $vRu, uRw, w : \Box p \vdash v : p \supset q$.

Remark 2. The $(\Diamond_r)$ and $(\Box_l)$ rules are instances of $(p_{\Diamond})$ and $(p_{\Box})$, respectively.

Definition 12 (Refined Labelled Calculus). *We define the* refined labelled calculus $\mathsf{IK}(\mathcal{A})\mathsf{L} := \mathbf{L}_{\Box\Diamond}(\mathcal{A}) + \{(p_{\Diamond}), (p_{\Box})\} - \{(S_{n,k}) \mid \phi(n,k) \in \mathcal{A}\}$.

We show that each calculus $\mathsf{IK}(\mathcal{A})\mathsf{L}$ is complete by means of a proof transformation procedure. That is, we show that through the elimination of structural rules we can transform a proof in $\mathbf{L}_{\Box\Diamond}(\mathcal{A})$ into a proof in $\mathsf{IK}(\mathcal{A})\mathsf{L}$. We note that Simpson proved a similar result, showing that labelled derivations with structural rules are transformable into derivations with his propagation rules $(\Diamond R)_{\mathcal{T}_H}$ and $(\Box L)_{\mathcal{T}_H}$ (see [31, Sect. 7.2]). In our context, the proof of structural rule eliminability requires more complex methods however due to the use of our new propagation rules that are parameterized with formal grammars. We first prove two crucial lemmata, and then show the elimination result.

Lemma 1. *Let* $\mathcal{R}_1 := \mathcal{R}, wR^n u, wR^k v, uRv$ *and* $\mathcal{R}_2 := \mathcal{R}, wR^n u, wR^k v$. *Suppose we are given a derivation in* $\mathbf{L}_{\Box\Diamond}(\mathcal{A}) + \{(p_\Diamond), (p_\Box)\}$ *ending with:*

$$\cfrac{\cfrac{\mathcal{R}, wR^n u, wR^k v, uRv, \Gamma \vdash z : A}{\mathcal{R}, wR^n u, wR^k v, uRv, \Gamma \vdash x : \Diamond A}\,(p_\Diamond)}{\mathcal{R}, wR^n u, wR^k v, \Gamma \vdash x : \Diamond A}\,(S_{n,k})$$

where the side condition $\exists \pi(x,z) \in PG(\mathcal{R}_1)(s_\pi(x,z) \in L_{g(\mathcal{A})}(\Diamond))$ *holds due to* $(p_\Diamond)$. *Then,* $\exists \pi'(x,z) \in PG(\mathcal{R}_2)(s_{\pi'}(x,z) \in L_{g(\mathcal{A})}(\Diamond))$, *that is to say, the* $(S_{n,k})$ *rule is permutable with the* $(p_\Diamond)$ *rule.*

Proof. We have two cases: either (i) the relational atom uRv is not active in the $(p_\Diamond)$ inference, or (ii) it is. Since (i) is easily resolved, we show (ii).

Let us suppose that the relational atom uRv is active in $(p_\Diamond)$, i.e. uRv occurs along the propagation path $\pi(x,z)$. To prove the claim, we need to show that $\exists \pi'(x,z) \in PG(\mathcal{R}_2)(s_{\pi'}(x,z) \in L_{g(\mathcal{A})}(\Diamond))$. Therefore, we construct such a propagation path by performing the following operations on $\pi(x,z)$:

- replace each occurrence of $u, \Diamond, v$ in $PG(\mathcal{R}_1)$ with

$$u, \blacklozenge, u_1, \ldots, u_{n-1}, \blacklozenge, w, \Diamond, w_1, \ldots, w_{k-1}, \Diamond, v;$$

- replace each occurrence of $v, \blacklozenge, u$ in $PG(\mathcal{R}_1)$ with

$$v, \blacklozenge, w_{k-1}, \ldots, w_1, \blacklozenge, w, \Diamond, u_{n-1}, \ldots, u_1, \Diamond, u.$$

We let $\pi'(x,z)$ denote the path obtained by performing the above operations on $\pi(x,z)$, and note that first half of the first propagation path and the second half of the second propagation path correspond to the edges $(u, \blacklozenge, u_1), \ldots, (u_{n-1}, \blacklozenge, w) \in PG(\mathcal{R}_1)$ and $(w, \Diamond, u_{n-1}), \ldots, (u_1, \Diamond, u) \in PG(\mathcal{R}_1)$, respectively, obtained from the relational atoms $wR^n u \in \mathcal{R}_1$, whereas the second half of the first propagation path and the first half of the second propagation path correspond to the edges $(w, \Diamond, w_1), \ldots, (w_{k-1}, \Diamond, v) \in PG(\mathcal{R}_1)$ and $(v, \blacklozenge, w_{k-1}), \ldots, (w_1, \blacklozenge, w) \in PG(\mathcal{R}_1)$, respectively, obtained from the edges $wR^k v \in \mathcal{R}_1$ (by Definition 13). Since the sole difference between $PG(\mathcal{R}_1)$ and $PG(\mathcal{R}_2)$ is that the former is guaranteed to contain the edges $(u, \Diamond, v)$ and $(v, \blacklozenge, u)$ obtained from uRv, while the latter is not, and since $\pi'(x,z)$ omits the use of such edges (i.e. $u, \Diamond, v$ and $v, \blacklozenge, u$ do not occur in $\pi'(x,z)$), we have that $\pi'(x,z)$ is a propagation path in $PG(\mathcal{R}_2)$.

To complete the proof, we need to additionally show that $s_{\pi'}(x,z) \in L_{g(\mathcal{A})}(\Diamond)$. By assumption, $s_\pi(x,z) \in L_{g(\mathcal{A})}(\Diamond)$, which implies that $\Diamond \longrightarrow^*_{g(\mathcal{A})} s_\pi(x,z)$ by Definition 8. Since $(S_{n,k})$ is a rule in $\mathbf{L}_{\Box\Diamond}(\mathcal{A})$, it follows that $\Diamond \longrightarrow \blacklozenge^n \Diamond^k$ and $\blacklozenge \longrightarrow \blacklozenge^k \Diamond^n \in g(\mathcal{A})$ by Definition 7. If we apply $\Diamond \longrightarrow \blacklozenge^n \Diamond^k$ to each occurrence of $\Diamond$ in $s_\pi(x,z)$ corresponding to the edge $(u, \Diamond, v)$ (and relational atom uRv), and apply $\blacklozenge \longrightarrow \blacklozenge^k \Diamond^n$ to each occurrence of $\blacklozenge$ in $s_\pi(x,z)$ corresponding to the edge $(v, \blacklozenge, u)$ (and relational atom uRv), we obtain the string $s_{\pi'}(x,z)$ and show that $\Diamond \longrightarrow^*_{g(\mathcal{A})} s_{\pi'}(x,z)$, i.e. $s_{\pi'}(x,z) \in L_{g(\mathcal{A})}(\Diamond)$. □

Lemma 2. *Let* $\mathcal{R}_1 := \mathcal{R}, wR^n u, wR^k v, uRv$ *and* $\mathcal{R}_2 := \mathcal{R}, wR^n u, wR^k v$. *Suppose we are given a derivation in* $\mathbf{L}_{\Box\Diamond}(\mathcal{A}) + \{(p_\Diamond), (p_\Box)\}$ *ending with:*

$$\dfrac{\dfrac{\mathcal{R}, wR^n u, wR^k v, uRv, x : \Box A, y : A, \Gamma \vdash z : C}{\mathcal{R}, wR^n u, wR^k v, uRv, x : \Box A, \Gamma \vdash z : C}\,(p_\Box)}{\mathcal{R}, wR^n u, wR^k v, x : \Box A, \Gamma \vdash z : C}\,(S_{n,k})$$

where the side condition $\exists \pi(x,y) \in PG(\mathcal{R}_1)(s_\pi(x,y) \in L_{g(\mathcal{A})}(\Diamond))$ *holds due to* $(p_\Box)$. *Then,* $\exists \pi'(x,y) \in PG(\mathcal{R}_2)(s_{\pi'}(x,y) \in L_{g(\mathcal{A})}(\Diamond))$, *that is to say, the* $(S_{n,k})$ *rule is permutable with the* $(p_\Box)$ *rule.*

Proof. Similar to the proof of Lemma 1 above. □

To improve the comprehensibility of the above lemmata, we provide an example of permuting an instance of the structural rule $(S_{n,k})$ above an instance of a propagation rule.

Example 2. Let $\mathcal{A} := \{(\Diamond\Box A \supset \Box A) \wedge (\Diamond A \supset \Box\Diamond A)\}$ so that the $\mathcal{A}$-grammar $g(\mathcal{A}) = \{\Diamond \longrightarrow \blacklozenge\Diamond, \blacklozenge \longrightarrow \blacklozenge\Diamond\}$. In the top derivation below, we assume that $(p_\Diamond)$ is applied due to the existence of the propagation path $\pi(u,v) = u, \Diamond, v$ in $PG(wRu, wRv, uRv)$, where $s_\pi(u,v) = \Diamond \in L_{g(\mathcal{A})}(\Diamond)$ by Definition 8. The propagation graph $PG(wRu, wRv, uRv)$ corresponding to the top sequent of the derivation shown below left is shown below right:

$$\dfrac{\dfrac{\dfrac{}{wRu, wRv, uRv, u : p \vdash u : p}\,(id)}{wRu, wRv, uRv, u : p \vdash v : \Diamond p}\,(p_\Diamond)}{wRu, wRv, u : p \vdash v : \Diamond p}\,(S_{1,1})$$

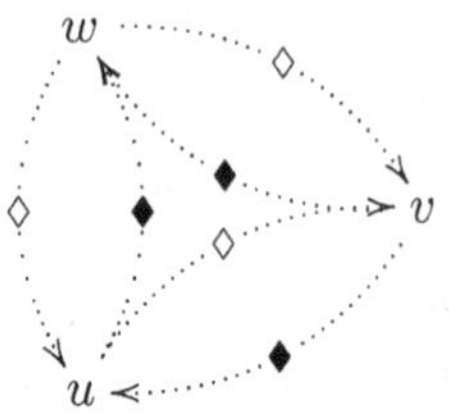

If we apply $\Diamond \longrightarrow \blacklozenge\Diamond \in g(\mathcal{A})$ to $s_\pi(u,v) = \Diamond$, then we obtain the string $\blacklozenge\Diamond$. Hence, $\Diamond \longrightarrow^*_{g(\mathcal{A})} \blacklozenge\Diamond$, i.e. $\blacklozenge\Diamond \in L_{g(\mathcal{A})}(\Diamond)$, meaning that a propagation path $\pi'(u,v)$ $(= u, \blacklozenge, w, \Diamond, v)$ exists in $PG(wRu, wRv)$ such that $s_{\pi'}(u,v) = \blacklozenge\Diamond \in L_{g(\mathcal{A})}(\Diamond)$. We may therefore apply $(S_{1,1})$ and then $(p_\Diamond)$ as shown below left; the propagation graph $PG(wRu, wRv)$ is shown below right:

$$\dfrac{\dfrac{\dfrac{}{wRu, wRv, uRv, u : p \vdash u : p}\,(id)}{wRu, wRv, u : p \vdash u : p}\,(S_{1,1})}{wRu, wRv, u : p \vdash v : \Diamond p}\,(p_\Diamond)$$

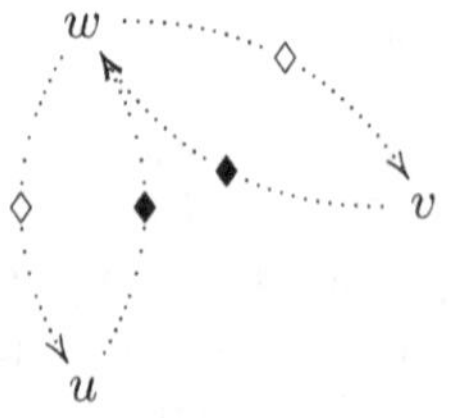

Theorem 3. *Every derivation in* $\mathbf{L}_{\Box\Diamond}(\mathcal{A})$ *can be algorithmically transformed into a derivation in* $\mathsf{IK}(\mathcal{A})\mathsf{L}$.

Proof. We consider a derivation in $\mathbf{L}_{\Box\Diamond}(\mathcal{A})$, which is a derivation in $\mathbf{L}_{\Box\Diamond}(\mathcal{A}) + \{(p_\Diamond), (p_\Box)\}$. By Remark 2, each instance of $(\Diamond_r)$ and $(\Box_l)$ can be replaced by a $(p_\Diamond)$ or $(p_\Box)$ instance, respectively, meaning we may assume our derivation in $\mathbf{L}_{\Box\Diamond}(\mathcal{A}) + \{(p_\Diamond), (p_\Box)\}$ is free of $(\Diamond_r)$ and $(\Box_l)$ instances. We show that the derivation can be transformed into a derivation in $\mathsf{IK}(\mathcal{A})\mathsf{L}$ by induction on its height, that is, we consider a topmost occurrence of a structural rule $(S_{n,k})$ and show that it can be eliminated. We obtain a derivation in $\mathsf{IK}(\mathcal{A})\mathsf{L}$ by successively eliminating topmost instances of $(S_{n,k})$ rules.

Base case. Observe that any application of $(S_{n,k})$ to (id) or $(\bot_l)$ yields another instance of the rule.

Inductive step. It is straightforward to verify that any instance of $(S_{n,k})$ freely permutes above instances of all rules in $\mathbf{L}_{\Box\Diamond}(\mathcal{A}) + \{(p_\Diamond), (p_\Box)\}$ with the exception of $(S_{n,k})$, $(p_\Diamond)$, and $(p_\Box)$ (this follows from the fact that all other rules do not have active relational atoms in their conclusion). Since we are considering a topmost application of $(S_{n,k})$, we need not consider the permutation of $(S_{n,k})$ above another instance of $(S_{n,k})$. The last two cases of permuting $(S_{n,k})$ above $(p_\Diamond)$ and $(p_\Box)$ follow from Lemma 1 and 2, respectively. □

Theorem 4 (**$\mathsf{IK}(\mathcal{A})\mathsf{L}$ Soundness and Completeness**). *$\mathcal{R}, \Gamma \vdash w : A$ is derivable in $\mathsf{IK}(\mathcal{A})\mathsf{L}$ iff $\mathcal{R}, \Gamma \vdash w : A$ is $\mathcal{A}$-valid.*

Proof. The forward direction (soundness) is shown by induction on the height of the given derivation, and the backward direction (completeness) follows from Theorem 2 and 3. □

6 Nested Sequent Systems

In our setting, nested sequents are taken to be trees of multisets of formulae containing a unique formula that occupies a special status. We utilize the nested sequents of [32], but note that the data structure underlying such sequents was originally used in [13], and is similar to the nested sequents for classical modal logics employed in [2]. Following [32], we mark the special, unique formula with a white circle $\circ$ indicating that the formula is of *output polarity*, and mark the other formulae with a black circle $\bullet$ indicating that the formulae are of *input polarity*. A nested sequent Σ is defined via the following BNF grammars:

$$\Sigma ::= \Delta, \Pi \qquad \Delta ::= A_1^\bullet, \ldots, A_n^\bullet, [\Delta_1], \ldots, [\Delta_k] \qquad \Pi ::= A^\circ \mid [\Sigma]$$

We assume that the comma operator associates and commutes, implying that such sequents are truly trees of multisets of formulae, and we let the *empty sequent* be the empty multiset $\emptyset$. We refer to a sequent in the shape of Δ (which contains only input formulae) as an *LHS-sequent*, a sequent in the shape of Π as an *RHS-sequent*, and a sequent Σ as a *full sequent.* We use both Σ and Δ to denote LHS- and full sequents with the context differentiating the usage.

As for classical modal logics (e.g. [2,17]), we define a *context* $\Sigma\{\ \}\cdots\{\ \}$ to be a nested sequent with some number of holes $\{\ \}$ in the place of formulae. This gives rise to two types of contexts: *input contexts*, which require holes to be filled with LHS-sequents to obtain a full sequent, and *output contexts*, which require a single hole to be filled with an RHS-sequent and the remaining holes to be filled with LHS-sequents to obtain a full sequent. We also define the *output pruning* of an input context $\Sigma\{\ \}\cdots\{\ \}$ or full sequent Σ, denoted $\Sigma^{\downarrow}\{\ \}\cdots\{\ \}$ and $\Sigma^{\downarrow}$ respectively, to be the same context or sequent with the unique output formula deleted. We note that all of the above terminology is due to [32].

Example 3. Let $\Sigma_1\{\} := p^{\bullet}, [\Diamond q^{\bullet}, \{\ \}]$, $\Sigma_2\{\} := p^{\bullet}, [\Diamond q^{\circ}, \{\ \}]$, $\Delta_1 := \bot^{\bullet}, [q \supset r^{\circ}]$, and $\Delta_2 := \bot^{\bullet}, [q \supset r^{\bullet}]$. Observe that neither $\Sigma_1\{\Delta_2\}$ nor $\Sigma_2\{\Delta_1\}$ are full sequents since the former has no output formula and the latter has two output formulae. Conversely, both $\Sigma_1\{\Delta_1\}$ and $\Sigma_2\{\Delta_2\}$ are full sequents.

Our nested sequent systems are presented in Fig. 4 and are generalizations of those for the the logics of the intuitionistic modal cube given in [32]. For example, a nested sequent system for the intuitionistic modal logic $\mathsf{IK} + \{(\Diamond^0 \Box A \supset \Box^3 A) \wedge (\Diamond^3 A \supset \Box^0 \Diamond A)\}$ incorporating the 3-to-1 transitivity axiom, which falls outside the intuitionistic modal cube, is obtained by employing the $\mathcal{A}$-grammar $g(\mathcal{A}) = \{\Diamond \longrightarrow \Diamond\Diamond\Diamond, \blacklozenge \longrightarrow \blacklozenge\blacklozenge\blacklozenge\}$ in the propagation rules $(p_{\Diamond})$ and $(p_{\Box})$. As in the previous section, our propagation rules $(p_{\Diamond})$ and $(p_{\Box})$ rely on auxiliary notions (e.g. propagation graphs and paths), which we define for nested sequents.

Definition 13 (Propagation Graph/Path). *Let w be the label assigned to the root of the nested sequent Σ. We define the* propagation graph $PG(\Sigma) := PG_w(\Sigma)$ *of a nested sequent Σ recursively on the structure of the nested sequent.*

- $PG_u(\emptyset) := (\emptyset, \emptyset, \emptyset)$;
- $PG_u(A) := (\{u\}, \emptyset, \{(u, A)\})$ *with* $A \in \{A^{\bullet}, A^{\circ}\}$;
- $PG_u(\Delta_1, \Delta_2) := (V_1 \cup V_2, E_1 \cup E_2, L_1 \cup L_2)$ *where* $PG_u(\Delta_i) = (V_i, E_i, L_i)$;
- $PG_u([\Sigma]) := (V \cup \{u\}, E \cup \{(u, \Diamond, v), (v, \blacklozenge, u)\}, L)$ *where* $PG_v(\Sigma) = (V, E, L)$ *and v is fresh.*

We will often write $u \in PG(\Sigma)$ to mean $u \in V$, and $(u, \langle ? \rangle, v) \in PG(\Sigma)$ to mean $(u, \langle ? \rangle, v) \in E$. Also, we define propagation paths, converses *of propagation paths, and the* string *of a propagation path as in Definition 11.*

For input or output formulae A and B, we use the notation $\Sigma\{A\}_w\{B\}_u$ to mean that $(w, A), (u, B) \in L$ in $PG(\Sigma)$. For example, if $\Sigma := p \supset q^{\circ}, [p^{\bullet}, [\Box p^{\bullet}]]$ with $PG(\Sigma) := (V, E, L)$ and $(v, p \supset q^{\circ}), (u, p^{\bullet}), (w, \Box p^{\bullet}) \in L$, then both $\Sigma\{p \supset q^{\circ}\}_v\{\Box p^{\bullet}\}_w$ and $\Sigma\{p^{\bullet}\}_u\{p \supset q^{\circ}\}_v$ are valid representations of Σ in our notation.

We now prove that proofs can be translated between our refined labelled and nested systems. In order to prove this fact, we make use of the following definitions, which are based on the work of [18,21].

Definition 14 (Labelled Tree Sequent/Derivation). *We define a* labelled tree sequent *to be a labelled sequent $\Lambda := \mathcal{R}, \Gamma \vdash w : A$ such that $\mathcal{R}$ forms a tree and all labels in $\Gamma, w : A$ occur in $\mathcal{R}$. We define a* labelled tree derivation *to be a proof containing only labelled tree sequents. We say that a labelled tree derivation has the* fixed root property *iff every labelled sequent in the derivation has the same root.*

$$\frac{}{\Sigma\{\bot^\bullet\}}(\bot^\bullet) \quad \frac{}{\Sigma\{p^\bullet, p^\circ\}}(id) \quad \frac{\Sigma\{A^\bullet, B^\bullet\}}{\Sigma\{A \land B^\bullet\}}(\land^\bullet) \quad \frac{\Sigma\{A^\circ\} \qquad \Sigma\{B^\circ\}}{\Sigma\{A \land B^\circ\}}(\land^\circ)$$

$$\frac{\Sigma\{A^\bullet\} \qquad \Sigma\{B^\bullet\}}{\Sigma\{A \lor B^\bullet\}}(\lor^\bullet) \quad \frac{\Sigma\{A^\bullet, B^\circ\}}{\Sigma\{A \supset B^\circ\}}(\supset^\circ) \quad \frac{\Sigma\{A_i^\circ\}}{\Sigma\{A_1 \lor A_2^\circ\}}(\lor^\circ)\ i \in \{1,2\}$$

$$\frac{\Sigma^\downarrow\{A \supset B^\bullet, A^\circ\} \qquad \Sigma\{B^\bullet\}}{\Sigma\{A \supset B^\bullet\}}(\supset^\bullet) \quad \frac{\Sigma\{[A^\circ]\}}{\Sigma\{\Box A^\circ\}}(\Box^\circ) \quad \frac{\Sigma\{[A^\bullet]\}}{\Sigma\{\Diamond A^\bullet\}}(\Diamond^\bullet) \quad \frac{\Sigma\{[\emptyset]\}}{\Sigma\{\emptyset\}}(d)$$

$$\frac{\Sigma\{\Delta_1\}_w\{A^\circ, \Delta_2\}_u}{\Sigma\{\Diamond A^\circ, \Delta_1\}_w\{\Delta_2\}_u}(p_\Diamond) \quad only\ if\ \exists\pi(w,u) \in PG(\Sigma)(s_\pi(w,u) \in L_{g(\mathcal{A})}(\Diamond))$$

$$\frac{\Sigma\{\Box A^\bullet, \Delta_1\}_w\{A^\bullet, \Delta_2\}_u}{\Sigma\{\Box A^\bullet, \Delta_1\}_w\{\Delta_2\}_u}(p_\Box) \quad only\ if\ \exists\pi(w,u) \in PG(\Sigma)(s_\pi(w,u) \in L_{g(\mathcal{A})}(\Diamond))$$

Fig. 4. The nested sequent calculi $\mathsf{NIK}(\mathcal{A})$. The (d) rule occurs in a calculus *iff* $\mathrm{D} \in \mathcal{A}$.

We now define our translation functions which transform a *full* nested sequent into a labelled tree sequent, and vice-versa. Our translations additionally depend on *sequent compositions* and *labelled restrictions*. If $\Lambda_1 := \mathcal{R}_1, \Gamma_1 \vdash \Gamma_1'$ and $\Lambda_2 := \mathcal{R}_2, \Gamma_2 \vdash \Gamma_2'$, then we define its sequent composition $\Lambda_1 \otimes \Lambda_2 := \mathcal{R}_1, \mathcal{R}_2, \Gamma_1, \Gamma_2 \vdash \Gamma_1', \Gamma_2'$. Given that Γ is a multiset of labelled formulae, we define the labelled restriction $\Gamma \restriction w := \{A \mid w : A \in \Gamma\}$, and we note that if w is not a label in Γ, then $\Gamma \restriction w := \emptyset$. Moreover, for a multiset $A_1, \ldots, A_n$ of formulae, we define $(A_1, \ldots, A_n)^* := A_1^*, \ldots, A_n^*$ and $(\emptyset)^* := \emptyset$, where $* \in \{\bullet, \circ\}$.

Definition 15 (Translation $\mathfrak{L}$). *We define $\mathfrak{L}_w(\Sigma) := \mathcal{R}, \Gamma \vdash u : A$ as follows:*

- $\mathfrak{L}_v(\emptyset) := \emptyset \vdash \emptyset$
- $\mathfrak{L}_v(A^\bullet) := v : A \vdash \emptyset$
- $\mathfrak{L}_v(A^\circ) := \emptyset \vdash v : A$
- $\mathfrak{L}_v(\Delta_1, \Delta_2) := \mathfrak{L}_v(\Delta_1) \otimes \mathfrak{L}_v(\Delta_2)$
- $\mathfrak{L}_v([\Sigma]) := (vRu \vdash \emptyset) \otimes \mathfrak{L}_u(\Sigma)$ *with u fresh*

We note that since Σ is a full sequent, the obtained labelled sequent will contain a single labelled formula in its consequent.

Example 4. We let $\Sigma := p \supset q^\circ, [p^\bullet, [\Box p^\bullet]]$ and show the output labelled sequent under the translation $\mathfrak{L}$.

$$\mathfrak{L}_w(\Sigma) = wRv, vRu, v : p, u : \Box p \vdash w : p \supset q$$

Definition 16 (Translation $\mathfrak{N}$). *Let $\Lambda := \mathcal{R}, \Gamma \vdash w : A$ be a labelled tree sequent with root u. We define $\Lambda_1 \subseteq \Lambda$ iff there exists a labelled tree sequent Λ_2 such that $\Lambda = \Lambda_1 \otimes \Lambda_2$. Let us further define Λ_u to be the unique labelled tree sequent rooted at the label u such that $\Lambda_u \subseteq \Lambda$. We define $\mathfrak{N}(\Lambda) := \mathfrak{N}_u(\Lambda)$ recursively on the tree structure of Λ:*

$$\mathfrak{N}_v(\Lambda) := \begin{cases} (\Gamma \restriction v)^\bullet, (w : A \restriction v)^\circ & \text{if } \mathcal{R} = \emptyset; \\ (\Gamma \restriction v)^\bullet, (w : A \restriction v)^\circ, [\mathfrak{N}_{z_1}(\Lambda_{z_1})], \ldots, [\mathfrak{N}_{z_n}(\Lambda_{z_n})] & \text{otherwise.} \end{cases}$$

$$\frac{\Sigma}{[\Sigma]}(n) \quad \frac{\Sigma\{\emptyset\}}{\Sigma\{\Delta\}}(w) \quad \frac{\Sigma\{A^{\bullet}, A^{\bullet}\}}{\Sigma\{A^{\bullet}\}}(c) \quad \frac{\Sigma\{[\Delta_1], [\Delta_2]\}}{\Sigma\{[\Delta_1, \Delta_2]\}}(m)$$

Fig. 5. Height-preserving (hp-)admissible structural rules.

In the second case above, we assume that $vRz_1, \ldots vRz_n$ are all of the relational atoms occurring in the input sequent which have the form vRx.

Example 5. We let $\Lambda := wRv, vRu, v : p, u : \Box p \vdash w : p \supset q$ and show the output nested sequent under the translation $\mathfrak{N}$.

$$\mathfrak{N}(\Lambda) = \mathfrak{N}_w(\Lambda) = p \supset q^{\circ}, [p^{\bullet}, [\Box p^{\bullet}]]$$

Lemma 3. *Every proof in* $\mathsf{IK}(\mathcal{A})\mathsf{L}$ *of a labelled tree sequent is a labelled tree proof with the fixed root property.*

Proof. The lemma follows from the observation that if any rule of $\mathsf{IK}(\mathcal{A})\mathsf{L}$ is applied bottom-up to a labelled tree sequent, then each premise is a labelled tree sequent with the same root. □

Theorem 5. *Every proof of a labelled tree sequent in* $\mathsf{IK}(\mathcal{A})\mathsf{L}$ *is transformable into a proof in* $\mathsf{NIK}(\mathcal{A})$*, and vice-versa.*

Proof. Follows from Lemma 3, and the fact that the rules of $\mathsf{IK}(\mathcal{A})\mathsf{L}$ and $\mathsf{NIK}(\mathcal{A})$ are translations of one another under the $\mathfrak{N}$ and $\mathfrak{L}$ functions. □

Theorem 6 **($\mathsf{NIK}(\mathcal{A})$ Soundness and Completeness).** *A formula A is derivable in* $\mathsf{NIK}(\mathcal{A})$ *iff A is* $\mathcal{A}$*-valid.*

Proof. Follows from Theorem 4 and 5. □

Theorem 7. *The rules (n), (w), (c), and (m) are hp-admissible in* $\mathsf{NIK}(\mathcal{A})$.

Proof. By induction on the height of the given derivation; the proofs are similar to those of [2, Lem. 1] and [32, Lem. 6.4]. For the (m) rule, we note that propagation paths are preserved from premise to conclusion (cf. [17, Fig. 12]), showing that the rule can be permuted above $(p_{\Diamond})$ and $(p_{\Box})$. □

7 Conclusion

In this paper, we employed the structural refinement methodology to extract nested sequent systems for a broad class of intuitionistic modal logics. The attainment of such systems answers the open problem of [25] to a large extent by showing how to transform axioms (namely, HSLs) into propagation/logical rules as well as how to obtain nested sequent systems for logics outside the intuitionistic modal cube. We aim to write proof-search algorithms in future work based on our nested systems which utilize saturation conditions and loop-checking (cf. [11,22,33]) to provide decision procedures for logics within the class considered. Our primary concern will be to establish the decidability of transitive extensions of IK, which has remained a longstanding open problem [15,31].

References

1. Bierman, G.M., de Paiva, V.C.V.: On an intuitionistic modal logic. Stud. Log. Int. J. Symb. Log. **65**(3), 383–416 (2000). http://www.jstor.org/stable/20016199
2. Brünnler, K.: Deep sequent systems for modal logic. Arch. Math. Log. **48**(6), 551–577 (2009). https://doi.org/10.1007/s00153-009-0137-3
3. Bull, R.A.: Cut elimination for propositional dynamic logic without *. Z. Math. Logik Grundlag. Math. **38**(2), 85–100 (1992)
4. Castilho, M.A., del Cerro, L.F., Gasquet, O., Herzig, A.: Modal tableaux with propagation rules and structural rules. Fundam. Inform. **32**(3, 4), 281–297 (1997)
5. Ciabattoni, A., Lyon, T., Ramanayake, R.: From display to labelled proofs for tense logics. In: Artemov, S., Nerode, A. (eds.) LFCS 2018. LNCS, vol. 10703, pp. 120–139. Springer, Cham (2018). https://doi.org/10.1007/978-3-319-72056-2_8
6. Ciabattoni, A., Lyon, T., Ramanayake, R., Tiu, A.: Display to labelled proofs and back again for tense logics. ACM Trans. Comput. Log. **22**(3), 1–31 (2021). https://doi.org/10.1145/3460492
7. Davies, R., Pfenning, F.: A modal analysis of staged computation. J. ACM **48**(3), 555–604 (2001). https://doi.org/10.1145/382780.382785
8. Fairtlough, M., Mendler, M.: An intuitionistic modal logic with applications to the formal verification of hardware. In: Pacholski, L., Tiuryn, J. (eds.) CSL 1994. LNCS, vol. 933, pp. 354–368. Springer, Heidelberg (1995). https://doi.org/10.1007/BFb0022268
9. Fitch, F.B.: Intuitionistic modal logic with quantifiers. Portugaliae Math. **7**(2), 113–118 (1948). http://eudml.org/doc/114664
10. Fitting, M.: Tableau methods of proof for modal logics. Notre Dame J. Form. Log. **13**(2), 237–247 (1972)
11. Fitting, M.: Proof Methods for Modal and Intuitionistic Logics, vol. 169. Springer Science & Business Media, Heidelberg (1983)
12. Fitting, M., Kuznets, R.: Modal interpolation via nested sequents. Ann. Pure Appl. Logic **166**(3), 274–305 (2015). https://doi.org/10.1016/j.apal.2014.11.002
13. Galmiche, D., Salhi, Y.: Label-free natural deduction systems for intuitionistic and classical modal logics. J. Appl. Non-Class. Log. **20**(4), 373–421 (2010). https://doi.org/10.3166/jancl.20.373-421
14. Galmiche, D., Salhi, Y.: Tree-sequent calculi and decision procedures for intuitionistic modal logics. J. Log. Comput. **28**(5), 967–989 (2015). https://doi.org/10.1093/logcom/exv039
15. Girlando, M., Straßburger, L.: MOIN: a nested sequent theorem prover for intuitionistic modal logics (system description). In: Peltier, N., Sofronie-Stokkermans, V. (eds.) IJCAR 2020. LNCS (LNAI), vol. 12167, pp. 398–407. Springer, Cham (2020). https://doi.org/10.1007/978-3-030-51054-1_25

16. Goré, R., Postniece, L., Tiu, A.: Cut-elimination and proof-search for bi-intuitionistic logic using nested sequents. In: Areces, C., Goldblatt, R. (eds.) Advances in Modal Logic 7, papers from the seventh conference on "Advances in Modal Logic," held in Nancy, France, 9–12 September 2008, pp. 43–66. College Publications (2008). http://www.aiml.net/volumes/volume7/Gore-Postniece-Tiu.pdf
17. Goré, R., Postniece, L., Tiu, A.: On the correspondence between display postulates and deep inference in nested sequent calculi for tense logics. Log. Methods Comput. Sci. **7**(2), 1–38 (2011). https://doi.org/10.2168/LMCS-7(2:8)2011
18. Goré, R., Ramanayake, R.: Labelled tree sequents, tree hypersequents and nested (deep) sequents. In: Bolander, T., Braüner, T., Ghilardi, S., Moss, L.S. (eds.) Advances in Modal Logic 9, papers from the ninth conference on "Advances in Modal Logic," held in Copenhagen, Denmark, 22–25 August 2012, pp. 279–299. College Publications (2012). http://www.aiml.net/volumes/volume9/Gore-Ramanayake.pdf
19. Kashima, R.: Cut-free sequent calculi for some tense logics. Stud. Log. **53**(1), 119–135 (1994)
20. Lemmon, E.J., Scott, D.S.: An Introduction to Modal Logic: The Lemmon Notes. Blackwell, Oxford (1977)
21. Lyon, T.: On the correspondence between nested calculi and semantic systems for intuitionistic logics. J. Log. Comput. **31**(1), 213–265 (2020). https://doi.org/10.1093/logcom/exaa078
22. Lyon, T.: Refining Labelled Systems for Modal and Constructive Logics with Applications. Ph.D. thesis, Technische Universität Wien (2021)
23. Lyon, T., van Berkel, K.: Automating agential reasoning: proof-calculi and syntactic decidability for STIT logics. In: Baldoni, M., Dastani, M., Liao, B., Sakurai, Y., Zalila Wenkstern, R. (eds.) PRIMA 2019. LNCS (LNAI), vol. 11873, pp. 202–218. Springer, Cham (2019). https://doi.org/10.1007/978-3-030-33792-6_13
24. Lyon, T., Tiu, A., Goré, R., Clouston, R.: Syntactic interpolation for tense logics and bi-intuitionistic logic via nested sequents. In: Fernández, M., Muscholl, A. (eds.) 28th EACSL Annual Conference on Computer Science Logic, CSL 2020, 13–16 January 2020, Barcelona, Spain. LIPIcs, vol. 152, pp. 28:1–28:16. Schloss Dagstuhl - Leibniz-Zentrum für Informatik (2020). https://doi.org/10.4230/LIPIcs.CSL.2020.28
25. Marin, S., Straßburger, L.: Label-free modular systems for classical and intuitionistic modal logics. In: Advances in Modal Logic 10, invited and contributed papers from the Tenth Conference on "Advances in Modal Logic," held in Groningen, The Netherlands, 5–8 August 2014, pp. 387–406 (2014). http://www.aiml.net/volumes/volume10/Marin-Strassburger.pdf
26. Pimentel, E.: A semantical view of proof systems. In: Moss, L.S., de Queiroz, R., Martinez, M. (eds.) WoLLIC 2018. LNCS, vol. 10944, pp. 61–76. Springer, Heidelberg (2018). https://doi.org/10.1007/978-3-662-57669-4_3
27. Pitts, A.M.: Evaluation logic. In: Birtwistle, G. (eds.) IV Higher Order Workshop, Banff 1990, pp. 162–189. Workshops in Computing. Springer, London (1991). https://doi.org/10.1007/978-1-4471-3182-3_11
28. Plotkin, G., Stirling, C.: A framework for intuitionistic modal logics: Extended abstract. In: Proceedings of the 1986 Conference on Theoretical Aspects of Reasoning about Knowledge, pp. 399–406. TARK 1986, Morgan Kaufmann Publishers Inc., San Francisco, CA, USA (1986)
29. Post, E.L.: Recursive unsolvability of a problem of Thue. J. Symb. Log. **12**(1), 1–11 (1947)

30. Servi, G.F.: Axiomatizations for some intuitionistic modal logics. Rend. Sem. Mat. Univers. Politec. Torino **42**(3), 179–194 (1984)
31. Simpson, A.K.: The proof theory and semantics of intuitionistic modal logic. Ph.D. thesis, University of Edinburgh. College of Science and Engineering. School of Informatics (1994)
32. Straßburger, L.: Cut elimination in nested sequents for intuitionistic modal logics. In: Pfenning, F. (ed.) FoSSaCS 2013. LNCS, vol. 7794, pp. 209–224. Springer, Heidelberg (2013). https://doi.org/10.1007/978-3-642-37075-5_14
33. Tiu, A., Ianovski, E., Goré, R.: Grammar logics in nested sequent calculus: proof theory and decision procedures. In: Bolander, T., Braüner, T., Ghilardi, S., Moss, L.S. (eds.) Advances in Modal Logic 9, papers from the ninth conference on "Advances in Modal Logic," held in Copenhagen, Denmark, 22–25 August 2012, pp. 516–537. College Publications (2012). http://www.aiml.net/volumes/volume9/Tiu-Ianovski-Gore.pdf

Game Semantics for Constructive Modal Logic

Matteo Acclavio[1(✉)], Davide Catta[2], and Lutz Straßburger[3]

[1] University of Luxembourg, Belval, Luxembourg
[2] LIRMM - Université de Montpellier, Montpellier, France
[3] INRIA-Saclay and LIX-École Polytechnique, Palaiseau, France

Abstract. In this paper we provide the first game semantics for the constructive modal logic CK. We first define arenas encoding modal formulas, we then define winning innocent strategies for games on these arenas, and finally we characterize the winning strategies corresponding to proofs in the logic CK. To prove the full-completeness of our semantics, we provide a sequentialization procedure of winning strategies. We conclude the paper by proving their compositionality and showing how our results can be extend to the constructive modal logic CD.

1 Introduction

Modal logics are extensions of classical logic making use of *modalities* to qualify the truth of a judgement. According to the interpretation of such modalities, modal logics find applications, for example, in knowledge representation [28], artificial intelligence [19] and formal verification [10]. More precisely, modal logics are obtained by extending classical logic with a modality operator □ (together with its dual operator ◇), which are usually interpreted as *necessity* (respectively *possibility*).

When we move from the classical to the intuitionistic setting, the modality ◇ is no longer the dual of the modality □ and by consequence the classical k-axiom $□(A ⊃ B) ⊃ (□A ⊃ □B)$ is no longer sufficient to express the behavior of the modality ◇. Depending on the chosen axioms, it is possible to define different flavors of "intuitionistic modal logics" (see, e.g., [4,6,8,22–24]). In this paper we consider the minimal approach obtained by adding only the axiom $□(A ⊃ B) ⊃ (◇A ⊃ ◇B)$, leading to what in the literature is now called *constructive modal logic* CK [4,7,9,13,18,23].

The study of the semantics of proofs in this logic is still rough and the only full complete denotational model for this logic is defined by the quotient of its $λ$-calculus with respect to $β$-reduction [3,4]. The purpose of this paper is to provide a full complete denotational semantics for CK in terms of a *game semantics* [1,11,17]. Thereby we provide a *concrete* denotational model for this logic, that is, a model whose elements are not obtained by the quotient on proofs induced by cut-elimination.

In game semantics proofs are denoted by winning strategies for two-player games played on a graph, called *modal arena*, that encodes a modal formula. We denote the players by ○ (white) and ● (black). In the literature the white player is called *opponent* (denoted by O) and the black player is called *proponent* (denoted by P). The motivations of our choices is due to the correspondence between players' moves, the parity of the

© Springer Nature Switzerland AG 2021
A. Das and S. Negri (Eds.): TABLEAUX 2021, LNAI 12842, pp. 428–445, 2021.
https://doi.org/10.1007/978-3-030-86059-2_25

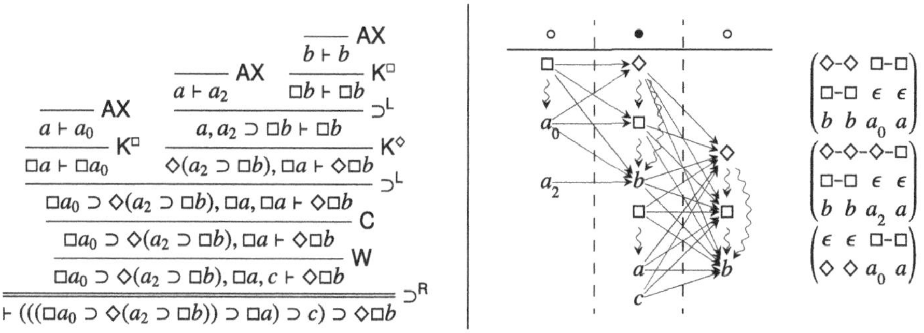

Fig. 1. A derivation $\mathcal{D}$ of the formula $F = (((\Box a_0 \supset \Diamond(a_2 \supset \Box b)) \supset \Box a) \supset c) \supset \Diamond\Box b$, the modal arena $[\![F]\!]$, and the maximal batched views in the CK-**WIS** $\{\!\{\mathcal{D}\}\!\}$ of F. We indexed some occurrences of the atom a to avoid ambiguity in the views.

depth in the corresponding vertex in the modal arena ($\circ$ for even and $\bullet$ for odd), and the polarities of the corresponding atoms in a polarized sequent calculus [2,15,16] where $\circ$ and $\bullet$ are usually used respectively for the positive and negative polarities.

Each play consists of an alternation of $\circ$-moves and $\bullet$-moves, that is, a play is represented by a list of occurrences of the vertices in the modal arena. The first move in a play is a $\circ$-move selected among the $\rightarrow$-roots of the modal arena. Each subsequent move of a player must be *justified* by a previous move of the other player, that is, the selected vertex must be the source of a $\rightarrow$-edge with target a vertex previously played by the other player. The game terminates when one player has no possible moves, losing the play. A *winning innocent strategy* (for $\bullet$) is a set of plays which takes into account every possible $\circ$-move, while each $\bullet$-move is uniquely determined (and justified) by one of the previous $\circ$-moves. Intuitively, a winning strategy is a complete description of all the possible plays always leading to the victory of $\bullet$. The adjective *innocent* is referred to the play-style of $\circ$ which chooses each of its non-initial moves only according with the previous $\bullet$-move in the play.

In [26] it is shown how the syntax of intuitionistic combinatorial proofs, a graphical proof system for propositional intuitionistic logic, provides intuitive insights about the winning innocent strategies (or **WIS**s) in a Hyland-Ong arena [11,21]. Following this intuition, in [2] we developed the syntax of intuitionistic combinatorial proofs for constructive modal logics allowing us to characterize the winning innocent strategies for this logic by extending this correspondence (see Fig. 1).

De facto, the presence of the modal axioms leads to the need of a new notion of *batches*[1] in a play in order to characterize winning innocent strategies corresponding to proofs in the constructive modal logic CK. By means of example consider the formulas $\Box a \supset a$ and $(\Box a \supset \Box b) \supset (\Box(a \supset b))$ which are not provable in CK. Their corresponding modal arenas are pictured below together with the unique maximal view in their winning innocent strategies. Instead of representing these views, we represent the corresponding *batched views*, which are matrices containing the view together with a decoration of each move given by the modalities in whose scope they occur.

[1] Batches can be interpreted as the nesting of a nested sequent calculi [5,25].

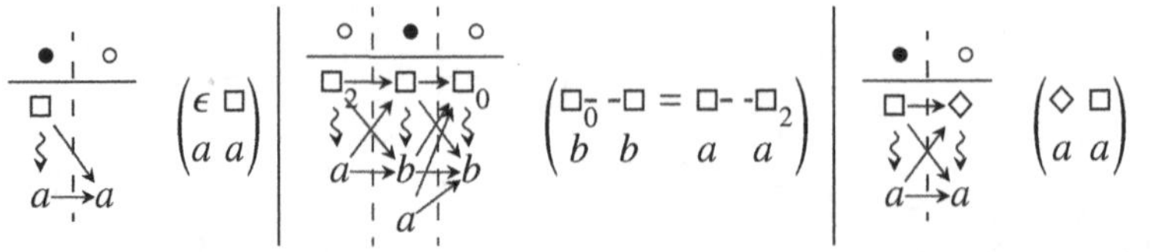

(1)

The strategies containing these views cannot be considered satisfactory since the modalities are not "properly batched" with respect to the modal rules in the sequent calculus for CK. In fact, the **WIS** containing these maximal views correspond to correct proofs in the intuitionistic propositional logic of the formulas obtained by removing the modalities, that is, $a \supset a$ and $(a \supset b) \supset (a \supset b)$.

In order to recover the correspondence between winning strategies and proofs, it suffices to consider two additional constraints on the accepted •-moves. We observe that each modality has a parity (the same of the corresponding node in the modal arena) and a height (defined as the number of the modalities in whose scope it belongs). The first constraint demands that each •-move must be in the scope of the same number of modalities of the previous ∘-move, ruling out the leftmost example in Eq. (1). This constraint allows us to define *sub-plays* (corresponding to sub-proofs): whenever a ∘-move is in the scope of a new ∘-modality, that is, a modality whose scope contains no previous moves of the play, then the successive moves are played in a same sub-play. A sub-play ends when a ∘-move is in the scope of no modalities or in the scope of a new ∘-modality with equal or smaller height with respect to the previous •-move. Note that sub-plays can be nested. This allows us to gather modalities having the same height and in whose scope there are moves of a sub-play into batches. The second constraint demands that these batches have a specific shape, that is, the same of the modalities in the rules of the sequent calculus: only one ∘ modality occurs, and either all modalities are boxes or there is exactly one •-diamond and one ∘-diamond. These conditions rule out the existence of winning strategies for the formulas from Eq. (1): in the first one the •-move has not the same height of the previous ∘-move, in the second one all the modalities are batched in the same set, which includes two ∘-modalities, in the third one the $\Diamond^\circ$ does not have the corresponding $\Diamond^\bullet$ in its batch.

Contribution of the Paper. In this paper we show a direct correspondence between the sequent system for CK and our winning innocent strategies (CK-**WIS**). In particular, we show that the CK-**WIS**s form a full-complete semantics for this logic. We then conclude the paper by showing that CK-**WIS**s are a denotational semantics by proving their compositionality.

Organisation of the Paper. In Sect. 2 we recall the definition of the constructive modal logic CK, its sound and complete sequent calculus and we recall the results from [2] on the encoding of modal arenas. In Sect. 3 we recall characterization of winning strategies encoding CK-proofs from [2] by providing a new detailed sequentialization procedure assuring the full-completeness of our model. In Sect. 4 we prove that our winning strategies compose. In Sect. 5 we collect the results allowing us to prove that we indeed define a full-complete denotational semantics for CK and we conclude in Sect. 6 where we discuss related works and some future research directions.

$$
\frac{}{a \vdash a}\,\mathsf{AX} \quad \frac{\Gamma, B \vdash A}{\Gamma \vdash B \supset A}\,\supset^{\mathsf{R}} \quad \frac{\Gamma, B, C \vdash A}{\Gamma, B \wedge C \vdash A}\,\wedge^{\mathsf{L}} \quad \frac{\Gamma \vdash A \quad \Delta \vdash B}{\Gamma, \Delta \vdash A \wedge B}\,\wedge^{\mathsf{R}} \quad \frac{\Gamma \vdash A \quad \Delta, B \vdash C}{\Gamma, \Delta, A \supset B \vdash C}\,\supset^{\mathsf{L}} \quad \Bigg| \quad \frac{\Gamma \vdash A \quad \Delta, A \vdash B}{\Gamma, \Delta \vdash B}\,\mathsf{cut}
$$

$$
\frac{}{\vdash \mathsf{1}}\,\mathsf{1} \quad \frac{\Gamma, B, B \vdash A}{\Gamma, B \vdash A}\,\mathsf{C} \quad \frac{\Gamma \vdash A}{\Gamma, B \vdash A}\,\mathsf{W} \quad \frac{\Gamma \vdash A}{\Box\Gamma \vdash \Box A}\,\mathsf{K}^{\Box} \quad \frac{B, \Gamma \vdash A}{\Diamond B, \Box\Gamma \vdash \Diamond A}\,\mathsf{K}^{\Diamond}
$$

Fig. 2. The rules for the sequent system LCK and the cut-rule

2 Background

In this section we recall some basic definition for the constructive modal logic CK together with some extensions of the definition from [2] allowing to encode formulas by means of specific directed graphs we call *modal arenas*.

2.1 Constructive Modal Logic

We consider the *(modal) formulas* generated by a countable set of (atomic) propositional variables $\mathcal{A} = \{a, b, \dots\}$ and the following grammar

$$A, B ::= a \mid \mathsf{1} \mid A \supset B \mid A \wedge B \mid \Box A \mid \Diamond A$$

We define the size $\|A\|$ of a formula A as the number of connectives and modalities in A and if $\Gamma = A_1, \dots, A_n$ then $\|\Gamma\| = \sum_{i=1}^{n} \|A_i\|$. We say that a formula is *modality-free* (respectively *unit-free*) if it contains no occurrences of $\Box$ and $\Diamond$ (respectively no occurrences of $\mathsf{1}$). A formula is a $\supset$-formula (resp. a $\wedge$-formula) if it is a formula of the form $A \supset B$ (resp. $A \wedge B$).

We define the *formula isomorphism* as the equivalence relation $\overset{\mathsf{f}}{\sim}$ over formulas generated by the following relations:

$$
\begin{array}{cccc}
A \wedge \mathsf{1} \overset{\mathsf{f}}{\sim} A & A \supset \mathsf{1} \overset{\mathsf{f}}{\sim} \mathsf{1} & \mathsf{1} \supset A \overset{\mathsf{f}}{\sim} A & \Box\mathsf{1} \overset{\mathsf{f}}{\sim} \mathsf{1} \\
A \wedge B \overset{\mathsf{f}}{\sim} B \wedge A & A \wedge (B \wedge C) \overset{\mathsf{f}}{\sim} (A \wedge B) \wedge C & & (A \wedge B) \supset C \overset{\mathsf{f}}{\sim} A \supset (B \supset C)
\end{array} \qquad (2)
$$

The constructive modal logic CK is obtained by extending the propositional intuitionistic logic [27] with the *necessitation rule*: “if F is provable, then so is $\Box F$”, and the following two modal axioms:

$$\mathsf{k}_1 : \Box(A \supset B) \supset (\Box A \supset \Box B) \qquad \mathsf{k}_2 : \Box(A \supset B) \supset (\Diamond A \supset \Diamond B)$$

The sequent system LCK, given in Fig. 2, is a sound and complete proof system for the logic CK [14]. We write $\overset{\mathsf{LCK}}{\vdash} F$ whenever $\vdash F$ is provable in LCK.

Theorem 2.1. *A formula F is provable in* LCK $\cup$ {cut} *iff is provable in* LCK.

2.2 Modal Arenas

A *directed graph* $\mathcal{G} = \langle V_{\mathcal{G}}, \overset{\mathcal{G}}{\to} \rangle$ is given by a set of vertices $V_{\mathcal{G}}$ and a set of direct edges $\overset{\mathcal{G}}{\to} \subseteq V_{\mathcal{G}} \times V_{\mathcal{G}}$. A vertex v is a $\overset{\mathcal{G}}{\to}$*-root*, denoted $v \not\to$ if there is no vertex w such that

$v\overset{\mathcal{G}}{\to}w$. We denote by $\vec{R}_{\mathcal{G}}$ the set of $\overset{\mathcal{G}}{\to}$-roots of $\mathcal{G}$. A *path* from v to w of length n is a sequence of vertices $x_0 \dots x_n$ such that $v = x_0$, $w = x_n$ and $x_i \overset{\mathcal{G}}{\to} x_{i+1}$ for $i \in \{0, \dots, n-1\}$. We write $v\overset{\mathcal{G}}{\to}{}^n w$ if there is a path from v to w of length n. A *directed acyclic graph* (or dag for short) is a direct graph such that $v\overset{\mathcal{G}}{\to}{}^n v$ implies $n = 0$ for all $v \in V$.

A *two-color directed acyclic graph* (or 2-dag for short) $\mathcal{G} = \langle V_{\mathcal{G}}, \overset{\mathcal{G}}{\to}, \overset{\mathcal{G}}{\rightsquigarrow}\rangle$ is given by a set of vertices $V_{\mathcal{G}}$ and two disjoint sets of edges $\overset{\mathcal{G}}{\to}$ and $\overset{\mathcal{G}}{\rightsquigarrow}$ such that the graph $\langle V_{\mathcal{G}}, \overset{\mathcal{G}}{\to} \cup \overset{\mathcal{G}}{\rightsquigarrow}\rangle$ is acyclic. We omit the superscript when clear from context and we denote by $\emptyset$ the empty 2-dag.

If $\mathcal{L}$ is a set, a 2-dag is *$\mathcal{L}$-labeled* if a *label* $\ell(v) \in \mathcal{L}$ is associated to each vertex $v \in V$. In this paper we fix the set of labels to be the set $\mathcal{L} = \mathcal{A} \cup \{\Box, \Diamond\}$, where $\mathcal{A}$ is the set of propositional variables occurring in formulas. We use the notation a, $\Box$ and $\Diamond$ to denote the graphs consisting of a single vertex labeled respectively by a, $\Box$ and $\Diamond$, and we denote by $V^{\mathcal{A}}_{\mathcal{G}}$, $V^{\Box}_{\mathcal{G}}$ and $V^{\Diamond}_{\mathcal{G}}$ the set of vertices of a graph $\mathcal{G}$ with labels respectively in $\mathcal{A}$, $\{\Box\}$ and $\{\Diamond\}$.

Definition 2.2. Let $\mathcal{G}, \mathcal{H}$ and $\mathcal{F} \neq \emptyset$ be 2-dags, we denote by $R^{\mathcal{G}}_{\mathcal{F}}$ the set of edges from the $\to$-roots of $\mathcal{G}$ to the $\to$-roots of $\mathcal{F}$, that is $R^{\mathcal{G}}_{\mathcal{F}} = \{(u, v) \mid u \in \vec{R}_{\mathcal{G}}, v \in \vec{R}_{\mathcal{F}}\}$.

We define the following operations on 2-dags:

$$
\begin{array}{lll}
\mathcal{G}+\mathcal{H} = \langle\, V_{\mathcal{G}} \cup V_{\mathcal{H}} \,, \overset{\mathcal{G}}{\to} \cup \overset{\mathcal{H}}{\to} & , \overset{\mathcal{G}}{\rightsquigarrow} \cup \overset{\mathcal{H}}{\rightsquigarrow} & \rangle \\
\mathcal{G}\mathrel{-\!\!\triangleright}\mathcal{F} = \langle\, V_{\mathcal{G}} \cup V_{\mathcal{F}} \,, \overset{\mathcal{G}}{\to} \cup \overset{\mathcal{F}}{\to} \cup R^{\mathcal{G}}_{\mathcal{F}} & , \overset{\mathcal{G}}{\rightsquigarrow} \cup \overset{\mathcal{F}}{\rightsquigarrow} & \rangle \\
\mathcal{G}\mathrel{\sim\!\!\triangleright}\mathcal{F} = \langle\, V_{\mathcal{G}} \cup V_{\mathcal{F}} \,, \overset{\mathcal{G}}{\to} \cup \overset{\mathcal{F}}{\to} & , \overset{\mathcal{G}}{\rightsquigarrow} \cup \overset{\mathcal{F}}{\rightsquigarrow} \cup R^{\mathcal{G}}_{\mathcal{F}} & \rangle \\
\mathcal{G}\mathrel{-\!\!\triangleright}\emptyset = \emptyset & \Box\mathrel{\sim\!\!\triangleright}\emptyset = \emptyset & \Diamond\mathrel{\sim\!\!\triangleright}\emptyset = \Diamond
\end{array}
$$

which can be pictured as follows, with ▸ representing the $\to$-roots of each graph.

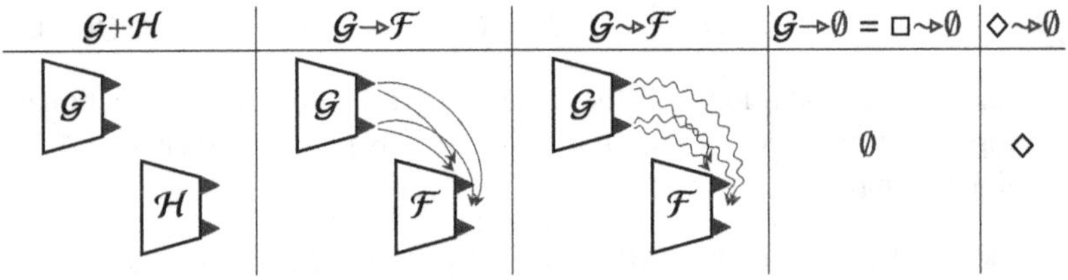

We can associate to each formula F a $\mathcal{L}$-labeled 2-dag $[\![F]\!]$ as follows:

$$
\begin{array}{rclrclrclrcl}
[\![a]\!] & = & a & [\![A \supset B]\!] & = & [\![A]\!]\mathrel{-\!\!\triangleright}[\![B]\!] & [\![A \wedge B]\!] & = & [\![A]\!]+[\![B]\!] & [\![1]\!] & = & \emptyset \\
 & & & [\![\Box A]\!] & = & \Box \mathrel{\sim\!\!\triangleright}[\![A]\!] & [\![\Diamond A]\!] & = & \Diamond \mathrel{\sim\!\!\triangleright}[\![A]\!] & & &
\end{array}
\tag{3}
$$

Moreover, if $\Gamma \vdash A$ is a sequent, we denote by $[\![\Gamma \vdash A]\!]$ the modal arena $[\![(\bigwedge_{B\in\Gamma} B) \supset A]\!]$.

Definition 2.3. A *modal arena* is a $\mathcal{L}$-labeled 2-dag $\mathcal{G}$ such that $\mathcal{G} = [\![F]\!]$ for a modal formula F[2].

[2] A geometrical characterization of the $\mathcal{L}$-labeled 2-dags which are modal arenas is out of the scope of this paper and can be found in [2].

In this paper we may say that a vertex in $[\![F]\!]$ *corresponds* to an occurrence of atom or modality in a formula F, or we may identify them. An *atomic vertex* is a vertex corresponding to an atom, and a *modal vertex* in a vertex corresponding to a modality.

Definition 2.4. Let $\mathcal{G} = [\![F]\!]$ be a modal arena and $v \in V_{\mathcal{G}}$. The *address* of v is the unique sequence of modal vertices $\mathsf{add}_v = m_1, \ldots, m_h$ in $V_{\mathcal{G}}$ which corresponds to the sequence of modalities in the path in the formula tree of F connecting the node of v to the root of F. If $\mathsf{add}_v = m_1, \ldots, m_h$, we denote by $\mathsf{add}_v^k = m_k$ its kth element and we call $h_v = |\mathsf{add}_v|$ the *height* of v, that is, the length of add_v.

Example 2.5. Consider the modal arena and the formula tree of $(a \supset \Box(b \wedge (c \supset \Diamond_1 d))) \supset \Diamond_2(e \supset f)$, then

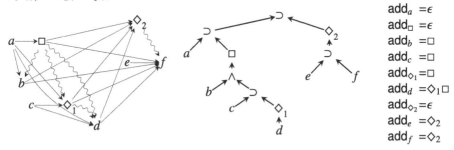

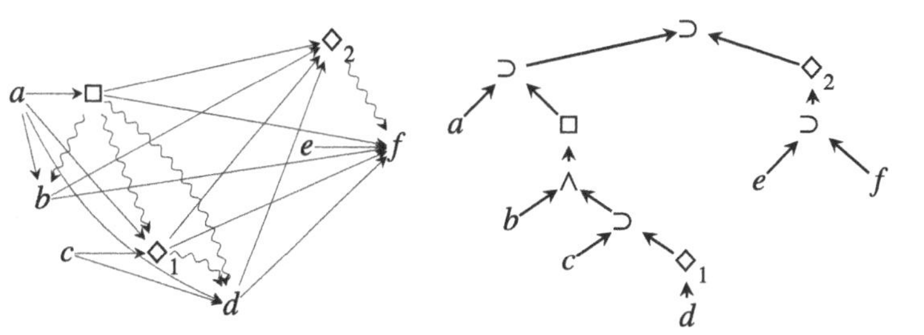

$\mathsf{add}_a = \epsilon$
$\mathsf{add}_\Box = \epsilon$
$\mathsf{add}_b = \Box$
$\mathsf{add}_c = \Box$
$\mathsf{add}_{\Diamond_1} = \Box$
$\mathsf{add}_d = \Diamond_1 \Box$
$\mathsf{add}_{\Diamond_2} = \epsilon$
$\mathsf{add}_e = \Diamond_2$
$\mathsf{add}_f = \Diamond_2$

If $\mathcal{G}$ is a modal arena and $v \in V_{\mathcal{G}}$, we define $d(v)$ as the length of the $\rightarrow$-paths from v to a $\rightarrow$-root $w \in \vec{R}_{\mathcal{G}}$. Note that the property that all paths in a modal arena from a vertex to any root have the same length is not trivial, but the proof can be found in [26, Lemma 9]. The *parity of a vertex* v is the parity of $d(v)$, which can be either *even* or *odd*. We denote by v° and $v^\bullet$ if the parity of v is respectively even or odd. Note that the players $\circ$ and $\bullet$ can only play vertices of the corresponding parity, but the parity of the modalities in which the vertex belongs may not be the same as the parity of the move. By means of example, consider the atom a_2 in Fig. 1 which is $\circ$ but it is in the scope of two $\bullet$-modalities.

We conclude the section by remarking that modal arenas identify formulas modulo the formula isomorphism $\overset{\mathsf{f}}{\sim}$ defined by the relations in Eq. (2).

Proposition 2.6. If F and G are two formulas, then $F \overset{\mathsf{f}}{\sim} G \iff [\![F]\!] = [\![G]\!]$.

Proof. If follows form the definition of the modal arenas operations $+$, $\multimap$ and $\rightsquigarrow$. $\Box$

3 Winning Strategies for CK

In this section we recall the definition of *winning innocent strategy* and we characterize the ones corresponding to correct CK-proofs. We then provide a direct proof of the correspondence between our winning innocent strategies and LCK-proofs by giving a *desequentialization* and a *sequentialization* procedure. The first procedure describes how to inductively define a winning strategy from a sequent calculus derivation. The second procedure defines a method to reconstruct a derivation in sequent calculus using the information contained in the winning strategy (and the proven formula).

Definition 3.1. Let F be a formula. A *move* is a vertex of $[\![F]\!]$. Let $\mathsf{p} = \mathsf{p}_0 \cdots \mathsf{p}_n$ be a sequence of distinct *moves* (we denote by ϵ the empty sequence). If v and w are two moves in p, we say that w *justifies* v whenever $v \xrightarrow{[\![F]\!]} w$. We call a move p_i in p a $\circ$-*move* or $\bullet$-*move* if i is respectively even or odd.

We say that p is a *view* in $[\![F]\!]$ if the following conditions are fulfilled:

1. p is a *play*: if $\mathsf{p} \neq \epsilon$, then $\mathsf{p}_0 \in \vec{R}_{[\![F]\!]}$;
2. p is *justified*: if $i > 0$, then $\mathsf{p}_i \xrightarrow{[\![F]\!]} \mathsf{p}_{i-(2k+1)}$ for a $k \in \mathbb{N}$;
3. p is $\circ$-*shortsighted*: if p°_{i+1} and $\mathsf{p}^\bullet_i$, then $\mathsf{p}_{i+1} \xrightarrow{[\![F]\!]} \mathsf{p}_i$;
4. p is $\bullet$-*uniform*: if $\mathsf{p}^\bullet_{i+1}$ and p°_i, then $\ell(\mathsf{p}_{i+1}) = \ell(\mathsf{p}_i)$;
5. p is *modal*: $\mathsf{p}_i \in V^{\mathcal{A}}_{[\![F]\!]} \cup V^{\diamond}_{[\![F]\!]}$.

Moreover, if p is a view, we say that

6. p is *well-batched*: $|\mathsf{add}_{\mathsf{p}_{2k}}| = |\mathsf{add}_{\mathsf{p}_{2k+1}}|$ for every $2k \in \{0, \ldots, n-1\}$.

The *predecessor* of a non-empty view p is the sequence obtained by removing the last move in p. The *successor* is the converse relation. A *winning innocent strategy* (or **WIS** for short) for F (or over $[\![F]\!]$) is a finite non-empty set $\mathcal{S}$ of views in $[\![F]\!]$ such that:

a. $\mathcal{S}$ is predecessor-closed: if $\mathsf{p} \cdot v \in \mathcal{S}$ then $\mathsf{p} \in \mathcal{S}$;
b. $\mathcal{S}$ is $\circ$-*complete*: if $\mathsf{p} \in \mathcal{S}$ has even length, then every successor of p is in $\mathcal{S}$;
c. $\mathcal{S}$ is $\bullet$-*deterministic* and $\bullet$-*total*: if $\mathsf{p} \in \mathcal{S}$ has odd length, then exactly one successor of p is in $\mathcal{S}$.

A view is *maximal* in $\mathcal{S}$ if it is not prefix of any other view in $\mathcal{S}$. We say that a **WIS** $\mathcal{S}$ is *trivial* if $\mathcal{S} = \{\epsilon\}$ and it is *well-batched* if all its views are.

Note that our definition of **WIS** on arenas of modality-free formulas is the same of the one given in [11,21,26] where the modal condition trivially holds. Moreover, it follows by definition of view (by the fact that is a play, justified and $\circ$-shortsighted) that $\circ$-moves and $\bullet$-moves can only be vertices with the corresponding parity.

Remark 3.2. If $\mathcal{G}$ is a non-empty modal arena, then a **WIS** $\mathcal{S}$ on $\mathcal{G}$ must contain all views of the form v with $v \in \vec{R}_{\mathcal{G}}$, that is, $\mathcal{S}$ is non-trivial.

Definition 3.3. Let $\mathsf{p} = \mathsf{p}_0 \cdots \mathsf{p}_{n-1}$ be a view on a modal arena $\mathcal{G}$. We write $h_\mathsf{p} = \max\{h_v \mid v \in \mathsf{p}\}$ and we define the *batched view* of p as the $h_\mathsf{p} \times n$ matrix $\mathcal{F}(\mathsf{p}) = (\mathcal{F}(\mathsf{p})_0, \ldots, \mathcal{F}(\mathsf{p})_n)$ with elements in $V_\mathcal{G} \cup \{\epsilon\}$ such that each column $\mathcal{F}(\mathsf{p})_i$ is defined as follows:

$$\mathcal{F}(\mathsf{p})_i = \begin{pmatrix} \mathcal{F}(\mathsf{p})_i^{h_\mathsf{p}} & = & \mathsf{add}_{\mathsf{p}_i}^{h_{\mathsf{p}_i}} \\ & \vdots & \\ \mathcal{F}(\mathsf{p})_i^{h_i+1} & = & \mathsf{add}_{\mathsf{p}_i}^{1} \\ \mathcal{F}(\mathsf{p})_i^{h_i} & = & \epsilon \\ & \vdots & \\ \mathcal{F}(\mathsf{p})_i^{1} & = & \epsilon \\ \mathcal{F}(\mathsf{p})_i^{0} & = & \mathsf{p}_i \end{pmatrix}$$

$$\left\{\!\!\left\{\frac{}{a\vdash a}\,\mathsf{AX}\right\}\!\!\right\}=\{a^{\circ}a^{\bullet}\}\qquad \left\{\!\!\left\{\frac{}{\vdash 1}\,\mathsf{1}\right\}\!\!\right\}=\{\epsilon\}\qquad \left\{\!\!\left\{\frac{\overset{\mathcal{D}_1}{\Gamma\vdash A}\quad \overset{\mathcal{D}_2}{\Delta\vdash B}}{\Gamma,\Delta\vdash A\wedge B}\,\wedge^{\mathsf{R}}\right\}\!\!\right\}=\{\!\{\mathcal{D}_1\}\!\}\cup\{\!\{\mathcal{D}_2\}\!\}$$

$$\left\{\!\!\left\{\frac{\overset{\mathcal{D}'}{\Gamma,B\vdash A}}{\Gamma\vdash B\supset A}\,\supset^{\mathsf{R}}\right\}\!\!\right\}=\{\!\{\mathcal{D}'\}\!\}\qquad \left\{\!\!\left\{\frac{\overset{\mathcal{D}'}{\Gamma,B,C\vdash A}}{\Gamma,B\wedge C\vdash A}\,\wedge^{\mathsf{L}}\right\}\!\!\right\}=\{\!\{\mathcal{D}'\}\!\}\qquad \left\{\!\!\left\{\frac{\overset{\mathcal{D}'}{\Gamma\vdash A}}{\Gamma,B\vdash A}\,\mathsf{W}\right\}\!\!\right\}=\{\!\{\mathcal{D}'\}\!\}$$

$$\left\{\!\!\left\{\frac{\overset{\mathcal{D}_1}{\Gamma\vdash A}\quad \overset{\mathcal{D}_2}{B,\Delta\vdash C}}{\Gamma,A\supset B,\Delta\vdash C}\,\supset^{\mathsf{L}}\right\}\!\!\right\}=\{\!\{\mathcal{D}_2\}\!\}\cup\left\{\rho\cdot\tau\mid \rho=\rho' b^{\bullet}\in\{\!\{\mathcal{D}_2\}\!\},\ \tau=a\tau'\in\{\!\{\mathcal{D}_1\}\!\},\ a\to b\right\}$$

$$\left\{\!\!\left\{\frac{\overset{\mathcal{D}'}{\Gamma,B,B\vdash A}}{\Gamma,B\vdash A}\,\mathsf{C}\right\}\!\!\right\}=\left\{f(\sigma)\mid \sigma\in\{\!\{\mathcal{D}'\}\!\}\text{ and } f: V_{[\![\Gamma,B,B\vdash A]\!]}\to V_{[\![\Gamma,B\vdash A]\!]}\text{ identifies the vertices on the } B\text{'s}\right\}$$

$$\left\{\!\!\left\{\frac{\overset{\mathcal{D}'}{\Gamma\vdash A}}{\Box\Gamma\vdash\Box A}\,\mathsf{K}^{\Box}\right\}\!\!\right\}=\{\!\{\mathcal{D}'\}\!\}\qquad \left\{\!\!\left\{\frac{\overset{\mathcal{D}'}{\Gamma,B\vdash A}}{\Box\Gamma,\Diamond^{\bullet}B\vdash\Diamond^{\circ}A}\,\mathsf{K}^{\Box}\right\}\!\!\right\}=\{\!\{\mathcal{D}'\}\!\}\cup\{\Diamond^{\circ}\Diamond^{\bullet}\}$$

Fig. 3. How to desequentialize a LCK-derivation of $\Gamma\vdash A$ into a CK-**WIS** for $\Gamma\vdash A$.

where $h_i = h_{\mathsf{p}} - h_{\mathsf{p}_i}$ for each $i \in \{0, \dots, n\}$.

Each view p induces an equivalence relation $\overset{\mathcal{G}_{\mathsf{p}}}{\sim}$ over $V_{\mathcal{G}}$ generated by the relation:

$$u\overset{\mathcal{G}_{\mathsf{p}}}{\sim}_1 w \quad\text{iff}\quad \begin{array}{l} u=\mathcal{F}(\mathsf{p})^h_{2k}\text{ and } w=\mathcal{F}(\mathsf{p})^h_{2k+1}\\ \text{for a } 2k<n-1 \text{ and a } h\leq h_{\mathsf{p}}\end{array}$$

Figure 1 and Eq. (1) show four examples of batched views.

Definition 3.4. Let $\mathcal{S}$ be a strategy on a modal arena $\mathcal{G}$. We say that $\mathcal{S}$ is *linked* if it is well-batched and for every $\mathsf{p} \in \mathcal{S}$ the $\overset{\mathcal{G}_{\mathsf{p}}}{\sim}$-classes are of the shape $\{v_1^{\bullet}, \dots, v_n^{\bullet}, w^{\circ}\}$. This induces the edge-relation $u\overset{\mathcal{G}_{\mathsf{p}}}{\rightharpoonup}w$ iff $u^{\bullet}\overset{\mathcal{G}_{\mathsf{p}}}{\sim}w^{\circ}$.

We say that $\mathcal{S}$ is CK-*batched* if it is linked and if for each modal vertex w° occurring in the address of a move in $\mathcal{S}$ the following conditions are fulfilled:

i. if $w^{\circ} \in V^{\Box}_{\mathcal{G}}$ and $v\overset{\mathcal{G}_{\mathsf{p}}}{\rightharpoonup}w$ for a $\mathsf{p} \in \mathcal{S}$, then $v \in V^{\Box}_{\mathcal{G}}$;

ii. if $w^{\circ} \in V^{\Diamond}_{\mathcal{G}}$, then there is a unique $u \in V^{\Diamond}_{\mathcal{G}}$ in the set $\{v \in V_{\mathcal{G}} \mid v\overset{\mathcal{G}_{\mathsf{p}}}{\rightharpoonup}w \text{ for a } \mathsf{p} \in \mathcal{S}\}$.

We call a CK-batched **WIS** a CK-*winning innocent strategy* (CK-**WIS** for short).

We can prove that CK-**WIS** are complete with respect to CK.

Lemma 3.5. *If a formula F is provable in* LCK*, then there is a* CK-**WIS** *for F.*

Proof. For each LCK-derivation $\mathcal{D}$ of F we define the CK-**WIS** $\{\!\{\mathcal{D}\}\!\}$ by induction over $\mathcal{D}$ according to the rules in Fig. 3. In fact, for each rule if its premise $\mathcal{D}'$ or both premises $\mathcal{D}_1$ and $\mathcal{D}_2$ are CK-**WIS**s, then also $\mathcal{D}$ is. □

In order to provide sequentialization we prove three preliminary lemmas. The first two lemmas give a way to sequentialize the CK-**WIS**s when a $\wedge$ in the right-hand side of the sequent or a $\supset$ in the left-hand side of the sequent occurs. In the sequent calculus LCK these connective require the use of rules splitting the context. In order to avoid to reprove the splitting lemmas from [21], we adopt a simpler approach relying on the presence of W and C in the sequent system. The third result proves that the presence of the two rules $\mathsf{K}^{\Box}$ and $\mathsf{K}^{\Diamond}$ can be easily recognized and sequentialized by only considering the shape of the conclusion sequent and the CK-framing conditions.

Lemma 3.6. *Let $\Gamma \vdash A_1 \wedge A_2$ such that Γ does not contain $\wedge$-formulas. If $\mathcal{S}$ is a* CK-**WIS** *for $\Gamma \vdash A_1 \wedge A_2$, then there are* CK-**WIS***s $\mathcal{S}_1$ and $\mathcal{S}_2$ for $\Gamma \vdash A_1$ and $\Gamma \vdash A_2$.*

Proof. For $i \in \{1,2\}$ we let $\mathcal{S}_i$ be the set of views in $\mathcal{S}$ starting form a move in A_i plus the empty view, that is, $\mathcal{S}_i = \{\mathsf{p} \in \mathcal{S} \mid \mathsf{p}_0 \in \vec{R}_{[\![A_i]\!]}\} \cup \{\epsilon\}$. By definition of the arena $[\![\Gamma \vdash A_1 \wedge A_2]\!]$ no move in A_i may occur in a view in $\mathcal{S}_j$ whenever $i \neq j$. Hence $\mathcal{S}_1$ and $\mathcal{S}_2$ are CK-**WIS**s for $\Gamma \vdash A_1$ and $\Gamma \vdash A_2$ respectively. □

Lemma 3.7. *Let $\mathcal{S}$ be a* CK-**WIS** *for $\Gamma' \vdash c^\circ$, hence $c^\circ c^\bullet \in \mathcal{S}$. If Γ' contains no $\wedge$-formulas and $\Gamma' \neq \Gamma, c^\bullet$, then $\Gamma' = \Gamma, A \supset B\{c^\bullet\}$ for a formula $A \supset B\{c^\bullet\} \neq c^\bullet$ containing the occurrence $c^\bullet$ of the atom c. Moreover there is a* CK-**WIS** *$\mathcal{T}$ for $\Gamma \vdash A$ and a* CK-**WIS** *$\mathcal{R}$ for $\Gamma, A \supset B\{c\}, B\{c\} \vdash c$.*

Proof. By $\bullet$-determinism and $\bullet$-totality, there is a uniquely determined vertex $c^\bullet$ such that $c^\circ c^\bullet \in \mathcal{S}$. Since $\Gamma' \neq \Gamma, c^\bullet$ does not contain $\wedge$-formulas, then Γ' contains a formula $A \supset B\{c^\bullet\}$ and, by definition of **WIS**, there is a view $c^\circ c^\bullet v \in \mathcal{S}$ for any $v \in \vec{R}_{[\![A]\!]}$.

We first show that for a $v \in \vec{R}_{[\![A]\!]}$ there is a maximal $\sigma \in \mathcal{S}$ such that $v = \sigma_{2k}$ and σ_i is not a move in $B\{c^\bullet\}$ for any $i > 2k$. If $k = 1$ the property holds. Otherwise, let $i > 2k$ such that σ_i is the first move in $B\{c^\bullet\}$, hence $\sigma_i \in \vec{R}_{[\![B\{c^\bullet\}]\!]}$. By $\circ$-completeness, there is a $\sigma' \in \mathcal{S}$ such that $\sigma' = \sigma_0 \cdots \sigma_i v$. By iterating this reasoning $\mathcal{S}$ should contain a view of infinite length. Hence the property holds.

Now observe that a σ^v with the previous property exists for a given $v \in \vec{R}_{[\![A]\!]}$. Thus, by $\circ$-completeness, for each $w \in \vec{R}_{[\![A]\!]}$ there is a σ^w with the same property and such that $\sigma_0^v \cdots \sigma_{2k-1}^v = \sigma_0^w \cdots \sigma_{2k-1}^w$. We define $\mathsf{Split}_{\mathcal{S}}^A$ to be the set containing such a view σ^w for each $w \in \vec{R}_{[\![A]\!]}$. All the σ^w share the same prefix. We use this $\mathsf{Split}_{\mathcal{S}}^A$ to define

$$\begin{aligned} \mathcal{T} &= \left\{\tau \mid \text{there are } \sigma \text{ and } \tau' \text{ such that } \sigma\tau\tau' \in \mathsf{Split}_{\mathcal{S}}^A\right\} \\ \mathcal{R} &= \left\{\rho \mid \text{there is no } \sigma \text{ such that } \rho\sigma \in \mathsf{Split}_{\mathcal{S}}^A\right\} \end{aligned}$$

By definition, $\mathcal{T}$ is a CK-**WIS** for $\Gamma \vdash A$ and $\mathcal{R}$ is a CK-**WIS** for $\Gamma, A \supset B\{c\}, B\{c\} \vdash c$ strictly smaller than $\mathcal{S}$. □

Lemma 3.8. *Let $\mathcal{S}$ be a* CK-**WIS***s for $\Gamma' \vdash A'$ such that Γ' contains no $\wedge$-formulas and at least one move from each formula in Γ' occurs in a view in $\mathcal{S}$.*

- *If $A' = \Box A$, then $\Gamma' \vdash A'$ is of the form $\Box\Gamma \vdash \Box A$ and $\mathcal{S}$ is also a* CK-**WIS** *for $\Gamma \vdash A$.*
- *If $A' = \Diamond A$, then $\Gamma' \vdash A'$ is of the form $\Box\Gamma, \Diamond^\bullet B \vdash \Diamond^\circ A$ and $\mathcal{S} = \mathcal{S}' \cup \{\Diamond^\circ, \Diamond^\circ\Diamond^\bullet\}$ where $\mathcal{S}'$ is a* CK-**WIS** *for $\Gamma \vdash A$.*

Sequent	Shape of $\mathcal{S}$	Shape of $\mathcal{D}_{\mathcal{S}}$
$\vdash 1$	$\mathcal{S} = \{\epsilon\}$	$\dfrac{}{\vdash 1}\,\mathsf{1}$
$a \vdash a$	$\mathcal{S} = \{\epsilon, a, aa\}$	$\dfrac{}{a \vdash a}\,\mathsf{AX}$
$\Gamma, B \wedge C \vdash A$	any	$\dfrac{\overset{\mathcal{D}_{\mathcal{S}}\,\Vert}{\Gamma, B, C \vdash A}}{\Gamma, B \wedge C \vdash A}\,\wedge^{\mathsf{L}}$
$\Gamma \vdash B \supset A$	any	$\dfrac{\overset{\mathcal{D}_{\mathcal{S}}\,\Vert}{\Gamma, B \vdash A}}{\Gamma \vdash B \supset A}\,\supset^{\mathsf{R}}$
$\Gamma \vdash A_1 \wedge A_2$ Γ contains no $\wedge$-formula	$\mathcal{S} = \mathcal{T} \cup \mathcal{R}$ $\mathcal{T} = \{\tau \in \mathcal{S} \mid \tau$ contains no moves in $A_2\}$ $\mathcal{R} = \{\rho \in \mathcal{S} \mid \rho$ contains no moves in $A_1\}$	$\dfrac{\dfrac{\overset{\mathcal{D}_{\mathcal{T}}\,\Vert}{\Gamma \vdash A_1} \quad \overset{\mathcal{D}_{\mathcal{R}}\,\Vert}{\Gamma \vdash A_2}}{\Gamma, \Gamma \vdash A_1 \wedge A_2}\,\wedge^{\mathsf{R}}}{\Gamma \vdash A_1 \wedge A_2}\,\mathsf{C}$
$\Gamma, A \supset B\{c^\bullet\} \vdash c^\circ$ c atomic and $A \supset B\{c^\bullet\} \neq c^\bullet$ $B\{c^\bullet\}$ contains the atom $c^\bullet$ Γ contains no $\wedge$-formulas	$c^\circ c^\bullet \in \mathcal{S}$ $\mathcal{T} = \{\tau \mid$ there are σ and τ' such that $\sigma\tau\tau' \in \mathsf{Split}^A_{\mathcal{S}}\}$ $\mathcal{R} = \{\rho \mid$ there is no σ such that $\rho\sigma \in \mathsf{Split}^A_{\mathcal{S}}\}$	$\dfrac{\dfrac{\overset{\mathcal{D}_{\mathcal{T}}\,\Vert}{\Gamma \vdash A} \quad \overset{\mathcal{D}_{\mathcal{R}}\,\Vert}{\Gamma, A \supset B\{c^\bullet\}, B\{c^\bullet\} \vdash c^\circ}}{\Gamma, \Gamma, A \supset B\{c^\bullet\}, A \supset B\{c^\bullet\} \vdash c^\circ}\,\supset^{\mathsf{L}}}{\Gamma, A \supset B\{c^\bullet\} \vdash c^\circ}\,\mathsf{C}$
$\Gamma, B \vdash A$	$\mathcal{S}$ contains no moves in B	$\dfrac{\overset{\mathcal{D}_{\mathcal{S}}\,\Vert}{\Gamma \vdash A}}{\Gamma, B \vdash A}\,\mathsf{W}$
$\Box\Gamma \vdash \Box A$	at least one move of each formula in $\Box\Gamma$ occurs in $\mathcal{S}$	$\dfrac{\overset{\mathcal{D}_{\mathcal{S}}\,\Vert}{\Gamma \vdash A}}{\Box\Gamma \vdash \Box A}\,\mathsf{K}^{\Box}$
$\Box\Gamma, \Diamond^\bullet B \vdash \Diamond^\circ A$	at least one move of each formula in $\Box\Gamma, \Diamond^\bullet B$ occurs in $\mathcal{S}$	$\dfrac{\overset{\mathcal{D}_{\mathcal{S} \setminus \{\Diamond^\circ, \Diamond^\circ\Diamond^\bullet\}}\,\Vert}{\Gamma, B \vdash A}}{\Box\Gamma, \Diamond B \vdash \Diamond A}\,\mathsf{K}^{\Diamond}$

Fig. 4. Sequentialization procedure

Proof. By the CK-batched condition, if at least one move from each formula in Γ' occurs in a view in $\mathcal{S}$, then each principal modality of a formula in Γ' must occur in the first row of a batched view of a $\mathsf{p} \in \mathcal{S}$. Moreover, all the principal modalities of the formulas in Γ' must be in $\overset{\mathcal{G}_{\mathsf{p}}}{\rightarrow}$-relation with the principal modality of A' for a $\mathsf{p} \in \mathcal{S}$. Hence $\Gamma' \vdash A'$ is either of the form $\Box\Gamma \vdash \Box A$ or $\Box\Gamma, \Diamond B \vdash \Diamond A$. In the first case, we conclude by remarking that if we remove the first row in any batched view $\mathcal{F}(\mathsf{p})$ with $\mathsf{p} \in \mathcal{S}$, then we obtain a batched view of the same p, but in $\Gamma \vdash A$. The second case is similar, but we here have to consider that the strategy also contains the two views $\Diamond^\circ$ and $\Diamond^\circ\Diamond^\bullet$. □

We can now prove the following correspondence between CK-proofs and CK-**WIS**s.

Theorem 3.9. *Let F be a formula. We have $\overset{\mathsf{LCK}}{\vdash} F$ iff there exists a* CK-**WIS** *for F.*

Proof. It $\mathcal{D}$ is a LCK-derivation of F, we can define a CK-**WIS** $\mathcal{S}_{\mathcal{D}}$ for F as in Lemma 3.5. To prove the converse, we define a LCK-derivation $\mathcal{D}_{\mathcal{S}}^{\Gamma \vdash A}$ for the sequent $\Gamma \vdash A$ by induction on the lexicographic order on the triple $\langle |\mathcal{S}|, ||A||, ||\Gamma|| \rangle$. We remark that if in no view in a CK-**WIS** $\mathcal{S}$ for $\Gamma, B \vdash A$ contains moves in B, then $\mathcal{S}$ is a CK-**WIS** also for $\Gamma \vdash A$. Observe that in case of $\Diamond$-formulas occurring in Γ, we may have that only one of these $\Diamond$s occurring in a view. In this case, we expect to observe in the final derivation a $\mathsf{K}^{\Diamond}$-rule preceded (bottom-up) by a W-rule.

Moreover, since $[\![\Gamma, B \wedge C \vdash A]\!] = [\![\Gamma, B, C \vdash A]\!]$, then each **CK-WIS** for the first sequent is a **CK-WIS** for the second one, but the size of the lhs sequent decreases. A similar reasoning applies to the sequents $\Gamma \vdash B \supset C$ and $\Gamma, B \vdash C$. We conclude by Lemmas 3.6, 3.7 and 3.8.

In Fig. 4 we give a table resuming the sequentialization step to apply according to the shape of the sequent and the shape of the **CK-WIS**. The conditions on the sequent (first column) can be checked in the given order, triggering the corresponding sequentialization step. □

4 Compositionality of Winning Strategies

In order to simplify the presentation of our compositionality result, we propose a slightly different approach to the proof of winning strategies compositionality with respect to the one normally used in the literature, e.g. [11, 17], where proofs are given by reasoning on specific sequences[3] over the arena $[\![A \supset (B \supset C)]\!] \overset{\mathsf{f}}{\sim} [\![A, B \vdash C]\!]$, such that these views can be projected on views over the arenas of $A \vdash B$ and $B \vdash C$. Instead, we here reason directly over (non $\circ$-shortsighted) views over the arena $[\![A, B \supset B \vdash C]\!]$. This allows us to preserve the parities of vertices when performing the projections.

To obtain an intuition behind the idea, consider the additional rule hide removing a formula of the shape $B \supset B$ occurring in the left-hand side of a sequent in order to simulate the cut as shown below.

$$\dfrac{\Gamma \vdash B \quad \Delta, B \vdash C}{\Gamma, \Delta \vdash C}\,\mathsf{cut} \quad \rightsquigarrow \quad \dfrac{\dfrac{\Gamma \vdash B \quad B, \Delta \vdash C}{\Gamma, \Delta, B \supset B \vdash C}\,\supset^{\mathsf{L}}}{\Gamma, \Delta \vdash C}\,\mathsf{hide}$$

This approach complies with the slogan "interaction + hide" often mentioned in the literature, e.g., [1, 17]. Here the interaction is represented by the $\supset^{\mathsf{L}}$-rule, while the hiding is performed by erasing the formula $A \supset A$ using the hide-rule.

In terms of views, our interaction is defined by composing views from the two corresponding strategies by "gluing" them using a *copycat* strategy on the cut-formula while the hiding consist of ignoring the moves in the hidden formulas.

Notation 4.1. If Δ is a list (of occurrences) of formulas in $\Gamma \vdash A$ and p is a sequence of moves in $[\![\Gamma \vdash A]\!]$, we denote by $\mathsf{p}|_{\Delta}$ the *projection* of p on Δ, that is, the sequence obtained by erasing from p any move not in Δ. By means of example, if $A = a \supset e$, $B = b \wedge d$ and $C = c$, then $baadcebda|_{A,C} = aacea$.

Whenever we consider two distinct occurrences B_1 and B_2 of the same formula B, we assume $\cdot^{\perp}$ to be the bijection between the vertices in $V_{[\![B_1]\!]}$ and in $V_{[\![B_2]\!]}$ corresponding to the same occurrence of the atom or modality in B. Note that b is a $\circ$-move (resp. $\bullet$-move) in B_1 iff $b^{\perp}$ is an $\bullet$-move (resp. $\circ$-move) in B_2.

[3] Note that these sequences are not views.

Definition 4.2. Let $\mathcal{T}$ and $\mathcal{R}$ be **WIS**s respectively for $A \vdash B_1$ and $B_2 \vdash C$ such that B_1 and B_2 are occurrences of the same formula B, and let $\tau \in \mathcal{T}$ and $\rho \in \mathcal{R}$.[4]

We define the *interaction* of τ ad ρ over B as the sequence of moves $\sigma = \tau \overset{B}{◐} \rho$ over $[\![A, B_1 \supset B_2 \vdash C]\!]$ following ρ (resp. τ) until a $\bullet$-move b in B_2 (resp. B_1) is reached; then it switches to the corresponding $\circ$-move $b^\perp$ in τ (resp. ρ), if it exists. That is,

$$\sigma_0 = \rho_0 \quad\text{and}\quad \sigma_{i+1} = \begin{cases} \tau_{k+1} & \text{where } \sigma_i = \tau_k \text{ is a move in } A \text{ or a } \circ\text{-move in } B_1 \\ \rho_{k+1} & \text{where } \sigma_i = \rho_k \text{ is a move in } C \text{ or a } \circ\text{-move in } B_2 \\ b^\perp & \text{where } \sigma_i = b \text{ is a } \bullet\text{-move in } B_1 \text{ and } b^\perp \text{ occurs in } \rho \\ b^\perp & \text{where } \sigma_i = b \text{ is a } \bullet\text{-move in } B_2 \text{ and } b^\perp \text{ occurs in } \tau \\ \text{not defined} & \text{otherwise} \end{cases}$$

We define the *composition* $\tau \overset{B}{*} \rho$ of τ and ρ over B as the projection of $\tau \overset{B}{◐} \rho$ over A and C, that is, $\tau \overset{B}{*} \rho = (\tau \overset{B}{◐} \rho)|_{A,C}$. We define the *composition* of $\mathcal{T}$ and $\mathcal{R}$ over B as the following set of sequences over $[\![A \vdash C]\!]$

$$\mathcal{T} \overset{B}{*} \mathcal{R} = \{\tau \overset{B}{*} \rho \mid \tau \in \mathcal{T}, \rho \in \mathcal{R}\}$$

Intuitively, when defining the interaction $◐$, the player $\circ$ changes way to play: whenever the player $\bullet$ plays a move b in B_1 (or B_2), its successive $\circ$-move is the corresponding $b^\perp$ in B_2 (resp. B_1) instead of playing according to $\circ$-shortsightedness. By definition $(\tau \overset{B}{◐} \rho)|_{A,B_1} = \tau$ and $(\tau \overset{B}{◐} \rho)|_{B_2,C} = \rho$, hence $(\tau \overset{B}{◐} \rho)$ is always finite. The rest of this section is devoted to prove that if $\mathcal{T}$ and $\mathcal{R}$ are **CK-WIS**s, then also is $\mathcal{T} \overset{B}{*} \mathcal{R}$.

Example 4.3. Consider the sequents $A \vdash B_1 = (c \supset a) \supset b \vdash (d \wedge (c \supset a)) \supset b$ and $B_2 \vdash C = (d \wedge (c \supset a)) \supset b \vdash (d \wedge ((e \supset e) \supset a)) \supset b$ and the view $\tau = bbaacc$ on $[\![A \vdash B_1]\!]$ and the views $\rho_1 = bbaaee$ and $\rho_2 = bbdd$ on $[\![B_2 \vdash C]\!]$. Note that these views are the unique maximal views in the unique **WIS**s for these sequents. Then we can picture the construction of $\tau \overset{B}{*} \rho_1$ as follows, where on the left-hand side we highlight the two occurrences of $[\![B]\!]$ on which the views interact, and the black arrows identify the sequences of moves on the arenas.

$\tau \overset{B}{◐} \rho_1 = bbbbaaaaee$ $\qquad\qquad$ $\tau \overset{B}{*} \rho_1 = bbaaee$

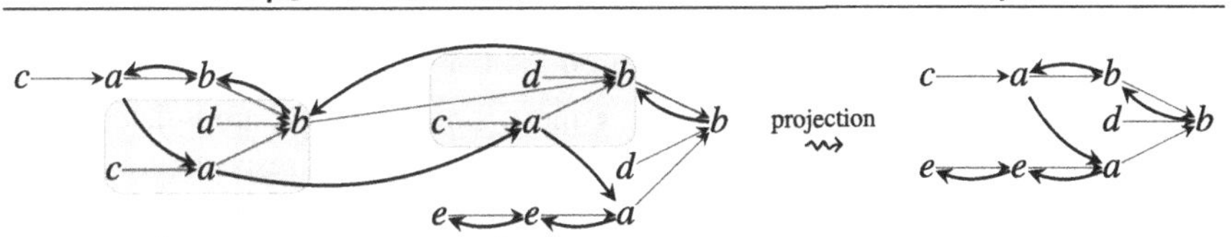

Similarly $\tau \overset{B}{◐} \rho_2 = bbbbaa$ and $\tau \overset{B}{*} \rho_2 = bba$. Note that in this case the definition of $\tau \overset{B}{◐} \rho_2$ stops because the successive should be $a^\perp$ but it does not occur in ρ.

Remark 4.4. If A, B_1, B_2 and C are formulas with B_1 and B_2 occurrences of the same formula B, then atoms and modalities in these formulas have the same parity in $[\![A, B_1 \supset B_2 \vdash C]\!]$ and in $[\![A \vdash B_1]\!]$ and $[\![B_2 \vdash C]\!]$.

[4] Note that a **CK-WIS** for $\Gamma, A \vdash B$ is also a **CK-WIS** for $A \vdash (\bigwedge \Gamma) \supset B$. This allows us to consider only **CK-WIS**s for sequents of the shape $A \vdash B$.

Our definitions allow us to show that the composition of well-batched **WIS**s is a well-batched **WIS**.

Lemma 4.5. *Let $\mathcal{T}$ and $\mathcal{R}$ be well-batched* **WIS** *for respectively $A \vdash B_1$ and $B_2 \vdash C$ such that $B = B_1 = B_2$. Then $\mathcal{S} = \mathcal{T} \overset{B}{*} \mathcal{R}$ is a well-batched* **WIS** *for $A \vdash C$.*

Proof. We first prove that for each $\tau \in \mathcal{T}$ and $\rho \in \mathcal{R}$ we have that $\tau \overset{B}{*} \rho$ is a well-batched view over $[\![A \vdash C]\!]$ since it verifies all conditions in Definition 3.1. For any $\sigma = \tau \overset{B}{*} \rho$ we have that

1. σ is a play: since $\sigma_0 \in \vec{R}_{[\![B \vdash C]\!]}$ and $\vec{R}_{[\![B \vdash C]\!]} = \vec{R}_{[\![C]\!]} = \vec{R}_{[\![A \vdash C]\!]}$.
2. σ is justified: if a move in $[\![A]\!]$ is justified in τ by a move in $[\![A]\!]$ or if a move in $[\![C]\!]$ is justified in ρ by a move in $[\![C]\!]$, then we can conclude. By definition of $[\![B \vdash C]\!]$ no move in $[\![C]\!]$ can be justified in ρ by a move in B. We conclude by remarking that if a move in $[\![A]\!]$ is justified in τ by a move in $[\![B]\!]$, then this move must be a root of $[\![A]\!]$, and then $v \overset{[\![A \vdash C]\!]}{\rightarrow} \sigma_0$ since $u \overset{[\![A \vdash C]\!]}{\rightarrow} w$ for all $u \in \vec{R}_{[\![A]\!]}$ and $w \in \vec{R}_{[\![C]\!]}$.
3. σ is $\circ$-shortsighted: by definition of σ we must have that both σ_{2k+1} and σ_{2k+2} are either in $[\![A]\!]$ or in $[\![C]\!]$. We conclude by hypothesis on ρ and τ.
4. σ is $\bullet$-uniform: by induction using the $\bullet$-uniformity of τ and ρ and the fact that $\ell(v) = \ell(v^\perp)$. In fact, let $\tilde{\sigma} = \tau \overset{B}{\between} \rho$. If $\tilde{\sigma}_i$ is a move in A (in C), $\tilde{\sigma}_{i+1} \cdots \tilde{\sigma}_{i+k-1}$ are moves over B_1 and B_2, and $\tilde{\sigma}_{i+k}$ is a move in C (respectively in A), then we can prove by induction that $\ell(\tilde{\sigma}_i) = \ell(\tilde{\sigma}_{i+j})$ for all $j \in \{1, \ldots, k\}$.
5. σ is modal: follows by the fact that no move in τ or ρ is a $\square$-vertex.
6. σ is well-batched: it suffices to remark that if $\mathsf{add}_v = m_1 \cdots m_k$, then $\mathsf{add}_{v^\perp} = m_1^\perp \cdots m_k^\perp$. We can conclude similarly to the proof of $\bullet$-uniformity since in $\tau \overset{B}{\between} \rho$ in all moves in a subsequence in B_1 and B_2 have constant height.

To conclude we show that $\mathcal{S}$ is

a. predecessor-closed: it follows by the fact that $\mathcal{T} \overset{B}{\between} \mathcal{R} = \{\tau \overset{B}{\between} \rho \mid \tau \in \mathcal{T}, \rho \in \mathcal{R}\}$ is predecessor closed.
b. $\circ$-complete: if $\sigma v^\bullet \in \mathcal{S}$ then $v^\bullet$ appears in a view $\tau \in \mathcal{T}$ or in a view $\rho \in \mathcal{R}$ as an $\bullet$-move. We conclude by the definition of the composition $*$ and by the fact that $\mathcal{S}$ and $\mathcal{R}$ are **WIS**.
c. $\bullet$-deterministic and $\bullet$-total: by induction on the length of $\tau \overset{B}{\between} \rho$ we can prove that each $v^\circ \in \tau \overset{B}{\between} \rho$ is followed by a unique $\bullet$-move since $\mathcal{T}$ and $\mathcal{R}$ are $\bullet$-deterministic and each $v^\perp \in [\![B_1]\!]$ and $w^\perp \in [\![B_2]\!]$ is uniquely determined respectively by a $v \in [\![B_2]\!]$ and a $w \in [\![B_1]\!]$. If $\bullet$-totality does not hold, then there should be a maximal view in $\mathcal{S}$ of odd length. That is, there should be $\tau \in \mathcal{T}$ and $\rho \in \mathcal{R}$ such that $\tau \overset{B}{\between} \rho = \tilde{\sigma} = \tilde{\sigma}' v^\circ s$ for a v° move in A or C, and a sequence s of moves in B_1 or in B_2. By $\bullet$-totality of $\mathcal{T}$ and $\mathcal{R}$ we can assume that $\tilde{\sigma}$ terminates with an $\bullet$-move $\tilde{\sigma}_n$. Moreover, $\tilde{\sigma}_n$ would be justified by a $\circ$-move $\tilde{\sigma}_h$ in B_1 or B_2 such that $\tilde{\sigma}_{h-1} = \tilde{\sigma}_h^\perp$. Thus we could find $\tau' \in \mathcal{T}$ and $\rho' \in \mathcal{R}$ such that $\tau' \overset{B}{\between} \rho' = \tilde{\sigma}_1 \ldots \tilde{\sigma}_n \tilde{\sigma}_n^\perp$, contradicting the maximality of $\tilde{\sigma}$. □

We can now prove that the composition of **CK-WIS**s is a **CK-WIS**.

Theorem 4.6. *Let $\mathcal{T}$ and $\mathcal{R}$ be* CK-**WIS** *for respectively $A \vdash B_1$ and $B_2 \vdash C$ such that B_1 and B_2 are occurrences of the same formula B. Then $\mathcal{S} = \mathcal{T} \overset{B}{*} \mathcal{R}$ is a* CK-**WIS**.

Proof. After Lemma 4.5 it suffices to prove that $\mathcal{S}$ is CK-batched[5]. To improve readability we write $\overset{\tau}{\sim}$, $\overset{\rho}{\sim}$, $\overset{\tau}{\rightharpoonup}$, and $\overset{\rho}{\rightharpoonup}$ instead of $\overset{[\![A\vdash B_1]\!]_\tau}{\sim}$, $\overset{[\![B_2\vdash C]\!]_\rho}{\sim}$, $\overset{[\![A\vdash B_1]\!]_\tau}{\rightharpoonup}$ and $\overset{[\![B_2\vdash C]\!]_\rho}{\rightharpoonup}$ respectively.

For this purpose we define for each $\sigma = \tau * \rho$ the relation $\overset{\tau\bullet\rho}{\rightharpoonup}$ on the vertices in $[\![A, B_1 \supset B_2 \vdash C]\!]$ as the transitive closure of the following relation

$$v \overset{\tau\bullet\rho}{\rightharpoonup}_1 w \iff v^\bullet \overset{\tau}{\rightharpoonup} w^\circ \ \text{ or } \ v^\bullet \overset{\rho}{\rightharpoonup} w^\circ \ \text{ or } \ v = w \ \text{ or } \ v^\circ = (w^\bullet)^\perp$$

where we write $w \overset{\perp}{\leftharpoondown} v$ if $v^\circ = (w^\bullet)^\perp$.

We use $\overset{\tau\bullet\rho}{\rightharpoonup}$ to prove the properties of $\overset{\sigma}{\sim}$. In particular, if $v \overset{\tau}{\sim}_1 w$ in $V_{[\![A]\!]}$ or $v \overset{\rho}{\sim}_1 w$ in $V_{[\![C]\!]}$, then $v \overset{\sigma}{\sim}_1 w$. Observe that if $\mathcal{T}$ and $\mathcal{R}$ are linked, then $\overset{\tau}{\rightharpoonup}$ and $\overset{\rho}{\rightharpoonup}$ can be considered as functions associating a vertex $v^\bullet$ a unique vertex w°. Then also $\overset{\tau\bullet\rho}{\rightharpoonup}$ can be considered as a function since $\overset{\perp}{\leftharpoondown}$ is a bijection.

If a $\overset{\sigma}{\sim}$-class contains only vertices either in A or in C, then we can conclude by hypothesis on $\mathcal{T}$ and $\mathcal{R}$. Otherwise, we only prove the case when $v \overset{\tau\bullet\rho}{\rightharpoonup} w$ with $v \in V_{[\![A]\!]}$ and $w \in V_{[\![C]\!]}$ since the case with $v \in V_{[\![C]\!]}$ and $w \in V_{[\![A]\!]}$ is proven symmetrically. By definition of $v \overset{\tau\bullet\rho}{\rightharpoonup} w$ we have $\tau\bullet\rho = \gamma_0 \cdots \gamma_i \beta_0 \cdots \beta_k \alpha_0 \cdots \alpha_j$ with $w = \mathsf{add}^h_{\gamma_i}$ and $v = \mathsf{add}^h_{\alpha_0}$, and $b_1 \ldots, b_n \in V_{[\![B_2]\!]}$ such that in the batched view of $\tau\bullet\rho$ we have the columns below, where at the bottom of each column we annotated the player playing the move and the formula in which the move and the vertices in its address belong.

$$\begin{array}{r|cccccccccccccccccccccc}
\mathsf{add}^h_{\mathsf{move}} & w^\circ & \overset{\rho}{\leftharpoondown} & b_1^\bullet & \overset{\perp}{\leftharpoondown} & b_1^\perp & \overset{\tau}{\sim} & b_2^\perp & \overset{\perp}{\leftharpoondown} & b_2 & \overset{\rho}{\sim} & b_3 & \overset{\perp}{\leftharpoondown} & b_4^\perp & \overset{\tau}{\sim} & \ldots & \overset{\rho}{\sim} & b_n & \overset{\perp}{\leftharpoondown} & (b_n^\perp)^\circ & \overset{\tau}{\leftharpoondown} & v^\bullet \\
 & \vdots & & \vdots & & \vdots & & \vdots & & \vdots & & \vdots & & \vdots & & & & \vdots & & \vdots & & \vdots \\
\mathsf{move} & \gamma_i & \leftarrow & \beta_0 & \overset{\perp}{\leftharpoondown} & \beta_1 & & \beta_2 & \overset{\perp}{\leftharpoondown} & \beta_3 & & \beta_4 & \overset{\perp}{\leftharpoondown} & \beta_5 & & \cdots & & \beta_{k-1} & \overset{\perp}{\leftharpoondown} & \beta_k & \leftarrow & \alpha_0 \\
\hline
\text{Player} & \circ & & \bullet & & \circ & & \bullet & & \circ & & \bullet & & \circ & & \cdots & & \bullet & & \circ & & \bullet \\
\text{Arena of} & C & & B_2 & & B_1 & & B_1 & & B_2 & & B_2 & & B_1 & & \cdots & & B_2 & & B_1 & & A
\end{array} \tag{4}$$

The proof that Conditions i and ii from Definition 3.4 hold follows by a similar reasoning on $\overset{\tau\bullet\rho}{\rightharpoonup}$ using the fact that $\mathcal{T}$ and $\mathcal{R}$ are CK-batched. More precisely, if $\ell(v) = \Diamond$ or $\ell(w) = \Box$, then we have $\ell(v) = \ell(b_i) = \ell(b_i^\perp) = \ell(w)$ for each $i \in \{1, \ldots, n\}$. □

Lemma 4.7. *Let A, B, C and D formulas. If $\mathcal{S}$ is a* CK-**WIS** *for $A \vdash B$ and $\mathcal{T}$ is a* CK-**WIS** *for $B \vdash C$ and $\mathcal{R}$ is a* CK-**WIS** *for $C \vdash D$, then $(\mathcal{S} \overset{B}{*} \mathcal{T}) \overset{C}{*} \mathcal{R} = \mathcal{S} \overset{B}{*} (\mathcal{T} \overset{C}{*} \mathcal{R})$.*

Proof. The operation $\bullet$ is associative by Definition 4.2. Moreover, for any Δ and Σ sequences of formulas, the projections on Δ and Σ permute, that is, $(s|_\Delta)|_\Sigma = s|_{\Delta,\Sigma} = (s|_\Sigma)|_\Delta$. We conclude by observing that for any $\sigma \in \mathcal{S}$, $\tau \in \mathcal{T}$ and $\rho \in \mathcal{R}$ we have

$$\begin{aligned}
\sigma \overset{B}{*} (\tau \overset{C}{*} \rho) = (\sigma \overset{A}{\bullet} (\tau \overset{B}{*} \rho))|_{A,D} &= (\sigma \overset{B}{\bullet} ((\tau \overset{C}{\bullet} \rho)|_{B,D}))|_{A,D} = \\
= \quad (\sigma \overset{B}{\bullet} (\tau \overset{C}{\bullet} \rho))|_{A,D} &= ((\sigma \overset{B}{\bullet} \tau) \overset{C}{\bullet} \rho)|_{A,D} \quad = \\
= (((\sigma \overset{B}{\bullet} \tau)|_{A,C}) \overset{C}{\bullet} \rho)|_{A,D} &= ((\sigma \overset{B}{*} \tau) \overset{C}{\bullet} \rho)|_{A,D} = (\sigma \overset{B}{*} \tau) \overset{C}{*} \rho
\end{aligned}$$

□

[5] This proof is similar to the one in [20].

5 Game Semantics for Constructive Modal Logic

In the previous sections, we provide various results on the correspondence between proofs in CK and CK-**WIS**s, as well as the compositionality properties of the latter. This allows us to formally state our full completeness result.

Theorem 5.1. *The* CK-**WIS**s *form a full-complete denotational semantics for* CK.

Proof. Let us consider the well-defined map

$$\{\!\{\cdot\}\!\}: \left\{\text{LCK-derivations of } F\right\} \quad\to\quad \left\{\text{CK-}\mathbf{WIS}\text{s for } F\right\}$$

from the proof of Lemma 3.5. After Theorem 3.9 we know that there is a map

$$\mathcal{D}^F_{(\cdot)}: \left\{\text{CK-}\mathbf{WIS}\text{s for } F\right\} \quad\to\quad \left\{\text{LCK-derivations of } F\right\}$$

which guarantees that each CK-**WIS** is the image of a LCK-derivation. In particular we have that $\{\!\{\mathcal{D}^F_S\}\!\} = S$, i.e., the map $\{\!\{\cdot\}\!\}$ is the left-adjoint of $\mathcal{D}^F_{(\cdot)}$. In Theorem 4.6 we prove that CK-**WIS**s compose. Moreover, by Lemma 4.7 composition is associative with neutral element the trivial strategy. □

5.1 Game Semantics for CD

The results presented in this paper can be straightforwardly extended to the constructive modal logic CD, which is obtained by extending CK with the modal axiom d shown below left:

$$\mathsf{d}: \Box A \supset \Diamond A \qquad\qquad \frac{\Gamma \vdash A}{\Box\Gamma \vdash \Diamond A}\,\mathsf{D}$$

A sound and complete (cut-free) sequent system for this logic can be obtained by adding the sequent rule above on the right to the sequent system for CK.

In order to define **WIS** capturing proofs in CD we need some additional definitions.

Definition 5.2. Let $\mathcal{S}$ be a **WIS** over an arena $\mathcal{G}$. We say that $\mathcal{S}$ is CD-*batched* if it is *atomic*, that is, the views in $\mathcal{S}$ contains only atomic vertices, linked, and if for each modal vertex w° occurring in the address of a move in $\mathcal{S}$ the following conditions are fulfilled:

i. if $w^\circ \in V^\Box_\mathcal{G}$ and $v \overset{\mathcal{G}_\mathsf{p}}{\rightharpoonup} w$ for a $\mathsf{p} \in \mathcal{S}$, then $v \in V^\Box_\mathcal{G}$;

ii. if $w^\circ \in V^\Diamond_\mathcal{G}$, then there is at most a $u \in V^\Diamond_\mathcal{G}$ in the set $\{v \in V_\mathcal{G} \mid v \overset{\mathcal{G}_\mathsf{p}}{\rightharpoonup} w \text{ for a } \mathsf{p} \in \mathcal{S}\}$.

Note that the first condition is the same first condition from Definition 3.4. The reason why we do not need the information about the diamonds in the strategies for CD depends on a property of the logic (see [2, Theorem 2]). The idea is that an instance of weakening can permute below $\mathsf{K}^\Diamond$-rules, transforming it into a an instance of the D-rule, as shown below (while in CK the information about the left-hand side diamond must be kept in some way):

$$\dfrac{\dfrac{\overset{\mathcal{D}}{\Gamma \vdash A}}{B, \Gamma \vdash A}\,\mathsf{W}}{\Diamond B, \Box\Gamma \vdash \Diamond A}\,\mathsf{K}^{\Diamond} \qquad \rightsquigarrow \qquad \dfrac{\dfrac{\overset{\mathcal{D}}{\Gamma \vdash A}}{\Box\Gamma \vdash \Diamond A}\,\mathsf{D}}{\Diamond B, \Box\Gamma \vdash \Diamond A}\,\mathsf{W}$$

We then define a CD-**WIS** as a CD-batched **WIS**. This allows to extend Theorems 3.9 and 4.6 with no effort, that is

Theorem 5.3. *The* CD-**WIS**s *form a full-complete denotational semantics for* CK.

6 Conclusion and Future Work

In this paper we have defined a game semantics for the constructive modal logic CK and have shown how it can be extended for the logic CD. We have proved full completeness and compositionality of our winning strategies, and thus have shown that our model provides a full complete denotational semantics for CK and CD.

We are currently investigating the possibility of extending our semantics to the logics CT and CS4, that are obtained by adding the modal axioms

$$\mathsf{T}\colon (A \supset \Diamond A) \wedge (\Box A \supset A) \qquad \text{and} \qquad \mathsf{4}\colon (\Diamond\Diamond A \supset \Diamond A) \wedge (\Box A \supset \Box\Box A)$$

However, the problem that arises is that for these logics also the $\Box$ should be allowed as move in order to keep track of the rules for T and 4. However, the $\bullet$-determinism of winning strategies depends on the fact that atoms and diamonds are paired by the rules which introduce them. This means that when boxes are allowed as moves, determinism cannot hold. We have to leave this issue for future work.

It is worth noticing that our result is strongly related to the game semantics for *light linear logic* as defined in [21]. In future work we will investigate the relation between our approach and this latter in order to provide a game semantics for elementary and light linear logic.

Finally, we conjecture the existence of a one-to-one correspondence between our CK-**WIS**s and the λ-calculi for constructive modal logics [3,4,12]. This investigation will also be object of future research.

Acknowledgements. We would like to thank Christian Fermüller, Robert Freiman, Yoni Zohar, and anonymous referees for the useful feedback which helped us to improve the final version of the manuscript.

References

1. Abramsky, S., Malacaria, P., Jagadeesan, R.: Full abstraction for PCF (extended abstract). In: Hagiya, M., Mitchell, J.C. (eds.) TACS 1994. LNCS, vol. 789, pp. 1–15. Springer, Heidelberg (1994). https://doi.org/10.1007/3-540-57887-0_87

2. Acclavio, M., Catta, D., Straßburger, L.: Towards a denotational semantics for proofs in constructive modal logic, April 2021. https://hal.archives-ouvertes.fr/hal-03201439 (preprint)
3. Bellin, G., De Paiva, V., Ritter, E.: Extended Curry-Howard correspondence for a basic constructive modal logic. In: Proceedings of Methods for Modalities, May 2001
4. Bierman, G.M., de Paiva, V.C.: On an intuitionistic modal logic. Stud. Logica **65**(3), 383–416 (2000)
5. Brünnler, K.: Deep sequent systems for modal logic. Arch. Math. Logic **48**(6), 551–577 (2009)
6. Davies, R., Pfenning, F.: A modal analysis of staged computation. J. ACM (JACM) **48**(3), 555–604 (2001)
7. Fairtlough, M., Mendler, M.: Propositional lax logic. Inf. Comput. **137**(1), 1–33 (1997)
8. Fitch, F.B.: Intuitionistic modal logic with quantifiers. Port. Math. **7**(2), 113–118 (1948)
9. Heilala, S., Pientka, B.: Bidirectional decision procedures for the intuitionistic propositional modal logic **IS4**. In: Pfenning, F. (ed.) CADE 2007. LNCS (LNAI), vol. 4603, pp. 116–131. Springer, Heidelberg (2007). https://doi.org/10.1007/978-3-540-73595-3_9
10. Horne, R., Ahn, K.Y., Lin, S.W., Tiu, A.: Quasi-open bisimilarity with mismatch is intuitionistic. In: Proceedings of the 33rd Annual ACM/IEEE Symposium on Logic in Computer Science, LICS 2018, New York, NY, USA, pp. 26–35. Association for Computing Machinery (2018). https://doi.org/10.1145/3209108.3209125
11. Hyland, J., Ong, C.H.: On full abstraction for PCF: I, II, and III. Inf. Comput. **163**(2), 285–408 (2000). https://doi.org/10.1006/inco.2000.2917. http://www.sciencedirect.com/science/article/pii/S0890540100929171
12. Kakutani, Y.: Call-by-name and call-by-value in normal modal logic. In: Shao, Z. (ed.) APLAS 2007. LNCS, vol. 4807, pp. 399–414. Springer, Heidelberg (2007). https://doi.org/10.1007/978-3-540-76637-7_27
13. Kojima, K.: Semantical study of intuitionistic modal logics. Ph.D. thesis, Kyoto University (2012)
14. Kuznets, R., Marin, S., Straßburger, L.: Justification logic for constructive modal logic *. In: 7th Workshop on Intuitionistic Modal Logic and Applications, IMLA 2017, July 2017. https://hal.inria.fr/hal-01614707
15. Lamarche, F.: Proof nets for intuitionistic linear logic: essential nets (2008). https://hal.inria.fr/inria-00347336
16. Marin, S., Straßburger, L.: Label-free modular systems for classical and intuitionistic modal logics. In: Advances in Modal Logic 10 (2014)
17. McCusker, G.: Games and full abstraction for FPC. Inf. Comput. **160**(1), 1–61 (2000). https://doi.org/10.1006/inco.1999.2845. http://www.sciencedirect.com/science/article/pii/S0890540199928456
18. Mendler, M., Scheele, S.: Cut-free Gentzen calculus for multimodal CK. Inf. Comput. **209**(12), 1465–1490 (2011)
19. Meyer, J.J., Veltmanw, F.: Intelligent agents and common sense reasoning. In: Blackburn, P., Van Benthem, J., Wolter, F. (eds.) Handbook of Modal Logic, Studies in Logic and Practical Reasoning, vol. 3, pp. 991–1029. Elsevier (2007). https://doi.org/10.1016/S1570-2464(07)80021-8. http://www.sciencedirect.com/science/article/pii/S1570246407800218
20. Murawski, A.S.: On semantic and type-theoretic aspects of polynomial-time computability (2001)
21. Murawski, A.S., Luke Ong, C.-H.: Evolving games and essential nets for affine polymorphism. In: Abramsky, S. (ed.) TLCA 2001. LNCS, vol. 2044, pp. 360–375. Springer, Heidelberg (2001). https://doi.org/10.1007/3-540-45413-6_28
22. Plotkin, G., Stirling, C.: A framework for intuitionistic modal logics. In: Proceedings of the 1st Conference on Theoretical Aspects of Reasoning about Knowledge (TARK), pp. 399–406 (1986)

23. Prawitz, D.: Natural Deduction: A Proof-Theoretical Study. Courier Dover Publications, Mineola (2006)
24. Simpson, A.K.: The proof theory and semantics of intuitionistic modal logic. Ph.D. thesis, University of Edinburgh, College of Science and Engineering (1994)
25. Straßburger, L.: Cut elimination in nested sequents for intuitionistic modal logics. In: Pfenning, F. (ed.) FoSSaCS 2013. LNCS, vol. 7794, pp. 209–224. Springer, Heidelberg (2013). https://doi.org/10.1007/978-3-642-37075-5_14
26. Straßburger, L., Heijltjes, W., Hughes, D.J.D.: Intuitionistic proofs without syntax. In: 34th Annual ACM/IEEE Symposium on Logic in Computer Science, LICS 2019, Vancouver, Canada, pp. 1–13. IEEE, June 2019. https://doi.org/10.1109/LICS.2019.8785827. https://hal.inria.fr/hal-02386878
27. Troelstra, A.S., Schwichtenberg, H.: Basic Proof Theory, vol. 43. Cambridge University Press, Cambridge (2000)
28. Vakarelov, D.: Modal logics for knowledge representation systems. Theor. Comput. Sci. **90**, 433–456 (1991)

The Došen Square Under Construction:
A Tale of Four Modalities

Michael Mendler, Stephan Scheele$^{(\boxtimes)}$, and Luke Burke

University of Bamberg, Bamberg, Germany
stephan.scheele@uni-bamberg.de

Abstract. In classical modal logic, necessity □A, possibility ◇A, impossibility □¬A and non-necessity ◇¬A form a Square of Oppositions (SO) whose corners are interdefinable using classical negation. The relationship between these modalities in intuitionistic modal logic is a more delicate matter since negation is weaker. Intuitionistic non-necessity ⊟ and impossibility ⊖, first investigated by Došen, have received less attention and—together with their positive counterparts □ and ◇—form a square we call the *Došen Square*. Unfortunately, the core property of constructive logic, the Disjunction Property (DP), fails when the modalities are combined and, interpreted in birelational Kripke structures à la Došen, the Square partially collapses. We introduce the constructive logic CKD, whose four semantically independent modalities □, ◇, ⊟, ⊖ prevent the Došen Square from collapsing under the effect of intuitionistic negation while preserving DP. The model theory of CKD involves a constructive Kripke frame interpretation of the modalities. A Hilbert deduction system and an equivalent cut-free sequent calculus are presented. Soundness, completeness and finite model property are proven, implying that CKD is decidable. The logics HK⊟, HK□, HK◇ and HK⊖ of Došen and other known theories of intuitionistic modalities are syntactic fragments or axiomatic extensions of CKD.

Being one world away from absurdity is very different from being in an absurd world. Being one step removed from disaster is often very different, and feels very different, from the disaster. (Routley 1983)

1 Introduction

The reader may recall the classical *square of opposition* (SO) [38] seen on the left side in Fig. 1, whose four corners express the distinction between contradictory and contrary oppositions, that were traditionally labelled with four letters A, E, I, O designating propositions, and connected by means of six edges. The SO has been applied to concepts in linguistics, mathematics and philosophy and can be generalised in a number of ways. From the vantage point of classical modal logic, the oppositions can be expressed in terms of the modal operators ◇ and □, which traditionally express *possibility* and *necessity*, and are interdefinable in terms of negation, i.e., ◇A = ¬□¬A and □A = ¬◇¬A. In

© Springer Nature Switzerland AG 2021
A. Das and S. Negri (Eds.): TABLEAUX 2021, LNAI 12842, pp. 446–465, 2021.
https://doi.org/10.1007/978-3-030-86059-2_26

constructive modal logic this is no longer the case, which results in four independent modal operators, complementing $\Diamond$ and $\Box$ with their opposing counterparts [10], namely *impossibility* $\ominus$ and *non-necessity* $\boxminus$. In this work we construct the *Došen square* (DS) seen on the right side in Fig. 1, by investigating the relationships between the modalities $\{\Diamond, \Box, \boxminus, \ominus\}$ in a constructive theory, in which they remain independent under (intuitionistic) negation ($\sim$) in the sense that they are not interdefinable anymore, unlike in classical logic. We will shortly discuss the interpretation of the DS.

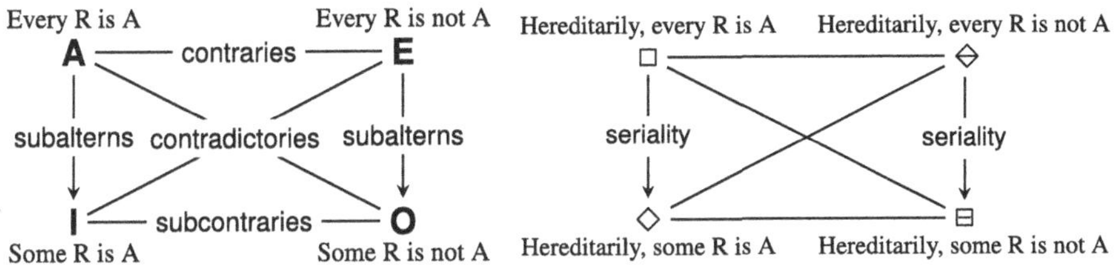

Fig. 1. The square of oppositions and the Došen Square.

1.1 State of the Art

In classical Kripke semantics, the modal operators $\Diamond$ and $\Box$ are interpreted w.r.t. frames $\mathfrak{F} = (S, R)$, consisting of a set of *states* S and a binary *accessibility* relation R on S. The satisfaction of formulas is defined relative to models $\mathfrak{M} = (\mathfrak{F}, V)$ extending a frame by a *valuation* $V : S \to \mathcal{P}(Var)$ that associates a set $V(s) \subseteq Var$ of propositional variables *satisfied at* a state s. Their interpretation is given by quantifying existentially and universally over states in the image of the relation R

$$\mathfrak{M}, s \models \Diamond A \Leftrightarrow \exists x. (sRx \;\&\; \mathfrak{M}, x \models A) \tag{1}$$

$$\mathfrak{M}, s \models \Box A \Leftrightarrow \forall x. (sRx \Rightarrow \mathfrak{M}, x \models A) \tag{2}$$

where $\mathfrak{M}, s \models A$ expresses that *A is satisfied at* state *s in* $\mathfrak{M}$. Standardly, in modal extensions of intuitionistic propositional logic (IPL), Kripke models are based on a birelational Kripke frame $\mathfrak{F} = (S, \sqsubseteq, R)$, where the accessibility relation R and the intuitionistic partial order $\sqsubseteq$ are relations on the same domain. Because the classical clauses (1) and (2) fail to ensure *intuitionistic heredity*:

$$s \sqsubseteq s' \text{ and } \mathfrak{M}, s \models A \text{ implies } \mathfrak{M}, s' \models A,$$

one common approach is to impose the frame conditions $(\sqsubseteq ; R) \subseteq (R ; \sqsupseteq)$ and $(\sqsubseteq ; R) \subseteq (R ; \sqsubseteq)$, where $R ; S =_{df} \{(x, z) \mid \exists y. x\, R\, y \text{ and } y\, S\, z\}$ denotes *sequential composition* of two binary relations R and S. In the Došen square we enforce heredity without any frame conditions by the following 'doubly quantified' (constructive) interpretation:

$$\mathfrak{M}, s \models \Diamond A \Leftrightarrow \forall s' \sqsupseteq s. \exists x. (s' \, R \, x \;\&\; \mathfrak{M}, x \models A) \tag{3}$$

$$\mathfrak{M}, s \models \Box A \Leftrightarrow \forall s' \sqsupseteq s. \forall x. (s' \, R \, x \Rightarrow \mathfrak{M}, x \models A). \tag{4}$$

We can pronounce $\Diamond A$ as "hereditarily, there is an R-accessible state at which A holds" and $\Box A$ as "hereditarily, for all R-accessible states A holds", hence the labelling of the Došen square in Fig. 1, in which such sentences have been still further abbreviated. The mainstream approach is to either adopt the 'singly quantified' approach (1) and (2) for both $\Box$ and $\Diamond$ [35,40,41] or to 'mix and match', adopting (1) for $\Diamond$ and (4) for $\Box$ [29,34]. The 'doubly quantified' approach for both modalities, first introduced by [39] and later used in the logic CK [3,20,25,33], is far less common, as it leads to non-normal modal logics invalidating the axiom $\Diamond(A \vee B) \rightarrow \Diamond A \vee \Diamond B$. Computationally, this makes sense (see [24,33]), and it has the consequence that $\sqsubseteq$ is not required to be antisymmetric as in standard intuitionistic Kripke frames. In CK, this gives rise to cyclic structures which are crucial in establishing the Finite Model Property (FMP) [25]. Furthermore, the nullary case $\sim \Diamond \bot$ is invalidated as well, because frames for CK include so-called *fallible* states which verify all formulas of the language. Fallible states may be accessible from other states via the modal accessibility relation in the clause for $\Diamond$ and so become 'visible' in the form of $\Diamond\bot$ statements and $\sqsubseteq$ is no longer reflexive. Constructive modal logics such as CK therefore allow for truth-value 'gluts' (i.e., they allow for the truth of formulas of the form $A \wedge {\sim}A$) as well as truth value 'gaps' (i.e., formulas of the form $A \vee {\sim}A$ fail to be verified at a state).

Consider now the *impossibility* and *non-necessity* operators [10] $\ominus$ and $\boxminus$ which occupy the right side of the squares in Fig. 1, where $\ominus$ (or $\boxminus$) is the negative counterpart of the positive modality $\Diamond$ (or $\Box$) and vice versa:[1]

$$\mathfrak{M}, s \models \ominus A \Leftrightarrow \forall x. (sRx \Rightarrow \mathfrak{M}, x \not\models A) \tag{5}$$

$$\mathfrak{M}, s \models \boxminus A \Leftrightarrow \exists x. (sRx \;\&\; \mathfrak{M}, x \not\models A). \tag{6}$$

Classically, these modalities can be expressed in terms of $\Diamond$ and $\Box$ as $\neg\Diamond A$ (or $\Box\neg A$) and $\neg\Box A$ (or $\Diamond\neg A$). Intuitionistically, this is no longer the case, because intuitionistic negation $\sim$ is weaker than classical negation $\neg$ as it fails Excluded Middle (EM).

To our knowledge, Došen was the first to pay extensive attention to the negative modalities in intuitionistic logic. For each $\otimes \in \{\Box, \Diamond, \boxminus, \ominus\}$, Došen produced

[1] Such negative modalities have been considered in the literature on FDE and Routley semantics as ways of capturing forms of negation [17–19,28,36] often called 'constructible' or 'strong' negation [26,37]. We do not suggest that the role of $\ominus$ and $\boxminus$ in the logic CKD is to capture forms of *negation*; rather, we are simply interested in how they behave in a constructive setting (i.e. in which the Disjunction Property holds) as *modal operators*.

a logic $HK\otimes$, combining $\otimes$ with IPL. In $HK\Box$, the classical truth conditions for $\Box$ in (2) are employed together with the frame condition $(\sqsubseteq; R) \subseteq (R; \sqsubseteq)$, whilst in $HK\Diamond$ the classical truth conditions for $\Diamond$ in (1) are employed together with $(\sqsupseteq; R) \subseteq (R; \sqsupseteq)$ [6]. In $HK\ominus$, the truth conditions (5) are employed for $\ominus$ and $(\sqsubseteq; R) \subseteq (R; \sqsupseteq)$ are imposed, and in $HK\boxminus$ the truth conditions (6) are employed for $\boxminus$ with the frame condition $(\sqsupseteq; R) \subseteq (R; \sqsubseteq)$ [9–11]. Each $HK\otimes$ for $\otimes \in \{\Box, \Diamond, \boxminus, \ominus\}$ is a conservative extension of IPL which is sound and complete with respect to birelational frames, subject to the associated frame conditions. The work of Došen was very much out on a limb with respect to the mainstream in intuitionistic logic, which concentrated on the positive modalities almost entirely [42], and only in recent years have the negative modalities been given more attention in the literature on intuitionistic and constructive logic [15,16,28]. Curiously, Došen did not produce a logic which combines $\ominus$, $\boxminus$, $\Diamond$ and $\Box$ with IPL on a single birelational frame $(S, \sqsubseteq, R)$ in which the modalities are interpreted with respect to the same R.

Some combinations of the modalities $\Box, \Diamond, \boxminus, \ominus$ with each other and negation $\sim$ have been explored. For example, [6] consider a system $HK\,\Box\,\Diamond$, combining $\Diamond$ and $\Box$. They give two equivalent axiomatisations of $HK\,\Box\,\Diamond$, yet the theory does not have the DP, nor is it conservative over either $HK\Diamond$ and $HK\Box$ (see [6] for discussion). Drobyschevich [15] investigates the properties of the combined modality $\sim\ominus A$ in an extension $\mathsf{N}^{\star}$ of IPL he calls $HKNR$ and he studies $\sim\ominus A$ in $HK\boxminus$ in an extension he calls $HKN\boxminus$. $\mathsf{N}^{\star}$ is an extension of $HK\ominus$ but without $\bot$, known as N [11]. In $\mathsf{N}^{\star}$, however, $\boxminus$ and $\ominus$ collapse into a single modality, since R is a functional accessibility relation, called the 'Routley star' operation. Addition of $\Diamond$ to $HK\ominus$ plus frame conditions imposed to ensure hereditariness, have the result that the modalities $\ominus$ and $\Diamond$ become interdefinable as $\Diamond A \leftrightarrow \sim\ominus A$ and $\ominus A \leftrightarrow \sim\Diamond A$ via intuitionistic negation. But, from a constructive point of view, the directions of $\sim\ominus A \rightarrow \Diamond A$ and $\sim\Diamond A \rightarrow \ominus A$ are suspicious. If we can prove the absurdity of something being impossible (i.e., $\sim\ominus A$), this doesn't mean we have a positive construction which will allow us to show that something is possible (i.e., $\Diamond A$). Likewise, if we can prove that a certain possibility is absurd (i.e., $\sim\Diamond A$), then we can't conclude that we have a proof that it is impossible. Similarly, addition of $\Box$ to $HK\boxminus$ plus frame conditions make $\Box$ and $\boxminus$ interdefinable ($\Box B \leftrightarrow \sim\boxminus B$ and $\boxminus B \leftrightarrow \sim\Box B$) and similar reservations regarding the constructive content of the implications $\sim\boxminus B \rightarrow \Box A$ and $\sim\Box B \rightarrow \boxminus B$ can be made. Adding $\Box$ and its associated heredity frame condition forces axiom $\boxminus B \vee \sim\Box B$ without $\boxminus B$ or $\sim\Box B$ being provable by itself. This breaks DP and thus constructiveness of non-necessity. This is a general side effect of the frame conditions: Each positive modality $\oplus$ induces the disjunction $\sim\ominus A \vee \ominus A$, where $\ominus$ is the corresponding negative modality, and each negative modality $\ominus$ induces the disjunction $\sim\oplus A \vee \oplus A$. Similar effects have been observed for $\mathsf{N}^{\star}$ [13], where the scheme $\ominus A \vee \ominus{\sim}A$ is valid and for $HK\,\Box\,\Diamond$, where $\Diamond A \vee \Box\neg A$ is an axiom, both in violation of the DP.

1.2 Contributions

The combination of the modalities $\Box$, $\Diamond$, $\ominus$ and $\boxminus$ so as to ensure a constructive logic is a delicate matter. Can the negative modalities $\ominus$ and $\boxminus$ live happily side-by-side with their 'positive' counterparts $\Diamond$ and $\Box$, within a constructive setting? According to consolidated tradition, a *constructive logic* means a logic in which the *Disjunction Property (DP)* holds: whenever $A \vee B$ is a theorem then either A is a theorem, or B is a theorem. Constructiveness thus construed is not a property of operators, but of logics. Our question is therefore whether we can combine the modalities whilst retaining the DP. In this paper we show that if we interpret $\ominus$ and $\boxminus$ constructively like $\Box$ and $\Diamond$ in (4) and (3),

$$\mathfrak{M}, s \models \ominus A \Leftrightarrow \forall s' \sqsupseteq s. \forall x. \,(s' \, R \, x \Rightarrow \mathfrak{M}, x \not\models A) \tag{7}$$

$$\mathfrak{M}, s \models \boxminus A \Leftrightarrow \forall s' \sqsupseteq s. \exists x. \,(s' \, R \, x \;\&\; \mathfrak{M}, x \not\models A) \tag{8}$$

then we can avoid the collapse of the modalities $\ominus$, $\boxminus$, $\Diamond$ and $\Box$, abandoning the frame conditions relating $\sqsubseteq$ and R:[2] The logic created by thus adding the negative modalities to CK [25,33], we dub CKD. CKD is both conservative over CK and constructive in the sense that it satisfies DP.

The Došen square is not supposed to be analogous to the SO; in fact, only certain features of the square of oppositions hold in CKD. The logic CKD will treat the relationships between the modalities in DS as follows. On the one hand, $\Diamond$ and $\ominus$ will be contradictories, i.e., $\sim(\Diamond A \wedge \ominus A)$ is valid. Similarly, necessity $\Box$ and unnecessity $\boxminus$ will be incompatible, i.e., $\sim(\Box A \wedge \boxminus A)$ is valid. Due to the absence of the Excluded Middle and fallibility, the modalities $\Diamond \sim A$ and $\boxminus A$ are independent in CKD, distinguishing the Došen square from the classical SO. In CKD $\Diamond \sim A \rightarrow \boxminus A$ follows from infallibility, expressed by $\ominus\bot$. Moreover, we have $\boxminus A \rightarrow \Diamond \sim A$ assuming $\Box(A \vee \sim A)$, which expresses the necessitation of the Excluded Middle. Similarly, $\Box \sim A$ and $\ominus A$ are independent. Again, the connection hinges on the absence of gluts and gaps: In CKD we have that infallibility $\ominus\bot$ entails $\Box \sim A \rightarrow \ominus A$ and similarly $\Box(A \vee \sim A)$ entails $\ominus{\sim}A \rightarrow \Box A$. Unless every state has an R-successor (seriality) – expressible by $\Diamond\top$ – the modality pairs $\Box$, $\Diamond$ and $\ominus$, $\boxminus$ are independent. However, like in the classical SO it holds that from seriality $\Diamond\top$ follows $\Box A \rightarrow \Diamond A$ and $\ominus A \rightarrow \boxminus A$.

In Sect. 2 the model theory of CKD is introduced and the DP is proven. In Sect. 3.1, an axiomatic Hilbert system, H_{CKD}, is provided for CKD, and its conservativity over CK and over N is sketched. In Sect. 3.2, a sequent calculus, G_{CKD}, for CKD is provided, proving its soundness and completeness with respect to C-frames , and its translation into H_{CKD} is obtained. As a corollary of completeness, it follows that the theory of CKD has the FMP, is cut-free and decidable. In Sect. 4 we end with Conclusions.

---

[2] Our claim is that the doubly quantified truth conditions are a neat way out of the bind, not that they are necessary in order to provide a logic which combines $\Box$, $\Diamond$, $\ominus$ and $\boxminus$ interpreted with respect to the same relation.

2 The Došen Square CKD of Constructive Modalities

We begin by introducing the frames and models we will make use of.

Definition 1 (C-frame). *A* C-frame $\mathfrak{F} = (S, \leq, F, R)$ *consists of a set* $S \neq \emptyset$ *of* states, *a preordering* $\leq$ *(reflexive & transitive) on* S, *a subset* $F \subseteq S$ *of* fallible *states, s.t.* $s_1 \leq s_2$ *and* $s_1 \in F$ *implies* $s_2 \in F$ *and a binary relation* R *on* S. *On a C-frame we define the ordering* $\sqsubseteq =_{df} \{(s, s') \mid s \leq s' \,\&\, s' \notin F\}$ *and if* $F = \emptyset$ *then* $\mathfrak{F}$ *is called* infallible.

C-frames are non-standard in three ways. Firstly, we do not require any frame property to constrain the interaction of $\leq$ and R. In this way, we obtain a minimal logic to fuse the modalities $\Diamond$, $\Box$, $\diamondminus$ and $\boxminus$ on a single accessibility relation. Secondly, we only require $\leq$ to be a preorder rather than a partial ordering, i.e., omitting antisymmetry allows for the possibility of cyclic structures which are crucial in establishing the FMP. Thirdly, by adding the fallibility set $F \subseteq S$ we can declare frame states as 'internally exploded' and make states $s \in S$ such that $s \; R \; s' \in F$ border states "one world away from absurdity". This is instrumental to preserve constructiveness for certain extensions of CKD and amounts to working with an intuitionistic accessibility $\sqsubseteq$ that is not only not antisymmetric but also not reflexive.

Definition 2 (C-model). *A* C-model $\mathfrak{M} = (\mathfrak{F}, V)$ *consists of a C-frame* $\mathfrak{F} = (S, \leq, F, R)$ *together with a* valuation *function* $V : S \to \mathcal{P}(Var)$ *from* S *to the subset of propositional variables subject to* heredity *and* explosion *conditions: if* $s_1 \leq s_2$ *then (i)* $V(s_1) \subseteq V(s_2)$ *and (ii) if* $s \in F$ *then* $V(s) = Var$.

The language $\mathcal{L}_{\mathsf{CKD}}$ of CKD coincides with that of intuitionistic propositional logic (IPL) extended by the four modalities $\{\Box, \Diamond, \diamondminus, \boxminus\}$.

Definition 3 (Language $\mathcal{L}_{\mathsf{CKD}}$). *The language* $\mathcal{L}_{\mathsf{CKD}}$ *is based on a denumerable set of propositional variables* $Var = \{p, q, \ldots\}$. *The set of well-formed* CKD-*formulas over* Var *is inductively defined by the following grammar:*

$$A, B ::= p \mid \top \mid \bot \mid A \wedge B \mid A \vee B \mid A \to B \mid \Box A \mid \Diamond A \mid \diamondminus A \mid \boxminus A$$

Note that $\sim A$ *abbreviates intuitionistic negation* $A \to \bot$, $A \leftrightarrow B$ *is expressed by* $(A \to B) \wedge (B \to A)$ *and implication* $\to$ *is right-associative.*

The interpretation of $\mathcal{L}_{\mathsf{CKD}}$ is by means of the following satisfaction relation:

Definition 4 (Satisfaction in C-models). *Let* $\mathfrak{M} = (S, \leq, F, R, V)$ *be a C-model. The notion of a formula* A *being* satisfied *in a C-model* $\mathfrak{M}$ *at a state* s *is* *defined inductively, for the modal operators as in* (3), (4), (7), (8) *and for the other operators as in* IPL.[3]

$$\begin{array}{ll} \mathfrak{M}, s \models \top, & \\ \mathfrak{M}, s \models \bot & \textit{iff } s \in F, \\ \mathfrak{M}, s \models p & \textit{iff } p \in V(s), \\ \mathfrak{M}, s \models A \wedge B & \textit{iff } \mathfrak{M}, s \models A \textit{ and } \mathfrak{M}, s \models B, \\ \mathfrak{M}, s \models A \vee B & \textit{iff } \mathfrak{M}, s \models A \textit{ or } \mathfrak{M}, s \models B, \\ \mathfrak{M}, s \models A \to B & \textit{iff for all } s' \sqsupseteq s, \textit{ if } \mathfrak{M}, s' \models A \textit{ then } \mathfrak{M}, s' \models B. \end{array}$$

The semantics of Definition 4 permits us to assume that each fallible state $f \in F$ is a dead end of the frame, i.e., there is no s with either $f\ R\ s$ or $f \sqsubseteq s$. Moreover, we may assume without loss of generality that every $f \in F$ is reachable by an R-step from a non-fallible state, i.e., there is $s \notin F$ with $s\ R\ f$. We call such frames $\bot$-*condensed.* In $\bot$-condensed frames we have $\mathfrak{M}, s \models \ominus\bot$ for all $s \in S$ iff $\mathfrak{M}$ is infallible, i.e., $F = \varnothing$.

Definition 5 (Validity). *A formula A is* valid in a C-model $\mathfrak{M}$*, written* $\mathfrak{M} \models A$*, if* $\mathfrak{M}, s \models A$ *for all* $s \in S$*. If* $\mathfrak{M}$ *is clear from the context, we will simply write* $s \models A$*. A formula A is* valid in a C-frame $\mathfrak{F}$*, written* $\mathfrak{F} \models A$*, if* $\mathfrak{M} \models A$ *for all models* $\mathfrak{M} = (\mathfrak{F}, V)$ *over* $\mathfrak{F}$*. We lift all the validity relations to sets of formulas* Γ *in the usual conjunctive way, for a state* $\mathfrak{M}, s \models \Gamma$*, a model* $\mathfrak{M} \models \Gamma$ *and frame* $\mathfrak{F} \models \Gamma$*.*

Lemma 1. *Satisfaction is hereditary and explosive, i.e., (i)* $s \models A$ *iff* $\forall s' \sqsupseteq s.\ s' \models A$ *and (ii)* $s \in F$ *implies* $s \models A$*.*

We define a semantic consequence relation axiomatising the semantic levels of the modal satisfaction relation at the frame, model and state level (global vs. local consequence) [21,31]. It allows us to map the semantic definition of a logical system to its syntactic axiomatisation in the form a Hilbert calculus, to be used in the discussion of the correspondences between Došen's logics and CKD (see Theorem 3).

Definition 6 (Semantic Entailment). *Let* Ω *(*frame hypotheses*),* Φ *(*model hypotheses*),* Γ *(*state hypotheses*) and* Π *(*state assertions*) be sets of formulas. We write* $\Omega; \Phi; \Gamma \models \Pi$ *iff for all C-frames* $\mathfrak{F} = (S, \leq, F, R)$ *with* $\mathfrak{F} \models \Omega$ *and all models* $\mathfrak{M} = (\mathfrak{F}, V)$ *with* $\mathfrak{M} \models \Phi$ *and all states* $s \in S$ *with* $\mathfrak{M}, s \models \Gamma$*, we have* $\mathfrak{M}, s \models \Pi$*.*

Let CKD be the set of all universally valid formulas, i.e., $\mathsf{CKD} = \{A \mid \emptyset; \emptyset; \emptyset \models A\}$. This set is a logical theory, i.e., closed under Modus Ponens and Substitution.

[3] As usual, we can take $\top =_{df} p \to p$ for a variable $p \in \mathit{Var}$. Interestingly, also absurdity $\bot$ is representable, viz. as the non-necessity of truth, i.e., $\bot =_{df} \boxminus\top$. First, $\mathfrak{M}, s \models \bot$ implies $\mathfrak{M}, s \models \boxminus\top$ since by definition there is no s' with $s \sqsubseteq s'$. Second, if $\mathfrak{M}, s \models \boxminus\top$ and $s \notin F$ we would have $s \sqsubseteq s$ and so by the truth condition for $\boxminus$ there must be s'' with $s\ R\ s''$ and $\mathfrak{M}, s'' \not\models \top$. This is impossible, hence $s \in F$ and so $\mathfrak{M}, s \models \bot$.

The theory CKD does not validate the axiom $\diamondminus A \vee \diamondminus{\sim}A$ of Drobyshevich nor any of the axiom schemes $\otimes A \vee {\sim} \otimes A$ for $\otimes \in \{\Diamond, \diamondminus, \Box, \boxminus\}$, as can be readily verified.

One of the hallmarks of constructive logics is the *disjunction property* (DP), stating that the proof of a disjunction $A \vee B$ requires positive evidence in the form of a proof of either A or B. The absence of frame conditions in CKD admits of a particularly simple model-theoretic argument for the Disjunction Property (Theorem 1) that proceeds completely analogously to IPL.

Theorem 1 (Disjunction Property). *The theory* CKD *has the Disjunction Property.*

A striking feature of CKD is that the Finite Model Property (Theorem 8) depends on permitting $\preceq$-cycles in C-frames. Consider the cyclic countermodel $\mathfrak{M}_c$ on the right in Fig. 2. The states s_0, s_1 each satisfy ${\sim}\boxminus A$, ${\sim}\boxminus B$ and $\boxminus(A \wedge B)$, being mutual $\sqsubseteq$-successors sharing the same theory. Yet, they cannot be condensed into a single state $s = \{s_0, s_1\}$, as s would have both s_0' and s_1' as immediate R-successors, and satisfy $s \models \boxminus A \wedge \boxminus B$ which is inconsistent with the properties of s_0 and s_1. Observe that $\mathfrak{M}_c$ does not satisfy Došen's HK$\boxminus$ frame condition [10] $(\sqsupseteq ; R) \subseteq (R; \sqsubseteq)$ that generates the constructively disputable scheme ${\sim}\boxminus A \to \Box A$. Even more, $\mathfrak{M}_c$ provides a countermodel for the distribution axioms $\boxminus(A \wedge B) \to (\boxminus A \vee \boxminus B)$ and $\Diamond(A \vee B) \to (\Diamond A \vee \Diamond B)$. Their absence is characteristic of CKD as a non-normal modal logic, due to the 'doubly-quantified' truth conditions in the existential modalities $\boxminus$ (8) and $\Diamond$ (3).

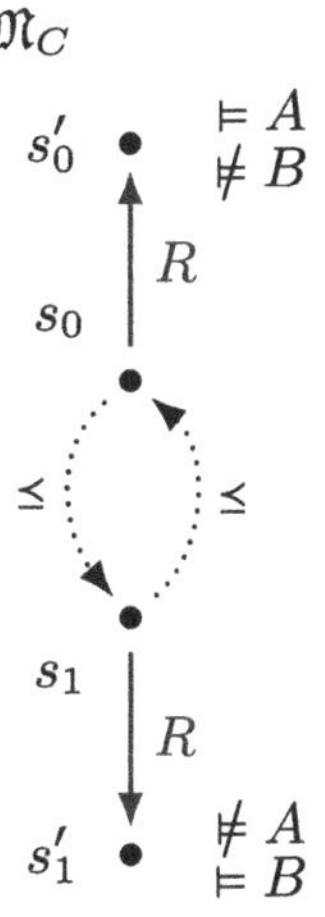

Fig. 2. Cyclic model.

Proposition 1. *The scheme* $({\sim}\boxminus A \wedge {\sim}\boxminus B) \to {\sim}\boxminus(A \wedge B)$ *is valid in* HK$\boxminus$ *[10] but not a theorem of* CKD. *Every* CKD *counter model for it is infinite or cyclic.*

3 Proof Systems for CKD

We develop the proof theory of CKD, in the form of the Hilbert calculus H_{CKD} and the Gentzen-style sequent calculus G_{CKD}. The calculus H_{CKD} captures semantic entailment $\Omega; \Phi; \Gamma \models \Pi$ where the set of state hypotheses $\Gamma = \varnothing$ is empty, which corresponds to the restriction [21] of rule *Nec* to apply to theorems only. In contrast, the sequent calculus G_{CKD} works entirely at the state level (i.e., $\Omega = \varnothing = \Phi$).

3.1 CKD Global Reasoning: The Hilbert Calculus H_{CKD}

Definition 7 (Hilbert Deduction and CKDAxioms). *Let* Ω *and* Φ *be sets of formulas. We write* $\Omega; \Phi \vdash_H A$ *if there is a sequence* $A_0, A_1, \ldots A_{n-1}$ *of formulas such that* $A_{n-1} = A$ *and each* A_i $(i \in n)$ *is either a* model hypothesis *from* Φ, *a substitution instance of some* frame hypothesis *or* axiom *in* Ω, *or arises by the rules of* Modus Ponens *(MP) or* Necessitation *(Nec) from formulas* A_j $(j < i)$ *appearing earlier. The set of axioms* CKD_{ax} *consist of those for* IPL *(see, e.g., [14]) and the modal axioms as depicted in the following. We write* $\mathsf{CKD}; \Phi \vdash_H A$ *for* $\mathsf{CKD}_{ax}; \Phi \vdash_H A$.

$$\Box K =_{df} \Box(A \to B) \to \Box A \to \Box B \qquad \diamondminus 2 =_{df} \diamondminus A \to \diamondminus B \to \diamondminus(A \vee B)$$
$$\Diamond K =_{df} \Box(A \to B) \to \Diamond A \to \Diamond B \qquad \boxminus 2 =_{df} \diamondminus A \to \boxminus B \to \boxminus(A \vee B)$$
$$\diamondminus K =_{df} \Box(A \to B) \to \diamondminus B \to \diamondminus A \qquad N5 =_{df} \diamondminus(A \wedge B) \to \Diamond A \to \boxminus B$$
$$\boxminus K =_{df} \Box(A \to B) \to \boxminus B \to \boxminus A \qquad N6 =_{df} \Box(A \vee B) \to \boxminus A \to \Diamond B$$
$$\Box 2 =_{df} \diamondminus A \to \Box(A \vee B) \to \Box B \qquad N7 =_{df} \boxminus \top \to \bot$$
$$\Diamond 2 =_{df} \diamondminus A \to \Diamond(A \vee B) \to \Diamond B$$

Theorem 2 (Hilbert Soundness). *If* $\mathsf{CKD}; \Phi \vdash_H A$ *then* $\varnothing; \Phi; \varnothing \models A$.

The axioms $\Box K$, $\Diamond K$, $\diamondminus K$, $\boxminus K$ in combination with *Nec* ensure that the logic is extensional, i.e., satisfies the *Replacement Principle*: If $\mathsf{CKD}; \Phi \vdash_H A \leftrightarrow B$ then $\mathsf{CKD}; \Phi \vdash_H \phi[A] \leftrightarrow \phi[B]$ where $\phi[.]$ is an arbitrary formula context. In the axiomatisation by [10] replacement is achieved with the *R-Rules*

$$\frac{\Omega; \Phi \vdash_H A \to B}{\Omega; \Phi \vdash_H \oplus A \to \oplus B}\, R\oplus \qquad \frac{\Omega; \Phi \vdash_H A \to B}{\Omega; \Phi \vdash_H \ominus B \to \ominus A}\, R\ominus$$

for $\oplus \in \{\Diamond, \Box\}$ and $\ominus \in \{\diamondminus, \boxminus\}$. These are derivable from our axioms $\Box K$, $\Diamond K$, $\diamondminus K$, $\boxminus K$, Modus Ponens *MP* and Necessitation *Nec*.

The axioms $\otimes K$ (for $\otimes \in \{\Diamond, \Box, \diamondminus, \boxminus\}$) deal with the consequences of a necessary implication $\Box(A \to B)$ for statements made under modalities. Analogously, the axioms $\otimes 2$ express the consequences of an impossible property $\diamondminus A$ for modalised statements. The import of axiom $\Box 2$ is that if a disjunction $A \vee B$ is necessary and one of the disjuncts is impossible, then the other disjunct is necessary. The axiom $\Diamond 2$ says that if a disjunction $A \vee B$ is possible and one of the disjuncts is impossible, then the other disjunct is possible. The axiom $\diamondminus 2$ states that if two properties are impossible, then their disjunction is impossible, too. The axiom $\boxminus 2$ says that if one property is impossible and another is non-necessary, then its disjunction is non-necessary. $N5$ implies that if a conjunction $A \wedge B$ is impossible while one of the conjuncts is possible then the other conjunct is non-necessary. $N6$ is the statement that if a disjunction is necessary and one disjunct non-necessary then the other disjunct is possible. The final axiom $N7$ gives a representation of absurdity as non-necessity of truth.

Let us verify that possibility $\Diamond A$ and impossibility $\diamondminus A$ are contradictory, i.e., $\vdash_H {\sim}(\Diamond A \wedge \diamondminus A)$. Since $\vdash_H A \leftrightarrow (A \wedge \top)$ we obtain $\vdash_H (\Diamond A \wedge \diamondminus A) \leftrightarrow (\Diamond A \wedge \diamondminus(A \wedge \top))$ by the Replacement Principle. Then, instantiating $N5$ as $\vdash_H \diamondminus(A \wedge \top) \to \Diamond A \to \boxminus\top$, we can derive $\vdash_H (\Diamond A \wedge \diamondminus A) \to \boxminus\top$ by IPL. Finally chaining up in IPL with the implication $N7$ this implies $\vdash_H (\Diamond A \wedge \diamondminus A) \to \bot$.

As explained above, in the standard Kripke model theory, the presence of frame conditions force a collapse of the modalities and the loss of DP. In CKD where we maintain their independence we can study existing theories as fragments and extensions. Došen's model theory of HK$\otimes$-frames [10] in the language $\mathcal{L}_{\otimes} = \{\bot, \wedge, \vee, \rightarrow, \otimes\}$ for fixed $\otimes \in \{\Diamond, \diamondminus, \Box, \boxminus\}$ generates the logic called HK$\otimes$. A HK$\otimes$-frame is an infallible C-frame satisfying the HK$\otimes$ frame condition (see Sect. 1). On such C-frames our truth conditions for $\otimes$ collapse to the ones of Došen for $\Diamond$, $\diamondminus$, $\Box$ and $\boxminus$. As a result, CKD is conservative over HK$\otimes$ in the language fragment $\mathcal{L}_{\otimes}$. However, the modalities $\otimes \in \{\diamondminus, \Diamond, \boxminus\}$ of CKD are weaker than the ones of HK$\otimes$. This is not surprising since we want to avoid the collapses arising from a naive fusion in the standard model theory. The properties of $\otimes$ in HK$\otimes$ can be regained in CKD by imposing frame conditions. Recall that N [11] is $HK\diamondminus$ in the language $\mathcal{L}_{\mathsf{N}} = \{\wedge, \vee, \rightarrow, \diamondminus\}$ without $\bot$. Now consider the axiom schemes:

$$(\boxminus 1) : \boxminus(A \wedge B) \rightarrow (\boxminus A \vee \boxminus B) \qquad (\Diamond 1) : \Diamond(A \vee B) \rightarrow (\Diamond A \vee \Diamond B)$$
$$(\diamondminus 2) : \diamondminus\bot \qquad (\Diamond 2) : {\sim}\Diamond\bot$$
$$(\Box\Diamond 1) : \Diamond A \vee \Box {\sim} A \qquad (\Box\Diamond 2) : {\sim}(\Diamond A \wedge \Box {\sim} A).$$

It can be shown that CKD in $\mathcal{L}_{\Box}$ corresponds to HK$\Box$ and in $\mathcal{L}_{\mathsf{N}}$ to N; HK$\diamondminus$ is CKD + $\diamondminus$2 restricted to $\mathcal{L}_{\diamondminus}$; CKD + $\boxminus$1 corresponds to HK$\boxminus$ in $\mathcal{L}_{\boxminus}$ and CKD + $\Diamond$1 + $\Diamond$2 generates the theory HK$\Diamond$ in $\mathcal{L}_{\Diamond}$. Finally, the extension CKD + $\diamondminus$2 + $\Box\Diamond$1 + $\Box\Diamond$2 coincides with the non-constructive theory HK$\Box\Diamond$ investigated by Božić & Došen [6] in $\mathcal{L}_{\Box\Diamond} =_{df} \{\bot, \wedge, \vee, \rightarrow, \Box, \Diamond\}$. In $\mathcal{L}_{\Box\Diamond}$ the logic CKD does not lose constructiveness like HK$\Box\Diamond$ does. In fact, CKD is conservative over CK [25] that combines the positive modalities $\Box$, $\Diamond$ by extending IPL with the axioms $\Box K$ and $\Diamond K$ and the *Nec* rule.

Theorem 3 (Conservativity). CKD *is a conservative extension of* N *and* CK *and* HK$\Box$. *The theories* HK$\otimes$ *for* $\otimes \in \{\Diamond, \diamondminus, \boxminus\}$ *and* HK $\Box\Diamond$ *are axiomatic extensions of* CKD:

For A in the language $\mathcal{L}_{\Box\Diamond}$: CK; $\varnothing \vdash_H A$ *iff* CKD; $\varnothing \vdash_H A$.
For A in the language $\mathcal{L}_{\Box\Diamond}$: $HK\Box\Diamond; \varnothing \vdash_H A$ *iff* CKD, $\diamondminus$2, $\Box\Diamond$1, $\Box\Diamond$2; $\varnothing \vdash_H A$.
For A in the language $\mathcal{L}_{\boxminus}$: $HK\boxminus; \varnothing \vdash_H A$ *iff* CKD, $\boxminus$1; $\varnothing \vdash_H A$.
For A in the language $\mathcal{L}_{\Box}$: $HK\Box; \varnothing \vdash_H A$ *iff* CKD; $\varnothing \vdash_H A$.
For A in the language $\mathcal{L}_{\diamondminus}$: $HK\diamondminus; \varnothing \vdash_H A$ *iff* CKD, $\diamondminus$2; $\varnothing \vdash_H A$.
For A in the language $\mathcal{L}_{\mathsf{N}}$: N; $\varnothing \vdash_H A$ *iff* CKD; $\varnothing \vdash_H A$.
For A in the language $\mathcal{L}_{\Diamond}$: $HK\Diamond; \varnothing \vdash_H A$ *iff* CKD, $\Diamond$1, $\Diamond$2; $\varnothing \vdash_H A$.

3.2 Landing at Došen Square: The Sequent Calculus G_{CKD}

The proof theory of CK has previously been investigated in terms of a Natural Deduction system [3], multisequent calculi [22–24], nested sequents [2] and a tableaux-based calculus [33]. Our sequent calculus G_{CKD} is a refinement of the multisequent calculus of Dragalin [12] for IPL, similar to [22], that is enriched by additional scopes to cover *local* and *global* properties. This is required for the interpretation of the four modalities, and is consonant with Poggiolesi's remark that

[...] the failures of the search for a sequent calculus for modal logic gave rise to the idea that the standard Gentzen calculus could only account for classical and intuitionistic logics and should therefore be enriched. [30][Sec. 2.3, p. 51]

In relation to the many variants explored in the literature (see [30]) G_{CKD} can be considered a *higher-arity* extension in the sense of Sato [32] and Blamey and Humberstone [5]. Notably, following Dragalin, we consider the *logical variant* of the Gentzen calculus (in the terminology of [30]) approach to sequents, where all structural rules are built into the axioms and logical rules. This is justified as we are dealing with a logical theory that has not been discussed before and thus are primarily interested in model-theoretic expressiveness, completeness, constructiveness and finite-model property.

A *sequent* in CKD is a structure $\Gamma \star \Delta \star \Theta \vdash \Pi \star \Sigma \star \Psi$ where the sets Γ and Π express direct truth and falsity at a state, as in a standard sequent. The sets Δ, Θ, Σ and Ψ are finite (possibly empty) sets of *signed* formulas each of which can be *strong* A^+ or *weak* A^-. With this structure, our sequents provide a formalisation of Došen square as visualised in Fig. 3. Note, that in Γ (Π) all formulas have no sign. Specifically, Δ and Θ contain positive existential and universal statements about modally reachable successors, while Σ and Ψ are negative existential and universal statements. Depending on the scope set, the sign $t \in \{+, -\}$ of a polarised formula A^t distinguishes *local* or hereditary *global* properties, where for a set X of signed formulas we write $X^t =_{df} \{A^t \mid A^t \in X\}$. For instance, $A^+ \in \Delta$ expresses the constraint that there *exists* an immediate R-successor satisfying A, while $A^- \in \Delta$ is the weaker statement that such a successor is reachable via $\sqsubseteq;R$, i.e., only after an initial intuitionistic step. Analogously, $A^- \in \Sigma$ says that A is false along immediate R-successors whereas $A^+ \in \Sigma$ is the stronger statement that A is false along all $\sqsubseteq;R$. This is captured by the following Definition 8.

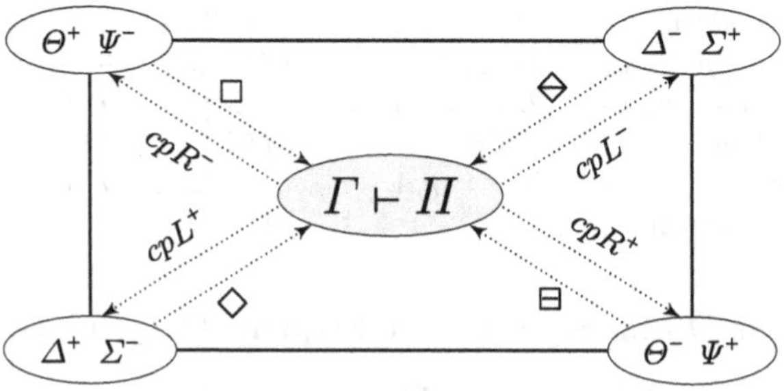

Fig. 3. The Došen square structure of G_{CKD} sequents.

Definition 8 (Refutability). *A sequent $\Gamma \star \Delta \star \Theta \vdash \Pi \star \Sigma \star \Psi$ is* refuted *in a state s of a C-model $\mathfrak{M} = (S, \leq, F, R, V)$ iff the following holds:*

- $\forall A \in \Gamma . \mathfrak{M}, s \models A$.
- $\forall B^- \in \Delta . \exists s' . s \sqsubseteq ; R\ s' \ \&\ \mathfrak{M}, s' \models B$; $\forall B^+ \in \Delta . \exists s' . s \sqsubseteq s\ R\ s' \ \&\ \mathfrak{M}, s' \models B$.
- $\forall C^- \in \Theta, s' . s \sqsubseteq s\ R\ s' \Rightarrow \mathfrak{M}, s' \models C$; $\forall C^+ \in \Theta, s' . s \sqsubseteq ; R\ s' \Rightarrow \mathfrak{M}, s' \models C$.
- $\forall D \in \Pi . \mathfrak{M}, s \not\models D$.
- $\forall E^- \in \Sigma, s' . s \sqsubseteq s\ R\ s' \Rightarrow \mathfrak{M}, s' \not\models E$; $\forall E^+ \in \Sigma, s' . s \sqsubseteq ; R\ s' \Rightarrow \mathfrak{M}, s' \not\models E$.
- $\forall F^- \in \Psi . \exists s' . s \sqsubseteq ; R\ s' \ \&\ \mathfrak{M}, s' \not\models F$; $\forall F^+ \in \Psi . \exists s' . s \sqsubseteq s\ R\ s' \ \&\ \mathfrak{M}, s \not\models F$.

A sequent is called refutable, *written* $\Gamma \star \Delta \star \Theta \not\models \Pi \star \Sigma \star \Psi$ *if there exists a C-model* $\mathfrak{M}$ *and a state* s *of* $\mathfrak{M}$ *in which it is refuted. A sequent is called* valid, *written* $\Gamma \star \Delta \star \Theta \models \Pi \star \Sigma \star \Psi$, *if it is not refutable.*

$$\dfrac{}{A, \Gamma \star \Delta \star \Theta \vdash A, \Pi \star \Sigma \star \Psi}\ Ax \qquad \dfrac{}{\bot, \Gamma \star \Delta \star \Theta \vdash \Pi \star \Sigma \star \Psi}\ \bot L^{\dagger} \qquad \dfrac{}{\Gamma \star \Delta \star \Theta \vdash \top, \Pi \star \Sigma \star \Psi}\ \top R$$

$$\dfrac{A, B, \Gamma \star \Delta \star \Theta \vdash \Pi \star \Sigma \star \Psi}{A \wedge B, \Gamma \star \Delta \star \Theta \vdash \Pi \star \Sigma \star \Psi}\ \wedge L \qquad \dfrac{\Gamma \star \Delta \star \Theta \vdash A, \Pi \star \Sigma \star \Psi \quad \Gamma \star \Delta \star \Theta \vdash B, \Pi \star \Sigma \star \Psi}{\Gamma \star \Delta \star \Theta \vdash A \wedge B, \Pi \star \Sigma \star \Psi}\ \wedge R$$

$$\dfrac{A, \Gamma \star \Delta \star \Theta \vdash \Pi \star \Sigma \star \Psi \quad B, \Gamma \star \Delta \star \Theta \vdash \Pi \star \Sigma \star \Psi}{A \vee B, \Gamma \star \Delta \star \Theta \vdash \Pi \star \Sigma \star \Psi}\ \vee L \qquad \dfrac{\Gamma \star \Delta \star \Theta \vdash A, B, \Pi \star \Sigma \star \Psi}{\Gamma \star \Delta \star \Theta \vdash A \vee B, \Pi \star \Sigma \star \Psi}\ \vee R$$

$$\dfrac{\Gamma \star \Delta \star \Theta \vdash A, \Pi \star \Sigma \star \Psi \quad B, \Gamma \star \Delta \star \Theta \vdash \Pi \star \Sigma \star \Psi}{A \to B, \Gamma \star \Delta \star \Theta \vdash \Pi \star \Sigma \star \Psi}\ {\to}L \qquad \dfrac{A, \Gamma \star \varnothing \star \Theta^+ \vdash B \star \Sigma^+ \star \varnothing}{\Gamma \star \Delta \star \Theta \vdash A \to B, \Pi \star \Sigma \star \Psi}\ {\to}R$$

$$\dfrac{B, \Theta^+ \star \varnothing \star \varnothing \vdash \Sigma^+ \star \varnothing \star \varnothing}{\Gamma \star B^-, \Delta \star \Theta \vdash \Pi \star \Sigma \star \Psi}\ cpL^- \qquad \dfrac{\Theta^+ \star \varnothing \star \varnothing \vdash F, \Sigma^+ \star \varnothing \star \varnothing}{\Gamma \star \Delta \star \Theta \vdash \Pi \star \Sigma \star F^-, \Psi}\ cpR^-$$

$$\dfrac{B, \Theta \star \varnothing \star \varnothing \vdash \Sigma \star \varnothing \star \varnothing}{\Gamma \star B^+, \Delta \star \Theta \vdash \Pi \star \Sigma \star \Psi}\ cpL^+ \qquad \dfrac{\Theta \star \varnothing \star \varnothing \vdash F, \Sigma \star \varnothing \star \varnothing}{\Gamma \star \Delta \star \Theta \vdash \Pi \star \Sigma \star F^+, \Psi}\ cpR^+$$

$$\dfrac{\Gamma \star A^+, \Delta \star \Theta \vdash \Pi \star \Sigma \star \Psi}{\Diamond A, \Gamma \star \Delta \star \Theta \vdash \Pi \star \Sigma \star \Psi}\ \Diamond L^{\dagger} \qquad \dfrac{\Gamma \star \varnothing \star \Theta^+ \vdash \bot \star D^-, \Sigma^+ \star \varnothing}{\Gamma \star \Delta \star \Theta \vdash \Diamond D, \Pi \star \Sigma \star \Psi}\ \Diamond R$$

$$\dfrac{\Gamma \star \Delta \star A^+, \Theta \vdash \Pi \star \Sigma \star \Psi}{\Box A, \Gamma \star \Delta \star \Theta \vdash \Pi \star \Sigma \star \Psi}\ \Box L \qquad \dfrac{\Gamma \star \Delta \star \Theta \vdash \Pi \star \Sigma \star D^-, \Psi}{\Gamma \star \Delta \star \Theta \vdash \Box D, \Pi \star \Sigma \star \Psi}\ \Box R$$

$$\dfrac{\Gamma \star \Delta \star \Theta \vdash \Pi \star A^+, \Sigma \star \Psi}{\diamondminus A, \Gamma \star \Delta \star \Theta \vdash \Pi \star \Sigma \star \Psi}\ \diamondminus L \qquad \dfrac{\Gamma \star D^-, \Delta \star \Theta \vdash \Pi \star \Sigma \star \Psi}{\Gamma \star \Delta \star \Theta \vdash \diamondminus D, \Pi \star \Sigma \star \Psi}\ \diamondminus R$$

$$\dfrac{\Gamma \star \Delta \star \Theta \vdash \Pi \star \Sigma \star A^+, \Psi}{\boxminus A, \Gamma \star \Delta \star \Theta \vdash \Pi \star \Sigma \star \Psi}\ \boxminus L^{\dagger} \qquad \dfrac{\Gamma \star \varnothing \star D^-, \Theta^+ \vdash \bot \star \Sigma^+ \star \varnothing}{\Gamma \star \Delta \star \Theta \vdash \boxminus D, \Pi \star \Sigma \star \Psi}\ \boxminus R$$

Fig. 4. G_{CKD} Sequent Rules. The sets Γ, Π are without sign. In the rules cpL^t and cpR^t all signs are dropped in the occurrences of the sets Θ, Θ^+ and Σ, Σ^+ in the premisses. Tagged rules (†) require its conclusion to be strict, i.e., $|\Delta \cup \Pi \cup \Psi| \geq 1$. We treat all scopes as sets with implicit duplication and permutation.

The sequent rules for CKD are seen in Fig. 4. In the top part, the rules Ax, $\bot L$, $\top R$, $\wedge L$, $\wedge R$, $\vee L$, $\vee R$, $\to L$ and $\to R$ are the left and right introduction rules for a (multisequent, logical [30]) Gentzen sequent calculus of IPL. These rules operate in the central $\Gamma \vdash \Pi$ scopes, leaving the corner scopes of the Došen square untouched. In the bottom part of Fig. 4 we list the left and right introduction rules $\Diamond L$, $\Diamond R$, $\Box L$, $\Box R$, $\diamondminus L$, $\diamondminus R$, $\boxminus L$ and $\boxminus R$ for the modalities.

These modal rules, applied in forward direction, take a signed formula from one of the corners Δ, Θ, Σ and Ψ of the Došen square (Fig. 3) and introduce an associated modal operator in the conclusion sequent, instead. From Ψ^- and Θ^+ we introduce the $\Box$ modalities in rules $\Box L$ and $\Box R$; From Ψ^+ and Θ^- we introduce $\boxminus$ via $\boxminus L$ and $\boxminus R$. No other rule depends on the presence of formulas in Ψ or Θ. From Δ^- and Σ^+ stem all occurrences of $\diamondminus$ through $\diamondminus R$ and $\diamondminus L$, while Δ^+ and Σ^- constitute a reservoir for $\Diamond$ introduced via $\Diamond L$ and $\Diamond R$. So far, G_{CKD} does not present surprises as a Gentzen-style calculus. The speciality of G_{CKD} lies in the four rules cpL^-, cpL^+, cpR^- and cpR^+ seen in the center of Fig. 4. The sign introduction rules cpL^t, cpR^t work in opposite direction to the modal introduction rules $\otimes L$, $\otimes R$. Together, they orchestrate the 'Grand Modal Dispatch' of the DS as suggested in Fig. 3.

Definition 9 (Derivability). *A derivation of a sequent $\Gamma \star \Delta \star \Theta \vdash \Pi \star \Sigma \star \Psi$ is either an axiom (rule Ax), an instance of $\bot L$ or $\top R$ or an application of a logical rule to derivations concluding its premises, that is built using the rules in Fig. 4. We say that a sequent is* underivable, *written $\Gamma \star \Delta \star \Theta \nvdash \Pi \star \Sigma \star \Psi$, if no derivation exists for it.*

G_{CKD} is conceived as a refutation system. Its purpose is to establish that a state specification (based on the six scopes) presented as a sequent is refutable. Refutability (Definition 8) and derivability (Definition 9) are linked in the sense that a sequent is underivable iff it is refutable, as established in the soundness and completeness proofs.

Theorem 4 (G_{CKD}Soundness). *If $\Gamma \star \Delta \star \Theta \not\models \Pi \star \Sigma \star \Psi$ then $\Gamma \star \Delta \star \Theta \nvdash \Pi \star \Sigma \star \Psi$.*

The proof of Theorem 4 is standard, by showing that for each sequent rule in Fig. 4 that if the conclusion is refutable then *at least one* of its premises is refutable as well.

$$
\begin{array}{cl}
\hline
A \star \varnothing \star \varnothing \vdash A \star \varnothing \star \varnothing & Ax \\
\hline
\varnothing \star A^+ \star \varnothing \vdash \bot \star A^+ \star \varnothing & cpL^+ \\
\hline
\Diamond A, \diamondminus A \star \varnothing \star \varnothing \vdash \bot \star \varnothing \star \varnothing & \diamondminus L\ \Diamond L \\
\hline
\Diamond A \wedge \diamondminus A \star \varnothing \star \varnothing \vdash \bot \star \varnothing \star \varnothing & \wedge L \\
\hline
\varnothing \star \varnothing \star \varnothing \vdash {\sim}(\Diamond A \wedge \diamondminus A) \star \varnothing \star \varnothing & {\sim}R
\end{array}
\qquad
\begin{array}{cl}
\text{cannot be closed} & \\
\hline
A \star \varnothing \star \varnothing \vdash A \wedge B \star \varnothing \star \varnothing & ?\,(2) \\
\hline
\varnothing \star \varnothing \star A^- \vdash \bot \star \varnothing \star (A \wedge B)^+ & cpR^+ \\
\hline
\boxminus(A \wedge B) \star \varnothing \star A^- \vdash \bot \star \varnothing \star \varnothing & \boxminus L \\
\hline
\boxminus(A \wedge B) \star \varnothing \star \varnothing \vdash \boxminus A, \boxminus B \star \varnothing \star \varnothing & \boxminus R\,(1) \\
\hline
\boxminus(A \wedge B) \star \varnothing \star \varnothing \vdash \boxminus A \vee \boxminus B \star \varnothing \star \varnothing & \vee R
\end{array}
$$

Fig. 5. A successful G_{CKD} derivation (left) and a non-completable derivation (right).

As examples consider the G_{CKD} derivations in Fig. 5. The left derivation demonstrates the incompatibility of $\Diamond$ and $\diamondminus$ and the right indicates why a proof of the distribution $\boxminus(A \wedge B) \rightarrow (\boxminus A \vee \boxminus B)$ is doomed to fail. The application (1) of rule $\boxminus R$ on the right of Fig. 5, corresponding to an intuitionistic

$\leq$-step in backwards direction, must clear the Π-scope and drop the constraint $\boxminus B$. Because of this, the formula B is missing in situation (2) so that the sequent cannot be derived.

Theorem 5. *For each H_{CKD} derivation $\varnothing;\varnothing \vdash_H D$ there is a G_{CKD} derivation of the sequent $\varnothing\star\varnothing\star\varnothing \vdash D\star\varnothing\star\varnothing$ using the rules of Fig. 4 plus the cut rule: From $\Gamma\star\Delta\star\Theta \vdash D, \Pi\star\Sigma\star\Psi$ and $D, \Gamma\star\Delta\star\Theta \vdash \Pi\star\Sigma\star\Psi$ infer $\Gamma\star\Delta\star\Theta \vdash \Pi\star\Sigma\star\Psi$.*

A sequent $\Gamma\star\Delta\star\Theta\vdash\Pi\star\Sigma\star\Psi$ is called *strict* if $|\Delta \cup \Pi \cup \Psi| \geq 1$ and *polarised* if $|\Theta^- \cup \Sigma^-| \leq 1$. One can show that every derivable sequent is strict and that polarised sequents can be proven only using polarised sequents. For polarised and strict sequents the following 'hilbertification' provides a *translation* of G_{CKD} back into H_{CKD}.

Definition 10 (Hilbertification). *Let each sequent $\Gamma\star\Delta\star\Theta\vdash\Pi\star\Sigma\star\Psi$ be translated into the formula $\left(\hat{\Gamma}\wedge\hat{\Diamond}\Delta\wedge\hat{\ominus}\Sigma\wedge\hat{\Box}\Theta\wedge\boxminus\Psi\right) \to \left(\check{\Pi}\vee\check{\ominus}\Delta\vee\check{\Diamond}\Sigma\vee\boxminus\Theta\vee\check{\Box}\Psi\right)$ where*

$$\begin{array}{ll}\hat{\Gamma} =_{df} \bigwedge_{A\in\Gamma} A, & \check{\Pi} =_{df} \bigvee_{D\in\Pi} D,\\ \hat{\Diamond}\Delta =_{df} \bigwedge_{B^+\in\Delta} \Diamond B, & \check{\ominus}\Delta =_{df} \bigvee_{B^-\in\Delta} \ominus B,\\ \hat{\ominus}\Sigma =_{df} \ominus\bigvee_{E^+\in\Sigma} E, & \check{\Diamond}\Sigma =_{df} \Diamond\bigvee_{E^-\in\Sigma} E,\\ \hat{\Box}\Theta =_{df} \bigwedge_{D^+\in\Theta} \Box D, & \boxminus\Theta =_{df} \check{\boxminus}\bigwedge_{D^-\in\Theta} D,\\ \boxminus\Psi =_{df} \bigwedge_{D^+\in\Psi} \boxminus F, & \check{\Box}\Psi =_{df} \bigvee_{D^-\in\Psi} \Box F,\end{array}$$

and for empty sets we put $\hat{\Gamma} =_{df} \top$ if $\Gamma = \varnothing$, $\check{\Pi} =_{df} \bot$ if $\Pi = \varnothing$, and for $\otimes \in \{\Box, \Diamond, \ominus, \boxminus\}$ and X a set of signed formulas: $\hat{\otimes}X = \top$ if $X^+ = \varnothing$ and $\check{\otimes}X = \bot$ if $X^- = \varnothing$.

Theorem 6 *Let $\Gamma\star\Delta\star\Theta\vdash\Pi\star\Sigma\star\Psi$ be a polarised sequent, derivable using the rules of Fig. 4. Then, there exists a Hilbert derivation of*

$$\mathsf{CKD};\varnothing \vdash_H \left(\hat{\Gamma}\wedge\hat{\Diamond}\Delta\wedge\hat{\ominus}\Sigma\wedge\hat{\Box}\Theta\wedge\boxminus\Psi\right) \to \left(\check{\Pi}\vee\check{\ominus}\Delta\vee\check{\Diamond}\Sigma\vee\boxminus\Theta\vee\check{\Box}\Psi\right).$$

Theorem 5 and 6 give us a back-and-forth translation of deductions in the Hilbert and Gentzen systems for CKD. However, this involves the *cut* rule, so neither calculus gives us a decision procedure. We address this by proving completeness of G_{CKD} and thus completeness of H_{CKD}, leading to our final completeness result that implies cut-elimination. First, let us introduce some technical definitions.

Definition 11 (Saturation). *A sequent $\Gamma\star\Delta\star\Theta \vdash \Pi\star\Sigma\star\Psi$ is called* saturated *if the following closure conditions hold:*

1. *If $M \wedge N \in \Gamma$ then both $M, N \in \Gamma$*
2. *If $M \vee N \in \Gamma$ then $M \in \Gamma$ or $N \in \Gamma$;*
3. *If $M \to N \in \Gamma$ then $M \in \Pi$ or $N \in \Gamma$*
4. *If $M \vee N \in \Pi$ then both $M, N \in \Pi$;*
5. *If $M \wedge N \in \Pi$ then $M \in \Pi$ or $N \in \Pi$*
6. *If $\ominus M \in \Gamma$ then $M^+ \in \Sigma$*
7. *If $\ominus M \in \Pi$ then $M^- \in \Delta$*
8. *If $\Box M \in \Gamma$ then $M^+ \in \Theta$*
9. *If $\Box M \in \Pi$ then $M^- \in \Psi$*
10. *If $\Pi = \varnothing$ and $\Delta = \varnothing$ then $\bot \in \Gamma$.*

In a saturated sequent the sets Γ and Π are coupled through the constraints (1)–(5). Closure conditions (6)–(9) are lower bounds on the presence of positive signs in Σ and Θ and on the negative signs in Δ and Ψ. If $\Gamma_1 \star \Delta_1 \star \Theta_1 \vdash \Pi \star \Sigma_1 \star \Psi_1$ is saturated then any sequent $\Gamma \star \Delta_2 \star \Theta_2 \vdash \Pi \star \Sigma_2 \star \Psi_2$ with $\Theta_1^+ \subseteq \Theta_2^+$, $\Sigma_1^+ \subseteq \Sigma_2^+$, $\Delta_1^- \subseteq \Delta_2^-$ and $\Psi_1^- \subseteq \Psi_2^-$ is saturated, too. In other words, we can add positive signs, or add and remove negative signs from Θ, Σ without losing saturation. Analogously, we can add negative signs or add and remove positive signs in Δ, Ψ and preserve saturation.

Definition 12. *A set SF of formulas is* subformula closed *if for every subformula A of a formula $M \in SF$ it holds that $A \in SF$. Let $SF^+ = SF \cup \{\bot\}$. We say that a sequent $\Gamma \star \Delta \star \Theta \vdash \Pi \star \Sigma \star \Psi$ is called a SF*-sequent *if $\Gamma \cup \Delta \cup \Theta \cup \Pi \cup \Sigma \cup \Psi \subseteq SF^+$. Moreover, a SF sequent is called* consistent *if it cannot be derived in the cut-free calculus. It is called SF*-complete *if for every $M \in SF^+$ we have $M \in \Gamma$ or $M \in \Pi$.*

For saturated, consistent and SF-complete sequents the essential information lies in Γ, in the positive signs $B^+ \in \Delta$, $F^+ \in \Psi$ and the negative signs $E^- \in \Sigma$, $C^- \in \Theta$. All of these express the existence and properties of *immediate* R-successors (see Definition 8).

Definition 13 (Canonical Interpretation). *Let SF be a subformula closed set. We define a basic* canonical *C-structure $\mathfrak{M}^c = (S^c, \leq^c, F^c, R^c, V^c)$ over SF as follows: The states $w \in S^c$ are the saturated and consistent SF sequents $w = \langle \Gamma \star \Delta \star \Theta \vdash \Pi \star \Sigma \star \Psi \rangle$. Relating these canonical states, we define the intuitionistic accessibility relation $\leq^c$ and the compatibility relation R^c on S^c as follows:*

$$\langle \Gamma \star \Delta \star \Theta \vdash \Pi \star \Sigma \star \Psi \rangle \ \leq^c \ \langle \Gamma' \star \Delta' \star \Theta' \vdash \Pi' \star \Sigma' \star \Psi' \rangle$$
$$\text{iff } \Gamma \subseteq \Gamma' \ \& \ \ \Theta^+ \subseteq \Theta' \ \ \Sigma^+ \subseteq \Sigma' \tag{9}$$

$$\langle \Gamma \star \Delta \star \Theta \vdash \Pi \star \Sigma \star \Psi \rangle \ R^c \ \langle \Gamma' \star \Delta' \star \Theta' \vdash \Pi' \star \Sigma' \star \Psi' \rangle$$
$$\text{iff } \Sigma \subseteq \Pi' \ \& \ \ \Theta \subseteq \Gamma'. \tag{10}$$

Let $w = \langle \Gamma \star \Delta \star \Theta \vdash \Pi \star \Sigma \star \Psi \rangle \in S^c$ be an arbitrary state. The valuation of propositional variables p is given by stipulating $p \in V^c(w)$ iff $p \in \Gamma$ or $\bot \in \Gamma$. The state w is fallible $w \in F^c$ iff $\bot \in \Gamma$.

Lemma 1. *The canonical structure $\mathfrak{M}^c =_{df} (S^c, F^c, \leq^c, R^c, V^c)$ in Definition 13 is a C-model in the sense of Definition 2 such that for every sequent $w \in S^c$ the pair $(\mathfrak{M}^c, w)$ refutes w according to Definition 8.*

Theorem 7 (Gentzen Completeness). *Every underivable sequent is refutable, i.e., if* $\Gamma \star \Delta \star \Theta \not\vdash \Pi \star \Sigma \star \Psi$ *then* $\Gamma \star \Delta \star \Theta \not\models \Pi \star \Sigma \star \Psi$.

The completeness proof proceeds in the standard fashion via canonical models (see Definition 13) constructed by saturation of unprovable end-sequents. Consistent saturation in all scopes Γ, Δ, Θ, Π, Σ and Ψ only involves subformulas (counting $\bot$ as a subformula) of the original sequent. The canonical model does not require maximal saturation or depends on the *cut* rule to achieve completeness of canonical states. Hence, the *cut* rule is admissible in CKD. Moreover, since all rules of CKD (not using *cut*) have the subformula property, it follows that CKD has the Finite Model Property. The Completeness Theorem 7 for our finite axiomatisation (Gentzen or Hilbert system) implies decidability. Therefore, we have the following theorem.

Theorem 8. *The theory* CKD *has the Finite Model Property, is cut-free and decidable.*

4 Conclusion

We have introduced a logic CKD, which combines the modalities $\Diamond, \Box, \ominus, \boxminus$ with IPL. CKD is constructive since it has the Disjunction Property, and it is a conservative extension of the logics CK [25], N [11] and HK$\Box$ [6]. Technically, this is a clear contribution, since many extensions of N are not constructive, and combining the modalities $\Diamond, \Box, \ominus, \boxminus$ with IPL can easily lead to loss of constructivity. But, we would add, this is also a contribution on another front: by combining the modalities $\Diamond, \Box, \ominus, \boxminus$ with IPL we have constructed a logic in which all parts of the Došen square are included. Moreover, Došen's logics HK$\otimes$ for $\otimes \in \{\Diamond, \ominus, \boxminus\}$ are axiomatic extensions of CKD.

The proof theory of CKD has been given in the form of a Hilbert calculus H_{CKD} and a sequent calculus G_{CKD}, and a constructive (bidirectional) translation between both proof systems is established. The soundness and completeness of H_{CKD} and G_{CKD} is proven, relative to a semantics based on C-frames and C-models. The structural complexity of G_{CKD} sequents arises from the aim to enforce the subformula property (analyticity) and to enable a Gentzen-style separation between left and right introduction rules for each operator (orthogonality). Finally, as a corollary of Gentzen completeness, it follows that the theory of CKD has the finite model property, is cut-free and decidable.

G_{CKD} is the first sequent calculus that combines all four modalities $\otimes \in \{\Box, \Diamond, \boxminus, \ominus\}$ preserving the disjunction property of intuitionistic logic. It is instructive to look at special fragments: In the modal-free fragment IPL, i.e., without the rules $\otimes L$, $\otimes R$ for $\otimes \in \{\Box, \Diamond, \boxminus, \ominus\}$, all scope sets except Γ and Π may be assumed empty. Hence, the dispatch rules cpL^t, cpR^t become obsolete and G_{CKD} reduces to the rules $\{Ax, \bot L, \top R, \wedge L, \wedge R, \vee L, \vee R, \to L, \to R\}$ corresponding to Dragalin's sequent calculus for IPL. In the $\Box$-fragment of G_{CKD} (i.e., IPL plus $\Box$), the modal rules $\Box L$, $\Box R$ generate only the positive signs Θ^+ and negative signs Ψ^- while $\Delta = \Sigma = \emptyset$. Hence, from the modal dispatch only cpR^- remains. The resulting sequents $\Gamma \star \emptyset \star \Theta^+ \vdash \Pi \star \emptyset \star \Psi^-$ correspond to an intuitionistic version of the 4-ary sequents $\Gamma \Rightarrow^{\Psi^-}_{\Theta^+} \Pi$ of Blamey and Humberstone's logic[4] K^4 [5], called H−ask by [30]. These K^4 sequents are translatable as formulas $(\bigwedge \Gamma \wedge \bigwedge \Box\Theta^+) \to (\bigvee \Pi \vee \bigvee \Box\Psi^-)$ (see [30] and also Definition 10). The constructive nature of CKD appears in the fact that the right introduction rules $\Diamond R$ and $\boxminus R$ are not obviously (locally) invertible, due to the restriction of the scopes in their premises. In classical logic, where $\sqsubseteq$ is the identity relation and there is no difference between positive and negative signs in the sequent's scope, the rule $\Diamond R$ could be replaced by the sound rule $\Gamma \star \Delta \star \Theta \vdash \Pi \star D, \Sigma \star \Psi \Rightarrow \Gamma \star \Delta \star \Theta \vdash \Diamond D, \Pi \star \Sigma \star \Psi$, which is invertible. Similarly, the rule $\boxminus R$ could be relaxed as the invertible rule $\Gamma \star \Delta \star D, \Theta \vdash \Pi \star \Sigma \star \Psi \Rightarrow \Gamma \star \Delta \star \Theta \vdash \boxminus D, \Pi \star \Sigma \star \Psi$. In such a classical collapse, G_{CKD} might be seen as a 6-ary multi-sequent calculus for the modalities $\otimes \in \{\Box, \Diamond, \boxminus, \ominus\}$ in the spirit of Blamey and Humberstone.

Two novel features of the semantics for CKD deserve to be highlighted for those unfamiliar with the literature on constructive logic: C-frames admit fallible states, and C-models adopt doubly-quantified truth conditions for modal operators, these latter explaining why $\Diamond$ does not distribute over disjunction, just like in CK [20,25,33]. We note that, fallible states appear to be relevant also in N. Došen [11] (see also [28,36]) proves completeness of N on HK$\ominus$-frames in the language $\mathcal{L}_{\mathsf{N}}$ which does not contain $\bot$. In the proof, however, canonical states with inconsistent theories must be permitted. As a result, the standard model theory via HK$\ominus$-frames is no longer adequate in the extended language $\mathcal{L}_{\mathsf{N}} \cup \{\bot\}$, since it would force the axiom $\ominus\bot$, which is not part of N. This problem does not re-occur in CKD since the definition of C-models permits fallible states to reject $\ominus\bot$. Hence, in CKD the fusion of N and *full* IPL can be studied.

There are various other logics in the vicinity of CKD which can be studied, too. For example, the theory of C-frames in which R is a transitive subrelation of $\leq$ that is reflexive on infallible states (if $s \notin F$ then $s\ R\ s$) generates *Propositional Lax Logic* PLL [20] also known as *Computational Logic* CL [4]. Both negative modalities $\ominus A$ and $\boxminus A$ collapse in this case, and become semantically equivalent to intuitionistic negation $\sim A$, whilst $\Box$ collapses since $\Box A \leftrightarrow A$. Only $\Diamond$ remains independent, yielding the (only) monadic modal operator $\bigcirc$ of Lax Logic, axiomatised by the single axiom $(A \to \bigcirc B) \leftrightarrow (\bigcirc A \to \bigcirc B)$, and the axiom $\sim \bigcirc \bot$ if additionally R is a subrelation of $\sqsubseteq$.

Other logics arise from CKD when the combined relation $\sqsubseteq;R$ is functional. C-frames in which $\sqsubseteq;R$ is functional collapse $\ominus A$ and $\boxminus A$ to a form of negation $\neg A$, known as *Routley negation* in the literature on FDE [17–19]. Routley negation is weaker than intuitionistic negation $\sim A$ in that it satisfies contraposition and DeMorgan laws while permitting gaps and gluts. In C-frames in which $\sqsubseteq;R$ is functional the theories $\mathsf{N}^\star$ and $\mathsf{N}^\star_i$ of Routley negation [27] can be developed.

[4] Blamey and Humberstone also use sets as scopes as we do, avoiding structural rules of duplication and permutation. However, [5] use an explicit weakening rule, which is built into the rules of G_{CKD}. Our dispatch rule cpR^- is named Switch in [5].

Specifically, if $\sqsubseteq;R$ is *weakly functional*[5] then we obtain the theory called N' [28] that extends IPL by axioms [27]

$$(N1) : \neg(A \wedge B) \rightarrow (\neg A \vee \neg B) \quad (N2) : (\neg A \wedge \neg B) \rightarrow \neg(A \vee B) \quad (N3) : \neg\top \rightarrow \bot$$

with derivation rules of Modus Ponens and Contraposition ("from $A \rightarrow B$ infer $\neg B \rightarrow \neg A$"). If we further assume that frames are infallible, the relation $\sqsubseteq;R$ becomes *functional*, and we arrive at Heyting-Ockham logic $\mathsf{N}^\star$ [7,27,28] (extended by quantifiers in [36]) that extends N' by the axiom $\neg\bot$. Note that CKD on functional frames also collapses the positive modalities $\Box A \leftrightarrow \Diamond A$ into a single modality $\Box$ that preserves the properties of $\Box$. This naturally generates an extension of $\mathsf{N}^\star$ with modality $\Box$ in a coherent theory that appears not to have been considered in the literature.

There are a number of open problems which could be considered in the future. The Correspondence Theory for CKD could be explored and a sequent calculus provided for extensions of CKD, such as $\mathsf{N}^\star$ and $\mathsf{N}_i^\star$ in language $\{\Box, \Diamond, \neg\}$ where $\neg$ collapses both $\ominus$ and $\boxminus$ into a single modality $\neg$. Following [36], the addition of quantifiers to CKD could be investigated. On the proof-theoretic front, means for termination control (such as invertibility of rules, duplication elimination, blocking conditions) of the sequent calculus G_{CKD} could be investigated, and the algorithmic complexity of the theory CKD determined. Since CKD is constructive, the question naturally arises of what lambda calculus is related to CKD via the Curry Howard isomorphism, and if there exists a natural deduction calculus for CKD. Recent work by [1] provides a novel semantics for proofs in CK, and could form the basis of constructing a semantics of proofs in CKD including negative modalities. Finally, it would be interesting to investigate if the neighbourhood semantics for CK and other non-normal extensions proposed by [8] could be used to interpret the negative modalities of CKD.

Acknowledgements. The authors would like to thank the anonymous referees and the PC, who provided useful and detailed comments on the submission version of the paper, and Stanislav Speranski, for sharing thoughts on constructive negation as a modality.

References

1. Acclavio, M., Catta, D., Straßburger, L.: Towards a denotational semantics for proofs in constructive modal logic. arXiv preprint arXiv:2104.09115 (2021)
2. Arisaka, R., Das, A., Straßburger, L.: On nested sequents for constructive modal logics. Logical Methods in Computer Science 11 (2015)
3. Bellin, G., de Paiva, V., Ritter, E.: Extended Curry-Howard correspondence for a basic constructive modal logic. In: Methods for Modalities II (2001)
4. Benton, N., Bierman, G., de Paiva, V.: Computational types from a logical perspective. J. Funct. Program. **8**(2), 177–193 (1998)

[5] A frame is *weakly functional* if $\forall s \in S \setminus F. \exists s'.\ s \sqsubseteq;R\ s'$ and $\forall s, s_1', s_2'.\ s \sqsubseteq;R\ s_1' \,\&\, s \sqsubseteq;R\ s_2' \Rightarrow s_1' \cong s_2'$, where $s_1' \cong s_2'$ iff $s_1' \leq s_2'$ and $s_2' \leq s_1'$. The frame is *functional* if the existence condition holds in the stronger form $\forall s \in S. \exists s'.\ s \sqsubseteq;R\ s'$.

5. Blamey, S., Humberstone, L.: A perspective on modal sequent logic. Publ. Res. Inst. Math. Sci. **27**, 763–782 (1991)
6. Božić, M., Došen, K.: Models for normal intuitionistic modal logics. Studia Logica **43**(3), 217–245 (1984)
7. Cabalar, P., Odintsov, S.P., Pearce, D.: Logical foundations of well-founded semantics. In: P.D. et al. (ed.) Proceedings of International Conference on Knowledge Representation and Reasoning (2006)
8. Dalmonte, T., Grellois, C., Olivetti, N.: Intuitionistic non-normal modal logics: a general framework. J. Philos. Logic **49**, 833–882 (2020)
9. Došen, K.: Negation in the light of modal logic. In: Gabbay, D.M., Wansing, H. (eds.) What is Negation?, pp. 77–86. Springer, Heidelberg (1999). https://doi.org/10.1007/978-94-015-9309-0_4
10. Došen, K.: Negative modal operators in intuitionistic logic. Publications de L'Institut Mathématique **35**(49), 3–14 (1984)
11. Došen, K.: Negation as a modal operator. Rep. Math. Logic **20**(1986), 15–27 (1986)
12. Dragalin, A.G.: Mathematical Intuitionism: Introduction to Proof Theory. American Mathematical Society (1988)
13. Drobyshevich, S.: Double negation operator in logic $N^{\star}$. J. Math. Sci. **205**(3) (2015)
14. Drobyshevich, S.A., Odintsov, S.P.: Finite model property for negative modalities. Sibirskie Elektronnye Matematicheskie Izvestiia 10 (2013)
15. Drobyshevich, S.A.: Composition of an intuitionistic negation and negative modalities as a necessity operator. Algebra Logic **52**, 1–19 (2013). https://doi.org/10.1007/s10469-013-9235-8
16. Drobyshevich, S.: On classical behavior of intuitionistic modalities. Logic Log. Philos. **24**(1), 79–104 (2015)
17. Dunn, J.M.: Star and perp: two treatments of negation. Philos. Perspect. **7**, 331–357 (1993)
18. Dunn, J.M.: Negation, a notion in focus, vol. 7, chap. Generalized Ortho Negation, pp. 3–26. Walter de Gruyter Berlin (1996)
19. Dunn, J.M., Zhou, C.: Negation in the context of gaggle theory. Studia Logica **80**(2–3), 235–264 (2005). https://doi.org/10.1007/s11225-005-8470-y
20. Fairtlough, M., Mendler, M.: Propositional lax logic. Inf. Comput. **137**(1), 1–33 (1997)
21. Fitting, M.: Basic modal logic. In: Gabbay, D.M., Hogger, C.J., Robinson, J.A. (eds.) Handbook of Logic in Artificial Intelligence and Logic Programming, vol. 1, pp. 368–448. Oxford University Press, New York (1993)
22. Mendler, M., Scheele, S.: Towards constructive DL for abstraction and refinement. J. Autom. Reason. **44**(3), 207–243 (2010). https://doi.org/10.1007/s10817-009-9151-8
23. Mendler, M., Scheele, S.: Cut-free Gentzen calculus for multimodal CK. Inf. Comput. **209**(12), 1465–1490 (2011)
24. Mendler, M., Scheele, S.: On the computational interpretation of CK_n. Fundamenta Informaticae **130**, 1–39 (2014)
25. Mendler, M., de Paiva, V.: Constructive CK for contexts. In: Proceedings of the First Workshop on Context Representation and Reasoning, CONTEXT 2005 (2005)
26. Nelson, D.: Constructible falsity. J. Symb. Logic **14**(1), 16–26 (1949)
27. Odintsov, S., Wansing, H.: Routley star and hyperintensionality. J. Philos. Logic **50**, 33–56 (2020)

28. Odintsov, S.P.: Combining intuitionistic connectives and Routley negation. In: Siberian Electronic Mathematical Reports (2005)
29. Plotkin, G., Stirling, C.: A framework for intuitionistic modal logics. In: Halpern, J. (ed.) Theoretical Aspects of Reasoning About Knowledge, pp. 399–406. Monterey (1986)
30. Poggiolesi, F.: Gentzen Calculi for Modal and Propositional Logic. Springer, Heidelberg (2011). https://doi.org/10.1007/978-90-481-9670-8
31. Popkorn, S.: First Steps in Modal Logic. Cambridge University Press, Cambridge (1994)
32. Sato, M.: A study of Kripke-type models for some modal logics by Gentzen's sequential method. Publ. Res. Inst. Math. Sci. **13**, 381–468 (1977)
33. Scheele, S.: Model and Proof Theory of Constructive ALC, Constructive Description Logics. Ph.D. thesis, University of Bamberg (2015)
34. Simpson, A.K.: The proof theory and semantics of intuitionistic modal logic. Ph.D. thesis, University of Edinburgh, Scotland (1994)
35. Sotirov, V.H.: Modal theories with intuitionistic logic. In: Proceedings of the Conference on Mathematical Logic, Sophia, pp. 139–171 (1980)
36. Speranski, S.O.: Negation as a modality in a quantified setting. J, Logic Comput. (2021)
37. Wansing, H.: On split negation, strong negation, information, falsification, and verification. In: Bimbó, K. (ed.) J. Michael Dunn on Information Based Logics. OCL, vol. 8, pp. 161–189. Springer, Cham (2016). https://doi.org/10.1007/978-3-319-29300-4_10
38. Westerståhl, D.: On the Aristotelian square of opposition. Kapten Mnemos Kolumbarium, en festskrift med anledning av Helge Malmgrens (2005)
39. Wijesekera, D.: Constructive modal logic I. Ann. Pure Appl. Logic **50**, 271–301 (1990)
40. Wolter, F., Zakharyaschev, M.: Intuitionistic modal logics as fragments of classical bimodal logics. Logic at work, pp. 168–186 (1997)
41. Wolter, F., Zakharyaschev, M.: The relation between intuitionistic and classical modal logics. Algebra Logic **36**(2), 73–92 (1997)
42. Wolter, F., Zakharyaschev, M.: Intuitionistic modal logic. In: Cantini, A., Casari, E., Minari, P. (eds.) Logic and Foundations of Mathematics, pp. 227–238. Springer, Heidelberg (1999). https://doi.org/10.1007/978-94-017-2109-7_17

Author Index

Author Index

Printed in the United States
by Baker & Taylor Publisher Services